MW01502643

HOLT
ELEMENTS OF
LITERATURE

Second Course

HOLT, RINEHART AND WINSTON

A Harcourt Education Company

Orlando • **Austin** • New York • San Diego • Toronto • London

EDITORIAL
Editorial Vice President: Ralph Tachuk
Executive Book Editors: Juliana Koenig, Katie Vignery
Senior Book Editors: Leslie Griffin, Kathryn Rogers
Senior Product Manager: Don Wulbrecht
Managing Editor: Marie Price
Editorial Staff: Gail Coupland, Randy Dickson, Ann Michelle Gibson, Kerry Johnson, Karen Kolar, Evan Wilson, Sari Wilson
Copyediting Manager: Michael Neibergall
Copyediting Supervisors: Kristen Azzara, Mary Malone
Copyeditors: Christine Altgelt, Elizabeth Dickson, Emily Force, Leora Harris, Anne Heausler, Julia Thomas Hu, Kathleen Scheiner, Nancy Shore
Associate Managing Editor: Elizabeth LaManna
Editorial Support: Christine Degollado, Betty Gabriel, Danielle Greer, Mark Koenig, Erik Netcher, Janet Jenkins, Gloria Shahan, Emily Stern
Editorial Permissions: Ann Farrar, Susan Lowrance

Index: Tamsin Nutter

ART, DESIGN, AND PRODUCTION
Director: Athena Blackorby
Senior Design Director: Betty Mintz
Series Design: Kirchoff/Wohlberg, Inc.
Design and Electronic Files: Peter Sawchuk, Paul Caullett
Photo Research: Mary Monaco, Susan Sato
Production Manager: Carol Trammel
Sr. Production Coordinator: Dolores Keller
Prepress: TSI Graphics, Inc.
Manufacturing: R. R. Donnelley & Sons Company, Willard, Ohio

COVER
Photo Credits: (inset) *The Rocket* (1909) by Edward Middleton Manigault. Oil on caras. Collection of Columbus Museum of Art, Ohio, Museum Purchase, Howard Fund II (81.009). (background) Photograph of fireworks, © Brian Stablyk/Getty Images.

Requests for permission to make copies of any part of the work should be mailed to the following address: Permissions Department, Holt, Rinehart and Winston, 10801 N. MoPac Expressw, Building 3, Austin, Texas 78759-5415.

Acknowledgments appear on pages 1009–1011, which are an extension of the copyright age.

Printed in the United States of America
ISBN 0-03-035703-9   5 048 06 05

Language Arts Standards

The following chart lists Virginia's **English Standards of Learning** for eighth-graders. The headings and left column contain the standards, as well as explanations of those standards. The right column contains specific examples of how *Elements of Literature* helps you master the standards.

ORAL LANGUAGE

8.1 The student will use interviewing techniques to gain information.

8.1.a Prepare and ask relevant questions for the interview. What you want to know will determine what you will ask. Prepare your questions beforehand.	**EXAMPLE:** Interviewing See "Preparing for the Interview" in "Interviewing" in the Speaking and Listening Handbook, page 994.
8.1.b Make notes of responses. Record the answers given to your questions, using an efficient note-taking technique.	**EXAMPLE:** Noting Responses to Questions Page 980 in the Communications Handbook gives tips on taking good notes.
8.1.c Compile and report responses. Organize the responses you receive so you may report them to others.	**EXAMPLE:** Reporting an Interview "Following Up the Interview" on page 995 of the Speaking and Listening Handbook suggests that you review your notes and summarize the main points soon after the interview.
8.1.d Evaluate the effectiveness of the interview. How well did the interview go? What could have been better? Review your original questions and your notes. Did you get the information you wanted?	**EXAMPLE:** Evaluating an Interview Evaluate the information you have received by following the steps for evaluating sources on page 219. You may want to confirm or clarify information by talking with your source again.

8.2 The student will develop and deliver oral presentations in groups and individually.

8.2.a Choose topic and purpose appropriate to the audience.

Your friends may want to know how to perform a specific skateboarding trick, while your teacher may want you to present a personal narrative about your favorite sport. Adapt your topic and purpose according to your audience.

EXAMPLE: Choosing Topic and Purpose to Match Audience

Every Speaking and Listening Handbook feature provides steps you can follow to match your topic and purpose to your audience. See the bulleted list on page 983 for tips in choosing a personal narrative that will appeal to your audience.

8.2.b Choose vocabulary and tone appropriate to the audience, topic, and purpose.

Would you describe the day's events to a friend the same way you would tell them to an older family member? The words you use will differ according to audience, topic, and purpose.

EXAMPLE: Choosing Appropriate Vocabulary and Tone

The chart "Narrative and Descriptive Strategies" on page 984 of the Speaking and Listening Handbook offers a number of techniques you can use to find just the right words.

8.2.c Use appropriate verbal and nonverbal presentation skills.

What you do not say, but show, is just as important as what you do say. Facial expressions, gestures, and the tone and pitch of your voice are all important.

EXAMPLE: Using Verbal and Nonverbal Skills

Each section of the Speaking and Listening Handbook emphasizes keeping eye contact. Why? See the discussion of audience's nonverbal cues on page 985.

8.2.d Respond to audience questions and comments.

Often when speaking in public, you will need to interact with your audience, answering their questions as best you can and responding politely to their comments.

EXAMPLE: Interacting with an Audience

The "Questions for Evaluating an Informative Speech" chart on page 991 suggests that an audience member ask questions to seek clarification from a speaker. Be prepared to support or rephrase any point you make.

8.2.e Use grammatically correct language.

Using grammatically correct language when speaking is just as important as when writing. Do not make your audience have to guess at your meaning.

EXAMPLE: Using Grammatically Correct Language When Speaking

If you have any grammar questions while you are preparing a speech, refer to the Language Handbook on pages 891–974.

8.2.f Critique oral presentations.

When critiquing anything, you first need to develop standards by which to judge it. You can use your standards for critiquing oral presentations to strengthen your own public speaking.

EXAMPLE: Critiquing Oral Presentations

You can use the bulleted list of items in the "Questions for Evaluating an Informative Speech" chart on page 991 to evaluate any oral presentation.

8.3 The student will analyze mass media messages.

8.3.a Evaluate the persuasive technique being used.

Speakers use persuasive techniques to achieve their goal of convincing you of their viewpoint. Be aware of these techniques so that you can become a critical listener and viewer.

EXAMPLE: Evaluating Persuasive Techniques

"Evaluating Persuasive Images in the Media" (pages 996–999 in the Media Handbook) offers a discussion of bias and point of view you can use to identify persuasive techniques in non-print sources.

8.3.b Describe the possible cause-effect relationships between mass media coverage and public opinion trends.

It is almost impossible to have a totally objective or neutral attitude in reporting events. Learn to determine how the media shapes public opinion on events and issues.

EXAMPLE: Identifying Cause-Effect Relationships in Media Messages

On pages 996–999 of the Media Handbook, the "Evaluating Persuasive Images in the Media" section asks you to consider the possible effects of every aspect of a media image or message. Refer to the section for discussion of specific techniques and tips for evaluation.

8.3.c Evaluate sources, including advertisements, editorials, and feature stories, for relationships between intent and factual content.

Does the message have an underlying bias or persuasive purpose? If so, you need to be very careful to analyze the facts in the message.

EXAMPLE: Evaluating Sources for Persuasive Purpose or Bias

Use the "Questions for Evaluating Media Images" chart on page 999 to evaluate any source for bias and persuasive techniques. The chart encourages the critical viewer to analyze content, color, light and shadow, point of view, and medium.

READING

8.4 The student will apply knowledge of word origins, derivations, inflections, analogies, and figurative language to extend vocabulary development.

8.4.a Identify simile, metaphor, personification, hyperbole, and analogy.

These are all types of figurative, or nonliteral, language used especially in description.

EXAMPLE: Recognizing Figurative Language

"Explaining Figures of Speech" on page 557 discusses similes, metaphors, and analogies. "Elements of Style: Literary Devices" on pages 530–532 discusses figures of speech.

8.4.b Use context, structure, and connotations to determine meaning of words and phrases.

Context, or the words and sentences surrounding an unfamiliar word, can help you determine the meaning of a word. A word's parts, or **structure,** can help you define a word. **Denotation** is a word's literal meaning. **Connotation** is the implied meaning of a word.

EXAMPLE: Determining Word Meanings

See the Vocabulary Development feature "Context Clues" on pages 192 and 264 for discussions of context. See "Word Ratings: Connotations" on page 461 for a discussion of the connotations of words. See "Using Word Parts" (pages 965–966) in the Language Handbook for help using roots, prefixes, and suffixes to determine a word's meaning.

8.5 The student will read and analyze a variety of narrative and poetic forms.

8.5.a Explain the use of symbols and figurative language.

Figurative language, which includes similes, metaphors, imagery, and symbols, encourages a reader to make good use of his or her imagination.

EXAMPLE: Analyzing Figurative Language

The "Elements of Style" essay on pages 530–532 discusses several types of figurative language, such as imagery, similes, metaphors, personification, and symbols, and gives examples of each.

8.5.b Describe inferred main ideas or themes, using evidence from the text as support.

An **inference** is a guess based on clues. Sometimes finding the main idea of a text requires guesswork.

EXAMPLE: Identifying Implied Main Idea or Theme

The essay "Theme" on pages 354–355 explains theme and how to identify the theme of a work by looking at different elements, such as the characters and the big scenes.

8.5.c Describe how authors use characters, conflict, point of view, and tone to create meaning.

Any story or poem contains specific elements you can analyze to explore the meaning of the work. Know which elements you can count on for good direction in finding your way and finding meaning in your reading.

EXAMPLE: Analyzing an Author's Use of Literary Elements

In the Author Study on Ray Bradbury on pages 298–330, you will investigate how the author uses character, conflict, point of view, tone, and other literary elements to create meaning in a number of works. You can get a preview by reading "Key Elements of Bradbury's Stories" on page 298.

8.5.d Compare and contrast the use of the poetic elements of word choice, dialogue, form, rhyme, rhythm, and voice.

Poets rely on sound to create sonic sculptures. Compare and contrast how different poets use sound elements to achieve distinct poetic effects.

EXAMPLE: Identifying Sound Effects in Poetry

Pages 616–618 focus on the sound effects of poetry, including rhythm, rhyme, alliteration, and onomatopoeia. Use these explanations and examples as a guide when you compare and contrast elements used in different poems.

8.5.e Compare and contrast authors' styles.

People have a certain style in the things they do, from the clothes they wear to the ways they speak. Determine an author's style so that you may compare it with that of another author.

EXAMPLE: Compare and Contrast Authors' Styles

In the Comparing Literature features throughout the book, you will compare and contrast works. See the feature on comparing humorous styles on pages 574–596.

8.6 The student will read, comprehend, and analyze a variety of informational sources.

8.6.a Draw on background knowledge and knowledge of text structure to understand selections.

Texts are like games: Each follows a set of rules that help guide the user. Rules in texts control how ideas are grouped and how they are connected.

EXAMPLE: Reading for Comprehension

You will find discussions of text structures on pages 156, 193, 275, and 724. The book also covers several text structures in specific detail, such as comparison and contrast on page 136.

8.6.b Analyze the author's credentials, viewpoint, and impact.

When deciding whether to trust what someone says, you will want to know all you can about that person and his or her claims to authority.

EXAMPLE: Analyzing an Author's Viewpoint

Analyzing an author's viewpoint is important when evaluating a source of information. Pages 979–980 in the Communications Handbook have tips on evaluating authors of Web sources.

8.6.c Analyze the author's use of text structure and word choice.

Writers should organize material so readers can find information easily. Note the organization in informational articles, and watch for loaded words and exaggeration.

EXAMPLE: Analyzing Text Structure

See "Analyzing Text Structures" on page 159. Also, a short exercise that covers exaggeration and loaded words is on page 183.

8.6.d Analyze details for relevance and accuracy.

Are a text's details all related to the main idea? Can you support and verify them?

EXAMPLE: Analyzing Details

Details and facts in informational materials must be accurate, supported, and relevant. See page 561 for practice in analyzing details.

8.6.e Read and follow instructions to complete an assigned task.

Being able to follow instructions is a skill you will use almost every day of your life, whether you are cooking a meal, fixing a car, or operating a computer.

EXAMPLE: Following Directions

Pages 828–834 in Collection 8 give practice in understanding technical directions. The Test Smarts section on pages 847–858 offers directions you can use to perform better on tests.

8.6.f Summarize and critique text.

Put a text into your own words so that you can understand it better and be able to evaluate it more thoroughly.

EXAMPLE: Summarizing

The Reading Focus feature on page 674 gives step-by-step instruction in summarizing an informational text.

8.6.g Evaluate and synthesize information to apply in written and oral presentations.

Synthesize means "to combine." Combine and organize information to evaluate it, and then share it through written or oral presentations.

EXAMPLE: Synthesizing and Evaluating

On pages 809–817, you will read several consumer, public, and workplace documents. After synthesizing and evaluating that information, you will use it to solve two different problems, sharing your suggestions for solving one problem through a letter.

8.6.h Draw conclusions based on explicit and implied information.

A text states some things directly, but you can often draw conclusions on what the text suggests.

EXAMPLE: Drawing Conclusions

Turn to page 294 for a discussion of strategies for drawing conclusions. See also "Conclusion" on page 877 in the Handbook of Reading and Informational Terms.

8.6.i Make inferences based on explicit and implied information.

An **inference** is an educated guess, a guess based on clues. Inferences should always be supported, or based on information.

EXAMPLE: Making Inferences

Pages 880–881 discuss supported and unsupported inferences. Page 296 contains a Test Practice feature that offers you the opportunity to make inferences.

WRITING

8.7 The student will write in a variety of forms, including narrative, expository, persuasive, and informational.

8.7.a Use prewriting strategies to generate and organize ideas.

Prewriting is that stage in which you brainstorm ideas, gather information, and organize your thoughts and notes to help you write your first draft.

EXAMPLE: Prewriting

Every Writing Workshop helps you generate and organize ideas. The workshop on pages 116–121, "Personal Narrative," suggests you explain the meaning of your experience in a sentence or two and refer to it often to stay on track as you draft.

8.7.b Organize details to elaborate the central idea.

Support your main ideas clearly and effectively by using logical, easy-to-follow organization to add details.

EXAMPLE: Organizing Details

The Writing Workshop on pages 516–521 suggests using a Venn diagram to chart similarities and differences. Then, it describes two effective ways to organize details in a comparison-contrast essay.

8.7.c Select specific vocabulary and information.

Vague ideas are dull and unconvincing. Choose your words thoughtfully, and check the facts you use carefully.

EXAMPLE: Selecting Specific Vocabulary

"Strategies for Elaboration" on page 119 of the Writing Workshop "Personal Narrative" will help you choose precise words and use figures of speech.

8.7.d Revise writing for word choice, sentence variety, and transitions among paragraphs.

No writer expects a first draft to be perfect. Revise your work to make it as clear and interesting as possible.

EXAMPLE: Revising Writing

Each of the Writing Workshops asks evaluation questions and gives tips and techniques for revision. See page 520 for a chart to help you revise a comparison-contrast essay. A Revision Model is shown on page 521.

8.7.e Use available technology.

The earliest writers used sticks, stones, and the walls of caves to write. Use the tools you have to help research, draft, and publish.

EXAMPLE: Using Technology When Writing

Turn to the Communications Handbook, pages 977–982, for suggestions on using technological tools to aid your research.

Standards of Learning

8.8 The student will edit writing for correct grammar, capitalization, punctuation, spelling, sentence structure, and paragraphing.

8.8.a Use a variety of graphic organizers, including sentence diagrams, to analyze and improve sentence formation and paragraph structure.

Well-structured sentences and paragraphs help to get your meaning across clearly.

EXAMPLE: Improving Structure

You will find graphic organizers useful in organizing and revising your ideas. Page 117 shows how to create a chronological chart of events. Page 517 features a Venn diagram that charts the similarities and differences of two subjects.

8.8.b Use and punctuate correctly varied sentence structures to include conjunctions and transition words.

Punctuation marks and transitional words are like traffic signals that tell users where they are, when they should pause, and when they can go.

EXAMPLE: Varying Sentences

Use "Kinds of Sentences" (pages 940–942), "Writing Effective Sentences" (pages 943–946), and "Punctuation" (pages 951–957) in the Language Handbook as a reference when revising your writing to introduce more varied sentence structures.

8.8.c Choose the correct case and number for pronouns in prepositional phrases with compound objects.

Prepositional phrases usually give additional information in a sentence. Make sure that the information is clear and that pronouns, their antecedents, and their objects are correctly structured.

EXAMPLE: Choosing the Correct Case and Number for Pronouns

See in the Language Handbook "Using Pronouns" on pages 916–919, "Agreement of Pronoun and Antecedent" and other pronoun problems on pages 905–907, and "The Prepositional Phrase" on pages 923–925. You might also find helpful the Grammar Link "Pronoun Reference" on page 293.

8.8.d Maintain consistent verb tense across paragraphs.

Verb tense tells the reader when the events the writer is describing took place. Keep a consistency in tense as you write so that you will not lose your reader.

EXAMPLE: Editing for Consistent Tense

See page 913 for a discussion of consistent verb tense. You will find there examples of consistent and inconsistent tense and a Quick Check to assess your understanding.

8.8.e Use comparative and superlative degrees in adverbs and adjectives.

Use the comparative degree when comparing two things; use the superlative degree when comparing more than two.

EXAMPLE: Using Comparative and Superlative Forms of Modifiers

Consult pages 920–922 of the Language Handbook for instruction and practice in using comparative and superlative forms of adjectives and adverbs.

Taking Virginia's Tests in Reading and Writing

You have probably been taking **standardized tests** throughout your school career. Later this year, you will take **Virginia's tests in reading and writing.** These tests measure how well you have mastered the skills and knowledge described in Virginia's **English Standards of Learning.**

The **Reading/Literature and Research** test contains a variety of reading passages followed by multiple-choice questions. Some of the questions test your grasp of the passage's content, purpose, and vocabulary. Other questions test your research skills.

The **Writing** test has two parts. The first part contains writing samples followed by multiple-choice questions. These questions test your understanding of good writing, including the writing process and correct grammar, usage, and mechanics. The second part of the test requires you to write an essay in response to a writing prompt.

Taking the Reading/Literature and Research Test

Here are some tips that can help you do well on standardized tests in reading. These tips are followed by sample passages and multiple-choice questions like those you will see on Virginia's reading test.

TIP 1   **Look ahead.** Quickly look over the reading passages and the questions. On this test you will find both literary and informational passages.

TIP 2   **This test is not timed.** You may take all the time you need to do your best.

TIP 3 **Read everything carefully.** Stay focused and alert as you read; do not skip anything. Pay careful attention to the directions, the reading passages, and each entire question.

TIP 4 **Make educated guesses.** Do not choose your answer until you have studied all of the answer choices. Eliminate the choices that you know to be wrong. Then, if you are still unsure of the answer, make an educated guess from the remaining choices. If you simply cannot answer a question, skip it and return to it later.

TIP 5 **Mark your answer carefully.** Be careful not to lose your place on the answer document. Match your answer carefully to each question's number.

TIP 6 **Review your work.** Check your work, and answer any questions that you skipped. Your score is based on the total number of correct responses, so try to answer every question. Erase any stray marks.

A PRACTICE TEST

The practice test that follows contains several reading passages. Following each passage are questions like those you will see on Virginia's reading test. On an actual exam, the number, length, and types of passages may differ from those on this practice test, as may the number of questions for each passage.

Directions: Read the passage and answer the questions that follow.

from The Open Window
Saki

1 "My aunt will be down presently, Mr. Nuttel," said a very self-possessed young lady of fifteen; "in the meantime you must try and put up with me."

2 Framton Nuttel endeavored to say the correct something which should duly flatter the niece of the moment without unduly discounting the aunt that

was to come. Privately he doubted more than ever whether these formal visits on a succession of total strangers would do much toward helping the nerve cure which he was supposed to be undergoing.

3   "I know how it will be," his sister had said when he was preparing to migrate to this rural retreat; "you will bury yourself down there and not speak to a living soul, and your nerves will be worse than ever from moping. I shall just give you letters of introduction to all the people I know there. Some of them, as far as I can remember, were quite nice."

4   Framton wondered whether Mrs. Sappleton, the lady to whom he was presenting one of the letters of introduction, came into the nice division.

5   "Do you know many of the people round here?" asked the niece, when she judged that they had had sufficient silent communion.

6   "Hardly a soul," said Framton. "My sister was staying here, at the rectory, you know, some four years ago, and she gave me letters of introduction to some of the people here."

7   He made the last statement in a tone of distinct regret.

8   "Then you know practically nothing about my aunt?" pursued the self-possessed young lady.

9   "Only her name and address," admitted the caller. He was wondering whether Mrs. Sappleton was in the married or widowed state. An undefinable something about the room seemed to suggest masculine habitation.

10   "Her great tragedy happened just three years ago," said the child; "that would be since your sister's time."

11   "Her tragedy?" asked Framton; somehow, in this restful country spot, tragedies seemed out of place.

12   "You may wonder why we keep that window wide open on an October afternoon," said the niece, indicating a large French window that opened onto a lawn.

13   "It is quite warm for the time of the year," said Framton, "but has that window got anything to do with the tragedy?"

14   "Out through that window, three years ago to a day, her husband and her two young brothers went off for their day's shooting. They never came back.

In crossing the moor to their favorite snipe-shooting ground, they were all three engulfed in a treacherous piece of <u>bog</u>. It had been that dreadful wet summer, you know, and places that were safe in other years gave way suddenly without warning. Their bodies were never recovered. That was the dreadful part of it." Here the child's voice lost its self-possessed note and became falteringly human. "Poor aunt always thinks that they will come back someday, they and the little brown spaniel that was lost with them, and walk in at that window just as they used to do. That is why the window is kept open every evening till it is quite dusk. Poor dear aunt, she has often told me how they went out, her husband with his white waterproof coat over his arm, and Ronnie, her youngest brother, singing 'Bertie, why do you bound?' as he always did to tease her, because she said it got on her nerves. Do you know, sometimes on still, quiet evenings like this, I almost get a creepy feeling that they will all walk in through that window——"

15   She broke off with a little shudder. It was a relief to Framton when the aunt bustled into the room with a whirl of apologies for being late in making her appearance. . . .

1 What adjective does the author use to describe the niece?

A Friendly
B Imaginative
C Self-possessed
D Intelligent

EXPLANATION: Skim the passage for the answer. The niece is obviously friendly (A), imaginative (B), and intelligent (D), but the author does not use those words. The correct answer, C, is in paragraphs 1 and 8.

2 Which of the following adjectives does *not* describe Framton Nuttel?

F Nervous
G Humorous
H Curious
J Worried

EXPLANATION: Watch for words like *not* and *except.* The only choice that does *not* apply to Framton Nuttel is G, which is the correct answer.

3 **The main purpose of the flashback in paragraph 3 is to—**
   A introduce an important character
   B introduce a universal theme—loneliness
   C explain an important mystery
   D explain the reason for Framton Nuttel's visit

EXPLANATION: Take a look at paragraph 3. You can eliminate A and C; the sister does not seem important, and there is no mention of a mystery. Although the flashback does touch on the loneliness of Framton Nuttel's isolation (B), the best answer is D.

4 **What is the "great tragedy" referred to in the story?**
   F One man's extreme loneliness
   G The disappearance of three men on a hunting trip
   H The death of a man who jumped through an open window
   J A young woman who catches pneumonia

EXPLANATION: You can eliminate F. Although Framton Nuttel can be described as lonely, his loneliness is not the tragedy. You can also rule out H and J, since they are not part of the story. In paragraph 14, the young woman explains the tragedy. The correct answer is G.

5 **From context clues in paragraph 14, you can conclude that a bog is probably a—**
   A swamp
   B lake
   C deep pit
   D cliff

EXPLANATION: From the context, you can tell that a bog has to do with unusually wet ground. Therefore, you can eliminate C and D. Since the characters were walking on the bog, B is also wrong. The correct answer is A.

6 **The third-person-limited point of view allows the reader to learn the thoughts and feelings of—**
   F the fifteen-year-old niece
   G Mrs. Sappleton
   H Framton Nuttel
   J all of the characters

EXPLANATION: By skimming the passage, you will see that the author reveals the thoughts and feelings of only one character, Framton Nuttel. The correct answer is H.

Directions: Read the poem. Then, choose the best answer to each question that follows the passage.

Desert Places
Robert Frost

1 Snow falling and night falling fast,
     oh, fast
   In a field I looked into going past,
   And the ground almost covered smooth
     in snow,
   But a few weeds and stubble showing
     last.

5 The woods around it have it—it is
     theirs.
   All animals are smothered in their lairs.
   I am too absent-spirited to count;
   The loneliness includes me unawares.

   And lonely as it is, that loneliness
10 Will be more lonely ere it will be less—
   A blanker whiteness of benighted snow
   With no expression, nothing to express.

   They cannot scare me with
     their empty spaces
   Between stars—on stars where
     no human race is.
15 I have it in me so much nearer home
   To scare myself with my own
     desert places.

"Desert Places" from *The Poems of Robert Frost*, edited by Edward Connery Lathem. Copyright © 1964 by Lesley Frost Ballantine. Reproduced by permission of **Henry Holt and Company, LLC.**

7 Which of the following *best* describes the first two stanzas of the poem?
A A man watches snow fall on a field.
B A man contemplates the meaning of the stars.
C A man observes animals hibernating.
D A man considers how the desert has changed.

EXPLANATION: Review the stanzas. The correct answer is A.

8 What is each stanza's rhyme pattern?
F *aabb*
G *abab*
H *aaba*
J *aabc*

EXPLANATION: Remember that repeated end rhymes are designated by the same letter and that nonrhyming lines are given a new letter. The correct answer is H.

9 The central feeling of this poem is—
A anger
B loneliness
C joy
D frustration

EXPLANATION: Read the poem again, trying to get an overall impression. The speaker does not express anger (A), joy (C), or frustration (D). The correct answer is B.

Directions: Read the letter to the editor and answer the questions that follow.

Dear Editor:

1   The paper we use is made from trees. To this, some might say, "So what? Paper must be cheap since it grows on trees." True, paper is inexpensive. However, the environmental cost of making new paper is quite high. I strongly believe our school should start a paper-recycling program.

2   One reason to start such a program is to conserve trees. Scientists estimate that in prehistoric times forests covered about 60 percent of the earth's land surface. Now, they cover only about 30 percent. Paper-recycling programs can help conserve remaining forests—forests filled with vital oxygen-producing trees. For every ton of paper made from recycled material, seventeen trees are saved. We use about six tons of paper each year at our school. So, if we recycle that paper, we can save more than one hundred trees.

3   Second, recycling paper is easy and inexpensive. Last year, North Lake Middle School started a successful recycling program. Each classroom has a box for white paper. All students have to do is throw white paper into the box; other trash goes into the regular trash can. Then, every Friday, students empty the white-paper boxes into the school's fifteen trash containers. These containers, which are just trash cans marked "white paper only," cost the school about $150. At the end of the week, the city collects the recycled paper at no charge.

4   Finally, a paper-recycling program would show that we are responsible and thoughtful. A recent survey in the school newspaper revealed that 58 percent of adults see teenagers as people who are mostly interested in dating and shopping. However, we are also interested in serious issues, and we know that what we do now affects the world we will live in tomorrow.

5   A schoolwide paper-recycling program is easy and inexpensive. It will not only make a difference but will also show that we care about the future of our planet. Let's get this program underway now.

Sincerely,
Lisa Wellington

10 **The writer supports her opinion with all of the following except—**
F a quotation from an expert
G statistics
H a specific example
J facts

EXPLANATION: Check the letter to find the kind of support that is *not* used. You will find statistics and facts, so G and J are incorrect. You can also eliminate H, since North Lake Middle School's paper-recycling program is a specific example. The correct answer is F.

11 **Where should the writer add the following sentence? "According to Marjorie Lamb, author of *2 Minutes a Day for a Greener Planet*, saving paper is one of the 'easiest and most beneficial contributions we can make to our environment.'"**
A At the beginning of paragraph 1
B Before the second sentence in paragraph 2
C After the first sentence in paragraph 3
D At the end of paragraph 4

EXPLANATION: Re-read the paragraphs, inserting the sentence where indicated in each choice. The most natural place to include the quotation is in paragraph 3, where the writer discusses how easy recycling can be. The best answer is C.

12 **The word prehistoric in paragraph 2 means—**
F after the nineteenth century
G during the time of the Roman Empire
H before the time of recorded history
J near the time of World War II

EXPLANATION: The key to this question is knowing that the Latin prefix *pre–* means "before." The word *prehistoric* literally means "before history." The correct answer is H.

13 **Where might you look to find the latest statistics on the amount of the earth's surface that is covered by forests?**
A The book *Vanishing Forests*, by Helen J. Challand, © 1991
B The book *Introduction to Forest Science,* by Raymond Allen Young, © 1990
C The Web site of the U.S. Department of Agriculture Forest Service
D The Web site of a Christmas tree company

EXPLANATION: When you are doing research, check the authors and copyright dates of possible sources. You can eliminate A and B, since the dates reveal that the statistics would not be current enough. You can also rule out D, since a Christmas tree company Web site, although probably current, would probably not address ecological issues. The best answer is C.

Standards of Learning

Directions: Read the passage. Then, answer the questions that follow.

Using a Floor Pump with a Built-in Gauge

The floor pump with a built-in gauge is a handy tool designed to inflate to the correct pressure bicycle tires, basketballs, soccer balls, or anything else that can be inflated with a human-powered pump (see figure below). The following steps explain the operation of the floor pump with a built-in gauge to inflate a bicycle tire.

1 **Remove the dust cap from your tire valve.** Tires are inflated through valves.

2 **Place the pump head onto the tire valve, and lift the pump head lever to the locked position.** Secure locking is important for efficient pumping. If you hear air releasing around the valve rather than through the valve as you pump, unlock the lever and try again.

3 **Check the sidewall of your tire to find the recommended tire pressure.** This number or range of numbers will be indicated in psi (pounds per square inch). Generally, narrower tires call for higher pressures than wider tires.

4 Now you are ready to inflate the tire. **First, place your feet on the pump's footrest and grasp the pump's T-handle with both hands. Next, pull the handle up as far as it will go to fill the pump with air. Finally, push the handle down to force air into the tire.**

5 **Watch the gauge, and pump the tire to the desired pressure.** Pumping will get more difficult as you reach the recommended psi. *Caution:* Do not pump more air into your tire than is indicated on the sidewall. An overinflated tire provides a rougher ride, has less traction, and is more prone to blowouts and damage.

6 **Move the pump head lever to the unlocked position, and quickly remove the pump head from the tire valve.** The more quickly you move, the less air you will lose from your tire.

7 **Place the dust cap on the tire valve.**

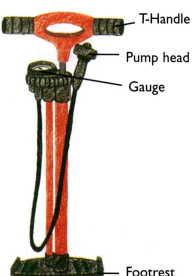

T-Handle

Pump head

Gauge

Footrest

Floor pump

VA22 Taking Virginia's Tests in Reading and Writing

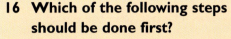
14 **Like most how-to articles, the information in this passage is organized in—**

   F chronological order

   G spatial order

   H comparison-contrast order

   J cause-effect order

EXPLANATION: To answer this question correctly, you need to know that *chronological order* means "time order," or the order in which events occur. The correct answer is F.

15 **Some sentences are written in boldface type because they indicate—**

   A important cautions about tire inflation

   B how to read a pressure gauge

   C the basic steps for tire inflation

   D directions on caring for a floor pump

EXPLANATION: This question asks you to understand the devices that writers use to help readers understand the text. The correct answer is C.

16 **Which of the following steps should be done first?**

   F Push the handle down to force air into the tire.

   G Place your feet on the pump's footrest.

   H Grasp the T-handle with both hands.

   J Pull the handle up as far as it will go.

EXPLANATION: Return to the passage, looking for the step that comes first. The correct answer is G.

17 **You need to know the psi so that—**

   A you can attach the pump to the tire

   B you can remove the pump head from the tire valve

   C you can pump air into the tire more easily

   D you do not pump too much air into the tire

EXPLANATION: Return to the passage. Information in step 3 (the definition of *psi*) and step 5 (the warning about overinflation) allows you to draw a conclusion about why psi is important: Overinflating a tire causes problems. The correct answer is D.

Directions: Read the passage. Then, answer the questions that follow.

A Strange, Funny-Looking Vegetable
by Milton Meltzer

1 One day in the 1530s a scouting party of Spaniards entered an Inca village, high in the Andes in what we now call Peru. Reports of cruel and greedy white invaders had already spread throughout the mountains, and the villagers had fled at word of their coming. The Spaniards went from empty house to empty house, hunting for loot. They found only maize (corn), beans, and a strange vegetable that was like nothing they had ever seen.

2 The vegetable came in many sizes, tiny as a nut to big as an apple. Its shape ranged from an irregular ball to a twisted oblong. Its skin was white, yellow, blue, purple, red, brown. Inside, its color could be white, yellow, purple, pink. The Spaniards were not impressed. They had come to the Andes searching for gold, silver, and precious stones. What good was this funny-looking vegetable?

3 Gradually they found out. First of all, it was the staple food of these mountain people. Secondly, the vegetable was believed to have healing powers. Raw slices were fixed to broken bones, pressed against the head to cure aching, eaten with other food to end a bellyache. The Incas also rubbed it on their bodies to cure skin diseases and carried slices to prevent rheumatism.

4 The Inca name for the vegetable was *papa*. It means a tuber, a short, fleshy underground stem or root. . . . When the Spaniards tasted the potato, they found it delicious—"a dainty dish even for Spaniards," one conquistador admitted.

5 The diet of the common people of Peru was mainly vegetarian. . . . The main diet was maize and other vegetables in the lowlands. In the highlands, where maize would not grow, it was the potato above all that people depended on. We now know that the native peoples living along the western coast of South America were growing and eating potatoes two thousand years before Columbus set sail. . . .

6 When the Spaniards discovered the rich silver mines of Potosí (now in Bolivia) in 1545, they were quick to see the use of the potato, fresh or freeze dried, as food for the Inca they forced to work for them. It didn't take long for

speculators in Spain to see a new way to get rich. They sailed across the Atlantic, bought up potatoes cheaply from the Inca farmers, and sold them at high prices to the native workers in the mines.

7   Here is a strange twist of history: The annual $100-billion value of the potato crop is three times greater than the value of all the gold and silver the Spanish lugged away from the Americas. The potatoes they took so lightly turned out to be worth far more than the gold and silver they killed for.

From *The Amazing Potato: A Story in Which the Incas, Conquistadors, Marie Antoinette, Thomas Jefferson, Wars, Famines, Immigrants, and French Fries All Play a Part* by Milton Meltzer. Copyright © 1992 by Milton Meltzer. Reproduced by permission of **Harold Ober Associates, Incorporated.**

18   What did the Spaniards hope to find in the Andes?
    F A lost civilization
    G Cheap labor for European factories
    H Gold, silver, and precious stones
    J Food for their starving soldiers

EXPLANATION: If you do not remember the answer, skim the passage to look for key words. The correct answer, H, is stated in paragraph 2.

19   The writer's attitude toward the Spanish conquistadors is—
    A sympathetic
    B critical
    C approving
    D admiring

EXPLANATION: The attitude is not directly stated; you have to infer it. Notice the words the writer uses to describe the Spanish conquistadors (*cruel, greedy*). The correct answer is B.

20   What is the main question that paragraph 7 answers?
    F Why is the potato a strange vegetable?
    G What is ironic about the conquistadors' discovery of the potato?
    H Why did the Spanish value the potato?
    J Why do we still eat potatoes?

EXPLANATION: F and J are not addressed in paragraph 7. You can also eliminate H, although it is addressed earlier in the passage. Even if you do not know the word *ironic* (which here means "the opposite from what is expected"), you can conclude that the correct answer is G.

Taking the Writing Test

For Virginia's writing test, you will answer multiple-choice questions and write an essay in response to a prompt. The multiple-choice questions measure what you know about writing; the essay measures how well you can apply what you know to your own work.

On the following pages, you will find sample multiple-choice questions, a sample writing prompt, and a sample essay.

Sports
Caroline's teacher has assigned a short essay about sports.

---

1 The first step Caroline should take is to—
A write a rough draft
B narrow down the topic to something more specific
C interview local sports celebrities
D research the history of sports

EXPLANATION: Sports is a broad topic. Therefore, Caroline should begin by narrowing down the topic to something more specific, such as a particular kind of sport. The correct answer is B.

Here is the first part of Caroline's rough draft of an essay about soccer. Use this rough draft to answer the questions that follow.

(1) Anyone can tell you that baseball, football, and basketball are popular sports in the United States. (2) My favorite sport is tennis. (3) However, soccer is the world's most popular sport. (4) It is played in almost every country.

(5) Historians say that games like soccer have been played for over two thousand years. (6) A professional soccer team has eleven players. (7) Only goalkeepers can use their arms or hands; the rest of the play-ers hit the ball with their feet, head, or other body parts. (8) Soccer has been an Olympic event since 1900, but the game goes back a very long way. (9) As in hockey, a point is scored when the ball enters the goal of the opposing team.

2 How can Caroline *best* combine sentences 3 and 4 without changing their meaning?

F However, soccer is the world's most popular sport, it is played in almost every country.

G However, soccer, which is played in almost every country, is the world's most popular sport.

H However, soccer is the world's most popular sport, although it is played in almost every country.

J However, soccer is the world's most popular sport and it is played in almost every country.

EXPLANATION: F, H, and J do not show how the ideas relate. Additionally, F and J contain comma errors. The correct answer is G.

3 Which transition fits *best* at the beginning of sentence 6?

A However,
B Therefore,
C As a result,
D Today,

EXPLANATION: Try out each transition. Only one makes sense in the context, tying together the ideas in sentences 5 and 6. The correct answer is D.

4 Sentence 8 is out of place. Where should it go?

F Before sentence 5
G After sentence 5
H After sentence 6
J After sentence 9

EXPLANATION: Try out sentence 8 in each of the suggested places. Because of the clause "but the game goes back a very long way," sentence 8 fits in only one place. The correct answer is F.

5 Which sentence should Caroline delete because it destroys the paragraph's unity?

A 2
B 3
C 4
D 7

EXPLANATION: Re-read the paragraphs. Then, check each answer choice. Although sentence 2 in the first paragraph is about sports, it does not fit in with the other sentences in the paragraph. The correct answer is A.

Read the next section of Caroline's rough draft. Then, answer the questions that follow. This section has groups of underlined words. The questions ask about these groups of underlined words.

(10) Women's soccer has had a much <u>harder time then men's</u> soccer. (11) In the 1920s, an English soccer organization actually prohibited women from playing, saying that soccer was "unsuitable for females." (12) Later, Holland and Germany also banned women from playing soccer. (13) <u>Since the 1970s however women have been</u> playing soccer in many countries.

(14) <u>Me and my cousin Rachel</u> have been playing soccer since the second grade. (15) Most of the girls in our school feel strongly that soccer is great. (16) It provides good exercise, develops team spirit, and makes us <u>feel really good about ourselves.</u>

6 In sentence 10, how is <u>harder time then men's</u> correctly written?

F more harder time then men's

G harder time then mens'

H harder time than men's

J As it is

EXPLANATION: In sentence 10, the only error is the incorrect use of *then* for *than*. The correct answer is H.

7 In sentence 13, how is <u>Since the 1970s however women have been</u> correctly written?

A Since the 1970s, however, women have been

B Since the1970s however women has been

C Since the 1970s, however women have been

D As it is

EXPLANATION: The error in this sentence involves the transition *however*, which should be set off by commas. The correct answer is A.

8 In sentence 14, how is <u>Me and my cousin Rachel</u> correctly written?

F My cousin Rachel and me

G My cousin Rachel and I

H I, my cousin, and Rachel

J As it is

EXPLANATION: The pronoun *me* should be *I*, since it is part of the subject of the sentence. Therefore, F and J are wrong. H is also wrong because as H is punctuated, *my cousin* and *Rachel* are two different persons. The correct answer is G.

9 In sentence 16, how is <u>feel really good about ourselves</u> correctly written?

A feel real good about ourselves

B feel really well about ourselves

C feel real well about ourselves

D As it is

EXPLANATION: Do not confuse the adverb *really* with the adjective *real*; also, do not use the adverb *well* when you should use the adjective *good*. The correct answer is D.

STEPS FOR WRITING AN ESSAY

The following steps will guide you through writing an essay from beginning to end.

STEP 1 **Analyze the prompt.** First, look for key verbs (such as *analyze, summarize, discuss, explain*) that define your writing task. Then, identify your purpose and audience. Be sure to cover the *entire* writing task; otherwise, you will lose points.

STEP 2 **Plan what you will say.** Brainstorm ideas. Use a cluster diagram or other graphic organizer to help you list and arrange main ideas and supporting details.

STEP 3 **Write your essay,** expressing your ideas as clearly as you can. Be sure to use plenty of descriptive details to support your main points. Also, include a strong opening paragraph and a definite closing.

STEP 4 **Edit and revise your essay.** Allow plenty of time to re-read your essay. Look for places where you can add transitions or combine sentences to make your sentences flow more smoothly. Strengthen your essay by inserting additional supporting details and by moving sentences or paragraphs to a more logical place.

STEP 5 **Proofread your essay.** Find and correct errors in grammar, usage, and mechanics.

A SAMPLE WRITING PROMPT

> Older generations have much to teach. They have experienced many of the situations that await you as you grow older. Write an essay about the life experiences of an older person you know.

CHECKLIST FOR WRITERS
(from the Virginia Standards of Learning Assessment)

____ I planned my paper before writing it.
____ I revised my paper to be sure that
    ____ the introduction captures the reader's attention;
    ____ the central idea is supported with specific information and examples that will be interesting to the reader;
    ____ the content relates to my central idea;
    ____ ideas are organized in a logical manner;
    ____ my sentences are varied in length;
    ____ my sentences are varied in the way that they begin; and
    ____ the conclusion brings my ideas together.
____ I edited my paper to be sure that
    ____ correct grammar is used;
    ____ words are capitalized when appropriate;
    ____ sentences are punctuated correctly;
    ____ words are spelled correctly; and
    ____ paragraphs are clearly indicated.
____ I checked my paper.

SAMPLE RESPONSE

Here is one writer's response to the sample prompt. It would likely receive a high score, according to Virginia's rubric.

This writer chose to write about her grandmother.

My Grandmother

Last year, I created a family tree for a history assignment. The tree showed four generations of relatives as well as their birthdays and where they were born. My dad had helped me gather some of the names and dates. However, even with his help, the tree looked a little bare. So, one day, I went to the one person who could help: my grandmother. She had all the information I needed—and more. I learned a lot about my family that day. Most of all, though, I learned what amazing experiences my grandmother has had.

The writer introduces the focus of her essay.

My grandmother went through some tough times when she was a young girl. She was born into a Jewish family in Hungary and, because of the Nazis, had to go into hiding during World War II. She and her family stayed with a farmer who hid them outside the city. My grandmother said she lived in constant fear that they would be caught. But she was strong, and they made it through. Once the war was over, they were finally able to go home.

The writer discusses a significant event in her grandmother's life.

Later, my grandmother and her family moved to a nice house in Budapest. For a while, they were safe and happy. Later, though, everything changed when the Russians invaded the country. People were not allowed to leave freely, so they had to escape. My grandmother said that on the night they left for Vienna, all they took was a change of clothes. The escape was very dangerous. As my grandmother and her family were walking across the border, there was gunfire all around them. Again, they made it through.

The writer discusses a second significant event.

When my grandmother was fourteen, she moved here. Moving here was hard for her because she had to leave her home and all of her friends again. She had gotten through difficult times before, though. In America, she worked hard in school and eventually went to college, where she met my grandfather. After they got married,

The writer discusses more significant events and continues to emphasize her grandmother's character.

she had a family of her own, two girls and two boys. Even with so much to do in helping to raise a family, she still somehow made the time to go to law school and then later to run her own law firm.

The writer concludes by restating the focus of the essay.

Today, my grandmother is still going strong. She is a great example. When she tells me stories about her life, I feel inspired. She went through such tough times to get to where she is now.

HOW THE WRITING TEST IS SCORED

Your essay will be scored in the three categories (domains) below. The lowest score is 1; the highest is 4. The bullet points, which are based on Virginia's scoring rubrics, describe an essay that would receive a 4 in each domain.

Domain 1: Composing

- The paper has a focused central idea.
- The paper fully elaborates the central idea with appropriate details.
- All ideas are well organized and logically connected.
- The paper has unity, with all parts contributing to the central idea.
- All ideas are logically connected.
- The paper has a strong beginning and ending.
- The point of view is consistent.

Domain 2: Written Expression (Style)

- The vocabulary is vivid and precise.
- The information is accurate and balanced.
- The writer's voice is strong.
- The tone has purpose and is appropriate for the audience.
- Sentences have varied beginnings, lengths, and constructions.

Domain 3: Usage and Mechanics

- Word order is natural and clearly shows the relationship between ideas.
- Each sentence is complete.
- The paper contains no fragments or run-on sentences.
- The verb tense is consistent.
- Usage is correct for subject-verb agreement, pronoun usage, noun and verb forms, and other conventions of standard written English.
- Words are correctly spelled and capitalized.
- Punctuation marks are used correctly.

EDITORIAL
Project Directors: Kathleen Daniel, Mescal Evler
Executive Editor: Juliana Koenig
Senior Book Editor: Leslie Griffin
Senior Product Manager: Don Wulbrecht
Managing Editor: Marie Price
Associate Managing Editor: Elizabeth LaManna
Editorial Staff: Kerry Johnson, Evan Wilson, Sari Wilson
Copyediting Manager: Michael Neibergall
Copyediting Supervisor: Mary Malone
Copyeditors: Christine Altgelt, Elizabeth Dickson, Emily Force, Leora Harris, Anne Heausler, Julia Thomas Hu, Kathleen Scheiner, Nancy Shore
Editorial Support: Christine Degollado, Betty Gabriel, Janet Jenkins, Mark Koenig, Erik Netcher, Gloria Shahan
Editorial Permissions: Mark Koenig, Sally Garland

Index: Tamsin Nutter

ART, DESIGN, AND PRODUCTION
Director: Athena Blackorby
Senior Design Director: Betty Mintz
Designer: Peter Sawchuk
Senior Picture Researcher: Mary Monaco
Picture Research: Susan Sato
Production Coordinator: Dolores Keller

COVER
Photo Credits: (inset) *The Rocket* (1909) by Edward Middleton Manigault. Oil on canvas. Collection of Columbus Museum of Art, Ohio, Museum Purchase, Howard Fund II (1981.009). (Background) Photograph of fireworks, © Brian Stablyk/Getty Images.

HOLT
ELEMENTS OF
LITERATURE

Second Course

HOLT, RINEHART AND WINSTON

A Harcourt Education Company

Orlando • **Austin** • New York • San Diego • Toronto • London

Program Author

Kylene Beers established the reading pedagogy for *Elements of Literature.* A former middle-school teacher, Dr. Beers has turned her commitment to helping readers having difficulty into the major focus of her research, writing, speaking, and teaching. Dr. Beers is currently Senior Reading Researcher at the Child Study Center of the School Development Program at Yale University and was formerly a Research Associate Professor at the University of Houston. Dr. Beers is also currently the editor of the National Council of Teachers of English journal *Voices from the Middle.* She is the author of *When Kids Can't Read: What Teachers Can Do* and the co-editor of *Into Focus: Understanding and Creating Middle School Readers.* Dr. Beers is the 2001 recipient of the Richard Halle Award from the NCTE for outstanding contributions to middle-level literacy education. She has served on the review boards of the *English Journal* and *The Alan Review.* Dr. Beers currently serves on the board of directors of the International Reading Association's Special Interest Group on Adolescent Literature.

Special Contributors

Flo Ota De Lange and **Sheri Henderson** helped plan and organize the program and played key roles in developing and preparing the informational materials. They also wrote Collection 8 Reading for Life and Test Smarts.

Flo Ota De Lange is a former teacher with a thirty-year second career in psychotherapy, during which she studied learning processes in children and adults. These careers have led to her third career, as a writer.

Sheri Henderson brings to the program twenty years of experience as a middle-school research practitioner and full-time reading and language arts teacher at La Paz Intermediate School in Saddleback Valley Unified School District in California. She regularly speaks at statewide and national conferences.

Since 1991, DeLangeHenderson LLC has published forty-three titles designed to integrate the teaching of literature with standards requirements and state and national tests.

Writers

John Malcolm Brinnin, author of six volumes of poetry that have received many prizes and awards, was a member of the American Academy and Institute of Arts and Letters. He was a critic of poetry and a biographer of poets and was for a number of years Director of New York's famous Poetry Center. His teaching career, begun at Vassar College, included long terms at the University of Connecticut and Boston University, where he succeeded Robert Lowell as Professor of Creative Writing and Contemporary Letters. Mr. Brinnin wrote *Dylan Thomas in America: An Intimate Journal* and *Sextet: T. S. Eliot & Truman Capote & Others.*

John Leggett is a novelist, biographer, and teacher. He went to the Writer's Workshop at the University of Iowa in the spring of 1969, expecting to work there for a single semester. In 1970, he assumed temporary charge of the program, and for the next seventeen years he was its director. Mr. Leggett's novels include *Wilder Stone, The Gloucester Branch, Who Took the Gold Away?, Gulliver House,* and *Making Believe.* He is also the author of the highly acclaimed biography *Ross and Tom: Two American Tragedies* and of a biography of William Saroyan, *A Daring Young Man.* Mr. Leggett lives in California's Napa Valley.

Joan Burditt is a writer and editor who has a master's degree in education with a specialization in reading. She taught for several years in Texas, where her experience included work in programs for readers having difficulty. Since then she has developed and written instructional materials for middle-school language arts texts.

Madeline Travers Hovland, who taught middle school for several years, is a writer of educational materials. She studied English at Bates College and received a master's degree in education from Harvard University.

Richard Kelso is a writer and editor whose children's books include *Building a Dream: Mary Bethune's School; Walking for Freedom: The Montgomery Bus Boycott; Days of Courage: The Little Rock Story;* and *The Case of the Amistad Mutiny.*

Mara Rockliff is a writer and editor with a degree in American civilization from Brown University. She has written dramatizations of classic stories for middle-school students, collected in a book called *Stories for Performance.* She has also published feature stories in national newspapers and is currently writing a novel for young adults.

Fannie Safier has worked as a teacher in New York City schools. She has been writing and editing educational materials for more than thirty years.

Program Consultants

READING CONSULTANT
Judith L. Irvin served as a reading consultant for the content-area readers: *The Ancient World; A World in Transition;* and *The United States: Change and Challenge.* Dr. Irvin is a Professor of Education at Florida State University. She writes a column, "What Research Says to the Middle Level Practitioner," for the *Middle School Journal* and serves as the literacy expert for the *Middle Level News*, published by the California League of Middle Schools. Her several books include the companion volumes *Reading and the Middle School Student: Strategies to Enhance Literacy* and *Reading and the High School Student: Strategies to Enhance Literacy* (with Buehl and Klemp).

SENIOR PROGRAM CONSULTANT
Carol Jago is the editor of CATE's quarterly journal, *California English.* She teaches English at Santa Monica High School, in Santa Monica, and directs the California Reading and Literature Project at UCLA. She also writes a weekly education column for the *Los Angeles Times.* She is the author of several books, including two in a series on contemporary writers in the classroom: *Alice Walker in the Classroom* and *Nikki Giovanni in the Classroom.* She is also the author of *With Rigor for All: Teaching the Classics to Contemporary Students* and *Beyond Standards: Excellence in the High School English Classroom.*

CRITICAL REVIEWERS

Dr. Julie M. T. Chan
Director of Literacy
   Instruction
Newport-Mesa Unified
   School District
Costa Mesa, California

Kathy Dubose
Murchison Junior High
   School
Austin, Texas

Pamela Dukes
Boude Storey Middle
   School
Dallas, Texas

Debra Hardick
Bennet Middle School
Manchester,
   Connecticut

Josephine M. Hayes
Costa Mesa High School
Costa Mesa, California

Cheri Howell
Reading Specialist
Covina-Valley Unified
   School District
Covina, California

José M. Ibarra-Tiznado
ELL Program Coordinator
Bassett Unified
   School District
La Puente, California

Stacy Kim
Rowland Unified
   School District
Rowland Heights,
   California

Dr. Ronald Klemp
Instructor
California State
   University, Northridge
Northridge, California

Colette F. McDonald
HB DuPont Middle
   School
Hockessin, Delaware

Jennifer Oehrlein
Tewinkle Middle School
Costa Mesa, California

Jeff Read
Oak Grove Middle
   School
Clearwater, Florida

Constance Ridenour
Ford Middle School
Brook Park, Ohio

Fern M. Sheldon
K–12 Curriculum and
   Instruction Specialist
Rowland Unified School
   District
Rowland Heights,
   California

Karen Simons
Slausen Middle School
Ann Arbor, Michigan

Beverly Sparks
John W. North High
   School
Riverside, California

FIELD-TEST PARTICIPANTS

Karen G. Armstrong
William Dandy
   Middle School
Fort Lauderdale, Florida

Joyce Patterson
Stewart Middle School
Tampa, Florida

Christina Scarpaci
South Hills Middle
   School
Pittsburgh,
   Pennsylvania

Sean Stromberg
South Hills Middle
   School
Pittsburgh,
   Pennsylvania

CONTENTS IN BRIEF

Collection 1

Telling Stories

LITERARY FOCUS
Analyzing Plot

INFORMATIONAL FOCUS
Analyzing Proposition and Support

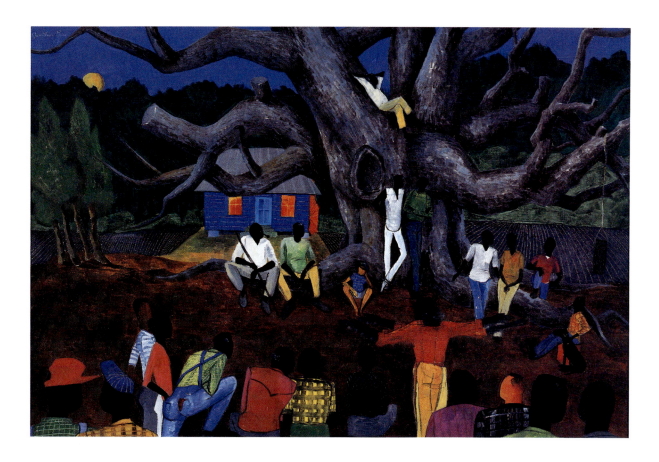

Do the Right Thing

LITERARY FOCUS
Analyzing Character

INFORMATIONAL FOCUS
Comparing and Contrasting Texts

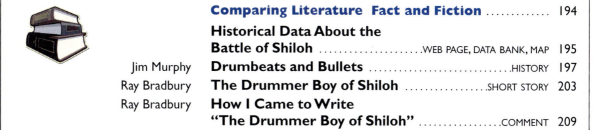

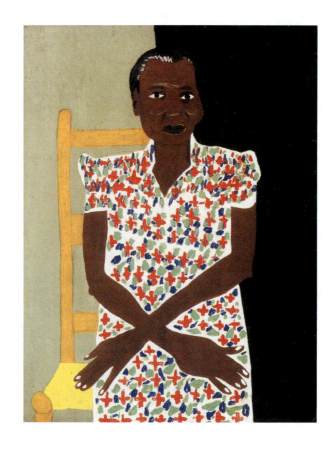

Collection 3

Being There

LITERARY FOCUS
Analyzing Setting and Its Influence on Mood and Tone

INFORMATIONAL FOCUS
Understanding Text Structures

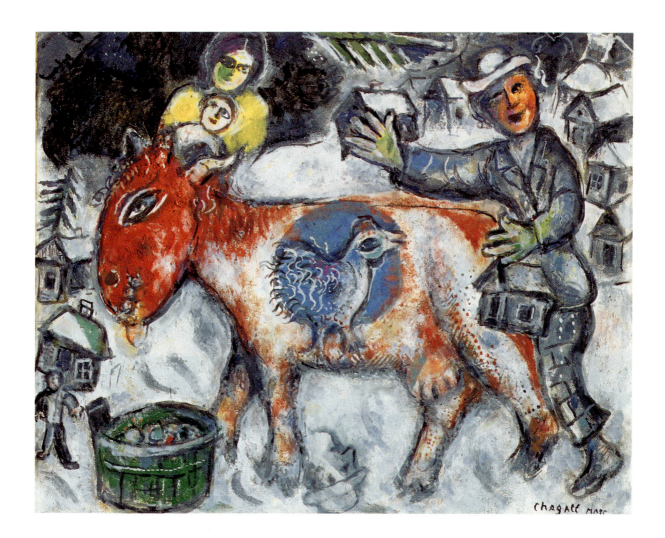

COLLECTION 3: SKILLS REVIEW

Collection 4

The Human Spirit

LITERARY FOCUS
Analyzing Theme
INFORMATIONAL FOCUS
Analyzing Main Idea

Collection 5

A Matter of Style

LITERARY FOCUS
Analyzing Literary Devices and Style

INFORMATIONAL FOCUS
Analyzing Unsupported Inferences
and Fallacious Reasoning

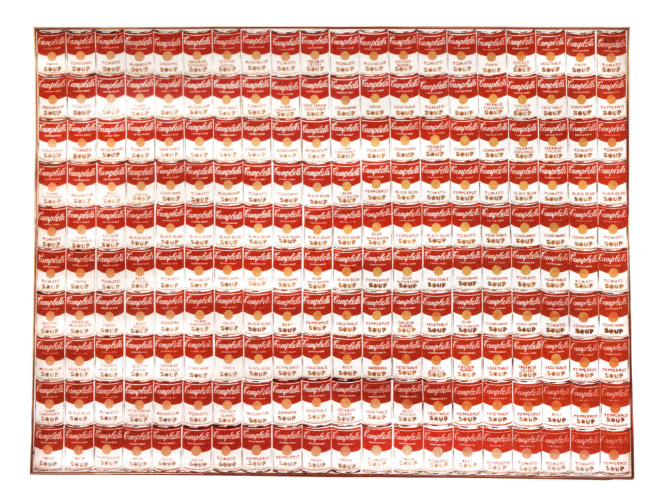

Collection 6

POETRY: SOUND AND SENSE

LITERARY FOCUS
Analyzing Poetry

INFORMATIONAL FOCUS
Analyzing Summaries

Collection 7

LITERARY CRITICISM: A BIOGRAPHICAL APPROACH

LITERARY FOCUS
Interpreting a Literary Work

INFORMATIONAL FOCUS
Analyzing Texts for Logic and Coherence

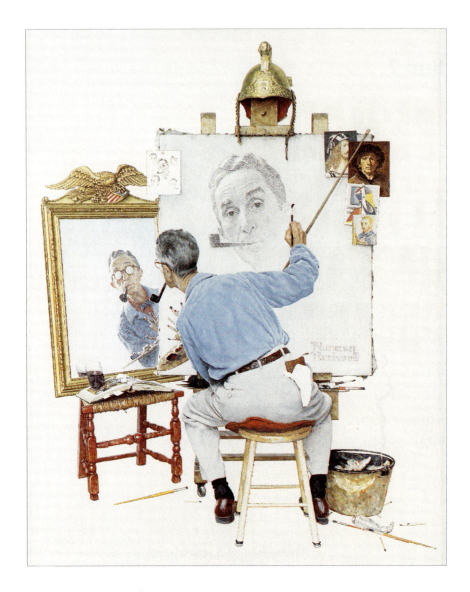

No Questions Asked

Leo Tolstoy   **The Old Grandfather and His Little Grandson** ....FOLK TALE   782

Writing Workshop Narrative Writing: Short Story   784

Collection 8

Reading for Life

INFORMATIONAL FOCUS

- Using Documents to Solve a Problem
- Analyzing Consumer Materials
- Explaining How to Use Technical Devices

Elements and Features of Consumer Materials

Resource Center

SKILLS, WORKSHOPS, AND FEATURES

SKILLS

ELEMENTS OF LITERATURE ESSAYS

READING SKILLS AND STRATEGIES LESSONS

LITERARY SKILLS

INFORMATIONAL TEXTS

INFORMATIONAL ARTICLES

MAGAZINE ARTICLES

NEWSPAPER ARTICLE

ENCYCLOPEDIA ARTICLE

PUBLIC, WORKPLACE, AND CONSUMER DOCUMENTS

Elements of Literature on the Internet

TO THE STUDENT

At the *Elements of Literature* Internet site, you can read texts by professional writers and learn the inside stories behind your favorite authors. You can also build your word power and analyze messages in the media. As you move through *Elements of Literature*, you will find the best online resources at **go.hrw.com.**

Here's how to log on:

1. Start your Web browser, and enter **go.hrw.com** in the Address or Location field.

2. Note the keyword in your textbook.

INTERNET
More About Plot
Keyword: LE5 8-1

3. Enter the keyword, and click "go."

More About the Writer
Author biographies provide the inside stories behind the lives and works of great writers.

More About the Literary Element
Animated graphics present visual representations of literary concepts.

Interactive Reading Model
Interactive Reading Workshops guide you through high-interest informational articles and allow you to share your opinions through pop-up questions and polls.

More Writer's Models
Interactive Writer's Models present annotations and reading tips to help you with your own writing. Printable Professional Models and Student Models provide you with quality writing by real writers and students from across the country.

Vocabulary Activity
Interactive vocabulary-building activities help you build your word power.

Cross-curricular Connection
Short informational readings relate the literature you read in your textbook to your other studies and to real life.

Projects and Activities
Projects and activities help you extend your study of literature through writing, research, art, and public speaking.

Speeches
Video clips from historical speeches provide you with the tools you need to analyze elements of great speechmaking.

Media Tutorials
Media tutorials help you dissect messages in the media and learn to create your own multimedia presentations.

Tales (1988) by Jonathan Green. Oil on masonite. 24" × 36".
Collection of Tom and Kyung Riihimaki.

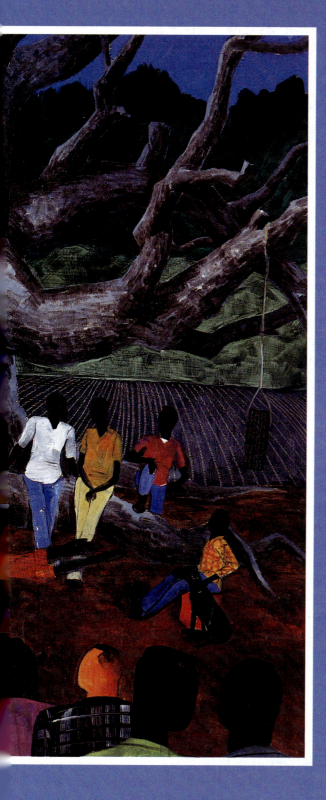

Collection 1

Telling Stories

Literary Focus:
Analyzing Plot

Informational Focus:
Analyzing Proposition and Support

Elements of Literature

Plot *by* Madeline Travers Hovland

A CHAIN OF EVENTS

Plot is the chain of related events that tells us what happens in a story. When a plot is well mapped out, it hooks us and we say we can't put the story down. The "hook" of the plot, the part that grabs us and keeps us reading, is usually a **conflict,** or problem faced by a character. The conflict might be a struggle with another character or with a force of nature, such as a tornado. We become curious and want to learn how the conflict is **resolved,** in other words, how the story turns out.

Here's an old story you may know:

Let's say three small pink pigs— Rupert, Rosemary, and Desmond—are building cottages when a wolf turns up and watches, his eyes yellow and shifty.

At once this storyteller hooks our curiosity by making us fear that a conflict will start between the pigs and the wolf. The pigs want to live in peace and safety. The wolf wants food.

The wolf says that the pigs are trespassing and should find another site. The pigs protest that they have a permit to build there. It was given to them by a rabbit who had come by earlier. The wolf declares that the permit is no good, swallows it in one gulp, and says that unless the swine are gone by evening, he will blow their cottages off the map.

Now **complications** are developing. We worry that the wolf will wreck the pigs' houses. Also, since the wolf is a carnivore, a meat-eating animal, there is a good chance the pigs will follow their permit down his throat.

Rupert hurries to finish his house with straw. Rosemary finishes hers with wood, and Desmond finishes his with fiberglass and aluminum siding. Then each pink pig goes inside to await developments.

The suspense is at a peak. What will happen to the pigs? The next event marks the **climax** of the story, when the outcome of the conflict is decided.

Just as he promised, the wolf turns up as the sun goes down. He huffs and puffs and blows Rupert's straw house to dust. Next he turns to Rosemary's house, and soon it too is blown to smithereens. But the wolf's deepest huffs and most violent puffs leave Desmond's fiberglass house unshaken.

The last part of a plot is the **resolution.** This is the end of the story, when all loose ends are tied up and we know what happens to the characters. In traditional fairy tales, as you know, villains like the wolf are punished, so that the story ends "happily ever after."

INTERNET

More About Plot

Keyword: LE5 8-1

SKILLS FOCUS

Literary Skills
Understand plot structure.

You may want to decide the resolution of this story yourself. What could possibly happen to the wolf? What could possibly happen to Rupert and Rosemary?

Subplots: Several Stories in One

If you think of movies and TV shows you've seen and of novels you've read, you know that stories often have subplots. **Subplots** are plots that are part of the larger story but are not as important. (The prefix *sub–* means "under" or "less important than.") In *The Diary of Anne Frank* (page 369), the major plot pits the Frank and Van Daan families against the Nazis. A subplot follows the growing attraction between Anne Frank and Peter Van Daan.

Parallel Episodes: Repeated Scenes

If you've read the traditional story of those three pigs, you might remember that the wolf goes to each house and says, "Little pig, little pig, let me come in." The plot repeats, with minor changes, each pig's response to that challenge. These are simple examples of **parallel episodes,** in which the story-teller repeats the main outline of an episode several times.

Map out the plot structure of a story you are familiar with. The story could be from a book or from TV or the movies. Use a graphic like this:

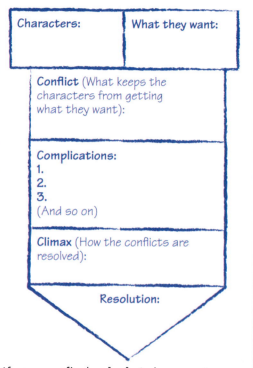

If you can find **subplots** in your story, fill out another chart just like this one.

It was a dark and stormy night. Suddenly, a shot rang out!

The maid screamed. A door slammed.

Suddenly, a pirate ship appeared on the horizon!

THIS TWIST IN THE PLOT WILL BAFFLE MY READERS...

PEANUTS reprinted by permission of United Feature Syndicate, Inc.

Retelling: Summarizing the Plot

by Kylene Beers

Here are two retellings of a traditional version of "The Three Little Pigs." Read each one, and decide which one is better.

1. Some pigs built some houses, and a wolf came to blow down their houses but couldn't. It's a story called "The Three Little Pigs."

2. This is the story of "The Three Little Pigs." No one knows who first told this story. The main characters are three pigs and a wolf. The three pigs each decide to build a house. The first one makes his house out of hay. A wolf comes along and blows it down, and that pig has to rush to the next pig's house. He had made his house out of sticks. Next, the wolf goes there and blows it down, and both pigs run to the third pig's house. The third one had made his house out of bricks. Finally, the wolf goes there and tries to blow it down, but can't. The wolf climbs down the chimney and falls into a pot of boiling water. He runs screaming out the front door and never bothers the pigs again. The three pigs live happily ever after.

INTERNET

More About Uchida

Keyword: LE5 8-1

SKILLS FOCUS

Reading Skills
Retell and summarize a story's plot.

Understanding Retelling

It's easy to recognize the second one as the better **retelling,** but exactly what makes it better than the first one? Use the Retelling Tips in the box to the right to evaluate the two summaries.

The Strategy Connection

The second retelling is better because it's organized and gives specific information in a certain order. A strategy called **retelling** helps you summarize a story. You'll practice retelling as you read the following story.

Retelling Tips

A good retelling should

1. state the title and author

2. identify the main character

3. describe the setting

4. relate the main events

5. use time-order words like *first, next,* and *finally*

6. keep events in the right order

7. explain how the story ends

THE WISE OLD WOMAN

traditional Japanese,
retold by **Yoshiko Uchida**

Many long years ago, there lived an arrogant and cruel young lord who ruled over a small village in the western hills of Japan.

"I have no use for old people in my village," he said haughtily. "They are neither useful nor able to work for a living. I therefore decree that anyone over seventy-one must be banished from the village and left in the mountains to die."

"What a dreadful decree! What a cruel and unreasonable lord we have," the people of the village murmured. But the lord fearfully punished anyone who disobeyed him, and so villagers who turned seventy-one were tearfully carried into the mountains, never to return. ❶ 📖

As you read, you'll find this open-book sign at certain points in the story: 📖 . Stop at these points, and think about what you've just read. Do what the prompt asks you to do.

RETELL

❶ Think about what you've learned so far. What's the title? Who's the author? Where does this story take place? Can you figure out what is going to cause a problem in this story?

Bamboo (1835) by Tani Bunchō. Folding fan; ink on paper.
Copyright The British Museum, London.

Gradually there were fewer and fewer old people in the village and soon they disappeared altogether. Then the young lord was pleased.

"What a fine village of young, healthy, and hard-working people I have," he bragged. "Soon it will be the finest village in all of Japan."

Now, there lived in this village a kind young farmer and his aged mother. They were poor, but the farmer was good to his mother, and the two of them lived happily together. However, as the years went by, the mother grew older, and before long she reached the terrible age of seventy-one.

"If only I could somehow deceive the cruel lord," the farmer thought. But there were records in the village books and everyone knew that his mother had turned seventy-one.

Peach Blossom Spring (detail) (1780s) by Tani Bunchō. Handscroll; ink, color, and gold on silk, after the Chinese artist Qiu Ying.

Each day the son put off telling his mother that he must take her into the mountains to die, but the people of the village began to talk. The farmer knew that if he did not take his mother away soon, the lord would send his soldiers and throw them both into a dark dungeon to die a terrible death.

"Mother——" he would begin, as he tried to tell her what he must do, but he could not go on.

Then one day the mother herself spoke of the lord's dread decree. "Well, my son," she said, "the time has come for you to take me to the mountains. We must hurry before the lord sends his soldiers for you." And she did not seem worried at all that she must go to the mountains to die. ❷

Copyright The British Museum, London.

RETELL

❷ Who are the characters you've met so far? What problem do they face?

"Forgive me, dear mother, for what I must do," the farmer said sadly, and the next morning he lifted his mother to his shoulders and set off on the steep path toward the mountains. Up and up he climbed, until the trees clustered close and the path was gone. There was no longer even the sound of birds, and they heard only the soft wail of the wind in the trees. The son walked slowly, for he could not bear to think of leaving his old mother in the mountains. On and on he climbed, not wanting to stop and leave her behind. Soon, he heard his mother breaking off small twigs from the trees that they passed.

"Mother, what are you doing?" he asked.

"Do not worry, my son," she answered gently. "I am just marking the way so you will not get lost returning to the village."

The son stopped. "Even now you are thinking of me?" he asked, wonderingly.

The mother nodded. "Of course, my son," she replied. "You will always be in my thoughts. How could it be otherwise?"

At that, the young farmer could bear it no longer. "Mother, I cannot leave you in the mountains to die all alone," he said. "We are going home and no matter what the lord does to punish me, I will never desert you again."

So they waited until the sun had set and a lone star crept into the silent sky. Then, in the dark shadows of night, the farmer carried his mother down the hill and they returned quietly to their little house. The farmer dug a deep hole in the floor of his kitchen and made a small room where he could hide his mother. From that day, she spent all her time in the secret room and the farmer carried meals to her there. The rest of the time, he was careful to work in the fields and act as though he lived alone. In this way, for almost two years he kept his mother safely hidden and no one in the village knew that she was there. ❸ 📖

Then one day there was a terrible commotion among the villagers, for Lord Higa of the town beyond the hills threatened to conquer their village and make it his own.

"Only one thing can spare you," Lord Higa announced. "Bring me a box containing one thousand ropes of ash and I will spare your village." ❹ 📖

The cruel young lord quickly gathered together all the wise men of his village. "You are men of wisdom," he said. "Surely you can tell me how to meet Lord Higa's demands so our village can be spared."

But the wise men shook their heads. "It is impossible to make even one rope of ash, sire," they answered. "How can we ever make one thousand?"

"Fools!" the lord cried angrily. "What good is your wisdom if you cannot help me now?"

And he posted a notice in the village square offering a great reward of gold to any villager who could help him save their village.

But all the people in the village whispered, "Surely, it is an impossible thing, for ash crumbles at the touch of the finger. How could anyone ever make a rope of ash?" They shook their heads and sighed, "Alas, alas, we must be conquered by yet another cruel lord."

The young farmer, too, supposed that this must be, and he wondered what would happen to his mother if a new lord even more terrible than their own came to rule over them.

When his mother saw the troubled look on his face, she asked, "Why are you so worried, my son?"

So the farmer told her of the impossible demand made by Lord Higa if the village was to be spared, but his mother did not seem troubled at all. Instead she laughed softly and said, "Why, that is not such an impossible task. All one has to do is soak ordinary rope in salt water and dry it well. When it is burned, it will hold its shape and there is your rope of ash! Tell the villagers to hurry and find one thousand pieces of rope."

The farmer shook his head in amazement. "Mother, you are wonderfully wise," he said, and he rushed to tell the young lord what he must do.

"You are wiser than all the wise men of the village," the lord said when he heard the farmer's solution, and he rewarded him with many pieces of gold. The thousand ropes of ash were quickly made and the village was spared. **5**

In a few days, however, there was another great commotion in the village as Lord Higa sent another threat. This time he sent a log with a small hole that curved and bent seven times through its length, and he demanded that a single piece of silk thread be threaded through the hole. "If you cannot perform this task," the lord threatened, "I shall come to conquer your village."

The young lord hurried once more to his wise men, but they all shook their heads in bewilderment. "A needle cannot bend its way

RETELL

5 Review what's happened so far. What does the cruel young lord require? What does the young farmer do?

The Wise Old Woman   **9**

through such curves," they moaned. "Again we are faced with an impossible demand."

"And again you are stupid fools!" the lord said, stamping his foot impatiently. He then posted a second notice in the village square asking the villagers for their help.

Once more the young farmer hurried with the problem to his mother in her secret room.

"Why, that is not so difficult," his mother said with a quick smile. "Put some sugar at one end of the hole. Then tie an ant to a piece of silk thread and put it in at the other end. He will weave his way in and out of the curves to get to the sugar and he will take the silk thread with him."

"Mother, you are remarkable!" the son cried, and he hurried off to the lord with the solution to the second problem. ❻ 📖

Once more the lord commended the young farmer and rewarded him with many pieces of gold. "You are a brilliant man and you have saved our village again," he said gratefully.

But the lord's troubles were not over even then, for a few days later Lord Higa sent still another demand. "This time you will undoubtedly fail and then I shall conquer your village," he threatened. "Bring me a drum that sounds without being beaten."

"But that is not possible," sighed the people of the village. "How can anyone make a drum sound without beating it?"

This time the wise men held their heads in their hands and moaned, "It is hopeless. It is hopeless. This time Lord Higa will conquer us all."

The young farmer hurried home breathlessly. "Mother, Mother, we must solve another terrible problem or Lord Higa will conquer our village!" And he quickly told his mother about the impossible drum.

His mother, however, smiled and answered, "Why, this is the easiest of them all. Make a drum with sides of paper and put a bumblebee inside. As it tries to escape, it will buzz and beat itself against the paper and you will have a drum that sounds without being beaten."

The young farmer was amazed at his mother's wisdom. "You are far wiser than any of the wise men of the village," he said, and he hurried to tell the young lord how to meet Lord Higa's third demand. ❼ 📖

When the lord heard the answer, he was greatly impressed. "Surely a young man like you cannot be wiser than all my wise men," he

RETELL

❻ What is Lord Higa's second threat? Who figures out a way around this one? How is it done?

RETELL

❼ What is Lord Higa's third threat? How is this one avoided? Who keeps getting the credit for resolving these threats?

Peach Blossom Spring (detail) (1780s) by Tani Bunchō.
Handscroll; ink, color, and gold on silk, after the Chinese
artist Qiu Ying.
Copyright The British Museum, London.

said. "Tell me honestly, who has helped you solve all these difficult problems?"

The young farmer could not lie. "My lord," he began slowly, "for the past two years I have broken the law of the land. I have kept my aged mother hidden beneath the floor of my house, and it is she who solved each of your problems and saved the village from Lord Higa."

He trembled as he spoke, for he feared the lord's displeasure and rage. Surely now the soldiers would be summoned to throw him into the dark dungeon. But when he glanced fearfully at the lord, he saw that the young ruler was not angry at all. Instead, he was silent and thoughtful, for at last he realized how much wisdom and knowledge old people possess.

"I have been very wrong," he said finally. "And I must ask the forgiveness of your mother and of all my people. Never again will I demand that the old people of our village be sent to the mountains to die. Rather, they will be treated with the respect and honor they deserve and share with us the wisdom of their years."

And so it was. From that day, the villagers were no longer forced to abandon their parents in the mountains, and the village became once more a happy, cheerful place in which to live. The terrible Lord Higa stopped sending his impossible demands and no longer threatened to conquer them, for he too was impressed. "Even in such a small village there is much wisdom," he declared, "and its people should be allowed to live in peace."

And that is exactly what the farmer and his mother and all the people of the village did for all the years thereafter. ❽

RETELL

❽ You should be able to identify two main problems in this story. You should also be able to list the three threats from Lord Higa and how they are overcome. Finally, you should be able to explain what happens to all the elderly people. Review the story if you aren't sure about some of these parts.

Meet the Writer

Yoshiko Uchida

Preserving the Magic

Yoshiko Uchida (1921–1992) was born in Alameda, California, and grew up in Berkeley. During World War II, Uchida and her family were imprisoned in one of the camps set up for the 110,000 Japanese Americans living on the West Coast. She later wrote about this experience in *The Invisible Thread.*

After the war, Uchida traveled to Japan to rediscover her roots and to collect Japanese folk tales. "The Wise Old Woman" is one of these tales.

Late in life, Uchida reflected on her lifelong love for the written word:

66 I was writing stories when I was ten, and being the child of frugal immigrant parents, I wrote them on brown wrapping paper which I cut up and bound into booklets, and because I am such a saver, I still have them. The first is titled 'Jimmy Chipmunk and His Friends: A Short Story for Small Children.'

I also kept a journal . . . which I began the day I graduated from elementary school. . . . [E]ven today I can read of the special events of my young life, such as . . . the day I got my first dog, or the sad day he died, when I drew a tombstone for him in my journal and decorated it with floral wreaths.

By putting these special happenings into words . . . I was trying to . . . preserve the magic, as well as the joy and sadness, of certain moments in my life, and I guess that's really what books and writing are all about. 99

For Independent Reading

If you enjoyed "The Wise Old Woman," look for other tales in Uchida's *The Sea of Gold and Other Tales from Japan.*

Practice the Strategy

Retelling the Story

Here's how one student started a retelling of "The Wise Old Woman." Read it, and then look at the Retelling Guide on this page. Is this a good beginning? Why or why not?

> The title of this story is "The Wise Old Woman." It's a traditional Japanese tale that has been retold by Yoshiko Uchida. It takes place in a small Japanese village a long time ago. The main characters are the cruel young lord, a young farmer, his mother, and Lord Higa.
>
> The cruel young lord decides that all people in his village who are seventy-one years old and older must be sent to the mountains to die. Anyone who does not do what he says is severely punished. One young farmer loves his mother so much that when she turns seventy-one, he cannot send her away to die.

PRACTICE

Finish this retelling yourself. Use the Retelling Guide on this page to help you. Then, ask a partner to listen to your retelling and to rate your retelling using the rating sheet on page 15.

SKILLS FOCUS

Reading Skills
Retell a story's plot.

Retelling Guide

1. **Introduction**
   Begin with the title and the author of the story. Then, tell where and when the story is set.

2. **Characters**
   Tell the characters' names, and explain how the characters are connected to one another. Tell what the main character wants.

3. **Conflict**
   What is the main character's problem or conflict? In other words, what's keeping the main character from getting what he or she wants?

4. **Complications**
   Tell the main events—what happens as the characters try to solve the conflict.

5. **Climax**
   Describe the climax, the most suspenseful moment in the story.

   > **Strategy Tip**
   > This is the moment when you are about to find out how the main character will overcome the conflict (or be defeated).

6. **Resolution**
   Tell what happens after the climax. How does the story end?

7. **Personal Response**
   Give your response to the story by telling what you thought of it.

Retelling Rating Sheet

Name _____

Text _____

Directions: Use the following checklist to have someone rate your retelling. Ask the listener to decide if you do each item listed below a little, some, a lot, or not at all. Work on those things that you don't do or only do a little.

0	1	2	3
Not at all	A little	Some	A lot

Does this retelling

1. have a good beginning that cites the title and author and describes the setting?

2. cite the characters' names and explain how the characters are connected?

3. tell what the main character wants?

4. identify the conflict or problem?

5. include the main events?

6. keep those main events in the correct sequence?

7. explain how the conflict or problem was resolved?

8. provide a personal comment about the story?

You can use the retelling strategy with the stories in this collection. If you want to review the elements of any plot, try **retelling.**

Broken Chain

Make the Connection
Quickwrite ✏️

This story is about a boy's first date. You'll see that his problems are like those many of us face—he worries a lot about how he looks—and everything seems to go wrong. Describe how you think most thirteen- and fourteen-year-olds feel about themselves.

Literary Focus
Conflict

Every story is built around a **plot,** a series of related events. The main ingredient in a plot is a **conflict** of some kind. Usually a conflict starts when a character wants something very badly and takes steps to get it. Along the way, problems develop: Somebody else wants the same thing, the boat capsizes, or a storm causes the electricity to go out. These are examples of **external conflicts:** The character struggles against outside forces. Conflicts can also be **internal:** A character might have to fight shyness, keep a terrible secret, or control fear. In many stories both kinds of conflict exist side by side. In this story, Alfonso has many conflicts. What internal conflict is revealed in the first two sentences?

INTERNET
Vocabulary
Activity
•
More About Soto
Keyword: LE5 8-1

**Literary
Skills**
Understand
conflict.

Reading Skills
Summarize a
story's plot.

Reading Skills
Summarizing a Plot

You can **summarize** most plots by using a strategy called **retelling**. Retelling means that you stop at key points in a text and retell what has happened so far. When you finish reading, you can use your retelling notes to summarize the story. As you read the following story, you will find open-book signs alongside the text. Stop at these points, and answer the questions about the story's plot.

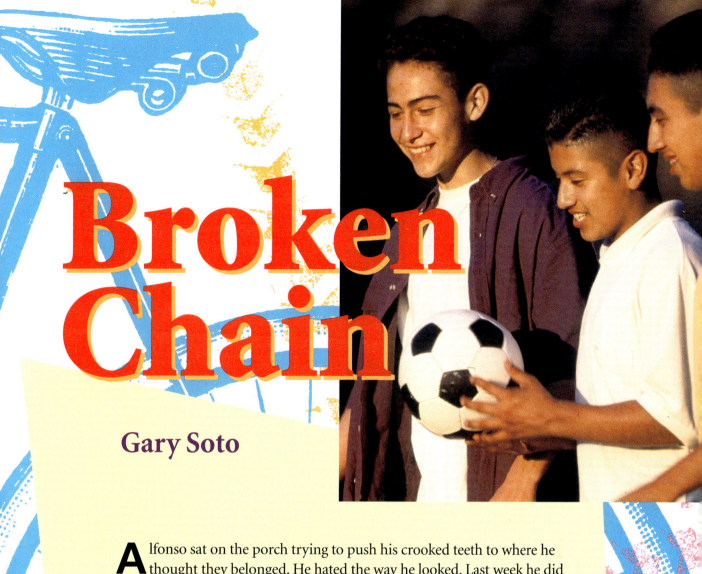

Broken Chain

Gary Soto

Alfonso sat on the porch trying to push his crooked teeth to where he thought they belonged. He hated the way he looked. Last week he did fifty sit-ups a day, thinking that he would burn those already <u>apparent</u> ripples on his stomach to even deeper ripples, dark ones, so when he went swimming at the canal next summer, girls in cut-offs would notice. And the guys would think he was tough, someone who could take a punch and give it back. He wanted "cuts" like those he had seen on a calendar of an Aztec[1] warrior standing on a pyramid with a woman in his arms. The calendar hung above the cash register at La Plaza. Orsua, the owner, said Alfonso could have the calendar at the end of the year if the waitress, Yolanda, didn't take it first.

---

1. **Aztec:** member of an American Indian people of what is now Mexico.

Vocabulary
apparent (ə·per′ənt) *adj.:* visible; easily seen; obvious.

Alfonso studied the magazine pictures of rock stars for a hairstyle. He liked the way Prince looked—and the bass player from Los Lobos. Alfonso thought he would look cool with his hair razored into a V in the back and streaked purple. But he knew his mother wouldn't go for it. And his father, who was puro Mexicano, would sit in his chair after work, <u>sullen</u> as a toad, and call him "sissy."

Alfonso didn't dare color his hair. But one day he had had it butched on the top, like in the magazines. His father had come home that evening from a softball game, happy that his team had drilled four homers in a thirteen-to-five bashing of Color Tile. He'd swaggered into the living room but had stopped cold when he saw Alfonso and asked, not joking but with real concern, "Did you hurt your head at school? ¿Qué pasó?"[2]

Alfonso had pretended not to hear his father and had gone to his room, where he studied his hair from all angles in the mirror. He liked what he saw until he smiled and realized for the first time that his teeth were crooked, like a pile of wrecked cars. He grew depressed and turned away from the mirror. He sat on his bed and leafed through the rock magazine until he came to the rock star with the butched top. His mouth was closed, but Alfonso was sure his teeth weren't crooked. ❶

Alfonso didn't want to be the handsomest kid at school, but he was determined to be

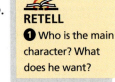

RETELL
❶ Who is the main character? What does he want?

better looking than average. The next day he spent his lawn-mowing money on a new shirt and, with a pocketknife, scooped the moons of dirt from under his fingernails.

He spent hours in front of the mirror trying to herd his teeth into place with his thumb. He asked his mother if he could have braces, like Frankie Molina, her god-son, but he asked at the wrong time. She was at the kitchen table licking the envelope to the house payment. She glared up at him. "Do you think money grows on trees?"

His mother clipped coupons from magazines and newspapers, kept a vegetable garden in the summer, and shopped at Penney's and Kmart. Their family ate a lot of frijoles,[3] which was OK because nothing else tasted so good, though one time Alfonso had had Chinese pot stickers[4] and thought they were the next best food in the world.

He didn't ask his mother for braces again, even when she was in a better mood. He decided to fix his teeth by pushing on them with his thumbs. After breakfast that Saturday he went to his room, closed the door quietly, turned the radio on, and pushed for three hours straight.

He pushed for ten minutes, rested for five, and every half hour, during a radio commercial, checked to see if his smile had improved. It hadn't.

Eventually he grew bored and went outside with an old gym sock to wipe down his bike, a ten-speed from Montgomery Ward. His thumbs were tired and wrinkled

---

3. **frijoles** (frē·hô′lās′) *n.*: Spanish for "beans."
4. **pot stickers** *n.*: dumplings.

Vocabulary
sullen (sul′ən) *adj.*: grumpy; resentful.

---

2. **¿Qué pasó?** (kā′ pä·sô′): Spanish for "What happened?"

and pink, the way they got when he stayed in the bathtub too long.

Alfonso's older brother, Ernie, rode up on *his* Montgomery Ward bicycle looking depressed. He parked his bike against the peach tree and sat on the back steps, keeping his head down and stepping on ants that came too close.

Alfonso knew better than to say anything when Ernie looked mad. He turned his bike over, balancing it on the handlebars and seat, and flossed the spokes with the sock. When he was finished, he pressed a knuckle to his teeth until they tingled.

Ernie groaned and said, "Ah, man."

Alfonso waited a few minutes before asking, "What's the matter?" He pretended not to be too interested. He picked up a wad of steel wool and continued cleaning the spokes.

Ernie hesitated, not sure if Alfonso would laugh. But it came out. "Those girls didn't show up. And you better not laugh."

"What girls?"

Then Alfonso remembered his brother bragging about how he and Frostie met two girls from Kings Canyon Junior High last week on Halloween night. They were dressed as Gypsies, the costume for all poor Chicanas[5]—they just had to borrow scarves and gaudy red lipstick from their abuelitas.[6]

Alfonso walked over to his brother. He compared their two bikes: His gleamed like a handful of dimes, while Ernie's looked dirty.

"They said we were supposed to wait at the corner. But they didn't show up. Me and Frostie waited and waited. . . . They were playing games with us."

Alfonso thought that was a pretty dirty trick but sort of funny too. He would have to try that someday.

"Were they cute?" Alfonso asked.

"I guess so."

"Do you think you could recognize them?"

"If they were wearing red lipstick, maybe."

Alfonso sat with his brother in silence, both of them smearing ants with their floppy high tops. Girls could sure act weird, especially the ones you meet on Halloween.

Later that day, Alfonso sat on the porch pressing on his teeth. Press, relax; press, relax. His portable radio was on, but not loud enough to make Mr. Rojas come down the steps and wave his cane at him.

Alfonso's father drove up. Alfonso could tell by the way he sat in his truck, a Datsun with a different-colored front fender, that his team had lost their softball game. Alfonso got off the porch in a hurry because he knew his father would be in a bad mood. He went to the backyard, where he unlocked his bike, sat on it with the kick-stand down, and pressed on his teeth. He punched himself in the stomach, and growled, "Cuts." Then he patted his butch and whispered, "Fresh."

After a while Alfonso pedaled up the street, hands in his pockets, toward Foster's Freeze, where he was chased by a ratlike Chihuahua.[7] At his old school, John Burroughs Elementary, he found a kid hanging upside down on the top of a

---

5. **Chicanas** (chi·kä′nəz): Mexican American girls and women.
6. **abuelitas** (ä′bwä·lē′täs) *n.*: in Spanish, an affectionate term for "grandmothers," like *grandmas* in English.

7. **Chihuahua** (chi·wä′wä): small dog with large, pointed ears.

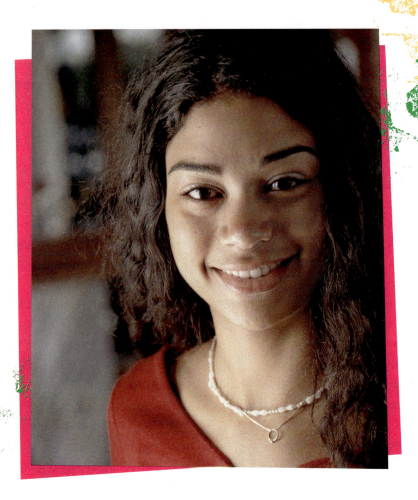

barbed-wire fence with a girl looking up at him. Alfonso skidded to a stop and helped the kid untangle his pants from the barbed wire. The kid was grateful. He had been afraid he would have to stay up there all night. His sister, who was Alfonso's age, was also grateful. If she had to go home and tell her mother that Frankie was stuck on a fence and couldn't get down, she would get scolded.

"Thanks," she said. "What's your name?"

Alfonso remembered her from his school and noticed that she was kind of cute, with ponytails and straight teeth. "Alfonso. You go to my school, huh?"

"Yeah. I've seen you around. You live nearby?"

"Over on Madison."

"My uncle used to live on that street, but he moved to Stockton."

"Stockton's near Sacramento, isn't it?"

"You been there?"

"No." Alfonso looked down at his shoes. He wanted to say something clever the way people do on TV. But the only thing he could think to say was that the governor lived in Sacramento. As soon as he shared this observation, he winced inside.

Alfonso walked with the girl and the boy as they started for home. They didn't talk much. Every few steps, the girl, whose name was Sandra, would look at him out of the corner of her eye, and Alfonso would look away. He learned that she was in seventh grade, just like him, and that she had a pet terrier named Queenie. Her father was a mechanic at Rudy's Speedy Repair, and her mother was a teacher's aide at Jefferson Elementary.

When they came to the street, Alfonso and Sandra stopped at her corner, but her brother ran home. Alfonso watched him stop in the front yard to talk to a lady he guessed was their mother. She was raking leaves into a pile.

"I live over there," she said, pointing.

Alfonso looked over her shoulder for a long time, trying to muster enough nerve to ask her if she'd like to go bike riding tomorrow.

Shyly, he asked, "You wanna go bike riding?"

"Maybe." She played with a ponytail and crossed one leg in front of the other. "But my bike has a flat."

"I can get my brother's bike. He won't mind."

She thought a moment before she said, "OK. But not tomorrow. I have to go to my aunt's."

"How about after school on Monday?"

"I have to take care of my brother until my mom comes home from work. How 'bout four-thirty?"

"OK," he said. "Four-thirty." Instead of parting immediately, they talked for a while, asking questions like "Who's your favorite group?" "Have you ever been on the Big Dipper at Santa Cruz?" and "Have you ever tasted pot stickers?" But the question-and-answer period ended when Sandra's mother called her home. ❷

Alfonso took off as fast as he could on his bike, jumped the curb, and, cool as he could

RETELL
❷ What else does Alfonso want?

be, raced away with his hands stuffed in his pockets. But when he looked back over his shoulder, the wind raking through his butch, Sandra wasn't even looking. She was already on her lawn, heading for the porch.

That night he took a bath, pampered his hair into place, and did more than his usual set of exercises. In bed, in between the push-and-rest on his teeth, he pestered his brother to let him borrow his bike.

"Come on, Ernie," he whined. "Just for an hour."

"Chale,[8] I might want to use it."

"Come on, man, I'll let you have my trick-or-treat candy."

"What you got?"

"Three baby Milky Ways and some Skittles."

"Who's going to use it?"

Alfonso hesitated, then risked the truth. "I met this girl. She doesn't live too far."

Ernie rolled over on his stomach and stared at the outline of his brother, whose head was resting on his elbow. "*You* got a girlfriend?"

"She ain't my girlfriend, just a girl."

"What does she look like?"

"Like a girl."

"Come on, what does she look like?"

"She's got ponytails and a little brother."

"Ponytails! Those girls who messed with Frostie and me had ponytails. Is she cool?"

"I think so."

Ernie sat up in bed. "I bet you that's her."

Alfonso felt his stomach knot up. "She's going to be my girlfriend, not yours!"

"I'm going to get even with her!"

"You better not touch her," Alfonso

---

8. **chale** (chä′lä): Spanish slang expression roughly meaning "it's not possible."

snarled, throwing a wadded Kleenex at him. "I'll run you over with my bike."

For the next hour, until their mother threatened them from the living room to be quiet or else, they argued whether it was the same girl who had stood Ernie up. Alfonso said over and over that she was too nice to pull a stunt like that. But Ernie argued that she lived only two blocks from where those girls had told them to wait, that she was in the same grade, and, the clincher, that she had ponytails. Secretly, however, Ernie was jealous that his brother, two years younger than himself, might have found a girlfriend. ❸

RETELL
❸ What complication has developed?

Sunday morning, Ernie and Alfonso stayed away from each other, though over breakfast they fought over the last tortilla. Their mother, sewing at the kitchen table, warned them to knock it off. At church they made faces at one another when the priest, Father Jerry, wasn't looking. Ernie punched Alfonso in the arm, and Alfonso, his eyes wide with anger, punched back.

Monday morning they hurried to school on their bikes, neither saying a word, though they rode side by side. In first period, Alfonso worried himself sick. How would he borrow a bike for her? He considered asking his best friend, Raul, for his bike. But Alfonso knew Raul, a paperboy with dollar signs in his eyes, would charge him, and he had less than sixty cents, counting the soda bottles he could cash.

Between history and math, Alfonso saw Sandra and her girlfriend huddling at their lockers. He hurried by without being seen.

During lunch Alfonso hid in metal shop so he wouldn't run into Sandra. What would he say to her? If he weren't mad at his brother, he could ask Ernie what girls and guys talk about. But he *was* mad, and anyway, Ernie was pitching nickels with his friends.

Alfonso hurried home after school. He did the morning dishes as his mother had asked and raked the leaves. After finishing his chores, he did a hundred sit-ups, pushed on his teeth until they hurt, showered, and combed his hair into a perfect butch. He then stepped out to the patio to clean his bike. On an impulse, he removed the chain to wipe off the gritty oil. But while he was unhooking it from the back sprocket, it snapped. The chain lay in his hand like a dead snake. ❹

RETELL
❹ What problem is caused by the broken chain?

Alfonso couldn't believe his luck. Now, not only did he not have an extra bike for Sandra, he had no bike for himself. Frustrated and on the verge of tears, he flung the chain as far as he could. It landed with a hard slap against the back fence and spooked his sleeping cat, Benny. Benny looked around, blinking his soft gray eyes, and went back to sleep.

Alfonso retrieved the chain, which was hopelessly broken. He cursed himself for being stupid, yelled at his bike for being cheap, and slammed the chain onto the cement. The chain snapped in another place and hit him when it popped up, slicing his hand like a snake's fang.

"Ow!" he cried, his mouth immediately going to his hand to suck on the wound.

After a dab of iodine, which only made his cut hurt more, and a lot of thought, he

Vocabulary
impulse (im′puls′) *n.:* urge.
retrieved (ri·trēvd′) *v.:* got back.

went to the bedroom to plead with Ernie, who was changing to his after-school clothes.

"Come on, man, let me use it," Alfonso pleaded. "Please, Ernie, I'll do anything."

Although Ernie could see Alfonso's desperation, he had plans with his friend Raymundo. They were going to catch frogs at the Mayfair canal. He felt sorry for his brother and gave him a stick of gum to make him feel better, but there was nothing he could do. The canal was three miles away, and the frogs were waiting.

Alfonso took the stick of gum, placed it in his shirt pocket, and left the bedroom with his head down. He went outside, slamming the screen door behind him, and sat in the alley behind his house. A sparrow landed in the weeds, and when it tried to come close, Alfonso screamed for it to scram. The sparrow responded with a squeaky chirp and flew away.

At four he decided to get it over with and started walking to Sandra's house, trudging slowly, as if he were waist-deep in water. Shame colored his face. How could he disappoint his first date? She would probably laugh. She might even call him menso.[9]

He stopped at the corner where they were supposed to meet and watched her house.

---

9. **menso** (men′sô) *adj.*: Spanish for "stupid."

But there was no one outside, only a rake leaning against the steps.

Why did he have to take the chain off? he scolded himself. He always messed things up when he tried to take them apart, like the time he tried to repad his baseball mitt. He had unlaced the mitt and filled the pocket with cotton balls. But when he tried to put it back together, he had forgotten how it laced up. Everything became tangled like kite string. When he showed the mess to his mother, who was at the stove cooking dinner, she scolded him but put it back together and didn't tell his father what a dumb thing he had done.

Now he had to face Sandra and say, "I broke my bike, and my stingy brother took off on his."

He waited at the corner a few minutes, hiding behind a hedge for what seemed like forever. Just as he was starting to think about going home, he heard footsteps and knew it was too late. His hands, moist from worry, hung at his sides and a thread of sweat raced down his armpit.

He peeked through the hedge. She was wearing a sweater with a checkerboard pattern. A red purse was slung over her shoulder. He could see her looking for him, standing on tiptoe to see if he was coming around the corner.

What have I done? Alfonso thought. He bit his lip, called himself menso, and pounded his palm against his forehead. Someone slapped the back of his head. He turned around and saw Ernie.

"We got the frogs, Alfonso," he said, holding up a wiggling plastic bag. "I'll show you later."

Ernie looked through the hedge, with one eye closed, at the girl. "She's not the one who messed with Frostie and me," he said finally. "You still wanna borrow my bike?"

Alfonso couldn't believe his luck. What a brother! What a pal! He promised to take Ernie's turn next time it was his turn to do the dishes. Ernie hopped on Raymundo's handlebars and said he would remember that promise. Then he was gone as they took off without looking back. ⑤

RETELL
⑤ How is one of Alfonso's problems resolved?

Free of worry now that his brother had come through, Alfonso emerged from behind the hedge with Ernie's bike, which was mud-splashed but better than nothing. Sandra waved.

"Hi," she said.

"Hi," he said back.

She looked cheerful. Alfonso told her his bike was broken and asked if she wanted to ride with him.

"Sounds good," she said, and jumped on the crossbar.

It took all of Alfonso's strength to steady the bike. He started off slowly, gritting his teeth, because she was heavier than he thought. But once he got going, it got easier. He pedaled smoothly, sometimes with only one hand on the handlebars, as they sped up one street and down another. Whenever he ran over a pothole, which was often, she screamed with delight, and once, when it looked like they were going to crash, she placed her hand over his, and it felt like love. ⑥

RETELL
⑥ Has Alfonso gotten everything he wanted?

Vocabulary
emerged (ē·murjd′) v.: came out.

Meet the Writer

Gary Soto

"Your Lives Are at Work, Too"

Gary Soto (1952–   ) was born and raised in Fresno, California, the setting of many of his stories, poems, and autobiographical pieces. In his writing, Soto tries to re-create the sights and sounds of the Mexican American neighborhood in which he grew up. He advises young writers to "look to your own lives," which is exactly what he does:

> 66 What are your life stories? Can you remember incidents from your childhood? Some of you will say that your lives are boring, that nothing has happened, that everything interesting happens far away. Not so. Your lives are at work, too. 99

Soto's poem "Oranges" (see page 696) is based on an incident in his life, but "Broken Chain" is more loosely drawn from his experience:

> 66 No, I'm not Alfonso in the story 'Broken Chain.' It's pure fiction, with the wild purpose of stirring in you—the reader—the feeling of one day latching onto a girlfriend or boyfriend. When I was Alfonso's age, I would have loved to have a girlfriend on my handlebars. Instead, I had my little brother, better known as chipped-tooth Jimmy, who often hopped onto my bike and cruised the streets of my hometown, Fresno, California. He was no 'Sandra.' Instead, Jimmy was a heavy problem, because it was my job to take care of him while my parents went off to work. 99

For Independent Reading

"Broken Chain" comes from *Baseball in April,* a book of short stories about growing up. You'll find "Oranges," along with other poems, in *A Fire in My Hands.*

First Thoughts

1. Finish one or both of these sentences:
   - I know how it feels to . . . because . . .
   - Alfonso reminds me of . . .

Thinking Critically

2. Explain how Alfonso feels about not having a bike for his date. Give details from the story that show his feelings.

3. In this story, Alfonso faces both **internal** and **external** **conflicts.** Describe four of his conflicts. Which do you think is his greatest challenge? Why?

4. Some stories have **subplots,** or minor plots that relate to the main plot. "Broken Chain" really has two plots: one involving Alfonso and the girl and one involving Alfonso and his brother. Which of those plots is the **subplot**? Explain your answer.

Reading Check

Use your retelling notes to **summarize** the **plot** of "Broken Chain." Cite the story's **title,** tell who the main **character** is and what he wants, describe the problems he has getting what he wants, list the main plot events, and tell how the story ends. To review the features of a good retelling, see Reading Skills and Strategies, pages 4–15.

Extending Interpretations

5. This story is told from a boy's viewpoint. In your experience, which of Alfonso's feelings are shared by girls?

6. How do Alfonso's feelings compare with the feelings you described in your Quickwrite? Do Alfonso's feelings and behavior seem realistic to you? Explain.

WRITING

Writing a Letter

Identify a problem that Alfonso has in the story (for example, worrying about his appearance or not knowing what to say to Sandra). Pretending you are Alfonso, write a **letter** to an advice column, explaining your problem. Then, switch papers with a classmate, and take the role of the columnist. Respond to Alfonso with practical, encouraging advice.

INTERNET

Projects and Activities

Keyword: LE5 8-1

SKILLS FOCUS

Literary Skills
Analyze conflict.

Reading Skills
Summarize a story's plot.

Writing Skills
Write a letter.

History of the English Language: Latin Roots

How Did Latin Get in There? When Alfonso worries that Sandra will call him *menso,* he is using the Spanish word for "stupid." If you know that a word is Spanish or comes from a Spanish word, you can be pretty sure it has a Latin root. Why? Because Spanish is a **Romance language.** No, not "romance" with flowers and violins. Romance languages developed from the language spoken by Roman soldiers who, for six hundred years, went about conquering the Western world, or at least most of Europe, North Africa, and the Middle East.

The Roman Armies Spread Latin. The Romans usually won their battles. They spoke Latin, and they made everyone else speak Latin too. Then they kept things peaceful for hundreds of years. In that peaceful time the language they spoke took on regional variations, so that eventually the modern languages of French, Spanish, Portuguese, Italian, and Romanian developed. Thus, when Alfonso speaks Spanish, he is actually speaking a modern version of Latin, as people do when they speak any of the Romance languages.

Latin Comes into English. Alfonso also speaks English, about 60 percent of which can be traced to Latin. However, English isn't a Romance language. Then how did so much Latin get into it? Well, thanks to the Romans and, later, the Roman Catholic Church, Latin got around. Just about every language in the Western world eventually borrowed from it. Latin was also the language of scholars for many centuries. But there was one other event that resulted in the addition of thousands of Latin words to the English language. That was the Norman Conquest of England.

In the year 1066, William the Conqueror, a Norman (from Normandy, in France) who spoke French, invaded England and became king. As a result, French—and, through it, Latin—became a major influence on the development of English.

(continued on next page)

SKILLS FOCUS

Vocabulary Skills
Understand the history of English.

(Vocabulary, continued)

PRACTICE

Study the following derivations, or origins, of the words in the Word Bank. (The abbreviation *L* stands for "Latin." *ME* stands for "Middle English.")

apparent	L *apparere*, "to appear"
sullen	L *solus*, "alone"
impulse	L *impellere*, "to drive"
retrieved	ME *retreven*, "to find again"
emerged	L *e–*, "out" + *mergere*, "to immerse"

> **Word Bank**
>
> apparent
> sullen
> impulse
> retrieved
> emerged

1. How is the Latin or Middle English meaning reflected in the modern meaning of each English word?
2. What other English words can you think of that come from *apparere, solus,* and *mergere*?

Grammar Link

When to Use Apostrophes

Apostrophes are used for two reasons: to show where letters in a word are missing (*it's* stands for "it is") and, in a noun, to show possession (*Alfonso's teeth*).

- Use an apostrophe in a contraction to show where letters have been left out. (A contraction is a combination of words from which letters have been omitted.)

  It's [it is] **broken. You're** [you are] **in trouble. They're** [they are] **furious. Who's** [who is] **going to fix it?**

- Use an apostrophe to form the possessive case of a noun (to show ownership).

  Sandra's hair [the hair of Sandra] **is in ponytails. The boys' bikes** [the bikes of the boys] **are broken. A boy's bike** [the bike of a boy] **is broken.**

- Do not use an apostrophe to form the plural of a noun.

  The girls never showed up.

- Do not use an apostrophe with the possessive form of a personal pronoun (*yours, hers, his, its, ours, theirs*).

  His bicycle is broken. May I borrow yours?

SKILLS FOCUS

Grammar Skills
Use apostrophes correctly.

PRACTICE

Correct any errors you find in the use of apostrophes.

1. Its broken.
2. Its chain is on the ground.
3. Your kidding!
4. You're girlfriend is here.
5. Your always late.
6. Who's bike are you riding?
7. Is the bike your's?
8. The boys took the girls bikes.

For more help, see Apostrophes, 15a–c, in the Language Handbook.

Analyzing Proposition and Support

Reading Focus
Proposition and Support

Some bikers might worry about the way Alfonso and his friends ride their bikes with no hands or balance their friends on the handlebars. The article on page 30 proposes some cycling rules that Alfonso and his pals might think about.

In the model below, the writer presents a **proposition,** an important idea or opinion, and **supports** the proposition with reasons. Reasons may be statistics, examples, anecdotes, and expert opinions.

■ After you've studied the model, read the following article on bike safety. Look for the writer's proposition in the first paragraph, and try to find at least one supporting reason in each paragraph that follows. Does the writer make a good case?

Kids Should Be Paid for Chores

I strongly believe that kids should be paid for doing chores around the house. Kids all across the country constantly nag their parents for money to go to the movies, buy CDs, go to McDonalds, and do many other things. Many parents complain about kids always asking for money.

Parents constantly complain that kids don't help out around the house enough. Lots of times parents nag kids until they clean up their rooms, put out the trash, cut the lawn, do the dishes, shovel the snow, and do many other chores.

Why can't kids and parents reach a compromise about money and chores? Parents would pay kids who remember to do their chores, without being reminded, a small fee for the work done. Kids would no longer ask for money.

This compromise teaches kids responsibility. They would learn that you don't get anything for doing nothing. When their chores are completed, with no nagging, they'd be paid whatever the parents had agreed to pay them. Kids could spend the money on things they like. They'd learn to save money for the expensive items.

No more nagging kids begging for money. No more nagging parents begging kids to clean up. Both kids and parents would be getting something they want.

—T. J. Wilson
Atlantic Middle School
North Quincy, Massachusetts

The writer states his **proposition** *twice—in the title and in the first sentence of the text.*

The writer gives **examples** *to illustrate the problem.*

The writer restates the issue as a question and gives **two reasons** *to support his proposition.*

The writer elaborates by giving several **more reasons** *to support his proposition.*

The writer ends with a strong **closing statement** *citing the benefits of the recommended course of action.*

SKILLS FOCUS

Reading Skills
Analyze proposition and support.

Road Warriors, Listen Up:
Some Rules for Streetwise Biking

When you ride a bike on city streets, you share the road with speeding fire engines, ambulances, and police cars. You see—but can't see around—giant-sized trucks with eighteen wheels instead of your two. Sports cars and SUVs zip in and out of lanes. Everyone's in a hurry, and there you are, with less protection than anyone else in a moving vehicle. Your best defense is your good sense. To ride a bike safely—on highways or byways—you've got to know and follow the rules of the road.

The consequences of not following bike-safety rules can be painful, if not fatal. Every year in the United States there are about eight hundred deaths due to bike accidents. More than half a million people end up in emergency rooms because of bike injuries.

To protect yourself against serious injury, wear a bike helmet whenever you hop on a bike, even for a short ride. A helmet that meets safety standards may seem expensive, but your intact brain is worth the investment. Bike helmets can reduce head injuries by as much as 80 percent.

To ride safely, you need to hear approaching traffic, barking dogs, and shouting drivers. Therefore, you should never ride wearing headphones. Wait to listen to music till you get where you're going. If you carry a cell phone or a pager, pull over to the side of the road before you take or make a call or check your beeper.

Biking safely also means obeying traffic signs and signals. Stop signs and red lights apply to everyone on the road, not just cars. State laws—and common sense—dictate that bicyclists ride on the right side of the road, in the same direction as all other traffic, not against it. When you come to an intersection, wait for the green light before you ride across. Remember that pedestrians always have the right of way, whether they are on the sidewalk or in the street.

Watch out for road hazards. (There are even more obstacles to worry about than cars and trucks and people.) Steer around potholes, bumps, gravel, piles of leaves, and grates covering storm drains. Use hand signals to alert drivers to your intentions. When you're not making a hand signal, be sure to keep both hands on your handlebars.

Biking is excellent practice for driving later on. Safe biking will help prepare you to be a safe driver. Even when you're old enough to drive a car, however, you'll probably still go biking. It's fun. It's an inexpensive way to travel. And it's great exercise. Whatever your age, always remember to follow the rules for streetwise biking. The life you save may be your own!

—Madeline Travers Hovland

Analyzing Proposition and Support

Road Warriors, Listen Up:
Some Rules for Streetwise Biking

Test Practice

1. Which sentence best states the writer's **proposition,** the main idea of the article?
   A Biking safely means obeying traffic signs and signals.
   B Watch out for road hazards.
   C Biking is excellent practice for driving later on.
   D To ride a bike safely, you've got to know and follow the rules of the road.

2. Which of the following is a statistic used to support the main idea of the article?
   F The consequences of not following bike-safety rules can be painful, if not fatal.
   G Bike helmets can reduce head injuries by as much as 80 percent.
   H When you come to an inter-section, wait for the green light before you ride across.
   J Safe biking will help prepare you to be a safe driver.

3. "More than half a million people end up in emergency rooms because of bike injuries." This sentence is an example of a —
   A personal experience
   B proposition
   C supporting detail
   D main idea

4. The overall **purpose** of the article is to —
   F discourage bikers
   G convince readers that bike safety is important
   H explain how to buy a good bike helmet
   J get readers interested in bike riding

5. Another good **title** for this article might be —
   A "Walk, Don't Bike"
   B "My Experiences as a Cyclist"
   C "Bike Now, Drive Later"
   D "Biking Safely: Your Best Defense on Two Wheels"

Constructed Response

1. What moving vehicle on the road has the least amount of protection?
2. According to the writer, what can happen if you don't follow bike-safety rules?
3. Why should you wear a bike helmet?
4. Who always has the right of way?
5. How does streetwise biking prepare riders for the future?

SKILLS FOCUS

Reading Skills
Analyze proposition and support.

Flowers for Algernon

Make the Connection

Quickwrite ✏️

Take a class poll: Would you rather be the most popular person in your school or the smartest person in your school?

On a small piece of paper, write either *S* for "smartest" or *P* for "most popular," and pass your response to a designated vote counter. (Even if you'd like to choose both, for now just choose one.) Tally the responses on the chalkboard. How close was the vote? Discuss what you think your classmates' reasons were for answering as they did.

Now, write a brief response to one of these questions:

- What are the advantages and disadvantages of popularity? of intelligence?

- What sacrifices do people make to fit in?

- What is good or bad about being unusual?

INTERNET

Vocabulary
Activity
•
Cross-curricular
Connection

Keyword: LE5 8-1

SKILLS FOCUS

Literary Skills
Understand subplots and parallel episodes.

Reading Skills
Use context clues.

Literary Focus

Subplots and Parallel Episodes

A long story, like the one that follows, might have a **subplot,** a minor plot that relates in some way to the major story. A long story might also have **parallel episodes,** in which the writer repeats certain elements of the plot. For example, you probably remember all those fairy tales that have three parallel episodes (writers back then seem to have liked the number three). The king might test his three daughters three times to see if they are loyal to him. Goldilocks tries the bears' beds three times to see which one is just right. Watch for both subplots and parallel episodes in "Flowers for Algernon."

Reading Skills 📖

Using Context Clues

Right at the start of "Flowers for Algernon," you'll notice that Charlie has trouble with spelling. To figure out what his misspelled words are meant to be, try sounding out each one. (Charlie usually spells words the way they sound.) If you're still stuck, check the word's context. The context will often give you enough **context clues,** or hints, to help you figure out the word's meaning. For example, on page 33, Charlie writes *faled*. You could figure out that this is his spelling of *failed* by sounding the word out or by looking at the context clue in the sentence just before it: "I had a test today."

Vocabulary Development

You'll have to know these words as you read "Flowers for Algernon":

misled (mis·led′) *v.:* fooled; led to believe something wrong. *Joe and Frank misled Charlie into thinking they were his friends.*

tangible (tan′jə·bəl) *adj.:* capable of being seen or felt. *An early tangible benefit of Charlie's operation was his improved skill at spelling.*

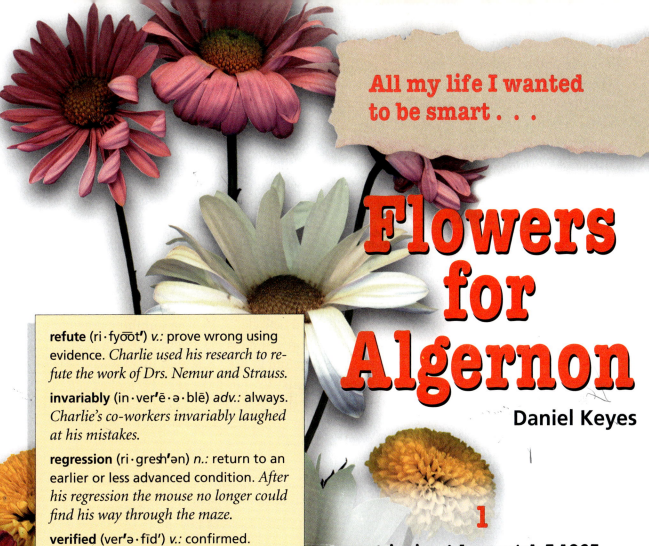

All my life I wanted to be smart . . .

Flowers for Algernon

Daniel Keyes

refute (ri·fyo͞ot′) *v.*: prove wrong using evidence. *Charlie used his research to refute the work of Drs. Nemur and Strauss.*

invariably (in·ver′ē·ə·blē) *adv.*: always. *Charlie's co-workers invariably laughed at his mistakes.*

regression (ri·gresh′ən) *n.*: return to an earlier or less advanced condition. *After his regression the mouse no longer could find his way through the maze.*

verified (ver′ə·fīd′) *v.*: confirmed. *Charlie wanted the results of his research verified by other scientists.*

obscure (əb·skyo͞or′) *v.*: hide. *Charlie wanted to obscure the fact that he was losing his intelligence.*

deterioration (dē·tir′ē·ə·rā′shən) *n.* used as *adj.*: worsening; decline. *Because of his mental deterioration, Charlie could no longer read German.*

hypothesis (hī·päth′ə·sis) *n.*: theory to be proved. *The doctors' hypothesis was that they could improve intelligence through surgery.*

introspective (in′trə·spek′tiv) *adj.*: looking inward. *Charlie kept an introspective journal of his thoughts and feelings.*

1

progris riport 1—martch 5 1965

Dr. Strauss says I shud rite down what I think and evrey thing that happins to me from now on. I dont know why but he says its importint so they will see if they will use me. I hope they use me. Miss Kinnian says maybe they can make me smart. I want to be smart. My name is Charlie Gordon. I am 37 years old and 2 weeks ago was my brithday. I have nuthing more to rite now so I will close for today.

progris riport 2—martch 6

I had a test today. I think I faled it. and I think that maybe now they wont use me. What happind is a nice young man was in the room and he had some white cards with ink spillled all over them. He sed Charlie what do you see on this card. I was very skared even tho I had my rabits foot[1] in my pockit because when I was a kid I always faled tests in school and I spillled ink to.

I told him I saw a inkblot. He said yes and it made me feel good. I thot that was all but when I got up to go he stopped me. He said now sit down Charlie we are not thru yet. Then I dont remember so good

---

1. **rabits foot:** The hind foot of a rabbit is sometimes used as a good-luck charm.

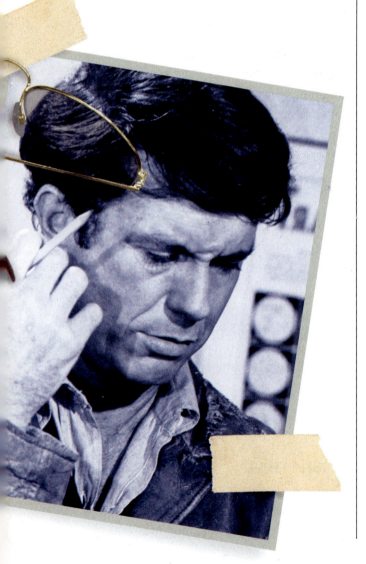

but he wantid me to say what was in the ink. I dint see nuthing in the ink but he said there was picturs there other pepul saw some picturs. I coudnt see any picturs. I reely tryed to see. I held the card close up and then far away. Then I said if I had my glases I coud see better I usally only ware my glases in the movies or TV but I said they are in the closit in the hall. I got them. Then I said let me see that card agen I bet Ill find it now.

I tryed hard but I still coudnt find the picturs I only saw the ink. I told him maybe I need new glases. He rote somthing down on a paper and I got skared of faling the test. I told him it was a very nice inkblot with littel points all around the eges. He looked very sad so that wasnt it. I said please let me try agen. Ill get it in a few minits becaus Im not so fast somtimes. Im a slow reeder too in Miss Kinnians class for slow adults but I'm trying very hard.

He gave me a chance with another card that had 2 kinds of ink spillled on it red and blue.

He was very nice and talked slow like Miss Kinnian does and he explaned it to me that it was a *raw shok*.[2] He said pepul see things in the ink. I said show me where. He said think. I told him I think a inkblot but that wasnt rite eather. He said what does it remind you—pretend something. I closd my eyes for a long time to pretend. I told him I pretned a fowntan pen with ink leeking all over a table cloth. Then he got up and went out.

I dont think I passd the *raw shok* test.

---

2. **raw shok:** Rorschach (rôr′shäk′) test, a psychological test in which people describe the images suggested to them by a series of inkblots.

He gave me a chance with another card that had 2 kinds of ink spilled on it red and blue.

progris report 3—martch 7

Dr Strauss and Dr Nemur say it dont matter about the inkblots. I told them I dint spill the ink on the cards and I couldn't see anything in the ink. They said that maybe they will still use me. I said Miss Kinnian never gave me tests like that one only spelling and reading. They said Miss Kinnian told that I was her bestist pupil in the adult nite scool becaus I tryed the hardist and I reely wantid to lern. They said how come you went to the adult nite scool all by yourself Charlie. How did you find it. I said I askd pepul and sumbody told me where I shud go to lern to read and spell good. They said why did you want to. I told them becaus all my life I wantid to be smart and not dumb. But its very hard to be smart. They said you know it will probly be tempirery. I said yes. Miss Kinnian told me. I dont care if it herts.

Later I had more crazy tests today. The nice lady who gave it me told me the name and I asked her how do you spellit so I can rite it in my progris riport. THEMATIC APPERCEPTION TEST. I dont know the frist 2 words but I know what *test* means. You got to pass it or you get bad marks. This test lookd easy becaus I coud see the pictures. Only this time she dint want me to tell her the picturs. That mixd me up. I said the man yesterday said I shoud tell him what I saw in the ink she said that dont make no difrence. She said make up storys about the pepul in the picturs.

I told her how can you tell storys about pepul you never met. I said why shud I make up lies. I never tell lies any more becaus I always get caut.

She told me this test and the other one the raw-shok was for getting personalty. I laffed so hard. I said how can you get that thing from inkblots and fotos. She got sore and put her picturs away. I dont care. It was sily. I gess I faled that test too.

Later some men in white coats took me to a difernt part of the hospitil and gave me a game to play. It was like a race with a white mouse. They called the mouse Algernon. Algernon was in a box with a lot of twists and turns like all kinds of walls and they gave me a pencil and a paper with lines and lots of boxes. On one side it said START and on the other end it said FINISH. They said it was *amazed* and that Algernon and me had the same *amazed* to do. I dint see how we could have the same *amazed* if Algernon had a box and I had a paper but I dint say nothing. Anyway there wasnt time because the race started.

One of the men had a watch he was trying to hide so I wouldnt see it so I tryed not to look and that made me nervus.

Anyway that test made me feel worser than all the others because they did it over 10 times with difernt *amazeds* and Algernon won every time. I dint know that mice were so smart. Maybe thats because Algernon is a white mouse. Maybe white mice are smarter then other mice.

progis riport 4—Mar 8

Their going to use me! Im so exited I can hardly write. Dr Nemur and Dr Strauss had a argament about it first. Dr Nemur was in the office when Dr Strauss brot me in. Dr Nemur was worryed about using me but Dr Strauss told him Miss Kinnian rekemmended me the best from all the people who she was teaching. I like Miss Kinnian becaus shes a very smart teacher. And she said Charlie your going to have a second chance. If you volenteer for this experament you mite get smart. They dont know if it will be perminint but theirs a chance. Thats why I said ok even when I was scared because she said it was an operashun. She said dont be scared Charlie you done so much with so little I think you deserv it most of all.

So I got scaird when Dr Nemur and Dr Strauss argud about it. Dr Strauss said I had something that was very good. He said I had a good *motor-vation*.[3] I never even knew I had that. I felt proud when he said that not every body with an eye-q of 68 had that thing. I dont know what it is or where I got it but he said Algernon had it too. Algernons *motor-vation* is the cheese they put in his box. But it cant be that because I didnt eat any cheese this week.

Then he told Dr Nemur something I dint understand so while they were talking I wrote down some of the words.

He said Dr Nemur I know Charlie is not what you had in mind as the first of your new brede of intelek** (coudnt get the word) superman. But most people of his low ment** are host** and uncoop** they are usualy dull apath** and hard to reach. He has a good natcher hes intristed and eager to please.

Dr Nemur said remember he will be the first human beeng ever to have his intelijence trippled by surgicle meens.

Dr Strauss said exakly. Look at how well hes lerned to read and write for his low mentel age its as grate an acheve** as you and I lerning einstines therey of **vity[4] without help. That shows the intenss motor-vation. Its comparat** a tremen** achev** I say we use Charlie.

I dint get all the words and they were talking to fast but it sounded like Dr Strauss was on my side and like the other one wasnt.

Then Dr Nemur nodded he said all right maybe your right. We will use Charlie.

---

3. **motor-vation:** motivation, the force or inner drive that makes someone want to do or accomplish something; here, Charlie's desire to learn.
4. **einstines therey of **vity:** Einstein's theory of relativity, which was developed by the German-born American physicist Albert Einstein (1879–1955) and deals with matter, time, space, and energy.

I asked Dr Strauss if Ill beat Algernon in the race after the operashun and he said maybe. If the operashun works Ill show that mouse I can be as smart as he is. Maybe smarter. Then Ill be abel to read better and spell the words good and know lots of things and be like other people. I want to be smart like other people. If it works perminint they will make everybody smart all over the wurld.

They dint give me anything to eat this morning. I dont know what that eating has to do with getting smart. Im very hungry and Dr Nemur took away my box of candy. That Dr Nemur is a grouch. Dr Strauss says I can have it back after the operashun. You cant eat befor a operashun . . .

Progress Report 6—Mar 15

The operashun dint hurt. He did it while I was sleeping. They took off the bandijis from my eyes and my head today so I can make a PROGRESS REPORT. Dr Nemur who looked at some of my other ones says I spell PROGRESS wrong and he told me how to spell it and REPORT too. I got to try and remember that.

I have a very bad memary for spelling. Dr Strauss says its ok to tell about all the things that happin to me but he says I shoud tell more about what I feel and what I think. When I told him I dont know how to think he said try. All the time when the bandijis were on my eyes I tryed to think. Nothing happened. I dont know what to think about. Maybe if I ask him he will tell me how I can think now that Im suppose to get smart. What do smart people think about. Fancy things I suppose. I wish I knew some fancy things alredy.

When he said that I got so exited I jumped up and shook his hand for being so good to me. I told him thank you doc you wont be sorry for giving me a second chance. And I mean it like I told him. After the operashun Im gonna try to be smart. Im gonna try awful hard.

progris ript 5—Mar 10

Im skared. Lots of people who work here and the nurses and the people who gave me the tests came to bring me candy and wish me luck. I hope I have luck. I got my rabits foot and my lucky penny and my horse shoe. Only a black cat crossed me when I was comming to the hospitil. Dr Strauss says dont be supersitis Charlie this is sience. Anyway Im keeping my rabits foot with me.

Their really my friends and they like me.

WEEKLY TIME CARD

DAY	IN	OUT	IN	OUT	IN	OUT	Total
M							
T							
W							
T							
F							
S							
S							
					REG.		
					O.T.		

HOURS

Foreman Signature

Progress Report 7—mar 19

Nothing is happining. I had lots of tests and different kinds of races with Algernon. I hate that mouse. He always beats me. Dr Strauss said I got to play those games. And he said some time I got to take those tests over again. Thse inkblots are stupid. And those pictures are stupid too. I like to draw a picture of a man and a woman but I wont make up lies about people.

I got a headache from trying to think so much. I thot Dr Strauss was my frend but he dont help me. He dont tell me what to think or when Ill get smart. Miss Kinnian dint come to see me. I think writing these progress reports are stupid too.

Progress Report 8—Mar 23

Im going back to work at the factery. They said it was better I shud go back to work but I cant tell anyone what the operashun was for and I have to come to the hospitil for an hour evry night after work. They are gonna pay me mony every month for lerning to be smart.

Im glad Im going back to work because I miss my job and all my frends and all the fun we have there.

Dr Strauss says I shud keep writing things down but I dont have to do it every day just when I think of something or something speshul happins. He says dont get discoridged because it takes time and it happins slow. He says it took a long time with Algernon before he got 3 times smarter then he was before. Thats why Algernon beats me all the time because he had that operashun too. That makes me feel better. I coud probly do that *amazed* faster than a reglar mouse. Maybe some day Ill beat Algernon. Boy that would be something. So far Algernon looks like he mite be smart perminent.

Mar 25 (I dont have to write PROGRESS REPORT on top any more just when I hand it in once a week for Dr Nemur to read. I just have to put the date on. That saves time)

We had a lot of fun at the factery today. Joe Carp said hey look where Charlie had his operashun what did they do Charlie put some brains in. I was going to tell him but I remembered Dr Strauss said no. Then Frank Reilly said what did you do Charlie forget your key and open your door the hard way. That made me laff. Their really my friends and they like me.

Sometimes somebody will say hey look at Joe or Frank or George he really pulled a Charlie Gordon. I don't know why they say that but they always laff. This morning Amos Borg who is the 4 man at Donnegans used my name when he shouted at Ernie the office boy. Ernie lost a packige. He said Ernie for godsake what are you trying to be a Charlie Gordon. I dont understand why he said that. I never lost any packiges.

Mar 28 Dr Strauss came to my room tonight to see why I dint come in like I was suppose to. I told him I dont like to race with Algernon any more. He said I dont have to for a while but I shud come in. He had a present for me only it wasnt a present but just for lend. I thot it was a little television but it wasnt. He said I got to turn it on when I go to sleep. I said your kidding why shud I turn it on when Im going to sleep. Who ever herd of a thing like that. But he said if I want to get smart I got to do what he says. I told him I dint think I was going to get smart and he put his hand on my sholder and said Charlie you dont know it yet but your getting smarter all the time. You wont notice for a while. I think he was just being nice to make me feel good because I dont look any smarter.

Oh yes I almost forgot. I asked him when I can go back to the class at Miss Kinnians school. He said I wont go their. He said that soon Miss Kinnian will come to the hospitil to start and teach me speshul. I was mad at her for not comming to see me when I got the operashun but I like her so maybe we will be frends again.

Mar 29 That crazy TV kept me up all night. How can I sleep with something yelling crazy things all night in my ears. And the nutty pictures. Wow. I dont know what it says when Im up so how am I going to know when Im sleeping.

Dr Strauss says its ok. He says my brains are lerning when I sleep and that will help me when Miss Kinnian starts my lessons in the hospitl (only I found out it isnt a hospitil its a labatory). I think its all crazy. If you can get smart when your sleeping why do people go to school. That thing I dont think will work. I use to watch the late show and the late late show on TV all the time and it never made me smart. Maybe you have to sleep while you watch it.

PROGRESS REPORT 9—April 3

Dr Strauss showed me how to keep the TV turned low so now I can sleep. I dont hear a thing. And I still dont understand what it says. A few times I play it over in the morning to find out what I lerned when I was sleeping and I dont think so. Miss Kinnian says Maybe its another langwidge or something. But most times it sounds american. It talks so fast faster then even Miss Gold who was my teacher in 6 grade and I remember she talked so fast I coudnt understand her.

I told Dr Strauss what good is it to get smart in my sleep. I want to be smart when Im awake. He says its the same thing and I have two minds. Theres the *subconscious* and the *conscious*[5] (thats how you spell it). And one dont tell the other one what its

doing. They don't even talk to each other. Thats why I dream. And boy have I been having crazy dreams. Wow. Ever since that night TV. The late late late late late show.

I forgot to ask him if it was only me or if everybody had those two minds.

(I just looked up the word in the dictionary Dr Strauss gave me. The word is *subconscious. adj. Of the nature of mental operations yet not present in consciousness; as, subconscious conflict of desires.*) Theres more but I still dont know what it means. This isnt a very good dictionary for dumb people like me.

Anyway the headache is from the party. My frends from the factery Joe Carp and Frank Reilly invited me to go with them to Muggsys Saloon for some drinks. I dont like to drink but they said we will have lots of fun. I had a good time.

Joe Carp said I shoud show the girls how I mop out the toilet in the factory and he got me a mop. I showed them and everyone laffed when I told that Mr Donnegan said I was the best janiter he ever had because I like my job and do it good and never come late or miss a day except for my operashun.

I said Miss Kinnian always said Charlie be proud of your job because you do it good.

Everybody laffed and we had a good time and they gave me lots of drinks and Joe said Charlie is a card when hes potted. I dont know what that means but everybody likes me and we have fun. I cant wait to be smart like my best frends Joe Carp and Frank Reilly.

I dont remember how the party was over but I think I went out to buy a newspaper and coffe for Joe and Frank and when I came back there was no one their. I looked for them all over till late. Then I dont remember so good but I think I got sleepy

---

5. **subconscious** (sub·kän′shəs) *n.:* mental activity that takes place below the level of the **conscious** (kän′shəs), or full awareness.

or sick. A nice cop brot me back home. Thats what my landlady Mrs Flynn says.

But I got a headache and a big lump on my head and black and blue all over. I think maybe I fell but Joe Carp says it was the cop they beat up drunks some times. I don't think so. Miss Kinnian says cops are to help people. Anyway I got a bad headache and Im sick and hurt all over. I dont think Ill drink anymore.

April 6 I beat Algernon! I dint even know I beat him until Burt the tester told me. Then the second time I lost because I got so exited I fell off the chair before I finished. But after that I beat him 8 more times. I must be getting smart to beat a smart mouse like Algernon. But I dont *feel* smarter.

I wanted to race Algernon some more but Burt said thats enough for one day. They let me hold him for a minit. Hes not so bad. Hes soft like a ball of cotton. He blinks and when he opens his eyes their black and pink on the eges.

I said can I feed him because I felt bad to beat him and I wanted to be nice and make frends. Burt said no Algernon is a very specshul mouse with an operashun like mine, and he was the first of all the animals to stay smart so long. He told me Algernon is so smart that every day he has to solve a test to get his food. Its a thing like a lock on a door that changes every time Algernon goes in to eat so he has to lern something new to get his food. That made me sad because if he couldnt lern he would be hungry.

I dont think its right to make you pass a test to eat. How woud Dr Nemur like it to have to pass a test every time he wants to eat. I think Ill be frends with Algernon.

April 9 Tonight after work Miss Kinnian was at the laboratory. She looked like she was glad to see me but scared. I told her dont worry Miss Kinnian Im not smart yet and she laffed. She said I have confidence in you Charlie the way you struggled so hard to read and right better than all the others. At werst you will have it for a littel wile and your doing somthing for sience.

We are reading a very hard book. I never read such a hard book before. Its called *Robinson Crusoe* about a man who gets merooned on a dessert Iland. Hes smart and figers out all kinds of things so he can have a house and food and hes a good swimmer. Only I feel sorry because hes all alone and has no frends. But I think their must be somebody else on the iland because theres a picture with his funny umbrella looking at footprints. I hope he gets a frend and not be lonely.

April 10 Miss Kinnian teaches me to spell better. She says look at a word and close your eyes and say it over and over until you remember. I have lots of truble with *through* that you say *threw* and *enough* and *tough* that you dont say *enew* and *tew*. You got to say *enuff* and *tuff*. Thats how I use to write it before I started to get smart. Im confused but Miss Kinnian says theres no reason in spelling.

Apr 14 Finished *Robinson Crusoe*. I want to find out more about what happens to him but Miss Kinnian says thats all there is. *Why*

Apr 15 Miss Kinnian says Im lerning fast. She read some of the Progress Reports and she looked at me kind of funny. She says Im a fine person and Ill show them all. I asked her why. She said never mind but I shoudnt feel bad if I find out that everybody isnt nice like I think. She said for a person who god gave so little to you done more then a lot of people with brains they never even used. I said all my frends are smart people but there good. They like me and they never did anything that wasnt nice. Then she got something in her eye and she had to run out to the ladys room.

Apr 16 Today, I lerned, the *comma*, this is a comma (,) a period, with a tail, Miss Kinnian, says its importent, because, it makes writing better, she said, sombeody, coud lose, a lot of money, if a comma, isnt, in the, right place, I dont have, any money, and I dont see, how a comma, keeps you from losing it,

But she says, everybody, uses commas, so Ill use, them too,

Apr 17 I used the comma wrong. Its punctuation. Miss Kinnian told me to look up long words in the dictionary to lern to spell them. I said whats the difference if you can read it anyway. She said its part of your education so now on Ill look up all the words Im not sure how to spell. It takes a long time to write that way but I think Im remembering. I only have to look up once and after that I get it right. Anyway thats how come I got the word *punctuation* right. (Its that way in the dictionary). Miss Kinnian says a period is punctuation too, and there are lots of other marks to lern. I told her I thot all the periods had to have tails but she said no.

You got to mix them up, she showed? me" how. to mix! them(up,. and now; I can! mix up all kinds" of punctuation, in! my writing? There, are lots! of rules? to lern; but Im gettin'g them in my head.

One thing I? like about, Dear Miss Kinnian: (thats the way it goes in a business letter if I ever go into business) is she, always gives me' a reason" when—I ask. She's a gen'ius! I wish! I cou'd be smart" like, her;

(Punctuation, is; fun!)

April 18 What a dope I am! I didn't even understand what she was talking about. I read the grammar book last night and it explanes the whole thing. Then I saw it was the same way as Miss Kinnian was trying to tell me, but I didn't get it. I got up in the middle of the night, and the whole thing straightened out in my mind.

Miss Kinnian said that the TV working in my sleep helped out. She said I reached a plateau. Thats like the flat top of a hill.

After I figgered out how punctuation worked, I read over all my old Progress Reports from the beginning. Boy, did I have crazy spelling and punctuation! I told Miss Kinnian I ought to go over the pages and fix all the mistakes but she said, "No, Charlie, Dr. Nemur wants them just as they are. That's why he let you keep them after they were photostated, to see your own progress. You're coming along fast, Charlie."

That made me feel good. After the lesson I went down and played with Algernon. We don't race anymore.

April 20 I feel sick inside. Not sick like for a doctor, but inside my chest it feels empty like getting punched and a heartburn at the same time.

I wasn't going to write about it, but I guess I got to, because it's important. Today was the first time I ever stayed home from work.

Last night Joe Carp and Frank Reilly invited me to a party. There were lots of girls and some men from the factory. I remembered how sick I got last time I drank too much, so I told Joe I didn't want anything to drink. He gave me a plain Coke instead. It tasted funny, but I thought it was just a bad taste in my mouth.

We had a lot of fun for a while. Joe said I should dance with Ellen and she would teach me the steps. I fell a few times and I couldn't understand why because no one else was dancing besides Ellen and me. And all the time I was tripping because somebody's foot was always sticking out.

Then when I got up I saw the look on Joe's face and it gave me a funny feeling in my stomack. "He's a scream," one of the girls said. Everybody was laughing.

Frank said, "I ain't laughed so much since we sent him off for the newspaper that night at Muggsy's and ditched him."

"Look at him. His face is red."

"He's blushing. Charlie is blushing."

"Hey, Ellen, what'd you do to Charlie? I never saw him act like that before."

I didn't know what to do or where to turn. Everyone was looking at me and laughing and I felt naked. I wanted to hide myself. I ran out into the street and I threw up. Then I walked home. It's a funny thing I never knew that Joe and Frank and the

Last night Joe Carp and Frank Reilly invited me to a party.

others liked to have me around all the time to make fun of me.

Now I know what it means when they say "to pull a Charlie Gordon."

I'm ashamed.

PROGRESS REPORT 10

April 21 Still didn't go into the factory. I told Mrs. Flynn my landlady to call and tell Mr. Donnegan I was sick. Mrs. Flynn looks at me very funny lately like she's scared of me.

I think it's a good thing about finding out how everybody laughs at me. I thought about it a lot. It's because I'm so dumb and I don't even know when I'm doing something dumb. People think it's funny when a dumb person can't do things the same way they can.

Anyway, now I know I'm getting smarter every day. I know punctuation and I can spell good. I like to look up all the hard words in the dictionary and I remember them. I'm reading a lot now, and Miss Kinnian says I read very fast. Sometimes I even understand what I'm reading about, and it stays in my mind. There are times when I can close my eyes and think of a page and it all comes back like a picture.

Besides history, geography, and arithmetic, Miss Kinnian said I should start to learn a few foreign languages. Dr. Strauss gave me some more tapes to play while I sleep. I still don't understand how that conscious and unconscious mind works, but Dr. Strauss says not to worry yet. He asked me to promise that when I start learning college subjects next week I wouldn't read any books on psychology—that is, until he gives me permission.

I feel a lot better today, but I guess I'm still a little angry that all the time people

were laughing and making fun of me because I wasn't so smart. When I become intelligent like Dr. Strauss says, with three times my I.Q. of 68, then maybe I'll be like everyone else and people will like me and be friendly.

I'm not sure what an I.Q. is. Dr. Nemur said it was something that measured how intelligent you were—like a scale in the drugstore weighs pounds. But Dr. Strauss had a big argument with him and said an I.Q. didn't weigh intelligence at all. He said an I.Q. showed how much intelligence you could get, like the numbers on the outside of a measuring cup. You still had to fill the cup up with stuff.

Then when I asked Burt, who gives me my intelligence tests and works with Algernon, he said that both of them were wrong (only I had to promise not to tell them he said so). Burt says that the I.Q. measures a lot of different things including some of the things you learned already, and it really isn't any good at all.

So I still don't know what I.Q. is except that mine is going to be over 200 soon. I didn't want to say anything, but I don't see how if they don't know *what* it is, or *where* it is—I don't see how they know *how much* of it you've got.

Dr. Nemur says I have to take a *Rorschach Test* tomorrow. I wonder what *that* is.

April 22 I found out what a *Rorschach* is. It's the test I took before the operation—the one with the inkblots on the pieces of cardboard. The man who gave me the test was the same one.

I was scared to death of those inkblots. I knew he was going to ask me to find the pictures and I knew I wouldn't be able to. I was thinking to myself, if only there was some way of knowing what kind of pictures were hidden there. Maybe there weren't any pictures at all. Maybe it was just a trick to see if I was dumb enough to look for something that wasn't there. Just thinking about that made me sore at him.

"All right, Charlie," he said, "you've seen these cards before, remember?"

"Of course I remember."

The way I said it, he knew I was angry, and he looked surprised. "Yes, of course. Now I want you to look at this one. What might this be? What do you see on this card? People see all sorts of things in these inkblots. Tell me what it might be for you— what it makes you think of."

I was shocked. That wasn't what I had expected him to say at all. "You mean there are no pictures hidden in those inkblots?"

He frowned and took off his glasses. "What?"

"Pictures. Hidden in the inkblots. Last time you told me that everyone could see them and you wanted me to find them too."

He explained to me that the last time he had used almost the exact same words he was using now. I didn't believe it, and I still have the suspicion that he misled me at the time just for the fun of it. Unless—I don't know any more—could I have been *that* feebleminded?

We went through the cards slowly. One of them looked like a pair of bats tugging at something. Another one looked like two men fencing with swords. I imagined all sorts of things. I guess I got carried away. But I didn't trust him any more, and I kept turning them around and even looking on the back to see if there was anything there I was supposed to catch. While he was making his notes, I peeked out of the corner of my eye to read it. But it was all in code that looked like this:

WF + A DdF-Ad orig. WF-A SF + obj

The test still doesn't make sense to me. It seems to me that anyone could make up lies about things that they didn't really see. How could he know I wasn't making a fool of him by mentioning things that I didn't really imagine? Maybe I'll understand it when Dr. Strauss lets me read up on psychology.

April 25 I figured out a new way to line up the machines in the factory, and Mr. Donnegan says it will save him ten thousand dollars a year in labor and increased production. He gave me a twenty-five-dollar bonus.

Vocabulary
misled (mis·led′) *v.*: fooled; led to believe something wrong.

I wanted to take Joe Carp and Frank Reilly out to lunch to celebrate, but Joe said he had to buy some things for his wife, and Frank said he was meeting his cousin for lunch. I guess it'll take a little time for them to get used to the changes in me. Everybody seems to be frightened of me. When I went over to Amos Borg and tapped him on the shoulder, he jumped up in the air.

People don't talk to me much anymore or kid around the way they used to. It makes the job kind of lonely.

April 27 I got up the nerve today to ask Miss Kinnian to have dinner with me tomorrow night to celebrate my bonus.

At first she wasn't sure it was right, but I asked Dr. Strauss and he said it was okay. Dr. Strauss and Dr. Nemur don't seem to be getting along so well. They're arguing all the time. This evening when I came in to ask Dr. Strauss about having dinner with Miss Kinnian, I heard them shouting. Dr. Nemur was saying that it was *his* experiment and *his* research, and Dr. Strauss was shouting back that he contributed just as much, because he found me through Miss Kinnian and he performed the operation. Dr. Strauss said that someday thousands of neurosurgeons might be using his technique all over the world.

Dr. Nemur wanted to publish the results of the experiment at the end of this month. Dr. Strauss wanted to wait a while longer to be sure. Dr. Strauss said that Dr. Nemur was more interested in the Chair of Psychology at Princeton than he was in the experiment. Dr. Nemur said that Dr. Strauss was nothing but an opportunist who was trying to ride to glory on *his* coattails.

When I left afterwards, I found myself trembling. I don't know why for sure, but it

was as if I'd seen both men clearly for the first time. I remember hearing Burt say that Dr. Nemur had a shrew of a wife who was pushing him all the time to get things published so that he could become famous. Burt said that the dream of her life was to have a big shot husband.

Was Dr. Strauss really trying to ride on his coattails?

April 28 I don't understand why I never noticed how beautiful Miss Kinnian really is. She has brown eyes and feathery brown hair

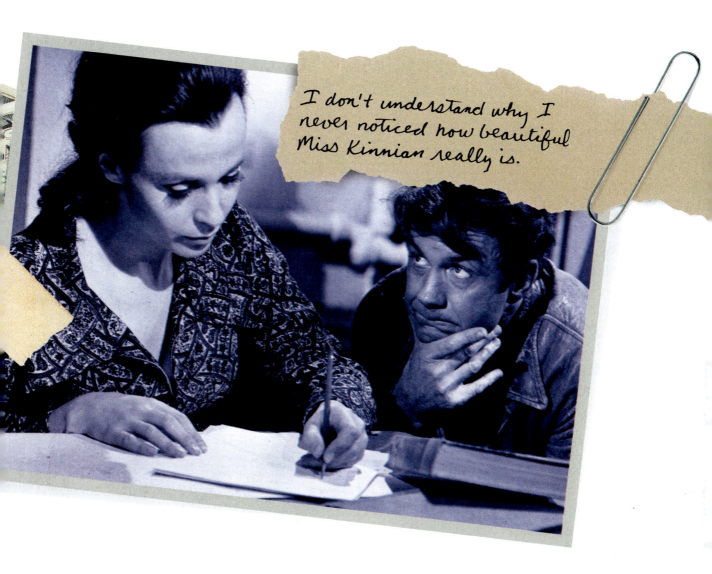

I don't understand why I never noticed how beautiful Miss Kinnian really is.

that comes to the top of her neck. She's only thirty-four! I think from the beginning I had the feeling that she was an unreachable genius—and very, very old. Now, every time I see her she grows younger and more lovely.

We had dinner and a long talk. When she said that I was coming along so fast that soon I'd be leaving her behind, I laughed.

"It's true, Charlie. You're already a better reader than I am. You can read a whole page at a glance while I can take in only a few lines at a time. And you remember every single thing you read. I'm lucky if I can recall the main thoughts and the general meaning."

"I don't feel intelligent. There are so many things I don't understand."

She took out a cigarette and I lit it for her. "You've got to be a *little* patient. You're accomplishing in days and weeks what it takes normal people to do in half a lifetime. That's what makes it so amazing. You're like a giant sponge now, soaking things in. Facts, figures, general knowledge. And soon you'll begin to connect them, too. You'll see how the different branches of learning are related. There are many levels, Charlie, like steps on a giant ladder that take you up higher and higher to see more and more of the world around you.

"I can see only a little bit of that, Charlie, and I won't go much higher than I am now, but you'll keep climbing up and up, and see more and more, and each step will open new worlds that you never even knew existed." She frowned. "I hope . . . I just hope to God—"

"What?"

"Never mind, Charles. I just hope I wasn't wrong to advise you to go into this in the first place."

I laughed. "How could that be? It worked, didn't it? Even Algernon is still smart."

We sat there silently for a while and I knew what she was thinking about as she watched me toying with the chain of my rabbit's foot and my keys. I didn't want to think of that possibility any more than elderly people want to think of death. I knew that this was only the beginning. I knew what she meant about levels because I'd seen some of them already. The thought of leaving her behind made me sad.

I'm in love with Miss Kinnian.

I'm in love with Miss Kinnian.

PROGRESS REPORT 11

April 30 I've quit my job with Donnegan's Plastic Box Company. Mr. Donnegan insisted that it would be better for all concerned if I left. What did I do to make them hate me so?

The first I knew of it was when Mr. Donnegan showed me the petition. Eight hundred and forty names, everyone connected with the factory, except Fanny Girden. Scanning the list quickly, I saw at once that hers was the only missing name. All the rest demanded that I be fired.

Joe Carp and Frank Reilly wouldn't talk to me about it. No one else would either, except Fanny. She was one of the few people I'd known who set her mind to something and believed it no matter what the rest of the world proved, said, or did—and Fanny did not believe that I should have been fired. She had been against the petition on principle and despite the pressure and threats she'd held out.

"Which don't mean to say," she remarked, "that I don't think there's something mighty strange about you, Charlie. Them changes. I don't know. You used to be a good, dependable, ordinary man—not too bright maybe, but honest. Who knows what you done to yourself to get so smart all of a sudden. Like everybody around here's been saying, Charlie, it's not right."

"But how can you say that, Fanny? What's wrong with a man becoming intelligent and wanting to acquire knowledge and understanding of the world around him?"

She stared down at her work and I turned to leave. Without looking at me, she said: "It was evil when Eve listened to the snake and ate from the tree of knowledge. It was evil when she saw that she was naked. If not for that none of us would ever have to grow old and sick, and die."

Once again now I have the feeling of shame burning inside me. This intelligence has driven a wedge between me and all the people I once knew and loved. Before, they laughed at me and despised me for my ignorance and dullness; now, they hate me for my knowledge and understanding. What in God's name do they want of me?

They've driven me out of the factory. Now I'm more alone than ever before . . .

April 30, 1965

Mr. Donnegan showed me the petition.

Dear Mr. Donnegan:

We, the undersigned employees of Donnegan's Plastic Box Company, request that Charlie Gordon

49

After You Read Response and Analysis

Part 1

First Thoughts

1. Re-read your Quickwrite. Then, add two or three sentences connecting what you wrote earlier with your thoughts about what has happened in the story so far.

Thinking Critically

2693

2. Go back to Charlie's March 7 entry (pages 35–36). What **context clues** did you use to figure out what "crazy tests" Charlie is taking (such as the "*amazed*" with Algernon)? Give some other examples of how you used context clues to figure out what Charlie is reporting.

3. Re-read Fanny's comments about the changes in Charlie (page 49). How are Charlie's experiences similar to those of Adam and Eve in the Bible? (Look especially at Charlie's entry for April 30. You may want to compare his description with the biblical account, in Genesis 2:25–3:24.)

4. Early in the story, Dr. Strauss tells Dr. Nemur that Charlie's learning to read and write is as much of an achievement as their learning a difficult scientific theory without help (page 36). What does he mean? Challenge or defend his statement.

Reading Check

a. What is the operation meant to do for Charlie?

b. Why does Dr. Strauss think Charlie would be a good subject for the experiment?

c. Who is Algernon? What happens when Charlie first races Algernon?

d. What are some signs that Charlie is changing now that he's had the operation?

Extending Interpretations

5. Re-read the last few lines in Part 1. What do you think about people who dislike others who are different from them?

WEEKLY TIME CARD

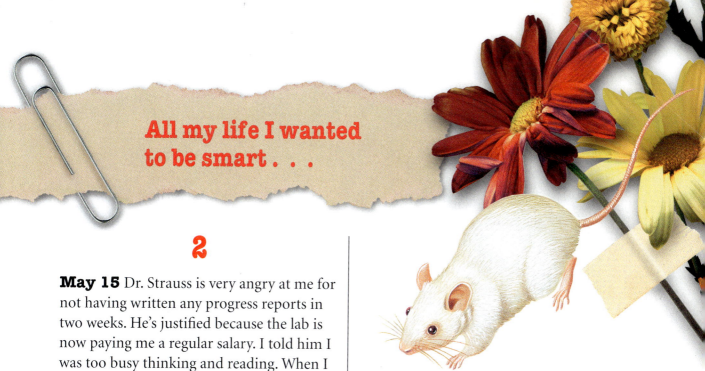

All my life I wanted to be smart . . .

2

May 15 Dr. Strauss is very angry at me for not having written any progress reports in two weeks. He's justified because the lab is now paying me a regular salary. I told him I was too busy thinking and reading. When I pointed out that writing was such a slow process that it made me impatient with my poor handwriting, he suggested that I learn to type. It's much easier to write now because I can type nearly seventy-five words a minute. Dr. Strauss continually reminds me of the need to speak and write simply so that people will be able to understand me.

I'll try to review all the things that happened to me during the last two weeks. Algernon and I were presented to the American Psychological Association sitting in convention with the World Psychological Association last Tuesday. We created quite a sensation. Dr. Nemur and Dr. Strauss were proud of us.

I suspect that Dr. Nemur, who is sixty—ten years older than Dr. Strauss—finds it necessary to see <u>tangible</u> results of his work. Undoubtedly the results of pressure by Mrs. Nemur.

Contrary to my earlier impressions of him, I realize that Dr. Nemur is not at all a genius. He has a very good mind, but it struggles under the specter of self-doubt. He wants people to take him for a genius. Therefore, it is important for him to feel that his work is acccpted by the world. I believe that Dr. Nemur was afraid of further delay because he worried that someone else might make a discovery along these lines and take the credit from him.

Dr. Strauss on the other hand might be called a genius, although I feel that his areas of knowledge are too limited. He was educated in the tradition of narrow specialization; the broader aspects of background were neglected far more than necessary—even for a neurosurgeon.

I was shocked to learn that the only ancient languages he could read were Latin, Greek, and Hebrew, and that he knows almost nothing of mathematics beyond the elementary levels of the calculus

Vocabulary
tangible (tanʹjə·bəl) *adj.:* capable of being seen or felt.

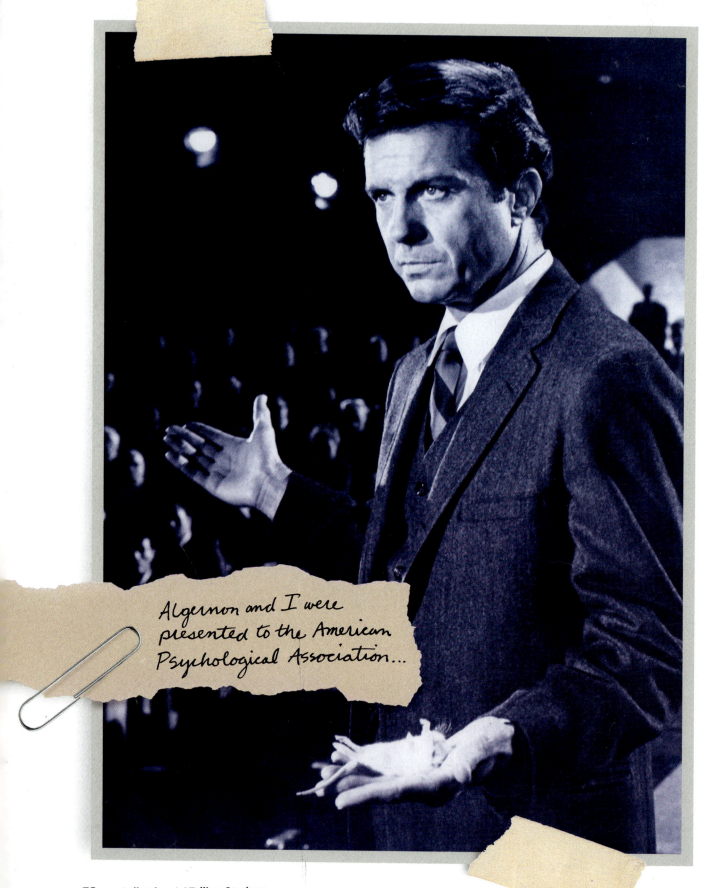

Algernon and I were presented to the American Psychological Association...

of variations. When he admitted this to me, I found myself almost annoyed. It was as if he'd hidden this part of himself in order to deceive me, pretending—as do many people, I've discovered—to be what he is not. No one I've ever known is what he appears to be on the surface.

Dr. Nemur appears to be uncomfortable around me. Sometimes when I try to talk to him, he just looks at me strangely and turns away. I was angry at first when Dr. Strauss told me I was giving Dr. Nemur an inferiority complex. I thought he was mocking me and I'm oversensitive at being made fun of.

How was I to know that a highly respected psychoexperimentalist like Nemur was unacquainted with Hindustani and Chinese? It's absurd when you consider the work that is being done in India and China today in the very field of his study.

I asked Dr. Strauss how Nemur could refute Rahajamati's attack on his method and results if Nemur couldn't even read them in the first place. That strange look on Dr. Strauss's face can mean only one of two things. Either he doesn't want to tell Nemur what they're saying in India, or else—and this worries me—Dr. Strauss doesn't know either. I must be careful to speak and write clearly and simply so that people won't laugh.

May 18 I am very disturbed. I saw Miss Kinnian last night for the first time in over a week. I tried to avoid all discussions of intellectual concepts and to keep the conversation on a simple, everyday level, but she just stared at me blankly and asked me what I meant about the mathematical variance equivalent in Dorbermann's Fifth Concerto.

When I tried to explain she stopped me and laughed. I guess I got angry, but I suspect I'm approaching her on the wrong level. No matter what I try to discuss with her, I am unable to communicate. I must review Vrostadt's equations on *Levels of Semantic Progression*. I find that I don't communicate with people much anymore. Thank God for books and music and things I can think about. I am alone in my apartment at Mrs. Flynn's boardinghouse most of the time and seldom speak to anyone.

May 20 I would not have noticed the new dishwasher, a boy of about sixteen, at the corner diner where I take my evening meals if not for the incident of the broken dishes.

They crashed to the floor, shattering and sending bits of white china under the tables. The boy stood there, dazed and frightened, holding the empty tray in his hand. The whistles and catcalls[1] from the customers (the cries of "Hey, there go the profits!". . . "Mazel tov!"[2] . . . and "Well, *he* didn't work here very long . . ." which invariably seem to follow the breaking of glass or dishware in a public restaurant) all seemed to confuse him.

When the owner came to see what the excitement was about, the boy cowered as if he expected to be struck and threw up his arms as if to ward off the blow.

---

1. **catcalls** *n.*: shouts and whistles made to express disapproval or ridicule, so called because people used to make noises like a cat's cry to show disapproval.
2. **mazel tov** (mä′zəl tōv′): Yiddish expression meaning "congratulations."

Vocabulary
refute (ri·fyo͞ot′) *v.*: prove wrong using evidence.
invariably (in·ver′ē·ə·blē) *adv.*: always.

"All right! All right, you dope," shouted the owner, "don't just stand there! Get the broom and sweep that mess up. A broom . . . a broom, you idiot! It's in the kitchen. Sweep up all the pieces."

The boy saw that he was not going to be punished. His frightened expression disappeared and he smiled and hummed as he came back with the broom to sweep the floor. A few of the rowdier customers kept up the remarks, amusing themselves at his expense.

"Here, sonny, over here there's a nice piece behind you . . ."

"C'mon, do it again . . ."

"He's not so dumb. It's easier to break 'em than to wash 'em . . ."

As his vacant eyes moved across the crowd of amused onlookers, he slowly mirrored their smiles and finally broke into an uncertain grin at the joke which he obviously did not understand.

I felt sick inside as I looked at his dull, vacuous smile, the wide, bright eyes of a child, uncertain but eager to please. They were laughing at him because he was mentally retarded.

And I had been laughing at him too.

Suddenly, I was furious at myself and all those who were smirking at him. I jumped up and shouted, "Shut up! Leave him alone! It's not his fault he can't understand! He can't help what he is! But for God's sake . . . he's still a human being!"

The room grew silent. I cursed myself for losing control and creating a scene. I tried not to look at the boy as I paid my check and walked out without touching my food. I felt ashamed for both of us.

How strange it is that people of honest feelings and sensibility, who would not take advantage of a man born without arms or legs or eyes—how such people think nothing of abusing a man born with low intelligence. It infuriated me to think that not too long ago I, like this boy, had foolishly played the clown.

And I had almost forgotten.

I'd hidden the picture of the old Charlie Gordon from myself because now that I was intelligent it was something that had to be pushed out of my mind. But today in looking at that boy, for the first time I saw what I had been. *I was just like him!*

Only a short time ago, I learned that people laughed at me. Now I can see that unknowingly I joined with them in laughing at myself. That hurts most of all.

I have often re-read my progress reports and seen the illiteracy, the childish naiveté,[3] the mind of low intelligence peering from a dark room, through the keyhole, at the dazzling light outside. I see that even in my dullness I knew that I was inferior, and that other people had something I lacked—something denied me. In my mental blindness, I thought that it was somehow connected with the ability to read and write, and I was sure that if I could get those skills I would automatically have intelligence too.

Even a feeble-minded man wants to be like other men.

A child may not know how to feed itself, or what to eat, yet it knows of hunger.

This then is what I was like. I never knew. Even with my gift of intellectual awareness, I never really knew.

This day was good for me. Seeing the past more clearly, I have decided to use my knowledge and skills to work in the field of increasing human intelligence levels. Who is better equipped for this work? Who else has lived in both worlds? These are my people. Let me use my gift to do something for them.

Tomorrow, I will discuss with Dr. Strauss the manner in which I can work in this area. I may be able to help him work out the problems of widespread use of the technique which was used on me. I have several good ideas of my own.

There is so much that might be done with this technique. If I could be made into a genius, what about thousands of others like myself? What fantastic levels might be achieved by using this technique on normal people? On *geniuses*?

3. **naiveté** (nä·ēv·tā′) *n.:* simplicity; foolish innocence.

There are so many doors to open. I am impatient to begin.

PROGRESS REPORT 12

May 23 It happened today. Algernon bit me. I visited the lab to see him as I do occasionally, and when I took him out of his cage, he snapped at my hand. I put him back and watched him for a while. He was unusually disturbed and vicious.

May 24 Burt, who is in charge of the experimental animals, tells me that Algernon is changing. He is less cooperative, he refuses to run the maze any more; general motivation has decreased. And he hasn't been eating. Everyone is upset about what this may mean.

May 25 They've been feeding Algernon, who now refuses to work the shifting-lock problem. Everyone identifies me with Algernon. In a way we're both the first of our kind. They're all pretending that Algernon's behavior is not necessarily significant for me. But it's hard to hide the fact that some of the other animals who were used in this experiment are showing strange behavior.

Dr. Strauss and Dr. Nemur have asked me not to come to the lab anymore. I know what they're thinking but I can't accept it. I am going ahead with my plans to carry their research forward. With all due respect to both of these fine scientists, I am well aware of their limitations. If there is an answer, I'll have to find it out for myself. Suddenly, time has become very important to me.

May 29 I have been given a lab of my own and permission to go ahead with the research. I'm on to something. Working day and night. I've had a cot moved into the lab. Most of my writing time is spent on the notes which I keep in a separate folder, but from time to time I feel it necessary to put down my moods and my thoughts out of sheer habit.

I find the *calculus of intelligence* to be a fascinating study. Here is the place for the application of all the knowledge I have acquired. In a sense it's the problem I've been concerned with all my life.

May 31 Dr. Strauss thinks I'm working too hard. Dr. Nemur says I'm trying to cram a lifetime of research and thought into a few weeks. I know I should rest, but I'm driven on by something inside that won't let me stop. I've got to find the reason for the sharp regression in Algernon. I've got to know *if* and *when* it will happen to me.

Vocabulary

regression (ri·gresh'ən) *n.*: return to an earlier or less advanced condition.

The Algernon-Gordon Effect:
A Study of Structure and Function

I have been given a lab of my own and permission to go ahead with the research.

June 4

LETTER TO DR. STRAUSS (copy)

Dear Dr. Strauss:

Under separate cover I am sending you a copy of my report entitled, "The Algernon-Gordon Effect: A Study of Structure and Function of Increased Intelligence," which I would like to have you read and have published.

As you see, my experiments are completed. I have included in my report all of my formulae, as well as mathematical analysis in the appendix. Of course, these should be verified.

Because of its importance to both you and Dr. Nemur (and need I say to myself, too?) I have checked and rechecked my results a dozen times in the hope of finding an error. I am sorry to say the results must stand. Yet for the sake of science, I am grateful for the little bit that I here add to the knowledge of the function of the human mind and of the laws governing the artificial increase of human intelligence.

I recall your once saying to me that an experimental *failure* or the *disproving* of a theory was as important to the advancement of learning as a success would be. I know now that this is true. I am sorry, however, that my own contribution to the field must rest upon the ashes of the work of two men I regard so highly.

    Yours truly,
    Charles Gordon
encl.: rept

June 5 I must not become emotional. The facts and the results of my experiments are clear, and the more sensational aspects of my own rapid climb cannot obscure the fact that the tripling of intelligence by the surgical technique developed by Drs. Strauss and Nemur must be viewed as having little or no practical applicability (at the present time) to the increase of human intelligence.

As I review the records and data on Algernon, I see that although he is still in his physical infancy, he has regressed mentally. Motor activity is impaired; there is a general reduction of glandular activity; there is an accelerated loss of coordination.

There are also strong indications of progressive amnesia.

As will be seen by my report, these and other physical and mental deterioration syndromes can be predicted with statistically significant results by the application of my formula.

The surgical stimulus to which we were both subjected has resulted in an intensification and acceleration of all mental processes. The unforeseen development, which I have taken the liberty of calling the *Algernon-Gordon Effect*, is the logical extension of the entire intelligence speed-up. The hypothesis here proven may be described simply in the following terms: Artificially increased intelligence deteriorates at a rate of time directly proportional to the quantity of the increase.

Vocabulary

verified (ver′ə·fīd′) *v.:* confirmed; checked or tested for correctness.

obscure (əb·skyoor′) *v.:* hide.

deterioration (dē·tir′ē·ə·rā′shən) *n.* used as *adj.:* worsening; decline.

hypothesis (hī·päth′ə·sis) *n.:* explanation or theory to be proved.

I feel that this, in itself, is an important discovery.

As long as I am able to write, I will continue to record my thoughts in these progress reports. It is one of my few pleasures. However, by all indications, my own mental deterioration will be very rapid.

I have already begun to notice signs of emotional instability and forgetfulness, the first symptoms of the burnout.

June 10 Deterioration progressing. I have become absent-minded. Algernon died two days ago. Dissection shows my predictions were right. His brain had decreased in weight and there was a general smoothing out of cerebral convolutions as well as a deepening and broadening of brain fissures.[4]

---

4. **brain fissures** (fish'ərz): grooves in the surface of the brain.

I guess the same thing is or will soon be happening to me. Now that it's definite, I don't want it to happen.

I put Algernon's body in a cheese box and buried him in the backyard. I cried.

June 15 Dr. Strauss came to see me again. I wouldn't open the door and I told him to go away. I want to be left to myself. I have become touchy and irritable. I feel the darkness closing in. It's hard to throw off thoughts of suicide. I keep telling myself how important this <u>introspective</u> journal will be.

It's a strange sensation to pick up a book that you've read and enjoyed just a few months ago and discover that you don't remember it. I remembered how great I thought John Milton was, but when I picked up *Paradise Lost* I couldn't understand it at all. I got so angry I threw the book across the room.

I've got to try to hold on to some of it. Some of the things I've learned. Oh, God, please don't take it all away.

June 19 Sometimes, at night, I go out for a walk. Last night I couldn't remember where I lived. A policeman took me home. I have the strange feeling that this has all happened to me before—a long time ago. I keep telling myself I'm the only person in the world who can describe what's happening to me.

June 21 Why can't I remember? I've got to fight. I lie in bed for days and I don't

Vocabulary
introspective (in'trə·spek'tiv) *adj.:* looking inward; observing one's own thoughts and feelings.

know who or where I am. Then it all comes back to me in a flash. Fugues of amnesia.[5] Symptoms of senility—second childhood. I can watch them coming on. It's so cruelly logical. I learned so much and so fast. Now my mind is deteriorating rapidly. I won't let it happen. I'll fight it. I can't help thinking of the boy in the restaurant, the blank expression, the silly smile, the people laughing at him. No—please—not that again . . .

June 22 I'm forgetting things that I learned recently. It seems to be following the classic pattern—the last things learned are the first things forgotten. Or is that the pattern? I'd better look it up again. . . .

I re-read my paper on the *Algernon-Gordon Effect* and I get the strange feeling that it was written by someone else. There are parts I don't even understand.

Motor activity impaired. I keep tripping over things, and it becomes increasingly difficult to type.

June 23 I've given up using the typewriter completely. My coordination is bad. I feel that I'm moving slower and slower. Had a terrible shock today. I picked up a copy of an article I used in my research, Krueger's *Uber psychische Ganzheit,* to see if it would help me understand what I had done. First I thought there was something wrong with my eyes. Then I realized I could no longer read German. I tested myself in other languages. All gone.

June 30 A week since I dared to write again. It's slipping away like sand through my fingers. Most of the books I have are too hard for me now. I get angry with them because I know that I read and understood them just a few weeks ago.

I keep telling myself I must keep writing these reports so that somebody will know what is happening to me. But it gets harder to form the words and remember spellings. I have to look up even simple words in the dictionary now and it makes me impatient with myself.

Dr. Strauss comes around almost every day, but I told him I wouldn't see or speak to anybody. He feels guilty. They all do. But I don't blame anyone. I knew what might happen. But how it hurts.

July 7 I don't know where the week went. Todays Sunday I know becuase I can see through my window people going to church. I think I stayed in bed all week but I remember Mrs. Flynn bringing food to me a few times. I keep saying over and over Ive got to do something but then I forget or maybe its just easier not to do what I say Im going to do.

I think of my mother and father a lot these days. I found a picture of them with me taken at a beach. My father has a big ball under his arm and my mother is holding me by the hand. I dont remember them the way they are in the picture. All I remember is my father drunk most of the time and arguing with mom about money.

He never shaved much and he used to scratch my face when he hugged me. My mother said he died but Cousin Miltie said he heard his mom and dad say that my father ran away with another woman. When I asked my mother she slapped my face and said my father was dead. I dont think I ever

---

5. **fugues** (fyo͞ogz) **of amnesia** (am·nē′zhə): temporary states of disturbed consciousness. A person who experiences fugues has no memory of them afterward.

found out which was true but I don't care much. (He said he was going to take me to see cows on a farm once but he never did. He never kept his promises . . .)

July 10 My landlady Mrs Flynn is very worried about me. She says the way I lay around all day and dont do anything I remind her of her son before she threw him out of the house. She said she doesn't like loafers. If Im sick its one thing, but if Im a loafer thats another thing and she wont have it. I told her I think Im sick.

I try to read a little bit every day, mostly stories, but sometimes I have to read the same thing over and over again because I dont know what it means. And its hard to write. I know I should look up all the words in the dictionary but its so hard and Im so tired all the time.

Then I got the idea that I would only use the easy words instead of the long hard ones. That saves time. I put flowers on Algernons grave about once a week. Mrs Flynn thinks Im crazy to put flowers on a mouses grave but I told her that Algernon was special.

July 14 Its sunday again. I dont have anything to do to keep me busy now because my television set is broke and I dont have any money to get it fixed. (I think I lost this months check from the lab. I dont remember)

I get awful headaches and asperin doesnt help me much. Mrs Flynn knows Im really sick and she feels very sorry for me. Shes a wonderful woman whenever someone is sick.

July 22 Mrs Flynn called a strange doctor to see me. She was afraid I was going to die.

I told the doctor I wasnt too sick and that I only forget sometimes. He asked me did I have any friends or relatives and I said no I dont have any. I told him I had a friend called Algernon once but he was a mouse and we used to run races together. He looked at me kind of funny like he thought I was crazy.

He smiled when I told him I used to be a genius. He talked to me like I was a baby and he winked at Mrs Flynn. I got mad and chased him out because he was making fun of me the way they all used to.

July 24 I have no more money and Mrs Flynn says I got to go to work somewhere and pay the rent because I havent paid for over two months. I dont know any work but the job I used to have at Donnegans Plastic Box Company. I dont want to go back there because they all knew me when I was smart and maybe theyll laugh at me. But I don't know what else to do to get money.

July 25 I was looking at some of my old progress reports and its very funny but I cant read what I wrote. I can make out some of the words but they dont make sense.

Miss Kinnian came to the door but I said go away I dont want to see you. She cried and I cried too but I wouldnt let her in because I didn't want her to laugh at me. I told her I didn't like her any more. I told her I didnt want to be smart any more. Thats not true. I still love her and I still want to be smart but I had to say that so shed go away. She gave Mrs Flynn money to pay the rent. I dont want that. I got to get a job.

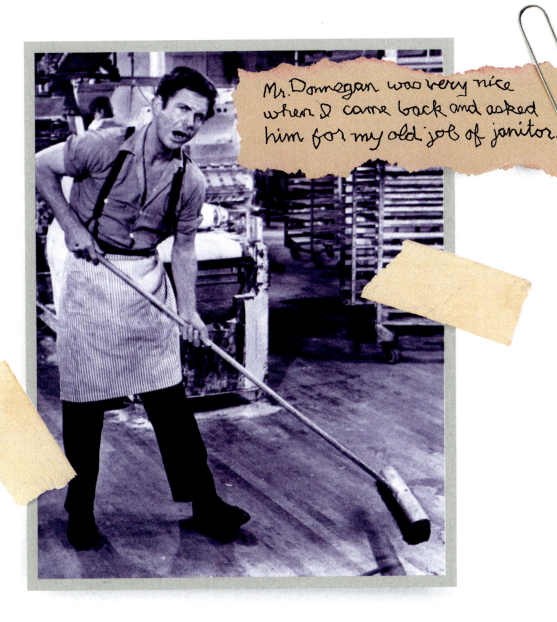

Mr. Donnegan was very nice when I came back and asked him for my old job of janitor.

Please . . . please let me not forget how to read and write . . .

July 27 Mr Donnegan was very nice when I came back and asked him for my old job of janitor. First he was very suspicious but I told him what happened to me then he looked very sad and put his hand on my shoulder and said Charlie Gordon you got guts.

Everybody looked at me when I came downstairs and started working in the toilet sweeping it out like I used to. I told myself Charlie if they make fun of you dont get sore because you remember their not so smart as you once thot they were. And besides they were once your friends and if they laughed at you that doesnt mean anything because they liked you too.

One of the new men who came to work there after I went away made a nasty crack he said hey Charlie I hear your a very smart fella a real quiz kid. Say something intelligent. I felt bad but Joe Carp came over and grabbed him by the shirt and said leave him alone you lousy cracker or Ill break your neck. I didn't expect Joe to take my part so I guess hes really my friend.

Later Frank Reilly came over and said Charlie if anybody bothers you or trys to take advantage you call me or Joe and we will set em straight. I said thanks Frank and I got choked up so I had to turn around and go into the supply room so he wouldnt see me cry. Its good to have friends.

July 28 I did a dumb thing today I forgot I wasnt in Miss Kinnians class at the adult center any more like I use to be. I went in and sat down in my old seat in the back of the room and she looked at me funny and she said Charles. I dint remember she ever called me that before only Charlie so I said hello Miss Kinnian Im redy for my lesin today only I lost my reader that we was using. She startid to cry and run out of the room and everybody looked at me and I saw they wasnt the same pepul who used to be in my class.

Then all of a suddin I rememberd some things about the operashun and me getting smart and I said holy smoke I reely pulled a Charlie Gordon that time. I went away before she come back to the room.

Thats why Im going away from New York for good. I dont want to do nothing like that agen. I dont want Miss Kinnian to feel sorry for me. Evry body feels sorry at the factery and I dont want that eather so Im going someplace where nobody knows that Charlie Gordon was once a genus and now he cant even reed a book or rite good.

Im taking a cuple of books along and even if I cant reed them Ill practise hard and maybe I wont forget every thing I lerned. If I try reel hard maybe Ill be a littel bit smarter then I was before the operashun. I got my rabits foot and my luky penny and maybe they will help me.

If you ever reed this Miss Kinnian dont be sorry for me Im glad I got a second chanse to be smart becaus I lerned a lot of things that I never even new were in this world and Im grateful that I saw it all for a littel bit. I dont know why Im dumb agen or what I did wrong maybe its becaus I dint try hard enuff. But if I try and practis very hard maybe Ill get a littl smarter and know what all the words are. I remember a littel bit how nice I had a feeling with the blue book that has the torn cover when I red it. Thats why Im gonna keep trying to get smart so I can have that feeling agen. Its a good feeling to know things and be smart. I wish I had it rite now if I did I would sit down and reed all the time. Anyway I bet Im the first dumb person in the world who ever found out somthing importent for sience. I remember I did somthing but I dont remember what. So I gess its like I did it for all the dumb pepul like me.

Good-by Miss Kinnian and Dr Strauss and evreybody. And P.S. please tell Dr Nemur not to be such a grouch when pepul laff at him and he woud have more frends. Its easy to make frends if you let pepul laff at you. Im going to have lots of frends where I go.

P.P.S. Please if you get a chanse put some flowrs on Algernons grave in the bakyard . . .

Meet the Writer

Daniel Keyes

"Fascinated by the . . . Human Mind"

Daniel Keyes (1927–   ) says that he is "fascinated by the complexities of the human mind." Many people share his interest, as the enormous popularity of "Flowers for Algernon" shows. The story won the 1959 Hugo Award, given by the Science Fiction Writers of America, and it has been widely translated. Keyes expanded it into a novel, which won another science fiction prize, the Nebula Award, in 1966. The story was also made into a movie, *Charly*, a television play, *The Two Worlds of Charlie Gordon*, and even a Broadway musical, *Charlie and Algernon*.

Daniel Keyes was born in Brooklyn, New York. He has worked as an English teacher, a merchant seaman, an editor, and a fashion photographer.

For Independent Reading

Keyes has written a book about the process of writing his famous story. It is called *Algernon, Charlie and I.*

Part 2

First Thoughts

1. What do you think becomes of Charlie after the story ends? Why?

Thinking Critically

2. Why is Algernon important to Charlie?

3. Charlie takes a Rorschach test twice. These two incidents can be called **parallel episodes.** What other parallel episodes can you find in this story?

4. An important **subplot** in this story involves Charlie's relationship with Miss Kinnian. What is the **resolution** of that subplot?

Extending Interpretations

5. Why would some people say that Charlie would be better off if he had not had the operation? What do you think?

6. At the end of the story, Charlie writes, "Its easy to make frends if you let pepul laff at you." Do you agree or disagree with Charlie's opinion? Explain.

7. Describe your feelings about human engineering—that is, using science to change a person's intelligence or personality.

Reading Check

a. At the beginning of Part 2, what **conflicts** is Charlie having with the doctors? with himself?

b. How does Charlie react when the boy in the diner drops the dishes?

c. What does Charlie's research reveal about the results of the experiment?

d. What are some of the signals that tell you that Charlie's mental state is getting worse?

e. At the end of the story, why does Charlie decide to leave New York?

go.hrw.com

INTERNET

Projects and Activities

Keyword: LE5 8-1

SKILLS FOCUS

Literary Skills
Analyze subplots and parallel episodes.

Reading Skills
Use context clues.

Writing Skills
Write a diary entry.

WRITING

Retelling from Another Point of View

This story is made up of Charlie's progress reports, which are like a diary or journal. Pick another character from the story, and write a diary entry for him or her corresponding to one of Charlie's reports. For example, what might Miss Kinnian have written the night she and Charlie had dinner? What might Frank Reilly have written the day Charlie returned to his former job at the factory? Use the first-person pronoun *I* to write from your character's **point of view.**

History of the English Language

Digging into the Past. Where did English come from? England, of course! Not entirely. People didn't wake up one morning speaking the English of today. Today's English developed over a long period of time. The history of English can be divided into three periods: **Old English** (A.D. 450–1066), **Middle English** (1066–1485), and **Modern English** (1485 to the present).

Old English. In the fifth century, the Anglo-Saxons migrated from northern Europe to the island of Britain. There they found the Britons, a Celtic people who had earlier been conquered by the Romans. The Anglo-Saxons settled in and proceeded to develop a new language, combining bits from their old Germanic language and bits from the Celtic language of the natives. Soon Britain was invaded again, this time by the fierce Northmen, or Vikings, from Scandinavia. Their language, Norse, also was added to the language of Britain. We call this new language Old English. It was a spoken, or oral, language. Anyone who wanted to write something down wrote it in Latin. Here are three Old English words that survive today: *horse, night, wife*.

Middle English. In the year 1066, William the Conqueror, who was from Normandy, in France, conquered England. Soon French words were added to the mix. Because French developed from Latin, Latin also became an important influence on English. For several hundred years, England was a bilingual country. French was spoken by the upper classes and used in courts and government. English was spoken by the lower classes and used for the purposes of daily life. Latin was used by the Church. Most people spoke English, but they were borrowing words from French at a rapid rate. English continued to grow and change with all these borrowings—from Anglo-Saxon, Norse, Latin, French—resulting today in a language with a huge vocabulary that is both rich and international. Here are three words derived from French: *government, justice, literature*.

(*continued on next page*)

SKILLS FOCUS

Vocabulary Skills
Understand the history of English.

Vocabulary Development

Modern English. In 1485, Henry VII, the first Tudor king, came to the throne of England. The House of Tudor helped to promote all things English—including the language. Printed books helped to make it possible for all English people to speak, read, and write the same language.

As you can see, there is more to an English word than its present-day definition. Our words have a past! You can dig into this past by looking up the **etymology** (et'ə·mäl'ə·jē), or origin and development of a word, in a dictionary. Consider this entry for the etymology of the word *obscure*. (The symbol < means "derived from" or "came from.")

> **obscure**   OFr *obscur* < L *obscurus*, "covered over"

Translated, this means "The word *obscure* evolved from the Old French word *obscur*, which in turn came from the Latin word *obscurus*, which means 'covered over.'"

PRACTICE

Dig into the past of three words from the Word Bank by using a good dictionary to look up their etymologies. You might have to go to more than one entry in the dictionary to get all your data for each word. Then, "translate" the story you discover behind each word. Make a word map, like the one below, based on the definitions and etymologies of the words. For each word, include a sentence that shows you understand the word's meaning.

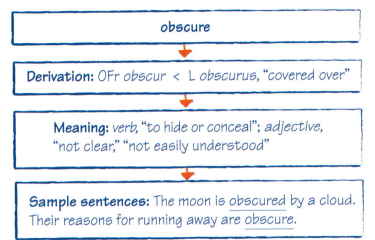

obscure

↓

Derivation: OFr *obscur* < L *obscurus*, "covered over"

↓

Meaning: *verb*, "to hide or conceal"; *adjective*, "not clear," "not easily understood"

↓

Sample sentences: The moon is obscured by a cloud. Their reasons for running away are obscure.

Word Bank

misled
tangible
refute
invariably
regression
verified
obscure
deterioration
hypothesis
introspective

Analyzing Proposition and Support

Reading Focus

Recognizing Proposition and Support

Suppose Charlie's doctors were to propose a treatment for his condition, based on one of their experiments. To evaluate that proposal, other scientists would have to determine how believable the doctors' arguments, or reasons, are.

Charlie's doctors would probably begin their proposal with a **proposition,** which is an opinion. The proposition should be clearly stated. Then it's up to the other scientists to evaluate each reason that **supports** the proposition. A **reason** answers the question *why?* about the proposition statement.

Recognizing Support

A proposition can be supported with the following evidence:

- **facts,** including the results of scientific research and surveys

- **statistics**—facts in number form

- **examples**—specific instances that illustrate reasons or facts

- **anecdotes**—brief stories, such as personal experiences

- **definitions**

- **opinions from experts** on the subject, especially with direct quotations

Facts Versus Opinions

When you read persuasion, you must determine which statements are facts and which are opinions.

- A **fact** is something that can be proved true by direct observation or by checking a reliable reference source, such as an encyclopedia.

The following statement is a **fact:**
I.Q. tests measure logical, verbal, and mathematical ability.

This statement is not a fact:
I.Q. tests are reliable measures of human ability. It might sound like a fact, but it's the kind of statement that is impossible to prove.

- An **opinion** is a belief or an attitude. An opinion cannot be proved true or false, but it can be supported with facts.

■ As you read the following article, you'll notice the proposition right away. How many kinds of support can you find?

Vocabulary Development

The following words appear in the next article:

inevitable (in·ev′i·tə·bəl) *adj.:* unavoidable.

crucial (kro͞o′shəl) *adj.:* highly important.

provocative (prə·väk′ə·tiv) *adj.:* stirring up thoughts or feelings.

irrevocably (i·rev′ə·kə·blē) *adv.:* in a way that cannot be undone or changed.

cognitive (käg′nə·tiv) *adj.:* having to do with the process of knowing and being able to remember.

INTERNET

Vocabulary Activity
•
Interactive Reading Model

Keyword: LE5 8-1

Reading Skills
Analyze proposition and support.

Memory a Matter of Brains and Brawn

Mental, Physical Exertion Needed to Preserve the Mind

By Lauran Neergaard
ASSOCIATED PRESS

The brain is like a muscle: Use it or lose it.

That is the growing conclusion from research that shows fogged memory and slowed wit are not inevitable consequences of getting old, and there are steps people can take to protect their brains.

Mental exercise seems crucial. Benefits start when parents read to tots and depend heavily on education, but scientists say it is never too late to start jogging the gray matter.

People have to get physical, too. Bad memory is linked to heart disease, diabetes, and a high-fat diet—all risks that people can counter by living healthier lives.

In fact, provocative new research suggests these brain-protective steps, mental and physical, may be strong enough even to help influence who gets Alzheimer's disease.

"There are some things that,

if you know you have a family history (of Alzheimer's) and you're just 20 to 30 years old, you can start doing to increase your protective factors," said Dr. Amir Soas of Case Western Reserve University Medical School in Cleveland.

It is also good advice for the average baby boomer hoping to stay sharp, or the mom priming her child for a lifelong healthy brain.

Most important: "Read, read, read," Soas said. Do crossword puzzles. Pull out the chessboard or Scrabble. Learn a foreign language or a new hobby. "Anything that stimulates the brain to think," he said.

And cut back on television, Soas insists. "When you watch television, your brain goes into neutral," he said.

Just a few years ago, scientists believed the brain was wired forever before age 5 and that over the ensuing decades, a person irrevocably lost neurons and crucial brain circuitry

until mental decline became noticeable.

Scientists now know the brain continually rewires and adapts itself, even in old age; large brain-cell growth continues into the teen years; and even seniors can grow at least some new neurons.

What keeps brains healthy? Clues come from Alzheimer's research.

Numerous studies show people with less education have higher risks of Alzheimer's than the better-educated. Lead researcher Mary Haan of the University of Michigan found less than a ninth-grade education a key threshold; other studies suggest a difference even between holders of bachelor's and master's degrees.

It's not just formal education. Reading habits between ages 6 and 18 appear crucial predictors of cognitive function decades later, said Dr. David Bennett of Chicago's Rush University.

—from the *San Francisco Chronicle*

Analyzing Proposition and Support

Memory a Matter of Brains and Brawn

Test Practice

1. Which of these statements is the **proposition** of this article?
   - A "The brain is like a muscle: Use it or lose it."
   - B Cut back on television.
   - C Formal education is very important in keeping the brain healthy.
   - D Alzheimer's disease can be prevented.

2. All of the following types of support are used in the article *except* —
   - F facts
   - G statistics
   - H anecdotes
   - J opinions

3. What is the writer's **attitude** about the possibility of increasing and preserving intelligence?
   - A Hopeful
   - B Neutral
   - C Pessimistic
   - D Angry

4. To keep the brain active, Dr. Amir Soas suggests all of the following *except* —
   - F reading
   - G playing chess
   - H watching educational television
   - J learning a foreign language

5. The experts quoted in this article agree on which one of the following statements?
   - A People who read will not get Alzheimer's disease.
   - B Reading and education can lower the risk of getting Alzheimer's disease.
   - C Physical exercise can prevent Alzheimer's disease.
   - D Memory is the most important function of the human mind.

Constructed Response

1. According to the article, how is the brain like a muscle?

2. At what point in life do the benefits of mental exercise begin?

3. What three factors are linked to bad memory?

4. According to one expert, what happens to people when they watch television?

5. What new brain-cell research makes scientists hopeful about preserving mental function?

6. Why is it important for people to get as much education as they can?

SKILLS FOCUS

Reading Skills
Analyze proposition and support.

After You Read   Vocabulary Development

Mapping Words

PRACTICE 1

Draw a word map like the one below for each word in the
Word Bank. Here is a word map for *provocative:*

provocative

> **Sample sentence:** The <u>provocative</u> remarks made us uneasy.

↑

> **Definition:** stirring up thoughts or feelings

→

> **Related words:** provoke, evoke, vocal

↓

> **Etymology:** L *pro–*, "forth," + *vocare*, "to call"

> **Word Bank**
>
> inevitable
> crucial
> provocative
> irrevocably
> cognitive

Comparisons in Informal Language

PRACTICE 2

This writer uses the informal language of popular culture.
Informal language is often vivid because it uses unexpected
connections. Think about the underlined word in each of
these sentences, and answer the question that follows:

1. "Research . . . shows <u>fogged</u> memory and slowed wit
   are not inevitable consequences of getting old. . . ."
   What is a poor memory compared to?

2. "Scientists say it is never too late to start <u>jogging</u>
   the gray matter." In using the word *jogging*, what
   is the writer comparing mental exercise to?

3. "'When you watch television, your brain goes
   into <u>neutral</u>.' . . ." What is Dr. Soas comparing
   an idle brain to?

4. "Scientists now know the brain continually <u>rewires</u>
   and adapts itself. . . ." In using the word *rewires*,
   what is the writer comparing the brain to?

SKILLS FOCUS

Vocabulary Skills
Map words; analyze comparisons in informal language.

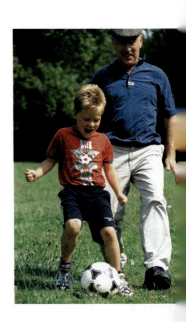

The Landlady

Make the Connection
How Do You Picture It?

Picture this: You've just arrived in a new town by train, and you're looking for a place to stay. As you walk down the street, you see this sign in a boardinghouse window:

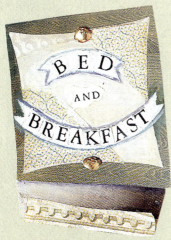

There are yellow flowers in a vase in the window and green curtains. You walk up to the window and look in. What do you see inside? What sort of a place is this boardinghouse?

   Draw an outline of a house like the one below. Fill it with words and symbols showing what—and whom—you imagine you would find in the boardinghouse.

Literary Focus
Foreshadowing

Writers make us feel suspense or anxiety by using **foreshadowing,** clues that hint at what will happen later. As you read "The Landlady," put yourself in the place of Billy, the main character. Pay close attention to what Billy sees and senses. Be on your toes—you may find yourself tripping over the many cleverly disguised clues.

Reading Skills
Making Predictions

As you read this story, you will probably find yourself **predicting,** or guessing, what will happen next. Your predictions might be based on what has already happened in the story and the clever clues the writer has left for you to figure out. They might also be based on similar events in other stories you know or in movies you have seen. As you read this story, look for the open-book signs after some paragraphs. Stop at those points, and jot down what you think is going to happen to Billy.

INTERNET

More About Dahl

Keyword: LE5 8-1

SKILLS FOCUS

Literary Skills
Understand foreshadowing.

Reading Skills
Make predictions.

The Landlady

Roald Dahl

Billy Weaver had traveled down from London on the slow afternoon train, with a change at Reading on the way, and by the time he got to Bath, it was about nine o'clock in the evening, and the moon was coming up out of a clear starry sky over the houses opposite the station entrance. But the air was deadly cold and the wind was like a flat blade of ice on his cheeks.

"Excuse me," he said, "but is there a fairly cheap hotel not too far away from here?"

"Try The Bell and Dragon," the porter[1] answered, pointing down the road. "They might take you in. It's about a quarter of a mile along on the other side."

Billy thanked him and picked up his suitcase and set out to walk the quarter-mile to The Bell and Dragon. He had never

---

1. **porter** *n.:* person hired to carry luggage.

been to Bath before. He didn't know anyone who lived there. But Mr. Greenslade at the head office in London had told him it was a splendid town. "Find your own lodgings," he had said, "and then go along and report to the branch manager as soon as you've got yourself settled."

Billy was seventeen years old. He was wearing a new navy-blue overcoat, a new brown trilby hat,[2] and a new brown suit, and he was feeling fine. He walked briskly down the street. He was trying to do everything briskly these days. Briskness, he had decided, was the one common characteristic of all successful businessmen. The big shots up at the head office were absolutely fantastically brisk all the time. They were amazing.

There were no shops on this wide street that he was walking along, only a line of tall houses on each side, all of them identical. They had porches and pillars and four or five steps going up to their front doors, and it was obvious that once upon a time they had been very swanky residences. But now, even in the darkness, he could see that the paint was peeling from the woodwork on their doors and windows and that the handsome white facades[3] were cracked and blotchy from neglect.

Suddenly, in a downstairs window that was brilliantly illuminated by a street lamp not six yards away, Billy caught sight of a printed notice propped up against the glass in one of the upper panes. It said "Bed and Breakfast." There was a vase of yellow chrysanthemums, tall and beautiful, standing just underneath the notice.

He stopped walking. He moved a bit closer. Green curtains (some sort of velvety

material) were hanging down on either side of the window. The chrysanthemums looked wonderful beside them. He went right up and peered through the glass into the room, and the first thing he saw was a bright fire burning in the hearth. On the carpet in front of the fire, a pretty little dachshund was curled up asleep with its nose tucked into its belly. The room itself, so far as he could see in the half darkness, was filled with pleasant furniture. There was a baby grand piano and a big sofa and several plump armchairs, and in one corner he spotted a large parrot in a cage. Animals were usually a good sign in a place like this, Billy told himself; and all in all, it looked to him as though it would be a pretty decent house to stay in. Certainly it would be more comfortable than The Bell and Dragon.

On the other hand, a pub would be more congenial[4] than a boardinghouse. There would be beer and darts in the evenings, and lots of people to talk to, and it would probably be a good bit cheaper, too. He had stayed a couple of nights in a pub once before and he had liked it. He had never stayed in any boardinghouses, and, to be perfectly honest, he was a tiny bit frightened of them. The name itself conjured up[5] images of watery cabbage, rapacious[6] landladies, and a powerful smell of kippers[7] in the living room.

After dithering about[8] like this in the cold for two or three minutes, Billy decided that he would walk on and take a look at

---

2. **trilby hat:** soft hat with the top deeply indented.
3. **facades** (fə·sädz′) *n.:* fronts of buildings.

4. **congenial** (kən·jēn′yəl) *adj.:* agreeable; pleasant.
5. **conjured** (kun′jərd) **up:** called to mind.
6. **rapacious** (rə·pā′shəs) *adj.:* greedy.
7. **kippers** *n.:* fish that have been salted and smoked. Kippers are commonly eaten for breakfast in Great Britain.
8. **dithering about:** acting nervous and confused.

him, compelling him, forcing him to stay where he was and not to walk away from that house, and the next thing he knew, he was actually moving across from the window to the front door of the house, climbing the steps that led up to it, and reaching for the bell. ❶

📖
PREDICT
❶ Where do you predict Billy will decide to stay?

He pressed the bell. Far away in a back room he heard it ringing, and then *at once*—it must have been at once because he hadn't even had time to take his finger from the bell button—the door swung open and a woman was standing there.

Normally you ring the bell and you have at least a half-minute's wait before the door opens. But this dame was like a jack-in-the-box. He pressed the bell—and out she popped! It made him jump.

She was about forty-five or fifty years old, and the moment she saw him, she gave him a warm, welcoming smile.

"*Please* come in," she said pleasantly. She stepped aside, holding the door wide open, and Billy found himself automatically starting forward. The compulsion or, more accurately, the desire to follow after her into that house was extraordinarily strong.

"I saw the notice in the window," he said, holding himself back.

"Yes, I know."

"I was wondering about a room."

"It's *all* ready for you, my dear," she said. She had a round pink face and very gentle blue eyes.

"I was on my way to The Bell and Dragon," Billy told her. "But the notice in your window just happened to catch my eye."

"My dear boy," she said, "why don't you come in out of the cold?"

The Bell and Dragon before making up his mind. He turned to go.

And now a queer thing happened to him. He was in the act of stepping back and turning away from the window when all at once his eye was caught and held in the most peculiar manner by the small notice that was there. BED AND BREAKFAST, it said. BED AND BREAKFAST, BED AND BREAKFAST, BED AND BREAKFAST. Each word was like a large black eye staring at him through the glass, holding

"How much do you charge?"

"Five and sixpence a night, including breakfast."

It was fantastically cheap. It was less than half of what he had been willing to pay.

"If that is too much," she added, "then perhaps I can reduce it just a tiny bit. Do you desire an egg for breakfast? Eggs are expensive at the moment. It would be sixpence less without the egg."

"Five and sixpence is fine," he answered. "I should like very much to stay here."

"I knew you would. Do come in."

She seemed terribly nice. She looked exactly like the mother of one's best school friend welcoming one into the house to stay for the Christmas holidays. Billy took off his hat and stepped over the threshold.

"Just hang it there," she said, "and let me help you with your coat."

There were no other hats or coats in the hall. There were no umbrellas, no walking sticks—nothing.

"We have it *all* to ourselves," she said, smiling at him over her shoulder as she led the way upstairs. "You see, it isn't very often I have the pleasure of taking a visitor into my little nest."

The old girl is slightly dotty,[9] Billy told himself. But at five and sixpence a night, who cares about that? "I should've thought you'd be simply swamped with applicants," he said politely.

"Oh, I am, my dear, I am, of course I am. But the trouble is that I'm inclined to be just a teeny-weeny bit choosy and particular—if you see what I mean."

"Ah, yes."

"But I'm always ready. Everything is al-

---

9. **dotty** *adj.*: crazy.

ways ready day and night in this house just on the off chance that an acceptable young gentleman will come along. And it is such a pleasure, my dear, such a very great pleasure when now and again I open the door and I see someone standing there who is just *exactly* right." She was halfway up the stairs, and she paused with one hand on the stair rail, turning her head and smiling down at him with pale lips. "Like you," she added, and her blue eyes traveled slowly all the way down the length of Billy's body, to his feet, and then up again.

On the second-floor landing she said to him, "This floor is mine."

They climbed up another flight. "And this one is *all* yours," she said. "Here's your room. I do hope you'll like it." She took him into a small but charming front bedroom, switching on the light as she went in.

"The morning sun comes right in the window, Mr. Perkins. It *is* Mr. Perkins, isn't it?"

"No," he said. "It's Weaver."

"Mr. Weaver. How nice. I've put a water bottle between the sheets to air them out, Mr. Weaver. It's such a comfort to have a hot-water bottle in a strange bed with clean sheets, don't you agree? And you may light the gas fire at any time if you feel chilly."

"Thank you," Billy said. "Thank you ever so much." He noticed that the bedspread had been taken off the bed and that the bedclothes had been neatly turned back on one side, all ready for someone to get in.

"I'm so glad you appeared," she said, looking earnestly into his face. "I was beginning to get worried."

"That's all right," Billy answered brightly. "You mustn't worry about me." He put his suitcase on the chair and started to open it.

"And what about supper, my dear? Did you manage to get anything to eat before you came here?"

"I'm not a bit hungry, thank you," he said. "I think I'll just go to bed as soon as possible because tomorrow I've got to get up rather early and report to the office."

"Very well, then. I'll leave you now so that you can unpack. But before you go to bed, would you be kind enough to pop into the sitting room on the ground floor and sign the book? Everyone has to do that because it's the law of the land, and we don't want to go breaking any laws at *this* stage in the proceedings, do we?" She gave him a little wave of the hand and went quickly out of the room and closed the door.

Now, the fact that his landlady appeared to be slightly off her rocker didn't worry Billy in the least. After all, she not only was harmless—there was no question about that—but she was also quite obviously a kind and generous soul. He guessed that she had probably lost a son in the war, or something like that, and had never gotten over it.

So a few minutes later, after unpacking his suitcase and washing his hands, he trotted downstairs to the ground floor and entered the living room. His landlady wasn't there, but the fire was glowing in the hearth, and the little dachshund was still sleeping soundly in front of it. The room was wonderfully warm and cozy. I'm a lucky fellow, he thought, rubbing his hands. This is a bit of all right. ❷ ⬱

> ⬱ **PREDICT**
> ❷ What prediction can you make about Billy's luck?

He found the guest book lying open on the piano, so he took out his pen and wrote down his name and address. There were only two other entries above his on the page, and as one always does with guest books, he started to read them. One was a Christopher Mulholland from Cardiff. The other was Gregory W. Temple from Bristol.

That's funny, he thought suddenly. Christopher Mulholland. It rings a bell.

Now where on earth had he heard that rather unusual name before?

Was it a boy at school? No. Was it one of his sister's numerous young men, perhaps, or a friend of his father's? No, no, it wasn't any of those. He glanced down again at the book.

Christopher Mulholland
231 Cathedral Road, Cardiff

Gregory W. Temple
27 Sycamore Drive, Bristol

As a matter of fact, now he came to think of it, he wasn't at all sure that the second name didn't have almost as much of a familiar ring about it as the first.

"Gregory Temple?" he said aloud, searching his memory. "Christopher Mulholland? . . ."

"Such charming boys," a voice behind him answered, and he turned and saw his landlady sailing into the room with a large silver tea tray in her hands. She was holding it well out in front of her, and rather high up, as though the tray were a pair of reins on a frisky horse.

"They sound somehow familiar," he said.

"They do? How interesting."

"I'm almost positive I've heard those names before somewhere. Isn't that odd? Maybe it was in the newspapers. They weren't famous in any way, were they? I mean famous cricketers[10] or footballers or something like that?"

"Famous," she said, setting the tea tray down on the low table in front of the sofa.

---

10. **cricketers** *n.*: people who play cricket, a game that is popular in Great Britain.

"Oh no, I don't think they were famous. But they were incredibly handsome, both of them, I can promise you that. They were tall and young and handsome, my dear, just exactly like you."

Once more, Billy glanced down at the book. "Look here," he said, noticing the dates.

"This last entry is over two years old."

"It is?"

"Yes, indeed. And Christopher Mulholland's is nearly a year before that—more than *three years* ago."

"Dear me," she said, shaking her head and heaving a dainty little sigh. "I would never have thought it. How time does fly away from us all, doesn't it, Mr. Wilkins?"

"It's Weaver," Billy said. "W-e-a-v-e-r."

"Oh, of course it is!" she cried, sitting down on the sofa. "How silly of me. I do apologize. In one ear and out the other, that's me, Mr. Weaver."

"You know something?" Billy said. "Something that's really quite extraordinary about all this?"

"No, dear, I don't."

"Well, you see, both of these names—Mulholland and Temple—I not only seem to remember each one of them separately, so to speak, but somehow or other, in some peculiar way, they both appear to be sort of connected together as well. As though they were both famous for the same sort of thing, if you see what I mean—like . . . well . . . like Dempsey and Tunney, for example, or Churchill and Roosevelt."[11]

"How amusing," she said. "But come over here now, dear, and sit down beside me on the sofa and I'll give you a nice cup of tea and a ginger biscuit[12] before you go to bed."

"You really shouldn't bother," Billy said. "I didn't mean you to do anything like that." He stood by the piano, watching her as she fussed about with the cups and saucers. He noticed that she had small, white, quickly moving hands and red fingernails.

"I'm almost positive it was in the newspapers I saw them," Billy said. "I'll think of it in a second. I'm sure I will."

There is nothing more tantalizing[13] than a thing like this that lingers just outside the borders of one's memory. He hated to give up.

"Now wait a minute," he said. "Wait just a minute. Mulholland . . . Christopher Mulholland . . . wasn't *that* the name of the Eton[14] schoolboy who was on a walking tour through the West Country, and then all of a sudden . . ."

"Milk?" she said. "And sugar?"

"Yes, please. And then all of a sudden . . ."

"Eton schoolboy?" she said. "Oh no, my dear, that can't possibly be right, because *my* Mr. Mulholland was certainly not an Eton schoolboy when he came to me. He was a Cambridge[15] undergraduate. Come over here now and sit next to me and warm yourself in front of this lovely fire. Come on. Your tea's all ready for you." She patted the empty place beside her on the sofa, and she sat there smiling at Billy and waiting for him to come over.

He crossed the room slowly and sat down on the edge of the sofa. She placed his teacup on the table in front of him.

"*There* we are," she said. "How nice and cozy this is, isn't it?"

Billy started sipping his tea. She did the same. For half a minute or so, neither of them spoke. But Billy knew that she was looking at him. Her body was half turned toward him, and he could feel her eyes resting on his face, watching him over the rim

---

11. **Dempsey and Tunney . . . Churchill and Roosevelt:** Jack Dempsey and Gene Tunney were American boxers who competed for the world heavyweight championship in 1926. Winston Churchill was prime minister of Great Britain, and Franklin D. Roosevelt was president of the United States, during World War II.

12. **biscuit** (bis′kit) *n.*: British term meaning "cookie."

13. **tantalizing** (tan′tə·līz′iŋ) *adj.*: teasing by remaining unavailable or by withholding something desired by someone; tempting. (In Greek mythology, Tantalus was a king condemned after death to stand in water that moved away whenever he tried to drink it and to remain under branches of fruit that were just out of reach.)

14. **Eton:** boys' prep school near London.

15. **Cambridge:** famous university in England.

of her teacup. Now and again, he caught a whiff of a peculiar smell that seemed to emanate[16] directly from her person. It was not in the least unpleasant, and it reminded him—well, he wasn't quite sure what it reminded him of. Pickled walnuts? New leather? Or was it the corridors of a hospital?

At length, she said, "Mr. Mulholland was a great one for his tea. Never in my life have I seen anyone drink as much tea as dear, sweet Mr. Mulholland."

"I suppose he left fairly recently," Billy said. He was still puzzling his head about the two names. He was positive now that he had seen them in the newspapers—in the headlines.

"Left?" she said, arching her brows. "But my dear boy, he never left. He's still here. Mr. Temple is also here. They're on the fourth floor, both of them together." ❸

INFER
❸ What do you think happened to Mr. Mulholland and Mr. Temple?

Billy set his cup down slowly on the table and stared at his landlady. She smiled back at him, and then she put out one of her white hands and patted him comfortingly on the knee. "How old are you, my dear?" she asked.

"Seventeen."

"Seventeen!" she cried. "Oh, it's the perfect age! Mr. Mulholland was also seventeen. But I think he was a trifle shorter than you are; in fact I'm sure he was, and his teeth weren't *quite* so white. You have the most beautiful teeth, Mr. Weaver, did you know that?"

"They're not as good as they look," Billy said. "They've got simply masses of fillings in them at the back."

"Mr. Temple, of course, was a little older,"

_____

16. **emanate** (em′ə·nāt′) *v.*: come forth.

she said, ignoring his remark. "He was actually twenty-eight. And yet I never would have guessed it if he hadn't told me, never in my whole life. There wasn't a *blemish* on his body."

"A what?" Billy said.

"His skin was *just* like a baby's."

There was a pause. Billy picked up his teacup and took another sip of his tea; then he set it down again gently in its saucer. He waited for her to say something else, but she seemed to have lapsed into another of her silences. He sat there staring straight ahead of him into the far corner of the room, biting his lower lip.

"That parrot," he said at last. "You know something? It had me completely fooled when I first saw it through the window. I could have sworn it was alive."

"Alas, no longer."

"It's most terribly clever the way it's been done," he said. "It doesn't look in the least bit dead. Who did it?"

"I did."

"*You* did?"

"Of course," she said. "And have you met my little Basil as well?" She nodded toward the dachshund curled up so comfortably in front of the fire. Billy looked at it. And suddenly, he realized that this animal had all the time been just as silent and motionless as the parrot. He put out a hand and touched it gently on the top of its back. The back was hard and cold, and when he pushed the hair to one side with his fingers, he could see the skin underneath, grayish black and dry and perfectly preserved.

"Good gracious me," he said. "How absolutely fascinating." He turned away from the dog and stared with deep admiration at the little woman beside him on the sofa.

"It must be most awfully difficult to do a thing like that."

"Not in the least," she said. "I stuff all my little pets myself when they pass away. Will you have another cup of tea?"

"No, thank you," Billy said. The tea tasted faintly of bitter almonds, and he didn't much care for it.

"You did sign the book, didn't you?"

"Oh, yes."

"That's good. Because later on, if I happen to forget what you were called, then I could always come down here and look it up. I still do that almost every day with Mr. Mulholland and Mr. . . . Mr. . . ."

"Temple," Billy said, "Gregory Temple. Excuse my asking, but haven't there been *any* other guests here except them in the last two or three years?"

Holding her teacup high in one hand, inclining her head slightly to the left, she looked up at him out of the corners of her eyes and gave him another gentle little smile.

"No, my dear," she said. "Only you." ❹

PREDICT
❹ What do you think happens now?

Meet the Writer

Roald Dahl

"A Persistent Muddler"

Roald (rōō′ôl) **Dahl** (1916–1990) was born in Wales, in Great Britain, to Norwegian parents. Many people believe that Dahl's dark humor had its source in his unpleasant experiences at boarding school. The brutal discipline at school apparently didn't help his writing at the time, however. One teacher said about young Roald, "A persistent muddler. Vocabulary negligible, sentences malconstructed. He reminds me of a camel."

For Independent Reading

Dahl wrote about boarding school and other childhood experiences in his autobiography *Boy*. Some of his most popular stories are in *The Wonderful Story of Henry Sugar and Six More*.

First Thoughts

1. Review your reading notes.
   - When did you first become suspicious that things in the boardinghouse were not quite normal?
   - What **predictions** did you make? Did events turn out as you predicted?

Thinking Critically

2. What seems to be the landlady's idea of a perfect guest? What happens to her guests, and how do you know?

3. One important fact you may not know is that potassium cyanide, a favorite poison in mystery and suspense stories, has a faint bitter-almond taste. Go back to the text, and find where the writer plants this clue. What other clues in the story **foreshadow** Billy's fate? (Can you find a hint in the very first paragraph?)

4. The **climax** of a story is its most exciting point. It is also the moment at which the outcome of the conflict is decided. What do you think is the climax of this story? When does the reader know what will happen to Billy? (Different interpretations are possible.)

5. Skim through the story to find the points at which Billy makes fateful decisions. Choose one of these moments, and describe what Billy does and why he does it. How might a different decision have changed the **resolution,** or outcome, of the story?

WRITING

Extending the Story

What happens just after the story ends? Does Billy realize the danger he faces? If he does, is it too late, or does he escape? Write a paragraph or two that describes Billy's (and the landlady's) fate.

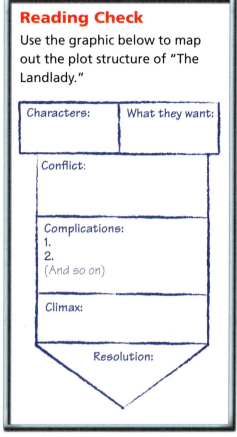

Reading Check

Use the graphic below to map out the plot structure of "The Landlady."

Characters: | What they want:

Conflict:

Complications:
1.
2.
(And so on)

Climax:

Resolution:

INTERNET

Projects and Activities

Keyword: LE5 8-1

SKILLS FOCUS

Literary Skills
Analyze foreshadowing.

Reading Skills
Make predictions.

Writing Skills
Extend the ending of the story.

English from England

"The Landlady" is set in England, as you have already figured out. How did you know? Well, the geographic name *London* tips you off right in the first paragraph. The name *London* is followed by the names of two other famous English cities, *Reading* and *Bath*.

But there is another clue that this story was written by someone from England. The story uses many words that are part of British English but are not used in American English.

Is there more than one kind of English? Indeed, yes. Even though the English language originally came to North America from England, we have been busily making our own brand of English on our side of the Atlantic Ocean for hundreds of years. Differences are bound to occur when the same language is spoken in countries so far apart. Folks in America and in England understand one another just fine, but they often use different words to describe the same things. For example, a truck is called a lorry in England. A sweater is a jumper, and a cookie is a biscuit. Even though we have no trouble understanding the "British English" words in "The Landlady," they do tip us off that, well, we are definitely not in Kansas.

PRACTICE

Each sentence that follows uses words from "The Landlady" that are common in British English. What might an American say instead of the underlined word in each of the sentences below?

1. Billy had to find his own <u>lodgings</u>.
2. "The old girl is slightly <u>dotty</u>. . . ."
3. "'<u>Pop into</u> the sitting room. . . .'"
4. "'Thank you <u>ever so</u> much.'"
5. "'This is <u>a bit of all right</u>.'"

Avoiding Double Comparisons

Billy thinks that the pub would be "cheaper" than a boardinghouse. He knows not to say "more cheaper." *More cheaper* is a double comparison, and it is wrong.

When you use an adjective to make a comparison, you should use only –*er* or *more,* and you should use only –*est* or *most.* You should never use both –*er* and *more* or –*est* and *most.* How do you know when to use one and when to use the other to form a comparison?

1. In general, add –*er* or –*est* to one-syllable modifiers, like *cheap.*
   cheap   cheaper   cheapest

2. Also add –*er* or –*est* to most two-syllable modifiers, like *pretty.*
   pretty   prettier   prettiest

3. Add *more* or *most* to adjectives of three or more syllables, like *beautiful.* (Think how hard it is to say "beautifuller" or "beautifullest.")
   beautiful   more beautiful   most beautiful

NONSTANDARD   **The landlady gave Billy her most warmest smile.**
STANDARD   **The landlady gave Billy her warmest smile.**

NONSTANDARD   **The landlady was more choosier than she had to be.**
STANDARD   **The landlady was more choosy than she had to be.**
STANDARD   **The landlady was choosier than she had to be.**

PRACTICE

Correct each nonstandard comparison.

1. most smelliest
2. smallest
3. more shorter
4. most intelligent
5. more comfortable
6. more warmer
7. terriblest
8. most nastiest
9. most happiest
10. more sadder

For more help, see Uses of Comparative and Superlative Forms, 5b–d, in the Language Handbook.

SKILLS FOCUS

Grammar Skills
Avoid double comparisons.

Comparing Literature

Literary Focus
Story Motifs

You're about to read and compare two stories in which each main character is offered three wishes— and then pays a price for getting what he wants.

You've probably read other stories that repeat the number three: *three* riddles, *three* choices, *three* tests of the hero. If you think of movies you've seen recently, you can probably identify some that include events that happen in threes.

The number three is called a **motif** (mō·tēf'). A motif in literature is an element that recurs in stories from many cultures and from many periods of history. The number three is used in stories from *The Arabian Nights* and in fairy tales and legends from Europe and India.

Storytellers around the world use many, many other motifs. A list of some storytelling motifs is in the box at the right. How many do you recognize?

Familiar Story Motifs

- the number three
- the use of magic and the supernatural
- metamorphoses, or marvelous transformations
- impossible tasks
- evil villains
- helpful or grateful animals
- maidens in danger and heroes who rescue them
- wicked stepmothers
- a perilous journey
- a door or box that should not be opened

Reading Skills
Comparing and Contrasting

When you **compare** and **contrast** two stories, you are looking for ways in which they are similar and ways in which they are different. As you read the two stories that follow, you will find that both share the motif of the "three wishes." Notes in the margin will alert you to other features the stories have in common and to certain ways in which they differ. As you read, pause to write your answers to the side questions on a separate piece of paper. After each story you will find a chart (see pages 100 and 108). Use this chart to record details about each story to keep for the comparison-contrast essay you will write at the end of this lesson.

SKILLS FOCUS

Literary Skills
Understand story motifs.

Reading Skills
Compare and contrast stories.

Before You Read

"The Monkey's Paw" is a masterpiece of suspense that has been popular for more than one hundred years. Read until just before the visitor walks through the door. Then, compare the story's two settings: the weather outside and the inside of the Whites' home. What moods do these settings create? What do you predict is going to happen to the Whites?

The Monkey's Paw

W. W. Jacobs

1

Without, the night was cold and wet, but in the small parlor of Laburnam Villa the blinds were drawn and the fire burned brightly. Father and son were at chess, the former, who possessed ideas about the game involving radical changes, putting his king into such sharp and unnecessary perils that it even provoked comment from the white-haired old lady knitting placidly by the fire. **1**

"Hark at the wind," said Mr. White, who, having seen a fatal mistake after it was too late, was amiably[1] desirous of preventing his son from seeing it.

"I'm listening," said the latter, grimly surveying the board as he stretched out his hand.

"Check."[2]

---

1. **amiably** (ā′mē·ə·blē) *adv.*: good-naturedly.
2. **check** *interj.*: in the game of chess, the situation of a king in danger of being captured when the opposing player makes his or her next move. **Checkmate** is a move that leaves the opponent's king unable to move safely and means winning the game. Both *check* and *checkmate* are announced by the player who has placed the opponent's king in those positions.

RETELL

1 Describe the scene in the Whites' home. Who is there? What are they doing?

"I should hardly think that he'd come tonight," said his father, with his hand poised over the board.

"Mate," replied the son.

"That's the worst of living so far out," bawled Mr. White, with sudden and unlooked-for violence; "of all the beastly, slushy, out-of-the-way places to live in, this is the worst. Pathway's a bog,[3] and the road's a torrent. I don't know what people are thinking about. I suppose because only two houses on the road are let,[4] they think it doesn't matter."

"Never mind, dear," said his wife soothingly; "perhaps you'll win the next one."

Mr. White looked up sharply, just in time to intercept a knowing glance between mother and son. The words died away on his lips, and he hid a guilty grin in his thin gray beard.

"There he is," said Herbert White, as the gate banged to loudly and heavy footsteps came toward the door. ❷

The old man rose with hospitable haste, and, opening the door, was heard condoling[5] with the new arrival. The new arrival also condoled with himself, so that Mrs. White said, "Tut, tut!" and coughed gently as her husband entered the room, followed by a tall burly man, beady of eye and rubicund of visage.[6]

"Sergeant Major Morris," he said, introducing him.

The sergeant major shook hands, and, taking the proffered seat by the fire, watched contentedly while his host got out whiskey and tumblers and stood a small copper kettle on the fire.

At the third glass his eyes got brighter, and he began to talk, the little family circle regarding with eager interest this visitor from distant parts, as he squared his broad shoulders in the chair and spoke of wild scenes and doughty[7] deeds, of wars and plagues and strange peoples.

"Twenty-one years of it," said Mr. White, nodding at his wife and son. "When he went away he was a slip of a youth in the warehouse. Now look at him."

"He don't look to have taken much harm," said Mrs. White politely.

---

3. **bog** *n.:* swamp; very wet ground.
4. **let** *v.:* rented.
5. **condoling** *v.* used as *adj.:* expressing sympathy (here, about the bad weather).
6. **rubicund** (rōō′bə·kund′) **of visage** (viz′ij): red-faced.
7. **doughty** (dout′ē) *adj.:* brave.

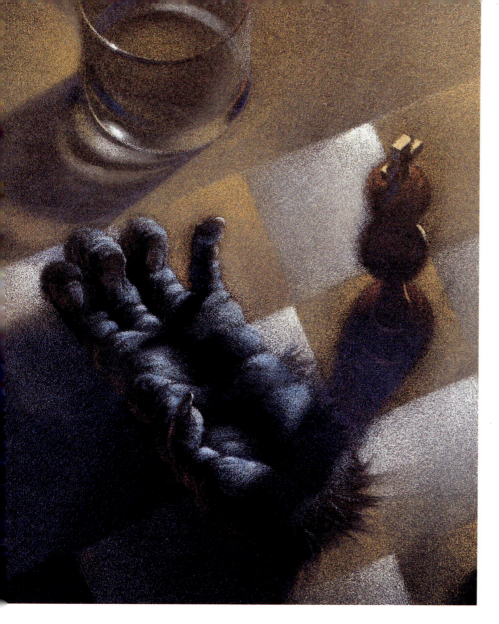

"I'd like to go to India myself," said the old man, "just to look around a bit, you know."

"Better where you are," said the sergeant major, shaking his head. He put down the empty glass and, sighing softly, shook it again.

"I should like to see those old temples and fakirs[8] and jugglers," said the old man. "What was that you started telling me the other day about a monkey's paw or something, Morris?"

"Nothing," said the soldier hastily. "Leastways, nothing worth hearing."

---

8. **fakirs** (fə·kirz′) *n. pl.:* Muslim or Hindu holy people, thought by some people to perform miracles.

COMPARE AND CONTRAST

❸ Compare Mrs. White's, Mr. White's, and Herbert's reactions to the paw.

INFER

❹ The first man's last wish was for death. What does this suggest about his first two wishes?

"Monkey's paw?" said Mrs. White curiously.

"Well, it's just a bit of what you might call magic, perhaps," said the sergeant major offhandedly.

His three listeners leaned forward eagerly. The visitor absent-mindedly put his empty glass to his lips and then set it down again. His host filled it for him.

"To look at," said the sergeant major, fumbling in his pocket, "it's just an ordinary little paw, dried to a mummy."

He took something out of his pocket and proffered it. Mrs. White drew back with a grimace, but her son, taking it, examined it curiously.

"And what is there special about it?" inquired Mr. White as he took it from his son and, having examined it, placed it upon the table. ❸

"It had a spell put on it by an old fakir," said the sergeant major, "a very holy man. He wanted to show that fate ruled people's lives, and that those who interfered with it did so to their sorrow. He put a spell on it so that three separate men could each have three wishes from it."

His manner was so impressive that his hearers were conscious that their light laughter jarred somewhat.

"Well, why don't you have three, sir?" said Herbert White cleverly.

The soldier regarded him in the way that middle age is wont to regard presumptuous[9] youth. "I have," he said quietly, and his blotchy face whitened.

"And did you really have the three wishes granted?" asked Mrs. White.

"I did," said the sergeant major, and his glass tapped against his strong teeth.

"And has anybody else wished?" inquired the old lady.

"The first man had his three wishes, yes," was the reply. "I don't know what the first two were, but the third was for death. That's how I got the paw." ❹

His tones were so grave that a hush fell upon the group.

"If you've had your three wishes, it's no good to you now, then, Morris," said the old man at last. "What do you keep it for?"

---

9. **presumptuous** (prē·zump′ch┤o͞o·əs) *adj.:* overly bold or confident; taking too much for granted.

The soldier shook his head. "Fancy,[10] I suppose," he said slowly. "I did have some idea of selling it, but I don't think I will. It has caused enough mischief already. Besides, people won't buy. They think it's a fairy tale, some of them, and those who do think anything of it want to try it first and pay me afterward."

"If you could have another three wishes," said the old man, eyeing him keenly, "would you have them?"

"I don't know," said the other. "I don't know."

He took the paw, and dangling it between his forefinger and thumb, suddenly threw it upon the fire. White, with a slight cry, stooped down and snatched it off.

"Better let it burn," said the soldier solemnly.

"If you don't want it, Morris," said the old man, "give it to me."

"I won't," said his friend doggedly. "I threw it on the fire. If you keep it, don't blame me for what happens. Pitch it on the fire again, like a sensible man."

The other shook his head and examined his new possession closely. "How do you do it?" he inquired.

"Hold it up in your right hand and wish aloud," said the sergeant major, "but I warn you of the consequences." ❺

"Sounds like *The Arabian Nights*," said Mrs. White, as she rose and began to set the supper. "Don't you think you might wish for four pairs of hands for me?"

Her husband drew the talisman[11] from his pocket and then all three burst into laughter as the sergeant major, with a look of alarm on his face, caught him by the arm.

"If you must wish," he said, gruffly, "wish for something sensible."

Mr. White dropped it back into his pocket, and placing chairs, motioned his friend to the table. In the business of supper, the talisman was partly forgotten, and afterward the three sat listening in an enthralled fashion to a second installment of the soldier's adventures in India.

"If the tale about the monkey's paw is not more truthful than those he has been telling us," said Herbert, as the door closed behind their guest, just in time for him to catch the last train, "we shan't make much out of it."

INFER

❺ Writers often create suspense by using **foreshadowing,** clues that hint at what will happen later. What clues so far suggest that the wishes will cause unhappiness for Mr. White and his family?

---

10. **fancy** *n.:* here, feeling that has no apparent cause. *Fancy* can also mean "imagination," as it does later in the story.
11. **talisman** (tal′is·mən) *n.:* something thought to have magic power.

❻ Why do you think Mr. White decides to keep the paw, despite his friend's warnings?

"Did you give him anything for it, Father?" inquired Mrs. White, regarding her husband closely.

"A trifle," said he, coloring slightly. "He didn't want it, but I made him take it. And he pressed me again to throw it away." ❻

"Likely," said Herbert, with pretended horror. "Why, we're going to be rich, and famous, and happy. Wish to be an emperor, Father, to begin with: then you can't be bossed around."

He darted round the table, pursued by the maligned Mrs. White armed with an antimacassar.[12]

Mr. White took the paw from his pocket and eyed it dubiously. "I don't know what to wish for, and that's a fact," he said slowly. "It seems to me I've got all I want."

"If you only cleared the house, you'd be quite happy, wouldn't you?" said Herbert, with his hand on his shoulder. "Well, wish for two hundred pounds,[13] then; that'll just do it."

His father, smiling shamefacedly at his own credulity,[14] held up the talisman, as his son, with a solemn face somewhat marred by a wink at his mother, sat down at the piano and struck a few impressive chords.

"I wish for two hundred pounds," said the old man distinctly. ❼

A fine crash from the piano greeted the words, interrupted by a shuddering cry from the old man. His wife and son ran toward him.

"It moved," he cried, with a glance of disgust at the object as it lay on the floor. "As I wished, it twisted in my hand like a snake."

"Well, I don't see the money," said his son, as he picked it up and placed it on the table, "and I bet I never shall."

"It must have been your fancy, Father," said his wife, regarding him anxiously.

He shook his head. "Never mind, though; there's no harm done, but it gave me a shock all the same."

They sat down by the fire again while the two men finished their pipes. Outside, the wind was higher than ever, and the old man started nervously at the sound of a door banging upstairs. A silence unusual and depressing settled upon all three, which lasted until the old couple rose to retire for the night.

"I expect you'll find the cash tied up in a big bag in the middle of your bed," said Herbert, as he bade them good night, "and something horrible squatting up on top of the wardrobe[15] watching you as you pocket your ill-gotten gains." ❽

---

12. **antimacassar** (an′ti·mə·kas′ər) *n.:* small cover placed on the back or arms of a chair to keep it clean. Macassar is a kind of hairdressing oil; antimacassars were originally used to protect furniture fabric from greasy heads.

13. **two hundred pounds:** British money equivalent to about one thousand dollars at the time of this story.

14. **credulity** (krə·dōō′lə·tē) *n.:* tendency to believe too readily.

15. **wardrobe** *n.:* movable closet.

EVALUATE

❼ Herbert suggests that his father wish for the money to pay off the mortgage on the house. Is Herbert's idea a good one? How should Mr. White phrase the wish to be sure he gets what he wants?

RETELL

❽ You have finished part one of this story. Stop and identify the main characters and the main events that have happened so far. What does each character want?

COMPARE AND CONTRAST

❾ How does the nighttime setting contrast with the morning setting? Why does Herbert feel less afraid in the morning?

PREDICT

❿ Do you think the money will arrive? If so, how do you think it might appear?

In the brightness of the wintry sun next morning as it streamed over the breakfast table Herbert laughed at his fears. There was an air of prosaic wholesomeness about the room which it had lacked on the previous night, and the dirty, shriveled little paw was pitched on the sideboard with a carelessness which betokened no great belief in its virtues.[16] **❾**

"I suppose all old soldiers are the same," said Mrs. White. "The idea of our listening to such nonsense! How could wishes be granted in these days? And if they could, how could two hundred pounds hurt you, Father?"

"Might drop on his head from the sky," said the frivolous Herbert.

"Morris said the things happened so naturally," said his father, "that you might if you so wished attribute it to coincidence."

"Well, don't break into the money before I come back," said Herbert, as he rose from the table. "I'm afraid it'll turn you into a mean, avaricious man, and we shall have to disown you." **❿**

His mother laughed, and followed him to the door, watched him down the road, and returning to the breakfast table, was very happy at the expense of her husband's credulity. All of which did not prevent her from scurrying to the door at the postman's knock, nor prevent her from referring somewhat shortly to retired sergeant majors of bibulous habits[17] when she found that the post brought a tailor's bill.

"Herbert will have some more of his funny remarks, I expect, when he comes home," she said, as they sat at dinner.

"I dare say," said Mr. White, pouring himself out some beer; "but for all that, the thing moved in my hand; that I'll swear to."

"You thought it did," said the old lady soothingly.

"I say it did," replied the other. "There was no thought about it. I had just—— What's the matter?"

His wife made no reply. She was watching the mysterious movements of a man outside, who, peering in an undecided fashion at the house, appeared to be trying to make up his mind to enter. In mental connection with the two hundred pounds, she noticed that

---

16. **virtues** *n.:* here, powers.
17. **bibulous** (bib′yōō·ləs) **habits:** tendency to drink heavily.

the stranger was well dressed and wore a silk hat of glossy newness. Three times he paused at the gate, and then walked on again. The fourth time he stood with his hand upon it, and then with sudden resolution flung it open and walked up the path. Mrs. White at the same moment placed her hands behind her, and hurriedly unfastening the strings of her apron, put that useful article of apparel beneath the cushion of her chair.

She brought the stranger, who seemed ill at ease, into the room. He gazed furtively at Mrs. White, and listened in a preoccupied fashion as the old lady apologized for the appearance of the room, and her husband's coat, a garment which he usually reserved for the garden. She then waited patiently for him to broach his business, but he was at first strangely silent. **⓫**

"I—was asked to call," he said at last, and stooped and picked a piece of cotton from his trousers. "I come from Maw and Meggins."

The old lady started. "Is anything the matter?" she asked breathlessly. "Has anything happened to Herbert? What is it? What is it?"

Her husband interposed. "There, there, Mother," he said hastily. "Sit down and don't jump to conclusions. You've not brought bad news, I'm sure, sir," and he eyed the other wistfully.

"I'm sorry——" began the visitor.

"Is he hurt?" demanded the mother wildly.

The visitor bowed in assent. "Badly hurt," he said quietly, "but he is not in any pain."

"Oh, thank God!" said the old woman, clasping her hands. "Thank God for that! Thank——" **⓬**

She broke off suddenly as the sinister meaning of the assurance dawned upon her and she saw the awful confirmation of her fears in the other's averted face. She caught her breath, and turning to her husband, laid her trembling old hand upon his. There was a long silence.

"He was caught in the machinery," said the visitor at length, in a low voice.

"Caught in the machinery," repeated Mr. White, in a dazed fashion, "yes."

He sat staring blankly out at the window, and taking his wife's hand between his own, pressed it as he had been wont to do in their old courting days nearly forty years before.

"He was the only one left to us," he said, turning gently to the visitor. "It is hard."

ANALYZE

⓫ What details about this stranger create suspense?

INFER

⓬ Can you answer these questions: What is Maw and Meggins? What has happened to Herbert? If you can't, read on and watch for clues to find out.

The other coughed, and, rising, walked slowly to the window. "The firm wished me to convey their sincere sympathy with you in your great loss," he said, without looking around. "I beg that you will understand I am only their servant and merely obeying orders."

There was no reply; the old woman's face was white, her eyes staring, and her breath inaudible; on the husband's face was a look such as his friend the sergeant might have carried into his first action.

"I was to say that Maw and Meggins disclaim all responsibility," continued the other. "They admit no liability at all, but in consideration of your son's services they wish to present you with a certain sum as compensation."

Mr. White dropped his wife's hand, and rising to his feet, gazed with a look of horror at his visitor. His dry lips shaped the words, "How much?"

"Two hundred pounds," was the answer.

Unconscious of his wife's shriek, the old man smiled faintly, put out his hands like a sightless man, and dropped, a senseless heap, to the floor. **13**

RETELL

13 Pause and retell the main events of part two. What **complication** has developed?

3

In the huge new cemetery, some two miles distant, the old people buried their dead, and came back to a house steeped in shadow and silence. It was all over so quickly that at first they could hardly realize it, and remained in a state of expectation as though of something else to happen—something else which was to lighten this load, too heavy for old hearts to bear. But the days passed, and expectations gave place to resignation—the hopeless resignation of the old, some-times miscalled apathy.[18] Sometimes they hardly exchanged a word, for now they had nothing to talk about, and their days were long to weariness. **14**

ANALYZE

14 The old soldier warned Mr. White of the consequences of using the monkey's paw. How has his warning come true?

It was about a week after that that the old man, waking suddenly in the night, stretched out his hand and found himself alone. The room was in darkness, and the sound of subdued weep-ing came from the window. He raised himself in bed and listened.

"Come back," he said tenderly. "You will be cold."

"It is colder for my son," said the old woman, and wept afresh.

The sound of her sobs died away on his ears. The bed was warm,

---

18. apathy (ap′ə·thē) *n.:* lack of emotion or interest.

and his eyes heavy with sleep. He dozed fitfully, and then slept until a sudden wild cry from his wife awoke him with a start.

"*The paw!*" she cried wildly. "The monkey's paw!"

He started up in alarm. "Where? Where is it? What's the matter?"

She came stumbling across the room toward him. "I want it," she said quietly. "You've not destroyed it?"

"It's in the parlor, on the bracket,"[19] he replied, marveling. "Why?"

She cried and laughed together, and bending over, kissed his cheek.

"I only just thought of it," she said hysterically. "Why didn't I think of it before? Why didn't *you* think of it?"

"Think of what?" he questioned.

"The other two wishes," she replied rapidly. "We've only had one."

"Was not that enough?" he demanded fiercely.

"No," she cried triumphantly; "we'll have one more. Go down and get it quickly, and wish our boy alive again." ⓕ

---

19. **bracket** *n.*: wall shelf held up by supports.

EVALUATE

ⓕ Do you think Mrs. White's idea is a good one? Why or why not?

Comparing
Literature

**COMPARE AND
CONTRAST**

16 Compare Mr. and
Mrs. White's reactions
to Herbert's death.

The man sat up in bed and flung the bedclothes from his quaking limbs. "You are mad!" he cried, aghast.

"Get it," she panted; "get it quickly, and wish—Oh, my boy, my boy!"

Her husband struck a match and lit the candle. "Get back to bed," he said unsteadily. "You don't know what you are saying."

"We had the first wish granted," said the old woman feverishly; "why not the second?"

"A coincidence," stammered the old man.

"Go and get it and wish," cried his wife, quivering with excitement.

The old man turned and regarded her, and his voice shook. "He has been dead ten days, and besides he—I would not tell you else, but—I could only recognize him by his clothing. If he was too terrible for you to see then, how now?"

"Bring him back," cried the old woman, and dragged him toward the door. "Do you think I fear the child I have nursed?" 16

He went down in the darkness, and felt his way to the parlor, and then to the mantelpiece. The talisman was in its place, and a horrible fear that the unspoken wish might bring his mutilated son before him ere he could escape from the room seized upon him, and he caught his breath as he found that he had lost the direction of the door. His brow cold with sweat, he felt his way round the table, and groped along the wall until he found himself in the small passage with the unwholesome thing in his hand.

Even his wife's face seemed changed as he entered the room. It was white and expectant, and to his fears seemed to have an unnatural look upon it. He was afraid of her.

"*Wish!*" she cried, in a strong voice.

"It is foolish and wicked," he faltered.

"*Wish!*" repeated his wife.

He raised his hand. "I wish my son alive again."

The talisman fell to the floor, and he regarded it fearfully. Then he sank trembling into a chair as the old woman, with burning eyes, walked to the window and raised the blind.

He sat until he was chilled with the cold, glancing occasionally at the figure of the old woman peering through the window. The candle end, which had burned below the rim of the china candlestick, was throwing pulsating shadows on the ceiling and walls,

until, with a flicker larger than the rest, it expired. The old man, with an unspeakable sense of relief at the failure of the talisman, crept back to his bed, and a minute or two afterward the old woman came silently and apathetically beside him. **17**

Neither spoke, but both lay silently listening to the ticking of the clock. A stair creaked, and a squeaky mouse scurried noisily through the wall. The darkness was oppressive, and after lying for some time screwing up his courage, the husband took the box of

COMPARE AND CONTRAST

17 The **conflict** in the first part of the story involves a close-knit family who are tempted by the dangerous, invading forces of magic. Now the **conflict** has shifted to struggles *within* the family. Compare Mr. and Mrs. White's relationship at the start of the story with the way they behave toward each other now.

IDENTIFY

18 What details in this paragraph increase the mood of mystery and terror? Write these words and phrases in your notebook.

INFER

19 Why does Mr. White say "it" and not "Herbert"?

IDENTIFY

20 The suspense increases as the **climax** of the story approaches. Read aloud the lines you find most suspenseful.

matches, and striking one, went downstairs for a candle.

At the foot of the stairs the match went out, and he paused to strike another, and at the same moment a knock, so quiet and stealthy as to be scarcely audible, sounded on the front door.

The matches fell from his hand. He stood motionless, his breath suspended until the knock was repeated. Then he turned and fled swiftly back to his room, and closed the door behind him. A third knock sounded through the house. **18**

"*What's that?*" cried the old woman, starting up.

"A rat," said the old man, in shaking tones—"a rat. It passed me on the stairs."

His wife sat up in bed listening. A loud knock resounded through the house.

"It's Herbert!" she screamed. "It's Herbert!"

She ran to the door, but her husband was before her, and catching her by the arm, held her tightly.

"What are you going to do?" he whispered hoarsely.

"It's my boy; it's Herbert!" she cried, struggling mechanically. "I forgot it was two miles away. What are you holding me for? Let go. I must open the door."

"For God's sake don't let it in," cried the old man, trembling. **19**

"You're afraid of your own son," she cried, struggling. "Let me go. I'm coming, Herbert; I'm coming."

There was another knock, and another. The old woman with a sudden wrench broke free and ran from the room. Her husband followed to the landing, and called after her appealingly as she hurried downstairs. He heard the chain rattle back and the bottom bolt drawn slowly and stiffly from the socket. Then the old woman's voice, strained and panting.

"The bolt," she cried loudly. "Come down. I can't reach it."

But her husband was on his hands and knees groping wildly on the floor in search of the paw. If he could only find it before the thing outside got in. A perfect fusillade[20] of knocks reverberated through the house, and he heard the scraping of a chair as his wife put it down in the passage against the door. He heard the creaking of the bolt as it came slowly back, and at the same moment he found the monkey's paw, and frantically breathed his third and last wish. **20**

---

20. fusillade (fyo͞o′sə·lād′) *n.:* here, something resembling a rapid, continuous series of gunshots.

The knocking ceased suddenly, although the echoes of it were still in the house. He heard the chair drawn back and the door opened. A cold wind rushed up the staircase, and a long loud wail of disappointment and misery from his wife gave him courage to run down to her side, and then to the gate beyond. The street lamp flickering opposite shone on a quiet and deserted road. ㉑

RETELL

㉑ Make sure you understand what has happened in the third and final part of this story. What is the story's **climax**? How are the **conflicts** finally resolved?

Meet the Writer

W. W. Jacobs

William Wymark Jacobs (1910) by Carton Moore-Park. Oil on canvas.

Watching the Ships Go By

The oldest child in a large family, **William Wymark Jacobs** (1863–1943) grew up in London, near the River Thames, where his father worked on the docks. As a teenager, Jacobs spent many hours on the docks, watching ships come and go and listening to the stories of the sailors. These experiences are reflected in his short stories and novels, many of which include seafaring characters. "The Monkey's Paw" is his most famous story.

First Thoughts

1. Complete the following sentence:
   • This story left me feeling . . .

Thinking Critically

2. Are the Whites' three wishes granted? Do they get what they really want? Explain.

3. In your opinion, has the fakir who put the spell on the paw made his point? Why or why not?

Comparing Literature

4. After you've read the next story, you'll write a comparison-contrast essay. You can begin to plan your essay by filling in the column under "The Monkey's Paw" in a chart like the one below. After you read "The Third Wish," you will add details about that story to this chart.

Reading Check

Use the following story map to outline the main parts of this story's **plot.** Keep your notes for the assignment on page 109.

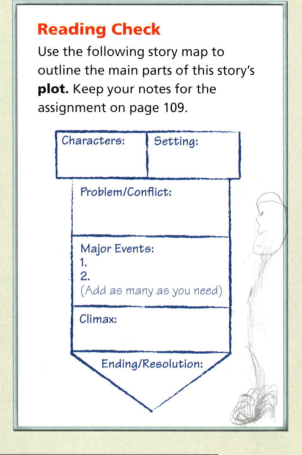

Characters: Setting:

Problem/Conflict:

Major Events:
1.
2.
(Add as many as you need)

Climax:

Ending/Resolution:

Comparing Stories		
	"The Monkey's Paw"	"The Third Wish"
Main character		
What does he want?		
First wish (and consequences)		
Second wish (and consequences)		
Third wish (and consequences)		
Mood of the story		
How does the story end?		
Lesson about life		

SKILLS FOCUS

Literary Skills
Analyze story motifs.

Reading Skills
Compare and contrast stories.

Before You Read

You may have read stories about people whose kindness to animals is rewarded with great gifts. In this story the reward is three wishes. Think about the wishes in "The Monkey's Paw"; what do you predict will happen to Mr. Peters and his three wishes in "The Third Wish"?

The Third Wish

Joan Aiken

Once there was a man who was driving in his car at dusk on a spring evening through part of the forest of Savernake. His name was Mr. Peters. The primroses were just beginning but the trees were still bare, and it was cold; the birds had stopped singing an hour ago. ❶

As Mr. Peters entered a straight, empty stretch of road he seemed to hear a faint crying, and a struggling and thrashing, as if somebody was in trouble far away in the trees. He left his car and climbed the mossy bank beside the road. Beyond the bank was an open slope of beech trees leading down to thorn bushes through which he saw the

IDENTIFY

❶ What details in this opening paragraph sound like a fairy tale? What elements seem out of place in a fairy tale?

gleam of water. He stood a moment waiting to try and discover where the noise was coming from, and presently heard a rustling and some strange cries in a voice which was almost human—and yet there was something too hoarse about it at one time and too clear and sweet at another. Mr. Peters ran down the hill and as he neared the bushes he saw something white among them which was trying to extricate[1] itself; coming closer he found that it was a swan that had become entangled in the thorns growing on the bank of the canal.

The bird struggled all the more frantically as he approached, looking at him with hate in its yellow eyes, and when he took hold of it to free it, hissed at him, pecked him, and thrashed dangerously with its wings which were powerful enough to break his arm. Nevertheless he managed to release it from the thorns, and carrying it tightly with one arm, holding the snaky head well away with the other hand (for he did not wish his eyes pecked out), he took it to the verge of the canal and dropped it in.

The swan instantly assumed great dignity and sailed out to the middle of the water, where it put itself to rights with much dabbling and preening, smoothing its feathers with little showers of drops. Mr. Peters waited, to make sure that it was all right and had suffered no damage in its struggles. Presently the swan, when it was satisfied with its appearance, floated in to the bank once more, and in a moment, instead of the great white bird, there was a little man all in green with a golden crown and long beard, standing by the water. He had fierce glittering eyes and looked by no means friendly.

"Well, Sir," he said threateningly, "I see you are presumptuous[2] enough to know some of the laws of magic. You think that because you have rescued—by pure good fortune—the King of the Forest from a difficulty, you should have some fabulous reward."

"I expect three wishes, no more and no less," answered Mr. Peters, looking at him steadily and with composure.[3] ❷

"Three wishes, he wants, the clever man! Well, I have yet to hear of the human being who made any good use of his three wishes—they mostly end up worse off than they started. Take your three wishes then—" he flung three dead leaves in the air "—don't blame me if you spend the last wish in undoing the work of the other two." ❸

---

1. **extricate** (eks′tri·kāt′) *v.:* free; release.
2. **presumptuous** (prē·zump′chōo·əs) *adj.:* overly bold or confident; taking too much for granted.
3. **composure** (kəm·pō′zhər) *n.:* calmness.

ANALYZE

❷ What is surprising about the King of the Forest's attitude toward Mr. Peters?

COMPARE AND CONTRAST

❸ In "The Monkey's Paw," Mr. White is warned of the danger of using his three wishes. How is the King of the Forest's warning similar?

Mr. Peters caught the leaves and put two of them carefully in his notecase. When he looked up the swan was sailing about in the middle of the water again, flicking the drops angrily down its long neck.

Mr. Peters stood for some minutes reflecting on how he should use his reward. He knew very well that the gift of three magic wishes was one which brought trouble more often than not, and he had no intention of being like the forester who first wished by mistake for a sausage, and then in a rage wished it on the end of his wife's nose, and then had to use his last wish in getting it off again. Mr. Peters had most of the things which he wanted and was very content with his life. The only thing that troubled him was that he was a little lonely, and had no companion for his old age. He decided to use his first wish and to keep the other two in case of an emergency. Taking a thorn he pricked his tongue with it, to remind himself not to utter rash[4] wishes aloud. ❹ Then holding the third leaf and gazing round him at the dusky undergrowth, the primroses, great beeches and the blue-green water of the canal, he said:

"I wish I had a wife as beautiful as the forest."

A tremendous quacking and splashing broke out on the surface of the water. He thought that it was the swan laughing at him. Taking no notice he made his way through the darkening woods to his car, wrapped himself up in the rug[5] and went to sleep.

When he awoke it was morning and the birds were beginning to call. Coming along the track toward him was the most beautiful creature he had ever seen, with eyes as blue-green as the canal, hair as dusky as the bushes, and skin as white as the feathers of swans.

"Are you the wife that I wished for?" asked Mr. Peters.

---

4. **rash** *adj.:* reckless; hasty.
5. **rug** *n.:* here, heavy blanket.

COMPARE AND CONTRAST

❹ Mr. Peters is more cautious about using his wishes than Mr. White is. What conclusions can you draw about these two characters based on their attitudes toward the wishes?

EVALUATE

5 Does Mr. Peters have a typical life for someone living in the modern world? Explain.

"Yes I am," she replied. "My name is Leita."

She stepped into the car beside him and they drove off to the church on the outskirts of the forest, where they were married. Then he took her to his house in a remote and lovely valley and showed her all his treasures—the bees in their white hives, the Jersey cows, the hyacinths, the silver candlesticks, the blue cups and the luster bowl for putting primroses in. She admired everything, but what pleased her most was the river which ran by the foot of his garden. **5**

"Do swans come up here?" she asked.

"Yes, I have often seen swans there on the river," he told her, and she smiled.

Leita made him a good wife. She was gentle and friendly, busied herself about the house and garden, polished the bowls, milked the cows and mended his socks. But as time went by Mr. Peters began to feel that she was not happy. She seemed restless, wandered much in the garden, and sometimes when he came back from the fields he would find the house empty and she would only return after half an hour or so with no explanation of where she had been. On these occasions she was always especially tender and would put out his slippers to warm and cook his favorite dish—Welsh rarebit[6] with wild strawberries—for supper.

One evening he was returning home along the river path when he saw Leita in front of him, down by the water. A swan had sailed up to the verge and she had her arms round its neck and the swan's head rested against her cheek. She was weeping, and as he came nearer he saw that tears were rolling, too, from the swan's eyes.

"Leita, what is it?" he asked, very troubled.

"This is my sister," she answered. "I can't bear being separated from her."

Now he understood that Leita was really a swan from the forest, and this made him very sad because when a human being marries a bird it always leads to sorrow. **6**

"I could use my second wish to give your sister human shape, so that she could be a companion to you," he suggested.

"No, no," she cried, "I couldn't ask that of her."

"Is it so very hard to be a human being?" asked Mr. Peters sadly.

"Very, very hard," she answered.

"Don't you love me at all, Leita?"

RETELL

6 How has Leita been spending her time away from Mr. Peters? Why is she so sad?

---

6. **Welsh rarebit** (rer′bit): melted cheese on crackers or toast.

"Yes, I do, I do love you," she said, and there were tears in her eyes again. "But I miss the old life in the forest, the cool grass and the mist rising off the river at sunrise and the feel of the water sliding over my feathers as my sister and I drifted along the stream." ❼

"Then shall I use my second wish to turn you back into a swan again?" he asked, and his tongue pricked to remind him of the old King's words, and his heart swelled with grief inside him.

"Who would darn your socks and cook your meals and see to the hens?"

"I'd do it myself as I did before I married you," he said, trying to sound cheerful.

She shook her head. "No, I could not be as unkind to you as that. I am partly a swan, but I am also partly a human being now. I will stay with you."

Poor Mr. Peters was very distressed on his wife's account and did his best to make her life happier, taking her for drives in the car, finding beautiful music for her to listen to on the radio, buying clothes for her and even suggesting a trip round the world. But she said no to that; she would prefer to stay in their own house near the river.

He noticed that she spent more and more time baking wonderful cakes—jam puffs, petits fours, éclairs and meringues. One day he saw her take a basketful down to the river and he guessed that she was giving them to her sister.

He built a seat for her by the river, and the two sisters spent hours together there, communicating in some wordless manner. For a time he thought that all would be well, but then he saw how thin and pale she was growing. ❽

One night when he had been late doing the accounts he came up to bed and found her weeping in her sleep and calling:

"Rhea! Rhea! I can't understand what you say! Oh, wait for me, take me with you!"

Then he knew that it was hopeless and she would never be happy as a human. He stooped down and kissed her goodbye, then took another leaf from his notecase, blew it out of the window, and used up his second wish.

Next moment instead of Leita there was a sleeping swan lying across the bed with its head under its wing. He carried it out of the house and down to the brink of the river, and then he said "Leita! Leita!" to waken her, and gently put her into the water. She gazed round her in astonishment for a moment, and then came up to him

INFER

❼ What **conflict** does Leita face?

PREDICT

❽ How do you think Mr. Peters will use his next wish?

and rested her head lightly against his hand; next instant she was flying away over the trees toward the heart of the forest.

He heard a harsh laugh behind him, and turning round saw the old King looking at him with a malicious[7] expression.

"Well, my friend! You don't seem to have managed so wonderfully with your first two wishes, do you? What will you do with the last? Turn yourself into a swan? Or turn Leita back into a girl?"

"I shall do neither," said Mr. Peters calmly. "Human beings and swans are better in their own shapes." ❾

But for all that he looked sadly over toward the forest where Leita had flown, and walked slowly back to his empty house.

Next day he saw two swans swimming at the bottom of the garden, and one of them wore the gold chain he had given Leita after their marriage; she came up and rubbed her head against his hand.

Mr. Peters and his two swans came to be well known in that part of the country; people used to say that he talked to the swans and they understood him as well as his neighbors. Many people were a little frightened of him. There was a story that once when thieves tried to break into his house they were set upon by two huge white birds which carried them off bodily and dropped them in the river.

As Mr. Peters grew old everyone wondered at his contentment. Even when he was bent with rheumatism[8] he would not think of moving to a drier spot, but went slowly about his work, milking the cows and collecting the honey and eggs, with the two swans always somewhere close at hand.

---

7. **malicious** (mə·lish′əs) *adj.*: deliberately harmful or mean.
8. **rheumatism** (rōō′mə·tiz′əm) *n.*: painful swelling of joints.

Comparing Literature

COMPARE AND CONTRAST

❾ Like Mr. White in the previous story, Mr. Peters ends up using his second wish to undo his first. How are the situations that lead each character to his second wish similar? How are they different?

Sometimes people who knew his story would say to him: "Mr. Peters, why don't you wish for another wife?"

"Not likely," he would answer serenely. "Two wishes were enough for me, I reckon. I've learned that even if your wishes are granted they don't always better you. I'll stay faithful to Leita." **10**

One autumn night, passers-by along the road heard the mournful sound of two swans singing. All night the song went on, sweet and harsh, sharp and clear. In the morning Mr. Peters was found peacefully dead in his bed with a smile of great happiness on his face. In between his hands, which lay clasped on his breast, were a withered leaf and a white feather.

IDENTIFY

10 What lesson does Mr. Peters say he has learned?

Meet the Writer

Joan Aiken

Alternate Worlds

Joan Aiken (1924–   ) began writing her first story on her fifth birthday and hasn't stopped since:

 " I spent my month's pocket money on a large blue note pad and started filling it with stories and poems. I still have it, and about a dozen successors; I was always writing something from then on. "

Aiken grew up in a literary household in England. Her father was the Pulitzer Prize–winning poet Conrad Aiken. Her mother, Jessie McDonald Aiken, read stories by Charles Dickens and James Thurber to her daughter. Aiken offers this description of short story writing:

 " [Y]ou get on course, and then some terrific power, like the power of gravity, takes command and whizzes you off to an unknown destination. "

For Independent Reading

Aiken has written a series of alternate-world fantasies, including *The Wolves of Willoughby Chase* and *Black Hearts in Battersea,* all starring the feisty Dido Twite. Aiken had Dido drown at the end of *Black Hearts in Battersea,* but a letter from a child protesting Dido's untimely end prompted her to bring Dido back to life in *Night Birds on Nantucket.*

First Thoughts

1. Respond to "The Third Wish" by completing the following sentence:
   - What surprised me most about the story was . . .

Thinking Critically

2. Why do you think Mr. Peters dies with a smile of happiness on his face?

3. The King of the Forest says that most human beings who use magic wishes "end up worse off than they started." Is this true of Mr. Peters? Support your answer with details from the story.

4. Think about what happens to Mr. Peters as a result of his wishes and what he learns. What lesson about the power of love do you find in "The Third Wish"?

5. Who uses his wishes more wisely—Mr. Peters or Mr. White? Explain.

Comparing Literature

6. Add information from "The Third Wish" to the chart you began on page 100. Then, use your completed chart to help you write the comparison-contrast essay assigned on the next page.

Reading Check

With a partner, **retell** the plot of "The Third Wish." Be sure to identify the story's title, author, setting, main characters, and key events. Have your partner evaluate your retelling using a retelling rating sheet like the one on page 15. If you need help in retelling a story, review the lesson on pages 4–15.

Comparing Stories		
	"The Monkey's Paw"	"The Third Wish"
Main character		
What does he want?		
First wish (and consequences)		
Second wish (and consequences)		
Third wish (and consequences)		
Mood of the story		
How does the story end?		
Lesson about life		

SKILLS FOCUS

Literary Skills
Analyze story motifs.

Reading Skills
Compare and contrast stories.

Writing a Comparison-Contrast Essay

Assignment

Write an essay comparing "The Monkey's Paw" with "The Third Wish." To help plan your essay, review the chart you completed after you read each story. The chart will help you focus on elements in the stories that are very similar or very different. You do not have to write about all of these elements in your essay.

Use the workshop on writing a Comparison-Contrast Essay, pages 516–521, for help with this assignment.

Here are two ways you can organize your essay:

1. You can organize your essay by the stories. That means that you will discuss one story at a time, explaining how certain elements are used in that story. If you organize by the stories, your first and second paragraphs might be outlined like this:

> **Paragraph 1:** How "The Monkey's Paw" uses two elements
> A. Resolution of plot in "The Monkey's Paw"
> B. Mood of "The Monkey's Paw"
> **Paragraph 2:** How "The Third Wish" uses two elements
> A. Resolution of plot in "The Third Wish"
> B. Mood of "The Third Wish"

2. You can organize your essay by the elements. That means that you will discuss each story element, one at a time, explaining how it is used in each story. If you organize by the elements, your first and second paragraphs might be focused on these topics:

> **Paragraph 1:** The resolution of the plot in each story
> A. "The Monkey's Paw"
> B. "The Third Wish"
> **Paragraph 2:** The mood in each story
> A. "The Monkey's Paw"
> B. "The Third Wish"

At the end of your essay, tell which story you prefer, and why. Which story challenged you more as a reader? Why?

Writing Skills
Write a comparison-contrast essay.

The Open Window

Saki

My aunt will be down presently, Mr. Nuttel," said a very self-possessed young lady of fifteen; "in the meantime you must try and put up with me."

Framton Nuttel endeavored to say the correct something which should duly flatter the niece of the moment without unduly discounting the aunt that was to come. Privately he doubted more than ever whether these formal visits on a succession of total strangers would do much toward helping the nerve cure which he was supposed to be undergoing.

"I know how it will be," his sister had said when he was preparing to migrate to this rural retreat; "you will bury yourself down there and not speak to a living soul, and your nerves will be worse than ever from moping. I shall just give you letters of introduction to all the people I know there. Some of them, as far as I can remember, were quite nice."

Framton wondered whether Mrs. Sappleton, the lady to whom he was presenting one of the letters of introduction, came into the nice division.

"Do you know many of the people round here?" asked the niece, when she judged that they had had sufficient silent communion.

"Hardly a soul," said Framton. "My sister was staying here, at the rectory,[1] you know, some four years ago, and she gave me letters of introduction to some of the people here."

He made the last statement in a tone of distinct regret.

"Then you know practically nothing about my aunt?" pursued the self-possessed young lady.

"Only her name and address," admitted the caller. He was wondering whether Mrs. Sappleton was in the married or widowed state. An undefinable something about the room seemed to suggest masculine habitation.

"Her great tragedy happened just three years ago," said the child; "that would be since your sister's time."

"Her tragedy?" asked Framton; somehow, in this restful country spot, tragedies seemed out of place.

"You may wonder why we keep that window wide open on an October afternoon," said the niece, indicating a large French window[2] that opened onto a lawn.

"It is quite warm for the time of the year," said Framton, "but has that window got anything to do with the tragedy?"

"Out through that window, three years ago to a day, her husband and her two young brothers went off for their day's shooting. They never came back. In crossing the moor to their favorite snipe-shooting[3] ground, they were all three engulfed in a treacherous piece of bog. It had been that dreadful wet summer, you know, and places that were safe in other years gave way suddenly without warning. Their bodies were never recovered. That was the dreadful part of it." Here the child's voice lost its self-possessed note and became falteringly human. "Poor aunt always thinks that they will come back someday, they and the little brown spaniel that was lost with them, and walk in at that window just as they used to do. That is why the window is kept open every evening till it is quite dusk. Poor dear aunt, she has often told me how they went out, her husband with his white waterproof coat over his arm, and Ronnie, her youngest brother, singing, 'Bertie, why do you bound?' as he always did to tease her, because she said it got on her nerves. Do you know, sometimes on still, quiet evenings like this, I almost get a creepy feeling that they will all walk in through that window——"

---

1. **rectory** *n.:* house in which the minister of a parish lives.
2. **French window:** pair of doors that have glass panes from top to bottom and open in the middle.
3. **snipe-shooting** *n.:* A snipe is a kind of bird that lives in swampy areas.

Miss Cicely Alexander: Harmony in Gray and Green (1872) by James McNeill Whistler. Oil on canvas.

She broke off with a little shudder. It was a relief to Framton when the aunt bustled into the room with a whirl of apologies for being late in making her appearance.

"I hope Vera has been amusing you?" she said.

"She has been very interesting," said Framton.

"I hope you don't mind the open window," said Mrs. Sappleton briskly; "my husband and brothers will be home directly from shooting, and they always come in this way. They've been out for snipe in the marshes today, so they'll make a fine mess over my poor carpets. So like you menfolk, isn't it?"

She rattled on cheerfully about the shooting and the scarcity of birds and the prospects for duck in the winter. To Framton, it was all purely horrible. He made a desperate but only partially successful effort to turn the talk onto a less ghastly topic; he was conscious that his hostess was giving him only a fragment of her attention, and her eyes were constantly straying past him to the open window and the lawn beyond. It was certainly an unfortunate coincidence that he should have paid his visit on this tragic anniversary.

"The doctors agree in ordering me complete rest, an absence of mental excitement, and avoidance of anything in the nature of violent physical exercise," announced Framton, who labored under the tolerably widespread delusion that total strangers and chance acquaintances are hungry for the least detail of one's ailments and infirmities, their cause and cure. "On the matter of diet they are not so much in agreement," he continued.

"No?" said Mrs. Sappleton, in a voice which only replaced a yawn at the last moment. Then she suddenly brightened into alert attention—but not to what Framton was saying.

"Here they are at last!" she cried. "Just in time for tea, and don't they look as if they were muddy up to the eyes!"

Framton shivered slightly and turned toward the niece with a look intended to convey sympathetic comprehension. The child was staring out through the open window with dazed horror in her eyes. In a chill shock of nameless fear Framton swung round in his seat and looked in the same direction.

In the deepening twilight three figures were walking across the lawn toward the window; they all carried guns under their arms, and one of them was additionally burdened with a white coat hung over his shoulders. A tired brown spaniel kept close at their heels. Noiselessly they neared the house, and then a hoarse young voice chanted out of the dusk: "I said, Bertie, why do you bound?"

Framton grabbed wildly at his stick and hat; the hall door, the gravel drive, and the front gate were dimly noted stages in his headlong retreat. A cyclist coming along the road had to run into the hedge to avoid imminent collision.

"Here we are, my dear," said the bearer of the white mackintosh, coming in through the window, "fairly muddy, but most of it's dry. Who was that who bolted out as we came up?"

"A most extraordinary man, a Mr. Nuttel," said Mrs. Sappleton; "could only talk about his illnesses and dashed off without a word of goodbye or apology when you arrived. One would think he had seen a ghost."

"I expect it was the spaniel," said the niece calmly; "he told me he had a horror of dogs. He was once hunted into a cemetery somewhere on the banks of the Ganges[4] by a pack of pariah dogs[5] and had to spend the night in a newly dug grave with the creatures snarling and grinning and foaming just above him. Enough to make anyone lose their nerve."

Romance at short notice was her specialty.

---

4. **Ganges** (gan′jēz): river in northern India and Bangladesh.
5. **pariah** (pə·rī′ə) **dogs**: wild dogs.

Meet the Writer

Saki

Mischief and Mayhem

Saki is the pen name of Hector Hugh Munro (1870–1916). He was born in Burma (now called Myanmar), where his father, a Scottish military officer, was posted. Saki's mother died when he was a toddler, and he and his brother and sister were sent to England to be raised by their grandmother and two strict aunts.

Sickly as a child, Saki received little formal education before he was sent to boarding school at age fourteen. He spent most of his time with his brother and sister, developing the mischievous sense of humor that later made his writing famous.

Although Saki was forty-three when World War I broke out, he enlisted in the British Army. He was killed by a German sniper two years later on a dark morning in France. His last words before he was shot were "Put that bloody cigarette out."

For Independent Reading

If you liked Vera's imaginative stories in "The Open Window," you'll enjoy watching her have fun with a stuffy politician in "The Lull." You can find this story in *The Complete Stories of Saki.* Also look for the mischief-making characters Reginald and Clovis.

Writing Workshop

SKILLS FOCUS

Writing Skills
Write a personal narrative.

NARRATIVE WRITING
Personal Narrative

A personal narrative is your account of an experience that was important to you. When you write a personal narrative, you tell what happened and you share your thoughts and feelings about the experience. A good personal narrative also reveals why this experience is important to the writer—and perhaps to the reader too.

Prewriting

1 Choosing a Topic

Read and think about the following **prompt:**

> Most of us love to tell about ourselves—our experiences, our feelings and memories, the details of our lives. Choose one important experience that has special meaning for you. Tell what happened, and share your thoughts and feelings with your readers. End by explaining why this experience means so much to you.

Now, ask yourself these questions as you decide on an experience to use as the subject of your personal narrative:

- Does my mind keep going back to one particular incident?
- Does the incident contain a conflict or surprise?
- Does the incident reveal something special about my personality?
- Am I willing to share my thoughts about the incident with readers?

2 Making Clear What the Experience Means

In a sentence or two, explain the special meaning this experience has for you. If you aren't sure, the experience may not be important enough to choose as a topic—or you may need to think about it more deeply or recall it more clearly. This explanation often appears near the end of a personal narrative—like the moral of a story. Here is an example from the Revision Model on page 121:

> I realized then how important it is to stick up for the victims of bullies.

As you draft, keep looking back at your statement to see whether what you've written is in line with it. If not, either rewrite your draft or rethink your statement.

Drafting

1 Getting Started

A first draft is a discovery piece, an experiment to find out what you have to say about your topic. Your object is to get your thoughts down as quickly as you can.

Use the *5W-How?* questions (*Who? What? When? Where? Why?* and *How?*) to recall details about an event. Answer questions such as "*What* happened?" "*Where* were you?" "*Who* was involved?" To be sure that you recall details clearly and coherently, create a chart of events in chronological order, like the one below.

Time	Event	Details
when sister was three years old	she received her Indian name	family lived in Wisconsin; medicine man gave name
when I was three years old	grandfather died	already had his Anglo name, now his Indian name was available
a few months after my tenth birthday	father suggested that I receive my Indian name	has to be given by medicine person

Finding More Ideas

- Look through photographs, journals, diaries, or letters.
- Ask family members or friends for stories about you.
- Examine souvenirs.
- Recall holidays and special birthdays.
- Think about the first time—or the last time—you did something.

Transitional Expressions

Use transitional words and phrases for greater coherence. Here are some common transitions to show time:

Chronological Order

afterward	later
at last	meanwhile
at once	next
before	soon
finally	then
first	when
in the past	while

Framework for a Personal Narrative

What the experience means to me: _____
_____

Introduction (in the words you'll actually use): _____
_____

Body

Order of events:

1. _____
2. _____
3. _____
4. _____

Conclusion (in the words you'll actually use, if possible): _____
_____

Writing Tip

Personal narratives are usually told in **chronological order,** from beginning to end. One alternative is to start with the most important moment, then tell the rest in **flashback.**

2 Developing a Framework

A writer's framework usually consists of an **introduction,** a **body,** and a **conclusion.** Grab your reader's attention with an interesting opener, and set your scene. Then, in the body of your paper, arrange events in the order in which they happened, and elaborate with vivid, specific details. In your conclusion, reveal the meaning the experience had for you.

3 Using Dialogue

If you use dialogue in your personal narrative, it should reflect the way people really talk. For instance, even though you avoid using sentence fragments in formal writing, it might be natural to use them when you're quoting someone.

Here is a passage of dialogue from the short story "Flowers for Algernon" (page 43). Joe Carp and Frank Reilly have invited Charlie to a party in order to make fun of him. Note how the author handles the speech of the factory workers.

> Frank said, "I ain't laughed so much since we sent him off for the newspaper that night at Muggsy's and ditched him."
>
> "Look at him. His face is red."
>
> "He's blushing. Charlie is blushing."
>
> "Hey, Ellen, what'd you do to Charlie? I never saw him act like that before."

(To review the rules for punctuating dialogue, see Quotation Marks, 14c–j, in the Language Handbook.)

4 Keeping Point of View Consistent

In a personal narrative you'll use the first-person pronouns (*I, me, my*) to refer to yourself. Be sure to use your natural voice—the words and phrases you would use when telling the story to your friends. Your tone reveals your attitude about your topic.

Student Model

from I Am Kwakkoli

A few months after my tenth birthday, my dad began to talk to me about receiving my Indian name. He said this had to be done in a ceremony by a medicine person or an elder in our tribe. My older sister, Megan, had received her Indian name, Maquegquay (Woman of the Woods), when she was only three. At that time my family lived on the Oneida Reservation just outside of Green Bay, Wisconsin. My grandfather was alive then, and he asked a medicine-man friend of his to name her and made the arrangements. I always thought my sister's Indian name was so perfect for her. I was told the medicine man meditated for three days before the name came to him.

There are many traditions connected to the Naming Ceremony. For one thing, there are a limited number of names among the Oneida people. When a person dies, that name returns to the pool of available names and can be given to someone else. The medicine person decides whose energy fits which available name, or a person may ask for a certain name. In my case, I was named after my grandfather through my Anglo name, but I also wanted to take his Indian name, which was available and had been waiting for me for seven years. I felt that if I had both of his names, it made a full circle and I was wholly connected to him and to my family. The name that was his is Kwakkoli, or "Whippoorwill" in English.

> —Bisco Hill
> Southern Hills Middle School
> Boulder, Colorado

*The first paragraph provides a strong **introduction** to the essay's main ideas.*

*The writer gives enough **background information** to prepare the reader to follow the story.*

*The writer reveals the importance of the subject. First, he gives **general information.** Then he provides **specific details** about himself.*

The writer describes his feelings about his subject.

Strategies for Elaboration

Precise Words

Precise words present specific ideas vividly. Consider these examples from Gary Soto's story "Broken Chain" (page 17):

- "an old gym sock" (instead of *rag*)
- "gaudy red lipstick" (instead of *makeup*)
- "ratlike Chihuahua" (instead of *small dog*)
- "pampered" his hair (instead of *combed*)

Figures of Speech

Writers use figures of speech to help us see everyday things in new ways. Note these examples from Soto's story:

Simile

- "his teeth were crooked, like a pile of wrecked cars."
- "His [bike] gleamed like a handful of dimes. . . ."

Metaphor

- "the wind raking through his butch"
- "a paperboy with dollar signs in his eyes"

INTERNET

More Writer's Models

Keyword: LE5 8-1

Evaluating and Revising

Use this chart to evaluate and revise your personal narrative.

Personal Narrative: Content and Organization Guidelines		
Evaluation Questions	▶ **Tips**	▶ **Revision Techniques**
❶ Does your introduction grab the reader's attention and set the scene?	▶ **Put stars** next to interesting or surprising statements. **Circle** details that show when and where the experience happened.	▶ **Add** an attention-getting quotation or statement. **Add** details about where and when the event took place.
❷ Are events in chronological order?	▶ **Number** the events in the narrative. Check that this sequence reflects the actual order of events.	▶ **Rearrange** events in the order in which they occurred, if necessary. **Add** transitions to link events.
❸ Do the details make people, places, and events seem real?	▶ **Highlight** sensory details and dialogue. In the margin, **note** which senses the sensory details appeal to.	▶ **Elaborate** with dialogue or sensory details, if necessary. **Delete** irrelevant details.
❹ Have you included your thoughts and feelings?	▶ **Put a check mark** next to statements of your feelings or thoughts.	▶ **Add** specific details about feelings and thoughts, if necessary.
❺ Does your conclusion reveal why the experience is meaningful?	▶ **Underline** your statement of why the experience is meaningful.	▶ **Add** a statement that explains why the experience is important, if needed.

Read the following revision model of a personal narrative and answer the questions that follow.

Revision Model

I had my first experience with a bully when I was in second

~~I had just been transferred to a new school and know none of~~

grade.

~~my classmates.~~ One day, ~~shortly after I arrived,~~ I was standing in

with red hair and freckles

the schoolyard during recess when a stocky girl approached me,

, at first,   To my surprise

smiling. I thought that she wanted to make friends. She asked

Unsuspecting,

me if I had any money. I put my hand into my coat pocket and

glared

brought out five pennies. She snatched the money and ~~looked~~ at

me with a warning, "Don't tell anybody or I'll beat you up!"

Luckily   who had been watching

I was terrified and began to cry. A sixth-grade monitor came

firmly

over and said to her, "If I catch you picking on anyone again, I'll

to the principal   defiantly

report you." The girl shrugged her shoulders and walked away.

Instead of stepping aside when we see kids in school being

mean or cruel to others, we should get involved. I realized then

how important it is to stick up for the victims of bullies.

PROOFREADING
TIPS

If you're working on a computer, use the spellchecker to catch spelling mistakes. It won't catch any words that are spelled correctly but used in the wrong way, however. Re-read your final draft carefully.

PUBLISHING
TIPS

Share your personal narrative with your audience. You may give a copy of your narrative to others or present it orally to a group. If you wish, add photographs or illustrations to your narrative.

Evaluating the Revision

1. Where has the writer added a sentence to grab the reader's attention?

2. Where has the writer elaborated with specific details or deleted irrelevant details?

Test Practice

DIRECTIONS: Read the story. Then, answer each question that follows.

Those Three Wishes

Judith Gorog

No one ever said that Melinda Alice was nice. That wasn't the word used. No, she was clever, even witty. She was called—never to her face, however—Melinda Malice. Melinda Alice was clever and cruel. Her mother, when she thought about it at all, hoped Melinda would grow out of it. To her father, Melinda's very good grades mattered.

It was Melinda Alice, back in the eighth grade, who had labeled the shy, myopic[1] new girl "Contamination" and was the first to pretend that anything or anyone touched by the new girl had to be cleaned, inoculated,[2] or avoided. High school had merely given Melinda Alice greater scope for her talents.

The surprising thing about Melinda Alice was her power; no one trusted her, but no one avoided her either. She was always

included, always in the middle. If you had seen her, pretty and witty, in the center of a group of students walking past your house, you'd have thought, "There goes a natural leader."

Melinda Alice had left for school early. She wanted to study alone in a quiet spot she had because there was going to be a big math test, and Melinda Alice was not prepared. That A mattered; so Melinda Alice walked to school alone, planning her studies. She didn't usually notice nature much, so she nearly stepped on a beautiful snail that was making its way across the sidewalk.

"Ugh. Yucky thing," thought Melinda Alice, then stopped. Not wanting to step on the snail accidentally was one thing, but now she lifted her shoe to crush it.

"Please don't," said the snail.

"Why not?" retorted Melinda Alice.

"I'll give you three wishes," replied the snail evenly.

1. **myopic** (mī·ăp′ik) *adj.:* nearsighted.
2. **inoculated** (i·năk′yə·lāt·id) *v.:* vaccinated.

SKILLS FOCUS

Literary Skills
Analyze plot structure.

"Agreed," said Melinda Alice. "My first wish is that my next," she paused a split second, "my next thousand wishes come true." She smiled triumphantly and opened her bag to take out a small notebook and pencil to keep track.

Melinda Alice was sure she heard the snail say, "What a clever girl," as it made it to the safety of an ivy bed beside the sidewalk.

During the rest of the walk to school, Melinda was occupied with wonderful ideas. She would have beautiful clothes. "Wish number two, that I will always be perfectly dressed," and she was just that. True, her new outfit was not a lot different from the one she had worn leaving the house, but that only meant that Melinda Alice liked her own taste.

After thinking awhile, she wrote, "Wish number three. I wish for pierced ears and small gold earrings." Her father had not allowed Melinda to have pierced

(*continued on next page*)

Test Practice

(*continued*)

ears, but now she had them anyway. She felt her new earrings and shook her beautiful hair in delight. "I can have anything: stereo, tapes, TV videodisc, moped, car, anything! All my life!" She hugged her books to herself in delight.

By the time she reached school, Melinda was almost an altruist;[3] she could wish for peace. Then she wondered, "Is the snail that powerful?" She felt her ears, looked at her perfect blouse, skirt, jacket, shoes. "I could make ugly people beautiful, cure cripples . . ." She stopped. The wave of altruism had washed past. "I could pay

---

3. **altruist** (al′tr$\overline{oo}$·ist) *n.*: person who helps others without expecting anything in return.

people back who deserve it!" Melinda Alice looked at the school, at all the kids. She had an enormous sense of power. "They all have to do what I want now." She walked down the crowded halls to her locker. Melinda Alice could be sweet; she could be witty. She could—The bell rang for homeroom. Melinda Alice stashed her books, slammed the locker shut, and just made it to her seat.

"Hey, Melinda Alice," whispered Fred. "You know that big math test next period?"

"Oh, no," grimaced Melinda Alice. Her thoughts raced; "That stupid snail made me late, and I forgot to study."

"I'll blow it," she groaned aloud. "I wish I were dead."

1. The writer leaves no doubt about what Melinda Alice is like. Which word does *not* describe her?
   - **A** Clever
   - **B** Pretty
   - **C** Nice
   - **D** Cruel

2. Which word best describes what Melinda Alice *wants*?
   - **F** Love
   - **G** Friends
   - **H** Knowledge
   - **J** Power

3. Why is Melinda Alice walking alone to school?
   - **A** No one likes her.
   - **B** She prefers to be alone.
   - **C** She wants to study.
   - **D** She is enjoying nature.

4. Melinda Alice does *not* step on the snail because —
   - **F** it is so beautiful
   - **G** it is too yucky
   - **H** it offers her three wishes
   - **J** she wants to be kind

5. Melinda Alice's wishes form **parallel episodes** in this short story. How many wishes does she make?
   - **A** A thousand
   - **B** Three
   - **C** Four
   - **D** Ten

6. Melinda Alice uses her wishes —
   - **F** for herself
   - **G** to benefit humanity
   - **H** to get even with enemies
   - **J** all of the above

7. Melinda Alice wishes for all of the following *except* —
   - **A** a thousand wishes
   - **B** to be perfectly dressed
   - **C** pierced ears and earrings
   - **D** a stereo, tapes, and a TV

8. The **climax** of a story is the moment when the outcome of the plot is decided. In "Those Three Wishes" the climax occurs when —
   - **F** the snail gives Melinda Alice three wishes
   - **G** Melinda Alice wishes for a thousand more wishes
   - **H** Melinda Alice wishes she were dead
   - **J** Fred reminds Melinda Alice of the math test

9. The **resolution** of the story —
   - **A** is described by the writer in great detail
   - **B** is left undecided
   - **C** happens after the story ends
   - **D** never happens

Constructed Response

10. In your opinion, what might be the **message** of this story? Explain how you know this is the message.

Test Practice

DIRECTIONS: Read the letter. Then, answer each question that follows.

Dear Councilman Duane:

More and more minors are smoking. When teens smoke, many problems arise. Something needs to be done to prove to minors that smoking is a bad thing. I am writing this letter to you in hopes that you will take steps to end this big problem.

Many problems develop when teenagers smoke. When teens smoke, laws are broken. Merchants break laws by intentionally selling cigarettes to minors. Teenage smokers damage their bodies permanently by smoking. Cigarettes cause addictions; even when teens want to quit, they often find they can't. Smoking can even affect a teenager's schooling. When a teenager needs a cigarette badly, he or she may ditch school to get one.

To help stop this problem, the city council could start a campaign against teenage smoking. You could make sure that schools with the sixth grade and older have a required class about the hazards of smoking, especially before the legal age. You could sponsor contests in each school for the best "Don't Smoke" posters, poems, essays, and stories. You could put the winners' posters and writing up around New York City. An educational campaign aimed at young teenagers would definitely help solve the problem of smoking by minors.

Some teenagers think, "It's my body; I can do what I want with it." Most smoking teenagers haven't fully matured emotionally. That means that what they believe now can change drastically in the following three to ten years of their lives. Therefore, as adults they may seriously regret decisions they made as teenagers.

Thank you for listening to my thoughts on this matter. I appreciate it and hope that you can do something to end the dilemma. Teenagers need to stop smoking, and you, as a person in power, can help them understand that it isn't all right to smoke.

—Hannah Fleury
St. Luke's School
New York, New York

SKILLS FOCUS

Reading Skills
Analyze proposition and support.

1. The writer's **purpose** in writing this letter is to —

   A   describe

   B   persuade

   C   entertain

   D   question

2. Which of the following sentences states the letter writer's **proposition**?

   F   "More and more minors are smoking."

   G   "When teens smoke, many problems arise."

   H   "Something needs to be done to prove to minors that smoking is a bad thing."

   J   "Cigarettes cause addictions."

3. Which of the following statements is an **opinion**?

   A   "When teens smoke, laws are broken."

   B   "More and more minors are smoking."

   C   "Merchants break laws by intentionally selling cigarettes to minors."

   D   "An educational campaign aimed at young teenagers would definitely help solve the problem of smoking by minors."

4. Which of the following sentences does *not* offer **support** for the letter writer's main idea?

   F   "When teens smoke, laws are broken."

   G   "Cigarettes cause addictions. . . ."

   H   "Smoking can even affect a teenager's schooling."

   J   "Teenagers need to stop smoking. . . ."

5. The **conclusion** of this letter —

   A   restates the proposition

   B   is a call to action

   C   both of the above

   D   none of the above

Constructed Response

6. How would you describe the **tone** of this letter? Use examples from the letter to explain your answer.

Collection 1: Skills Review

Vocabulary Skills

Test Practice

Multiple-Meaning Words

DIRECTIONS: Choose the answer in which the underlined word is used in the same way it is used in the passage from "Flowers for Algernon."

1. "'You used to be a good, dependable, ordinary man—not too bright maybe, but honest. Who knows what you done to yourself to get so <u>smart</u> all of a sudden.'"
   A Your new outfit looks <u>smart</u>.
   B How <u>smart</u> do you think you are?
   C Don't be <u>smart</u> with me, young man!
   D Does the cut on your finger still <u>smart</u>?

2. "He hasn't been eating. Everyone is upset about what this may <u>mean</u>."
   F Charlie's friends were very <u>mean</u> to him.
   G The <u>mean</u> rainfall in that part of the world is one inch a year.
   H David Wells throws a <u>mean</u> fastball.
   J High intelligence doesn't necessarily <u>mean</u> high achievement.

3. "'I am grateful for the little bit that I here add to the knowledge of the function of the human <u>mind</u>.' . . ."
   A Did Charlie <u>mind</u> being teased?
   B Who will <u>mind</u> the lab tonight?
   C A <u>mind</u> is a terrible thing to waste.
   D That nasty dog should <u>mind</u> its owner.

4. "Then Frank Reilly said what did you do Charlie forget your <u>key</u> and open your door the hard way."
   F Play that song in the <u>key</u> of G major, please.
   G The homecoming game was a <u>key</u> event for everyone.
   H Ken locked the car door but left the <u>key</u> in the ignition.
   J Someone took the answer <u>key</u> to the test.

5. "I tried not to look at the boy as I paid my <u>check</u> and walked out without touching my food."
   A This test will <u>check</u> your word power.
   B Waiter, <u>check</u>, please.
   C The doctors tried to <u>check</u> Algernon's decline.
   D Have you cashed that <u>check</u> yet?

SKILLS FOCUS

Vocabulary Skills
Understand multiple-meaning words.

Collection 1: Skills Review
Writing Skills

Test Practice

DIRECTIONS: Read the following paragraph from a personal narrative. Then, answer each question that follows.

(1) It was a cool October evening as I stood backstage all dressed up in my black leotard and tights with a gold-sequined belt. (2) My hair was pulled back in a bun, and a strong flowery smell of hair spray wafted around me. (3) My brother had teased me and called my outfit "silly," but I felt beautiful. (4) I was seven years old, and I knew that my first dance performance would be perfect. (5) I had eaten spaghetti, my favorite meal, for dinner. (6) As I pranced proudly onto the stage and into the hot, bright stage lights, I swelled with confidence. (7) Just as I neared my position on stage, my enthusiasm interfered with my footing, and I tripped. (8) On my knees on the stage floor, I could hear my brother's distinctive laugh and feel the heat rushing to my face. (9) I remembered my dance teacher's advice, "If you make a mistake, keep smiling and move on." (10) I held back my tears and jumped up from the floor like a graceful ballerina. (11) I wouldn't let a little fall stop me from enjoying my night in the spotlight.

1. Which of the following strategies would help the writer develop the ideas introduced in this paragraph?
   A Description of the main character's mother
   B Description of the main character's expressions
   C Description of the actions of the other dancers
   D Description of the car ride to the performance

2. Which of the following sentences is least necessary for the paragraph's coherence?
   F 2
   G 3
   H 5
   J 7

3. What should the writer add to this paragraph or to a later passage to make the personal narrative complete?
   A A reflection on the importance of the event
   B An explanation of the history of dance recitals
   C An analysis of dance choreography
   D A summary of the events leading up to the fall

4. The **tone** of this story would best be described as a mixture of —
   F embarrassment and sadness
   G anger and confidence
   H confusion and sadness
   J embarrassment and confidence

SKILLS FOCUS

Writing Skills
Analyze aspects of a personal narrative.

Fiction

Can Heroes Rise?

Can you solve the mystery of *Jackaroo*? In this Cynthia Voigt novel, Gwen hears tales of Jackaroo, a swash-buckling hero who helps the hopeless and fights for justice, but she is too realistic to believe them to be true. Then a series of events changes her life, and she learns there may be more to Jackaroo than stories.

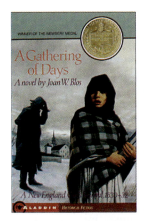

A Memorable Time

In Joan W. Blos's *A Gathering of Days*, teenaged Catherine Hall receives a journal and chronicles an eventful time of her life in it. Beginning in 1830, Catherine learns about racial prejudice from a man fleeing slavery, loses a close friend, and assumes greater responsibility on her family's New Hampshire farm as she journeys toward adulthood.

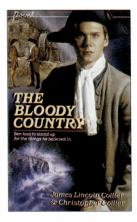

The Ties That Bind

In *The Bloody Country* by James Lincoln Collier and Christopher Collier, Ben Buck and his eighteenth-century Pennsylvania family may lose their home because of the threat of war. They also may lose Joe, a half-black, half–American Indian boy whom they hold as a slave. Ben considers Joe his best friend.

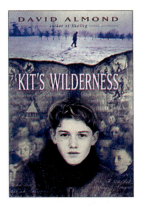

Searching for Sympathy

When a well-behaved thirteen-year-old named Kit Watson moves to Stoneygate, he encounters John Askew, a boy with a knack for getting into trouble. As they get to know each other, Kit finds they have something in common: Both can see ghosts of children who have died in Stoneygate's mines. In David Almond's *Kit's Wilderness*, Kit hopes this bond will help reveal John's goodness.

Nonfiction

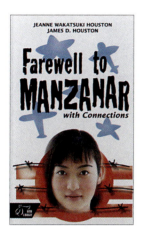

Punishment Without Crime

In 1942, seven-year-old Jeanne Wakatsuki and her family were sent to the Manzanar internment camp. Jeanne Wakatsuki Houston and James D. Houston's *Farewell to Manzanar* is the true story of a native-born American who grew up behind barbed wire in her own country.

This title is available in the HRW Library.

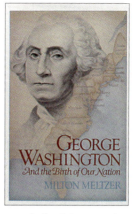

More Than a Dollar Bill

You know he was the first president, but have you ever wondered what George Washington was really like? Milton Meltzer answers that question in *George Washington and the Birth of Our Nation*. Meltzer looks at Washington's formative years as a surveyor and soldier in colonial Virginia, his role in the American Revolution, and his retirement in Mount Vernon.

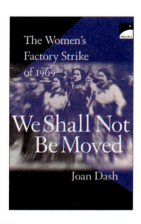

Taking a Stand

In 1909, young women throughout the United States worked in factories under unhealthy conditions for low pay. In *We Shall Not Be Moved*, Joan Dash tells how a group of women in the shirtwaist industry in New York City battled for fair treatment by going on strike and struggling to form a union.

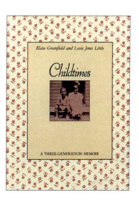

Days Gone By

In *Childtimes* by Eloise Greenfield and Lessie Jones Little, African American women from three generations look back on their child-hoods. Some of their memories, such as the smell of home-baked rolls on a Sunday morning, are pleasant. But the writers also recall confrontations with racism at a very young age.

Signs (1961) by Robert Vickrey. Tempera on board (27¾" × 41¾").
The Corcoran Gallery of Art, Gift of Ray C. Markus through the FRIENDS of the Corcoran.
© Robert Vickrey/Licensed by VAGA, New York, N.Y.

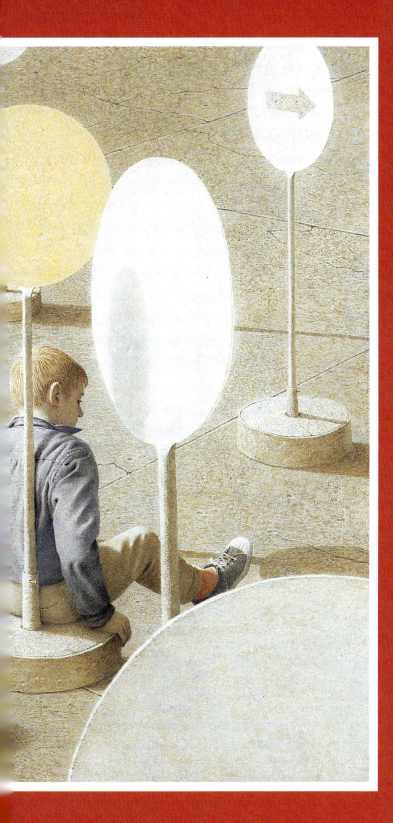

Do the Right Thing

Literary Focus:
Analyzing Character

Informational Focus:
Comparing and
Contrasting Texts

INTERNET

Collection
Resources

Keyword: LE5 8-2

Elements of Literature

Characters *by* John Leggett
THE HUMAN EXPERIENCE

Most of us are fascinated by other people. We like to know how other people deal with problems, disappointments, and temptations. A good story, whether it's true, made-up, or somewhere in between, reveals some truth about human experience. It does this through the people who live in its pages—its **characters.**

Characterization: The Breath of Life

The way a writer reveals character is called **characterization.** Poor characterization can make even a real person uninteresting. Good characterization can make readers feel that even fantasy characters—a bumbling teddy bear or a girl who is tossed by a tornado into an emerald city—live and breathe.

Creating Characters

A writer may simply *tell* us directly that a character is mean tempered or thrifty or brave or honest. This kind of characterization, called **direct characterization,** was often used by writers years ago. Present-day writers generally prefer to *show* their characters in action and let us decide for ourselves what kinds of people we are meeting. This method is called **indirect characterization.**

INTERNET

More About Characterization

Keyword: LE5 8-2

Literary Skills
Understand characterization.

Direct Characterization

1 **Stating directly what the character is like.**

Sergeant Randolph was the cruelest drillmaster in the regiment.

Indirect Characterization

2 **Describing the appearance of the character.**

Wanda's hair was pink, and every pink hair stuck up from her head. Underneath all that pink hair, though, was a pair of innocent blue eyes.

3 **Showing the character in action.**

Toni glanced around, then tossed the empty soda can on the grass and kept walking.

4 **Allowing us to hear the character speak.**

"I don't have to do what you say," declared Darlene, pinching the new baby sitter.

5 **Revealing the character's thoughts and feelings.**

Ashley didn't like the looks of the squash pudding but decided to eat some to please the cook.

PEANUTS reprinted by permission of United Feature Syndicate, Inc.

6 **Showing how others react to the character.**

"Go wake up my sister?" Lulu said. "Sure, Mom. Just give me armor and a twenty-foot pole, and I'll be all set to go."

How Could You Do That? Motivation

Why did your best friend suddenly get a crush on the biggest jerk in school? What could possibly have possessed your brother to think he could climb Mount McKinley?

We always wonder about people's **motivation**—that is, we wonder what makes people behave the way they do. In real life we may never learn the answer. Literature is different. In literature you'll find plenty of clues to characters' **motives**—why they do the things they do. One of the pleasures of literature is using these clues to figure out what makes people tick.

Practice

Choose a character from a story or novel you have read recently, and fill in a chart like the one below:

Character Profile of _____	
Method of Characterization	Details in Story
Appearance:	
Actions:	
Words spoken by character:	
Thoughts:	
Other characters' responses:	
Writer's direct comments:	

Reading Skills and Strategies

Comparing and Contrasting

by Kylene Beers

Comparisons and contrasts—you make them all the time, whenever you talk about how things are similar **(comparisons)** and how they are different **(contrasts).** Teachers ask you to find and discuss comparisons and contrasts constantly. Your English teacher asks you to discuss how two stories are similar or different. Your history teacher asks you to explain how the Civil War was different from the Revolutionary War. Your science teacher asks you to compare and contrast the ways mountains form.

A Strategy: Looking for Signal Words

Writers often help you understand comparisons and contrasts by introducing ideas with words that act as signals. For instance, the phrase "just like" can be used to signal a comparison: "Gary Paulsen writes adventure books just like Will Hobbs does." The word *although* tells you to look for a contrast: "*Although* Paulsen writes about boys having adventures, girls can enjoy his stories."

Applying the Strategy

As you read the next article about Thanksgiving, look for the signal words or phrases that help you compare and contrast Thanksgiving traditions today with the original feast.

Signal Words	
Comparisons	**Contrasts**
additionally	except
moreover	despite the fact
in the same way	but
similarly	although
both	by contrast
correspondingly	instead of
as well as	nevertheless
besides	however
further	on the other hand
too	otherwise
also	

SKILLS FOCUS

Reading Skills
Understand comparing and contrasting.

Thanksgiving

A Meal Without Forks

and Other Feast Facts ❶

In 1621 the Plymouth colonists and the Wampanoag[1] shared an autumn harvest feast which is now known as the first Thanksgiving. While cooking methods and table etiquette have changed as the holiday has evolved, the meal is still consumed today with the same spirit of celebration and overindulgence. ❷

---

1. **Wampanoag** (wäm′pə·nō′ag′).

Using the Strategy

As you read, you'll find this open-book sign at certain points in the story: . Stop at these points, and think about what you've just read. Do what the prompt asks you to do.

COMPARE AND CONTRAST

❶ This article tells you about the first Thanksgiving. Look for signal words that help you compare and contrast the pilgrims' feast to today's celebration.

COMPARE AND CONTRAST

❷ Look at the second sentence. What's changed in the way we celebrate Thanksgiving? What's stayed the same? Remember that *etiquette* means "manners." Is that sentence telling you that table manners have changed or stayed the same?

Using the Strategy

COMPARE AND CONTRAST

❸ Look again at that second sentence on page 137, which contrasts what we do today with what the pilgrims did. Who's eating that pumpkin pie and playing with those potatoes?

COMPARE AND CONTRAST

❹ This section points out lots of differences (contrasts) between what and how pilgrims ate and what and how we eat. You might make a two-column list, and write *1621 Pilgrims* at the top of one column and *Americans Today* at the top of the other one. As you read through the various items in the article, put information in the correct column.

What Was Actually on the Menu?

What foods topped the table at the first harvest feast? Historians aren't completely certain about the full bounty, but it's safe to say the pilgrims weren't gobbling up pumpkin pie or playing with their mashed potatoes. ❸ 📖 [T]he only two items that historians know for sure were on the menu are venison and wild fowl, which are mentioned in primary sources. The most detailed description of the first Thanksgiving comes from Edward Winslow.[2]

Seventeenth-Century Table Manners ❹ 📖

- The pilgrims didn't use forks; they ate with spoons, knives, and their fingers. They wiped their hands on large cloth napkins which they also used to pick up hot morsels of food.
- Salt would have been on the table at the harvest feast, and people would have sprinkled it on their food. Pepper, however, was

---

2. **Edward Winslow** (1595–1655): One of the founders and leaders of Plymouth Colony.

First Thanksgiving (1942) by Newell Convers Wyeth.

something that they used for cooking but wasn't available on the table.

- In the seventeenth century, a person's social standing determined what he or she ate. The best food was placed next to the most important people. People didn't tend to sample everything that was on the table (as we do today); they just ate what was closest to them.
- Serving in the seventeenth century was very different from serving today. People weren't served their meals individually. Foods were served onto the table and then people took the food from the table and ate it. All the servers had to do was move the food from the place where it was cooked onto the table.
- Pilgrims didn't eat in courses as we do today. All of the different types of foods were placed on the table at the same time and people ate in any order they chose. Sometimes there were two courses, but each of them would contain both meat dishes, puddings, and sweets.

Using the Strategy

COMPARE AND CONTRAST

5 In the sentence you just read, what signal word indicates a contrast?

COMPARE AND CONTRAST

6 What happened to the sugar brought on the *Mayflower*? What word signals that the pilgrims didn't have much sugar by the time of the feast?

COMPARE AND CONTRAST

7 In the first sentence of this paragraph the word *but* signals a contrast. Look back at the list of contrast words on page 136, and find other words that would work as well.

More Meat, Fewer Vegetables

- Our modern Thanksgiving repast[3] is centered around the turkey, but that certainly wasn't the case at the pilgrims' feasts. **5** Their meals included many different meats. Vegetable dishes, one of the main components of our modern celebration, didn't really play a large part in the feast mentality of the seventeenth century. Depending on the time of year, many vegetables weren't available to the colonists.

- The pilgrims probably didn't have pies or anything sweet at the harvest feast. They had brought some sugar with them on the *Mayflower* but by the time of the feast, the supply had dwindled. Also, they didn't have an oven so pies and cakes and breads were not possible at all. **6**

- The food that was eaten at the harvest feast would have seemed fatty by today's standards, but it was probably more healthy for the pilgrims than it would be for people today. **7** The colonists were more active and needed more protein. Heart attack was the least of their worries. They were more concerned about the plague and pox.[4]

---

3. **repast** (ri·past´) *n.*: meal.
4. **pox** *n.*: smallpox.

Practice the Strategy

Using Signal Words to Make Comparisons and Contrasts

PRACTICE 1

Here's how one student compared the first Thanksgiving feast with the feast her family celebrates each year. As you read, look at how she signals the comparisons and contrasts she wants to make. Then, make a list of the signal words used in the paragraph.

> Both the pilgrims and my family have celebrated Thanksgiving. However, our celebration looks very different from the pilgrims' celebration. We use forks to eat our wonderful meal. By contrast, the pilgrims used their fingers! My mom makes us use napkins to wipe our messy mouths, while the pilgrims used their napkins to pick up hot food. We put everything on the table and pass it around to everyone instead of just eating what is near the way the pilgrims did.

PRACTICE 2

Write your own paragraph about how the pilgrims' Thanksgiving is similar to and different from yours. Organize your thoughts by making an H-map to help you see what you do at Thanksgiving, what the pilgrims did, and how those two feasts are the same and different. First, draw a big capital letter H on a piece of paper. Then, to the left of the first vertical line, write what the pilgrims did. To the right of the second vertical line, write what you do. Underneath the horizontal line, write what you both do.

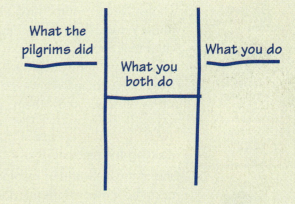

What the pilgrims did

What you both do

What you do

PRACTICE 3

Now, take the information from your H-map, and put it into paragraph form. Show your comparisons and contrasts by using some of the signal words in the box on page 136.

You can use an H-map to organize your thoughts about any of the stories in this collection. Any time you need to **compare** and **contrast,** try using an **H-map.**

SKILLS FOCUS

Reading Skills
Compare and contrast.

Before You Read The Biography

from Harriet Tubman

Make the Connection
Quickwrite 🖉

What have people over the centuries endured for the sake of freedom? What have people endured because their freedom was taken away? In your journal, jot down notes on these questions.

Literary Focus
Characters in Biography

When we read a **biography**—the story of someone's life written by another person—we get to know the real people in the story. We get acquainted with the characters in a biography the same way we get to know people in our own lives. We observe their **actions**—what they say and do. We think about their **motivations,** the reasons for their actions. We learn something about their values. We watch the way they interact with other people. We compare these characters with the people we know (or with other people we have read about). Soon we feel we know them.

Reading Skills 📖
Making Inferences

One of the pleasures of reading is making our own inferences about characters. **Inferences** are conclusions we come to based on information in the text and what we already know. An inference is an educated guess. As you read this biography, look for the open-book signs. These signs indicate places where you must make inferences.

Vocabulary Development

These are the words you'll need to know as you read the biography:

fugitives (fyo͞oʹji·tivz) *n.:* people fleeing from danger. *The fugitives escaped to the North, traveling by night.*

incomprehensible (in·käm'prē·hen'sə·bəl) *adj.:* impossible to understand. *The Fugitive Slave Law had once been an incomprehensible set of words.*

incentive (in·sentʹiv) *n.:* reason to do something; motivation. *The incentive of a warm house and good food kept the fugitives going.*

dispel (di·spelʹ) *v.:* scatter; drive away. *Harriet tried to dispel the fugitives' fear of capture.*

eloquence (elʹə·kwəns) *n.:* ability to write or speak gracefully and convincingly. *Frederick Douglass was known for his eloquence in writing and speaking.*

INTERNET

Vocabulary Activity

•

More About Petry

Keyword: LE5 8-2

SKILLS FOCUS

Literary Skills
Understand characterization.

Reading Skills
Make inferences.

Background
Literature and Religion

In the biblical Book of Exodus, Moses is chosen by God to lead the people of Israel out of slavery in Egypt. Moses takes his people on a long, perilous desert journey and leads them to the Promised Land. As you read this biography, look for reasons why Harriet Tubman was called the Moses of her people.

Roots (1964) by Charles White. Chinese ink.

from **Harriet Tubman**

Conductor on the Underground Railroad

Ann Petry

If they were caught, she would probably be hanged.

The Railroad Runs to Canada

Along the Eastern Shore of Maryland, in Dorchester County, in Caroline County, the masters kept hearing whispers about the man named Moses, who was running off slaves. At first they did not believe in his existence. The stories about him were fantastic, unbelievable. Yet they watched for him. They offered rewards for his capture.

They never saw him. Now and then they heard whispered rumors to the effect that he was in the neighborhood. The woods were searched. The roads were watched. There was never anything to indicate his whereabouts. But a few days afterward, a goodly number of slaves would be gone from the plantation. Neither the master nor the overseer had heard or seen anything unusual in the quarter.[1] Sometimes one or the other would vaguely remember having heard a whippoorwill call somewhere in the woods, close by, late at night. Though it was the wrong season for whippoorwills.

Sometimes the masters thought they had heard the cry of a hoot owl, repeated, and would remember having thought that the intervals between the low moaning cry were wrong, that it had been repeated four times in succession instead of three. There was never anything more than that to suggest that all was not well in the quarter. Yet, when morning came, they invariably discovered that a group of the finest slaves had taken to their heels.

Unfortunately, the discovery was almost always made on a Sunday. Thus a whole day was lost before the machinery of pursuit could be set in motion. The posters offering rewards for the fugitives could not be printed until Monday. The men who made a living hunting for runaway slaves were out of reach, off in the woods with their dogs and their guns, in pursuit of four-footed game, or they were in camp meetings saying their prayers with their wives and families beside them.

Harriet Tubman could have told them that there was far more involved in this matter of running off slaves than signaling the would-be runaways by imitating the call of a whippoorwill, or a hoot owl, far more involved than a matter of waiting for a clear night when the North Star[2] was visible.

In December 1851, when she started out with the band of fugitives that she planned to take to Canada, she had been in the vicinity of the plantation for days, planning the trip, carefully selecting the slaves that she would take with her.

She had announced her arrival in the quarter by singing the forbidden spiritual[3]— "Go down, Moses, 'way down to Egypt Land"—singing it softly outside the door of a slave cabin, late at night. The husky voice was beautiful even when it was barely more than a murmur borne on the wind.

Once she had made her presence known,

---

1. **quarter** *n.*: area in a plantation where enslaved blacks lived. It consisted of windowless, one-room cabins made of logs and mud.

2. **North Star:** Runaways fleeing north used the North Star (Polaris) to help them stay on course.
3. **forbidden spiritual:** Spirituals are religious songs, some of which are based on the biblical story of the Israelites' escape from slavery in Egypt. Plantation owners feared that the singing of spirituals might lead to rebellion.

Vocabulary

fugitives (fyōō′ji·tivz) *n.*: people fleeing from danger.

word of her coming spread from cabin to cabin. The slaves whispered to each other, ear to mouth, mouth to ear, "Moses is here." "Moses has come." "Get ready. Moses is back again." The ones who had agreed to go North with her put ashcake[4] and salt herring in an old bandanna, hastily tied it into a bundle, and then waited patiently for the signal that meant it was time to start.

There were eleven in this party, including one of her brothers and his wife. It was the largest group that she had ever conducted, but she was determined that more and more slaves should know what freedom was like.

She had to take them all the way to Canada. The Fugitive Slave Law[5] was no longer a great many incomprehensible words written down on the country's lawbooks. The new law had become a reality. It was Thomas Sims, a boy, picked up on the streets of Boston at night and shipped back to Georgia. It was Jerry and Shadrach, arrested and jailed with no warning. ❶

INFER
❶ What does it mean that the new law was Thomas Sims or Jerry and Shadrach?

She had never been in Canada. The route beyond Philadelphia was strange to her. But she could not let the runaways who accompanied her know this. As they walked along, she told them stories of her own first flight; she kept painting vivid word pictures of what it would be like to be free.

But there were so many of them this time. She knew moments of doubt, when she was half afraid and kept looking back over her shoulder, imagining that she heard the sound of pursuit. They would certainly be pursued. Eleven of them. Eleven thousand dollars' worth of flesh and bone and muscle that belonged to Maryland planters. If they were caught, the eleven runaways would be whipped and sold South, but she—she would probably be hanged.

They tried to sleep during the day but they never could wholly relax into sleep. She could tell by the positions they assumed, by their restless movements. And they walked at night. Their progress was slow. It took them three nights of walking to reach the first stop. She had told them about the place where they would stay, promising warmth and good food, holding these things out to them as an incentive to keep going.

When she knocked on the door of a farmhouse, a place where she and her parties of runaways had always been welcome, always been given shelter and plenty to eat, there was no answer. She knocked again, softly. A voice from within said, "Who is it?" There was fear in the voice.

She knew instantly from the sound of the voice that there was something wrong. She said, "A friend with friends," the password on the Underground Railroad.

The door opened, slowly. The man who stood in the doorway looked at her coldly, looked with unconcealed astonishment and

---

4. **ashcake** *n.:* cornmeal bread baked in hot ashes.
5. **Fugitive Slave Law:** harsh federal law passed in 1850 stating that fugitives who escaped from slavery to free states could be forced to return to their owners. As a result, those who escaped were safe only in Canada. The law also made it a crime for a free person to help fugitives or to prevent their return.

Vocabulary

incomprehensible (in·käm′prē·hen′sə·bəl) *adj.:* impossible to understand.

incentive (in·sent′iv) *n.:* reason to do something; motivation.

fear at the eleven disheveled[6] runaways who were standing near her. Then he shouted, "Too many, too many. It's not safe. My place was searched last week. It's not safe!" and slammed the door in her face.

She turned away from the house, frowning. She had promised her passengers food and rest and warmth, and instead of that, there would be hunger and cold and more walking over the frozen ground. Somehow she would have to instill courage into these eleven people, most of them strangers, would have to feed them on hope and bright dreams of freedom instead of the fried pork and corn bread and milk she had promised them.

They stumbled along behind her, half dead for sleep, and she urged them on, though she was as tired and as discouraged as they were. She had never been in Canada, but she kept painting wondrous word pictures of what it would be like. She managed to dispel their fear of pursuit so that they would not become hysterical, panic-stricken. Then she had to bring some of the fear back, so that they would stay awake and keep walking though they drooped with sleep.

Yet, during the day, when they lay down deep in a thicket, they never really slept, because if a twig snapped or the wind sighed in the branches of a pine tree, they jumped to their feet, afraid of their own shadows, shivering and shaking. It was very cold, but they dared not make fires because someone would see the smoke and wonder about it.

She kept thinking, eleven of them. Eleven thousand dollars' worth of slaves. And she had to take them all the way to Canada. Sometimes she told them about Thomas Garrett, in Wilmington.[7] She said he was their friend even though he did not know them. He was the friend of all fugitives. He called them God's poor. He was a Quaker[8] and his speech was a little different from that of other people. His clothing was different, too. He wore the wide-brimmed hat that the Quakers wear.

She said that he had thick white hair, soft, almost like a baby's, and the kindest eyes she had ever seen. He was a big man and strong, but he had never used his strength to harm anyone, always to help people. He would give all of them a new pair of shoes. Everybody. He always did. Once they reached his house in Wilmington, they would be safe. He would see to it that they were. ❷

She described the house where he lived, told them about the store where he sold shoes. She said he kept a pail of milk and a loaf of bread in the drawer of his desk so that he would have food ready at hand for any of God's poor who should suddenly appear before him, fainting with hunger. There was a hidden room in the store. A whole wall swung open, and behind it was a room where he could hide fugitives. On the wall there were shelves filled with small boxes—boxes of shoes—so that you would never guess that the wall actually opened.

While she talked, she kept watching

> **INFER**
> ❷ Why would shoes be so important to the fugitives?

---

7. **Wilmington:** city in Delaware.
8. **Quaker:** member of the Society of Friends, a religious group active in the movement to end slavery.

---

6. **disheveled** (di·shev′əld) *adj.:* untidy; rumpled.

Vocabulary
dispel (di·spel′) *v.:* scatter; drive away.

them. They did not believe her. She could tell by their expressions. They were thinking. New shoes, Thomas Garrett, Quaker, Wilmington—what foolishness was this? Who knew if she told the truth? Where was she taking them anyway?

That night they reached the next stop—a farm that belonged to a German. She made the runaways take shelter behind trees at the edge of the fields before she knocked at the door. She hesitated before she approached the door, thinking, suppose that he too should refuse shelter, suppose— Then she thought, *Lord, I'm going to hold steady on to You and You've got to see me through*—and knocked softly. ❸

> **📖 INFER**
> ❸ What inferences can you make about Tubman from this paragraph?

She heard the familiar guttural voice say, "Who's there?"

She answered quickly, "A friend with friends."

He opened the door and greeted her warmly. "How many this time?" he asked.

"Eleven," she said and waited, doubting, wondering.

He said, "Good. Bring them in."

He and his wife fed them in the lamp-lit kitchen, their faces glowing as they offered food and more food, urging them to eat, saying there was plenty for everybody, have more milk, have more bread, have more meat.

They spent the night in the warm kitchen. They really slept, all that night and until dusk the next day. When they left, it was with reluctance. They had all been warm and safe and well-fed. It was hard to exchange the security offered by that clean, warm kitchen for the darkness and the cold of a December night.

Go Down, Moses

traditional African American spiritual

When Israel was in Egypt land—
Let my people go.
Oppressed so hard they could not
    stand
Let my people go.
    CHORUS:
    Go down, Moses, way down in
      Egypt land;
    tell ole Pharaoh to let my people go.

Thus saith the Lord, bold Moses
    said—
Let my people go.
If not I'll smite your firstborn dead—
Let my people go.
    CHORUS

No more shall they in bondage toil—
Let my people go.
Let them come out with Egypt's
    spoil—
Let my people go.
    CHORUS

We need not always weep and
    mourn—
Let my people go.
And wear those slavery's chains
    forlorn—
Let my people go.
    CHORUS

"Go On or Die"

Harriet had found it hard to leave the warmth and friendliness, too. But she urged them on. For a while, as they walked, they seemed to carry in them a measure of contentment; some of the serenity and the cleanliness of that big, warm kitchen lingered on inside them. But as they walked farther and farther away from the warmth and the light, the cold and the darkness entered into them. They fell silent, sullen, suspicious. She waited for the moment when some one of them would turn mutinous.[9] It did not happen that night.

Two nights later, she was aware that the feet behind her were moving slower and slower. She heard the irritability in their voices, knew that soon someone would refuse to go on.

She started talking about William Still and the Philadelphia Vigilance Committee.[10] No one commented. No one asked any questions. She told them the story of William and Ellen Craft and how they escaped from Georgia. Ellen was so fair that she looked as though she were white, and so she dressed up in a man's clothing and she looked like a wealthy young planter. Her husband, William, who was dark, played the role of her slave. Thus they traveled from Macon, Georgia, to Philadelphia, riding on the trains, staying at the finest hotels. Ellen pretended to be very ill—her right arm was in a sling and her right hand was bandaged because she was supposed to have rheumatism.[11] Thus she avoided having to sign the register at the hotels, for she could not read or write. They finally arrived safely in Philadelphia and then went on to Boston.

No one said anything. Not one of them seemed to have heard her.

She told them about Frederick Douglass, the most famous of the escaped slaves, of his eloquence, of his magnificent appearance. Then she told them of her own first, vain effort at running away, evoking the memory of that miserable life she had led as a child, reliving it for a moment in the telling.

But they had been tired too long, hungry too long, afraid too long, footsore too long. One of them suddenly cried out in despair, "Let me go back. It is better to be a slave than to suffer like this in order to be free."

She carried a gun with her on these trips. She had never used it—except as a threat. Now, as she aimed it, she experienced a feeling of guilt, remembering that time, years ago, when she had prayed for the death of Edward Brodas, the Master, and then, not too long afterward, had heard that great wailing cry that came from the throats of the field hands, and knew from the sound that the Master was dead.

One of the runaways said again, "Let me go back. Let me go back," and stood still, and then turned around and said, over his shoulder, "I am going back."

She lifted the gun, aimed it at the

---

9. **mutinous** (myoot'n·əs) *adj.:* rebellious. *Mutiny* usually refers to a revolt of sailors against their officer.
10. **Philadelphia Vigilance Committee:** group that offered help to people escaping slavery. **William Still,** a free African American, was chairman of the committee.

---

11. **rheumatism** (roo'mə·tiz'əm) *n.:* painful swelling and stiffness of the joints or muscles.

Vocabulary

eloquence (el'ə·kwəns) *n.:* ability to write or speak gracefully and convincingly.

Harriet (1972) by Charles White. Oil wash.
© 1973 The Charles White Archives.

despairing slave. She said, "Go on with us or die." The husky, low-pitched voice was grim. ④

INFER
④ Why does Harriet Tubman make this threat?

He hesitated for a moment and then he joined the others. They started walking again. She tried to explain to them why none of them could go back to the plantation. If a runaway returned, he would turn traitor; the master and the overseer would force him to turn traitor. The returned slave would disclose the stopping places, the hiding places, the corn stacks they had used with the full knowledge of the owner of the farm, the name of the German farmer who had fed them and sheltered them. These people who had risked their own security to help runaways would be ruined, fined, imprisoned.

She said, "We got to go free or die. And freedom's not bought with dust."

This time she told them about the long agony of the Middle Passage[12] on the old slave ships, about the black horror of the holds, about the chains and the whips. They too knew these stories. But she wanted to remind them of the long, hard way they had come, about the long, hard way they had yet to go. She told them about Thomas Sims, the boy picked up on the streets of Boston and sent back to Georgia. She said when they got him back to Savannah, got him in prison there, they whipped him until a doctor who was standing by watching said, "You will kill him if you strike him again!" His master said, "Let him die!"

Thus she forced them to go on. Sometimes she thought she had become nothing but a voice speaking in the darkness, cajoling,[13] urging, threatening. Sometimes she told them things to make them laugh; sometimes she sang to them and heard the eleven voices behind her blending softly with hers, and then she knew that for the moment all was well with them.

She gave the impression of being a short, muscular, indomitable woman who could never be defeated. Yet at any moment she was liable to be seized by one of those curious fits of sleep, which might last for a few minutes or for hours.[14]

Even on this trip, she suddenly fell asleep in the woods. The runaways, ragged, dirty, hungry, cold, did not steal the gun as they might have and set off by themselves or turn back. They sat on the ground near her and waited patiently until she awakened. They had come to trust her implicitly, totally. They, too, had come to believe her repeated statement, "We got to go free or die." She was leading them into freedom, and so they waited until she was ready to go on.

Finally, they reached Thomas Garrett's house in Wilmington, Delaware. Just as Harriet had promised, Garrett gave them all new shoes, and provided carriages to take them on to the next stop.

By slow stages they reached Philadelphia, where William Still hastily recorded their names, and the plantations whence they

---

12. **Middle Passage:** route traveled by ships carrying captured Africans across the Atlantic Ocean to the Americas. The captives endured the horrors of the Middle Passage crammed into **holds,** airless cargo areas below deck.

13. **cajoling** (kə·jōl′iŋ) *v.* used as *adj.*: coaxing.
14. Harriet's losses of consciousness were caused by a serious head injury that she had suffered as a teenager. Harriet had tried to protect someone else from punishment, and an enraged overseer threw a two-pound weight at her head.

The Underground Railroad runs to Canada.

had come, and something of the life they had led in slavery. Then he carefully hid what he had written, for fear it might be discovered. In 1872 he published this record in book form and called it *The Underground Railroad.* In the foreword to his book he said: "While I knew the danger of keeping strict records, and while I did not then dream that in my day slavery would be blotted out, or that the time would come when I could publish these records, it used to afford me great satisfaction to take them down, fresh from the lips of fugitives on the way to freedom, and to preserve them as they had given them."

William Still, who was familiar with all the station stops on the Underground Railroad, supplied Harriet with money and sent her and her eleven fugitives on to Burlington, New Jersey.

Harriet felt safer now, though there were danger spots ahead. But the biggest part of her job was over. As they went farther and farther north, it grew colder; she was aware of the wind on the Jersey ferry and aware of the cold damp in New York. From New York they went on to Syracuse,[15] where the temperature was even lower.

In Syracuse she met the Reverend J. W. Loguen, known as "Jarm" Loguen. This was the beginning of a lifelong friendship. Both Harriet and Jarm Loguen were to become friends and supporters of Old John Brown.[16]

From Syracuse they went north again, into a colder, snowier city—Rochester. Here they almost certainly stayed with Frederick Douglass, for he wrote in his autobiography:

"On one occasion I had eleven fugitives at the same time under my roof, and it was necessary for them to remain with me until I could collect sufficient money to get them to Canada. It was the largest number I ever had at any one time, and I had some difficulty in providing so many with food and shelter, but, as may well be imagined, they were not very fastidious[17] in either direction, and were well content with very plain food, and a strip of carpet on the floor for a bed, or a place on the straw in the barn loft."

Late in December 1851, Harriet arrived in St. Catharines, Canada West (now Ontario), with the eleven fugitives. It had taken almost a month to complete this journey.

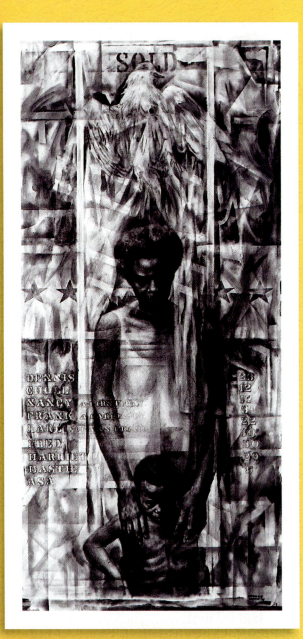

Wanted Poster Series #17 (1971) by Charles White. Oil wash.
© 1971 The Charles White Archives.

---

15. **Syracuse:** city in central New York.
16. **John Brown** (1800–1859): abolitionist (opponent of slavery) who was active in the Railroad. In 1859, Brown led a raid on the federal arsenal at Harpers Ferry, then in Virginia, in hopes of inspiring a slave uprising. Federal troops overpowered Brown and his followers, and Brown was convicted of treason and was hanged.
17. **fastidious** (fa·stid′ē·əs) *adj.:* fussy; hard to please.

Meet the Writer

Ann Petry

"A Message in the Story"

A native of Old Saybrook, Connecticut, **Ann Petry** (1908–1997) was the granddaughter of a man who escaped from slavery on a Virginia plantation and came north by way of the Underground Railroad. As a young woman she worked as a pharmacist in her family's drugstores before moving to New York, where she became a writer of books for young people and adults. About her writing she said:

> ❝My writing has, of course, been influenced by the books I've read but it has been much more influenced by the circumstances of my birth and my growing up, by my family. . . .
>
> We always had relatives visiting us. They added excitement to our lives. They brought with them the aura and the customs of a very different world. They were all storytellers, spinners of yarns. So were my mother and my father.
>
> Some of these stories had been handed down from one generation to the next, improved, embellished, embroidered. Usually there was a message in the story, a message for the young, a message that would help a young black child survive, help convince a young black child that black is truly beautiful.❞

For Independent Reading

Tituba of Salem Village is based on the true story of another heroic woman of African descent, who was accused of witchcraft in 1692.

First Thoughts

1. Why might someone like Harriet Tubman, who was already free, risk her life to lead other people to freedom?

Thinking Critically

2. How was Tubman like Moses in the Bible? What was *her* Promised Land?

3. We sense **irony** when we notice that something is the opposite of what is expected. Why do we sense irony when we read that the men who hunted fugitives for money said prayers with their families on Sundays (page 144)?

4. What **inference** about Harriet Tubman's **character** can you draw from the incident with the gun? What other inferences can you make about the character of Harriet Tubman? Consider her words, her actions, and her effect on others.

5. Go back to the text, and find two **primary sources** (firsthand accounts) mentioned by Petry. What other firsthand sources might she have used to get all this factual information?

Extending Interpretations

6. Think about another period in history when people were forced to leave behind everything they knew and loved. How would their experiences compare with the experiences of Harriet Tubman and her eleven fugitives? Think about your responses to the Quickwrite before you answer.

Reading Check

a. List at least five **facts** about the workings of the Underground Railroad that you learned from this biography.

b. List at least five **facts** you learned about Harriet Tubman.

INTERNET

Projects and Activities

Keyword: LE5 8-2

WRITING

Writing a Biographical Sketch

Most people would agree that Harriet Tubman is a hero. Heroism is also found in people who aren't famous. Maybe there is someone in your family who has heroic qualities. Perhaps a teacher, a coach, or a friend is a real hero to you. Write a brief **biographical sketch** of someone you think is a hero. Your sketch should tell where and when the person was born, where the person lives (or lived, if now dead), and what he or she does (or did). Be sure to explain why this person is a hero to you.

SKILLS FOCUS

Literary Skills
Analyze characterization.

Reading Skills
Make inferences.

Writing Skills
Write a biographical sketch.

Influences on English: All in the Family

The histories of English words can give us a glimpse of the history of the English-speaking peoples themselves. Thousands of words that we use every day have come into English from other languages. Some countries, such as France and Germany, have tried to prevent their languages from borrowing foreign words. English, however, has always been like a giant sponge, absorbing words from every group it comes in contact with. The Vocabulary words in Petry's biography of Harriet Tubman all come from Latin. Latin is an ancient language that is no longer spoken. Because of its rich literature and its influence on English, however, it is still taught in some schools. The Word Bank, below, contains a list of the Vocabulary words and the Latin words they come from.

Word Bank

fugitives < L *fugere*, "to flee"

incomprehensible < L *prehendere*, "to seize, grasp, get hold of"

incentive < L *canere*, "to sing"

dispel < L *pellere*, "to drive, beat"

eloquence < L *loqui*, "to speak or talk"

PRACTICE

Study the meaning of the words above, all of which come from Latin, and then look at the list called Related Words. The **related words** and some of the Vocabulary words have Latin roots in common. Make word trees grouping the words from each list that come from the same Latin word. One word tree has already been done for you. (Some trees will have just a few branches!)

Related Words

apprehend: capture; understand.

compel: force; overpower; control.

enchant: charm; bewitch.

expulsion: banishment.

impel: push; drive; urge; require.

loquacious: very talkative.

propel: send forcefully outward.

recant: take back one's words.

refuge: place safe from danger.

soliloquy: speech made by an actor alone onstage.

subterfuge: actions used to escape the consequences of one's misdeeds.

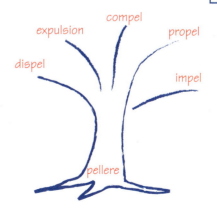

Vocabulary Skills
Understand word origins.

Harriet Tubman   **155**

Understanding Text Structures

Reading Focus
Using Text Structures to Organize Ideas

"Get organized!" Has anyone ever said that to you? What exactly does it mean? Let's look at the CDs floating around your room. If you have five CDs, you can probably stack them in one place. Then all the CDs are together—end of problem. If you have a lot of CDs, though, you may want to broaden the scope of your organization. You could alphabetize your CDs by artist or group, or you might put all the hip-hop together and all the classical together. As long as you are willing to live with it, almost anything you do will be fine.

Writers have a different problem. They have to organize ideas not just for themselves but also for their readers. So writers rely on certain **text structures** to help convey their ideas. Recognizing those structures can help you understand how the ideas are grouped and how they are connected.

Kinds of Text Structures

There are many kinds of text structures, but among the most commonly used are the following ones:

- **enumeration** (ē·nōō'mər·ā'shən) or **sequence**—explaining things first, second, third, and so on
- **chronology** (krə·näl'ə·jē)—describing events in the order in which they happen
- **comparison and contrast**—showing how one thing is similar to or different from another thing
- **cause and effect**—showing how one event causes another event, and so on

Background
Social Studies

The text that follows is a summary of two laws that were important in the lives of Harriet Tubman and all blacks in America (whether held in slavery or free), slave owners, and citizens of the Northern states. The laws are called the Fugitive Slave Acts of 1793 and 1850.

The **Fugitive Slave Act of 1793** was a law with no provisions for enforcement. It did set a legal precedent, however. In the year 1850, the North and the South agreed to a compromise on the issue of slavery. The North got California admitted to the Union as a free state. The South got the **Fugitive Slave Act of 1850,** which required the federal government to capture fugitives from slavery in the North and return them to the South. The consequences of the 1850 act would soon echo in the gunfire of the Civil War.

■ What kinds of text structures are used to organize the text that begins on page 157?

SKILLS FOCUS

Reading Skills
Understand text structures.

The Fugitive Slave Acts of 1793 and 1850

The Fugitive Slave Act of 1793 stated that a person could not offer any form of protection to a fugitive from slavery; in fact, the law required that all runaways be captured and returned to the states they had fled from. The person protecting the fugitive was subject to a fine and was liable for any damages that the "owner" of the person might claim. This law was strongly opposed in the North, however, and was only loosely enforced. As a result, the South demanded that more severe legislation be passed—hence, the Fugitive Slave Act of 1850.

THE FUGITIVE SLAVE ACT OF 1850 HAD TEN SECTIONS, AS FOLLOWS:

SECTIONS 1, 2, AND 3 established the rules by which federal commissioners were appointed. These commissioners were then "authorized and required to exercise and discharge all the powers and duties conferred by this act."

SECTION 4 gave the appointed federal commissioners the authority to arrest and return alleged fugitives to the state or territory from which they had supposedly fled. This meant that the federal appointees who decided an alleged fugitive's fate did not belong to the community. Rather, they were strangers who came into the community to hold a hearing. Since the federal government was in charge, the local courts had no say in determining what would happen to the alleged fugitive.

SECTION 5 listed the penalties for failure to comply with warrants issued under the act: A federal marshal or deputy marshal who refused to serve a warrant was subject, on conviction, to a one-thousand-dollar fine. In 1850, one thousand dollars was enough to buy a good-sized house on a ten-acre plot of land.

This section also said that if an arrested person escaped a marshal's custody, the marshal was liable for "the full value of the service or labor of said fugitive in the State, Territory, or District whence he escaped."

In addition, this section empowered federal commissioners to deputize any bystander to serve on a posse or to do whatever was necessary to apprehend an alleged fugitive. The deputized person could not refuse to serve, although this would seem to have been a violation of the person's rights as a U.S. citizen.

SECTION 6 held that a fugitive from slavery was still a slave no matter where he or she was. This meant that fugitives crossing the Mason-Dixon line from the South into the North were no longer free. They now carried the legal status of slave. Free blacks in the North understood that this change in the law meant they were not safe in the "cradle of liberty," and thousands of them fled to Canada.

Section 6 also prohibited an alleged fugitive from testifying at his or her own trial. This meant that the defendant could not defend herself or himself. The only admissible evidence was testimony from the slave owner or his representative. The federal commissioners then judged whether that testimony was believable. In a speech on the Fugitive Slave Law of 1850, Frederick Douglass said that under this law the oaths of "any two villains" were sufficient to confine a free man to slavery for life.

SECTION 7 established penalties for interfering with the capture of an alleged fugitive: a fine "not exceeding one thousand dollars, and imprisonment not exceeding six months."

SECTION 8 dealt with fees paid to officials for their part in the arrest, custody, and delivery of a fugitive to his or her owner. It specified that these officials would not earn a salary. Instead, the more people they arrested, the more money they earned.

SECTION 9 stated that if the claimant suspected that an attempt would be made to rescue the fugitive by force, the arresting officer was required to keep the fugitive in custody, take him back to the state he fled, and deliver him to his "owner." This section more or less acknowledged that while many Northerners might not be particularly concerned about slavery as long as it was down South, they felt different when it affected their own communities. Seeing armed men on horses running down an unarmed person on foot forced them to make a choice between abiding by the law of the land and helping a fellow human being in trouble. Many ordinary Northerners, even those who did not consider themselves abolitionists,° chose to help.

SECTION 10 detailed the legal procedures to be followed when someone was claimed as a fugitive and handed over to his or her "owner."

—Flo Ota De Lange

° **abolitionists** *n.:* people dedicated to ending (abolishing) slavery.

The Harriet Tubman Series (1939–1940), No. 20, by Jacob Lawrence.

In 1850, the Fugitive Slave Law was passed, which bound the people north of the Mason and Dixon Line to return to bondage any fugitives found in their territories—forcing Harriet Tubman to lead her escaped slaves into Canada.

Hampton University Museum, Hampton, Virginia. Artwork copyright 2003 Gwendolyn Knight Lawrence, Courtesy of the Jacob and Gwendolyn Lawrence Foundation.

Analyzing Text Structures

The Fugitive Slave Acts of 1793 and 1850

Test Practice

1. How did the Fugitive Slave Act of 1850 differ from the Fugitive Slave Act of 1793?
   A   It was broader in scope.
   B   It gave fugitives more rights.
   C   It had less severe penalties.
   D   It opposed slavery.

2. Although Northerners could and did ignore the 1793 Fugitive Slave Act, the passage of the law was significant because —
   F   it set a legal precedent
   G   it caused the Civil War
   H   it was a step toward abolishing slavery
   J   blacks had voted for its passage

3. Section 6 of the Fugitive Slave Act of 1850 made it unsafe for black persons, whether free or fugitive, to be in any of the places below *except* —
   A   the South
   B   the North
   C   the United States
   D   Canada

4. The Fugitive Slave Acts were enacted to benefit —
   F   the cause of justice
   G   slave owners
   H   all humanity
   J   fugitives

5. To **organize** the ideas in this selection, the author used —
   A   sequence
   B   chronology
   C   both of the above
   D   none of the above

Constructed Response

1. Under the Fugitive Slave Act of 1793, what would happen to someone who knowingly helped a person running away from slavery?

2. Under the Fugitive Slave Act of 1850, what would happen to a person who knowingly helped someone running away from slavery?

3. Under the Fugitive Slave Act of 1850, who was, and who was not, allowed to testify at the trial of an alleged runaway? (See Section 6.)

4. Under the Fugitive Slave Act of 1850, who was required to help catch a suspected runaway?

5. How did many Northerners react to the provisions of the Fugitive Slave Act of 1850?

SKILLS FOCUS

Reading Skills
Analyze text structures.

After You Read Vocabulary Development

Latin and the Law

The language of law and government uses many words derived from Latin. This reliance on Latin-based words sometimes makes reading legal materials a bit difficult, so let's take a closer look at some commonly used Latin words and their modern uses.

agere, "to act or do"	*jurare,* "to swear"
clamare, "to call out; to shout"	*legare,* "to send"
dicere, "to say; to tell"	*lex,* "law"

PRACTICE

Each passage below contains words formed from one of the Latin words listed above. First, identify the Latin root that is common to all the underlined words in each passage. Next, define each underlined word.

1. The enactment of the Fugitive Slave Act of 1850 pitted Northern and Southern activists against each other.
2. Abolitionists proclaimed the act unconstitutional and immoral. Slave owners wanted to reclaim their "property" in courts of law.
3. Abolitionists declared the Fugitive Slave Act of 1850 illegal because it threatened the safety of legitimately free persons.
4. Section 6 states that a black person would be arrested if someone alleged ownership. This allegation was legal and binding until a federal commissioner decided the case in court.
5. The law dictated that only the alleged "owner" could speak in court. The indicted person was thus left to the mercy of a prejudiced judicial proceeding.
6. Because a black person could not speak in his or her own defense, any "owner" could easily commit perjury by lying and obtaining an unjust verdict.

SKILLS FOCUS

Vocabulary Skills
Understand word origins.

Regular and Irregular Verbs

A **regular verb** forms its past tense and past participle by simply adding *–d* or *–ed* to its base form:

Base Form	Past Tense	Past Participle
escape	escaped	(have) escaped
disappear	disappeared	(have) disappeared

Irregular verbs are more complicated:

Base Form	Past Tense	Past Participle
leave	left	(have) left
eat	ate	(have) eaten
know	knew	(have) known

There are hundreds of irregular verbs, each with its own forms. Three of the most difficult irregular pairs follow.

Lie and *Lay*, *Sit* and *Set*, *Rise* and *Raise*

Lie and *lay*, *sit* and *set*, and *rise* and *raise* are pairs of irregular verbs that often cause confusion. Remember that the second verb in each pair expresses an action directed toward an object—a person or a thing named in the sentence; the first verb simply expresses an action. (For example, you *lie* down, but first you *lay* your schoolbag on the table.) Below are some of the forms of these six verbs.

Base Form	Present Participle	Past Participle
lie	lying	(have) lain
lay	laying	(have) laid
sit	sitting	(have) sat
set	setting	(have) set
rise	rising	(have) risen
raise	raising	(have) raised

PRACTICE 1

Proofread the following paragraph, and correct all the incorrect verb forms.

The fugitives had leaved the plantation after they ate their evening meal. They knowed that the way would be hard but thinked that if they getted help along the way, they would be able to make it.

For more help, see Regular Verbs and Irregular Verbs, 3b–c, in the Language Handbook.

PRACTICE 2

Copy the following paragraph, choosing the correct verb from each underlined pair.

The fugitives (1) sat/set on the ground and (2) lay/laid their bundles down for pillows. Soon they were (3) lying/laying fast asleep. They were sad when it was time to (4) rise/raise again; they wished they could have (5) lain/laid there longer.

For more help, see Irregular Verbs, 3c, in the Language Handbook.

SKILLS FOCUS

Grammar Skills
Understand regular and irregular verbs.

Barbara Frietchie

Make the Connection
Quickwrite ✏️

Many of the people we most admire and think of as heroes have had to stand up for their beliefs. Use a chart like the one that follows to make a list of some of these individuals (contemporary, historical, fictional).

Name	Action	Belief

Literary Focus
A Character's Character

How a person reacts to a challenge can be considered a test of character. In that sentence the word *character* means "a person's essential quality or personality." A person's **character** can be described as kind, self-centered, outgoing, honest, brave, selfish, and so on. The word *character* can also mean "a person in a story, play, or poem." In the following poem, see what the *character* Barbara Frietchie reveals about her *character* when she decides to be different from the crowd.

INTERNET

Vocabulary Activity
•
Cross-curricular Connection

Keyword: LE5 8-2

Reading Skills 📖
Paraphrasing: Saying It Your Way

Paraphrasing means restating a writer's text in your own words. A paraphrase differs from a **summary,** which retells only the most important points in a text. Here is a paraphrase of lines 1–4 of Whittier's poem: *The church spires of Frederick rise up from the cornfields, clear in the September morning. The spires are surrounded by the green hills of Maryland.*

Vocabulary Development

These words look familiar, but their use in the poem may surprise you:

staff (staf) *n.*: pole. *Frietchie hung the flag from a staff outside her window.*

tread (tred) *n.*: step. *The tread of the soldiers was echoed through the town.*

rent (rent) *v.*: tore. *The rifle blast rent a hole in the flag.*

stirred (sturd) *v.*: woke up. *The old woman stirred Jackson's feelings.*

host (hōst) *n.*: army. *The rebel host marched into Frederick, Maryland.*

SKILLS FOCUS

Literary Skills
Understand character.

Reading Skills
Paraphrase a poem.

Background
Literature and Social Studies

"Barbara Frietchie" is set during the Civil War. In 1862, after defeating Union forces at the Second Battle of Bull Run, Confederate troops moved north into Maryland. Led by Generals Robert E. Lee and "Stonewall" Jackson, the troops marched into the town of Frederick. Lee and his men were expecting a warm welcome, but the people of Frederick were loyal to the Union. Whittier based "Barbara Frietchie" on these events.

Barbara Frietchie

John Greenleaf Whittier

Up from the meadows rich with corn,
Clear in the cool September morn,

The clustered spires of Frederick stand
Green-walled by the hills of Maryland.

5   Round about them orchards sweep,
Apple and peach tree fruited deep,

Fair as the garden of the Lord
To the eyes of the famished rebel horde,°

On that pleasant morn of the early fall
10   When Lee marched over the mountain wall;

Over the mountains winding down,
Horse and foot, into Frederick town.

Forty flags with their silver stars,
Forty flags with their crimson bars,

15   Flapped in the morning wind: the sun
Of noon looked down, and saw not one.

Up rose old Barbara Frietchie then,
Bowed with her fourscore years and ten;

Bravest of all in Frederick town,
20   She took up the flag the men hauled down

In her attic window the staff she set,
To show that one heart was loyal yet.

Up the street came the rebel tread,
Stonewall Jackson riding ahead.

8. horde (hôrd) *n.:* crowd.

Barbara Frietchie (1876) (detail) by Dennis Malone Carter (1827–1881). Oil on canvas (36¼" × 46¼").

Vocabulary

staff (staf) *n.:* pole; stick. *Staff* also means "group of workers" and "lines on which musical notes are written."

tread (tred) *n.:* act of stepping or walking. *Tread* also means "the outer part of tires or of shoe soles."

25   Under his slouched hat left and right
    He glanced; the old flag met his sight.

    "Halt!"—the dust-brown ranks stood fast.
    "Fire!"—out blazed the rifle blast.

    It shivered the window, pane and sash;
30   It <u>rent</u> the banner with seam and gash.

    Quick, as it fell, from the broken staff
    Dame Barbara snatched the silken scarf.

    She leaned far out on the windowsill,
    And shook it forth with a royal will.

35   "Shoot, if you must, this old gray head,
    But spare your country's flag," she said.

    A shade of sadness, a blush of shame,
    Over the face of the leader came;

    The nobler nature within him <u>stirred</u>
40   To life at that woman's deed and word;

    "Who touches a hair of yon gray head
    Dies like a dog! March on!" he said.

    All day long through Frederick street
    Sounded the tread of marching feet:

45   All day long that free flag tossed
    Over the heads of the rebel <u>host</u>.

    Ever its torn folds rose and fell
    On the loyal winds that loved it well;

    And through the hill gaps sunset light
50   Shone over it with a warm good night.

    Barbara Frietchie's work is o'er,
    And the Rebel rides on his raids no more.

Vocabulary

rent (rent) *v.* (past tense of *rend*, meaning "tear"): tore;
  ripped. *Rent* also means "pay money for use of a house or
  apartment or of things such as bowling shoes or ice skates."

stirred (sturd) *v.:* arose; woke up. *Stirred* also means "mixed a
  liquid or loose ingredients, as in a recipe."

host (hōst) *n.:* army; large number; crowd. *Host* also means
  "someone who entertains guests, at home or on TV."

Honor to her! and let a tear
Fall, for her sake, on Stonewall's bier.°

55   Over Barbara Frietchie's grave,
Flag of Freedom and Union, wave!

Peace and order and beauty draw
Round thy symbol of light and law;

And ever the stars above look down
60   On thy stars below in Frederick town!

54. bier (bir) *n.:* coffin and the platform on which it rests. Stonewall Jackson died in 1863 after being wounded in battle.

Meet the Writer

John Greenleaf Whittier

Dedicated to Freedom

John Greenleaf Whittier (1807–1892) was born and raised on a farm in Haverhill, Massachusetts, where his Quaker family had lived since 1688. Whittier devoted most of his life to the antislavery movement. His poems reflect his dedication to freedom and justice and his deep religious faith. Whittier was born in the same year as Henry Wadsworth Longfellow (whose poem "Paul Revere's Ride" begins on page 629). Like Longfellow, Whittier was one of the hugely popular Fireside Poets, whose works sold the way best-selling novels do today.

John Greenleaf Whittier (1833) by Robert Peckham. Oil on canvas.
Courtesy Trustees of the Whittier Homestead, Haverhill, Massachusetts.

After You Read   Response and Analysis

First Thoughts

1. Would you have done what Barbara Frietchie did if you were in her place? Explain.

Thinking Critically

2. When writers use **allusions,** they refer to events, characters, or places in literature, history, or current events, and they expect us to understand what they are alluding to. What is the speaker alluding to in line 7, when he says the orchards of Maryland are as "fair as the garden of the Lord"?

3. In lines 15 and 16, something important happens, but we have to **infer** what it is. The speaker expects us to know, based on what he says next. What has happened by noontime in Frederick?

4. One definition of a hero is a person who does the right thing even though he or she might have to act alone. Could this definition apply to Barbara Frietchie and to Harriet Tubman (page 143)? How about Stonewall Jackson? Could it apply to those heroes you cited in your Quickwrite notes? Consider the words and actions of these people in your responses. ✏

Extending Interpretations

5. Suppose Whittier were alive today. Who might make a good subject for his next **narrative poem**?

SPEAKING AND LISTENING

Giving a Dramatic Reading

Alone or with a small group, prepare a **dramatic reading** of "Barbara Frietchie." You might want to have one person read Barbara Frietchie's lines, another person read Stonewall Jackson's, and a chorus read the rest. You could use props and sound effects. After your reading, ask your audience for feedback.

> ### Reading Check
> a. **Paraphrase** lines 26–42, which describe the most important actions in the poem.
>
> b. In lines 55–60, the speaker addresses the flag. What does he ask the flag to do in lines 55–56? How would you **paraphrase** lines 57–60?

INTERNET

Projects and Activities

Keyword: LE5 8-2

SKILLS FOCUS

Literary Skills
Analyze character.

Reading Skills
Paraphrase a poem.

Speaking and Listening Skills
Present a dramatic reading.

Vocabulary Development

History of the English Language: Finding Our Roots

The written record of English dates back about fourteen hundred years, but the ancestry of English goes back much further. Long ago, people living near the Caspian Sea (between what is now Asia and the Middle East) spoke a language we call Proto-Indo-European. (*Proto*– means "original or earliest." *Indo*– refers to India.) These people were fighters, farmers, and herders, and they had an urge to travel. Eventually they took to their great four-wheeled carts and spread east through modern-day Iran and India and west through Turkey and most of Europe. As groups settled in different areas, their language changed into the languages we now call Persian, Hindi, Armenian, Sanskrit, Greek, Russian, Polish, Irish, Italian, French, Spanish, German, Dutch, Swedish, Norwegian—and English. All these languages share ancient roots and are called Indo-European.

Word Bank

staff
tread
rent
stirred
host

PRACTICE 1

Look up *staff* and *tread* in a dictionary to discover their **Indo-European** (IE) **roots.** Then, with a small group of class-mates, try to figure out how each word's different meanings might have derived from its one root.

Multiple-Meaning Words

PRACTICE 2

To practice using the **multiple meanings** of the Word Bank words, fill in the blanks in the paragraph below with the appropriate words. Then, write sentences of your own, using *another* meaning of each word. For extra credit, see if you can use all five words in one paragraph.

   At daybreak the enemy _____, which was camped on the plain, _____ into action. The _____ of their massive formations could be heard for miles around as they marched to battle. On the hilltop the lieutenant proudly planted the _____ holding the company flag, which was _____ and bloodied from the fighting.

SKILLS FOCUS

Vocabulary Skills
Understand word roots; use multiple-meaning words.

Barbara Frietchie   **167**

Keeping Tenses Consistent

Many writers tell their stories in the past tense, showing that the events have already happened.

> **The townspeople huddled indoors. Only Barbara Frietchie hung out the U.S. flag as the Confederate troops marched by.**

Writers sometimes tell their stories in the present tense instead, to give their readers the feeling that the events are happening right now.

> **The townspeople are huddling indoors. Only Barbara Frietchie hangs out the U.S. flag as the Confederate troops march by.**

Whichever tense you choose to write in, use it consistently. Either the events happened before, or they are happening now. You'll confuse your readers if you keep switching tenses.

Active and Passive Voice

When a verb is in the **active voice,** the subject of the verb does something. When a verb is in the **passive voice,** something is done to its subject.

ACTIVE **The father told a story to his sons.**
[The action is done *by* the subject, the father.]

PASSIVE **The sons were told a story by their father.**
[The action is done *to* the subject, the sons.]

Those two sentences convey the same information, but with different emphases. The first sentence stresses the doer of the action; the second sentence stresses the receiver of the action.

Try always to use the active voice, to give your writing a direct, lively tone.

SKILLS FOCUS

Grammar Skills
Use consistent tenses; use active and passive voice.

PRACTICE 1

Select a story in this book, and rewrite its opening paragraph using a different tense. You might turn to "Raymond's Run" (page 547). How does the story sound when you rewrite the first paragraph in the past tense? How does "Broken Chain" (page 17) sound when you rewrite the first paragraph in the present tense?

For more help, see Verb Tense, 3d–e, in the Language Handbook.

PRACTICE 2

Change the following sentences from the passive to the active voice. We think you'll like the difference.

(1) Her flag was waved by Barbara Frietchie. (2) Their rifles were fired by the troops. (3) Her now famous words were said by Barbara Frietchie. (4) Shame was felt by "Stonewall" Jackson.

For more help, see Voice, 3f, in the Language Handbook.

Too Soon a Woman

Make the Connection

Quickwrite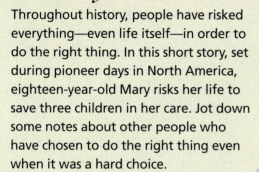

Throughout history, people have risked everything—even life itself—in order to do the right thing. In this short story, set during pioneer days in North America, eighteen-year-old Mary risks her life to save three children in her care. Jot down some notes about other people who have chosen to do the right thing even when it was a hard choice.

Literary Focus

Motivation

What makes people do the things they do? In literature as in life, a person's **motivation,** or reason for behavior, is not always clear. As you read this story, decide if the characters' actions make sense to you. Does each character's motivation become clearer as the story continues?

Reading Skills

Summarizing: Keep It Simple

A summary is a short restatement of the main events and essential ideas in a work. When you **summarize** a story, briefly identify the major characters.

Then, in your own words, describe the characters' problems, state the main events, and explain how the problems are finally resolved. Remember to keep your summary simple and to leave out minor details. As you read "Too Soon a Woman," think about which events you would include if you had to summarize it for a friend.

Vocabulary Development

You'll find these words in the story:

skimpy (skim′pē) *adj.:* less than enough. *Their skimpy supplies wouldn't last long.*

grudging (gruj′iŋ) *v.* used as *adj.:* reluctant; unwilling. *Hungry travelers are glad for even a grudging bit of food.*

gaunt (gônt) *adj.:* very thin and bony. *The weary traveler had a gaunt face.*

rummaged (rum′ijd) *v.:* searched through the contents of a box, a drawer, and so on. *She rummaged around in the box for something to eat.*

savoring (sā′vər·iŋ) *v.* used as *adj.:* enjoying with great delight. *She sat up late at night, savoring life to the full.*

INTERNET

Vocabulary Activity

Keyword: LE5 8-2

SKILLS FOCUS

Literary Skills Understand character motivation.

Reading Skills Summarize a story.

Background

Literature and Social Studies

In 1803, with the Louisiana Purchase, the size of the United States doubled. By the 1880s, about one quarter of the nation's population lived in the West. In large part this mass resettlement was a result of the Homestead Act of 1862, which allowed a settler to earn up to 160 acres of land by living on it for five years and improving it. Of the 400,000 families or more that homesteaded, nearly 60 percent failed.

Too Soon a Woman

Dorothy M. Johnson

We left the home place behind, mile by slow mile, heading for the mountains, across the prairie where the wind blew forever.

At first there were four of us with the one-horse wagon and its skimpy load. Pa and I walked, because I was a big boy of eleven. My two little sisters romped and trotted until they got tired and had to be boosted up into the wagon bed.

That was no covered Conestoga,[1] like Pa's folks came West in, but just an old farm wagon, drawn by one weary horse, creaking and rumbling westward to the mountains, toward the little woods town where Pa thought he had an old uncle who owned a little two-bit sawmill.

Two weeks we had been moving when we picked up Mary, who had run away from somewhere that she wouldn't tell. Pa didn't want her along, but she stood up to him with no fear in her voice.

"I'd rather go with a family and look after kids," she said, "but I ain't going back. If you won't take me, I'll travel with any wagon that will."

Pa scowled at her, and her wide blue eyes stared back.

"How old are you?" he demanded.

"Eighteen," she said. "There's teamsters[2] come this way sometimes. I'd rather go with you folks. But I won't go back."

"We're prid' near out of grub," my father told her. "We're clean out of money. I got all I can handle without taking anybody else." He turned away as if he hated the sight of her. "You'll have to walk," he said.

So she went along with us and looked after the little girls, but Pa wouldn't talk to her.

On the prairie, the wind blew. But in the mountains, there was rain. When we stopped at little timber claims along the way, the homesteaders said it had rained all

---

1. **Conestoga** (kän′ə·stō′gə): covered wagon with wide wheels, used by American settlers to cross the prairies.

2. **teamsters** *n.:* people who drive teams of horses.

summer. Crops among the blackened stumps were rotted and spoiled. There was no cheer anywhere, and little hospitality. The people we talked to were past worrying. They were scared and desperate.

So was Pa. He traveled twice as far each day as the wagon, ranging through the woods with his rifle, but he never saw game. He had been depending on venison,[3] but we never got any except as a grudging gift from the homesteaders.

He brought in a porcupine once, and that was fat meat and good. Mary roasted it in chunks over the fire, half crying with the smoke. Pa and I rigged up the tarp[4] sheet for shelter to keep the rain from putting the fire clean out.

The porcupine was long gone, except for some of the tried-out fat[5] that Mary had saved, when we came to an old, empty cabin. Pa said we'd have to stop. The horse was wore out, couldn't pull anymore up those grades on the deep-rutted roads in the mountains.

At the cabin, at least there was shelter. We had a few potatoes left and some cornmeal. There was a creek that probably had fish in it, if a person could catch them. Pa tried it for half a day before he gave up. To this day I don't care for fishing. I remember my father's sunken eyes in his gaunt, grim face.

He took Mary and me outside the cabin to talk. Rain dripped on us from branches overhead.

"I think I know where we are," he said. "I calculate to get to old John's and back in about four days. There'll be grub in the town, and they'll let me have some whether old John's still there or not."

He looked at me. "You do like she tells you," he warned. It was the first time he had admitted Mary was on earth since we picked her up two weeks before.

"You're my pardner," he said to me, "but it might be she's got more brains. You mind what she says."

He burst out with bitterness, "There ain't anything good left in the world or people to care if you live or die. But I'll get grub in the town and come back with it."

He took a deep breath and added, "If you get too all-fired hungry, butcher the horse. It'll be better than starvin'."

He kissed the little girls good-bye and plodded off through the woods with one blanket and the rifle.

The cabin was moldy and had no floor. We kept a fire going under a hole in the roof, so it was full of blinding smoke, but we had to keep the fire so as to dry out the wood.

The third night we lost the horse. A bear scared him. We heard the racket, and Mary and I ran out, but we couldn't see anything in the pitch dark.

In gray daylight I went looking for him, and I must have walked fifteen miles. It seemed

---

3. **venison** (ven′i·sən) *n.:* deer meat.
4. **tarp** *n.:* short for *tarpaulin* (tär·pô′lin), or waterproof canvas.
5. **tried-out fat:** fat that has been melted down.

Too Soon a Woman 171

like I had to have that horse at the cabin when Pa came or he'd whip me. I got plumb lost two or three times and thought maybe I was going to die there alone and nobody would ever know it, but I found the way back to the clearing.

That was the fourth day, and Pa didn't come. That was the day we ate up the last of the grub.

The fifth day, Mary went looking for the horse. My sisters whimpered, huddled in a quilt by the fire, because they were scared and hungry.

I never did get dried out, always having to bring in more damp wood and going out to yell to see if Mary would hear me and not get lost. But I couldn't cry like the little girls did, because I was a big boy, eleven years old.

It was near dark when there was an answer to my yelling, and Mary came into the clearing.

Mary didn't have the horse—we never saw hide nor hair of that old horse again—

but she was carrying something big and white that looked like a pumpkin with no color to it.

She didn't say anything, just looked around and saw Pa wasn't there yet, at the end of the fifth day.

"What's that thing?" my sister Elizabeth demanded.

"Mushroom," Mary answered. "I bet it hefts[6] ten pounds."

"What are you going to do with it now?" I sneered. "Play football here?"

"Eat it—maybe," she said, putting it in a corner. Her wet hair hung over her shoulders. She huddled by the fire.

My sister Sarah began to whimper again. "I'm hungry!" she kept saying.

"Mushrooms ain't good eating," I said. "They can kill you."

"Maybe," Mary answered. "Maybe they can. I don't set up to know all about everything, like some people."

---

6. **hefts** *v.:* weighs.

"What's that mark on your shoulder?" I asked her. "You tore your dress on the brush."

"What do you think it is?" she said, her head bowed in the smoke.

"Looks like scars," I guessed.

"'Tis scars. They whipped me. Now mind your own business. I want to think."

Elizabeth whimpered, "Why don't Pa come back?"

"He's coming," Mary promised. "Can't come in the dark. Your pa'll take care of you soon's he can."

She got up and rummaged around in the grub box.

"Nothing there but empty dishes," I growled. "If there was anything, we'd know it."

Mary stood up. She was holding the can with the porcupine grease.

"I'm going to have something to eat," she said coolly. "You kids can't have any yet. And I don't want any squalling, mind."

It was a cruel thing, what she did then. She sliced that big, solid mushroom and heated grease in a pan.

The smell of it brought the little girls out of their quilt, but she told them to go back in so fierce a voice that they obeyed. They cried to break your heart.

I didn't cry. I watched, hating her.

I endured the smell of the mushroom frying as long as I could. Then I said, "Give me some."

"Tomorrow," Mary answered. "Tomorrow, maybe. But not tonight." She turned to me with a sharp command: "Don't bother me! Just leave me be."

She knelt there by the fire and finished frying the slice of mushroom.

If I'd had Pa's rifle, I'd have been willing to kill her right then and there.

She didn't eat right away. She looked at the brown, fried slice for a while and said, "By tomorrow morning, I guess you can tell whether you want any."

The little girls stared at her as she ate. Sarah was chewing an old leather glove.

When Mary crawled into the quilts with them, they moved away as far as they could get.

I was so scared that my stomach heaved, empty as it was.

Mary didn't stay in the quilts long. She took a drink out of the water bucket and sat down by the fire and looked through the smoke at me.

She said in a low voice, "I don't know how it will be if it's poison. Just do the best you can with the girls. Because your pa will come back, you know. . . . You better go to bed. I'm going to sit up."

And so would you sit up. If it might be your last night on earth and the pain of death might seize you at any moment, you would sit up by the smoky fire, wide awake, remembering whatever you had to remember, savoring life.

We sat in silence after the girls had gone to sleep. Once I asked, "How long does it take?"

Vocabulary

rummaged (rum′ijd) *v.*: searched through the contents of a box or another container.

savoring (sā′vər·in) *v.* used as *adj.*: enjoying or appreciating with great delight.

"I never heard," she answered. "Don't think about it."

I slept after a while, with my chin on my chest. Maybe Peter dozed that way at Gethsemane as the Lord knelt praying.[7]

Mary's moving around brought me wide awake. The black of night was fading.

"I guess it's all right," Mary said. "I'd be able to tell by now, wouldn't I?"

I answered gruffly, "I don't know."

Mary stood in the doorway for a while, looking out at the dripping world as if she found it beautiful. Then she fried slices of the mushroom while the little girls danced with anxiety.

We feasted, we three, my sisters and I,

until Mary ruled, "That'll hold you," and would not cook any more. She didn't touch any of the mushroom herself.

That was a strange day in the moldy cabin. Mary laughed and was gay; she told stories, and we played "Who's Got the Thimble?" with a pine cone.

In the afternoon we heard a shout, and my sisters screamed and I ran ahead of them across the clearing.

The rain had stopped. My father came plunging out of the woods leading a pack horse—and well I remember the treasures of food in that pack.

He glanced at us anxiously as he tore at the ropes that bound the pack.

"Where's the other one?" he demanded.

Mary came out of the cabin then, walking sedately. As she came toward us, the sun began to shine.

My stepmother was a wonderful woman.

---

7. **Maybe Peter . . . knelt praying:** According to Matthew 26:36–46, Jesus spent an entire night praying in the Garden of Gethsemane, outside Jerusalem, knowing he would be arrested in the morning. He asked Peter and two other followers to stay awake with him, but they kept falling asleep.

Meet the Writer

Dorothy M. Johnson

"Kills-Both-Places"

Dorothy M. Johnson (1905–1984) was born in McGregor, Iowa, but made the West her home—in both a physical and a literary sense. After graduating from the University of Montana, she moved to New York City to work as a magazine editor but eventually returned to Montana to write the stories that would make her famous. Johnson is known for her sensitive, realistic portrayals of the American West. Three of her stories— "The Hanging Tree," "The Man Who Shot Liberty Valance," and "A Man Called Horse"—were made into movies.

The Blackfoot people of Montana made Johnson an honorary member and gave her the name Kills-Both-Places.

First Thoughts

1. Does Mary seem like a typical teenager? Explain.

Thinking Critically

2. List three **conflicts** (internal or external) in this story. Which conflict is the main one?

3. Think about the **title** of the story. In what way is Mary "too soon a woman"?

4. Explain the character's **motivation** for the actions involved in each of these questions:

- At the beginning of the story, why does Pa refuse to talk to Mary?
- Why does Mary refuse to give the children any of the mushroom at first?
- Why does Mary laugh and tell stories and play games the day after she eats the mushroom?
- Why does Pa ask about Mary when he returns?

Extending Interpretations

5. Most people would consider Mary a hero because she risked her life for others. Do you think any teenagers today are heroes? What have they done to show their bravery? (You may want to consult your Quickwrite notes.) 🖉

WRITING

Analyzing a Character

What kind of a person is Mary? Write a paragraph in which you analyze Mary's character. In your character analysis, consider the following aspects:

- how Mary responds to the conflicts in her life
- why she makes the choices she does
- how people respond to her
- how she reacts to their responses

Use details from the text to support your analysis of Mary.

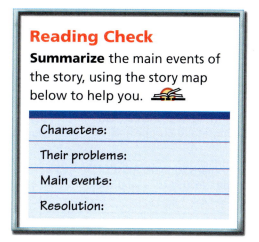

Reading Check

Summarize the main events of the story, using the story map below to help you.

Characters:
Their problems:
Main events:
Resolution:

INTERNET

Projects and Activities

Keyword: LE5 8-2

Literary Skills
Analyze character motivation.

Reading Skills
Summarize a story.

Writing Skills
Analyze a character.

History of the English Language: Review

Here is a time line to help you review some highlights in the development of the English language.

Historic Event	Time Frame	Effect on the English Language
Tribes living near the Caspian Sea migrate to Europe and Asia.	c. third millennium B.C.	Proto-Indo-European gradually changes into many languages.
The Romans conquer most of Europe, North Africa, and the Middle East.	27 B.C.– A.D. 476	Latin, the language of Roman soldiers, influences the language of the Britons.
Anglo-Saxons arrive in Britain, driving out the Britons.	fifth century A.D.	The Germanic language of the Anglo-Saxons replaces the Celtic spoken by the Britons.
Saint Augustine arrives in Britain to do missionary work on behalf of the Roman Catholic Church.	597	The Anglo-Saxons borrow many words from Latin, the language of the Roman Catholic Church.
Vikings from Scandinavia invade Britain.	end of the eighth century	Norse combines with the language of Britain to form what we now call **Old English.**
William the Conqueror, a Norman from France, conquers England.	1066	French and Latin influence the English language, and the period of **Middle English** begins.
William Caxton prints the first book in English.	1475	Written English reaches a large number of people.
Henry VII is crowned king of England.	1485	Henry VII promotes pride in all things English, including the language. The era of **Modern English** begins.
William Shakespeare is born.	1564	Shakespeare adds thousands of words and numerous phrases to the language.
Noah Webster publishes the *American Dictionary of the English Language*.	1828	Webster includes new American words and new meanings for older English words.
Americans move westward into territories originally settled by the Spanish.	middle of the nineteenth century	English-speaking Americans adopt many words of Spanish origin.
Science and technology advance at an unprecedented rate.	present	Use of English continues to spread around the world through the World Wide Web.

SKILLS FOCUS

Vocabulary Skills
Understand the history of English.

Romans.

Use the words from the Word Bank to solve the mystery-word questions below. You'll notice several of the historical influences listed in the time line on the previous page.

1. This word is from Middle English, perhaps coming from the Icelandic word *gandur*, meaning "stick." Today it describes anyone who is overly thin and bony. *What word is it?*

2. This word is probably related to the Swedish word *skrympa*, meaning "to shrink." It describes quantities that are too small or that are less than what is needed. *What word is it?*

3. This word can be traced back to Middle English, from there to Old French, and finally to the Latin *sapor*, meaning "flavor." Today it has come to mean "enjoying and appreciating." *What word is it?*

4. This word is related to the Middle High German word *grogezen*, meaning "to howl or lament." It means "done or given unwillingly." *What word is it?*

5. This word comes from the Middle French verb *arrimer*, meaning "to pack or arrange cargo." Today's English word means "to search in or through something." *What word is it?*

Word Bank

skimpy
grudging
gaunt
rummaged
savoring

Vikings.

Conestoga wagon.

William Shakespeare.

Too Soon a Woman   **177**

Comparing Texts: A Historical Document and an Article

Reading Focus

Comparing Texts: Treatment and Scope of Ideas

Home on the Range
Oh give me a home
Where the buffalo roam
Where the deer and the antelope play
Where seldom is heard
A discouraging word
And the skies are not cloudy all day

"Home on the Range" makes the prairie sound like a paradise, doesn't it? That must have been another prairie, not the one Mary encountered. Perhaps the ballad was written by a lonesome cowboy long after he'd left the prairie for the comforts of running tap water and home cooking.

But let's not be too hard on our singing cowboy, even though he has given us a **biased,** or one-sided, treatment of his subject. He has conveniently forgotten all unpleasant memories in order to paint a beautiful picture of the life he longs for.

An **objective,** or balanced, treatment presents all sides of a subject so that readers can draw their own conclusions. When the treatment covers many aspects of a topic, it is said to have a **broad scope,** unlike our ballad, which has a **limited scope.**

■ As you read the poster from the Union Pacific Railroad and the article "Home, Sweet Soddie," think about what each text says and how it says it.

- Is there evidence of bias, or is the treatment balanced and objective?

- Is the focus on the big picture or on a small snapshot?

- How are the selections similar in their scope and treatment of ideas?

- How are they different?

SKILLS FOCUS

Reading Skills
Compare texts.

RICH FARMING LANDS!

ON THE LINE OF THE
Union Pacific Railroad!

Located in the GREAT CENTRAL BELT of POPULA-TION, COMMERCE and WEALTH, and adjoining the WORLD'S HIGHWAY from OCEAN TO OCEAN.

12,000,000 ACRES!

3,000,000 Acres in Central and Eastern Nebraska, in the Platte Valley, now for sale!

We invite the attention of all parties seeking a HOME, to the LANDS offered for sale by this Company.

The Vast Quantity of Land from which to select enables everyone to secure such a location as he desires, suitable to any branch of farming or stock raising.

The Prices are Extremely Low. The amount of land owned by the Company is so large that they are determined to sell at the cheapest possible rates, ranging from $1.50 to $8.00 per acre.

The Terms of Payment are Easy. Ten years' credit at six percent interest. A deduction of ten percent for cash.

The Location is Central, along the 41st parallel, the favorite latitude of America. Equally well adapted to corn or wheat; free from the long, cold winters of the Northern, and the hot, unhealthy influences of the Southern States.

The Face of the Country is diversified with hill and dale, grain land and meadow, rich bottoms, low bluffs, and undulating tables, all covered with a thick growth of sweet nutritious grasses.

The Soil is a dark loam, slightly impregnated with lime, free from stone and gravel, and eminently adapted to grass, grain, and root crops; the subsoil is usually light and porous, retaining moisture with wonderful tenacity.

The Climate is mild and healthful; the atmosphere dry and pure. Epidemic diseases never prevail; Fever and Ague are unknown. The greatest amount of rain falls between March and October. The Winters are dry with but little snow.

Timber is found on the streams and grows rapidly.

The Title given the purchaser is absolute, in fee simple, and free from all encumbrances, derived directly from the United States.

Soldiers of the Late War are entitled to a Homestead of one hundred and sixty acres, within Railroad limits, which is equal to a bounty of $400.

Persons of Foreign Birth are also entitled to the benefits of the Free Homestead Law, on declaring their intentions of becoming citizens of the United States; this they may do immediately on their arrival in this country. . . .

Full information in regard to lands, prices, terms of sale, etc., together with pamphlets, circulars and maps, may be obtained from the Agents of the Department, also the **"PIONEER."**

A handsome ILLUSTRATED PAPER, with maps, etc., and containing the HOMESTEAD LAW. Mailed free to all applicants. Address

O. F. DAVIS,
Land Commissioner, U. P. R. R.
OMAHA, NEB.

Home, Sweet Soddie

Here you are, a pioneer on the prairie, settled for your first night in your new Home Sweet Home. After you've traveled overland so many miles that it felt as though you'd gone halfway around the world, your straw mattress feels like heaven. But it sure is dark in here. Even though your fingers are right in front of your nose, you can't see them. The dark here is absolutely dark. There are no lights from other houses or from a town or city to reflect on the horizon. Outside there might be stars, but inside there is nothing but the velvety-black black.

Thousands of Worms

So when the first crack of dawn comes, you're anxious to check out your new world. But what's that? It looks like the ceiling above your head is moving. No, it couldn't be. Look again. Now it looks like the wall is moving too. Shut those eyes quick! While you're lying there trying to muster your forces to take another look, your parents wake up. Your mother exclaims, "This place is alive with worms!" You look again, and, sure enough, there are worms suspended from the ceiling, worms waving at you from the walls, and—what's that all over the floor? More worms! Hundreds—no, thousands of worms!

Houses Built of Soil

Where did all those worms

come from? Since there are hardly any trees out on the prairie, the pioneers built their first houses out of sod bricks cut from the surface layer of soil and including all the grasses and roots growing in it. It wasn't easy to build a house of sod. A twelve-by-fourteen-foot shelter required an acre of sod and a great deal of hard work. Because of the thick root system in the prairie grassland, walls built of sod were strong and long lasting. This was one of the advantages. Other advantages of sod houses included the fact that they were better insulated than wood houses, so they were cooler in summer and warmer in winter. They also offered more protection from tornadoes, wind, and fire.

No Sense Cleaning It!

What were the disadvantages? These: Sod blocks were essentially compacted soil, which tended to sift down from the ceiling and walls, making it hard, if not impossible, to keep the house clean. Sod also wasn't waterproof. In fact, it was quite the opposite. Whenever there was a heavy rain, water followed the root systems in the sod bricks right on down through the sod ceiling, soaking everything in the room and turning the sod floor to mud. All this dripping didn't stop when the rains stopped either. The roof could leak for days, and that meant people sometimes had to use boots and umbrellas indoors while the sun was shining brightly outside!

Bugs and Weather

The drawbacks of sod houses were not the only difficulties you would have faced as a pioneer on the prairie. Others included the unaccustomed vastness of the wide-open spaces, the endless blue sky, and the almost total lack of neighbors. There were also fleas, flies, mosquitoes, moths, bedbugs, field mice, rattlesnakes, grasshoppers, tornadoes, floods, hail, blizzards, prairie fires, dust storms, and drought. In summer the ground baked, and in winter it froze. The wind blew constantly, and water was as scarce as hens' teeth. One pioneer who couldn't take it anymore left this hard-earned lesson scrawled across the cabin door of his deserted homestead: "250 miles to the nearest post office, 100 miles to wood, 20 miles to water, 6 inches to hell. Gone to live with wife's folks."

No Warranties

Yes, sirree, homesteading on the prairie was hard work, and there were no warranties on claimed land. The buyers had to take all the risks upon themselves. The term for this arrangement is *caveat emptor*—"let the buyer beware." So what can you do but sweep all those worms out the front door and back onto the prairie? What else can happen, after all?

Well, newly cut sod is home to fleas, and bedbugs come crawling out of it at night. So every morning you have to take your bitten self and your infested bedding out-of-doors and pick off all those bugs. Then you head back inside armed with chicken

feathers dipped in kerosene to paint every crack and every crevice in every bit of that sod ceiling, wall, and floor.

Blizzards of Grasshoppers

One creature that doesn't come *out of* the sod, but instead comes *onto* the sod, is the grasshopper. You know, of course, about blizzards of snow. But what about a blizzard of grasshoppers? Enough grasshoppers to block out the sun? So many millions of grasshoppers that they can strip a farm bare in a matter of hours? Did you know that grasshoppers can chew their way through a plow handle? Did you know that grasshoppers are capable of eating almost everything in sight, including fences, bark, and that bedding that you just picked clean of fleas and bedbugs? If a pioneer family had dug 150 feet down for a well—the height of a thirteen-story building—grasshoppers falling into it could sour the water for weeks upon weeks. Grasshoppers could even stop a Union Pacific Railroad train from running. Piled some six inches deep on the tracks, their bodies so greased the rails that a train's wheels would spin but not move.

So, welcome to the good life out on the prairie, where "the skies are not cloudy all day." By the way, do you know what constantly blue skies mean for the average farmer?

—Flo Ota De Lange

PIONEER LIFE IN 1887

Comparing a Historical Document and an Article

Union Pacific Railroad Poster
Home, Sweet Soddie

Test Practice

1. The **purpose** of the Union Pacific Railroad poster was to —
   - A entertain railroad travelers passing through Nebraska
   - B persuade people to buy land in Nebraska
   - C provide information on Nebraska to scientists
   - D describe the good and bad qualities of Nebraska

2. The **purpose** of "Home, Sweet Soddie" is to —
   - F encourage people to move to the prairie
   - G praise the heroism of pioneers
   - H teach people how to build sod houses
   - J describe some of the difficulties of life on the prairie

3. The poster and the article are **similar** in that they both offer —
   - A an unbiased treatment
   - B a biased treatment
   - C an objective treatment
   - D a discouraging word

4. Which statement accurately describes the **tone** of these texts—that is, their attitudes toward their topics?
   - F "Home, Sweet Soddie" is humorous; the poster is enthusiastic.
   - G "Home, Sweet Soddie" is romantic; the poster is satiric.
   - H Both are romantic.
   - J Both are sarcastic.

5. The Union Pacific Railroad poster was intended as —
   - A a newspaper editorial
   - B an encyclopedia entry
   - C a travel magazine article
   - D an advertisement

Constructed Response

1. What is the **main point** of the Union Pacific Railroad poster?

2. What is the **main point** of "Home, Sweet Soddie"?

3. List at least five details in the poster that would have motivated pioneers to buy land in Nebraska.

4. List at least five details in "Home, Sweet Soddie" that might have discouraged pioneers from buying land in Nebraska.

5. **Exaggeration** is overstating something for an effect. What examples of exaggeration can you find in the poster and the article?

6. **Loaded words** are words that evoke a strong emotional reaction in the reader. What examples can you find in the poster?

SKILLS FOCUS

Reading Skills
Compare texts.

Who Am I? Diverse Derivations

No single person could travel the whole of the United States during the pioneer days, but the English language could and did. Some of the words commonly associated with the pioneers actually originated in far-off places. Play the word game below.

PRACTICE

Match the following words with the riddles that describe their origins:

beef jerky	muslin	siesta
calico	paddock	wilderness

1. I am a cotton fabric named for the place where I originated, Mosul, in what is now Iraq. My name came into English from Arabic, first through Italian (*mussolina*), then through French (*mousseline*).

2. If you take a nap in the afternoon, you know my name, but you might not know my origin. I came through Spanish from the Latin *sexta hora*, meaning "sixth hour," which refers to noon. Figure that one out.

3. I come from the American Spanish word *charqui,* which came from the Quechua *ch'arki*. I have nothing to do with tics or odd movements.

4. If you had a horse, you would keep it corralled in me. I came into use from the Old English *pearruc,* meaning "enclosure."

5. I am the cotton fabric used for most pioneer dresses. I come in many patterns, and I was named after the town in India where I originated, Calicut (now Kozhikode).

6. If you think I belong to America, think again. I existed in the English language long before anyone knew about the Wild West. I originally came from Old English and described the place where wild deer lived. (The word *deer* originally referred to any wild animals.)

SKILLS FOCUS

Vocabulary Skills
Identify word origins.

Mrs. Flowers

Make the Connection
Class Survey

Rate each of the statements that follow with a number from 0 to 4.

disagree   0   1   2   3   4   agree

1. Young people need older role models.
2. Friends should be the same age.
3. Adults can't understand how young people feel.
4. Everyone deserves to feel special.

Record your ratings on a sheet of paper. Then, with your class, tally the responses to each statement on the board.

Literary Focus
A Character's Influence

People often reveal their character—what they are made of—in hard times, when they face tough conflicts. People can also show their character in the way they live their everyday lives—especially in the way they treat other people. In this autobiographical story a woman named Mrs. Flowers has an important influence on a young girl named Marguerite.

Reading Skills
Determining the Main Idea: What's It All About?

The **main idea** is the message, opinion, or insight that is the focus of a piece of nonfiction writing. To find the main idea, look for key statements made by the writer. Look also at the details that the writer gives, and think about what the details add up to. Then, try to put the main idea into your own words.

Vocabulary Development

You'll learn these words as you read this autobiography:

taut (tôt) *adj.:* tightly stretched. *Though she was thin, Mrs. Flowers's skin was not taut.*

benign (bi·nīn′) *adj.:* kindly. *Marguerite loved Mrs. Flowers's benign smile.*

infuse (in·fyo͞oz′) *v.:* fill. *When Mrs. Flowers read aloud, she could infuse the words with great meaning.*

intolerant (in·täl′ər·ənt) *adj.:* unwilling to accept something. *Mrs. Flowers was intolerant of rudeness and ignorance.*

illiteracy (i·lit′ər·ə·sē) *n.:* inability to read or write. *Mrs. Flowers said we should be understanding of illiteracy.*

go.
hrw.
.com

INTERNET

Vocabulary Activity
•
More About Angelou

Keyword: LE5 8-2

SKILLS FOCUS

Literary Skills
Understand character.

Reading Skills
Identify the main idea.

Background   Literature and Real Life

"Mrs. Flowers" is from a volume of Maya Angelou's autobiography. When Angelou (born Marguerite Johnson) was a little girl, her parents separated. She and her brother, Bailey, were sent to Stamps, Arkansas, to live with their grandmother (called Momma), who owned a general store. A year before meeting Mrs. Flowers, Marguerite had been violently assaulted by a friend of her mother's. In reaction she became depressed and withdrawn, and she stopped speaking.

Mrs. Flowers

from I Know Why the Caged Bird Sings

Maya Angelou

For nearly a year, I sopped around the house, the Store, the school, and the church, like an old biscuit, dirty and inedible. Then I met, or rather got to know, the lady who threw me my first lifeline.

Mrs. Bertha Flowers was the aristocrat of Black Stamps. She had the grace of control to appear warm in the coldest weather, and on the Arkansas summer days it seemed she had a private breeze which swirled around, cooling her. She was thin without the taut look of wiry people, and her printed voile[1] dresses and flowered hats were as right for her as denim overalls for a farmer. She was our side's answer to the richest white woman in town.

Her skin was a rich black that would have peeled like a plum if snagged, but then no one would have thought of getting close enough to Mrs. Flowers to ruffle her dress, let alone snag her skin. She didn't encourage familiarity. She wore gloves too.

I don't think I ever saw Mrs. Flowers laugh, but she smiled often. A slow widening of her thin black lips to show even, small white teeth, then the slow effortless closing. When she chose to smile on me, I always wanted to thank her. The action was so graceful and inclusively benign.

She was one of the few gentlewomen I have ever known, and has remained throughout my life the measure of what a human being can be.

One summer afternoon, sweet-milk fresh in my memory, she stopped at the Store to buy provisions. Another Negro woman of her health and age would have been expected to carry the paper sacks home in one hand, but Momma said, "Sister Flowers, I'll send Bailey up to your house with these things."

She smiled that slow dragging smile, "Thank you, Mrs. Henderson. I'd prefer Marguerite, though." My name was beautiful when she said it. "I've been meaning to talk to her, anyway." They gave each other age-group looks.

There was a little path beside the rocky road, and Mrs. Flowers walked in front swinging her arms and picking her way over the stones.

She said, without turning her head, to me, "I hear you're doing very good schoolwork, Marguerite, but that it's all written. The teachers report that they have trouble getting you to talk in class." We passed the triangular farm on our left and the path widened to allow us to walk together. I hung back in the separate unasked and unanswerable questions.

"Come and walk along with me,

---

1. **voile** (voil) *n.* used as *adj.:* thin, sheer fabric.

Vocabulary

taut (tôt) *adj.:* tightly stretched.
benign (bi·nīn′) *adj.:* kindly. *Benign* can also mean "harmless."

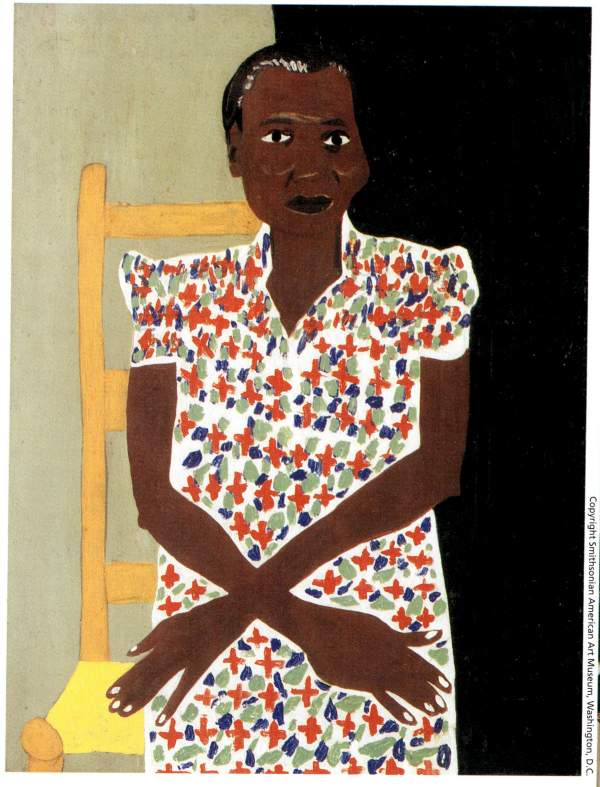

Woman in Calico (1944) by William H. Johnson. Oil.

Marguerite." I couldn't have refused even if I wanted to. She pronounced my name so nicely. Or more correctly, she spoke each word with such clarity that I was certain a foreigner who didn't understand English could have understood her.

"Now no one is going to make you talk— possibly no one can. But bear in mind, language is man's way of communicating with his fellow man and it is language alone which separates him from the lower animals." That was a totally new idea to me, and I would need time to think about it.

"Your grandmother says you read a lot. Every chance you get. That's good, but not good enough. Words mean more than what is set down on paper. It takes the human voice to <u>infuse</u> them with the shades of deeper meaning."

I memorized the part about the human voice infusing words. It seemed so valid and poetic.

She said she was going to give me some books and that I not only must read them, I must read them aloud. She suggested that I try to make a sentence sound in as many different ways as possible.

"I'll accept no excuse if you return a book to me that has been badly handled." My imagination boggled at the punishment I would deserve if in fact I did abuse a book of Mrs. Flowers's. Death would be too kind and brief.

The odors in the house surprised me. Somehow I had never connected Mrs. Flowers with food or eating or any other common experience of common people. There must have been an outhouse, too, but my mind never recorded it.

The sweet scent of vanilla had met us as she opened the door.

"I made tea cookies this morning. You see, I had planned to invite you for cookies and lemonade so we could have this little chat. The lemonade is in the icebox."

It followed that Mrs. Flowers would have ice on an ordinary day, when most families in our town bought ice late on Saturdays only a few times during the summer to be used in the wooden ice cream freezers.

She took the bags from me and disappeared through the kitchen door. I looked around the room that I had never in my wildest fantasies imagined I would see. Browned photographs leered or threatened from the walls and the white, freshly done curtains pushed against themselves and against the wind. I wanted to gobble up the room entire and take it to Bailey, who would help me analyze and enjoy it.

"Have a seat, Marguerite. Over there by the table." She carried a platter covered with a tea towel. Although she warned that she hadn't tried her hand at baking sweets for some time, I was certain that like everything else about her the cookies would be perfect.

They were flat round wafers, slightly browned on the edges and butter-yellow in the center. With the cold lemonade they were sufficient for childhood's lifelong diet. Remembering my manners, I took nice little ladylike bites off the edges. She said she had made them expressly for me and that she had a few in the kitchen that I could take home to my brother. So I jammed one whole cake in my mouth and the rough crumbs scratched the insides of my jaws, and if I hadn't had to swallow, it would have been a dream come true.

Vocabulary
infuse (in·fyo͞oz′) *v.*: fill; inspire.

As I ate she began the first of what we later called "my lessons in living." She said that I must always be intolerant of ignorance but understanding of illiteracy. That some people, unable to go to school, were more educated and even more intelligent than college professors. She encouraged me to listen carefully to what country people called mother wit. That in those homely sayings was couched the collective wisdom of generations.

When I finished the cookies she brushed off the table and brought a thick, small book from the bookcase. I had read *A Tale of Two Cities* and found it up to my standards as a romantic novel. She opened the first page and I heard poetry for the first time in my life.

"It was the best of times, it was the worst of times. . . ." Her voice slid in and curved down through and over the words. She was nearly singing. I wanted to look at the pages. Were they the same that I had read? Or were there notes, music, lined on the pages, as in a hymn book? Her sounds began cascading gently. I knew from listening to a thousand preachers that she was nearing the end of her reading, and I hadn't really heard, heard to understand, a single word.

"How do you like that?"

It occurred to me that she expected a response. The sweet vanilla flavor was still on my tongue and her reading was a wonder in my ears. I had to speak.

I said, "Yes, ma'am." It was the least I could do, but it was the most also.

"There's one more thing. Take this book of poems and memorize one for me. Next time you pay me a visit, I want you to recite."

I have tried often to search behind the sophistication of years for the enchantment I so easily found in those gifts. The essence escapes but its aura[2] remains. To be allowed, no, invited, into the private lives of strangers, and to share their joys and fears, was a chance to exchange the Southern bitter wormwood[3] for a cup of mead with Beowulf[4] or a hot cup of tea and milk with Oliver Twist. When I said aloud, "It is a far, far better thing that I do, than I have ever done . . ."[5] tears of love filled my eyes at my selflessness.

On that first day, I ran down the hill and into the road (few cars ever came along it) and had the good sense to stop running before I reached the Store.

I was liked, and what a difference it made. I was respected not as Mrs. Henderson's grandchild or Bailey's sister but for just being Marguerite Johnson.

Childhood's logic never asks to be proved (all conclusions are absolute). I didn't question why Mrs. Flowers had singled me out for attention, nor did it occur to me that Momma might have asked her to give me a little talking-to. All I cared about was that she had made tea cookies for *me* and read to *me* from her favorite book. It was enough to prove that she liked me.

---

2. **aura** (ô′rə) *n.:* feeling or mood that seems to surround something like a glow.

3. **wormwood** *n.:* bitter-tasting plant. Angelou is referring to the harshness of life for African Americans in the South at that time.

4. **Beowulf** (bā′ə·wŏŏlf′): hero of an Old English epic. During the period portrayed in the epic, people drank **mead,** a drink made with honey.

5. **"It is . . . ever done":** another quotation from Charles Dickens's *A Tale of Two Cities.* One of the characters says these words as he goes voluntarily to die in place of another man.

Vocabulary

intolerant (in·tăl′ər·ənt) *adj.:* unwilling to accept something.

illiteracy (i·lit′ər·ə·sē) *n.:* inability to read or write.

Meet the Writer

Maya Angelou

"When You Get, Give"

On January 20, 1993, **Maya Angelou** (1928–   ) stood at a podium on Capitol Hill and recited her poem "On the Pulse of Morning" in honor of Bill Clinton's presidential inauguration. She may have thought at that moment that she had come a long way from her childhood in Stamps, Arkansas. Angelou has been an actor, a teacher, a speaker, a civil rights worker, and, above all, a writer—of poems, plays, songs, screenplays, and newspaper and magazine articles, as well as four autobiographies.

Angelou says that the two writers who have had the greatest influence on her work are William Shakespeare and the African American poet Paul Laurence Dunbar. (The title *I Know Why the Caged Bird Sings* is from Dunbar's poem "Sympathy.")

Angelou has in turn influenced the lives of many young people, both in person and through her writing. Six feet tall, gracious, and commanding, Angelou is as much a gentlewoman as her childhood friend Mrs. Flowers was. In an interview with *Essence* magazine, Angelou tells about a time when she was able to "throw a lifeline" to a young man she found cursing and fighting on a movie set in California:

"I went over and I said, 'Baby, may I speak to you for a minute?' He dropped his head, and I said, 'Come on, let's walk.'

And I started talking to him and started crying. I said, 'Do you know how much at risk you are? Do you know how valuable you are to us? You're all we've got, baby.'

He started crying and said to me, 'Don't cry.' I don't know who has cried for him. And let him see how much he means. . . .

Black people say, when you get, give; when you learn, teach. As soon as that healing takes place, then we have to go out and heal somebody, and pass on the idea of a healing day—so that somebody else gets it and passes it on."

After You Read Response and Analysis

First Thoughts

1. How does Mrs. Flowers compare with one of your own role models?

Thinking Critically

2. At the beginning of "Mrs. Flowers," Maya Angelou says that she "sopped around" until Mrs. Flowers threw her a "lifeline." What **main idea** does Angelou suggest here? Find some passages from the story that support this point she makes about her experience.

3. Go back to the text, and find the only two words that Marguerite speaks. What do you think Angelou means when she writes, "It was the least I could do, but it was the most also" (page 189)? What does this tell you about Marguerite's **character**?

4. Throughout history, people have had to respond to difficult situations. Take three of the characters from this collection, and compare their challenges and the ways they handled them.

Extending Interpretations

5. What do you think Mrs. Flowers meant when she told Marguerite that she "must always be intolerant of ignorance but understanding of illiteracy" (page 189)? Is that good advice for today? Draw on your own experience to support your answer.

WRITING

Comparing Messages

Re-read Meet the Writer on page 190, and pay special attention to what Maya Angelou says about the young man in California. What words in this passage connect with the story of Mrs. Flowers? Write a paragraph in which you tell how Mrs. Flowers's talk with Marguerite is like what Angelou says here. Be sure to quote details from both the autobiography and Angelou's comments to show how each memory offers a similar message.

> ### Reading Check
> This selection is taken from an **autobiography,** the story of the writer's own life. Angelou tells her story in **narrative form,** that is, as a series of related events. On a sheet of paper, identify the main events of the narrative, and sum up the resolution. You should be able to find five key events.

INTERNET
Projects and Activities
Keyword: LE5 8-2

Literary Skills
Analyze character.

Reading Skills
Identify the main idea.

Writing Skills
Compare messages.

After You Read Vocabulary Development

Context Clues: They Can Help

Sometimes (if you're lucky) the **context** of an unfamiliar word—the words, sentences, and paragraphs surrounding it—can help you figure out what the word means. The following terms are various kinds of **context clues**. (Which kind of context clue is used right here in the first sentence of this paragraph?)

> **Word Bank**
>
> taut
> benign
> infuse
> intolerant
> illiteracy

- **Definitions and restatements.** Look for words that define the unfamiliar word or that restate it in other terms. *People should be intolerant of ignorance—they should not put up with it.*
- **Synonyms.** Look for words in the context that mean the same thing as the unfamiliar word. *Mrs. Flowers had a kindly, benign manner.*
- **Antonyms.** Look for words in the context that mean the opposite of the unfamiliar word. *Mrs. Flowers did not have the taut look thin people often have; she seemed relaxed and gracious.*
- **Cause and effect.** Look for words in the context that indicate that an unfamiliar word is the cause or the effect of some action. *Mrs. Flowers's benign smile caused Marguerite to glow with pleasure.*
- **Examples.** Look for examples that hint at the meaning of the unfamiliar word. *Mrs. Flowers's benign actions—giving Marguerite attention, baking cookies for her, lending her books—made the girl feel special.*

PRACTICE

Search for context clues that help you choose the correct meaning of the underlined words from "Mrs. Flowers."

1. Mrs. Flowers was the aristocrat of Black Stamps. Her noble behavior caused everyone to look up to her. *The word* aristocrat *means upper-class person / dictator / poor person.*
2. No one would have thought of getting close enough to touch Mrs. Flowers. She didn't encourage familiarity. *The word* familiarity *means family / closeness / distance.*
3. She stopped at the store to buy provisions, such as sugar, flour, and milk. *The word* provisions *means property / paper / food.*
4. Although they are not expressed in fancy language, the homely sayings of ordinary people often contain great wisdom. *The word* homely *means awful / simple / elegant.*

SKILLS FOCUS

Vocabulary Skills
Use context clues.

LINK TO "MRS. FLOWERS"

Understanding Text Structures: Recipes

Reading a Text Carefully

When you read most informational materials, you have to pay very close attention to every detail. This is especially true of recipes. If you don't read very carefully, you could easily confuse teaspoon (*tsp*) and tablespoon (*tbsp*). If you don't put the right amount of baking powder in Mrs. Flowers's cookies, they might come out like rocks.

There'll be no questions asked about these recipes, but we hope you'll try them out. You may want to get together with a few classmates and make enough for the class. Note that the cookies take two days to make. Once you and your classmates have eaten cookies and drunk lemonade, you all can answer this:

BONUS QUESTION

How did they taste?

✳ Lemonade ✳

4–6 medium-sized lemons
1–2 cups sugar
2 quarts water
sprigs of mint (optional)

Squeeze lemons. Discard seeds. Add water. Add sugar to taste, stirring constantly until sugar is dissolved. (Note: Do not use chilled water, as sugar may clump instead of dissolving fully.) Chill and serve alone or over ice. (Optional: Garnish with sprigs of mint.)

✳ Crisp Sugar Cookies ✳

1/2 cup butter or margarine
1 cup sugar
1 egg

1 tbsp heavy cream
1 tsp vanilla
2 cups sifted all-purpose flour

1/2 tsp salt
1 tsp baking powder
extra sugar for topping (optional)

Cream butter or margarine with sugar in mixing bowl until light and fluffy. Add egg, heavy cream, and vanilla. Beat well. Sift flour with salt and baking powder. Add to creamed mixture, beating until well combined. Chill dough overnight. (Note: This step is essential. If not chilled, the dough will be too sticky to be rolled out smoothly.)

When ready to bake, preheat oven to 350° F (moderate).

Roll out the dough with a rolling pin until it is very thin, using only a small amount at a time, on a lightly floured board. Cut with a round cookie cutter or a glass. (Optional: Sprinkle cookies lightly with the extra sugar.) Place on ungreased cookie sheets.

Bake five minutes or until done. Makes 36–50 large cookies or about six dozen small cookies.

Comparing Literature

Literary Focus

Historical Fiction

If you have read *Little House on the Prairie* or *My Brother Sam Is Dead*, **historical fiction** is a form you are already familiar with. Historical fiction combines an imaginative story with facts about events that happened in the past. Some historical fiction uses actual historical figures along with fictional characters.

Writers of historical fiction are storytellers of a special kind. They weave fact and fiction together, so that you imagine you are back in time with the people you are reading about. The best writers of historical fiction teach us about the past by showing us how people of that time lived, how they thought and felt, and what their problems were.

Reading Skills

Checking for Historical Accuracy

In your literature and social studies classes, you might be asked to compare a piece of historical fiction (a short story or a novel, for example) with historical data. Your aim would be to see how accurate the factual elements are. For example, you might want to check the details of the setting, the way the historical characters are presented, or the accounts of certain real events. You will get a chance to work on these skills as you read the following historical material and historical fiction. You will be checking a famous short story about a Civil War battle against the historical record. Then you'll make your own judgments.

SKILLS FOCUS

Literary Skills
Understand historical fiction.

Reading Skills
Evaluate historical accuracy; compare and contrast texts.

Elements of Historical Fiction

- set during a real historical era
- contains historically accurate details
- includes fictional characters
- often includes characters based on actual historical figures

Examples of Historical Fiction

- *Across Five Aprils* by Irene Hunt
- *Catherine, Called Birdy* by Karen Cushman
- *The Witch of Blackbird Pond* by Elizabeth George Speare
- *Bud, Not Buddy* by Christopher Paul Curtis

Before You Read

You're about to read a number of factual sources about the Battle of Shiloh, an important Civil War battle, including an encyclopedia Web page entry, a Data Bank (a list of facts about the battle), a map, and a photo. Then, you will read a chapter of a nonfiction book on one aspect of the Battle of Shiloh—the Civil War drummer boys. Study each source carefully. You will use the facts from these sources to assess the accuracy of "The Drummer Boy of Shiloh," a short story by Ray Bradbury, which begins on page 203.

HISTORICAL DATA ABOUT THE

Battle of Shiloh

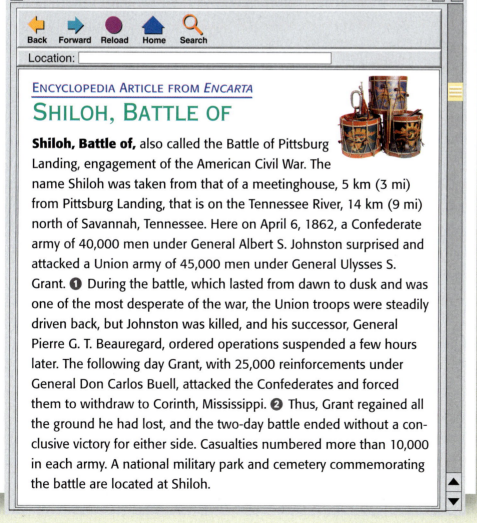

Back Forward Reload Home Search

Location:

ENCYCLOPEDIA ARTICLE FROM *ENCARTA*

SHILOH, BATTLE OF

Shiloh, Battle of, also called the Battle of Pittsburg Landing, engagement of the American Civil War. The name Shiloh was taken from that of a meetinghouse, 5 km (3 mi) from Pittsburg Landing, that is on the Tennessee River, 14 km (9 mi) north of Savannah, Tennessee. Here on April 6, 1862, a Confederate army of 40,000 men under General Albert S. Johnston surprised and attacked a Union army of 45,000 men under General Ulysses S. Grant. ❶ During the battle, which lasted from dawn to dusk and was one of the most desperate of the war, the Union troops were steadily driven back, but Johnston was killed, and his successor, General Pierre G. T. Beauregard, ordered operations suspended a few hours later. The following day Grant, with 25,000 reinforcements under General Don Carlos Buell, attacked the Confederates and forced them to withdraw to Corinth, Mississippi. ❷ Thus, Grant regained all the ground he had lost, and the two-day battle ended without a conclusive victory for either side. Casualties numbered more than 10,000 in each army. A national military park and cemetery commemorating the battle are located at Shiloh.

INFER

❶ What advantage did the Confederate army have on the first day of fighting?

INFER

❷ What advantage did the Union army have on the second day of fighting?

Company H, 44th Indiana Volunteers outside a camp in Tennessee (c. 1863).

DATA BANK

The Battle of Shiloh

Date: April 6–7, 1862

Location

• In Tennessee near the Mississippi border beside the Tennessee River (Shiloh was a nearby church) at the site of a peach orchard, owned by Sarah Bell, in bloom at the time of the battle. (Observers compared peach blossoms cut down by bullets to snow.)

Generals

• Union—Ulysses S. Grant with 45,000 troops. (On second day, 25,000 reinforcements participated under General Don Carlos Buell.)

• Confederate—Albert Sidney Johnston with 40,000 troops.

Casualties: 23,746

Largest, bloodiest battle of the Civil War to that point. (Larger battles, like Gettysburg, were still to come.) ❸

IDENTIFY

❸ It is always a good idea to consult more than one source when you're researching a topic. What does the Data Bank tell you that the Web page does not?

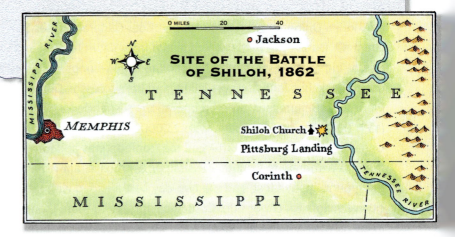

0 MILES 20 40

Jackson

SITE OF THE BATTLE OF SHILOH, 1862

T E N N E S S E E

MISSISSIPPI RIVER

MEMPHIS

Shiloh Church

Pittsburg Landing

Corinth

TENNESSEE RIVER

M I S S I S S I P P I

Before You Read

Do you think teenagers today are given too much or too little responsibility? Currently, the minimum age for enlistment in the U.S. Armed Forces is seventeen. During the Civil War, boys as young as twelve enlisted in the army (often lying about their age) and found themselves fighting alongside grown men—often as drummers. Many of these drummer boys were runaways or were homeless. Read on to find out how these boys faced life and death on the battlefield during the Civil War.

Drumbeats and Bullets

Jim Murphy

Johnny Clem, the twelve-year-old drummer boy of Shiloh.

THE GROGGY SOLDIER woke up to a persistent, brain-rattling drumming noise. *Thrump. Thrump. Thrump.* He rolled over in an attempt to ignore the sound and pulled his blanket up over his head. The drumming went on and intensified as drummers all over camp signaled the call to muster.[1] There was no escaping it, and eventually—and usually with a grumble—the soldier got up to start another day. ❶

Soldiers probably came to hate the sound of the drums, especially when they heard them on a drizzly, cold morning. Yet drummer boys who served during the Civil War provided valuable service to the armies of both sides, although some didn't realize it at first.

"I wanted to fight the Rebs," a twelve-year-old boy wrote, "but I was very small and they would not give me a musket. The next day I went back and the man behind the desk said I looked as if I could hold a drum and if I wanted I could join that way. I did, but I was not happy to change a musket for a stick." ❷

This boy was disappointed at being assigned a "nonfighting" and, to him, dull job. Most likely, he saw himself always drumming in parades or in the safety of camp. He would soon learn differently.

---

1. **muster** *v.*: assemble; come together.

IDENTIFY

❶ What role did the drummers play in the morning ritual of an army camp?

INFER

❷ This twelve-year-old uses some slang words and phrases of his day. Based on context clues, can you guess what "Rebs" is short for? What is the "stick" he refers to?

❸ What important role did the drummer boy play in battle?

The beat of the drum was one of the most important means of communicating orders to soldiers in the Civil War. Drummers did find themselves in camp sounding the routine calls to muster or meals and providing the beat for marching drills. But more often than not, they were with the troops in the field, not just marching to the site of the battle but in the middle of the fighting. It was the drumbeat that told the soldiers how and when to maneuver[2] as smoke poured over the battlefield. And the sight of a drummer boy showed soldiers where their unit was located, helping to keep them close together. ❸

Drummers were such a vital part of battle communication that they often found themselves the target of enemy fire. "A ball hit my drum and bounced off and I fell over," a Confederate drummer at the Battle of Cedar Creek recalled. "When I got up, another ball tore a hole in the drum and another came so close to my ear that I heard it sing."

Naturally, such killing fire alarmed many drummer boys at first. But like their counterparts with rifles, they soon learned how to face enemy shells without flinching. Fourteen-year-old Orion Howe was struck by several Confederate bullets during the Battle of

---

2. **maneuver** (mə·n$\overline{oo}$′vər) *v.*: move as a troop.

Drummer boys of the 61st New York Infantry (1863).

Vicksburg in 1863. Despite his wounds, he maintained his position and relayed the orders given him. For his bravery, Howe would later receive the Medal of Honor.

Drumming wasn't the only thing these boys did, either. While in camp, they would carry water, rub down horses, gather wood, or cook for the soldiers. There is even evidence that one was a barber for the troops when he wasn't drumming. After a battle, most drummers helped carry wounded soldiers off the field or assisted in burial details. And many drummer boys even got their wish to fight the enemy. ❹

Fighting in the Civil War was particularly bloody. Of the 900 men in the First Maine Heavy Artillery, 635 became casualties *in just seven minutes* of fighting at the Battle of Petersburg. A North Carolina regiment saw 714 of its 800 soldiers killed at Gettysburg. At such a time, these boys put down their drums and took up whatever rifle was handy. One such drummer was Johnny Clem.

Clem ran away from home in 1861 when he was eleven years old. He enlisted, and the Twenty-second Michigan Regiment took him in as their drummer, paying him thirteen dollars a month for his services. Several months later, at the Battle of Shiloh, Clem earned the nickname of "Johnny Shiloh" when a piece of cannon shell bounced off a tree stump and destroyed his drum. When another drum was shattered in battle, Clem found a musket and fought bravely for the rest of the war, becoming a sergeant[3] in the fall of 1863. ❺

The Civil War would be the last time drummer boys would be

---

3. **sergeant** (sär′jənt) *n.:* noncommissioned officer in the military.

IDENTIFY

❹ What other duties—besides drumming—did drummer boys perform?

IDENTIFY

❺ How old was Johnny Clem when he became a sergeant? What circumstances led to his becoming a sergeant at such a young age?

IDENTIFY

6 List some of the factors that led to the disappearance of the drummer boy from the battlefield.

IDENTIFY

7 Review this text, and note where the writer quotes from primary sources—that is, documents such as letters or interviews that give firsthand accounts of events.

used in battle. The roar of big cannons and mortars, the rapid firing of thousands of rifles, and the shouts of tens of thousands of men made hearing a drumbeat difficult. More and more, bugles were being used to pass along orders. Military tactics were changing, too. Improved weapons made it impractical to have precise lines of soldiers face their enemy at close range. Instead, smaller, fast-moving units and trench warfare, neither of which required drummers, became popular. **6**

Even as their role in the fighting was changing, Civil War drummers stayed at their positions signaling orders to the troops. Hundreds were killed and thousands more wounded. "A cannon ball came bouncing across the corn field," a drummer boy recalled, "kicking up dirt and dust each time it struck the earth. Many of the men in our company took shelter behind a stone wall, but I stood where I was and never stopped drumming. An officer came by on horseback and chastised the men, saying 'this boy puts you all to shame. Get up and move forward.' We all began moving across the cornfield. . . . Even when the fighting was at its fiercest and I was frightened, I stood straight and did as I was ordered. . . . I felt I had to be a good example for the others." **7**

Members of the drum corps of the 93rd New York Infantry Regiment (1863).

Meet the Writer

Jim Murphy

A Sense of Adventure

Jim Murphy (1947–   ) grew up in Kearny, New Jersey, a small town where he and his friends would often play football and baseball when they weren't "roaming around town . . . inventing various 'adventures.'"

Murphy has retained that sense of adventure in a number of his books that focus on dramatic historical events. The idea for *The Boys' War* (the book that features "Drumbeats and Bullets") originated while Murphy was researching an unrelated project at the library:

> 66 I spotted a book sitting in the middle of a big table . . . picked it up and discovered it was the Civil War diary of a fifteen-year-old Union soldier named Elisha Stockwell, Jr. Hmmm, I thought, I didn't know kids so young had fought in that war. . . . Elisha described his years in the Union Army in an amazingly vivid, detailed, and funny way. Why not let him and other young soldiers talk about the war in their own words? This started my search for other Union and Confederate voices. . . . 99

Murphy found his own voice as a writer after working at a publishing company, where he assisted authors with their writing. Although he enjoyed the work, Murphy realized that he wanted to focus on his own writing. Murphy continues to write in New Jersey, where he lives with his family.

For Independent Reading

The Boys' War isn't the only book in which Jim Murphy presents exciting firsthand accounts. *The Great Fire* (a portrayal of the devastating Chicago fire of 1871) and *The Long Road to Gettysburg* are two other award-winning books containing vivid accounts that will transport you to another time and place.

Civil War regulation drums.

After You Read   "Drumbeats and Bullets"

First Thoughts

1. Respond to "Drumbeats and Bullets" by completing the following sentence:
   - I was surprised to learn that . . .

Thinking Critically

2. Based on the information in the encyclopedia article (page 195), was the Union general or the Confederate general better prepared for the Battle of Shiloh? Explain.

3. "Drumbeats and Bullets" comes from a book called *The Boys' War.* Based on the selection you just read, explain what the title of the book means.

4. Review Johnny Clem's story (see page 199). What conclusions can you draw about the way boys were treated during the Civil War period? Are boys treated differently today? If so, how?

Comparing Literature

5. The next selection you will read is Ray Bradbury's fictional portrait of a drummer boy. To evaluate the historical accuracy of Bradbury's short story, begin a chart like the one below. Make notes under the column heading "Drumbeats and Bullets." Consider what you've learned about the typical drummer boy. This chart will be repeated after "The Drummer Boy of Shiloh," on page 212, where you'll add details from that story.

Reading Check

Fill in the outline below with details or quotations from "Drumbeats and Bullets." One detail has been filled in for you.

I. Drummer boys' duties in war
   A. helped keep unit together
   B.
II. Other duties
   A.
   B.
   C.
III. Risk to drummer boys
   A.
   B.
IV. Johnny Clem
   A.
   B.
V. End of drummer boys' use in war
   A.
   B.

Comparing Fact and Fiction: The Drummer Boys		
	"Drumbeats and Bullets"	"The Drummer Boy of Shiloh"
Age and background		
Role in battle		
Dangers faced		
Attitude toward war		

SKILLS FOCUS

Reading Skills
Evaluate historical accuracy; compare and contrast texts.

Before You Read

You are about to read a famous short story about a drummer boy. It takes place during the American Civil War, the night before the Battle of Shiloh. As you read this story, you might have many questions: Did this really happen? Was there really a drummer boy at the Battle of Shiloh? Does this story match the historical record of the Battle of Shiloh? Who could the general be? Before he wrote this story, Bradbury did his research. You've also done yours—think of all you've learned about the Battle of Shiloh and drummer boys. As you read, consider how your prior reading of the historical article and the other historical sources widens your comprehension of this story.

The Drummer Boy of Shiloh

Ray Bradbury

"I'm the one of all the rest who won't die. I'll live through it."

In the April night, more than once, blossoms fell from the orchard trees and lighted with rustling taps on the drumhead. At midnight a peach stone, left miraculously on a branch through winter, flicked by a bird, fell swift and unseen; it struck once, like panic, and jerked the boy upright. In silence he listened to his own heart ruffle away, away—at last gone from his ears and back in his chest again. ❶

After that he turned the drum on its side, where its great lunar face peered at him whenever he opened his eyes.

VISUALIZE

❶ **Imagery** is language that appeals to the senses. What **images,** or pictures, do you *see* as you read this first paragraph?

Comparing Literature

IDENTIFY

❷ Look back at the map and Data Bank on page 196. When and where does this story take place?

His face, alert or at rest, was solemn. It was a solemn time and a solemn night for a boy just turned fourteen in the peach orchard near Owl Creek, not far from the church at Shiloh.

"... thirty-one ... thirty-two ... thirty-three." Unable to see, he stopped counting.

Beyond the thirty-three familiar shadows, forty thousand men, exhausted by nervous expectation and unable to sleep for romantic dreams of battles yet unfought, lay crazily askew[1] in their uniforms. A mile farther on, another army was strewn helter-skelter, turning slowly, basting themselves with the thought of what they would do when the time came—a leap, a yell, a blind plunge their strategy, raw youth their protection and benediction.[2] ❷

Now and again the boy heard a vast wind come up that gently stirred the air. But he knew what it was—the army here, the army there, whispering to itself in the dark. Some men talking to others, others murmuring to themselves, and all so quiet it was like a natural element arisen from South or North with the motion of the earth toward dawn.

What the men whispered the boy could only guess, and he guessed that it was "Me, I'm the one, I'm the one of all the rest who won't die. I'll live through it. I'll go home. The band will play. And I'll be there to hear it."

"Yes," thought the boy, *"that's all very well for them, they can give as good as they get!"*

For with the careless bones of the young men, harvested by night and bindled[3] around campfires, were the similarly strewn steel bones of their rifles with bayonets fixed like eternal lightning lost in the orchard grass.

"Me," thought the boy, *"I got only a drum, two sticks to beat it, and no shield."*

There wasn't a man-boy on this ground tonight who did not have a shield he cast, riveted, or carved himself on his way to his first attack, compounded of remote but nonetheless firm and fiery family devotion, flag-blown patriotism, and cocksure immortality, strengthened by the touchstone of very real gunpowder, ramrod,

---

1. **askew** (ə·skyoo′) *adv.*: crookedly; not in straight lines.
2. **benediction** (ben′ə·dik′shən) *n.*: blessing.
3. **bindled** *v.* used as *adj.*: bundled together.

Minié ball,[4] and flint. ❸ But without these last, the boy felt his family move yet farther off in the dark, as if one of those great prairie-burning trains had chanted them away, never to return—leaving him with this drum, which was worse than a toy in the game to be played tomorrow or someday much too soon.

The boy turned on his side. A moth brushed his face, but it was peach blossom. A peach blossom flicked him, but it was a moth. Nothing stayed put. Nothing had a name. Nothing was as it once was.

If he stayed very still when the dawn came up and the soldiers put on their bravery with their caps, perhaps they might go away, the war with them, and not notice him lying small here, no more than a toy himself.

"Well, by thunder now," said a voice. The boy shut his eyes to hide inside himself, but it was too late. Someone, walking by in the night, stood over him. "Well," said the voice quietly, "here's a soldier crying before the fight. Good. Get it over. Won't be time once it all starts." ❹

And the voice was about to move on when the boy, startled, touched the drum at his elbow. The man above, hearing this, stopped. The boy could feel his eyes, sense him slowly bending near. A hand must have come down out of the night, for there was a little *rat-tat* as the fingernails brushed and the man's breath fanned the boy's face.

"Why, it's the drummer boy, isn't it?"

The boy nodded, not knowing if his nod was seen. "Sir, is that you?" he said.

"I assume it is." The man's knees cracked as he bent still closer. He smelled as all fathers should smell, of salt-sweat, tobacco, horse and boot leather, and the earth he walked upon. He had many eyes. No, not eyes, brass buttons that watched the boy.

He could only be, and was, the general. "What's your name, boy?" he asked.

"Joby, sir," whispered the boy, starting to sit up.

"All right, Joby, don't stir." A hand pressed his chest gently, and the boy relaxed. "How long you been with us, Joby?"

"Three weeks, sir."

"Run off from home or join legitimate, boy?"

Silence.

---

4. **Minié** (min′ē) **ball** *n.:* cone-shaped rifle bullet, used in the 1800s.

ANALYZE

❸ The writer tells us that the soldiers all have "shields." What does he say these shields are made of? Are they real shields? Explain.

INFER

❹ Why is the drummer boy crying?

ANALYZE

❺ **Figures of speech** are comparisons between two unlike things. In this story, Bradbury uses figures of speech to create setting and mood. In this paragraph, what does the general compare the boy's cheek to? Why does he make this comparison?

EVALUATE

❻ What does the general predict will happen in the coming battle? According to the historical facts, is his prediction well-founded? (See encyclopedia entry and Data Bank, pages 195–196.)

"Darn-fool question," said the general. "Do you shave yet, boy? Even more of a fool. There's your cheek, fell right off the tree overhead. And the others here, not much older. Raw, raw, darn raw, the lot of you. You ready for tomorrow or the next day, Joby?" ❺

"I think so, sir."

"You want to cry some more, go on ahead. I did the same last night."

"You, sir?"

"God's truth. Thinking of everything ahead. Both sides figuring the other side will just give up, and soon, and the war done in weeks and us all home. Well, that's not how it's going to be. And maybe that's why I cried."

"Yes, sir," said Joby.

The general must have taken out a cigar now, for the dark was suddenly filled with the Indian smell of tobacco—unlighted yet, but chewed as the man thought what next to say.

"It's going to be a crazy time," said the general. "Counting both sides, there's a hundred thousand men—give or take a few thousand—out there tonight, not one as can spit a sparrow off a tree or knows a horse clod from a Minié ball. Stand up, bare the breast, ask to be a target, thank them, and sit down, that's us, that's them. We should turn tail and train four months; they should do the same. But here we are, taken with spring fever and thinking it blood lust, taking our sulfur with cannons instead of with molasses,[5] as it should be—going to be a hero, going to live forever. And I can see all them over there nodding agreement, save the other way around. It's wrong, boy, it's wrong as a head put on hind-side front and a man marching backward through life. Sometime this week more innocents will get shot out of pure Cherokee enthusiasm than ever got shot before. Oil Creek was full of boys splashing around in the noonday sun just a few hours ago. I fear it will be full of boys again, just floating, at sundown tomorrow, not caring where the current takes them." ❻

The general stopped and made a little pile of winter leaves and twigs in the dark, as if he might at any moment strike fire to them to see his way through the coming days when the sun might not show its face because of what was happening here and just beyond.

The boy watched the hand stirring the leaves and opened his lips

---

5. Sulfur and molasses was used to treat constipation and other discomforts.

to say something, but did not say it. The general heard the boy's breath and spoke himself.

"Why am I telling you this? That's what you wanted to ask, eh? Well, when you got a bunch of wild horses on a loose rein somewhere, somehow you got to bring order, rein them in. These lads, fresh out of the milkshed, don't know what I know; and I can't tell them—men actually die in war. So each is his own army. I got to make one army of them. And for that, boy, I need you." ❼

"Me!" The boy's lips barely twitched.

"You, boy," said the general quietly. "You are the heart of the army. Think about that. You are the heart of the army. Listen to me, now."

And lying there, Joby listened. And the general spoke. If he, Joby, beat slow tomorrow, the heart would beat slow in the men. They would lag by the wayside. They would drowse in the fields on their muskets. They would sleep forever after that—in those same fields, their hearts slowed by a drummer boy and stopped by enemy lead.

But if he beat a sure, steady, ever-faster rhythm, then, then, their knees would come up in a long line down over that hill, one knee after the other, like a wave on the ocean shore. Had he seen the ocean ever—seen the waves rolling in like a well-ordered cavalry charge to the sand? Well, that was it, that's what he wanted; that's what was needed. Joby was his right hand and his left. He gave the orders, but Joby set the pace.

So bring the right knee up and the right foot out and the left knee up and the left foot out, one following the other in good time, in brisk time. Move the blood up the body, and make the head proud and the spine stiff and the jaw resolute.[6] Focus the eye and set the teeth; flare the nostril and tighten the hands; put steel armor all over the men, for blood moving fast in them does indeed make men feel as if they'd put on steel. He must keep at it, at it! Long and steady, steady and long! Then, even though shot or torn, those

---

6. **resolute** (rez′ə·lo͞ot′) *adj.:* purposeful; determined.

INFER

❼ What do you know about the generals in this battle from the online encyclopedia entry on page 195? Who could this general be? Does Bradbury give you any clues as to who might be talking to Joby?

wounds got in hot blood—in blood he'd helped stir—would feel less pain. If their blood was cold, it would be more than slaughter: It would be murderous nightmare and pain best not told and no one to guess.

The general spoke and stopped, letting his breath slack off. Then, after a moment, he said, "So there you are, that's it. Will you do that, boy? Do you know now you're general of the army when the general's left behind?"

The boy nodded mutely.

"You'll run them through for me then, boy?"

"Yes, sir."

"Good. And, God willing, many nights from tonight, many years from now, when you're as old or far much older than me, when they ask you what you did in this awful time, you will tell them—one part humble and one part proud—I was the drummer boy at the battle of Owl Creek or of the Tennessee River, or maybe they'll just name it after the church there. I was the drummer boy at Shiloh. Good grief, that has a beat and sound to it fitting for Mr. Longfellow.[7] 'I was the drummer boy at Shiloh.' Who will ever hear those words and not know you, boy, or what you thought this night, or what you'll think tomorrow or the next day when we must get up on our legs and move." ❽

The general stood up. "Well, then, God bless you, boy. Good night."

"Good night, sir." And tobacco, brass, boot polish, salt-sweat, and leather, the man moved away through the grass.

Joby lay for a moment staring, but unable to see where the man had gone. He swallowed. He wiped his eyes. He cleared his throat. He settled himself. Then, at last, very slowly and firmly, he turned the drum so it faced up toward the sky.

He lay next to it, his arm around it, feeling the tremor,[8] the touch, the muted thunder as all the rest of the April night in the year 1862, near the Tennessee River, not far from the Owl Creek, very close to the church named Shiloh, the peach blossoms fell on the drum. ❾

---

7. **Mr. Longfellow:** Henry Wadsworth Longfellow (1807–1882), popular American poet who was known for writing poems with strong, regular rhythms. (See "Paul Revere's Ride," page 629.)
8. **tremor** (trem′ər) *n.:* quiver; vibration.

COMPARE AND CONTRAST

❽ Look back at the facts of Johnny Clem's life (page 199). How is Joby like, and unlike, Johnny Clem?

VISUALIZE

❾ What do you visualize when you read this final sentence?

How I Came to Write "The Drummer Boy of Shiloh"

Ray Bradbury

I was browsing through the morning newspaper forty years ago when I came across an obituary of an actor named Olin Howland who had appeared in dozens of films.

Along with the facts about his sickness and departure, it mentioned the fact that his great-grandfather was the drummer boy at Shiloh.

I cannot possibly tell you the impact of those words. This often happens with me.

On one occasion many years ago my wife quoted "There Will Come Soft Rains" by Sara Teasdale, and the sound of that title caused me to write a story. [This story is on page 266.]

So here I was with the drummer boy of Shiloh. The sound of it was so poetic and so haunting that I rushed to the typewriter and, lacking full knowledge about the War between the States, nevertheless, in a white-hot passion wrote the first draft of "The Drummer Boy of Shiloh" in one afternoon.

When I finished, I was in tears because something had been waiting in me for many years to be released: my feelings about North and South and the terrible war that ensued between them.

Glancing at the story, I realized how ignorant I was as to the facts surrounding that drummer boy on that particular day so many, many years ago.

I had to go and do some research and make sure there was a peach orchard and that it was the proper time of year for blossoms to fall on the drum and to see which generals were lined up and how many troops there were, even if I didn't use all of the facts.

When I finished doing my research, I went back to the story and applied my knowledge.

In later years I wrote a one-act play about this story and have seen it performed many times. It never ceases to bring me to tears. It is one of the most deeply felt stories I have ever written.

I am much pleased that you contain it here in this collection.

Peach orchard at Shiloh National Military Park.

Meet the Writer

Ray Bradbury

"My Stories Have Led Me Through My Life"

At the age of twelve, **Ray Bradbury** (1920–   ) wrote his first short stories, in pencil on brown wrapping paper. He's been writing stories—and novels, poems, plays, and screenplays—ever since. Their settings range from Mars and Venus to Ireland and Greentown, a fictional town based on his birthplace, Waukegan, Illinois. Bradbury notes that he has written about Waukegan in many of his works, but his realistic novel *Dandelion Wine* is the work most closely associated with the small town.

Bradbury has also explored the realm of nonfiction. One of his notable works of nonfiction is *Zen in the Art of Writing*, a collection of essays that captures the complete joy Bradbury experiences whenever he writes. In this book, he encourages aspiring writers to view writing as an exciting venture.

As Bradbury once said:

> **If you write a hundred short stories and they're all bad, that doesn't mean you've failed. You fail only if you stop writing. I've written about two thousand short stories; I've only published about three hundred, and I feel I'm still learning.**

He follows his own advice and writes nearly every day. Although he has been writing for over seventy years, Bradbury says he is still having fun.

> **Writing is supposed to be difficult, agonizing, a dreadful exercise, a terrible occupation. But, you see, my stories have led me through my life. They shout, I follow. They run up and bite me on the leg—I respond by writing down everything that goes on during the bite. When I finish, the idea lets go and runs off.**

For more information on Bradbury and his work, see the Author Study on pages 298–330.

First Thoughts

1. Respond to "The Drummer Boy of Shiloh" by completing the following sentence:

- This story left me feeling . . .

Thinking Critically

2. Why is the boy so afraid? (What do the soldiers have that he does not have?)

3. After the Battle of Shiloh, the orchards and fields near Owl Creek were littered with the bodies of more than 23,000 soldiers. Find passages in which the general indicates that he knows the battle will be a bad one. Do you think the drummer boy survives? Why or why not?

4. How do you think the writer wants you to feel about the drummer boy, the general, and the war itself?

5. With a partner, trace the emotional state of the main character during his long conversation with the general. What is his state of mind at the start of the story? What is his state of mind at the end?

6. Look back at Bradbury's comment about "The Drummer Boy of Shiloh." What details in the story did Bradbury research to ensure historical accuracy?

Reading Check

Check your comprehension by **retelling** this story to a partner. Start with the title and author. Describe the main characters and the setting. Then, cite the main events in the story. Tell what the drummer boy's main conflict, or problem, is. Finally, explain the resolution of this conflict.

Comparing Literature

7. Complete the chart below by adding information about Joby from "The Drummer Boy of Shiloh."

Comparing Fact and Fiction: The Drummer Boys		
	"Drumbeats and Bullets"	"The Drummer Boy of Shiloh"
Age and background		
Role in battle		
Dangers faced		
Attitude toward war		

Evaluating Historical Accuracy

Assignment

Would a drummer boy act the way Joby does? Would a general say the things the general does? Based on what you've read, how much of "The Drummer Boy of Shiloh" is based on real events, people, and places from the past? In an essay, use your knowledge of the historical record to form an opinion and evaluate the historical accuracy of Bradbury's story. You can begin your essay with one of these statements:

• Based on the historical facts, Bradbury's story "The Drummer Boy of Shiloh" presents (or does not present) a believable portrait of a Civil War drummer boy.

• Based on the historical facts, Bradbury's story is a believable (or is not a believable) account of events the night before the battle of Shiloh.

   Whichever position you take, you should cite at least one way in which the story is either historically believable or not believable. Then you should support your statement with at least one specific detail from one of the historical texts on pages 195–200. You should also refer to at least one detail from Bradbury's story, and you may also want to cite some of Bradbury's comments from pages 209–210.

   Before you write, review the chart you made after you read "Drumbeats and Bullets" and "The Drummer Boy of Shiloh." Then, gather notes for your evaluation in a chart like the one below. In the first column, fill in details about the fictional setting, characters, and events from the story. Then, fill in the second column with information you learned from the historical sources in this feature. Finally, compare the two columns to see where they match up—and where they don't. (That is, *if* they don't; you may decide the story is an accurate reflection of the historical record.)

Use the workshop on writing a Comparison-Contrast Essay, pages 516–521, for help with this assignment.

	"The Drummer Boy of Shiloh"	Details from Historical Record
Setting (time, place, etc.)		
Characters (Joby, the general)		
Events		

GREEN GULCH

Loren Eiseley

We stood in a wide flat field at sunset. For the life of me I can remember no other children before them. I must have run away and been playing by myself until I had wandered to the edge of the town. They were older than I and knew where they came from and how to get back. I joined them.

They were not going home. They were going to a place called Green Gulch. They came from some other part of town, and their clothes were rough, their eyes worldly and sly. I think, looking back, that it must have been a little like a child following goblins home to their hill at nightfall, but nobody threatened me. Besides, I was very small and did not know the way home, so I followed them.

Presently we came to some rocks. The place was well named. It was a huge pool in a sandstone basin, green and dark with the evening over it and the trees leaning secretly inward above the water. When you looked down, you saw the sky. I remember that place as it was when we came there. I remember the quiet and the green ferns touching the green water. I remember we played there, innocently at first.

But someone found the spirit of the place, a huge old turtle, asleep in the ferns. He was the last lord of the green water before the town poured over it. I saw his end. They pounded him to death with stones on the other side of the pool while I looked on in stupefied horror. I had never seen death before.

Suddenly, as I stood there small and uncertain and frightened, a grimy, splattered gnome who had been stooping over the turtle stood up with a rock in his hand. He looked at me, and around that little group some curious evil impulse passed like a wave. I felt it and drew back. I was alone there. They were not human.

I do not know who threw the first stone, who splashed water over my suit, who struck me first, or even who finally, among that ring of vicious faces, put me on my feet, dragged me to the roadside, pointed and said, roughly, "There's your road, kid, follow the street lamps. They'll take you home."

They stood in a little group watching me, nervous now, ashamed a little at the ferocious pack impulse toward the outsider that had swept over them.

I never forgot that moment.

I went because I had to, down that road with the wind moving in the fields. I went slowly from one spot of light to another and in between I thought the things a child thinks, so that I did not stop at any house nor ask anyone to help me when I came to the lighted streets.

I had discovered evil. It was a monstrous and corroding knowledge. It could not be told to adults because it was the evil of childhood in which no one believes. I was alone with it in the dark.

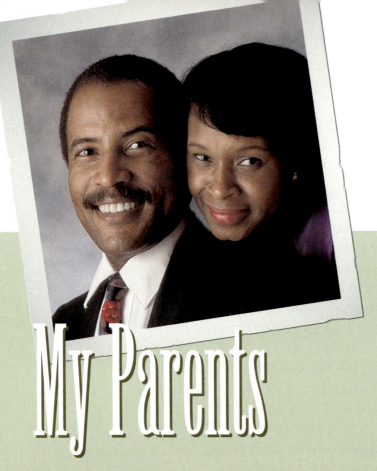

My Parents

Stephen Spender

My parents kept me from children who were rough
Who threw words like stones and wore torn clothes
Their thighs showed through rags they ran in the street
And climbed cliffs and stripped by the country streams.

5   I feared more than tigers their muscles like iron
Their jerking hands and their knees tight on my arms
I feared the salt coarse pointing of those boys
Who copied my lisp behind me on the road.

They were lithe they sprang out behind hedges
10   Like dogs to bark at my world. They threw mud
While I looked the other way, pretending to smile.
I longed to forgive them but they never smiled.

Meet the Writers

Loren Eiseley

A Mysterious World

The archaeologist **Loren Eiseley** (1907–1977) wrote many popular books about the mysteries of existence. His first book, called *The Immense Journey,* was a series of essays about how flowers transformed the earth and prepared it for human life. "The Green Gulch" is from a book called *The Night Country,* an autobiographical account of his childhood experiences in Nebraska. Ray Bradbury commented in his review of *The Night Country* that it "can be read . . . in about three hours. The vibrations from those three hours, however, might well last the rest of your life. . . ." Eiseley's mother was deaf, and Eiseley, an only child, often felt he shared her silent, lonely world.

Stephen Spender

A Poet of His Time

As a member of the Oxford Poets, a group of young British poets who first achieved recognition during the 1930s, **Stephen Spender** (1909–1995) tried to incorporate the modern world into his poetry. He sought to discover beauty and order in a world shaken by an economic depression and the advance of World War II.

Spender once said:

> **❝I began to realize that unpoetic-seeming things were material for poetry. . . . The poet, instead of having to set himself apart from his time, could create out of an acceptance of it.❞**

Spender was born and raised in London, England, where he attended school. As a teenager he had his own small-scale hand-run printing press. He printed his first collection of poems on this press, as well as the first poetry collection of the famed poet W. H. Auden. Spender met him while attending the University of Oxford, where Auden served as his mentor.

Writing Workshop

SKILLS FOCUS

Writing Skills
Write an informative report.

EXPOSITORY WRITING
Informative Report

Research frequently begins with a question about some subject that interests you. The answers to your question may be found in a variety of informational sources that you will need to locate and investigate. The success of your report will depend on how well you select and use evidence to support your **thesis,** the controlling idea of your paper. In this workshop you'll find, organize, and present information about someone or something from history.

Prewriting

1 Choosing a Subject

Consider the following **prompt:**

> The past is the key to the present. Through understanding people and events that have helped to shape history, we gain insight into our own times. Think of an influential individual or event to investigate as the subject of your informative report.

Brainstorm a list of possible historical figures or events to research. To keep your subject focused and manageable—not too broad—frame a question that will guide your research. For example, if you were to choose as your subject the Indian leader Mohandas K. Gandhi, you might ask this question: *How did Gandhi develop his philosophy of nonviolent resistance?* (See Student Model, pages 220–221.)

CALVIN AND HOBBES © Watterson.
Reprinted with permission of UNIVERSAL PRESS SYNDICATE. All Rights Reserved.

Freewriting is a very good way to begin discovering your answer to this guide question. Remember, no one will see your freewrite but you, so you have complete freedom to explore your ideas. You'll find that you know more than you think you do about some aspects of your topic; you'll also find that you have gaps and lingering questions that will help you direct your research.

2 Finding and Evaluating Sources

Plan to use at least three sources of information for your report. Whenever possible, use **primary sources,** such as maps, diaries, and letters. **Secondary sources** are interpretations of primary materials. They include encyclopedia entries, newspaper articles, and documentaries. You can access both primary and secondary sources on a computer, and you may be able to get additional historical information from colleges, museums, government offices, and experts in the field.

Evaluate every source before you begin taking notes, using the following questions:

- Is the source factual (nonfiction)?
- Is the information up-to-date?
- Is the information trustworthy?

3 Taking Notes

- As you take notes, make a list of your sources, and give each source a number. Record each fact or idea on a separate note card or sheet of paper. Label every note with its source number and the page number(s) on which the information is located in that source.

- **Paraphrase,** or restate, information in your own words. If you wish to copy any material word for word, be sure to put quotation marks around it in your notes. You'll need to give credit to the original source for each quotation you use in your report and for each idea that is not your own.

- Keep your research question in mind as you write down facts, statistics, examples, and quotations that help answer the research question. Remember to stay focused on a very specific aspect of your subject area.

Questions to Guide Your Research

- How were our lives changed by a single individual or event?
- How did this individual contribute to or affect a moment in history?
- Why is this historical event important and memorable?

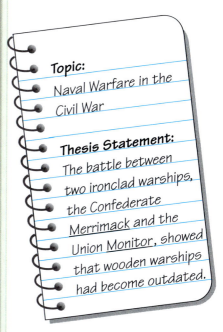

Topic:
Naval Warfare in the Civil War

Thesis Statement:
The battle between two ironclad warships, the Confederate Merrimack and the Union Monitor, showed that wooden warships had become outdated.

Framework for an Informative Report

- **Introduction:** Hooks reader's interest; clearly identifies subject of report
- **Body:** Discusses each main idea in one or more paragraphs; supports each main idea with facts, examples, and quotations
- **Conclusion:** Summarizes or restates main idea(s); draws conclusions
- **Bibliography:** Lists sources alphabetically

Communications Handbook
H E L P

Listing Sources and Taking Notes

Summarizing, Paraphrasing, and Outlining

INTERNET

More Writer's Models

Keyword: LE5 8-2

4 Writing a Thesis Statement

Your **thesis statement** tells what the point of the paper will be. It usually appears in your introductory paragraph. Your thesis should state both the topic of your paper and the most important conclusion you've drawn from your research.

5 Organizing the Report

Organize important information in an outline. Sort your notes into several major categories; then, divide them further into subtopics, each to be developed into a full paragraph. Decide how you will organize the information in your report—by order of importance or in chronological (time) order—and record your plan.

Your report should include an introduction, a body, and a conclusion. In your conclusion, summarize and draw conclusions from the information you gathered. You may also raise unanswered questions.

Drafting

1 Getting Started

As you write, you may decide to rearrange your ideas, take out information, or add new information. Keep referring to your notes, and go back to your sources if you need more information.

Use your own words. If you quote from a source, be sure to give the writer credit. Using a writer's words without crediting the source is called **plagiarism,** or literary theft.

Student Model

This is an excerpt from a report about the Indian leader Mohandas K. Gandhi.

Gandhi was educated as a lawyer. Born in India, a country that was under British rule,

Introduces and describes **subject:** *Gandhi.*

he became the principal leader of the drive for India's independence from Britain. Gandhi was a deeply religious man who believed in eliminating the oppression of his people by the British without the use of force.

According to the *World Book Encyclopedia,* Gandhi was educated in London and spent over twenty years practicing law in South Africa. During this period in South Africa, he chose to claim his rights as a British subject, but since he was Indian, he was discriminated against by the government. As was the custom, Gandhi was married at age thirteen to a wife chosen for him by his family. He was assassinated in 1948 at the age of seventy-eight.

The discrimination that Gandhi experienced during his life, and in particular the treatment he received while in South Africa, led him to believe that persons of all faiths, cultures, creeds, and beliefs should be able to live together equally. He used fasting to express this belief and once fasted for one week to get the Hindus and Muslims of India to stop fighting. As a result of that fast, the fighting stopped. Gandhi believed people could work out their disagreements through nonviolent confrontation, that is, without fighting.

— Spencer Duncan,
Topeka West High School,
Topeka, Kansas

*States **main idea:** Gandhi's belief in non-violence.*

*Mentions **source** for more facts about Gandhi's life.*

Tells what caused his beliefs.

*Describes his use of fasting with a **specific example** and its results.*

*Restates **main idea:** Gandhi's belief in non-violence.*

Strategies For Elaboration

In order to elaborate each main idea, look through your notes to find relevant

- facts
- explanations
- specific examples
- quotations
- descriptions
- comparisons

Works Cited

Chatterjee, Patricia. Gandhi. New York: S.A.R. Publications, 1996.

Gandhi, Mohandas. Gandhi: An Autobiography. Boston: Beacon Press, 1957.

"Gandhi, Mohandas Karamchand." The World Book Encyclopedia. 1998 ed.

2 Listing Sources

A **bibliography**—a list of works cited—should appear on a separate sheet of paper at the end of your report. You may use the Modern Language Association (MLA) style shown in the Communications Handbook, which gives detailed instructions and examples for citing different kinds of electronic, print, and audiovisual sources. List your sources in alphabetical order by authors' last names. When no author (or editor) is cited, list sources alphabetically by the first word of the title.

Notice how the student writer has represented his sources for his report on Gandhi in the works-cited list on page 221.

Evaluating and Revising

Use this chart to evaluate and revise the content and organization of your report.

Informative Report: Content and Organization Guidelines		
Evaluation Questions	▶ **Tips**	▶ **Revision Techniques**
❶ Does your introduction contain a clear statement of your topic and your thesis?	▶ **Put a star** next to your statement of the report's topic and main point.	▶ **Add** a thesis statement, or **add** to the statement the main point about the topic.
❷ Does each paragraph in the body of your paper develop one subtopic?	▶ **Label** the margin of each paragraph with the subtopic it develops.	▶ **Delete** unrelated ideas, or **rearrange** information into separate paragraphs. **Link** ideas with transitions.
❸ Does each paragraph contain supporting evidence, such as facts, examples, and quotations?	▶ **Highlight** the facts, examples, and quotations that elaborate the subtopic.	▶ **Elaborate,** if necessary, with additional facts and explanations from your notes.
❹ Does your final paragraph adequately sum up your overall findings or conclusions?	▶ **Put a check mark** next to the question or final statement.	▶ **Add** a question that your research did not answer, or **revise** your final statement for clarity.
❺ Have you included at least three sources in the list of works cited?	▶ **Number** the sources listed.	▶ **Add** sources to the works-cited list, if needed, and **add** information from those sources to your report.

On the next page, you'll see the opening paragraphs of an informative report that the writer has revised. Following the model are questions to help you evaluate the revisions.

Revision Model

Before the Civil War, American naval campaigns were fought in wooden warships. The course of naval history changed *, however,* in 1862, when a battle between two ironclad warships, the Confederate <u>Merrimack</u> and the Union <u>Monitor</u>, showed that wooden warships had become outdated.

The <u>Merrimack</u> was equipped with iron-plated armor. *No gunfire could destroy it.* The Union navy retaliated with their own iron-plated ship, the <u>Monitor</u>. *Nevertheless,* Their combat revolutionized naval warfare. The two ships met at Hampton Roads *, Virginia,* on March 9, 1862, and engaged in a four-hour duel. Neither ship was able to damage the other seriously.

PROOFREADING
TIPS

- Check the spelling and capitalization of all proper names in your sources—people, places, and events.
- Follow the correct style for citations, using underlining or quotation marks as necessary.
- Search for errors in grammar and mechanics. A partner can help you double-check your final draft.

PUBLISHING
TIPS

File a copy of your report in your school library for other students' reference.

Evaluating the Revision

1. What details have been added? Why?
2. Where have transitional words or phrases been added? Do they improve the flow of the text? Explain.
3. How have elements been reorganized? Does this reorganization result in greater effectiveness?

Literary Skills

Test Practice

DIRECTIONS: Read this excerpt from an autobiography. Then, answer each question that follows.

This excerpt from an autobiography takes place in Sweden soon after World War II. The narrator, a Polish Jewish girl, and her younger brother had been in Nazi concentration camps. There they both contracted tuberculosis, a lung disease. The children were rescued from the camps and taken to a sanitarium in the Swedish countryside. The narrator has now recovered from her illness and is on her way to a shelter for Polish children in Stockholm, the capital of Sweden.

from No Pretty Pictures: A Child of War
Anita Lobel

It had been explained to me that I had recovered from my illness. I couldn't stay at a house for sick people anymore. When Herr[1] Nillson came to gather me up at the sanitarium, I had to accept that I was going with him alone. My brother was still sick. Lucky, I thought, to be allowed to stay for a little while longer at the sanitarium.

Herr Nillson was taking me to a shelter for Polish refugee kids. "You will like being with people from your own country again," he said. He must have sensed instantly that he had not reassured me. "It is a fine place," he said quietly. "You will see. And it is only temporary," he added. "Don't be frightened."

The trip to Stockholm had taken several hours. My recovery to good health was sending me into unwanted exile, but the journey did not feel like a deportation[2] or a flight. I loved sitting on a train with upholstered seats and watching the winter landscape rush by through the pristinely[3] polished window. In the January cold of Sweden there had been no possibility of sticking my head out an open window and letting the wind whip my face and hair. The hair that had grown to shoulder length and was at last braided into two thick, stubby braids. They were still too short. But there was no more concentration camp stubble to be ashamed of.

We came to a quiet street away from the tramways and neon lights. After a

---

1. **Herr:** Swedish for "Mr."

2. **deportation** (dē'pôr·tā'shən) *n.:* forcible removal; banishment.
3. **pristinely** (pris'tēn'lē) *adv.:* here, to the point of perfect cleanliness.

SKILLS FOCUS

Literary Skills
Understand character motivation.

ride to the third floor in a small cage elevator, we stood in front of a door with a brass plaque with "A. Nillson" engraved on it. Herr Nillson rang the bell. The door was opened by a gaunt lady, in a prim white apron over a brown dress. Except that her gray hair was tightly wound into a bun and her head was not covered in a wimple, she made me think of a Benedictine nun. She curtsied to Herr Nillson. I curtsied to her. She took my little suitcase and my coat and scarf.

"If Miss Stina would be so kind," Herr Nillson said, "our young traveler will have some tea and sandwiches."

I was twelve years old that late January afternoon when I was ushered into A. Nillson's elegant apartment in Stockholm, Sweden. For seven years, in or out of danger, I had lived and slept in hovels[4] or public rooms with many other people. The convent. The concentration camp barracks. The sanitarium. Institutions. Since we had fled with Niania[5] away from Kraków,[6] I had not been in a private place where people had properly arranged tables and chairs and rugs and lamps. And servants.

---

4. **hovels** (huv′əlz) *n.*: small, miserable dwellings; huts.
5. **Niania:** the writer's nanny (a person who cares for young children).
6. **Kraków** (krä′kou′): city in Poland.

"You may sit down," Herr Nillson smiled. In the beautiful sitting room I eased myself cautiously onto the edge of a wooden chair that stood by the door. There were pots with plants by the windows. There were lace curtains. Several paintings on twisted silk cords hung from moldings. There was a rug on the floor that made me think of the old kilim in my parents' apartment in Kraków. One whole wall was covered with books. I heard the sounds of piano music from somewhere in the building.

"No, sit here," Herr Nillson said, pointing to an elegant chair covered in a silky blue striped fabric.

I wished I had been a doll or a puppet. I wished someone would come and bend my arms and legs into the right angles so that I knew how to fit myself properly into the seat of the beautiful chair I had been asked to occupy. I had seen a movie one afternoon in the big hall in the sanitarium. It took place in France. The people moved and posed gracefully in splendid rooms. Ladies in gowns of silk sat on silk sofas and took little sips of tea out of pretty porcelain cups and delicate bites of little cakes. Gentlemen bowed and kissed the hands of the ladies.

I knew my body was clean. There were no lice in my newly grown hair. Or in the seams of the skirt and blouse

Test Practice

and sweater that had come out of a freshly donated bundle. When I carefully eased myself down onto the seat, I could feel my wool stockings pull around my thighs as the home-sewn garters with the buttons dug into my buttocks. I sat on Herr Nillson's silk chair, still fearing that shameful dirt would seep through. In my head there were echoes of the Nazis' shouts.

Herr Nillson sank easily into a large upholstered chair with curved arms.

Stina brought buttered bread and ham and tea on a tray. And cups and linen napkins. I took little bites of my sandwich and held my teacup as delicately as I could. I wanted to stay there with Herr Nillson forever.

Behind him I saw a half-opened door to a small room with a bed. Herr Nillson followed my gaze. "For tonight that is your room," he said. "Early tomorrow we will continue our journey." We both sipped from our teacups.

Herr Nillson told me about the work he did with refugees who had come to Sweden after the war. And about the interesting times I could expect at the Polish shelter and beyond. When it was time to go to bed, Herr Nillson took down a book from his crowded bookshelf. "This is for you," he said. "You may keep this."

Safely tucked in my suitcase were some catechism magazines that had been given out during Sunday school lessons at the sanitarium. And my miniature copy of the New Testament with pages thin and delicate and filled with beautiful pictures of the Holy Family, the gift from Sister Svea. Now I would add another book to my belongings. I thanked Herr Nillson for the volume of Selma Lagerlöf stories. I thanked the stern-looking Stina for the food. Everyone said, "*God natt.*"

I went into my private room and closed the door. Tomorrow I was going to a place that would have no barbed wire around it. There would be no Nazis with guns. There would be no shooting. But again I would be living in an institution. Under the large soft bolster with my head on a pillow edged with lace, I fell asleep reading a tale by Selma Lagerlöf.

1. In this selection from an **autobiography,** the narrator visits —
   A a shelter for Polish refugees
   B Herr Nillson's apartment
   C a Nazi concentration camp
   D a tuberculosis sanitarium

2. The narrator of this story is grateful for the special attention she receives. A character from another autobiography in this chapter is also appreciative of special attention. That **character** is —
   F Harriet Tubman
   G Barbara Frietchie
   H Mrs. Flowers
   J Marguerite

3. The narrator of this story fled with her brother and nanny to escape from the Nazis. Another character in this chapter also ran away from tyranny. That **character** is —
   A Harriet Tubman
   B Barbara Frietchie
   C Mrs. Flowers
   D Marguerite

4. The narrator of this story and Marguerite in "Mrs. Flowers" have similar reactions when they receive a book as a gift. Both girls —
   F are pleased with the gift
   G wish they were able to read
   H refuse to accept the book
   J spill their drinks on the book

5. Although they lived in different times, the narrator of this story and Barbara Frietchie have an experience in common. Both —
   A told off a general
   B protected their flag
   C lived through a war
   D recovered from tuberculosis

6. The writer doesn't tell you what a *sanitarium* is. The word is mentioned twice in the first paragraph. Re-read the surrounding sentences, and use **context clues** to determine which of the following best defines *sanitarium*.
   F Shelter for Polish children
   G Place for sick people
   H Train
   J Concentration camp

7. Both "Mrs. Flowers" and this extract from a book called *No Pretty Pictures* feature all of the following characters *except* a —
   A kind adult who helps a child
   B child who cannot talk
   C child who has suffered from violence
   D child who loves books

Constructed Response

8. What is the **main idea** of this extract from an autobiography?

Test Practice

DIRECTIONS: Read the following two passages. Then, answer each question that follows.

Fragment on Slavery, 1854
Abraham Lincoln

If A can prove, however conclusively, that he may of right enslave B—why may not B snatch the same argument, and prove equally that he may enslave A?

You say A is white, and B is black. It is color, then, the lighter having the right to enslave the darker? Take care. By this rule you are to be slave to the first man you meet with a fairer skin than your own.

You do not mean color exactly? You mean the whites are intellectually the superior of the blacks and, therefore, have the right to enslave them? Take care again. By this rule, you are to be slave to the first man you meet with an intellect superior to your own.

But, say you, it is a question of interest; and, if you can make it your interest, you have the right to enslave another. Very well. And if he can make it his interest, he has the right to enslave you.

from What to the Slave Is the Fourth of July?
From an oration at Rochester, July 5, 1852
Frederick Douglass

Would you have me argue that man is entitled to liberty? that he is the rightful owner of his own body? . . . To do so, would be to make myself ridiculous, and to offer an insult to your understanding. There is not a man beneath the canopy of heaven that does not know that slavery is wrong for him.

What! am I to argue that it is wrong to make men brutes, to rob them of their liberty, to work them without wages, to keep them ignorant of their relations to their fellowmen, to beat them with sticks, to flay[1] their flesh with the lash, to load their limbs with irons, to hunt them with dogs, to sell them at auction, to sunder[2] their families, to knock out their teeth, to burn their flesh, to starve them into obedience and submission to their

---

1. **flay** *v.:* strip the skin off, as by whipping.
2. **sunder** *v.:* drive apart; separate.

SKILLS FOCUS

Reading Skills
Compare texts.

masters? Must I argue that a system, thus marked with blood and stained with pollution, is wrong? No; I will not. . . .

At a time like this, scorching irony, not convincing argument, is needed. . . . We need the storm, the whirlwind, and the earthquake. The feeling of the nation must be quickened; the conscience of the nation must be roused; the

propriety[3] of the nation must be startled; the hypocrisy[4] of the nation must be exposed; and its crimes against God and man must be proclaimed and denounced.

_____

3. **propriety** (prə·prī′ə·tē) *n.:* sense of correct behavior.
4. **hypocrisy** (hi·päk′rə·sē) *n.:* pretense of virtue or goodness.

1. The passage by Abraham Lincoln presents an argument —
   A for light skin
   B against personal interest
   C for slavery
   D against slavery

2. Which of the following statements *best* expresses what Frederick Douglass is saying?
   F Arguments won't work against slavery; passions must be aroused.
   G We should sit down and talk calmly about the evils of slavery.
   H We don't need to do anything; everyone knows slavery is wrong.
   J The world needs more stormy weather and earthquakes.

3. The passage by Abraham Lincoln was intended as a —
   A personal narrative
   B persuasive argument
   C newspaper advertisement
   D poetic description

4. Douglass's passage was intended to do all of the following *except* to —
   F convince
   G rouse to action
   H affect listeners' feelings
   J amuse

5. The **tone** of the passage by Douglass is —
   A detached
   B emotional
   C unfeeling
   D silly

6. The **subject** of both texts is —
   F the Union
   G the Civil War
   H slavery
   J the Fourth of July

Constructed Response

7. What is the **tone** of the passage by Abraham Lincoln?

Collection 2: Skills Review

Vocabulary Skills

Test Practice

Synonyms

DIRECTIONS: Choose the word or phrase that is the best synonym of each underlined word from the literary selections in this collection.

1. Something that is incomprehensible is —
   A not understandable
   B unconvincing
   C invented
   D misspelled

2. To have an incentive is to have —
   F incense
   G a motive
   H an interest
   J an invention

3. If you dispel a crowd, you _____ it.
   A join
   B challenge
   C scatter
   D control

4. A man who is gaunt is —
   F thin
   G heavy
   H disabled
   J muscular

5. If you go someplace with friends but you are grudging about it, you are —
   A unwilling
   B enthusiastic
   C annoyed
   D slow

6. If a rope is pulled taut, it is —
   F loose
   G tight
   H frayed
   J broken

7. If someone is benign, she is —
   A kindly
   B hostile
   C boring
   D sick

8. Lincoln could infuse speeches with feeling. *Infuse* means —
   F omit
   G lengthen
   H fill
   J ruin

9. If a student is intolerant of others, she is _____.
   A accepting
   B unaccepting
   C interested
   D uninterested

SKILLS FOCUS

Vocabulary Skills
Identify synonyms.

Collection 2: Skills Review

Writing Skills

Test Practice

DIRECTIONS: Read this passage from an informative report. Then, answer each question that follows.

(1) Some parasites make their hosts behave strangely. (2) A kind of wasp can make a spider build a home for its larva. (3) According to <u>Nature</u> magazine, the wasp stings the spider to paralyze it and then lays an egg on the spider's abdomen. (4) After the larva hatches, it feeds on the living spider's blood. (5) Then, the larva injects a chemical into the spider that makes the spider spin a special kind of web, one very different from its usual web. (6) In a BBC News Online article, Dr. William Eberhard, a scientist who studies these insects, calls it "the ideal web from the wasp-larva point of view" because it provides "a very solid and durable support." (7) When the web is finished, the larva kills and eats the spider, and then builds its cocoon in the spider's last web. (8) As scientist Fritz Vollrath comments in a Discovery.com article, "The irony is that the poor thing that fed this larva builds it a little shelter as its last act. (9) It makes a gruesome fairy tale."

1. Which of the following would be the **best** thesis for this informative report analyzing the effects of parasites on their hosts?
   A There are many types of parasites found all over the world.
   B A parasite is an organism that lives off another species without providing any benefit to that species.
   C After the larva hatches, it feeds on the living spider's blood.
   D While all parasites benefit from their hosts, their effects on those hosts vary from strange to deadly.

2. Which of the following is a **primary source** the writer could consult for more information on this topic?
   F Dr. Eberhard's Web site containing his research notes
   G an encyclopedia article on the effects of parasites on hosts
   H a newspaper article reporting on how wasps benefit gardeners
   J a magazine article analyzing Dr. Eberhard's research results

3. Which transition might be added to the beginning of sentence 2 to show the relationship of ideas in sentences 1 and 2?
   A By the way,
   B On the other hand,
   C For example,
   D As a result,

4. Which visual resource would **best** support this paragraph?
   F a map showing the habitats of the wasp and spider
   G a chart showing different types of wasps from all over the world
   H a time line showing the stages in the life cycle of the average wasp
   J illustrations showing the two types of webs made by the spider

SKILLS FOCUS

Writing Skills
Analyze an informative report.

Fiction

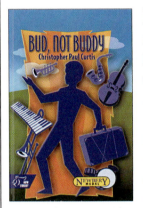

Hard Travelin'

Bud—not Buddy—has had enough bad treatment in orphanages and foster homes, so he runs off in search of his father. Bud has never seen his dad, but he thinks he is a member of the famous jazz band the Dusky Devastators of the Depression!!!!!! Bud finds adventure and trouble in *Bud, Not Buddy.* This heartwarming and hilarious novel by Christopher Paul Curtis won a Newbery Medal.

This title is available in the HRW Library.

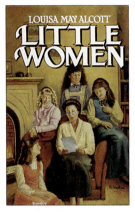

Civil War Sisters

In Louisa May Alcott's *Little Women,* Meg, Jo, Beth, and Amy March—four sisters—grow up in Massachusetts during the Civil War. This rich American classic of family love, a favorite of readers for more than a century, has been made into a movie four times (most recently in 1994).

A Helping Hand

Katherine Ayres's *North by Night: A Story of the Underground Railroad* is made up of fictional journal entries and letters written by sixteen-year-old Lucy Spenser. Lucy has been helping fugitives from slavery reach Canada for four years. When one of the fugitives dies while giving birth to a baby, Lucy is faced with a difficult decision.

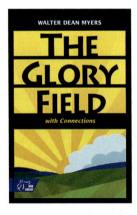

History Lesson

Walter Dean Myers covers 250 years in the lives of an African American family in *The Glory Field.* From the family's early time in Africa until the end of segregation, the members of the Lewis family have supported one another despite persecution. Can they persuade one lost relative to return to their South Carolina home?

This title is available in the HRW Library.

Nonfiction

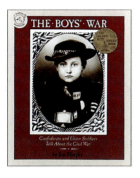

The Eyes of a Child

Grizzled men were not the only soldiers who fought in the Civil War. Many teenagers signed up to fight for both the Union and the Confederate causes. In *The Boys' War,* Jim Murphy tells of the excitement the young soldiers felt as they entered on this new experience and the horror they felt when they came face to face with the grim reality of war.

Master of Disguise

Determined to be a member of the Union army, Emma Edmonds presents herself as a man named Franklin Thompson and is made a private. Seymour Reit details her adventures in *Behind Rebel Lines.* When Edmonds is sent across Confederate lines to spy, she learns not just military secrets but the hardships of being a soldier on any side of a battle.

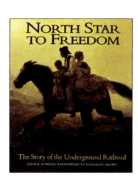

The Path to Freedom

Gena K. Gorrell offers a comprehensive history of the Underground Railroad in *North Star to Freedom: The Story of the Underground Railroad.* You will learn about the importance of figures such as William Lloyd Garrison and Frederick Douglass in the battle against slavery. Newspapers and photographs from the time depict acts of heroism during a tragic period in American history.

Problems in the Pacific

More than a hundred years ago Hawaii was an independent territory that the United States was eager to acquire. However, Hawaii's seventeen-year-old Princess Ka'iulani cherished her country's independence. In *Princess Ka'iulani: Hope of a Nation, Heart of a People,* Sharon Linnéa describes the princess's struggle with the U.S. government and even with members of her own family.

In the Village (1973) by Marc Chagall.
© 2005, Artists Rights Society (ARS), New York/ADAGP, Paris.

CHAGALL MARC

Being There

Literary Focus:
Analyzing Setting and
Its Influence on
Mood and Tone

Informational Focus:
Understanding
Text Structures

go.
hrw
.com

INTERNET
Collection
Resources
Keyword: LE5 8-3

Elements of Literature
Setting *by* Mara Rockliff

YOU ARE THERE

Shipwrecked on a desert island in the novel *Robinson Crusoe*. Hiding from the Nazis in an Amsterdam attic during World War II in the play called *The Diary of Anne Frank*. Wandering through the crazy upside-down world of Lewis Carroll's *Alice's Adventures in Wonderland*. Where and when these famous works of literature take place— their **settings**—are at the heart of everything that happens. Without a setting, there simply would be no story.

Hey, Where Am I?

Opening a new book can be like dropping down the rabbit hole into Wonderland. One minute we're flopped in our favorite chair, feet up, one hand in a bowl of popcorn. The next minute we're in a spaceship on the cold, dark, silent surface of Pluto—or right in the middle of the Battle of Bull Run, bullets whistling past our ears.

Wherever we end up, we count on the writer to make it seem real. The writer can't tell us, "This story takes place in an eighteenth-century Mexican village," and then let the main character, Alfredo, order a large pepperoni pizza on his cell phone. The **customs** in the story have to fit the **time** and **place**.

Writers build believable settings by appealing to our senses. We *see* Alfredo's brightly dyed serape and *feel* the rough texture of the wool as he pulls it over his head. We *hear* his mother calling him down for breakfast and *smell* the sweet tamales in their corn husks before we *taste* them. These details make us feel that we are right there with Alfredo, ready to share whatever adventures come his way.

It Could Only Happen Here

Setting isn't just scenery, a colorful backdrop for the characters to stand in front of as they act out the plot. Setting, character, plot—they're all woven together as closely as the threads in Alfredo's serape. A teenage girl working in a mill factory in New England in the 1840s will not face the same challenges or make the same choices as a teenager trapped in a Chicago bank lobby during an armed robbery.

Sometimes the setting is responsible for the story's main **conflict.** A boy crash-lands alone in the Canadian wilderness, carrying nothing but a hatchet. A group of climbers is determined to reach the summit of Mount Everest, unaware of the deadly storm rolling in. In these situations, setting acts almost like another character, troubling and terrifying the main characters as no human villain ever could.

INTERNET
More About Setting
Keyword: LE5 8-3

SKILLS FOCUS

Literary Skills Analyze setting and its influence on mood and tone.

This Place Has Great Atmosphere

Even when the setting isn't the center of the action, it can still play a key role in creating **tone** and **mood,** or atmosphere. There will always be a murder in a murder mystery—but compare the coziness of a solution arrived at in an English drawing room with the gritty, edgy feel of clues dredged in the sewers. An August afternoon in a Mississippi swamp, a glamorous Hollywood premiere—setting can set a mood.

Language is what creates that setting. When you read a story with a vivid setting, look for words that help you use your senses. Find words that let you *see* the purple towers or the littered street, *smell* the arsenic poison or the musty closets, *hear* the sounds of creaky doors and droning bees, *taste* the hot chilies or the pancake syrup, *feel* the tropical breezes or the Arctic blasts.

Somewhere a Time and Place for Us . . .

When you're picking out something to read, the setting is often the first thing that helps you decide. Would you rather read a story set in a commune in rural America during the 1960s or one set in an Iroquois village in the 1690s? Would you rather immerse yourself in Renaissance Italy or in Tokyo in 2200? We all have special times and places that capture our imaginations. What are your favorites?

Practice

Choose a story you've read recently, perhaps one in this book or a novel you are reading independently. Describe its setting (both time and place) in a sentence or two. Now, choose a different setting for the story—your own neighborhood, for example, or another planet. List three important aspects of the story that would be affected by the switch in settings, and explain how they would change.

Title: _____

Setting: _____

Alternative setting: _____

Changes to the story:

1. _____
2. _____
3. _____

THERE'S NOTHING PRETTIER THAN NEW FALLEN SNOW ON A CLEAR, FREEZING MOONLIT NIGHT.

... THROUGH A WINDOW, THAT IS.

WATTERSON 12·26

CALVIN AND HOBBES ©1988 Watterson. Reprinted with permission of UNIVERSAL PRESS SYNDICATE. All rights reserved.

Making Inferences

by Kylene Beers

Sam gave the lady behind the window $10. She gave him back $2. He went in and gave his ticket to the kid standing by a rope. The kid then moved the rope, and Sam went in another door and started looking for a place to sit. Soon it got dark, so everyone in there got quiet.

Where is Sam? Why did he give the lady $10? Why did she give him back $2? Who was the kid by the rope? Why did the room get dark? To answer those questions, you have to be able to make **inferences.**

So What's an Inference?

Inferring is a way of thinking. You make an **inference** when you take new information, add it to something you already know, and then make an educated guess about what's going on.

Your new information in the top paragraph is that a boy named Sam has $10, he spends $8, the room he sits in gets dark, and then people stop talking. The information you already have is how to subtract (gives $10; gets back $2), where you'd be to need a ticket that costs about $8, and then what kind of place holds a lot of people who all sit in a dark room. You combine the new information with what you already know, and you probably already inferred that Sam went to a movie that cost $8.

INTERNET
More About Dahl
Keyword: LE5 8-3

Reading Skills
Make inferences.

Hints for Making Inferences

1. As you read, ask yourself, "What's the writer telling me about these characters or events that he or she isn't saying directly?"

2. Next, ask yourself what information you could add to what you've read in the story. For instance, if you read that a character suddenly felt afraid, but the writer doesn't tell you why, you'll think of what you know about the character and about what makes us fearful, and you'll guess at all the things he or she could be afraid of.

3. Finally, keep your guesses in mind as you keep reading. Use other information you find to decide if your inferences are correct. In some cases you'll have to revise your inferences as you go along.

"The Green Mamba" is from Roald Dahl's autobiography *Going Solo.* When Dahl was only eighteen, he was hired to work for the eastern staff of the Shell Oil Company. When he was twenty, the company sent him to work in Tanganyika, where he stayed from 1937 to 1939. "The Green Mamba" takes place during this time.

The Green Mamba

Roald Dahl

Oh, those snakes! How I hated them! They were the only fearful thing about Tanganyika,[1] and a newcomer very quickly learned to identify most of them and to know which were deadly and which were simply poisonous. ❶ The killers, apart from the black mambas, were the green mambas, the cobras and the tiny little puff adders that looked very much like small sticks lying motionless in the middle of a dusty path, and so easy to step on. ❷

One Sunday evening I was invited to go and have a sundowner[2] at the house of an Englishman called Fuller who worked in the

---

1. **Tanganyika** (tanʹgən·yēʹkə): former British-controlled territory on the east coast of Africa that joined with Zanzibar in 1964 to form Tanzania.
2. **sundowner** *n.:* evening drink.

As you read, you'll find this open-book sign at certain points in the story: Stop at these points, and do what the prompt asks you to do.

INFER

❶ As you read this selection, think about the information the author gives you and the information you must supply on your own. When you combine what's in the text with what you already know, you are making an **inference.**

INFER

❷ You've just read that snakes "were the only fearful thing about Tanganyika." From that comment, what inference can you make about how the narrator feels about this place?

INFER

❸ Why does the narrator run around to the back of the house while yelling to the family?

Customs office in Dar es Salaam.[3] He lived with his wife and two small children in a plain white wooden house that stood alone some way back from the road in a rough grassy piece of ground with coconut trees scattered about. I was walking across the grass toward the house and was about twenty yards away when I saw a large green snake go gliding straight up the veranda steps of Fuller's house and in through the open front door. The brilliant yellowy-green skin and its great size made me certain it was a green mamba, a creature almost as deadly as the black mamba, and for a few seconds I was so startled and dumbfounded and horrified that I froze to the spot. Then I pulled myself together and ran round to the back of the house shouting, "Mr. Fuller! Mr. Fuller!" ❸ 🔖

Mrs. Fuller popped her head out of an upstairs window. "What on earth's the matter?" she said.

"You've got a large green mamba in your front room!" I shouted. "I saw it go up the veranda steps and right in through the door!"

"Fred!" Mrs. Fuller shouted, turning round. "Fred! Come here!"

Freddy Fuller's round red face appeared at the window beside his wife. "What's up?" he asked.

"There's a green mamba in your living room!" I shouted.

Without hesitation and without wasting time with more questions, he said to me, "Stay there. I'm going to lower the children down to you one at a time." He was completely cool and unruffled. He didn't even raise his voice.

A small girl was lowered down to me by her wrists and I was able to catch her easily by the legs. Then came a small boy. Then Freddy Fuller lowered his wife and I caught her by the waist and put her on the ground. Then came Fuller himself. He hung by his hands from the windowsill and when he let go he landed neatly on his two feet.

We stood in a little group on the grass at the back of the house and I told Fuller exactly what I had seen.

The mother was holding the two children by the hand, one on each side of her. They didn't seem to be particularly alarmed.

"What happens now?" I asked.

"Go down to the road, all of you," Fuller said. "I'm off to fetch the snake-man." He trotted away and got into his small ancient black car and drove off. Mrs. Fuller and the two

---

3. **Dar es Salaam** (där′es sä·läm′): largest city in Tanzania; former capital of Tanganyika.

small children and I went down to the road and sat in the shade of a large mango tree.

"Who is this snake-man?" I asked Mrs. Fuller.

"He is an old Englishman who has been out here for years," Mrs. Fuller said. "He actually *likes* snakes. He understands them and never kills them. He catches them and sells them to zoos and laboratories all over the world. Every native for miles around knows about him and whenever one of them sees a snake, he marks its hiding place and runs, often for great distances, to tell the snake-man. Then the snake-man comes along and captures it. The snake-man's strict rule is that he will never buy a captured snake from the natives."

"Why not?" I asked.

"To discourage them from trying to catch snakes themselves," Mrs. Fuller said. "In his early days he used to buy caught snakes, but so many natives got bitten trying to catch them, and so many died, that he decided to put a stop to it. Now any native who brings in a caught snake, no matter how rare, gets turned away." ❹

"That's good," I said.

"What is the snake-man's name?" I asked.

"Donald Macfarlane," she said. "I believe he's Scottish."

"Is the snake in the house, Mummy?" the small girl asked.

"Yes, darling. But the snake-man is going to get it out."

"He'll bite Jack," the girl said.

INFER

❹ Does the snake-man think he needs to protect the native people?

INFER

❺ Do you think Jack is hiding? Why do you think the mother told the children that?

"Oh, my God!" Mrs. Fuller cried, jumping to her feet. "I forgot about Jack!" She began calling out, "Jack! Come here, Jack! Jack! . . . Jack! . . . Jack!"

The children jumped up as well and all of them started calling to the dog. But no dog came out of the open front door.

"He's bitten Jack!" the small girl cried out. "He must have bitten him!" She began to cry and so did her brother who was a year or so younger than she was. Mrs. Fuller looked grim.

"Jack's probably hiding upstairs," she said. "You know how clever he is." ❺

Mrs. Fuller and I seated ourselves again on the grass, but the children remained standing. In between their tears they went on calling to the dog.

"Would you like me to take you down to the Maddens' house?" their mother asked.

"No!" they cried. "No, no, no! We want Jack!"

"Here's Daddy!" Mrs. Fuller cried, pointing at the tiny black car coming up the road in a swirl of dust. I noticed a long wooden pole sticking out through one of the car windows.

The children ran to meet the car. "Jack's inside the house and he's been bitten by the snake!" they wailed. "We know he's been bitten! He doesn't come when we call him!"

Mr. Fuller and the snake-man got out of the car. The snake-man was small and very old, probably over seventy. He wore leather boots made of thick cowhide and he had long gauntlet-type gloves on his hands made of the same stuff. The gloves reached above his elbows. In his right hand he carried an extraordinary implement, an eight-foot-long wooden pole with a forked end. The two prongs of the fork were made, so it seemed, of black rubber, about an inch thick and quite flexible, and it was clear that if the fork was pressed against the ground the two prongs would bend outward, allowing the neck of the fork to go down as close to the ground as necessary. In his left hand he carried an ordinary brown sack.

Donald Macfarlane, the snake-man, may have been old and small but he was an impressive-looking character. His eyes were pale blue, deep-set in a face round and dark and wrinkled as a walnut. Above the blue eyes, the eyebrows were thick and startlingly white but the hair on his head was almost

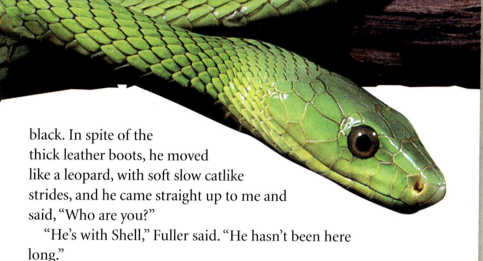

black. In spite of the thick leather boots, he moved like a leopard, with soft slow catlike strides, and he came straight up to me and said, "Who are you?"

"He's with Shell," Fuller said. "He hasn't been here long."

"You want to watch?" the snake-man said to me.

"Watch?" I said, wavering. "Watch? How do you mean watch? I mean where from? Not in the house?"

"You can stand out on the veranda and look through the window," the snake-man said.

"Come on," Fuller said. "We'll both watch."

"Now don't do anything silly," Mrs. Fuller said.

The two children stood there forlorn and miserable, with tears all over their cheeks.

The snake-man and Fuller and I walked over the grass toward the house, and as we approached the veranda steps the snake-man whispered, "Tread softly on the wooden boards or he'll pick up the vibration. Wait until I've gone in, then walk up quietly and stand by the window."

The snake-man went up the steps first and he made absolutely no sound at all with his feet. He moved soft and catlike onto the veranda and straight through the front door and then he quickly but very quietly closed the door behind him.

I felt better with the door closed. What I mean is I felt better for myself. I certainly didn't feel better for the snake-man. I figured he was committing suicide. I followed

INFER

6 Why does the narrator feel better after he sees the mosquito netting over the open window?

INFER

7 Jack died from the snake's bite. Re-read the sentences that describe where Jack is. Do you think he knew the snake was in the room? What clues in those sentences help you make your decision?

Fuller onto the veranda and we both crept over to the window. The window was open, but it had a fine mesh mosquito netting all over it. That made me feel better still. We peered through the netting. **6**

The living room was simple and ordinary, coconut matting on the floor, a red sofa, a coffee table and a couple of armchairs. The dog was sprawled on the matting under the coffee table, a large Airedale with curly brown and black hair. He was stone dead. **7**

The snake-man was standing absolutely still just inside the door of the living room. The brown sack was now slung over his left shoulder and he was grasping the long pole with both hands, holding it out in front of him, parallel to the ground. I couldn't see the snake. I didn't think the snake-man had seen it yet either.

A minute went by . . . two minutes . . . three . . . four . . . five. Nobody moved. There was death in that room. The air was heavy with death and the snake-man stood as motionless as a pillar of stone, with the long rod held out in front of him.

And still he waited. Another minute . . . and another . . . and another.

And now I saw the snake-man beginning to bend his knees. Very slowly he bent his knees until he was almost squatting on the floor, and from that position he tried to peer under the sofa and the armchairs.

And still it didn't look as though he was seeing anything.

Slowly he straightened his legs again, and then his head began to swivel around the room. Over to the right, in the far corner, a staircase led up to the floor above. The snake-man looked at the stairs, and I knew very well what was going through his head. Quite abruptly, he took one step forward and stopped.

Nothing happened.

A moment later I caught sight of the snake. It was lying full-length along the skirting of the right-hand wall, but hidden from the snake-

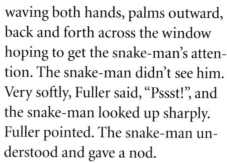

man's view by the back of the sofa. It lay there like a long, beautiful, deadly shaft of green glass, quite motionless, perhaps asleep. It was facing away from us who were at the window, with its small triangular head resting on the matting near the foot of the stairs.

I nudged Fuller and whispered, "It's over there against the wall." I pointed and Fuller saw the snake. At once, he started waving both hands, palms outward, back and forth across the window hoping to get the snake-man's attention. The snake-man didn't see him. Very softly, Fuller said, "Pssst!", and the snake-man looked up sharply. Fuller pointed. The snake-man understood and gave a nod.

Now the snake-man began working his way very very slowly to the back wall of the room so as to get a view of the snake behind the sofa. He never walked on his toes as you or I would have done. His feet remained flat on the ground all the time. The cowhide boots were like moccasins, with neither soles nor heels. Gradually, he worked his way over to the back wall, and from there he was able to see at least the head and two or three feet of the snake itself. ❽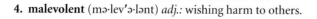

But the snake also saw him. With a movement so fast it was invisible, the snake's head came up about two feet off the floor and the front of the body arched backwards, ready to strike. Almost simultaneously, it bunched its whole body into a series of curves, ready to flash forward.

The snake-man was just a bit too far away from the snake to reach it with the end of his pole. He waited, staring at the snake and the snake stared back at him with two small malevolent[4] black eyes.

Then the snake-man started speaking to the snake. "Come along,

---

4. **malevolent** (mə·lev′ə·lənt) *adj.:* wishing harm to others.

INFER

❽ Why does Macfarlane wear cowhide boots "like moccasins, with neither soles nor heels"? If you need a hint, look back on page 243 at what Macfarlane tells the narrator about walking.

The Green Mamba **245**

my pretty," he whispered in a soft wheedling voice. "There's a good boy. Nobody's going to hurt you. Nobody's going to harm you, my pretty little thing. Just lie still and relax . . ." He took a step forward toward the snake, holding the pole out in front of him.

What the snake did next was so fast that the whole movement couldn't have taken more than a hundredth of a second, like the flick of a camera shutter. There was a green flash as the snake darted forward at least ten feet and struck at the snake-man's leg. Nobody could have got out of the way of that one. I heard the snake's head strike against the thick cowhide boot with a sharp little *crack,* and then at once the head was back in that same deadly backward-curving position, ready to strike again.

"There's a good boy," the snake-man said softly. "There's a clever boy. There's a lovely fellow. You mustn't get excited. Keep calm and everything's going to be all right." As he was speaking, he was slowly lowering the end of the pole until the forked prongs were about twelve inches above the middle of the snake's body. "There's a lovely fellow," he whispered. "There's a good kind little chap. Keep still now, my beauty. Keep still, my pretty. Keep quite still. Daddy's not going to hurt you."

I could see a thin dark trickle of venom running down the snake-man's right boot where the snake had struck.

The snake, head raised and arcing backwards, was as tense as a tight-wound spring and ready to strike again. "Keep still, my lovely," the snake-man whispered. "Don't move now. Keep still. No one's going to hurt you." ❾

Then *wham,* the rubber prongs came down right across the snake's body, about midway along its length, and pinned it to the floor. All I could see was a green blur as the snake thrashed around furiously in an effort to free itself. But the snake-man kept up the pressure on the prongs and the snake was trapped.

What happens next? I wondered. There was no way he could catch hold of that madly twisting flailing length of green muscle with his hands, and even if he could have done so, the head would surely have flashed around and bitten him in the face.

Holding the very end of the eight-foot pole, the snake-man began to work his way round the room until he was at the tail

INFER

❾ The snake-man constantly whisper-talks to the green mamba. Do you think that talking helps the snake calm down? If so, why? If not, then why does the snake-man do it?

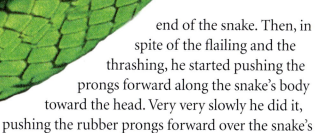

end of the snake. Then, in spite of the flailing and the thrashing, he started pushing the prongs forward along the snake's body toward the head. Very very slowly he did it, pushing the rubber prongs forward over the snake's flailing body, keeping the snake pinned down all the time and pushing, pushing, pushing the long wooden rod forward millimeter by millimeter. It was a fascinating and frightening thing to watch, the little man with white eyebrows and black hair carefully manipulating his long implement and sliding the fork ever so slowly along the length of the twisting snake toward the head. The snake's body was thumping against the coconut matting with such a noise that if you had been upstairs you might have thought two big men were wrestling on the floor.

Then at last the prongs were right behind the head itself, pinning it down, and at that point the snake-man reached forward with one gloved hand and grasped the snake very firmly by the neck. He threw away the pole. He took the sack off his shoulder with his free hand. He lifted the great still-twisting length of the deadly green snake and pushed the head into the sack. Then he let go the head and bundled the rest of the creature in and closed the sack. The sack started jumping about as though there were fifty angry rats inside it, but the snake-man was now totally relaxed and he held the sack casually in one hand as if it contained no more than a few pounds of potatoes. He stooped and picked up his pole from the floor, then he turned and looked toward the window where we were peering in.

"Pity about the dog," he said. "You'd better get it out of the way before the children see it." **10**

For a biography of Roald Dahl, see page 80.

For a biography of Roald Dahl, see page 80.

INFER

10 The snake-man doesn't seem upset about Jack's death. What might his matter-of-fact attitude tell you about how often he's seen what a snake can do?

Making Inferences

PRACTICE 1

Read the three questions below. Then, decide which one you can answer by just referring to the story, which one you can answer based on your own thoughts, and which one requires you to combine information from the story with your own knowledge.

1. Where does Mr. Fuller work?

2. Why does Mr. Fuller lower his children, wife, and himself out of the window and to the ground?

3. Would you like to hold a snake?

Each question requires you to do a different kind of thinking to form the answer. You can answer question 1 by just locating information in the text. Questions like this one test your ability to recall where specific information is located. The second question requires you to make an **inference.** In order to answer it, you have to know from the text that Mr. Fuller thinks there's a very dangerous snake in a room on the first floor of his house and combine that with your knowledge that parents want to protect their children. Question 3 asks you to reflect on your own feelings.

SKILLS FOCUS

Reading Skills
Make inferences.

When you need to make an **inference** to answer a question, try making a chart that looks like this:

It Says	I Say	And So

In the first column, write down the information in the text that helps you answer the question. In the second column, write down what you already know about that topic. In the third column, combine what the text says with what you know to come up with the answer—that will be your **inference**. Here's an example for question 2 from page 248:

It Says	I Say	And So
The text says that newcomers quickly learn which snakes are poisonous and that Fuller has lived there long enough to know this too.	When you know something is dangerous, you'll do anything to keep your family from the danger.	Fuller lowers his family to the ground because he knows how dangerous the snake is. He is afraid to pass through the living room downstairs.

Try answering these questions using a chart like the one above:

1. Why doesn't Mr. Fuller start yelling when he hears that there is a green mamba in his home?

2. Why does Mrs. Fuller tell the children Jack is hiding upstairs?

3. Why does the snake-man keep talking to the snake?

4. How does the snake-man feel about what happened to the dog?

You can use the **It Says, I Say, And So strategy** with the stories in this collection. If you want to make inferences about any story, try this strategy.

In Trouble

Make the Connection

Quickwrite ✏️

Think about settings that have had a strong effect on you. Where were you once very hot or very cold or very scared? What place made you feel especially safe and happy? Pick a setting you have strong feelings about, and jot down details that describe what you saw, heard, smelled, touched, and tasted.

Literary Focus

Setting

Setting is often the first thing a writer tells you about. Here is the opening sentence of "The Landlady": "Billy Weaver had traveled down from London . . . and by the time he got to Bath, it was about nine o'clock in the evening. . . ." Setting can put you in a specific time and place or plunk you down in the middle of another culture. Setting can also affect the story's **mood,** or feeling. You may feel cheerful if you read that it's a sunny day, but you'll probably expect something bad to happen if you read that it's been raining for a week. Sometimes the setting goes even further and takes an active role in the **plot.** This happens when the character is in conflict with a force of nature—a mountain, a parched desert, bitterly cold weather. Setting is key in "In Trouble," as you'll learn in the very first sentence.

INTERNET

Vocabulary Activity

•

More About Paulsen

Keyword: LE5 8-3

Literary Skills
Analyze setting and mood.

Reading Skills
Visualize setting.

Reading Skills 📖

Visualizing Setting

In a story in which setting is key, you have to use your imagination to try to *see* where you are and what is happening. In other words, you have to try to **visualize** what the writer is describing. As you read this story, try to picture where the man is and what his problem is. It may help if you draw a rough sketch of what you see.

Vocabulary Development

You'll meet up with these words as you read the story:

steeped (stēpt) *v.* used as *adj.:* filled with. *The sky was steeped in brilliant colors.*

alleviate (ə·lē′vē·āt′) *v.:* relieve. *Dogs need activities to alleviate boredom.*

contention (kən·ten′shən) *n.:* conflict. *There was contention among the dogs.*

exaltation (eg′zôl·tā′shən) *n.:* great joy. *Paulsen felt a sense of exaltation when he was with his dogs.*

chagrin (shə·grin′) *n.:* embarrassment. *Paulsen felt chagrin over his mistake.*

In Trouble

from *Woodsong*

Gary Paulsen

Background

Literature and Real Life

This selection is taken from *Woodsong*, a book Gary Paulsen wrote about his adventures with dogs. Earlier in the book, Paulsen tells about how he had been trapping coyotes and beavers in Minnesota. He had been covering the sixty miles of his route on foot or on skis until a friend gave him a team of four sled dogs. Those dogs would change his life. "In Trouble" is about some of these changes.

Cold can be very strange. Not the cold felt running from the house to the bus or the car to the store, not the chill in the air on a fall morning, but deep cold.

Serious cold.

Forty, fifty, even sixty below zero—actual temperature, not windchill—seems to change everything. Steel becomes brittle and breaks, shatters; breath taken straight into the throat will freeze the lining and burst blood vessels; eyes exposed too long will freeze; fingers and toes freeze, turn black, and break off. These are all known, normal parts of intense cold.

But it changes beauty as well. Things are steeped in a new clarity, a clear focus. Sound seems to ring and the very air seems to be filled with diamonds when ice crystals form.

On a river in Alaska, while training, I once saw a place where a whirlpool had frozen into a cone, open at the bottom, like a beautiful trap waiting to suck the whole team down. When I stopped to look at it, with the water roaring through at the bottom, the dogs became nervous and stared down into the center as if mystified and were very glad when we moved on.

After a time I stopped trapping. That change—as with many changes—occurred because of the dogs. As mentioned, I had hunted when I was young, trapping and killing many animals. I never thought it wrong until the dogs came. And then it was a simple thing, almost a silly thing, that caused the change.

Columbia had a sense of humor and I saw it.

In the summer the dogs live in the kennel area, each dog with his own house, on a chain that allows him to move in a circle.

They can run only with the wheeled carts on cool nights, and sometimes they get bored being tied up. To alleviate the boredom, we give the dogs large beef bones to chew and play with. They get a new bone every other day or so. These bones are the center of much contention—we call them Bone Wars. Sometimes dogs clear across the kennel will hold their bones up in the air, look at each other, raise their hair, and start growling at each other, posturing and bragging about their bones.

But not Columbia.

Usually Columbia just chewed on his bone until the meat was gone. Then he buried it and waited for the next bone. I never saw him fight or get involved in Bone Wars and I always thought him a simple—perhaps a better word would be primitive—dog, basic and very wolflike, until one day when I was sitting in the kennel.

I had a notebook and I was sitting on the side of Cookie's roof, writing—the dogs are good company for working—when I happened to notice Columbia doing something strange.

He was sitting quietly on the outside edge of his circle, at the maximum length of his chain. With one paw he was pushing his bone—which still had a small bit of meat on it—out and away from him, toward the next circle.

Next to Columbia was a dog named Olaf.

Vocabulary

steeped (stēpt) *v.* used as *adj.*: filled with; saturated; soaked.

alleviate (ə·lē′vē·āt′) *v.*: relieve; reduce.

contention (kən·ten′shən) *n.*: conflict; struggle. Paulsen is playing on the phrase *bone of contention*, meaning "subject about which there is disagreement."

While Columbia was relatively passive, Olaf was very aggressive. Olaf always wanted to fight and he spent much time arguing over bones, females, the weather—anything and everything that caught his fancy. He was much scarred from fighting, with notched ears and lines on his muzzle, but he was a very good dog—strong and honest—and we liked him.

Being next to Columbia, Olaf had tried many times to get him to argue or bluster, but Columbia always ignored him.

Until this morning.

Carefully, slowly, Columbia pushed the bone toward Olaf's circle.

And of all the things that Olaf was—tough, strong, honest—he wasn't smart. As they say, some are smarter than others, and some are still not so smart, and then there was Olaf. It wouldn't be fair to call Olaf dumb—dogs don't measure those things like people—but even in the dog world he would not be known as a whip. Kind of a big bully who was also a bit of a doofus.

When he saw Columbia pushing the bone toward him, he began to reach for it. Straining against his chain, turning and trying to get farther and farther, he reached as far as he could with the middle toe on his right front foot, the claw going out as far as possible.

But not quite far enough. Columbia had measured it to the millimeter. He slowly pushed the bone until it was so close that Olaf's claw—with Olaf straining so hard his eyes bulged—just barely touched it.

Columbia sat back and watched Olaf straining and pushing and fighting, and when this had gone on for a long time—many minutes—and Olaf was still straining for all he was worth, Columbia leaned back and laughed.

"Heh, heh, heh . . ."

Then Columbia walked away.

And I could not kill or trap any longer.

It happened almost that fast. I had seen dogs with compassion for each other and their young and with anger and joy and hate and love, but this humor went into me more than the other things.

It was so complicated.

To make the joke up in his mind, the joke with the bone and the bully, and then set out to do it, carefully and quietly, to do it, then laugh and walk away—all of it was so complicated, so complex, that it triggered a chain reaction in my mind.

If Columbia could do that, I thought, if a dog could do that, then a wolf could do that. If a wolf could do that, then a deer could do that. If a deer could do that, then a beaver, and a squirrel, and a bird, and, and, and . . .

And I quit trapping then.

It was wrong for me to kill.

But I had this problem. I had gone over some kind of line with the dogs, gone back into some primitive state of exaltation that I wanted to study. I wanted to run them and learn from them. But it seemed to be wasteful (the word *immature* also comes to mind) to just run them. I thought I had to have a trap line to justify running the dogs, so I kept the line.

But I did not trap. I ran the country and camped and learned from the dogs and studied where I would have trapped if I were going to trap. I took many imaginary beaver and muskrat but I did no more sets and killed no more animals. I will not kill anymore.

Vocabulary

exaltation (eg′zôl·tā′shən) *n.:* great joy.

Yet the line existed. Somehow in my mind—and until writing this I have never told another person about this—the line still existed and when I had "trapped" in one area, I would extend the line to "trap" in another, as is proper when you actually trap. Somehow the phony trapping gave me a purpose for running the dogs and would until I began to train them for the Iditarod, a dog-sled race across Alaska, which I had read about in *Alaska* magazine.

But it was on one of these "trapping" runs that I got my third lesson,[1] or awakening.

There was a point where an old logging trail went through a small, sharp-sided gully—a tiny canyon. The trail came down one wall of the gully—a drop of fifty or so feet— then scooted across a frozen stream and up the other side. It might have been a game trail that was slightly widened or an old foot trail that had not caved in. Whatever it was, I came onto it in the middle of January. The dogs were very excited. New trails always get them tuned up and they were fairly smoking as we came to the edge of the gully.

I did not know it was there and had been letting them run, not riding the sled brake to slow them, and we virtually shot off the edge.

The dogs stayed on the trail, but I immediately lost all control and went flying out into space with the sled. As I did, I kicked sideways, caught my knee on a sharp snag, and felt the wood enter under the kneecap and tear it loose.

I may have screamed then.

The dogs ran out on the ice of the stream but I fell onto it. As these things often seem to happen, the disaster snowballed.

_____

1. **my third lesson:** The first two lessons are described in the two previous chapters of *Woodsong*.

The trail crossed the stream directly at the top of a small frozen waterfall with about a twenty-foot drop. Later I saw the beauty of it, the falling lobes[2] of blue ice that had grown as the water froze and refroze, layering on itself. . . .

But at the time I saw nothing. I hit the ice of the streambed like dropped meat, bounced once, then slithered over the edge of the waterfall and dropped another twenty feet onto the frozen pond below, landing on the torn and separated kneecap.

I have been injured several times running dogs—cracked rib, a broken left leg, a broken left wrist, various parts frozen or cut or bitten while trying to stop fights—but nothing ever felt like landing on that knee.

I don't think I passed out so much as my brain simply exploded.

Again, I'm relatively certain I must have screamed or grunted, and then I wasn't aware of much for two, perhaps three minutes as I squirmed around trying to regain some part of my mind.

When things settled down to something I could control, I opened my eyes and saw that my snow pants and the jeans beneath were ripped in a jagged line for about a foot. Blood was welling out of the tear, soaking the cloth and the ice underneath the wound.

Shock and pain came in waves and I had to close my eyes several times. All of this was in minutes that seemed like hours, and I realized that I was in serious trouble. Contrary to popular belief, dog teams generally do not stop and wait for a musher[3] who falls off. They keep going, often for many miles.

Lying there on the ice, I knew I could not walk. I didn't think I could stand without some kind of crutch, but I knew I couldn't walk. I was a good twenty miles from home, at least eight or nine miles from any kind of farm or dwelling.

It may as well have been ten thousand miles.

There was some self-pity creeping in, and not a little chagrin at being stupid enough to just let them run when I didn't know the country. I was trying to skootch myself up to the bank of the gully to get into a more comfortable position when I heard a sound over my head.

I looked up, and there was Obeah looking over the top of the waterfall, down at me.

I couldn't at first believe it.

He whined a couple of times, moved back and forth as if he might be going to drag the team over the edge, then disappeared from view. I heard some more whining and growling, then a scrabbling sound, and was amazed to see that he had taken the team back up the side of the gully and dragged them past the waterfall to get on the gully wall just over me.

Vocabulary

chagrin (shə·grin′) *n.*: embarrassment and annoyance caused by disappointment or failure.

---

2. **lobes** *n.*: rounded pieces that jut out.
3. **musher** (mush′ər) *n.*: person who travels over snow by dog sled.

They were in a horrible tangle, but he dragged them along the top until he was well below the waterfall, where he scrambled down the bank with the team almost literally falling on him. They dragged the sled up the frozen streambed to where I was lying.

On the scramble down the bank Obeah had taken them through a thick stand of cockleburs. Great clumps of burs wadded between their ears and down their backs.

He pulled them up to me, concern in his eyes and making a soft whine, and I reached into his ruff and pulled his head down and hugged him and was never so happy to see anybody probably in my life. Then I felt something and looked down to see one of the other dogs—named Duberry—licking the wound in my leg.

She was licking not with the excitement that prey blood would cause but with the gentle licking that she would use when cleaning a pup, a wound lick.

I brushed her head away, fearing infection, but she persisted. After a moment I lay back and let her clean it, still holding on to Obeah's ruff, holding on to a friend.

And later I dragged myself around and untangled them and unloaded part of the sled and crawled in and tied my leg down. We made it home that way, with me sitting in the sled; and later, when my leg was sewed up and healing and I was sitting in my cabin with the leg propped up on pillows by the woodstove; later, when all the pain was gone and I had all the time I needed to think of it . . . later I thought of the dogs.

How they came back to help me, perhaps to save me. I knew that somewhere in the dogs, in their humor and the way they thought, they had great, old knowledge; they had something we had lost.

And the dogs could teach me.

Meet the Writer

Gary Paulsen

"I Had Been Dying of Thirst"

Gary Paulsen (1939–   ) lived all over the United States, as well as in the Philippines, when he was growing up. His father was an army officer who moved the family with each new assignment. Paulsen calls his boyhood a "rough run":

66 The longest time I spent in one school was for about five months. I was an 'Army brat,' and it was a miserable life. School was a nightmare because I was unbelievably shy, and terrible at sports. I had no friends, and teachers ridiculed me. . . .

One day, as I was walking past the public library in twenty-below temperatures, I could see the reading room bathed in a beautiful golden light. I went in to get warm, and to my absolute astonishment the librarian walked up to me and asked if I wanted a library card. She didn't care if I looked right, wore the right clothes, dated the right girls, was popular at sports—none of those prejudices existed in the public library. When she handed me the card, she handed me the world. I can't even describe how liberating it was. She recommended westerns and science fiction but every now and then would slip in a classic. I roared through everything she gave me and in the summer read a book a day. It was as though I had been dying of thirst and the librarian had handed me a five-gallon bucket of water. I drank and drank. 99

For Independent Reading

Woodsong is an autobiography, but Paulsen is best known for his young adult novels. These are two of the most popular:

- *Hatchet*, a thirteen-year-old boy survives alone in the Canadian wilderness.
- *Dogsong*, an Inuit youth treks across Alaska by dog sled.

First Thoughts

1. In your opinion, what is the most important sentence in "In Trouble"? Explain your choice.

Thinking Critically

2. Make a rough diagram illustrating the trick that Columbia plays on Olaf. Explain Columbia's plan in terms of **causes** and **effects.**

3. How does the **setting** contribute to Paulsen's accident and make it worse?

4. Paulsen says of the frozen waterfall he fell over, "Later I saw the beauty of it. . . ." Why doesn't he notice that beauty during the accident?

5. What can you **infer** that Paulsen learns from his accident and from the way his dogs responded?

Reading Check

a. What do you learn about the **setting** in the first three paragraphs of this story?

b. Why does Paulsen stop trapping animals?

c. What mistake leads to Paulsen's accident?

d. How do the dogs react to the accident?

e. Why is Paulsen surprised by the dogs' behavior?

Extending Interpretations

6. As you read about Paulsen's terrible accident, are you able to **visualize** exactly where he is and why he is in such trouble? As you consider this question, discuss the story's illustrations: Do they help you visualize this setting? Did you try drawing this setting yourself? If so, compare your visual interpretation with the artist's.

7. Paulsen concludes by saying of the dogs that "they had great, old knowledge; they had something we had lost." What do you think he means by this?

WRITING

Writing a Descriptive Essay

Write a brief descriptive essay about a place you know very well. Help your readers visualize the place by including details that help them *see* the setting, *smell* it, *hear* it, and perhaps *taste* it and *touch* it. Open your description with a topic statement that tells your readers what place you are going to describe and how you feel about it. Be sure to check your Quickwrite notes before you write.

INTERNET
Projects and Activities
Keyword: LE5 8-3

SKILLS FOCUS

Literary Skills
Analyze setting and mood.

Reading Skills
Visualize setting.

Writing Skills
Write a descriptive essay.

After You Read   Vocabulary Development

Verify Meanings

PRACTICE 1

Show that you understand the words in the Word Bank by answering the following questions.

1. What might cause <u>contention</u> between a person and a dog?

2. How would you <u>alleviate</u> someone's fear of dogs?

3. How would a dog show <u>chagrin</u>? How would you?

4. How would a dog show <u>exaltation</u>? How would you?

5. What is <u>steeped</u> every morning to drink for breakfast?

Word Bank

steeped
alleviate
contention
exaltation
chagrin

Sound-Alikes and Look-Alikes

Homophones (häm′ə·fōnz′) are words that sound the same but have different meanings and spellings. *Bear* and *bare* are homophones. **Homographs** (häm′ə·grafs′) are words that are spelled the same but have different meanings and origins and sometimes different pronunciations. *Wind* (rhymes with *pinned*) and *wind* (rhymes with *mind*) are homographs.

PRACTICE 2

For each sentence below, select the correct word from the two underlined **homophones.**

1. Paulsen felt the <u>would/wood</u> enter under his kneecap.

2. Paulsen hit the ice like a piece of dropped <u>meat/meet</u>.

3. The shock and <u>pain/pane</u> were hard to bear.

4. To steady himself, Paulsen held on to Obeah's <u>ruff/rough</u>.

Answer the question in parentheses about each **homograph.** Be sure to read each sentence <u>aloud</u> (or <u>allowed</u>?).

5. Paulsen felt the sharp snag <u>tear</u> his kneecap loose. (Does *tear* rhyme here with *pear* or *near*?)

6. One of the dogs was licking the <u>wound</u> in Paulsen's leg. (Does *wound* here rhyme with *sound* or *tuned*?)

SKILLS FOCUS

Vocabulary Skills
Verify word meanings by example; understand homophones and homographs.

260   Collection 3 / Being There

Understanding Comparison and Contrast

Reading Focus

Text Structure: Comparison and Contrast

Gary Paulsen describes his dogs as a team and also as individuals. Think for a moment about the dogs you have known. Do you agree that no two dogs are ever alike in personality, even those that have been raised together? Take a moment to complete a Venn diagram for two dogs—or cats or cows—you have known. In each circle, note the animals' differences. In the center, where the circles overlap, note the similarities.

When you note similarities, you are **comparing** features. When you note differences, you are **contrasting** features.

Differences   Similarities   Differences

■ As you read the next selection, watch for the ways in which the writer provides you with information about each breed. Where is comparison used? Where is contrast used?

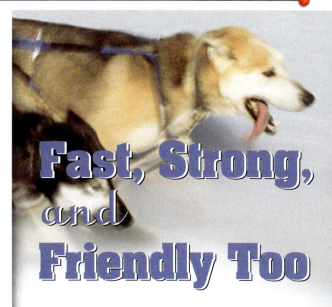

Fast, Strong, and Friendly Too

In October 1999, a team of 230 huskies hauled a big-rig Kenworth flatbed truck with a huge load up Front Street in Whitehorse, Yukon Territory, Canada. The truck and load weighed 110,000 pounds.

Who were these dogs that performed this amazing feat? Huskies are thick-coated working dogs of the Arctic, often used as sled dogs. They can be of a number of breeds, including Siberian husky, Samoyed, and Alaskan malamute.

Siberian huskies are the typical sled dog. They were bred originally by the Chukchi people of Siberia, in northeastern Asia. The Chukchi trained them to run at a fast pace over great distances. That background probably accounts for the ability of the

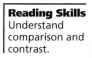

Reading Skills
Understand comparison and contrast.

Siberian huskies to win races. For many years they won most of the dog-team-racing titles in Alaska. Their great endurance makes them ideally suited to take on the rugged terrain of the North.

The Chukchi upbringing may also account for the dogs' friendly nature. Siberian huskies are particularly good with children, and Chukchi tots were encouraged to play with the dogs.

Of all modern dog breeds the Samoyed is the one most closely related to the first ancestor dog. No wolf or fox bloodlines run in the Samoyed strain. For centuries the Samoyed has been bred true in its homeland—the vast stretches of tundra reaching from the White Sea to the Yenisei River in central Siberia. There they served as sled dogs, reindeer guards, and household companions.

Many dog lovers believe the Samoyed to be the ultimate canine companion. After centuries of living with humankind, this white-furred, smiling-faced dog has developed an almost uncanny understanding of people. Samoyeds are intelligent and good-natured; they always protect and never hurt their human families. Some people consider Samoyeds to be the most beautiful dogs in existence.

Alaskan malamutes are the largest of the sled dogs, standing some twenty-four inches high. These powerful-looking dogs have remarkable endurance and fortitude. They were bred in upper western Alaska by an Inuit people called Mahlemuts, or Malemutes. Like Siberian huskies and Samoyeds, Alaskan malamutes are known for their loyalty, understanding, and intelligence.

While Alaskan malamutes are the largest of the sled dogs, the smallest dog that *looks* like one is the American Eskimo dog. No one knows why the Eskie is called an Eskimo dog. This miniature animal probably couldn't find its way out of a tall northern snowbank. At nine inches short, the toy-sized Eskie looks like a full-sized sled dog in the same way that a toy version of a big-rig Kenworth flatbed truck looks like a full-sized one. Can't you just see it? Two hundred thirty less-than-one-foot-tall Eskies hauling a toy-sized big rig up Front Street in Whitehorse, Yukon Territory, Canada.

—Flo Ota De Lange

Analyzing a Comparison–Contrast Article

Fast, Strong, and Friendly Too

Test Practice

1. The writer says that all the following breeds have been used as sled dogs *except* the —
   A Alaskan malamute
   B Siberian husky
   C Samoyed
   D American Eskimo dog

2. Samoyeds are different from Siberian huskies and Alaskan malamutes in that they —
   F have no wolf bloodlines in their strain
   G are intelligent and loyal
   H are strong and hardworking
   J like to play with children

3. The largest sled dog is the —
   A Alaskan malamute
   B Siberian husky
   C Samoyed
   D American Eskimo dog

4. The smallest dog that looks like a sled dog is the —
   F Siberian husky
   G Samoyed
   H Alaskan malamute
   J American Eskimo dog

Constructed Response

To **compare** and **contrast** the four breeds of dog you have just read about, complete a chart like the one below. It works on the same principle as the Venn diagram you filled in before reading the article, but it allows you to compare and contrast four things instead of just two.

Breed of Dog	Distinct Features	Similarities to Other Breeds
Siberian husky		
Samoyed		
Alaskan malamute		
American Eskimo dog		

SKILLS FOCUS

Reading Skills
Analyze a comparison-contrast article.

Context Clues: Reading Closely

Using a word's context—or surrounding words—to discover its meaning is especially useful when you're reading unfamiliar factual material.

PRACTICE

For each underlined word in the following passages from "Fast, Strong, and Friendly Too," fill in a chart like the one below. On a separate sheet of paper, write down your best guess at the word's meaning, and list the context clues in the passage that led you to that guess. Then, look up the dictionary definition. How close did you come? The first item has been completed for you.

1. "Of all modern dog breeds the Samoyed is the one most closely related to the first <u>ancestor</u> dog. No wolf or fox bloodlines run in the Samoyed strain. For centuries the Samoyed has been bred true in its homeland. . . ."

ancestor	My best guess: original (very first)
Context clues: first dog bred true no wolf or fox bloodlines	Dictionary definition: forefather; forebear further back in generations than a grandparent

2. "For many years [Siberian huskies] won most of the dog-team-racing titles in Alaska. Their great <u>endurance</u> makes them ideally suited to take on the rugged <u>terrain</u> of the north."

3. "For centuries the Samoyed has been bred true in its home-land—the <u>vast</u> stretches of <u>tundra</u> reaching from the White Sea to the Yenisei River in central Siberia."

4. "Many dog lovers believe the Samoyed to be the ultimate <u>canine</u> companion."

5. "After centuries of living with humankind, this white-furred, smiling-faced dog has developed an almost <u>uncanny</u> understanding of people."

6. "[Alaskan malamutes] were bred in upper western Alaska by an <u>Inuit</u> people called Mahlemuts, or Malemutes."

SKILLS FOCUS

Vocabulary Skills
Use context clues.

There Will Come Soft Rains

Make the Connection
Quickwrite 🖍

New technology changes the way people live. At the start of the twentieth century, most people had no cars, no electricity, no telephones. Most people didn't even have indoor toilets or running water. If someone had predicted an invention like the World Wide Web, people would have laughed. No one at that time could have imagined the way we live today. Jot down your ideas about what life might be like a hundred years from now. How do you think new technology will affect our lives?

Literary Focus
Setting as Character

The setting of Gary Paulsen's "In Trouble" plays a major role in the story. An accident on a frozen riverbank miles from human habitation creates a life-threatening situation. In some stories the setting is even more important; it becomes a **character** in the story. If the dogs had not returned to rescue him, Paulsen might have been forced to battle a deadly opponent—the frozen setting. As you read "There Will Come Soft Rains," you may be surprised at just how important a role the setting plays.

Reading Skills 📖
Text Structures: Chronology

Have you ever asked a question like this after seeing a movie: "Did the holdup take place *before* or *after* the phone rang?" If you have, you were asking about chronology. **Chronology** is time order—what happens first, next, and last. A story written in **chronological order** presents events in the time sequence in which they occurred, one after the other.

As you read "There Will Come Soft Rains," use your reading notes to keep track of what's happening from hour to hour.

Vocabulary Development

You'll learn these words as you read this story:

paranoia (par′ə·noi′ə) *n.:* mental disorder that causes people to feel unreasonable distrust and suspicion. *The house was so concerned with self-protection that it almost seemed to suffer from paranoia.*

cavorting (kə·vôrt′iŋ) *v.* used as *adj.:* leaping about. *Images of panthers could be seen cavorting on the walls of the nursery.*

tremulous (trem′yo͞o·ləs) *adj.:* trembling. *The tremulous branches swayed in the night breezes.*

oblivious (ə·bliv′ē·əs) *adj.:* unaware. *The mechanical house was oblivious of events in the world outside.*

sublime (sə·blīm′) *adj.:* majestic; grand. *The sublime poetry was recited until the very end.*

INTERNET

Vocabulary Activity
•
Cross-curricular Connection

Keyword: LE5 8-3

SKILLS FOCUS

Literary Skills
Understand the role of setting.

Reading Skills
Understand chronological order.

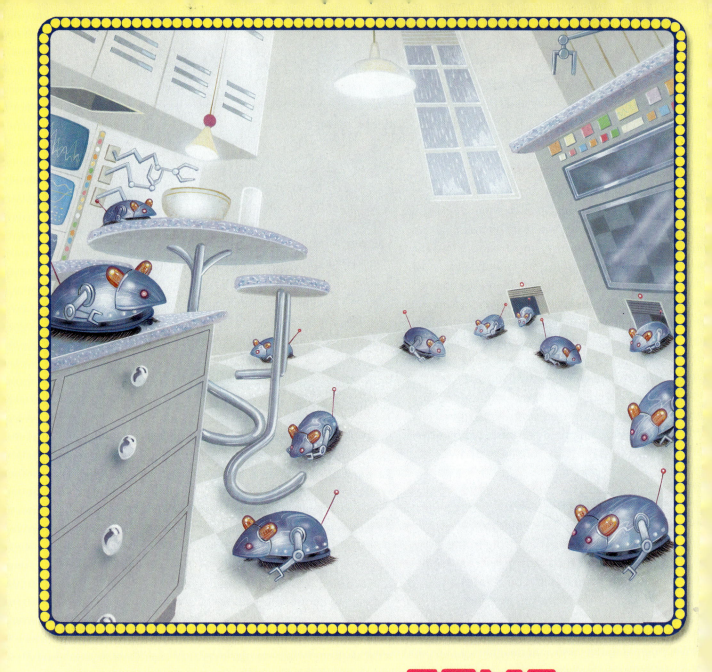

THERE WILL COME SOFT RAINS

Ray Bradbury

7:00 In the living room the voice-clock sang, *Ticktock, seven o'clock, time to get up, time to get up, seven o'clock!* as if it were afraid that nobody would. The morning house lay empty. The clock ticked on, repeating and repeating its sounds into the emptiness. *Seven-nine, breakfast time, seven-nine!*

In the kitchen the breakfast stove gave a hissing sigh and ejected from its warm interior eight pieces of perfectly browned toast, eight eggs sunny side up, sixteen slices of bacon, and two coffees.

"Today is August 4, 2026," said a second voice from the kitchen ceiling, "in the city of Allendale, California." It repeated the date three times for memory's sake. "Today is Mr. Featherstone's birthday. Today is the anniversary of Tilita's marriage. Insurance is payable, as are the water, gas, and light bills."

Somewhere in the walls, relays clicked, memory tapes glided under electric eyes.

8:01 *Eight-one, tick-tock, eight-one o'clock, off to school, off to work, run, run, eight-one!* But no doors slammed, no carpets took the soft tread of rubber heels. It was raining outside. The weather box on the front door sang quietly: "Rain, rain, go away; rubbers, raincoats for today . . ." And the rain tapped on the empty house, echoing.

Outside, the garage chimed and lifted its door to reveal the waiting car. After a long wait the door swung down again.

At eight-thirty the eggs were shriveled and the toast was like stone. An aluminum wedge scraped them into the sink, where hot water whirled them down a metal throat which digested and flushed them away to the distant sea. The dirty dishes were dropped into a hot washer and emerged twinkling dry.

Nine-fifteen, sang the clock, *time to clean.*

Out of warrens[1] in the wall, tiny robot mice darted. The rooms were acrawl with the small cleaning animals, all rubber and metal. They thudded against chairs, whirling their moustached runners, kneading the rug nap, sucking gently at hidden dust. Then, like mysterious invaders, they popped into their burrows. Their pink electric eyes faded. The house was clean.

10:00 *Ten o'clock.* The sun came out from behind the rain. The house stood alone in a city of rubble and ashes. This was the one house left standing. At night the ruined city gave off a radioactive glow which could be seen for miles.

Ten-fifteen. The garden sprinklers whirled up in golden founts, filling the soft morning air with scatterings of brightness. The water pelted windowpanes, running down the charred west side where the house had been burned evenly free of its white paint. The entire west face of the house was black, save for five places. Here the silhouette in paint of a man mowing a lawn. Here, as in a photograph, a woman bent to pick flowers. Still farther over, their images burned on wood in one titanic instant, a small boy, hands flung into the air; higher up, the image of a thrown ball, and opposite him a girl, hands raised to catch a ball which never came down.

The five spots of paint—the man, the woman, the children, the ball—remained. The rest was a thin charcoaled layer.

The gentle sprinkler rain filled the garden with falling light.

Until this day, how well the house had

---

1. **warrens** *n.:* small, crowded spaces. The little holes in the ground in which rabbits live are called warrens.

kept its peace. How carefully it had inquired, "Who goes there? What's the password?" and, getting no answer from lonely foxes and whining cats, it had shut up its windows and drawn shades in an old-maidenly preoccupation with self-protection which bordered on a mechanical paranoia.

It quivered at each sound, the house did. If a sparrow brushed a window, the shade snapped up. The bird, startled, flew off! No, not even a bird must touch the house!

The house was an altar with ten thousand attendants, big, small, servicing, attending, in choirs. But the gods had gone away, and the ritual of the religion continued senselessly, uselessly.

12:00 *Twelve noon.*
A dog whined, shivering, on the front porch.

The front door recognized the dog voice and opened. The dog, once huge and fleshy, but now gone to bone and covered with sores, moved in and through the house, tracking mud. Behind it whirred angry mice, angry at having to pick up mud, angry at inconvenience.

For not a leaf fragment blew under the door but what the wall panels flipped open and the copper scrap rats flashed swiftly out. The offending dust, hair, or paper, seized in miniature steel jaws, was raced back to the burrows. There, down tubes which fed into the cellar, it was dropped into the sighing vent of an incinerator which sat like evil Baal[2] in a dark corner.

The dog ran upstairs, hysterically yelping to each door, at last realizing, as the house realized, that only silence was here.

---

2. **Baal** (bā′əl): in the Bible, the god of Canaan, whom the Israelites came to regard as a false god.

It sniffed the air and scratched the kitchen door. Behind the door, the stove was making pancakes which filled the house with a rich baked odor and the scent of maple syrup.

The dog frothed at the mouth, lying at the door, sniffing, its eyes turned to fire. It ran wildly in circles, biting at its tail, spun in a frenzy, and died. It lay in the parlor for an hour.

2:00 *Two o'clock,* sang a voice.
Delicately sensing decay at last, the regiments of mice hummed out as softly as blown gray leaves in an electrical wind.

Two-fifteen.
The dog was gone.

In the cellar, the incinerator glowed suddenly and a whirl of sparks leaped up the chimney.

Two thirty-five.
Bridge tables sprouted from patio walls. Playing cards fluttered onto pads in a shower of pips.[3] Martinis manifested on an oaken bench with egg-salad sandwiches. Music played.

But the tables were silent and the cards untouched.

At four o'clock the tables folded like great butterflies back through the paneled walls.

Four-thirty.
The nursery walls glowed. Animals took shape: yellow giraffes, blue lions, pink antelopes, lilac panthers cavorting in crystal

---

3. **pips** *n.:* figures on cards.

Vocabulary

paranoia (par′ə·noi′ə) *n.:* mental disorder that causes people to believe they are being persecuted; false suspicions.

cavorting (kə·vôrt′iŋ) *v.* used as *adj.:* leaping about; frolicking.

substance. The walls were glass. They looked out upon color and fantasy. Hidden films clocked through well-oiled sprockets,[4] and the walls lived. The nursery floor was woven to resemble a crisp cereal[5] meadow. Over this ran aluminum roaches and iron crickets, and in the hot, still air butterflies of delicate red tissue wavered among the sharp aromas of animal spoors![6] There was the sound like a great matted yellow hive of bees within a dark bellows, the lazy bumble of a purring lion. And there was the patter of okapi[7] feet and the murmur of a fresh jungle rain, like other hoofs, falling upon the summer-starched grass. Now the walls dissolved into distances of parched weed, mile on mile, and warm endless sky. The animals drew away into thorn brakes[8] and water holes.

It was the children's hour.

 Five o'clock. The bath filled with clear hot water.

Six, seven, eight o'clock. The dinner dishes manipulated like magic tricks, and in the study a *click.* In the metal stand opposite the hearth where a fire now blazed up warmly, a cigar popped out, half an inch of soft gray ash on it, smoking, waiting.

Nine o'clock. The beds warmed their hidden circuits, for nights were cool here.

Nine-five. A voice spoke from the study ceiling:

"Mrs. McClellan, which poem would you like this evening?"

The house was silent.

The voice said at last, "Since you express no preference, I shall select a poem at random." Quiet music rose to back the voice. "Sara Teasdale. As I recall, your favorite. . . .

> *There will come soft rains and the smell of*
> *the ground,*
> *And swallows circling with their shimmer-*
> *ing sound;*
>
> *And frogs in the pools singing at night,*
> *And wild plum trees in <u>tremulous</u> white;*
>
> *Robins will wear their feathery fire,*
> *Whistling their whims on a low fence-wire;*
>
> *And not one will know of the war, not one*
> *Will care at last when it is done.*
>
> *Not one would mind, neither bird nor tree,*
> *If mankind perished utterly;*
>
> *And Spring herself, when she woke at dawn*
> *Would scarcely know that we were gone."*

The fire burned on the stone hearth, and the cigar fell away into a mound of quiet ash on its tray. The empty chairs faced each other between the silent walls, and the music played.

At ten o'clock the house began to die.

The wind blew. A falling tree bough crashed through the kitchen window. Cleaning solvent,[9] bottled, shattered over the stove. The room was ablaze in an instant!

"Fire!" screamed a voice. The house lights flashed, water pumps shot water from the

---

4. **sprockets** *n.:* wheels with points designed to fit into the holes along the edges of a filmstrip.
5. **cereal** *n.:* grasses that produce grain.
6. **spoors** *n.:* animal tracks or droppings.
7. **okapi** (ō·kä′pē) *n.:* African animal related to the giraffe but with a much shorter neck.
8. **thorn brakes:** clumps of thorn bushes; thickets.

---

9. **solvent** *n.:* something that can dissolve something else (here, something that dissolves dirt). *Solvent, dissolve,* and *solution* have the same Latin root, *solvere,* which means "to loosen."

Vocabulary
tremulous (trem′yoo·ləs) *adj.:* trembling.
Tremulous also means "fearful" or "timid."

ceilings. But the solvent spread on the linoleum, licking, eating, under the kitchen door, while the voices took it up in chorus: "Fire, fire, fire!"

The house tried to save itself. Doors sprang tightly shut, but the windows were broken by the heat and the wind blew and sucked upon the fire.

The house gave ground as the fire in ten billion angry sparks moved with flaming ease from room to room and then up the stairs. While scurrying water rats squeaked from the walls, pistoled their water, and ran for more. And the wall sprays let down showers of mechanical rain.

But too late. Somewhere, sighing, a pump shrugged to a stop. The quenching rain ceased. The reserve water supply which had filled baths and washed dishes for many quiet days was gone.

The fire crackled up the stairs. It fed upon Picassos and Matisses[10] in the upper halls, like delicacies, baking off the oily flesh, tenderly crisping the canvases into black shavings.

Now the fire lay in beds, stood in windows, changed the colors of drapes!

And then, reinforcements.

From attic trapdoors, blind robot faces peered down with faucet mouths gushing green chemical.

The fire backed off, as even an elephant must at the sight of a dead snake. Now there were twenty snakes whipping over the floor, killing the fire with a clear cold venom of green froth.

---

10. **Picassos and Matisses:** paintings by Pablo Picasso (1881–1973), a famous Spanish painter and sculptor who worked in France, and by Henri Matisse (än·rē′ mà·tēs′) (1869–1954), a famous French painter.

But the fire was clever. It had sent flame outside the house, up through the attic to the pumps there. An explosion! The attic brain which directed the pumps was shattered into bronze shrapnel on the beams.

The fire rushed back into every closet and felt of the clothes hung there.

The house shuddered, oak bone on bone, its bared skeleton cringing from the heat, its wire, its nerves revealed as if a surgeon had torn the skin off to let the red veins and capillaries quiver in the scalded air. Help, help! Fire! Run, run! Heat snapped mirrors like the first brittle winter ice. And the voices wailed, Fire, fire, run, run, like a tragic nursery rhyme, a dozen voices, high, low, like children dying in a forest, alone, alone. And the voices fading as the wires popped their sheathings[11] like hot chestnuts. One, two, three, four, five voices died.

In the nursery the jungle burned. Blue lions roared, purple giraffes bounded off. The panthers ran in circles, changing color, and ten million animals, running before the fire, vanished off toward a distant steaming river. . . .

Ten more voices died. In the last instant under the fire avalanche, other choruses, oblivious, could be heard announcing the time, playing music, cutting the lawn by remote-control mower, or setting an umbrella frantically out and in, the slamming and opening front door, a thousand things happening, like a clock shop when each clock strikes the hour insanely before or after the other, a scene of maniac confusion, yet unity; singing, screaming, a few last cleaning mice darting bravely out to carry the horrid ashes away! And one voice, with sublime disregard for the situation, read

poetry aloud in the fiery study, until all the film spools burned, until all the wires withered and the circuits cracked.

The fire burst the house and let it slam flat down, puffing out skirts of spark and smoke.

In the kitchen, an instant before the rain of fire and timber, the stove could be seen making breakfasts at a psychopathic[12] rate, ten dozen eggs, six loaves of toast, twenty dozen bacon strips, which, eaten by fire, started the stove working again, hysterically hissing!

The crash. The attic smashing into kitchen and parlor. The parlor into cellar, cellar into subcellar. Deep freeze, armchair, film tapes, circuits, beds, and all like skeletons thrown in a cluttered mound deep under.

Smoke and silence. A great quantity of smoke.

Dawn showed faintly in the east. Among the ruins, one wall stood alone. Within the wall, a last voice said, over and over again and again, even as the sun rose to shine upon the heaped rubble and steam:

"Today is August 5, 2026, today is August 5, 2026, today is . . ."

---

11. **sheathings** *n.*: protective coverings.

12. **psychopathic** (sī′kō·path′ik) *adj.*: insane.

Vocabulary
oblivious (ə·bliv′ē·əs) *adj.*: unaware.
sublime (sə·blīm′) *adj.*: majestic; grand.

Meet the Writer

Ray Bradbury

"My Stories Have Led Me Through My Life"

At the age of twelve, **Ray Bradbury** (1920–   ) wrote his first short stories, in pencil on brown wrapping paper. He's been writing stories—and novels, poems, plays, and screenplays—ever since. Their settings range from Mars and Venus to Ireland and Green Town, a fictional town based on his birthplace, Waukegan, Illinois. Much of Bradbury's writing, like "There Will Come Soft Rains," expresses his belief that advances in science and technology should never come at the expense of human beings.

Bradbury advises young writers to keep writing:

66If you write a hundred short stories and they're all bad, that doesn't mean you've failed. You fail only if you stop writing. I've written about two thousand short stories; I've only published about three hundred, and I feel I'm still learning.99

He follows his own advice and writes nearly every day. Although he has been writing for more than seventy years, he says he is still having fun.

66Writing is supposed to be difficult, agonizing, a dreadful exercise, a terrible occupation. But, you see, my stories have led me through my life. They shout, I follow. They run up and bite me on the leg—I respond by writing down everything that goes on during the bite. When I finish, the idea lets go and runs off.99

For Independent Reading

Try *The Martian Chronicles,* the book in which "There Will Come Soft Rains" appears. Other popular books by Bradbury include the short story collection *The Illustrated Man* and the novel *Fahrenheit 451.*

After You Read   Response and Analysis

First Thoughts

1. Complete the following statement:
   - I thought this story was . . .

Thinking Critically

2. In this story the house, the fire, and the appliances are **personified**—that is, they are described as if they were living, even human, beings. Find three examples of such personification in the text.

3. A fully automated house is not only the **setting** of this story; it is also the main **character.** What does the house do as its life is threatened and then destroyed?

4. On page 267, Bradbury writes, "At night the ruined city gave off a radioactive glow. . . ." What **inference,** or guess based on evidence, can you make to explain what caused this glow and destroyed the house?

5. Compare Bradbury's vision of the future with Sara Teasdale's, on page 269. Why might Bradbury have chosen to include Teasdale's poem in his story?

Extending Interpretations

6. When Bradbury published this story back in 1950, the year 2026 seemed a lot further off than it does today. Describe what you think life in 2026 will be like. Go back to your Quickwrite notes for ideas. ✏

WRITING
Creating an Invention

Invent a new toy or labor-saving device for Bradbury's world of 2026 or for the world you imagined in your Quickwrite. Make a drawing of your invention, and attach a written explanation of what it does and how it works. ✏

> ### Reading Check
> Review the story by listing, in **chronological order,** the main events that take place in the house on August 4, 2026. Now, look at the little digital clocks that indicate the hours. How long does it take for the house to be destroyed?

INTERNET
Projects and Activities
Keyword: LE5 8-3

Dog-wash machine, designed by Kimberly Swift, Canyon Vista Middle School, Austin, Texas.

SKILLS FOCUS

Literary Skills
Analyze the role of setting.

Reading Skills
Analyze chronological order.

Writing Skills
Create and explain an invention.

After You Read   Vocabulary Development

Word Analogies

A **word analogy** (ə·nal′ə·jē) is a word puzzle based on two pairs of words that have the same relationship. The words in each pair might have the same meaning or an opposite meaning, or they might share some other relationship, such as cause and effect or whole to part. For example, in the analogy "*Start* is to *stop* as *hate* is to _____," *start* and *stop* are opposites, so the word that would show the same relationship in the second pair is *love*, the opposite of *hate*.

> **Word Bank**
>
> paranoia
> cavorting
> tremulous
> oblivious
> sublime

PRACTICE 1

On a separate sheet of paper, complete each analogy by writing down the word from the Word Bank that best fits in the blank. These pairs are words with the same meanings or words with opposite meanings.

1. *Weary* is to *tired* as *shaky* is to _____.
2. *Depression* is to *sadness* as _____ is to *suspicion*.
3. *Afraid* is to *frightened* as *majestic* is to _____.
4. *Hit* is to *miss* as *aware* is to _____.
5. *Crying* is to *weeping* as _____ is to *frolicking*.

Words in Context

PRACTICE 2

On a separate sheet of paper, write down the words from the Word Bank that correctly fill the blanks.

The elderly man watched the boys and girls _____ in the meadow. The setting was _____, with mountains rising in all directions. However, instead of enjoying the happy scene, the man was _____ to its charm. In his _____, he imagined that the boys and girls were making fun of him. He shook his cane, _____ with rage, and yelled at them to leave him alone. So they did.

SKILLS FOCUS

Vocabulary Skills
Understand word analogies; use context clues.

274   Collection 3 / Being There

LINK TO "THERE WILL COME SOFT RAINS"

Understanding Text Structures: A Magazine

Reading Focus

Text Structures: Magazines

Some magazines—like *Time* and *Newsweek*—cover a broad range of topics. Others deal with specific topics, such as astronomy and technology (topics that might appeal to Ray Bradbury). No matter what you're interested in, you can probably find a magazine devoted to it.

All About Magazines

Magazines have structural features that tell you what's inside:

- **The cover.** A magazine's cover art and its main headline tell you what the lead article is. Often the cover will have one or two smaller headlines that announce other featured stories.

- **The contents page.** Usually found within the first few pages of a magazine, the contents page lists articles and regular features and tells you what page they are on. *National Geographic World* (now called *National Geographic Kids*), the magazine that the article you are about to read comes from, calls its contents page "Inside this issue."

■ Before you read your next magazine article, take some time to look at the way it's structured. Along with the text, a magazine article may include the following features:

- **A title.** A magazine article usually has a title that is cleverly worded to get your attention.

- **A subtitle.** An article often has a subtitle—a secondary title that tells you more about the article.

- **Illustrations.** An article is usually illustrated with art or photographs that explain or enrich the text. **Captions** usually explain illustrations.

- **Sidebars.** Many articles feature a sidebar or two, short articles set off within the main article that focus on a topic related to the main story.

SKILLS FOCUS

Reading Skills
Understand text structures of magazines.

Destination: MARS

Aline Alexander Newman

IN THE 21ST CENTURY THERE WILL BE LIFE ON MARS— HUMAN LIFE!

SO FAR only robots have visited Mars. Robots are safer and cheaper than manned missions. Scientists used to think sending humans would require hauling three years' worth of oxygen and water (for the round trip as well as the time spent on Mars) and enough rocket fuel to get them home. That's a bulky and expensive way to travel.

However, scientists are studying new ideas that would be less costly and also allow astronauts to "pack light." Using inflatable habitats, producing oxygen and rocket fuel on Mars instead of lugging it all from Earth, and recycling air and water would all lighten the load.

In 1997, engineer John Lewis took part in an experiment designed to see whether four people could survive in a closed-loop life-support system. That means nothing goes to waste—not even a drop of water—no matter where it comes from.

For about three months the crew was sealed inside a three-story chamber at Johnson Space Center in Houston, Texas. They washed their hands in recycled sweat, measured and weighed how much they went to the bathroom, and even drank each other's urine! Sounds disgusting, right? It wasn't. All the body wastes were collected and purified. "Our drinking water was cleaner than water out of a tap," says Lewis....

The Earthlings are coming! The Earthlings are coming!

Engineers at the National Aeronautics and Space Administration (NASA), in Houston, Texas, are preparing to send people to Mars. The mission is not official yet. "But it will happen," says John Connolly, NASA mission designer. "Probably before 2020."

Scientists give many reasons for going: to explore, to learn new things, to find important minerals, and maybe eventually to establish colonies so people can live there. But perhaps the most exciting reason to go is to search for evidence of past or present life, probably microscopic, on Mars.

"I want to believe it's there," says Connolly. "But the surface of Mars is a pretty nasty place. We may have to dig down to where we think it's wetter and warmer."

The mission will require an extended stay on a frozen planet that lacks breathable oxygen and has only trace amounts of water on its surface. Keep reading to learn how NASA is planning to get humans there and then keep them alive and safe.

"OUR EVENTUAL GOAL," explains aerospace engineer Scott Baird, "is to live off the land." In preparation for the astronauts' arrival, a cargo carrier will reach Mars first and drop off a large chemical maker° and inflatable habitat.

It will take six months for astronauts to travel to Mars. Once there, they will study and explore Mars for 500 days before returning to Earth. Their landing craft, expanded with the attached inflatable habitat, will serve as their home away from home.

"It'll be a blast," says Baird. "And by the time the kids of today grow up, they may be able to go."

° **chemical maker:** device that produces oxygen and fuel.

Inside the "can," the nickname for the simulated capsule, the crew lived as they would during a long space voyage. Cut off from the world, they kept busy by exercising, maintaining the life-support systems, and keeping written logs.

COMPARING EARTH AND MARS

Earth	Mars
Nickname: the Blue Planet	Nickname: the Red Planet
Length of day: 23 hours, 56 minutes	Length of day: 24 hours, 37 minutes
Length of year: 365 days	Length of year: 687 Earth days
Moons: one	Moons: two
Planet surface: mostly wet and warm	Planet surface: cold and dry
Atmosphere: 98 percent oxygen and nitrogen mix	Atmosphere: 95 percent carbon dioxide
Weather highlights: temperatures range from below −100°F to above 120°F; most storms wet	Weather highlights: almost always below freezing; dry dust storms

Analyzing a Magazine Article

Destination:

1. In what part of "Destination: Mars" do you learn that the surface of Mars is "a pretty nasty place"?
   - **A** The title
   - **B** The subtitle
   - **C** The caption
   - **D** The sidebar

2. The explanation that accompanies the photo of the "can" is called —
   - **F** a caption
   - **G** a subtitle
   - **H** an illustration
   - **J** a sidebar

3. It is clear that the author of the article got some information from —
   - **A** personal experience
   - **B** interviews
   - **C** photographs
   - **D** travel magazines

4. All of the following statements about Mars are true *except* —
   - **F** it lacks breathable oxygen
   - **G** its surface is warm
   - **H** it has more than one moon
   - **J** it's nicknamed "the Red Planet"

5. According to the article, why have only robots traveled to Mars so far?
   - **A** They are more efficient than humans.
   - **B** They are safer and cheaper to send.
   - **C** They produce their own oxygen and fuel.
   - **D** They are not affected by dry dust storms.

Constructed Response

1. What is the **subtitle** of the article?

2. According to information in the **sidebar,** when is it likely that people will land on Mars?

3. Give some reasons for scientists' wanting to travel to Mars. Where do you find this information?

4. What new ideas are scientists implementing to allow astronauts to "travel light"?

5. Name three differences between Earth and Mars. Where do you find this information?

SKILLS FOCUS

Reading Skills
Analyze a magazine article.

The Circuit

Make the Connection
Quickwrite ✏️

The United States is often called a nation of immigrants, because almost every family has roots in other parts of the world. Draw a line down the middle of a page in your notebook. On the left, list the reasons you think families come to the United States today. On the right, list some of the difficulties you think they face.

Literary Focus
Tone

Tone usually refers to the way a writer feels about a place or a character. Tone is revealed through word choice. In describing a **setting,** for example, a writer might use words that reveal his love for the twisty streets of his neighborhood. His tone will be upbeat, positive. Another writer might use words that suggest her hatred for the muddy fields and pig odor of the farm where she was born. Her tone will be negative. Notice how Francisco Jiménez describes the places where he and his family picked crops in California. How does he feel about these settings?

Reading Skills
Making Inferences

Part of the power of this story comes from the fact that the writer doesn't always tell you exactly what is happening. He depends on you to make **inferences,** or educated guesses based

on clues in the story. As you read, look for the little open-book signs at the end of some paragraphs. Stop at those points to answer the questions that require you to make inferences.

Literary Skills
Analyze tone and setting.

Reading Skills
Make inferences.

Vocabulary Development

These words are used in Francisco Jiménez's story:

circuit (sur′kit) *n.:* regular route of a person doing a certain job. *Panchito and his family followed a crop-picking circuit.*

detect (dē·tekt′) *v.:* discover; notice. *His father did not detect any problems with the car.*

populated (päp′yə·lāt′id) *v.* used as *adj.:* lived in. *The dirt floor was populated by earthworms.*

drone (drōn) *n.:* continuous buzzing sound. *The drone of the insects made the hot day seem hotter.*

instinctively (in·stiŋk′tiv·lē) *adv.:* automatically. *Panchito instinctively hid when he saw the school bus.*

THE CIRCUIT

Cajas de cartón

Francisco Jiménez

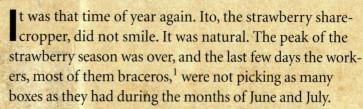

It was that time of year again. Ito, the strawberry share-cropper, did not smile. It was natural. The peak of the strawberry season was over, and the last few days the workers, most of them braceros,[1] were not picking as many boxes as they had during the months of June and July.

As the last days of August disappeared, so did the number of braceros. Sunday, only one—the best picker—came to work. I liked him. Sometimes we talked during our half-hour lunch break. That is how I found out he was from Jalisco,[2] the same state in Mexico my family was from. That Sunday was the last time I saw him.

When the sun had tired and sunk behind the mountains, Ito signaled us that it was time to go home. "Ya esora,"[3] he yelled in his broken Spanish. Those were the words I waited for twelve hours a day, every day, seven days a week, week after week. And the thought of not hearing them again saddened me.

As we drove home, Papá did not say a word. With both hands on the wheel, he stared at the dirt road. My older brother, Roberto, was also silent. He leaned his head back and closed his eyes. Once in a while he cleared from

---

1. **braceros** (brə·ser′ōz) *n.:* Mexican farm laborers brought into the United States for limited periods to harvest crops. *Bracero* comes from the Spanish word *brazo,* meaning "arm."
2. **Jalisco** (hä·lēs′kô).
3. **Ya esora** (yä es·ô′rä): *Ya es hora,* Spanish for "It's time."

---

his throat the dust that blew in from outside.

Yes, it was that time of year. When I opened the front door to the shack, I stopped. Everything we owned was neatly packed in cardboard boxes. Suddenly I felt even more the weight of hours, days, weeks, and months of work. I sat down on a box. The thought of having to move to Fresno and knowing what was in store for me there brought tears to my eyes. ❶

📖 **INFER**
❶ Why is the narrator so sad?

That night I could not sleep. I lay in bed thinking about how much I hated this move.

A little before five o'clock in the morning, Papá woke everyone up. A few minutes later, the yelling and screaming of my little brothers and sisters, for whom the move was a great adventure, broke the silence of dawn. Shortly, the barking of the dogs accompanied them.

While we packed the breakfast dishes, Papá went outside to start the "Carcanchita." That was the name Papá gave his old '38 black Plymouth. He bought it in a used-car lot in Santa Rosa in the winter of 1949. Papá was very proud of his little jalopy. He had a right to be proud of it. He spent a lot of time looking at other cars before buying this one. When he finally chose the Carcanchita, he checked it thoroughly before driving it out of the car lot. He examined every inch of the car. He listened to the motor, tilting his head from side to side like a parrot, trying to detect any noises that spelled car trouble. After being satisfied with the looks and sounds of the car, Papá then insisted on knowing who the original owner was. He never did find out from the car salesman, but he bought the car anyway. Papá figured the original owner must have been an important man, because behind the rear seat of the car he found a blue necktie.

Papá parked the car out in front and left the motor running. "Listo,"[4] he yelled. Without saying a word, Roberto and I began to carry the boxes out to the car. Roberto carried the two big boxes and I carried the two smaller ones. Papá then threw the mattress on top of the car roof and tied it with ropes to the front and rear bumpers.

Everything was packed except Mamá's pot. It was an old, large galvanized pot[5] she had picked up at an army surplus store in Santa María the year I was born. The pot had many dents and nicks, and the more dents and nicks it acquired the more Mamá liked it. "Mi olla,"[6] she used to say proudly.

I held the front door open as Mamá carefully carried out her pot by both handles, making sure not to spill the cooked beans. When she got to the car, Papá reached out to help her with it. Roberto opened the rear car door and Papá gently placed it on the floor behind the front seat. All of us then climbed in. Papá sighed, wiped the sweat off his forehead with his sleeve, and said wearily: "Es todo."[7]

As we drove away, I felt a lump in my throat. I turned around and looked at our little shack for the last time.

At sunset we drove into a labor camp near Fresno. Since Papá did not speak English, Mamá asked the camp foreman if he needed any more workers. "We don't need no more," said the foreman, scratching his head. "Check with Sullivan down the road. Can't

---

4. **listo** (lēs′tô): Spanish for "ready."
5. **galvanized pot:** metal pot plated with zinc.
6. **mi olla** (mē ð′yä): Spanish for "my pot."
7. **Es todo** (es tô′dô): Spanish for "That's all."

Vocabulary
detect (dē·tekt′) v.: discover; notice.

miss him. He lives in a big white house with a fence around it."

When we got there, Mamá walked up to the house. She went through a white gate, past a row of rosebushes, up the stairs to the front door. She rang the doorbell. The porch light went on and a tall, husky man came out. They exchanged a few words. After the man went in, Mamá clasped her hands and hurried back to the car. "We have work! Mr. Sullivan said we can stay there the whole season," she said, gasping and pointing to an old garage near the stables.

The garage was worn out by the years. It had no windows. The walls, eaten by termites, strained to support the roof, full of holes. The dirt floor, populated by earthworms, looked like a gray road map. ❷

INFER
❷ How does the garage contrast with the Sullivans' house? How do you suppose this makes the family feel?

That night, by the light of a kerosene lamp, we unpacked and cleaned our new home. Roberto swept away the loose dirt, leaving the hard ground. Papá plugged the holes in the walls with old newspapers and tin can tops. Mamá fed my little brothers and sisters. Papá and Roberto then brought in the mattress and placed it on the far corner of the garage. "Mamá, you and the little ones sleep on the mattress. Roberto, Panchito, and I will sleep outside under the trees," Papá said.

Early next morning Mr. Sullivan showed us where his crop was, and after breakfast, Papá, Roberto, and I headed for the vineyard to pick.

Around nine o'clock the temperature had risen to almost one hundred degrees. I was completely soaked in sweat and my mouth felt as if I had been chewing on a handkerchief. I walked over to the end of the row, picked up the jug of water we had brought, and began drinking. "Don't drink too much; you'll get sick," Roberto shouted. No sooner had he said that than I felt sick to my stomach. I dropped to my knees and let the jug roll off my hands. I remained motionless with my eyes glued on the hot sandy ground. All I could hear was the drone of insects. Slowly I began to recover. I poured water over my face and neck and watched the dirty water run down my arms to the ground.

I still felt a little dizzy when we took a break to eat lunch. It was past two o'clock, and we sat underneath a large walnut tree that was on the side of the road. While we ate, Papá jotted down the number of boxes we had picked. Roberto drew designs on the ground with a stick. Suddenly I noticed Papá's face turn pale as he looked down the road. "Here comes the school bus," he whispered loudly in alarm. Instinctively, Roberto and I ran and hid in the vineyards. We did not want to get in trouble for not going to school. The neatly dressed boys about my age got off. They carried books under their arms. After they crossed the street, the bus drove away. Roberto and I came out from hiding and joined Papá. "Tienen que tener cuidado,"[8] he warned us. ❸

INFER
❸ Why is Papá alarmed when he sees the school bus?

8. **Tienen que tener cuidado** (tē·e′nen kā te·nār′ kwē·dä′ð): Spanish for "You have to be careful."

Vocabulary

populated (păp′yə·lāt′id) *v.* used as *adj.*: inhabited; lived in or on.

drone (drōn) *n.*: continuous and monotonous buzzing or humming sound.

instinctively (in·stiŋk′tiv·lē) *adv.*: automatically; without thinking.

After lunch we went back to work. The sun kept beating down. The buzzing insects, the wet sweat, and the hot, dry dust made the afternoon seem to last forever. Finally the mountains around the valley reached out and swallowed the sun. Within an hour it was too dark to continue picking. The vines blanketed the grapes, making it difficult to see the bunches.

"Vámonos,"[9] said Papá, signaling to us that it was time to quit work. Papá then took out a pencil and began to figure out how much we had earned our first day. He wrote down numbers, crossed some out, wrote down some more. "Quince,"[10] he murmured.

When we arrived home, we took a cold shower underneath a water hose. We then sat down to eat dinner around some wooden crates that served as a table. Mamá had cooked a special meal for us. We had rice and tortillas with carne con chile, my favorite dish.

The next morning I could hardly move. My body ached all over. I felt little control over my arms and legs. This feeling went on every morning for days until my muscles finally got used to the work.

It was Monday, the first week of November. The grape season was over and I could now go to school. I woke up early that morning and lay in bed, looking at the stars and savoring[11] the thought of not going to work and of starting sixth grade for the first time that year. Since I could not sleep, I decided to get up and join Papá and Roberto at breakfast. I sat at the table across from Roberto, but I kept my head down. I did not want to look up and face him. I knew he was sad. He was not going to school today. He was not going tomorrow, or next week, or next month. He would not go until the cotton season was over, and that was sometime in February. I rubbed my hands together and watched the dry, acid-stained skin fall to the floor in little rolls. ❹

When Papá and Roberto left for work, I felt relief. I walked to the top of a small grade[12] next to the shack and watched the Carcanchita disappear in the distance in a cloud of dust.

📖 **INFER**

❹ What do you infer about the amount of time Roberto can spend in school? How does Roberto feel about it?

---

9. **Vámonos** (vä′mô·nôs): Spanish for "Let's go."
10. **quince** (kēn′sä): Spanish for "fifteen."

11. **savoring** (sā′vər·iŋ) *v.* used as *adj.*: enjoying, as if tasting something delicious.
12. **grade** *n.*: here, hill.

Two hours later, around eight o'clock, I stood by the side of the road waiting for school bus number twenty. When it arrived, I climbed in. Everyone was busy either talking or yelling. I sat in an empty seat in the back.

When the bus stopped in front of the school, I felt very nervous. I looked out the bus window and saw boys and girls carrying books under their arms. I put my hands in my pant pockets and walked to the principal's office. When I entered, I heard a woman's voice say: "May I help you?" I was startled. I had not heard English for months. For a few seconds I remained speechless. I looked at the lady, who waited for an answer. My first instinct was to answer her in Spanish, but I held back. Finally, after struggling for English words, I managed to tell her that I wanted to enroll in the sixth grade. After answering many questions, I was led to the classroom.

Mr. Lema, the sixth-grade teacher, greeted me and assigned me a desk. He then introduced me to the class. I was so nervous and scared at that moment when everyone's eyes were on me that I wished I were with Papá and Roberto picking cotton. After taking roll, Mr. Lema gave the class the assignment for the first hour. "The first thing we have to do this morning is finish reading the story we began yesterday," he said enthusiastically. He walked up to me, handed me an English book, and asked me to read. "We are on page 125," he said politely. When I heard this, I felt my blood rush to my head; I felt dizzy. "Would you like to read?" he asked hesitantly. I opened the book to page 125. My mouth was dry. My eyes began to water. I could not begin. "You can read later," Mr. Lema said understandingly.

For the rest of the reading period I kept getting angrier and angrier with myself. *I should have read,* I thought to myself.

During recess I went into the restroom and opened my English book to page 125. I began to read in a low voice, pretending I was in class. There were many words I did not know. I closed the book and headed back to the classroom.

Mr. Lema was sitting at his desk correcting papers. When I entered he looked up at me and smiled. I felt better. I walked up to him and asked if he could help me with the new words. "Gladly," he said.

The rest of the month I spent my lunch hours working on English with Mr. Lema, my best friend at school.

One Friday, during lunch hour, Mr. Lema asked me to take a walk with him to the music room. "Do you like music?" he asked me as we entered the building.

"Yes, I like corridos,"[13] I answered. He then picked up a trumpet, blew on it, and handed it to me. The sound gave me goose bumps. I knew that sound. I had heard it in many corridos. "How would you like to learn how to play it?" he asked. He must have read my face because before I could answer, he added: "I'll teach you how to play it during our lunch hours."

That day I could hardly wait to get home to tell Papá and Mamá the great news. As I got off the bus, my little brothers and sisters ran up to meet me. They were yelling and screaming. I thought they were happy to see me, but when I opened the door to our shack, I saw that everything we owned was neatly packed in cardboard boxes. ❺

INFER
❺ What do these cardboard boxes reveal?

---

13. **corridos** (cō·rē'dôs) *n.*: Mexican folk ballads.

Meet the Writer

Francisco Jiménez

Francisco Jiménez (1943–   ) was born in Mexico and came to the United States when he was four years old. At the age of six, he started working in the fields. The crop cycle took his family all over southern California. After many difficult years, Jiménez acquired U.S. citizenship and a doctoral degree in Latin American literature. Jiménez has won several awards for his short stories. He writes:

66 'The Circuit' is an autobiographical short story based on my experiences as a child growing up in a family of migrant farm workers. The setting is the San Joaquin Valley, a rich agricultural area in California, where my family made a living working in the fields....

I actually wrote the first version of the story in Spanish when I was a graduate student at Columbia University in 1972, and published it in a Spanish literary magazine in New York City. Later I expanded it and named it 'Cajas de cartón' ('Cardboard Boxes'), which I then translated into English under the title 'The Circuit.' I retitled 'Cajas de cartón' 'The Circuit' rather than 'Cardboard Boxes' because 'Cardboard Boxes' did not sound right to me.

I wrote the original version of 'The Circuit' in Spanish because it was the language in which the events I describe occurred. In fact, I had difficulty finding the exact English words to translate the story because the events I describe in it were not experienced in the English language. This is why I kept some of the Spanish words in the translation. I write in both Spanish and English, but the language I write in is determined by what period in my life I write about. Since Spanish was the dominant language during my childhood, I generally write about those experiences in Spanish. 99

First Thoughts

1. Work with a small group of classmates to illustrate the struggles and dreams of Panchito and his family. (Brainstorm first.)

Thinking Critically

2. Draw a large version of the thought bubble on the left. Fill it with words and symbols showing what Panchito might be thinking and feeling at one of the following points in the story:

• as he enters the school for the first time

• when he comes home and sees the cardboard boxes again

3. The narrator takes time to describe two **settings:** the old garage the family lives in and Mr. Sullivan's vineyard, where they pick grapes. Make two lists of the words that help you feel you are there in each setting. After you have completed each list, write at least one word describing the **tone** of the writer's description.

4. **Setting** is not only a time and a place. What does the setting in this story tell you about the customs, foods, activities, clothing, and lifestyle of the migrant worker?

5. Go back to your Quickwrite chart. Circle any items in either column that you think apply to the family in the story. Then, in a different color, add any new information that you learned from the story.

WRITING

Writing a Letter

What does the **title** of the story mean to you? Do you agree with Jiménez's statement in Meet the Writer that "The Circuit" is a better title than "Cardboard Boxes"? Write a letter to the author giving your responses to these questions. For the "inside address" of your letter, write the name and address of your school.

Reading Check

Fill out this time line to show the main events in Panchito's story. At each point in the time line, sum up what happens to Panchito.

June–
July   Last days
             in August   November   December

INTERNET

Projects and
Activities

Keyword: LE5 8-3

Literary Skills
Analyze tone.

Writing Skills
Write a letter.

Verify Meanings

PRACTICE

1. Which word is related to the word *circuit*?
   a. circumference   **b.** pursuit   **c.** citrus   **d.** electric

2. If Papá <u>detects</u> noises in the car's engine, has he discovered noises, or has he repaired them?

3. Which of these words is related to the word *detect*?
   a. defect   **b.** defeat   **c.** detective   **d.** defective

4. Is Mr. Sullivan's garage fit to be <u>populated</u> by a family? Why or why not?

5. What would the <u>drone</u> of insects sound like? What other sounds could be described as drones?

6. If people act <u>instinctively</u>, are they acting automatically or thoughtfully?

Word Bank

circuit
detect
populated
drone
instinctively

Grammar Link

Personal Pronouns

Here are some rules for choosing between the personal pronoun forms *I* and *me, she* and *her, he* and *him, we* and *us,* and *they* and *them:*

- When the pronoun is the **subject** of the verb, use *I, she, he, we,* or *they.*

  <u>I</u> worked with my family.

  <u>We</u> picked strawberries.

- When the pronoun is the **object** of the verb (the receiver of the action) or the **object** of a preposition, use *me, her, him, us,* or *them.*

  The long hours tired <u>us</u>.

  The hot sun beat down on <u>me</u>.

PRACTICE

For each of the following sentences, choose the correct pronoun from the underlined pair.

1. Papa was proud when <u>he/him</u> bought Carcanchita.

2. The garage served as a home for <u>they/them</u> all.

3. Roberto and <u>I/me</u> hid when the school bus came.

4. Panchito's teacher offered to teach <u>he/him</u> to play the trumpet.

For more help, see Personal Pronouns, 1b, in the Language Handbook.

Understanding Cause and Effect

Reading Focus

Text Structure: Cause and Effect

Human beings are naturally curious (OK, nosy). We like to know the reason (**cause**) for an action or reaction (**effect**). We want to know why (**cause**) something happened (**effect**). We make sense of events (**effects**) by looking carefully at what caused them. We sometimes even want to know what caused our mistakes.

Cause and Effect: It Happens in Real Life

Let's look back at "The Circuit" (page 281) and Panchito's life for a moment. The hardships he faces are familiar to thousands of migrant farmworkers in California: poor working and living conditions, low wages, lack of education. One of those thousands of workers, Cesar Chavez, set out to change things for the farmworkers by forming a union in order to fight for fair wages and better working conditions. In 1962, he organized the National Farm Workers Association (later called the United Farm Workers of America). It took years of difficult and sometimes frightening struggle, but the farmworkers eventually prevailed.

Why did the farmworkers succeed despite all the odds against them? There was no single cause, but a major one was Chavez's belief in the power of nonviolence. Chavez knew that resorting to violence would lead to defeat for the farmworkers. His decision to use nonviolent means was important to their success.

We might also wonder, "Why was Cesar Chavez so determined to change things, even to the point of risking his life? Why, out of the thousands of migrant workers in California, did this man make a difference? What goes into the making of such a person?"

■ As you read the following biographical article, see if you can spot some **causes** and **effects** of Chavez's actions.

Mexican migratory workers in the fields of southern California, drinking soda pop. Photograph taken between 1945 and 1960.

SKILLS FOCUS

Reading Skills
Understand cause and effect.

CESAR CHAVEZ: He Made a Difference

WHAT IS IT ABOUT THE PERSONAL experience of injustice that makes some people decide to help others while other people help only themselves?

One of the people who decided to help others was Cesar Chavez (1927–1993). When Chavez was growing up, his family members were migrant farmworkers. They traveled from region to region in California and worked long hours picking crops in the hot sun for very low wages. Since the whole family had to work to make enough money to survive, Chavez was able to go to school only when the harvests were in, and he had to quit school after eighth grade.

One year his father saw an opportunity to own his own land. He made an agreement with a landowner to clear eighty acres of the man's land and to take forty other acres of the man's land as payment for his work. Chavez's father cleared the eighty acres as promised, but when the time came for him to be paid, the landowner refused to give him the deed to the promised forty acres. Instead, he sold the land to another person.

When Cesar Chavez's father saw a lawyer about the matter, the lawyer advised him to borrow some money and buy the land from the other person. Chavez's father did just that. But cash was a difficult thing for his father to come by, and one day he didn't have the money to make an interest payment. The lawyer not only took the forty acres back but also sold it to the original owner—the man who had cheated Chavez's father in the first place.

Cesar Chavez says that he never forgot the injustice those men did to his father. For more than a hundred years, people like his father had been

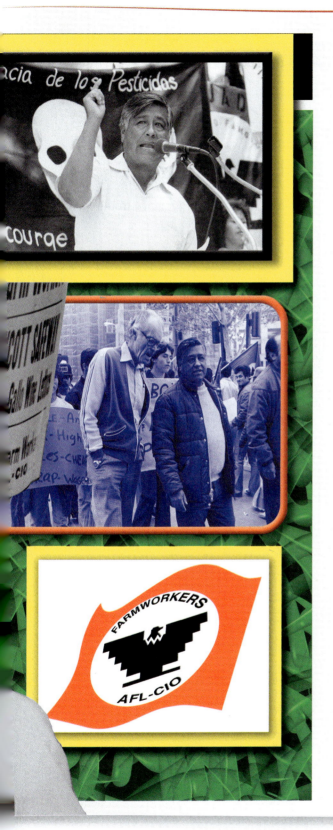

allowed to toil in the fields but had not been allowed to enjoy the fruits of their toil. Chavez hoped to change this, a task many regarded as hopeless.

Chavez believed that migrant farmworkers needed a union to help them get fair wages and better working conditions. In 1962, he organized the National Farm Workers Association, later called the United Farm Workers of America. The union's five-year strike against California's grape growers drew support from around the country. Many people across the United States refused to buy or eat grapes until the strike was settled.

The union's actions were based on the nonviolent principles of Mohandas K. Gandhi and Martin Luther King, Jr. However, many farmworkers were angry and believed that they could not win against the growers without violence. After all, the growers were using scare tactics and violence against them. Chavez met the threat of violence with a radical plan. He was willing to sacrifice his own life by going on a hunger strike to prevent violence and to ensure that the union would continue. His example won the angry workers over. By practicing nonviolence himself, Chavez inspired others in the farmworkers' movement to recommit themselves to the struggle for justice through nonviolence.

When Cesar Chavez died in 1993, more than fifty thousand mourners gathered to honor him at the United Farm Workers' field office in Delano, California. The field office is called Forty Acres.

—Flo Ota De Lange

Analyzing a Cause-and-Effect Article

CESAR CHAVEZ: He Made a Difference

Test Practice

1. Which of the following situations was *not* a **cause** of Cesar Chavez's dedication to bettering the lives of migrant workers?
   - **A** The way the landowner treated Chavez's father
   - **B** The way the lawyer treated Chavez's father
   - **C** The opportunity to purchase the Forty Acres field office
   - **D** The possibility of achieving justice through nonviolent means

2. An **effect** of Cesar Chavez's dedication to bettering the lives of farmworkers was that the —
   - **F** United Farm Workers was formed
   - **G** farmworkers became angry
   - **H** landowner cheated his father
   - **J** lawyer gave his father advice

3. The **cause** of Cesar Chavez's hunger strike was —
   - **A** imprisonment of strikers
   - **B** possibility of violence from farmworkers
   - **C** love of his father
   - **D** deep religious beliefs

4. *Nonviolence* means —
   - **F** "being too afraid to fight"
   - **G** "being afraid of violence"
   - **H** "refusing to use violence on principle"
   - **J** "not wanting to be caught"

5. Cesar Chavez gave the name Forty Acres to the site of the United Farm Workers' field office at Delano. The name was —
   - **A** symbolic
   - **B** offensive
   - **C** literal
   - **D** humorous

Constructed Response

This account of the life of Cesar Chavez is built on a series of **causes** and **effects.** Think about the succession of events, how one thing leads to another. Copy the chart on the right onto a separate sheet of paper, adding other examples from the article to complete the chart.

Cause	Effect
1. Family earns low wages.	1. All have to work.
2. Father sees chance to own land.	2.
3. [And so on]	3.

SKILLS FOCUS

Reading Skills
Analyze a cause-and-effect article.

After You Read   Vocabulary Development

Spanish and English: All in the Family

Thousands of words from Spanish have become part of the English language, and more words from Spanish are entering English all the time. Many Spanish words were absorbed into the English language in the sixteenth and seventeenth centuries, when explorers from Spain gave Spanish names to mountains, rivers, lakes, and new settlements in North America.

PRACTICE

Copy the chart on the right, and fill in the meanings of the Spanish names. Use a dictionary if you need to.

Spanish Name	Meaning
Colorado	
Florida	
Los Angeles	
San Francisco	
Fresno	

SKILLS FOCUS

Vocabulary Skills
Identify the origins and meanings of foreign words.

Grammar Skills
Use pronouns correctly.

Grammar Link

Pronoun Reference

When you use pronouns in your writing, make sure their **antecedents** (words they refer to) are clear.

UNCLEAR   **Chavez's father saw a lawyer, and he advised buying the land.** [Who advised buying the land, Chavez's father or the lawyer?]

CLEAR   **Chavez's father saw a lawyer, who advised buying the land.**

UNCLEAR   **The landowner made a promise to Chavez's father, but it didn't happen.** [What didn't happen?]

CLEAR   **The landowner made a promise to Chavez's father, but didn't keep the promise.**

PRACTICE

Find a piece of writing you've been working on, and exchange papers with a classmate. Circle every pronoun your partner used, and underline its antecedent. If you can't identify the antecedent, put a question mark in the margin. Exchange papers again, and revise any sentences with unclear pronoun references.
For more help, see Agreement of Pronoun and Antecedent, 2o, in the Language Handbook.

Drawing Inferences, Drawing Conclusions and Making Generalizations

Reading Focus
Take a Guess

Here's the beginning of a story about a boy whose life is quite different from Panchito's:

Lance opened his eyes, glanced lazily at the clock, and was suddenly wide awake. Nine-thirty! Good grief, he must have overslept.... A slow smile spread across Lance's face and turned into a wide grin, which soon turned into a yawn. He stretched once, turned over, and thought, "Two weeks! No alarms, no bus, no homework." Ahhhhh . . . mmmmmmm . . . zzzzzzzzz.

Even though the writer of the passage above has left out quite a few details, it isn't difficult to figure out the situation. You don't need to have every fact spelled out to understand what is happening. That is because, like any good reader, you have made inferences and generalizations and drawn conclusions on your own.

Drawing Inferences

When you draw **inferences,** you make educated guesses based on the clues the writer gives and your own experience or knowledge. You can probably supply the following information about the passage above even though the writer has not given it to you directly:

- a possible time of year
- the situation
- why Lance doesn't have to worry
- Lance's feelings

Drawing Conclusions

A **conclusion** is your final thought or judgment about what you have read. It takes into account all the facts and all your inferences. A conclusion is **valid** (both true and logical) if it can be supported with information from the text and if no information in the text contradicts it. Let's return to Lance. You probably concluded that Lance is enjoying the first day of a two-week vacation. Absolutely.

Making Generalizations

A **generalization** is a broad statement that can apply to many situations. To be valid, generalizations, like conclusions, have to be supported by facts. For the "story" about Lance, one generalization might be "Waking up on the first morning of a two-week vacation is a pleasure." Generalizations unsupported by facts are untrue. "All vacations are relaxing" would be too general, since some vacations are hectic.

■ As you read the following article about picking strawberries, think about the inferences you might draw from it. Also think about any conclusions or generalizations you might make based on facts in the article.

SKILLS FOCUS

Reading Skills
Understand inferences, conclusions, and generalizations.

PICKING STRAWBERRIES:

Could You Do It?

The following experiment will give you an idea of what it is like to pick strawberries for a living. One problem with picking a strawberry is that a ripe berry is easily bruised by handling, and if it is bruised, no one will buy it. So the strawberry picker must find a way to pluck the berry off the plant without hurting it. Sound easy? Well, maybe so—if you have all the time in the world and are picking only one berry. But what if, in order to earn enough money to provide your family with the basics, you have to pick about ten thousand strawberries in a twelve-hour workday? That increase in numbers turns strawberry picking into a very different situation, doesn't it?

To pick ten thousand strawberries in twelve hours, you have to pick about

- 1 strawberry every four seconds
- 14 strawberries every minute
- 840 strawberries every hour

So how can we get an idea of what the strawberry picker's hands are doing as she or he picks a berry? In the absence of a real strawberry plant, let's settle for a twelve-inch length of string. Anchor this piece of string around something stable, like a chair back or a door handle. Then, tie a granny knot. Have someone time you while you are doing it. How fast can you tie it? Practice doing it until you can tie a granny knot in four seconds or less. Then, try doing the same thing with fourteen separate lengths of twelve-inch string. The idea is to get fourteen separate knots tied in less than a minute. Now, imagine tying 840 knots in an hour and 10,080 knots in twelve hours. Are you getting an idea of what strawberry picking is like?

—Flo Ota De Lange

Drawing Inferences, Conclusions and Making Generalizations

PICKING STRAWBERRIES: Could You Do It?

Test Practice

1. "But what if, in order to earn enough money to provide your family with the basics, you have to pick about ten thousand strawberries in a twelve-hour workday?" One **inference** that can be made from this sentence is that —
   A strawberry pickers and their families are wealthy
   B strawberry picking is slow and leisurely
   C strawberry pickers are paid by quantity
   D strawberry pickers are paid by the hour

2. All of the following **inferences** can be made from the knot-tying experiment *except* —
   F a strawberry picker needs to know many knot-tying styles
   G a strawberry picker must have good coordination
   H strawberry picking is repetitive work
   J a strawberry picker must be fast

3. Which of the following **conclusions** about strawberry picking could be drawn from this text?
   A It is easy money.
   B It is harder than you might think.
   C It requires maturity and strength.
   D It is impossible.

4. One **generalization** that could be made from this reading is that —
   F strawberries taste good
   G strawberry picking is hard
   H strawberries are hard to grow
   J strawberry pickers are nice

5. Based on this article, which **conclusion** could you make about the writer's beliefs?
   A Strawberry pickers work too hard.
   B Strawberry pickers could work harder.
   C Strawberry pickers should seek other work.
   D Management takes unfair advantage of strawberry pickers.

SKILLS FOCUS

Reading Skills
Draw inferences, conclusions, and make generalizations.

Constructed Response

1. How many strawberries must a worker pick in an hour to support his or her family?

2. Why does the writer suggest that you try tying the knots?

Vocabulary Development

Context Clues: Multiple Meanings

The following exercise will give you practice in using context clues to figure out a word's meaning. In this exercise the words are simple. As you will see, however, they have multiple meanings.

PRACTICE

Each sentence below contains one underlined word followed by several definitions of that word. Choose the definition that best fits the sentence. Then, explain which words in the sentence led you to choose that definition. The first item has been done for you.

1. "The following experiment will give you an idea of what it is like to <u>pick</u> strawberries for a living."
   a. gather   **b.** choose   **c.** criticize

   Answer: The definition that works best is **a,** *gather.* The writer uses *pick* in the sense of gathering strawberries and carrying them away. This is not like choosing one special strawberry, and it certainly wouldn't make sense to criticize them!

2. "But what if, in order to earn enough money to provide your family with the basics, you <u>have</u> to pick about ten thousand strawberries in a twelve-hour workday?"
   a. own   **b.** get; acquire   **c.** are required

3. "That increase in numbers turns strawberry picking into a very different <u>situation</u>, doesn't it?"
   a. rank   **b.** location   **c.** circumstance

4. "In the absence of a real strawberry plant, let's settle for a twelve-inch <u>length</u> of string."
   a. distance   **b.** segment   **c.** duration

SKILLS FOCUS

Vocabulary Skills
Use context clues.

Author Study   Ray Bradbury

Literary Focus

A Writer's Messages

Ray Bradbury is one of the best-loved writers of our time. In more than seventy years of writing, he has published more than seven hundred works—short stories, novels, plays, screenplays, television scripts, and poetry. His stories may be set just about anywhere—small towns in Illinois, the surface of Mars, ancient China. Bradbury moves effortlessly between past, present, and future. Whatever he is writing about, his stories are marked by the fantastic, the mysterious, and the magical. His stories are somewhat like old fables: They always contain a powerful message or lesson.

Reading Skills

Making Generalizations

A **generalization** is a broad statement about something. When you make a generalization, you combine evidence in the text with what you already know. After you read the following stories, you'll be asked to develop a broad statement about Bradbury's messages. To collect evidence for your generalization, follow these steps:

- Decide what the **conflict** in the story is.
- Decide who wins the conflict (if anyone).
- Decide what the **characters** have learned by the end of the story.
- Think about the **messages** the story reveals.

SKILLS FOCUS

Literary Skills
Recognize a writer's message.

Reading Skills
Make generalizations.

Key Elements of Bradbury's Stories

- **Settings** are strange and mysterious places, a combination of fantasy and reality. The past, the present, and the future may blend together in a single story.

- **Plots** are often built around conflicts between characters and powerful forces. Characters may confront monsters, the sinister side of technology, or tyranny.

- **Messages** often focus on our fascination with and fear of technology. They often celebrate heroism and individual freedoms.

from

RAY BRADBURY IS ON FIRE!

an interview by
James Hibberd

Today Bradbury continues to criticize modern innovations, putting him in the seemingly contradictory position of being a sci-fi writer who's also a technophobe. He famously claims to have never driven a car (Bradbury finds accident statistics appallingly unacceptable; he witnessed a deadly car accident as a teen). He is scornful of the Internet (telling one reporter it's "a big scam" by computer companies) and ATMs (asking, "Why go to a machine when you can go to a human

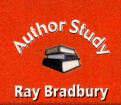
being?") and computers ("A computer is a typewriter," he says, "I have two typewriters, I don't need another one").

By mocking the electronic shortcuts and distracting entertainment that replace human contact and active thinking, Bradbury shows his science-fiction label is misplaced. He cares little for science or its fictions. The author of more than thirty books, six hundred short stories, and numerous poems, essays, and plays, Bradbury is a consistent champion of things human and real. There is simply no ready label for a writer who mixes poetry and mythology with fantasy and technology to create literate tales of suspense and social criticism; no ideal bookstore section for the author whose stories of rockets and carnivals and Halloween capture the fascination of twelve-year-olds, while also stunning adult readers with his powerful

Bradbury browses through spacesuits for possible television series (1959).

A Ray Bradbury Time Line

Publishes stories in pulp magazines such as *Black Mask, Amazing Stories,* and *Weird Tales* throughout the 1940s.

At age fourteen, moves with his family to Los Angeles, where he develops a love for the movies.

In 1957, publishes *Dandelion Wine* an autobiographical novel about his boyhood.

1920   1930   1940   1950   1960

Born on August 22, 1920, in Waukegan, Illinois.

At age twelve, decides to become a writer.

When he is twenty, his first story is accepted by the magazine *Script*.

In 1950, publishes *The Martian Chronicles,* which becomes a bestseller.

Wins critical acclaim for his novel *Fahrenheit 451* (1953).

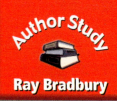
prose and knowing grasp of the human condition.

   One secret to Bradbury's lifelong productivity is that his play and his work are the same. When asked, "How often do you write?" Bradbury replies, "Every day of my life—you got to be in love or you shouldn't do it."

   . . . When I phoned his Los Angeles home for a 9:00 A.M. interview, Bradbury was thoughtful and cranky, and told me he'd already written a short story.

James Hibberd.	**What makes a great story?**
Ray Bradbury.	If you're a storyteller, that's what makes a great story. I think the reason my stories have been so successful is that I have a strong sense of metaphor. . . . I grew

Bradbury at the National Book Awards in New York (2000).

Twenty-six years after *The Martian Chronicles* is published, the first U.S. spacecraft lands on Mars.

Publishes *Something Wicked This Way Comes* in 1983.

1970   1980   1990   2000

Receives a World Fantasy Award for lifetime achievement in 1977.

Ray Bradbury Theater, a popular TV show, airs from 1985 to 1992.

Receives medal for Distinguished Contribution to American Letters from the National Book Foundation.

An Apollo 11 astronaut names a moon crater *Dandelion Crater,* after Bradbury's novel.

301

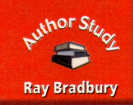
up on Greek myths, Roman myths, Egyptian myths, and the Norse Eddas. So when you have influences like that, your metaphors are so strong that people can't forget them.

James Hibberd. **You've been critical of computers in the past. But what about programs that aid creativity? Do you think using a word processor handicaps a writer?**

Ray Bradbury. There is no one way of writing. Pad and pencil, wonderful. Typewriter, wonderful. It doesn't matter what you use. In the last month I've written a new screenplay with a pad and pen. There's no one way to be creative. Any old way will work. . . .

James Hibberd. **What's an average workday like for you?**

Ray Bradbury. Well, I've already got my work done. At 7:00 A.M., I wrote a short story.

James Hibberd. **How long does that usually take?**

Ray Bradbury. Usually about a morning. If an idea isn't exciting you shouldn't do it. I usually get an idea around 8 o'clock in the morning, when I'm getting up, and by noon it's finished. And if it isn't done quickly you're going to begin to lie. So as quickly as you can, you emotionally react to an idea. That's how I write short stories. They've all been done in a single morning when I felt passionately about them. . . .

James Hibberd. **There's so much competition for a young person's attention nowadays. For the record, why is reading still important?**

Ray Bradbury. Are you kidding? You can't have a civilization without that, can you? If you can't read and write you can't think. Your thoughts are dispersed if you don't know how to read and write. You've got to be able to look at your thoughts on paper and discover what a fool you were. . . .

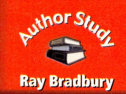

Before You Read

Ray Bradbury says he tells tales to warn people about dangers in the world around them. You are about to read a fairy-tale-like story that takes place in the distant past. As you read, think about how this story connects to our world today. Stop for a moment and think about the title. What do you think of when you see the term *flying machine*?

The Flying Machine

Ray Bradbury

Blue and Green Landscapes by Li Qing.

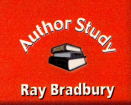

Ancestor Portrait (late 17th or early 18th century) by Chinese School.
Private collection.

IDENTIFY

❶ Where and when is this story set?

IN THE YEAR A.D. 400, the Emperor Yuan held his throne by the Great Wall of China, and the land was green with rain, readying itself toward the harvest, at peace, the people in his dominion[1] neither too happy nor too sad. ❶

Early on the morning of the first day of the first week of the second month of the new year, the Emperor Yuan was sipping tea and fanning himself against a warm breeze when a servant ran across the scarlet and blue garden tiles, calling, "Oh, Emperor, Emperor, a miracle!"

---

1. **dominion** *n.:* country; territory.

"Yes," said the Emperor, "the air *is* sweet this morning."

"No, no, a miracle!" said the servant, bowing quickly.

"And this tea is good in my mouth, surely that is a miracle."

"No, no, Your Excellency."

"Let me guess then—the sun has risen and a new day is upon us. Or the sea is blue. *That* now is the finest of all miracles."

"Excellency, a man is flying!" ❷

"What?" The Emperor stopped his fan.

"I saw him in the air, a man flying with wings. I heard a voice call out of the sky, and when I looked up, there he was, a dragon in the heavens with a man in its mouth, a dragon of paper and bamboo, colored like the sun and the grass."

"It is early," said the Emperor, "and you have just wakened from a dream."

"It is early, but I have seen what I have seen! Come, and you will see it too."

"Sit down with me here," said the Emperor. "Drink some tea. It must be a strange thing, if it is true, to see a man fly. You must have time to think of it, even as I must have time to prepare myself for the sight."

They drank tea.

"Please," said the servant at last, "or he will be gone."

The Emperor rose thoughtfully. "Now you may show me what you have seen."

They walked into a garden, across a meadow of grass, over a small bridge, through a grove of trees, and up a tiny hill.

"There!" said the servant.

The Emperor looked into the sky.

And in the sky, laughing so high that you could hardly hear him laugh, was a man; and the man was clothed in bright papers and reeds to make wings and a beautiful yellow tail, and he was soaring all about like the largest bird in a universe of birds, like a new dragon in a land of ancient dragons. ❸

The man called down to them from high in the cool winds of morning. "I fly, I fly!"

The servant waved to him. "Yes, *yes!*"

The Emperor Yuan did not move. Instead he looked at the Great Wall of China now taking shape out of the farthest mist in the green hills, that splendid snake of stones which writhed with majesty across the entire land. That wonderful wall which had protected

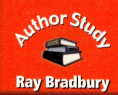
RETELL

❷ What does the Emperor say are miracles? What does the servant say is a miracle?

VISUALIZE

❸ **Imagery** is language that appeals to the senses. What **images,** or word pictures, does Bradbury create to help you see the man flying?

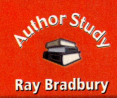
them for a timeless time from enemy hordes[2] and preserved peace for years without number. ❹ He saw the town, nestled to itself by a river and a road and a hill, beginning to waken.

"Tell me," he said to his servant, "has anyone else seen this flying man?"

"I am the only one, Excellency," said the servant, smiling at the sky, waving.

The Emperor watched the heavens another minute and then said, "Call him down to me."

"Ho, come down, come down! The Emperor wishes to see you!" called the servant, hands cupped to his shouting mouth.

The Emperor glanced in all directions while the flying man soared down the morning wind. He saw a farmer, early in his fields, watching the sky, and he noted where the farmer stood.

The flying man alit with a rustle of paper and a creak of bamboo reeds. He came proudly to the Emperor, clumsy in his rig, at last bowing before the old man.

"What have you done?" demanded the Emperor.

"I have flown in the sky, Your Excellency," replied the man.

"What *have* you done?" said the Emperor again.

"I have just told you!" cried the flier.

"You have told me nothing at all." The Emperor reached out a thin hand to touch the pretty paper and the birdlike keel of the apparatus. It smelled cool, of the wind.

"Is it not beautiful, Excellency?"

"Yes, too beautiful."

"It is the only one in the world!" smiled the man. "And I am the inventor."

"The *only* one in the world?"

"I swear it!"

"Who else knows of this?"

"No one. Not even my wife, who would think me mad with the sun. She thought I was making a kite. I rose in the night and walked to the cliffs far away. And when the morning breezes blew and the sun rose, I gathered my courage, Excellency, and leaped from the cliff. I flew! But my wife does not know of it."

---

2. **hordes** *n.*: moving crowds.

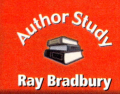

"Well for her, then," said the Emperor. "Come along." **5**

They walked back to the great house. The sun was full in the sky now, and the smell of the grass was refreshing. The Emperor, the servant, and the flier paused within the huge garden.

The Emperor clapped his hands. "Ho, guards!" **6**

The guards came running.

"Hold this man."

The guards seized the flier.

"Call the executioner," said the Emperor.

"What's this!" cried the flier, bewildered. "What have I done?" He began to weep, so that the beautiful paper apparatus rustled.

"Here is the man who has made a certain machine," said the Emperor, "and yet asks us what he has created. He does not know himself. It is only necessary that he create, without knowing why he has done so, or what this thing will do."

The executioner came running with a sharp silver ax. He stood with his naked, large-muscled arms ready, his face covered with a serene[3] white mask.

---

3. **serene** *adj.:* calm; undisturbed.

ANALYZE

5 What do you think the **conflict,** or struggle, in this story will be?

PREDICT

6 What do you think the Emperor will do to the flying man?

Ornamental Chinese dragon.

Spring Morning in the Palace of Han (detail).

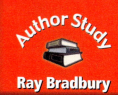

"One moment," said the Emperor. He turned to a nearby table upon which sat a machine that he himself had created. The Emperor took a tiny golden key from his own neck. He fitted his key to the tiny, delicate machine and wound it up. Then he set the machine going.

The machine was a garden of metal and jewels. Set in motion, the birds sang in tiny metal trees, wolves walked through miniature forests, and tiny people ran in and out of sun and shadow, fanning themselves with miniature fans, listening to tiny emerald birds, and standing by impossibly small but tinkling fountains.

"Is *it* not beautiful?" said the Emperor. "If you asked me what I have done here, I could answer you well. I have made birds sing, I have made forests murmur, I have set people to walking in this woodland, enjoying the leaves and shadows and songs. That is what I have done."

"But, oh, Emperor!" pleaded the flier, on his knees, the tears pouring down his face. "I have done a similar thing! I have found beauty. I have flown on the morning wind. I have looked down on all the sleeping houses and gardens. I have smelled the sea and even *seen* it, beyond the hills, from my high place. And I have soared like a bird; oh, I cannot say how beautiful it is up there, in the sky, with the wind about me, the wind blowing me here like a feather, there like a fan, the way the sky smells in the morning! And how free one feels! *That* is beautiful, Emperor, that is beautiful too!" ❼

"Yes," said the Emperor sadly, "I know it must be true. For I felt my heart move with you in the air and I wondered: What is it like? How does it feel? How do the distant pools look from so high? And how my houses and servants? Like ants? And how the distant towns not yet awake?"

"Then spare me!"

"But there are times," said the Emperor, more sadly still, "when one must lose a little beauty if one is to keep what little beauty one already has. I do not fear you, yourself, but I fear another man."

"What man?"

RETELL

❼ On what grounds does the flying man ask for mercy?

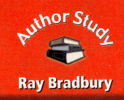

IDENTIFY

8 What does the Emperor fear?

"Some other man who, seeing you, will build a thing of bright papers and bamboo like this. But the other man will have an evil face and an evil heart, and the beauty will be gone. It is this man I fear."

"Why? Why?"

"Who is to say that someday just such a man, in just such an apparatus of paper and reed, might not fly in the sky and drop huge stones upon the Great Wall of China?" said the Emperor. **8**

No one moved or said a word.

"Off with his head," said the Emperor.

The executioner whirled his silver ax.

"Burn the kite and the inventor's body and bury their ashes together," said the Emperor.

The servants retreated to obey.

The Emperor turned to his hand-servant, who had seen the man flying. "Hold your tongue. It was all a dream, a most sorrowful and beautiful dream. And that farmer in the distant field who also saw, tell him it would pay him to consider it only a vision. If ever the word passes around, you and the farmer die within the hour."

"You are merciful, Emperor."

INFER

9 How does the Emperor justify his treatment of the flying man?

"No, not merciful," said the old man. Beyond the garden wall he saw the guards burning the beautiful machine of paper and reeds that smelled of the morning wind. He saw the dark smoke climb into the sky. "No, only very much bewildered and afraid." He saw the guards digging a tiny pit wherein to bury the ashes. "What is the life of one man against those of a million others? I must take solace[4] from that thought." **9**

He took the key from its chain about his neck and once more wound up the beautiful miniature garden. He stood looking out across the land at the Great Wall, the peaceful town, the green fields, the rivers and streams. He sighed. The tiny garden whirred its hidden and delicate machinery and set itself in motion; tiny people walked in forests, tiny faces loped through sun-speckled glades in beautiful shining pelts, and among the tiny trees flew little bits of high song and bright blue and yellow color, flying, flying, flying in that small sky.

INTERPRET

10 Why do you think the narrator ends the story with the Emperor watching the birds in his mechanical garden?

"Oh," said the Emperor, closing his eyes, "look at the birds, look at the birds!" **10**

---

4. **solace** (säl′is) *n.*: comfort.

First Thoughts

1. Finish this sentence: *The Emperor was right/wrong to . . .*

Thinking Critically

2. How do you think Bradbury wants you to feel about the Emperor? Use details from the story to explain your answer.

3. The Emperor fears that the beautiful flying machine will be used by a man with "an evil face and an evil heart" to destroy the Great Wall. What inventions have been used for both good and evil purposes in our own world?

Bradbury's Message

4. Think of this story as a fable with a **message** for our time. State which of the following messages you think is the most important in the story, and explain why:

- Some inventions can be used for both good and evil.
- Progress cannot be stopped.
- The beauty of nature is far superior to that of mechanical objects.
- It is justifiable to take one life to save a whole people.

In a chart like the one below, record your notes and your response to the message you find in this story. You will use these notes to write an essay after you have read all the Bradbury stories.

Reading Check

Retell "The Flying Machine" to a partner. Start with the **title, author, main characters,** and **setting.** Then, retell the main events in the order in which they occur. Be sure to state what the story's **conflict,** or problem, is and explain how it is resolved. You will find help in retelling a story on pages 14–15.

Chinese Astronomer by Peter Verbiest.
Bibliotheque Nationale, Paris, France.

Bradbury's message in "The Flying Machine":

_____

My response to the message:

SKILLS FOCUS

Literary Skills
Analyze a writer's message.

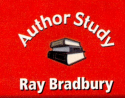

Author Study

Ray Bradbury

Before You Read

Here is what Ray Bradbury has said about "The Dragon":

 It is hard to talk about 'The Dragon' without giving away its secret, telling you the surprise. So all I can talk about is the boy I was that became the young man who thought about, and the older man who wrote, this story. I loved dinosaurs from the age of five, when I saw the film *The Lost World*, filled with prehistoric monsters. I became even more enamored with these beasts when at age thirteen, *King Kong* fell off the Empire State and landed on me in the front row of the Elite Theater. I never recovered. Later, I met and became friends with Ray Harryhausen, who built and film-animated dinosaurs in his garage when we were both eighteen. We dedicated our lives to these monsters, to dragons in all their shapes and forms. Simultaneously, we loved airplanes, rocket ships, trolley cars, and trains. From this amalgam of loves came our lives and careers. We wound up doing *The Beast from 20,000 Fathoms* as our first film. Not very good, but a beginning. He went on to *Mighty Joe Young* and I to *Moby Dick* and its great sea-beast. When I was in my thirties I wrote 'The Dragon' and combined two of these loves. You'll have to read the story to find out which ones. Read on. 99

Ray

The Dragon

Ray Bradbury

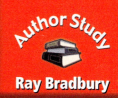

IDENTIFY

❶ Use what you see in the illustration to describe the setting. Who are the characters? What problem do they face?

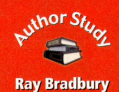

PREDICT

❷ What do you think the knights are going to do?

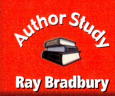

THERE,... OH, LORD. IN THE DISTANCE.

THE DRAGON ROARED NEARER, NEARER. ITS FLASHING YELLOW GLARE SPURTED ABOVE A HILL.

QUICK! THIS IS WHERE IT PASSES.!

THEY SEIZED THEIR LANCES WITH MAILED FISTS AND URGED THEIR HORSES FORWARD.

THE DRAGON ROUNDED A HILL. WITH A TERRIBLE WAILING CRY AND A GRINDING RUSH IT FLUNG ITSELF FORWARD.

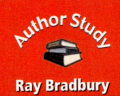

Author Study

Ray Bradbury

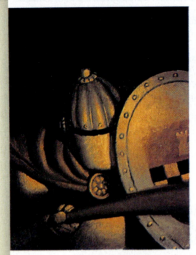

LORD HAVE MERCY!

THE LANCE STRUCK THE UNLIDDED YELLOW EYE, BUCKLED, TOSSED THE MAN THROUGH THE AIR.

RETELL

❸ What happens when the knights attack the dragon?

THE BLACK BRUNT OF ITS SHOULDER SMASHED THE REMAINING HORSE AND RIDER A HUNDRED FEET AGAINST THE SIDE OF A BOULDER. THE DRAGON'S WAIL BECAME A SHRIEK. THERE WAS FIRE ALL ABOUT.

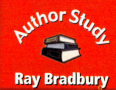

DID YOU SEE IT? JUST LIKE I TOLD YOU!

AS YOU SAID, A KNIGHT IN ARMOR. AND WE HIT HIM. ARE YOU GOING TO STOP?

DID ONCE. FOUND NOTHING. DON'T LIKE TO STOP ON THIS MOOR. IT GIVES ME THE WILLIES.

BUT WE HIT SOMETHING!

GAVE HIM PLENTY OF WHISTLE— CHAP WOULDN'T BUDGE.

THE NIGHT TRAIN, IN FIRE AND FURY, SHOT THROUGH THE GULLY, UP A RISE, AND VANISHED— LEAVING SMOKE AND STEAM TO DISSOLVE IN THE NUMBED AIR AFTER IT HAD PASSED AND GONE FOREVER.

WE'LL MAKE IT TO STOKELY ON TIME, MORE COAL, eh, FRED?

INFER

❹ What important information do you learn from the dialogue and illustrations on this page?

The Dragon   **317**

First Thoughts

1. Finish these sentences:

- In "The Dragon," I was surprised when . . .
- I like/dislike graphic stories because . . .

Thinking Critically

2. In "The Dragon," Bradbury's descriptions of the dragon take on new meaning once you know the dragon's real identity. What do the following descriptions of the dragon refer to?

- "unlidded yellow eye"
- "his breath a white gas"
- "see him burn across the dark lands"

Reading Check

A simple way of summarizing a plot is to fill in a graphic called Somebody Wanted But So. *Somebody* is the main character or characters. *Wanted* names the thing they want. *But* names the problem they have getting it. *So* describes the outcome of the struggle. Fill out this simple chart to show the basic plot of "The Dragon."

Somebody	Wanted	But	So

Bradbury's Message

3. Which of these **messages** do you think Bradbury is trying to convey in "The Dragon"?

- Our machines are as powerful as the mythical dragons of old.
- It is heroic to fight against monsters even when they are not real.
- People of earlier times would see our lives as full of terrifying dangers.

In the chart below, write down the message you find in this graphic story and your response to it. You'll refer to this chart when you write your essay about Bradbury's stories.

Bradbury's message in "The Dragon":
My response to the message:

SKILLS FOCUS

Literary Skills
Analyze a writer's message.

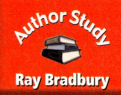
Before You Read

Bradbury writes about all sorts of monsters. These monsters are often more like us than we would like to think. We see ourselves in the monster, and the monster in us. How does Bradbury make you feel about the monster in this story?

THE FOG HORN

Ray Bradbury

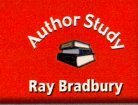

Author Study

Ray Bradbury

Out there in the cold water, far from land, we waited every night for the coming of the fog, and it came, and we oiled the brass machinery and lit the fog light up in the stone tower. Feeling like two birds in the gray sky, McDunn and I sent the light touching out, red, then white, then red again, to eye the lonely ships. And if they did not see our light, then there was always our Voice, the great deep cry of our Fog Horn shuddering through the rags of mist to startle the gulls away like decks of scattered cards and make the waves turn high and foam.

"It's a lonely life, but you're used to it now, aren't you?" asked McDunn.

"Yes," I said. "You're a good talker, thank the Lord."

"Well, it's your turn on land tomorrow," he said, smiling, "to dance the ladies and drink gin."

"What do you think, McDunn, when I leave you out here alone?"

"On the mysteries of the sea." McDunn lit his pipe. It was a quarter past seven of a cold November evening, the heat on, the light switching its tail in two hundred directions, the Fog Horn bumbling in the high throat of the tower. There wasn't a town for a hundred miles down the coast, just a road which came lonely through dead country to the sea, with few cars on it, a stretch of two miles of cold water out to our rock, and rare few ships. ❶

ANALYZE

❶ List details of the **setting.** How would you describe the **mood** of the story so far?

320

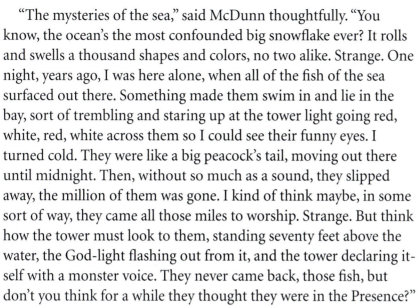

"The mysteries of the sea," said McDunn thoughtfully. "You know, the ocean's the most confounded big snowflake ever? It rolls and swells a thousand shapes and colors, no two alike. Strange. One night, years ago, I was here alone, when all of the fish of the sea surfaced out there. Something made them swim in and lie in the bay, sort of trembling and staring up at the tower light going red, white, red, white across them so I could see their funny eyes. I turned cold. They were like a big peacock's tail, moving out there until midnight. Then, without so much as a sound, they slipped away, the million of them was gone. I kind of think maybe, in some sort of way, they came all those miles to worship. Strange. But think how the tower must look to them, standing seventy feet above the water, the God-light flashing out from it, and the tower declaring itself with a monster voice. They never came back, those fish, but don't you think for a while they thought they were in the Presence?"

I shivered. I looked out at the long gray lawn of the sea stretching away into nothing and nowhere. ❷

"Oh, the sea's full." McDunn puffed his pipe nervously, blinking. He had been nervous all day and hadn't said why. "For all our engines and so-called submarines, it'll be ten thousand centuries before we set foot on the real bottom of the sunken lands, in the fairy kingdoms there, and know *real* terror. Think of it, it's still the year 300,000 Before Christ down under there. While we've paraded around with trumpets, lopping off each other's countries and heads, they have been living beneath the sea twelve miles deep and cold in a time as old as the beard of a comet." ❸

"Yes, it's an old world."

"Come on. I got something special I been saving up to tell you."

We ascended the eighty steps, talking and taking our time. At the top, McDunn switched off the room lights so there'd be no reflection in the plate glass. The great eye of the light was humming, turning easily in its oiled socket. The Fog Horn was blowing steadily, once every fifteen seconds.

"Sounds like an animal, don't it?" McDunn nodded to himself. "A big lonely animal crying in the night. Sitting here on the edge of ten billion years called out to the Deeps, I'm here, I'm here, I'm here. And the Deeps do answer, yes, they do. You been here now for three

INTERPRET

❷ Why do you think the narrator shivers?

PREDICT

❸ Writers use **foreshadowing** to hint at events to come. What might be foreshadowed in this paragraph?

The Fog Horn   **321**

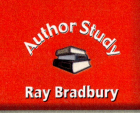

months, Johnny, so I better prepare you. About this time of year," he said, studying the murk and fog, "something comes to visit the lighthouse."

"The swarms of fish like you said?"

"No, this is something else. I've put off telling you because you might think I'm daft. But tonight's the latest I can put it off, for if my calendar's marked right from last year, tonight's the night it comes. I won't go into detail, you'll have to see it yourself. Just sit down there. If you want, tomorrow you can pack your duffel and take the motorboat in to land and get your car parked there at the dinghy pier on the cape and drive on back to some little inland town and keep your lights burning nights. I won't question or blame you. It's happened three years now, and this is the only time anyone's been here with me to verify it. You wait and watch." ❹

Half an hour passed with only a few whispers between us. When we grew tired of waiting, McDunn began describing some of his ideas to me. He had some theories about the Fog Horn itself.

"One day many years ago a man walked along and stood in the sound of the ocean on a cold sunless shore and said, "We need a voice to call across the water, to warn ships. I'll make one. I'll make a voice like all of time and all of that fog that ever was; I'll make a

PREDICT

❹ What do you predict will happen tonight?

voice that is like an empty bed beside you all night long, and like an empty house when you open the door, and like trees in autumn with no leaves. A sound like the birds flying south, crying, and a sound like November wind and the sea on the hard, cold shore. I'll make a sound that's so alone that no one can miss it, that whoever hears it will weep in their souls, and hearths will seem warmer, and being inside will seem better to all who hear it in the distant towns. I'll make me a sound and an apparatus and they'll call it a Fog Horn and whoever hears it will know the sadness of eternity and the briefness of life." ❺

The Fog Horn blew.

"I made up that story," said McDunn quietly, "to try to explain why this thing keeps coming back to the lighthouse every year. The Fog Horn calls it, I think, and it comes. . . ."

"But—" I said.

"Sssst!" said McDunn. "There!" He nodded out to the Deeps.

Something was swimming toward the lighthouse tower.

It was a cold night, as I have said; the high tower was cold, the light coming and going, and the Fog Horn calling and calling through the raveling mist. You couldn't see far and you couldn't see plain, but there was the deep sea moving on its way about the night

IDENTIFY

❺ McDunn uses a string of **similes,** or comparisons, to help us imagine the sound of the fog horn. What does he compare it to?

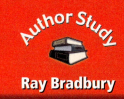
earth, flat and quiet, the color of gray mud, and here were the two of us alone in the high tower, and there, far out at first, was a ripple, followed by a wave, a rising, a bubble, a bit of froth. And then, from the surface of the cold sea came a head, a large head, dark-colored, with immense eyes, and then a neck. And then—not a body—but more neck and more! The head rose a full forty feet above the water on a slender and beautiful dark neck. Only then did the body, like a little island of black coral and shells and crayfish, drip up from the subterranean. There was a flicker of tail. In all, from head to tip of tail, I estimated the monster at ninety or a hundred feet.

I don't know what I said. I said something.

"Steady, boy, steady," whispered McDunn.

"It's impossible!" I said.

"No, Johnny, *we're* impossible. *It's* like it always was ten million years ago. *It* hasn't changed. It's *us* and the land that've changed, become impossible. *Us!*"

It swam slowly and with a great dark majesty out in the icy waters, far away. The fog came and went about it, momentarily erasing its shape. One of the monster eyes caught and held and flashed back our immense light, red, white, red, white, like a disk held high and sending a message in primeval° code. It was as silent as the fog through which it swam.

"It's a dinosaur of some sort!" I crouched down, holding to the stair rail.

"Yes, one of the tribe."

"But they died out!"

"No, only hid away in the Deeps. Deep, deep down in the deepest Deeps. Isn't *that* a word now, Johnny, a real word, it says so much: the Deeps. There's all the coldness and darkness and deepness in a word like that."

"What'll we do?"

"Do? We got our job, we can't leave. Besides, we're safer here than in any boat trying to get to land. That thing's as big as a destroyer and almost as swift."

° **primeval** (prī·mēʹvəl) *adj.:* of the earliest times; ancient.

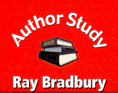
"But here, why does it come *here?*"

The next moment I had my answer.

The Fog Horn blew.

And the monster answered.

A cry came across a million years of water and mist. A cry so anguished and alone that it shuddered in my head and my body. The monster cried out at the tower. The Fog Horn blew. The monster roared again. The Fog Horn blew. The monster opened its great toothed mouth and the sound that came from it was the sound of the Fog Horn itself. Lonely and vast and far away. The sound of isolation, a viewless sea, a cold night, apartness. That was the sound.

"Now," whispered McDunn, "do you know why it comes here?" ❻

I nodded.

"All year long, Johnny, that poor monster there lying far out, a thousand miles at sea, and twenty miles deep maybe, biding its time, perhaps it's a million years old, this one creature. Think of it, waiting a million years; could *you* wait that long? Maybe it's the last of its kind. I sort of think that's true. Anyway, here come men on land and build this lighthouse, five years ago. And set up their Fog Horn and sound it and sound it out toward the place where you bury yourself in sleep and sea memories of a world where there were thousands like yourself, but now you're alone, all alone in a world not made for you, a world where you have to hide.

"But the sound of the Fog Horn comes and goes, comes and goes, and you stir from the muddy bottom of the Deeps, and your eyes open like the lenses of two-foot cameras and you move, slow, slow, for you have the ocean sea on your shoulders, heavy. But that Fog Horn comes through a thousand miles of water, faint and familiar, and the furnace in your belly stokes up, and you begin to rise, slow, slow. You feed yourself on great slakes of cod and minnow, on rivers of jellyfish, and you rise slow through the autumn months, through September when the fogs started, through October with more fog and the horn still calling you on,

INTERPRET

❻ Why does the monster come to the tower? How does Bradbury describe its voice?

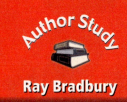
RETELL

7 How does McDunn explain the monster's attraction to the fog horn?

IDENTIFY

8 What episodes in natural history are hinted at in this paragraph?

PREDICT

9 What do you think the monster will do when it no longer hears the fog horn?

and then, late in November, after pressurizing yourself day by day, a few feet higher every hour, you are near the surface and still alive. You've got to go slow; if you surfaced all at once you'd explode. So it takes you all of three months to surface, and then a number of days to swim through the cold waters to the lighthouse. And there you are, out there, in the night, Johnny, the biggest monster in creation. And here's the lighthouse calling to you, with a long neck like your neck sticking way up out of the water, and a body like your body, and, most important of all, a voice like your voice. Do you understand now, Johnny, do you understand?" **7**

The Fog Horn blew.

The monster answered.

I saw it all, I knew it all—the million years of waiting alone, for someone to come back who never came back. The million years of isolation at the bottom of the sea, the insanity of time there, while the skies cleared of reptile-birds, the swamps dried on the continental lands, the sloths and saber-tooths had their day and sank in tar pits, and men ran like white ants upon the hills. **8**

The Fog Horn blew.

"Last year," said McDunn, "that creature swam round and round, round and round, all night. Not coming too near, puzzled, I'd say. Afraid, maybe. And a bit angry after coming all this way. But the next day, unexpectedly, the fog lifted, the sun came out fresh, the sky was as blue as a painting. And the monster swam off away from the heat and the silence and didn't come back. I suppose it's been brooding on it for a year now, thinking it over from every which way."

The monster was only a hundred yards off now, it and the Fog Horn crying at each other. As the lights hit them, the monster's eyes were fire and ice, fire and ice.

"That's life for you," said McDunn. "Someone always waiting for someone who never comes home. Always someone loving some thing more than that thing loves them. And after a while, you want to destroy whatever that thing is, so it can't hurt you no more."

The monster was rushing at the lighthouse.

The Fog Horn blew.

"Let's see what happens," said McDunn.

He switched the Fog Horn off. **9**

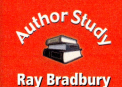

The ensuing minute of silence was so intense that we could hear our hearts pounding in the glassed area of the tower, could hear the slow greased turn of the light.

The monster stopped and froze. Its great lantern eyes blinked. Its mouth gaped. It gave a sort of rumble, like a volcano. It twitched its head this way and that, as if to seek the sounds now dwindled off into the fog. It peered at the lighthouse. It rumbled again. Then its eyes caught fire. It reared up, threshed the water, and rushed at the tower, its eyes filled with angry torment. ❿

"McDunn!" I cried. "Switch on the horn!"

McDunn fumbled with the switch. But even as he flicked it on, the monster was rearing up. I had a glimpse of its gigantic paws, fishskin glittering in webs between the finger-like projections, clawing at the tower. The huge eyes on the right side of its anguished head glittered before me like a caldron into which I might drop, screaming. The tower shook. The Fog Horn cried; the monster cried. It seized the tower and gnashed at the glass, which shattered in upon us.

McDunn seized my arm. "Downstairs!"

The tower rocked, trembled, and started to give. The Fog Horn and the monster roared. We stumbled and half fell down the stairs. "Quick!"

We reached the bottom as the tower buckled down toward us. We ducked under the stairs into the small stone cellar. There were a thousand concussions as the rocks rained down; the Fog Horn stopped abruptly. The monster crashed upon the tower. The tower fell. We knelt together, McDunn and I, holding tight, while our world exploded. ⓫

Then it was over, and there was nothing but darkness and the wash of the sea on the raw stones.

That and the other sound.

"Listen," said McDunn quietly. "Listen."

We waited a moment. And then I began to hear it. First a great vacuumed sucking of air, and then the lament, the bewilderment, the loneliness of the great monster, folded over and upon us, above us, so that the sickening reek of its body filled the air, a stone's thickness away from our cellar. The monster gasped and cried. The tower was gone. The light was gone. The thing that had called to it across a million years was gone. And the monster was opening its mouth and sending out great sounds. The sounds of a Fog Horn, again and again. And ships far at sea, not finding the light, not seeing anything,

INFER

❿ What does the monster do after McDunn switches off the fog horn? What words describe the monster's feelings?

RETELL

⓫ The **climax** of a story is the exciting moment when the outcome of the **conflict** is revealed. Retell what happens at the climax of this story.

but passing and hearing late that night, must've thought: There it is, the lonely sound, the Lonesome Bay horn. All's well. We've rounded the cape.

And so it went for the rest of that night.

The sun was hot and yellow the next afternoon when the rescuers came out to dig us from our stoned-under cellar.

"It fell apart, is all," said Mr. McDunn gravely. "We had a few bad knocks from the waves and it just crumbled." He pinched my arm. **⓬**

There was nothing to see. The ocean was calm, the sky blue. The only thing was a great algaic stink from the green matter that covered the fallen tower stones and the shore rocks. Flies buzzed about. The ocean washed empty on the shore.

The next year they built a new lighthouse, but by that time I had a job in the little town and a wife and a good small warm house that glowed yellow on autumn nights, the doors locked, the chimney puffing smoke. As for McDunn, he was master of the new lighthouse, built to his own specifications, out of still-reinforced concrete. "Just in case," he said.

The new lighthouse was ready in November. I drove down alone one evening late and parked my car and looked across the gray waters and listened to the new horn sounding, once, twice, three, four times a minute far out there, by itself.

The monster?

It never came back.

"It's gone away," said McDunn. "It's gone back to the Deeps. It's learned you can't love anything too much in this world. It's gone into the deepest Deeps to wait another million years. Ah, the poor thing! Waiting out there, and waiting out there, while man comes and goes on this pitiful little planet. Waiting and waiting." **⓭**

I sat in my car, listening. I couldn't see the lighthouse or the light standing out in Lonesome Bay. I could only hear the Horn, the Horn, the Horn. It sounded like the monster calling.

I sat there wishing there was something I could say.

First Thoughts

1. Finish these sentences:
   - I was surprised when . . .
   - This story made me think about . . .

Thinking Critically

2. Why does the monster destroy the lighthouse?

3. A **quest** is a long, perilous journey undertaken to win something of great value. How could this be seen as a quest story? Explain your response.

4. Bradbury likes to imagine the existence of other worlds. In "The Dragon," Bradbury imagines that the ghosts of people from the past still live on the lonely moors. What other world does he depict in "The Fog Horn"?

Reading Check

Check your comprehension by retelling "The Fog Horn" to a partner. Start with the **title, author, main characters,** and **setting.** Identify the main **conflict**— what the main character wants and the problems he faces in trying to get it. (The main character doesn't have to be human.) Then, retell the main events of the story in the order in which they occur. Finally, describe the story's **climax,** the point at which you discover what happens to the main character. Have your partner fill out a Retelling Rating Sheet (see page 15) to give you feedback on your retelling.

Bradbury's Message

5. Which of the following messages do you think Bradbury is trying to convey in this story of a monster and his doomed quest?

   - Everyone, even a monster, needs love and will take great risks to find it.
   - The world contains mysteries that we can't begin to imagine.
   - The past still exists in a parallel universe, and it sometimes crosses boundaries and appears in the present.

   In the chart below, write down what you think Bradbury's message is. Then, write your response to that message. You'll refer to the chart when you write your essay at the end of this section.

Bradbury's message in "The Fog Horn":

_____

My response to the message:

SKILLS FOCUS

Literary Skills
Analyze a writer's message.

Author Study: Ray Bradbury

Assignment

1. Writing an Expository Essay

Write an essay in which you discuss Bradbury's **messages** in the stories you have just read. Before you write, review the charts you filled in after you read "The Flying Machine," "The Dragon," and "The Fog Horn." Write three paragraphs. In the first paragraph, write a **generalization** about the messages conveyed by the stories. In the second paragraph, state the messages you found in "The Flying Machine," "The Dragon," and "The Fog Horn." In the third paragraph, describe your responses to these stories and their messages. You may want to quote from the interview on page 299 to support your interpretations. If you wish, include a discussion of "There Will Come Soft Rains" (page 266) in your essay.

Assignment

2. Designing a Graphic Story

If you enjoyed the graphic story "The Dragon," you may want to create your own graphic version of another Bradbury story.

Most graphic stories are created by a writer and an artist working together. The writer divides the story into panels and decides how many panels will go on a page. The writer must consider how to pace the story so that it holds the reader's attention. Then the writer creates a script that shows which words will appear in each panel. Next the writer and artist discuss which images would best bring the story to life. At this point, the artist takes over.

Choose one of the four other Bradbury stories you have read so far—"The Drummer Boy of Shiloh" (page 203), "There Will Come Soft Rains" (page 266), "The Flying Machine" (page 303), or "The Fog Horn" (page 319). Then, with a partner, follow the steps just described to create a graphic version of that story. Display your story on a bulletin board in your classroom.

SKILLS FOCUS

Writing Skills
Write an expository essay; design a graphic story; analyze metaphors.

Assignment

3. Analyzing Metaphors

In the interview on page 299, Bradbury talks about his use of **metaphor**. In an essay, show how Bradbury uses metaphors in the stories you have read. Be sure to quote passages in which metaphors are used to help you imagine the monsters in "The Fog Horn" and "The Dragon."

SHIPWRECK AT THE BOTTOM OF THE WORLD

Jennifer Armstrong

Ernest Shackleton.

The Boss

Imagine yourself in the most hostile place on earth. It's not the Sahara or the Gobi Desert. It's not the Arctic. The most hostile place on earth is the Antarctic, the location of the South Pole. When winter descends on the southern continent, the seas surrounding the land begin to freeze at the terrifying rate of two square miles every minute, until the frozen sea reaches an area of seven million square miles, about twice the size of the United States. Just imagine yourself stranded in such a place. In 1915, a British crew of 28 men *was* stranded there, with no ship and no way to contact the outside world. Fortunately they were led by Ernest Shackleton, a polar explorer famous for bringing his men home alive.

The crew was somewhat in awe of Ernest Shackleton, whom they all called Boss. Shackleton was a master at keeping his crew working together. Whenever he found two men who had quarreled and were not speaking to each other, he told them, "Stop and forget it," and made them shake hands.

Shipwreck: Stuck in the Ice

The last stop the expedition's ship, *Endurance,* made before taking on the challenge of the Antarctic was a whaling station on South Georgia Island. Soon after leaving the station on December 5, 1914, *Endurance* was caught in pack ice in the Weddell Sea and then frozen in place for the winter. All the crew could do was wait and hope that the drifting ice pack, which was slowly moving north, would carry them closer to land.

Toward the spring, great masses of ice pushed by the wind first toppled and then crushed the ship, forcing the men onto the ice. They tried to drag their three lifeboats toward land, but the boats weighed a ton each and enormous slabs of ice jutted out of the pack at all angles, blocking their way. Instead they made a camp and waited for the ice pack to break up. More than a year after *Endurance* first became stuck in the ice, the crew was able to row the lifeboats into the open ocean. At this point their lives depended on their making land at either Elephant or Clarence Island, the tiny islands at the tip of the Antarctic peninsula. If they missed the islands the nearest land was South America, and they would almost certainly die at sea. After six horrific days in the lifeboats, they reached Elephant Island on April 16, 1916. But the island was barren and many of the men were near collapse. It was clear that somebody would have to try to reach the whaling station on South Georgia Island before winter set in.

Shipwreck: The Open Boat Journey

Shackleton handpicked five men for the relief party he would lead. The ship's carpenter refitted one of the lifeboats, the *James Caird,* for the journey. The men loaded it with bags of stone to keep it steady, boxes of food, a hand pump, a cook pot, a camp stove, two kegs of drinking water, and six reindeer-skin sleeping bags. As they shoved off, the 22 men left behind cheered and waved. "Good luck, Boss!" they shouted.

The living arrangements on board were uncomfortable and cramped. It was a tossup which was worse—being pounded up and down in the bow of the boat in a sorry excuse for sleep, or huddling in the cockpit as icy seas swept across thwarts[1] and gunwales.[2] The men were dressed in wool, which got wet and stayed wet for the duration of the voyage. With temperatures below freezing, and no room to move around to get their blood stirred up, they were always cold. Miserably cold. Waves broke over the bows, where bucketfuls of water streamed through the flimsy decking. The bottom of the boat was constantly full of water, and the two men on watch who weren't steering were always bailing or pumping. The reindeer-skin sleeping bags were soaking wet all the time, and beginning to rot. Loose reindeer hair found its way into the men's nostrils and mouths as they breathed, into their water and food as they ate.

On their seventh day at sea, the wind turned into a gale roaring up from the Pole; the temperature plummeted. The men began to fear that the sails would freeze up and cake with ice, becoming heavier and heavier until the boat toppled upside down. With the gale howling around their ears, they took down their sails.

Throughout the night, waves crashed over the *James Caird* and quickly turned to ice. At first the crew was relieved, since it meant the flimsy decking was sealed against further leaks. But when they awoke on the eighth day, they felt the clumsy, heavy motion of the boat beneath them and knew they were in trouble: 15 inches of ice encased the boat above the waterline, and she was rolling badly.

The ice had to come off. Taking turns, the men crawled on hands and knees over the deck, hacking away with an ax. "First you chopped a handhold, then a kneehold, and then chopped off ice

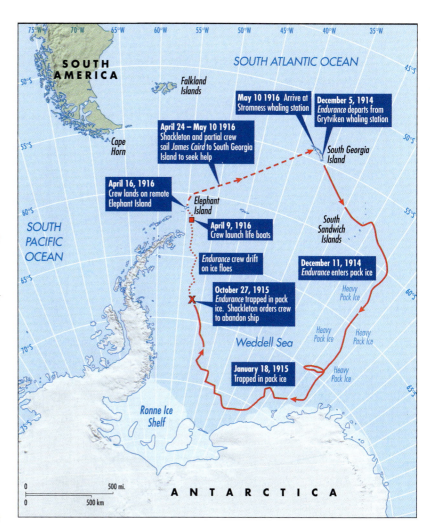

The route of Shackleton's expedition.

---

1. **thwarts** *n.:* rowers' seats extending across a boat.
2. **gunwales** (gun′əlz) *n.:* upper edges of the sides of a boat.

Endurance trapped in pack ice.

hastily but carefully with an occasional sea washing over you," one of the men explained. Each man could stand only five minutes or so of this cold and perilous job at a time. Then it was the next man's turn.

By the time the gale ended, everything below was thoroughly soaked. The sleeping bags were so slimy and revolting that Shackleton had the two worst of them thrown overboard. Exposure was beginning to wear the men down. They were cold, frostbitten, and covered with salt-water blisters. Their legs were rubbed raw from the chafing of their wet pants, and they were exhausted from lack of sleep.

When someone looked particularly bad, the Boss ordered a round of hot milk for all hands. The one man he really wanted to get the hot drink into never realized that the break was for his benefit and so wasn't embarrassed, and all of the men were better off for having the warmth and nourishment.

The night after the gale ended, Shackleton was at the tiller, hunched against the cold. He glanced back toward the south and saw a line of white along the horizon. "It's clearing, boys!" he shouted. But when he looked again, he yelled, "For God's sake, hold on! It's got us!" Instead of a clearing sky, the white line to the south was the foaming crest of an enormous storm wave bearing down on them. When the wave struck, for a few moments the entire boat seemed to be submerged. Then for the next hour the men frantically pumped and bailed, laboring to keep the water from capsizing the *Caird.* They could hardly believe they had not foundered.[3]

On the twelfth day out from Elephant Island, they discovered that salt water had gotten into one of the two kegs of drinking water. Shackleton reduced the water ration to half a cup a day. The water had to be strained through gauze to remove the reindeer hair that had gotten into it—the hair had gotten into everything.

On their fifteenth day out from Elephant Island they reached South Georgia Island, but it was obvious they were in for a storm. By noon the gale had blown up into hurricane force, lashing them with snow, rain, hail, and sleet. The howling winds were driving them straight toward the rocky coast.

Their only hope lay in trying to sail out of reach. The boat began clawing offshore, directly into the onrushing waves. Each wave now smashed into the *Caird* with such force that the bow planks opened and lines of water spurted in from every seam. All afternoon and into the night, the punishment continued.

---

3. **foundered** *v.:* sank.

Finally the hurricane began to decrease. With the storm over, the first watch crawled into the bows to try to catch some sleep. A meal was out of the question: the water was gone, and their mouths and tongues were so swollen with thirst that they could hardly swallow. When the sun rose, the men stared bleary-eyed at the coast of South Georgia. They had to land that day. Shackleton thought the weakest man among them would probably die if they didn't.

Shipwreck: The Rescue

They landed that evening, but they were on the wrong side of the island, the side opposite the whaling station. Afraid to take the battered boat to sea again, the three strongest men—Shackleton, Worsley, who was captain of *Endurance,* and second officer Crean—set out to cross the mountains that lay between them and the station. They stumbled into the station on May 19, 1916, 17 months after they had begun their expedition. They were so changed by their experience they were not recognized.

For the next four months Shackleton tried desperately to get a rescue ship to Elephant Island, where the men who had been left behind were huddled in a hut made of the remaining two lifeboats. Each time, the winter ice turned him back. Finally on August 30, more than four months after the *James Caird* had sailed away, the rescue ship arrived at the island. As soon as a boat lowered from the ship got within shouting distance, Shackleton called out, "Are all well?" "Yes!" someone shouted back. "We knew you'd come back," one of the men later told Shackleton, who said it was the highest compliment anyone ever paid him.

Rescue is at hand as Shackleton and his men return to Elephant Island.

Meet the Writer

Jennifer Armstrong

"I Was Always, First and Last, an Author"

Jennifer Armstrong (1961–) was motivated to write *Shipwreck at the Bottom of the World,* the book that inspired the article you just read, after reading an account of the explorer Ernest Shackleton's ill-fated journey in Antarctica. As she recalls:

> **I always thought it was one of the greatest adventures I had ever heard about. At the time, nobody had written a book about the voyage for kids, so when I decided I'd like to try writing nonfiction I picked this story to write.**

From an early age, Armstrong was certain that she wanted to be a writer:

> **By the time I was in first grade, I knew I was going to be an author.... I was always, first and last, an author.**

This conviction has led Armstrong to write many award-winning books for young adults, including popular works of historical fiction and nonfiction.

For Independent Reading

Read Armstrong's powerful novel *Steal Away,* set in pre–Civil War America, in which two young girls make a daring escape together in search of freedom. Susannah longs to leave her slave-owning uncle's farm and return to her original home in Vermont, while Bethlehem, Susannah's personal servant, seeks freedom from the bondage of slavery.

Writing Workshop

Assignment

Write an essay supporting your position on an important issue.

Audience

Your classmates, teachers, parents, or school board, or the readers of a school or local newspaper.

RUBRIC
Evaluation Criteria

A good persuasive essay

1. includes a thesis statement that clearly states a position on an issue

2. presents at least two strong reasons to support the position

3. supports each reason with evidence, logical arguments, and possibly emotional appeals

4. is clearly organized

5. concludes with a restatement of the writer's position and possibly a call to action

Writing Skills
Write an essay supporting a position.

PERSUASIVE WRITING

Supporting a Position

In your everyday conversations you probably spend a lot of time explaining and defending your ideas—maybe about school rules, homework, or people and events in the news. In this workshop you'll write an essay in which you present your position on an important issue and try to persuade an audience to agree with you.

Prewriting

1 Choosing a Topic

Read and respond to the following **prompt:**

> You may have strong opinions about a number of issues. To get others to see things your way, however, you need to use the tools of persuasion to convince your audience that your point of view is the right one. Take a stand on an important issue that concerns you. Write an essay in which you state and offer support for your position.

Brainstorm issues with a partner or small group. The issue you choose should meet these criteria:

- You have strong feelings about the issue.
- There are reasonable arguments on both sides of the issue.
- You can do research on the issue.

Freewrite for a few minutes about one or more possible topics for your essay.

2 Identifying Your Audience

To identify your audience, ask yourself questions like these: Which groups of people are concerned about the topic? How much are they likely to know about it? Who might disagree with my opinion, and why?

3 Writing a Thesis Statement

Your **thesis statement,** or opinion statement, should identify the issue and make your position clear. A good thesis is focused and consistent; it establishes a tone that will prepare the reader to consider your point of view.

4 Appealing to Reason

The key to successful persuasion is developing a strong argument. Once you have stated your thesis, your task is to find two or three strong **reasons** to support your position.

The framework on the right outlines the structure of a persuasive essay. Each paragraph begins with a **topic sentence** that clearly states the reason presented in that paragraph. The rest of the paragraph contains **supporting evidence** that backs up and develops the reason. Such evidence may include

- **examples**
- **research and survey results**
- **statistics**—facts in numerical form
- **anecdotes**—brief true stories that may be drawn from personal experiences
- **interviews**
- **direct quotations from experts**

5 Appealing to Emotions

It's OK to use **emotional appeals** to stir the feelings of your audience. **Loaded words**—words that have strong positive or negative connotations—can be powerful persuasive tools when used thoughtfully and in moderation. *Propaganda,* for example, is a loaded word that has negative connotations; it suggests deception. The word *integrity,* by contrast, is a loaded word with positive connotations; it suggests honesty and sincerity.

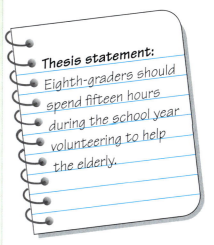

Thesis statement:
Eighth-graders should
spend fifteen hours
during the school year
volunteering to help
the elderly.

Framework for an Essay Supporting a Position

Introduction

Thesis statement presenting issue and position.

Body

Paragraph 1: reason 1
- topic sentence
- supporting evidence (examples, statistics, anecdotes, quotations)

Paragraph 2: reason 2
- topic sentence
- supporting evidence

Paragraph 3: reason 3
- topic sentence
- supporting evidence

Conclusion

Restatement of position, possibly ending with a call to action.

Resources for Support

- books
- magazines
- newspapers
- news programs
- informational videos
- Web sites
- leaders and experts

Strategies for Elaboration

You can elaborate on your ideas by

- **defining words** that your readers may not know
- **explaining a reason** or the way a piece of evidence supports a reason
- **adding evidence,** such as an example, a statistic, or a quotation to support a reason
- **using a comparison** to illustrate an idea

Drafting

1 Organizing Your Argument

Organize your argument logically. One effective way to present an argument is **order of importance,** in which you give the most important reason first and follow it with less important reasons *or* you begin with the least important reason and build up to the most important one.

2 Addressing Counterarguments

Anticipate and deal with any counterarguments that might be raised against your position. Present the other side fairly so that your reader will accept your own ideas as reasonable.

3 Ending with a Bang

End your paper forcefully with a **call to action.** Ask your audience to take a specific action, such as voting a certain way or joining a volunteer group. The Student Model below concludes with a call to action.

Student Model

Distinguished Members of the School Board:

I am in favor of the proposed require-ments that eighth-graders spend fifteen hours during the school year volunteering to help the elderly.

Thesis statement.

One reason this would be a good idea is that I feel it would be an awesome learn-ing experience. Students could learn how to work with and relate to older people. My mother works at a nursing home, so I have had the opportunity to help her in the summer. I have learned to help with the residents there, and I also learned interesting

Reason 1— topic sentence.

Personal experience.

What writer learned.

things from the people themselves and things about their lives.

Another reason I think this rule would be magnificent is that it is a good way to help others. Eighth-graders can help people who cannot do things for themselves. Students could do yardwork, housework, run errands, or just spend time with the elderly so they would not be alone.

Reason 2— topic sentence.

Specific examples.

Finally, I think just spending at least fifteen hours a school year with the elderly would improve students' people skills. Students would learn to talk to and relate to others. They would learn how to be less shy, too. In a recent *Time* magazine poll, sixty percent of people becoming nurses in care homes said they learned how to be able to talk to residents and their families more confidently. A woman who works with my mother did volunteer work when she was in high school and has told me she is grateful for that experience.

Reason 3— topic sentence.

Supporting evidence: survey results, statistic.

Anecdote.

For all these reasons, I believe the proposed requirements for volunteering would make a good rule. I hope that you will consider my reasons and vote to accept the proposed requirement.

Conclusion.

Call to action.

> —Teresa Lacey
> Franklin Middle School
> Abilene, Texas

Writing Tips

Transitional Words and Phrases

Remember to use transitional words and phrases in your essay to make the relationship between ideas clear. Here are some useful transitions:

also

another

because

but

finally

first

however

likewise

moreover

most important

next

then

therefore

to begin with

INTERNET

More Writer's Models

Keyword: LE5 8-3

Evaluating and Revising

Use the following chart to evaluate and revise your persuasive essay.

Supporting a Position: Content and Organization Guidelines		
Evaluation Questions ▶	**Tips** ▶	**Revision Techniques** ▶
❶ Does your introduction contain a clear thesis statement?	▶ **Circle** the sentence or sentences that state the issue and your position.	▶ If necessary, **add** a thesis statement or **revise** the statement to clarify your point of view.
❷ Are the paragraphs in the essay arranged in order of importance?	▶ **Number** the paragraphs in order of importance.	▶ **Rearrange** the paragraphs if necessary.
❸ Have you provided reasons and evidence to support your opinion?	▶ **Put a star** next to each reason, and **highlight** the evidence for each reason.	▶ **Add** reasons, or **add** an example, statistic, anecdote, comparison, or expert opinion to support each reason, if needed.
❹ Does the body of your paper include elaboration to clarify reasons or evidence? Have you addressed counterarguments?	▶ **Put a box** around anything that needs to be clarified. **List** any counterarguments that have not been addressed.	▶ **Elaborate** by adding explanations and addressing reader concerns.
❺ Does your paper present a consistent point of view?	▶ **Draw a wavy line** under any sentence that does not support the position expressed in the thesis statement.	▶ **Cut** any lines of argument that do not support your position.
❻ Does your conclusion restate your opinion and summarize your reasons? Is there a call to action?	▶ **Underline** the restatement of opinion and the summary of reasons. **Underline** the call to action.	▶ If necessary, **add** a restatement of your opinion, a summary of reasons, and a call to action.

On the next page you will find the opening paragraph of a persuasive essay that has been revised. Read the paragraph, and then respond to the questions that follow.

Revision Model

Should students have a say in what the school

Parents and dietitians

cafeteria offers for lunch? ~~Some people~~ may be

alarmed   *Given the freedom to choose,*

~~scared~~ by this prospect. ~~Wouldn't~~ students

gorge   *deep-fried foods and candy?*

~~pig out~~ on ~~junk food?~~

I believe that if students knew more about the

and their daily calorie needs

nutritional value of foods, they would choose a

sensible diet. Schools would have fewer problems

avoid

getting students to ~~cut out~~ foods high in calories and

to eat more fruits, vegetables, and whole grains.

A committee of students should be appointed in

each school to keep the student body informed about

on diet and nutrition

current research and to make recommendations for

tasty, nourishing meals.

Evaluating the Revision

1. How has the writer changed the language to make it more appropriate for a wide audience?

2. Where has the writer elaborated on any statements? Do these changes clarify ideas? Explain.

3. Has the rearrangement of material improved coherence? Explain why or why not.

4. What additional changes would you recommend?

Communications Handbook
H E L P

See Proofreaders' Marks.

Literary Skills

Test Practice

DIRECTIONS: Read the passage. Then, answer each question that follows.

from The Cay

Theodore Taylor

In the novel The Cay, *Phillip, an eleven-year-old boy who is blind, is shipwrecked on a very small island, or cay, with a West Indian seaman named Timothy and a cat. Timothy dies while protecting Phillip during a hurricane. In this part of the story, Phillip is trying to make it on his own.*

The sun came out strong in the morning. I could feel it on my face. It began to dry the island, and toward noon, I heard the first cry of a bird. They were returning.

By now, I had taught myself to tell time, very roughly, simply by turning my head toward the direct warmth of the sun. If the angle was almost overhead, I knew it was around noon. If it was low, then of course, it was early morning or late evening.

There was so much to do that I hardly knew where to start. Get a campfire going, pile new wood for a signal fire, make another rain catchment for the water keg, weave a mat of palm fibers to sleep on. Then make a shelter of some kind, fish the hole on the reef, inspect the palm trees to see if any coconuts

were left—I didn't think any could be up there—and search the whole island to discover what the storm had deposited. It was enough work for weeks, and I said to Stew Cat, "I don't know how we'll get it all done." But something told me I must stay very busy and not think about myself.

I accomplished a lot in three days, even putting a new edge on Timothy's knife by honing it on coral. I jabbed it into the palm nearest my new shelter, so that I would always know where it was if I needed it. Without Timothy's eyes, I was finding that in my world, everything had to be very precise; an exact place for everything.

On the fifth day after the storm, I began to scour the island to find out what had been cast up. It was exciting, and I knew it would take days or weeks to accomplish. I had made another cane and beginning with east beach, I felt my way back and forth, reaching down to touch everything that my cane struck; sometimes having to spend a long time trying to decide what it was that I held in my hands.

I found several large cans and used one of them to start the "time" can again, dropping five pebbles into it so that the reckoning would begin again from the night of the storm. I discovered

SKILLS FOCUS

Literary Skills
Analyze setting and mood.

an old broom, and a small wooden crate that would make a nice stool. I found a piece of canvas, and tried to think of ways to make pants from it, but I had no needle or thread.

Other than that, I found many shells, some bodies of dead birds, pieces of cork, and chunks of sponge, but nothing I could really put to good use.

It was on the sixth day after the storm, when I was exploring on south beach, that I heard the birds. Stew Cat was with me, as usual, and he growled when they first screeched. Their cries were angry, and I guessed that seven or eight might be in the air.

I stood listening to them; wondering what they were. Then I felt a beat of wing past my face, and an angry cry as the bird dived at me. I lashed out at it with my cane, wondering why they were attacking me.

Another dived down, screaming at me, and his bill nipped the side of my head. For a moment, I was confused, not knowing whether to run for cover under sea grape, or what was left of it, or try to fight them off with my cane. There seemed to be a lot of birds.

Then one pecked my forehead sharply, near my eyes, and I felt blood run down my face. I started to walk back toward camp, but had taken no more than three or four steps when I tripped over a log. I fell into the sand, and at the same time, felt a sharp pain in the back of my head. I heard a raging screech as the bird soared up again. Then another bird dived at me.

I heard Stew Cat snarling and felt him leap up on my back, his claws digging into my flesh. There was another wild screech, and Stew Cat left my back, leaping into the air.

His snarls and the wounded screams of the bird filled the stillness over the cay. I could hear them battling in the sand. Then I heard the death caw of the bird.

I lay still a moment. Finally, I crawled to where Stew Cat had his victim. I touched him; his body was rigid and his hair was still on edge. He was growling, low and muted.

Then I touched the bird. It had sounded large, but it was actually rather small. I felt the beak; it was very sharp.

Slowly, Stew Cat began to relax.

Wondering what had caused the birds to attack me, I felt around in the sand. Soon, my hand touched a warm shell. I couldn't blame the birds very much. I'd accidentally walked into their new nesting ground.

They were fighting for survival, after the storm, just as I was. I left Stew Cat to his unexpected meal and made my way slowly back to camp.

Literary Skills

1. What details tell you that the **setting** of this story is a tropical island?

   A Palm trees and coconuts

   B Warm sun

   C A wooden crate

   D Returning birds

2. Being blind and alone on a small island is scary enough for Phillip, but what detail of the setting adds horror to the **mood**?

   F Timothy's knife

   G Stew Cat

   H A signal fire

   J Attacking birds

3. Which sentence shows that Phillip is optimistic in spite of his troubles?

   A "There was so much to do that I hardly knew where to start."

   B "It was enough work for weeks, and I said to Stew Cat, 'I don't know how we'll get it all done.'"

   C "I accomplished a lot in three days, even putting a new edge on Timothy's knife. . . ."

   D "I found a piece of canvas, and tried to think of ways to make pants from it, but I had no needle or thread."

4. Which of the following **conclusions** can you reasonably make about Phillip's character?

   F Phillip is self-pitying.

   G Phillip is brave and intelligent.

   H Phillip is fun-loving and lazy.

   J Phillip lacks self-esteem.

5.

Phillip hears birds screeching.		Stew Cat kills a bird.

   If you were arranging the events of this passage in **chronological order,** which of the following events would you place in the empty box?

   A Birds attack Phillip.

   B Birds lay eggs in the sand.

   C Stew Cat eats the bird.

   D Phillip returns to camp.

6. Phillip says he accomplished a lot, "even putting a new edge on Timothy's knife by honing it on coral." *Honing* probably means —

   F breaking

   G sharpening

   H coloring

   J ruining

7. What does Phillip discover was the **cause** of the bird attack?

   A The birds hate humans.

   B The birds were hungry.

   C The birds were protecting their eggs.

   D The birds wanted to eat the cat.

Constructed Response

8. What **inference** can you make about Stew Cat and the bird at the end of the story? Support your inference with evidence from the text and with your own prior knowledge.

Collection 3: Skills Review

Vocabulary Skills

Test Practice

Context Clues

DIRECTIONS: Use context clues to guess the meaning of each underlined word or phrase in the following sentences.

1. "The <u>peak</u> of the strawberry season was over, and the last few days the workers, most of them braceros, were not picking as many boxes as they had during the months of June and July." In this sentence, *peak* means —
   A part of a baseball cap
   B crest of a hill
   C worst period
   D highest point

2. "The yelling and screaming of my little brothers and sisters . . . broke the silence of dawn. Shortly, the barking of the dogs <u>accompanied</u> them." In this sentence, *accompanied* means —
   F joined in with
   G fought against
   H quieted
   J awoke

3. "While we ate, Papá <u>jotted down</u> the number of boxes we had picked." In this sentence, *jotted down* means —
   A wrote a brief note about
   B analyzed completely
   C stacked up
   D summed up

4. "The vines <u>blanketed</u> the grapes, making it difficult to see the bunches." In this sentence, *blanketed* means —
   F revealed
   G destroyed
   H covered
   J exposed

5. "Papá sighed, wiped the sweat off his forehead with his sleeve, and said <u>wearily</u>: 'Es todo [That's all].'" In this sentence, *wearily* means —
   A weirdly
   B tiredly
   C meanly
   D angrily

SKILLS FOCUS

Vocabulary Skills
Use context clues.

Collection 3: Skills Review

Vocabulary Skills

Test Practice

Synonyms

DIRECTIONS: Choose the word or group of words that has the same or about the same meaning as the underlined word. You studied some of these words in previous collections.

1. Apparent means —
    A   unknown
    B   outrageous
    C   visible
    D   hidden

2. Someone who is sullen is —
    F   grumpy
    G   wealthy
    H   jealous
    J   funny

3. Someone who has been misled has been —
    A   employed
    B   fooled
    C   deserted
    D   ignored

4. A disheveled person is —
    F   angry
    G   prepared
    H   easygoing
    J   untidy

5. Sublime means —
    A   grand
    B   ancient
    C   destructive
    D   fortunate

6. To obscure something is to —
    F   sell it
    G   hide it
    H   throw it
    J   taste it

7. Intolerant means —
    A   incurable
    B   unaccepting
    C   unbelievable
    D   insincere

8. Someone who is gaunt is —
    F   ill
    G   quiet
    H   thin
    J   bright

SKILLS FOCUS

Vocabulary Skills
Identify synonyms.

Collection 3: Skills Review
Writing Skills

Test Practice

DIRECTIONS: Read the following passage from an essay supporting a position. Then, answer each question that follows.

(1) Although more American students are getting high school diplomas than at any other time in the past, the high school dropout rate is still too high. (2) Various estimates place it between 12 and 25 percent. (3) The unemployment rate for high school dropouts is greater than that for graduates. (4) Dropping out of high school reduces one's employment opportunities. (5) Since many jobs today require specialized skills, dropouts may be forced into a labor market that is unstable.

(6) To help "at risk" students stay in school, we need to consider a range of proposals. (7) First, we need to offer career counseling to students, beginning in the ninth grade. (8) Second, we should provide stimulating quality education that will give students incentives to complete their schooling. (9) And third, we must get parents more involved in school programs and policies.

1. What sources might this writer consult to get statistics to support the statements in Paragraph 1?
   - **A** Census Bureau
   - **B** Educational Resources Information Center
   - **C** National Center for Education Statistics
   - **D** All of the above

2. Which of the following statements might the writer use to elaborate on sentence 5?
   - **F** "A technical education can increase one's chances of qualifying for a well-paying job."
   - **G** "Many dropouts become discouraged about work."
   - **H** "Dropouts should consider getting their general equivalency diplomas."
   - **J** "For example, one area of employment for dropouts has been the construction industry, which is strongly affected by changes in the economy."

3. Which sentence is repetitive and can be dropped?
   - **A** Sentence 2
   - **B** Sentence 4
   - **C** Sentence 8
   - **D** Sentence 9

4. The audience for this essay probably includes all of the following groups *except* —
   - **F** parent-teacher associations
   - **G** local community boards
   - **H** conservation groups
   - **J** guidance counselors

SKILLS FOCUS

Writing Skills
Analyze an essay supporting a position.

Fiction

Consequences of War

As World War II comes to a close, Yuki Sakane and her family are finally released from an internment camp and allowed to return home to Berkeley, California. However, the Sakanes quickly find that Berkeley has changed. Because of the war, former friends and other residents have become suspicious of returning Japanese Americans. Yuki and her family try to overcome this hostility in Yoshiko Uchida's novel *Journey Home*.

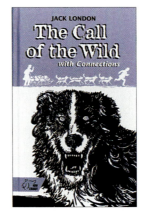

Change of Scenery

In Jack London's classic adventure story *The Call of the Wild*, Buck is stolen from his comfortable home and forced into service as a sled dog in the Alaskan wilderness. As he struggles to adapt to his new surroundings, Buck learns to draw on his instincts to survive among brutal owners and fierce competition.

This title is available in the HRW Library.

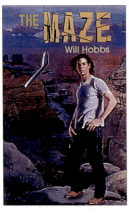

Lost and Found

Rick Walker doesn't know where to turn when he is lost and alone. Luckily, a biologist named Lon Peregrino befriends Rick. Lon is dedicated to preserving the nearly extinct California condors who reside by the Maze, a landscape of beautiful deep canyons. In Will Hobbs's novel *The Maze*, Rick helps Lon protect the condors from extinction while following his own dreams of flight.

Triumph and Tragedy

Patricia A. Cochrane's *Purely Rosie Pearl* tells the story of twelve-year-old Rosie Pearl Bush and her family, migrant workers in the Sacramento Valley. Rosie thinks her family's future looks bright after her father replaces the disagreeable Jake Porter as field boss. But her joy turns to sadness when a terrible event takes place.

Nonfiction

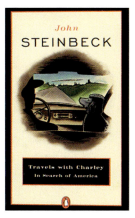

Across the Country

By the time John Steinbeck turned fifty-eight, he had written the classic American novels *Of Mice and Men* and *The Grapes of Wrath*. He continued his career by writing the eloquent nonfiction book *Travels with Charley* about his journey across the country. With his French poodle, Charley, by his side, Steinbeck encounters all the sides of America in the 1960s: beauty at Niagara Falls, racism in New Orleans, companionship in California.

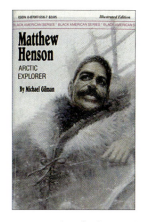

Overdue Recognition

When Robert Peary was searching for men to join him on the first expedition to the North Pole, he knew Matthew Henson would be a worthy partner. Peary recognized this African American's determination and resourcefulness, and their association led to a lifetime of exciting Arctic exploration for both men. Discover Henson's little-known contributions to a remarkable journey in Michael Gilman's *Matthew Henson: Arctic Explorer.*

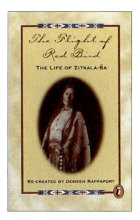

Cruel Decisions

When Gertrude Bonnin was eight years old, she was removed from her Sioux reservation in the Dakotas and placed in a boarding school in Indiana. Gertrude resisted when her instructors tried to make her renounce her Native American customs. Instead, she renamed herself Zitkala-Ša (Red Bird). As an adult, Zitkala-Ša made people aware of the harsh treatment of American Indians. Doreen Rappaport tells this brave woman's story in *The Flight of Red Bird: The Life of Zitkala-Ša.*

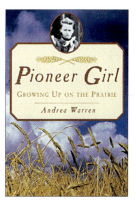

Nebraska Landscapes

Although living on the prairie could be physically and mentally grueling, Grace McCance loved it. Andrea Warren documents McCance's life on the Nebraska prairie in *Pioneer Girl: Growing Up on the Prairie.* Even when blizzards or thunderstorms damaged their land, Grace and her family found a way to survive, and even to triumph.

The Human Spirit

Literary Focus:
Analyzing Theme

Informational Focus:
Analyzing Main Idea

go.
hrw
.com

INTERNET
Collection
Resources
Keyword: LE5 8-4

I Never Saw Another Butterfly Here
(1944) by Nely Silvínová, age 12,
Theresienstadt Concentration Camp,
Terezin, Czechoslovakia. The artist
died before her thirteenth birthday.
Collection, The Jewish Museum, Prague.

353

Elements of Literature

Theme *by* Mara Rockliff

TRUTHS ABOUT OUR LIVES

People read fiction for excitement, emotion, suspense, laughs, and the chance to meet interesting people doing interesting things. Yet when a story touches us, it usually has taught us something. The stories that have a meaning beyond the people and events on their pages—a meaning that *we* can use—are the ones that change our lives. This deeper meaning is called **theme.**

Most writers say they don't know their theme when they begin to write. They often start with just a character or a situation. "What would motivate someone to risk everything?" they wonder, or "How would a thirteen-year-old boy deal with his parents' divorce?" Then they start to write.

A theme will often emerge naturally from the story as it progresses and from what the writer believes about life. A writer who believes that a single mistake can haunt a person forever, for example, will write one kind of story. Someone who believes that what matters most is to learn from our mistakes and move on will write another kind. We, the readers, discover a truth about life as we share the characters' experiences. At the end of the story, what the characters have discovered we have discovered also.

Finding Meaning in It All

Like the truths we discover in real life, themes in stories can be complicated, open to interpretation, and sometimes difficult to put into words.

Theme is the special message that a reader takes away from a story. Usually no two readers state a theme in exactly the same way. In fact, readers may even differ on what they see as the story's theme.

You might read about a family hiding from the Nazis and come away thinking the theme is: *Even in extraordinary circumstances, people still do ordinary things, like fight, make up, and fall in love*. One of your classmates might say the theme is: *The human spirit can triumph over evil*. You both could be right. The meaning of a story comes from both the writer and the individual reader.

So how do you put your finger on a story's theme? Try looking at these elements:

The title. Often, but not always, writers use titles to hint at the story's theme. Consider what the title suggests. Why do you think the writer chose this title?

The characters. How do the main characters change in the course of the story? What do they discover that could

SKILLS FOCUS

Literary Skills Identify and analyze themes.

have meaning for other people's lives—including your own?

The big moments. Which scenes or passages in the story seem especially important? What revelations about life do they suggest to you?

The resolution. How are conflicts or problems in the story settled? How do you feel about the outcome? Does the resolution give you an idea of what the story means?

Recurring Themes the World Over

People all over the world share the same dreams and fears: They long for a vision of human life that gives meaning to their own existence. They long for heroes who will come to their rescue in times of danger. It is not surprising, then, that all over the world people tell the same stories—more or less. Characters change and settings change, but themes recur. The same themes can be found in ancient myths, in short stories published in today's magazines, in movies, and even on TV shows.

Practice

To begin your exploration of recurring themes, look again at the two themes mentioned on page 354: *Even in extraordinary circumstances, people still do ordinary things, like fight, make up, and fall in love* and *The human spirit can triumph over evil*. Then, think of novels, stories, poems, and plays you have studied or read on your own. Think also of movies, plays, and TV shows you have seen. With a group of classmates, brainstorm titles of works that reflect those two themes.

Reprinted with Special Permission of King Features Syndicate.

Theme: A Message, Not a Summary

by Kylene Beers

Aesop, a legendary storyteller from centuries ago, told a fable about a dog crossing a bridge holding a bone in his mouth. The dog looked at his reflection in the water and saw a dog holding a bone. He wanted that dog's bone, so he growled. The dog in the reflection growled back. Then the dog shook his head, and the dog in the water shook his head in response. Finally the dog on the bridge jumped into the water, barking at the reflection in the water. When he came up, his bone was gone, and so was the dog in the water.

Summary Versus Theme

A **summary** explains what happens in a story. A **theme** is the truth about life revealed in a story.

What is Aesop's fable about? You can come up with a good summary by using these four words: *Somebody, Wanted, But, So.*

First, decide who is the most important **somebody** in this fable. (That would be the dog on the bridge.) Then, ask yourself what that dog **wanted; but** what happened to keep the dog from getting what he wanted? Finally, ask yourself, "**So** what was the outcome?" You might come up with a statement like this: *A dog on a bridge wants another dog's bone, but he doesn't realize that the other dog is his own reflection, so he jumps in to get the other dog's bone and loses his own.*

This is a summary of what happens in the fable. Now let's figure out a **theme.**

SKILLS FOCUS

Reading Skills
Understand summary and theme.

Tips for Finding Theme

Here are two possible themes for Aesop's fable:

1. Greed causes problems and may leave us with less than what we originally had.

2. Be happy with what you have, and don't compare your life with someone else's.

After you read a story, you can use the "Somebody Wanted But So" strategy to write a summary. When you've finished the summary, ask yourself, "What message or truth about life have I gotten from this story?" Turn your response into a statement, and you have a theme.

Try creating a theme statement after you read "The People Could Fly."

THE PEOPLE COULD FLY

Virginia Hamilton

Using the Strategy

As you read, you'll find this open-book sign at certain points in the story: . Stop at these points, and think about what you've just read.

They say the people could fly. Say that long ago in Africa, some of the people knew magic. And they would walk up on the air like climbin up on a gate. And they flew like blackbirds over the fields. Black, shiny wings flappin against the blue up there.

Then, many of the people were captured for Slavery. The ones that could fly shed their wings. They couldn't take their wings across the water on the slave ships. Too crowded, don't you know.

The folks were full of misery, then. Got sick with the up and down of the sea. So they forgot about flyin when they could no longer breathe the sweet scent of Africa.

Say the people who could fly kept their power, although they shed their wings. They kept their secret magic in the land of slavery. They looked the same as the other people from Africa who had been comin over, who had dark skin. Say you couldn't tell anymore one who could fly from one who couldn't. ❶ 🔖

One such who could was an old man, call him Toby. And standin tall, yet afraid, was a young woman who once had wings. Call her Sarah. Now Sarah carried a babe tied to her back. She trembled to be so hard worked and scorned.

The slaves labored in the fields from sunup to sundown. The owner of the slaves callin himself their Master. Say he was a hard lump of clay. A hard, glinty coal. A hard rock pile, wouldn't be moved. His Overseer on horseback pointed out the slaves who were slowin down. So the one called Driver cracked his whip over the slow ones to make them move faster. That whip was a slice-open cut of pain. So they did move faster. Had to.

Sarah hoed and chopped the row as the babe on her back slept.

Say the child grew hungry. That babe started up bawlin too loud. Sarah couldn't stop to feed it. Couldn't stop to soothe and quiet it down. She let it cry. She didn't want to. She had no heart to croon to it.

"Keep that thing quiet," called the Overseer. He pointed his finger at the babe. The woman scrunched low. The Driver cracked his whip across the babe anyhow. The babe hollered like any hurt child, and the woman fell to the earth.

The old man that was there, Toby, came and helped her to her feet.

"I must go soon," she told him.

"Soon," he said.

Sarah couldn't stand up straight any longer. She was too weak. The sun burned her face. The babe cried and cried, "Pity me, oh, pity me," say it sounded like. Sarah was so sad and starvin, she sat down in the row.

"Get up, you black cow," called the Overseer. He pointed his hand, and the Driver's whip snarled around Sarah's legs. Her sack dress tore into rags. Her legs bled onto the earth. She couldn't get up.

Toby was there where there was no one to help her and the babe.

"Now, before it's too late," panted Sarah. "Now, Father!"

IDENTIFY

❶ This African American folk tale was passed on from one generation to the next. What details in the first few paragraphs make it seem like a story someone would tell aloud to someone else?

PREDICT

❷ Sarah tells Toby she must go soon. Where do you think she will go? The narrator tells you that she has started flying. What else might "she rose just as free as a bird" mean?

INFER

❸ The Overseer and the Driver want to control the slaves. What can't they control? If the people aren't actually flying away, what are they doing?

INTERPRET

❹ Why do you think these words from Toby are important for the people left behind to hear?

"Yes, Daughter, the time is come," Toby answered. "Go, as you know how to go!"

He raised his arms, holdin them out to her. "Kum . . . yali, kum buba tambe," and more magic words, said so quickly, they sounded like whispers and sighs.

The young woman lifted one foot on the air. Then the other. She flew clumsily at first, with the child now held tightly in her arms. Then she felt the magic, the African mystery. Say she rose just as free as a bird. As light as a feather. ❷

The Overseer rode after her, hollerin. Sarah flew over the fences. She flew over the woods. Tall trees could not snag her. Nor could the Overseer. She flew like an eagle now, until she was gone from sight. No one dared speak about it. Couldn't believe it. But it was, because they that was there saw that it was.

Say the next day was dead hot in the fields. A young man slave fell from the heat. The Driver come and whipped him. Toby come over and spoke words to the fallen one. The words of ancient Africa once heard are never remembered completely. The young man forgot them as soon as he heard them. They went way inside him. He got up and rolled over on the air. He rode it awhile. And he flew away.

Another and another fell from the heat. Toby was there. He cried out to the fallen and reached his arms out to them. "Kum kunka yali, kum . . . tambe!" Whispers and sighs. And they too rose on the air. They rode the hot breezes. The ones flyin were black and shinin sticks, wheelin above the head of the Overseer. They crossed the rows, the fields, the fences, the streams, and were away. ❸

"Seize the old man!" cried the Overseer. "I heard him say the magic *words.* Seize him!"

The one callin himself Master come runnin. The Driver got his whip ready to curl around old Toby and tie him up. The slaveowner took his hip gun from its place. He meant to kill old, black Toby.

But Toby just laughed. Say he threw back his head and said, "Hee, hee! Don't you know who I am? Don't you know some of us in this field?" He said it to their faces. "We are ones who fly!" ❹

And he sighed the ancient words that were a dark promise. He said them all around to the others in the field under the whip, ". . . buba yali . . . buba tambe. . . ."

There was a great outcryin. The bent backs straighted up. Old and young who were called slaves and could fly joined hands. Say like they would ring-sing. But they didn't shuffle in a circle. They didn't

sing. They rose on the air. They flew in a flock that was black against the heavenly blue. Black crows or black shadows. It didn't matter, they went so high. Way above the plantation, way over the slavery land. Say they flew away to *Free-dom.*

And the old man, old Toby, flew behind them, takin care of them. He wasn't cryin. He wasn't laughin. He was the seer. His gaze fell on the plantation where the slaves who could not fly waited.

"Take us with you!" Their looks spoke it but they were afraid to shout it. Toby couldn't take them with him. Hadn't the time to teach them to fly. They must wait for a chance to run.

"Goodie-bye!" The old man called Toby spoke to them, poor souls! And he was flyin gone.

So they say. The Overseer told it. The one called Master said it was a lie, a trick of the light. The Driver kept his mouth shut. ❺

The slaves who could not fly told about the people who could fly to their children. When they were free. When they sat close before the fire in the free land, they told it. They did so love firelight and *Free-dom,* and tellin.

They say that the children of the ones who could not fly told their children. And now, me, I have told it to you. ❻

INTERPRET

❺ Why does the one called Master say this was a lie? Why does the Driver keep silent?

INTERPRET

❻ What message do you think people held in slavery took from this story?

Meet the Writer

Virginia Hamilton

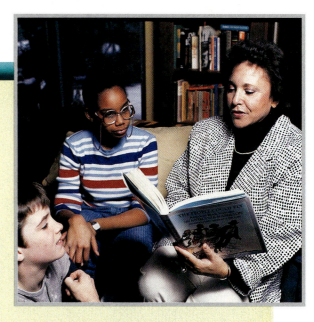

"I Wanted You to Understand the Horrors of Slavery"

Virginia Hamilton (1936–2002) grew up in Yellow Springs, Ohio, an Underground Railroad stop where her grandfather had settled after escaping from slavery in Virginia. Hamilton grew up to be a celebrated writer of books for children and young adults, including the award-winning folk-tale collection *The People Could Fly: American Black Folktales* (1986). "I wrote this tale," she tells readers, "because I wanted you to understand the horrors of slavery and to be touched by these courageous human beings."

66 'The People Could Fly' is one of the most extraordinary, moving tales in black folklore. It almost makes us believe that the people could fly. There are numerous separate accounts of flying Africans and slaves in the black folk-tale literature. Such accounts are often combined with tales of slaves disappearing. A plausible explanation might be the slaves running away from slavery, slipping away while in the fields or under cover of darkness. In code language murmured from one slave to another, 'Come fly away!' might have been the words used. Another explanation is the wish-fulfillment motif.

'The People Could Fly' is a detailed fantasy of suffering, of magic power exerted against the so-called Master and his underlings. Finally, it is a powerful testament to the millions of slaves who never had the opportunity to 'fly' away. They remained slaves, as did their children. 'The People Could Fly' was first told and retold by those who had only their imaginations to set them free. 99

Practice the Strategy

Developing Summary and Theme Statements

PRACTICE 1

Sometimes, when you're trying to come up with a theme, it helps to write a summary first. That way you won't mistakenly use a summary statement for a theme statement. Use the "Somebody Wanted But So" chart below to write a summary statement for "The People Could Fly."

Somebody	Wanted	But	So

Strategy Tip

Themes are generally statements, not just single words. For example, *greed* is a topic; *Greed can lead to trouble* is a theme. *Freedom* is a topic; *Hope can set you free* is a theme.

PRACTICE 2

Read each of the following statements, and decide whether it is a summary or a theme of "The People Could Fly." Be able to explain your decisions.

1. Your imagination can help set you free.

2. The Overseer wants the slaves to work harder, but they can't, so he punishes them.

3. Toby uses magic words to set the slaves free.

4. In the midst of despair, hope can be a powerful type of freedom.

5. The master of your body does not have to be the master of your mind.

PRACTICE 3

Now, write your own theme statement for this story. One student did this by first jotting down words that came to mind as she read the story. Her list included the following important words: *slavery, freedom, pain, magic, belief, escape, flying.* What words would you add to this list? Now, choose one of the starters below (or write your own), and form your own theme statement.

• Freedom is a result of . . .   • You can be free if . . .

You can use "Somebody Wanted But So" with the texts in this collection and with any text you want to summarize.

SKILLS FOCUS

Reading Skills
Develop summary and theme statements.

The Diary of Anne Frank

Literary Focus

Theme

Plot answers the question "What happens?" Theme answers the question "What does this reveal?" **Theme** is the general idea or insight about human existence that is revealed in a story, poem, or play. It's what the writer is saying about life. Most works of literature have more than one theme; a long work will often reveal many themes. See what themes you discover in this play as you experience with the characters the terror of hiding from enemies who want to destroy you.

Reading Skills

Using Resources

In the following pages you'll find many **resources** that contain facts about the true story of Anne Frank and about the play. Those resources include **maps**, a **time line**, historical **photographs**, and entries from Anne Frank's diary. (The diary is an example of a **primary source,** that is, firsthand information.) As you read, use those background resources to deepen your understanding of what is happening in the play. The time line especially will help you trace what is going on in the war-torn world beyond Anne's attic. The stage design will help you visualize the action of the play.

go.
hrw
.com

INTERNET

Vocabulary
Activity
•
Cross-curricular
Connection

Keyword: LE5 8-4

Literary Skills
Identify and analyze themes.

Reading Skills
Use resources to understand the historical background of a play.

Vocabulary Development

These are some of the words you will learn as you read the play:

conspicuous (kən·spik′yoo·əs) *adj.:* noticeable. *The Nazis required all Jews to wear a conspicuous yellow Star of David on their clothing.*

unabashed (un′ə·basht′) *adj.:* unembarrassed. *Anne's unabashed comments sometimes embarrassed her mother.*

loathe (lōth) *v.:* hate. *Anne loathed having her mother treat her like a baby.*

indignantly (in·dig′nənt·lē) *adv.:* with anger caused by something felt to be unjust. *Anne indignantly claimed she had not been rude.*

fortify (fôrt′ə·fī′) *v.:* strengthen. *Mr. Dussel took pills to fortify himself.*

zeal (zēl) *n.:* great enthusiasm; devotion to a cause. *The Maccabees showed great zeal in their fight against tyranny.*

tyranny (tir′ə·nē) *n.:* cruel and unjust use of power. *The Maccabees' fight against tyranny and oppression two thousand years ago still inspires people today.*

gingerly (jin′jər′lē) *adv.:* cautiously. *Peter held Anne's gift gingerly, afraid it might jump out and hit him.*

ostentatiously (äs′tən·tā′shəs·lē) *adv.:* in a showy way. *Peter held his coat ostentatiously to pretend he was hiding his cat there.*

appalled (ə·pôld′) *v.* used as *adj.:* horrified. *Dussel's alarming news was met with a moment of appalled silence.*

disgruntled (dis·grunt′ʹld) v. used as *adj.*: displeased; annoyed. *Mr. Dussel, disgruntled, listened to the conversation.*

inarticulate (in′är·tik′yōō·lit) *adj.*: unable to speak. *Peter was so furious at Dussel that he became inarticulate.*

forlorn (fôr·lôrn′) *adj.*: abandoned and lonely. *Dussel felt forlorn when Peter and Anne both closed their doors on him.*

animation (an′i·mā′shen) *n.*: liveliness. *Anne's animation could both delight and annoy her family.*

remorse (ri·môrs′) *n.*: deep feeling of guilt. *Mrs. Frank felt remorse for her angry outburst.*

Background
Literature and Real Life

" I hope I shall be able to confide in you completely, as I have never been able to do in anyone before, and I hope that you will be a great support and comfort to me. "

So begins the diary of a thirteen-year-old Jewish girl named Anne Frank. Anne's diary opens in 1942 with stories of boyfriends, parties, and school life. It closes two years later, just days before Anne is captured and imprisoned in a Nazi concentration camp.

Anne Frank was born in Frankfurt, Germany, in 1929. When she was four years old, her family immigrated to Amsterdam, the Netherlands, to escape the anti-Jewish measures being introduced in Germany. In Amsterdam, Otto Frank, Anne's father, managed a company that sold pectin, a substance used in making jams and jellies. Anne and her older sister, Margot, enjoyed a happy, carefree childhood until May 1940, when the Netherlands capitulated (surrendered) to the invading German army. Anne wrote in her diary about the Nazi occupation that followed:

" After May 1940, good times rapidly fled: first the war, then the capitulation, followed by the arrival of the Germans, which is when the sufferings of us Jews really began. Anti-Jewish decrees followed each other in quick succession. Jews must wear a yellow star, Jews must hand in their bicycles, Jews are banned from trains and are forbidden to drive. Jews are only allowed to do their shopping between three and five o'clock and then only in shops which bear the placard 'Jewish shop.' Jews must be indoors by eight o'clock and cannot even sit in their own gardens after that hour. Jews are forbidden to visit theaters, cinemas, and other places of entertainment. Jews may not take part in public sports. Swimming baths, tennis courts, hockey fields, and other sports grounds are all prohibited to them. Jews may not visit Christians. Jews must go to Jewish schools, and many more restrictions of a similar kind.

So we could not do this and were forbidden to do that. But life went on in spite of it all. "

Soon, however, the situation in the Netherlands grew much worse. As in other German-occupied countries, the Nazis began rounding up Jews and transporting them to concentration camps and death camps, where prisoners died from overwork, starvation, or disease or were murdered in gas chambers. Escaping Nazi-occupied territory became nearly impossible. Like many other Jews

Europe Before World War II

See also the maps on page 443.

trapped in Europe at the time, Anne and her family went into hiding to avoid capture. Others were not so lucky, as Anne knew:

" Countless friends and acquaintances have gone to a terrible fate. Evening after evening the green and gray army lorries [trucks] trundle past. The Germans ring at every front door to inquire if there are any Jews living in the house. If there are, then the whole family has to go at once. If they don't find any, they go on to the next house. No one has a chance of evading them unless one goes into hiding. Often they go around with lists and only ring when they know they can get a good haul. Sometimes they let them off for cash—so much per head. It seems like the slave hunts of olden times. . . . In the evenings when it's dark, I often see rows of good, innocent people accompanied by crying children, walking on and on, in the charge of a couple of these chaps, bullied and knocked about until they almost drop. No one is spared—old people, babies, expectant mothers, the sick—each and all join in the march of death. "

The Frank family and four other Jews lived for more than two years hidden in a few cramped rooms (now known as the Secret Annex) behind Mr. Frank's office and warehouse. In August 1944, the Nazi police raided their hiding place and sent all eight of its occupants to concentration camps. Of the eight, only Otto Frank survived. Anne died of typhus in a camp in Germany called Bergen-Belsen. She was fifteen years old.

When she began her diary, Anne didn't intend to show it to anyone unless she found a "real friend." Through its dozens of translations and the stage adaptation you are about to read, Anne's diary has found her generations of friends all over the world.

ANNE FRANK'S LIFE

June 12: Anne Frank is born in Frankfurt, Germany.

Anne in 1933.

The Franks decide to leave Germany to escape Nazi persecution. While Mr. Frank looks for a new home in Amsterdam, the Netherlands, the rest of the family stays with relatives in Aachen, Germany.

Anne with her father at Miep Santrouschitz and Jan Gies's wedding.

Summer: The Van Pels family (called the Van Daans in Anne's diary) flee Germany for the Netherlands.

December 8: Fritz Pfeffer (called Albert Dussel in Anne's diary) flees Germany for the Netherlands.

Anne playing with her friend Sanne Ledermann in Amsterdam.

The Granger Collection, New York.

WORLD EVENTS

1929

1930 to 1932
The National Socialist German Workers' (Nazi) party begins its rise to power. The Nazis proclaim the superiority of the German "master race" and blame Jews for the German defeat in World War I and for the troubled economy.

1933
January 30: The Nazi party leader, Adolf Hitler, becomes chancellor (head of the government) of Germany.

March 10: The first concentration camp is established by the Nazis, at Dachau, Germany.

April: The Nazis pass their first anti-Jewish law, banning the public employment of Jews.

Adolf Hitler.

1934

1935
September 15: The Nuremberg Laws are passed, denying Jews German citizenship and forbidding marriage between Jews and non-Jews.

1936
October 25: Germany and Italy form an alliance (the Axis).

1937

1938
March 12–13: The German army invades and annexes Austria.

September 29: The Munich Agreement, granting Germany the right to annex part of Czechoslovakia, is drafted and signed by representatives of France, Great Britain, Italy, and Germany.

November 9–10: Kristallnacht (Night of the Broken Glass). Led by the SS, the Nazi special police, Germans beat and kill Jews, loot Jewish stores, and burn synagogues.

ANNE FRANK'S LIFE

Anne, second from left, with friends on her tenth birthday.

The Granger Collection, New York.

June 12: Anne receives a diary for her thirteenth birthday.

July 6: The Franks go into hiding after Margot receives an order to appear for deportation to a labor camp in Germany. The Van Pels family joins them one week later.

November 16: Fritz Pfeffer becomes the eighth occupant of the Secret Annex.

August 4: Nazi police raid the Secret Annex; the occupants are sent to concentration camps.

September: Mr. Van Pels dies in Auschwitz.

December 20: Fritz Pfeffer dies in Neuengamme.

Anne's mother, Edith Frank, dies in Auschwitz. Three weeks later Otto Frank is freed when Auschwitz is liberated by the Soviet army. Anne and Margot die in Bergen-Belsen a few weeks before British soldiers liberate the camp. Peter Van Pels dies in Mauthausen. Mrs. Van Pels dies in Theresienstadt.

WORLD EVENTS

1939

March: Germany invades and occupies most of Czechoslovakia.

September 1: Germany invades Poland; World War II begins. France and Great Britain declare war on Germany two days later.

1940

Spring: Germany invades Denmark, Norway, the Netherlands, Belgium, Luxembourg, and France.

September 27: Japan joins the Axis.

1941

June 22: Germany invades the Soviet Union.

December: The United States enters the war on the side of the Allied nations (including Great Britain, the Soviet Union, and other countries) after Japan attacks the U.S. naval base at Pearl Harbor.

1942

January: The "Final Solution" is secretly announced at a conference of Nazi officials: Europe's Jews are to be "exterminated," or murdered. Construction of death camps begins in Poland. Millions of people (Jews and non-Jews) will die in those camps.

1943

1944

June 6: D-day. Allied forces land in Normandy, in northern France, and launch an invasion of western Europe.

Bombing of Hiroshima.

1945

May 8: The war in Europe ends with Germany's unconditional surrender to the Allies.

September 2: Japan surrenders after the United States drops atomic bombs on the Japanese cities of Hiroshima and Nagasaki. World War II ends one week later.

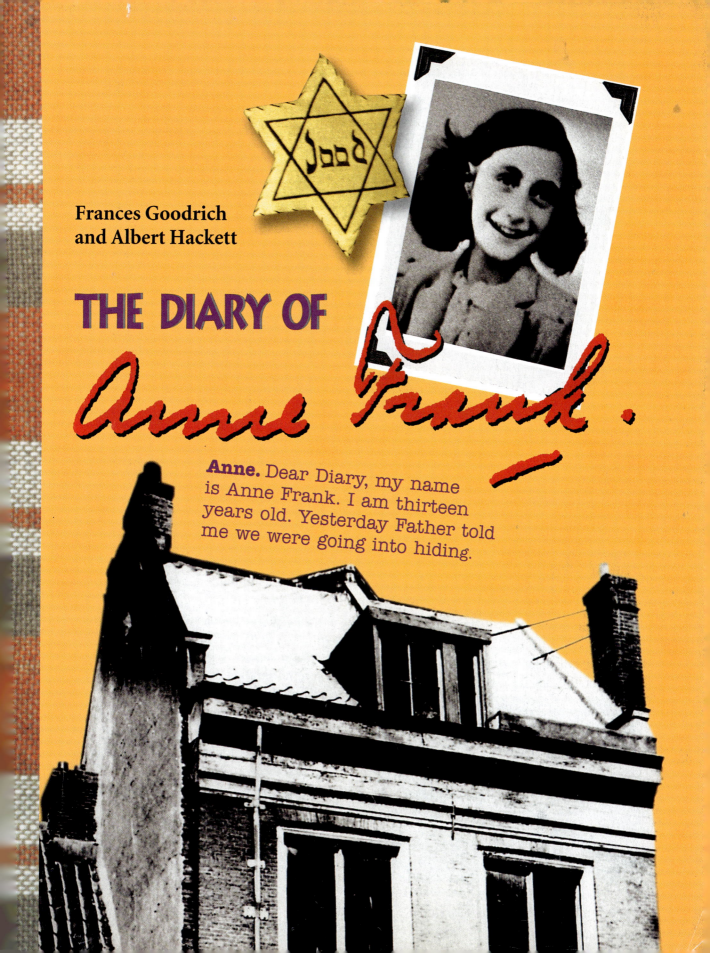

**Frances Goodrich
and Albert Hackett**

THE DIARY OF
Anne Frank.

Anne. Dear Diary, my name
is Anne Frank. I am thirteen
years old. Yesterday Father told
me we were going into hiding.

Stage Set for *The Diary of Anne Frank*

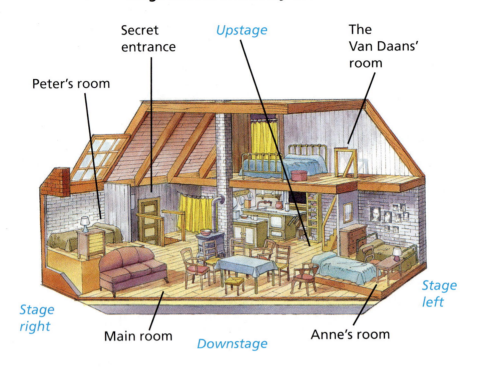

Peter's room

Secret entrance

Upstage

The Van Daans' room

Stage right

Main room

Downstage

Anne's room

Stage left

Characters

Occupants of the Secret Annex:
Anne Frank
Margot Frank, her older sister
Mr. Frank, their father
Mrs. Frank, their mother
Peter Van Daan
Mr. Van Daan, his father
Mrs. Van Daan, his mother
Mr. Dussel, a dentist

Workers in Mr. Frank's Business:
Miep Gies,[1] a young Dutchwoman
Mr. Kraler,[2] a Dutchman

Setting: Amsterdam, the Netherlands, July 1942 to August 1944; November 1945.

---

1. **Miep Gies** (mēp khēs).
2. **Kraler** (krä′lər).

Act One

■ SCENE 1

The scene remains the same throughout the play. It is the top floor of a warehouse and office building in Amsterdam, Holland. The sharply peaked roof of the building is outlined against a sea of other rooftops stretching away into the distance. Nearby is the belfry of a church tower, the Westertoren, whose carillon[3] rings out the hours. Occasionally faint sounds float up from below: the voices of children playing in the street, the tramp of marching feet, a boat whistle from the canal.[4]

---

3. **carillon** (kar′ə·län′) *n.:* set of bells, each of which produces a single tone.
4. **canal** *n.:* artificial waterway. Amsterdam, which was built on soggy ground, has more than one hundred canals, built to help drain the land. The canals are used like streets.

The three rooms of the top floor and a small attic space above are exposed to our view. The largest of the rooms is in the center, with two small rooms, slightly raised, on either side. On the right is a bathroom, out of sight. A narrow, steep flight of stairs at the back leads up to the attic. The rooms are sparsely furnished, with a few chairs, cots, a table or two. The windows are painted over or covered with makeshift blackout curtains. In the main room there is a sink, a gas ring for cooking, and a wood-burning stove for warmth.

The room on the left is hardly more than a closet. There is a skylight in the sloping ceiling. Directly under this room is a small, steep stairwell, with steps leading down to a door. This is the only entrance from the building below. When the door is opened, we see that it has been concealed on the outer side by a bookcase attached to it.

The curtain rises on an empty stage. It is late afternoon, November 1945.

The rooms are dusty, the curtains in rags. Chairs and tables are overturned.

The door at the foot of the small stairwell swings open. MR. FRANK *comes up the steps into view. He is a gentle, cultured European in his middle years. There is still a trace of a German accent in his speech.*

He stands looking slowly around, making a supreme effort at self-control. He is weak, ill. His clothes are threadbare.

After a second he drops his rucksack on the couch and moves slowly about. He opens the door to one of the smaller rooms and then abruptly closes it again, turning away. He goes to the window at the back, looking off at the Westertoren as its carillon strikes the hour of six; then he moves restlessly on.

From the street below we hear the sound of a barrel organ and children's voices at play.

There is a many-colored scarf hanging from a nail. MR. FRANK *takes it, putting it around his neck. As he starts back for his rucksack, his eye is caught by something lying on the floor. It is a woman's white glove. He holds it in his hand and suddenly all of his self-control is gone. He breaks down crying.*

We hear footsteps on the stairs. MIEP GIES *comes up, looking for* MR. FRANK. MIEP *is a Dutchwoman of about twenty-two. She wears a coat and hat, ready to go home. She is pregnant. Her attitude toward* MR. FRANK *is protective, compassionate.*

Miep. Are you all right, Mr. Frank?

Mr. Frank (*quickly controlling himself*). Yes, Miep, yes.

Miep. Everyone in the office has gone home . . . It's after six. (*Then, pleading*) Don't stay up here, Mr. Frank. What's the use of torturing yourself like this?

Mr. Frank. I've come to say goodbye . . . I'm leaving here, Miep.

Miep. What do you mean? Where are you going? Where?

Mr. Frank. I don't know yet. I haven't decided.

Miep. Mr. Frank, you can't leave here! This is your home! Amsterdam is your home. Your business is here, waiting for you. . . . You're needed here. . . . Now that the war is over, there are things that . . .

Mr. Frank. I can't stay in Amsterdam, Miep. It has too many memories for me. Everywhere, there's something . . . the house we lived in . . . the school . . . that street organ playing out there . . . I'm not the person you used to know, Miep. I'm a bitter old man. (*Breaking off*) Forgive me. I shouldn't speak to you like this . . . after all that you did for us . . . the suffering . . .

Miep. No. No. It wasn't suffering. You can't say we suffered. (*As she speaks, she straightens a chair which is overturned.*)

Mr. Frank. I know what you went through, you and Mr. Kraler. I'll remember it as long as I live. (*He gives one last look around.*) Come, Miep. (*He starts for the steps, then remembers his rucksack, going back to get it.*)

Miep (*hurrying up to a cupboard*). Mr. Frank, did you see? There are some of your papers here. (*She brings a bundle of papers to him.*) We found them in a heap of rubbish on the floor after . . . after you left.

Mr. Frank. Burn them. (*He opens his rucksack to put the glove in it.*)

Miep. But, Mr. Frank, there are letters, notes . . .

Mr. Frank. Burn them. All of them.

Miep. Burn *this*? (*She hands him a paperbound notebook.*)

Mr. Frank (*quietly*). Anne's diary. (*He opens the diary and begins to read.*) "Monday, the sixth of July, nineteen forty-two." (*To* MIEP) Nineteen forty-two. Is it possible, Miep? . . . Only three years ago. (*As he continues his reading, he sits down on the couch.*) "Dear Diary, since you and I are going to be great friends, I will start by telling you about myself. My name is Anne Frank. I am thirteen years old. I was born in Germany the twelfth of June, nineteen twenty-nine. As my family is Jewish, we emigrated to Holland when Hitler came to power."

[*As* MR. FRANK *reads on, another voice joins his, as if coming from the air. It is* ANNE'*s voice.*]

Mr. Frank and Anne's Voice. "My father

Miep Gies and Otto Frank.

started a business, importing spice and herbs. Things went well for us until nineteen forty. Then the war came, and the Dutch capitulation, followed by the arrival of the Germans. Then things got very bad for the Jews."

[MR. FRANK'*s voice dies out.* ANNE'*s voice continues alone. The lights dim slowly to darkness. The curtain falls on the scene.*]

Anne's Voice. You could not do this and you could not do that. They forced Father out of his business. We had to wear yellow stars.[5] I had to turn in my bike. I couldn't go to a Dutch school anymore. I couldn't go to the movies or ride in an automobile or even on a streetcar, and a million other things. But somehow we children still managed to have fun. Yesterday Father told me we were going into hiding. Where, he wouldn't say. At five o'clock this morning Mother woke me and told me to hurry and get dressed. I was to put on as many clothes as I could. It would look too suspicious if we walked along carrying suitcases. It wasn't until we were on our way that I learned where we were going. Our hiding place was to be upstairs in the building where Father used to have his business. Three other people were coming in with us . . . the Van Daans and their son Peter . . . Father knew the Van Daans but we had never met them . . .

---

5. **yellow stars:** The Nazis ordered all Jews to sew a large Star of David (a six-pointed star) on their outer clothing so that they could be easily recognized as Jews.

[*During the last lines the curtain rises on the scene. The lights dim on.* ANNE's *voice fades out.*]

■ SCENE 2

It is early morning, July 1942. The rooms are bare, as before, but they are now clean and orderly.

MR. VAN DAAN, *a tall, portly man in his late forties, is in the main room, pacing up and down, nervously smoking a cigarette. His clothes and overcoat are expensive and well cut.*

MRS. VAN DAAN *sits on the couch, clutching her possessions: a hatbox, bags, etc. She is a pretty woman in her early forties. She wears a fur coat over her other clothes.*

PETER VAN DAAN *is standing at the window of the room on the right, looking down at the street below. He is a shy, awkward boy of sixteen. He wears a cap, a raincoat, and long Dutch trousers, like plus fours.[6] At his feet is a black case, a carrier for his cat.*

The yellow Star of David is conspicuous *on all of their clothes.*

Mrs. Van Daan (*rising, nervous, excited*). Something's happened to them! I know it!

Mr. Van Daan. Now, Kerli!

Mrs. Van Daan. Mr. Frank said they'd be here at seven o'clock. He said . . .

Mr. Van Daan. They have two miles to walk. You can't expect . . .

Mrs. Van Daan. They've been picked up. That's what's happened. They've been taken . . .

[MR. VAN DAAN *indicates that he hears someone coming.*]

Mr. Van Daan. You see?

---

6. **plus fours** *n.*: baggy trousers that end in cuffs just below the knees.

[PETER *takes up his carrier and his school bag, etc., and goes into the main room as* MR. FRANK *comes up the stairwell from below.* MR. FRANK *looks much younger now. His movements are brisk, his manner confident. He wears an overcoat and carries his hat and a small cardboard box. He crosses to the* VAN DAANS, *shaking hands with each of them.*]

Mr. Frank. Mrs. Van Daan, Mr. Van Daan, Peter. (*Then, in explanation of their lateness*) There were too many of the Green Police[7] on the streets . . . we had to take the long way around.

[*Up the steps come* MARGOT FRANK, MRS. FRANK, MIEP (*not pregnant now*), *and* MR. KRALER. *All of them carry bags, packages, and so forth. The Star of David is conspicuous on all of the* FRANKS' *clothing.* MARGOT *is eighteen, beautiful, quiet, shy.* MRS. FRANK *is a young mother, gently bred, reserved. She, like* MR. FRANK, *has a slight German accent.* MR. KRALER *is a Dutchman, dependable, kindly.*

As MR. KRALER *and* MIEP *go upstage to put down their parcels,* MRS. FRANK *turns back to call* ANNE.]

Mrs. Frank. Anne?

[ANNE *comes running up the stairs. She is thirteen, quick in her movements, interested in everything, mercurial[8] in her emotions. She wears a cape and long wool socks and carries a school bag.*]

---

7. **Green Police:** Nazi police, who wore green uniforms.
8. **mercurial** (mər·kyoor'ē·əl) *adj.*: changeable.

Vocabulary

conspicuous (kən·spik'yoo·əs) *adj.*: obvious; noticeable.

Stage scene showing the Secret Annex in a 1997 adaptation of *The Diary of Anne Frank*.

Mr. Frank (*introducing them*). My wife, Edith. Mr. and Mrs. Van Daan (MRS. FRANK *hurries over, shaking hands with them.*) . . . their son, Peter . . . my daughters, Margot and Anne.

[ANNE *gives a polite little curtsy as she shakes* MR. VAN DAAN'*s hand. Then she immediately starts off on a tour of investigation of her new home, going upstairs to the attic room.*

MIEP *and* MR. KRALER *are putting the various things they have brought on the shelves.*]

Mr. Kraler. I'm sorry there is still so much confusion.

Mr. Frank. Please. Don't think of it. After all, we'll have plenty of leisure to arrange everything ourselves.

Miep (*to* MRS. FRANK). We put the stores of food you sent in here. Your drugs are here . . . soap, linen here.

Mrs. Frank. Thank you, Miep.

Miep. I made up the beds . . . the way Mr. Frank and Mr. Kraler said. (*She starts out.*) Forgive me. I have to hurry. I've got to go to the other side of town to get some ration books[9] for you.

Mrs. Van Daan. Ration books? If they see our names on ration books, they'll know we're here.

Mr. Kraler. There isn't anything . . .

Miep. Don't worry. Your names won't be on them. (*As she hurries out*) I'll be up later.

Together

Mr. Frank. Thank you, Miep.

Mrs. Frank (*to* MR. KRALER). It's illegal, then, the ration books? We've never done anything illegal.

---

9. **ration books:** books of stamps or coupons issued by the government during wartime. People could purchase scarce items, such as food, clothing, and gasoline, only with these coupons.

Mr. Frank. We won't be living here exactly according to regulations.

[*As* MR. KRALER *reassures* MRS. FRANK, *he takes various small things, such as matches and soap, from his pockets, handing them to her.*]

Mr. Kraler. This isn't the black market,[10] Mrs. Frank. This is what we call the white market . . . helping all of the hundreds and hundreds who are hiding out in Amsterdam.

[*The carillon is heard playing the quarter-hour before eight.* MR. KRALER *looks at his watch.* ANNE *stops at the window as she comes down the stairs.*]

Anne. It's the Westertoren!

Mr. Kraler. I must go. I must be out of here and downstairs in the office before the workmen get here. (*He starts for the stairs leading out.*) Miep or I, or both of us, will be up each day to bring you food and news and find out what your needs are. Tomorrow I'll get you a better bolt for the door at the foot of the stairs. It needs a bolt that you can throw yourself and open only at our signal. (*To* MR. FRANK) Oh . . . You'll tell them about the noise?

Mr. Frank. I'll tell them.

Mr. Kraler. Goodbye, then, for the moment. I'll come up again, after the workmen leave.

Mr. Frank. Goodbye, Mr. Kraler.

Mrs. Frank (*shaking his hand*). How can we thank you?

[*The others murmur their goodbyes.*]

Mr. Kraler. I never thought I'd live to see the day when a man like Mr. Frank would

---

10. **black market** *n.:* place or system for buying and selling goods illegally, without ration stamps.

---

have to go into hiding. When you think—

[*He breaks off, going out.* MR. FRANK *follows him down the steps, bolting the door after him. In the interval before he returns,* PETER *goes over to* MARGOT, *shaking hands with her. As* MR. FRANK *comes back up the steps,* MRS. FRANK *questions him anxiously.*]

Mrs. Frank. What did he mean, about the noise?

Mr. Frank. First let us take off some of these clothes.

[*They all start to take off garment after garment. On each of their coats, sweaters, blouses, suits, dresses is another yellow Star of David.* MR. *and* MRS. FRANK *are underdressed quite simply. The others wear several things: sweaters, extra dresses, bathrobes, aprons, nightgowns, etc.*]

Mr. Van Daan. It's a wonder we weren't arrested, walking along the streets . . . Petronella with a fur coat in July . . . and that cat of Peter's crying all the way.

Anne (*as she is removing a pair of panties*). A cat?

Mrs. Frank (*shocked*). Anne, please!

Anne. It's all right. I've got on three more.

[*She pulls off two more. Finally, as they have all removed their surplus clothes, they look to* MR. FRANK, *waiting for him to speak.*]

Mr. Frank. Now. About the noise. While the men are in the building below, we must have complete quiet. Every sound can be heard down there, not only in the workrooms but in the offices too. The men come at about eight-thirty and leave at about five-thirty. So, to be perfectly safe, from eight in the morning until six in the evening we must move only when it is necessary, and then in stockinged feet. We must not speak above a whisper. We must not run any water. We cannot use the sink or even, forgive me, the w.c.[11] The pipes go down through the workrooms. It would be heard. No trash . . . (MR. FRANK *stops abruptly as he hears the sound of marching feet from the street below. Everyone is motionless, paralyzed with fear.* MR. FRANK *goes quietly into the room on the right to look down out of the window.* ANNE *runs after him, peering out with him. The tramping feet pass without stopping. The tension is relieved.* MR. FRANK, *followed by* ANNE, *returns to the main room and resumes his instructions to the group.*) . . . No trash must ever be thrown out which might reveal that someone is living up here . . . not even a potato paring. We must burn everything in the stove at night. This is the way we must live until it is over, if we are to survive.

[*There is silence for a second.*]

Mrs. Frank. Until it is over.

Mr. Frank (*reassuringly*). After six we can move about . . . we can talk and laugh and have our supper and read and play games . . . just as we would at home. (*He looks at his watch.*) And now I think it would be wise if we all went to our rooms, and we settled before eight o'clock. Mrs. Van Daan, you and your husband will be upstairs. I regret that there's no room for Peter. But he will be here, near us. This will be our common room, where we'll meet to talk and eat and read like one family.

Mr. Van Daan. And where do you and Mrs. Frank sleep?

Mr. Frank. This room is also our bedroom.

Mrs. Van Daan. That isn't right. We'll sleep here and you take the room upstairs. } *Together*

Mr. Van Daan. It's your place.

Mr. Frank. Please. I've thought this out for weeks. It's the best arrangement. The only arrangement.

Mrs. Van Daan (*to* MR. FRANK). Never, never can we thank you. (*Then, to* MRS. FRANK) I don't know what would have happened to us, if it hadn't been for Mr. Frank.

Mr. Frank. You don't know how your husband helped me when I came to this country . . . knowing no one . . . not able to speak the language. I can never repay him for that. (*Going to* MR. VAN DAAN) May I help you with your things?

Mr. Van Daan. No. No. (*To* MRS. VAN DAAN) Come along, liefje.[12]

Mrs. Van Daan. You'll be all right, Peter? You're not afraid?

Peter (*embarrassed*). Please, Mother.

[*They start up the stairs to the attic room above.* MR. FRANK *turns to* MRS. FRANK.]

Mr. Frank. You too must have some rest, Edith. You didn't close your eyes last night. Nor you, Margot.

Anne. I slept, Father. Wasn't that funny? I knew it was the last night in my own bed, and yet I slept soundly.

Mr. Frank. I'm glad, Anne. Now you'll be able to help me straighten things in here. (*To* MRS. FRANK *and* MARGOT) Come with me. . . . You and Margot rest in this room for the time being. (*He picks up their clothes, starting for the room on the right.*)

Mrs. Frank. You're sure . . . ? I could help

---

11. **w.c.:** short for "water closet," or toilet.

12. **liefje** (lēf′hyə): Dutch for "little dear one."

. . . And Anne hasn't had her milk . . .

Mr. Frank. I'll give it to her. (*To* ANNE *and* PETER) Anne, Peter . . . it's best that you take off your shoes now, before you forget. (*He leads the way to the room, followed by* MARGOT.)

Mrs. Frank. You're sure you're not tired, Anne?

Anne. I feel fine. I'm going to help Father.

Mrs. Frank. Peter, I'm glad you are to be with us.

Peter. Yes, Mrs. Frank.

[MRS. FRANK *goes to join* MR. FRANK *and* MARGOT.

During the following scene MR. FRANK *helps* MARGOT *and* MRS. FRANK *to hang up their clothes. Then he persuades them both to lie down and rest. The* VAN DAANS, *in their room above, settle themselves. In the main room* ANNE *and* PETER *remove their shoes.* PETER *takes his cat out of the carrier.*]

Anne. What's your cat's name?

Peter. Mouschi.[13]

Anne. Mouschi! Mouschi! Mouschi! (*She picks up the cat, walking away with it. To* PETER) I love cats. I have one . . . a darling little cat. But they made me leave her behind. I left some food and a note for the neighbors to take care of her . . . I'm going to miss her terribly. What is yours? A him or a her?

Peter. He's a tom. He doesn't like strangers. (*He takes the cat from her, putting it back in its carrier.*)

Anne (*unabashed*). Then I'll have to stop being a stranger, won't I? Is he fixed?

Peter (*startled*). Huh?

Anne. Did you have him fixed?

Peter. No.

---

13. **Mouschi** (mo͞o′shē).

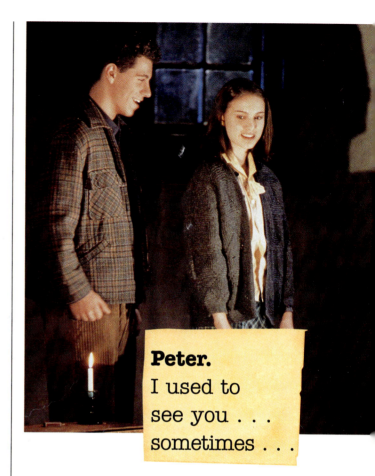

Peter.
I used to
see you . . .
sometimes . . .

Anne. Oh, you ought to have him fixed—to keep him from—you know, fighting. Where did you go to school?

Peter. Jewish Secondary.

Anne. But that's where Margot and I go! I never saw you around.

Peter. I used to see you . . . sometimes . . .

Anne. You did?

Peter. . . . in the schoolyard. You were always in the middle of a bunch of kids. (*He takes a penknife from his pocket.*)

Anne. Why didn't you ever come over?

Peter. I'm sort of a lone wolf. (*He starts to rip off his Star of David.*)

Vocabulary
unabashed (un′ə·basht′) *adj.:* unembarrassed; unashamed.

Anne. What are you doing?

Peter. Taking it off.

Anne. But you can't do that. They'll arrest you if you go out without your star.

[*He tosses his knife on the table.*]

Peter. Who's going out?

Anne. Why, of course! You're right! Of course we don't need them anymore. (*She picks up his knife and starts to take her star off.*) I wonder what our friends will think when we don't show up today?

Peter. I didn't have any dates with anyone.

Anne. Oh, I did. I had a date with Jopie to go and play ping-pong at her house. Do you know Jopie de Waal?[14]

Peter. No.

Anne. Jopie's my best friend. I wonder what she'll think when she telephones and there's no answer? . . . Probably she'll go over to the house. . . . I wonder what she'll think . . . we left everything as if we'd suddenly been called away . . . breakfast dishes in the sink . . . beds not made . . . (*As she pulls off her star, the cloth underneath shows clearly the color and form of the star.*) Look! It's still there! (PETER *goes over to the stove with his star.*) What're you going to do with yours?

Peter. Burn it.

Anne (*she starts to throw hers in, and cannot*). It's funny, I can't throw mine away. I don't know why.

Peter Van Pels
("Peter Van Daan").

Peter. You can't throw . . . ? Something they branded you with . . . ? That they made you wear so they could spit on you?

Anne. I know. I know. But after all, it *is* the Star of David, isn't it?

[*In the bedroom, right,* MARGOT *and* MRS. FRANK *are lying down.* MR. FRANK *starts quietly out.*]

Peter. Maybe it's different for a girl.

[MR. FRANK *comes into the main room.*]

Mr. Frank. Forgive me, Peter. Now let me see. We must find a bed for your cat. (*He goes to a cupboard.*) I'm glad you brought your cat. Anne was feeling so badly about hers. (*Getting a used small washtub*) Here we are. Will it be comfortable in that?

Peter (*gathering up his things*). Thanks.

Mr. Frank (*opening the door of the room on the left*). And here is your room. But I warn you, Peter, you can't grow anymore. Not an inch, or you'll have to sleep with your feet out of the skylight. Are you hungry?

Peter. No.

Mr. Frank. We have some bread and butter.

Peter. No, thank you.

Mr. Frank. You can have it for luncheon then. And tonight we will have a real supper . . . our first supper together.

Peter. Thanks. Thanks. (*He goes into his room. During the following scene he arranges his possessions in his new room.*)

Mr. Frank. That's a nice boy, Peter.

Anne. He's awfully shy, isn't he?

---

14. **Jopie de Waal** (yō′pē də väl′).

Mr. Frank. You'll like him, I know.

Anne. I certainly hope so, since he's the only boy I'm likely to see for months and months.

[MR. FRANK *sits down, taking off his shoes.*]

Mr. Frank. Annele,[15] there's a box there. Will you open it?

[*He indicates a carton on the couch.* ANNE *brings it to the center table. In the street below, there is the sound of children playing.*]

Anne (*as she opens the carton*). You know the way I'm going to think of it here? I'm going to think of it as a boardinghouse. A very peculiar summer boardinghouse, like the one that we— (*She breaks off as she pulls out some photographs.*) Father! My movie stars! I was wondering where they were! I was looking for them this morning . . . and Queen Wilhelmina![16] How wonderful!

Mr. Frank. There's something more. Go on. Look further. (*He goes over to the sink, pouring a glass of milk from a thermos bottle.*)

Anne (*pulling out a pasteboard-bound book*). A diary! (*She throws her arms around her father.*) I've never had a diary. And I've always longed for one. (*She looks around the room.*) Pencil, pencil, pencil, pencil. (*She starts down the stairs.*) I'm going down to the office to get a pencil.

Mr. Frank. Anne! No! (*He goes after her, catching her by the arm and pulling her back.*)

Anne (*startled*). But there's no one in the building now.

Mr. Frank. It doesn't matter. I don't want you ever to go beyond that door.

Anne (*sobered*). Never . . . ? Not even at nighttime, when everyone is gone? Or on Sundays? Can't I go down to listen to the radio?

Mr. Frank. Never. I am sorry, Anneke.[17] It isn't safe. No, you must never go beyond that door.

[*For the first time* ANNE *realizes what "going into hiding" means.*]

Anne. I see.

Mr. Frank. It'll be hard, I know. But always remember this, Anneke. There are no walls, there are no bolts, no locks that anyone can put on your mind. Miep will bring us books. We will read history, poetry, mythology. (*He gives her the glass of milk.*) Here's your milk. (*With his arm about her, they go over to the couch, sitting down side by side.*) As a matter of fact, between us, Anne, being here has certain advantages for you. For instance, you remember the battle you had with your mother the other day on the subject of overshoes? You said you'd rather die than wear overshoes? But in the end you had to wear them? Well now, you see, for as long as we are here, you will never have to wear overshoes! Isn't that good? And the coat that you inherited from Margot, you won't have to wear that anymore. And the piano! You won't have to practice on the piano. I tell you, this is going to be a fine life for you!

[ANNE's *panic is gone.* PETER *appears in the doorway of his room, with a saucer in his hand. He is carrying his cat.*]

Peter. I . . . I . . . I thought I'd better get some water for Mouschi before . . .

---

15. **Annele** (än′ə·lə): Yiddish for "little Anne" (like "Annie").
16. **Queen Wilhelmina** (vil′hel·mē′nä) (1880–1962): queen of the Netherlands from 1890 to 1948.

17. **Anneke** (än′ə·kə): another affectionate nickname for Anne.

Mr. Frank. . . . you must never go beyond that door.

Mr. Frank. Of course.

[*As he starts toward the sink, the carillon begins to chime the hour of eight. He tiptoes to the window at the back and looks down at the street below. He turns to* PETER, *indicating in pantomime that it is too late.* PETER *starts back for his room. He steps on a creaking board. The three of them are frozen for a minute in fear. As* PETER *starts away again,* ANNE *tiptoes over to him and pours some of the milk from her glass into the saucer for the cat.* PETER *squats on the floor, putting the milk before the cat.* MR. FRANK *gives* ANNE *his fountain pen and then goes into the room at the right. For a second* ANNE *watches the cat; then she goes over to the center table and opens her diary.*

In the room at the right, MRS. FRANK *has sat up quickly at the sound of the carillon.* MR. FRANK *comes in and sits down beside her on the settee,[18] his arm comfortingly around her.*

---

18. **settee** (se·tē′) *n.*: small couch.

Upstairs, in the attic room, MR. *and* MRS. VAN DAAN *have hung their clothes in the closet and are now seated on the iron bed.* MRS. VAN DAAN *leans back, exhausted.* MR. VAN DAAN *fans her with a newspaper.*

ANNE *starts to write in her diary. The lights dim out; the curtain falls.*

In the darkness ANNE's *voice comes to us again, faintly at first and then with growing strength.*]

Anne's Voice. I expect I should be describing what it feels like to go into hiding. But I really don't know yet myself. I only know it's funny never to be able to go outdoors . . . never to breathe fresh air . . . never to run and shout and jump. It's the silence in the nights that frightens me most. Every time I hear a creak in the house or a step on the street outside, I'm sure they're coming for us. The days aren't so bad. At least we know that Miep and Mr. Kraler are down there below us in the office. Our protectors, we call them. I asked Father what would happen to them if the Nazis found out they were hiding us. Pim[19] said that they would suffer the same fate that we would. . . . Imagine! They know this, and yet when they come up here, they're always cheerful and gay, as if there were nothing in the world to bother them. . . . Friday, the twenty-first of August, nineteen forty-two. Today I'm going to tell you our general news. Mother is unbearable. She insists on treating me like a baby, which I loathe. Otherwise things are going better. The weather is . . .

[*As* ANNE's *voice is fading out, the curtain rises on the scene.*]

---

19. **Pim:** family nickname for Mr. Frank.

■ SCENE 3

It is a little after six o'clock in the evening, two months later.

MARGOT *is in the bedroom at the right, studying.* MR. VAN DAAN *is lying down in the attic room above.*

The rest of the "family" is in the main room. ANNE *and* PETER *sit opposite each other at the center table, where they have been doing their lessons.* MRS. FRANK *is on the couch.* MRS. VAN DAAN *is seated with her fur coat, on which she has been sewing, in her lap. None of them are wearing their shoes.*

Their eyes are on MR. FRANK, *waiting for him to give them the signal which will release them from their day-long quiet.* MR. FRANK, *his shoes in his hand, stands looking down out of the window at the back, watching to be sure that all of the workmen have left the building below.*

After a few seconds of motionless silence, MR. FRANK *turns from the window.*

Mr. Frank (*quietly, to the group*). It's safe now. The last workman has left.

[*There is an immediate stir of relief.*]

Anne (*her pent-up energy explodes*). WHEE!
Mrs. Frank (*startled, amused*). Anne!
Mrs. Van Daan. I'm first for the w.c.

[*She hurries off to the bathroom.* MRS. FRANK *puts on her shoes and starts up to the sink to prepare supper.* ANNE *sneaks* PETER's *shoes from under the table and hides them behind her back.* MR. FRANK *goes into* MARGOT's *room.*]

Mr. Frank (*to* MARGOT). Six o'clock. School's over.

[MARGOT *gets up, stretching.* MR. FRANK *sits down to put on his shoes. In the main room* PETER *tries to find his.*]

Peter. (*to* ANNE). Have you seen my shoes?
Anne (*innocently*). Your shoes?
Peter. You've taken them, haven't you?
Anne. I don't know what you're talking about.
Peter. You're going to be sorry!
Anne. Am I?

[PETER *goes after her.* ANNE, *with his shoes in her hand, runs from him, dodging behind her mother.*]

Mrs. Frank (*protesting*). Anne, dear!
Peter. Wait till I get you!
Anne. I'm waiting! (PETER *makes a lunge for her. They both fall to the floor.* PETER *pins her down, wrestling with her to get the shoes.*) Don't! Don't! Peter, stop it. Ouch!
Mrs. Frank. Anne! . . . Peter!

[*Suddenly* PETER *becomes self-conscious. He grabs his shoes roughly and starts for his room.*]

Anne (*following him*). Peter, where are you going? Come dance with me.
Peter. I tell you I don't know how.
Anne. I'll teach you.
Peter. I'm going to give Mouschi his dinner.
Anne. Can I watch?
Peter. He doesn't like people around while he eats.
Anne. Peter, please.
Peter. No!

[*He goes into his room.* ANNE *slams his door after him.*]

Mrs. Frank. Anne, dear, I think you shouldn't play like that with Peter. It's not dignified.
Anne. Who cares if it's dignified? I don't want to be dignified.

[MR. FRANK *and* MARGOT *come from the room on the right.* MARGOT *goes to help her mother.* MR. FRANK *starts for the center table to correct* MARGOT's *school papers.*]

Mrs. Frank (*to* ANNE). You complain that I don't treat you like a grown-up. But when I do, you resent it.
Anne. I only want some fun . . . someone to laugh and clown with . . . After you've sat still all day and hardly moved, you've got to have some fun. I don't know what's the matter with that boy.
Mr. Frank. He isn't used to girls. Give him a little time.
Anne. Time? Isn't two months time? I could cry. (*Catching hold of* MARGOT) Come on, Margot . . . dance with me. Come on, please.
Margot. I have to help with supper.
Anne. You know we're going to forget how to dance . . . When we get out, we won't remember a thing.

[*She starts to sing and dance by herself.* MR. FRANK *takes her in his arms, waltzing with her.* MRS. VAN DAAN *comes in from the bathroom.*]

Mrs. Van Daan. Next? (*She looks around as she starts putting on her shoes.*) Where's Peter?
Anne (*as they are dancing*). Where would he be!
Mrs. Van Daan. He hasn't finished his lessons, has he? His father'll kill him if he catches him in there with that cat and his work not done. (MR. FRANK *and* ANNE *finish their dance. They bow to each other with*

extravagant formality.) Anne, get him out of there, will you?

Anne (*at* PETER's *door*). Peter? Peter?

Peter (*opening the door a crack*). What is it?

Anne. Your mother says to come out.

Peter. I'm giving Mouschi his dinner.

Mrs. Van Daan. You know what your father says. (*She sits on the couch, sewing on the lining of her fur coat.*)

Peter. For heaven's sake, I haven't even looked at him since lunch.

Mrs. Van Daan. I'm just telling you, that's all.

Anne. I'll feed him.

Peter. I don't want you in there.

Mrs. Van Daan. Peter!

Peter (*to* ANNE). Then give him his dinner and come right out, you hear?

[*He comes back to the table.* ANNE *shuts the door of* PETER's *room after her and disappears behind the curtain covering his closet.*]

Mrs. Van Daan (*to* PETER). Now is that any way to talk to your little girlfriend?

Peter. Mother . . . for heaven's sake . . . will you please stop saying that?

Mrs. Van Daan. Look at him blush! Look at him!

Peter. Please! I'm not . . . anyway . . . let me alone, will you?

Mrs. Van Daan. He acts like it was something to be ashamed of. It's nothing to be ashamed of, to have a little girlfriend.

Peter. You're crazy. She's only thirteen.

Mrs. Van Daan. So what? And you're six-

Mrs. Van Pels
("Mrs. Van Daan").

teen. Just perfect. Your father's ten years older than I am. (*To* MR. FRANK) I warn you, Mr. Frank, if this war lasts much longer, we're going to be related and then . . .

Mr. Frank. Mazel tov![20]

Mrs. Frank (*deliberately changing the conversation*). I wonder where Miep is. She's usually so prompt.

[*Suddenly everything else is forgotten as they hear the sound of an automobile coming to a screeching stop in the street below. They are tense, motionless in their terror. The car starts away. A wave of relief sweeps over them. They pick up their occupations again.* ANNE *flings open the door of* PETER's *room, making a dramatic entrance. She is dressed in* PETER's *clothes.* PETER *looks at her in fury. The others are amused.*]

Anne. Good evening, everyone. Forgive me if I don't stay. (*She jumps up on a chair.*) I have a friend waiting for me in there. My friend Tom. Tom Cat. Some people say that we look alike. But Tom has the most beautiful whiskers, and I have only a little fuzz. I am hoping . . . in time . . .

Peter. All right, Mrs. Quack Quack!

Anne (*outraged—jumping down*). Peter!

Peter. I heard about you . . . how you talked so much in class they called you Mrs. Quack Quack. How Mr. Smitter made you write a composition . . . "'Quack, quack,' said Mrs. Quack Quack."

---

20. **mazel tov** (mä′zəl tōv′): Yiddish expression meaning "congratulations."

Anne. Well, go on. Tell them the rest. How it was so good he read it out loud to the class and then read it to all his other classes!
Peter. Quack! Quack! Quack . . . Quack . . . Quack . . .

[ANNE *pulls off the coat and trousers.*]

Anne. You are the most intolerable, insufferable boy I've ever met!

[*She throws the clothes down the stairwell.* PETER *goes down after them.*]

Peter. Quack, quack, quack!
Mrs. Van Daan (*to* ANNE). That's right, Anneke! Give it to him!
Anne. With all the boys in the world . . . why I had to get locked up with one like you! . . .
Peter. Quack, quack, quack, and from now on stay out of my room!

[*As* PETER *passes her,* ANNE *puts out her foot, tripping him. He picks himself up and goes on into his room.*]

Mrs. Frank (*quietly*). Anne, dear . . . your hair. (*She feels* ANNE's *forehead.*) You're warm. Are you feeling all right?
Anne. Please, Mother. (*She goes over to the center table, slipping into her shoes.*)
Mrs. Frank (*following her*). You haven't a fever, have you?
Anne (*pulling away*). No. No.
Mrs. Frank. You know we can't call a doctor here, ever. There's only one thing to do . . . watch carefully. Prevent an illness before it comes. Let me see your tongue.
Anne. Mother, this is perfectly absurd.
Mrs. Frank. Anne, dear, don't be such a baby. Let me see your tongue. (*As* ANNE *refuses,* MRS. FRANK *appeals to* MR. FRANK.) Otto . . . ?

Mr. Frank. You hear your mother, Anne.

[ANNE *flicks out her tongue for a second, then turns away.*]

Mrs. Frank. Come on—open up! (*As* ANNE *opens her mouth very wide*) You seem all right . . . but perhaps an aspirin . . .
Mrs. Van Daan. For heaven's sake, don't give that child any pills. I waited for fifteen minutes this morning for her to come out of the w.c.
Anne. I was washing my hair!
Mr. Frank. I think there's nothing the matter with our Anne that a ride on her bike or a visit with her friend Jopie de Waal wouldn't cure. Isn't that so, Anne?

[MR. VAN DAAN *comes down into the room. From outside we hear faint sounds of bombers going over and a burst of ack-ack.*][21]

Mr. Van Daan. Miep not come yet?
Mrs. Van Daan. The workmen just left, a little while ago.
Mr. Van Daan. What's for dinner tonight?
Mrs. Van Daan. Beans.
Mr. Van Daan. Not again!
Mrs. Van Daan. Poor Putti! I know. But what can we do? That's all that Miep brought us.

[MR. VAN DAAN *starts to pace, his hands behind his back.* ANNE *follows behind him, imitating him.*]

Anne. We are now in what is known as the "bean cycle." Beans boiled, beans en casserole, beans with strings, beans without strings . . .

---

21. **ack-ack** *n.:* slang for "antiaircraft gunfire."

[PETER *has come out of his room. He slides into his place at the table, becoming immediately absorbed in his studies.*]

Mr. Van Daan (*to* PETER). I saw you . . . in there, playing with your cat.

Mrs. Van Daan. He just went in for a second, putting his coat away. He's been out here all the time, doing his lessons.

Mr. Frank (*looking up from the papers*). Anne, you got an "excellent" in your history paper today . . . and "very good" in Latin.

Anne (*sitting beside him*). How about algebra?

Mr. Frank. I'll have to make a confession. Up until now I've managed to stay ahead of you in algebra. Today you caught up with me. We'll leave it to Margot to correct.

Anne. Isn't algebra vile, Pim!

Mr. Frank. Vile!

Margot (*to* MR. FRANK). How did I do?

Anne (*getting up*). Excellent, excellent, excellent, excellent!

Mr. Frank (*to* MARGOT). You should have used the subjunctive here . . .

Margot. Should I? . . . I thought . . . look here . . . I didn't use it here . . .

[*The two become absorbed in the papers.*]

Anne. Mrs. Van Daan, may I try on your coat?

Mrs. Frank. No, Anne.

Mrs. Van Daan (*giving it to* ANNE). It's all right . . . but careful with it. (ANNE *puts it on and struts with it.*) My father gave me that the year before he died. He always bought the best that money could buy.

Anne. Mrs. Van Daan, did you have a lot of boyfriends before you were married?

Mrs. Frank. Anne, that's a personal question. It's not courteous to ask personal questions.

Mrs. Van Daan. Oh, I don't mind. (*To* ANNE) Our house was always swarming with boys. When I was a girl, we had . . .

Mr. Van Daan. Oh, God. Not again!

Mrs. Van Daan (*good-humored*). Shut up! (*Without a pause, to* ANNE. MR. VAN DAAN *mimics* MRS. VAN DAAN, *speaking the first few words in unison with her.*) One summer we had a big house in Hilversum. The boys came buzzing round like bees around a jam pot. And when I was sixteen! . . . We were wearing our skirts very short those days and I had good-looking legs. (*She pulls up her skirt, going to* MR. FRANK.) I still have 'em. I may not be as pretty as I used to be, but I still have my legs. How about it, Mr. Frank?

Mr. Van Daan. All right. All right. We see them.

Mrs. Van Daan. I'm not asking you. I'm asking Mr. Frank.

Peter. Mother, for heaven's sake.

Mrs. Van Daan. Oh, I embarrass you, do I? Well, I just hope the girl you marry has as good. (*Then, to* ANNE) My father used to worry about me, with so many boys hanging round. He told me, if any of them gets fresh, you say to him . . . "Remember, Mr. So-and-So, remember I'm a lady."

Anne. "Remember, Mr. So-and-So, remember I'm a lady." (*She gives* MRS. VAN DAAN *her coat.*)

Mr. Van Daan. Look at you, talking that way in front of her! Don't you know she puts it all down in that diary?

Mrs. Van Daan. So, if she does? I'm only telling the truth!

[ANNE *stretches out, putting her ear to the floor, listening to what is going on below. The sound of the bombers fades away.*]

Mrs. Frank (*setting the table*). Would you mind, Peter, if I moved you over to the couch?

Anne (*listening*). Miep must have the radio on.

[PETER *picks up his papers, going over to the couch beside* MRS. VAN DAAN.]

Mr. Van Daan (*accusingly, to* PETER). Haven't you finished yet?

Peter. No.

Mr. Van Daan. You ought to be ashamed of yourself.

Peter. All right. All right. I'm a dunce. I'm a hopeless case. Why do I go on?

Mrs. Van Daan. You're not hopeless. Don't talk that way. It's just that you haven't anyone to help you, like the girls have. (*To* MR. FRANK) Maybe you could help him, Mr. Frank?

Mr. Frank. I'm sure that his father . . .?

Mr. Van Daan. Not me. I can't do anything with him. He won't listen to me. You go ahead . . . if you want.

Mr. Frank (*going to* PETER). What about it, Peter? Shall we make our school co-educational?

Mrs. Van Daan (*kissing* MR. FRANK). You're an angel, Mr. Frank. An angel. I don't know why I didn't meet you before I met that one there. Here, sit down, Mr. Frank . . . (*She forces him down on the couch beside* PETER.) Now, Peter, you listen to Mr. Frank.

Mr. Frank. It might be better for us to go into Peter's room.

[PETER *jumps up eagerly, leading the way.*]

Mrs. Van Daan. That's right. You go in there, Peter. You listen to Mr. Frank. Mr. Frank is a highly educated man.

[*As* MR. FRANK *is about to follow* PETER *into*

Anne Frank.

his room, MRS. FRANK *stops him and wipes the lipstick from his lips. Then she closes the door after them.*]

Anne (*on the floor, listening*). Shh! I can hear a man's voice talking.

Mr. Van Daan (*to* ANNE). Isn't it bad enough here without your sprawling all over the place?

[ANNE *sits up.*]

Mrs. Van Daan (*to* MR. VAN DAAN). If you didn't smoke so much, you wouldn't be so bad-tempered.

Mr. Van Daan. Am I smoking? Do you see me smoking?

Mrs. Van Daan. Don't tell me you've used up all those cigarettes.

Mr. Van Daan. One package. Miep only brought me one package.

Mrs. Van Daan. It's a filthy habit anyway. It's a good time to break yourself.

Mr. Van Daan. Oh, stop it, please.

Mrs. Van Daan. You're smoking up all our money. You know that, don't you?

Mr. Van Daan. Will you shut up? (*During this,* MRS. FRANK *and* MARGOT *have studiously kept their eyes down. But* ANNE, *seated on the floor, has been following the discussion interestedly.* MR. VAN DAAN *turns to see her staring up at him.*) And what are you staring at?

Anne. I never heard grown-ups quarrel before. I thought only children quarreled.

Mr. Van Daan. This isn't a quarrel! It's a discussion. And I never heard children so rude before.

Anne (*rising, indignantly*). I, rude!

Mr. Van Daan. Yes!

Mrs. Frank (*quickly*). Anne, will you get me my knitting? (ANNE *goes to get it.*) I must remember, when Miep comes, to ask her to bring me some more wool.

Margot (*going to her room*). I need some hairpins and some soap. I made a list. (*She goes into her bedroom to get the list.*)

Mrs. Frank (*to* ANNE). Have you some library books for Miep when she comes?

Anne. It's a wonder that Miep has a life of her own, the way we make her run errands for us. Please, Miep, get me some starch. Please take my hair out and have it cut. Tell me all the latest news, Miep. (*She goes over, kneeling on the couch beside* MRS. VAN DAAN.) Did you know she was engaged? His name is Dirk, and Miep's afraid the Nazis will ship him off to Germany to work in one of their war plants. That's what they're doing with some of the young Dutchmen . . . they pick them up off the streets—

Mr. Van Daan (*interrupting*). Don't you ever get tired of talking? Suppose you try keeping still for five minutes. Just five minutes.

[*He starts to pace again. Again* ANNE *follows him, mimicking him.* MRS. FRANK *jumps up and takes her by the arm up to the sink and gives her a glass of milk.*]

Mrs. Frank. Come here, Anne. It's time for your glass of milk.

Mr. Van Daan. Talk, talk, talk. I never heard such a child. Where is my . . . ? Every evening it's the same, talk, talk, talk. (*He looks around.*) Where is my . . . ?

Mrs. Van Daan. What're you looking for?

Mr. Van Daan. My pipe. Have you seen my pipe?

Mrs. Van Daan. What good's a pipe? You haven't got any tobacco.

Mr. Van Daan. At least I'll have something to hold in my mouth! (*Opening* MARGOT's *bedroom door*) Margot, have you seen my pipe?

Margot. It was on the table last night.

[ANNE *puts her glass of milk on the table and picks up his pipe, hiding it behind her back.*]

Mr. Van Daan. I know. I know. Anne, did you see my pipe? . . . Anne!

Mrs. Frank. Anne, Mr. Van Daan is speaking to you.

Anne. Am I allowed to talk now?

Mr. Van Daan. You're the most aggravating . . . The trouble with you is, you've been spoiled. What you need is a good old-fashioned spanking.

Anne (*mimicking* MRS. VAN DAAN). "Remember, Mr. So-and-So, remember I'm a lady." (*She thrusts the pipe into his mouth, then picks up her glass of milk.*)

Mr. Van Daan (*restraining himself with difficulty*). Why aren't you nice and quiet like your sister Margot? Why do you have to show off all the time? Let me give you a little advice, young lady. Men don't like that kind of thing in a girl. You know that? A man likes a girl who'll listen to him once in a while . . . a domestic girl, who'll keep her house shining for her husband . . . who loves to cook and sew and . . .

Anne. I'd cut my throat first! I'd open my veins! I'm going to be remarkable! I'm going to Paris . . .

Mr. Van Daan (*scoffingly*). Paris!

Anne . . . . to study music and art.

Mr. Van Daan. Yeah! Yeah!

Vocabulary

indignantly (in·dig′nənt·lē) *adv.*: with anger caused by something felt to be unjust.

Anne. I'm going to be a famous dancer or singer . . . or something wonderful.

[*She makes a wide gesture, spilling the glass of milk on the fur coat in* MRS. VAN DAAN's *lap.* MARGOT *rushes quickly over with a towel.* ANNE *tries to brush the milk off with her skirt.*]

Mrs. Van Daan. Now look what you've done . . . you clumsy little fool! My beautiful fur coat my father gave me . . .

Anne. I'm so sorry.

Mrs. Van Daan. What do you care? It isn't yours. . . . So go on, ruin it! Do you know what that coat cost? Do you? And now look at it! Look at it!

Anne. I'm very, very sorry.

Mrs. Van Daan. I could kill you for this. I could just kill you!

[MRS. VAN DAAN goes *up the stairs, clutching the coat.* MR. VAN DAAN *starts after her.*]

Mr. Van Daan. Petronella . . . liefje! Liefje! . . . Come back . . . the supper . . . come back!

Mrs. Frank. Anne, you must not behave in that way.

Anne. It was an accident. Anyone can have an accident.

Mrs. Frank. I don't mean that. I mean the answering back. You must not answer back. They are our guests. We must always show the greatest courtesy to them. We're all living under terrible tension. (*She stops as* MARGOT *indicates that* MR. VAN DAAN *can hear. When he is gone, she continues.*) That's why we must control ourselves . . . You don't hear Margot getting into arguments with them, do you? Watch Margot. She's always courteous with them. Never familiar. She keeps her distance. And they respect her for it. Try to be like Margot.

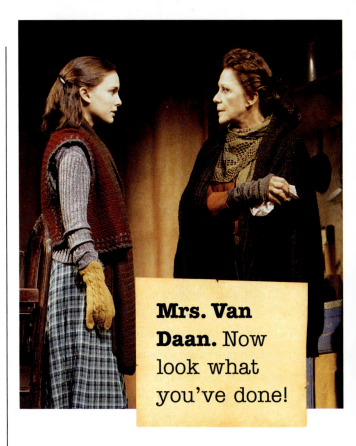

Mrs. Van Daan. Now look what you've done!

Anne. And have them walk all over me, the way they do her? No, thanks!

Mrs. Frank. I'm not afraid that anyone is going to walk all over you, Anne. I'm afraid for other people, that you'll walk on them. I don't know what happens to you, Anne. You are wild, self-willed. If I had ever talked to my mother as you talk to me . . .

Anne. Things have changed. People aren't like that anymore. "Yes, Mother." "No, Mother." "Anything you say, Mother." I've got to fight things out for myself! Make something of myself!

Mrs. Frank. It isn't necessary to fight to do it. Margot doesn't fight, and isn't she . . . ?

Anne (*violently rebellious*). Margot! Margot! Margot! That's all I hear from everyone . . . how wonderful Margot is . . . "Why aren't you like Margot?"

Margot (*protesting*). Oh, come on, Anne, don't be so . . .

Anne (*paying no attention*). Everything she does is right, and everything I do is wrong! I'm the goat around here! . . . You're all against me! . . . And you worst of all!

[*She rushes off into her room and throws herself down on the settee, stifling her sobs.* MRS. FRANK *sighs and starts toward the stove.*]

Mrs. Frank (*to* MARGOT). Let's put the soup on the stove . . . if there's anyone who cares to eat. Margot, will you take the bread out? (MARGOT *gets the bread from the cupboard.*) I don't know how we can go on living this way . . . I can't say a word to Anne . . . she flies at me . . .

Margot. You know Anne. In half an hour she'll be out here, laughing and joking.

Mrs. Frank. And . . . (*She makes a motion upward, indicating the* VAN DAANS.) . . . I told your father it wouldn't work . . . but no . . . no . . . he had to ask them, he said . . . he owed it to him, he said. Well, he knows now that I was right! These quarrels! . . . This bickering!

Margot (*with a warning look*). Shush. Shush.

[*The buzzer for the door sounds.* MRS. FRANK *gasps, startled.*]

Mrs. Frank. Every time I hear that sound, my heart stops!

Margot (*starting for* PETER's *door*). It's Miep. (*She knocks at the door.*) Father?

[MR. FRANK *comes quickly from* PETER's *room.*]

Mr. Frank. Thank you, Margot. (*As he goes down the steps to open the outer door*) Has everyone his list?

Margot. I'll get my books. (*Giving her mother a list*) Here's your list. (MARGOT *goes into her and* ANNE's *bedroom on the*

right. ANNE *sits up, hiding her tears, as* MARGOT *comes in.*) Miep's here.

[MARGOT *picks up her books and goes back.* ANNE *hurries over to the mirror, smoothing her hair.*]

Mr. Van Daan (*coming down the stairs*). Is it Miep?

Margot. Yes. Father's gone down to let her in.

Mr. Van Daan. At last I'll have some cigarettes!

Mrs. Frank (*to* MR. VAN DAAN). I can't tell you how unhappy I am about Mrs. Van Daan's coat. Anne should never have touched it.

Mr. Van Daan. She'll be all right.

Mrs. Frank. Is there anything I can do?

Mr. Van Daan. Don't worry.

[*He turns to meet* MIEP. *But it is not* MIEP *who comes up the steps. It is* MR. KRALER, *followed by* MR. FRANK. *Their faces are grave.* ANNE *comes from the bedroom.* PETER *comes from his room.*]

Mrs. Frank. Mr. Kraler!

Mr. Van Daan. How are you, Mr. Kraler?

Margot. This is a surprise.

Mrs. Frank. When Mr. Kraler comes, the sun begins to shine.

Mr. Van Daan. Miep is coming?

Mr. Kraler. Not tonight. (MR. KRALER *goes to* MARGOT *and* MRS. FRANK *and* ANNE, *shaking hands with them.*)

Mrs. Frank. Wouldn't you like a cup of coffee? . . . Or, better still, will you have supper with us?

Mr. Frank. Mr. Kraler has something to talk over with us. Something has happened, he says, which demands an immediate decision.

Mrs. Frank (*fearful*). What is it?

[MR. KRALER *sits down on the couch. As he*

talks he takes bread, cabbages, milk, etc., from his briefcase, giving them to MARGOT *and* ANNE *to put away.*]

Mr. Kraler. Usually, when I come up here, I try to bring you some bit of good news. What's the use of telling you the bad news when there's nothing that you can do about it? But today something has happened. . . . Dirk . . . Miep's Dirk, you know, came to me just now. He tells me that he has a Jewish friend living near him. A dentist. He says he's in trouble. He begged me, could I do anything for this man? Could I find him a hiding place? . . . So I've come to you . . . I know it's a terrible thing to ask of you, living as you are, but would you take him in with you?

Mr. Frank. Of course we will.

Mr. Kraler (*rising*). It'll be just for a night or two . . . until I find some other place. This happened so suddenly that I didn't know where to turn.

Mr. Frank. Where is he?

Mr. Kraler. Downstairs in the office.

Mr. Frank. Good. Bring him up.

Mr. Kraler. His name is Dussel[22] . . .

Mr. Frank. Dussel . . . I think I know him.

Mr. Kraler. I'll get him.

[*He goes quickly down the steps and out.* MR. FRANK *suddenly becomes conscious of the others.*]

Mr. Frank. Forgive me. I spoke without consulting you. But I knew you'd feel as I do.

Mr. Van Daan. There's no reason for you to consult anyone. This is your place. You have a right to do exactly as you please. The only thing I feel . . . there's so little food as it is . . . and to take in another person . . .

───────────
22. **Dussel** (dŏŏs′əl).

[PETER *turns away, ashamed of his father.*]

Mr. Frank. We can stretch the food a little. It's only for a few days.

Mr. Van Daan. You want to make a bet?

Mrs. Frank. I think it's fine to have him. But, Otto, where are you going to put him? Where?

Peter. He can have my bed. I can sleep on the floor. I wouldn't mind.

Mr. Frank. That's good of you, Peter. But your room's too small . . . even for you.

Anne. I have a much better idea. I'll come in here with you and Mother, and Margot can take Peter's room and Peter can go in our room with Mr. Dussel.

Margot. That's right. We could do that.

Mr. Frank. No, Margot. You mustn't sleep in that room . . . neither you nor Anne. Mouschi has caught some rats in there. Peter's brave. He doesn't mind.

Anne. Then how about *this*? I'll come in here with you and Mother, and Mr. Dussel can have my bed.

Mrs. Frank. No. No. *No!* Margot will come in here with us and he can have her bed. It's the only way. Margot, bring your things in here. Help her, Anne.

[MARGOT *hurries into her room to get her things.*]

Anne (*to her mother*). Why Margot? Why can't I come in here?

Mrs. Frank. Because it wouldn't be proper for Margot to sleep with a . . . Please, Anne. Don't argue. Please.

[ANNE *starts slowly away.*]

Mr. Frank (*to* ANNE). You don't mind sharing your room with Mr. Dussel, do you, Anne?

Anne. No. No, of course not.

Mr. Frank. Good. (ANNE *goes off into her bedroom, helping* MARGOT. MR. FRANK *starts to search in the cupboards.*) Where's the cognac?²³

Mrs. Frank. It's there. But, Otto, I was saving it in case of illness.

Mr. Frank. I think we couldn't find a better time to use it. Peter, will you get five glasses for me?

[PETER *goes for the glasses.* MARGOT *comes out of her bedroom, carrying her posses- sions, which she hangs behind a curtain in the main room.* MR. FRANK *finds the cognac and pours it into the five glasses that* PETER *brings him.* MR. VAN DAAN *stands looking on sourly.* MRS. VAN DAAN *comes downstairs and looks around at all the bustle.*]

Mrs. Van Daan. What's happening? What's going on?

Mr. Van Daan. Someone's moving in with us.

Mrs. Van Daan. In here? You're joking.

Margot. It's only for a night or two . . . until Mr. Kraler finds him another place.

Mr. Van Daan. Yeah! Yeah!

[MR. FRANK *hurries over as* MR. KRALER *and* DUSSEL *come up.* DUSSEL *is a man in his late fifties, meticulous, finicky . . . bewildered now. He wears a raincoat. He carries a briefcase, stuffed full, and a small medicine case.*]

Mr. Frank. Come in, Mr. Dussel.

Mr. Kraler. This is Mr. Frank.

Dussel. Mr. Otto Frank?

Fritz Pfeffer ("Dussel").

Mr. Frank. Yes. Let me take your things. (*He takes the hat and briefcase, but* DUSSEL *clings to his medicine case.*) This is my wife, Edith . . . Mr. and Mrs. Van Daan . . . their son, Peter . . . and my daughters, Margot and Anne.

[DUSSEL *shakes hands with everyone.*]

Mr. Kraler. Thank you, Mr. Frank. Thank you all. Mr. Dussel, I leave you in good hands. Oh . . . Dirk's coat.

[DUSSEL *hurriedly takes off the raincoat, giving it to* MR. KRALER. *Underneath is his white dentist's jacket, with a yellow Star of David on it.*]

Dussel (*to* MR. KRALER). What can I say to thank you . . . ?

Mrs. Frank (*to* DUSSEL). Mr. Kraler and Miep . . . They're our lifeline. Without them we couldn't live.

Mr. Kraler. Please. Please. You make us seem very heroic. It isn't that at all. We simply don't like the Nazis. (*To* MR. FRANK, *who offers him a drink*) No, thanks. (*Then, going on*) We don't like their methods. We don't like . . .

Mr. Frank (*smiling*). I know. I know. "No one's going to tell us Dutchmen what to do with our damn Jews!"

Mr. Kraler (*to* DUSSEL). Pay no attention to Mr. Frank. I'll be up tomorrow to see that they're treating you right. (*To* MR. FRANK) Don't trouble to come down again. Peter will bolt the door after me, won't you, Peter?

Peter. Yes, sir.

Mr. Frank. Thank you, Peter. I'll do it.

Mr. Kraler. Good night. Good night.

---

23. **cognac** (kōn′yak′) *n.:* type of brandy (distilled wine).

Group. Good night, Mr. Kraler. We'll see you tomorrow. (*Etc., etc.*)

[MR. KRALER *goes out with* MR. FRANK. MRS. FRANK *gives each one of the "grown-ups" a glass of cognac.*]

Mrs. Frank. Please, Mr. Dussel, sit down.

[DUSSEL *sinks into a chair.* MRS. FRANK *gives him a glass of cognac.*]

Dussel. I'm dreaming. I know it. I can't believe my eyes. Mr. Otto Frank here! (*To* MRS. FRANK) You're not in Switzerland, then? A woman told me . . . She said she'd gone to your house . . . the door was open, everything was in disorder, dishes in the sink. She said she found a piece of paper in the wastebasket with an address scribbled on it . . . an address in Zurich.[24] She said you must have escaped to Zurich.

Anne. Father put that there purposely . . . just so people would think that very thing!

Dussel. And you've been *here* all the time?

Mrs. Frank. All the time . . . ever since July.

[ANNE *speaks to her father as he comes back.*]

Anne. It worked, Pim . . . the address you left! Mr. Dussel says that people believe we escaped to Switzerland.

Mr. Frank. I'm glad. . . . And now let's have a little drink to welcome Mr. Dussel. (*Before they can drink,* DUSSEL *bolts his drink.* MR. FRANK *smiles and raises his glass.*) To Mr. Dussel. Welcome. We're very honored to have you with us.

Mrs. Frank. To Mr. Dussel, welcome.

[*The* VAN DAANS *murmur a welcome. The "grown-ups" drink.*]

Mrs. Van Daan. Um. That was good.

Mr. Van Daan. Did Mr. Kraler warn you that you won't get much to eat here? You can imagine . . . three ration books among the seven of us . . . and now you make eight.

[PETER *walks away, humiliated. Outside, a street organ is heard dimly.*]

Dussel (*rising*). Mr. Van Daan, you don't realize what is happening outside that you should warn me of a thing like that. You don't realize what's going on. . . . (*As* MR. VAN DAAN *starts his characteristic pacing,* DUSSEL *turns to speak to the others.*) Right here in Amsterdam every day hundreds of Jews disappear. . . . They surround a block and search house by house. Children come home from school to find their parents gone. Hundreds are being deported[25] . . . people that you and I know . . . the Hallensteins . . . the Wessels . . .

Mrs. Frank (*in tears*). Oh, no. No!

Dussel. They get their call-up notice . . . come to the Jewish theater on such and such a day and hour . . . bring only what you can carry in a rucksack. And if you refuse the call-up notice, then they come and drag you from your home and ship you off to Mauthausen. The death camp!

Mrs. Frank. We didn't know that things had got so much worse.

Dussel. Forgive me for speaking so.

Anne (*coming to* DUSSEL). Do you know the de Waals? . . . What's become of them? Their daughter Jopie and I are in the same class. Jopie's my best friend.

---

24. **Zurich** (zoor′ik): Switzerland's largest city. Because Switzerland remained neutral during World War II, many refugees sought safety there.

---

25. **deported** *v.:* forcibly sent away (to concentration camps and death camps).

Dussel. They are gone.
Anne. Gone?
Dussel. With all the others.
Anne. Oh, no. Not Jopie!

[*She turns away, in tears.* MRS. FRANK *motions to* MARGOT *to comfort her.* MARGOT *goes to* ANNE, *putting her arms comfortingly around her.*]

Mrs. Van Daan. There were some people called Wagner. They lived near us . . . ?
Mr. Frank (*interrupting, with a glance at* ANNE). I think we should put this off until later. We all have many questions we want to ask. . . . But I'm sure that Mr. Dussel would like to get settled before supper.
Dussel. Thank you. I would. I brought very little with me.
Mr. Frank (*giving him his hat and briefcase*). I'm sorry we can't give you a room alone. But I hope you won't be too uncomfortable. We've had to make strict rules here . . . a schedule of hours . . . We'll tell you after supper. Anne, would you like to take Mr. Dussel to his room?
Anne (*controlling her tears*). If you'll come with me, Mr. Dussel? (*She starts for her room.*)
Dussel (*shaking hands with each in turn*). Forgive me if I haven't really expressed my gratitude to all of you. This has been such a shock to me. I'd always thought of myself as Dutch. I was born in Holland. My father was born in Holland, and my grandfather. And now . . . after all these years . . . (*He breaks off.*) If you'll excuse me.

[DUSSEL *gives a little bow and hurries off after* ANNE. MR. FRANK *and the others are subdued.*]

Anne (*turning on the light*). Well, here we are.

[DUSSEL *looks around the room. In the main room* MARGOT *speaks to her mother.*]

Margot. The news sounds pretty bad, doesn't it? It's so different from what Mr. Kraler tells us. Mr. Kraler says things are improving.
Mr. Van Daan. I like it better the way Kraler tells it.

[*They resume their occupations, quietly.* PETER *goes off into his room. In* ANNE's *room,* ANNE *turns to* DUSSEL.]

Anne. You're going to share the room with me.
Dussel. I'm a man who's always lived alone. I haven't had to adjust myself to others. I hope you'll bear with me until I learn.
Anne. Let me help you. (*She takes his briefcase.*) Do you always live all alone? Have you no family at all?
Dussel. No one. (*He opens his medicine case and spreads his bottles on the dressing table.*)
Anne. How dreadful. You must be terribly lonely.
Dussel. I'm used to it.
Anne. I don't think I could ever get used to it. Didn't you even have a pet? A cat, or a dog?
Dussel. I have an allergy for fur-bearing animals. They give me asthma.
Anne. Oh, dear. Peter has a cat.
Dussel. Here? He has it here?
Anne. Yes. But we hardly ever see it. He keeps it in his room all the time. I'm sure it will be all right.
Dussel. Let us hope so. (*He takes some pills to* fortify *himself.*)
Anne. That's Margot's bed, where you're going to sleep. I sleep on the sofa there. (*Indicating the clothes hooks on the wall*) We cleared these off for your things. (*She goes over to the window.*) The best part about this

Vocabulary
fortify (fôrt′ə·fī′) *v.:* strengthen.

room . . . you can look down and see a bit of the street and the canal. There's a houseboat . . . you can see the end of it . . . a bargeman lives there with his family . . . They have a baby and he's just beginning to walk and I'm so afraid he's going to fall into the canal someday. I watch him . . .

Dussel (*interrupting*). Your father spoke of a schedule.

Anne (*coming away from the window*). Oh, yes. It's mostly about the times we have to be quiet. And times for the w.c. You can use it now if you like.

Dussel (*stiffly*). No, thank you.

Anne. I suppose you think it's awful, my talking about a thing like that. But you don't know how important it can get to be, especially when you're frightened. . . . About this room, the way Margot and I did . . . she had it to herself in the afternoons for studying, reading . . . lessons, you know . . . and I took the mornings. Would that be all right with you?

Dussel. I'm not at my best in the morning.

Anne. You stay here in the mornings, then. I'll take the room in the afternoons.

Dussel. Tell me, when you're in here, what happens to me? Where am I spending my time? In there, with all the people?

Anne. Yes.

Dussel. I see. I see.

Anne. We have supper at half past six.

Dussel (*going over to the sofa*). Then, if you don't mind . . . I like to lie down quietly for ten minutes before eating. I find it helps the digestion.

Anne. Of course. I hope I'm not going to be too much of a bother to you. I seem to be able to get everyone's back up.

[DUSSEL *lies down on the sofa, curled up, his back to her.*]

Dussel. I always get along very well with children. My patients all bring their children to me, because they know I get on well with them. So don't you worry about that.

[ANNE *leans over him, taking his hand and shaking it gratefully.*]

Anne. Thank you. Thank you, Mr. Dussel.

[*The lights dim to darkness. The curtain falls on the scene.* ANNE'*s voice comes to us, faintly at first and then with increasing power.*]

Anne's Voice. . . . And yesterday I finished Cissy Van Marxvelt's latest book. I think she is a first-class writer. I shall definitely let my children read her. Monday, the twenty-first of September, nineteen forty-two. Mr. Dussel and I had another battle yesterday. Yes, Mr. Dussel! According to him, nothing, I repeat . . . nothing is right about me . . . my appearance, my character, my manners. While he was going on at me, I thought . . . sometime I'll give you such a smack that you'll fly right up to the ceiling! Why is it that every grown-up thinks he knows the way to bring up children? Particularly the grown-ups that never had any. I keep wishing that Peter was a girl instead of a boy. Then I would have someone to talk to. Margot's a darling, but she takes everything too seriously. To pause for a moment on the subject of Mrs. Van Daan. I must tell you that her attempts to flirt with Father are getting her nowhere. Pim, thank goodness, won't play.

[*As she is saying the last lines, the curtain rises on the darkened scene.* ANNE'*s voice fades out.*]

Act One, Scenes 1–3

First Thoughts

1. What do you think would be the hardest part of life in the Secret Annex? Explain.

Thinking Critically

2. A **flashback** interrupts a story to take you back to earlier times and events. Most of this play is told in an extended flashback, framed by the opening and closing scenes. Where in Scene 1 does the flashback begin? What do we learn about the characters and their basic situation before the flashback begins?

3. When does Anne begin to understand what going into hiding will mean? Describe some of the ways life in the Secret Annex is different from life outside.

4. Sounds from outside the Secret Annex play an important part in the play. Some remind us of ordinary life in the city. Others punctuate the scene with reminders of the danger outside. List four of the sounds heard so far. Which sounds are pleasant? Which are threatening?

5. Do Anne and Peter seem to have typical teenage attitudes toward their families? Use examples from the text to support your response.

6. List the **conflicts** that have developed among the characters by the end of Scene 3. Why are these conflicts dangerous for the people in the Secret Annex? What other conflicts do you **predict** might arise?

7. **Compare** Mr. Frank's and Mr. Van Daan's reactions to the arrival of Albert Dussel. Which seems like the right way to respond? Why?

Extending Interpretations

8. Mr. Frank tells Anne, "There are no walls, there are no bolts, no locks that anyone can put on your mind" (page 379). What does he mean? Do you agree? Support your opinion with examples from your own knowledge or experiences.

Reading Check

By the end of Scene 3, we have met all ten **characters** who appear in the play. List those characters, and choose two or three adjectives to describe each one.

SKILLS FOCUS

Literary Skills
Identify flashback and conflicts.

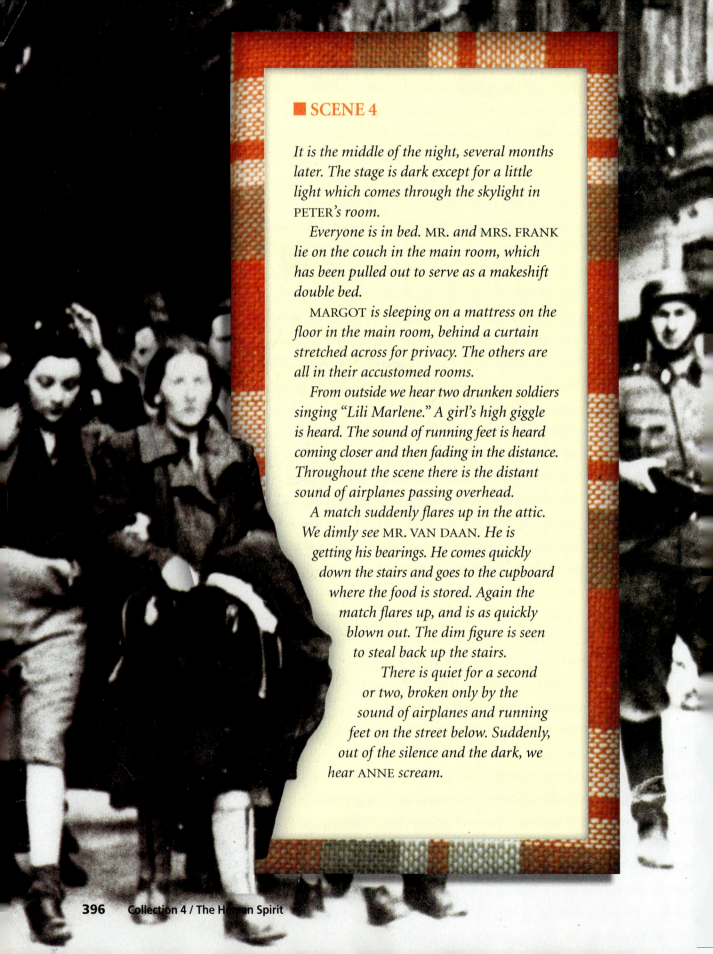

■ SCENE 4

It is the middle of the night, several months later. The stage is dark except for a little light which comes through the skylight in PETER's *room.*

Everyone is in bed. MR. *and* MRS. FRANK *lie on the couch in the main room, which has been pulled out to serve as a makeshift double bed.*

MARGOT *is sleeping on a mattress on the floor in the main room, behind a curtain stretched across for privacy. The others are all in their accustomed rooms.*

From outside we hear two drunken soldiers singing "Lili Marlene." A girl's high giggle is heard. The sound of running feet is heard coming closer and then fading in the distance. Throughout the scene there is the distant sound of airplanes passing overhead.

A match suddenly flares up in the attic. We dimly see MR. VAN DAAN. *He is getting his bearings. He comes quickly down the stairs and goes to the cupboard where the food is stored. Again the match flares up, and is as quickly blown out. The dim figure is seen to steal back up the stairs.*

There is quiet for a second or two, broken only by the sound of airplanes and running feet on the street below. Suddenly, out of the silence and the dark, we hear ANNE *scream.*

Mrs. Frank. It was just a dream.

Anne (*screaming*). No! No! Don't . . . don't take me!

[*She moans, tossing and crying in her sleep. The other people wake, terrified.* DUSSEL *sits up in bed, furious.*]

Dussel. Shush! Anne! Anne, for God's sake, shush!

Anne (*still in her nightmare*). Save me! Save me!

[*She screams and screams.* DUSSEL *gets out of bed, going over to her, trying to wake her.*]

Dussel. For God's sake! Quiet! Quiet! You want someone to hear?

[*In the main room* MRS. FRANK *grabs a shawl and pulls it around her. She rushes in to* ANNE, *taking her in her arms.* MR. FRANK *hurriedly gets up, putting on his overcoat.* MARGOT *sits up, terrified.* PETER's *light goes on in his room.*]

Mrs. Frank (*to* ANNE, *in her room*). Hush, darling, hush. It's all right. It's all right. (*Over her shoulder, to* DUSSEL) Will you be kind enough to turn on the light, Mr. Dussel? (*Back to* ANNE) It's nothing, my darling. It was just a dream.

[DUSSEL *turns on the light in the bedroom.* MRS. FRANK *holds* ANNE *in her arms. Gradually* ANNE *comes out of her nightmare, still trembling with horror.* MR. FRANK *comes into the room, and goes quickly to the window, looking out to be sure that no one outside has heard* ANNE's *screams.* MRS. FRANK *holds* ANNE, *talking softly to her. In the main room* MARGOT *stands on a chair, turning on the center hanging lamp. A light goes on in the* VAN DAANS' *room overhead.* PETER *puts his robe on, coming out of his room.*]

Dussel (*to* MRS. FRANK, *blowing his nose*). Something must be done about that child, Mrs. Frank. Yelling like that! Who knows but there's somebody on the streets? She's endangering all our lives.

Mrs. Frank. Anne, darling.

Dussel. Every night she twists and turns. I don't sleep. I spend half my night shushing her. And now it's nightmares!

[MARGOT *comes to the door of* ANNE'*s room, followed by* PETER. MR. FRANK *goes to them, indicating that everything is all right.* PETER *takes* MARGOT *back.*]

Mrs. Frank (*to* ANNE). You're here, safe, you see? Nothing has happened. (*To* DUSSEL) Please, Mr. Dussel, go back to bed. She'll be herself in a minute or two. Won't you, Anne?

Dussel (*picking up a book and a pillow*). Thank you, but I'm going to the w.c. The one place where there's peace!

[*He stalks out.* MR. VAN DAAN, *in underwear and trousers, comes down the stairs.*]

Mr. Van Daan (*to* DUSSEL). What is it? What happened?

Dussel. A nightmare. She was having a nightmare!

Mr. Van Daan. I thought someone was murdering her.

Dussel. Unfortunately, no.

[*He goes into the bathroom.* MR. VAN DAAN *goes back up the stairs.* MR. FRANK, *in the main room, sends* PETER *back to his own bedroom.*]

Mr. Frank. Thank you, Peter. Go back to bed.

[PETER *goes back to his room.* MR. FRANK *follows him, turning out the light and looking out the window. Then he goes back to the main room, and gets up on a chair, turning out the center hanging lamp.*]

Mrs. Frank (*to* ANNE). Would you like some water? (ANNE *shakes her head.*) Was it a very bad dream? Perhaps if you told me . . . ?

Anne. I'd rather not talk about it.

Mrs. Frank. Poor darling. Try to sleep, then. I'll sit right here beside you until you fall asleep. (*She brings a stool over, sitting there.*)

Anne. You don't have to.

Mrs. Frank. But I'd like to stay with you . . . very much. Really.

Anne. I'd rather you didn't.

Mrs. Frank. Good night, then. (*She leans down to kiss* ANNE. ANNE *throws her arm up over her face, turning away.* MRS. FRANK, *hiding her hurt, kisses* ANNE'*s arm.*) You'll be all right? There's nothing that you want?

Anne. Will you please ask Father to come.

Mrs. Frank (*after a second*). Of course, Anne dear. (*She hurries out into the other room.* MR. FRANK *comes to her as she comes in.*) Sie verlangt nach Dir![1]

Mr. Frank (*sensing her hurt*). Edith, Liebe, schau . . .[2]

Mrs. Frank. Es macht nichts! Ich danke dem lieben Herrgott, dass sie sich wenigstens an Dich wendet, wenn sie Trost braucht! Geh hinein, Otto, sie ist ganz hysterisch vor Angst.[3] (*As* MR. FRANK *hesitates*) Geh zu ihr.[4] (*He looks at her for a second and then goes to get a cup of water for* ANNE. MRS. FRANK *sinks down on the bed, her face in her hands, trying to keep from sobbing aloud.* MARGOT *comes over to her, putting*

---

1. **Sie . . . Dir:** German for "She's asking for you."
2. **Liebe, schau:** "Dear, look."
3. **Es . . . Angst:** "It doesn't matter! I thank the dear Lord that she turns at least to you when she needs comfort! Go to her, Otto, she's completely hysterical with fear."
4. **Geh zu ihr:** "Go to her."

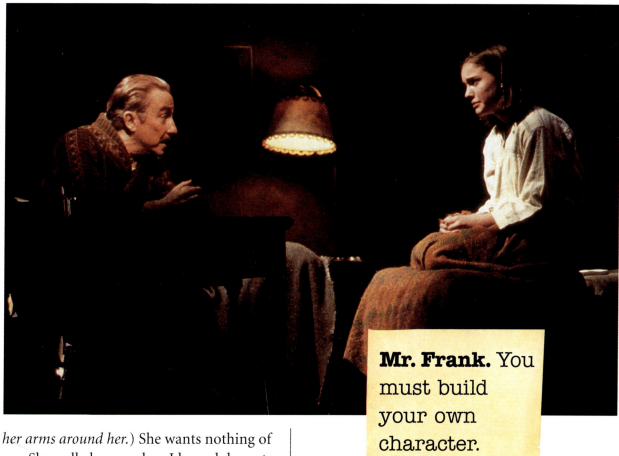

Mr. Frank. You must build your own character.

her arms around her.) She wants nothing of me. She pulled away when I leaned down to kiss her.

Margot. It's a phase . . . You heard Father. . . Most girls go through it . . . they turn to their fathers at this age . . . they give all their love to their fathers.

Mrs. Frank. You weren't like this. You didn't shut me out.

Margot. She'll get over it. . . .

[*She smooths the bed for* MRS. FRANK *and sits beside her a moment as* MRS. FRANK *lies down. In* ANNE's *room* MR. FRANK *comes in, sitting down by* ANNE. ANNE *flings her arms around him, clinging to him. In the distance we hear the sound of ack-ack.*]

Anne. Oh, Pim. I dreamed that they came to get us! The Green Police! They broke down the door and grabbed me and started to drag me out the way they did Jopie.

Mr. Frank. I want you to take this pill.

Anne. What is it?

Mr. Frank. Something to quiet you.

[*She takes it and drinks the water. In the main room* MARGOT *turns out the light and goes back to her bed.*]

Mr. Frank (*to* ANNE). Do you want me to read to you for a while?

Anne. No. Just sit with me for a minute. Was I awful? Did I yell terribly loud? Do you think anyone outside could have heard?

Mr. Frank. No. No. Lie quietly now. Try to sleep.

Anne. I'm a terrible coward. I'm so disappointed in myself. I think I've conquered my fear . . . I think I'm really grown-up . . . and then something happens . . . and I run to you like a baby. . . . I love you, Father. I don't love anyone but you.

Mr. Frank (*reproachfully*). Annele!

Anne. It's true. I've been thinking about it for a long time. You're the only one I love.

Mr. Frank. It's fine to hear you tell me that you love me. But I'd be happier if you said you loved your mother as well. . . . She needs your help so much . . . your love . . .

Anne. We have nothing in common. She doesn't understand me. Whenever I try to explain my views on life to her, she asks me if I'm constipated.

Mr. Frank. You hurt her very much just now. She's crying. She's in there crying.

Anne. I can't help it. I only told the truth. I didn't want her here . . . (*Then, with sudden change*) Oh, Pim, I was horrible, wasn't I? And the worst of it is, I can stand off and look at myself doing it and know it's cruel and yet I can't stop doing it. What's the matter with me? Tell me. Don't say it's just a phase! Help me.

Mr. Frank. There is so little that we parents can do to help our children. We can only try to set a good example . . . point the way. The rest you must do yourself. You must build your own character.

Anne. I'm trying. Really I am. Every night I think back over all of the things I did that day that were wrong . . . like putting the wet mop in Mr. Dussel's bed . . . and this thing now with Mother. I say to myself, that was wrong. I make up my mind, I'm never going to do that again. Never! Of course, I may do something worse . . . but at least I'll never do *that* again! . . . I have a nicer side, Father . . . a sweeter, nicer side. But I'm scared to show it. I'm afraid that people are going to laugh at me if I'm serious. So the mean Anne comes to the outside and the good Anne stays on the inside, and I keep on trying to switch them around and have the good Anne outside and the bad Anne inside and be what I'd like to be . . . and might be . . . if only . . . only . . .

[*She is asleep.* MR. FRANK *watches her for a moment and then turns off the light, and starts out. The lights dim out. The curtain falls on the scene.* ANNE's *voice is heard, dimly at first and then with growing strength.*]

Anne's Voice. . . . The air raids[5] are getting worse. They come over day and night. The noise is terrifying. Pim says it should be music to our ears. The more planes, the sooner will come the end of the war. Mrs. Van Daan pretends to be a fatalist.[6] What will be, will be. But when the planes come over, who is the most frightened? No one else but Petronella! . . . Monday, the ninth of November, nineteen forty-two. Wonderful news! The Allies have landed in Africa. Pim says that we can look for an early finish to the war. Just for fun, he asked each of us what was the first thing we wanted to do when we got out of here. Mrs. Van Daan longs to be home with her own things, her needlepoint chairs, the Bechstein piano her father gave her . . . the best that money

---

5. **air raids** *n.:* Allied aircraft conducted air raids, or bombing attacks on ground targets, in the Netherlands because the country was occupied by the Germans.

6. **fatalist** (fāt″l·ist) *n.:* person who believes that all events are determined by fate and therefore cannot be prevented or affected by people's actions.

could buy. Peter would like to go to a movie. Mr. Dussel wants to get back to his dentist's drill. He's afraid he is losing his touch. For myself, there are so many things . . . to ride a bike again . . . to laugh till my belly aches . . . to have new clothes from the skin out . . . to have a hot tub filled to overflowing and wallow in it for hours . . . to be back in school with my friends . . .

[*As the last lines are being said, the curtain rises on the scene. The lights dim on as* ANNE'*s voice fades away.*]

■ SCENE 5

It is the first night of the Hanukkah[7] celebration. MR. FRANK *is standing at the head of the table on which is the menorah.[8] He lights the shamas, or servant candle, and holds it as he says the blessing. Seated, listening, are all of the "family," dressed in their best. The men wear hats;* PETER *wears his cap.*

Mr. Frank (*reading from a prayer book*). "Praised be Thou, oh Lord our God, Ruler of the universe, who has sanctified us with Thy commandments and bidden us kindle the Hanukkah lights. Praised be Thou, oh Lord our God, Ruler of the universe, who has wrought wondrous deliverances for our fa-

thers in days of old. Praised be Thou, oh Lord our God, Ruler of the universe, that Thou has given us life and sustenance and brought us to this happy season." (MR. FRANK *lights the one candle of the menorah as he continues.*) "We kindle this Hanukkah light to celebrate the great and wonderful deeds wrought through the zeal with which God filled the hearts of the heroic Maccabees, two thousand years ago. They fought against indifference, against tyranny and oppression, and they restored our Temple to us. May these lights remind us that we should ever look to God, whence cometh our help." Amen. (*Pronounced "o-mayn"*)

All. Amen.

[MR. FRANK *hands* MRS. FRANK *the prayer book.*]

Mrs. Frank (*reading*). "I lift up mine eyes unto the mountains, from whence cometh my help. My help cometh from the Lord who made heaven and earth. He will not suffer thy foot to be moved. He that keepeth thee will not slumber. He that keepeth Israel doth neither slumber nor sleep. The Lord is thy keeper. The Lord is thy shade upon thy right hand. The sun shall not smite thee by day, nor the moon by night. The Lord shall keep thee from all evil. He shall keep thy soul. The Lord shall guard thy going out and thy coming in, from this time forth and forevermore."[9] Amen.

All. Amen.

---

7. **Hanukkah** (khä**'**nʊʊ·kä′): joyous eight-day Jewish holiday, usually falling in December, celebrating the rededication of the holy Temple in Jerusalem in 164 B.C. The Temple had been taken over by the Syrians, who had conquered Jerusalem. The Maccabee family led the Jews in a successful rebellion against the Syrians and retook the Temple.

8. **menorah** (mə·nō**'**rə) *n.:* Hebrew for "lamp." Mr. Frank is lighting a menorah that holds nine candles: eight candles, one for each of the eight nights of Hanukkah, and the shamas, the candle used to light the others.

---

9. Mrs. Frank is reading Psalm 121 from the Bible.

Vocabulary

zeal (zēl) *n.:* great enthusiasm; devotion to a cause.

tyranny (tir**'**ə·nē) *n.:* cruel and unjust rule or use of power.

Anne.
Presents!

[MRS. FRANK *puts down the prayer book and goes to get the food and wine.* MARGOT *helps her.* MR. FRANK *takes the men's hats and puts them aside.*]

Dussel (*rising*). That was very moving.
Anne (*pulling him back*). It isn't over yet!
Mrs. Van Daan. Sit down! Sit down!
Anne. There's a lot more, songs and presents.
Dussel. Presents?
Mrs. Frank. Not this year, unfortunately.
Mrs. Van Daan. But always on Hanukkah everyone gives presents . . . everyone!

Dussel. Like our St. Nicholas's Day.[10]

[*There is a chorus of no's from the group.*]

Mrs. Van Daan. No! Not like St. Nicholas! What kind of a Jew are you that you don't know Hanukkah?

---

10. **St. Nicholas's Day:** Christian holiday celebrated in the Netherlands and other European countries on December 5, on which small gifts are given, especially to children.

Mrs. Frank (*as she brings the food*). I remember particularly the candles . . . First, one, as we have tonight. Then, the second night, you light two candles, the next night three . . . and so on until you have eight candles burning. When there are eight candles, it is truly beautiful.

Mrs. Van Daan. And the potato pancakes.

Mr. Van Daan. Don't talk about them!

Mrs. Van Daan. I make the best latkes[11] you ever tasted!

Mrs. Frank. Invite us all next year . . . in your own home.

Mr. Frank. God willing!

Mrs. Van Daan. God willing.

Margot. What I remember best is the presents we used to get when we were little . . . eight days of presents . . . and each day they got better and better.

Mrs. Frank (*sitting down*). We are all here, alive. That is present enough.

Anne. No, it isn't. I've got something. . . . (*She rushes into her room, hurriedly puts on a little hat improvised from the lampshade, grabs a satchel bulging with parcels, and comes running back.*)

Mrs. Frank. What is it?

Anne. Presents!

Mrs. Van Daan. Presents!

Dussel. Look!

Mr. Van Daan. What's she got on her head?

Peter. A lampshade!

Anne (*she picks out one at random*). This is for Margot. (*She hands it to* MARGOT, *pulling her to her feet.*) Read it out loud.

Margot (*reading*).

You have never lost your temper.
You never will, I fear,

You are so good.
But if you should,
Put all your cross words here.

(*She tears open the package.*) A new crossword puzzle book! Where did you get it?

Anne. It isn't new. It's one that you've done. But I rubbed it all out, and if you wait a little and forget, you can do it all over again.

Margot (*sitting*). It's wonderful, Anne. Thank you. You'd never know it wasn't new.

[*From outside we hear the sound of a streetcar passing.*]

Anne (*with another gift*). Mrs. Van Daan.

Mrs. Van Daan (*taking it*). This is awful . . . I haven't anything for anyone . . . I never thought . . .

Mr. Frank. This is all Anne's idea.

Mrs. Van Daan (*holding up a bottle*). What is it?

Anne. It's hair shampoo. I took all the odds and ends of soap and mixed them with the last of my toilet water.[12]

Mrs. Van Daan. Oh, Anneke!

Anne. I wanted to write a poem for all of them, but I didn't have time. (*Offering a large box to* MR. VAN DAAN) Yours, Mr. Van Daan, is *really* something . . . something you want more than anything. (*As she waits for him to open it*) Look! Cigarettes!

Mr. Van Daan. Cigarettes!

Anne. Two of them! Pim found some old pipe tobacco in the pocket lining of his coat . . . and we made them . . . or rather, Pim did.

Mrs. Van Daan. Let me see . . . Well, look at that! Light it, Putti! Light it.

[MR. VAN DAAN *hesitates.*]

---

11. **latkes** (lätʼkəz) *n.*: potato pancakes, a traditional Hanukkah food.

---

12. **toilet water** *n.*: cologne.

Anne. It's tobacco, really it is! There's a little fluff in it, but not much.

[*Everyone watches intently as* MR. VAN DAAN *cautiously lights it. The cigarette flares up. Everyone laughs.*]

Peter. It works!
Mrs. Van Daan. Look at him.
Mr. Van Daan (*spluttering*). Thank you, Anne. Thank you.

[ANNE *rushes back to her satchel for another present.*]

Anne (*handing her mother a piece of paper*). For Mother, Hanukkah greeting. (*She pulls her mother to her feet.*)
Mrs. Frank (*she reads*).

> Here's an IOU that I promise to pay.
> Ten hours of doing whatever you say.
> Signed, Anne Frank.

(MRS. FRANK, *touched, takes* ANNE *in her arms, holding her close.*)
Dussel (*to* ANNE). Ten hours of doing what you're told? *Anything* you're told?
Anne. That's right.
Dussel. You wouldn't want to sell that, Mrs. Frank?
Mrs. Frank. Never! This is the most precious gift I've ever had!

[*She sits, showing her present to the others.* ANNE *hurries back to the satchel and pulls out a scarf, the scarf that* MR. FRANK *found in the first scene.*]

Anne (*offering it to her father*). For Pim.
Mr. Frank. Anneke . . . I wasn't supposed to have a present! (*He takes it, unfolding it and showing it to the others.*)
Anne. It's a muffler . . . to put round your neck . . . like an ascot, you know. I made it myself out of odds and ends. . . . I knitted it in the dark each night, after I'd gone to bed. I'm afraid it looks better in the dark!
Mr. Frank (*putting it on*). It's fine. It fits me perfectly. Thank you, Annele.

[ANNE *hands* PETER *a ball of paper with a string attached to it.*]

Anne. That's for Mouschi.
Peter (*rising to bow*). On behalf of Mouschi, I thank you.
Anne (*hesitant, handing him a gift*). And . . . this is yours . . . from Mrs. Quack Quack. (*As he holds it gingerly in his hands*) Well . . . open it . . . Aren't you going to open it?
Peter. I'm scared to. I know something's going to jump out and hit me.
Anne. No. It's nothing like that, really.
Mrs. Van Daan (*as he is opening it*). What is it, Peter? Go on. Show it.
Anne (*excitedly*). It's a safety razor!
Dussel. A what?
Anne. A razor!
Mrs. Van Daan (*looking at it*). You didn't make that out of odds and ends.
Anne (*to* PETER). Miep got it for me. It's not new. It's secondhand. But you really do need a razor now.
Dussel. For what?
Anne. Look on his upper lip . . . you can see the beginning of a moustache.
Dussel. He wants to get rid of that? Put a little milk on it and let the cat lick it off.
Peter (*starting for his room*). Think you're funny, don't you.
Dussel. Look! He can't wait! He's going in to try it!

Vocabulary
gingerly (jin′jər′lē) *adv.*: carefully; cautiously.

Peter. I'm going to give Mouschi his present! (*He goes into his room, slamming the door behind him.*)

Mr. Van Daan (*disgustedly*). Mouschi, Mouschi, Mouschi.

[*In the distance we hear a dog persistently barking.* ANNE *brings a gift to* DUSSEL.]

Anne. And last but never least, my roommate, Mr. Dussel.

Dussel. For me? You have something for me? (*He opens the small box she gives him.*)

Anne. I made them myself.

Dussel (*puzzled*). Capsules! Two capsules!

Anne. They're earplugs!

Dussel. Earplugs?

Anne. To put in your ears so you won't hear me when I thrash around at night. I saw them advertised in a magazine. They're not real ones. . . . I made them out of cotton and candle wax. Try them . . . See if they don't work . . . See if you can hear me talk . . .

Dussel (*putting them in his ears*). Wait now until I get them in . . . so.

Anne. Are you ready?

Dussel. Huh?

Anne. Are you ready?

Dussel. Good God! They've gone inside! I can't get them out! (*They laugh as* DUSSEL *jumps about, trying to shake the plugs out of his ears. Finally he gets them out. Putting them away*) Thank you, Anne! Thank you!

Mr. Van Daan. A real Hanukkah!
Mrs. Van Daan. Wasn't it cute of her? } *Together*
Mrs. Frank. I don't know when she did it.
Margot. I love my present.

Anne (*sitting at the table*). And now let's have the song, Father . . . please . . . (*To

DUSSEL*) Have you heard the Hanukkah song, Mr. Dussel? The song is the whole thing! (*She sings*) "Oh, Hanukkah! Oh, Hanukkah! The sweet celebration . . ."

Mr. Frank (*quieting her*). I'm afraid, Anne, we shouldn't sing that song tonight. (*To* DUSSEL) It's a song of jubilation, of rejoicing. One is apt to become too enthusiastic.

Anne. Oh, please, please. Let's sing the song. I promise not to shout!

Mr. Frank. Very well. But quietly, now . . . I'll keep an eye on you and when . . .

[*As* ANNE *starts to sing, she is interrupted by* DUSSEL, *who is snorting and wheezing.*]

Dussel (*pointing to* PETER). You . . . You! (PETER *is coming from his bedroom, ostentatiously holding a bulge in his coat as if he were holding his cat, and dangling* ANNE'*s present before it.*) How many times . . . I told you . . . Out! Out!

Mr. Van Daan (*going to* PETER). What's the matter with you? Haven't you any sense? Get that cat out of here.

Peter (*innocently*). Cat?

Mr. Van Daan. You heard me. Get it out of here!

Peter. I have no cat.

[*Delighted with his joke, he opens his coat and pulls out a bath towel. The group at the table laugh, enjoying the joke.*]

Dussel (*still wheezing*). It doesn't need to be the cat . . . his clothes are enough . . . when he comes out of that room . . .

Mr. Van Daan. Don't worry. You won't be bothered anymore. We're getting rid of it.

Vocabulary
ostentatiously (äs′tən·tā′shəs·lē) *adv.*: in a showy or exaggerated way.

Dussel. At last you listen to me. (*He goes off into his bedroom.*)

Mr. Van Daan (*calling after him*). I'm not doing it for you. That's all in your mind . . . all of it! (*He starts back to his place at the table.*) I'm doing it because I'm sick of seeing that cat eat all our food.

Peter. That's not true! I only give him bones . . . scraps . . .

Mr. Van Daan. Don't tell me! He gets fatter every day! Damn cat looks better than any of us. Out he goes tonight!

Peter. No! No!

Anne. Mr. Van Daan, you can't do that! That's Peter's cat. Peter loves that cat.

Mrs. Frank (*quietly*). Anne.

Peter (*to* MR. VAN DAAN). If he goes, I go.

Mr. Van Daan. Go! Go!

Mrs. Van Daan. You're not going and the cat's not going! Now please . . . this is Hanukkah . . . Hanukkah . . . this is the time to celebrate . . . What's the matter with all of you? Come on, Anne. Let's have the song.

Anne (*singing*).

> Oh, Hanukkah!
> Oh, Hanukkah!
> The sweet celebration.

Mr. Frank (*rising*). I think we should first blow out the candle . . . then we'll have something for tomorrow night.

Margot. But, Father, you're supposed to let it burn itself out.

Mr. Frank. I'm sure that God understands shortages. (*Before blowing it out*) "Praised be Thou, oh Lord our God, who hast sustained us and permitted us to celebrate this joyous festival."

[*He is about to blow out the candle when suddenly there is a crash of something falling below. They all freeze in horror, motionless. For a few seconds there is complete silence.* MR. FRANK *slips off his shoes. The others noiselessly follow his example.* MR. FRANK *turns out a light near him. He motions to* PETER *to turn off the center lamp.* PETER *tries to reach it, realizes he cannot, and gets up on a chair. Just as he is touching the lamp, he loses his balance. The chair goes out from under him. He falls. The iron lampshade crashes to the floor. There is a sound of feet below running down the stairs.*]

Mr. Van Daan (*under his breath*). God Almighty! (*The only light left comes from the Hanukkah candle.* DUSSEL *comes from his room.* MR. FRANK *creeps over to the stairwell and stands listening. The dog is heard barking excitedly.*) Do you hear anything?

Mr. Frank (*in a whisper*). No. I think they've gone.

Mrs. Van Daan. It's the Green Police. They've found us.

Mr. Frank. If they had, they wouldn't have left. They'd be up here by now.

Mrs. Van Daan. I know it's the Green Police. They've gone to get help. That's all. They'll be back!

Mr. Van Daan. Or it may have been the Gestapo,[13] looking for papers . . .

Mr. Frank (*interrupting*). Or a thief, looking for money.

Mrs. Van Daan. We've got to do something . . . Quick! Quick! Before they come back.

Mr. Van Daan. There isn't anything to do. Just wait.

[MR. FRANK *holds up his hand for them to be quiet. He is listening intently. There is complete silence as they all strain to hear any sound from below. Suddenly* ANNE *begins to sway.*]

---

13. **Gestapo** (gə·stäʹpō): Nazi secret police.

With a low cry she falls to the floor in a faint. MRS. FRANK *goes to her quickly, sitting beside her on the floor and taking her in her arms.*]

Mrs. Frank. Get some water, please! Get some water!

[MARGOT *starts for the sink.*]

Mr. Van Daan (*grabbing* MARGOT). No! No! No one's going to run water!
Mr. Frank. If they've found us, they've found us. Get the water. (MARGOT *starts again for the sink.* MR. FRANK, *getting a flashlight*) I'm going down.

[MARGOT *rushes to him, clinging to him.* ANNE *struggles to consciousness.*]

Margot Frank.

Margot. No, Father, no! There may be someone there, waiting. . . . It may be a trap!
Mr. Frank. This is Saturday. There is no way for us to know what has happened until Miep or Mr. Kraler comes on Monday morning. We cannot live with this uncertainty.
Margot. Don't go, Father!
Mrs. Frank. Hush, darling, hush. (MR. FRANK *slips quietly out, down the steps, and out through the door below.*) Margot! Stay close to me.

[MARGOT *goes to her mother.*]

Mr. Van Daan. Shush! Shush!

[MRS. FRANK *whispers to* MARGOT *to get the water.* MARGOT *goes for it.*]

Mrs. Van Daan. Putti, where's our money? Get our money. I hear you can buy the Green Police off, so much a head. Go upstairs quick! Get the money!
Mr. Van Daan. Keep still!
Mrs. Van Daan (*kneeling before him, pleading*). Do you want to be dragged off to a concentration camp? Are you going to stand there and wait for them to come up and get you? Do something, I tell you!
Mr. Van Daan (*pushing her aside*). Will you keep still!

[*He goes over to the stairwell to listen.* PETER *goes to his mother, helping her up onto the sofa. There is a second of silence; then* ANNE *can stand it no longer.*]

Anne. Someone go after Father! Make Father come back!
Peter (*starting for the door*). I'll go.
Mr. Van Daan. Haven't you done enough?

[*He pushes* PETER *roughly away. In his anger against his father* PETER *grabs a chair as if to hit him with it, then puts it down, burying his face in his hands.* MRS. FRANK *begins to pray softly.*]

Anne. Please, please, Mr. Van Daan. Get Father.
Mr. Van Daan. Quiet! Quiet!

[ANNE *is shocked into silence.* MRS. FRANK *pulls her closer, holding her protectively in her arms.*]

Mrs. Frank (*softly, praying*). "I lift up mine eyes unto the mountains, from whence cometh my help. My help cometh from the Lord who made heaven and earth. He will not suffer thy foot to be moved . . . He that keepeth thee will not slumber . . ."

[*She stops as she hears someone coming. They all watch the door tensely.* MR. FRANK *comes quietly in.* ANNE *rushes to him, holding him tight.*]

Mr. Frank. It was a thief. That noise must have scared him away.

Mrs. Van Daan. Thank God.

Mr. Frank. He took the cash box. And the radio. He ran away in such a hurry that he didn't stop to shut the street door. It was swinging wide open. (*A breath of relief sweeps over them.*) I think it would be good to have some light.

Margot. Are you sure it's all right?

Mr. Frank. The danger has passed. (MARGOT *goes to light the small lamp.*) Don't be so terrified, Anne. We're safe.

Dussel. Who says the danger has passed? Don't you realize we are in greater danger than ever?

Mr. Frank. Mr. Dussel, will you be still! (MR. FRANK *takes* ANNE *back to the table, making her sit down with him, trying to calm her.*)

Dussel (*pointing to* PETER). Thanks to this clumsy fool, there's someone now who knows we're up here! Someone now knows we're up here, hiding!

Mrs. Van Daan (*going to* DUSSEL). Someone knows we're here, yes. But who is the someone? A thief! A thief! You think a thief is going to go to the Green Police and say . . . "I was robbing a place the other night and I heard a noise up over my head?" You think a thief is going to do that?

Dussel. Yes. I think he will.

Mrs. Van Daan (*hysterically*). You're crazy! (*She stumbles back to her seat at the table.* PETER *follows protectively, pushing* DUSSEL *aside.*)

Dussel. I think someday he'll be caught and then he'll make a bargain with the Green Police . . . if they'll let him off, he'll tell them where some Jews are hiding!

[*He goes off into the bedroom. There is a second of appalled silence.*]

Mr. Van Daan. He's right.

Anne. Father, let's get out of here! We can't stay here now . . . Let's go . . .

Mr. Van Daan. Go! Where?

Mrs. Frank (*sinking into her chair at the table*). Yes. Where?

Mr. Frank (*rising, to them all*). Have we lost all faith? All courage? A moment ago we thought that they'd come for us. We were sure it was the end. But it wasn't the end. We're alive, safe. (MR. VAN DAAN *goes to the table and sits.* MR. FRANK *prays*) "We thank Thee, oh Lord our God, that in Thy infinite mercy Thou hast again seen fit to spare us." (*He blows out the candle, then turns to* ANNE.) Come on, Anne. The song! Let's have the song! (*He starts to sing.* ANNE *finally starts falteringly to sing, as* MR. FRANK *urges her on. Her voice is hardly audible at first.*)

Anne (*singing*).

Oh, Hanukkah! Oh, Hanukkah!
The sweet . . . celebration . . .

[*As she goes on singing, the others gradually join in, their voices still shaking with fear.* MRS. VAN DAAN *sobs as she sings.*]

Vocabulary
appalled (ə·pôld′) *v.* used as *adj.:* horrified; shocked.

Group.

> Around the feast . . . we . . . gather
> In complete . . . jubilation . . .
> Happiest of sea . . . sons
> Now is here.
> Many are the reasons for good cheer.

[DUSSEL *comes from the bedroom. He comes over to the table, standing beside* MARGOT, *listening to them as they sing.*]

> Together
> We'll weather
> Whatever tomorrow may bring.

[*As they sing on with growing courage, the lights start to dim.*]

> So hear us rejoicing
> And merrily voicing
> The Hanukkah song that we sing.
> Hoy!

[*The lights are out. The curtain starts slowly to fall.*]

> Hear us rejoicing
> And merrily voicing
> The Hanukkah song that we sing.

[*They are still singing as the curtain falls.*]

> *Curtain*

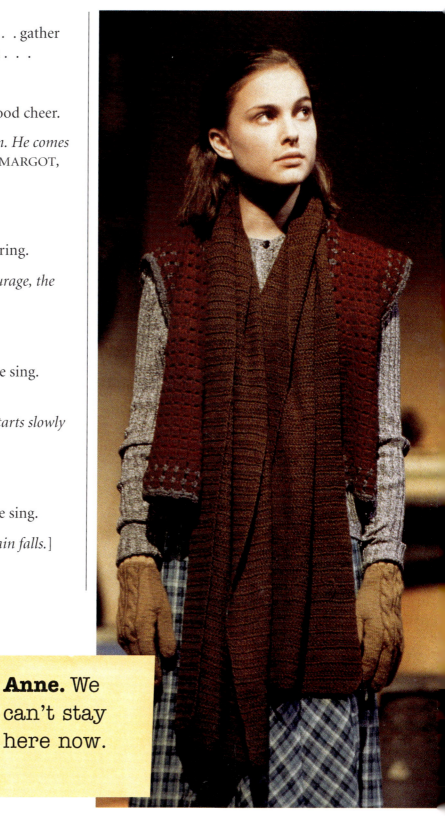

Anne. We can't stay here now.

After You Read | Response and Analysis

Act One, Scenes 4–5

First Thoughts

1. Go back to the list of **characters** you made after you read Scenes 1–3. Which adjectives, if any, would you change now? Why?

Thinking Critically

2. Anne is a **dynamic character;** that is, she changes in the course of the play. How does she hurt her mother in Scene 4? How do her gifts to her mother and Peter show that she has changed?

3. Many events in our lives involve rituals: birthdays, wedding anniversaries, Christmas, Hanukkah. When we take part in those rituals, we remember the past and look to the future. How does the Hanukkah celebration contrast with the harsh reality outside the hiding place? What is the **mood** of this Hanukkah scene?

4. Describe the **reversal**—the sudden change in the characters' fortunes—that occurs in Scene 5. How did it make you feel?

5. Imagine that you are watching this play in a theater. What questions do you have as the curtain comes down on Act One? What do you **predict** will happen in Act Two?

6. Re-read Anne's conversation with her father on page 400. What does she say that reminds you the most—or the least—of yourself? Explain.

Reading Check

a. The events that take place in Scene 4 reveal tensions between Anne and two other members of the household. What tensions does the scene reveal?

b. Describe how the Hanukkah celebration in Scene 5 is interrupted. What does Peter do that makes matters worse? According to Dussel, how will this incident lead to the household's discovery by the police?

Extending Interpretations

7. During World War II, when England stood alone against the Nazis, the English took courage from these words of their prime minister, Winston Churchill: "We shall fight on the beaches, we shall fight on the landing grounds, we shall fight in the fields and in the streets, we shall fight in the hills, we shall never surrender." At what point in the play does a group of people take courage from the words of a song? Can you think of other episodes in plays or movies (or real life) in which people facing danger summon up courage from a speech or song?

SKILLS FOCUS

Literary Skills
Analyze character.

Reading Skills
Make predictions.

410   Collection 4 / The Human Spirit

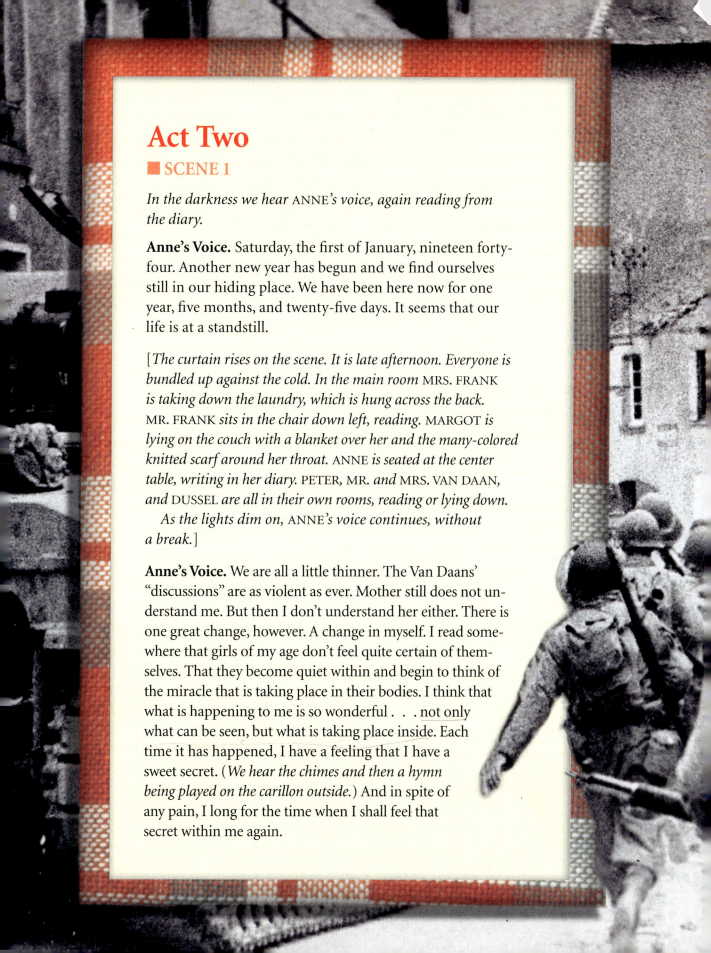

Act Two

■ SCENE 1

In the darkness we hear ANNE's *voice, again reading from the diary.*

Anne's Voice. Saturday, the first of January, nineteen forty-four. Another new year has begun and we find ourselves still in our hiding place. We have been here now for one year, five months, and twenty-five days. It seems that our life is at a standstill.

[*The curtain rises on the scene. It is late afternoon. Everyone is bundled up against the cold. In the main room* MRS. FRANK *is taking down the laundry, which is hung across the back.* MR. FRANK *sits in the chair down left, reading.* MARGOT *is lying on the couch with a blanket over her and the many-colored knitted scarf around her throat.* ANNE *is seated at the center table, writing in her diary.* PETER, MR. *and* MRS. VAN DAAN, *and* DUSSEL *are all in their own rooms, reading or lying down.*

As the lights dim on, ANNE's *voice continues, without a break.*]

Anne's Voice. We are all a little thinner. The Van Daans' "discussions" are as violent as ever. Mother still does not understand me. But then I don't understand her either. There is one great change, however. A change in myself. I read somewhere that girls of my age don't feel quite certain of themselves. That they become quiet within and begin to think of the miracle that is taking place in their bodies. I think that what is happening to me is so wonderful . . . not only what can be seen, but what is taking place inside. Each time it has happened, I have a feeling that I have a sweet secret. (*We hear the chimes and then a hymn being played on the carillon outside.*) And in spite of any pain, I long for the time when I shall feel that secret within me again.

[*The buzzer of the door below suddenly sounds. Everyone is startled.* MR. FRANK *tiptoes cautiously to the top of the steps and listens. Again the buzzer sounds, in* MIEP'S *V-for-victory signal.*][1]

Mr. Frank. It's Miep!

[*He goes quickly down the steps to unbolt the door.* MRS. FRANK *calls upstairs to the* VAN DAANS *and then to* PETER.]

Mrs. Frank. Wake up, everyone! Miep is here! (ANNE *quickly puts her diary away.* MARGOT *sits up, pulling the blanket around her shoulders.* DUSSEL *sits on the edge of his bed, listening, disgruntled.* MIEP *comes up the steps, followed by* MR. KRALER. *They bring flowers, books, newspapers, etc.* ANNE *rushes to* MIEP, *throwing her arms affectionately around her.*) Miep . . . and Mr. Kraler . . . What a delightful surprise!

Mr. Kraler. We came to bring you New Year's greetings.

Mrs. Frank. You shouldn't . . . you should have at least one day to yourselves. (*She goes quickly to the stove and brings down teacups and tea for all of them.*)

Anne. Don't say that, it's so wonderful to see them! (*Sniffing at* MIEP'S *coat*) I can smell the wind and the cold on your clothes.

Miep (*giving her the flowers*). There you are. (*Then to* MARGOT, *feeling her forehead*) How are you, Margot? . . . Feeling any better?

Margot. I'm all right.

Anne. We filled her full of every kind of pill so she won't cough and make a noise.

[*She runs into her room to put the flowers in water.* MR. *and* MRS. VAN DAAN *come from upstairs. Outside there is the sound of a band playing.*]

Mrs. Van Daan. Well, hello, Miep. Mr. Kraler.

Mr. Kraler (*giving a bouquet of flowers to* MRS. VAN DAAN). With my hope for peace in the New Year.

Peter (*anxiously*). Miep, have you seen Mouschi? Have you seen him anywhere around?

Miep. I'm sorry, Peter. I asked everyone in the neighborhood had they seen a gray cat. But they said no.

[MRS. FRANK *gives* MIEP *a cup of tea.* MR. FRANK *comes up the steps, carrying a small cake on a plate.*]

Mr. Frank. Look what Miep's brought for us!

Mrs. Frank (*taking it*). A cake!

Mr. Van Daan. A cake! (*He pinches* MIEP'S *cheeks gaily and hurries up to the cupboard.*) I'll get some plates.

[DUSSEL, *in his room, hastily puts a coat on and starts out to join the others.*]

Mrs. Frank. Thank you, Miepia. You shouldn't have done it. You must have used all of your sugar ration for weeks. (*Giving it to* MRS. VAN DAAN) It's beautiful, isn't it?

Mrs. Van Daan. It's been ages since I even saw a cake. Not since you brought us one last year. (*Without looking at the cake, to* MIEP) Remember? Don't you remember, you gave us one on New Year's Day? Just this time last year? I'll never forget it because you had "Peace in nineteen forty-three" on it.

---

1. **V-for-victory signal:** three short rings and one long ring, Morse code for the letter *V*, the Allied symbol for victory.

Vocabulary
disgruntled (dis·grunt'ld) *v.* used as *adj.:* displeased; annoyed.

(*She looks at the cake and reads*) "Peace in nineteen forty-four!"

Miep. Well, it has to come sometime, you know. (*As* DUSSEL *comes from his room*) Hello, Mr. Dussel.

Mr. Kraler. How are you?

Mr. Van Daan (*bringing plates and a knife*). Here's the knife, liefje. Now, how many of us are there?

Miep. None for me, thank you.

Mr. Frank. Oh, please. You must.

Miep. I couldn't.

Mr. Van Daan. Good! That leaves one . . . two . . . three . . . seven of us.

Dussel. Eight! Eight! It's the same number as it always is!

Mr. Van Daan. I left Margot out. I take it for granted Margot won't eat any.

Anne. Why wouldn't she!

Mrs. Frank. I think it won't harm her.

Mr. Van Daan. All right! All right! I just didn't want her to start coughing again, that's all.

Dussel. And please, Mrs. Frank should cut the cake.

Mr. Van Daan. What's the difference? } *Together*

Mrs. Van Daan. It's not Mrs. Frank's cake, is it, Miep? It's for all of us.

Dussel. Mrs. Frank divides things better.

Mrs. Van Daan (*going to* DUSSEL). What are you trying to say? } *Together*

Mr. Van Daan. Oh, come on! Stop wasting time!

Mr. Kraler.

Mrs. Van Daan (*to* DUSSEL). Don't I always give everybody exactly the same? Don't I?

Mr. Van Daan. Forget it, Kerli.

Mrs. Van Daan. No. I want an answer! Don't I?

Dussel. Yes. Yes. Everybody gets exactly the same . . . except Mr. Van Daan always gets a little bit more.

[MR. VAN DAAN *advances on* DUSSEL, *the knife still in his hand.*]

Mr. Van Daan. That's a lie!

[DUSSEL *retreats before the onslaught of the* VAN DAANS.]

Mr. Frank. Please, please! (*Then, to* MIEP) You see what a little sugar cake does to us? It goes right to our heads!

Mr. Van Daan (*handing* MRS. FRANK *the knife*). Here you are, Mrs. Frank.

Mrs. Frank. Thank you. (*Then, to* MIEP, *as she goes to the table to cut the cake*) Are you sure you won't have some?

Miep (*drinking her tea*). No, really, I have to go in a minute.

[*The sound of the band fades out in the distance.*]

Peter (*to* MIEP). Maybe Mouschi went back to our house . . . they say that cats . . . Do you ever get over there . . . ? I mean . . . do you suppose you could . . . ?

Miep. I'll try, Peter. The first minute I get, I'll try. But I'm afraid, with him gone a week . . .

Dussel. Make up your mind, already someone has had a nice big dinner from that cat!

[PETER *is furious, inarticulate. He starts toward* DUSSEL *as if to hit him.* MR. FRANK *stops him.* MRS. FRANK *speaks quickly to ease the situation.*]

Mrs. Frank (*to* MIEP). This is delicious, Miep!
Mrs. Van Daan (*eating hers*). Delicious!
Mr. Van Daan (*finishing it in one gulp*). Dirk's in luck to get a girl who can bake like this!
Miep (*putting down her empty teacup*). I have to run. Dirk's taking me to a party tonight.
Anne. How heavenly! Remember now what everyone is wearing and what you have to eat and everything, so you can tell us tomorrow.
Miep. I'll give you a full report! Goodbye, everyone!
Mr. Van Daan (*to* MIEP). Just a minute. There's something I'd like you to do for me. (*He hurries off up the stairs to his room.*)
Mrs. Van Daan (*sharply*). Putti, where are you going? (*She rushes up the stairs after him, calling hysterically.*) What do you want? Putti, what are you going to do?
Miep (*to* PETER). What's wrong?
Peter (*his sympathy is with his mother*). Father says he's going to sell her fur coat. She's crazy about that old fur coat.
Dussel. Is it possible? Is it possible that anyone is so silly as to worry about a fur coat in times like this?
Peter. It's none of your darn business . . . and if you say one more thing . . . I'll, I'll take you and I'll . . . I mean it . . . I'll . . .

[*There is a piercing scream from* MRS. VAN DAAN, *above. She grabs at the fur coat as* MR. VAN DAAN *is starting downstairs with it.*]

Mrs. Van Daan. No! No! No! Don't you dare take that! You hear? It's mine! (*Downstairs* PETER *turns away, embarrassed, miserable.*) My father gave me that! You didn't give it to me. You have no right. Let go of it . . . you hear?

[MR. VAN DAAN *pulls the coat from her hands and hurries downstairs.* MRS. VAN DAAN *sinks to the floor, sobbing. As* MR. VAN DAAN *comes into the main room, the others look away, embarrassed for him.*]

Mr. Van Daan (*to* MR. KRALER). Just a little—discussion over the advisability of selling this coat. As I have often reminded Mrs. Van Daan, it's very selfish of her to keep it when people outside are in such desperate need of clothing. . . . (*He gives the coat to* MIEP.) So if you will please to sell it for us? It should fetch a good price. And by the way, will you get me cigarettes. I don't care what kind they are . . . get all you can.
Miep. It's terribly difficult to get them, Mr. Van Daan. But I'll try. Goodbye.

[*She goes.* MR. FRANK *follows her down the steps to bolt the door after her.* MRS. FRANK *gives* MR. KRALER *a cup of tea.*]

Mrs. Frank. Are you sure you won't have some cake, Mr. Kraler?
Mr. Kraler. I'd better not.
Mr. Van Daan. You're still feeling badly? What does your doctor say?
Mr. Kraler. I haven't been to him.
Mrs. Frank. Now, Mr. Kraler! . . .
Mr. Kraler (*sitting at the table*). Oh, I tried. But you can't get near a doctor these days . . . they're so busy. After weeks I finally

Vocabulary
inarticulate (in'är·tik'yōō·lit) *adj.:* unable to speak. *Inarticulate* also means "unable to speak understandably or effectively."

managed to get one on the telephone. I told him I'd like an appointment . . . I wasn't feeling very well. You know what he answers . . . over the telephone . . . "Stick out your tongue!" (*They laugh. He turns to* MR. FRANK *as* MR. FRANK *comes back.*) I have some contracts here . . . I wonder if you'd look over them with me . . .

Mr. Frank (*putting out his hand*). Of course.

Mr. Kraler (*he rises*). If we could go downstairs . . . (MR. FRANK *starts ahead;* MR. KRALER *speaks to the others.*) Will you forgive us? I won't keep him but a minute. (*He starts to follow* MR. FRANK *down the steps.*)

Margot (*with sudden foreboding*). What's happened? Something's happened! Hasn't it, Mr. Kraler?

[MR. KRALER *stops and comes back, trying to reassure* MARGOT *with a pretense of casualness.*]

Mr. Kraler. No, really. I want your father's advice . . .

Margot. Something's gone wrong! I know it!

Mr. Frank (*coming back, to* MR. KRALER). If it's something that concerns us here, it's better that we all hear it.

Mr. Kraler (*turning to him, quietly*). But . . . the children . . . ?

Mr. Frank. What they'd imagine would be worse than any reality.

[*As* MR. KRALER *speaks, they all listen with intense apprehension.* MRS. VAN DAAN *comes down the stairs and sits on the bottom step.*]

Mr. Kraler. It's a man in the storeroom . . . I don't know whether or not you remember him . . . Carl, about fifty, heavyset, nearsighted . . . He came with us just before you left.

Mr. Frank. He was from Utrecht?

Mr. Kraler. That's the man. A couple of weeks ago, when I was in the storeroom, he closed the door and asked me . . . "How's Mr. Frank? What do you hear from Mr. Frank?" I told him I only knew there was a rumor that you were in Switzerland. He said he'd heard that rumor too, but he thought I might know something more. I didn't pay any attention to it . . . but then a thing happened yesterday . . . He'd brought some invoices to the office for me to sign. As I was going through them, I looked up. He was standing staring at the bookcase . . . your bookcase. He said he thought he remembered a door there . . . Wasn't there a door there that used to go up to the loft? Then he told me he wanted more money. Twenty guilders[2] more a week.

Mr. Van Daan. Blackmail!

Mr. Frank. Twenty guilders? Very modest blackmail.

Mr. Van Daan. That's just the beginning.

Dussel (*coming to* MR. FRANK). You know what I think? He was the thief who was down there that night. That's how he knows we're here.

Mr. Frank (*to* MR. KRALER). How was it left? What did you tell him?

Mr. Kraler. I said I had to think about it. What shall I do? Pay him the money? . . . Take a chance on firing him . . . or what? I don't know.

Dussel (*frantic*). For God's sake, don't fire him! Pay him what he asks . . . keep him here where you can have your eye on him.

Mr. Frank. Is it so much that he's asking? What are they paying nowadays?

Mr. Kraler. He could get it in a war plant. But

---

2. **guilders** (gil′dərz) *n.:* Dutch money.

this isn't a war plant. Mind you, I don't know if he really knows . . . or if he doesn't know.

Mr. Frank. Offer him half. Then we'll soon find out if it's blackmail or not.

Dussel. And if it is? We've got to pay it, haven't we? Anything he asks we've got to pay!

Mr. Frank. Let's decide that when the time comes.

Mr. Kraler. This may be all my imagination. You get to a point, these days, where you suspect everyone and everything. Again and again . . . on some simple look or word, I've found myself . . .

[*The telephone rings in the office below.*]

Mrs. Van Daan (*hurrying to* MR. KRALER). There's the telephone! What does that mean, the telephone ringing on a holiday?

Mr. Kraler. That's my wife. I told her I had to go over some papers in my office . . . to call me there when she got out of church. (*He starts out.*) I'll offer him half, then. Goodbye . . . we'll hope for the best!

[*The group call their goodbyes halfheartedly.* MR. FRANK *follows* MR. KRALER *to bolt the door below. During the following scene,* MR. FRANK *comes back up and stands listening, disturbed.*]

Dussel (*to* MR. VAN DAAN). You can thank your son for this . . . smashing the light! I tell you, it's just a question of time now. (*He goes to the window at the back and stands looking out.*)

Margot. Sometimes I wish the end would come . . . whatever it is.

Mrs. Frank (*shocked*). Margot!

[ANNE *goes to* MARGOT, *sitting beside her on the couch with her arms around her.*]

Margot. Then at least we'd know where we were.

Mrs. Frank. You should be ashamed of yourself! Talking that way! Think how lucky we are! Think of the thousands dying in the war, every day. Think of the people in concentration camps.

Anne (*interrupting*). What's the good of that? What's the good of thinking of misery when you're already miserable? That's stupid!

Mrs. Frank. Anne!

[*As* ANNE *goes on raging at her mother,* MRS. FRANK *tries to break in, in an effort to quiet her.*]

Anne. We're young, Margot and Peter and I! You grown-ups have had your chance! But look at us . . . If we begin thinking of all the horror in the world, we're lost! We're trying to hold on to some kind of ideals . . . when everything . . . ideals, hopes . . . everything is being destroyed! It isn't our fault that the world is in such a mess! We weren't around when all this started! So don't try to take it out on us! (*She rushes off to her room, slamming the door after her. She picks up a brush from the chest and hurls it to the floor. Then she sits on the settee, trying to control her anger.*)

Mr. Van Daan. She talks as if we started the war! Did we start the war? (*He spots* ANNE'S *cake. As he starts to take it,* PETER *anticipates him.*)

Peter. She left her cake. (*He starts for* ANNE'S *room with the cake. There is silence in the main room.* MRS. VAN DAAN *goes up to her room, followed by* MR. VAN DAAN. DUSSEL *stays looking out the window.* MR. FRANK *brings* MRS. FRANK *her cake. She eats it slowly, without relish.* MR. FRANK *takes his cake to* MARGOT *and sits quietly on the sofa beside her.* PETER *stands* *in the doorway of* ANNE's *darkened room, looking at her, then makes a little movement to let her know he is there.* ANNE *sits up quickly, trying to hide the signs of her tears.* PETER *holds out the cake to her.*) You left this.

Anne (*dully*). Thanks.

[PETER *starts to go out, then comes back.*]

Peter. I thought you were fine just now. You know just how to talk to them. You know just how to say it. I'm no good . . . I never can think . . . especially when I'm mad . . . That Dussel . . . when he said that about Mouschi . . . someone eating him . . . all I could think is . . . I wanted to hit him. I wanted to give him such a . . . a . . . that he'd . . . That's what I used to do when there was an argument at school. . . . That's the way I . . . but here . . . And an old man like that . . . it wouldn't be so good.

Anne. You're making a big mistake about me. I do it all wrong. I say too much. I go too far. I hurt people's feelings. . . .

[DUSSEL *leaves the window, going to his room.*]

Peter. I think you're just fine . . . What I want to say . . . if it wasn't for you around here, I don't know. What I mean . . .

[PETER *is interrupted by* DUSSEL's *turning on the light.* DUSSEL *stands in the doorway, startled to see* PETER. PETER *advances toward him forbiddingly.* DUSSEL *backs out of the room.* PETER *closes the door on him.*]

Anne. Do you mean it, Peter? Do you really mean it?

Peter. I said it, didn't I?

Anne. Thank you, Peter!

[*In the main room* MR. *and* MRS. FRANK *collect the dishes and take them to the sink, washing them.* MARGOT *lies down again on the couch.* DUSSEL, *lost, wanders into* PETER's *room and takes up a book, starting to read.*]

Peter (*looking at the photographs on the wall*). You've got quite a collection.

Anne. Wouldn't you like some in your room? I could give you some. Heaven knows you spend enough time in there . . . doing heaven knows what . . .

Peter. It's easier. A fight starts, or an argument . . . I duck in there.

Anne. You're lucky, having a room to go to. His Lordship is always here . . . I hardly ever get a minute alone. When they start in on me, I can't duck away. I have to stand there and take it.

Peter. You gave some of it back just now.

Anne. I get so mad. They've formed their opinions . . . about everything . . . but we . . . we're still trying to find out . . . We have problems here that no other people our age have ever had. And just as you think you've solved them, something comes along and bang! You have to start all over again.

Peter. At least you've got someone you can talk to.

Anne. Not really. Mother . . . I never discuss anything serious with her. She doesn't understand. Father's all right. We can talk about everything . . . everything but one thing. Mother. He simply won't talk about her. I don't think you can be really intimate with anyone if he holds something back, do you?

Peter. I think your father's fine.

Anne. Oh, he is, Peter! He is! He's the only one who's ever given me the feeling that I have any sense. But anyway, nothing can take the place of school and play and friends of your own age . . . or near your age . . . can it?

Peter. I suppose you miss your friends and all.

Anne. It isn't just . . . (*She breaks off, staring up at him for a second.*) Isn't it funny, you and I? Here we've been seeing each other every minute for almost a year and a half, and this is the first time we've ever really talked. It helps a lot to have someone to talk to, don't you think? It helps you to let off steam.

Peter (*going to the door*). Well, any time you want to let off steam, you can come into my room.

Anne (*following him*). I can get up an awful lot of steam. You'll have to be careful how you say that.

Peter. It's all right with me.

Anne. Do you mean it?

Peter. I said it, didn't I?

[*He goes out.* ANNE *stands in her doorway looking after him. As* PETER *gets to his door, he stands for a minute looking back at her. Then he goes into his room.* DUSSEL *rises as he comes in, and quickly passes him, going out. He starts across for his room.* ANNE *sees him coming and pulls her door shut.* DUSSEL *turns back toward* PETER'*s room.* PETER *pulls his door shut.* DUSSEL *stands there, bewildered, forlorn.*

The scene slowly dims out. The curtain falls on the scene. ANNE'*s voice comes over in the darkness . . . faintly at first and then with growing strength.*]

Anne's Voice. We've had bad news. The people from whom Miep got our ration books have been arrested. So we have had to cut down on our food. Our stomachs are so empty that they rumble and make strange noises, all in different keys. Mr. Van Daan's is deep and low, like a bass fiddle. Mine is high, whistling like a flute. As we all sit around waiting for supper, it's like an orchestra tuning up. It only needs Toscanini[3] to raise his baton and we'd be off in the "Ride of the Valkyries."[4] Monday, the sixth of March, nineteen forty-four. Mr. Kraler is in the hospital. It seems he has ulcers. Pim says we are his ulcers. Miep has to run the business and us too. The Americans have landed on the southern tip of Italy. Father looks for a quick finish to the war. Mr. Dussel is waiting every day for the warehouse man to demand more money. Have I been skipping too much from one subject to another? I can't help it. I feel that spring is coming. I feel it in my whole body and soul. I feel utterly confused. I am longing . . . so longing . . . for everything . . . for friends . . . for someone to talk to . . . someone who understands . . . someone young, who feels as I do . . .

[*As these last lines are being said, the curtain rises on the scene. The lights dim on.* ANNE'*s voice fades out.*]

■ SCENE 2

It is evening, after supper. From outside we hear the sound of children playing. The "grown-ups," with the exception of MR. VAN DAAN, *are all in the main room.* MRS.

---

3. **Toscanini** (täs′kə·nē′nē): Arturo Toscanini (1867–1957), a famous orchestra conductor.
4. **"Ride of the Valkyries"** (val·kir′ēz): lively piece of music from an opera by the German composer Richard Wagner (1813–1883).

Vocabulary
forlorn (fôr·lôrn′) *adj.:* abandoned and lonely.

FRANK *is doing some mending.* MRS. VAN DAAN *is reading a fashion magazine.* MR. FRANK *is going over business accounts.* DUSSEL, *in his dentist's jacket, is pacing up and down, impatient to get into his bedroom.* MR. VAN DAAN *is upstairs working on a piece of embroidery in an embroidery frame.*

In his room PETER *is sitting before the mirror, smoothing his hair. As the scene goes on, he puts on his tie, brushes his coat and puts it on, preparing himself meticulously for a visit from* ANNE. *On his wall are now hung some of* ANNE's *motion picture stars.*

In her room ANNE *too is getting dressed. She stands before the mirror in her slip, trying various ways of dressing her hair.* MARGOT *is seated on the sofa, hemming a skirt for* ANNE *to wear.*

In the main room DUSSEL *can stand it no longer. He comes over, rapping sharply on the door of his and* ANNE's *bedroom.*

Anne (*calling to him*). No, no, Mr. Dussel! I am not dressed yet. (DUSSEL *walks away, furious, sitting down and burying his head in his hands.* ANNE *turns to* MARGOT.) How is that? How does that look?
Margot (*glancing at her briefly*). Fine.
Anne. You didn't even look.
Margot. Of course I did. It's fine.
Anne. Margot, tell me, am I terribly ugly?
Margot. Oh, stop fishing.
Anne. No. No. Tell me.
Margot. Of course you're not. You've got nice eyes . . . and a lot of animation, and . . .
Anne. A little vague, aren't you?

[*She reaches over and takes a brassiere out of* MARGOT's *sewing basket. She holds it up to herself, studying the effect in the mirror. Outside,* MRS. FRANK, *feeling sorry for* DUSSEL, *comes over, knocking at the girls' door.*]

Mrs. Frank (*outside*). May I come in?
Margot. Come in, Mother.
Mrs. Frank (*shutting the door behind her*). Mr. Dussel's impatient to get in here.
Anne (*still with the brassiere*). Heavens, he takes the room for himself the entire day.
Mrs. Frank (*gently*). Anne, dear, you're not going in again tonight to see Peter?
Anne (*dignified*). That is my intention.
Mrs. Frank. But you've already spent a great deal of time in there today.
Anne. I was in there exactly twice. Once to get the dictionary, and then three quarters of an hour before supper.
Mrs. Frank. Aren't you afraid you're disturbing him?
Anne. Mother, I have some intuition.
Mrs. Frank. Then may I ask you this much, Anne. Please don't shut the door when you go in.
Anne. You sound like Mrs. Van Daan! (*She throws the brassiere back in* MARGOT's *sewing basket and picks up her blouse, putting it on.*)
Mrs. Frank. No. No. I don't mean to suggest anything wrong. I only wish that you wouldn't expose yourself to criticism . . . that you wouldn't give Mrs. Van Daan the opportunity to be unpleasant.
Anne. Mrs. Van Daan doesn't need an opportunity to be unpleasant!
Mrs. Frank. Everyone's on edge, worried about Mr. Kraler. This is one more thing . . .
Anne. I'm sorry, Mother. I'm going to Peter's room. I'm not going to let Petronella Van Daan spoil our friendship.

Vocabulary
animation (an'i·mā'shen) *n.:* liveliness.

[MRS. FRANK *hesitates for a second, then goes out, closing the door after her. She gets a pack of playing cards and sits at the center table, playing solitaire. In* ANNE's *room* MARGOT *hands the finished skirt to* ANNE. *As* ANNE *is putting it on,* MARGOT *takes off her high-heeled shoes and stuffs paper in the toes so that* ANNE *can wear them.*]

Margot (*to* ANNE). Why don't you two talk in the main room? It'd save a lot of trouble. It's hard on Mother, having to listen to those remarks from Mrs. Van Daan and not say a word.
Anne. Why doesn't she say a word? I think it's ridiculous to take it and take it.
Margot. You don't understand Mother at all, do you? She can't talk back. She's not like you. It's just not in her nature to fight back.
Anne. Anyway . . . the only one I worry about is you. I feel awfully guilty about you. (*She sits on the stool near* MARGOT, *putting on* MARGOT's *high-heeled shoes.*)
Margot. What about?
Anne. I mean, every time I go into Peter's room, I have a feeling I may be hurting you. (MARGOT *shakes her head.*) I know if it were me, I'd be wild. I'd be desperately jealous, if it were me.
Margot. Well, I'm not.
Anne. You don't feel badly? Really? Truly? You're not jealous?
Margot. Of course I'm jealous . . . jealous that you've got something to get up in the morning for . . . But jealous of you and Peter? No.

[ANNE *goes back to the mirror.*]

Anne. Maybe there's nothing to be jealous of. Maybe he doesn't really like me. Maybe I'm just taking the place of his cat . . . (*She picks up a pair of short white gloves, putting them on.*) Wouldn't you like to come in with us?
Margot. I have a book.

[*The sound of the children playing outside fades out. In the main room* DUSSEL *can stand it no longer. He jumps up, going to the bedroom door and knocking sharply.*]

Dussel. Will you please let me in my room!
Anne. Just a minute, dear, dear Mr. Dussel. (*She picks up her mother's pink stole and adjusts it elegantly over her shoulders, then gives a last look in the mirror.*) Well, here I go . . . to run the gantlet.[5] (*She starts out, followed by* MARGOT.)
Dussel (*as she appears—sarcastic*). Thank you so much.

[DUSSEL *goes into his room.* ANNE *goes toward* PETER's *room, passing* MRS. VAN DAAN *and her parents at the center table.*]

Mrs. Van Daan. My God, look at her! (ANNE *pays no attention. She knocks at* PETER's *door.*) I don't know what good it is to have a son. I never see him. He wouldn't care if I killed myself. (PETER *opens the door and stands aside for* ANNE *to come in.*) Just a minute, Anne. (*She goes to them at the door.*) I'd like to say a few words to my son. Do you mind? (PETER *and* ANNE *stand waiting.*) Peter, I don't want you staying up till all hours tonight. You've got to have your sleep. You're a growing boy. You hear?
Mrs. Frank. Anne won't stay late. She's going to bed promptly at nine. Aren't you, Anne?
Anne. Yes, Mother . . . (*To* MRS. VAN DAAN) May we go now?

---

5. **run the gantlet** (gônt′lit): proceed while under attack from both sides.

Mrs. Van Daan. Are you asking me? I didn't know I had anything to say about it.

Mrs. Frank. Listen for the chimes, Anne dear.

[*The two young people go off into* PETER's *room, shutting the door after them.*]

Mrs. Van Daan (*to* MRS. FRANK). In my day it was the boys who called on the girls. Not the girls on the boys.

Mrs. Frank. You know how young people like to feel that they have secrets. Peter's room is the only place where they can talk.

Mrs. Van Daan. Talk! That's not what they called it when I was young.

[MRS. VAN DAAN *goes off to the bathroom.* MARGOT *settles down to read her book.* MR. FRANK *puts his papers away and brings a chess game to the center table. He and* MRS. FRANK *start to play. In* PETER's *room,* ANNE *speaks to* PETER, *indignant, humiliated.*]

Anne. Aren't they awful? Aren't they impossible? Treating us as if we were still in the nursery.

[*She sits on the cot.* PETER *gets a bottle of pop and two glasses.*]

Peter. Don't let it bother you. It doesn't bother me.

Anne. I suppose you can't really blame them . . . they think back to what *they* were like at our age. They don't realize how much more advanced we are. . . . When you think what wonderful discussions we've

Mrs. Frank.

had! . . . Oh, I forgot. I was going to bring you some more pictures.

Peter. Oh, these are fine, thanks.

Anne. Don't you want some more? Miep just brought me some new ones.

Peter. Maybe later. (*He gives her a glass of pop and, taking some for himself, sits down facing her.*)

Anne (*looking up at one of the photographs*). I remember when I got that . . . I won it. I bet Jopie that I could eat five ice-cream cones. We'd all been playing ping-pong . . . We used to have heavenly times . . . we'd finish up with ice cream at the Delphi or the Oasis, where Jews were allowed . . . there'd always be a lot of boys . . . we'd laugh and joke . . . I'd like to go back to it for a few days or a week. But after that I know I'd be bored to death. I think more seriously about life now. I want to be a journalist . . . or something. I love to write. What do you want to do?

Peter. I thought I might go off someplace . . . work on a farm or something . . . some job that doesn't take much brains.

Anne. You shouldn't talk that way. You've got the most awful inferiority complex.

Peter. I know I'm not smart.

Anne. That isn't true. You're much better than I am in dozens of things . . . arithmetic and algebra and . . . well, you're a million times better than I am in algebra. (*With sudden directness*) You like Margot, don't you? Right from the start you liked her, liked her much better than me.

Peter (*uncomfortably*). Oh, I don't know.

[*In the main room* MRS. VAN DAAN *comes from the bathroom and goes over to the sink, polishing a coffeepot.*]

Anne. It's all right. Everyone feels that way. Margot's so good. She's sweet and bright and beautiful and I'm not.
Peter. I wouldn't say that.
Anne. Oh, no, I'm not. I know that. I know quite well that I'm not a beauty. I never have been and never shall be.
Peter. I don't agree at all. I think you're pretty.
Anne. That's not true!
Peter. And another thing. You've changed . . . from at first, I mean.
Anne. I have?
Peter. I used to think you were awful noisy.
Anne. And what do you think now, Peter? How have I changed?
Peter. Well . . . er . . . you're . . . quieter.

[*In his room* DUSSEL *takes his pajamas and toilet articles and goes into the bathroom to change.*]

Anne. I'm glad you don't just hate me.
Peter. I never said that.
Anne. I bet when you get out of here, you'll never think of me again.
Peter. That's crazy.
Anne. When you get back with all of your friends, you're going to say . . . now what did I ever see in that Mrs. Quack Quack.
Peter. I haven't got any friends.
Anne. Oh, Peter, of course you have. Everyone has friends.
Peter. Not me. I don't want any. I get along all right without them.
Anne. Does that mean you can get along without me? I think of myself as your friend.

Peter. No. If they were all like you, it'd be different.

[*He takes the glasses and the bottle and puts them away. There is a second's silence and then* ANNE *speaks, hesitantly, shyly.*]

Anne. Peter, did you ever kiss a girl?
Peter. Yes. Once.
Anne (*to cover her feelings*). That picture's crooked. (PETER *goes over, straightening the photograph.*) Was she pretty?
Peter. Huh?
Anne. The girl that you kissed.
Peter. I don't know. I was blindfolded. (*He comes back and sits down again.*) It was at a party. One of those kissing games.
Anne (*relieved*). Oh. I don't suppose that really counts, does it?
Peter. It didn't with me.
Anne. I've been kissed twice. Once a man I'd never seen before kissed me on the cheek when he picked me up off the ice and I was crying. And the other was Mr. Koophuis, a friend of Father's, who kissed my hand. You wouldn't say those counted, would you?
Peter. I wouldn't say so.
Anne. I know almost for certain that Margot would never kiss anyone unless she was engaged to them. And I'm sure too that Mother never touched a man before Pim. But I don't know . . . things are so different now . . . What do you think? Do you think a girl shouldn't kiss anyone except if she's engaged or something? It's so hard to try to think what to do, when here we are with the whole world falling around our ears and you think . . . well . . . you don't know what's going to happen tomorrow and . . . What do you think?
Peter. I suppose it'd depend on the girl. Some girls, anything they do's wrong. But

others . . . well . . . it wouldn't necessarily be wrong with them. (*The carillon starts to strike nine o'clock.*) I've always thought that when two people . . .

Anne. Nine o'clock. I have to go.

Peter. That's right.

Anne (*without moving*). Good night.

[*There is a second's pause; then* PETER *gets up and moves toward the door.*]

Peter. You won't let them stop you coming?

Anne. No. (*She rises and starts for the door.*) Sometime I might bring my diary. There are so many things in it that I want to talk over with you. There's a lot about you.

Peter. What kind of thing?

Anne. I wouldn't want you to see some of it. I thought you were a nothing, just the way you thought about me.

Peter. Did you change your mind, the way I changed my mind about you?

Anne. Well . . . You'll see . . .

[*For a second* ANNE *stands looking up at* PETER, *longing for him to kiss her. As he* makes no move, she turns away. Then suddenly PETER *grabs her awkwardly in his arms, kissing her on the cheek.* ANNE *walks out dazed. She stands for a minute, her back to the people in the main room. As she regains her poise, she goes to her mother and father and* MARGOT, *silently kissing them. They murmur their good nights to her. As she is about to open her bedroom door, she catches sight of* MRS. VAN DAAN. *She goes quickly to her, taking her face in her hands and kissing her, first on one cheek and then on the other. Then she hurries off into her room.* MRS. VAN DAAN *looks after her and then looks over at* PETER's *room. Her suspicions are confirmed.*]

Mrs. Van Daan (*she knows*). Ah hah!

[*The lights dim out. The curtain falls on the scene. In the darkness* ANNE's *voice comes, faintly at first and then with growing strength.*]

Anne's Voice. By this time we all know each other so well that if anyone starts to tell a story, the rest can finish it for him. We're having to cut down still further on our

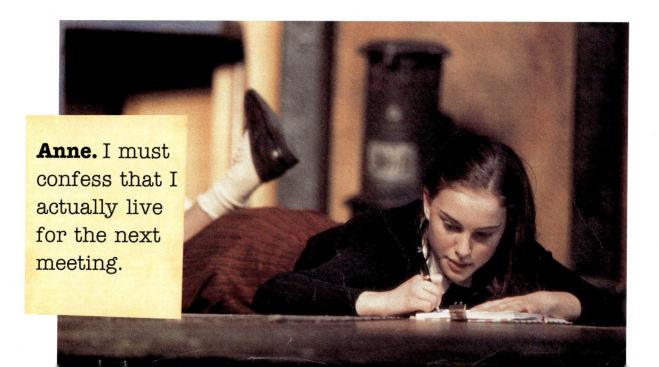

Anne. I must confess that I actually live for the next meeting.

meals. What makes it worse, the rats have been at work again. They've carried off some of our precious food. Even Mr. Dussel wishes now that Mouschi was here. Thursday, the twentieth of April, nineteen forty-four. Invasion fever is mounting every day. Miep tells us that people outside talk of nothing else. For myself, life has become much more pleasant. I often go to Peter's room after supper. Oh, don't think I'm in love, because I'm not. But it does make life more bearable to have someone with whom you can exchange views. No more tonight. P.S. . . . I must be honest. I must confess that I actually live for the next meeting. Is there anything lovelier than to sit under the skylight and feel the sun on your cheeks and have a darling boy in your arms? I admit now that I'm glad the Van Daans had a son and not a daughter. I've outgrown another dress. That's the third. I'm having to wear Margot's clothes after all. I'm working hard on my French and am now reading *La Belle Nivernaise*.[6]

[*As she is saying the last lines, the curtain rises on the scene. The lights dim on as* ANNE'*s voice fades out.*]

■ SCENE 3

It is night, a few weeks later. Everyone is in bed. There is complete quiet. In the VAN DAANS' *room a match flares up for a moment and then is quickly put out.* MR. VAN DAAN, *in bare feet, dressed in underwear and trousers, is dimly seen coming stealthily down*

the stairs and into the main room, where MR. *and* MRS. FRANK *and* MARGOT *are sleeping. He goes to the food safe and again lights a match. Then he cautiously opens the safe, taking out a half loaf of bread. As he closes the safe, it creaks. He stands rigid.* MRS. FRANK *sits up in bed. She sees him.*

Mrs. Frank (*screaming*). Otto! Otto! Komme schnell![7]

[*The rest of the people wake, hurriedly getting up.*]

Mr. Frank. Was ist los? Was ist passiert?[8]

[DUSSEL, *followed by* ANNE, *comes from his room.*]

Mrs. Frank (*as she rushes over to* MR. VAN DAAN). Er stiehlt das Essen![9]
Dussel (*grabbing* MR. VAN DAAN). You! You! Give me that.
Mrs. Van Daan (*coming down the stairs*). Putti . . . Putti . . . what is it?
Dussel (*his hands on* MR. VAN DAAN'*s neck*). You dirty thief . . . stealing food . . . you good-for-nothing . . .
Mr. Frank. Mr. Dussel! For God's sake! Help me, Peter!

[PETER *comes over, trying, with* MR. FRANK, *to separate the two struggling men.*]

Peter. Let him go! Let go!

[DUSSEL *drops* MR. VAN DAAN, *pushing him away. He shows them the end of a loaf of bread that he has taken from* MR. VAN DAAN.]

Dussel. You greedy, selfish . . . !

---

6. *La Belle Nivernaise* (nē·ver'nez'): children's story by the French writer Alphonse Daudet (1840–1897).

7. **Komme schnell:** German for "Come quickly."
8. **Was . . . passiert:** "What's going on? What happened?"
9. **Er . . . Essen:** "He is stealing the food."

[MARGOT *turns on the lights.*]

Mrs. Van Daan. Putti . . . what is it?

[*All of* MRS. FRANK'*s gentleness, her self-control, is gone. She is outraged, in a frenzy of indignation.*]

Mrs. Frank. The bread! He was stealing the bread!
Dussel. It was you, and all the time we thought it was the rats!
Mr. Frank. Mr. Van Daan, how could you!
Mr. Van Daan. I'm hungry.
Mrs. Frank. We're all of us hungry! I see the children getting thinner and thinner. Your own son Peter . . . I've heard him moan in his sleep, he's so hungry. And you come in the night and steal food that should go to them . . . to the children!
Mrs. Van Daan (*going to* MR. VAN DAAN *protectively*). He needs more food than the rest of us. He's used to more. He's a big man.

[MR. VAN DAAN *breaks away, going over and sitting on the couch.*]

Mrs. Frank (*turning on* MRS. VAN DAAN). And you . . . you're worse than he is! You're a mother, and yet you sacrifice your child to this man . . . this . . . this . . .
Mr. Frank. Edith! Edith!

[MARGOT *picks up the pink woolen stole, putting it over her mother's shoulders.*]

Mrs. Frank (*paying no attention, going on to* MRS. VAN DAAN). Don't think I haven't seen you! Always saving the choicest bits for him! I've watched you day after day and I've held my tongue. But not any longer! Not after this! Now I want him to go! I want him to get out of here!

Mr. Frank. Edith!
Mr. Van Daan. Get out of here? ⎫
Mrs. Van Daan. What do you mean? ⎭ *Together*
Mrs. Frank. Just that! Take your things and get out!
Mr. Frank (*to* MRS. FRANK). You're speaking in anger. You cannot mean what you are saying.
Mrs. Frank. I mean exactly that!

[MRS. VAN DAAN *takes a cover from the* FRANKS' *bed, pulling it about her.*]

Mr. Frank. For two long years we have lived here, side by side. We have respected each other's rights . . . we have managed to live in peace. Are we now going to throw it all away? I know this will never happen again, will it, Mr. Van Daan?
Mr. Van Daan. No. No.
Mrs. Frank. He steals once! He'll steal again!

[MR. VAN DAAN, *holding his stomach, starts for the bathroom.* ANNE *puts her arms around him, helping him up the step.*]

Mr. Frank. Edith, please. Let us be calm. We'll all go to our rooms . . . and afterwards we'll sit down quietly and talk this out . . . we'll find some way . . .
Mrs. Frank. No! No! No more talk! I want them to leave!
Mrs. Van Daan. You'd put us out, on the streets?
Mrs. Frank. There are other hiding places.
Mrs. Van Daan. A cellar . . . a closet. I know. And we have no money left even to pay for that.
Mrs. Frank. I'll give you money. Out of my own pocket I'll give it gladly. (*She gets her*

purse from a shelf and comes back with it.)

Mrs. Van Daan. Mr. Frank, you told Putti you'd never forget what he'd done for you when you came to Amsterdam. You said you could never repay him, that you . . .

Mrs. Frank (*counting out money*). If my husband had any obligation to you, he's paid it, over and over.

Mr. Frank. Edith, I've never seen you like this before. I don't know you.

Mrs. Frank. I should have spoken out long ago.

Dussel. You can't be nice to some people.

Mrs. Van Daan (*turning on* DUSSEL). There would have been plenty for all of us, if *you* hadn't come in here!

Mr. Frank. We don't need the Nazis to destroy us. We're destroying ourselves.

[*He sits down, with his head in his hands.* MRS. FRANK *goes to* MRS. VAN DAAN.]

Mrs. Frank (*giving* MRS. VAN DAAN *some money*). Give this to Miep. She'll find you a place.

Anne. Mother, you're not putting *Peter* out. Peter hasn't done anything.

Mrs. Frank. He'll stay, of course. When I say I must protect the children, I mean Peter too.

[PETER *rises from the steps where he has been sitting.*]

Peter. I'd have to go if Father goes.

[MR. VAN DAAN *comes from the bathroom.* MRS. VAN DAAN *hurries to him and takes him to the couch. Then she gets water from the sink to bathe his face.*]

Mrs. Frank (*while this is going on*). He's no father to you . . . that man! He doesn't know what it is to be a father!

Peter (*starting for his room*). I wouldn't feel

right. I couldn't stay.

Mrs. Frank. Very well, then. I'm sorry.

Anne (*rushing over to* PETER). No, Peter! No! (PETER *goes into his room, closing the door after him.* ANNE *turns back to her mother, crying.*) I don't care about the food. They can have mine! I don't want it! Only don't send them away. It'll be daylight soon. They'll be caught . . .

Margot (*putting her arms comfortingly around* ANNE). Please, Mother!

Mrs. Frank. They're not going now. They'll stay here until Miep finds them a place. (*To* MRS. VAN DAAN) But one thing I insist on! He must never come down here again! He must never come to this room where the food is stored! We'll divide what we have . . . an equal share for each! (DUSSEL *hurries over to get a sack of potatoes from the food safe.* MRS. FRANK *goes on, to* MRS. VAN DAAN) You can cook it here and take it up to him.

[DUSSEL *brings the sack of potatoes back to the center table.*]

Margot. Oh, no. No. We haven't sunk so far that we're going to fight over a handful of rotten potatoes.

Dussel (*dividing the potatoes into piles*). Mrs. Frank, Mr. Frank, Margot, Anne, Peter, Mrs. Van Daan, Mr. Van Daan, myself . . . Mrs. Frank . . .

[*The buzzer sounds in* MIEP's *signal.*]

Mr. Frank. It's Miep! (*He hurries over, getting his overcoat and putting it on.*)

Margot. At this hour?

Mrs. Frank. It is trouble.

Mr. Frank (*as he starts down to unbolt the door*). I beg you, don't let her see a thing like this!

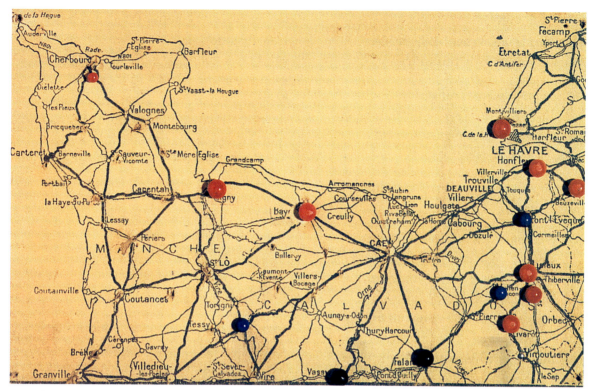

Map kept by Mr. Frank after the Allied invasion of Normandy. Colored pins show the progress of the Allied forces.

Dussel (*counting without stopping*). . . . Anne, Peter, Mrs. Van Daan, Mr. Van Daan, myself . . .

Margot (*to* DUSSEL). Stop it! Stop it!

Dussel. . . . Mr. Frank, Margot, Anne, Peter, Mrs. Van Daan, Mr. Van Daan, myself, Mrs. Frank . . .

Mrs. Van Daan. You're keeping the big ones for yourself! All the big ones . . . Look at the size of that! . . . And that! . . .

[DUSSEL *continues with his dividing.* PETER, *with his shirt and trousers on, comes from his room.*]

Margot. Stop it! Stop it!

[*We hear* MIEP's *excited voice speaking to* MR. FRANK *below.*]

Miep. Mr. Frank . . . the most wonderful news! . . . The invasion[10] has begun!

Mr. Frank. Go on, tell them! Tell them!

[MIEP *comes running up the steps, ahead of* MR. FRANK. *She has a man's raincoat on over her nightclothes and a bunch of orange-colored flowers in her hand.*]

Miep. Did you hear that, everybody? Did you hear what I said? The invasion has begun! The invasion!

[*They all stare at* MIEP, *unable to grasp what she is telling them.* PETER *is the first to recover his wits.*]

---

10. **the invasion:** On June 6, 1944, Allied forces landed in Normandy, a region of northern France, to launch a military campaign against the Germans.

Peter. Where?

Mrs. Van Daan. When? When, Miep?

Miep. It began early this morning . . .

[*As she talks on, the realization of what she has said begins to dawn on them. Everyone goes crazy. A wild demonstration takes place.* MRS. FRANK *hugs* MR. VAN DAAN.]

Mrs. Frank. Oh, Mr. Van Daan, did you hear that?

[DUSSEL *embraces* MRS. VAN DAAN. PETER *grabs a frying pan and parades around the room, beating on it, singing the Dutch national anthem.* ANNE *and* MARGOT *follow him, singing, weaving in and out among the excited grown-ups.* MARGOT *breaks away to take the flowers from* MIEP *and distribute them to everyone. While this pandemonium is going on,* MRS. FRANK *tries to make herself heard above the excitement.*]

Mrs. Frank (*to* MIEP). How do you know?

Miep. The radio . . . The BBC![11] They said they landed on the coast of Normandy!

Peter. The British?

Miep. British, Americans, French, Dutch, Poles, Norwegians . . . all of them! More than four thousand ships! Churchill[12] spoke, and General Eisenhower![13] D-day, they call it!

Mr. Frank. Thank God, it's come!

Mrs. Van Daan. At last!

Miep (*starting out*). I'm going to tell Mr.

---

11. **BBC:** British Broadcasting Corporation. People listened to the BBC, illegally, for news of the war that was more accurate than what German-controlled broadcasters offered.

12. **Churchill:** Sir Winston Churchill (1874–1965), British prime minister during World War II.

13. **General Eisenhower:** Dwight D. Eisenhower (1890–1969), commander of the Allied forces in western Europe. He later became president of the United States (1953–1961).

Kraler. This'll be better than any blood transfusion.

Mr. Frank (*stopping her*). What part of Normandy did they land, did they say?

Miep. Normandy . . . that's all I know now . . . I'll be up the minute I hear some more! (*She goes hurriedly out.*)

Mr. Frank (*to* MRS. FRANK). What did I tell you? What did I tell you?

[MRS. FRANK *indicates that he has forgotten to bolt the door after* MIEP. *He hurries down the steps.* MR. VAN DAAN, *sitting on the couch, suddenly breaks into a convulsive sob. Everybody looks at him, bewildered.*]

Mrs. Van Daan (*hurrying to him*). Putti! Putti! What is it? What happened?

Mr. Van Daan. Please. I'm so ashamed.

[MR. FRANK *comes back up the steps.*]

Dussel. Oh, for God's sake!

Mrs. Van Daan. Don't, Putti.

Margot. It doesn't matter now!

Mr. Frank (*going to* MR. VAN DAAN). Didn't you hear what Miep said? The invasion has come! We're going to be liberated! This is a time to celebrate! (*He embraces* MRS. FRANK *and then hurries to the cupboard and gets the cognac and a glass.*)

Mr. Van Daan. To steal bread from children!

Mrs. Frank. We've all done things that we're ashamed of.

Anne. Look at me, the way I've treated Mother . . . so mean and horrid to her.

Mrs. Frank. No, Anneke, no.

[ANNE *runs to her mother, putting her arms around her.*]

Anne. Oh, Mother, I was. I was awful.

Mr. Van Daan. Not like me. No one is as

bad as me!

Dussel (*to* MR. VAN DAAN). Stop it now! Let's be happy!

Mr. Frank (*giving* MR. VAN DAAN *a glass of cognac*). Here! Here! Schnapps![14] L'chaim![15]

[MR. VAN DAAN *takes the cognac. They all watch him. He gives them a feeble smile.* ANNE *puts up her fingers in a V-for-victory sign. As* MR. VAN DAAN *gives an answering V sign, they are startled to hear a loud sob from behind them. It is* MRS. FRANK, *stricken with remorse. She is sitting on the other side of the room.*]

Mrs. Frank (*through her sobs*). When I think of the terrible things I said . . .

[MR. FRANK, ANNE, *and* MARGOT *hurry to her, trying to comfort her.* MR. VAN DAAN *brings her his glass of cognac.*]

Mr. Van Daan. No! No! You were right!

Mrs. Frank. That I should speak that way to you! . . . Our friends! . . . Our guests! (*She starts to cry again.*)

Dussel. Stop it, you're spoiling the whole invasion!

[*As they are comforting her, the lights dim out. The curtain falls.*]

Anne's Voice (*faintly at first and then with growing strength*). We're all in much better spirits these days. There's still excellent news of the invasion. The best part about it is that I have a feeling that friends are coming. Who knows? Maybe I'll be back in school by fall. Ha, ha! The joke is on us! The warehouse man doesn't know a thing and we are paying him all that money! . . . Wednesday, the second of July, nineteen forty-four. The invasion seems temporarily to be bogged down. Mr. Kraler has to have an operation, which looks bad. The Gestapo have found the radio that was stolen. Mr. Dussel says they'll trace it back and back to the thief, and then, it's just a matter of time till they get to us. Everyone is low. Even poor Pim can't raise their spirits. I have often been downcast myself . . . but never in despair. I can shake off everything if I write. But . . . and that is the great question . . . will I ever be able to write well? I want to so much. I want to go on living even after my death. Another birthday has gone by, so now I am fifteen. Already I know what I want. I have a goal, an opinion.

[*As this is being said, the curtain rises on the scene, the lights dim on, and* ANNE's *voice fades out.*]

■ SCENE 4

It is an afternoon a few weeks later. . . . Everyone but MARGOT *is in the main room. There is a sense of great tension.*

Both MRS. FRANK *and* MR. VAN DAAN *are nervously pacing back and forth.* DUSSEL *is standing at the window, looking down fixedly at the street below.* PETER *is at the center table, trying to do his lessons.* ANNE *sits opposite him, writing in her diary.* MRS. VAN DAAN *is seated on the couch, her eyes on* MR. FRANK *as he sits reading.*

---

14. **schnapps** (shnäps) *n.:* strong liquor.
15. **l'chaim** (lə khä′yim) *interj.:* Hebrew toast meaning "to life."

Vocabulary
remorse (ri·môrs′) *n.:* deep feeling of guilt; self-reproach.

The sound of a telephone ringing comes from the office below. They all are rigid, listening tensely. DUSSEL *rushes down to* MR. FRANK.

Dussel. There it goes again, the telephone! Mr. Frank, do you hear?

Mr. Frank (*quietly*). Yes. I hear.

Dussel (*pleading, insistent*). But this is the third time, Mr. Frank! The third time in quick succession! It's a signal! I tell you it's Miep, trying to get us! For some reason she can't come to us and she's trying to warn us of something!

Mr. Frank. Please. Please.

Mr. Van Daan (*to* DUSSEL). You're wasting your breath.

Dussel. Something has happened, Mr. Frank. For three days now Miep hasn't been to see us! And today not a man has come to work. There hasn't been a sound in the building!

Mrs. Frank. Perhaps it's Sunday. We may have lost track of the days.

Mr. Van Daan (*to* ANNE). You with the diary there. What day is it?

Dussel (*going to* MRS. FRANK). I don't lose track of the days! I know exactly what day it is! It's Friday, the fourth of August. Friday, and not a man at work. (*He rushes back to* MR. FRANK, *pleading with him, almost in tears.*) I tell you Mr. Kraler's dead. That's the only explanation. He's dead and they've closed down the building, and Miep's trying to tell us!

Mr. Frank. She'd never telephone us.

Dussel (*frantic*). Mr. Frank, answer that! I beg you, answer it!

Mr. Frank. No.

Mr. Van Daan. Just pick it up and listen. You don't have to speak. Just listen and see if it's Miep.

Dussel (*speaking at the same time*). For God's sake . . . I ask you.

Mr. Frank. No. I've told you, no. I'll do nothing that might let anyone know we're in the building.

Peter. Mr. Frank's right.

Mr. Van Daan. There's no need to tell us what side you're on.

Mr. Frank. If we wait patiently, quietly, I believe that help will come.

[*There is silence for a minute as they all listen to the telephone ringing.*]

Dussel. I'm going down. (*He rushes down the steps.* MR. FRANK *tries ineffectually to hold him.* DUSSEL *runs to the lower door, unbolting it. The telephone stops ringing.* DUSSEL *bolts the door and comes slowly back up the steps.*) Too late.

[MR. FRANK *goes to* MARGOT *in* ANNE's *bedroom.*]

Mr. Van Daan. So we just wait here until we die.

Mrs. Van Daan (*hysterically*). I can't stand it! I'll kill myself! I'll kill myself!

Mr. Van Daan. For God's sake, stop it!

[*In the distance, a German military band is heard playing a Viennese waltz.*]

Mrs. Van Daan. I think you'd be glad if I did! I think you want me to die!

Mr. Van Daan. Whose fault is it we're here? (MRS. VAN DAAN *starts for her room. He follows, talking at her.*) We could've been safe somewhere . . . in America or Switzerland. But no! No! You wouldn't leave when I wanted to. You couldn't leave your things. You couldn't leave your precious furniture.

Mrs. Van Daan. Don't touch me!

[*She hurries up the stairs, followed by* MR. VAN DAAN. PETER, *unable to bear it, goes to his room.* ANNE *looks after him, deeply concerned.* DUSSEL *returns to his post at the window.* MR. FRANK *comes back into the main room and takes a book, trying to read.* MRS. FRANK *sits near the sink, starting to peel some potatoes.* ANNE *quietly goes to* PETER's *room, closing the door after her.* PETER *is lying face down on the cot.* ANNE *leans over him, holding him in her arms, trying to bring him out of his despair.*]

Anne. Look, Peter, the sky. (*She looks up through the skylight.*) What a lovely, lovely day! Aren't the clouds beautiful? You know what I do when it seems as if I couldn't stand being cooped up for one more minute? I *think* myself out. I think myself on a walk in the park where I used to go with Pim. Where the jonquils and the crocuses and the violets grow down the slopes. You know the most wonderful part about *thinking* yourself out? You can have it any way you like. You can have roses and violets and chrysanthemums all blooming at the same time. . . . It's funny . . . I used to take it all for granted . . . and now I've gone crazy about everything to do with nature. Haven't you?

Peter. I've just gone crazy. I think if something doesn't happen soon . . . if we don't get out of here . . . I can't stand much more of it!

Anne (*softly*). I wish you had a religion, Peter.

Peter. No, thanks! Not me!

Anne. Oh, I don't mean you have to be Orthodox[16] . . . or believe in Heaven and Hell and Purgatory and things . . . I just

---

16. **Orthodox:** Orthodox Jews strictly observe Jewish law.

mean some religion . . . it doesn't matter what. Just to believe in something! When I think of all that's out there . . . the trees . . . and flowers . . . and sea gulls . . . When I think of the dearness of you, Peter . . . and the goodness of the people we know . . . Mr. Kraler, Miep, Dirk, the vegetable man, all risking their lives for us every day . . . When I think of these good things, I'm not afraid anymore . . . I find myself, and God, and I . . .

[PETER *interrupts, getting up and walking away.*]

Peter. That's fine! But when I begin to think, I get mad! Look at us, hiding out for two years. Not able to move! Caught here like . . . waiting for them to come and get us . . . and all for what?

Anne. We're not the only people that've had to suffer. There've always been people that've had to . . . sometimes one race . . . sometimes another . . . and yet . . .

Peter. That doesn't make me feel any better!

Anne (*going to him*). I know it's terrible, trying to have any faith . . . when people are doing such horrible . . . But you know what I sometimes think? I think the world may be going through a phase, the way I was with Mother. It'll pass, maybe not for hundreds of years, but someday . . . I still believe, in spite of everything, that people are really good at heart.

Peter. I want to see something now . . . not a thousand years from now! (*He goes over, sitting down again on the cot.*)

Anne. But, Peter, if you'd only look at it as part of a great pattern . . . that we're just a little minute in the life . . . (*She breaks off.*) Listen to us, going at each other like a couple

Anne. And so it seems our stay here is over.

of stupid grown-ups! Look at the sky now. Isn't it lovely? (*She holds out her hand to him.* PETER *takes it and rises, standing with her at the window looking out, his arms around her.*) Someday, when we're outside again, I'm going to . . .

[*She breaks off as she hears the sound of a car, its brakes squealing as it comes to a sudden stop. The people in the other rooms also be-* come aware of the sound. They listen tensely. Another car roars up to a screeching stop. ANNE and PETER come from PETER's room. MR. and MRS. VAN DAAN creep down the stairs. DUSSEL comes out from his room. Everyone is listening, hardly breathing. A doorbell clangs again and again in the building *below.* MR. FRANK *starts quietly down the steps to the door.* DUSSEL *and* PETER *follow him. The others stand rigid, waiting, terrified.*

In a few seconds DUSSEL *comes stumbling back up the steps. He shakes off* PETER's *help and goes to his room.* MR. FRANK *bolts the door below and comes slowly back up the steps. Their eyes are all on him as he stands there for a minute. They realize that what they feared has happened.* MRS. VAN DAAN *starts to whimper.* MR. VAN DAAN *puts her gently in a chair and then hurries off up the stairs to their room to collect their things.* PETER *goes to comfort his mother. There is a sound of violent pounding on a door below.*]

Mr. Frank (*quietly*). For the past two years we have lived in fear. Now we can live in hope.

[*The pounding below becomes more insistent. There are muffled sounds of voices, shouting commands.*]

Men's Voices. Aufmachen! Da drinnen! Aufmachen! Schnell! Schnell! Schnell![17] (*Etc., etc.*)

[*The street door below is forced open. We hear the heavy tread of footsteps coming up.* MR. FRANK *gets two school bags from the shelves and gives one to* ANNE *and the other to* MARGOT. *He goes to get a bag for* MRS. FRANK. *The sound of feet coming up grows louder.* PETER *comes to* ANNE, *kissing her goodbye; then he goes to his room to collect his things. The buzzer of their door starts to ring.* MR. FRANK *brings* MRS. FRANK *a bag. They stand together, waiting. We hear the thud of gun butts on the door, trying to break it down.*

---

17. **Aufmachen . . . Schnell:** German for "Open up! You in there! Open up! Quickly! Quickly! Quickly!"

ANNE *stands, holding her school satchel, looking over at her father and mother with a soft, reassuring smile. She is no longer a child, but a woman with courage to meet whatever lies ahead.*

The lights dim out. The curtain falls on the scene. We hear a mighty crash as the door is shattered. After a second ANNE's *voice is heard.*]

Anne's Voice. And so it seems our stay here is over. They are waiting for us now. They've allowed us five minutes to get our things. We can each take a bag and whatever it will hold of clothing. Nothing else. So, dear Diary, that means I must leave you behind. Goodbye for a while. P.S. Please, please, Miep, or Mr. Kraler, or anyone else. If you should find this diary, will you please keep it safe for me, because someday I hope . . .

[*Her voice stops abruptly. There is silence. After a second the curtain rises.*]

■ SCENE 5

It is again the afternoon in November 1945. The rooms are as we saw them in the first scene. MR. KRALER *has joined* MIEP *and* MR. FRANK. *There are coffee cups on the table. We see a great change in* MR. FRANK. *He is calm now. His bitterness is gone. He slowly turns a few pages of the diary. They are blank.*

Mr. Frank. No more. (*He closes the diary and puts it down on the couch beside him.*)
Miep. I'd gone to the country to find food. When I got back, the block was surrounded by police . . .
Mr. Kraler. We made it our business to learn how they knew. It was the thief . . . the thief who told them.

[MIEP *goes up to the gas burner, bringing back a pot of coffee.*]

Mr. Frank (*after a pause*). It seems strange to say this, that anyone could be happy in a concentration camp. But Anne was happy in the camp in Holland where they first took us. After two years of being shut up in these rooms, she could be out . . . out in the sunshine and the fresh air that she loved.

Miep (*offering the coffee to* MR. FRANK). A little more?

Mr. Frank (*holding out his cup to her*). The news of the war was good. The British and

Americans were sweeping through France. We felt sure that they would get to us in time. In September we were told that we were to be shipped to Poland. . . . The men to one camp. The women to another. I was sent to Auschwitz. They went to Belsen. In January we were freed, the few of us who were left. The war wasn't yet over, so it took us a long time to get home. We'd be sent here and there behind the lines where we'd be safe. Each time our train would stop . . . at a siding or a crossing . . . we'd all get out and go from group to group . . . Where were you? Were you at Belsen? At Buchenwald? At Mauthausen? Is it possible that you knew my wife? Did you ever see my husband? My son? My daughter? That's how I found out about my wife's death . . . of Margot, the Van Daans . . . Dussel. But Anne . . . I still hoped . . . Yesterday I went to Rotterdam. I'd heard of a woman there . . . She'd been in Belsen with Anne . . . I know now.

[*He picks up the diary again and turns the pages back to find a certain passage. As he finds it, we hear* ANNE's *voice.*]

Anne's Voice. In spite of everything, I still believe that people are really good at heart.

[MR. FRANK *slowly closes the diary.*]

Mr. Frank. She puts me to shame.

[*They are silent.*]

Curtain

Meet the Writers

Frances Goodrich and Albert Hackett

The Making of a Masterpiece

Frances Goodrich (1890–1984) and **Albert Hackett** (1900–1995) both started out as actors. They began writing plays and screenplays together and were married soon after. Working at desks facing in opposite directions in the same room, they would each write a version of a scene, then read and comment on the other's version before revising. In this way, Goodrich and Hackett created the scripts for many hit movies, including *Easter Parade, Father of the Bride*, and *It's a Wonderful Life*.

The Diary of Anne Frank, a work totally different from their other plays, is considered their masterpiece. Before they wrote the play, the playwrights spent ten days in Amsterdam visiting the Secret Annex, studying the neighborhood, and questioning Otto Frank (who came from Switzerland to help) on his memories and impressions. It took them two years and eight drafts to complete the play, which opened on Broadway in 1955 to great acclaim. The play won a Pulitzer Prize in 1956 and has since been performed countless times in countries around the world.

For Independent Reading

In addition to her diary, Anne wrote many short stories and autobiographical sketches during her time in hiding. You'll find a selection of these in *Anne Frank's Tales from the Secret Annex.*

Anne Frank Remembered is the story of Anne and the other occupants of the Secret Annex as told by their helper and protector, Miep Gies.

Act Two and the Play as a Whole

First Thoughts

1. Do you agree with Anne that "people are really good at heart"? Why or why not?

Thinking Critically

2. The **climax** of a play is its moment of greatest tension, the point at which the main conflict is about to be resolved. What is this play's climax? How did you feel at that moment?

3. In Act One, Scene 4, Mr. Frank tells Anne, "You must build your own character." Has Anne done this by the end of the play? Explain.

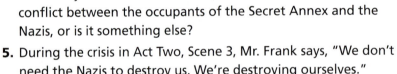

Reading Check

a. How does Anne and Peter's relationship change in Act Two, Scene 1? In Scene 2, how do Mrs. Frank and Mrs. Van Daan respond to this change?

b. What news does Miep bring in Act Two, Scene 3?

c. At the beginning of Act Two, Scene 4, what is causing tension and fear in the household?

4. What do you think is the main **conflict** in the play? Is it the conflict between the occupants of the Secret Annex and the Nazis, or is it something else?

5. During the crisis in Act Two, Scene 3, Mr. Frank says, "We don't need the Nazis to destroy us. We're destroying ourselves." How would you describe the forces destroying the characters from inside? Do you think, given their desperate situation, that such behavior was inevitable?

6. On page 429, Anne says, "I want to go on living even after my death." How has her wish come true?

7. Which of the **resources** that accompany the play—the maps, Anne's diary entries, the historical photographs, the time line—did you find most helpful? Are there other resources you think should have been included? Explain your answers.

Extending Interpretations: The Play as a Whole

8. What do you think this play reveals about our need for freedom? about the power of love? about courage and hope? about good and evil? In your answers, consider how the play's **themes** relate to the themes of another work, such as Ann Petry's story about Harriet Tubman (page 143).

go.hrw.com

INTERNET
Projects and Activities
Keyword: LE5 8-4

SKILLS FOCUS

Literary Skills
Identify and analyze themes.

Reading Skills
Use resources to understand the historical background of a play.

9. Before *The Diary of Anne Frank* was first performed, Otto Frank wrote in a letter to the actor who would portray him, "Please don't play me as a 'hero.' . . . Nothing happened to me that did not happen to thousands upon thousands of other people." Do you see anyone in the play as a hero? In your answer, cite the qualities or actions that you think make someone a hero.

10. The play's version of events differs in many ways from what actually happened. For example:

- In real life, Anne was given the diary as a present for her thirteenth birthday, several weeks before her family went into hiding.

- The Frank family moved into the Secret Annex a week before the Van Daan family did.

- Margot was sixteen, not eighteen, when the Franks went into hiding.

- The occupants of the Secret Annex often went down to the lower floors of the office building after working hours.

- There is no evidence in Anne's diary that Mr. Van Daan stole food.

Why might the writers have chosen to change or invent these details? Do you think it's acceptable for writers to change details in works based on real people and real events? Discuss your responses.

WRITING

Comparing and Contrasting Characters

When you **compare** two people or things, you tell how they're alike. When you **contrast** them, you point out their differences. Choose any two characters in this play who have at least one thing in common—young people (Anne, Margot, and Peter), for instance, or the two mothers or fathers. Think about how they're alike and how they're different, and jot down your ideas in a Venn diagram like the one at the right. In the area where the circles overlap, list ways in which your characters are alike. Then, write a brief essay explaining how your characters are alike and how they are different. A model of a student's essay comparing and contrasting Anne and Margot appears on pages 518–519.

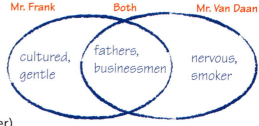

Mr. Frank — cultured, gentle | Both — fathers, businessmen | Mr. Van Daan — nervous, smoker

SKILLS FOCUS

Writing Skills
Compare and contrast characters.

After You Read — Vocabulary Development

Verify Meanings

PRACTICE

With two classmates, divide up the list of words in the Word Bank. Write down your five words. Then, match each word with the name of a character or an event in the play. For example, you might make this match:

loathe—the way the residents of the Secret Annex feel toward the Nazis

Word Bank

conspicuous
unabashed
loathe
indignantly
fortify
zeal
tyranny
remorse

gingerly
ostentatiously
appalled
disgruntled
inarticulate
forlorn
animation

Grammar Link

Dangling and Misplaced Modifiers

A modifying phrase or clause that doesn't clearly modify a word in a sentence is called a **dangling modifier.**

DANGLING   **Peeking out the window, *the church tower* could be seen.**

The church tower isn't peeking out the window. Rearranging and adding or changing words in the sentence can make the meaning clear.

CLEAR   **Peeking out the window, *Anne* could see the church tower.**

A **misplaced modifier** causes confusion because it seems to modify the wrong word in a sentence.

MISPLACED   **My grandmother *told* me about her experiences in Nazi-occupied Europe last week.**

CLEAR   **My grandmother *told* me last week about her experiences in Nazi-occupied Europe.**

The best way to catch dangling and misplaced modifiers, as with any error that causes confusion for readers, is to ask other people to read your drafts.

PRACTICE

Each of the following sentences contains a dangling or misplaced modifier. Rewrite each sentence so that it makes sense.

1. Anne watched the canal boats hiding in the Secret Annex.
2. Coughing and sneezing, Peter's cat was a problem for Dussel.
3. Hoping for a better future, the cake read, "Peace in 1944."

For more help, see Placement of Modifiers, 5e, in the Language Handbook.

SKILLS FOCUS

Vocabulary Skills
Verify word meanings.

Grammar Skills
Use modifiers correctly.

438   Collection 4 / The Human Spirit

from The Diary of a Young Girl

Literary Focus

Comparing Characterization

The writers of *The Diary of Anne Frank* based their play on Anne's actual diary, which her father had published after the war, under the title *The Diary of a Young Girl*. The playwrights drew the character of Anne from their own interpretation of the person revealed in the diary. They considered the opinions Anne expressed, the way she described herself, and the way she interacted with other people. They also talked with Anne's father, Otto Frank. Some critics have felt that the playwrights did not capture the real Anne. As you read the following excerpts from Anne's diary, try to decide what kind of person Anne might have been. How close do you think the playwrights came to portraying the real Anne?

Reading Skills

Comparing and Contrasting

When you **compare** people or things, you show their similarities—how they are alike. When you **contrast** people or things, you show how they are different. As you read the excerpts from Anne's diary, notice how this Anne is similar to or different from the Anne in the play.

INTERNET

More About Frank

Keyword: LE5 8-4

SKILLS FOCUS

Literary Skills
Analyze characterization.

Reading Skills
Compare and contrast types of characterization.

from The Diary of a Young Girl

Anne Frank

Wednesday, 3 May, 1944

. . . Since Saturday we've changed over, and have lunch at half past eleven in the mornings, so we have to last out with one cupful of porridge; this saves us a meal. Vegetables are still very difficult to obtain; we had rotten boiled lettuce this afternoon. Ordinary lettuce, spinach, and boiled lettuce, there's nothing else. With these we eat rotten potatoes, so it's a delicious combination!

As you can easily imagine, we often ask ourselves here despairingly: "What, oh, what is the use of the war? Why can't people live peacefully together? Why all this destruction?"

The question is very understandable, but no one has found a satisfactory answer to it so far. Yes, why do they make still more gigantic planes, still heavier bombs, and, at the same time, prefabricated houses for reconstruction? Why should millions be spent daily on the war and yet there's not a penny available for medical services, artists, or poor people?

Why do some people have to starve while there are surpluses rotting in other parts of the world? Oh, why are people so crazy?

I don't believe that the big men, the politicians and the capitalists alone, are guilty of the war. Oh no, the little man is just as guilty; otherwise the peoples of the world would have risen in revolt long ago! There's in people simply an urge to destroy, an urge to kill, to murder and rage, and until all mankind, without exception, undergoes a great change, wars will be waged, everything that has been built up, cultivated, and grown will be destroyed and disfigured, after which mankind will have to begin all over again.

I have often been downcast, but never in despair; I regard our hiding as a dangerous adventure, romantic and interesting at the same time. In my diary I treat all the privations° as amusing. I have made up my mind now to lead a different life from other girls and, later on, different from ordinary housewives. My start has been so very full of interest, and that is the sole reason why I have to laugh at the humorous side of the most dangerous moments.

I am young and I possess many buried qualities; I am young and strong and am living a great adventure; I am still in the midst of it and can't grumble the whole day long. I have been given a lot: a happy nature, a great deal of cheerfulness and strength. Every day I feel that I am developing inwardly, that the liberation is drawing nearer, and how beautiful nature is, how good the

---

° **privations** (prī·vā′shənz) *n.:* lack of necessities.

people are about me, how interesting this adventure is! Why, then, should I be in despair?

Yours,

Anne

Saturday, 15 July, 1944

. . . "For in its innermost depths youth is lonelier than old age." I read this saying in some book and I've always remembered it, and found it to be true. Is it true, then, that grown-ups have a more difficult time here than we do? No. I know it isn't. Older people have formed their opinions about everything and don't waver before they act. It's twice as hard for us young ones to hold our ground and maintain our opinions in a time when all ideals are being shattered and destroyed, when people are showing their worst side and do not know whether to believe in truth and right and God.

Anyone who claims that the older ones have a more difficult time here certainly doesn't realize to what extent our problems weigh down on us, problems for which we are probably much too young but which thrust themselves upon us continually, until, after a long time, we think we've found a solution, but the solution doesn't seem able to resist the facts which reduce it to nothing again. That's the difficulty in these times: Ideals, dreams, and cherished hopes rise within us, only to meet the horrible truth and be shattered.

It's really a wonder that I haven't dropped

Anne in 1940.

all my ideals, because they seem so absurd and impossible to carry out. Yet I keep them, because in spite of everything I still believe that people are really good at heart. I simply can't build up my hopes on a foundation consisting of confusion, misery, and death. I see the world gradually being turned into a wilderness, I hear the ever approaching thunder, which will destroy us too, I can feel the sufferings of millions, and yet, if I look up into the heavens, I think that it will all come right, that this cruelty too will end, and that peace and tranquility will return again.

In the meantime, I must uphold my ideals, for perhaps the time will come when I shall be able to carry them out.

Yours,

Anne

After You Read Response and Analysis

First Thoughts

1. What questions does Anne ask in these diary entries that could still be asked today? What answers would you give to those questions?

Reading Check

a. How does Anne describe herself in the first entry?

b. In the second entry, what reasons does Anne give for keeping her ideals?

Thinking Critically

2. In **dramatic irony** the audience or reader knows something a character does not know. What do we know as we read Anne's diary that Anne does not know? How does the dramatic irony make you feel?

3. In the first entry, Anne writes, "There's in people simply an urge to destroy, an urge to kill, to murder and rage. . . ." In the second entry she says that "in spite of everything I still believe that people are really good at heart." How do you think Anne could reconcile these seemingly contradictory opinions? (Cite evidence from the text in your response.) How do you feel about Anne's beliefs?

Extending Interpretations

INTERNET

Projects and Activities

Keyword: LE5 8-4

4. In her diary, Anne says that "the little man" is as guilty of the war as the politicians and the capitalists. What does she mean? What experiences did she have, according to the play, that might have led her to that conclusion?

5. After reading these excerpts, decide if you think the play captures the real Anne, or if you think important aspects of Anne's personality are missing from the character in the play. What can a play do that a diary cannot do? What can a diary tell us that a play cannot tell us?

WRITING

Writing a Poem

Using details from the play and the diary, as well as your own ideas, write an "I am" poem for Anne Frank, using this framework:

I am . . .	I am . . .	I hear . . .
I feel . . .	I see . . .	I try . . .
I say . . .	I dream . . .	I am . . .

SKILLS FOCUS

Literary Skills
Analyze characterization.

Reading Skills
Compare and contrast types of characterization.

Writing Skills
Write a poem.

Before You Read | The Article

A Tragedy Revealed: A Heroine's Last Days

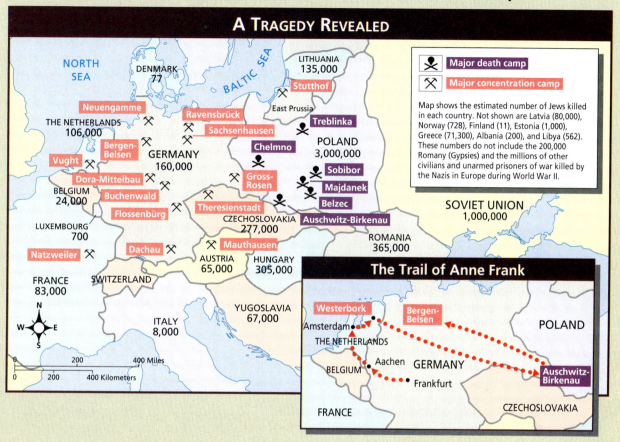

A TRAGEDY REVEALED

NORTH SEA

BALTIC SEA

DENMARK 77

LITHUANIA 135,000

East Prussia

Stutthof

Neuengamme

THE NETHERLANDS 106,000

Ravensbrück

Sachsenhausen

Treblinka

Bergen-Belsen

Chelmno

POLAND 3,000,000

GERMANY 160,000

Vught

Dora-Mittelbau

Gross-Rosen

Sobibor

BELGIUM 24,000

Buchenwald

Majdanek

Flossenbürg

Theresienstadt

Belzec

LUXEMBOURG 700

CZECHOSLOVAKIA 277,000

Auschwitz-Birkenau

SOVIET UNION 1,000,000

Natzweiler

Dachau

Mauthausen

ROMANIA 365,000

FRANCE 83,000

SWITZERLAND

AUSTRIA 65,000

HUNGARY 305,000

YUGOSLAVIA 67,000

ITALY 8,000

N W E S

0 200 400 Miles
0 200 400 Kilometers

☠ **Major death camp**

⚒ **Major concentration camp**

Map shows the estimated number of Jews killed in each country. Not shown are Latvia (80,000), Norway (728), Finland (11), Estonia (1,000), Greece (71,300), Albania (200), and Libya (562). These numbers do not include the 200,000 Romany (Gypsies) and the millions of other civilians and unarmed prisoners of war killed by the Nazis in Europe during World War II.

The Trail of Anne Frank

Westerbork

Amsterdam

Bergen-Belsen

POLAND

THE NETHERLANDS

Aachen

GERMANY

Auschwitz-Birkenau

BELGIUM

Frankfurt

FRANCE

CZECHOSLOVAKIA

Make the Connection

Quickwrite ✏️

If you could interview survivors of the Holocaust who knew Anne Frank, what would you ask them? Jot down some of your questions.

Literary Focus

Factual Reporting: What's the Main Idea?

The factual article you're about to read, which was first published in 1958, starts where Anne Frank's diary and the play end—with the discovery of the Secret Annex and the arrest of its occupants. In articles like this one, writers often provide **key passages** or **key statements** that reveal their feelings about the topic. These key statements can clue you in to the writer's main idea.

SKILLS FOCUS

Literary Skills Understand main ideas in factual reporting.

A Tragedy Revealed 443

Reading Skills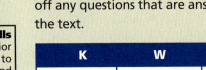
Using Prior Knowledge

Suppose you saw this item on the front page of a newspaper:

INSIDE

Never Again. In Holocaust Remembrance Day speech, community leader urges students to wipe out racial prejudice and violence.

From your knowledge of history and your understanding of current events, you'd probably have some idea of what to expect in the article.

The more you know about the topic of a text, of course, the easier it is to understand the text. Before reading a text, you might ask yourself these questions:

- What do I know about this topic?
- When I think about this topic, what words and ideas come to mind?
- Do I expect to agree or disagree with the ideas expressed in this text? Why?

Make a **KWL chart** like the one that follows. In the K column, jot down what you already **k**now about Anne Frank's life. In the W column, write down what you **w**ant to know about Anne's fate after the discovery of the Secret Annex.

Then, as you read, note in the L column any new information that you **l**earn that adds to or contradicts your **prior knowledge.** In the W column, check off any questions that are answered in the text.

go.hrw.com

INTERNET

Vocabulary Activity

Keyword: LE5 8-4

SKILLS FOCUS

Reading Skills
Use prior knowledge to understand factual reporting.

K	W	L

Vocabulary Development

These are the words you'll learn as you read the article:

indomitable (in·däm′i·tə·bəl) *adj.:* unconquerable. *Anne Frank's spirit was indomitable.*

annihilation (ə·nī′ə·lā′shən) *n.:* complete destruction. *We still mourn the Nazi annihilation of six million Jews.*

refuge (ref′yo͞oj) *n.:* place of safety. *The Franks found refuge for two years in the Secret Annex.*

reconciliations (rek′ən·sil′ē·ā′shənz) *n.:* acts of making up after arguments. *After the arguments in the Secret Annex came the tearful reconciliations.*

inexplicable (in·eks′pli·kə·bəl) *adj.:* incapable of being explained. *There were inexplicable sounds coming from the building.*

dispirited (di·spir′it·id) *v.* used as *adj.:* sad and discouraged. *The residents were often dispirited during their long confinement in the Secret Annex.*

premonition (prem′ə·nish′ən) *n.:* feeling that something bad will happen. *When the lamp crashed, the residents of the Secret Annex had a premonition that they would be discovered.*

emaciated (ē·mā′shē·āt′id) *v.* used as *adj.:* extremely thin, as from starvation or illness. *Anne's emaciated face showed suffering and hunger.*

raucous (rô′kəs) *adj.:* loud and rough. *They were frightened by the raucous shouting outside the window.*

clamorous (klam′ər·əs) *adj.:* loud and demanding. *They heard the clamorous voices of the Gestapo in the stairway.*

A Tragedy Revealed:
A Heroine's Last Days

Ernst Schnabel

Statue of Anne Frank by Pieter L'Hont, Utrecht, the Netherlands.

Last year in Amsterdam I found an old reel of movie film on which Anne Frank appears. She is seen for only ten seconds and it is an accident that she is there at all.

The film was taken for a wedding in 1941, the year before Anne Frank and seven others went into hiding in their "Secret Annex." It has a flickering, Chaplinesque[1] quality, with people popping suddenly in and out of doorways, the nervous smiles and hurried waves of the departing bride and groom.

Then, for just a moment, the camera seems uncertain where to look. It darts to the right, then to the left, then whisks up a wall, and into view comes a window

---

1. **Chaplinesque** (chap′lin·esk′): like the old silent movies starring Charlie Chaplin (1889–1977).

Last year I set out to follow the fading trail of this girl who has become a legend.

crowded with people waving after the departing automobiles. The camera swings farther to the left, to another window. There a girl stands alone, looking out into space. It is Anne Frank.

Just as the camera is about to pass on, the child moves her head a trifle. Her face flits more into focus, her hair shimmers in the sun. At this moment she discovers the camera, discovers the photographer, discovers us watching seventeen years later, and laughs at all of us, laughs with sudden merriment and surprise and embarrassment all at the same time.

I asked the projectionist to stop the film for a moment so that we could stand up to examine her face more closely. The smile stood still, just above our heads. But when I walked forward close to the screen, the smile ceased to be a smile. The face ceased to be a face, for the canvas screen was granular and the beam of light split into a multitude of tiny shadows, as if it had been scattered on a sandy plain.

Anne Frank, of course, is gone too, but her spirit has remained to stir the conscience of the world. Her remarkable diary has been read in almost every language. I have seen a letter from a teenaged girl in Japan who says she thinks of Anne's Secret Annex as her second home. And the play based on the diary has been a great success wherever it is produced. German audiences, who invariably greet the final curtain of *The Diary of Anne Frank* in stricken silence, have jammed the theaters in what seems almost a national act of penance.

Last year I set out to follow the fading trail of this girl who has become a legend. The trail led from Holland to Poland and back to Germany, where I visited the moss-grown site of the old Bergen-Belsen concentration camp at the village of Belsen and saw the common graves shared by Anne Frank and thirty thousand others. I interviewed forty-two people who knew Anne or who survived the ordeal that killed her. Some had known her intimately in those last tragic months. In the recollections of others she appears only for a moment. But even these fragments fulfill a promise. They make explicit a truth implied in the diary. As we somehow knew she must be, Anne Frank, even in the most frightful extremity, was indomitable.

The known story contained in the diary is a simple one of human relationships, of the poignant maturing of a perceptive girl who is thirteen when her diary begins and only fifteen when it ends. It is a story without violence, though its background is the most dreadful act of violence in the history of man, Hitler's annihilation of six million European Jews.

In the summer of 1942, Anne Frank, her father, her mother, her older sister, Margot, and four others were forced into hiding during the Nazi occupation of Holland. Their refuge was a tiny apartment they called the Secret Annex, in the back of an Amsterdam office building. For twenty-five months the Franks, the Van Daan family, and later a dentist, Albert Dussel,[2] lived in

---

2. In her diary, Anne made up names. The Van Daans were really named Van Pels, and Albert Dussel was really Fritz Pfeffer.

Vocabulary
indomitable (in·däm′i·tə·bəl) *adj.*: unconquerable.
annihilation (ə·nī′ə·lā′shən) *n.*: complete destruction.
refuge (ref′yōōj) *n.*: place of safety.

the Secret Annex, protected from the Gestapo[3] only by a swinging bookcase which masked the entrance to their hiding place and by the heroism of a few Christians who knew they were there. Anne Frank's diary recounts the daily pressures of their cramped existence: the hushed silences when strangers were in the building, the diminishing food supply, the fear of fire from the incessant Allied air raids, the hopes for an early invasion, above all the dread of capture by the pitiless men who were hunting Jews from house to house and sending them to concentration camps. Anne's diary also describes with sharp insight and youthful humor the bickerings, the wounded pride, the tearful reconciliations of the eight human beings in the Secret Annex. It tells of Anne's wishes for the understanding of her adored father, of her despair at the gulf between her mother and herself, of her tremulous and growing love for young Peter Van Daan.

The actual diary ends with an entry for August 1, 1944, in which Anne Frank, addressing her imaginary friend Kitty, talks of her impatience with her own unpredictable personality. The stage version goes further: It attempts to reconstruct something of the events of August 4, 1944, the day the Secret Annex was violated and its occupants finally taken into a captivity from which only one returned.

What really happened on that August day fourteen years ago was far less dramatic than what is now depicted on the stage. The automobiles did not approach with howling sirens, did not stop with screaming brakes in front of the house on the Prinsengracht canal in Amsterdam. No rifle butt pounded against the door until it reverberated, as it now does in the theater every night somewhere in the world. The truth was, at first, that no one heard a sound.

It was midmorning on a bright summer day. In the hidden apartment behind the secret bookcase there was a scene of relaxed domesticity. The Franks, the Van Daans, and Mr. Dussel had finished a poor breakfast of ersatz[4] coffee and bread. Mrs. Frank and Mrs. Van Daan were about to clear the table. Mr. Van Daan, Margot Frank, and Mr. Dussel were resting or reading. Anne Frank was very likely at work on one of the short stories she often wrote when she was not busy with her diary or her novel. In Peter Van Daan's tiny attic room Otto Frank was chiding the eighteen-year-old boy for an error in his English lesson. "Why, Peter," Mr. Frank was saying, "you know that *double* is spelled with only one *b*."

In the main part of the building four other people, two men and two women, were working at their regular jobs. For more than two years these four had risked their lives to protect their friends in the hide-out, supplied them with food, and brought them news of a world from which they had disappeared. One of the women was Miep, who had just got married a few months earlier. The other was Elli, a pretty typist of twenty-three. The men were Kraler and Koophuis,

---

3. **Gestapo** (gə·stä′pō): Nazi secret police force, known for its use of terror.

4. **ersatz** (er′zäts′) *adj.*: artificial. Regular coffee beans were unavailable because of severe wartime shortages.

Vocabulary
reconciliations (rek′ən·sil′ē·ā′shənz) *n.*: acts of making up after arguments or disagreements.

middle-aged spice merchants who had been business associates of Otto Frank's before the occupation. Mr. Kraler was working in one office by himself. Koophuis and the two women were in another.

I spoke to Miep, Elli, and Mr. Koophuis in Amsterdam. The two women had not been arrested after the raid on the Secret Annex. Koophuis had been released in poor health after a few weeks in prison, and Kraler, who now lives in Canada, had eventually escaped from a forced labor camp.

Elli, now a mother, whose coloring and plump good looks are startlingly like those of the young women painted by the Dutch masters,[5] recalled: "I was posting entries in the receipts book when a car drove up in front of the house. But cars often stopped, after all. Then the front door opened, and someone came up the stairs. I wondered who it could be. We often had callers. Only this time I could hear that there were several men. . . ."

Miep, a delicate, intelligent, still young-looking woman, said: "The footsteps moved along the corridor. Then a door creaked, and a moment later the connecting door to Mr. Kraler's office opened, and a fat man thrust his head in and said in Dutch: 'Quiet. Stay in your seats.' I started and at first did not know what was happening. But then, suddenly, I knew."

Mr. Koophuis is now in very poor health, a gaunt, white-haired man in his sixties. He added: "I suppose I did not hear them because of the rumbling of the spice mills in the warehouse. The fat man's head was the first thing I knew. He came in and planted himself in front of us. 'You three stay here, understand?' he barked. So we stayed in the office and listened as someone else went upstairs, and doors rattled, and then there were footsteps everywhere. They searched the whole building."

Mr. Kraler wrote me this account from Toronto: "A uniformed staff sergeant of the Occupation Police[6] and three men in civilian clothes entered my office. They wanted to see the storerooms in the front part of the building. All will be well, I thought, if they don't want to see anything else. But after the sergeant had looked at everything, he went out into the corridor, ordering me again to come along. At the end of the corridor they drew their revolvers all at once and the sergeant ordered me to push aside the bookcase and open the door behind it. I said: 'But there's only a bookcase there!' At that he turned nasty, for he knew everything. He took hold of the bookcase and pulled. It yielded and the secret door was exposed. Perhaps the hooks had not been properly fastened. They opened the door and I had to precede them up the steps. The policemen followed me. I could feel their pistols in my back. I was the first to enter the Franks' room. Mrs. Frank was standing at the table. I made a great effort and managed to say: 'The Gestapo is here.'"

Otto Frank, now sixty-eight, has remarried and lives in Switzerland. Of the eight who lived in the Secret Annex, he is the only survivor. A handsome, soft-spoken man of obviously great intelligence, he regularly answers correspondence that comes to him

---

5. **Dutch masters:** seventeenth-century painters including Rembrandt, Frans Hals (fräns häls), and Jan Vermeer (yän vər·mer′).

6. **Occupation Police:** police organized by the German forces while they occupied the Netherlands.

Bookcase hiding the entrance to the Secret Annex.

"It yielded and the secret door was exposed."

about his daughter from all over the world. He recently went to Hollywood for consultation on the movie version of *The Diary of Anne Frank.* About the events of that August morning in 1944 Mr. Frank told me: "I was showing Peter Van Daan his spelling mistakes when suddenly someone came running up the stairs. The steps creaked, and I started to my feet, for it was morning, when everyone was supposed to be quiet. But then the door flew open and a man stood before us holding his pistol aimed at my chest.

"In the main room the others were already assembled. My wife and the children and Van Daans were standing there with raised hands. Then Albert Dussel came in, followed by another stranger. In the middle of the room stood a uniformed policeman. He stared into our faces.

"'Where are your valuables?' he asked. I pointed to the cupboard where my cash box was kept. The policeman took it out. Then he looked around and his eye fell on the leather briefcase where Anne kept her diary and all her papers. He opened it and shook everything out, dumped the contents on the floor so that Anne's papers and notebooks and loose sheets lay scattered at our feet. No one spoke, and the policeman didn't even glance at the mess on the floor as he put our valuables into the briefcase and closed it. He asked us whether we had any weapons. But we had none, of course. Then he said, 'Get ready.'"

Who betrayed the occupants of the Secret Annex? No one is sure, but some suspicion centers on a man I can only call M., whom the living remember as a crafty and disagreeable sneak. He was a warehouse clerk hired after the Franks moved into the building, and he was never told of their presence. M. used to come to work early in the mornings, and he once found a locked briefcase which Mr. Van Daan had carelessly left in the office, where he sometimes worked in the dead of night. Though Kraler claimed it was his own briefcase, it is possible the clerk suspected. Little signs lead to bigger conclusions. In the course of the months he had worked in the building, M. might have gathered many such signs: the dial on the office radio left at BBC[7] by nocturnal listeners, slight rearrangements in the office furniture, and, of course, small <u>inexplicable</u> sounds from the back of the building.

M. was tried later by a war crimes court, denied everything, and was acquitted. No one knows where he is now. I made no effort to find him. Neither did I search out Silberthaler, the German police sergeant who made the arrest. The betrayers would have told me nothing.

Ironically enough, the occupants of the Secret Annex had grown optimistic in the last weeks of their self-imposed confinement. The terrors of those first nights had largely faded. Even the German army communiqués[8] made clear that the war was approaching an end. The Russians were well into Poland. On the Western front Americans had broken through at Avranches and were pouring into the heart of France. Holland must be liberated soon. In her diary Anne Frank wrote that she thought she might be back in school by fall.

Now they were all packing. Of the capture Otto Frank recalled: "No one wept. Anne was very quiet and composed, only just as <u>dispirited</u> as the rest of us. Perhaps that was why she did not think to take along her notebooks, which lay scattered about on the floor. But maybe she too had the <u>premonition</u> that all was lost now, everything, and so she walked back and forth and did not even glance at her diary."

As the captives filed out of the building, Miep sat listening. "I heard them going," she said, "first in the corridor and then down the stairs. I could hear the heavy boots and the footsteps, and then the very light footsteps of Anne. Through the years she had taught herself to walk so softly that you could hear her only if you knew what to listen for. I did not see her, for the office door was closed as they all passed by."

---

8. **communiqués** (kə·myōō′ni·kāz′) *n.:* official bulletins.

Vocabulary

inexplicable (in·eks′pli·kə·bəl) *adj.:* incapable of being explained.

dispirited (di·spir′it·id) *v.* used as *adj.:* sad and discouraged.

premonition (prem′ə·nish′ən) *n.:* feeling that something, especially something bad, will happen.

---

7. **BBC:** British Broadcasting Corporation.

At Gestapo headquarters the prisoners were interrogated only briefly. As Otto Frank pointed out to his questioners, it was unlikely, after twenty-five months in the Secret Annex, that he would know the whereabouts of any other Jews who were hiding in Amsterdam.

The Franks, the Van Daans, and Dussel were kept at police headquarters for several days, the men in one cell, the women in the other. They were relatively comfortable there. The food was better than the food they had had in the Secret Annex and the guards left them alone.

Suddenly, all eight were taken to the railroad station and put on a train. The guards named their destination: Westerbork, a concentration camp for Jews in Holland, about eighty miles from Amsterdam. Mr. Frank said: "We rode in a regular passenger train. The fact that the door was bolted did not matter very much. We were together and had been given a little food for the journey. We were actually cheerful. Cheerful, at least, when I compare that journey to our next. We had already anticipated the possibility that we might not remain in Westerbork to the end. We knew what was happening to Jews in Auschwitz. But weren't the Russians already deep into Poland? We hoped our luck would hold.

"As we rode, Anne would not move from the window. It was summer outside. Meadows, stubble fields, and villages flew by. The telephone wires along the right of way curved up and down along the windows. After two years it was like freedom for her. Can you understand that?"

Among the names given me of survivors who had known the Franks at Westerbork was that of a Mrs. de Wiek, who lives in Apeldoorn, Holland. I visited Mrs. de Wiek in her home. A lovely, gracious woman, she told me that her family, like the Franks, had been in hiding for months before their capture. She said: "We had been at Westerbork three or four weeks when the word went around that there were new arrivals. News of that kind ran like wildfire through the camp, and my daughter Judy came running to me, calling, 'New people are coming, Mama!'

"The newcomers were standing in a long row in the mustering square,[9] and one of the clerks was entering their names on a list. We looked at them, and Judy pressed close against me. Most of the people in the camp were adults, and I had often wished for a

9. **mustering square:** place of assembly for inspection and roll call.

"As we rode, Anne would not move from the window. After two years it was like freedom for her."

young friend for Judy, who was only fifteen. As I looked along the line, fearing I might see someone I knew, I suddenly exclaimed, 'Judy, see!'

"In the long line stood eight people whose faces, white as paper, told you at once that they had been hiding and had not been in the open air for years. Among them was this girl. And I said to Judy, 'Look, there is a friend for you.'

"I saw Anne Frank and Peter Van Daan every day in Westerbork. They were always together, and I often said to my husband, 'Look at those two beautiful young people.'

"Anne was so radiant that her beauty flowed over into Peter. Her eyes glowed and her movements had a lilt to them. She was very pallid at first, but there was something so attractive about her frailty and her expressive face that at first Judy was too shy to make friends.

"Anne was happy there, incredible as it seems. Things were hard for us in the camp. We 'convict Jews' who had been arrested in hiding places had to wear blue overalls with a red bib and wooden shoes. Our men had their heads shaved. Three hundred people lived in each barracks. We were sent to work at five in the morning, the children to a cable workshop and the grown-ups to a shed where we had to break up old batteries and salvage the metal and the carbon rods. The food was bad, we were always kept on the run, and the guards all screamed 'Faster, faster!' But Anne was happy. It was as if she had been liberated. Now she could see new people and talk to them and could laugh. She could laugh while the rest of us thought nothing but: Will they send us to the camps in Poland? Will we live through it?

"Edith Frank, Anne's mother, seemed numbed by the experience. She could have been a mute. Anne's sister Margot spoke little and Otto Frank was quiet too, but his was a reassuring quietness that helped Anne and all of us. He lived in the men's barracks, but once when Anne was sick, he came over to visit her every evening and would stand beside her bed for hours, telling her stories. Anne was so like him. When another child, a twelve-year-old boy named David, fell ill, Anne stood by his bed and talked to him. David came from an Orthodox family, and he and Anne always talked about God."

Anne Frank stayed at Westerbork only three weeks. Early in September a thousand of the "convict Jews" were put on a freight train, seventy-five people to a car. Brussels fell to the Allies, then Antwerp, then the Americans reached Aachen. But the victories were coming too late. The Franks and their friends were already on the way to Auschwitz, the camp in Poland where four million Jews died.

Mrs. de Wiek was in the same freight car as the Franks on that journey from Westerbork to Auschwitz. "Now and then when the train stopped," she told me, "the SS guards[10] came to the door and held out their caps and we had to toss our money and valuables into the caps. Anne and Judy sometimes pulled themselves up to the small barred window of the car and described the villages we were passing through. We made the children repeat the addresses where we could meet after the war if we became separated in the camp. I remember that the Franks chose a meeting place in Switzerland.

"I sat beside my husband on a small box.

---

10. **SS guards:** Nazi special police, who ran the concentration camps.

On the third day in the train, my husband suddenly took my hand and said, 'I want to thank you for the wonderful life we have had together.'

"I snatched my hand away from his, crying, 'What are you thinking about? It's not over!'

"But he calmly reached for my hand again and took it and repeated several times, 'Thank you. Thank you for the life we have had together.' Then I left my hand in his and did not try to draw it away."

On the third night, the train stopped, the doors of the car slid violently open, and the first the exhausted passengers saw of Auschwitz was the glaring searchlights fixed on the train. On the platform, kapos (criminal convicts who were assigned to positions of authority over the other prisoners) were running back and forth shouting orders. Behind them, seen distinctly against the light, stood the SS officers, trimly built and smartly uniformed, many of them with huge dogs at their sides. As the people poured out of the train, a loudspeaker roared, "Women to the left! Men to the right!"

Mrs. de Wiek went on calmly: "I saw them all as they went away, Mr. Van Daan and Mr. Dussel and Peter and Mr. Frank. But I saw no sign of my husband. He had vanished. I never saw him again.

"'Listen!' the loudspeaker bawled again. 'It is an hour's march to the women's camp. For the children and the sick there are trucks waiting at the end of the platform.'

"We could see the trucks," Mrs. de Wiek said. "They were painted with big red crosses. We all made a rush for them. Who among us was not sick after those days on the train? But we did not reach them.

People were still hanging on to the backs of the trucks as they started off. Not one person who went along on that ride ever arrived at the women's camp, and no one has ever found any trace of them."

Mrs. de Wiek, her daughter, Mrs. Van Daan, Mrs. Frank, Margot, and Anne survived the brutal pace of the night march to the women's camp at Auschwitz. Next day their heads were shaved; they learned that the hair was useful as packing for pipe joints in U-boats.[11] Then the women were put to work digging sods of grass, which they placed in great piles. As they labored each day, thousands of others were dispatched with maniacal efficiency in the gas chambers, and smoke rising from the stacks of the huge crematoriums[12] blackened the sky.

Mrs. de Wiek saw Anne Frank every day at Auschwitz. "Anne seemed even more beautiful there," Mrs. de Wiek said, "than she had at Westerbork. Of course her long hair was gone, but now you could see that her beauty was in her eyes, which seemed to grow bigger as she grew thinner. Her gaiety had vanished, but she was still alert and sweet, and with her charm she sometimes secured things that the rest of us had long since given up hoping for.

"For example, we each had only a gray sack to wear. But when the weather turned cold, Anne came in one day wearing a suit of men's long underwear. She had begged it somewhere. She looked screamingly funny with those long white legs but somehow still delightful.

"Though she was the youngest, Anne was

---

11. **U-boats** *n.:* submarines.
12. **crematoriums** (krē'mə·tôr'ē·əmz) *n.:* furnaces in which prisoners' bodies were cremated (burned to ashes).

Prisoners arriving at Auschwitz.

the leader in her group of five people. She also gave out the bread to everyone in the barracks and she did it so fairly there was none of the usual grumbling.

"We were always thirsty at Auschwitz, so thirsty that at roll call we would stick out our tongues if it happened to be raining or snowing, and many became sick from bad water. Once, when I was almost dead because there was nothing to drink, Anne suddenly came to me with a cup of coffee. To this day I don't know where she got it.

"In the barracks many people were dying, some of starvation, others of weakness and despair. It was almost impossible not to give up hope, and when a person gave up, his face became empty and dead. The Polish woman doctor who had been caring for the sick said to me, 'You will pull through. You still have your face.'

"Anne Frank, too, still had her face, up to the very last. To the last also she was moved by the dreadful things the rest of us had somehow become hardened to. Who bothered to look when the flames shot up into the sky at night from the crematoriums? Who was troubled that every day new people were being selected and gassed? Most of us were beyond feeling. But not Anne. I can still see her standing at the door and looking down the camp street as a group of naked Gypsy girls were driven by on their way to the crematorium. Anne watched them going and cried. And she also cried when we marched past the Hungarian children who had been waiting half a day in the rain in front of the gas chambers. And Anne nudged me and said, 'Look, look! Their eyes!' Anne cried. And you cannot imagine how soon most of us came to the end of our tears."

Late in October the SS selected the healthiest of the women prisoners for work in a munitions factory in Czechoslovakia. Judy de Wiek was taken from her mother, but Anne and her sister Margot were rejected because they had contracted scabies.[13] A few days later there was another selection for shipment from Auschwitz. Stripped, the women waited naked for hours on the mustering ground outside the barracks. Then, one by one, they filed into the barracks, where a battery of powerful lights had been set up and an SS doctor waited to check them over. Only those able to stand a trip and do hard work were being chosen for this new shipment, and many of the women lied about their age and condition in the hope that they would escape the almost certain death of Auschwitz. Mrs. de Wiek was rejected and so was Mrs. Frank. They waited, looking on.

"Next it was the turn of the two girls, Anne and Margot," Mrs. de Wiek recalled. "Even under the glare of that light Anne still had her face, and she encouraged Margot, and Margot walked erect into the light. There they stood for a moment, naked and shaven-headed, and Anne looked at us with her unclouded face, looked straight and stood straight, and then they were approved

---

13. **scabies** *n.:* skin disease that causes severe itching.

and passed along. We could not see what was on the other side of the light. Mrs. Frank screamed, 'The children! Oh, God!'"

The chronicle of most of the other occupants of the Secret Annex ends at Auschwitz. Mrs. Frank died there of malnutrition two months later. Mr. Frank saw Mr. Van Daan marched to the gas chambers. When the SS fled Auschwitz before the approaching Russians in January 1945, they took Peter Van Daan with them. It was bitter cold and the roads were covered with ice and Peter Van Daan, Anne Frank's shy beloved, was never heard of again.

From Auschwitz, Mr. Dussel, the dentist, was shipped to a camp in Germany, where he died. Only Otto Frank remained there alive until liberation. Anne Frank and Mrs. Van Daan and Margot had been selected for shipment to Bergen-Belsen.

Last year I drove the 225 miles from Amsterdam to Belsen and spent a day there walking over the heath.[14] The site of the old camp is near the city of Hannover, in the state of Lower Saxony. It was June when I arrived, and lupine was in flower in the scrubland.

My guide first showed me the cemetery where fifty thousand Russian prisoners of war, captured in one of Hitler's great early offensives, were buried in 1941. Next to them is a cemetery for Italians. No one knows exactly whether there are three hundred or three thousand in that mass grave.

About a mile farther we came to the main site of the Bergen-Belsen camp. Amid the low growth of pine and birches many large rectangular patches can be seen on the heath. The barracks stood on these, and between them the worn tracks of thousands of bare feet are still visible. There are more mass graves nearby, low mounds overgrown with heath grass or new-planted dwarf pines. Boards bearing the numbers of the dead stand beside some mounds, but others are unmarked and barely discernible. Anne Frank lies there.

The train that carried Anne from Auschwitz to Belsen stopped at every second station because of air raids. At Bergen-Belsen there were no roll calls, no organization, almost no sign of the SS. Prisoners lived on the heath without hope. The fact that the Allies had reached the Rhine encouraged no one. Prisoners died daily—of hunger, thirst, sickness.

The Auschwitz group had at first been assigned to tents on the Bergen-Belsen heath, tents which, one survivor recalls, gave an oddly gay, carnival aspect to the camp. One night that fall a great windstorm brought the tents crashing down, and their occupants were then put in wooden barracks. Mrs. B. of Amsterdam remembered about Anne: "We lived in the same block and saw each other often. In fact, we had a party together at Christmastime. We had saved up some stale bread, and we cut this up and put onions and boiled cabbage on the pieces. Over our feast we nearly forgot our misery for a few hours. We were almost happy. I know that it sounds ghastly now, but we really were a little happy in spite of everything."

One of Anne Frank's dearest childhood friends in Amsterdam was a girl named Lies Goosens.[15] Lies is repeatedly mentioned in

---

14. **heath** (hēth) *n.*: area of open wasteland covered with low-growing plants.

15. **Lies Goosens** (lēs khō′sins).

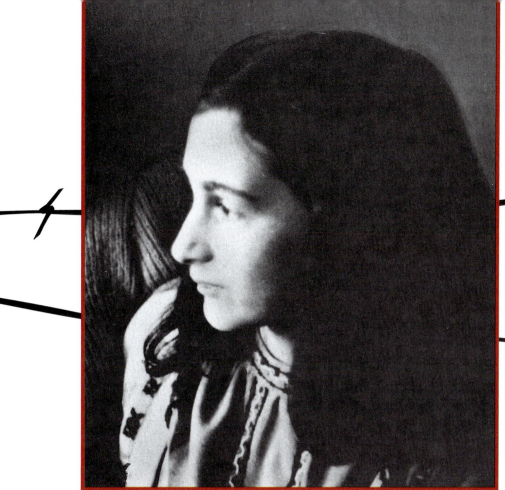

Anne in 1942. This may be the last photograph of her ever taken.

the diary. She was captured before the Franks were found in the Secret Annex, and Anne wrote of her great fears for the safety of her friend. Now the slim and attractive wife of an Israeli army officer, Lies lives in Jerusalem. But she was in Bergen-Belsen in February 1945, when she heard that a group of Dutch Jews had been moved into the next compound.

Lies said, "I waited until night. Then I stole out of the barracks and went over to the barbed wire which separated us from the newcomers. I called softly into the darkness, 'Is anyone there?'

"A voice answered, 'I am here. I am Mrs. Van Daan.'

"We had known the Van Daans in Amsterdam. I told her who I was and asked whether Margot or Anne could come to the fence. Mrs. Van Daan answered in a breathless voice that Margot was sick but that Anne could probably come and that she would go look for her.

"I waited, shivering in the darkness. It took a long time. But suddenly I heard a voice: 'Lies? Lies? Where are you?'

"I ran in the direction of the voice, and then I saw Anne beyond the barbed wire. She was in rags. I saw her <u>emaciated</u>, sunken

---

Vocabulary

emaciated (ē·mā′shē·āt′id) v. used as *adj.*:
extremely thin, as from starvation or illness.

face in the darkness. Her eyes were very large. We cried and cried as we told each other our sad news, for now there was only the barbed wire between us, nothing more, and no longer any difference in our fates.

"But there was a difference after all. My block still had food and clothing. Anne had nothing. She was freezing and starving. I called to her in a whisper, 'Come back to-morrow. I'll bring you something.'

"And Anne called across, 'Yes, tomorrow. I'll come.'

"I saw Anne again when she came to the fence on the following night," Lies continued. "I had packed up a woolen jacket and some zwieback[16] and sugar and a tin of sardines for her. I called out, 'Anne, watch now!' Then I threw the bundle across the barbed wire.

"But I heard only screams and Anne crying. I shouted, 'What's happened?' And she called back, weeping, 'A woman caught it and won't give it to me.' Then I heard rapid footsteps as the woman ran away. Next night I had only a pair of stockings and zwieback, but this time Anne caught it."

In the last weeks at Bergen-Belsen, as Germany was strangled between the Russians and the Western Allies, there was almost no food at all. The roads were blocked, the railroads had been bombed, and the SS commander of the camp drove around the district trying unsuccessfully to requisition supplies. Still, the crematoriums worked night and day. And in the midst of the starvation and the murder there was a great epidemic of typhus.

Both Anne and Margot Frank contracted the disease in late February or early March of 1945. Margot lay in a coma for several days. Then, while unconscious, she somehow rolled from her bed and died. Mrs. Van Daan also died in the epidemic.

The death of Anne Frank passed almost without notice. For Anne, as for millions of others, it was only the final anonymity, and I met no one who remembers being with her in that moment. So many were dying. One woman said, "I feel certain she died because of her sister's death. Dying is easy for anyone left alone in a concentration camp." Mrs. B., who had shared the pitiful Christmastide feast with Anne, knows a little more: "Anne, who was very sick at the time, was not informed of her sister's death. But a few days later she sensed it and soon afterward she died, peacefully."

Three weeks later British troops liberated Bergen-Belsen.

Miep and Elli, the heroic young women who had shielded the Franks for two years, found Anne's papers during the week after the police raid on the Secret Annex. "It was terrible when I went up there," Miep recalled. "Everything had been turned upside down. On the floor lay clothes, papers, letters, and school notebooks. Anne's little wrapper hung from a hook on the wall. And among the clutter on the floor lay a notebook with a red-checked cover. I picked it up, looked at the pages, and recognized Anne's handwriting."

Elli wept as she spoke to me: "The table was still set. There were plates, cups, and spoons, but the plates were empty, and I was so frightened I scarcely dared take a step. We sat down on the floor and leafed through all the papers. They were all Anne's, the notebooks and the colored duplicate paper from the office too. We

---

16. **zwieback** (swē′bak′) *n*.: sweetened bread that is sliced and toasted after it is baked.

gathered all of them and locked them up in the main office.

"A few days later M. came into the office, M. who now had the keys to the building. He said to me, 'I found some more stuff upstairs,' and he handed me another sheaf of Anne's papers. How strange, I thought, that *he* should be the one to give these to me. But I took them and locked them up with the others."

Miep and Elli did not read the papers they had saved. The red-checked diary, the office account books into which it over-flowed, the 312 tissue-thin sheets of colored paper filled with Anne's short stories and the beginnings of a novel about a young girl who was to live in freedom—all these were kept in the safe until Otto Frank finally returned to Amsterdam alone. Thus Anne Frank's voice was preserved out of the millions that were silenced. No louder than a child's whisper, it speaks for those millions and has outlasted the <u>raucous</u> shouts of the murderers, soaring above the <u>clamorous</u> voices of passing time.

Vocabulary
raucous (rô′kəs) *adj.:* loud and rowdy.
clamorous (klam′ər·əs) *adj.:* loud and demanding.

Meet the Writer

Ernst Schnabel

Following the Trail

As a young man, **Ernst Schnabel** (1913–1986) left his birthplace of Zittau, Germany, to become a sailor and travel the world. He served in the German marines during World War II, then gave up the seafaring life for a writing career. He was well-known in Germany for his radio plays, tales of his adventures at sea, and books linking classical mythology with modern-day situations. Schnabel's adventures didn't end when he began writing: In 1951, he flew around the world in nine days, then turned his experience into a novel.

For Independent Reading

"I have followed the trail of Anne Frank. It leads out of Germany and back into Germany, for there was no escape." So begins *Anne Frank: A Portrait in Courage* (1958). Based on interviews with forty-two people whose lives touched Anne's, this book enlarges on the story told in the article.

Response and Analysis

First Thoughts

1. Did reading this article change your feelings about Anne Frank's story or help you understand the events in the play? Explain.

Thinking Critically

2. Fill in the L column of your **KWL** chart. Then, choose one or two interesting facts that you learned, and discuss them with a partner.

3. Choose two quotations from the people Schnabel interviewed, and write the question you think he asked to get each response. Are any of these questions similar to ones you wrote in your Quickwrite notes?

4. This writer wanted to discover what happened to Anne Frank after her arrest. But he certainly had other **purposes** in writing this factual article. What do you think his purposes were? What would you say is the **main idea** of the article? Find at least one passage in the article that supports the main idea.

5. Now that you've read Schnabel's article, how do you feel about Anne's statement that "people are really good at heart"? Explain.

Reading Check

This article contains a **chronological account** of what happened to Anne and the other residents of the Secret Annex after their arrest by the Gestapo. Draw a time line that shows what Ernst Schnabel discovered. Start with August 4, 1944, and end with March 1945. For a model time line, see pages 367–368.

Extending Interpretations

6. In his factual article, Schnabel uses the names that Anne made up for Mr. and Mrs. Van Pels (Mr. and Mrs. Van Daan) and Fritz Pfeffer (Albert Dussel). Why do you think he chose to do this? Do you think he should have used their real names? Why or why not?

WRITING

Presenting a Report

Read one of the books about the Holocaust or World War II recommended on pages 526–527. Write a brief report on that book, and present it to the class. Include a comparison of the new book with the other materials in this chapter. What new information did you find in the new book? Which work did you like the best?

INTERNET
Projects and Activities
Keyword: LE5 8-4

Literary Skills
Analyze main ideas in factual reporting.

Reading Skills
Use prior knowledge to analyze factual reporting.

Writing Skills
Write and present a report.

Word Ratings: Connotations

Connotations are the feelings associated with a word, feelings that go beyond its strict dictionary definition, or **denotation.** Often connotations show shades of meaning or intensity.

PRACTICE

Use the symbol "+" if the word on the right seems stronger than the numbered Word Bank word on the left. Use "−" if it seems weaker. Use a dictionary for help. (Try this exercise with a partner. You may not agree!)

1. indomitable ( ) strong
2. annihilation ( ) ruin
3. refuge ( ) shelter
4. reconciliations ( ) agreements
5. inexplicable ( ) mysterious
6. dispirited ( ) hopeless
7. premonition ( ) dread
8. emaciated ( ) skinny
9. raucous ( ) noisy
10. clamorous ( ) loud

Word Bank

indomitable
annihilation
refuge
reconciliations
inexplicable
dispirited
premonition
emaciated
raucous
clamorous

Grammar Link

Joining Independent Clauses

Use a semicolon between independent clauses joined by words and phrases such as these:

after all   in fact   otherwise
besides   instead   still
for example   meanwhile   therefore
however   on the other hand   unfortunately

The play tells the story of life in the Secret Annex; however, it does not always stick to what really happened.

The playwrights invented the howling siren and pounding rifle butt for the arrest scene; after all, it's more dramatic that way.

Note that a comma always follows a connecting word.

PRACTICE

Choose three of the words or phrases listed on the left. Use each one in a sentence of your own. Be sure your semicolons and commas are in the right places.
For more help, see Semicolons, 13l–n, in the Language Handbook.

SKILLS FOCUS

Vocabulary Skills
Analyze connotations.

Grammar Skills
Join independent clauses correctly.

Identifying and Connecting Main Ideas

Reading Focus

Identifying the Main Idea

The **main idea** is the message, opinion, or insight that is the focus or key concept in a piece of writing. It's the most important idea that the writer wants you to remember. This important idea is developed with **supporting details.** To find the main idea, follow these steps:

- Look for direct statements made by the writer.
- Look closely at the details presented by the writer. (*Who, what, when, where,* and *why* questions will help you identify the important details.)
- Think about what the details add up to.
- Try to put the main idea into your own words.

Connecting Main Ideas

Why is it important to connect main ideas? It's important because seeing how one idea relates to another deepens your understanding of our rich and complex world.

Some people say that the best readers are able to find connections between all the texts they read.

■ As you read this personal essay, called "Walking with Living Feet," look for Dara Horn's **main idea**—the message, opinion, or insight that is central to a piece of nonfiction. Then, think about what you learned from "A Tragedy Revealed" by Ernst Schnabel (page 445). How does Schnabel's factual report deepen your understanding of Horn's personal essay?

Train destination sign.

WALKING WITH LIVING FEET

I had a very unusual fifteenth birthday. During my birthday week, at the end of April, I was traveling with five thousand high school students from around the world, visiting concentration camps in Poland. I learned more there than I learned during my entire life in school; once I stepped out of a gas chamber, I became a different person. When I turned fifteen, I discovered that no matter how much you read about the Holocaust, nothing can ever be like seeing it with your own eyes. The day after my fifteenth birthday was the turning point of my life. I was at Majdanek, one of the largest Nazi concentration camps. And I will never forget it.

Majdanek has been left exactly as it was when it was in use, so intact that if it were to be "plugged in," it could start gassing people tomorrow.

I stood in a gas chamber there, at Majdanek. I saw the blue stains of Zyklon B streaking the ceilings and walls, the poison used to kill the people who were crushed into this tiny, gray cement room. I could see how their fingers had scraped off the white paint, trying to escape. The cement floor that I sat on was cold and clammy; the air in the room seemed made of chills. When I first sat down, I did not notice, but soon those chilling waves were seeping into my skin, like so many tiny fingers trying to pull at my nerves and make my bones quiver. All around me, kids were crying hysterically, yet the chills that rankled the air around me hadn't reached my mind, and I could not feel. I hated myself for it. Anger, fear, pain, and shock—I could have felt all of those and more, but instead I felt nothing. That void was far worse: All the other emotions around me showed the presence of human hearts, but I was almost not there at all. I wanted to feel; I hated the guilt I had at my lack of reaction as much as I hated what happened there. Only my squirming skin could attest to my surroundings, and the crawling air made my lungs tighten. I wished I could cry, but I couldn't break down my mental blockade. Why?

The camp of Majdanek extends for miles, but one of the worst things about it is that it's right in a town, almost a city, called Lublin. There are actually houses right next to the barbed wire, the fence with its thorns that stabbed my frightened eyes, enough to separate a universe. The people of that city would have had to be dead not to notice the death which struck daily, right behind their backyards, where I saw children playing. People marched through Lublin from the train station, entered through the same barbed wire gate that I did, and left through the chimney. Nobody in Lublin noticed, because if they had, their fate would have been the same. And today the camp's long gray, barnlike barracks still extend forever, in endless rows, the sky a leaden weight blocking the colors that grace free life. Gray is the color of hell.

Inside each of the barracks is a new horror. Some are museum exhibits, with collections of people's toothbrushes (they were told that they were being "relocated" and to bring one suitcase, the contents of which were confiscated) and people's hair. All of the walls in one barracks are covered with people's hats, hanging in rows. But the worst were the shoes.

About five of the barracks are filled with nothing but the shoes of some of the people who were killed there—over 850,000 pairs. In one barracks, I sat on a platform about five feet off the ground, and surrounding it was an ocean of shoes, five feet deep. In the gas chamber I could not feel, but in that room filled with shoes, my mental blockade cracked. The photographs meant nothing to me, the history lessons and names and numbers were never strong enough. But here each shoe is different, a different size and shape: a high heel, a sandal, a baby's shoe so tiny that its owner couldn't have been old enough to walk, and shoes like mine. Each pair of those shoes walked a path all its own, guided its owner through his or her life and to all of their deaths. Thousands and thousands of shoes, each pair different, each pair silently screaming someone's murdered dreams. No book can teach me what I saw there with my own eyes!

I glanced at my own shoe, expecting it to be far different from those in that ocean of death, and my breath caught in my throat as I saw that my shoe seemed to be almost the same style as one, no, two, three, of the shoes I saw; it seemed as if every shoe there was my shoe. I touched the toe of one nearby and felt its dusty texture, certain that mine would be different. But as I touched my own toe, tears welled in my eyes as my fingers traced the edges of my dusty, living shoes. Eight hundred and fifty thousand pairs of shoes, but now I understood: They weren't numbers; they were people.

Soon I was crying, but for someone else: for the child whose mother's sandals rested on that pile, for the woman whose husband's shoes swam motionless in that sea, like the tears that streaked my face, for the girl whose best friend's slippers were buried in that ocean of grayness and silence. I was lost to the shoes there. I wished I could throw my shoes into that pile, to grasp and feel each shoe, to jump into the sea of shoes, to become a part of it, to take it with me. I wanted to add my own shoes to that ocean, but all I could leave there were my salty tears. My feet clumped on the wooden platform as I left, and I had never been more conscious of how my shoes fit my living feet.

At the very end of the camp was another gas chamber and the crematorium, its smokestack jutting through the leaden sky. This gas chamber did not have the blue poison stains that streaked the walls in the one I saw first, or maybe it did: The only light in that cement room was from dozens of memorial candles. It was too dark to see. The air inside was damp and suffocating, like a burial cave, and yet the air was savagely alive. It crawled down my neck and compressed me as the walls and ceiling seemed to move closer. No words can express how it felt to step out of that gas chamber alive, wearing my living shoes.

And I saw the crematorium where the corpses were burned, ovens shaped to fit a person. As I touched the brick furnaces with trembling fingers, my tears froze in my eyes and I could not cry. It was here that I felt my soul go up in flames, leaving me an empty shell.

Majdanek reeks of death everywhere. Even the reminders and signs of life that exist in a cemetery, like a footprint or rustling leaves, are absent here, every image of life erased. Even the wind does not ruffle the grass, which never used to grow here because the prisoners would eat it. But in the crematorium, I felt something I cannot express. No words exist to describe how I felt. It was someone else's nightmare, a nightmare that turned real before I even noticed it. It was a stark and chilling reality that struck me there, standing where people were slaughtered and burned, and my mind simply stopped. Have you ever been to Planet Hell? My people are numbers here, struck from a list and sent out the chimney, their children's bodies roasting. And I was there. You cannot visit this planet through any film or book; photographs cannot bring you here. Planet Hell is beyond the realm of tears. This is why I could not cry.

I left the camp. How many people, who had walked in those 850,000 pairs of shoes, once dreamed of doing what I had just done? And did they, too, forget how to cry?

In Israel I planted a tree with soil I had taken from concentration camps. In the soil were white specks, human bone ash. I am fifteen years old, and I know I can never forget.

—Dara Horn
Millburn High School
Millburn, New Jersey

First appeared in *Merlyn's Pen: Fiction, Essays, and Poems by America's Teens.*

Analyzing Main Ideas

WALKING WITH LIVING FEET

Test Practice

1. The writer's **purpose** in writing about her visit to Majdanek was most likely to —
   - **A** tell how it felt
   - **B** entertain the reader
   - **C** persuade the reader to take a stand
   - **D** teach the history of the camp

2. Which of the following sentences do you think *best* states the writer's **main idea**?
   - **F** "I had a very unusual fifteenth birthday."
   - **G** "No matter how much you read about the Holocaust, nothing can ever be like seeing it with your own eyes."
   - **H** "Nobody in Lublin noticed. . . ."
   - **J** "No words exist to describe how I felt."

3. The writer says that no Lublin residents noticed anyone entering the camp through the barbed wire gate and leaving through the chimney because —
   - **A** if they had, their fate would have been the same as the prisoners' fate
   - **B** they could not see over the high walls around the camp
   - **C** the camp was so far from town they could not see what went on inside
   - **D** they did not want to know what was happening in the camp

4. Planting a tree in soil taken from a concentration camp is a **symbol** of —
   - **F** good land management
   - **G** good growing out of evil
   - **H** a need for revenge
   - **J** a misuse of resources

Constructed Response

1. Why does the writer finally cry when she sees the room full of shoes?

2. The writer calls the crematorium "Planet Hell." What evidence does she give to support this **analogy** comparing the crematorium to hell?

3. Think back to what you learned from "A Tragedy Revealed" by Ernst Schnabel (page 445). What connections do you see between Schnabel's main idea and the main idea of "Walking with Living Feet"?

SKILLS FOCUS

Reading Skills
Connect main ideas across texts.

Context Clues

PRACTICE 1

In the following passages from this essay, context clues for the underlined words are in italic type. Use the context clues to identify the meaning of each underlined word.

1. "The cement floor that I sat on was *cold* and clammy; *the air in the room seemed made of chills.*" *Clammy* means
   a. cold and damp   **c.** flooded
   b. warm and damp   **d.** rough

2. "Anger, fear, pain, and shock—I could have felt all of those and more, but instead *I felt nothing.* That void was far worse. . . ." *Void* means
   a. pit   **c.** space
   b. vista   **d.** emptiness

3. "I wished I could cry, but I couldn't *break down* my mental blockade." *Blockade* means
   a. barrier   **c.** agony
   b. bombardment   **d.** illness

4. "The air was savagely alive. It crawled down my neck and compressed me *as the walls and ceiling seemed to move closer.*" *Compressed* means
   a. squeezed together from pressure
   b. comforted by a parent
   c. released from prison
   d. relieved from anxiety

Words in Context

PRACTICE 2

The underlined words above can be used in other contexts. See if you can answer these questions:

1. How would a cave explorer use the word *clammy*?
2. How would a physicist use the word *void*?
3. How would a naval officer use the word *blockade*?
4. How would a pipe fitter use the word *compressed*?

SKILLS FOCUS

Vocabulary Skills
Use context clues.

Camp Harmony *and*
In Response to Executive Order 9066

Make the Connection
Quickwrite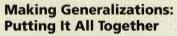

Look at the paintings on pages 471 and 476. Freewrite in response to one of them. You might use this starter: "The first thing I noticed was . . ."

Literary Focus
Recurring Themes

Because **themes** are general ideas about human experience, they have been repeated again and again in literature throughout the ages. For instance, a theme such as *Good can triumph over evil* can be found in ancient texts as well as in contemporary novels. As you read the following selections, look for themes you recognize from other works, including *The Diary of Anne Frank*.

Reading Skills
Making Generalizations: Putting It All Together

A **generalization** is a broad statement based on several particular situations. When you make a generalization, you combine new evidence in a text with what you already know. For example, after you have read about Monica Sone's experiences, you might make a generalization about the treatment of Japanese Americans during World War II.

Vocabulary Development

You will learn these words as you read "Camp Harmony":

tersely (tʉrsʹlē) *adv.:* briefly and clearly. *The child tersely stated, "Pigs—dirty."*

laconically (lə·kän'ik·lē) *adv.:* with few words. *He answered laconically: "Soup."*

breach (brēch) *n.:* opening. *The narrator squeezed into a breach in the wall of people.*

riveted (rivʹit·id) *v.:* fastened; held firmly. *The family watched, riveted with fear, as the stove turned red hot.*

vigil (vijʹəl) *n.:* watch. *Armed guards kept an around-the-clock vigil in the camp.*

INTERNET

Vocabulary Activity

Keyword: LE5 8-4

SKILLS FOCUS

Literary Skills
Understand recurring themes.

Reading Skills
Make generalizations.

Background
Literature and Social Studies

In 1942, many thousands of Japanese Americans living on the West Coast were sent to internment camps. They had committed no crime, but the United States had gone to war with Japan. Executive Order 9066 made their confinement legal. Ironically, many of the evacuated families had sons or brothers serving with the U.S. Army in the war overseas. Most of the 120,000 Japanese Americans detained spent three years behind barbed wire. Released in 1945, at the end of World War II, they returned home to find their property stolen and their livelihoods gone. They had to wait more than forty years for an apology and compensation from the U.S. government.

Camp Harmony

from **Nisei Daughter**
Monica Sone

What was I doing behind a fence, like a criminal?

When our bus turned a corner and we no longer had to smile and wave, we settled back gravely in our seats. Everyone was quiet except for a chattering group of university students, who soon started singing college songs. A few people turned and glared at them, which only served to increase the volume of their singing. Then suddenly a baby's sharp cry rose indignantly above the hubbub. The singing stopped immediately, followed by a guilty silence. Three seats behind us, a young mother held a wailing red-faced infant in her arms, bouncing it up and down. Its angry little face emerged from multiple layers of kimonos, sweaters, and blankets, and it, too, wore the white pasteboard tag[1]

---

1. **white pasteboard tag:** All Japanese American families registering for evacuation were given numbered tags to wear and to attach to their luggage. Monica's family became family number 10710.

pinned to its blanket. A young man stammered out an apology as the mother gave him a wrathful look. She hunted frantically for a bottle of milk in a shopping bag, and we all relaxed when she had found it.

We sped out of the city southward along beautiful stretches of farmland, with dark, newly turned soil. In the beginning we devoured every bit of scenery which flashed past our window and admired the massive-muscled workhorses plodding along the edge of the highway, the rich burnished copper color of a browsing herd of cattle, the vivid spring green of the pastures, but eventually the sameness of the country landscape palled[2] on us. We tried to sleep to escape from the restless anxiety which kept bobbing up to the surface of our minds. I awoke with a start when the bus filled with excited buzzing. A small group of straw-hatted Japanese farmers stood by the highway, waving at us. I felt a sudden warmth toward them, then a twinge of pity. They would be joining us soon.

About noon we crept into a small town. Someone said, "Looks like Puyallup, all right." Parents of small children babbled excitedly, "Stand up quickly and look over there. See all the chick-chicks and fat little piggies?" One little city boy stared hard at the hogs and said tersely, "They're bachi—dirty!"

Our bus idled a moment at the traffic signal, and we noticed at the left of us an entire block filled with neat rows of low shacks, resembling chicken houses. Someone commented on it with awe, "Just look at those chicken houses. They sure go in for poultry in a big way here." Slowly the bus made a left turn, drove through a wire-fence gate, and to our dismay, we were inside the oversized chicken farm. The bus driver opened the door, the guard stepped out and stationed himself at the door again. Jim, the young man who had shepherded us into the buses, popped his head inside and sang out, "OK, folks, all off at Yokohama, Puyallup."

We stumbled out, stunned, dragging our bundles after us. It must have rained hard the night before in Puyallup, for we sank ankle deep into gray, glutinous[3] mud. The receptionist, a white man, instructed us courteously, "Now, folks, please stay together as family units and line up. You'll be assigned your apartment."

We were standing in Area A, the mammoth parking lot of the state fairgrounds. There were three other separate areas, B, C, and D, all built on the fairgrounds proper, near the baseball field and the racetracks. This camp of army barracks was hopefully called Camp Harmony.

We were assigned to apartment 2–I–A, right across from the bachelor quarters. The apartments resembled elongated,[4] low stables about two blocks long. Our home was one room, about eighteen by twenty feet, the size of a living room. There was one small window in the wall opposite the one door. It was bare except for a small, tinny wood-burning stove crouching in the center. The flooring consisted of two-by-fours laid directly on the earth, and dandelions were already pushing their way up through the cracks. Mother was delighted when she saw their shaggy yellow heads. "Don't anyone pick them. I'm going to cultivate them."

---

3. **glutinous** (glо̄о̄t′n·əs) *adj.:* sticky; gluey.
4. **elongated** (ē·lôŋ′gāt′id) *v.* used as *adj.:* lengthened.

Vocabulary
tersely (tŭrs′lē) *adv.:* briefly and clearly; without unnecessary words.

---

2. **palled** (pôld) *v.:* became boring or tiresome.

Topaz, August 1943 (1943) by Suiko Mikami. Watercolor.

Father snorted, "Cultivate them! If we don't watch out, those things will be growing out of our hair."

Just then Henry stomped inside, bringing the rest of our baggage. "What's all the excitement about?"

Sumi replied laconically, "Dandelions."

Henry tore off a fistful. Mother scolded, "Arra! Arra! Stop that. They're the only beautiful things around here. We could have a garden right in here."

"Are you joking, Mama?"

I chided Henry, "Of course she's not. After all, she has to have some inspiration to write poems, you know, with all the 'nari keri's.'[5] I can think of a poem myself right now:

Oh, Dandelion, Dandelion,
Despised and uprooted by all,
Dance and bob your golden heads
For you've finally found your home
With your yellow fellows, nari keri, amen!"

Henry said, thrusting the dandelions in Mother's black hair, "I think you can do ten times better than that, Mama."

Sumi reclined on her sea bag[6] and fretted, "Where do we sleep? Not on the floor, I hope."

"Stop worrying," Henry replied disgustedly. Mother and Father wandered out to see

---

5. *Nari keri* (nä·rē ke·rē) is a phrase used to end many Japanese poems. It is meant to convey wonder and awe.

6. sea bag *n.:* large canvas bag like the ones sailors use to carry their personal belongings. Each person was allowed to bring only one sea bag of bedding and two suitcases of clothing to the internment camps.

Vocabulary

laconically (lə·kän′ik·lē) *adv.:* with few words. *Laconically* and *tersely* are synonyms.

what the other folks were doing and they found people wandering in the mud, wondering what other folks were doing. Mother returned shortly, her face lit up in an ecstatic smile, "We're in luck. The latrine is right nearby. We won't have to walk blocks."

We laughed, marveling at Mother who could be so poetic and yet so practical. Father came back, bent double like a wood-cutter in a fairy tale, with stacks of scrap lumber over his shoulder. His coat and trouser pockets bulged with nails. Father dumped his loot in a corner and explained, "There was a pile of wood left by the carpenters and hundreds of nails scattered loose. Everybody was picking them up, and I hustled right in with them. Now maybe we can live in style, with tables and chairs."

The block leader knocked at our door and announced lunchtime. He instructed us to take our meal at the nearest mess hall. As I untied my sea bag to get out my pie plate, tin cup, spoon, and fork, I realized I was hungry. At the mess hall we found a long line of people. Children darted in and out of the line, skiing in the slithery mud. The young stood impatiently on one foot, then the other, and scowled, "The food had better be good after all this wait." But the issei[7] stood quietly, arms folded, saying very little. A light drizzle began to fall, coating bare black heads with tiny sparkling raindrops. The chow line inched forward.

Lunch consisted of two canned sausages, one lob of boiled potato, and a slab of bread. Our family had to split up, for the hall was too crowded for us to sit together. I wandered up and down the aisles, back and forth along the crowded tables and benches, looking for a few inches to squeeze into. A small issei woman finished her meal, stood up, and hoisted her legs modestly over the bench, leaving a space for one. Even as I thrust myself into the breach, the space had shrunk to two inches, but I worked myself into it. My dinner companion, hooked just inside my right elbow, was a baldheaded, gruff-looking issei man who seemed to resent nestling at mealtime. Under my left elbow was a tiny, mud-spattered girl. With busy, runny nose, she was belaboring her sausages, tearing them into shreds and mixing them into the potato gruel which she had made with water. I choked my food down.

We cheered loudly when trucks rolled by, distributing canvas army cots for the young and hardy, and steel cots for the older folks. Henry directed the arrangement of the cots. Father and Mother were to occupy the corner nearest the woodstove. In the other corner, Henry arranged two cots in an L shape and announced that this was the combination living room–bedroom area, to be occupied by Sumi and myself. He fixed a male den for himself in the corner nearest the door. If I had had my way, I would have arranged everyone's cots in one neat row, as in Father's hotel dormitory.

We felt fortunate to be assigned to a room at the end of the barracks, because we had just one neighbor to worry about. The partition wall separating the rooms was only seven feet high, with an opening of four feet at the top, so at night, Mrs. Funai next door could tell when Sumi was still sitting up in bed in the dark, putting her hair

---

7. **issei** (ē′sā′) *n.:* Japanese who immigrated to North America. Issei were forbidden by law to become U.S. citizens.

Vocabulary

breach (brēch) *n.:* opening. *Breach* usually refers to a breakthrough in a wall or in a line of defense.

I stared at our little window, unable to sleep.

up. "Mah, Sumi-chan," Mrs. Funai would say through the plank wall, "are you curling your hair tonight, again? Do you put it up every night?" Sumi would put her hands on her hips and glare defiantly at the wall.

The block monitor, an impressive nisei[8] who looked like a star tackle, with his crouching walk, came around the first night to tell us that we must all be inside our room by nine o'clock every night. At ten o'clock, he rapped at the door again, yelling, "Lights out!" and Mother rushed to turn the light off not a second later.

Throughout the barracks, there was a medley[9] of creaking cots, whimpering infants, and explosive night coughs. Our attention was riveted on the intense little woodstove, which glowed so violently I feared it would melt right down to the floor. We soon learned that this condition lasted for only a short time, after which it suddenly turned into a deep freeze. Henry and Father took turns at the stove to produce the harrowing[10] blast which all but singed our army blankets but did not penetrate through them. As it grew quieter in the barracks, I could hear the light patter of rain. Soon I felt the *splat! splat!* of raindrops digging holes into my face. The dampness on my pillow spread like a mortal bleeding, and I finally had to get out and haul my cot toward the center of the room. In a short while, Henry was up. "I've got multiple leaks, too. Have to complain to the landlord first thing in the morning."

All through the night I heard people getting up, dragging cots around. I stared at our little window, unable to sleep. I was glad Mother had put up a makeshift curtain on the window, for I noticed a powerful beam of light sweeping across it every few seconds. The lights came from high towers placed around the camp, where guards with tommy guns kept a twenty-four-hour vigil. I remembered the wire fence encircling us, and a knot of anger tightened in my breast. What was I doing behind a fence, like a criminal? If there were accusations to be made, why hadn't I been given a fair trial? Maybe I wasn't considered an American anymore. My citizenship wasn't real, after all. Then what was I? I was certainly not a citizen of Japan, as my parents were. On second thought, even Father and Mother were more alien residents of the United States than Japanese nationals, for they had little tie with their mother country. In their twenty-five years in America, they had worked and paid their taxes to their adopted government as any other citizen.

Of one thing I was sure. The wire fence was real. I no longer had the right to walk out of it. It was because I had Japanese ancestors. It was also because some people had little faith in the ideas and ideals of democracy. They said that after all these were but words and could not possibly ensure loyalty. New laws and camps were surer devices. I finally buried my face in my pillow to wipe out burning thoughts and snatch what sleep I could.

---

8. **nisei** (nē′sā′) *n.:* native U.S. or Canadian citizen born of Japanese immigrant parents.
9. **medley** (med′lē) *n.:* jumble; mixture.
10. **harrowing** (har′ō·iŋ) *adj.:* extremely distressing.

Vocabulary

riveted (riv′it·id) *v.:* fastened or held firmly, as if by rivets (metal bolts or pins).

vigil (vij′əl) *n.:* watch; act of staying awake to keep watch.

Meet the Writer

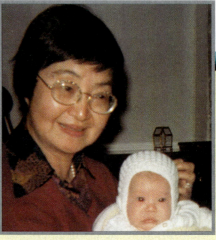

Monica Sone with her granddaughter, Mariko Davison.

Monica Sone

"I Wanted to Tell Our Story"

Monica Sone (1919–   ) was born in Seattle, Washington. This is her explanation of how she came to write *Nisei Daughter:*

❝In the spring of 1942, shortly after Pearl Harbor [site of the U.S. naval base bombed by Japan], I was forced to leave my home in Seattle under U.S. Army orders. I was sent away to a prison camp built inside a state fairground in Puyallup, Washington. This camp, for some strange reason, was called Camp Harmony.

While incarcerated there, I wrote letters to my friend Betty McDonald [an author of children's books], describing our living conditions, which were mind-boggling to me. I had gone from a fairly normal life to being herded into a camp with thousands of others, surrounded with barbed wire and armed guards. This occurred even though we were Americans and we had not been charged with any crime.

Betty had apparently preserved all of my letters. One day she showed the packet of letters to an editor from Little, Brown and Co. He immediately became interested in my camp experiences, especially since at that time no details had come out of camp to be reported in the media. The editor reacted to my letters, sensing in them a human-interest story as well as a major historical event in our country.

The editor contacted me and inquired if I would be interested in expanding on my letters and writing a book. I was eager to do so. This was because after I eventually left camp and moved to the eastern part of the country, I discovered that the general public knew nothing about our evacuation and imprisonment of tens of thousands of Americans. I wanted to tell our story.❞

In Response to Executive Order 9066:

All Americans of Japanese Descent Must Report to Relocation Centers

Dwight Okita

Dear Sirs:
Of course I'll come. I've packed my galoshes
and three packets of tomato seeds. Denise calls them
"love apples." My father says where we're going
5   they won't grow.

I am a fourteen-year-old girl with bad spelling
and a messy room. If it helps any, I will tell you
I have always felt funny using chopsticks
and my favorite food is hot dogs.
10   My best friend is a white girl named Denise—
we look at boys together. She sat in front of me
all through grade school because of our names:
O'Connor, Ozawa. I know the back of Denise's head very well.
I tell her she's going bald. She tells me I copy on tests.
15   We're best friends.

I saw Denise today in Geography class.
She was sitting on the other side of the room.
"You're trying to start a war," she said, "giving secrets away
to the Enemy. Why can't you keep your big mouth shut?"
20   I didn't know what to say.
I gave her a packet of tomato seeds
and asked her to plant them for me, told her
when the first tomato ripened
she'd miss me.

Meet the Writer

Dwight Okita

Controversial Issues in a Charming Style

Dwight Okita (1958–   ) frequently looks to events from his own life as material for his poetry. His parents had to report to a Japanese American internment camp during World War II, a traumatic event that inspired "In Response to Executive Order 9066."

Okita does not shy away from controversial social and political issues, but he maintains a light, charming style that has made his writing popular with American readers. His poems also look at personal issues with a keen sense of humor. *Crossing with the Light*, the collection from which "In Response to Executive Order 9066" is taken, was published in 1992.

Progress After One Year, the Mess Hall (1943) by Kango Takamura. Collection 99, M-16.

Department of Special Collections, Charles E. Young Research Library, UCLA.

After You Read   Response and Analysis

First Thoughts

1. Discuss your reactions to the autobiography and the poem, using one of these starters:
   - I realized . . .
   - I felt . . .

Thinking Critically

2. Sone says her camp "was hopefully called Camp Harmony" (see page 470). Do you think the name is appropriate? Support your opinion with evidence from the text.

3. Find several details that describe the conditions in Sone's camp. Using these details, make a **generalization** about the Japanese American internment camps.

4. What details in Okita's poem show that the narrator feels she is a real American? How is she betrayed by her friend?

5. The paintings on pages 471 and 476 were made by Japanese Americans living in internment camps during World War II. Choose one, and explain how it reminds you of, or seems different from, what you read in "Camp Harmony" or "In Response to Executive Order 9066." You may want to re-read your Quickwrite.

Extending Interpretations

6. *People often bear the burden of blame for things they did not do.* Discuss how this **theme** is revealed in "Camp Harmony," in "In Response to Executive Order 9066," and in another story, movie, or TV show. How are the treatments of the theme similar? How are they different?

WRITING

Composing a Letter

Pretend you are Sone or the speaker of "In Response to Executive Order 9066." Write a letter to President Franklin D. Roosevelt to persuade him to cancel Executive Order 9066 and allow you and your family to go home. Use practical, moral, or legal arguments to make your case, supporting them with details from the text.

Reading Check

a. Write a one-paragraph **summary** of the main events in "Camp Harmony."

b. Write a brief **summary** of the main events in "In Response to Executive Order 9066."

go.
hrw
.com

INTERNET

Projects and Activities

Keyword: LE5 8-4

SKILLS FOCUS

Literary Skills
Analyze recurring themes.

Reading Skills
Make generalizations.

Writing Skills
Write a persuasive letter.

Verify Meanings: Restatement

PRACTICE

Change each of the following sentences so that you say the same thing using words that are different from the underlined words. You can restate just the underlined word or rewrite the whole sentence.

1. One little boy stared at the hogs and said tersely, "They're dirty."
2. Sumi answered laconically, "Dandelions."
3. Guards with tommy guns kept a twenty-four-hour vigil around the camp.
4. The narrator thrust herself into the tiny breach between two people sitting on the bench.
5. The family's attention was riveted on the stove.

> **Word Bank**
>
> tersely
> laconically
> vigil
> breach
> riveted

Grammar Link

Avoiding Double Negatives

A **double negative** occurs when two negative words express one negative idea. Avoid using double negatives in formal writing and speaking.

These are some commonly used negative words:

barely	never	none	nothing
hardly	no	no one	nowhere
neither	nobody	not or –n't	scarcely

NONSTANDARD	The room *did*n't *have* no furniture.
STANDARD	The room *had* no furniture.
	The room *did*n't *have* any furniture.
NONSTANDARD	It was so crowded they *could*n't hardly *sit* down.
STANDARD	It was so crowded they *could* hardly *sit* down.

PRACTICE

Correct all double negatives:

Monica and her family couldn't hardly believe dandelions were growing up through their floor. Nobody didn't like it when the rain came through the roof. Scarcely no one in the family slept the first night. They didn't have no privacy.

For more help, see Uses of Comparative and Superlative Forms, 5b–d, in the Language Handbook.

SKILLS FOCUS

Vocabulary Skills
Use restatement to verify meanings.

Grammar Skills
Avoid double negatives.

Before You Read · The Speech

The Gettysburg Address

Make the Connection
A Class Quilt

Think about what America means to you. On an unlined sheet of paper, draw a symbol that represents your thoughts and feelings. Tape or staple your paper to your classmates' papers to create a class quilt, and explain the meaning of your symbol.

Literary Focus
Refrain

Like poets, good speakers appeal to our sense of hearing. One way they do this is by using refrains, which create echoes in listeners' ears. A **refrain** is a repeated sound, word, phrase, line, or group of lines. Refrains are used to build rhythm and emphasize important themes or messages. As you read the Gettysburg Address, look for the words and phrases that Lincoln chose to repeat.

Reading Skills
Dialogue with the Text: Slow Down to Understand

Read the Gettysburg Address at least twice. Read slowly and carefully, just as you'd read any difficult text. Record, in one column, any comments and questions suggested by your first reading. Then, in a second column, write down answers to your questions and additional thoughts as you read the speech a second time.

Background
Literature and Social Studies

The Battle of Gettysburg, which took place in Pennsylvania in 1863, was a turning point of the Civil War. In that bloody three-day battle, Union forces prevented Confederate forces from moving north, thus confining the war mainly to the South. The battle left at least 51,000 soldiers dead, wounded, or missing.

On November 19, 1863, part of the battlefield was dedicated as a military cemetery. President Abraham Lincoln was asked to make some remarks at the dedication. Although very brief, Lincoln's Gettysburg Address is considered one of the greatest speeches by a U.S. political leader. It is notable especially for its vision of American democracy.

SKILLS FOCUS

Literary Skills
Understand refrain.

Reading Skills
Dialogue with the text.

Executive Mansion,

*Washington, _____, 186_*

Four score and seven years ago our fathers brought forth, upon this continent, a new nation, conceived in liberty, and dedicated to the proposition that "all men are created equal"

Now we are engaged in a great civil war, testing ... nation so conceiving,

First draft of the Gettysburg Address, in Lincoln's handwriting.

The Granger Collection, New York.

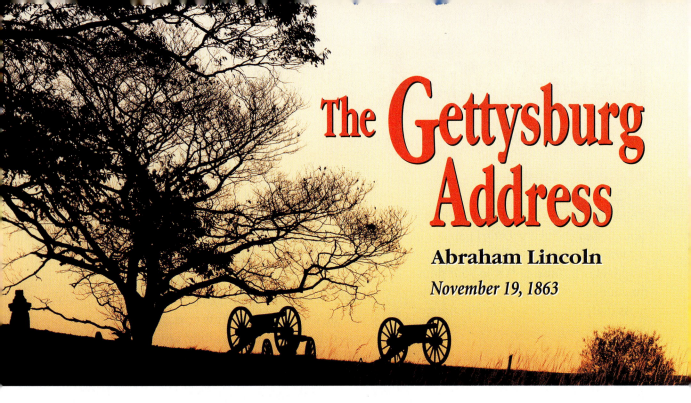

The Gettysburg Address

Abraham Lincoln

November 19, 1863

Four score and seven years ago our fathers brought forth on this continent a new nation, conceived in liberty, and dedicated to the proposition that all men are created equal.

Now we are engaged in a great civil war, testing whether that nation, or any nation so conceived and so dedicated, can long endure. We are met on a great battlefield of that war. We have come to dedicate a portion of that field, as a final resting place for those who here gave their lives that that nation might live. It is altogether fitting and proper that we should do this.

But, in a larger sense, we cannot dedicate—we cannot consecrate—we cannot hallow°—this ground. The brave men, living and dead, who struggled here, have consecrated it, far above our poor power to add or detract. The world will little note nor long remember what we say here, but it can never forget what they did here. It is for us the living, rather, to be dedicated here to the unfinished work which they who fought here have thus far so nobly advanced. It is rather for us to be here dedicated to the great task remaining before us—that from these honored dead we take increased devotion to that cause for which they gave the last full measure of devotion—that we here highly resolve that these dead shall not have died in vain—that this nation, under God, shall have a new birth of freedom—and that government of the people, by the people, for the people, shall not perish from the earth.

The Battle of Gettysburg (detail) (1870) by Peter Frederick Rothermel. Oil on canvas.

The State Museum of Pennsylvania, Pennsylvania Historical and Museum Commission.

° *Consecrate* and *hallow* are synonyms meaning "make or declare holy." Lincoln is using repetition to create rhythm and emphasize his point.

Meet the Writer

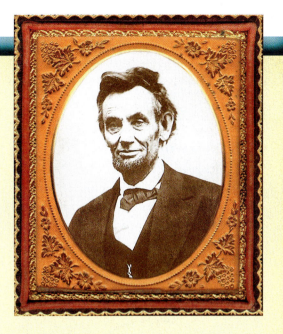

Abraham Lincoln

Plain Speaking

Abraham Lincoln (1809–1865) was born in rural Kentucky. He spent his childhood there and in Indiana. At the age of twenty-one, he moved with his family to Illinois, where he taught himself law.

Lincoln soon became involved in politics, first at the state level and then at the national level. He was elected president in 1860, during a period of crisis that quickly erupted into war between the Northern and Southern states. In 1863, during the Civil War, he issued the Emancipation Proclamation. This proclamation led to the adoption of the Thirteenth Amendment to the Constitution, outlawing slavery.

Although Lincoln led the Union to victory, he did not live to see his country reunited. As he sat in a Washington theater, watching a play, Lincoln was shot by an assassin, John Wilkes Booth.

Lincoln believed in speaking and writing as clearly and simply as he could, so that people could understand exactly what he meant. He once explained:

❝Among my earliest recollections I remember how, when a mere child, I used to get irritated when anybody talked to me in a way I could not understand. . . . I can remember going to my little bedroom, after hearing the neighbors talk of an evening with my father, and spending the night walking up and down and trying to make out what was the exact meaning of some of their, to me, dark sayings. I could not sleep when I got on such a hunt after an idea, until I had caught it; and when I thought I had got it, I was not satisfied until I had put it in language plain enough, as I thought, for any boy I knew to comprehend. This was a kind of passion with me, and it has stuck by me.❞

from I Have a Dream

Make the Connection
Quickwrite ✏️

Pick one of the words from the list below, and create a **cluster map**, in which you write what you think of when you hear that word. Draw as many circles on your map as you like.

- freedom
- democracy
- equality
- liberty

from allusions to texts familiar to many Americans, such as this famous passage from the Bible, from Isaiah 40:4–5:

❝Every valley shall be exalted, and every mountain and hill shall be made low: And the crooked shall be made straight, and the rough places plain.❞

As you read "I Have a Dream," see what other allusions you recognize.

Cluster map: fair teachers — justice — Supreme Court — right to trial by jury

Literary Focus
Allusion

An **allusion** is a reference to features of a culture that people share—literature, religion, history, mythology, sports. "I Have a Dream," a speech by Martin Luther King, Jr., draws much of its power

Vocabulary Development

Martin Luther King, Jr., uses these words in his "I Have a Dream" speech:

creed (krēd) *n.:* statement of belief or principles. *The Declaration of Independence is our nation's creed.*

oasis (ō·ā′sis) *n.:* place or thing offering relief. *King hopes to transform the United States into an oasis of freedom and justice.*

exalted (eg·zôlt′id) *v.:* lifted up. *King's stirring speech exalted his audience.*

discords (dis′kôrdz′) *n.:* conflicts. *King urges us to turn discords into harmony.*

prodigious (prō·dij′əs) *adj.:* huge; amazing. *King's dream involves a prodigious task: bringing justice to all people.*

SKILLS FOCUS

Literary Skills
Understand allusion.

Background
Literature and Social Studies

On August 28, 1963, more than 200,000 Americans of all races and from almost every state in the Union took part in a march in Washington, D.C. The marchers demanded full equality for African Americans.

Late in the day, Martin Luther King, Jr., rose to speak. His words, which were heard by people across the country on TV and radio, deeply moved his listeners. King's concluding words are reprinted here as "I Have a Dream."

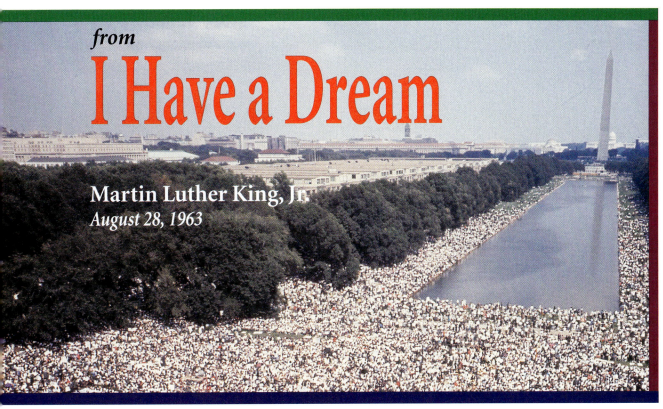

from

I Have a Dream

Martin Luther King, Jr.
August 28, 1963

Marchers gather in front of the Lincoln Memorial in Washington, D.C., with the Washington Monument in the distance.

I say to you today, my friends, that in spite of the difficulties and frustrations of the moment I still have a dream. It is a dream deeply rooted in the American Dream.

I have a dream that one day this nation will rise up and live out the true meaning of its creed: "We hold these truths to be self-evident; that all men are created equal."

I have a dream that one day on the red hills of Georgia the sons of former slaves and the sons of former slave owners will be able to sit down together at the table of brotherhood.

I have a dream that one day even the state of Mississippi, a desert state sweltering with the heat of injustice and oppression, will be transformed into an oasis of freedom and justice.

I have a dream that my four little children will one day live in a nation where they will not be judged by the color of their skin but by the content of their character.

I have a dream today.

I have a dream that one day every valley shall be exalted, every hill and mountain shall be made low, the rough places will be made plain, and the crooked places will be made straight, and the glory of the Lord shall be revealed, and all flesh shall see it together.

This is our hope. This is the faith with which I return to the South. With this faith

Vocabulary

creed (krēd) *n.:* statement of belief or principles.
oasis (ō·ā′sis) *n.:* place in a desert with plants and a supply of water; place or thing offering relief.
exalted (eg·zôlt′id) *v.:* raised; lifted up.

Martin Luther King, Jr., delivers his "I Have a Dream" speech.

we will be able to hew out of the mountain of despair a stone of hope. With this faith we will be able to transform the jangling discords of our nation into a beautiful symphony of brotherhood. With this faith we will be able to work together, to pray together, to struggle together, to go to jail together, to stand up for freedom together, knowing that we will be free one day.

This will be the day when all of God's children will be able to sing with new meaning "My country 'tis of thee, sweet land of liberty, of thee I sing. Land where my fathers died, land of the pilgrim's pride, from every mountainside, let freedom ring."

And if America is to be a great nation, this must become true. So let freedom ring from the prodigious hilltops of New Hampshire. Let freedom ring from the mighty mountains of New York. Let freedom ring from the heightening Alleghenies of Pennsylvania! Let freedom ring from the snowcapped Rockies of Colorado!

Let freedom ring from the curvaceous peaks of California!

But not only that; let freedom ring from Stone Mountain of Georgia!

Let freedom ring from Lookout Mountain of Tennessee!

Let freedom ring from every hill and molehill of Mississippi. From every mountainside, let freedom ring.

When we let freedom ring, when we let it ring from every village and every hamlet, from every state and every city, we will be able to speed up that day when all of God's children, black men and white men, Jews and Gentiles, Protestants and Catholics, will be able to join hands and sing in the words of the old Negro spiritual, "Free at last! Free at last! Thank God almighty, we are free at last!"

Vocabulary

discords (dis′kôrdz′) *n.:* conflicts; disagreements.
prodigious (prō·dij′əs) *adj.:* huge; amazing.

Meet the Writer

Martin Luther King, Jr.

Martin Luther King, Jr., with picture of Gandhi.

"Nonviolence Is the Answer"

Martin Luther King, Jr. (1929–1968), grew up in Atlanta, Georgia. He started college at the age of fifteen. After he graduated, he went on to Crozer Theological Seminary in Pennsylvania to become a Baptist minister, like his father and grandfather. King continued his studies in Boston, where he received a doctorate degree. He then returned to the South to take a position as pastor of a church in Montgomery, Alabama. King was shocked by the intense racism and the strict segregation he saw in Montgomery. He helped organize the Montgomery bus boycott and went on to become a national leader in the civil rights movement, facing violence and risking arrest to spread his message of nonviolent resistance. In 1964, four years before he was assassinated, he accepted the Nobel Peace Prize with these words:

> **"Nonviolence is the answer to the crucial political and moral questions of our time; the need for man to overcome oppression and violence without resorting to oppression and violence."**

King with the civil rights activist Stokely Carmichael at a protest, 1966.

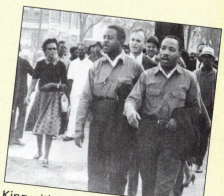

King with his chief aide, Ralph Abernathy, 1963.

First Thoughts

1. What two American ideals seem most important to Abraham Lincoln? Do you agree with him? Explain.

Thinking Critically

2. What challenge does Lincoln propose for the future? How is honoring the dead connected to that challenge?

3. Find two examples of **refrains** in Lincoln's speech. What idea is he trying to emphasize in each case?

4. In his speech, King makes **allusions,** or references, to the Declaration of Independence and to the patriotic hymn "My Country, 'Tis of Thee." Why would King want to remind his audience of those texts?

5. Find several examples of **refrain** (repeated words or sentences) in King's speech. What important ideas are being emphasized?

6. Describe in a sentence or two what you think the **theme,** or message, of the Gettysburg Address is. How is it similar to King's theme? How is it different?

Reading Check

a. What is happening in the present (1863)? How is that related to the past, according to Lincoln?

b. List three important things Martin Luther King, Jr., hopes to see come about.

Extending Interpretations

7. In Meet the Writer on page 481, Lincoln describes his efforts to express ideas in plain language. Do you think the Gettysburg Address is easy to understand? Support your opinion with examples from the text. Which passages, if any, gave you trouble? (Refer to the notes you made as you read.)

WRITING

Writing from Another Point of View

Both Abraham Lincoln and Martin Luther King, Jr., were assassinated. Using the Internet or a library, research the life history of Lincoln or King or of another political leader who was assassinated, such as John F. Kennedy, Malcolm X, or Mohandas Gandhi. Write a poem, a letter, or a eulogy (a speech praising a person who has died) from the point of view of one of that person's followers.

INTERNET
Projects and Activities
Keyword: LE5 8-4

SKILLS FOCUS

Literary Skills
Analyze refrains and allusions.

Reading Skills
Use dialogue-with-the-text notes.

Writing Skills
Write a poem, letter, or eulogy from another point of view.

After You Read   Vocabulary Development

Word Analogies

A **word analogy** is a puzzle that consists of two pairs of words that have the same relationship. (For a review of the types of analogies, see page 274.)

(For a review of the types of analogies, see page 274.)

Word Bank

creed
oasis
exalted
discords
prodigious

PRACTICE 1

Complete each sentence below with the word from the Word Bank that fits best. Use each word only once.

1. *Suffering* is to *relief* as *desert* is to _____.
2. _____ is to *tiny* as *bright* is to *dim*.
3. *Arguments* is to _____ as *agreements* is to *harmonies*.
4. *Dream* is to *vision* as _____ is to *belief*.
5. *Raised* is to *sunken* as _____ is to *lowered*.

Words in Context

PRACTICE 2

Practice using word meanings within the appropriate context by filling in the blanks in the following paragraphs with the best word from the Word Bank. (Hint: You'll have to use each word twice.) You may recognize two characters from a famous novel, which has been made into many movies for screen and TV.

Ebenezer Scrooge took it as his _____ that money should be made and saved, not spent. For him the most _____ task of humankind was making money. His _____ talent for getting rich was legendary, as were his many _____ with anyone who tried to get money from him. He sought no _____ in which to rest from struggle and strife.

Bob Cratchit's _____ was to do the best he could in life, at work and at home. He put in a(n) _____ effort at his job, which was never appreciated by his stingy boss. He got through the trials and _____ of his workday by remembering his home, his _____. Cratchit's spirits were soothed and _____ each evening when he walked through his door and was greeted by his loving family.

What is the book (or movie)?

SKILLS FOCUS

Vocabulary Skills
Complete word analogies; use words in context.

Taking Notes and Making Outlines

Reading Focus

Taking Notes and Outlining

Good informational material is fascinating when you read it, but when you try to share your interest with a friend, you often cannot remember the details. You might even have forgotten the writer's main idea. Here are two good ways to keep track of important ideas and interesting details: (1) take notes, and (2) make an outline.

Note cards. Gather a stack of three-by-five-inch index cards. (You can substitute slips of paper of a similar size.)

Main ideas. As you read each paragraph, stop and ask yourself, "What is the main idea?" Some paragraphs may offer a new idea, while others will offer supporting evidence for an idea presented in a previous paragraph. Write each main idea at the top of a note card.

Details. On each card containing a main idea, write all the important supporting details. Try to use your own words. If you do use the writer's words, put quotation marks around them.

Outline. Once your cards are filled, you can organize your notes in an outline. Here is how an **informal outline** is set up:

> Informal Outline
> I. First main idea
>   A. Supporting detail
>   B. Supporting detail
>   C. Supporting detail
> II. Second main idea
> [Etc.]

A formal outline is useful when you are preparing notes for a composition of your own, especially a research paper. Here is how a **formal outline** is set up:

> Formal Outline
> I. First main idea
>   A. Supporting point
>   1. Detail
>   2. Detail
>   B. Supporting point
> II. Second main idea
>   A. Supporting point
>   1. Detail
>   2. Detail
>   B. Supporting point
> [Etc.]

A formal outline must always have at least two items at each level. That is, if there is a I, there must be at least a II, if not a III; if there is an A, there must be at least a B, and so on.

■ Here's the start of an informal outline of the interview with the civil rights activist John Lewis that you are about to read. It's up to you to outline the rest.

> I. Childhood experience of segregation
>   A. Encountered separate water fountains
>   B. Encountered separate seating in movie theaters
>   C. Found experience differed from religious teaching

SKILLS FOCUS

Reading Skills
Take notes; create an outline.

from **The Power of Nonviolence**

John Lewis, *interviewed by Joan Morrison and Robert K. Morrison*

When I was a boy, I would go downtown to the little town of Troy, and I'd see the signs saying "White" and "Colored" on the water fountains. There'd be a beautiful, shining water fountain in one corner of the store marked "White," and in another corner was just a little spigot marked "Colored." I saw the signs saying "White Men," "Colored Men," and "White Women," "Colored Women." And at the theater we had to go upstairs to go to a movie. You bought your ticket at the same window that the white people did, but they could sit downstairs, and you had to go upstairs.

Lunch-counter segregation protest.

I wondered about that, because it was not in keeping with my religious faith, which taught me that we were all the same in the eyes of God. And I had been taught that all men are created equal.

It really hit me when I was fifteen years old, when I heard about Martin Luther King, Jr., and the Montgomery bus boycott. Black people were walking the streets for more than a year rather than riding segregated buses. To me it was like a great sense of hope, a light. Many of the teachers at the high school that I attended were from Montgomery, and they would tell us about what was happening there. That, more than any other event, was the turning point for me, I think. It gave me a way out. . . .

Lewis went on to college, where he attended workshops and studied the philosophy of nonviolence.

In February 1960, we planned the first mass lunch-counter sit-in. About five hundred students, black and white, from various colleges showed up and participated in a nonviolent workshop the night before the sit-in. Some of them came from as far away as Pomona College in California and Beloit College in Wisconsin.

We made a list of what we called the "Rules of the Sit-in"—the do's and don'ts—and we mimeographed it on an old machine and passed it out to all the students. I wish I had a copy of this list today. I remember it said things like, "Sit up straight. Don't talk back. Don't laugh. Don't strike back." And at the end it said, "Remember the teachings of Jesus, Gandhi, Thoreau, and Martin Luther King, Jr."

Lunch-counter sit-in.

Then the next day it began. We wanted to make a good impression. The young men put on their coats and ties, and the young ladies their heels and stockings. We selected seven stores to go into, primarily the chain stores — Woolworth's, Kresge's, and the

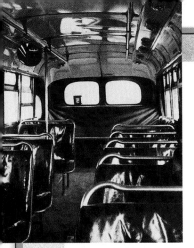

Empty bus during the Montgomery bus boycott.

Walgreen drugstore—and we had these well-dressed young people with their books going to the lunch counters. They would sit down in a very orderly, peaceful, nonviolent fashion and wait to be served. They would be reading a book or doing their homework or whatever while they were waiting.

I was a spokesperson for one of these groups. I would ask to be served, and we would be told that we wouldn't be served. The lunch counter would be closed, and they would put up a sign saying "Closed—not serving." Sometimes they would lock the door, leave us in there, and turn out all the lights, and we would continue to sit.

After we had been doing this for a month, it was beginning to bother the business community and other people in Nashville. We heard that the city had decided to allow the police officials to stand by and allow the hoodlum element to come in and attack us—and that the police would arrest us—to try to stop the sit-ins. We had a meeting after we heard that, to decide did we still want to go down on this particular day. And we said yes.

I was with the group that went into the Woolworth's there. The lunch counter was upstairs—just a long row of stools in front of a counter. My group went up to sit there, and after we had been there for half an hour or so, a group of young white men came in and began pulling people off the lunch-counter stools, putting lighted cigarettes out in our hair or faces or down our backs, pouring ketchup and hot sauce all over us, pushing us down to the floor and beating us. Then the police came in and started arresting *us.* They didn't arrest a single person that beat us, but they arrested all of us and charged us with disorderly conduct.

That was the first mass arrest of students in the South for participating in a sit-in. Over one hundred of us were arrested that day. We were sentenced, all of us, to a fifty-dollar fine or thirty days in jail, and since we wouldn't pay the fine, we were put in jail. . . .

Lewis and his fellow students were jailed, but they continued their protests when they were released. In April 1960, the mayor of Nashville agreed that the lunch counters should be desegregated.

And so Nashville became the first major city in the South to desegregate its downtown lunch counters and restaurants. That was the power of nonviolence. . . .

I think one thing the movement did for all of us in the South, black and white alike, was to have a cleansing effect on our psyche. I think it brought up a great deal of the dirt and a great deal of the guilt from under the rug to the top, so that we could deal with it, so that we could see it in the light. And I think that in a real sense, we are a different people. We are better people. It freed even those of us who didn't participate—black people, white people alike—to be a little more human.

Civil rights activists march in Selma, Alabama.

Analyzing an Outline

from **The Power of Nonviolence**

Test Practice

1. Suppose an **outline** of this article listed these main ideas:

   > **I.** Experiences of segregation
   > **II.**
   > **III.** Lunch-counter sit-ins
   > **IV.** Effect of the movement

   Which **main idea** should be II?
   A Segregated water fountains
   B Montgomery bus boycott
   C Rules of the sit-in
   D Woolworth's lunch counter

2. Suppose an **outline** of this article has a main heading that reads "Hoodlums Attack Demonstrators." Which of these details does *not* support that main idea?
   F Pulled demonstrators off stools
   G Poured hot sauce on demonstrators
   H Beat up demonstrators
   J Fined demonstrators fifty dollars

3. John Lewis said that the police "didn't arrest a single person that beat us, but they arrested all of us and charged us with disorderly conduct." This shows that the police were —
   A trying to keep law and order
   B prejudiced against the protesters
   C just doing their job
   D fair to everyone involved

4. Which of the following is the *best* statement of John Lewis's **main idea** in this article?
   F Nonviolence makes us all better people.
   G All men are created equal.
   H Police arrest protesters unfairly.
   J Injustice can be overcome with nonviolence.

Constructed Response

1. What were the "Rules of the Sit-in"?
2. What did the students do to make a good impression?
3. How did the lunch-counter workers respond to the sit-ins?
4. How did the city officials respond to the sit-ins?
5. What was the result of the sit-ins?
6. According to John Lewis, how did the nonviolent movement affect black people and white people?
7. Complete the outline started for you on page 488.

SKILLS FOCUS

Reading Skills
Analyze an outline; identify main ideas.

Comparing Literature

Literary Focus

Theme: The American Dream

Today freedom and equality are guaranteed to people of all races, religions, and genders, according to the laws of the United States. The promise of freedom and equality has long inspired waves of immigrants to come to the United States in search of the American dream.

Before even the Pilgrims came to America, this vast continent held millions of native peoples. These people have struggled for years to gain equality and attain their dreams.

The first immigrants from England to settle in North America, in the 1600s, dreamed of establishing a society where they could experience religious freedom. Later, in the 1800s, millions of Europeans poured through the open doors of America. These often desperately poor and persecuted people dreamed of a society where their children would not be judged by their language or religion.

At the same time, the millions of people from Africa who were still being held in slavery dreamed of living in freedom, without fearing oppression because of their skin color.

> ### The American Dream
>
> - America offers endless opportunity to those willing to work hard.
> - People can find freedom in America.
> - All Americans are equal under the law.
> - Americans respect one another and celebrate their differences as well as their similarities.
> - America offers a refuge for people fleeing oppression.

SKILLS FOCUS

Literary Skills Understand theme.

Reading Skills Compare and contrast texts.

Reading Skills

Comparing and Contrasting

After you read the three texts that follow, you'll compare their views of the American dream. What does the American dream mean to you?

Before You Read

In 1886, the Statue of Liberty, a gift from France to the United States, was erected in New York Harbor. In 1903, a poem by Emma Lazarus called "The New Colossus" was engraved on a bronze plaque that was placed inside the pedestal of the statue. The title of the poem refers to the Colossus, a huge bronze (or brazen) statue of the Greek god Helios that towered over the harbor of the Greek city of Rhodes from 280 to 225 B.C. Lazarus contrasts the imposing Greek statue with "the new Colossus," the Statue of Liberty, a woman whose torch lights the golden door of America, offering refuge to those seeking freedom.

Think about what the Statue of Liberty means to you. Then, write down three words that come to mind when you think of America.

The New Colossus

Emma Lazarus

Not like the brazen giant of Greek fame,
With conquering limbs astride from land to land; **❶**
Here at our sea-washed, sunset gates shall stand
A mighty woman with a torch, whose flame
5 Is the imprisoned lightning, and her name
Mother of Exiles. From her beacon-hand **❷**
Glows world-wide welcome; her mild eyes command
The air-bridged harbor that twin cities frame.
"Keep, ancient lands, your storied pomp!"° cries she
10 With silent lips. "Give me your tired, your poor,
Your huddled masses yearning to breathe free,
The wretched refuse of your teeming° shore.
Send these, the homeless, tempest-tost° to me.
I lift my lamp beside the golden door!" **❸**

---

9. **pomp** *n.:* splendor; magnificence.
12. **teeming** *v* used as *adj.:* crowded.
13. **tempest-tost:** upset by storm. *Tempest* here refers to other hardships as well.

IDENTIFY

❶ What details tell you that the old Colossus was huge and probably warlike in appearance?

ANALYZE

❷ What name does the speaker give the Statue of Liberty? In what way does the statue differ from the old Colossus?

INTERPRET

❸ In your own words, restate what the speaker imagines the statue is saying.

Meet the Writer

Emma Lazarus

"Mother of Exiles"

"The New Colossus" is the one poem that **Emma Lazarus** (1849–1887) is remembered for today. In 1903, the words of the poem were engraved on a bronze plaque that was placed inside the Statue of Liberty's pedestal.

Lazarus was born into a wealthy and cultured family in New York City. She noted that she had been "brought up exclusively under American institutions, amid liberal influences, in a society where all differences of race and faith were fused."

From an early age, Lazarus was privately tutored in the classics and foreign languages. She also exhibited talent as a poet: Her first collection of poetry was published when she was a teenager. These poems were praised by the famed philosopher and poet Ralph Waldo Emerson, who would become an important mentor to Lazarus.

Lazarus's early poetry reflects a fascination with Romantic themes. She would later write in defense of the Jews being persecuted in Russia during the 1880s. After the Statue of Liberty committee read an article by Lazarus in support of Jewish refugees from Russia, they asked her to write a poem for the statue's pedestal. The result was the powerful sonnet "The New Colossus," in which she refers to the Statue of Liberty as the "Mother of Exiles." The dedication ceremony for the statue took place in 1886. Unfortunately, Lazarus died before she could see the statue.

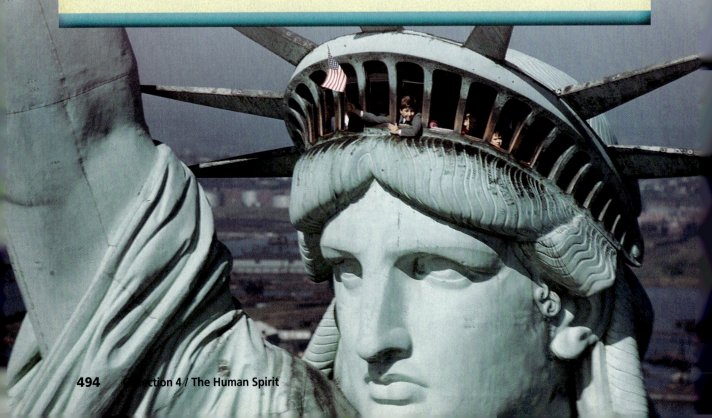

First Thoughts

1. Which words spoken by the statue do you think are the most important? Read those lines aloud.

2. Think about the words you wrote down to describe what America makes you think of. Would you change any of these words after reading this poem?

Thinking Critically

3. In the late 1800s, immigrants from Europe poured into America. What do you think the statue means when she tells these countries to keep their "storied pomp"? Read this line aloud the way you think the statue would say it.

4. The statue calls the people coming to America "huddled masses." What do they long for?

5. Do you think the people the statue addresses have found what they sought in America? Explain your response.

Comparing Literature

6. Think about what the poem, particularly the statue's words to people coming to the United States, reveals about the American dream. In the chart below, write down what the poem says about that dream. You'll finish the chart after you have read the next two selections.

Comparing Expressions of the American Dream	
	Expressions of the American Dream
"The New Colossus"	
"Refugee in America"	
"The First Americans"	

Reading Check

a. In lines 3–8, how does the speaker describe the statue that stands at New York's "gates"?

b. According to lines 9–14, what does the statue seem to say?

c. Whom is the statue talking to? What line tells you?

SKILLS FOCUS

Literary Skills
Analyze theme.

Reading Skills
Compare and contrast texts.

By the Gate (1953) by Ernest Crichlow. Oil on board.

The Harmon and Harriet Kelley Foundation for the Arts. Collection of Harmon and Harriet Kelley, San Antonio, Texas.

INTERPRET

❶ What might this speaker have experienced that makes him feel like crying?

Before You Read

This poem about the American dream was written around 1947 by the African American poet Langston Hughes. Before you read, think for a minute about the way you feel when you hear the words *freedom* and *liberty*.

Refugee in America

Langston Hughes

There are words like *Freedom*
Sweet and wonderful to say.
On my heart-strings freedom sings
All day everyday.

There are words like *Liberty*
That almost make me cry.
If you had known what I knew
You would know why. ❶

Meet the Writer

Langston Hughes

"Poems Are Like Rainbows"

Born in Joplin, Missouri, **Langston Hughes** (1902–1967) began writing poetry in his early teens. As a young man he traveled around the world and held many jobs. One day in 1925, Hughes discovered that the famous poet Vachel Lindsay was staying at the Washington, D.C., hotel where he was working as a busboy. Hughes left some of his poems beside Lindsay's dinner plate. That night, Lindsay read them aloud at a poetry reading, announcing that he had discovered a great new poet. (Hughes was actually already a published poet and had a contract with Alfred Knopf, a major publisher in New York. Still, Lindsay's endorsement helped.)

In his autobiography *The Big Sea* (1940), Hughes describes his writing process:

66 There are seldom many changes in my poems, once they're down. Generally, the first two or three lines come to me from something I'm thinking about, or looking at, or doing, and the rest of the poem (if there is to be a poem) flows from those first few lines, usually right away. If there is a chance to put the poem down then, I write it down. If not, I try to remember it until I get to a pencil and paper; for poems are like rainbows: They escape you quickly. 99

First Thoughts

1. Suppose the speaker of this poem was talking to you. How would you respond to what he says?

Thinking Critically

2. The title suggests that the speaker sees himself as a refugee. What is a refugee? Why does the speaker consider himself a refugee in his own country?

3. The speaker has different reactions to two words that mean nearly the same thing. Do you see any differences in meaning between the words *liberty* and *freedom*? How do the words make you feel? Explain.

Reading Check

a. What words does the speaker use to describe the word *freedom* in stanza 1?

b. What happens to the speaker when he hears the word *liberty*?

Comparing Literature

4. In the chart that follows, write down your answers to these questions:

- Which aspects of the American dream does the speaker of this poem refer to?
- What does he think America promises us?
- What does he think about the way America has kept that promise?

Add any other ideas you have about the way the poem comments on the American dream. After you respond to the next selection, your chart will be complete with details from all three texts.

Comparing Expressions of the American Dream	
	Expressions of the American Dream
"The New Colossus"	
"Refugee in America"	
"The First Americans"	

SKILLS
FOCUS

Literary Skills
Analyze theme.

Reading Skills
Compare and contrast texts.

In 1927, an organization called the Grand Council Fire of American Indians sent a group of representatives from the Chippewa, Ottawa, Navajo, Sioux, and Winnebago peoples to address the mayor of Chicago. Their goal was to persuade him that American Indians should be more fairly and accurately represented in textbooks and classrooms. Mayor William Hale Thompson, who had been reelected just a month before the council met with him, had campaigned on the slogan "America First." (Thompson opposed U.S. involvement in world affairs and claimed that the British government influenced the U.S. government's policies.) "The First Americans" comments on this slogan and on other patriotic slogans of the time which unthinkingly excluded many Americans from the American dream.

Before you read, think about the way various groups in America are portrayed in your textbooks. Do you think the portrayals are fair? Jot down some responses to this question.

The First Americans

The Grand Council Fire of American Indians
December 1, 1927

To the mayor of Chicago:
You tell all white men "America First." We believe in that. We are the only ones, truly, that are one hundred percent. We therefore ask you, while you are teaching

IDENTIFY

❶ What is the council asking of the mayor?

EVALUATE

❷ According to the council, what words do white people use to describe American Indians? Note the date when this speech was delivered. Are Indians still spoken of this way today?

Pueblo owl pottery (20th century).

schoolchildren about America First, teach them truth about the First Americans. ❶

We do not know if school histories are pro-British, but we do know that they are unjust to the life of our people—the American Indian. They call all white victories battles and all Indian victories massacres. The battle with Custer[1] has been taught to schoolchildren as a fearful massacre on our part. We ask that this, as well as other incidents, be told fairly. If the Custer battle was a massacre, what was Wounded Knee?[2]

History books teach that Indians were murderers—is it murder to fight in self-defense? Indians killed white men because white men took their lands, ruined their hunting grounds, burned their forests, destroyed their buffalo. White men penned[3] our people on reservations, then took away the reservations. White men who rise to protect their property are called patriots—Indians who do the same are called murderers.

White men call Indians treacherous—but no mention is made of broken treaties on the part of the white man. White men say that Indians were always fighting. It was only our lack of skill in white man's warfare that led to our defeat. An Indian mother prayed that her boy be a great medicine man rather than a great warrior. It is true that we had our own small battles, but in the main we were peace loving and home loving.

White men called Indians thieves—and yet we lived in frail skin lodges and needed no locks or iron bars. White men call Indians savages. What is civilization? Its marks are a noble religion and philosophy, original arts, stirring music, rich story and legend. We had these. Then we were not savages, but a civilized race. ❷

We made blankets that were beautiful, that the white man with all his machinery has never been able to duplicate. We made baskets that were beautiful. We wove in beads and colored quills designs that were not just decorative motifs but were the outward expression of our very thoughts. We made pottery—pottery that was useful, and beautiful as

---

1. **battle with Custer:** the Battle of the Little Bighorn, which took place in 1876 in what is now Montana. General George A. Custer (1839–1876) led an attack on an Indian village and was killed along with all of his troops by Sioux and Cheyenne warriors.
2. **Wounded Knee:** Wounded Knee Creek, in South Dakota, was the site of a battle in 1890 between U.S. soldiers and Sioux whom they had captured. About two hundred Sioux men, women, and children were killed by the soldiers.
3. **penned** v.: confined or enclosed. (A pen is a fenced area where animals are kept.)

well. Why not make schoolchildren acquainted with the beautiful handicrafts in which we were skilled? Put in every school Indian blankets, baskets, pottery.

We sang songs that carried in their melodies all the sounds of nature—the running of waters, the sighing of winds, and the calls of the animals. Teach these to your children that they may come to love nature as we love it.

We had our statesmen—and their oratory[4] has never been equaled. Teach the children some of these speeches of our people, remarkable for their brilliant oratory.

We played games—games that brought good health and sound bodies. Why not put these in your schools? We told stories. Why not teach schoolchildren more of the wholesome proverbs and legends of our people? Tell them how we loved all that was beautiful. That we killed game only for food, not for fun. Indians think white men who kill for fun are murderers. ❸

Tell your children of the friendly acts of Indians to the white people who first settled here. Tell them of our leaders and heroes and their deeds. Tell them of Indians such as Black Partridge, Shabbona, and others who many times saved the people of Chicago at great danger to themselves. Put in your history books the Indian's part in the World War. Tell how the Indian fought for a country of which he was not a citizen, for a flag to which he had no claim, and for a people that have treated him unjustly. ❹

The Indian has long been hurt by these unfair books. We ask only that our story be told in fairness. We do not ask you to overlook what we did, but we do ask you to understand it. A true program of America First will give a generous place to the culture and history of the American Indian.

We ask this, Chief, to keep sacred the memory of our people.

---

4. **oratory** (ôr′ə·tôr′ē) *n.*: skill in public speaking; the art of public speaking.

Pomo feathered basket (c. 1810).

IDENTIFY

❸ What evidence does the council present to demonstrate the richness of American Indian culture? Name seven facts about the Indians that the council wants children to be taught.

EVALUATE

❹ Review the suggestions in this paragraph. Do you think students learn these facts about Indians today?

Hopewell artifact.

First Thoughts

1. If you heard this speech delivered today, how would you respond to it?

Thinking Critically

2. A **stereotype** is a fixed idea about a group of people. "Athletes are not intellectual" is a stereotype. So is "Girls are not good at fixing plumbing." Stereotypes are often offensive. What stereotypes about American Indians can you find in this speech?

3. This speech was delivered in 1927. Have any of its suggestions been put into effect? Are parts of the speech still relevant today? Discuss your responses.

Comparing Literature

4. In the chart below, write down how this speech reflects the American dream. Be sure to consider the information presented in the box on page 492. You'll use your finished chart, including the notes you added after reading "The New Colossus" and "Refugee in America," to plan an essay comparing views of the American dream expressed in these three texts.

Reading Check

To review the arguments presented in this speech, complete the outline that follows:

1. Purpose of speech (paragraph l):

2. Ways in which school history books are unjust to the American Indian:

    A.

    B.

    etc.

3. Evidence that American Indians are highly civilized people:

    A.

    B.

    etc.

4. What children should be taught about American Indians:

    A.

    B.

    etc.

Comparing Expressions of the American Dream	
	Expressions of the American Dream
"The New Colossus"	
"Refugee in America"	
"The First Americans"	

SKILLS FOCUS

Literary Skills
Analyze theme.

Reading Skills
Compare and contrast texts.

Comparing "The New Colossus," "Refugee in America," and "The First Americans"

Assignment

1. Writing a Comparison-Contrast Essay

Write an essay of four paragraphs comparing views of the American dream expressed in "The New Colossus," "Refugee in America," and "The First Americans." To find points of comparison for your essay, review the chart you filled in after you read each selection. Also check the box on page 492 that lists aspects of the American dream.

Organize your essay in the following way:

Paragraph 1: Explain how "The New Colossus" reflects the American dream.

Paragraph 2: Explain how "Refugee in America" reflects the American dream.

Paragraph 3: Explain how "The First Americans" reflects the American dream.

Paragraph 4: Describe your response, whether positive or negative, to one of the selections.

> Use the workshop on writing a Comparison-Contrast Essay, pages 516–521, for help with this assignment.

Assignment

2. Presenting an Oral Reading

Prepare one of these three selections for an oral presentation. You might have each selection read by an individual reader or use several voices for each one. Before you begin, copy the selection on a separate piece of paper. Note the punctuation marks that indicate where in your reading you should pause briefly and where you should come to a complete stop. At which points will you show special feeling?

Assignment

3. Researching the Statue

Using history texts and reliable Internet sites, research the history of the Statue of Liberty. Why did France have it made as a gift to the United States? What is the statue holding? What are its dimensions and weight? (How large is one finger, for example?) If you have the equipment, do a multimedia presentation called "Mother of Exiles."

SKILLS FOCUS

Reading Skills
Compare and contrast texts.

First Stop: Ellis Island

As they sailed into New York Harbor, immigrants spotted the Statue of Liberty in the distance and, nearby, Ellis Island. Ellis Island was their first stop in America. Here they were given medical examinations and officially permitted to enter the country. More than twelve million people arrived through this gateway between 1892 and 1954. The peak year was 1907—when more than one million newcomers entered through the "Golden Door."

"Well, I came to America because I heard the streets were paved with gold. When I got here, I found out three things: first, the streets weren't paved with gold; second, they weren't paved at all; and third, I was expected to pave them."

—*Old Italian Story*

"We naturally were in steerage. Everyone had smelly food, and the atmosphere was so thick and dense with smoke and bodily odors that your head itched, and when you went to scratch your head you got lice in your hands. We had six weeks of that."

—Sophia Kreitzberg, a Russian Jewish immigrant in 1908

By courtesy of the Ellis Island Immigration Museum.

"I can remember only the hustle and bustle of those last weeks in Pinsk, the farewells from the family, the embraces and the tears. Going to America then was almost like going to the moon."

—Golda Meir, a Russian Jewish immigrant in 1906

(Opposite, inset) The faces of three immigrants.

(Opposite, top) View of Ellis Island in 1905.

(Opposite, bottom) Jewish war orphans arriving from eastern Europe in 1921.

(Top) A Slovakian mother and daughter wait to be admitted to Ellis Island, about 1915.

(Center) Children's playground, Ellis Island roof garden.

(Left) Women from Guadeloupe, French West Indies, at Ellis Island on April 6, 1911.

"Those who are loudest in their cry of 'America for Americans' do not have to look very far back to find an ancestor who was an immigrant."

—New Immigrants' Protective League, 1906

COMING TO

from **New Kids on the Block: Oral Histories of Immigrant Teens**

Janet Bode

AMITABH, AGE 15, FROM INDIA

It is really bad for us in the beginning. We were five in a two-room apartment. Every day my parents would get up and go out to look for jobs. They knew they had to start all the way at the bottom, that people here didn't count any experience from India. But my father had been a biologist. My mother was a chemistry professor at a university. In India they were both making good money.

Now, though, they would come home every evening and they wouldn't have found anything. They would be very, very sad. They didn't know the bus systems or the subway systems here. They'd get lost. They'd get to someplace and it would be too late. The job would be gone. They'd go to another place and the answer would be no. One day, my parents said, "This is a dead end. We can't find

I think Americans must be the same as us inside.

AMERICA

jobs. We don't have any more money. Nothing. We're going to have to jump into the river." I want to think that they were not being serious, but I still would feel so sad for them and so sad for us.

I couldn't always understand why we had come here. Why would they leave the country where they had been born, where their children had been born? Bhavnagar was a modernized city on the northwest side of India. It had a lot of factories, apartment houses, and private homes. Our home was three stories high, and we lived together with my uncle, my aunt, and my grandparents. My grandparents had another house in a small city called Mehsana. Every summer and during other vacations, we'd go there.

The weather was very warm. In the winters it would get cool enough to wear sweaters, but that was it. No snow. It also used to

Bombay, India.

rain quite a bit. There was a dry and a rainy season, with monsoons° that occurred every year at a certain time. We had a good life there.

I know that people think that in India everybody is poor, that everything is backward. It's not that backward, and it's probably improved since I've been here. We had electricity and running water and traffic jams. I went to a good school. They taught the same subjects as over here, like art, general science, and math, and also some of the different languages of India. I think there are fifteen or sixteen languages. At home we spoke Gujarati, and I learned how to speak Hindi, too.

I knew the food. I loved cooked okra, the vegetable, and pouri, the bread. I had a favorite kind of curry. I knew my future. I knew that when I got married, I would bring my wife to live with my parents. The bride's family would provide a dowry, money and silverware and things like that.

My parents said, though, that we would move to America because us kids would have more opportunities for the future. This was a long time planning. I don't even remember the first time they told me. At first it went so slow. I did not know anything about America. Once, a friend of mine who was Christian took me to this place to get American hot dogs. At that time I had no idea what they were. I took a bite and I spit it out. It tasted disgusting!

But then sometimes I would get interested in coming here. I heard there were big buildings and fast cars. My older brother told me, "Over there in the United States you never see the sun. It's always snowing. When the sun does shine, it's a holiday." I thought, Like WOW! About a month before we left, my parents said, "We're moving to America." That's how they told me. And I said, "Yes." I told my friends in school, and they said, "Yeah, sure, sure." I said, "Really. Watch."

After the first few months my parents found jobs, but the work was very tough on them. My father worked as a messenger, more a job for a boy than a man. He delivered letters and carried packages all over the city. Again, he would get lost the way he had when he was looking

---

° **monsoons** (män·sōōnz′) *n.*: seasonal winds that bring heavy rains to India and other countries in southern Asia for several months of the year.

(Left) Indian neighborhood in Chicago.

for work. He lasted about three or four months doing that until he found another job, and another job. All small jobs. Then he met an Indian man who owned a laboratory who hired him. Now he's sort of back in the area of biology, where he used to work.

My mother started working at a store. She had to fold clothes, mostly. Then she got a better job watching patients at a senior citizens' home. Eventually, she became the dietitian there. And now it's OK for me, too. Kids don't look at me strangely the way they did in the beginning. I had my first hamburger and said, "Forget it!" I threw it out. Eventually, though, I got used to it. Now I eat anything. I eat hot dogs, hamburgers, chicken, and french fries. I love pizza. In India I remember that once we had a fair and they had pizza, a small triangle, for eight rupees, about twenty-five cents. "It was better than the hot dog," I thought then.

Now we live in the suburbs in a big house with four bedrooms. I have my own bedroom, with military posters all over the place. My middle brother and I have a computer. We have more than six hundred games for it. He wants to work in computers. My older brother is in college, the University of Maryland. He wants to be a surgeon.

I'm in the tenth grade. ROTC is my favorite class. I'm planning to go into the military right after I finish high school. It should help me out a lot because ROTC trains us for the military. Since when I was in India, my ambition was to make the military a career. I remember every time my father would take us to a shop, I'd want to buy military-colored clothes. Just yesterday I was looking at some photographs taken at my aunt and uncle's wedding in India. There I was, just a kid, in a military uniform. I don't know why I'm into it so much.

I'm more Americanized than my parents. I still speak Gujarati at home, but now there's English mixed in a lot. I'm trying to get out of my accent as much as possible. And now I have what I guess you could call an American mouth: I have braces. I'd never seen braces in India. I hate wearing them!!! Just like American kids.

XIAOJUN/ "DEBBIE," AGE 13, FROM CHINA

We had a relative, a second uncle, who lived in the United States. He sent us a tape. We all sat in the living room, put it on a tape recorder, and listened. He said we should come to the United States. He told us to bring "lots of clothes because it's really cold, but no cups or plates because they have them. And bring a blanket."

I didn't know any history of America, except someone had told me that everybody had a slave. I thought, great! I'd come here and get my very own slave. I would not have to carry water anymore!

I'm my parents' oldest daughter. I have a younger brother and a younger sister. We lived in a small village in a house made of brick. It had a big room in the middle, and all the way in the back we could go up a ladder to the two bedrooms. We shared the house with my uncle and his family, ten of us all together. Sometimes my parents and my uncle and aunt would talk about their early life. My father and mother came from the city. He was an architect and built houses. I don't know why they all moved to the country. They didn't talk about that.

We had no running water in the house, but we were lucky because we lived near the river. Every morning at 5:00 A.M. I would go and— pant, pant—get water. I used a big stick and carried the water in buckets balanced on it. The water we used for cooking and for bathing.

We slept on hard wooden beds with no mattresses. There was no telephone, no television, no VCR. There was no "I want my MTV." The most we could get was a radio. We had electricity in the house but used it only when my parents said we could. Usually we used candles.

There was a little houselike building with the cooking fire inside. We didn't have much wood, just sticks, so instead we used the stalks from the wheat. First we put them in the sun to dry or we boiled them with other things like carrots for feed for the pigs. We used every part of everything. Mostly my mother and I did the cooking. That was one of the duties of the oldest daughter. We ate mostly rice and vegetables, sometimes my favorite, bok choy. Only at New Year's would we have chicken and soup.

I had other chores. I had to clean the bathroom. Well, that is, it was a sort of bathroom. It was a bucket behind the bed or outside. (In big, big, big houses in the village, they have, like, latrines.) I had to change my brother's diapers. I had to help him take a bath and wash his hair. I had to take care of him and my sister after school. Sometimes I really got mad at them and yelled at them. In China the

Xi'an, Shaanxi province, China.

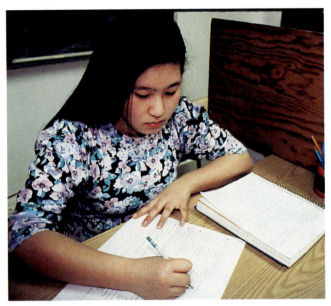
Chinese American student in New Jersey.

oldest starts cooking at five; you change diapers at six.

My mother—she was the oldest daughter in her family, too—had to feed the chickens, collect the eggs, and clean the coop. She and I helped tend the village's pigs. We had a garden; everybody did. And everybody worked on the village farm. Together we grew wheat and rice and other stuff; I forget what.

The weather and the crops were very important. If the weather got bad, oh, oh, we were in trouble. We worried and worried. When it was harvest time, we had to cut this and cut that. The adults were so busy they couldn't even stop to make lunch for the littlest kids.

We helped our families and we went to school. In China our parents were turning us over to the teachers to educate. They could use the same punishment as our parents. That meant the teachers were strict. If we were late, we had to stand outside the door for one hour. If the teachers didn't think we were paying attention, they took a stick and beat us. Or they took a ruler and smacked our hand until it turned red and black and blue. They pulled our ears like they were stretching them. When we talked, monitors wrote our name on the blackboard, or they made us sit without a chair, on an invisible chair. It was really painful when we didn't do good at school, and this was just elementary school!

After school, I would visit and play with my girlfriends. There weren't any games, no toys, no swings. We didn't have bicycles; only my father did. But we did have lots of homework, even for little kids. At my house we would all sit around the table and my mother would help us.

There was a nice thing about school, though. That's where the one TV was. Whole families would go together to watch television, like you might go to the movies together here.

If you want to move from China, it is very difficult. A lot of people sneak out. My father sneaked out using the ID card of my second uncle. First you take a plane. When those people ask you where you are going, you don't say America. You say Thailand, or something like that. Then you go to one place, change planes, and fly to either Mexico or Canada. If you go to Mexico, you have to climb through the mountains at the border, show the fake ID, and say you are just traveling. If you go to Canada, you just drive across. They don't check you a lot. If you're caught, you're in big trouble. They can even put you behind bars.

After my father got here, he began to work and to send money home. My mom used some of it to get fake ID cards for us. Then one day she was piercing my ears and using ginger and oil to help them heal. "Your father wrote a letter," she said. "He's earned enough money and he got an apartment for us."

It was real different in New York. It looked almost nothing like China. No foreigners ever came to my village. I had never seen a black person before. I'd never seen any Americans. My mother told me, "People kidnap and kill each other. You have to watch the window and the door all the time to make sure nobody comes in." I could hardly sleep.

The first night my parents prayed for good luck. They took strings and then put matches to them. And they prayed that I go to school and do well. I was very scared to go. The teacher said, "What's her name?" and my mom told him Xiaojun, my Chinese name. He said, "Does she have an English name? No? Well, what about Debbie?"

"Okay," said my mother and that's how I got my name.

Coming to America has changed my life. Now my parents work too much and too hard and I never see them. But we do have a TV, a radio, a microwave, and a washing machine. I still have things to do, like sweep and mop the floor, do the dishes, mop the table, clean the mirrors, wash the fans when they're dirty, wash the clothes in the washing machine, and take care of my brother. For this I get five dollars a week allowance.

I get up around 7:00 A.M. I leave for school between 7:30 and 8:00. School is over at 3:00. I have to go straight home every day after class. I can't go out at night. They know where I am right this minute. Once I'm home, I study for four hours. Before I eat dinner, my father gives me a little lecture. He says, "Work hard so when you grow up, it will be easier to get a good job and make money. If you don't get a good education and a scholarship, you might have to beg for money. You don't want that."

Middle school on a farm commune near Suzhou, Jiangsu province, China.

I think of being a doctor, help people get healthier and make their lives easier. I also think about being a model, like Christie Brinkley, or maybe an actress or a lawyer or a cop or a singer. My parents say, "Be a secretary." They tell me, too, "Stay involved with our Chinese community," and I do. But, of course, I'm not an ABC, an American-born Chinese. The ABCs sometimes curse at us and call me and my friends FOBs, "fresh off the boat." I don't like that. I turn my eyes away.

I cry at night sometimes. My father says, "What are you doing?" I say, "Nothing. Nothing." I get real confused. In China my father went with me to the school to watch movies on television. We had time together. I used to tell him my problems. Now there is no time. Here I can watch TV anytime and I don't have to get the water or take care of the pigs. I guess I like it better in America.

Meet the Writer

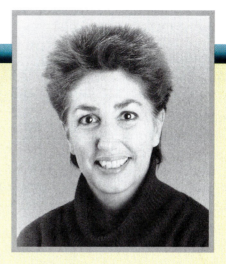

Janet Bode

"We Are a Nation of Immigrants"

"Coming to America" is from *New Kids on the Block: Oral Histories of Immigrant Teens* by **Janet Bode** (1943–1999), a nonfiction writer who lived in New York City. In addition to Amitabh's and Xiaojun's stories, the book includes interviews with teenagers from Afghanistan, El Salvador, Cuba, the Philippines, Mexico, South Korea, Greece, and Vietnam. In her introduction, Bode explained what led her to write her book:

66 We are a nation of immigrants with a national makeup that's forever shifting. We continue to be the American Dream, the land of opportunity. In the mid-1800s, when my German ancestors set sail for America, they were taking the same gamble that brings people here today. Then, nearly all immigrants were from northern and western Europe. Now only five percent come from that part of the world.

Then, if you wanted to come here, you came. But today immigration is more difficult. Over the last hundred-plus years, laws have been passed and extended and changed and amended. Now, once again, Congress is debating the issue of who should be allowed in and who should be left out. And to this day, some of our residents—some of the children and grandchildren of yesterday's immigrants—want to close the borders to our future arrivals. Once inside, some people develop a kind of collective amnesia, forgetting their own immigrant roots. We forget that our country's power and beauty stem from the very fact that we are a collection of different cultures. 99

Writing Workshop

Assignment
Write an essay comparing and contrasting two characters, literary works, or subjects.

Audience
Your teacher, your classmates, and other students in your school.

RUBRIC
Evaluation Criteria

A good comparison-contrast essay

1. introduces the subject clearly and states the essay's main idea

2. discusses at least one similarity and one difference

3. is organized according to either the block method or the point-by-point method

4. presents details and examples to support statements

5. concludes by restating the main idea

SKILLS FOCUS

Writing Skills
Write a comparison-contrast essay.

EXPOSITORY WRITING
Comparison-Contrast Essay

Often the best way to understand something is to compare it with something else. When you **compare,** you look for similarities; when you **contrast,** you look for differences. Comparing and contrasting is particularly useful in the analysis of literature.

Prewriting

1 Choosing a Topic

Consider the following **prompt:**

> One way to gain insight into a literary work is to compare and contrast it with another, similar work. Select a pair of characters, literary selections, or stylistic elements that have some points in common as well as some differences. Examine the characteristics of the two subjects, and write an essay analyzing their similarities and differences. Be sure to state your conclusions.

A good way to find works with a common **subject** or **theme** is to choose two selections from one of the collections in this book. The works you choose don't have to be in the same form, but they must be similar in some way. You can compare and contrast these elements: the themes of a poem and of a short story or essay; a character in a novel or a play and the same character in a movie based on the story or play; or two settings in a short story or a novel.

CALVIN AND HOBBES © Watterson. Reprinted with permission of UNIVERSAL PRESS SYNDICATE. All rights reserved.

2 Finding Similarities and Differences

Decide which features or characteristics to compare and contrast. If you choose to compare and contrast two short stories, discuss the same aspect of both works: theme, setting, or point of view, for example. If you're comparing and contrasting two characters in the same work or in two different works, you might discuss each character's appearance, traits, motivation, and actions.

Use a Venn diagram to collect ideas about your subjects' similarities and differences. List similarities in the area where the two circles overlap; list differences in the nonoverlapping areas. The following diagram compares and contrasts Anne Frank with her sister, Margot.

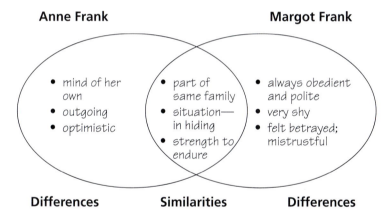

Anne Frank   **Margot Frank**

- mind of her own
- outgoing
- optimistic

- part of same family
- situation—in hiding
- strength to endure

- always obedient and polite
- very shy
- felt betrayed; mistrustful

Differences   **Similarities**   **Differences**

3 Organizing Your Information

There are two basic ways to organize a comparison-contrast essay: the **block method** and the **point-by-point method.** The block method focuses on all points of comparison, or features, for one subject at a time. A block comparison is organized by subject. The point-by-point method alternates between the two subjects, discussing the same point of comparison in each. Both methods are illustrated in the chart on the right.

Block Method

Subject 1:   Anne Frank

Feature 1:   behavior

Feature 2:   personality

Feature 3:   feelings

Subject 2:   Margot Frank

Feature 1:   behavior

Feature 2:   personality

Feature 3:   feelings

Point-by-Point Method

Feature 1:   behavior

Subject 1:   Anne

Subject 2:   Margot

Feature 2:   personality

Subject 1:   Anne

Subject 2:   Margot

Feature 3:   feelings

Subject 1:   Anne

Subject 2:   Margot

Framework for a Comparison–Contrast Essay

Introduction (description of the subjects and clear statement of your main idea about their relationship to each other):

_____

Body (organized according to either the block method or the point-by-point method):

_____

Conclusion (summary of your main idea, noting its importance or usefulness):

_____

Writing Tips

A good **conclusion** is more than just a summary. Expand on the main idea stated in your introduction, and explain its importance. You might also connect the subjects with your own or your readers' experiences or extend the discussion to larger topics related to the subjects.

go.
hrw
.com

INTERNET

More Writer's Models

Keyword: LE5 8-4

Drafting

Construct your essay in three parts:

- **Introduction.** Briefly describe the two subjects of your paper. Identify characters or works by author and title. Include one or two sentences that summarize your main idea about the subjects' similarities and differences.

- **Body.** Discuss the two or three most important similarities and differences. Use either the block method or the point-by-point method of organization.

- **Conclusion.** Leave your readers with a sense of completeness by restating your main idea. You might also add a personal response or comment, as in the student model.

Student Model

Thirteen-year-old Anne Frank and eighteen-year-old Margot Frank are sisters growing up in Amsterdam during World War II. Anne and Margot are alike and different in many ways, and in the play version of *The Diary of Anne Frank,* they are often compared to each other.

Margot is a mature, beautiful young lady. Even through the hardest times in the war, she would keep quiet. She was always obedient and polite; she did everything that she was told, like helping with supper and setting the table. Anne, on the other hand, had a mind of her own. She did not need people to tell her what to do. She was often active, loud, and curious. Anne was a daydreamer, and sometimes her dreams caused people to see her as a troublemaker. A perfect example is when Anne tried on Mrs. Van Daan's fur coat. While pretending she was a young Mrs. Van Daan, Anne spilled milk all over the coat.

Identifies **characters.**

States **main idea.**

Identifies **title.**

Paragraph **elaborates** *first difference: their behavior.*

Uses **transition** *and* **point-by-point method.**

Cites **specific example.**

Mrs. Frank would always compare Anne and Margot, which sometimes made Anne feel insecure. Margot was always known as the ladylike one, whereas Anne was known as the childish one. I do not think that Anne was treated like other girls her age because of Margot's maturity.

Summarizes a character's views of the two girls.

Anne was always outgoing. She had many school friends and grew to be Peter Van Daan's good friend. Margot was charming and polite, but very shy, so it was hard for her to be sociable. When Anne went to see Peter, Margot would always stay in her room and read a book.

Paragraph elaborates second difference: their personalities.

Throughout the play Anne was usually cheerful and peppy. It might have been her way of making the war less painful. Though she would never say it, I think that Margot felt like she had been betrayed and had trouble trusting people. I also think that she felt that she should keep quiet and let others sort things out.

Paragraph elaborates third difference: their feelings.

All in all, I believe that Anne and Margot are different, but they do share one thing: the strength to survive through the harsh times in the Secret Annex. I think they should have forgotten their petty differences and concentrated on what they believed in because they were all fighting for the same reasons.

Conclusion.

Similarity.

Personal response.

—Hanna Jamal
United Nations International School
New York, New York

Clue Words

Transition words and phrases that signal similarities:

also, another, as well as, both, in addition, in the same way, just as, like, neither, not only . . . but also, similarly, too

Transition words and phrases that signal differences:

although, but, however, in contrast, instead, in spite of, on the other hand, unlike, yet

Strategies For Elaboration

Provide **details** and **examples** to back up general statements. The writer of the student model, for instance, refers to a specific incident in the play to support a statement about Anne's behavior. Search for passages to quote and specific details to support the statements you make.

Evaluating and Revising

Use the following chart to evaluate and revise your comparison-contrast essay.

Comparison–Contrast Essay: Content and Organization Guidelines		
▶ **Evaluation Questions**	▶ **Tips**	▶ **Revision Techniques**
❶ **Does your introduction state your main idea? Have you identified works by title and author?**	▶ **Put stars** next to your main idea statement. **Circle** titles and authors.	▶ **Add** a statement of the essay's main idea. **Add** titles of works and authors' names.
❷ **Have you discussed at least one similarity and one difference?**	▶ **Put a check mark** next to each example of comparison or contrast.	▶ If necessary, **add** examples of comparison or contrast. **Delete** irrelevant statements.
❸ **Is your essay organized according to either the block method or the point-by-point method?**	▶ **Label** the method of organization. **Put the letter *A*** above each point about the first subject. **Put the letter *B*** above each point about the second subject.	▶ **Rearrange** sentences into either block order or point-by-point order.
❹ **Have you used transitional words and phrases to signal comparison or contrast?**	▶ **Highlight** transitional words and phrases.	▶ **Add** transitional words that indicate similarities or differences.
❺ **Does your essay provide details and examples to back up general statements?**	▶ **Underline** supporting details and examples.	▶ If necessary, **elaborate** with additional details and examples.
❻ **Does your conclusion restate and expand on the main idea stated in the introduction?**	▶ **Bracket** the main idea. **Underline** statements that expand on your main idea.	▶ **Elaborate** on statements that summarize or evaluate.

Read the following Revision Model. Following the model are questions to help you evaluate the writer's changes.

Revision Model

, by Abraham Lincoln,
Both the Gettysburg Address and "I Have a Dream"
by Martin Luther King, Jr.,
are eloquent speeches that make skillful use of

repetition, parallelism, and allusion
~~stylistic techniques~~ to express a belief in the

of liberty and equality
American dream. ~~In some ways the speeches are~~

~~similar~~. However, Lincoln's point of view is strikingly

Whereas
different from King's. Lincoln emphasizes the concept

the personal pronoun
of unity by using we, King uses I to emphasize his

While
personal vision. King's references to the Bible and to

African American
spirituals reveal the evangelistic preaching tradition

that shaped his style. Both writers allude to the

Declaration of Independence.

Evaluating the Revision

1. What changes has the writer made in the opening sentence? How do these changes clarify the essay's subject matter?
2. How do the writer's deletions improve the flow of the paragraph?
3. Has the writer organized the essay according to either the block method or the point-by-point method?
4. What other changes would you recommend?

PROOFREADING TIPS

- *Check the spelling of authors' names and of titles.*
- *Be sure to underline the titles of books and long works and to enclose the titles of short works, like poems and essays, in quotation marks.*
- *For correct style of literary titles, see 14a and 14k in the Language Handbook.*

Communications Handbook HELP

See Proofreaders' Marks.

PUBLISHING TIPS

- *Place copies of your essays in a binder, to be filed in your school library or media center for other students' reference.*
- *Collaborate with other students on a desktop publishing program, and create a collection of essays for the class.*

DIRECTIONS: Read the two stories. Then, answer each question that follows.

The Dog and the Wolf
Aesop (sixth century B.C.)

One cold and snowy winter the Wolf couldn't find enough to eat. She was almost dead with hunger when a House Dog happened by.

"Ah, Cousin," said the Dog, "you are skin and bones. Come, leave your life of roaming and starving in the forest. Come with me to my master and you'll never go hungry again."

"What will I have to do for my food?" said the Wolf.

"Not much," said the House Dog. "Guard the property, keep the Fox from the henhouse, protect the children. It's an easy life."

That sounded good to the Wolf, so the Dog and the Wolf headed to the village. On the way the Wolf noticed a ring around the Dog's neck where the hair had been rubbed off.

"What's that?" she asked.

"Oh, it's nothing," said the Dog. "It's just where the collar is put on at night to keep me chained up. I'm used to it."

"Chained up!" exclaimed the Wolf, as she ran quickly back to the forest.

Better to starve free than to be a well-fed slave.

The Puppy
Aleksandr Solzhenitsyn (twentieth century)

In our backyard a boy keeps his little dog Sharik chained up, a ball of fluff shackled since he was a puppy.

One day I took him some chicken bones that were still warm and smelt delicious. The boy had just let the poor dog off his lead to have a run round the yard. The snow there was deep and feathery; Sharik was bounding about like a hare, first on his hind legs, then on his front ones, from one corner of the yard to the other, back and forth, burying his muzzle in the snow.

He ran towards me, his coat all shaggy, jumped up at me, sniffed the bones—then off he went again, belly-deep in the snow.

I don't need your bones, he said. Just give me my freedom. . . .

—*translated by* Michael Glenny

SKILLS FOCUS

Literary Skills
Identify and understand recurring themes.

1. In the fable "The Dog and the Wolf," the Wolf decides to go to the village with the House Dog because she —

   A is hungry

   B wants an easier life

   C wants to be chained up

   D likes children

2. What does the Wolf notice on the way to the village?

   F Children playing happily

   G Well-fed people

   H A ring on the Dog's neck

   J The Dog limping

3. In "The Puppy," where is the little dog, Sharik, usually kept?

   A Chained in the yard

   B In a doghouse

   C In the living room

   D In the boy's bedroom

4. What do the House Dog and Sharik have in common?

   F They both are chained at times.

   G They both run away from home.

   H They both are starving.

   J They both hate their masters.

5. What do both the Wolf and Sharik want more than food?

   A Love

   B Freedom

   C Security

   D Fame

6. In the first paragraph of "The Puppy," the writer uses the word *shackled*. Using context clues, you can guess that *shackled* means —

   F punished

   G chained up

   H fed

   J fenced in

Constructed Response

7. What **theme** do the fable from ancient Greece and the story from modern-day Russia have in common?

Collection 4: Skills Review

Vocabulary Skills

Test Practice

Multiple-Meaning Words

DIRECTIONS: Choose the answer in which the underlined word is used in the same way it is used in the quoted sentence. Items 1–3 are from *The Diary of Anne Frank.* Items 4–6 are from "Camp Harmony."

1. "The rooms are sparsely furnished, with a few chairs, cots, a <u>table</u> or two."
   - **A** The <u>table</u> of contents shows no listing for "Holocaust."
   - **B** The vote was to <u>table</u> the measure until the next meeting.
   - **C** The family gathered at the <u>table</u> as a platter of latkes was brought in.
   - **D** Because of the drought, the area's water <u>table</u> has dropped.

2. "Tomorrow I'll get you a better <u>bolt</u> for the door at the foot of the stairs."
   - **F** Please cut me three yards from this <u>bolt</u> of cloth.
   - **G** Hang on, or that horse will <u>bolt</u>.
   - **H** He installed a new double-<u>bolt</u> lock.
   - **J** That last lightning <u>bolt</u> struck the birdbath.

3. "I tell you, this is going to be a <u>fine</u> life for you!"
   - **A** What we need is a <u>fine</u> grade of sandpaper.
   - **B** The <u>fine</u> for littering has gone up.
   - **C** He's taking a course in <u>fine</u> wines.
   - **D** We all had a <u>fine</u> time.

4. "When our bus turned a corner and we no longer had to smile and <u>wave</u>, we settled back gravely in our seats."
   - **F** There was a <u>wave</u> of prejudice, and we could not escape it.
   - **G** Sometimes you just have to wait and see what comes in on the next <u>wave</u>.
   - **H** A <u>wave</u> of disapproval followed on our heels.
   - **J** <u>Wave</u> goodbye.

5. "Then suddenly a baby's <u>sharp</u> cry rose indignantly above the hubbub."
   - **A** Being deprived of one's rights is a very <u>sharp</u> blow.
   - **B** We tried to look <u>sharp</u> boarding the bus, but none of us felt that way.
   - **C** Barbed-wire fencing has <u>sharp</u> points.
   - **D** His voice gets <u>sharp</u> when he talks about those times.

6. "I awoke with a <u>start</u> when the bus filled with excited buzzing."
   - **F** The bombing of Pearl Harbor was more of an ending than a <u>start</u> for many of us.
   - **G** During the internment we had to <u>start</u> doing without many things.
   - **H** Sometimes I realized with a <u>start</u> that I was no longer free.
   - **J** When we came out of camp we literally had to <u>start</u> all over again.

SKILLS FOCUS

Vocabulary Skills
Analyze multiple-meaning words.

Collection 4: Skills Review
Writing Skills

DIRECTIONS: Read the following paragraph from a comparison-contrast essay. Then, answer each question that follows.

(1) The simile and the analogy are both forms of comparison, but they shouldn't be confused. (2) A **simile** draws an imaginative comparison between two dissimilar things by using a word such as *like, as,* or *resembles.* (3) A **metaphor** makes a direct comparison between two unlike things without the use of *like, as,* or *resembles.* (4) "I wandered lonely as a cloud" is a well-known simile from a poem by William Wordsworth, in which the poet emphasizes one point of similarity—the solitary wandering of the poet and of the cloud. (5) By contrast, an **analogy** reveals several points of comparison between things that seem dissimilar. (6) A common analogy compares the game of chess to a military campaign in which various strategies are used to overcome an opponent. (7) An analogy is often used to explain something unfamiliar by comparing it to something familiar.

1. The paragraph focuses chiefly on —
   - **A** the resemblance of simile to analogy
   - **B** the literary uses of simile and analogy
   - **C** the difference between simile and analogy
   - **D** the confusion between simile and analogy

2. Which sentence does not fit in the paragraph and should be deleted?
   - **F** sentence 3
   - **G** sentence 4
   - **H** sentence 5
   - **J** sentence 6

3. Transitional words are used in —
   - **A** sentence 1
   - **B** sentence 3
   - **C** sentence 5
   - **D** all of the above

4. The best position for sentence 7 would be —
   - **F** following sentence 1
   - **G** following sentence 3
   - **H** following sentence 4
   - **J** following sentence 5

5. The rest of this essay will probably discuss —
   - **A** uses of analogy and simile in writing
   - **B** different chess moves
   - **C** definitions of analogy and simile
   - **D** other figures of speech

6. This paragraph is an example of —
   - **F** narration
   - **G** exposition
   - **H** description
   - **J** persuasion

SKILLS FOCUS

Writing Skills
Analyze a comparison-contrast essay.

Fiction

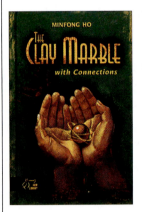

Never Tear Us Apart

Twelve-year-old Dara and her family flee war-torn Cambodia and find a haven at the refugee camp of Nong Chan. In *The Clay Marble* by Minfong Ho, Dara finds a new friend, Jantu, and for a short while their lives are peaceful. When the war brings chaos to the camp, however, Dara is separated from her family and Jantu. Now she must find the courage to reunite the people she loves.

This title is available in the HRW Library.

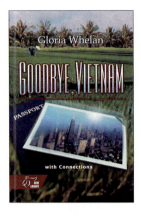

Another Dream

One of the messages in Martin Luther King's famous speech is that freedom does not come easily for everyone; some people must face injustice and treachery before they can be free. You'll find a character determined to find freedom no matter how dire the situation in Gloria Whelan's *Goodbye, Vietnam*. Thirteen-year-old Mai and her family are forced to leave Vietnam for Hong Kong. Although faced with unspeakable horrors on their voyage, they are determined to persevere so that they can reach their ultimate goal: a new life in America.

This title is available in the HRW Library.

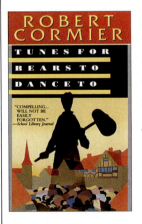

Aftermath

The Holocaust continues to affect people after all these years. In Robert Cormier's novel *Tunes for Bears to Dance To*, Henry is lonely until he meets Mr. Levine, a Holocaust survivor who continually works on a miniature re-creation of his old village. The two take comfort in one another. Then Mr. Hairston, Henry's racist employer, promises Henry a better life for his family if he ends the friendship.

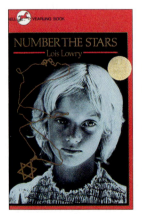

Perilous Mission

How far would you go to save a friend's life? In the 1990 Newbery Medal book by Lois Lowry, *Number the Stars*, Annemarie Johansen and Ellen Rosen, best friends living in peaceful Copenhagen, Denmark, don't concern themselves with questions like this—until the Nazis come for Ellen.

Nonfiction

Regrettable Action

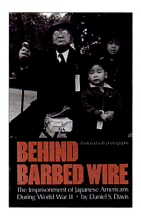

After the bombing of Pearl Harbor, Japanese Americans were forced to abandon their homes and businesses and live in internment camps. Families were crowded into tiny, one-room apartments in long barracks behind fences guarded twenty-four hours a day by armed soldiers. Japanese Americans were essentially stripped of their human and civil rights. In *Behind Barbed Wire*, Daniel S. Davis describes the many difficulties they faced during World War II and the courage they showed in making a new start when they were finally released from the camps.

Persecuted

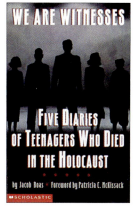

Jacob Boas looks at excerpts from the diaries of five teenagers who lived during World War II. Although they lived in different countries, each received a death sentence under Hitler's reign of terror. *We Are Witnesses: Five Diaries of Teenagers Who Died in the Holocaust* shows how the teenagers dealt with the worst kind of pain and oppression.

Real-Life Heroes

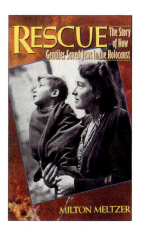

Under Nazi rule, even to be seen talking to a Jew was dangerous—yet all over Europe, non-Jews risked their lives to save neighbors and friends from the death camps. In *Rescue: The Story of How Gentiles Saved Jews in the Holocaust*, Milton Meltzer tells of their heroism.

Undercover

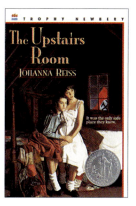

In the Netherlands during World War II, Anne and Margot Frank went into hiding with their parents. At the same time, another pair of sisters escaped to the country to live through the war with a Dutch family in their farmhouse. *The Upstairs Room* and its sequel, *The Journey Back*, tell the true story of Johanna Reiss and her sister Sini.

Two Hundred Campbell's Soup Cans (1962) by Andy Warhol.

A Matter of Style

Literary Focus:
Analyzing Literary Devices and Style

Informational Focus:
Analyzing Unsupported Inferences and Fallacious Reasoning

INTERNET
Collection Resources
Keyword: LE5 8-5

Elements of Literature
Elements of Style *by* Mara Rockliff
LITERARY DEVICES

Poem 1

from **Green Eggs and Ham**

I would not like them
here or there.
I would not like them
anywhere.
I do not like
green eggs and ham.
I do not like them,
Sam-I-am. . . .

Poem 2

who are you,little i

who are you,little i

(five or six years old)
peering from some high

window;at the gold

of november sunset

(and feeling:that if day
has to become night

this is a beautiful way)

**go.
hrw
.com**

INTERNET

**More About
Literary Devices**

Keyword: LE5 8-5

**SKILLS
FOCUS**

Literary Skills
Understand
style.

If somebody gave you these two poems and told you one was written by E. E. Cummings and one by Dr. Seuss, would you be able to tell which was which? If you've ever read anything by either writer, you almost certainly would know the first is by Dr. Seuss and the second is by E. E. Cummings. But *how* would you know?

The answer is **style**—the way a writer uses language. The regular rhythm and the rhyme pattern we expect in a Dr. Seuss book, along with his silly-sounding invented words, make up his unique style. E. E. Cummings's use of lowercase letters, words that bump into each other, and unusual punctuation make up another style.

Every writer has a style, though some styles are more distinctive than others. Generations of beginning writers have tried to copy the unmistakable "plain style" of Ernest Hemingway. In fact, every year there's an Imitation Hemingway Contest, in which writers try to create the best "really good page of really bad Hemingway."

Unexpected Connections

Most writers don't self-consciously try to come up with a style. But style comes naturally from the choices writers make when they put words on a page. A long word or a short one? A simple sentence or one that's long and complex? A sarcastic and biting tone or one that is passionately sincere?

An important part of many writers' style is their use of **figures of speech,** expressions that are not literally true but that suggest similarities between usually unrelated things. Some figures of speech are so common that we use them without even noticing they're not literally true.

- He was tied up in traffic.
- That check you wrote bounced!
- I sat at the foot of the bed.

The bed doesn't actually have a foot; we're comparing it to a body, which has feet at the bottom. The check didn't really bounce like a rubber ball, and the man tied up in traffic wasn't tied with ropes—though he may have felt as if he were.

Here are some of the types of figurative language you're likely to come across:

Similes compare two unlike things using a word of comparison such as *like, than, as,* or *resembles.*

- Her hands were like ice.
- I feel lower than a snake in a ditch.

Metaphors compare two unlike things directly, without using a specific word of comparison.

- His heart is made of stone.
- Lewis is a rotten skunk!

In an **extended metaphor** the comparison is extended as far as the writer wants to take it.

> Fame is a bee.
> It has song—
> It has a sting—
> Ah, too, it has a wing.
> —Emily Dickinson

Personification speaks of a nonhuman or inanimate thing as if it had human or lifelike qualities.

- A falling leaf danced on the breeze.
- The train eats up the miles.
- The sun smiled on our cookout.

Symbols, in literature, are people, places, or events that have meaning in themselves but that also stand for something beyond themselves. Moby-Dick is a white whale hunted by Captain Ahab in the novel *Moby-Dick*, but he is also a symbol of evil. In everyday life we have many symbols. They are called public symbols because everyone knows what they mean: A dove with an olive branch symbolizes peace; a skull and crossbones symbolizes poison; a bearded man called Uncle Sam symbolizes the U.S. government.

(*continued on next page*)

Writers try to create fresh figures of speech to help us to see everyday things in a new way. "Her hands were as cold as ice" is a cliché—everyone's heard it before. But what about "Her handshake would make a snowman put on gloves"? or "Her hands were colder than a lizard in an ice chest"?

Unexpected Events

Another way writers create a fresh and exciting style is by playing with our expectations. When reality contradicts what we expect, it's called **irony.**

Verbal irony occurs when we say one thing and mean something else. "That's just great," your friend says in a disgusted tone, and you know she means it's *not* great at all.

Situational irony is a situation that turns out to be just the opposite of what we'd expect. The son of the police chief is arrested for burglary. The firehouse burns to the ground. The prize encyclopedia goes to the kid who never studied for the exam.

Dramatic irony occurs when we know something that a character in a book (or a movie or play) doesn't know. "Don't go down that dark hallway!" we want to scream, but the heroine goes anyway, and we know what she'll find there.

Putting Us There

Style also comes from the way a writer uses words so that they spring to life from the page. Vivid **imagery**—language that creates word pictures and appeals to the senses—makes us feel that we are seeing (or hearing, touching, tasting, or smelling) what the writer is describing. The poet John Greenleaf Whittier helps us experience the start of a New England blizzard with this image: "The sun that bleak December day / Rose cheerless over hills of gray."

Writers can also appeal to the ear with **dialect,** a way of speaking that's characteristic of a particular place or group of people. "Y'all come back now" tells us we're in the South. In older movies we'd hear a New York City cabdriver say: "Dat bum wanted me to take him and huh all da way to Noo Joisey."

Practice

Prepare a "literary devices" wall display for your classroom. You can keep adding to this display as your experience with literary devices grows. Here is how you do it:

Get seven poster boards, and give them the following labels:

- Symbols
- Images
- Irony
- Dialect
- Similes
- Metaphors
- Personification

Under each term, write its definition. Then, under each definition, write in examples that you think are interesting. You can find your examples in newspapers and magazines, as well as in the stories, poems, and novels you are reading in class and independently. Be sure to cite the author and title of the work you take each quotation from.

Reading Skills and Strategies

Fallacious Reasoning

by Kylene Beers

It's Friday night and you want to go to a concert. You tell your parents or guardian that *everyone* will be going, that it is supposed to be the safest concert that your city has ever had, that if you don't get to go, you won't be invited to any parties for the rest of your teenage years, and that if your parents trust you they will let you go. Your parents tell you that they think your argument is filled with fallacious reasoning. You aren't sure if that's a compliment until you find out that **fallacious reasoning** means "false thinking." People reason fallaciously when they draw incorrect or false conclusions. Such conclusions may be illogical, or they may be based on incomplete information.

For an argument to be convincing, it must be based on **logic,** or correct reasoning. Opinions should be supported by reasons and evidence, such as **facts, statistics, examples,** or **expert testimony.**

Fallacious or faulty reasoning can be hard to spot, so it's important to watch for it whenever you evaluate an argument.

Types of Fallacious Reasoning

- **Hasty generalizations**—conclusions drawn from weak or insufficient evidence: *Your friend said the concert you're attending would have extra security. Obviously, this will be the safest concert your city has ever had.*

- **False cause and effect**—assuming that event A caused event B simply because A came first: *After I went to the concert, I was invited to a party. Going to concerts will make me more popular.*

- **Either/or fallacy**—the assumption that a problem or situation has only one possible cause or resolution when there may be several: *If your parents don't let you go to the concert, then they don't trust you.*

- **Stereotyping**—believing that all members of a group share a certain characteristic: *All concerts are unsafe.*

- **Name-calling**—attacking the person who's making the argument rather than the argument itself: *Your parents don't want you to go to the concert. They obviously don't know anything about anything.*

SKILLS FOCUS

Reading Skills
Understand fallacious reasoning.

As you read, you'll find this open-book sign at certain points in the essay: ![icon]. Stop at these points, and think about what you've just read. Do what the prompt asks you to do.

ANALYZE

❶ The first sentence is a negative statement about Poe. What information would the author need to provide next to support that statement? In the second sentence, the author says that "every single story" is about insane people. Could this statement be supported? Explain.

ANALYZE

❷ Why is the last sentence in this paragraph an example of **name-calling**? Look back to page 533 to review the definition of name-calling.

*Grade F =
An example
of fallacious
reasoning.*

Edgar Allan Poe: His Life Revealed in His Work

Edgar Allan Poe was a very, very disturbed man. Every single story and poem he ever wrote is about disturbed, usually insane people. He writes about murderers, people buried alive, people being tortured, people killed by the Black Death. ❶ His characters imagine weird things, like a raven that croaks in English and plunges his beak into someone's heart.

No one could write stories like this without being crazy. How else could Poe have known what it is like to be insane? The only way he could have known is by being insane himself. ❷

Poe's stories also show that he was a drug addict or an alcoholic. We know that he was always drunk. That probably accounts for the strange style of his writing. His stories are often very choppy. They use a lot of dashes and exclamation points, which suggests that a very nervous person wrote them, or someone on drugs.

We know that all writers are strange anyway, especially writers who specialize in horror.

I hope I have convinced you that Poe's writing reflects his sick mind.

(Despite all this, I love Poe's stories!)

—F. Reasoner

Practice the Strategy

PRACTICE 1

Identifying Types of Fallacious Reasoning

In the selection "Edgar Allan Poe: His Life Revealed in His Work," there are several types of fallacious reasoning, or arguments that are not logical. Review the types of fallacious reasoning on page 533. Then, answer the questions below.

1. "Every single story and poem he ever wrote is about disturbed, usually insane people" is a hasty generalization because the writer —

   a. probably hasn't read everything Poe wrote

   b. is not of Poe's generation

2. "The only way he could have known is by being insane himself" is another hasty generalization because —

   a. the statement assumes we all agree on something

   b. there is insufficient evidence to support the statement

3. By saying that Poe's use of dashes and exclamation points suggests that a very nervous person or someone on drugs wrote the text, the writer is —

   a. using false cause and effect

   b. name-calling

4. By implying that we shouldn't take Poe's stories seriously because he was always drunk, the writer is —

   a. using the either/or fallacy

   b. name-calling

PRACTICE 2

Practice recognizing different types of fallacious reasoning by completing the following statements:

1. **Hasty generalization:** She would not loan me a pencil. Everyone obviously…

2. **False cause and effect:** After I used this new toothpaste, I got invited to a party. This new toothpaste…

3. **Either/or fallacy:** If we don't elect a girl for class president, then girls…

4. **Stereotyping:** All teenagers are…

5. **Name-calling:** Ray's in favor of school uniforms. That's no surprise because Ray…

> **Strategy Tip**
> Look for examples of fallacious reasoning as you read ads, listen to commercials, or write persuasive papers. Remember to use logic, facts, examples, or expert testimony when trying to convince someone of a point.

The Tell-Tale Heart

Make the Connection

Conduct a Survey: Top-Ten Terrors

Many people like a good scare now and then. Conduct a class poll to come up with a list of your top-ten terrors—choose details from scary TV shows, movies, books, and events.

Literary Focus

Narrator: Who Says So?

When we read a story, we rely on the **narrator** (the person telling the story) to let us know what is going on. But what if the narrator can't be trusted? As you begin reading this story, decide if the narrator seems to be a reliable source of information.

Irony: The Unexpected!

Much of the horror in "The Tell-Tale Heart" comes from Poe's use of **irony.** There are three kinds of irony:

- **Verbal irony**—we say just the opposite of what we mean.
- **Situational irony**—what happens is different from what we expect.
- **Dramatic irony**—we know something a character doesn't know.

Poe's skillful use of irony in many of his stories helps define his unique style. Which types of irony work on your emotions in "The Tell-Tale Heart"? Pay particular attention to the narrator.

INTERNET

Vocabulary Activity
•
More About Poe

Keyword: LE5 8-5

SKILLS FOCUS

Literary Skills
Understand narrator; understand irony.

Reading Skills
Preview the story.

Reading Skills

Previewing: What's Ahead?

Preview this famous story by looking at the title and the illustrations. What do you think might happen in this story?

Vocabulary Development

You'll learn these good, ordinary words as you read this strange story:

acute (ə·kyo͞ot′) *adj.:* sharp. *His nervousness increased his acute sense of hearing.*

vexed (vekst) *v.:* disturbed. *He was vexed by the old man's eye.*

sagacity (sə·gas′ə·tē) *n.:* intelligence and good judgment. *He was proud of his powers and of his sagacity.*

refrained (ri·frānd′) *v.:* held back. *Though furious, he refrained from action.*

wary (wer′ē) *adj.:* cautious. *He was too wary to make a careless mistake.*

suavity (swäv′ə·tē) *n.:* smooth manner. *The police showed perfect suavity.*

audacity (ô·das′ə·tē) *n.:* boldness. *He was impressed with his own audacity.*

vehemently (vē′ə·mənt·lē) *adv.:* forcefully. *He talked more vehemently, but he couldn't drown out the sound.*

gesticulations (jes·tik′yo͞o·lā′shənz) *n.:* energetic gestures. *His violent gesticulations did not disturb the policemen.*

derision (di·rizh′ən) *n.:* ridicule. *He hated the smiling derision of the police.*

Why will you say that I am mad?

The Tell-Tale Heart

Edgar Allan Poe

True!—nervous—very, very dreadfully nervous I had been and am; but why *will* you say that I am mad? The disease had sharpened my senses—not destroyed—not dulled them. Above all was the sense of hearing acute. I heard all things in the heaven and in the earth. I heard many things in hell. How, then, am I mad? Hearken! and observe how healthily—how calmly I can tell you the whole story. ❶

It is impossible to say how first the idea entered my brain; but once conceived, it haunted me day and night. Object[1] there was none. Passion there was none. I loved the old man. He had never wronged me. He had never given me insult. For his gold I had no desire. I think it was his eye! Yes, it was this! One of his eyes resembled that

---

1. object (äb′jikt) *n.:* purpose or goal.

Vocabulary
acute (ə·kyo͞ot′) *adj.:* sharp; sensitive; severe.

of a vulture—a pale blue eye, with a film over it. Whenever it fell upon me, my blood ran cold; and so by degrees—very gradually—I made up my mind to take the life of the old man and thus rid myself of the eye forever.

Now this is the point. You fancy me mad. Madmen know nothing. But you should have seen *me.* You should have seen how wisely I proceeded—with what caution—with what foresight—with what dissimulation[2] I went to work! I was never kinder to the old man than during the whole week before I killed him. And every night, about midnight, I turned the latch of his door and opened it—oh, so gently! And then, when I had made an opening sufficient for my head, I put in a dark lantern, all closed, closed, so that no light shone out, and then I thrust in my head. Oh, you would have laughed to see how cunningly I thrust it in! I moved it slowly—very, very slowly, so that I might not disturb the old man's sleep. It took me an hour to place my whole head within the opening so far that I could see him as he lay upon his bed. Ha! Would a madman have been so wise as this? And then, when my head was well in the room, I undid the lantern cautiously—oh, so cautiously—cautiously (for the hinges creaked)—I undid it just so much that a single thin ray fell upon the vulture eye. And this I did for seven long nights—every night just at midnight—but I found the eye always closed; and so it was impossible to do the work; for it was not the old man who vexed me, but his Evil Eye. And

every morning, when the day broke, I went boldly into the chamber and spoke courageously to him, calling him by name in a hearty tone and inquiring how he had passed the night. So you see he would have been a very profound[3] old man, indeed, to suspect that every night, just at twelve, I looked in upon him while he slept. ❷

📖 **INFER**
❷ The narrator is talking to someone. Who might "you" be?

Upon the eighth night I was more than usually cautious in opening the door. A watch's minute hand moves more quickly than did mine. Never before that night had I *felt* the extent of my own powers—of my sagacity. I could scarcely contain my feelings of triumph. To think that there I was, opening the door, little by little, and he not even to dream of my secret deeds or thoughts. I fairly chuckled at the idea; and perhaps he heard me; for he moved on the bed suddenly, as if startled. Now you may think that I drew back—but no. His room was as black as pitch with the thick darkness (for the shutters were close fastened, through fear of robbers), and so I knew that he could not see the opening of the door, and I kept pushing it on steadily, steadily. ❸

📖 **STYLE**
❸ Why is it ironic that the old man feared robbers? (What should he have feared?)

I had my head in, and was about to open the lantern, when my thumb slipped upon

---

2. **dissimulation** (di·sim′yo͞o·lā′shen) *n.:* disguising of intentions or feelings. (Look for a similar word at the end of the story.)

---

3. **profound** (prō·found′) *adj.:* deeply intellectual.

Vocabulary
vexed (vekst) *v.:* disturbed; annoyed.
sagacity (sə·gas′ə·tē) *n.:* intelligence and good judgment.

The illustrations on pages 539 and 542 are from a short movie based on "The Tell-Tale Heart."

the tin fastening, and the old man sprang up in the bed, crying out—"Who's there?"

I kept quite still and said nothing. For a whole hour I did not move a muscle, and in the meantime I did not hear him lie down. He was still sitting up in the bed listening—just as I have done, night after night, hearkening to the deathwatches[4] in the wall.

Presently I heard a slight groan, and I knew it was the groan of mortal terror. It was not a groan of pain or of grief—oh, no!—it was the low, stifled sound that arises from the bottom of the soul when over-charged with awe. I knew the sound well. Many a night, just at midnight, when all the world slept, it has welled up from my own bosom, deepening, with its dreadful echo, the terrors that distracted me. I say I knew it well. I knew what the old man felt, and pitied him, although I chuckled at heart. I knew that he had been lying awake ever since the first slight noise, when he had turned in the bed. His fears had been ever since growing upon him. He had been trying to fancy them causeless but could not. He had been saying to himself—"It is nothing but the wind in the chimney—it is only

---

4. **deathwatches** *n.:* beetles that burrow into wood and make tapping sounds, which some people believe are a sign of approaching death.

a mouse crossing the floor," or "It is merely a cricket which has made a single chirp." Yes, he had been trying to comfort himself with these suppositions; but he had found all in vain. *All in vain;* because Death, in approaching him, had stalked with his black shadow before him and enveloped the victim. And it was the mournful influence of the unperceived shadow that caused him to feel—although he neither saw nor heard—to *feel* the presence of my head within the room.

When I had waited a long time, very patiently, without hearing him lie down, I resolved to open a little—a very, very little crevice in the lantern. So I opened it—you cannot imagine how stealthily, stealthily—until, at length, a single dim ray, like the thread of the spider, shot from out the crevice and full upon the vulture eye. ❹

It was open—wide, wide open—and I grew furious as I gazed upon it. I saw it with perfect distinctness—all a dull blue, with a hideous veil over it that chilled the very marrow in my bones; but I could see nothing else of the old man's face or person, for I had directed the ray, as if by instinct, precisely upon the damned spot.

And now have I not told you that what you mistake for madness is but overacuteness of the senses?—now, I say, there came to my ears a low, dull, quick sound, such as a watch makes when enveloped in cotton. I knew *that* sound well too. It was the beating of the old man's heart. It increased my fury, as the beating of a drum stimulates the soldier into courage.

But even yet I refrained and kept still. I scarcely breathed. I held the lantern motionless. I tried how steadily I could maintain the ray upon the eye. Meantime the hellish tattoo[5] of the heart increased. It grew quicker and quicker and louder and louder every instant. The old man's terror *must* have been extreme! It grew louder, I say, louder every moment!—do you mark me well? I have told you that I am nervous: So I am. And now at the dead hour of the night, amid the dreadful silence of that old house, so strange a noise as this excited me to uncontrollable terror. Yet for some minutes longer I refrained and stood still. But the beating grew louder, louder! I thought the heart must burst. And now a new anxiety seized me—the sound would be heard by a neighbor! The old man's hour had come! With a loud yell, I threw open the lantern and leaped into the room. He shrieked once—once only. In an instant I dragged him to the floor and pulled the heavy bed over him. I then smiled gaily to find the deed so far done. But, for many minutes, the heart beat on with a muffled sound. This, however, did not vex me; it would not be heard through the wall. At length it ceased. The old man was dead. I removed the bed and examined the corpse. Yes, he was stone, stone dead. I placed my hand upon the heart and held it there many minutes. There was no pulsation. He was stone dead. His eye would trouble me no more. ❺

---

5. **tattoo** *n.*: steady beat.

Vocabulary
refrained (ri·frānd′) *v.*: held back.

STYLE
❹ What simile does Poe use to help us see the ray of light from the lantern?

STYLE
❺ Where does Poe use repetition in this paragraph? Read the paragraph aloud to emphasize the repeated words.

If still you think me mad, you will think so no longer when I describe the wise precautions I took for the concealment of the body. The night waned,[6] and I worked hastily but in silence. First of all I dismembered the corpse. I cut off the head and the arms and the legs.

I then took up three planks from the flooring of the chamber and deposited all between the scantlings.[7] I then replaced the boards so cleverly, so cunningly, that no human eye—not even *his*—could have detected anything wrong. There was nothing to wash out—no stain of any kind—no blood spot whatever. I had been too wary for that. A tub had caught all—ha! ha!

When I had made an end of these labors, it was four o'clock—still dark as midnight. As the bell sounded the hour, there came a knocking at the street door. I went down to open it with a light heart—for what had I *now* to fear? There entered three men, who introduced themselves, with perfect suavity, as officers of the police. A shriek had been heard by a neighbor during the night; suspicion of foul play had been aroused; information had been lodged at the police office, and they (the officers) had been deputed[8] to search the premises.

I smiled—for *what* had I to fear? I bade the gentlemen welcome. The shriek, I said, was my own in a dream. The old man, I mentioned, was absent in the country. I took my visitors all over the house. I bade them search—search *well*. I led them, at length, to *his* chamber. I showed them his treasures, secure, undisturbed. In the enthusiasm of my confidence, I brought chairs into the room and desired them *here* to rest from their fatigues, while I myself, in the wild audacity of my perfect triumph, placed my own seat upon the very spot beneath which reposed the corpse of the victim.

The officers were satisfied. My *manner* had convinced them. I was singularly at ease. They sat, and while I answered cheerily, they chatted of familiar things. But, ere long, I felt myself getting pale and wished them gone. My head ached, and I fancied a ringing in my ears; but still they sat and still they chatted. The ringing became more distinct—it continued and became more distinct: I talked more freely to get rid of the feeling: but it continued and gained definitiveness—until, at length, I found that the noise was *not* within my ears.

No doubt I now grew *very* pale—but I talked more fluently and with a heightened voice. Yet the sound increased—and what could I do? It was *a low, dull, quick sound— much such a sound as a watch makes when enveloped in cotton*. I gasped for breath— and yet the officers heard it not. I talked more quickly—more vehemently; but the noise steadily increased. I arose and argued about trifles, in a high key and with violent gesticulations, but the noise steadily increased. Why *would* they not be gone? I paced the floor to and fro with heavy strides, as if excited to fury by the observation of the men—but the noise steadily increased. Oh

---

6. **waned** (wānd) *v.:* gradually drew to a close.
7. **scantlings** *n.:* small beams of wood.
8. **deputed** (dē·pyoot′id) *v.:* appointed.

Vocabulary
wary (wer′ē) *adj.:* cautious.
suavity (swäv′ə·tē) *n.:* smoothness; politeness.
audacity (ô·das′ə·tē) *n.:* boldness.
vehemently (vē′ə·mənt·lē) *adv.:* forcefully; passionately.
gesticulations (jes·tik′yoo·lā′shənz) *n.:* energetic gestures.

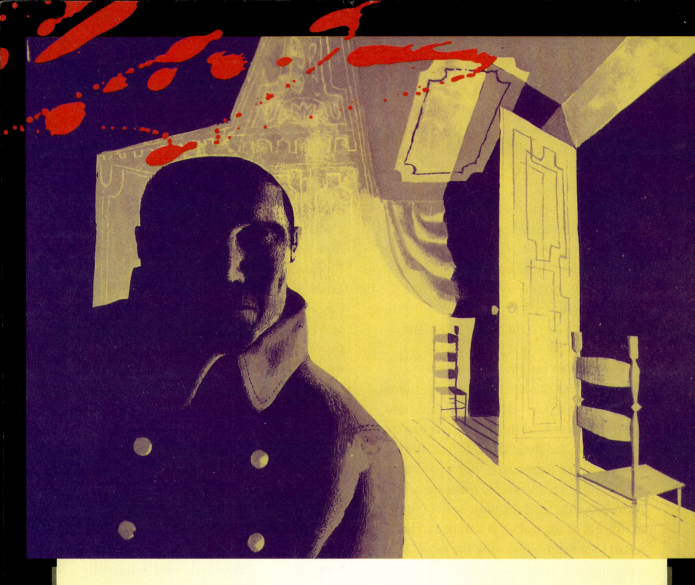

God! what *could* I do? I foamed—I raved—I swore! I swung the chair upon which I had been sitting and grated it upon the boards, but the noise arose over all and continually increased. It grew louder—louder—*louder!* And still the men chatted pleasantly, and smiled. Was it possible they heard not? Almighty God!—no, no! They heard!—they suspected!—they *knew!*—they were making a mockery of my horror!—this I thought, and this I think. But anything was better than this agony! Anything was more tolerable than this derision! I could bear those hypocritical smiles no longer! I felt that I must scream or die!—and now—again!—hark! louder! *louder!* louder! louder!— **6**

"Villains!" I shrieked, "dissemble no more! I admit the deed!—tear up the planks!—here, here!—it is the beating of his hideous heart!"

STYLE

6 How do punctuation and repetition build a sense of horror in this paragraph? What do you imagine the police are really thinking by now?

Vocabulary
derision (di·rizh′ən) *n.:* contempt; ridicule.

Meet the Writer

Edgar Allan Poe

The Dark Side

Born in Boston, **Edgar Allan Poe** (1809–1849) was the son of traveling actors. When Poe was a baby, his father deserted the family; his mother died before his third birthday. Poe was taken in by the wealthy Allan family of Richmond, Virginia, and given a first-class education. At the age of twelve, he had already written enough poems (mainly love poems to girls he knew) to fill a book. By the time he was twenty, he had published two volumes of poetry.

Poe constantly argued with his foster father, John Allan, about money. Allan eventually broke all ties with Poe, leaving him penniless. In 1831, Poe moved in with his aunt, Maria Clemm, and her children in Baltimore, probably in an attempt to find a new family. He married his young cousin Virginia Clemm five years later.

Poe became as celebrated for his tales of horror and mystery as for his poetry. He made very little money from his writing, though—one of his most famous poems, "The Raven," earned him only about fifteen dollars. He seemed to live on the brink of disaster. His wife's death from tuberculosis in 1847 brought on a general decline in his physical and emotional health. He was found very ill and probably flooded with drink in a Baltimore tavern on a rainy day in 1849; he died four days later of unknown causes.

For Independent Reading

Poe was one of the first American writers to explore the dark side of the imagination. His horror tales include "The Masque of the Red Death," "The Pit and the Pendulum," and "The Fall of the House of Usher."

After You Read   Response and Analysis

First Thoughts

1. Go back to your reading notes. Did **previewing** the story help you make accurate predictions? Why or why not?

Thinking Critically

2. We feel a strong sense of **dramatic irony** in this story: The narrator keeps claiming to be sane, but we become more and more certain that he is insane. What details in the story indicate that the narrator is insane?

3. How does the opening paragraph **foreshadow,** or hint at, the events of the story?

4. What is your explanation for the "heartbeat" noise that drives the narrator to confess?

5. **Mood,** or atmosphere, is the overall feeling in a story. How would you describe the mood of this story? What details does Poe use to create that mood?

6. The final paragraph of the story builds to a kind of mad **climax.** How does the writer use words and punctuation to create tension—and even the rhythm of a heartbeat?

7. To whom could the narrator be telling this horrible story?

8. Why is the story called "The Tell-Tale Heart"? (Could the title have more than one meaning?)

Extending Interpretations

9. How is this story like other stories that scare people? Refer to your class survey of top-ten terrors for examples.

WRITING
Evaluating Style

Poe wrote that every word in a story should help create a "single overwhelming impression." How well has he done that in "The Tell-Tale Heart"? In a paragraph, describe the story's impact on you. Mention at least three details from the story that help create this impression.

> ### Reading Check
> Some of the information in Poe's story is suspect because the only source is an unreliable **narrator.** Write down three questions you would like to ask a more reliable source. Explain how each question would help you better understand the **motivations** behind the murder.

go.
hrw
.com

INTERNET
Projects and Activities
Keyword: LE5 8-5

SKILLS FOCUS

Literary Skills
Analyze the narrator; analyze irony.

Reading Skills
Preview the story.

Writing Skills
Evaluate style.

After You Read Vocabulary Development

Searching for Synonyms

PRACTICE 1

Imagine that you are the editor of a magazine for teenagers. You want to include "The Tell-Tale Heart" in your Spooky Stories issue, but you think Poe's vocabulary is too hard and old-fashioned. Divide the words in the Word Bank with a partner (five apiece). Find the sentences in the story in which your words appear, and copy the sentences onto a blank sheet of paper. Rewrite each sentence to make it easier for today's teens to understand. Substitute more familiar words or phrases for the Word Bank words as well as for any other difficult words in the sentence. To locate **synonyms**—words with similar meanings—use a **thesaurus** (a dictionary of synonyms), a **synonym finder,** or a thesaurus that is part of your computer's **software.**

Word Bank

acute
vexed
sagacity
refrained
wary
suavity
audacity
vehemently
gesticulations
derision

Explaining Figures of Speech

PRACTICE 2

Each underlined phrase below contains a figure of speech from the story. Tell what two things are being compared in each sentence. Then, explain what each figure of speech means.

1. The narrator says the old man's eye resembled that of a vulture.
2. He said the eye makes his blood run cold.
3. He is moving in a room as black as pitch.
4. He sees the single ray of light from his lantern shoot out like the thread of the spider.
5. The heartbeat caused fury in the narrator the way the beating of a drum stimulates the soldier into courage.

Choose one of the phrases above, and make a drawing to illustrate its literal meaning. For example, if you were going to illustrate the figure of speech *I feel like a million bucks,* you might draw a person with money sprouting from her head, hands, and feet. Got the idea? Give it a try.

Vocabulary Skills
Identify synonyms; explain figures of speech.

Raymond's Run

Make the Connection
Quickwrite ✏️

Squeaky, the narrator of the story you are about to read, is a tough, smart, funny, streetwise girl with strong opinions. She thinks she can tell what other people are like just from the way they look and talk. Like many of us, she sometimes forgets that there's much more to people than what appears on the surface. Have you ever been surprised to discover something new about someone? Take a few minutes to jot down what you've discovered.

Literary Focus
Style: Allusions

Squeaky, the girl who tells this story, likes allusions, especially to mythology and to an old TV show called *Gunsmoke*. An **allusion** is a reference to something in current events, on TV, in history, in literature, and so on. When writers use allusions, they expect readers to understand what they are referring to. Usually allusions refer to an aspect of culture that people share—literature, history, religion, mythology, politics, sports. The risk in using allusions is that some people may not make the connection. Sometimes allusions become dated. Footnotes in "Raymond's Run" explain a few allusions that may not make sense to you.

Style: Dialect

When you read this story, you hear Squeaky's own true voice—her dialect. A **dialect** is a way of speaking that is characteristic of a certain geographical area or a certain group of people. Dialect can involve special pronunciation, vocabulary, and grammar. Everyone speaks a dialect of some kind. No matter how close your dialect is to standard English, it will still show regional or group differences. Dialect is used by writers to capture the voice of a particular person. Squeaky and most of the other characters in "Raymond's Run" speak in a dialect used in Harlem, a neighborhood in New York City.

Reading Skills 📖
Making Judgments

As you read, you continually make **judgments** about what you are reading. You form opinions about the story's characters, plot, and style. You decide if the plot or characters are believable. You find that you like or dislike individual characters or the way the story is told. As the story goes on, you might revise your judgments. As you read "Raymond's Run," make notes on your judgments about the story's characters, events, and style. See if your feelings change as the story progresses.

go.hrw.com

INTERNET

More About Bambara

Keyword: LE5 8-5

SKILLS FOCUS

Literary Skills
Understand allusions and dialect.

Reading Skills
Make judgments.

RAYMOND'S RUN

Toni Cade Bambara

I don't have much work to do around the house like some girls. My mother does that. And I don't have to earn my pocket money by hustling; George runs errands for the big boys and sells Christmas cards. And anything else that's got to get done, my father does. All I have to do in life is mind my brother Raymond, which is enough.

Sometimes I slip and say my little brother Raymond. But as any fool can see he's much bigger and he's older too. But a lot of people call him my little brother cause he needs looking after cause he's not quite right. And a lot of smart mouths got lots to say about that too, especially when George was minding him. But now, if anybody has anything to say to Raymond, anything to say about his big head, they have to come by me. And I don't play the dozens[1] or believe in standing around with somebody in my face doing a lot of talking. I much rather just knock you down and take my chances even if I am a little girl with skinny arms and a squeaky voice, which is how I got the name Squeaky. And if things get too rough, I run. And as anybody can tell you, I'm the fastest thing on two feet. ❶ 📖

📖 **INFER**
❶ What details in Squeaky's comments here reveal her special personality? What kind of person is Squeaky?

There is no track meet that I don't win the first-place medal. I used to win the twenty-yard dash when I was a little kid in kindergarten. Nowadays, it's the fifty-yard dash. And tomorrow I'm subject to run the quarter-meter relay all by myself and come in first, second, and third. The big kids call me

---

1. **play the dozens:** slang for "trade insults."

I'm the fastest and that goes for Gretchen, too, who says she's going to win this year. Ridiculous.

Mercury[2] cause I'm the swiftest thing in the neighborhood. Everybody knows that—except two people who know better, my father and me. He can beat me to Amsterdam Avenue with me having a two-fire-hydrant head start and him running with his hands in his pockets and whistling. But that's private information. Cause can you imagine some thirty-five-year-old man stuffing himself into PAL[3] shorts to race little kids? So as far as everyone's concerned, I'm the fastest and that goes for Gretchen, too, who has put out the tale that she is going to win the first-place medal this year. Ridiculous. In the second place, she's got short legs. In the third place, she's got freckles. In the first place, no one can beat me and that's all there is to it.

I'm standing on the corner admiring the weather and about to take a stroll down Broadway so I can practice my breathing exercises, and I've got Raymond walking on the inside close to the buildings, cause he's subject to fits of fantasy and starts thinking he's a circus performer and that the curb is a tightrope strung high in the air. And sometimes after a rain he likes to step down off his tightrope right into the gutter and slosh around getting his shoes and cuffs wet. Then I get hit when I get home. Or sometimes if you don't watch him he'll dash across traffic to the island[4] in the middle of Broadway and give the pigeons a fit. Then I have to go behind him apologizing to all the old people sitting around trying to get some sun and getting all upset with the pigeons fluttering

around them, scattering their newspapers and upsetting the waxpaper lunches in their laps. So I keep Raymond on the inside of me, and he plays like he's driving a stagecoach which is OK by me so long as he doesn't run me over or interrupt my breathing exercises, which I have to do on account of I'm serious about my running, and I don't care who knows it. ❷ 📖

📖 **INFER**
❷ What details does Squeaky use here to help you see Raymond and understand how tough it is to watch him?

Now some people like to act like things come easy to them, won't let on that they practice. Not me. I'll high-prance down 34th Street like a rodeo pony

---

2. **Mercury:** in Roman mythology, messenger of the gods, known for his speediness.
3. **PAL:** Police Athletic League.
4. **island** *n.:* traffic island, a car-free area in the middle of the street.

to keep my knees strong even if it does get my mother uptight so that she walks ahead like she's not with me, don't know me, is all by herself on a shopping trip, and I am somebody else's crazy child. Now you take Cynthia Procter for instance. She's just the opposite. If there's a test tomorrow, she'll say something like, "Oh, I guess I'll play handball this afternoon and watch television tonight," just to let you know she ain't thinking about the test. Or like last week when she won the spelling bee for the millionth time, "A good thing you got 'receive,' Squeaky, cause I would have got it wrong. I completely forgot about the spelling bee." And she'll clutch the lace on her blouse like it was a narrow escape. Oh, brother. But of course when I pass her house on my early morning trots around the block, she is practicing the scales on the piano over and over and over and over. Then in music class she always lets herself get bumped around so she falls accidentally on purpose onto the piano stool and is so surprised to find herself sitting there that she decides just for fun to try out the ole keys. And what do you

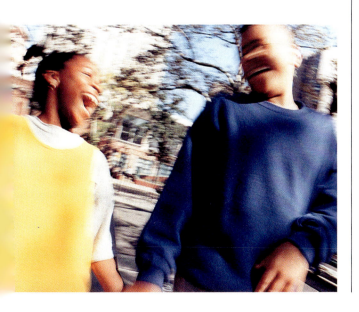

know—Chopin's[5] waltzes just spring out of her fingertips and she's the most surprised thing in the world. A regular prodigy. I could kill people like that. I stay up all night studying the words for the spelling bee. And you can see me any time of day practicing running. I never walk if I can trot, and shame on Raymond if he can't keep up. But of course he does, cause if he hangs back someone's liable to walk up to him and get smart, or take his allowance from him, or ask him where he got that great big pumpkin head. People are so stupid sometimes.

So I'm strolling down Broadway breathing out and breathing in on counts of seven, which is my lucky number, and here comes Gretchen and her sidekicks: Mary Louise, who used to be a friend of mine when she

---

5. **Chopin's:** Frédéric François Chopin (shō′pan) (1810–1849), Polish composer and pianist.

first moved to Harlem from Baltimore and got beat up by everybody till I took up for her on account of her mother and my mother used to sing in the same choir when they were young girls, but people ain't grateful, so now she hangs out with the new girl Gretchen and talks about me like a dog; and Rosie, who is as fat as I am skinny and has a big mouth where Raymond is concerned and is too stupid to know that there is not a big deal of difference between herself and Raymond and that she can't afford to throw stones. So they are steady coming up Broadway and I see right away that it's going to be one of those Dodge City scenes[6] cause the street ain't that big and they're close to the buildings just as we are. First I think I'll step into the candy store and look over the new comics and let them pass. But that's chicken and I've got a reputation to consider. So then I think I'll just walk straight on through thcm or even over them if necessary. But as they get to me, they slow down. I'm ready to fight, cause like I said I don't feature a whole lot of chit-chat, I much prefer to just knock you down right from the jump and save everybody a lotta precious time.

"You signing up for the May Day races?" smiles Mary Louise, only it's not a smile at all. A dumb question like that doesn't deserve an answer. Besides, there's just me and Gretchen standing there really, so no use wasting my breath talking to shadows.

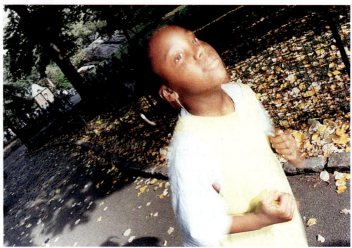

"I don't think you're going to win this time," says Rosie, trying to signify[7] with her hands on her hips all salty, completely forgetting that I have whupped her behind many times for less salt than that.

"I always win cause I'm the best," I say straight at Gretchen who is, as far as I'm concerned, the only one talking in this ventriloquist-dummy routine. Gretchen smiles, but it's not a smile, and I'm thinking that girls never really smile at each other because they don't know how and don't want to know how and there's probably no one to teach us how, cause grown-up girls don't know either. Then they all look at Raymond who has just brought his mule team to a standstill. And they're about to see what trouble they can get into through him. ❸ 📖

"What grade you in now, Raymond?"
"You got anything to say to my brother,

📖 **STYLE**
❸ Explain the comparison Squeaky makes between Rosie and Gretchen and the "ventriloquist-dummy routine."

---

6. **Dodge City scenes:** showdowns like those in the television western *Gunsmoke*, which was set in Dodge City, Kansas. In a typical scene a marshal and an outlaw face off with pistols on an empty street.

---

7. **signify** *v.:* slang for "act boastful or insult someone."

you say it to me, Mary Louise Williams of Raggedy Town, Baltimore."

"What are you, his mother?" sasses Rosie.

"That's right, Fatso. And the next word out of anybody and I'll be their mother too." So they just stand there and Gretchen shifts from one leg to the other and so do they. Then Gretchen puts her hands on her hips and is about to say something with her freckle-face self but doesn't. Then she walks around me looking me up and down but keeps walking up Broadway, and her sidekicks follow her. So me and Raymond smile at each other and he says, "Gidyap" to his team and I continue with my breathing exercises, strolling down Broadway toward the iceman on 145th with not a care in the world cause I am Miss Quicksilver[8] herself.

I take my time getting to the park on May Day because the track meet is the last thing on the program. The biggest thing on the program is the May Pole dancing, which I can do without, thank you, even if my mother thinks it's a shame I don't take part and act like a girl for a change. You'd think my mother'd be grateful not to have to make me a white organdy dress with a big satin sash and buy me new white baby-doll shoes that can't be taken out of the box till the big day. You'd think she'd be glad her daughter ain't out there prancing around a May Pole getting the new clothes all dirty and sweaty and trying to act like a fairy or a flower or whatever you're supposed to be when you should be trying to be yourself, whatever that is, which is, as far as I am concerned, a poor black girl who really can't afford to buy shoes and a new dress you only wear once a lifetime cause it won't fit next year.

I was once a strawberry in a Hansel and Gretel pageant when I was in nursery school and didn't have no better sense than to dance on tiptoe with my arms in a circle over my head doing umbrella steps and being a perfect fool just so my mother and father could come dressed up and clap. You'd think they'd know better than to encourage that kind of nonsense. I am not a strawberry. I do not dance on my toes. I run. That is what I am all about. So I always come late to the May Day program, just in time to get my number pinned on and lay in the grass till they announce the fifty-yard dash.

I put Raymond in the little swings, which is a tight squeeze this year and will be impossible next year. Then I look around for Mr. Pearson, who pins the numbers on. I'm really looking for Gretchen if you want to know the truth, but she's not around. The park is jam-packed. Parents in hats and corsages and breast-pocket handkerchiefs peeking up. Kids in white dresses and light-blue suits. The parkees unfolding chairs and chasing the rowdy kids from Lenox[9] as if they had no right to be there. The big guys with their caps on backwards, leaning against the fence swirling the basketballs on the tips of their fingers, waiting for all these crazy people to clear out the park so they can play. Most of the kids in my class are carrying bass drums and glockenspiels[10] and flutes. You'd think they'd put in a few bongos or something for real like that.

Then here comes Mr. Pearson with his

---

8. **Quicksilver:** another name for mercury, a silver-colored liquid metal that flows rapidly.

9. **Lenox:** Lenox Avenue, a major street in Harlem.
10. **glockenspiels** (gläk'ən·spēlz´) *n.:* musical instruments with flat metal bars that are struck with small hammers and produce bell-like sounds. Glockenspiels are often used in marching bands.

clipboard and his cards and pencils and whistles and safety pins and fifty million other things he's always dropping all over the place with his clumsy self. He sticks out in a crowd because he's on stilts. We used to call him Jack and the Beanstalk to get him mad. But I'm the only one that can outrun him and get away, and I'm too grown for that silliness now.

"Well, Squeaky," he says, checking my name off the list and handing me number seven and two pins. And I'm thinking he's got no right to call me Squeaky, if I can't call him Beanstalk.

"Hazel Elizabeth Deborah Parker," I correct him and tell him to write it down on his board.

"Well, Hazel Elizabeth Deborah Parker, going to give someone else a break this year?" I squint at him real hard to see if he is seriously thinking I should lose the race on purpose just to give someone else a break. "Only six girls running this time," he continues, shaking his head sadly like it's my fault all of New York didn't turn out in sneakers. "That new girl should give you a run for your money." He looks around the park for Gretchen like a periscope in a submarine movie. "Wouldn't it be a nice gesture if you were . . . to ahhh . . ."

I give him such a look he couldn't finish putting that idea into words. Grown-ups got a lot of nerve sometimes. I pin number seven to myself and stomp away, I'm so burnt. And I go straight for the track and stretch out on the grass while the band winds up with "Oh, the Monkey Wrapped His Tail Around the Flag Pole," which my teacher calls by some other name. The man on the loudspeaker is calling everyone over

to the track and I'm on my back looking at the sky, trying to pretend I'm in the country, but I can't, because even grass in the city feels hard as sidewalk, and there's just no pretending you are anywhere but in a "concrete jungle" as my grandfather says. ❹

INFER
❹ What values does Squeaky reveal in her remarks about Mr. Pearson and other grown-ups? How do you think she feels when she makes her last remark?

The twenty-yard dash takes all of two minutes cause most of the little kids don't know no better than to run off the track or run the wrong way or run smack into the fence and fall down and cry. One little kid, though, has got the good sense to run straight for the white ribbon up ahead so he wins. Then the second-graders line up for the thirty-yard dash and I don't even bother to turn my head to watch cause Raphael Perez always wins. He wins before he even begins by psyching the runners, telling them they're going to trip on their shoelaces and fall on their faces or lose their shorts or something, which he doesn't really have to do since he is very fast, almost as fast as I am. After that is the forty-yard dash which I used to run when I was in first grade. Raymond is hollering from the swings cause he knows I'm about

to do my thing cause the man on the loudspeaker has just announced the fifty-yard dash, although he might just as well be giving a recipe for angel food cake cause you can hardly make out what he's sayin for the static. I get up and slip off my sweat pants and then I see Gretchen standing at the starting line, kicking her legs out like a pro. Then as I get into place I see that ole Raymond is on line on the other side of the fence, bending down with his fingers on the ground just like he knew what he was doing. I was going to yell at him but then I didn't. It burns up your energy to holler.

Every time, just before I take off in a race, I always feel like I'm in a dream, the kind of dream you have when you're sick with fever and feel all hot and weightless. I dream I'm flying over a sandy beach in the early morning sun, kissing the leaves of the trees as I fly by. And there's always the smell of apples, just like in the country when I was little and used to think I was a choo-choo train, running through the fields of corn and chugging up the hill to the orchard. And all the time I'm dreaming this, I get lighter and lighter until I'm flying over the beach again, getting blown through the sky like a feather that weighs nothing at all. But once I spread my fingers in the dirt and crouch over the Get on Your Mark, the dream goes and I am solid again and am telling myself, Squeaky you must win, you must win, you are the fastest thing in the world, you can even beat your father up Amsterdam if you really try. And then I feel my weight coming back just behind my knees then down to my feet then into the earth and the pistol shot explodes in my blood and I am off and weightless again, flying past the other runners, my arms pumping up and down and the whole world is quiet except for the crunch as I zoom over the gravel in the track. I glance to my left and there is no one. To the right, a blurred Gretchen, who's got her chin jutting out as if it would win the race all by itself. And on the other side of the fence is Raymond with his arms down to his side and the palms tucked up behind him, running in his very own style, and it's the first time I ever saw that and I almost stop to watch my brother Raymond on his first run. But the white ribbon is bouncing toward me and I tear past it, racing into the distance till my feet with a mind of their own start digging up footfuls of dirt and brake me short. Then all the kids standing on the side pile on me, banging me on the back and slapping my head with their May Day programs, for I have won again and everybody on 151st Street can walk tall for another year. ❺ ◿◺

"In first place . . ." the man on the loudspeaker is clear as a bell now. But then he pauses and the loudspeaker starts to whine. Then static. And I lean down to catch my breath and here comes Gretchen walking back, for she's overshot the finish line too, huffing and puffing with her hands on her hips taking it slow, breathing in steady time like a real pro and I sort of like her a little for the first time. "In first place . . ." and then three or four voices get all mixed up on the loudspeaker and I dig my sneaker into the grass and stare at Gretchen who's staring back, we both wondering just who did win. I can hear old Beanstalk arguing with the man on the loudspeaker and then a few others running their mouths about

STYLE
❺ Read parts of this paragraph aloud to hear how the sentences imitate the rhythm of Squeaky's run.

what the stopwatches say. Then I hear Raymond yanking at the fence to call me and I wave to shush him, but he keeps rattling the fence like a gorilla in a cage like in them gorilla movies, but then like a dancer or something he starts climbing up nice and easy but very fast. And it occurs to me, watching how smoothly he climbs hand over hand and remembering how he looked running with his arms down to his side and with the wind pulling his mouth back and his teeth showing and all, it occurred to me that Raymond would make a very fine runner. Doesn't he always keep up with me on my trots? And he surely knows how to breathe in counts of seven cause he's always doing it at the dinner table, which drives my brother George up the wall. And I'm smiling to beat the band cause if I've lost this race, or if me and Gretchen tied, or even if I've won, I can always retire as a runner and begin a whole new career as a coach with Raymond as my champion. After all, with a little more study I can beat Cynthia and her phony self at the spelling bee. And if I bugged my mother, I could get piano lessons and become a star. And I have a big rep[11] as the baddest thing around. And I've got a roomful of ribbons and medals and awards. But what has Raymond got to call his own?

So I stand there with my new plans, laughing out loud by this time as Raymond jumps down from the fence and runs over with his teeth showing and his arms down to the side, which no one before him has quite mastered as a running style. And by the time he comes over I'm jumping up

and down so glad to see him—my brother Raymond, a great runner in the family tradition. But of course everyone thinks I'm jumping up and down because the men on the loudspeaker have finally gotten themselves together and compared notes and are announcing "In first place—Miss Hazel Elizabeth Deborah Parker." (Dig that.) "In second place—Miss Gretchen P. Lewis." And I look over at Gretchen wondering what the "P" stands for. And I smile. Cause she's good, no doubt about it. Maybe she'd like to help me coach Raymond; she obviously is serious about running, as any fool can see. And she nods to congratulate me and then she smiles. And I smile. We stand there with this big smile of respect between us. It's about as real a smile as girls can do for each other, considering we don't practice real smiling every day, you know, cause maybe we too busy being flowers or fairies or strawberries instead of something honest and worthy of respect . . . you know . . . like being people. ❻

STYLE
❻ What parts of this paragraph show Squeaky's special way of talking?

---

11. **rep** *n.*: slang for "reputation." People often create slang by clipping off parts of words.

Meet the Writer

Toni Cade Bambara

"I Deal in Straight-Up Fiction Myself"

Toni Cade Bambara (1939–1995) grew up in New York City, where "Raymond's Run" takes place. Bambara's writing drew on the voices of her childhood: street-corner speechmakers, barbershop storytellers, performers at Harlem's legendary Apollo Theater. She said her stories came from her imagination, though:

> ❝It does no good to write autobiographical fiction, cause the minute the book hits the stand here comes your mama screamin how could you. . . . And it's no use using bits and snatches even of real events and real people, even if you do cover, guise, switch-around, and change-up, cause next thing you know your best friend's laundry cart is squeaking past but your bell ain't ringing so you trot down the block after her and there's this drafty cold pressure front the weatherman surely did not predict and your friend says in this chilly way that it's really something when your own friend stabs you in the back with a pen. . . . So I deal in straight-up fiction myself, cause I value my family and friends, and mostly cause I lie a lot anyway. ❞

Toni Cade adopted the name Bambara from a signature on a sketchbook she found in her great-grandmother's trunk. The Bambara are a people of northwestern Africa known for their skill in woodcarving.

For Independent Reading

"Raymond's Run" comes from a collection of short stories called *Gorilla, My Love*. Other stories in the collection with characters like Squeaky are "Blues Ain't No Mockin Bird" and the title story, "Gorilla, My Love."

First Thoughts

1. Complete the following statement:
   - If I were Squeaky, I would/would not have . . .

Thinking Critically

2. What do you think is the most important **conflict** in this story? Why?

3. Squeaky and Gretchen almost get into a fight before the race. Why, then, do they smile at each other after the race?

4. Go back to the notes you made while reading the story. Which of your **judgments** changed over the course of the story? Explain why you first made them and why you changed your mind. If you didn't change your mind, describe one of your judgments, and explain why it did not change.

5. Find Squeaky's **allusions** (references to literature, history, sports, and so on), and explain what they reveal about Squeaky's interests and education.

6. In a **dialect,** words can have special meanings, pronunciations, or spellings. What do you think the italicized words in the following sentence from "Raymond's Run" mean? "'I don't think you're going to win this time,' says Rosie, trying to *signify* with her hands on her hips *all salty,* completely forgetting that I have *whupped* her behind many times for less *salt* than that" (page 550). Rewrite the sentence as someone in your neighborhood might say it.

Reading Check

a. Explain why taking care of Raymond is not an easy job. How does Squeaky protect Raymond?

b. What does Squeaky decide to do for Raymond?

Extending Interpretations

7. Is it ever necessary to fight or use threats to defend someone? Explain.

WRITING

Writing a Personal Narrative

Write a brief narrative about an incident in your life in which a first impression turned out to be wrong or someone you thought you knew well did something that surprised you. Explain what happened during this incident and why this incident is important to you.

---

go.
hrw
.com

INTERNET

Projects and Activities

Keyword: LE5 8-5

SKILLS FOCUS

Literary Skills
Analyze allusions; analyze dialect.

Reading Skills
Make judgments.

Writing Skills
Write a personal narrative.

Explaining Figures of Speech

Squeaky speaks in a colorful way and uses a lot of slang. The slang terms are usually based on **metaphors,** in which one thing is compared to something quite different. Squeaky also sprinkles her talk with **similes,** in which she compares one thing to another using *like, as, than*, or *resembles*. She also uses an **analogy,** a comparison of two things to show how they are alike. Analogies are often used to explain one concept by showing how it is similar to another concept, perhaps one that is more easily understood. Squeaky uses an analogy when she helps us understand her state of mind before the race by comparing it to a dream of flying.

PRACTICE 1

Identify each figure of speech that follows as a metaphor or as a simile. (Hint: Two are similes; two are metaphors.) Then, explain the comparison each figure of speech is based on.

1. Squeaky prances down the street like a rodeo pony to keep her knees strong.
2. Squeaky gets angry when people ask Raymond where he got that great big pumpkin head.
3. She thinks it is chicken to hide from the girls in the candy store.
4. She says that Mr. Pearson looks around the park like a periscope in a submarine movie.

PRACTICE 2

In a long paragraph on page 553, Squeaky uses an **analogy** to compare her state of mind before the race to a dream of flying. Re-read this analogy. Then, write an analogy of your own. You might compare playing football to playing a game of chess, or you might compare being sent to your room to being sent to jail. Open your analogy with words like these: "Playing football is like . . ." or "Being sent to my room is like . . ." Try to describe at least two ways in which your analogy works.

SKILLS FOCUS

Vocabulary Skills
Identify and explain figures of speech; write an analogy.

Understanding Supported and Unsupported Inferences

Reading Focus

Supported and Unsupported Inferences

"Hi, Mrs. Johnson. Got a minute?"

"Sure, Ted. What's up?"

"I was just wondering about this grade on my essay. I thought I did better than that."

"Well, Ted, you really went out on a limb with unsupported inferences."

"Unsupported what?"

"Inferences. You know, when you take the writer's clues and put two and two together."

"I did it wrong?"

"Well, in this essay you sometimes took two and two and came up with twenty-two. At other times you took two and two into orbit."

SKILLS FOCUS

Reading Skills
Analyze supported and unsupported inferences.

An **inference** is an educated guess. When you read, you make inferences by combining information in the text with what you already know. When you're evaluating a text or presenting an argument, make sure your inferences are supported—make sure you base them on information in the text and on reasonable prior knowledge. Ted's problem was that he made unsupported inferences. Instead of basing his inferences on the text, he went "into orbit."

Supported inferences are based on details in a writer's text. You can pose any number of possibilities as long as you can find evidence in the text to support your ideas. In "Raymond's Run" you could support an inference that Squeaky and Gretchen will become friends because of the new respect they feel for each other at the end of the race. You could not find evidence to support an inference that Squeaky resents Raymond. Nothing in the story supports that inference. When making inferences about a character in a story, you cannot ignore facts in the text.

Unsupported inferences are not based on details in the text. They might ignore facts or misinterpret details. They might draw conclusions that are not logical. Unsupported inferences can also go too far.

■ You'll find two readings in the pages that follow. One is an encyclopedia article about the Olympic Games. The second, a report based on the first article, is full of **unsupported inferences.** See how many you can find.

Olympic Games

THE ANCIENT GAMES. Athletics played an important role in the religious festivals of ancient Greece. Historians believe the ancient Greeks first organized athletic games as part of funeral ceremonies for important people. This practice probably existed by the 1200s B.C. Later, games became part of religious festivals honoring the gods. Many Greek cities held festivals every two or four years.

Over time, four great religious festivals developed that brought together people from throughout the Greek world. These festivals were the Isthmian, Nemean, Pythian, and Olympic games. The Olympic Games, which ranked as the most important, honored Zeus, the king of the gods.

The first recorded Olympic contest took place in 776 B.C. at Olympia in western Greece. The first winner was Koroibos (later spelled Coroebus), a cook from Elis. The Olympic Games were held every four years. They were so important to the ancient Greeks that time was measured in *Olympiads*, the four-year intervals between games. The only event in the first thirteen games was the *stadion,* a running race of 192 meters (210 yards). Through the years, longer running races were added.

Other types of competition became part of the ancient Olympics. In 708 B.C., wrestling and the pentathlon were added. The pentathlon was a combination of jumping, running, the discus throw, the javelin throw, and wrestling. Boxing joined the program in 688 B.C., and the four-horse chariot race was added in 680 B.C. Horse racing was included in 648 B.C., as was the *pancratium* (also spelled *pankration*), a combination of boxing, wrestling, and kicking. Some unusual events were included in the Olympics, such as a race in armor, a chariot race called the *apene*, in which two mules pulled the chariot, and a competition for trumpeters. . . .

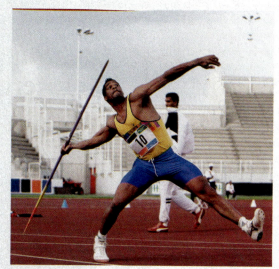

Javelin thrower.

The Romans conquered Greece during the 140s B.C., and the games soon lost their religious meaning. In A.D. 393, Emperor Theodosius I banned the games.

THE MODERN GAMES. In 1857, a group of German archaeologists began to excavate the ruins of the stadium and temples of Olympia, which had been destroyed by an earthquake and buried by a landslide and floods. Their discoveries inspired Baron Pierre de Coubertin, a French educator, to organize a modern international Olympics. He first proposed the idea publicly in 1892. In 1894, the first IOC was formed.

The first modern Olympic Games were held in Athens, Greece, in 1896. The athletes competed in nine sports: (1) cycling, (2) fencing, (3) gymnastics, (4) lawn tennis, (5) shooting, (6) swimming, (7) track and field, (8) weight lifting, and (9) wrestling. James B. Connolly of the United States became the first modern Olympic champion, winning the triple jump (then known as the hop, step, and jump).

—from *The World Book Encyclopedia*

The Old Olympic Games: A Report

The Olympic Games began in Greece a long time ago, before anyone knew how to write or play basketball. People weren't as smart back then as we are today. They played games for dead people, and they believed in lots of gods. They even thought the gods had a king, named Zeus. They didn't have clocks or watches, either, so they told time by counting games.

At first the only thing the old Greeks could do was race. They weren't very strong, so they could run only 210 yards. Later they got stronger and ran farther. Then they learned how to wrestle, jump, and throw things. They didn't play fair, though, and kicked each other when they were boxing and wrestling. They also raced chariots using four horses, which seems like three too many to me. Some of them raced chariots using mules! If they were that silly, it's no wonder the Romans conquered them and banned the games.

An earthquake and a landslide buried the old stadium. After a German dug it up, for some reason—I don't know what—a Frenchman decided to hold games again. The modern games began in 1896. They had nine cool events but no winter sports because it is too hot in Greece. An American won the hop, step, and jump. It's nice that an American won, but I don't get why winning a dance contest made him a champion.

—Anonymous

The Discus Thrower. An ancient Roman copy of a 2nd-century B.C. sculpture by Myron.

Analyzing Supported and Unsupported Inferences

The Old Olympic Games: A Report
An Example of Unsupported Inferences

Test Practice

1. Which of the following statements from the report can be **supported** by details in the encyclopedia article?

   A "The Olympic Games began in Greece. . . ."

   B "People weren't as smart back then. . . ."

   C "They played games for dead people. . . ."

   D "They didn't have clocks or watches. . . ."

2. Which of the following statements from the report is an **unsupported inference**?

   F "The only thing the old Greeks could do was race."

   G "They also raced chariots using four horses. . . ."

   H "The Romans conquered them. . . ."

   J "The modern games began in 1896."

3. The following statements from the report are all **unsupported inferences** *except* —

   A "They even thought the gods had a king, named Zeus."

   B "They told time by counting games."

   C "They weren't very strong. . . ."

   D "They didn't play fair, though. . . ."

4. The report ends with the **unsupported inference** that the hop, step, and jump was —

   F a triple jump

   G a track-and-field event

   H a dance contest

   J won by an American

Constructed Response

Base your answers to the following questions on "Olympic Games," the article from *The World Book Encyclopedia.*

1. When was the first recorded Olympic contest held?

2. Why were the ancient Olympic Games held?

3. List four events in the ancient Olympic Games.

4. Why did the ancient Olympic Games end?

5. When did the modern Olympic Games begin?

SKILLS FOCUS

Reading Skills
Analyze supported and unsupported inferences.

My Mother Pieced Quilts *and* Suéter / Sweater

Make the Connection

Quickwrite ✏️

Teresa Palomo Acosta has her mother's quilt, and Alberto Forcada has his grandmother's sweater. Is there an object in your life that symbolizes something important to you? It could be an old toy or a favorite book or maybe a food that brings back memories. Your object may represent happy times or sad times. Jot down some notes about this important object. How does it make you feel?

Literary Focus

Symbolism

People are symbol makers. A **symbol** is a person, a place, a thing, or an event that stands for something beyond itself. Some of our symbols are traditional. We easily understand them because people have agreed on their meaning. For example, a blindfolded woman holding scales symbolizes justice. In cartoons a lightbulb over someone's head symbolizes a bright idea.

Literary symbols are created by individual writers. Literary symbols stand for themselves in a story or a poem, but they stand for something else as well. Here is what writer Gary Soto (see "Broken Chain," page 17) says about symbols in poetry:

❝Poetry is a concentrated form of writing; so much meaning is packed into such a little space. Therefore, each word in a poem is very important and is chosen very carefully to convey just the right meaning. For example, the word *tree* might stand for more than a tree in an orchard. It might symbolize life itself, or it might symbolize the strength of your grandfather or your father. *Rain* may symbolize tears; *dusk* may symbolize approaching death.❞

Reading Skills 📖

Reading Poetry: Watch the Sense of the Lines

Poetry is written in lines—some long and some very short. Some poets use punctuation in their lines; some poets do not. When you read a poem that does not use punctuation, you have to read the lines as thought units. That means you do not come to a dead stop at the end of every line. You have to see if the sense of the line carries over to the next line. In the first two lines of "My Mother Pieced Quilts," for example, you should not stop at the end of line 1. Instead, you should read on to line 2, which completes the meaning.

Read the poem three times. The second time, note where you should not pause and where you should make brief or full pauses. The third time, read the poem aloud.

Woman Sewing (1948) by Jacob Lawrence.

My Mother Pieced Quilts

Teresa Palomo Acosta

they were just meant as covers
in winters
as weapons
against pounding january winds

5   but it was just that every morning I awoke to these
october ripened canvases
passed my hand across their cloth faces
and began to wonder how you pieced
all these together
these strips of gentle communion cotton and flannel
10   nightgowns
wedding organdies
dime store velvets

how you shaped patterns square and oblong and round
positioned
15 balanced
then cemented them
with your thread
a steel needle
a thimble

20   how the thread darted in and out
      galloping along the frayed edges, tucking them in
      as you did us at night
      oh how you stretched and turned and rearranged
      your michigan spring faded curtain pieces
25   my father's santa fe work shirt
      the summer denims, the tweeds of fall

      in the evening you sat at your canvas
      —our cracked linoleum floor the drawing board
      me lounging on your arm
30   and you staking out the plan:
      whether to put the lilac purple of easter against the red plaid of
          winter-going-
      into-spring
      whether to mix a yellow with blue and white and paint the
      corpus christi noon when my father held your hand
35   whether to shape a five-point star from the
      somber black silk you wore to grandmother's funeral

      you were the river current
      carrying the roaring notes . . .
      forming them into pictures of a little boy reclining
40   a swallow flying
      you were the caravan master at the reins
      driving your threaded needle artillery across the mosaic cloth bridges
      delivering yourself in separate testimonies°

      oh mother you plunged me sobbing and laughing
45   into our past
      into the river crossing at five
      into the spinach fields
      into the plainview cotton rows
      into tuberculosis wards
50   into braids and muslin dresses
      sewn hard and taut to withstand the thrashing of twenty-five years

      stretched out they lay
      armed/ready/shouting/celebrating

      knotted with love
55   the quilts sing on

---

43. testimonies *n.:* declarations. For example, people make testimonies of faith or of love.

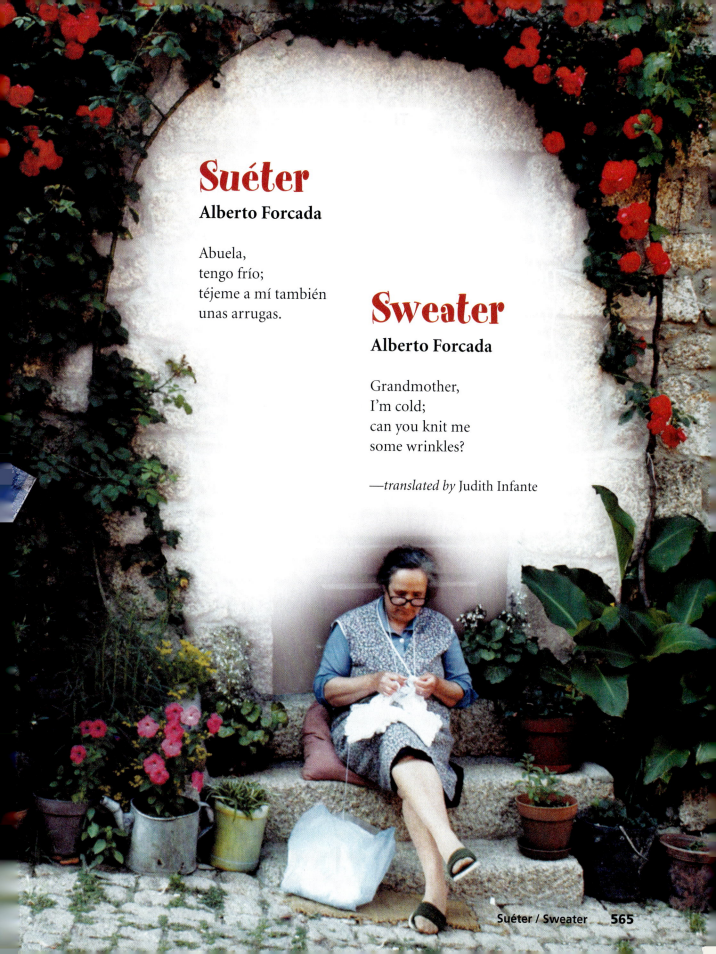

Suéter

Alberto Forcada

Abuela,
tengo frío;
téjeme a mí también
unas arrugas.

Sweater

Alberto Forcada

Grandmother,
I'm cold;
can you knit me
some wrinkles?

—*translated by* Judith Infante

Teresa Palomo Acosta

A Love of Poetry

Teresa Acosta (1949–   ) began writing poetry when she was sixteen and published her first poem in 1976. As a teenager she enjoyed European and early American poetry. Later she was inspired by African American and Mexican American poetry, when it became available to her. Acosta grew up in McGregor, Texas.

Alberto Forcada

Despertar

The poems of **Alberto Forcada** (1969–   ) that appear in *Despertar (Awaking)*—"Suéter" is one of them—describe the dreams and fantasies of children. Forcada has a degree in philosophy from the National University of Mexico. His poems have been collected in three books and have been published in such magazines as *De Polanco para Polanco*, which serves a neighborhood in Mexico City.

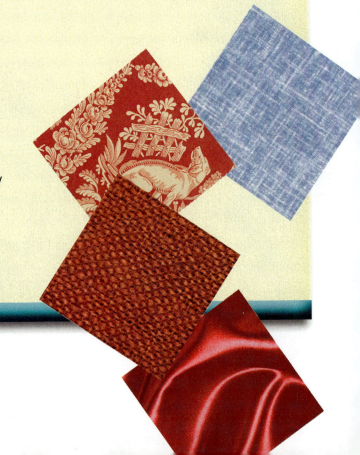

First Thoughts

1. Complete the following statement:
   - These poems made me think about . . .

Thinking Critically

2. In lines 44–51, the speaker says that the quilts make her remember her family history. From the details in these lines, what can you **infer,** or guess, about that history?

3. **Personification** is a figure of speech in which an inanimate object is given human or lifelike qualities. List three or more examples of personification in Acosta's description of the quilts.

4. What would you say the quilts **symbolize** for the speaker of "My Mother Pieced Quilts"?

5. What does the speaker of "Sweater" compare the sweater to? Do you think he would have used this comparison if the poem had been addressed to his sister?

Reading Check

a. When the speaker of "My Mother Pieced Quilts" wakes up in the morning, what does she wonder about her mother's quilts?

b. What decisions does her mother have to make as she plans her quilts? See lines 30–36.

c. Beginning in line 37 of "My Mother Pieced Quilts," the speaker identifies her mother with two things. What are they?

d. Who is speaking in "Sweater"?

e. What does the speaker of "Sweater" ask the grandmother to do?

Extending Interpretations

6. If you know Spanish, check the translation of "Suéter." What word has the translator omitted from the English translation? What do you think of this omission?

WRITING

Describing an Object

In your Quickwrite you took notes on an object that symbolizes something important to you. In a paragraph or a poem, describe the object, and tell what you remember when you see it, taste it, smell it, or feel it. If you write a poem, you might imitate Acosta's style. Try to use figures of speech in your poem or paragraph.

SKILLS FOCUS

Literary Skills
Analyze symbolism.

Writing Skills
Describe an object.

More on Metaphors

Metaphors are an important part of everyday speech. They make our language colorful and fun. They are even more essential to poetry. It would be unusual to find a poem without at least one metaphor in it.

PRACTICE 1

The following statements refer to metaphors in "My Mother Pieced Quilts." For each statement, tell what is being compared to what. Then, explain how the metaphor works—what is the poet *saying* about the quilts and the quilter in each metaphor? In some cases you will have to use your imagination. The first one has been completed for you.

1. Quilts were meant as weapons against pounding january winds.

    Answer: Quilts are compared to weapons. The metaphor means that the quilts protect the sleeper against the cold winds of January, just as weapons may protect someone from harm.

2. Quilts are october ripened canvases.

3. The quilter is said to have cemented the quilt pieces with her thread.

4. The thread is described as galloping along the frayed edges.

5. The speaker says the quilt maker was the river current / carrying the roaring notes.

6. The speaker says the quilt maker was the caravan master at the reins / driving your threaded needle artillery across the mosaic cloth bridges.

7. The quilts are said to be armed/ready/shouting/celebrating.

8. In the last line, the quilts sing on.

PRACTICE 2

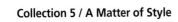

For fun, make a drawing of the literal meanings of one or more of the images above. For example, for item 8, you could draw several quilts with faces, singing into microphones.

SKILLS FOCUS

Vocabulary Skills
Analyze metaphors.

A word is dead *and*
The Word / La palabra

Make the Connection
Quickwrite

We all use words every day to communicate our needs, our thoughts, our feelings. But what do words themselves mean to you? Are they tools you use without thinking about them? Do you hate them for their hidden meanings or because you forget their definitions when you have to take a test? Do you delight in their possibilities and their variety? Jot down whatever comes into your mind when you think about words.

Literary Focus
Figures of Speech

Figures of speech are important tools of poetry—and all imaginative writing. Figures of speech are built on comparisons and are not literally true. The two most common figures of speech are the metaphor and the simile.

- A **metaphor** directly compares two very different things: *The moon was a golden grapefruit high up in the sky.*

- A **simile** also compares two distinct things, but it does so using a word or phrase of comparison—such as *like, such as, as, than,* or *resembles: The moon looked like a gleaming new penny.*

A third common figure of speech is **personification,** in which a nonhuman or inanimate (not living) thing is described as if it were human or alive and did something that only living things do: *The moon smiled down on all the creatures of the forest. The wind tapped at my window.*

INTERNET

More About Dickinson

Keyword: LE5 8-5

Literary Skills
Understand figures of speech.

A word is dead

Emily Dickinson

A word is dead
When it is said,
Some say.

I say it just
Begins to live
That day.

Sketch of a rabbit by
Seiho Takeuchi.

The Word

Manuel Ulacia

comes out from the pen
like a rabbit from a magician's hat
astronaut who knows itself alone
and weightless suspended on a line
in space

—*translated by* Jennifer Clement

La palabra

Manuel Ulacia

sale de la pluma
como el conejo del sombrero de un mago
astronauta que se sabe sola y sin peso
suspendida en una línea
en el espacio

Meet the Writers

Emily Dickinson

"Letter to the World"

Although today **Emily Dickinson** (1830–1886) is one of the most respected poets in the world, her work was almost completely unknown during her lifetime. Dickinson led an extremely private life in her family home in Amherst, Massachusetts. After she died, her sister Lavinia discovered the poems—almost eighteen hundred—that Dickinson had gathered into handmade booklets. Dickinson said that her poems were her "letter to the world" that never wrote to her.

The Granger Collection, New York.

Manuel Ulacia

Professor and Poet

When **Manuel Ulacia** (1954–2001) was a student, he studied architecture as well as literature. He went on to become a professor at Yale University and also taught at Mexico City's Universidad Autónoma. In addition to his own poetry, Ulacia studied and wrote about the work of his mentor, Octavio Paz, a Latin American poet and essayist who won the Nobel Prize in 1990.

First Thoughts

1. Do you agree with either Dickinson's or Ulacia's point of view about words? Explain.

Thinking Critically

2. Dickinson uses **personification** when she says that a word begins to "live." How do you think a word can begin to live after it has been spoken?

3. What do the **similes** in lines 2–4 of Ulacia's poem make you see?

4. A children's rhyme goes, "Sticks and stones / Can break my bones / But names can never hurt me." How would Dickinson feel about that saying? How do you feel about it?

Extending Interpretations

5. If you know Spanish, read the original text of Ulacia's poem aloud. Does it contain rhyme? What is your evaluation of the translation into English?

WRITING

Expressing an Opinion

Before you read these poems, you took notes on your own feelings about words. Refer to your notes now, and write a paragraph—or a poem—expressing your feelings about words. Try to use comparisons in your work: What do words remind *you* of? You might start off with Dickinson's beginning: "A word is . . ." 🖉

Writing a Short Story

Write a brief story for children, using a word as a character. It could be a particular word—*blue,* for example. Think of your word as a person; let your word explain how he or she is used and how he or she feels about other people and the way they use language. You can tell your story in the form of a poem or a brief narrative. Illustrations would be more than acceptable.

Reading Check

a. What is the subject of each poem?

b. In Emily Dickinson's poem, what do some people say happens to a word when it is spoken? What does the speaker say happens?

SKILLS FOCUS

Literary Skills
Analyze figures of speech.

Writing Skills
Express an opinion; write a short story.

Vocabulary Development

Metaphors, Similes, and Personification

The most common figures of speech are metaphors, similes, and personification. **Metaphors** directly compare two unlike things. **Similes** also compare two unlike things but use *like*, *than*, *as*, or *resembles* to introduce the comparison. **Personification** gives human or lifelike qualities or behavior to nonhuman things.

PRACTICE

The following lines from famous poems include figures of speech. Decide if each quotation uses a metaphor, a simile, or personification. (Watch out: Personification is a type of metaphor.) Then, tell what two things are being compared.

1. "'Hope' is the thing with feathers" —Emily Dickinson
2. "I wandered lonely as a cloud" —William Wordsworth
3. "The road was a ribbon of moonlight" —Alfred Noyes
4. "O my Luve is like a red, red rose" —Robert Burns
5. "I hear America singing . . ." —Walt Whitman
6. "The sea is a hungry dog, / Giant and gray. /
   He rolls on the beach all day." —James Reeves
7. "The fog comes / on little cat feet" —Carl Sandburg
8. "I stepped on the toe / Of an unemployed hoe.
   It rose in offense / And struck me a blow. . . ."
   —Robert Frost

SKILLS FOCUS

Literary Skills
Identify and analyze metaphors, similes, and personification.

Comparing Literature

Literary Focus
The Elements of Humor

Why do we laugh? Most situations that make us laugh involve the *unexpected.* We laugh at an elephant dressed in a tutu. We laugh at the comedian Charlie Chaplin when he puts an old shoe on his plate and proceeds to eat it as if it were a delicious steak. We laugh at two tough men who are scared of a little kid.

Here are five techniques that are often used to get a laugh:

1. **Exaggeration:** the use of overstatement for comic effect.

2. **Understatement:** a description of something as less than it is (the opposite of exaggeration).

3. **Comic language:** the use of nonsense words where they don't belong.

4. **Verbal irony:** a contrast between what is said and what is actually meant.

5. **Situational irony:** a situation that is the opposite of what we expect or of what seems appropriate.

Reading Skills
Comparing Humorous Styles

When you **compare,** you look for ways in which things are alike. When you compare humorous styles, you look at the way different texts use similar techniques of humor.

After you read each story that follows, you'll complete a chart that will help you gather material for your comparison.

Elements and Examples of Humor

Exaggeration

The Senator hit the ceiling when he read the headlines.

Understatement

When she saw Lake Michigan, my mom remarked, "Nice little pond they have there."

Comic Language

The animals didn't mess with Brer Rabbit again till the "forty-eleventh of Octorerarry."

Verbal Irony

Nick played a great game; he struck out ten times.

Situational Irony

In O. Henry's story a little kid terrifies two tough kidnappers.

SKILLS FOCUS

Literary Skills
Understand elements of humor.

Reading Skills
Compare humorous styles.

Before You Read

"Brer Rabbit and Brer Lion" is a trickster tale. The figure of the trickster is a motif that has appeared in different forms throughout history and in oral traditions all over the world. Jot down the kinds of things you think a trickster would do. Then, after you finish reading this folk tale, see how Brer Rabbit measures up to your expectations of a trickster.

Brer Rabbit and Brer Lion

traditional African American, retold by **Julius Lester**

Illustration (1987) by Jerry Pinkney.

HUMOR

To enjoy the humor in this story, you must read it aloud or listen to someone reading it aloud.

HUMOR

❶ Do any of the words in the second paragraph strike you as funny? If so, which ones?

INFER

❷ Who seems smarter, the rabbit or the lion?

INFER

❸ Why is Brer Rabbit afraid to untie Brer Lion?

HUMOR

❹ What exaggeration do you find in this paragraph?

INFER

❺ What is Brer Rabbit pretending at the end of the story?

Brer Rabbit was in the woods one afternoon when a great wind came up. It blew on the ground and it blew in the tops of the trees. It blew so hard that Brer Rabbit was afraid a tree might fall on him, and he started running.

He was trucking through the woods when he ran smack into Brer Lion. Now, don't come telling me ain't no lions in the United States. Ain't none here now. But back in yonder times, all the animals lived everywhere. The lions and tigers and elephants and foxes and what 'nall run around with each other like they was family. So that's how come wasn't unusual for Brer Rabbit to run up on Brer Lion like he done that day. ❶

"What's your hurry, Brer Rabbit?"

"Run, Brer Lion! There's a hurricane coming."

Brer Lion got scared. "I'm too heavy to run, Brer Rabbit. What am I going to do?"

"Lay down, Brer Lion. Lay down! Get close to the ground!"

Brer Lion shook his head. "The wind might pick me up and blow me away."

"Hug a tree, Brer Lion! Hug a tree!"

"But what if the wind blows all day and into the night?"

"Let me tie you to the tree, Brer Lion. Let me tie you to the tree."

Brer Lion liked that idea. Brer Rabbit tied him to the tree and sat down next to it. After a while, Brer Lion got tired of hugging the tree. ❷

"Brer Rabbit? I don't hear no hurricane."

Brer Rabbit listened. "Neither do I."

"Brer Rabbit? I don't hear no wind."

Brer Rabbit listened. "Neither do I."

"Brer Rabbit? Ain't a leaf moving in the trees."

Brer Rabbit looked up. "Sho' ain't."

"So untie me."

"I'm afraid to, Brer Lion." ❸

Brer Lion began to roar. He roared so loud and so long, the foundations of the Earth started shaking. Least that's what it seemed like, and the other animals came from all over to see what was going on. ❹

When they got close, Brer Rabbit jumped up and began strutting around the tied-up Brer Lion. ❺ When the animals saw what Brer

Rabbit had done to Brer Lion, you'd better believe it was the forty-eleventh of Octorerarry before they messed with him again. **6**

Wooden Rabbit (1981) by Felipe Archuleta. Cottonwood, sisal, and latex house paint.

Comparing Literature

HUMOR

6 What humorous detail does the story-teller use to end this tale—to emphasize that the animals will not mess with the rabbit for a very long time?

Meet the Writer

Julius Lester

"Trust the Tale"

Julius Lester (1939–   ) was born in St. Louis, Missouri, but lived in Kansas, Tennessee, and Arkansas as a child and a teenager. Lester says he "absorbed so much of Southern rural black traditions, particularly music and stories," from his father, a Methodist minister. Growing up in the segregated South of the 1940s and 1950s shaped Lester's goals and beliefs. He became a political activist and folk musician in the 1960s, then turned to writing for young people as a way of passing on African American history and traditions.

"The tales will live only if they flow through your voice," Lester tells his readers.

66 If the language you speak is different from the language I speak, tell the tale in your language. Tell the tale as you would, not I, and believe in the tale. It will communicate its riches and its wonders, regardless of who you are. Trust the tale. Trust your love for the tale. That is all any good storyteller can do. **99**

For Independent Reading

"Brer Rabbit and Brer Lion" appears in *The Tales of Uncle Remus.* The adventures of Brer Rabbit and his friends continue in *More Tales of Uncle Remus, Further Tales of Uncle Remus,* and *The Last Tales of Uncle Remus.*

First Thoughts

1. Why didn't the animals ever mess with Brer Rabbit again?

Thinking Critically

2. In **trickster tales** a smaller, less powerful character outwits a larger, stronger one. How does this tale qualify as a trickster tale?

3. Trickster tales are told around the world. This one comes from the American South and was first told by Africans who were held in slavery. Why do you think such stories were popular among the people who told them and laughed at them? What were the people really laughing at?

Reading Check

The following graphic organizer already lists the first event of this folk tale and the last event. Fill in four events that take place in the middle.

```
┌─────────────────────────────┐
│      A wind comes up.        │
└─────────────────────────────┘
              ↓
┌─────────────────────────────┐
│                             │
└─────────────────────────────┘
              ↓
┌─────────────────────────────┐
│                             │
└─────────────────────────────┘
              ↓
┌─────────────────────────────┐
│                             │
└─────────────────────────────┘
              ↓
┌─────────────────────────────┐
│                             │
└─────────────────────────────┘
              ↓
┌─────────────────────────────┐
│ The animals don't mess with │
│     Brer Rabbit again.      │
└─────────────────────────────┘
```

Comparing Literature

4. Fill out a chart like the one that follows, in order to pinpoint the elements of humor in this tale. (All these elements may not appear in the story.) When you finish the next story, you will complete the chart.

Comparing Elements of Humor		
	"Brer Rabbit and Brer Lion"	"The Ransom of Red Chief"
Exaggeration		
Understatement		
Comic language		
Verbal irony		
Situational irony		

SKILLS FOCUS

Literary Skills
Analyze elements of humor.

Reading Skills
Compare humorous styles.

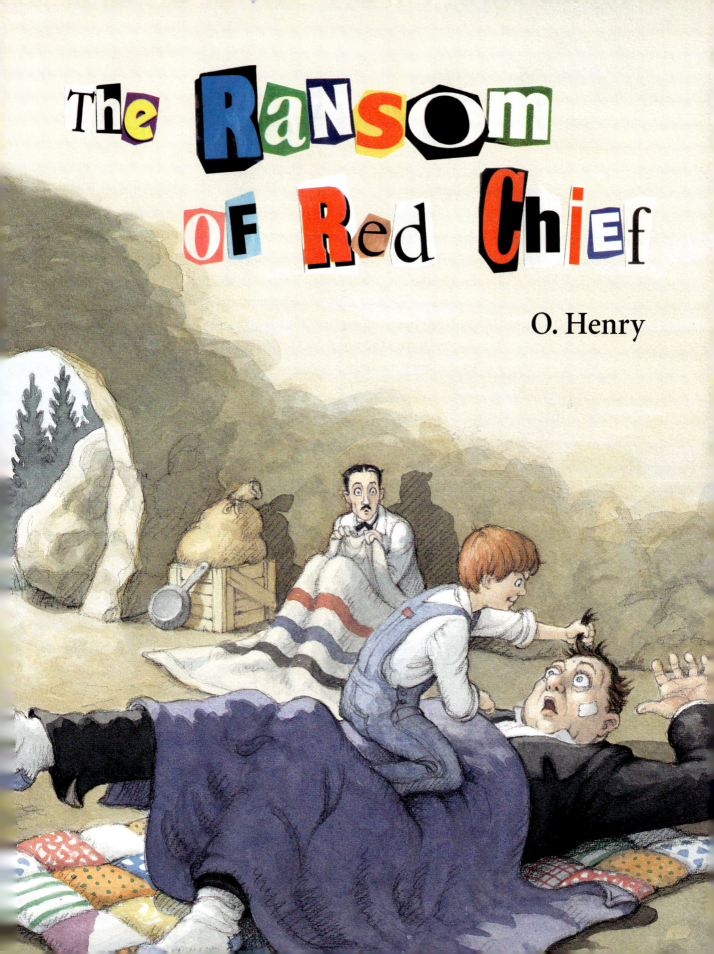

Comparing Literature

Before You Read

"The Ransom of Red Chief" is a long joke about a pair of kidnappers who make off with a nine-year-old boy who proves so ornery that *they* become *his* victims.

The story's fun has two sources. The first is the ability of an energetic nine-year-old child to drive his elders crazy with a flood of questions and activities.

The second source of fun is the notion of the bungling criminal. Sam, the narrator, has only a slight edge in intelligence on his partner. But Bill Driscoll is a model of the bumbling outlaw. Their greatest threat is to themselves.

As you read the story, decide where your sympathies lie—with the kidnappers or with the kidnap victim.

It looked like a good thing: but wait till I tell you. We were down South, in Alabama—Bill Driscoll and myself—when this kidnapping idea struck us. It was, as Bill afterward expressed it, "during a moment of temporary mental apparition";[1] but we didn't find that out till later. ❶

There was a town down there, as flat as a flannel cake, and called Summit, of course. It contained inhabitants of as undeleterious[2] and self-satisfied a class of peasantry as ever clustered around a Maypole. ❷

Bill and me had a joint capital of about six hundred dollars, and we needed just two thousand dollars more to pull off a fraudulent town-lot scheme in Western Illinois with. We talked it over on the front steps of the Hotel. Philoprogenitiveness,[3] says we, is strong in semirural communities; therefore, and for other reasons, a

---

1. **apparition** (ap′ə·rish′ən) *n.:* appearance of a ghost. Bill means *aberration* (ab′ər·ā′shən), a departure from what is normal.
2. **undeleterious** (un·del′ə·tir′ē·əs) *adj.:* harmless.
3. **philoprogenitiveness** (fil′ō·prō·jen′ə·tiv·nis) *n.:* parents' love for their children.

kidnapping project ought to do better there than in the radius[4] of newspapers that send reporters out in plain clothes to stir up talk about such things. ❸ We knew that Summit couldn't get after us with anything stronger than constables and, maybe, some lackadaisical bloodhounds and a diatribe[5] or two in the *Weekly Farmers' Budget.* So, it looked good.

We selected for our victim the only child of a prominent citizen named Ebenezer Dorset. The father was respectable and tight, a mortgage fancier and a stern, upright collection-plate passer and forecloser. The kid was a boy of ten, with bas-relief[6] freckles and hair the color of the cover of the magazine you buy at the newsstand when you want to catch a train. Bill and me figured that Ebenezer would melt down for a ransom of two thousand dollars to a cent. But wait till I tell you.

---

4. **radius** *n.:* range; area of activity.
5. **diatribe** (dī′ə·trīb′) *n.:* condemnation; harsh, abusive criticism.
6. **bas-relief** (bä′ri·lēf′) *n.* used as *adj.:* slightly raised. *Bas-relief* usually refers to a kind of sculpture in which figures are carved in a flat surface so that they project only slightly from the background.

COMIC LANGUAGE

❸ Restate Bill's long sentence beginning "Philoprogenitiveness" in plain English.

FORESHADOWING

❹ What details in these passages hint at the idea that the boy will not be an easy victim to handle?

EXAGGERATION

❺ Buffalo Bill used to take his exciting Wild West show, with cowboys and Indians and horses, around the country, even around the world. What does Bill mean when he says the boy's game makes "Buffalo Bill's show look like magic-lantern views" in the town hall?

About two miles from Summit was a little mountain, covered with a dense cedar brake. On the rear elevation of this mountain was a cave. There we stored provisions.

One evening after sundown, we drove in a buggy past old Dorset's house. The kid was in the street, throwing rocks at a kitten on the opposite fence.

"Hey, little boy!" says Bill, "would you like to have a bag of candy and a nice ride?"

The boy catches Bill neatly in the eye with a piece of brick. ❹

"That will cost the old man an extra five hundred dollars," says Bill, climbing over the wheel.

That boy put up a fight like a welterweight cinnamon bear; but, at last, we got him down in the bottom of the buggy and drove away. We took him up to the cave, and I hitched the horse in the cedar brake. After dark I drove the buggy to the little village, three miles away, where we had hired it, and walked back to the mountain.

Bill was pasting court plaster[7] over the scratches and bruises on his features. There was a fire burning behind the big rock at the entrance of the cave, and the boy was watching a pot of boiling coffee, with two buzzard tail feathers stuck in his red hair. He points a stick at me when I come up, and says:

"Ha! cursed paleface, do you dare to enter the camp of Red Chief, the terror of the plains?"

"He's all right now," says Bill, rolling up his trousers and examining some bruises on his shins. "We're playing Indian. We're making Buffalo Bill's show look like magic-lantern views[8] of Palestine in the town hall. I'm Old Hank, the Trapper, Red Chief's captive, and I'm to be scalped at daybreak. By Geronimo! that kid can kick hard." ❺

Yes, sir, that boy seemed to be having the time of his life. The fun of camping out in a cave had made him forget that he was a captive himself. He immediately christened me Snake-eye, the Spy, and announced that when his braves returned from the warpath, I was to be broiled at the stake at the rising of the sun.

---

7. **court plaster:** cloth that sticks to the skin, used for covering cuts and scratches.
8. **magic-lantern views:** slides. A magic lantern is an early type of projector. Years ago, travelers to places like Palestine used to show slides of their trips in town halls.

Then we had supper; and he filled his mouth full of bacon and bread and gravy and began to talk. He made a during-dinner speech something like this:

"I like this fine. I never camped out before; but I had a pet 'possum once, and I was nine last birthday. I hate to go to school. Rats ate up sixteen of Jimmy Talbot's aunt's speckled hen's eggs. Are there any real Indians in these woods? I want some more gravy. Does the trees moving make the wind blow? We had five puppies. What makes your nose so red, Hank? My father has lots of money. Are the stars hot? I whipped Ed Walker twice, Saturday. I don't like girls. You dassent⁹ catch toads unless with a string. Do oxen make any noise? Why are oranges round? Have you got beds to sleep on in this cave? Amos Murray has got six toes. A parrot can talk, but a monkey or a fish can't. How many does it take to make twelve?" ❻

Every few minutes he would remember that he was a pesky redskin, and pick up his stick rifle and tiptoe to the mouth of the cave to rubber¹⁰ for the scouts of the hated paleface. Now and then he would let out a war whoop that made Old Hank the Trapper shiver. That boy had Bill terrorized from the start.

"Red Chief," says I to the kid, "would you like to go home?"

"Aw, what for?" says he. "I don't have any fun at home. I hate to go to school. I like to camp out. You won't take me back home again, Snake-eye, will you?"

"Not right away," says I. "We'll stay here in the cave awhile."

"All right!" says he. "That'll be fine. I never had such fun in all my life."

We went to bed about eleven o'clock. We spread down some wide blankets and quilts and put Red Chief between us. We weren't afraid he'd run away. He kept us awake for three hours, jumping up and reaching for his rifle and screeching: "Hist! pard," in mine and Bill's ears, as the fancied crackle of a twig or the rustle of a leaf revealed to his young imagination the stealthy approach of the outlaw band. At last, I fell into a troubled sleep, and dreamed that I had been kidnapped and chained to a tree by a ferocious pirate with red hair. ❼

---

9. **dassent** *v.*: dare not.
10. **rubber** *v.*: short for *rubberneck*, meaning "stretch the neck to look at something curiously." Traffic reports often mention delays caused by rubbernecking—drivers slow down to stare at accidents and create jams.

FLUENCY

❻ Read aloud the boy's during-dinner speech. Use your voice to show how the boy leaps from subject to subject and drives Bill and the narrator crazy.

SITUATIONAL IRONY

❼ We laugh when a situation is exactly the reverse of what we expect. What comic reversal of a kidnapping situation is happening here?

Just at daybreak, I was awakened by a series of awful screams from Bill. They weren't yells, or howls, or shouts, or whoops, or yawps, such as you'd expect from a manly set of vocal organs—they were simply indecent, terrifying, humiliating screams, such as women emit when they see ghosts or caterpillars. It's an awful thing to hear a strong, desperate, fat man scream incontinently[11] in a cave at daybreak.

I jumped up to see what the matter was. Red Chief was sitting on Bill's chest, with one hand twined in Bill's hair. In the other he had the sharp case knife we used for slicing bacon; and he was industriously and realistically trying to take Bill's scalp, according to the sentence that had been pronounced upon him the evening before.

I got the knife away from the kid and made him lie down again. But, from that moment, Bill's spirit was broken. He laid down on his side of the bed, but he never closed an eye again in sleep as long as that boy was with us. I dozed off for a while, but along toward sunup I remembered that Red Chief had said I was to be burned at the stake at the rising of the sun. I wasn't nervous or afraid; but I sat up and lit my pipe and leaned against a rock. **8**

"What you getting up so soon for, Sam?" asked Bill.

"Me?" says I. "Oh, I got a kind of pain in my shoulder. I thought sitting up would rest it."

"You're a liar!" says Bill. "You're afraid. You was to be burned at sunrise, and you was afraid he'd do it. And he would, too, if he could find a match. Ain't it awful, Sam? Do you think anybody will pay out money to get a little imp like that back home?"

"Sure," said I. "A rowdy kid like that is just the kind that parents dote on. Now, you and the Chief get up and cook breakfast, while I go up on the top of this mountain and reconnoiter."

I went up on the peak of the little mountain and ran my eye over the contiguous vicinity.[12] Over toward Summit I expected to see the sturdy yeomanry of the village armed with scythes and pitchforks beating the countryside for the dastardly kidnappers. But what I saw was a peaceful landscape dotted with one man plowing with a dun mule. Nobody was dragging the creek; no couriers dashed hither and yon, bringing tidings of no news to the distracted parents. There was

VERBAL IRONY

8 Does Bill mean what he says—that he isn't nervous or afraid?

---

11. **incontinently** (in·känt′n·ənt·lē) *adv.:* uncontrollably.
12. **contiguous vicinity:** nearby area.

a sylvan[13] attitude of somnolent[14] sleepiness pervading that section of the external outward surface of Alabama that lay exposed to my view. "Perhaps," says I to myself, "it has not yet been discovered that the wolves have borne away the tender lambkin from the fold. Heaven help the wolves!" says I, and I went down the mountain to breakfast. ❾

When I got to the cave, I found Bill backed up against the side of it, breathing hard, and the boy threatening to smash him with a rock half as big as a coconut.

"He put a red-hot boiled potato down my back," explained Bill, "and then mashed it with his foot; and I boxed his ears. Have you got a gun about you, Sam?"

I took the rock away from the boy and kind of patched up the argument. "I'll fix you," says the kid to Bill. "No man ever yet struck the Red Chief but he got paid for it. You better beware!"

After breakfast the kid takes a piece of leather with strings wrapped around it out of his pocket and goes outside the cave unwinding it.

"What's he up to now?" says Bill, anxiously. "You don't think he'll run away, do you, Sam?"

"No fear of it," says I. "He don't seem to be much of a homebody. But we've got to fix up some plan about the ransom. There don't seem to be much excitement around Summit on account of his disappearance; but maybe they haven't realized yet that he's gone. His folks may think he's spending the night with Aunt Jane or one of the neighbors. Anyhow, he'll be missed today. Tonight we must get a message to his father demanding the two thousand dollars for his return."

Just then we heard a kind of war whoop, such as David might have emitted when he knocked out the champion Goliath. It was a sling that Red Chief had pulled out of his pocket, and he was whirling it around his head.

I dodged, and heard a heavy thud and a kind of a sigh from Bill, like a horse gives out when you take his saddle off. A rock the size of an egg had caught Bill just behind his left ear. He loosened himself all over and fell in the fire across the frying pan of hot water for

---

13. **sylvan** (sil′vən) *adj.:* like a forest.
14. **somnolent** (säm′nə·lənt) *adj.:* drowsy.

VERBAL IRONY

❾ Who is really the "wolf"? Who is really the "lambkin"?

washing the dishes. I dragged him out and poured cold water on his head for half an hour.

By and by, Bill sits up and feels behind his ear and says: "Sam, do you know who my favorite Biblical character is?"

"Take it easy," says I. "You'll come to your senses presently."

"King Herod,"[15] says he. "You won't go away and leave me here alone, will you, Sam?"

I went out and caught that boy and shook him until his freckles rattled. ❿

"If you don't behave," says I, "I'll take you straight home. Now, are you going to be good, or not?"

"I was only funning," says he, sullenly. "I didn't mean to hurt Old Hank. But what did he hit me for? I'll behave, Snake-eye, if you won't send me home and if you'll let me play the Black Scout today." ⓫

"I don't know the game," says I. "That's for you and Mr. Bill to decide. He's your playmate for the day. I'm going away for a while, on business. Now, you come in and make friends with him and say you are sorry for hurting him, or home you go, at once."

I made him and Bill shake hands, and then I took Bill aside and told

15. **King Herod** (her′əd): Herod, ruler of Judea from 37 B.C. to 4 B.C., ordered the killing of all boys in Bethlehem two years old and younger (Matthew 2:16).

EXAGGERATION

❿ What is exaggerated about the description of the freckles?

SITUATIONAL IRONY

⓫ The victim doesn't want to go home. How is this a comic reversal of the usual situation in a kidnapping?

him I was going to Poplar Grove, a little village three miles from the cave, and find out what I could about how the kidnapping had been regarded in Summit. Also, I thought it best to send a peremptory[16] letter to old man Dorset that day, demanding the ransom and dictating how it should be paid.

"You know, Sam," says Bill, "I've stood by you without batting an eye in earthquakes, fire, and flood—in poker games, dynamite outrages, police raids, train robberies, and cyclones. I never lost my nerve yet till we kidnapped that two-legged skyrocket of a kid. He's got me going. You won't leave me long with him, will you, Sam?" **12**

"I'll be back sometime this afternoon," says I. "You must keep the boy amused and quiet till I return. And now we'll write the letter to old Dorset."

---

16. **peremptory** (pər·emp′tə·rē) *adj.*: commanding; allowing no debate or delay.

SITUATIONAL IRONY

12 What reversal do you see here—in the behavior of the kidnapper?

Bill and I got paper and pencil and worked on the letter while Red Chief, with a blanket wrapped around him, strutted up and down, guarding the mouth of the cave. Bill begged me tearfully to make the ransom fifteen hundred dollars instead of two thousand. "I ain't attempting," says he, "to decry[17] the celebrated moral aspect of parental affection, but we're dealing with humans, and it ain't human for anybody to give up two thousand dollars for that forty-pound chunk of freckled wildcat. I'm willing to take a chance at fifteen hundred dollars. You can charge the difference up to me."

So, to relieve Bill, I acceded,[18] and we collaborated a letter that ran this way:

> EBENEZER DORSET, ESQ.:
>
> We have your boy concealed in a place far from Summit. It is useless for you or the most skillful detectives to attempt to find him. Absolutely the only terms on which you can have him restored to you are these: We demand fifteen hundred dollars in large bills for his return; the money to be left at midnight tonight at the same spot and in the same box as your reply—as hereinafter described. If you agree to these terms, send your answer in writing by a solitary messenger tonight at half-past eight o'clock. After crossing Owl Creek on the road to Poplar Grove, there are three large trees about a hundred yards apart, close to the fence of the wheat field on the right-hand side. At the bottom of the fence post, opposite the third tree, will be found a small pasteboard box.
>
> The messenger will place the answer in this box and return immediately to Summit.
>
> If you attempt any treachery or fail to comply with our demand as stated, you will never see your boy again.
>
> If you pay the money as demanded, he will be returned to you safe and well within three hours. These terms are final, and if you do not accede to them, no further communication will be attempted.
>
> TWO DESPERATE MEN ⑬

DOUBLE MEANING

⑬ Are the men desperate to get the money or to get rid of their victim?

I addressed this letter to Dorset and put it in my pocket. As I was about to start, the kid comes up to me and says:

---

17. **decry** *v.*: speak out against.
18. **acceded** (ak·sēd′id) *v.*: gave in; consented.

"Aw, Snake-eye, you said I could play the Black Scout while you was gone."

"Play it, of course," says I. "Mr. Bill will play with you. What kind of a game is it?"

"I'm the Black Scout," says Red Chief, "and I have to ride to the stockade to warn the settlers that the Indians are coming. I'm tired of playing Indian myself. I want to be the Black Scout."

"All right," says I. "It sounds harmless to me. I guess Mr. Bill will help you foil the pesky savages."

"What am I to do?" asks Bill, looking at the kid suspiciously.

"You are the hoss," says Black Scout. "Get down on your hands and knees. How can I ride to the stockade without a hoss?"

"You'd better keep him interested," said I, "till we get the scheme going. Loosen up."

Bill gets down on his all fours, and a look comes in his eye like a rabbit's when you catch it in a trap.

"How far is it to the stockade, kid?" he asks, in a husky manner of voice.

"Ninety miles," says the Black Scout. "And you have to hump[19] yourself to get there on time. Whoa, now!"

The Black Scout jumps on Bill's back and digs his heels in his side.

"For Heaven's sake," says Bill, "hurry back, Sam, as soon as you can. I wish we hadn't made the ransom more than a thousand. Say, you quit kicking me or I'll get up and warm you good."

I walked over to Poplar Grove and sat around the post office and store, talking with the chaw-bacons that came in to trade. One whiskerando says that he hears Summit is all upset on account of Elder Ebenezer Dorset's boy having been lost or stolen. That was all I wanted to know. I bought some smoking tobacco, referred casually to the price of black-eyed peas, posted my letter surreptitiously,[20] and came away. The postmaster said the mail carrier would come by in an hour to take the mail to Summit.

When I got back to the cave, Bill and the boy were not to be found. I explored the vicinity of the cave and risked a yodel or two, but there was no response.

So I lighted my pipe and sat down on a mossy bank to await developments.

---

19. hump *v.*: here, hurry.
20. surreptitiously (sur′əp·tish′əs·lē) *adv.*: in a secret or sneaky way.

In about half an hour I heard the bushes rustle, and Bill wabbled out into the little glade in front of the cave. Behind him was the kid, stepping softly like a scout, with a broad grin on his face. Bill stopped, took off his hat, and wiped his face with a red handkerchief. The kid stopped about eight feet behind him.

"Sam," says Bill, "I suppose you'll think I'm a renegade, but I couldn't help it. I'm a grown person with masculine proclivities and habits of self-defense, but there is a time when all systems of egotism and predominance fail. The boy is gone. I sent him home. All is off. There was martyrs in old times," goes on Bill, "that suffered death rather than give up the particular graft they enjoyed. None of 'em ever was subjugated to such supernatural tortures as I have been. I tried to be faithful to our articles of depredation;[21] but there came a limit." **14**

"What's the trouble, Bill?" I asks him.

"I was rode," says Bill, "the ninety miles to the stockade, not barring an inch. Then, when the settlers was rescued, I was given oats. Sand ain't a palatable substitute. And then, for an hour I had to try to explain to him why there was nothin' in holes, how a road can run both ways, and what makes the grass green. I tell you, Sam, a human can only stand so much. I takes him by the neck of his clothes and drags him down the mountain. On the way he kicks my legs black and blue from the knees down; and I've got to have two or three bites on my thumb and hand cauterized.[22]

"But he's gone"—continues Bill—"gone home. I showed him the road to Summit and kicked him about eight feet nearer there at one kick. I'm sorry we lose the ransom; but it was either that or Bill Driscoll to the madhouse."

Bill is puffing and blowing, but there is a look of ineffable[23] peace and growing content on his rose-pink features.

"Bill," says I, "there isn't any heart disease in your family, is there?"

"No," says Bill, "nothing chronic except malaria and accidents. Why?"

"Then you might turn around," says I, "and have a look behind you."

---

21. **depredation** (dep′rə·dā′shən) *n.:* robbery; looting. The phrase *articles of depredation* is a pun on *Articles of Confederation,* the name of the first U.S. constitution.
22. **cauterized** *v.:* burned to prevent infection.
23. **ineffable** (in·ef′ə·bəl) *adj.:* indescribable; too great to describe.

Bill turns and sees the boy, and loses his complexion and sits down plump on the ground and begins to pluck aimlessly at grass and little sticks. For an hour I was afraid of his mind. And then I told him that my scheme was to put the whole job through immediately and that we would get the ransom and be off with it by midnight if old Dorset fell in with our proposition. So Bill braced up enough to give the kid a weak sort of a smile and a promise to play the Russian in a Japanese war[24] with him as soon as he felt a little better.

I had a scheme for collecting that ransom without danger of being caught by counterplots that ought to commend itself to professional kidnappers. The tree under which the answer was to be left—and the money later on—was close to the road fence, with big, bare fields on all sides. If a gang of constables should be watching for anyone to come for the note, they could see him a long way off crossing the fields or in the road. But no, sirree! At half-past eight I was up in that tree as well hidden as a tree toad, waiting for the messenger to arrive.

Exactly on time, a half-grown boy rides up the road on a bicycle, locates the pasteboard box at the foot of the fence post, slips a folded piece of paper into it, and pedals away again back toward Summit.

I waited an hour and then concluded the thing was square. I slid down the tree, got the note, slipped along the fence till I struck the woods, and was back at the cave in another half an hour. I opened the note, got near the lantern, and read it to Bill. It was written with a pen in a crabbed hand,[25] and the sum and substance of it was this:

> *TWO DESPERATE MEN:*
>
> *Gentlemen: I received your letter today by post, in regard to the ransom you ask for the return of my son. I think you are a little high in your demands, and I hereby make you a counter-proposition, which I am inclined to believe you will accept. You bring Johnny home and pay me two hundred and fifty dollars in cash, and I agree to take him off your hands. You had better come at night, for the neighbors believe he is lost, and I couldn't be responsible for what they would do to anybody they saw bringing him back. Very respectfully,*
>
> *EBENEZER DORSET* **⑮**

---

24. **Russian in a Japanese war:** reference to the 1904–1905 Russo-Japanese War, in which Japan defeated Russia.
25. **crabbed** (krab′id) **hand:** handwriting that is hard to read.

SITUATIONAL IRONY

⑮ What would you expect the father of a kidnap victim to say? What does this father say?

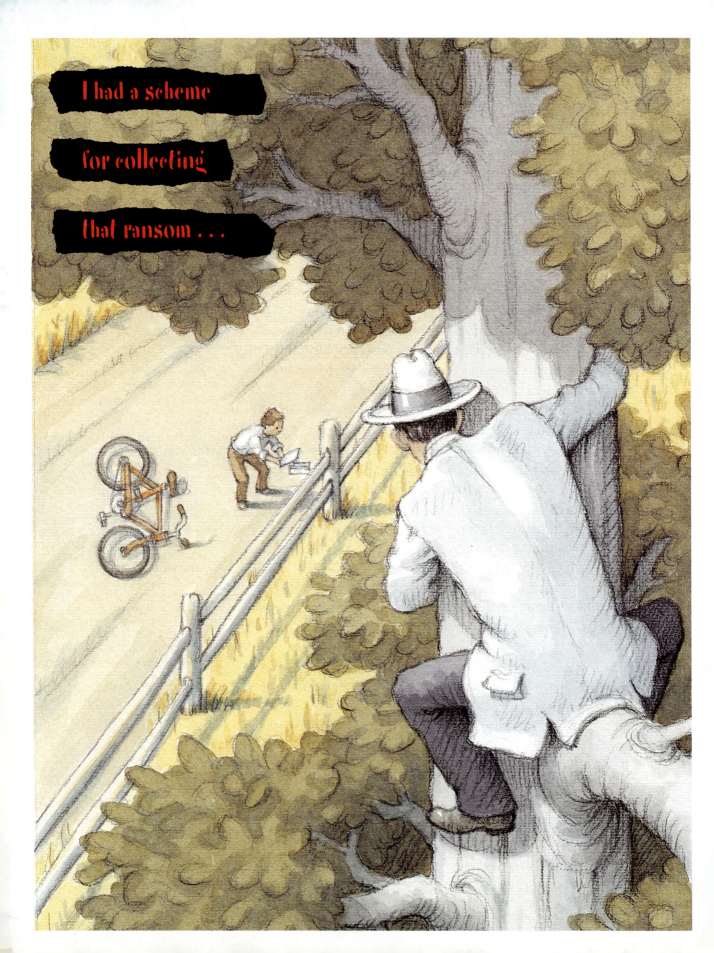

I had a scheme

for collecting

that ransom . . .

"Great Pirates of Penzance," says I; "of all the impudent——"

But I glanced at Bill, and hesitated. He had the most appealing look in his eyes I ever saw on the face of a dumb or a talking brute.

"Sam," says he, "what's two hundred and fifty dollars, after all? We've got the money. One more night of this kid will send me to a bed in Bedlam.²⁶ Besides being a thorough gentleman, I think Mr. Dorset is a spendthrift for making us such a liberal offer. You ain't going to let the chance go, are you?"

"Tell you the truth, Bill," says I, "this little he–ewe lamb has somewhat got on my nerves too. We'll take him home, pay the ransom, and make our getaway." ❶❻

We took him home that night. We got him to go by telling him that his father had bought a silver-mounted rifle and a pair of moccasins for him and we were to hunt bears the next day.

It was just twelve o'clock when we knocked at Ebenezer's front door. Just at the moment when I should have been abstracting the fifteen hundred dollars from the box under the tree, according to the original proposition, Bill was counting out two hundred and fifty dollars into Dorset's hand.

When the kid found out we were going to leave him at home, he started up a howl like a calliope²⁷ and fastened himself as tight as a leech to Bill's leg. His father peeled him away gradually, like a porous plaster.

"How long can you hold him?" asks Bill.

"I'm not as strong as I used to be," says old Dorset, "but I think I can promise you ten minutes."

"Enough," says Bill. "In ten minutes I shall cross the Central, Southern, and Middle Western States and be legging it trippingly for the Canadian border." ❶❼

And as dark as it was, and as fat as Bill was, and as good a runner as I am, he was a good mile and a half out of Summit before I could catch up with him.

SITUATIONAL IRONY

❶❻ Who is paying the ransom—the father or the kidnappers?

EXAGGERATION

❶❼ How does Bill exaggerate the speed with which he'll escape?

---

26. **Bedlam:** an insane asylum.
27. **calliope** (kə·lī′ə·pē′) *n.:* keyboard instrument like an organ, with a series of whistles sounded by steam or compressed air.

O. Henry

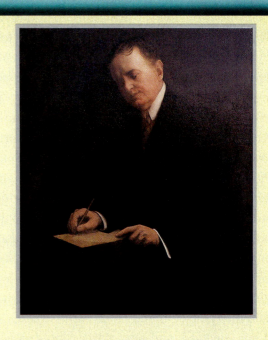

"I Have to Get a Story off My Chest"

O. Henry is the pen name of William Sydney Porter (1862–1910), who wrote almost three hundred short stories in his relatively brief life. O. Henry grew up in Greensboro, North Carolina. His mother died when he was young, and his aunt, who ran a private school, took over his education.

When he was twenty years old, O. Henry moved to Texas. In 1896, facing charges of embezzling money from a bank where he had worked, he fled the country and sailed to Honduras. He returned to Texas because his wife was ill, and he was obliged to stand trial. He was convicted of embezzlement and sent to jail for three years. Some people believe that he took his pen name from the name of a prison guard, Orrin Henry; others say that he found the name in a book.

O. Henry moved to New York in 1902. He took to life in the city, prowling streets, cafes, and stores and recording snatches of conversation. He turned many of his experiences into fiction, often locking himself in a room for three or four days to write. When a friend expressed amazement at this habit, O. Henry responded:

> **"**I have to get a story off my chest as soon as possible.... I have to top it off while my interest is still hot. Once I begin to yarn, I must finish it without stopping or it kinda goes dead on me.**"**

For Independent Reading

"The Ransom of Red Chief" and other popular stories by O. Henry, including "A Retrieved Reformation" and "After Twenty Years," appear in his *Selected Stories*.

After You Read "The Ransom of Red Chief"

First Thoughts

1. Did you sympathize with the kidnappers or the victim? Why?

Thinking Critically

2. What is Johnny doing when we first meet him? How do his actions **foreshadow,** or hint at, the trouble he'll make for his kidnappers?

3. Check the notes you took as you read the story. Describe two **inferences** you made as you read the story—that is, what did you expect to happen? In each case, what actually happened?

4. The story of Brer Rabbit that begins on page 575 is an old **trickster tale**—the story of a little character who uses his wit to outsmart a bigger, stronger character. Does Johnny qualify as a trickster character? Explain why or why not.

Comparing Literature

5. Fill out a chart like the following with examples of humorous devices used in "The Ransom of Red Chief." An assignment asking you to write about this story and the one on page 575 follows.

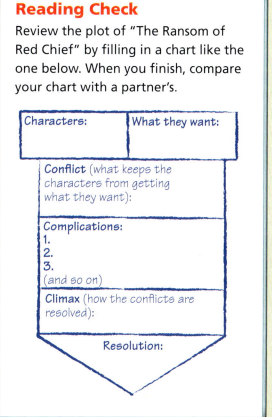

Reading Check

Review the plot of "The Ransom of Red Chief" by filling in a chart like the one below. When you finish, compare your chart with a partner's.

Characters: / What they want:

Conflict (what keeps the characters from getting what they want):

Complications:
1.
2.
3.
(and so on)

Climax (how the conflicts are resolved):

Resolution:

Comparing Elements of Humor		
	"Brer Rabbit and Brer Lion"	"The Ransom of Red Chief"
Exaggeration		
Understatement		
Comic language		
Verbal irony		
Situational irony		

SKILLS FOCUS

Literary Skills
Analyze elements of humor.

Reading Skills
Compare humorous styles.

The Ransom of Red Chief   **595**

Writing a Comparison Essay

Use the workshop on writing a Comparison-Contrast Essay, pages 516–521, for help with this assignment.

Assignment

Julius Lester and O. Henry both use traditional elements of humor to make us laugh. Write an essay comparing Lester's use of humor with O. Henry's. Before you begin, review the charts you filled in after you finished each story.

There are two ways you can organize your essay:

1. You can organize your essay by the stories: First, you would discuss Julius Lester's use of humor; then, you would discuss O. Henry's use of humor. Your first and second paragraphs might be organized like this:

Paragraph 1:	How Julius Lester creates humor
	A. Comic language
	B. Situational irony
Paragraph 2:	How O. Henry creates humor
	A. Comic language
	B. Situational irony

2. You can organize your essay by the elements of humor. That means you would discuss two or three elements of humor and show how each storyteller uses those elements.

Paragraph 1:	The use of irony in each story
	A. "Brer Rabbit and Brer Lion"
	B. "The Ransom of Red Chief"
Paragraph 2:	The use of comic language in each story
	A. "Brer Rabbit and Brer Lion"
	B. "The Ransom of Red Chief"

At the end of your essay, include a third paragraph that tells which story you enjoyed more and why.

SKILLS FOCUS

Writing Skills
Write a comparison essay.

Brer Possum's Dilemma

traditional African American, retold by **Jackie Torrence**

Back in the days when the animals could talk, there lived ol' Brer Possum. He was a fine feller. Why, he never liked to see no critters in trouble. He was always helpin' out, a-doin' somethin' for others.

Ever' night, ol' Brer Possum climbed into a persimmon tree, hung by his tail, and slept all night long. And each mornin', he climbed outa the tree and walked down the road to sun 'imself.

One mornin', as he walked, he come to a big hole in the middle of the road. Now, ol' Brer Possum was kind and gentle, but he was also nosy, so he went over to the hole and looked in. All at once, he stepped back, 'cause layin' in the bottom of that hole was ol' Brer Snake with a brick on his back.

Black and Tan (1939–1942) by Bill Traylor. Pencil, crayon, and gouache on paper.

Brer Possum said to 'imself, "I best git on outa here, 'cause ol' Brer Snake is mean and evil and lowdown, and if I git to stayin' around 'im, he jist might git to bitin' me."

So Brer Possum went on down the road.

But Brer Snake had seen Brer Possum, and he commenced to callin' for 'im.

"Help me, Brer Possum."

Brer Possum stopped and turned around. He said to 'imself, "That's ol' Brer Snake a-callin' me. What do you reckon he wants?"

Well, ol' Brer Possum was kindhearted, so he went back down the road to the hole, stood at the edge, and looked down at Brer Snake.

"Was that you a-callin' me? What do you want?"

Brer Snake looked up and said, "I've been down here in this hole for a mighty long time with this brick on my back. Won't you help git it offa me?"

Brer Possum thought.

"Now listen here, Brer Snake. I knows you. You's mean and evil and lowdown, and if'n I was to git down in that hole and git to liftin' that brick offa your back, you wouldn't do nothin' but bite me."

Ol' Brer Snake just hissed.

"Maybe not. Maybe not. Maaaaaaaybe not."

Brer Possum said, "I ain't sure 'bout you at all. I jist don't know. You're a-goin' to have to let me think about it."

So ol' Brer Possum thought—he thought high, and he thought low—and jist as he was thinkin', he looked up into a tree and saw a dead limb a-hangin' down. He climbed into the tree, broke off the limb, and with that ol' stick, pushed that brick offa Brer Snake's back. Then he took off down the road.

Brer Possum thought he was away from ol' Brer Snake when all at once he heard somethin'.

"Help me, Brer Possum."

Brer Possum said, "Oh, no, that's him agin."

But bein' so kindhearted, Brer Possum turned around, went back to the hole, and stood at the edge.

"Brer Snake, was that you a-callin' me? What do you want now?"

Ol' Brer Snake looked up outa the hole and hissed.

"I've been down here for a mighty long time, and I've gotten a little weak, and the sides of this ol' hole are too slick for me to climb. Do you think you can lift me outa here?"

Brer Possum thought.

"Now, you jist wait a minute. If'n I was to git down into that hole and lift you outa there, you wouldn't do nothin' but bite me."

Brer Snake hissed.

"Maybe not. Maybe not. Maaaaaaaybe not."

Brer Possum said, "I jist don't know. You're a-goin' to have to give me time to think about this."

So ol' Brer Possum thought.

Snake (1939–1942)
by Bill Traylor.
Pencil, crayon, and
gouache on paper.

And as he thought, he jist happened to look down there in that hole and see that ol' dead limb. So he pushed the limb underneath ol' Brer Snake and he lifted 'im outa the hole, way up into the air, and throwed 'im into the high grass.

Brer Possum took off a-runnin' down the road.

Well, he thought he was away from ol' Brer Snake when all at once he heard somethin'.

"Help me, Brer Possum."

Brer Possum thought, "That's him agin."

But bein' so kindhearted, he turned around, went back to the hole, and stood there a-lookin' for Brer Snake. Brer Snake crawled outa the high grass just as slow as he could, stretched 'imself out across the road, rared up, and looked at ol' Brer Possum.

Then he hissed. "I've been down there in that ol' hole for a mighty long time, and I've gotten a little cold 'cause the sun didn't shine. Do you think you could put me in your pocket and git me warm?"

Brer Possum said, "Now you listen here, Brer Snake. I knows you. You's mean and evil and lowdown, and if'n I put you in my pocket you wouldn't do nothin' but bite me."

Brer Snake hissed.

"Maybe not. Maybe not. Maaaaaaaybe not."

"No, sireee, Brer Snake. I knows you. I jist ain't a-goin' to do it."

But jist as Brer Possum was talkin' to Brer Snake, he happened to git a real good look at 'im. He was a-layin' there lookin' so pitiful, and Brer Possum's great big heart began to feel sorry for ol' Brer Snake.

"All right," said Brer Possum. "You must be cold. So jist this once I'm a-goin' to put you in my pocket."

So ol' Brer Snake coiled up jist as little as he could, and Brer Possum picked 'im up and put 'im in his pocket.

Brer Snake laid quiet and still—so quiet and still that Brer Possum even forgot that he was a-carryin' 'im around. But all of a sudden,

Meet the Writer

Jackie Torrence

"She Told Me This Story"

A professional storyteller, **Jackie Torrence** (1944–   ) learned her art by telling Bible stories in church and entertaining small children at the public library where she worked. Many of her most popular stories are traditional African American tales she heard while growing up in North Carolina. Torrence has her Aunt Mildred to thank for "Brer Possum's Dilemma," as she explains:

66 When I was in high school, my best friend promised for months to buy me a sweater. 'I'm goin' to git you that sweater for Christmas,' she told me. 'I've done laid it away.' Her mother was a teacher and her father was a professional band director, and I knew that she could afford to buy me the sweater.

Then she took me shopping downtown and showed me a bracelet and ring that she wanted. Since she had promised me the sweater, I knew that I had to give her something just as nice. The bracelet and ring cost $25, and I begged Aunt

Brer Snake commenced to crawlin' out, and he turned and faced Brer Possum and hissed.

"I'm a-goin' to bite you."

But Brer Possum said, "Now wait a minute. Why are you a-goin' to bite me? I done took that brick offa your back, I got you outa that hole, and I put you in my pocket to git you warm. Why are you a-goin' to bite me?"

Brer Snake hissed.

"You knowed I was a snake before you put me in your pocket."

And when you're mindin' your own business and you spot trouble, don't never trouble trouble 'til trouble troubles you.

Mildred to help me buy it for my friend for Christmas. We were poor, and Aunt Mildred refused.

'I've got to get that bracelet for her!'

Aunt Mildred just said, 'I know her and I know her mama, and she's not goin' to git you that sweater. She's jist talkin'.'

I spent nights awake, wondering where I was going to get the money to buy that jewelry, and finally I persuaded my uncle Nesbit to give me $25. And I bought the bracelet and ring.

Christmas came, and I couldn't wait to get my sweater. Sure enough, my friend called.

'I'm comin' to see you with your Christmas present.'

I said, 'That's great, 'cause I've got your present too.'

But when she walked into my house, I didn't see a box. I looked at her, puzzled.

She said, 'I've got your gift right here.'

And from her purse, she pulled a little box and gave it to me. I ripped it open, and instead of the sweater, I found rocks glued to a piece of paper—something you could buy for fifty cents.

I gave her the bracelet and ring. And when she left, I cried. But Aunt Mildred took me in her arms and said, 'I warned you of her nature.' And she told me this story. "

Writing Workshop

SKILLS FOCUS

Writing Skills
Write a character analysis.

EXPOSITORY WRITING
Character Analysis

Have you ever thought, "I don't want this book (or movie) to end" because you cared about a character so much? Have you ever gotten hooked on a series of books because you wanted to keep following the adventures of a character you liked?

Some fictional characters seem so real that we feel we know them. In this workshop you'll write an essay analyzing a fictional character who has made an impression on you.

Prewriting

1 Choosing a Character

Read and respond to the following **prompt:**

> Who is the most unforgettable character you've met in a book, movie, or television show? Is it the main character in a classic like *The Adventures of Tom Sawyer* or *Anne of Green Gables*? Is it Brian, who is stranded in the Canadian wilderness in *Hatchet*? Or Miyax, the Inuit teenager in *Julie of the Wolves*? Perhaps it is a memorable animal character, like Rikki-tikki-tavi, the mongoose of Rudyard Kipling's story, or Buck, the dog hero in Jack London's *The Call of the Wild*. Choose a character that really interests you. Write an essay in which you tell what makes that character tick.

Get together with classmates and brainstorm a list of unforgettable or favorite characters from books, stories, comic books, movies, or television shows. Pick a character who really interests you—who seems as real as a flesh-and-blood person.

PEANUTS reprinted by permission of United Feature Syndicate, Inc.

2 Analyzing a Character

To **analyze** something means to break it down into parts in order to understand how it works. When you analyze a character, you examine what the character says, does, and thinks in order to gain an overall understanding or insight into him or her.

Before you begin your character analysis, re-read the essay "Characters: The Human Experience" on pages 134–135. Then, for the character you have chosen, take notes on the following:

- **What the character looks like.** This is not always important.

- **How the character behaves or acts.** This is very important. Think about what *motivates* your character—that is, why does the character behave the way he or she does? What does your character *want*? What does he or she do to get it? How does the character *change* in the story? What has the character *learned* or *discovered* by the end of the story?

- **What the character says.** Look for key speeches that reveal the character's wants or fears or conflicts.

- **What the character thinks.** Sometimes we don't know this.

- **How other people in the story respond to the character.** This is important. It tells you whether the character is well liked or hated, if people avoid him or her, and so on.

- **What the writer tells us directly about the character.** Look for direct statements, such as "Harold was mean." However, not all writers tell us directly what a character is like. Many let us figure it out for ourselves, which is much more fun.

- **How believable your character is.** Does he or she behave the way real people behave? Does your character have a mixture of good and bad traits, the way most people do? Is he or she instead only one-dimensional—all good or all bad?

A Box of Character Traits

You may want to use some of these words to describe your character:

calm	important
clever	intelligent
conceited	kind
courageous	lazy
cruel	loyal
curious	nervous
dishonest	patient
friendly	proud
helpful	sincere
honest	sinister
humorous	timid

Framework for a Character Analysis

Introduction

Identify **character** and **work** (title, author). Include a sentence that states the essay's **main idea**.

Body

Give at least three **details** supporting your main idea.

Conclusion

Summarize or restate your main idea. Add a final comment.

Writing Tip

When the material you quote runs for more than four lines in your essay, set the quotation in **block style**. A block quotation begins on a new line. Each line of the quotation should be indented about ten spaces. A quotation set off in this way does not need quotation marks.

INTERNET

More Writer's Models

Keyword: LE5 8-5

Put these details in a chart like the one below. (Don't worry about filling in every row; some won't apply.)

Character Profile of _____

Method of Characterization	Details
Appearance	
Actions	
Words spoken by character	
Thoughts	
Other characters' responses	
Writer's direct comments	
Character's believability	

3 Finding a Main Idea

After you have explored your character, review your notes and decide on a statement that will serve as your main idea. The **thesis statement** sums up what you will discuss in your essay. Here is an example:

> In Roald Dahl's "The Landlady," the main character, Billy Weaver, is so polite and unquestioning and really *dim* that he is not like a real-life person.

4 Elaborating: Finding Supporting Details

Once you are satisfied with your main idea, you can begin to gather details to elaborate and support it. Your chart should help you here. You should be able to cite at least three details from the story that support your main idea.

Drafting

Keep your chart and notes in front of you as you write. Remember to focus on the character, not the plot. If you need to summarize the plot for an audience unfamiliar with the work, keep your plot summary brief.

Student Model

An Insane Narrator

Edgar Allan Poe had a very hard life, and maybe that's why he wrote so many dark stories. In the first paragraph of Poe's short story "The Tell-Tale Heart," the narrator tells someone (a psychiatrist?) that he will "calmly" tell his whole story to prove that he is not insane. Poe reveals what the narrator is really like just by letting us hear how he speaks. He tries to prove that he is *not* insane, but then he says the idea of murder "haunted me day and night." This leads me to believe that the idea to murder the old man was conceived by the narrator's insanity itself.

When the story begins, the narrator has killed the old man he has been living with, an old man with a strange eye. The murder is motivated by the old man's eye. At first, the narrator is very annoyed by the eye, and then it drives him to murder.

First, I think the narrator was already insane before the murder because a little thing like an eye couldn't possibly lead him to murder an old man he says he loved: "I loved the old man. He had never wronged me. He had never given me insult. For his gold I had no desire. I think it was his eye! Yes, it was this!" This makes no sense.

Second, the narrator becomes increasingly nervous and strange after the officers come to his door. Then, he begins to hear the beating of the old man's heart. It isn't really there, but in his mind it is.

Finally, by the end of his story, the narrator can't take it anymore. He breaks down completely, shows the officers the body, and yells, "It is the beating of his hideous heart!" He has given himself away.

This story is very dark and eerie, like all of Poe's work. I enjoyed reading "The Tell-Tale Heart." It's classic Poe. The use of an insane narrator is also classic Poe.

—Taylor Roderick
Martin Junior High School
Austin, Texas

Begins with attention-grabbing **opener.**

Identifies character, story, and writer.

Thesis statement.

Brief **plot summary.**

First detail *supporting thesis statement.*

Quotation *from story to elaborate.*

Second detail *supporting thesis statement.*

Third detail *supporting thesis statement.*

Summation *of main idea.*

Strategies For Elaboration

Collect more details to support your main idea by completing the following chart.

Character's Appearance

Details:

Character's Actions

Details:

Character's Words

Details:

Character's Thoughts

Details:

Reactions of Other Characters

Details:

Writer's Direct Comments

Details:

Evaluating and Revising

Use this chart to evaluate and revise your essay.

Character Analysis: Content and Organization Guidelines		
Evaluation Questions	▶ **Tips**	▶ **Revision Techniques**
❶ Does your opening capture the reader's attention?	▶ **Underline** the sentences that hook the reader. **Revise** if no sentences are underlined.	▶ **Add** a quotation, a question, or a personal connection to the character.
❷ Are the author, title, and character named in your introduction?	▶ **Highlight** the title, author, and character.	▶ **Add** a sentence or phrase naming the author, title, and character, if needed.
❸ Does your introduction have a clear thesis? Are elements of characterization introduced?	▶ **Underline** the thesis statement. **Circle** the key literary elements.	▶ If necessary, **add** a sentence stating the theme. **Introduce** key elements.
❹ Is the main idea of each body paragraph clear, and does it support the thesis?	▶ **Bracket** the key element, such as **conflict** or **motivation,** that is discussed in each paragraph in the body.	▶ **Revise** the body paragraphs so that each discusses a key literary element.
❺ Is the main idea of each body paragraph supported with evidence and explanations?	▶ **Draw a box** around each supporting quotation or detail. **Draw a wavy line** under elaborations.	▶ **Add** details or quotations, if needed. **Elaborate** on each detail or quotation with commentary.
❻ Does your conclusion restate the thesis and summarize key points? Does it leave readers with something to consider?	▶ **Highlight** the sentence in the conclusion that restates the thesis. **Circle** the summary of key points.	▶ **Add** a sentence restating the thesis. **Add** a sentence that applies the thesis to human experience.

The model on the next page is from a character analysis of the main character in "Raymond's Run" (page 547). Following the model are questions to help you evaluate the writer's revisions.

Revision Model

Squeaky isn't her real name, but there's nothing

phony about the main character ~~and narrator~~ of Toni Cade

Bambara's story "Raymond's Run." Squeaky

likes to act tough and sassy, and her attitude

gets her into trouble with the neighborhood

girls, who make fun of Raymond **her brother** **, who is "not quite right."**

Squeaky begins to mature when she ~~begins to~~ **learns**

~~see~~ that other people **, including her brother,** have special skills and

talents. Before the May Day race, she has no

respect for her competitors and boasts that she

always wins "cause I'm the best."

Evaluating the Revision

1. How has the writer elaborated on key details?
2. Where has the writer rearranged text? Does this improve the passage?
3. What additional changes would improve this writer's work?

PROOFREADING
TIPS

- Pay particular attention to the punctuation of the title of the work.

- Use quotation marks at the beginning and the end of material quoted directly. Block quotations, however, do not need quotation marks.

- Proofread your work at least twice, and ask another student to work with you, checking for errors in grammar, spelling, and punctuation.

Communications Handbook
H E L P

See Proofreaders' Marks.

PUBLISHING
TIPS

- Publish your analysis on a Web site that accepts student writing.

- Tape-record a reading of your essay for a class audio library.

Literary Skills

Test Practice

DIRECTIONS: Read the following little story. Then, answer each question that follows.

Gil's Furniture Bought & Sold

Sandra Cisneros

There is a junk store. An old man owns it. We bought a used refrigerator from him once, and Carlos sold a box of magazines for a dollar. The store is small with just a dirty window for light. He doesn't turn the lights on unless you got money to buy things with, so in the dark we look and see all kinds of things, me and Nenny. Tables with their feet upside-down and rows and rows of refrigerators with round corners and couches that spin dust in the air when you punch them and a hundred T.V.'s that don't work probably. Everything is on top of everything so the whole store has skinny aisles to walk through. You can get lost easy.

The owner, he is a black man who doesn't talk much and sometimes if you didn't know better you could be in there a long time before your eyes notice a pair of gold glasses floating in the dark. Nenny who thinks she is smart and talks to any old man, asks lots of questions. Me, I never said nothing to him except once when I bought the Statue of Liberty for a dime.

But Nenny, I hear her asking one time how's this here and the man says, This, this is a music box, and I turn around quick thinking he means a *pretty* box with flowers painted on it, with a ballerina inside. Only there's nothing like that where this old man is pointing, just a wood box that's old and got a big brass record in it with holes. Then he starts it up and all sorts of things start happening. It's like all of a sudden he let go a million moths all over the dusty furniture and swan-neck shadows and in our bones. It's like drops of water. Or like marimbas only with a funny little plucked sound to it like if you were running your fingers across the teeth of a metal comb.

And then I don't know why, but I have to turn around and pretend I don't care about the box so Nenny won't see how stupid I am. But Nenny, who is stupider, already is asking how much and I can see her fingers going for the quarters in her pants pocket.

This, the old man says shutting the lid, this ain't for sale.

SKILLS FOCUS

Literary Skills
Analyze literary devices.

Collection 5: Skills Review

1. Cisneros writes: "Me, I never said nothing to him" and "I hear her asking one time how's this here." She uses **dialect** to do all of the following *except* —
   - **A** give her characters a voice
   - **B** make her characters come alive
   - **C** make fun of her characters
   - **D** show how her characters really speak

2. The narrator of this story says, "It's like all of a sudden he let go a million moths all over the dusty furniture and swan-neck shadows and in our bones." She uses these **figures of speech** to describe —
   - **F** the magical power of music
   - **G** how dirty the owner keeps his store
   - **H** how creepy she thinks insects are
   - **J** the animal shadows on the walls of the store

3. When the narrator says that the music is "like drops of water," she is using —
   - **A** a simile
   - **B** a metaphor
   - **C** personification
   - **D** irony

4. This little story is told by —
   - **F** Nenny
   - **G** Gil, the store owner
   - **H** a young narrator who speaks as "I"
   - **J** Carlos

5. The narrator turns around "so Nenny won't see how stupid I am." She is embarrassed —
   - **A** because she has no money for the music box
   - **B** by how much she likes the music
   - **C** to be in such a dusty junk shop
   - **D** to be seen with Nenny

6. When the narrator says that Nenny is "stupider" than she is, she is using **verbal irony.** What she really means is that —
   - **F** Nenny is as moved by the music as she is
   - **G** she's mad because Nenny has enough money to buy the box
   - **H** she doesn't think Nenny is smart
   - **J** she is embarrassed to be seen with Nenny

7. The **situational irony** in this story involves the fact that —
   - **A** the girls are in an uncomfortable situation
   - **B** the girls find beauty in a dirty, messy junk store
   - **C** the junk store is dirty and crowded
   - **D** the junk store is full of moths

Constructed Response

8. What is the music box a **symbol** of for the narrator, the store owner, and Nenny?

Collection 5: Skills Review

Vocabulary Skills

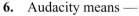

Test Practice

Synonyms

DIRECTIONS: Choose the word or words that mean the same, or about the same, as the underlined word. These are the words you learned while reading "The Tell-Tale Heart."

1. Acute means —
   - **A** heavy
   - **B** sharp
   - **C** full
   - **D** attractive

2. Sagacity means —
   - **F** intelligence
   - **G** sneakiness
   - **H** safety
   - **J** innocence

3. Refrained means —
   - **A** redid
   - **B** directed
   - **C** held back
   - **D** trained

4. Vexed means —
   - **F** cursed
   - **G** voted
   - **H** annoyed
   - **J** announced

5. Derision means —
   - **A** decision
   - **B** ridicule
   - **C** division
   - **D** pleasure

6. Audacity means —
   - **F** boldness
   - **G** bitterness
   - **H** speediness
   - **J** niceness

7. Wary means —
   - **A** nice
   - **B** very
   - **C** annoyed
   - **D** cautious

8. Vehemently means —
   - **F** forcefully
   - **G** verbally
   - **H** viciously
   - **J** gently

9. Suavity means —
   - **A** smoothness
   - **B** safety
   - **C** seriousness
   - **D** carelessness

10. Gesticulations are —
    - **F** funny jokes
    - **G** energetic gestures
    - **H** angry words
    - **J** math problems

SKILLS FOCUS

Vocabulary Skills
Identify synonyms.

Collection 5: Skills Review

Writing Skills

Test Practice

DIRECTIONS: Read the following paragraph from an essay analyzing character. Then, answer each question that follows.

(1) Framton Nuttel, in Saki's story "The Open Window," is an awkward, timid bachelor who has been bullied by his sister. (2) He suffers from a nervous disorder and has been sent to the country to recover. (3) Since Framton is new to this part of the country, his sister gives him letters of introduction to people who are complete strangers. (4) Framton doesn't know many people in those parts. (5) He calls upon Mrs. Sappleton and is greeted by her niece Vera. (6) Vera is a self-possessed teenager who finds him an easy target for mischief. (7) Framton is totally absorbed in his own illness and assumes that others are interested in the details of his ailments. (8) He is so gullible that he believes Vera's story about her aunt's delusions and is frightened half to death when the "ghosts" appear through the open window.

1. Which sentence is unnecessary and should be deleted?
   - **A** Sentence 2
   - **B** Sentence 3
   - **C** Sentence 4
   - **D** Sentence 7

2. Which of the following sentences does not provide insight into Framton's character?
   - **F** Sentence 1
   - **G** Sentence 2
   - **H** Sentence 5
   - **J** Sentence 8

3. This passage could be improved by
   - **A** a description of the setting
   - **B** details of the hunting party
   - **C** discussion of the niece's motivation
   - **D** elaboration of Framton's responses

4. What would be the best way to combine Sentences 5 and 6?
   - **F** "He calls upon Mrs. Sappleton and is greeted by her niece Vera, who is a self-possessed teenager who finds him an easy target for mischief."
   - **G** "He calls upon Mrs. Sappleton and is greeted by her niece Vera, a self-possessed teenager who finds him an easy target for mischief."
   - **H** "He calls upon Mrs. Sappleton and is greeted by her niece Vera; her niece Vera is a self-possessed teenager who finds him an easy target for mischief."
   - **J** "Calling upon Mrs. Sappleton, he finds himself greeted by Vera, a self-possessed niece who finds him an easy target for mischief."

SKILLS FOCUS

Writing Skills
Analyze a character analysis.

Fiction *and* Poetry

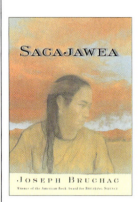

A Historic Journey

It's quite possible that the explorers Lewis and Clark never would have completed their famous journey from the Mississippi to the Pacific Ocean if they had not been guided by a young Native American woman, Sacajawea. In his historical novel, *Sacajawea,* award-winning author Joseph Bruchac recounts the danger and excitement of the journey through Sacajawea's and William Clark's eyes.

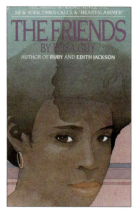

The Loner

You know her: the new kid in class no one wants for a friend. In *The Friends* by Rosa Guy, the new girl is Phyllisia Cathy, and she is from the West Indies. The only person who will befriend her is Edith, a Harlem-born girl trying to keep her family together despite the hardships of poverty.

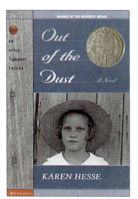

Picking Up the Pieces

While dust storms are devastating her family's Oklahoma farm in 1934, Billie Jo finds joy only in playing the piano. Then a terrible accident takes that joy away and changes her life forever. *Out of the Dust,* Karen Hesse's Newbery Medal–winning novel, tells the story of Billie Jo's coming to terms with her struggles and misfortunes. The story is told through a series of free-verse poems written in everyday language.

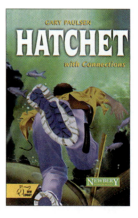

Survival of the Fittest

Young Brian finds himself stranded alone in the Canadian wilderness after a plane crash. With only his wits and a hatchet to rely on for survival, Brian learns some memorable lessons about nature, growing up, and himself in Gary Paulsen's Newbery Honor book *Hatchet.*

This title is available in the HRW Library.

Nonfiction

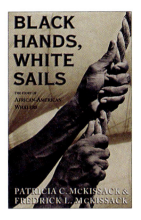

Finally Recognized

In *Black Hands, White Sails,* Patricia C. and Fredrick L. McKissack bring attention to African Americans who worked in the whaling industry from Colonial times until the nineteenth century. Some were to become captains and shipowners, and others played key roles in the Civil War and the Underground Railroad.

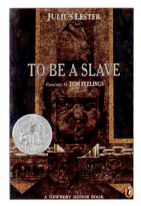

From Slavery to Freedom

In *To Be a Slave,* a Newbery Honor book by Julius Lester, men and women who lived through slavery tell their stories in their own words. Lester's *Long Journey Home,* six true stories of freedom, is an uplifting sequel.

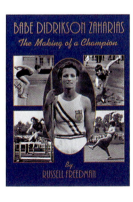

Battling the Odds

The athletic achievements of Babe Didrikson Zaharias could probably fill a book as large as this one! For starters, she was a championship golfer, a gold medalist in track and field, and an outstanding basketball player. More impressive, her accomplishments took place at a time when women had few opportunities for competition. Russell Freedman tells her story in *Babe Didrikson Zaharias: The Making of a Champion.*

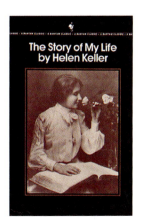

A Portrait of Bravery

Even though Helen Keller was left blind and deaf by an illness when she was nineteen months old, she was determined to read and write. In *The Story of My Life,* Keller writes about her refusal to give up in the face of unthinkable adversity. The book includes letters she wrote to friends and personal records that will lead readers to a greater understanding of her life.

Our Song by Alfredo Castañeda (1999).
Courtesy of Mary-Anne Martin/Fine Art, New York.

POETRY: SOUND AND SENSE

Literary Focus:

Analyzing Poetry

Informational Focus:

Analyzing Summaries

INTERNET

Collection Resources

Keyword: LE5 8-6

Elements of Literature

Poetry *by* Mara Rockliff
SOUND AND SENSE

Words with Their Own Music

Did you ever unwrap a new CD and read the song lyrics before playing the disc? Often the words by themselves don't seem all that special. It takes music to bring them to life.

Poetry is different. The words in a good poem create their own music. The English poet Samuel Taylor Coleridge once defined poetry as "the best words in their best order." Listen to how one of his own poems begins:

In Xanadu did Kubla Khan
A stately pleasure-dome decree:
Where Alph, the sacred river, ran
Through caverns measureless to man
Down to a sunless sea.

                              —from "Kubla Khan"

All Coleridge gave us were words on a page, and yet more than two centuries after he wrote them down, the music still comes through. How did he do it?

Moving to the Beat

If words can create the haunting music of a poem, **rhythm**—the repetition of stressed and unstressed syllables—provides the poem's beat. Like many other languages, English is accented: Certain syllables get a stronger beat than other syllables. The beat of a poem comes from the patterns made by the stressed and unstressed syllables. If you

say a few English words aloud, you'll hear the beat built into them: MOUN-tain, be-CAUSE, Cin-cin-NAT-i. Say your name aloud, and notice its beat.

Read aloud this limerick (a **limerick** is a short, humorous poem with a definite pattern of rhythm). Listen to the way your voice rises and falls as you pronounce the stressed and unstressed syllables.

A gentleman dining at Crewe
Found quite a large mouse in his stew
  Said the waiter, "Don't shout,
  And wave it about,
Or the rest will be wanting one too!"

You probably stressed the words this way ($'$ indicates a stressed syllable; $\smile$ indicates an unstressed syllable):

Ă gen´tlĕmăn dín´ĭng ăt Cré´we

A regular pattern of stressed and unstressed syllables is called **meter**. The metric pattern for lines 1, 2, and 5 of the limerick is the same:

$$\smile \; ' \; \smile \; \smile \; ' \; \smile \; \smile \; '$$

The pattern for lines 3 and 4 is slightly different. Re-read lines 3 and 4 to hear the difference.

Chiming Sounds

The chiming effect of **rhyme** adds to the music of a poem, like the tinkling of a bell or the clash of cymbals. Most rhymes

INTERNET
More About
Sounds of Poetry
Keyword: LE5 8-6

Literary Skills
Understand elements of poetry.

in poetry are **end rhymes.** In the limerick the end rhymes are *Crewe, stew,* and *too* (lines 1, 2, and 5) and *shout* and *about* (lines 3 and 4). When the two rhyming lines are consecutive, they're called a **couplet.** Here is a couplet with end rhymes that are spelled differently— but they rhyme:

> The panther is like a leopard,
> Except it hasn't been peppered.
> —Ogden Nash,
> from "The Panther"

Rhymes can also occur within lines; these are called **internal rhymes.**

> While I nodded, nearly napping,
> suddenly there came a tapping,
> As of someone gently rapping, rapping
> at my chamber door—
>
> —Edgar Allan Poe,
> from "The Raven"

Napping, tapping, and *rapping* are **exact rhymes,** as are *leopard* and *peppered.* Many modern poets prefer **approximate rhymes** (also called near rhymes, off rhymes, imperfect rhymes, or slant rhymes). Approximate rhymes use sounds that are similar but not exactly the same, like *fellow* and *hollow* or *cat* and *catch* or *bat* and *bit.*

Some people think approximate rhymes sound less artificial than exact rhymes, more like real speech. Some poets use approximate rhymes because they feel that all the good exact rhymes have already been used too many times.

The Beat Goes On

Many poets today prefer to work in **free verse.** With free verse they do not have to write in meter or use a regular rhyme scheme, but that doesn't mean that "anything goes." Even when they write free verse, poets work to make their lines rhythmic. One way they do this is by repeating sentence patterns. You can't miss the rhythm in these lines by Walt Whitman, one of the first American poets to use free verse:

> Give me the splendid silent sun with
> all his beams full-dazzling,
> Give me juicy autumnal fruit ripe and
> red from the orchard,
> Give me a field where the unmowed
> grass grows,
> Give me an arbor, give me the trellised
> grape . . .
>
> —from "Give Me the
> Splendid Silent Sun"

Meter and rhyme aren't the only ways in which a poet can create music with words. Note all the *s* sounds as you read aloud this line from "The Raven":

> And the silken, sad, uncertain rustling
> of each purple curtain

Do you hear the rustling of that curtain in all those *s* sounds? This is **alliteration** (ə·lit′ər·ā′shən), the repetition of consonant sounds in several words that are close together. When vowel sounds are repeated, it's called **assonance** (as′ə·nəns).

(continued)

Poe's line also provides an example of **onomatopoeia** (än′ō·mat′ō·pē′ə), a long word that refers to the use of words with sounds that imitate or suggest their meaning—such as *rustle*. Doesn't *sizzle* sound like bacon frying on the grill? How about *snap*, *crackle*, *pop*? Words like these help poets bring sound and sense together.

Some Types of Poems

ballad: songlike poem that tells a story, often a sad story of betrayal, death, or loss. Ballads usually have a regular, steady rhythm, a simple rhyme pattern, and a refrain, all of which make them easy to memorize.

epic: long narrative poem about the many deeds of a great hero. Epics are closely connected to a particular culture. The hero of an epic embodies the important values of the society he comes from. (Heroes of epics have— so far—been male.)

narrative poem: poem that tells a story—a series of related events.

lyric poem: poem that does not tell a story but expresses the personal feelings of a speaker.

ode: long lyric poem, usually praising some subject, and written in dignified language.

sonnet: fourteen-line lyric poem that follows strict rules of structure, meter, and rhyme.

Practice

Find a poem you like, and prepare it for reading aloud. Here are some tips:

- Be aware of punctuation, especially periods and commas. A period signals the end of a sentence—which is not always at the end of a line. You should make a full stop when you come to a period.
- If a line of poetry doesn't end with punctuation, don't stop. Continue reading until you reach a punctuation mark.
- If the poem is written in meter, don't read it in a singsong way. Read the poem for its meaning, using a natural voice. Let the music come through on its own.

"I think that I shall never see, a poem as lovely as a bee, flea, sea, ski, plea, key . . ."

How to Read a Poem

by Kylene Beers

Robert Frost once said that a poem "begins in delight and ends in wisdom." I think he meant that as we read a poem, we delight in its rhythms, rhymes, images, and comparisons and in the story or experience it shares. But, by the end of the poem, we've often had an "aha" experience: We've found wisdom that touches our own lives.

Finding the "Aha" in a Poem

- **Read from the inside out.** If you read a poem and worry about finding metaphors or identifying rhyme schemes, then you've missed the point of the poem. You've read it from the outside in. Don't do that! First, enjoy the poem. Then, ask yourself *why* you liked it. If you enjoyed the sounds, you've probably picked up on **rhyme.** If you liked the beat of the lines, you liked the **rhythm.** If you liked the poet's unusual comparisons, you've noticed **metaphors** or **similes.** These elements of the poem—what's on the outside—help you enjoy the poem and then discover its wisdom on the inside.

- **Read the poem aloud at least once.** Pay special attention to punctuation. Don't stop just because you've come to the end of a line. Stop only when there is a punctuation mark. Pause briefly at commas and at dashes, which indicate a break in thought. Pause a little longer at periods. Each poem has its own pulse, which you can hear more distinctly by reading it aloud.

- **Pay attention to each word.** Poets generally use few words, so each word is important. If you aren't sure what a word in a poem means, look it up.

- **Pay attention to the title.** Sometimes—but not always—the meaning of the poem is hinted at in the title.

SKILLS FOCUS

Reading Skills
Use specific strategies to read and analyze a poem.

Every poem is a message from its writer. In the past, poets often stated that message openly, tacking it on at the end of the poem.

Today poets generally try to let their readers discover the messages for themselves. In this way, poets invite us to join directly in their experience. Read "Riding Lesson" aloud at least once. Then, read the questions and responses in the margins. They will help you discover the poem's wisdom or message.

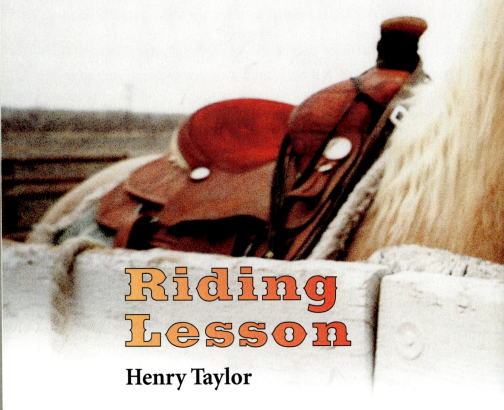

Riding Lesson

Henry Taylor

I learned two things
from an early riding teacher.
He held a nervous filly
in one hand and gestured
5   with the other, saying, "Listen.
Keep one leg on one side,
the other leg on the other side,
and your mind in the middle."
He turned and mounted.
10   She took two steps, then left

IDENTIFY

What does the title suggest the poem will be about?

It will be about someone learning how to ride something— maybe a horse.

INFER

Who is speaking in the poem? What do you think the speaker will talk about in the poem? (lines 1–2)

The speaker is someone who has taken riding lessons. He or she will probably talk about the lessons.

IDENTIFY

What does the word *filly* (line 3) mean?

A filly is a young female horse.

the ground, I thought for good.
But she came down hard, humped
her back, swallowed her neck,
and threw her rider as you'd
15 throw a rock. He rose, brushed
his pants and caught his breath,
and said, "See that's the way
to do it. When you see
they're gonna throw you, get off."

Practice the Strategy

PRACTICE

Finding the "Aha" Moment

Read this poem about reading poetry, and answer the questions alongside it. Do any lines in the poem provide that "aha" moment for you? If so, which ones?

INFER

In line 1, who is "I"? Who is "them"? What clue does the title offer?

IDENTIFY

In which lines does the poet compare a poem to a beehive? to a maze? to a dark room? to a body of water?

SKILLS FOCUS

Reading Skills
Use specific strategies to read and analyze a poem.

Introduction to Poetry
Billy Collins

I ask them to take a poem
and hold it up to the light
like a color slide

or press an ear against its hive.

5   I say drop a mouse into a poem
and watch him probe his way out,

or walk inside the poem's room
and feel the walls for a light switch.

I want them to water-ski
10   across the surface of a poem
waving at the author's name on the shore.

But all they want to do
is tie the poem to a chair with rope
and torture a confession out of it.

15   They begin beating it with a hose
to find out what it really means.

INFER

How would *you* "torture" a poem (line 14)? What might a poem's "confession" be?

COMPARE AND CONTRAST

Compare what the speaker wants "them" to do with what "they" want to do (lines 9–16). Which methods do you think will reveal a poem's message? Explain.

Meet the Writers

Henry Taylor

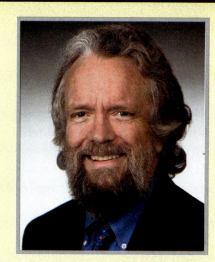

A Lover of Horses

The Pulitzer Prize–winning poet **Henry Taylor** (1942–   ) grew up in rural Virginia; his father was a dairy farmer. Although Taylor decided at an early age not to follow in his father's footsteps, he was strongly influenced by his surroundings. He says,

> 66 Horses, in fact, were central to my life until I was in my early twenties; my sisters and I had various ponies and horses around the place, and our parents . . . started us foxhunting, showing in small local horse and pony shows, and generally being as horsy as we could be. . . . Many of my poems draw heavily on that experience. 99

Billy Collins

A "Lifter of Chalk"

When **Billy Collins** (1941–   ) was named poet laureate of the United States in 2001, he said, "It came completely out of the blue, like a soft wrecking ball from outer space." Surprising and playful images like this one are typical of Collins's poetry.

Collins was born in New York City. For more than thirty years, he has been a professor of English at the City University of New York—or, as he modestly puts it, a "lifter of chalk in the Bronx." His poetry has brought him many awards as well as wide popularity. Some have called him the most popular poet in America.

Valentine for Ernest Mann

Make the Connection

Quickwrite

Think about the poems you have read or heard. Do you have any favorites? What do you think most poems are about? Jot down some of your feelings about poetry. Then, see if the poem that follows surprises you.

Literary Focus

Lyric Poetry

Poems can tell stories, or they can just express the feelings or thoughts of the speaker. Poems that express feelings and do not tell stories are called **lyrics.** Lyric poems are usually short, and they imply—rather than state directly—a single, strong emotion. The word *lyric* comes from the word *lyre* (lĭr), which refers to a stringed instrument something like a small harp. In ancient Greece, people used to recite poems to the strumming of a lyre. (At poetry readings today music is still sometimes used to set the beat or create atmosphere.)

Reading Skills

More Tips for Reading a Poem

All reading requires skill, but you may have to work a little harder to read a poem well. You'll find it easier if you use these strategies:

1. **Be aware of punctuation,** especially commas and periods. Periods signal the beginnings and ends of sentences (which are not always at ends of lines).

2. **Let the rhythm come through.** If a poem has a steady beat—da-DUM, da-DUM, da-DUM, da-DUM—try to avoid reading the poem in a singsong way. Read the poem in a normal voice, as if you were speaking to a friend. The poem's music will emerge naturally.

3. **Look for figures of speech.** Figurative language is at the heart of most poems. Look for **metaphors** and **similes.** What comparisons are they revealing to you?

4. **Find the subject and verb.** When you are confused by a passage, look for the subject and verb. Then, decide how the other words in the sentence are used. Usually you'll find that they are modifiers.

5. **Read it again.** After you finish reading a poem, think about it. Then, read it a second and even a third time. With each re-reading you'll probably discover something new.

6. **Have fun.** Poems are not written to torment you. Even the most serious poem, written to express the deepest emotion, involves a kind of play. Poets play with words, sounds, rhythms, rhymes. As you work at interpreting a poem, you are playing a game with the poet.

SKILLS FOCUS

Literary Skills
Understand the characteristics of lyric poetry.

Reading Skills
Use specific strategies to read a poem.

Valentine for Ernest Mann

Naomi Shihab Nye

You can't order a poem like you order a taco.
Walk up to the counter, say, "I'll take two"
and expect it to be handed back to you
on a shiny plate.

5   Still, I like your spirit.
Anyone who says, "Here's my address,
write me a poem," deserves something in reply.
So I'll tell a secret instead:
poems hide. In the bottoms of our shoes,
10   they are sleeping. They are the shadows
drifting across our ceilings the moment
before we wake up. What we have to do
is live in a way that lets us find them.

Once I knew a man who gave his wife
15   two skunks for a valentine.
He couldn't understand why she was crying.
"I thought they had such beautiful eyes."
And he was serious. He was a serious man
who lived in a serious way. Nothing was ugly
20   just because the world said so. He really
liked those skunks. So, he re-invented them
as valentines and they became beautiful.
At least, to him. And the poems that had been hiding
in the eyes of skunks for centuries
25   crawled out and curled up at his feet.

Maybe if we re-invent whatever our lives give us
we find poems. Check your garage, the odd sock
in your drawer, the person you almost like, but not quite.
And let me know.

Meet the Writer

Naomi Shihab Nye

A Poet of the Familiar

Naomi Shihab Nye (1952–   ) often runs workshops in schools to help students find the poetry hidden in their imaginations. Nye grew up in St. Louis, lived in Jerusalem with her father's family for a year, and settled in San Antonio, Texas. Since Nye was born to an American mother and a Palestinian father, it's not surprising that she often celebrates in her writing the diversity of American culture. Wherever she lived, Nye carefully observed the activities of her friends and neighbors:

66 For me the primary source of poetry has always been local life, random characters on the streets, our own ancestry sifting down to us by small essential daily tasks. 99

These "daily tasks" have continually inspired some of Nye's most powerful work. She can make the tiniest details seem exceptional. She once said:

66 Familiar sights, sounds, smells have always been my necessities. Let someone else think about future goals and professional lives! I will keep track of the bucket and the hoe, billowing leaves, and clouds drifting in from the horizon. 99

For Independent Reading

Nye's first young-adult novel, *Habibi*, is autobiographical, about an American teenager who, on moving to Jerusalem, finds that suddenly *she* is the immigrant.

First Thoughts

1. Where do you find poems in your life—in the garage, your sock drawer, somewhere else?

Thinking Critically

2. In the first stanza the poet uses a **simile.** What two very different things is she comparing? What is she saying about poems by using this simile?

3. In the second stanza the poet **personifies** poems. What human things does she say poems can do? What is she telling us about poems by using this figure of speech?

4. The second stanza also includes a **metaphor.** What are poems compared to? What does this metaphor tell us about poems?

5. Why does the speaker tell us about the man and the skunks in the third stanza? (What do skunks have to do with poetry?)

6. What final advice does the speaker give Ernest Mann?

WRITING

Writing a Lyric Poem

Follow Naomi Shihab Nye's advice, and try to find a lyric poem in your life. Use words that will help your reader see, hear, touch, or smell an object or person the way you do. Help your reader feel the way you feel about the object or person. For a structure you might spell out the name of your subject and start each line with a letter of the word, as in this example:

Soggy socks hang on the line,

Or rest in my drawer rolled up and dry.

Crew socks once smelly,

Kneesocks once fuzzy,

Soon will look like new!

SKILLS FOCUS

Literary Skills
Analyze a lyric poem.

Reading Skills
Use specific strategies to read a poem.

Writing Skills
Write a lyric poem.

Paul Revere's Ride

tells an exciting story about a historical event.

Galloping Rhythm

People love rhythm. We love the rhythm of music, the rhythm of dance, the rhythm of our language. Rhythm is not only pleasing to the ear (and eye); it also affects our moods. A slow rhythm can make us feel sad or dreamy. A fast rhythm can make us feel like dancing. Rhythm is as essential to language as it is to music. In language, **rhythm** is the rise and fall of the voice, produced by sounds. When the sounds occur in a particular pattern, we call it **meter.**

"Paul Revere's Ride" is written with a strong meter. Notice, when you read it aloud, how the meter sounds like a galloping horse: da-da-DUM da-da-DUM da-da-DUM da-da-DUM. The story of Paul Revere has been told many times and in many different ways, but this poem is the most famous version of what happened on that fateful night. What makes everyone remember this poem is its rhythm.

Make the Connection
Quickwrite ✏️

Many countries have heroes whom they honor for their courage in standing up for justice and freedom. Work with a partner to make a list of some of these heroes. Tell who they are, what country honors them, and what they did to help their people.

Literary Focus
Narrative Poem

A **narrative poem** is a poem that tells a story. The poem you are about to read

Literary Skills
Understand the characteristics of narrative poetry; understand rhythm and meter.

Background
Literature and Social Studies

This poem is based loosely on historical events. On the night of April 18, 1775, Paul Revere, William Dawes, and Dr. Samuel Prescott set out from Boston to warn American colonists of a planned British raid on Concord, Massachusetts. The British wanted to arrest two Americans who were calling for armed resistance to England. The British also wanted to destroy a supply of arms in Concord. The next day armed volunteers known as minutemen confronted the British at Lexington and Concord. These were the first battles of the American Revolution.

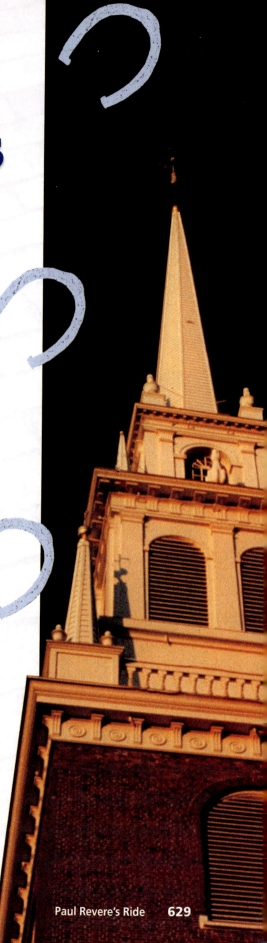

Paul Revere's Ride

Henry Wadsworth Longfellow

Listen, my children, and you shall hear
Of the midnight ride of Paul Revere,
On the eighteenth of April, in Seventy-five;
Hardly a man is now alive
5   Who remembers that famous day and year.

He said to his friend, "If the British march
By land or sea from the town tonight,
Hang a lantern aloft in the belfry° arch
Of the North Church tower as a signal light—
10   One, if by land, and two, if by sea;
And I on the opposite shore will be,
Ready to ride and spread the alarm
Through every Middlesex village and farm,
For the country folk to be up and to arm."

15   Then he said, "Good night!" and with muffled oar
Silently rowed to the Charlestown shore,
Just as the moon rose over the bay,
Where swinging wide at her moorings° lay
The Somerset, British man-of-war;
20   A phantom ship, with each mast and spar°
Across the moon like a prison bar,
And a huge black hulk, that was magnified
By its own reflection in the tide.

---

8. belfry (bel′frē) *n.* used as *adj.*: steeple of a church where bells are hung.
18. moorings *n.*: cables holding a ship in place so that it doesn't float away.
20. mast and spar: poles supporting a ship's sails.

Meanwhile, his friend, through alley and street,
25   Wanders and watches with eager ears,
Till in the silence around him he hears
The muster° of men at the barrack door,
The sound of arms, and the tramp of feet,
And the measured tread of the grenadiers,°
30   Marching down to their boats on the shore.

Then he climbed the tower of the Old North Church,
By the wooden stairs, with stealthy tread,
To the belfry chamber overhead,
And startled the pigeons from their perch
35   On the somber rafters, that round him made
Masses and moving shapes of shade—
By the trembling ladder, steep and tall,
To the highest window in the wall,
Where he paused to listen and look down
40   A moment on the roofs of the town,
And the moonlight flowing over all.

Beneath, in the churchyard, lay the dead,
In their night encampment on the hill,
Wrapped in silence so deep and still
45   That he could hear, like a sentinel's° tread,
The watchful night wind, as it went
Creeping along from tent to tent,
And seeming to whisper, "All is well!"
A moment only he feels the spell
50   Of the place and the hour, and the secret dread
Of the lonely belfry and the dead;
For suddenly all his thoughts are bent
On a shadowy something far away,
Where the river widens to meet the bay—
55   A line of black that bends and floats
On the rising tide, like a bridge of boats.

---

27. muster *n.:* assembly; gathering.
29. grenadiers (gren'ə·dirz') *n.:* foot soldiers who carry and throw grenades.
45. sentinel's: guard's.

The Midnight Ride of Paul Revere (detail) (1985) by Barbara Olsen. Oil on canvas.

Meanwhile, impatient to mount and ride,
Booted and spurred, with a heavy stride
On the opposite shore walked Paul Revere.
60   Now he patted his horse's side,
Now gazed at the landscape far and near,
Then, impetuous,° stamped the earth,
And turned and tightened his saddle girth;
But mostly he watched with eager search
65   The belfry tower of the Old North Church,
As it rose above the graves on the hill,
Lonely and spectral° and somber and still.
And lo! as he looks, on the belfry's height

---

62. impetuous (im·pech′o͞o·əs) *adj.:* impulsive; eager.
67. spectral *adj.:* ghostly.

A glimmer, and then a gleam of light!
70 He springs to the saddle, the bridle he turns,
But lingers and gazes, till full on his sight
A second lamp in the belfry burns!

A hurry of hoofs in a village street,
A shape in the moonlight, a bulk in the dark,
75 And beneath, from the pebbles, in passing, a spark
Struck out by a steed flying fearless and fleet:
That was all! And yet, through the gloom and the light,
The fate of a nation was riding that night;
And the spark struck out by that steed, in his flight,
80 Kindled the land into flame with its heat.

He has left the village and mounted the steep,
And beneath him, tranquil and broad and deep,
Is the Mystic, meeting the ocean tides;
And under the alders° that skirt its edge,
85 Now soft on the sand, now loud on the ledge,
Is heard the tramp of his steed as he rides.

It was twelve by the village clock,
When he crossed the bridge into Medford town.
He heard the crowing of the cock,
90 And the barking of the farmer's dog,
And felt the damp of the river fog,
That rises after the sun goes down.

It was one by the village clock,
When he galloped into Lexington.
95 He saw the gilded weathercock°
Swim in the moonlight as he passed,
And the meetinghouse windows, blank and bare,
Gaze at him with a spectral glare,
As if they already stood aghast°
100 At the bloody work they would look upon.

---

84. alders (ôl'dərz) *n.:* shrubs and trees of the birch family.
95. weathercock *n.:* weathervane made to look like a rooster (cock).
    Weathervanes indicate the direction in which the wind is blowing.
99. aghast (ə·gast') *adj.:* shocked; horrified.

It was two by the village clock,
When he came to the bridge in Concord town.
He heard the bleating of the flock,
And the twitter of birds among the trees,
105   And felt the breath of the morning breeze
Blowing over the meadows brown.
And one was safe and asleep in his bed
Who at the bridge would be first to fall,
Who that day would be lying dead,
110   Pierced by a British musket ball.

You know the rest. In the books you have read,
How the British Regulars fired and fled—
How the farmers gave them ball for ball,
From behind each fence and farmyard wall,
115   Chasing the redcoats down the lane,
Then crossing the fields to emerge again
Under the trees at the turn of the road,
And only pausing to fire and load.

So through the night rode Paul Revere;
120   And so through the night went his cry of alarm
To every Middlesex village and farm—
A cry of defiance and not of fear,
A voice in the darkness, a knock at the door,
And a word that shall echo forevermore!
125   For, borne on the night wind of the Past,
Through all our history, to the last,
In the hour of darkness and peril and need,
The people will waken and listen to hear
The hurrying hoofbeats of that steed,
130   And the midnight message of Paul Revere.

Meet the Writer

Henry Wadsworth Longfellow

"Footprints on the Sands of Time"

If you went to school a hundred years ago, you and all your friends would probably be able to recite by heart several of the poems of **Henry Wadsworth Longfellow** (1807–1882). Born in Portland, Maine, Longfellow became the most popular poet of his day. Many of Longfellow's poems, such as *Evangeline* (1847), *The Song of Hiawatha* (1855), and *The Courtship of Miles Standish* (1858), were inspired by people and events in American history. As "Paul Revere's Ride" shows, Longfellow believed that one person's actions could make a difference. In an early piece of verse, he wrote:

> **"Lives of great men all remind us
> We can make our lives sublime.
> And, departing, leave behind us
> Footprints on the sands of time."**

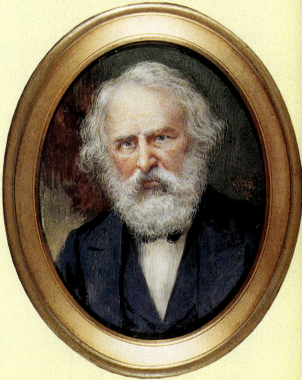

Henry Wadsworth Longfellow (1871) by Theodore Wust. Watercolor on ivory.
Copyright National Portrait Gallery, Smithsonian Institution/Art Resource, NY.

First Thoughts

1. Do you think Paul Revere is a hero? Is his friend? Explain why or why not.

Thinking Critically

2. Read aloud the first stanza. Then, mark its stressed and unstressed syllables to indicate its **meter.** Notice that the poet varies the pattern to avoid monotony. One thing that never varies is the stress on the last syllable of each line. (For help in marking the syllables, see page 616.)

3. What does "The fate of a nation was riding that night" (line 78) mean? What does the poet mean by saying that the spark struck by the horse's hoof "Kindled the land into flame" (line 80)?

4. What do you think the word or words are "that shall echo forevermore" (line 124)? Write what Revere might have said as he knocked on each door.

5. Re-read the last six lines of the poem. Why does the poet believe that "in the hour of darkness and peril and need," Americans will remember Paul Revere's message? What significance do you think this story has today?

Extending Interpretations

6. What other Paul Reveres, from history or living today, have rallied their people with cries "of defiance and not of fear" (line 122)? ✏️

WRITING

Writing a Reflection

Write a paragraph or two responding to the quotation from a verse by Longfellow in Meet the Writer. You might start by considering this question: What historical figures or people living today remind you that people can accomplish great things?

Reading Check

a. What is the purpose of Paul Revere's ride?

b. What signal does Revere finally see?

c. A **narrative poem** relates a series of events. Trace the main events of Revere's ride, as it is described in lines 81–106.

d. According to Longfellow, what were the results of Revere's midnight ride?

INTERNET
Projects and Activities
Keyword: LE5 8-6

SKILLS FOCUS

Literary Skills
Analyze a narrative poem; analyze meter.

Writing Skills
Write a reflection.

The Cremation of Sam McGee *and*
The Dying Cowboy *and*
Maiden-Savin' Sam

Make the Connection
Quickwrite ✏️

Two of the ballads you are about to read are tall tales. A **tall tale** is an exaggerated, farfetched story that is obviously untrue but is told as though it were absolutely factual.

Exaggerations, which stretch the truth about as high and wide as it will go, are generally used for humor. Can you top this old standard: It was so hot, you could fry an egg on the sidewalk? Choose two of the starters below, and make up your own humorous exaggerations.

- It was so cold . . .
- It rained so hard . . .
- The snow was so deep . . .

Literary Focus
Ballad

A **ballad** is a song or a songlike poem that tells a story, usually about lost love or betrayal or death. Ballads can be sad or humorous. They usually use simple language and a great deal of repetition, including a refrain. Their simple, regular meters and their rhyme patterns make them easy to memorize. All those sound patterns also make ballads fun to sing or read aloud.

The most famous ballads are old songs that were passed on orally for many years before they were written down. The authors of these old ballads are unknown, and the songs were often changed as they were handed down. That's why the most popular ballads come in many versions.

The strange story of Sam McGee is not a ballad in this traditional sense. After all, we know who wrote the poem. However, its writer calls it a ballad, and as you will see, he has told his story in a form that imitates the old ballads. Two other ballads follow: a traditional ballad by our old friend Anonymous and a student's ballad that includes a lot of exaggeration and a refrain.

INTERNET
Cross-curricular Connection
Keyword: LE5 8-6

Literary Skills
Understand the characteristics of ballads.

Background
Literature and Geography

In the 1890s, thousands of fortune hunters rushed north, braving bitter cold and deep snow. Gold had been found in northwestern Canada, in the Klondike region of the Yukon Territory. The town of Dawson, at the center of the region, became the Yukon's capital.

Like many other gold seekers, Sam McGee is unprepared for the Klondike's seven-month winter, when the temperature sometimes falls as low as minus sixty-eight degrees Fahrenheit. This poem tells his story. (Cremation is the burning of a body to ashes.)

The Cremation of Sam McGee

Robert W. Service

> There are strange things done in the midnight sun
>   By the men who moil° for gold;
> The Arctic trails have their secret tales
>   That would make your blood run cold;
> 5 The Northern Lights have seen queer sights,
>   But the queerest they ever did see
> Was that night on the marge° of Lake Lebarge
>   I cremated Sam McGee.

2. moil *v.:* labor.

7. marge *n.:* edge.

Now Sam McGee was from Tennessee, where the
    cotton blooms and blows.
Why he left his home in the South to roam 'round the
10   Pole, God only knows.
He was always cold, but the land of gold seemed to
    hold him like a spell;
Though he'd often say in his homely way that he'd
    "sooner live in hell."

On a Christmas Day we were mushing our way over the
    Dawson trail.
Talk of your cold! through the parka's fold it stabbed
    like a driven nail.
If our eyes we'd close, then the lashes froze till some-
15   times we couldn't see;
It wasn't much fun, but the only one to whimper was
    Sam McGee.

And that very night, as we lay packed tight in our robes
    beneath the snow,
And the dogs were fed, and the stars o'erhead were
    dancing heel and toe,
He turned to me, and "Cap," says he, "I'll cash in this
    trip, I guess;
And if I do, I'm asking that you won't refuse my last
20   request."

Well, he seemed so low that I couldn't say no; then he
    says with a sort of moan:
"It's the cursèd cold, and it's got right hold till I'm
    chilled clean through to the bone.
Yet 'tain't being dead—it's my awful dread of the icy
    grave that pains;
So I want you to swear that, foul or fair, you'll cremate
    my last remains."

A pal's last need is a thing to heed, so I swore I would
25   not fail;
And we started on at the streak of dawn; but God! he
    looked ghastly pale.

He crouched on the sleigh, and he raved all day of his
    home in Tennessee;
And before nightfall a corpse was all that was left of
    Sam McGee.

There wasn't a breath in that land of death, and I
    hurried, horror-driven,
With a corpse half hid that I couldn't get rid, because
30   of a promise given;
It was lashed to the sleigh, and it seemed to say: "You
    may tax your brawn and brains,
But you promised true, and it's up to you to cremate
    those last remains."

Now a promise made is a debt unpaid, and the trail has
    its own stern code.
In the days to come, though my lips were dumb, in my
    heart how I cursed that load.
In the long, long night, by the lone firelight, while the
35   huskies, round in a ring,
Howled out their woes to the homeless snows—
    O God! how I loathed° the thing.

And every day that quiet clay seemed to heavy and
    heavier grow;
And on I went, though the dogs were spent° and the
    grub was getting low;
The trail was bad, and I felt half mad, but I swore I
    would not give in;
And I'd often sing to the hateful thing, and it
40   hearkened° with a grin.

Till I came to the marge of Lake Lebarge, and a
    derelict° there lay;
It was jammed in the ice, but I saw in a trice it was
    called the "Alice May."
And I looked at it, and I thought a bit, and I looked at
    my frozen chum;
Then "Here," said I, with a sudden cry, "is my cre-ma-
    tor-ium."

36. loathed (lō*th*d) *v.*:
hated.

38. spent *adj.*: worn-out.

40. hearkened
(här**'**kənd) *v.*:
listened carefully.

41. derelict (der**'**ə·likt')
n.: abandoned ship.

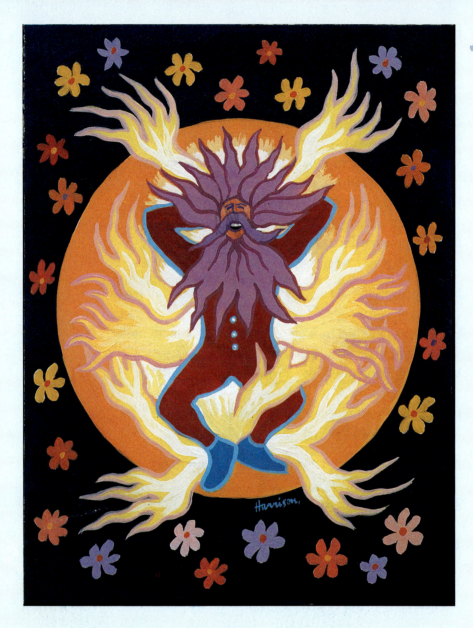

Some planks I tore from the cabin floor, and I lit the
    boiler fire;
Some coal I found that was lying around, and I heaped
    the fuel higher;
The flames just soared, and the furnace roared—such a
    blaze you seldom see;
And I burrowed a hole in the glowing coal, and I
    stuffed in Sam McGee.

Then I made a hike, for I didn't like to hear him sizzle
      so;
And the heavens scowled, and the huskies howled, and
50   the wind began to blow.
It was icy cold, but the hot sweat rolled down my
      cheeks, and I don't know why;
And the greasy smoke in an inky cloak went streaking
      down the sky.

I do not know how long in the snow I wrestled with
      grisly° fear;
But the stars came out and they danced about ere again
      I ventured near;
I was sick with dread, but I bravely said: "I'll just take a
55   peep inside.
I guess he's cooked, and it's time I looked"; . . . then
      the door I opened wide.

And there sat Sam, looking cool and calm, in the heart
      of the furnace roar;
And he wore a smile you could see a mile, and he said:
      "Please close that door.
It's fine in here, but I greatly fear you'll let in the cold
      and storm—
Since I left Plumtree, down in Tennessee, it's the first
60   time I've been warm."

There are strange things done in the midnight sun
  By the men who moil for gold;
The Arctic trails have their secret tales
  That would make your blood run cold;
65 *The Northern Lights have seen queer sights,*
  But the queerest they ever did see
Was that night on the marge of Lake Lebarge
  I cremated Sam McGee.

53. grisly *adj.:* here, caused by something horrible.

Meet the Writer

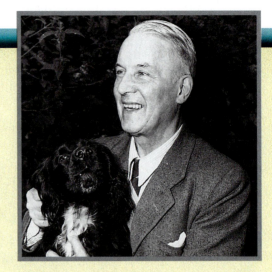

Robert W. Service

"A Story Jack London Never Got"

Born in Lancashire, England, **Robert W. Service** (1874–1958) immigrated to Canada in his early twenties. After traveling along the Canadian Pacific coast, he took a job with a bank and was transferred to the Yukon Territory. He wrote his most popular poems there, including "The Cremation of Sam McGee." The poem was inspired by a story Service heard at a party where he was feeling awkward and out of place:

> 66 I was staring gloomily at a fat fellow across the table. He was a big mining man from Dawson, and he scarcely acknowledged his introduction to a little bank clerk. Portly and important, he was smoking a big cigar with a gilt band. Suddenly he said: 'I'll tell you a story Jack London never got.' Then he spun a yarn of a man who cremated his pal. It had a surprise climax which occasioned much laughter. I did not join, for I had a feeling that here was a decisive moment of destiny. I still remember how a great excitement usurped me. Here was a perfect ballad subject. The fat man who ignored me went his way to bankruptcy, but he had pointed me the road to fortune. 99

Service left the party and spent the next six hours wandering through the frozen woods in the bright moonlight, writing verse after verse in his head. When he finally went to bed, the poem was complete and Service was satisfied; he didn't even put it on paper until the next day.

For Independent Reading

You'll find "The Cremation of Sam McGee," along with "The Shooting of Dan McGrew" and other poems, in *The Best of Robert Service*.

Ballads like this one were sung by cowboys in the American West. They helped make the long, lonely nights on the prairie pass more quickly. This ballad is based on an eighteenth-century Irish tune, and it gave rise to the famous blues song "St. James Infirmary." The ballad also provided the title and the haunting theme music for *Bang the Drum Slowly,* a movie about the death of a young baseball player.

The Dying Cowboy
traditional American ballad

As I rode out by Tom Sherman's barroom,
As I rode out so early one day,
'Twas there I espied a handsome young cowboy,
All dressed in white linen, all clothed for the grave.

5   "I see by your outfit that you are a cowboy,"
These words he did say as I boldly stepped by.
"Come sit down beside me and hear my sad story,
For I'm shot in the breast and I know I must die.

"Then beat your drum slowly and play your fife lowly,
10   And play the dead march as you carry me along,
And take me to the graveyard and throw the sod o'er me,
For I'm a young cowboy and I know I've done wrong.

"'Twas once in the saddle I used to go dashing,
'Twas once in the saddle I used to go gay,
15   But I first took to drinking and then to card playing,
Got shot in the body and I'm dying today.

"Let sixteen gamblers come handle my coffin,
Let sixteen young cowboys come sing me a song,
Take me to the green valley and lay the sod o'er me,
20   For I'm a poor cowboy and I know I've done wrong.

"Go bring me back a cup of cool water
To cool my parched lips," this cowboy then said.
Before I returned, his soul had departed
And gone to his Maker—the cowboy lay dead.

25   We swung our ropes slowly and rattled our spurs lowly,
And gave a wild whoop as we carried him on,
For we all loved our comrade, so brave, young and handsome,
We all loved our comrade, although he'd done wrong.

The Cowboy (c. 1897) by Frederic Remington. Watercolor on paper.
Museum of Fine Arts, Houston, Texas, USA/Hogg Brothers Collection, Gift of Miss Ima Hogg.

Maiden-Savin' Sam

In the wild ol' West there lived a man,
A man by the title of Maiden-Savin' Sam.
Saving maidens was his hobby and he did it
   very well,
Bragged about his victories—great stories
   did he tell.

> *Sam, Sam, Maiden-Savin' Sam,*
> *Greatest maiden saver in all of the land.*
> *Saved all the short ones, all the tall ones,*
>   *too,*
> *With his hat on his head and spurs on*
>   *his shoes.*

"One day a herd of buffalo crossed the land,
Biggest gaw-darned herd in all the land!
I was a-watchin' them, watchin' was I,"
Sam began the story, with a twinkle in his
   eye.

> *Sam, Sam, Maiden-Savin' Sam . . .*

"Now as I was watchin'—'Uh-oh,' says I,
'In the herd's way a pretty maiden does lie.
She's gonna get trampled,' I thought to
   myself.
'No longer will she be in such radiatin'
   health.'"

> *Sam, Sam, Maiden-Savin' Sam . . .*

"I looked all around, and what did I see?
A big, shiny pitchfork just a-waitin' for me.
I picked it up, threw it far and wide,
And now them buffalo are buffalo hide."

> *Sam, Sam, Maiden-Savin' Sam . . .*

Sam now lies deep in his grave,
Chased one too many bears into a cave.
But never we'll forget him—he was the very
   best
Of all the maiden savers in all of the West!

> —Jenny Ellison
>   Webb School of Knoxville
>   Knoxville, Tennessee

First Thoughts

1. What did you like best (or least) about "The Cremation of Sam McGee"? Why has it been popular for so long, in your opinion?

Thinking Critically

2. List two or three details from "The Cremation of Sam McGee" that help you picture the frozen landscape or feel the cold.

3. The poem about Sam McGee uses both end rhymes and **internal rhymes**—rhymes contained within lines, such as *done* and *sun* in line 1. List three more pairs of internal rhymes in the poem.

4. Sam McGee's story is fun to read aloud because of its sound effects. Look at the use of alliteration in the poem. **Alliteration** is the repetition of consonant sounds in words close together in a text. The repeated sounds can be in the beginning or middle of the word: "In the *l*ong, *l*ong night, by the *l*one fire*l*ight . . ." See how many uses of alliteration you can find in this poem. Be sure to read the lines aloud to *hear* the sound effects.

5. Traditional **ballads** usually

- tell a story
- are written in simple language
- generally have a refrain, usually at the end of each stanza
- have simple rhymes
- have a regular meter
- describe supernatural events

Using this list, compare, point by point, Sam McGee's story with "The Dying Cowboy" and with "Maiden-Savin' Sam." Which poem is closest to the old ballad form?

(continued)

Reading Check

a. Why is Sam McGee in the Klondike?

b. What does Sam ask the speaker to do? Why?

c. What surprise does the speaker meet with after he carries out Sam's request?

INTERNET
Projects and Activities
Keyword: LE5 8-6

Literary Skills
Analyze ballads.

WRITING

Writing Exaggerations

Refer to the examples of **exaggeration** you made up for the Quickwrite. Can you top yourself? Write at least three more based on those statements about the weather. Then, exchange your exaggerations in class. Which exaggeration is—well—the most exaggerated? 🖊️

SPEAKING AND LISTENING

A Choral Reading

The story of Sam McGee's fantastic rebirth has been recited around many campfires over the years. Now it's your chance to prepare the poem for a **choral reading.** First, form a group, and assign different stanzas or lines to different people. (You might want to use a chorus for the refrain.) Then, prepare the script, carefully marking on each person's copy the points at which he or she is to start and stop reading. As you rehearse, work on your presentation until you are satisfied that you have it right. It will help to assign a group of students to act as critics. These students should prepare a list of standards for an oral presentation. After each rehearsal, ask for feedback from your listeners. You may want to wear costumes or use props in your reading.

SKILLS FOCUS

Writing Skills
Write exaggerations.

Speaking and Listening Skills
Present a choral reading.

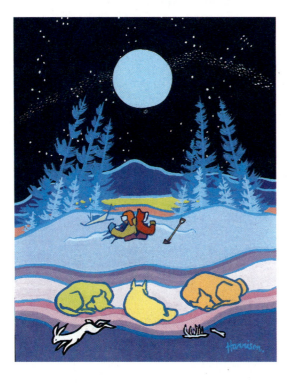

from Beowulf *and* Casey at the Bat

Make the Connection
Quickwrite ✏️

The old epic heroes were larger-than-life warriors. They were usually the saviors of their people. What do our sports heroes today have in common with those epic heroes? How are they different? Jot down your ideas.

Literary Focus
Epic

An **epic** is a long narrative poem written in formal, elegant language that tells about a series of quests undertaken by a great hero. In the ancient epics this hero is a warrior who embodies the values cherished by the culture that recites the epic.

The oldest stories in the world are epics. In ancient Mesopotamia around 2000 B.C., people told the epic of the hero Gilgamesh, who was searching for the secret of immortal life. In ancient Greece around 500 B.C., children learned values by studying the *Iliad* and the *Odyssey*, Homer's great epics about the Trojan War heroes. In India, children know the adventures of the heroes in the *Mahabharata* and *Ramayana*. In Anglo-Saxon England around A.D. 700, people passed the long, dark nights listening to bards tell the story of the hero Beowulf, who saved a kingdom from two swamp monsters.

Sutton Hoo helmet (7th century) from the Sutton Hoo ship treasure, Suffolk, England.
Copyright The British Museum, London.

A mock-heroic story. "Casey at the Bat" is a short narrative poem that imitates the old epic tales, but in a comical way. Instead of a warrior we have a small-town baseball player. Instead of a quest focused on saving a great kingdom, we have a quest for a home run to save Mudville's home team. Instead of the epic poet's elegant similes, metaphors, and alliteration, we have sports slang.

SKILLS FOCUS

Literary Skills
Understand the characteristics of epics and the mock-heroic narrative.

Beowulf is the first great work of English literature. Since it was written in Old English, which is very different from the English used today, the epic has been translated into Modern English many times. In the excerpt that follows, Beowulf, a warrior from the land of the Geats (in Scandinavia), has arrived at the court of Hrothgar, a Danish king. Beowulf gives his credentials; that is, he tells the king why he should be chosen to face Grendel, a huge monster who has been devouring Hrothgar's followers. Beowulf is speaking to the king in the section that follows.

Beowulf and the Dragon (1932) by Rockwell Kent. Lithograph.
The Granger Collection, New York.

from BEOWULF

"Hail, Hrothgar!
Higlac is my cousin° and my king; the days
Of my youth have been filled with glory. Now Grendel's
Name has echoed in our land: Sailors
5   Have brought us stories of Herot, the best
Of all mead-halls,° deserted and useless when the moon
Hangs in skies the sun had lit,
Light and life fleeing together.
My people have said, the wisest, most knowing
10   And best of them, that my duty was to go to the Danes'
Great King. They have seen my strength for themselves,
Have watched me rise from the darkness of war,
Dripping with my enemies' blood. I drove

2. cousin *n.*: any relative. Higlac is Beowulf's uncle and his king.

6. mead-halls: Mead is a drink made from honey, water, yeast, and malt. The hall was a central gathering place where warriors could feast, listen to a bard's stories, and sleep in safety.

Five great giants into chains, chased
15 All of that race from the earth. I swam
In the blackness of night, hunting monsters
Out of the ocean, and killing them one
By one; death was my errand and the fate
They had earned. Now Grendel and I are called
20 Together, and I've come. Grant me, then,
Lord and protector of this noble place,
A single request! I have come so far,
Oh shelterer of warriors and your people's loved friend,
That this one favor you should not refuse me—
25 That I, alone and with the help of my men,
May purge all evil from this hall. I have heard,
Too, that the monster's scorn of men
Is so great that he needs no weapons and fears none.
Nor will I. My lord Higlac
30 Might think less of me if I let my sword
Go where my feet were afraid to, if I hid
Behind some broad linden shield:° My hands
Alone shall fight for me, struggle for life
Against the monster. God must decide
Who will be given to death's cold grip.

—*translated by* Burton Raffel

A knight, from a chess set carved from walrus ivory (12th century).
British Museum, London.

32. linden shield: shield made from wood of the linden tree.

Gundestrup caldron.
National Museum, Copenhagen.

Casey at the Bat

Ernest Lawrence Thayer

The outlook wasn't brilliant for the Mudville nine that day;
The score stood four to two, with but one inning more to play;
And so, when Cooney died at first, and Burrows did the same,
A sickly silence fell upon the patrons of the game.

5   A straggling few got up to go in deep despair. The rest
Clung to the hope which springs eternal in the human breast;
They thought, if only Casey could but get a whack, at that,
They'd put up even money now, with Casey at the bat.

But Flynn preceded Casey, as did also Jimmy Blake,
10   And the former was a pudding, and the latter was a fake;

So upon that stricken multitude grim melancholy sat,
For there seemed but little chance of Casey's getting to the bat.

But Flynn let drive a single, to the wonderment of all,
And Blake, the much-despised, tore the cover off the ball;
15 And when the dust had lifted, and they saw what had occurred,
There was Jimmy safe on second, and Flynn a-hugging third.

Then from the gladdened multitude went up a joyous yell;
It bounded from the mountaintop, and rattled in the dell;
It struck upon the hillside, and recoiled upon the flat;
20 For Casey, mighty Casey, was advancing to the bat.

There was ease in Casey's manner as he stepped into his place;
There was pride in Casey's bearing, and a smile on Casey's face;
And when, responding to the cheers, he lightly doffed his hat,
No stranger in the crowd could doubt 'twas Casey at the bat.

25 Ten thousand eyes were on him as he rubbed his hands with dirt;
Five thousand tongues applauded when he wiped them on his shirt;
Then while the writhing pitcher ground the ball into his hip,
Defiance gleamed in Casey's eye, a sneer curled Casey's lip.

And now the leather-covered sphere came hurtling through the air,
30 And Casey stood a-watching it in haughty grandeur there;
Close by the sturdy batsman the ball unheeded sped.
"That ain't my style," said Casey. "Strike one," the umpire said.

From the benches, black with people, there went up a muffled roar,
Like the beating of the storm waves on a stern and distant shore;
35 "Kill him! Kill the umpire!" shouted someone on the stand;
And it's likely they'd have killed him had not Casey raised his hand.

With a smile of Christian charity great Casey's visage shone;
He stilled the rising tumult; he bade the game go on;
He signaled to the pitcher, and once more the spheroid flew;
40 But Casey still ignored it, and the umpire said, "Strike two."

"Fraud!" cried the maddened thousands, and the echo answered, "Fraud!"
But a scornful look from Casey, and the audience was awed;
They saw his face grow stern and cold, they saw his muscles strain,

And they knew that Casey wouldn't let that ball go by again.

45 The sneer is gone from Casey's lips, his teeth are clenched in hate,
He pounds with cruel violence his bat upon the plate;
And now the pitcher holds the ball, and now he lets it go,
And now the air is shattered by the force of Casey's blow.

Oh! somewhere in this favored land the sun is shining bright;
50 The band is playing somewhere, and somewhere hearts are light;
And somewhere men are laughing, and somewhere children shout,
But there is no joy in Mudville—mighty Casey has struck out!

Meet the Writer

Ernest Lawrence Thayer

Shunning the Limelight

When the journalist **Ernest Lawrence Thayer** (1863–1940) submitted "Casey at the Bat" to the San Francisco *Examiner* in 1888, he had no idea it would become the most famous baseball poem ever written. In fact, he didn't even sign his own name to his work, choosing instead to use a nickname from his Harvard college days, Phin.

Shortly after the poem appeared in the California newspaper, a copy was given to a vaudeville entertainer named William De Wolf Hopper, who was about to appear in a Baseball Night performance in New York. Hopper must have recognized a winner. After quickly memorizing the poem, he went onstage and recited it; the audience went wild. Hopper went on to make a successful career of touring the country reciting "Casey at the Bat."

Despite the poem's popularity, Thayer considered it badly written and for years would not admit authorship. Many people tried to take credit for writing the poem, and a number of baseball players claimed the dubious distinction of having been the model for Casey. When the author was finally identified, he refused to take money for the poem's many reprintings. "All I ask," he said, "is never to be reminded of it again."

First Thoughts

1. Do Beowulf or Casey remind you of any of today's heroes, either in real life, in movies or books, or on television? Explain.

Thinking Critically

2. Beowulf is a typical **epic hero** in that he is enormously strong and has come to save a kingdom. Identify lines where the poet makes Casey seem like an epic hero.

3. Epic heroes embody the values that their society holds dear—traits like courage, humility, strength, generosity, and selflessness. What values do you think Casey embodies? Do you think these values are typically American? ✏️

4. Beowulf has come to Herot, the great hall of Hrothgar, where he expects to perform mighty deeds. Casey is expected to perform his mighty deeds in a baseball stadium. How is this **setting** like Herot? How is it different?

5. The epics of ancient Greece and Rome are marked by long, beautiful similes and metaphors. Ernest Lawrence Thayer also uses figures of speech to describe Casey and the ballgame in heroic language. The poem includes **similes** (comparisons of different things, using *like* or *as*), **metaphors** (direct comparisons of different things, without using *like* or *as*), and **personification** (speaking of something that is not human as if it had human qualities). Find figures of speech in lines 3, 6, 10, and 33–34. In each instance, identify the things being compared.

Reading Check

a. What request does Beowulf make of Hrothgar?

b. At the beginning of "Casey at the Bat," why are the Mudville fans in despair?

c. What happens when the mighty Casey comes to bat?

Animal head from Viking ship (c. 800).
© University Museum of Cultural Heritage, University of Oslo, Norway.

WRITING

Writing a Mock Epic

Try your hand at writing a **mock epic.** Pick an everyday event in your life—such as getting ready for school—and describe it in the heightened language of an epic. A regular meter and rhymes would make it more fun, but if those are too hard to come up with, write your mock epic in free verse. That means that you don't have to use rhymes, but you do have to pay attention to the sound and rhythm of your poem.

SKILLS FOCUS

Literary Skills
Analyze an epic and a mock-heroic poem.

Writing Skills
Write a mock epic.

Understanding Summaries: "Casey at the Bat"

Reading Focus
What Goes into a Summary

"Hey, did you read that story? It's due tomorrow."

"I read it. But it had so many details! What's the point of it, anyway?"

Details. Which are critical? Which are not so critical? How do you tell the difference? A **critical detail** is one that must be included for the summary of a text to make sense. If the detail is not included, the summary falls apart, has a big gap, or is illogical.

■ A good summary of a story can help you understand important elements like **main events, cause and effect,** and **theme.** Here is a checklist of elements to look for in a summary of a story, including a story told as a narrative poem, like "Casey at the Bat." Keep these items in mind as you read the following summaries.

INTERNET
Interactive
Reading Model
Keyword: LE5 8-6

Reading Skills
Understand
summaries.

Summary of a Story: A Checklist

1. The summary of a story should cite the story's **author** and **title.**

2. The summary should identify the **main characters,** the **problem** or **conflict** in the story, the **main events,** and the **resolution** of the problem.

3. The summary should list the main events of the plot, in the **order** in which they occur and in a way that shows the relationship of one event to another. (In other words, the summary should show **cause-and-effect** relationships. This means it should use words and phrases like *because, as a result of, since, therefore, so.*)

4. The summary should state the story's **theme.**

5. If the writer's words are quoted exactly in the summary, quotation marks should be used.

"Casey at the Bat"

SUMMARY 1

In the bottom of the ninth, Mudville trails. The last outs go to Cooney, Burrows, and Casey. Mudville loses 4–2.

"Casey at the Bat"

SUMMARY 2

The poem "Casey at the Bat" by Ernest Lawrence Thayer is about a baseball hero named Casey who plays for the Mudville nine. At the opening the game looks bad for Mudville. They are losing 4–2 in the bottom of the ninth. Then Cooney and Burrows are both out at first. If Casey gets to bat, he'll surely save the day; but Flynn and Blake go to bat first, and neither is likely to score. But, look! Each player bags a hit, and the crowd goes wild with joy. With two men on, up steps the mighty Casey. Strike one! Then strike two! The crowd screams. Casey signals for silence. His smile turns to a frown; his anger signals his resolve. He'll slam the next ball out of the park. But the air is shattered by his swing. Somewhere men are laughing, the poet says. But there is no joy in Mudville—mighty Casey has struck out! "Casey at the Bat" in its comic way reminds us that even the mighty can fall.

Analyzing Summaries

"Casey at the Bat"
SUMMARIES 1 AND 2

Test Practice

1. Summary 1 should be made stronger by doing all of the following *except* —

   A conveying the main ideas more clearly

   B adding more critical details

   C conveying the author's underlying meaning

   D using fewer details and sticking to the details in the poem

2. Which of the following **critical details** from the poem is included in both summaries?

   F Mudville is losing in the bottom of the ninth.

   G Cooney and Burrows are out at first.

   H Casey strikes out.

   J Even the mighty can fall.

3. Which of the following sentences from Summary 2 is not an important detail?

   A "They are losing 4–2 in the bottom of the ninth."

   B "Then Cooney and Burrows are both out at first."

   C "The crowd goes wild with joy."

   D "Mighty Casey has struck out!"

4. Which passage in Summary 2 should be put in quotation marks because it is a direct quote from the poem?

   F "The game looks bad for Mudville."

   G "He'll surely save the day."

   H "The crowd screams."

   J "Somewhere men are laughing."

Constructed Response

1. Which summary contains all or most of the poem's **critical details**? List three of these details.

2. Which summary states a **theme,** or **underlying meaning,** of the poem? What is that theme?

SKILLS FOCUS

Reading Skills
Analyze summaries by comparing the original text with the summary.

Oda a las gracias / Ode to Thanks *and*
Birdfoot's Grampa *and*
Ode to a Toad

Make the Connection

Quickwrite ✏️

What would you like to celebrate in your life? It could be a person, place, or thing. *Thing* may include many things—animals, food, flowers, machines, laughter, justice. Make a list of five subjects worthy of celebration.

Literary Focus

Ode

The **ode** originated in ancient Greece. For centuries, poets imitated these long, complex poems, which celebrated, in elegant language, one person or thing. Over the centuries famous odes have been written to nightingales, Greek vases, autumn, melancholy, joy, Britain, solitude, and winners in the Olympic Games.

Today odes are looser in form and subject matter, but they still celebrate a particular person or thing. The great Chilean poet Pablo Neruda has written several books of odes, most of which celebrate ordinary objects and everyday experiences.

Neruda dedicates "Ode to Thanks" to a word that most of us use every day. (The first twenty-two lines of the Spanish original are at the right.) The two other poems in this grouping are about toads. Only one of them is an ode; the other is a lyric (the titles will tell you which).

from **Oda a las gracias**

Pablo Neruda

Gracias a la palabra
que agradece.
Gracias a *gracias*
por
5   cuanto esta palabra
derrite nieve o hierro.

El mundo parecía amenazante
hasta que suave
como pluma
10   clara,
o dulce como pétalo de azúcar,
de labio en labio
pasa,
gracias,
15   grandes a plena boca
o susurrantes,
apenas murmulladas,
y el ser volvió a ser hombre
y no ventana,
20   alguna claridad
entró en el bosque:
fue posible cantar bajo las
    hojas. . . .

INTERNET

More About Neruda

Keyword: LE5 8-6

Literary Skills
Understand the characteristics of an ode.

Ode to Thanks

Pablo Neruda

Thanks to the word
that says *thanks!*
Thanks to *thanks,*
word
5　that melts
iron and snow!

The world is a threatening place
until
thanks
10　makes the rounds
from one pair of lips to another,
soft as a bright
feather
and sweet as a petal of sugar,
15　filling the mouth with its sound
or else a mumbled
whisper.
Life becomes human again:
it's no longer an open window.
20　A bit of brightness
strikes into the forest,
and we can sing again beneath the leaves.
Thanks, you're the medicine we take
to save us from
25　the bite of scorn.
Your light brightens the altar of harshness.
Or maybe
a tapestry
known
30　to far distant peoples.
Travelers
fan out
into the wilds,
and in that jungle
35　of strangers,

merci°
rings out
while the hustling train
changes countries,
40　sweeping away borders,
then *spasibo*°
clinging to pointy
volcanoes, to fire and freezing cold,
or *danke,*° yes! and *gracias,*° and
45　the world turns into a table:
a single word has wiped it clean,
plates and glasses gleam,
silverware tinkles,
and the tablecloth is as broad as a
　　plain.

50　Thank you, *thanks,*
for going out and returning,
for rising up
and settling down.
We know, *thanks,*
55　that you don't fill every space—
you're only a word—
but
where your little petal
appears
60　the daggers of pride take cover,
and there's a penny's worth of
　　smiles.

—*translated by* Ken Krabbenhoft

---

36. *merci* (mer·sē′): French for "thanks."
41. *spasibo* (spa·sē′bə): Russian for "thanks."
44. *danke* (dän′kə): German for "thanks."
　　gracias (grä′sē·äs′): Spanish for "thanks."

Birdfoot's Grampa

Joseph Bruchac

The old man
must have stopped our car
two dozen times to climb out
and gather into his hands
5   the small toads blinded
by our lights and leaping,
live drops of rain.

The rain was falling,
a mist about his white hair
10   and I kept saying
you can't save them all
accept it, get back in
we've got places to go.

But, leathery hands full
15   of wet brown life,
knee deep in the summer
roadside grass,
he just smiled and said
they have places to go to
20   *too.*

Ode to a Toad

I was out one day for my usual jog
(I go kinda easy, rarely full-hog)
When I happened to see right there on the road
The squishy remains of a little green toad.

5   I thought to myself, where is his home?
Down yonder green valley, how far did he
    roam?
From out on the pond I heard sorrowful croaks,
Could that be the wailing of some of his folks?

I felt for the toad and his pitiful state,
But the day was now fading, and such was his
10   fate.
In the grand scheme of things, now I confess,
What's one little froggie more or less?

—Anne-Marie Wulfsberg
     Concord-Carlisle High School
     Concord, Massachusetts

First appeared in *Merlyn's Pen: Fiction,
Essays, and Poems by America's Teens*

Meet the Writers

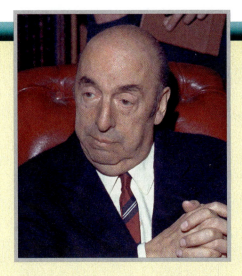

Pablo Neruda

A Poet for All People

Pablo Neruda (1904–1973) was born and died in his beloved Chile, but he lived many years abroad, sometimes as a diplomat for his country and sometimes in political exile. Neruda won the Nobel Prize in literature in 1971, but he was only in his twenties when he first became famous—for his love poems. Those poems are recited often throughout the Spanish-speaking world. In his odes, Neruda gave up a complex, formal style and adopted a plainer one, using simple words and short lines so that his poems could be enjoyed by all people. He said of his new style:

> 66 My poetry became clear and happy when it branched off toward humbler subjects and things. 99

Joseph Bruchac

"One Lesson I Was Taught"

Joseph Bruchac (1942–   ) was born in Saratoga Springs, New York, and was raised there by his grandmother and his grandfather, who was a member of the Abenaki people. Bruchac studied wildlife conservation in college. Today he is a well-known editor, publisher, poet, and collector of folk tales. Bruchac says that "Birdfoot's Grampa" describes one lesson he was taught "in the way most good lessons come to you—when you least expect them."

First Thoughts

1. Which of the three poems you've just read do you like best? Why?

Thinking Critically

2. What do you think the speaker of "Ode to Thanks" means when he says in lines 3–6 that *thanks* "melts iron and snow"?

3. What does the speaker compare *thanks* to in lines 12–15? How is a thank-you like these things?

4. In lines 31–44 of "Ode to Thanks," what effect does the poem say the word *thanks* has all over the world?

5. The last line of "Ode to Thanks" is "and there's a penny's worth of smiles." What do you think this line means?

6. Review the definition of *ode* on page 657. How is "Ode to Thanks" like classical odes? How is it different? Cite details from the poem to support your answer.

Extending Interpretations

7. If you know Spanish, compare this translation with the original Spanish of lines 1–22 on page 657. Would you make any changes in word choice?

8. How is the jogger in "Ode to a Toad" (page 659) different from Birdfoot's Grampa? Whose attitude is closer to your own?

9. Many people, like Birdfoot's Grampa, believe that their actions can make a difference, even if they can't save everyone. Think of someone you know (or someone you know of) who has acted on that belief. What actions has this person taken? Do you believe the actions were worth doing?

INTERNET

Projects and
Activities

Keyword: LE5 8-6

WRITING

Writing an Ode

Pick a person, place, or thing you would like to celebrate, and write an **ode.** Your purpose is to express strong, positive feelings about many aspects of your subject. Talk directly to your subject, as Neruda does.

Writing from a New Point of View

Write a short rhymed or unrhymed poem describing the incident in the road in "Birdfoot's Grampa" from the toads' **point of view.** Be sure to include the toads' feelings toward Birdfoot's Grampa. You might begin, "We were on our way to. . . ."

SKILLS FOCUS

Literary Skills
Analyze an ode.

Writing Skills
Write an ode;
write a poem
from a new
point of view.

On the Grasshopper and the Cricket

Make the Connection
Quickwrite ✏️

Nineteenth-century writers, like many others through the ages, shared their ideas and feelings about nature. How do you feel about nature? What do you see in nature that scares or disgusts you? What scenes, creatures, and patterns in nature fill you with wonder and awe? Think about the natural world for a minute or two, and jot down some of your thoughts.

Literary Focus
Sonnet

Imagine that you live in nineteenth-century England. You're a well-educated young person, and you want to impress a friend. Forget gifts of flowers. You would write your friend a poem. You'd most likely write a sonnet.

Every sonnet has fourteen lines, usually in iambic pentameter. **Iambic** refers to verse in which the beat or stress is on every other syllable, starting with the unstressed beat, like this:

From hedge to hedge.

Pentameter is verse in which there are five stressed beats in every line (*pente* is Greek for "five"). Occasional variations are OK. On top of that, if you were writing an **Italian sonnet** (also called **Petrarchan,** for the fourteenth-century Italian poet Petrarch, who mastered the form), you'd pose a question or make a point in the first eight lines. Then, in the last six lines, you'd respond to your own question or point.

Another sonnet form, called the **English,** or **Shakespearean, sonnet,** is made up of three units with four lines in each one. Each unit expresses related ideas. Two rhymed lines (called a **couplet**) sum up the poem.

John Keats, a great English poet, wrote many sonnets and sent them to friends. "On the Grasshopper and the Cricket" is one of his early sonnets. He wrote it in the Italian form.

Reading Skills 📖
Using Form to Find Meaning

Knowing the form of a poem helps you figure out its meaning. You know that "On the Grasshopper and the Cricket" is a sonnet written in the Italian form. That means you can divide it into two chunks of meaning. First you look for a problem, a question, or an idea in the first eight lines. Then you see how the final six lines resolve the problem, answer the question, or comment on the idea.

(Opposite)
Landscape (detail) (19th century)
by Patrick Nasmyth.
Ray Miles Gallery, London.

SKILLS FOCUS

Literary Skills
Understand the characteristics of a sonnet.

Reading Skills
Use a poem's form to find its meaning.

On the Grasshopper and the Cricket

John Keats

The poetry of earth is never dead:
    When all the birds are faint with the hot sun,
    And hide in cooling trees, a voice will run
From hedge to hedge about the new-mown mead;°
5   That is the Grasshopper's—he takes the lead
In summer luxury—he has never done
With his delights; for when tired out with fun
He rests at ease beneath some pleasant weed.
The poetry of earth is ceasing never:
10   On a lone winter evening, when the frost
      Has wrought a silence, from the stove there shrills
The Cricket's song, in warmth increasing ever,
    And seems to one in drowsiness half lost,
      The Grasshopper's among some grassy hills.

——————
4. mead (mēd) *n.:* meadow.

Meet the Writer

John Keats

John Keats by Charles Armitage Brown.
By courtesy of the National Portrait Gallery, London.

He Won the Contest

"On the Grasshopper and the Cricket" was the result of a sonnet-writing contest that **John Keats** (1795–1821) had with another poet, his friend Leigh Hunt. Snug indoors on a winter's night in 1816, the two poets heard the chirping of a cricket. Hunt challenged Keats to see which of them could write the best sonnet on the subject of the grasshopper and the cricket—within fifteen minutes.

At that time, Keats had only begun to write sonnets. He had trained to be a doctor for six years and had passed his examinations for a license to practice medicine, but he disliked surgery. What he really wanted was to become a poet.

Keats did become a poet, one of the greatest in the English language, although he lived for only twenty-five years. In physical size, Keats was a small man. When fully grown, he was barely five feet tall, and he was always slender. At school he was strong and athletic, however, admired by his many friends for having the courage and fighting spirit of a terrier.

The oldest of four children, John Keats was born into a middle-class family. Shortly after he was sent away to boarding school, at the age of eight, his father was killed in an accident. His mother died of tuberculosis when Keats was only fourteen. That event ended his formal education. Keats was apprenticed to a surgeon shortly afterward.

Keats's first book of poetry (1817) was not received well by critics, but despite many personal difficulties he continued to write. His beloved brother Tom died of tuberculosis in 1818, and then Keats himself began to show early signs of the disease. Meanwhile, he had fallen deeply in love with a young woman named Fanny Brawne. He knew, however, that his sickness would keep them from marrying. Even though he was dying, Keats continued to write poems of such beauty and depth of meaning that they are still read and admired today.

First Thoughts

1. Listen to Keats's poem read aloud, and sketch the image that appeals to you most. Compare your sketch with the sketches of other students. Did you and your classmates see different things?

Thinking Critically

2. In this Italian **sonnet,** Keats describes two "poets" of the natural world. Who is the poet of summer in the first eight lines? Who is the poet of winter in the last six lines?

3. What simple words does Keats use to describe the hot, sleepy feeling of a summer day? What words does he use to describe a winter evening?

4. Which line of the poem echoes the first line? How do the changed words affect the meaning?

5. In this brief sonnet, Keats makes points about nature, sound and silence, the heat of summer (and life), the cold of winter (and death). Sum up in your own words *one* point that the poet makes in the first eight lines of the sonnet. What point, related to the one you discussed, does he make in the last six lines?

WRITING

Writing a Nature Poem

Look back at your Quickwrite notes, and choose one thing in nature that has special meaning for you. Write a poem in which you help your reader *picture* something in the world of nature and understand how you feel about it. You can either use a regular meter and rhyme in your poem or write in free verse, without a regular meter or rhyme. You may want to try writing an Italian sonnet—and challenge a friend to a sonnet-writing contest!

SKILLS FOCUS

Literary Skills
Analyze a sonnet.

Reading Skills
Use a poem's form to find its meaning.

Writing Skills
Write a nature poem.

O Captain! My Captain!

Make the Connection
Quickwrite

Although you are still young, you have probably lost someone or something you cared about. A person you were close to may have died. Perhaps you have lost a beloved pet. Maybe you had to move away from a place you loved. Perhaps a favorite hill or stream has been lost to a housing development. Think about someone or something that meant a lot to you and is now gone. Jot down some quick notes about how that loss affected you.

Abraham Lincoln.

Literary Focus
Elegy

An **elegy** (el′ə · jē) is a poem of mourning. Most elegies are about someone who has died. Some elegies mourn a way of life that is gone forever. "O Captain! My Captain!" mourns the tragic death of President Abraham Lincoln. This elegy uses an **extended metaphor.** That means that a metaphor is stated, and the comparison is extended as far as the poet can take it— in this case, through the entire poem! As you read, decide who the captain really is and what the ship represents.

Background
Literature and Real Life

Walt Whitman lived in Washington, D.C., during the Civil War. He worked as a government clerk and a war correspondent. He also served as a volunteer nurse, caring for the thousands of wounded soldiers who filled the nearby military hospitals. The Saturday before Lincoln's second inauguration, Whitman attended a reception at the White House. On inauguration day, March 4, 1865, Whitman twice saw Lincoln pass by in his carriage. He commented that the president "looked very much worn and tired; the lines, indeed, of vast responsibilities, intricate questions, and demands of life and death, cut deeper than ever upon his dark brown face; yet all the old goodness, tenderness, sadness, and canny shrewdness, underneath the furrows." The president was assassinated just a month later, on April 14, 1865. The country had just concluded a terrible civil war. The difficult job of healing had just begun.

SKILLS FOCUS

Literary Skills
Understand the characteristics of an elegy.

O Captain! My Captain!

Walt Whitman

O Captain! my Captain! our fearful trip is done,
The ship has weathered every rack,° the prize we sought is won,
The port is near, the bells I hear, the people all exulting,°
While follow eyes the steady keel, the vessel grim and daring;
5   But O heart! heart! heart!
        O the bleeding drops of red,
          Where on the deck my Captain lies,
            Fallen cold and dead.

O Captain! my Captain! rise up and hear the bells;
10 Rise up—for you the flag is flung—for you the bugle trills,
For you bouquets and ribboned wreaths—for you the shores a-crowding,
For you they call, the swaying mass, their eager faces turning;
        Here Captain! dear father!
        The arm beneath your head!
15   It is some dream that on the deck,
            You've fallen cold and dead.

My Captain does not answer, his lips are pale and still,
My father does not feel my arm, he has no pulse nor will,
The ship is anchored safe and sound, its voyage closed and done,
20 From fearful trip the victor° ship comes in with object won:
        Exult O shores, and ring O bells!
        But I with mournful tread,
          Walk the deck my Captain lies,
            Fallen cold and dead.

---

2. **rack** *n.*: here, violent change or disorder, like that caused by a storm.
3. **exulting** (eg·zult′iŋ) *v.* used as *adj.*: rejoicing.
20. **victor** *n.* used as *adj.*: winner.

Meet the Writer

Walt Whitman

An American Original

Walt Whitman (1819–1892) is one of the finest and most original American poets. Born on Long Island, New York, Whitman had to leave school at age eleven to go to work. On weekends he continued his education by reading widely. He would sit on the beach and read Sir Walter Scott, the Bible, and Shakespeare. Whitman dressed and behaved in a manner all his own.

According to one story, Whitman once drove a horse-drawn carriage along Broadway, reciting Shakespeare at the top of his lungs. Whitman was also very talented and very persistent. When he couldn't find a publisher for *Leaves of Grass*, he published it himself, in 1855. He even wrote his own reviews. Whitman never stopped working on his "leaves." He revised his book and added poems to it until his death.

With *Leaves of Grass*, Whitman became an original voice of the still-new United States. Whitman embraced and celebrated all aspects of his country and its people—especially its workers. In "I Hear America Singing" (see page 671), he celebrates mechanics, carpenters, masons, woodcutters, shoemakers, girls sewing or washing. In *Song of Myself,* he sings of boatmen, clam diggers, trappers, and men fleeing slavery.

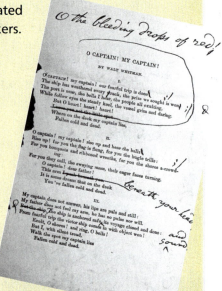

Leaves of Grass is now recognized as a masterpiece, but that wasn't always so. At first many readers criticized Whitman's poems because they were about common people and common experiences. Readers also hated the poems because they were written in free verse instead of strictly rhymed and metered lines. For more than a century now, however, Americans and people all over the world have been strengthened and inspired by the poetry of Walt Whitman. We take great joy in it.

After You Read | Response and Analysis

First Thoughts

1. In your opinion, what is the most memorable word or phrase in this poem? Why?

Thinking Critically

2. "O Captain! My Captain!" is built on an **extended metaphor.** The poet speaks of a captain and a ship all the way through the poem, but we sense that he is not talking about an actual captain and an actual ship. What clues tell you who the captain is? What does the ship represent?

A sketch of Lincoln dying, by Hermann Faber.

3. The poet uses a second **metaphor** in lines 13 and 18. What is it, and how does this metaphor make the poem even sadder?

4. In line 20, the poet says, "From fearful trip the victor ship comes in with object won." If the ship is a metaphor for the country, what "fearful trip" has the country made? What "object" has it won?

5. What **refrain,** or repeated line, appears at the end of each stanza? Why is the situation it describes **ironic** or not what we would expect when a captain has brought his ship home victorious?

WRITING

Writing an Elegy

Write a brief **elegy** for someone or something you cared deeply about but lost. You may want to use your notes from your Quickwrite, or you may prefer to choose another topic. Let the reader understand why the subject is important to you. Try writing your elegy in free verse without using rhyme and a strict meter.

SPEAKING AND LISTENING

Presenting a Dramatic Reading

Prepare and present a **dramatic reading** of "O Captain! My Captain!" Your delivery should be loud, slow, and clear. Emphasize the **rhythm** of the words, and pay special attention to **refrains.**

I Hear America Singing
and I, Too

Make the Connection

Quickwrite ✏️

Think about the sounds you hear around you. If you live in a city, you may hear the rumble of a subway, the roar of traffic, people arguing, pigeons cooing. In the suburbs you might hear a gentler whoosh of traffic, kids shouting, birds singing, the drone of a lawn mower. In the country you might hear the wind blowing, a meadowlark singing, cicadas humming. Wherever you are, sit quietly and listen. Then, jot down all the sounds you hear.

Literary Focus

Free Verse

Free verse does not follow a regular rhyme scheme or meter, but that doesn't mean that anything goes. Without a strict pattern to follow, poets writing free verse have to rely on their own sense of balance and measure. Poets writing free verse also use the following devices (for more information on these devices, turn to the definitions in the Handbook of Literary Terms in the back of this book):

- **alliteration** (ə·lit′ər·ā′shən)— repetition of consonant sounds (snow *falling fast*)

- **onomatopoeia** (än′ō·mat′ō·pē′ə)— the use of words whose sounds echo their meaning (the chain saw's *buzz*)

- **imagery**—language that evokes sensations of sight, sound, smell, taste, and touch

- **figures of speech**—language that is based on comparisons and is not literally true (metaphors, similes, personification)

- **rhythm**—a musical quality produced by repetition

Walt Whitman was the first American poet to use free verse. Today many poets write in free verse, so we take it for granted. In Whitman's day, however, people were used to poems written in "poetic" language, which used strict rhyme schemes and meters. These people were shocked by Whitman's sprawling lines and use of slang. In time many critics came to feel that Walt Whitman was the first and greatest poet to "give voice" to America. "I Hear America Singing" offers a good example of why they came to think so.

SKILLS FOCUS

Literary Skills
Understand the characteristics of free verse.

I Hear America Singing

Walt Whitman

I hear America singing, the varied carols I hear,
Those of mechanics, each one singing his as it should
    be blithe° and strong,
The carpenter singing his as he measures his plank or
    beam,
The mason singing his as he makes ready for work, or
    leaves off work,
The boatman singing what belongs to him in his boat,
5   the deckhand singing on the steamboat deck,
The shoemaker singing as he sits on his bench, the
    hatter singing as he stands,
The woodcutter's song, the plowboy's on his way in
    the morning, or at noon intermission or at sundown,
The delicious singing of the mother, or of the young
    wife at work, or of the girl sewing or washing,
Each singing what belongs to him or her and to none
    else,
The day what belongs to the day—at night the party of
10   young fellows, robust, friendly,
Singing with open mouths their strong melodious
    songs.

---

2. blithe (blīth) *adj.:* lighthearted.

*For biographical information on
Walt Whitman, see page 668.*

Walt Whitman.
Courtesy of the Bayley-Whitman Collection,
Ohio Wesleyan University
Delaware, Ohio, 43015.

I, Too

Langston Hughes

I, too, sing America.

I am the darker brother.
They send me to eat in the kitchen
When company comes,
5   But I laugh,
And eat well,
And grow strong.

Tomorrow,
I'll sit at the table
10 When company comes.
Nobody'll dare
Say to me,
"Eat in the kitchen,"
Then.

15 Besides,
They'll see how beautiful I am
And be ashamed—

I, too, am America.

*For biographical
information
on Langston Hughes,
see page 497.*

First Thoughts

1. In your opinion, what is the most important word or phrase in each poem? Explain your choices.

Thinking Critically

2. "I, Too" was written in response to "I Hear America Singing." Whitman's poem is a celebration of the American worker. What is Hughes's poem about?

3. Do any of the people in Whitman's poem sing about disturbing or unpleasant subjects, such as poor working conditions? Is Whitman painting too rosy a picture of working-class life in nineteenth-century America? Explain your answers.

4. "I Hear America Singing" and "I, Too" are both **free-verse** poems—they do not have a regular rhyme scheme or meter. They do, however, use repetition to create **rhythm.** In each poem, find examples of repeated words, lines, and sentence patterns.

Extending Interpretations

5. Imagine what kinds of singing Whitman might hear if he were alive today. In what ways might these "songs" be different from those he heard in his own time? In what ways would they be similar?

City Building, from American Today, 1930 by Thomas Hart Benton. Distemper and egg tempera on gessoed linen with oil glaze (92″ × 117″).

Collection, AXA Financial, Inc. through its subsidiary The Equitable Life Assurance Society of the U.S.

WRITING

Writing a Free-Verse Poem

Write a free-verse poem about the sounds you hear around you. Go back to your Quickwrite for ideas. Structure your poem as a list the way Whitman did, and try to make most of your sentences similar in structure. (The repetition of sentence patterns will give your poem rhythm.) In your poem, simply describe the sounds you hear, or include your feelings about the "songs." Whatever your plan, be sure to use words and images that will help your reader hear the sounds.

SKILLS FOCUS

Literary Skills
Analyze free verse.

Writing Skills
Write a free-verse poem.

Understanding a Summary

Reading Focus

What Goes into a Summary

Writing a good **summary** of an informational text is not easy. You have to restate the main ideas, include critical details, and sum up the underlying meaning of the text. Here is a list of elements to look for in a good summary of informational nonfiction:

> ### Summary of an Informational Text: A Checklist
>
> 1. The summary should open with the **title** and **author** of the text.
> 2. The summary should state the **topic** of the text.
> 3. The summary should state the **main ideas,** in the **order** in which they occur in the text.
> 4. The summary should include important **supporting details.**
> 5. Quotation marks should be put around any words from the text that are quoted exactly.

Reading Skills
Understand how to summarize an informational text.

■ Read the biography of Langston Hughes and the summary that follows. What makes the summary a good—or bad—summary?

Langston Hughes: A Biography

Langston Hughes was born in 1902 in Joplin, Missouri, but he spent most of his childhood in Lawrence, Kansas, with his grandmother. When he was twelve, he moved to Lincoln, Illinois, and then to Cleveland, Ohio, to live with his mother and stepfather. Hughes died in 1967 in his home in his beloved Harlem, in New York City.

According to a popular story, Langston Hughes first tasted fame when he was twenty-three years old. When the poet Vachel Lindsay came to dine at the Wardman Park Hotel in Washington, D.C., where Hughes was working as a busboy, Hughes left three poems by Lindsay's plate. Lindsay was so impressed by the poems that he presented them that night at a reading, saying he had discovered a true poet, a young black man who was working as a busboy in a nearby restaurant. For the next few days, newspapers up and down the East Coast ran articles acclaiming the "busboy poet."

That story is a good one, but it's a little misleading. Hughes was not really an overnight success. He had already put in a long apprenticeship as a writer. He had written his first poem when he was in eighth grade and was first published in his high school literary magazine. Hughes had also read a great deal of poetry, especially the works of Edgar Lee Masters, Vachel Lindsay, Amy Lowell, Carl Sandburg, and Walt Whitman. Whitman and Sandburg had a strong influence on Hughes because they celebrated the humanity of all people regardless of age, gender, race, or class. Hughes had already seen many of his own poems published in journals and magazines. What's more, a book of his poetry, *The Weary Blues,* was soon to be published by a famous New York publisher.

As the anecdote about Vachel Lindsay shows, Hughes was energetic and ambitious. Before he met Lindsay, he had attended Columbia University and had worked as a crew member on a freighter crossing the Atlantic to Africa and back. He spoke German and Spanish and had lived in Mexico (where his father also lived), France, and Italy. After meeting Lindsay, Hughes went on to earn a college degree at Lincoln University and to write fifteen volumes of poetry, six novels, three books of short stories, eleven plays, and a variety of nonfiction works. Hughes worked in Harlem during the heady days of the Harlem Renaissance, when that New York City neighborhood was teeming with talent—poets, musicians, artists.

Langston Hughes outside his house in Harlem.

About his poetry, Hughes said, "Perhaps the mission of an artist is to interpret beauty to the people—the beauty within themselves." Hughes also interpreted—and celebrated—the experiences of African Americans. Some of his most famous poems imitated jazz rhythms and the repetitive structure of the blues. Later in life he wrote poems specifically designed for jazz accompaniment. He also helped found several black theater companies and wrote and translated plays for them to perform. Langston Hughes is perhaps the most famous and original of all African American poets. He said his work was an attempt to "explain and illuminate the Negro condition in America." Hughes succeeded in that and more: His work illuminates the condition of all people everywhere.

"Langston Hughes": A Summary

"Langston Hughes: A Biography" focuses on the life and works of the poet Langston Hughes. The main point made in this biographical sketch is that Langston Hughes wrote about the experiences of African Americans but his work "illuminates the condition of all people everywhere." Hughes became famous when he was twenty-three, when the poet Vachel Lindsay read his poems at a poetry reading. Hughes had been writing since eighth grade, however, and had published a poem in a high school literary magazine. He was especially influenced by Whitman and Sandburg because they celebrated all humanity. Hughes accomplished a lot both before and after meeting Lindsay. He attended Columbia and graduated from Lincoln University. He traveled widely and spoke three languages. He was part of the Harlem Renaissance and published many books of poetry, plays, fiction, and nonfiction. Langston Hughes is probably the most famous and original of all African American poets.

Analyzing a Summary

"Langston Hughes":
A Summary

Test Practice

1. Which of the following **details** is included in *both* the summary and the biography?
   A Hughes was influenced by Whitman and Sandburg.
   B Hughes read Masters, Lindsay, Lowell, Sandburg, and Whitman.
   C Hughes spoke German and Spanish.
   D Hughes traveled to Africa, Mexico, France, and Italy.

2. Which detail in the summary is probably *not* important and could have been omitted?
   F Hughes became famous at age twenty-three.
   G Hughes was part of the Harlem Renaissance.
   H Hughes wrote about African Americans.
   J Hughes was published in a high school literary magazine.

3. Which **critical details** from the biography does the summary omit?
   A Hughes's birth and death dates
   B Influences on Hughes
   C Colleges Hughes attended
   D Hughes's subject matter

4. Which passage in the summary should be placed in **quotation marks** because it uses the exact words of the writer of the biography?
   F attended Columbia and graduated from Lincoln University
   G accomplished a lot both before and after meeting Lindsay
   H traveled widely and spoke three languages
   J the most famous and original of all African American poets

Constructed Response

Langston Hughes: A Biography

1. According to the biography, how did Vachel Lindsay help Langston Hughes?

2. According to the biography, which poets most influenced Hughes?

3. How did Hughes use the experiences of African Americans in his poetry?

4. What did Hughes say was the mission of an artist?

5. What did Hughes say he attempted to do in his work?

SKILLS FOCUS

Reading Skills
Analyze a summary of an informational text.

Comparing Literature

Literary Focus
Theme: From Generation to Generation

The family is a universal topic in literature. Families influence us through much of our lives and leave us with many legacies: the way we look, the way we act, the things we value. Older generations also pass down the wisdom they've gained through years of experience.

The two poems you're about to read offer insights into the speakers' relationships with a grandparent. As you read, think about what each speaker gains from this relationship. What **theme,** or message, about relationships between generations emerges from these poems?

Reading Skills and Strategies
Comparing and Contrasting

When you **compare** and **contrast** two poems, you look for similarities and differences between them. The two poems that follow are both about a bond between a grandchild and a grandparent. In the margins are questions about each poem. As you read, pause to write your answers to the questions on a separate piece of paper. After each poem you will find a chart (see pages 681 and 684). Record details of the poem in the chart; you'll use it when you write a comparison-contrast essay at the end of this lesson.

More Poems About Family Ties

- "Sisters" by Rita Dove
- "For My Sister Molly Who in the Fifties" by Alice Walker
- "Birdfoot's Grampa" by Joseph Bruchac
- "Abuelito Who" by Sandra Cisneros
- "4 daughters" by Lucille Clifton
- "To a Daughter Leaving Home" by Linda Pastan
- "The Courage That My Mother Had" by Edna St. Vincent Millay
- "Mother to Son" by Langston Hughes
- "My Father's Song" by Simon J. Ortiz

SKILLS FOCUS

Literary Skills
Understand theme.

Reading Skills
Compare and contrast poems.

Before You Read

Has anyone ever told you that you have your great-grandfather's nose or that you're going to be as tall as your aunt? The special connection of a resemblance can cause mixed feelings. You may be proud to look so much like your sister, but you probably also want everyone to realize that you're a unique person with your own identity. Do people say you look like someone else? (The person doesn't have to be a family member; you may be told you resemble a friend or someone famous.) If so, who? How do you feel about the resemblance?

Grandma Ling

Amy Ling

If you dig that hole deep enough,
you'll reach China, they used to tell me,
a child in a back yard in Pennsylvania.
Not strong enough to dig that hole,
5   I waited twenty years,
then sailed back, half way around the world. ❶

In Taiwan I first met Grandma.
Before she came to view, I heard
her slippered feet softly measure
10   the tatami° floor with even step;
the aqua paper-covered door slid open
and there I faced
my five foot height, sturdy legs and feet,
square forehead, high cheeks and wide-set eyes;
15   my image stood before me,
acted on by fifty years. ❷

She smiled, stretched her arms
to take to heart the eldest daughter
of her youngest son a quarter century away.
20   She spoke a tongue I knew no word of,
and I was sad I could not understand,
but I could hug her. ❸

---

10. **tatami** (tə·tä′mē): floor mat woven of rice straw.

IDENTIFY

❶ Where does the speaker go when she goes "half way around the world"? Why does she go?

INFER

❷ What does the speaker mean by "my image" in line 15?

INTERPRET

❸ How can the speaker and her grandmother share their thoughts and feelings without words?

Meet the Writer

Amy Ling

Between Worlds

As a child, **Amy Ling** (1939–1999) had a special reason for wanting to reach China: She'd be going home. Ling, whose name was originally Ling Ying Ming, was born in Beijing, China, and moved to the United States with her family at the age of six.

"Grandma Ling" was inspired by a trip to Taiwan the poet made in the early 1960s. The photo shown here was taken during that visit.

> "This is a photo of my grandmother, my cousin May Li Ling (in the yellow dress, on the right), and me (in pale blue, on the left). We are celebrating our twenty-fourth birthday—my cousin is five days older than I—in my aunt's home in Da Ling Sugar Factory in Taiwan. See the tatami mats on the floor and the sliding paper doors. I thought this photo would be particularly appropriate, since this is the paternal grandmother I was writing about meeting in my poem."

Ling studied and wrote about other American writers who are "between worlds," especially Asian American women writers.

After You Read   "Grandma Ling"

First Thoughts

1. Briefly describe or draw an **image** that this poem calls to mind.

Thinking Critically

2. Draw a thought bubble like the one on the right. Fill it in with symbols and words showing what the speaker might have been thinking and feeling at the moment when "my image stood before me, acted on by fifty years" (lines 15–16).

3. The speaker in the poem cannot understand her grandmother's words. What do you think the grandmother is saying to her granddaughter?

4. Look at the adults around you. Do you see in them any clues about what you might be like when you're older? Which traits do you hope to share? Which would you like to change?

Comparing Literature

5. After you've read the next poem, you'll write a brief comparison-contrast essay. You can begin to plan your writing by filling in the column under the heading "Grandma Ling" in a chart like the one below. After you read "Legacy II," you will add details from that poem to the chart.

Comparing Poems		
	"Grandma Ling"	"Legacy II"
Characteristics of speaker		
Characteristics of grandparent		
What speaker wants		
What speaker learns from grandparent		
Theme		

SKILLS FOCUS

Literary Skills
Analyze theme.

Reading Skills
Compare and contrast poems.

Before You Read

Usually we think of a legacy as money or property handed down from a relative who has died. Before you read this poem, think about all the kinds of legacies people might pass on. Can people pass on nonmaterial things—values like wisdom, faith, or honesty?

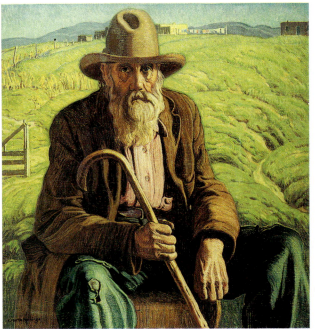

Spanish Octogenarian by E. Martin Hennings. Oil on canvas.

Stark Museum of Art, Orange, Texas.

Legacy II
Leroy V. Quintana

Grandfather never went to school
spoke only a few words of English

a quiet man; when he talked
talked about simple things
5   planting corn or about the weather
sometimes about herding sheep as a child ❶

One day pointed to the four directions
taught me their names
                    El Norte
10   Poniente   Oriente
                El Sur

IDENTIFY

❶ What have you learned about Grandfather so far?

He spoke their names as if they were
one of only a handful of things
a man needed to know

15 Now I look back
only two generations removed
realize I am nothing but a poor fool
who went to college

trying to find my way back
20 to the center of the world
where Grandfather stood
that day ❷

**COMPARE AND
CONTRAST**

❷ What is the speaker
trying to do now?
How is this action
similar to what the
speaker does in
"Grandma Ling"?

Meet the Writer

Leroy V. Quintana

Family Ties

Leroy V. Quintana (1944–   ) was
born in Albuquerque, New Mexico, and
was raised by his grandparents. Many of
his poems contrast his Mexican
ancestors' traditional way of life with
the way people live in big cities today.
"In many ways I'm still basically a small-
town New Mexico boy carrying on the
oral tradition," he says.

❝I heard Grandmother tell me the
old stories hundreds of times, over
and over. To me it was like turning
on the TV. She had the nuances of
language, though she had no education; she knew the inflections, how

to tell the story, how to keep you in
suspense. You know, that seems to
be lost, and I would hope that I
could at least put a little bit of that
on paper.❞

"Legacy II" builds on the theme of
another poem by Quintana, "A Legacy,"
about an educated man who longs to
return to the time when his grandfather
told him *cuentos* (kwen′tôs), Mexican
American folk tales.

First Thoughts

1. Do you think it's possible for qualities like wisdom to be handed down as legacies? Why or why not?

Thinking Critically

2. What legacy did the speaker receive? When does he learn to appreciate it?

3. How does the speaker feel about his grandfather?

4. What do you think the speaker means when he says that his grandfather stood at the center of the world that day (lines 20–22)?

5. Look at lines 9–11. How does the placement of the words in these lines help you to understand the Spanish words? What do the words mean?

6. What **theme,** or message, is the poet sharing with you? Does this message apply to your own life? Explain.

Comparing Literature

7. Add information about "Legacy II" to the chart you began on page 681. You'll use the chart to complete the comparison-contrast assignment on the next page.

Comparing Poems		
	"Grandma Ling"	"Legacy II"
Characteristics of speaker		
Characteristics of grandparent		
What speaker wants		
What speaker learns from grandparent		
Theme		

SKILLS FOCUS

Literary Skills
Analyze theme.

Reading Skills
Compare and contrast poems.

Assignment

1. Writing a Comparison-Contrast Essay

Write three paragraphs comparing "Grandma Ling" with "Legacy II." To plan your essay, review the chart you filled in after you read each poem. The chart will help you identify similarities and differences between the poems. (You do not have to write about all the elements listed in the chart.)

Assignment

2. Interviewing a Family Member

Interview an older family member about his or her life before you were born. You may want to concentrate on one or two of these areas: education; career plans; or talents, interests, and hobbies.

Write up the interview either in a question-and-answer format or in paragraph form, using a combination of your words and the words of the person you're interviewing.

Assignment

3. Writing a Thank-you Note

Think of a gift someone gave you that was *not* an object—perhaps knowledge, love, or just attention when you needed someone to listen. Write a **thank-you note** explaining what the gift meant to you.

Assignment

4. Drawing a Self-portrait

What will you look like in fifty years? Draw yourself as sixty-something.

SKILLS FOCUS

Writing Skills
Write a comparison-contrast essay; write a thank-you note.

Speaking and Listening Skills
Interview a family member.

The Naming of Cats

T. S. Eliot

The Naming of Cats is a difficult matter,
　　It isn't just one of your holiday games;
You may think at first I'm as mad as a hatter
When I tell you, a cat must have THREE DIFFERENT NAMES.
5　First of all, there's the name that the family use daily,
　　Such as Peter, Augustus, Alonzo or James,
Such as Victor or Jonathan, George or Bill Bailey—
　　All of them sensible everyday names.
There are fancier names if you think they sound sweeter,
10　Some for the gentlemen, some for the dames:
Such as Plato, Admetus, Electra, Demeter—
　　But all of them sensible everyday names.
But I tell you, a cat needs a name that's particular,
　　A name that's peculiar, and more dignified,
15　Else how can he keep up his tail perpendicular,
　　Or spread out his whiskers, or cherish his pride?
Of names of this kind, I can give you a quorum,°
　　Such as Munkustrap, Quaxo, or Coricopat,
Such as Bombalurina, or else Jellylorum—
20　Names that never belong to more than one cat.
But above and beyond there's still one name left over,
　　And that is the name that you never will guess;

---

17. quorum (kwôr′əm): here, a select group.

The name that no human research can discover—
    But THE CAT HIMSELF KNOWS, and will never confess.
25 When you notice a cat in profound meditation,
    The reason, I tell you, is always the same;
  His mind is engaged in a rapt contemplation
    Of the thought, of the thought, of the thought of his name:
      His ineffable° effable
30   Effanineffable
  Deep and inscrutable° singular Name.

---

29. ineffable (in·ef′ə·bəl): too awesome to be spoken.
31. inscrutable (in·skrōōt′ə·bəl): mysterious; can't be understood.

Cat drawings by Edward Gorey from
Old Possum's Book of Practical Cats by T. S. Eliot.

Meet the Writer

T. S. Eliot

Drawing, 1930 by Powys Evans, The Granger Collection.

The Poet's Secret Name Is . . .

George Pushdragon. That's the alias **Thomas Stearns Eliot** (1888–1965) used when entering crossword competitions; it was also the name of one of his beloved cats. (Wiscus and Pittipaws were others.) Eliot, an American who moved to England in 1914 and later became a British citizen, was a truly revolutionary poet who won a Nobel Prize in 1948. Eliot wrote the humorous *Old Possum's Book of Practical Cats* for his godchildren—and perhaps for his father, who liked drawing cats.

Eliot himself loved nonsense verse and music-hall shows, so he would probably have wanted a front-row seat for the smash Broadway hit *Cats,* which was based on his cat poems.

Media Workshop

Assignment

Plan and present a poetry reading.

Audience

Your classmates, teacher, friends, and other students.

RUBRIC
Evaluation Criteria

A successful poetry performance

1. has a clear focus or topic
2. captures the audience's attention
3. includes a variety of selections
4. consists of expressive and natural oral readings
5. uses different media, such as sound effects, slides, dance, and music, to enhance the reading
6. has a dramatic conclusion

SKILLS FOCUS

Speaking and Listening Skills
Present a poetry performance.

MULTIMEDIA PRESENTATION
Poetry in Performance

In recent years, poetry readings and poetry slams have become popular. In some performances, poets read their own work; other performances combine poetry readings with music, dance, and visual arts.

In this workshop you will plan and present a poetry reading. You can be as creative as you like in finding ways to bring poetry to your public.

Planning Your Performance

 1 **Choosing a Focus**

Before you select poems for your reading, decide on a focus for your performance. To hold your audience's attention, choose a topic that will create suspense, elicit a variety of moods, or appeal to their sense of humor. Like any form of theater, a poetry reading should be dramatic.

Here are some possible topics paired with poems that appear in this anthology.

Topic	Poems
Famous characters in poetry	"Barbara Frietchie" (page 163) "Paul Revere's Ride" (page 629) "Casey at the Bat" (page 650)
America the beautiful	"The New Colossus" (page 493) "I Hear America Singing" (page 671)

Poems to make you laugh	"The Cremation of Sam McGee" (page 637) "Casey at the Bat" (page 650) "The Naming of Cats" (page 686)
Short and sweet	"Fame is a bee" (page 531) "who are you,little i" (page 530) "A word is dead" (page 570) "The Word" (page 570)
Walt Whitman: An American original	"O Captain! My Captain!" (page 667) "I Hear America Singing" (page 671)

Consider reading some of your own poetry as well.

2 Preparing Background Material

Learn as much as you can about the poems you are presenting. Find out if there are special circumstances surrounding the composition of the poems. See if anything in the poet's own life gives you clues to the poems' meanings. You may want to share this information with your audience.

3 Interpreting and Reading Poems

After you choose a topic and poems to read, prepare your oral interpretation by following these steps:

- Read and re-read each poem aloud, concentrating on its meaning. Jot down ideas on ways to communicate your thoughts and feelings to an audience.
- Aim for a natural reading of the lines. Follow the punctuation of the poem, varying your **pauses, volume, tone,** and the **emphasis** you put on certain words.
- Copy the poems, and add notes and marks to guide you in your reading. Underline words or phrases to be emphasized. Use slashes to represent pauses.
- Practice reading the poems aloud with a few classmates as your audience. Note which vocal effects work best.
- Tape-record or videotape your practice reading. Study the recording to see whether you need to make any changes.

Research Tips

- Most libraries now have online catalogs on which you can search for sources. Use **electronic databases** to get information.
- If your computer is equipped with a CD-ROM player, you can use **CD-ROMs** to find recordings of poems.
- To do research on the World Wide Web, you will need a **Web browser.**

For guidance in doing research, see the Communications Handbook.

Presentation Tips

- Check the pronunciation of each poet's name and of any unfamiliar words or names in the poems.
- Do not pause automatically at the end of each line, even if the poem contains rhyme. Let the punctuation guide your pauses (pause at commas and semicolons; pause a little longer at dashes and periods).
- Phrase your reading so that it is not choppy.

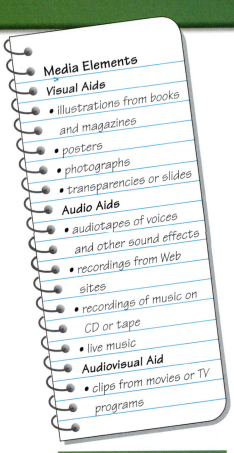

Media Elements

Visual Aids
- illustrations from books and magazines
- posters
- photographs
- transparencies or slides

Audio Aids
- audiotapes of voices and other sound effects
- recordings from Web sites
- recordings of music on CD or tape
- live music

Audiovisual Aid
- clips from movies or TV programs

Framework for a Poetry Performance

Introduction
- attention-getting opener
- titles of poems and authors
- presentation of topic

Body
- poem 1: interpretation, media elements
- poem 2: interpretation, media elements

Conclusion
- restatement of topic
- media elements

4 Using Different Media

In a multimedia presentation you can use recorded music, visual aids, sound effects, and even dance. Try incorporating background music into your presentation or pairing poems with songs. Display fine art or photographs that evoke the ideas or feelings similar to those expressed in the poems. If you wish, pair published poems with poems of your own. You might even want to act out certain lines in a poem. For more possibilities, see the list of media elements at the left.

Developing a Script

The script for your performance should include an introduction, a body, and a conclusion. You should have a fairly accurate idea of how long your presentation will be so that you don't run out of time.

Your **introduction** should get the audience's attention. Think of an imaginative way to open your presentation. A quotation or question is a good way to engage your listeners; you might also use music, a transparency, or a video clip if the technology is available. State the topic of your presentation, identify the poems you will read by title and author, and tell your audience how you intend to proceed.

In the **body** of your presentation, give your oral interpretations of the poems you have chosen. You may comment on the poems before or after you read or recite them, emphasizing the connection with your topic. Accompany your readings with other media to provide background or help convey the mood and content of the works.

In your **conclusion,** restate the topic of your presentation and talk about its significance. End with a quotation, a musical excerpt, or a slide that leaves your audience with a dramatic impression.

Remember that an effective presentation makes poetry come alive for listeners. Your insights into the poems you have chosen can help your audience appreciate the poets' skills.

On the following pages you will find a script for a presentation of poems by Walt Whitman.

Model Presentation

Walt Whitman: An American Original

Visuals
- photograph of Walt Whitman by Mathew Brady (c. 1866)
- title page of Leaves of Grass (1855)
- painting: The Jolly Flatboatmen in Port (1857) by George Caleb Bingham
- photograph of Lincoln's funeral (1882)

Music
- "O Captain! My Captain!" excerpt from Memories of Lincoln by John Church (available on CD)

Recordings
- wax cylinder recording by Thomas Edison of Whitman reading his own poetry (available on CD or Web site)

Texts
- "I Hear America Singing" by Walt Whitman
- "O Captain! My Captain!" by Walt Whitman
- excerpt from preface to Leaves of Grass
- excerpt from Specimen Days

List of media elements and poems to be used in presentation.

[Present visual: Photograph of Walt Whitman by Mathew Brady]

Today Walt Whitman is recognized as one of America's greatest poets. His work has been translated into many languages. In my presentation I'm going to focus on two well-known poems that show his individuality and genius.

Visuals used as background.

Introduction presents focus of presentation.

[Present visual: Title page of Leaves of Grass]

When Whitman published the first edition of his volume of poetry, Leaves of Grass, in 1855, many readers didn't know what to make of it. No one had ever written poetry like it before. Some readers did recognize its worth, though, and in the years since then, Whitman has found his place as a great original poet.

Paragraph develops topic: Whitman's originality.

What was so new about Whitman's poetry? Most American poets of the time wrote in a fairly formal style, using blank verse and rhyme, but Whitman wrote in free verse. Poetry written in this style mimics the sound of natural speech: It lacks a regular meter and rhyme scheme. Whitman's subject matter was also unconventional: He wrote about himself and about Americans from all walks of life. Listen to "I Hear America Singing."

[Recite: "I Hear America Singing"]

[Present visual: The Jolly Flatboatmen in Port]

In his preface to Leaves of Grass, Whitman wrote:

[Quotations] "Here is not merely a nation but a teeming nation of nations." He celebrated the vitality and diversity of America: "The United States themselves are essentially the greatest poem."

Abraham Lincoln admired Whitman's Leaves of Grass and kept a copy of the book in his office. During the Civil War, Whitman, too old to enlist, volunteered in hospitals in Washington, D.C., caring for sick and wounded soldiers. While passing to and from his lodgings, he sometimes saw the president. In Specimen Days, Whitman wrote of

[Quotation] "Abraham Lincoln's dark brown face, with the deep-cut lines, always to me with a deep latent sadness in the expression."

After Lincoln's assassination, Whitman wrote a moving elegy in his memory. In "O Captain! My Captain!" Whitman uses the metaphor of the ship of state, with Lincoln as its fallen captain. The poem is unusual for Whitman because of its regular structure and use of rhyme.

[Recite: "O Captain! My Captain!"]

This famous poem has been set to music by John Church.

[Play: Musical excerpt]

A photograph of Lincoln's funeral has survived.

[Present visual: Photograph of Lincoln's funeral]

Whitman's influence is seen in the work of many modern poets who could never have written their poems without Whitman's example. Fortunately, Whitman recorded some of his poetry. I would like to close my presentation by letting you hear his voice.

[Play: Audiotape or CD of Edison's wax cylinder recording]

Visual provides **context** *for poem.*

Quotations *offer insights into poet's ideas.*

Paragraph **transitions** *to second poem.*

Quotation *gives firsthand impression of Lincoln.*

Paragraph **explains metaphor** *of poem.*

Musical excerpt *provides another interpretation.*

Photograph *is firsthand* **evidence.**

Whitman's own reading is used in **conclusion** *for dramatic effect.*

Evaluating Your Performance

Poetry in Performance: Guidelines for Evaluation

Content and Organization

❶ Did you use an effective introduction? **Underline** the focus of your presentation.

❷ Did you develop your theme in the body of your script? **Put a star** next to each subtopic sentence.

❸ Did you supply details to support your main points? **Bracket** the details.

❹ **Put a check mark** next to each form of media used in the presentation.

❺ Did you identify poems by title and author? **Highlight** the title of each work used.

❻ Did you provide a dramatic conclusion? **Underline** the restatement of topic or your comment.

Delivery

❶ Did you **speak clearly** so that everyone in the audience could understand you?

❷ Did you **look at your audience** while you were speaking?

❸ Did you **maintain a good pace**—not too fast or too slow?

❹ Did you vary your presentation by using **different media**?

❺ Did you use **appropriate language**? Did you define or explain any terms that your listeners might not understand?

❻ Did you **show enthusiasm** for your subject?

Peer Evaluation

- Have members of your audience respond to your presentation by summarizing their overall reaction. Ask them to focus on your effectiveness as a speaker and to discuss elements like pace, clarity of expression, facial expressions, gestures, and eye contact.

- Invite the audience to discuss issues raised by your presentation.

INTERNET

Media Tutorials
Keyword: LE5 8-6

Collection 6: Skills Review

Literary Skills

Test Practice

POETRY

DIRECTIONS: Answer each question that follows.

1. Many old songs survive from the Middle Ages in England. These old songs often tell stories of betrayal, murder, and love. They have simple meters, use simple rhymes, and include a refrain. These old songs are called —

   A ballads
   B sonnets
   C epics
   D couplets

2. Read this short poem by Langston Hughes, and answer the question that follows.

   O God of dust and rainbows help us see
   That without dust the rainbow would not be.

   This poem could *best* be described as —

   F a ballad
   G a sonnet
   H an epic
   J a lyric

3. In the poem above, the rhyme could *best* be described as —

   A free verse
   B a couplet
   C meter
   D approximate rhyme

4. Homer's great stories of the heroes of the Trojan War, the *Iliad* and the *Odyssey;* the ancient Mesopotamian story of the hero-king Gilgamesh; the story of the warrior Beowulf, who saves a people from monsters—all of these are called —

   F ballads
   G epics
   H lyrics
   J elegies

5. Read these famous lines from the Bible, and answer the question that follows.

   To every thing there is a season,
   And a time to every purpose under the heaven:
   A time to be born, and a time to die;
   A time to plant, and a time to pluck up that which is planted. . . .
   —Ecclesiastes 3:1–2

   Which of the following comments about these lines is correct?

   A The lines are in free verse.
   B The lines are in couplets.
   C The lines are a ballad.
   D The lines are written in strict meter.

SKILLS FOCUS

Literary Skills
Analyze forms of poetry.

6. Read the following poem, and answer the question that follows. (Be sure to note the number of lines in the poem. Also note that *D.R.* in line 6 means "Dominican Republic.")

> **I've heard said that among the eskimos**
>
> **there are over a hundred words for snow:**
>
> **the soft kind, the hard-driving kind, the roll**
>
> **a snowball kind: snow being such a force**
>
> **in their lives, it needs a blizzard**
> 5 **of words.**
>
> **In my own D.R. we have many rains:**
>
> **the sprinkle, the shower, the hurricane,**
>
> **the tears, the many tears for our many dead.**
>
> **I've asked around and find that in all tongues**
>
> **there are at least a dozen words**
> 10 **for talk:**
>
> **the heart-to-heart, the chat, the confession,**
>
> **the juicy gossip, the quip, the harangue—**
>
> **no matter where we're from we need to talk**
>
> **about snow, rain, about being human.**
> —Julia Alvarez

This poem is an example of —

F an elegy

G an ode

H a ballad

J a sonnet

7. Which of the following statements *best* expresses the **main idea** of Julia Alvarez's poem? (See item 6.)

A Eskimos have many words for snow.

B People in the Dominican Republic have many words for rain.

C All languages have many words for talk.

D Communication is important for all people.

8. If you read a poem called "Ode to the West Wind," you could expect —

F a poem that was light and humorous

G a song with a refrain

H a mournful poem about someone who has died

J a serious poem written in formal language

Constructed Response

9. If you were reading a serious poem written to mourn someone who has died, what kind of poem would you be reading? Explain.

Test Practice

DIRECTIONS: Read the poem and the summary. Then, answer each question that follows.

Oranges

Gary Soto

The first time I walked
With a girl, I was twelve,
Cold, and weighted down
With two oranges in my jacket.
5　December. Frost cracking
Beneath my steps, my breath
Before me, then gone,
As I walked toward
Her house, the one whose
10　Porch light burned yellow
Night and day, in any weather.
A dog barked at me, until
She came out pulling
At her gloves, face bright
15　With rouge. I smiled,
Touched her shoulder, and led
Her down the street, across
A used car lot and a line
Of newly planted trees,
20　Until we were breathing
Before a drugstore. We
Entered, the tiny bell
Bringing a saleslady
Down a narrow aisle of goods.
25　I turned to the candies
Tiered like bleachers,
And asked what she wanted—
Light in her eyes, a smile
Starting at the corners

30　Of her mouth. I fingered
A nickel in my pocket,
And when she lifted a chocolate
That cost a dime,
I didn't say anything.
35　I took the nickel from
My pocket, then an orange,
And set them quietly on
The counter. When I looked up,
The lady's eyes met mine,
40　And held them, knowing
Very well what it was all
About.

　　　Outside,
A few cars hissing past,
Fog hanging like old
45　Coats between the trees.
I took my girl's hand
In mine for two blocks,
Then released it to let
Her unwrap the chocolate.
50　I peeled my orange
That was so bright against
The gray of December
That, from some distance,
Someone might have thought
55　I was making a fire in my hands.

SKILLS FOCUS

Reading Skills
Analyze a
summary of a
poem.

"Oranges": A Summary

The poem "Oranges" by Gary Soto is about the experience of a first date. As the boy walks to the girl's house, with a nickel and two oranges in his pocket, his breath is visible in the December chill. A dog barks at him till the girl appears; then all is well. They walk together to the drugstore. Offered her choice, the girl picks a chocolate that costs a dime. The boy pays for the candy with his nickel, which is all the money he has, and offers an orange as well. The saleslady understands, her eyes holding his for a moment. Back on the street again, the boy takes his girl's hand for two blocks and then releases it so she can unwrap her chocolate. He peels his orange, which is so bright in the darkness he says someone might have thought I was making a fire in my hands. The brightness of that moment will live in his memory like a flame.

1. Which phrase from the summary contains a **critical detail**?

   A "As the boy walks"

   B "with a nickel and two oranges in his pocket"

   C "his breath is visible"

   D "Back on the street again"

2. Which item below contains a less important detail, one that could have been omitted from the summary?

   F "A dog barks at him. . . ."

   G "They walk together to the drugstore."

   H "The saleslady understands. . . ."

   J "The boy takes his girl's hand. . . ."

3. Which passage from the summary is a **direct quote** and should be in quotation marks?

   A the bittersweet experience of a first date

   B all is well

   C The saleslady understands

   D someone might have thought I was making a fire in my hands

Constructed Response

4. Which passage from the summary suggests the poem's **underlying meaning,** or **main idea**?

Collection 6: Skills Review

Vocabulary Skills

Test Practice

Multiple-Meaning Words

DIRECTIONS: Choose the answer in which the underlined word is used the way it is used in the quotation from "The Cremation of Sam McGee."

1. "Now Sam McGee was from Tennessee, where the cotton blooms and blows."
   A   The boxer's blows were swift and deadly.
   B   The milkweed seed blows over the fields.
   C   Joshua blows his trumpet, and the walls come tumbling down.
   D   The boy blows his nose in his handkerchief.

2. "Talk of your cold! through the parka's fold it stabbed like a driven nail."
   F   Jake had no friends because of his cold personality.
   G   The ponies shivered all night in the cold.
   H   When Angela got a cold, she couldn't stop sneezing.
   J   Mara prefers cold colors, like blue, to warm ones, like red.

3. "And that very night, as we lay packed tight in our robes beneath the snow . . ."
   A   No one knew who would win the tight race for class president.
   B   Scrooge was so tight he wouldn't pay fair wages.
   C   The puppies snuggled tight against their mother.
   D   The salesclerk said, "Sit tight. I'll be right with you."

4. "And the dogs were fed, and the stars o'erhead were dancing heel and toe . . ."
   F   Maria got a blister on her heel while hiking in the woods.
   G   Jim felt like a heel when he was mean to his brother.
   H   The well-behaved dog would heel behind his trainer.
   J   Paulie threw the heel of bread to the hungry ducks.

5. "Some planks I tore from the cabin floor, and I lit the boiler fire. . . ."
   A   The candidate had twelve planks in her platform.
   B   Ivan built his cabin out of oak planks.
   C   The pirates made their prisoners walk the plank.
   D   Mary served the fish on a wooden plank.

SKILLS FOCUS

Vocabulary Skills
Understand multiple-meaning words.

Collection 6: Skills Review

Writing Skills

Test Practice

DIRECTIONS: Read the following paragraph. Then, answer each question that follows.

(1) To improve your technique in reciting poetry, attend poetry readings and listen to studio recordings of poetry. (2) You can learn effective techniques by listening to skillful readers interpret poems. (3) Poetry readings are given regularly at libraries, bookstores, colleges, and theaters. (4) Many Web sites and CDs offer recordings of poems and of poets reading their own work. (5) You can listen to recordings made more than a century ago. (6) The invention of wax cylinders allowed people to record their voices. (7) Thomas Edison invented wax cylinders. (8) It became possible to record famous poets of the day. (9) You now can hear Alfred, Lord Tennyson, Robert Browning, and Walt Whitman reciting their own works.

1. How might the writer support the statement in sentence 2?
   A Explain how to write poetry
   B List effective techniques
   C Include techniques to avoid
   D List famous poems

2. If you were revising the paragraph, which sentence might you delete as unnecessary?
   F Sentence 2
   G Sentence 3
   H Sentence 4
   J Sentence 7

3. Which of the following transitions would be the best one to use at the beginning of sentence 4?
   A In addition
   B By contrast
   C For example
   D At last

4. What would be the best way to combine sentences 8 and 9?
   F Once it became possible to record famous poets of the day, the works of Alfred, Lord Tennyson, Robert Browning, and Walt Whitman could be recited.
   G Because it became possible to record famous poets of the day, you can now hear Alfred, Lord Tennyson, Robert Browning, and Walt Whitman reciting their own works.
   H You can now hear Alfred, Lord Tennyson, Robert Browning, and Walt Whitman reciting their own works after recording famous poets of the day became possible.
   J It became possible to record famous poets of the day, and so now you can hear reciting their own works Alfred, Lord Tennyson, Robert Browning, and Walt Whitman.

SKILLS FOCUS

Writing Skills
Analyze a paragraph.

Skills Review   **699**

Fiction *and* Poetry

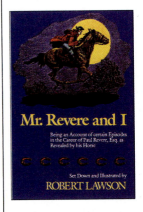

Full Speed Ahead!

Robert Lawson presents a different perspective on Paul Revere's ride in his novel *Mr. Revere and I.* Lawson writes about Revere's famous ride from the point of view of the horse! The book contains humor as well as useful historical information about the beginning of the American Revolution.

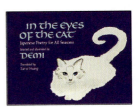

Wonders of Nature

You will gain an appreciation of Japanese poetry in *In the Eyes of the Cat.* The editor and illustrator Demi has selected short poems about animals, from the gnat to the monkey, and arranged them according to the seasons. The illustrations help make this a thoroughly enjoyable book for all readers.

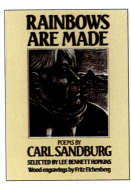

An American Icon

Carl Sandburg's interest in America was boundless. He composed poems about American workers and cities, played folk songs, and wrote a six-volume biography of Abraham Lincoln. *Rainbows Are Made* is a collection of Sandburg's poems. They are sometimes funny, occasionally grim, and always enlightening.

The Power of Imagination

The popular poet Naomi Shihab Nye chose the poems that make up the bilingual collection called *The Tree Is Older Than You Are.* Famous poets such as Octavio Paz and Alberto Blanco take scenes from everyday life and make them extraordinary. Illustrations by Mexican painters complement the poems.

Nonfiction

Cultural Revolution

In *The Harlem Renaissance,* Veronica Chambers looks back at a special time in American history. During the 1920s, African American musicians such as Duke Ellington, writers such as Zora Neale Hurston, and painters such as William H. Johnson produced visionary art. Their work continues to influence American society to this day.

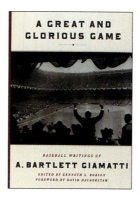

The National Pastime

Baseball was more than a game to A. Bartlett Giamatti; each game was a drama that gave insight into the American character. *A Great and Glorious Game* collects some of Giamatti's writings about the game he loved, from the time he was a literature professor at Yale University through the period when he served as commissioner of baseball.

Honest Abe

Russell Freedman's *Lincoln: A Photo-biography* takes an intimate look at the man who has been called our greatest president. Freedman writes about Abraham Lincoln's childhood, his legendary debates with Stephen Douglas, and his struggles as president during the years of the Civil War. The photographs and text of this Newbery Medal winner are complemented by illustrations and historical documents.

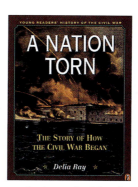

A Nation Divided

Delia Ray looks at the forces that created the Civil War in *A Nation Torn: The Story of How the Civil War Began.* In the years leading up to the war, the North and the South were growing increasingly passionate about their opposing views of slavery, which finally made war inevitable. Ray also highlights the major political figures involved in the war.

LITERARY CRITICISM: A BIOGRAPHICAL APPROACH

Literary Focus:
Interpreting a Literary Work

Informational Focus:
Analyzing Texts for Logic and Coherence

INTERNET

Collection Resources

Keyword: LE5 8-7

Triple Self-Portrait by Norman Rockwell.
Collection of The Norman Rockwell Museum at Stockbridge, Norman Rockwell Art Collection Trust. Printed by permission of the Norman Rockwell Family Agency. © 1960 the Norman Rockwell Family Entities.

Elements of Literature

Literary Criticism *by* Mara Rockliff

DOES FICTION REFLECT THE WRITER'S LIFE?

The Person on the Page

The great French essayist Michel de Montaigne once wrote, "Everyone recognizes me in my book, and my book in me." Other writers, however, have complained that readers are mistaken when they believe that a fictional character is actually the writer.

Using Their Lives

There is no question that writers' lives often influence their subject matter. Gary Paulsen wasn't stranded alone in the Canadian wilderness at the age of thirteen, as was his hero in *Hatchet*. However, his adult adventures training sled dogs in Alaska surely made their way into his novel *Dogsong,* about a boy's trek across Alaska by dog sled.

Writers' lives can play into their writing in a multitude of ways. A British writer might set a story in a location he knows well—perhaps an English country home or a boarding school—and then fill his plot with bizarre, completely imaginary events. A fantasy writer might set her story in a place and time that never existed, but her hero's mother might behave very much like someone she once knew—her great-aunt, for example.

However, it's important not to mistake fiction for autobiography. Many of Gary Soto's stories and poems take place in the Mexican American neighborhood where he grew up, but not everything he writes about really happened to him. For example, he says he would have loved to have a girlfriend riding on the handlebars of his bicycle, as Alfonso does in Soto's story "Broken Chain." Instead, he had only his little brother, Jimmy, to share his bike.

Still, it can be intriguing to connect what we know about a writer's life with his or her work. Why does one writer make all of her teenage characters outsiders and rebels? Why does another seem especially interested in divorce? Only the writer can answer these questions for sure.

Writing from Experience

At one time almost all the books published in America were written by people of European descent. These writers wrote not just about their own lives and traditions but about everyone else's too.

Today if you want to read about Native American experiences, you might choose a book by Virginia Driving Hawk Sneve or Joseph Bruchac. A hundred years ago it would have been James Fenimore Cooper's *The Last of the Mohicans.* Today if you want to read about African American experiences, you might pick up a book by Virginia

go.hrw.com

INTERNET

More About Literary Criticism

Keyword: LE5 8-7

SKILLS FOCUS

Literary Skills
Understand literary criticism.

Hamilton or Christopher Paul Curtis. A hundred years ago it might have been Harriet Beecher Stowe's wildly popular *Uncle Tom's Cabin.* Today if you want to read about Asian experiences, you might pick up a book by Amy Tan or Laurence Yep. Years ago it would have been *The Good Earth* by Pearl Buck.

Writing from Imagination

There are limits to the idea that writers should write about only what they know. In Laurence Yep's science fiction novel *Sweetwater,* for example, none of the main characters are Asian, like the writer. Some aren't even human! But Yep *is* writing about what he knows— the fear we all may feel in the face of the unknown.

Over a hundred years ago, sitting in her room in Amherst, Massachusetts, the poet Emily Dickinson wrote:

I never saw a moor,
I never saw the sea;
Yet know I how the heather looks.
And what a wave must be.

Can a person who has spent her whole life far from the sea write about the ocean? Can a grown woman write from the point of view of a little boy? Can a writer who's never solved a crime write convincingly, book after book, about all kinds of mysteries?

In fact, good writers deal successfully with challenges like these all the time. Research helps. So does the ability to take what they *know* about life—how people think, act, feel—and apply it to an imagined situation. Today, as they have for thousands of years, writers

start with some basic truths, and their imaginations fill in the rest.

Practice

Each school year you are expected to read a variety of books. In your reading you have almost certainly found a special writer whose stories you love. As the school year goes on, keep records of your favorite reading experiences on note cards like the one below. You can find answers to the last three items below by reading about the writer's life.

Author:

Favorite titles:

What he/she writes about:

How stories show author's
  heritage:
  beliefs:
  experiences:

Taking a Biographical Approach to Literary Criticsm

by Kylene Beers

Read this conversation that I once had with a group of eighth-graders. See if you've ever had a reaction like Adam's:

> "So, what did you think about the story?" I asked.
>
> "I liked it," some said. Others just nodded. Some just sat.
>
> "Well, what can you tell me about the author from reading this story?" I asked.
>
> Silence for a while and finally Adam said, "I didn't read anything about the author, I just read the story."

Adam was right—he did just read the story—but he was also wrong. When reading a story, you can sometimes make **inferences,** or guesses, about its writer. Consider this situation: You read a story about a character who suffers through a tough experience, but in the end is celebrated for her bravery. You can guess that the author believes that bravery should be rewarded.

You can't always presume, however, that a writer has had the same experiences that she writes about. You can't presume that Sandra Cisneros lived through the events described by the eleven-year-old girl who narrates the short story "Eleven," even though Cisneros was once eleven herself. You *can* conclude that Sandra Cisneros understands what it is *like* to be an eleven-year-old girl.

Authors bring their education, experiences, and interests with them to the page. A **biographical approach** to literary criticism means that you think about an author's life experiences as you respond to and analyze a text.

You can practice using a biographical approach to literary criticsm by reading the following biography of Robert Frost and by applying what you learn about him as you respond to his poem "Out, Out—" on page 708.

INTERNET

More About Frost

Keyword: LE5 8-7

Reading Skills
Understand a biographical approach to literary criticism.

Robert Frost

The New England Poet

Winner of four Pulitzer Prizes for poetry, **Robert Frost** (1874–1963) was for years the best-known poet in America. Frost was born in San Francisco, but he was raised in New England, which became the setting for almost all of his poetry. As a young man, Frost had tried raising chickens on a farm that his grandfather had given him, but he was unsuccessful. He also had a difficult time selling his poems. In 1912, after the deaths of two of his children, he and his family moved to England. There, Frost met with success: He found a publisher for his first two collections of poems (*A Boy's Will* and *North of Boston*). The books were popular immediately, and by the time Frost returned to the United States, publishers were interested in his work.

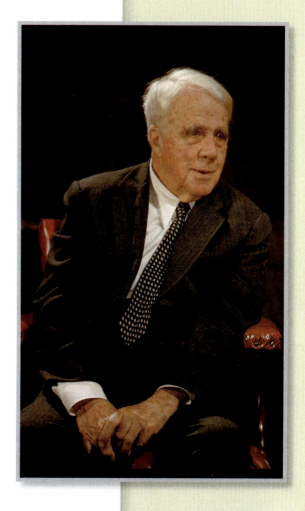

Frost lived in New England for most of his life and was known as the New England poet. He found his subjects in the landscapes and people of New England, especially in New Hampshire and Vermont. He deliberately used the everyday language he heard in conversations with farmers in his poems. The plain speech and simple, everyday subjects of his poems disguise their complex thoughts. Frost once wrote that a subject for poetry " . . . should be common in experience and uncommon in books. . . . It should have happened to everyone but it should have occurred to no one before as material."

Frost spent the rest of his long life farming, writing poetry, giving lectures, and reading his poems to audiences. As he put it, he liked to "say" rather than to recite his poetry. However, Frost never read "Out, Out—" (page 708) in public because he felt it was "too cruel."

As you read, you'll
find this open-book
sign at certain points
in the poem: .
Stop at these points,
and think about what
you've just read.

"Out, Out—"

Robert Frost

The buzz saw snarled and rattled in the yard
And made dust and dropped stove-length sticks of wood,
Sweet-scented stuff when the breeze drew across it.
And from there those that lifted eyes could count
5   Five mountain ranges one behind the other
Under the sunset far into Vermont. ❶
And the saw snarled and rattled, snarled and rattled,
As it ran light, or had to bear a load.
And nothing happened: day was all but done.
10 Call it a day, I wish they might have said
To please the boy by giving him the half hour
That a boy counts so much when saved from work.
His sister stood beside them in her apron
To tell them "Supper." At the word, the saw, ❷
15 As if to prove saws knew what supper meant,

ANALYZE

❶ What is the **setting**
of this poem? Did
Frost live somewhere
similar? Explain.

RETELL

❷ Re-read lines 10–14.
What have you learned
about the poem's
speaker? What does
he or she wish?

Leaped out at the boy's hand, or seemed to leap—
He must have given the hand. However it was,
Neither refused the meeting. But the hand!
The boy's first outcry was a rueful laugh,
20   As he swung toward them holding up the hand,
Half in appeal, but half as if to keep
The life from spilling. Then the boy saw all—
Since he was old enough to know, big boy
Doing a man's work, though a child at heart—
25   He saw all spoiled. "Don't let him cut my hand off—
The doctor, when he comes. Don't let him, sister!"
So. But the hand was gone already. ❸
The doctor put him in the dark of ether.°
He lay and puffed his lips out with his breath.
30   And then—the watcher at his pulse took fright.
No one believed. They listened at his heart.
Little—less—nothing!—and that ended it.
No more to build on there. And they, since they
Were not the one dead, turned to their affairs. ❹

---

28. ether (ē′thər) *n.:* chemical compound used as an anesthetic.

INFER

❸ What has happened to the boy? Do you think this incident could be based on an event Frost witnessed or experienced? Explain.

INFER

❹ The poem ends with a surprising matter-of-fact **tone.** Why do you think no one shows any signs of grief or horror? Could this reaction be based on Frost's knowledge of rural life? Explain.

Practicing a Biographical Approach

PRACTICE 1

Frost based his poem on an actual accident recorded in the *Littleton Courier,* a New Hampshire newspaper, on March 31, 1901. Compare and contrast Frost's poem with this newspaper account. Make a list of all the similarities and differences you find.

SAD TRAGEDY AT BETHLEHEM
Raymond Fitzgerald a Victim of Fatal Accident

Raymond Tracy Fitzgerald, one of the twin sons of Michael G. and Margaret Fitzgerald of Bethlehem, died at his home Thursday afternoon, March 24, as the result of an accident by which one of his hands was badly hurt in a sawing machine. The young man was assisting in sawing up some wood in his own dooryard [yard] with a sawing machine and accidentally hit the loose pulley, causing the saw to descend upon his hand, cutting and lacerating it badly. Raymond was taken into the house and a physician was immediately summoned, but he died very suddenly from the effects of the shock, which produced heart failure. . . .

Using "It Says, I Say, And So"

PRACTICE 2

Biographical criticism sounds like something that's very difficult to do. Not true! The term *biographical* comes from *biography,* and you know what a biography is—the story of a person's life. In this case, that person is an author. *Criticism,* in this phrase, means "evaluation." So, ***biographical criticism*** means "evaluating how the author's life is evident in what he or she wrote."

It's helpful to use a strategy called **It Says, I Say, And So** to keep track of what's in the text and how you think it relates to the author's life.

To practice this strategy, write "It Says," "I Say," "And So," in three columns. In the "It Says" column, write down what the text says in a particular passage. Under the "I Say" column, write what you think the passage might reflect about the writer. Under the "And So" column, write your final inference about what the passage reveals.

Here's the beginning of an It Says, I Say, And So chart for "Out, Out—." Complete the first section, and then add thoughts and inferences of your own. Be sure to consider information from Frost's biography on page 707.

> You can use the It Says, I Say, And So strategy with the selections in this collection. If you want to connect any text to the author's life, try using this strategy.

It Says	I Say	And So
The wood that's cut is "stove-length."	I bet Frost cut lots of wood to use for cooking and heating.	These details sound realistic.
[Add your own notes.]	[Add your own thoughts.]	[Add your own inferences.]

Ribbons

Make the Connection
Quickwrite ✏️

The grandmother and granddaughter in this story grew up in very different cultures. How is your childhood different from the childhoods of your parents, grandparents, or any other adults you know well?

Literary Focus
The Speaker

The **speaker** in a story or poem is the person who tells you the story or talks to you in the poem. It is important to remember, though, that the speaker is not always the writer. In "Ribbons," the speaker is a young girl named Stacy. A man named Laurence Yep wrote the story, so obviously the speaker is not the writer.

No matter how a writer tells a story, it usually reveals something about the writer's background or experiences. As you read this story, look for details that reflect Laurence Yep's heritage. Why do you think he chose a girl to tell you about an ancient Chinese custom that left millions of women with horribly deformed feet that made walking painful?

Reading Skills
Asking Questions

As a reader you do not have to know anything about the writer to appreciate or understand a story. Sometimes, though, you may want to be sure that a writer really knows the subject he or she is writing about. As you read "Ribbons," note any questions you have about the historical or factual details in the story.

Vocabulary Development

You'll come across these words as you read this short story:

harassed (har′əst, hə·rast′) v. used as adj.: troubled; bothered. *Father looked harassed by all the work he had to do.*

laborious (lə·bôr′ē·əs) adj.: hard; difficult. *With difficulty, Grandma made the laborious climb up the stairs.*

exotic (eg·zät′ik) adj.: foreign; strange in a fascinating way. *Stacy noticed the exotic scent of her grandmother's belongings.*

exertion (eg·zʉr′shən) n.: hard work or effort. *Stacy's father was tired from the exertion of carrying many boxes.*

exile (ek′sīl′) n.: living away from one's country or community. Exile is usually forced. *Stacy felt she was in exile from ballet classes. Her grandma lived in exile from her home.*

INTERNET

More About Yep
•
Vocabulary Activity

Keyword: LE5 8-7

SKILLS FOCUS

Literary Skills
Understand speaker.

Reading Skills
Ask questions about historical or factual details in the story.

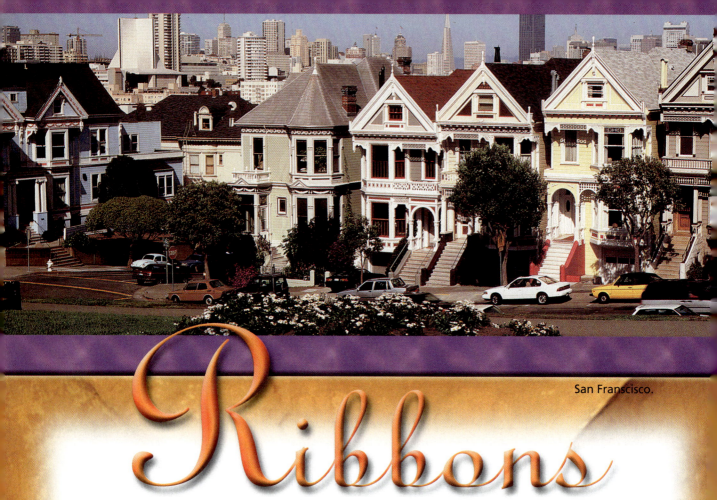

San Franscisco.

Ribbons

Laurence Yep

The sunlight swept over the broad grassy square, across the street, and onto our living room rug. In that bright, warm rectangle of light, I practiced my ballet. Ian, my little brother, giggled and dodged around me while I did my exercises.

A car stopped outside, and Ian rushed to the window. "She's here! She's here!" he shouted excitedly. "Paw-paw's here!" *Paw-paw* is Chinese for grandmother—for "mother's mother."

I squeezed in beside Ian so I could look out the window, too. Dad's head was just disappearing as he leaned into the trunk of the car. A pile of luggage and cardboard boxes wrapped in rope sat by the curb. "Is that all Grandmother's?" I said. I didn't see how it would fit into my old bedroom.

Mom laughed behind me. "We're lucky she had to leave her furniture behind in Hong Kong." Mom had been trying to get her mother to come to San Francisco for years. Grandmother had finally agreed, but only because the British were going to return the city to the Chinese Communists in 1997. Because Grandmother's airfare and legal expenses had been so high, there wasn't room in the family budget for Madame Oblomov's ballet school. I'd had to stop my daily lessons.

The rear car door opened, and a pair of carved black canes poked out like six-shooters. "Wait, Paw-paw," Dad said, and slammed the trunk shut. He looked sweaty and <u>harassed</u>.

Grandmother, however, was already using her canes to get to her feet. "I'm not helpless," she insisted to Dad.

Ian was relieved. "She speaks English," he said.

"She worked for a British family for years," Mom explained.

Turning, Ian ran toward the stairs. "I've got the door," he cried. Mom and I caught up with him at the front door and made him wait on the porch. "You don't want to knock her over," I said. For weeks, Mom had been rehearsing us for just this moment. Ian was supposed to wait, but in his excitement he began bowing to Grandmother as she struggled up the outside staircase.

Grandmother was a small woman in a padded silk jacket and black slacks. Her hair was pulled back into a bun behind her head. On her small feet she wore a pair of quilted cotton slippers shaped like boots, with furred tops that hid her ankles.

"What's wrong with her feet?" I whispered to Mom.

"They've always been that way. And don't mention it," she said. "She's sensitive about them."

I was instantly curious. "But what happened to them?"

"Wise grandchildren wouldn't ask," Mom warned.

Mom bowed formally as Grandmother

reached the porch. "I'm so glad you're here," she said.

Grandmother gazed past us to the stairway leading up to our second-floor apartment. "Why do you have to have so many steps?" she said.

Mom sounded as meek as a child. "I'm sorry, Mother," she said.

Dad tried to change the subject. "That's Stacy, and this little monster is Ian."

"*Joe sun, Paw-paw,*" I said. "Good morning, Grandmother." It was afternoon, but that was the only Chinese I knew, and I had been practicing it.

Mother had coached us on a proper Chinese greeting for the last two months, but I thought Grandmother also deserved an American-style bear hug. However, when I tried to put my arms around her and kiss

---

Vocabulary
harassed (har′əst, hə·rast′) *v.* used as *adj.*: troubled; bothered.

her, she stiffened in surprise. "Nice children don't drool on people," she snapped at me.

To Ian, anything worth doing was worth repeating, so he bowed again. *"Joe sun, Paw-paw."*

Grandmother brightened in an instant. "He has your eyes," she said to Mom.

Mom bent and hefted Ian into her arms. "Let me show you our apartment. You'll be in Stacy's room."

Grandmother didn't even thank me. Instead, she stumped up the stairs after Mom, trying to coax a smile from Ian, who was staring at her over Mom's shoulder.

Grandmother's climb was long, slow, laborious. *Thump, thump, thump.* Her canes struck the boards as she slowly mounted the steps. It sounded like the slow, steady beat of a mechanical heart.

Mom had told us her mother's story often enough. When Mom's father died, Grandmother had strapped my mother to her back and walked across China to Hong Kong to escape the Communists who had taken over her country. I had always thought her trek was heroic, but it seemed even braver when I realized how wobbly she was on her feet.

I was going to follow Grandmother, but Dad waved me down to the sidewalk. "I need you to watch your grandmother's things until I finish bringing them up," he said. He took a suitcase in either hand and set off, catching up with Grandmother at the foot of the first staircase.

While I waited for him to come back, I inspected Grandmother's pile of belongings. The boxes, webbed with tight cords, were covered with words in Chinese and English. I could almost smell their exotic scent, and in my imagination I pictured sunlit waters lapping at picturesque docks. Hong Kong was probably as exotic to me as America was to Grandmother. Almost without thinking, I began to dance.

Dad came back out, his face red from exertion. "I wish I had half your energy," he said. Crouching, he used the cords to lift a box in each hand.

I pirouetted,[1] and the world spun round and round. "Madame Oblomov said I should still practice every day." I had waited for this day not only for Grandmother's sake but for my own. "Now that Grandmother's here, can I begin my ballet lessons again?" I asked.

Dad turned toward the house. "We'll see, hon."

Disappointment made me protest. "But you said I had to give up the lessons so we could bring her from Hong Kong," I said. "Well, she's here."

Dad hesitated and then set the boxes down. "Try to understand, hon. We've got to set your grandmother up in her own apartment. That's going to take even more money. Don't you want your room back?"

Poor Dad. He looked tired and worried. I should have shut up, but I loved ballet almost as much as I loved him. "Madame put

---

1. **pirouetted** (pir′o͞o·et′id) *v.*: whirled around on one foot or on the point of the toe.

Vocabulary

laborious (lə·bôr′ē·əs) *adj.*: hard; difficult.

exotic (eg·zät′ik) *adj.*: foreign; strange in a fascinating way.

exertion (eg·zur′shən) *n.*: hard work or effort.

Street in Hong Kong.

me in the fifth division even though I'm only eleven. If I'm absent much longer, she might make me start over again with the beginners."

"It'll be soon. I promise." He looked guilty as he picked up the boxes and struggled toward the stairs.

Dad had taken away the one hope that had kept me going during my exile from Madame. Suddenly I felt lost, and the following weeks only made me more confused. Mom started laying down all sorts of new rules. First, we couldn't run around or make noise because Grandmother had to rest. Then, we couldn't watch our favorite TV shows because Grandmother couldn't understand them.

Instead, we had to watch westerns on one of the cable stations because it was easier for her to figure out who was the good guy and who was the bad one.

Worst of all, Ian got all of her attention— and her candy and anything else she could bribe him with. It finally got to me on a warm Sunday afternoon a month after she had arrived. I'd just returned home from a long walk in the park with some friends. I was looking forward to something cool and sweet when I found her giving Ian an ice-cream bar I'd bought for myself. "But that was *my* ice-cream bar," I complained as he gulped it down.

Vocabulary

exile (ek′sīl′) *n.:* living away from one's country, usually not by choice.

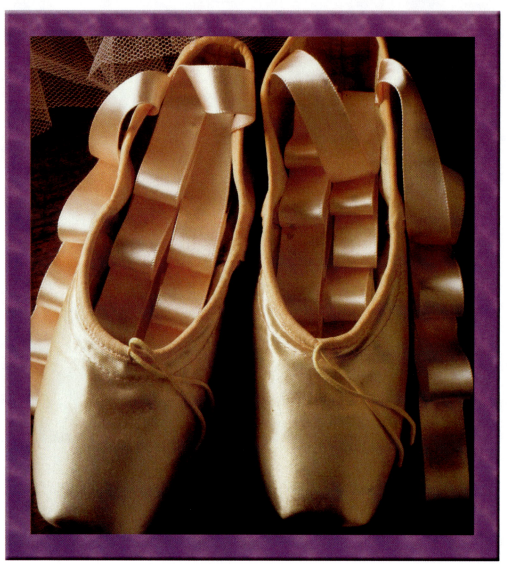

Still Life of Satin Ballet Shoes, Tutu Frill, Wooden Background
by Tony Hutchings. Photograph.

"Big sisters need to share with little brothers," Grandmother said, and she patted him on the head to encourage him to go on eating.

When I complained to Mom about how Grandmother was spoiling Ian, she only sighed. "He's a boy, Stacy. Back in China, boys are everything."

It wasn't until I saw Grandmother and Ian together the next day that I thought I really understood why she treated him so much better. She was sitting on a kitchen chair with her head bent over next to his. She had taught Ian enough Chinese so that they could hold short, simple conversations. With their faces so close, I could see how much alike they were.

Ian and I both have the same brown eyes, but his hair is black, while mine is brown, like Dad's. In fact, everything about Ian looks more Chinese. Except for the shape of my eyes, I look as Caucasian as Dad. And yet people sometimes stare at me as if I were a freak. I've always told myself that it's because they're ignorant and never learned manners, but it was really hard to have my own grandmother make me feel that way.

Even so, I kept telling myself: Grandmother is a hero. She saved my mother. She'll like me just as much as she likes Ian once she gets to know me. And, I thought in a flash, the best way to know a person is to know what she loves. For me, that was the ballet.

Ever since Grandmother had arrived, I'd been practicing my ballet privately in the room I now shared with Ian. Now I got out the special box that held my satin toeshoes. I had been so proud when Madame said I was ready to use them. I was the youngest girl on *pointe* [2] at Madame's school. As I lifted them out, the satin ribbons fluttered down around my wrists as if in a welcoming caress. I slipped one of the shoes onto my foot, but when I tried to tie the ribbons around my ankles, the ribbons came off in my hands.

I could have asked Mom to help me re-attach them, but then I remembered that at one time Grandmother had supported her family by being a seamstress.

Grandmother was sitting in the big re-cliner in the living room. She stared uneasily out the window as if she were gazing not upon the broad, green lawn of the square but upon a Martian desert.

"Paw-paw," I said, "can you help me?"

Grandmother gave a start when she turned around and saw the ribbons dangling from my hand. Then she looked down at my bare feet, which were calloused from three years of daily lessons. When she looked back at the satin ribbons, it was with a hate and disgust that I had never seen before. "Give those to me." She held out her hand.

I clutched the ribbons tightly against my stomach. "Why?"

"They'll ruin your feet." She lunged toward me and tried to snatch them away.

Angry and bewildered, I retreated a few steps and showed her the shoe. "No, they're for dancing!"

All Grandmother could see, though, was the ribbons. She managed to totter to her feet without the canes and almost fell forward on her face. Somehow, she regained her balance. Arms reaching out, she stumbled clumsily after me. "Lies!" she said.

"It's the truth!" I backed up so fast that I bumped into Mom as she came running from the kitchen.

Mom immediately assumed it was my fault. "Stop yelling at your grandmother!" she said.

By this point, I was in tears. "She's taken everything else. Now she wants my toeshoe ribbons."

Grandmother panted as she leaned on Mom. "How could you do that to your own daughter?"

"It's not like you think," Mom tried to explain.

However, Grandmother was too upset to listen. "Take them away!"

Mom helped Grandmother back to her easy chair. "You don't understand," Mom said.

All Grandmother did was stare at the ribbons as she sat back down in the chair. "Take them away. Burn them. Bury them."

Mom sighed. "Yes, Mother."

---

2. ***pointe*** (point) *n.*: ballet position on the tip of the toe. In French the pronunciation is pwa*nt*.

As Mom came over to me, I stared at her in amazement. "Aren't you going to stand up for me?"

But she acted as if she wanted to break any ties between us. "Can't you see how worked up Paw-paw is?" she whispered. "She won't listen to reason. Give her some time. Let her cool off." She worked the ribbons away from my stunned fingers. Then she also took the shoe.

For the rest of the day, Grandmother just turned away every time Mom and I tried to raise the subject. It was as if she didn't want to even think about satin ribbons.

That evening, after the dozenth attempt, I finally said to Mom, "She's so weird. What's so bad about satin ribbons?"

"She associates them with something awful that happened to her," Mom said.

That puzzled me even more. "What was that?"

She shook her head. "I'm sorry. She made me promise never to talk about it to anyone."

The next morning, I decided that if Grandmother was going to be mean to me, then I would be mean to her. I began to ignore her. When she entered a room I was in, I would deliberately turn around and leave.

For the rest of the day, things got more and more tense. Then I happened to go into the bathroom early that evening. The door wasn't locked, so I thought it was unoccupied, but Grandmother was sitting fully clothed on the edge of the bathtub. Her slacks were rolled up to her knees, and she had her feet soaking in a pan of water.

"Don't you know how to knock?" she snapped, and dropped a towel over her feet.

However, she wasn't quick enough, because I saw her bare feet for the first time. Her feet were like taffy that someone had stretched out and twisted. Each foot bent downward in a way that feet were not meant to, and her toes stuck out at odd angles, more like lumps than toes. I didn't think she had all ten of them, either.

"What happened to your feet?" I whispered in shock.

Looking ashamed, Grandmother flapped a hand in the air for me to go. "None of your business. Now get out."

She must have said something to Mom, though, because that night Mom came in and sat on my bed. Ian was outside playing with Grandmother. "Your grandmother's very upset, Stacy," Mom said.

"I didn't mean to look," I said. "It was horrible." Even when I closed my eyes, I could see her mangled feet.

I opened my eyes when I felt Mom's hand on my shoulder. "She was so ashamed of them that she didn't like even me to see them," she said.

"What happened to them?" I wondered.

Mom's forehead furrowed as if she wasn't sure how to explain things. "There was a time back in China when people thought women's feet had to be shaped a certain way to look beautiful. When a girl was about five, her mother would gradually bend her toes under the sole of her foot."

"Ugh." Just thinking about it made my own feet ache. "Her own mother did that to her?"

Mom smiled apologetically. "Her mother and father thought it would make their little girl attractive so she could marry a rich man. They were still doing it in some of the back areas of China long after it was outlawed in the rest of the country."

I shook my head. "There's nothing lovely about those feet."

"I know. But they were usually bound up in silk ribbons." Mom brushed some of the hair from my eyes. "Because they were a symbol of the old days, Paw-paw undid the ribbons as soon as we were free in Hong Kong—even though they kept back the pain."

I was even more puzzled now. "How did the ribbons do that?"

Mom began to brush my hair with quick, light strokes. "The ribbons kept the blood from circulating freely and bringing more feeling to her feet. Once the ribbons were gone, her feet ached. They probably still do."

I rubbed my own foot in sympathy. "But she doesn't complain."

"That's how tough she is," Mom said.

Finally the truth dawned on me. "And she mistook my toeshoe ribbons for her old ones."

Mom lowered the brush and nodded solemnly. "And she didn't want you to go through the same pain she had."

I guess Grandmother loved me in her own way. When she came into the bedroom with Ian later that evening, I didn't leave. However, she tried to ignore me—as if I had become tainted by her secret.

When Ian demanded a story, I sighed. "All right. But only one."

Naturally, Ian chose the fattest story he could, which was my old collection of fairy tales by Hans Christian Andersen. Years of

Private collection.

Illustration (late 19th century) by E. S. Hardy, from "The Little Mermaid" by Hans Christian Andersen.

reading had cracked the spine so that the book fell open automatically in his hands to the story that had been my favorite when I was small. It was the original story of "The Little Mermaid"—not the cartoon. The picture illustrating the tale showed the mermaid posed like a ballerina in the middle of the throne room.

"This one," Ian said, and pointed to the picture of the Little Mermaid.

When Grandmother and Ian sat down on my bed, I began to read. However, when I got to the part where the Little Mermaid could walk on land, I stopped.

Ian was impatient. "Come on, read," he ordered, patting the page.

"After that," I went on, "each step hurt her as if she were walking on a knife." I couldn't help looking up at Grandmother.

This time she was the one to pat the page. "Go on. Tell me more about the mermaid."

So I went on reading to the very end, where the Little Mermaid changes into sea foam. "That's a dumb ending," Ian said. "Who wants to be pollution?"

"Sea foam isn't pollution. It's just bubbles," I explained. "The important thing was that she wanted to walk even though it hurt."

"I would rather have gone on swimming," Ian insisted.

"But maybe she wanted to see new places and people by going on the land," Grandmother said softly. "If she had kept her tail, the land people would have thought she was odd. They might even have made fun of her."

When she glanced at her own feet, I thought she might be talking about herself— so I seized my chance. "My satin ribbons aren't like your old silk ones. I use them to tie my toeshoes on when I dance." Setting the book down, I got out my other shoe. "Look."

Grandmother fingered the dangling ribbons and then pointed at my bare feet. "But you already have calluses there."

I began to dance before Grandmother could stop me. After a minute, I struck a pose on half-toe. "See? I can move fine."

She took my hand and patted it clumsily. I think it was the first time she had showed me any sign of affection. "When I saw those ribbons, I didn't want you feeling pain like I do."

I covered her hands with mine. "I just wanted to show you what I love best— dancing."

"And I love my children," she said. I could hear the ache in her voice. "And my grandchildren. I don't want anything bad to happen to you."

Suddenly I felt as if there were an invisible ribbon binding us, tougher than silk and satin, stronger even than steel; and it joined her to Mom and Mom to me.

I wanted to hug her so badly that I just did. Though she was stiff at first, she gradually softened in my arms.

"Let me have my ribbons and my shoes," I said in a low voice. "Let me dance."

"Yes, yes," she whispered fiercely.

I felt something on my cheek and realized she was crying, and then I began crying, too.

"So much to learn," she said, and began hugging me back. "So much to learn."

Meet the Writer

Laurence Yep

"Being an Outsider"

Laurence Yep (1948–   ) believes his sympathy for the outcast is the main reason for his success, particularly with younger readers. He says:

> 66 I'm always pursuing the theme of being an outsider—an alien—and many teenagers feel they're aliens. 99

Indeed, Yep's ability to relate to these feelings has made him popular with readers from all backgrounds for nearly thirty years.

Laurence Yep was born in San Francisco and grew up in an African American neighborhood while commuting to an elementary school in Chinatown. He then went to a predominantly white high school. Although Yep was exposed to many cultures, he felt he had no culture to call his own. His family had lost touch with the traditions of China, their homeland. Perhaps this is why much of Yep's fiction deals with the quest for identity. In *Child of the Owl* the heroine is an American girl named Casey who yearns to connect with her Chinese background. In *Sea Glass* a boy named Craig feels excluded from both white and Chinese American cultures before he finds his own identity.

Maxine Hong Kingston once wrote that Laurence Yep makes readers "gasp with recognition. 'Hey! that happened to me! I did that. I saw that,' the young reader will say, and be glad that a writer set it down, and feel comforted, less eccentric, less alone."

For Independent Reading

Dragonwings is one of Yep's most beloved novels. Set in San Francisco in the early twentieth century, it features a boy who dreams of building the ideal flying machine with his father. *Dragon's Gate* is a more challenging book. It tells the story of fourteen-year-old Otter, a Chinese immigrant who works on the transcontinental railroad under brutal conditions.

First Thoughts

1. Does Stacy's relationship with her grandmother remind you of a relationship you have with someone in your own family or with a friend? Explain.

Thinking Critically

2. Why does Stacy's grandmother favor Stacy's brother, Ian?

3. What misunderstanding about the ribbons causes the **conflict** between Stacy and her grandmother? How is this conflict between Stacy and her grandmother finally resolved?

4. Think about questions you have after reading this story. Consider the following details, which are presented as facts. Where could you go to check them out—to find out if they are accurate?

   • Foot binding was once practiced in China.

   • "Back in China, boys are everything."

   • The Communists took over China.

   • Many Chinese fled to Hong Kong.

   • In 1997, Hong Kong was returned to Chinese control.

Reading Check

Map out the structure of this story, using a graphic like the one that follows:

Main characters:
Their problem or conflict:
Main events (list as many as you need):
Climax:
Resolution:

Extending Interpretations

5. Why, in your opinion, did Yep choose a girl to be the **speaker**? Do you think Stacy is a believable character—that is, does she speak and behave the way girls her age actually speak and behave? Support your evaluation with specific details from the story.

SKILLS FOCUS

Literary Skills
Analyze speaker.

Reading Skills
Ask questions about historical or factual details in the story.

Writing Skills
Write a comparison essay.

WRITING

Comparing Childhoods

Write an essay comparing two childhoods: your own childhood and the childhood of an adult you know. Try to show how they are different and how they are similar. You could compare things such as homes, games, chores, schools, clothes, music, and fads.

Verify Meanings: Examples

PRACTICE

1. Describe three situations in which someone would feel harassed. Describe three situations in which someone would *not* feel harassed.
2. How would someone feel after a laborious day? What is the opposite of a laborious day?
3. Name an animal, a plant, and a food that you see as exotic. Name an animal, a plant, and a food that do *not* seem exotic to you.
4. Name three tasks that require exertion. Name three that do *not* require any exertion at all.
5. The term *political exile* is often used today. What does it mean? Give an example of a famous person who was in political exile.

Word Bank

harassed
laborious
exotic
exertion
exile

Grammar Link

Its or *It's*?

Confusing *its* and *it's* is one of the most common errors writers make.

- *Its* is the **possessive** form of *it.* A possessive form shows ownership or belonging.

  Stacy held her toeshoe, with its [the shoe's] **satin ribbons, in her hand.**

The possessive form of a noun—such as *shoe's*—has an apostrophe. The possessive form of a personal pronoun—such as *its*—does not.

- *It's* is a **contraction** of *it is* or *it has.* A contraction shortens words by replacing one letter or more with an apostrophe.

  Stacy loves dancing on *pointe* even though it's hard work.

If you're not sure which form is correct, try using *it is* in the sentence. You'll see right away that *Stacy held her toeshoe, with it is satin ribbons, in her hand* doesn't make sense.

PRACTICE

Copy the following sentences, filling in the correct word: *its* or *it's.*

1. When her grandmother comes to live with them, _____ hard for Stacy to adjust.
2. She gives Ian the ice-cream bar even though _____ Stacy's.
3. Ian loves the book, with _____ pretty illustrations.
4. The fairy tale and _____ message help Stacy and her grandmother to understand each other.

For more help, see Contractions, 15b, in the Language Handbook.

SKILLS FOCUS

Vocabulary Skills
Verify word meanings by example.

Grammar Skills
Use contractions correctly.

Understanding Unity and Text Structure: An Article

Reading Focus

Unity and Text Structure

A friend calls to tell you about her ballet class, but her story is so confusing that you ask her to start over again. You can't follow what your friend is saying because she's having trouble with the unity and structure of her story. Here's what to look for in a text when you're evaluating its unity and structure:

A Text Should Have Unity

When a text has **unity,** all its details support the main idea or topic. If your friend's story is about ballet, all the details should involve ballet. She shouldn't add details about her math test. If she sticks to her topic, her story will be unified.

A Text Should Have Structure

A text should have a clear structure. Most texts are organized according to one of the following **structural patterns:**

- **Chronological order.** In chronological order, events are described in the order in which they happen. This pattern is often used in narrative writing. Chronological order is also often used in historical writing and in compositions that explain a process. "Mrs. Flowers's Recipes," on page 193, uses chronological order to explain how to bake sugar cookies. When a text uses chronological order, it usually makes **cause-and-effect** relationships clear. If you are writing about the Communist takeover of China, for example, you might want to make clear what **caused** the takeover and what **effect** it had on the country.

- **Order of importance.** When you use the order of importance to express your opinion, you give your strongest reason first and then move through less important reasons. For example, you might say, "Getting an education is important because you learn things that will help you all through life. You also need education to get a good job and to earn people's respect." You could also reverse the order, giving the weakest reason first, followed by the stronger ones, saving your strongest point for last.

- **Logical order.** You use logical order when you arrange your supporting details in related groups so that their connections are clear. For example, an article about a dog show might describe first how the dogs are groomed and then how they are paraded before the judges. Next it might list the standards for judging different breeds. When it talks about breed standards, similar breeds might be grouped together and compared. This would be a logical order.

■ You can use printed texts as models for writing well-organized texts of your own. Start by evaluating the unity and structure of the following article.

go.hrw.com
INTERNET
Interactive Reading Model
Keyword: LE5 8-7

SKILLS FOCUS

Reading Skills
Understand unity and text structure.

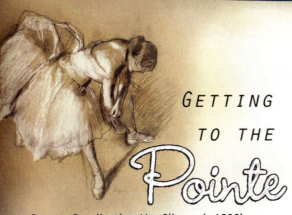

GETTING TO THE *Pointe*

Dancer Readjusting Her Slipper (c.1890)
by Edgar Degas. Pastel and charcoal.

❶ When you think of extreme sports, what's on your list? Snowboarding? Rock climbing? Ballet? . . . What? Not ballet? Think again. Although we think of dancers primarily as artists, they also need the skills of an extreme athlete. A ballet dancer must have the strength of a rock climber, the balance of a snowboarder, and the flexibility of a gymnast. As artists, ballet dancers are capable of casting a spell on an audience; but to cast that spell, they need to be first-rate athletes.

The *Pointe*—A Platform the Size of a Silver Dollar

❷ Gymnasts perform tremendous feats of balance. Ballet dancers, however, perform on the *pointe* of their toeshoes—a platform about the size of a silver dollar. During a performance the force on the *pointe* of their shoes can equal ten times their body's weight. And what about those shoes? If someone hit you on the head with a brand-new ballet shoe, you might think it had a block of wood in its toe. What's really in it? Most *pointe* shoes are made from paper or burlap that has been soaked in glue, shaped, and covered in satin. Although the shoes are stiff at first, they break down quickly when used. Makers of *pointe* shoes are testing materials that are now used in athletic shoes, but most dancers still prefer the old-fashioned paper-and-glue version. These shoes don't give the foot much padding or protection, but they allow the dancer to "feel" the floor in much the same way that rock climbers must feel the surfaces of the rocks they are climbing. Footing is particularly important to ballet dancers because of the surfaces they perform on.

The *Floor*—It Should Protect the Dancer

❸ Most of the stages that dancers perform on were designed for opera, not dance. Their wood floors are often laid directly on concrete or steel beams. Thus, they lack the spring, or resilience, that could protect a dancer's legs and feet. To see for yourself, try doing jumping jacks on a concrete driveway and then on dirt or a lawn. (You can also try the basketball floor at your school, since most basketball floors are designed to "float" over concrete foundations.) It won't be difficult for your legs, ankles, and feet to feel the differences in these surfaces. Good ballet studios have sprung-wood floors with an inch or two of space between the floor and its concrete foundation. However, since most stages do not offer such a specialized floor, the quality of a ballet studio's flooring is less important than the excellence of the studio's training.

Ballet—A Risky Art

❹ Ballet dancers must follow a long, demanding training program because tremendous risks are built into this extreme art form. Ballet training does more than just build strength; it changes the shape of the body. You may have observed that dancers walk, move, and carry their weight differently. This difference reflects the way they must move to stay strong and healthy as they dance. The importance of correct form and technique cannot be overstated. If a dancer shifts balance even slightly to one side rather than directly over the ankle, an additional forty pounds of pressure may be transferred to the delicate foot and ankle. Over time that can lead to stress fractures, tendonitis, and ankle strains or sprains—and a great deal of pain. A good ballet teacher corrects the tiniest errors in foot placement, and ballet students come to welcome such corrections as a means to avoid injury. As much as young dancers long for toeshoes, good ballet teachers know that this step should not be rushed. Experts suggest that *pointe* work should not begin before ages ten to twelve, while a dancer's feet are still growing, and once begun, it should proceed very slowly.

Dance—A Conversation Between Dancer and Audience

❺ Though their movements are carefully controlled, ballet dancers must learn to make it all look effortless. Dance is an art form, so it is not judged by the same standards that athletic contests are. The longest leap doesn't win a medal. The best dancers may not have the longest leaps, but they have something else: They are able to enchant an audience with the power, grace, and courage of their movement. The length of a leap is less important than the story the dancer tells in leaping. Thus, a leap becomes a sentence in a conversation between the dancer and the audience. When audience members are so involved in the conversation that they forget to notice that the leap itself is spectacular, the dancer has been successful.

Why Do It?

❻ If you were to ask any extreme athletes why they do what they do, despite the risks of pain and injury, they would probably tell you about the freedom and joy that come with defying gravity, with challenging one's limits, with beating the odds. There is a thrill that comes with holding an audience spellbound. For ballet dancers the joy of performing their art well is as necessary as breathing.

—Sheri Henderson

Analyzing an Article's Unity and Text Structure

Getting to the *Pointe*

Test Practice

1. Which sentence *best* expresses the **main idea** of the entire article?
   - **A** Ballet dancers are better athletes than gymnasts are.
   - **B** A ballet dancer is both an extreme athlete and an artist.
   - **C** It is really hard to be a ballet dancer.
   - **D** Ballet dancing is a dangerous profession.

2. Which of the following sentences could be added to paragraph 2 without destroying its **unity**?
   - **F** Dancers wear many types of warm-up gear.
   - **G** A sprung-wood floor is the best kind for ballet.
   - **H** Dancers soften brand-new *pointe* shoes by hitting them with hammers or slamming them into doors.
   - **J** Tap shoes can badly damage a wood floor.

3. Which of the following sentences could be added to paragraph 4 without destroying its **unity**?
   - **A** Exercises on *pointe* should be increased gradually.
   - **B** Dance costumes should not get in the dancer's way.
   - **C** Try to do fifty jumping jacks every day.
   - **D** Basketball is also a good sport to learn.

4. You can tell that the details in this article are organized in a **logical order** because —
   - **F** the details are organized into related groups
   - **G** the text uses cause-and-effect arguments
   - **H** the text relates events in the order in which they happen
   - **J** the text starts with the most important point and ends with the least important point

Contructed Response

To review the **structure** of this article, make an **outline** that shows the main topic of each paragraph and its supporting details. The outline is begun for you here:

I. Ballet is an extreme sport
   A. It requires strength
   B. It requires balance
   C. It requires flexibility
II. [And so on]

For help in making an outline, see page 488.

SKILLS FOCUS

Reading Skills
Analyze an article's unity and text structure.

Context Clues

PRACTICE

Use **context** clues to guess at the meaning of each underlined word in the following sentences from "Getting to the *Pointe*."

1. "Gymnasts perform tremendous feats of balance." *Feats* are —
   a. sly tricks
   b. remarkable acts
   c. tasty meals
   d. toeholds

2. "Their wood floors are often laid directly on concrete or steel beams. Thus, they lack the spring, or resilience. . . ." *Resilience* means —
   a. ability to bounce back into position
   b. ability to change shape
   c. warmth when touched
   d. hardness and firmness

3. "If a dancer shifts balance even slightly to one side rather than directly over the ankle, an additional forty pounds of pressure may be transferred to the delicate foot and ankle." *Transferred* means —
   a. moved from one place to another
   b. changed completely
   c. sent to a new job
   d. lost on the way

4. "They would probably tell you about the freedom and joy that come with defying gravity. . . ." *Defying* means —
   a. obeying fearfully
   b. defining carefully
   c. defending strongly
   d. resisting boldly

SKILLS FOCUS

Vocabulary Skills
Analyze context clues.

Dancers (detail) by Edgar Degas (1834–1917).

The Treasure of Lemon Brown

Make the Connection
Quickwrite ✏️

Everyone's background is unique. Jot down some notes about your own background: where you live, the customs of your family, the beliefs you live by. What do you treasure most about your background?

Literary Focus
A Biographical Approach: The Writer's Background

Writers often draw on their own backgrounds to create a story. The setting may be a place they once lived. The characters may be based on people they knew. The theme may involve issues that especially concern them. The plot might even include events from their own lives. The setting of "The Treasure of Lemon Brown" is Harlem, the neighborhood in New York City where Walter Dean Myers grew up in the 1940s. Myers describes Harlem this way:

❝Thinking back to my boyhood days, I remember the bright sun on Harlem streets, the easy rhythms of black and brown bodies moving along the tar-and-asphalt pavement, the sounds of hundreds of children streaming in and out of red-brick tenements. . . . I remember playing basketball in Morningside Park until it was too dark to see the basket and then climbing over the fence to go home.

Harlem was a place of affirmation. The excitement of city living exploded in the teeming streets.❞

After you have finished the story and read Myers's biography, think about how the writer has used aspects of his life experiences to write this fictional story.

Reading Skills 📖
Retelling

To be certain you understand what you are reading, stop from time to time and **retell** what has happened so far. As you read this story, stop at the open-book signs alongside the text. Tell a partner what has happened.

Vocabulary Development

Review these words before you read "The Treasure of Lemon Brown":

impromptu (im·prämp′to͞o′) *adj.:* unplanned. *Greg's friends had an impromptu checkers tournament.*

tentatively (ten′tə·tiv·lē) *adv.:* in an uncertain or hesitant way. *Greg pushed tentatively on the tenement door.*

intently (in·tent′lē) *adv.:* with close attention. *Greg listened intently to the sounds in the room.*

brittle (brit′l) *adj.:* having a sharp, hard quality; ready to break. *The man's voice sounded high and brittle.*

ominous (äm′ə·nəs) *adj.:* threatening. *After the crash, Greg heard only an ominous silence.*

INTERNET

Vocabulary Activity

Keyword: LE5 8-7

SKILLS FOCUS

Literary Skills
Understand a biographical approach to literary criticism.

Reading Skills
Retell the story.

Studio View (1977) by Gilbert Fletcher (24" × 20").
© Gilbert Fletcher.

The Treasure of Lemon Brown

Walter Dean Myers

The dark sky, filled with angry, swirling clouds, reflected Greg Ridley's mood as he sat on the stoop of his building. His father's voice came to him again, first reading the letter the principal had sent to the house, then lecturing endlessly about his poor efforts in math.

"I had to leave school when I was thirteen," his father had said; "that's a year younger than you are now. If I'd had half the chances that you have, I'd . . ."

Greg had sat in the small, pale-green kitchen listening, knowing the lecture would end with his father saying he couldn't play ball with the Scorpions. He had asked his father the week before, and his father had said it depended on his next report card. It wasn't often the Scorpions took on new players, especially fourteen-year-olds, and this was a chance of a lifetime for Greg. He hadn't been allowed to play high school ball, which he had really wanted to do, but playing for the Community Center team was the next best thing. Report cards were due in a week, and Greg had been hoping for the best. But the principal had ended the suspense early when she sent that letter saying Greg would probably fail math if he didn't spend more time studying.

"And you want to play *basketball*?" His father's brows knitted over deep-brown eyes. "That must be some kind of a joke. Now you just get into your room and hit those books." ❶

That had been two nights before. His father's words, like the distant thunder that now echoed through the streets of Harlem, still rumbled softly in his ears.

It was beginning to cool. Gusts of wind made bits of paper dance between the parked cars. There was a flash of nearby lightning, and soon large drops of rain splashed onto his jeans. He stood to go upstairs, thought of the lecture that probably awaited him if he did anything except shut himself in his room with his math book, and started walking down the street instead. Down the block there was an old tenement that had been abandoned for some months. Some of the guys had held an impromptu checkers tournament there the week before, and Greg had noticed that the door, once boarded over, had been slightly ajar.

Pulling his collar up as high as he could, he checked for traffic and made a dash across the street. He reached the house just as another flash of lightning changed the night to day for an instant, then returned the graffiti-scarred building to the grim shadows. He vaulted over the outer stairs and pushed tentatively on the door. It was open, and he let himself in.

The inside of the building was dark except for the dim light that filtered through the dirty windows from the street lamps. There

"And you want to play basketball?"

Vocabulary

impromptu (im·prämp′tōō′) *adj.:* unplanned; made or done without preparation.

tentatively (ten′tə·tiv·lē) *adv.:* in an uncertain or hesitant way.

was a room a few feet from the door, and from where he stood at the entrance, Greg could see a squarish patch of light on the floor. He entered the room, frowning at the musty smell. It was a large room that might have been someone's parlor at one time. Squinting, Greg could see an old table on its side against one wall, what looked like a pile of rags or a torn mattress in the corner, and a couch, with one side broken, in front of the window. ❷

📖 **RETELL**
❷ How does Greg end up in this old tenement?

He went to the couch. The side that wasn't broken was comfortable enough, though a little creaky. From this spot he could see the blinking neon sign over the bodega[1] on the corner. He sat awhile, watching the sign blink first green, then red, allowing his mind to drift to the Scorpions, then to his father. His father had been a postal worker for all Greg's life and was proud of it, often telling Greg how hard he had worked to pass the test. Greg had heard the story too many times to be interested now.

For a moment Greg thought he heard something that sounded like a scraping against the wall. He listened carefully, but it was gone.

Outside, the wind had picked up, sending the rain against the window with a force that shook the glass in its frame. A car passed, its tires hissing over the wet street and its red taillights glowing in the darkness.

Greg thought he heard the noise again. His stomach tightened as he held himself still and listened intently. There weren't any more scraping noises, but he was sure he had heard something in the darkness—something breathing!

---

1. **bodega** (bō·dā′gə) *n.:* small grocery store.

He tried to figure out just where the breathing was coming from; he knew it was in the room with him. Slowly he stood, tensing. As he turned, a flash of lightning lit up the room, frightening him with its sudden brilliance. He saw nothing, just the overturned table, the pile of rags, and an old newspaper on the floor. Could he have been imagining the sounds? He continued listening, but heard nothing and thought that it might have just been rats. Still, he thought, as soon as the rain let up he would leave. He went to the window and was about to look out when he heard a voice behind him.

"Don't try nothin', 'cause I got a razor here sharp enough to cut a week into nine days!"

Greg, except for an involuntary tremor in his knees, stood stock-still. The voice was high and brittle, like dry twigs being broken, surely not one he had ever heard before. There was a shuffling sound as the person who had been speaking moved a step closer. Greg turned, holding his breath, his eyes straining to see in the dark room.

The upper part of the figure before him was still in darkness. The lower half was in the dim rectangle of light that fell unevenly from the window. There were two feet, in cracked, dirty shoes from which rose legs that were wrapped in rags.

"Who are you?" Greg hardly recognized his own voice.

"I'm Lemon Brown," came the answer. "Who're you?"

"Greg Ridley."

Vocabulary
intently (in·tent′lē) *adv.:* with close attention.
brittle (brit′l) *adj.:* having a sharp, hard quality. *Brittle* also means "touchy or unbending."

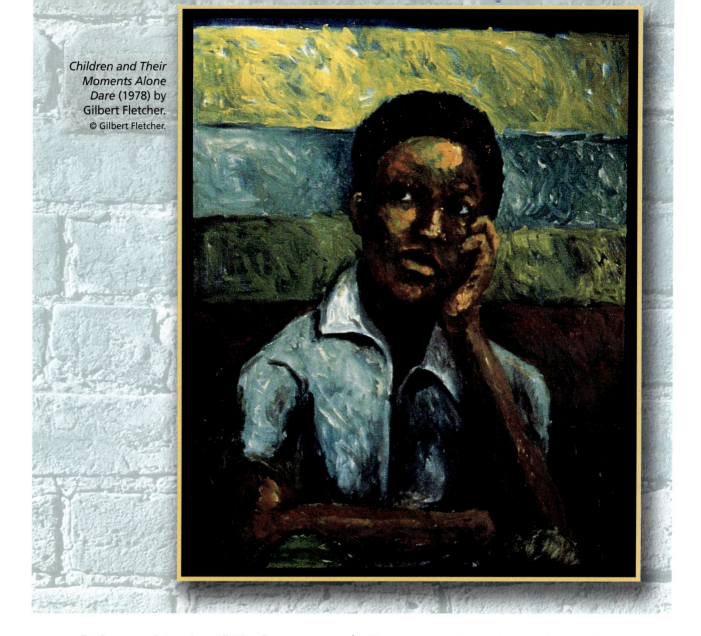

Children and Their Moments Alone Dare (1978) by Gilbert Fletcher.
© Gilbert Fletcher.

"What you doing here?" The figure shuffled forward again, and Greg took a small step backward.

"It's raining," Greg said.

"I can see that," the figure said.

The person who called himself Lemon Brown peered forward, and Greg could see him clearly. He was an old man. His black, heavily wrinkled face was surrounded by a halo of crinkly white hair and whiskers that seemed to separate his head from the layers of dirty coats piled on his smallish frame.

His pants were bagged to the knee, where they were met with rags that went down to the old shoes. The rags were held on with strings, and there was a rope around his middle. Greg relaxed. He had seen the man before, picking through the trash on the corner and pulling clothes out of a Salvation Army box. There was no sign of the razor that could "cut a week into nine days."

"What are you doing here?" Greg asked.

"This is where I'm staying," Lemon Brown said. "What you here for?"

"Told you it was raining out," Greg said, leaning against the back of the couch until he felt it give slightly.

"Ain't you got no home?"

"I got a home," Greg answered.

"You ain't one of them bad boys looking for my treasure, is you?" Lemon Brown cocked his head to one side and squinted one eye. "Because I told you I got me a razor."

"I'm not looking for your treasure," Greg answered, smiling. "*If* you have one."

"What you mean, *if* I have one," Lemon Brown said. "Every man got a treasure. You don't know that, you must be a fool!"

"Sure," Greg said as he sat on the sofa and put one leg over the back. "What do you have, gold coins?"

"Don't worry none about what I got," Lemon Brown said. "You know who I am?"

"You told me your name was orange or lemon or something like that."

"Lemon Brown," the old man said, pulling back his shoulders as he did so, "they used to call me Sweet Lemon Brown."

"Sweet Lemon?" Greg asked.

"Yessir. Sweet Lemon Brown. They used to say I sung the blues so sweet that if I sang at a funeral, the dead would commence to rocking with the beat. Used to travel all over Mississippi and as far as Monroe, Louisiana, and east on over to Macon, Georgia. You mean you ain't never heard of Sweet Lemon Brown?"

"Afraid not," Greg said. "What . . . what happened to you?"

"Hard times, boy. Hard times always after a poor man. One day I got tired, sat down to rest a spell and felt a tap on my shoulder. Hard times caught up with me."

"Sorry about that."

"What you doing here? How come you didn't go on home when the rain come? Rain don't bother you young folks none."

"Just didn't." Greg looked away.

"I used to have a knotty-headed boy just like you." Lemon Brown had half walked, half shuffled back to the corner and sat down against the wall. "Had them big eyes like you got. I used to call them moon eyes. Look into them moon eyes and see anything you want."

"How come you gave up singing the blues?" Greg asked.

"Didn't give it up," Lemon Brown said. "You don't give up the blues; they give you up. After a while you do good for yourself, and it ain't nothing but foolishness singing about how hard you got it. Ain't that right?"

"I guess so." ❸

"What's that noise?" Lemon Brown asked, suddenly sitting upright.

Greg listened, and he heard a noise outside. He looked at Lemon Brown and saw the old man was pointing toward the window.

Greg went to the window and saw three men, neighborhood thugs, on the stoop. One was carrying a length of pipe. Greg looked back toward Lemon Brown, who moved quietly across the room to the window. The old man looked out, then beckoned frantically for Greg to follow him. For a moment Greg couldn't move. Then he found himself following Lemon Brown into the hallway and up darkened stairs. Greg followed as closely as he could. They reached the top of the stairs, and Greg felt Lemon Brown's hand first lying on his

> **RETELL**
> ❸ Who is Lemon Brown? What is *his* problem?

Street Person (1982)
by Tom McKinney.
Watercolor
(16″ × 20″).
Courtesy of the artist.

shoulder, then probing down his arm until he finally took Greg's hand into his own as they crouched in the darkness.

"They's bad men," Lemon Brown whispered. His breath was warm against Greg's skin.

"Hey! Ragman!" a voice called. "We know you in here. What you got up under them rags? You got any money?"

Silence.

"We don't want to have to come in and hurt you, old man, but we don't mind if we have to."

Lemon Brown squeezed Greg's hand in his own hard, gnarled fist.

There was a banging downstairs and a light as the men entered. They banged around noisily, calling for the ragman.

"We heard you talking about your treasure." The voice was slurred. "We just want to see it, that's all."

"You sure he's here?" One voice seemed to come from the room with the sofa.

"Yeah, he stays here every night."

"There's another room over there; I'm going to take a look. You got that flashlight?"

"Yeah, here, take the pipe too."

Greg opened his mouth to quiet the sound of his breath as he sucked it in uneasily. A beam of light hit the wall a few feet opposite him, then went out.

"Ain't nobody in that room," a voice said. "You think he gone or something?"

"I don't know," came the answer. "All I know is that I heard him talking about some kind of treasure. You know they found that shopping-bag lady with that money in her bags."

"Yeah. You think he's upstairs?"

"HEY, OLD MAN, ARE YOU UP THERE?"

Silence.

"Watch my back, I'm going up." ❹

RETELL
❹ What has happened to put Greg and Lemon Brown in danger?

There was a footstep on the stairs, and the beam from the flashlight danced crazily along the peeling wallpaper. Greg held his breath. There was another step and a loud crashing noise as the man banged the pipe against the wooden banister. Greg could feel his temples throb as the man slowly neared them. Greg thought about the pipe, wondering what he would do when the man reached them—what he *could* do.

Then Lemon Brown released his hand and moved toward the top of the stairs. Greg looked around and saw stairs going up to the next floor. He tried waving to Lemon Brown, hoping the old man would see him in the dim light and follow him to the next floor. Maybe, Greg thought, the man wouldn't follow them up there. Suddenly, though, Lemon Brown stood at the top of the stairs, both arms raised high above his head.

"There he is!" a voice cried from below.

"Throw down your money, old man, so I won't have to bash your head in!"

Lemon Brown didn't move. Greg felt himself near panic. The steps came closer, and still Lemon Brown didn't move. He was an eerie sight, a bundle of rags standing at the top of the stairs, his shadow on the wall looming over him. Maybe, the thought came to Greg, the scene could be even eerier.

Greg wet his lips, put his hands to his mouth, and tried to make a sound. Nothing came out. He swallowed hard, wet his lips once more, and howled as evenly as he could.

"What's that?"

As Greg howled, the light moved away from Lemon Brown, but not before Greg saw him hurl his body down the stairs at the men who had come to take his treasure. There was a crashing noise, and then footsteps. A rush of warm air came in as the downstairs door opened; then there was only an ominous silence.

Greg stood on the landing. He listened, and after a while there was another sound on the staircase.

"Mr. Brown?" he called.

"Yeah, it's me," came the answer. "I got their flashlight." ❺

RETELL
❺ How do Lemon Brown and Greg scare off the men?

Greg exhaled in relief as Lemon Brown made his way slowly back up the stairs.

"You OK?"

"Few bumps and bruises," Lemon Brown said.

"I think I'd better be going," Greg said, his breath returning to normal. "You'd

Vocabulary
ominous (ăm′ə·nəs) *adj.*: threatening; seeming to indicate that something bad will happen.

better leave, too, before they come back."

"They may hang around outside for a while," Lemon Brown said, "but they ain't getting their nerve up to come in here again. Not with crazy old ragmen and howling spooks. Best you stay awhile till the coast is clear. I'm heading out west tomorrow, out to East St. Louis."

"They were talking about treasures," Greg said. "You *really* have a treasure?"

"What I tell you? Didn't I tell you every man got a treasure?" Lemon Brown said. "You want to see mine?"

"If you want to show it to me," Greg shrugged.

"Let's look out the window first, see what them scoundrels be doing," Lemon Brown said.

They followed the oval beam of the flashlight into one of the rooms and looked out the window. They saw the men who had tried to take the treasure sitting on the curb near the corner. One of them had his pants leg up, looking at his knee.

"You sure you're not hurt?" Greg asked Lemon Brown.

"Nothing that ain't been hurt before," Lemon Brown said. "When you get as old as me, all you say when something hurts is, 'Howdy, Mr. Pain, sees you back again.' Then when Mr. Pain see he can't worry you none, he go on mess with somebody else."

Greg smiled.

"Here, you hold this." Lemon Brown gave Greg the flashlight.

He sat on the floor near Greg and carefully untied the strings that held the rags on his right leg. When he took the rags away, Greg saw a piece of plastic. The old man carefully took off the plastic and unfolded it. He revealed some yellowed newspaper clippings and a battered harmonica.

"There it be," he said, nodding his head. "There it be."

Greg looked at the old man, saw the distant look in his eye, then turned to the clippings. They told of Sweet Lemon Brown, a blues singer and harmonica player who was appearing at different theaters in the South. One of the clippings said he had been the hit of the show, although not the headliner. All of the clippings were reviews of shows Lemon Brown had been in more than fifty years ago. Greg looked at the harmonica. It was dented badly on one side, with the reed holes on one end nearly closed.

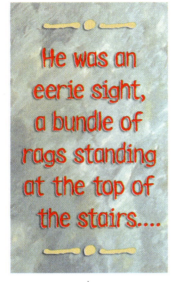

He was an eerie sight, a bundle of rags standing at the top of the stairs....

"I used to travel around and make money for to feed my wife and Jesse—that's my boy's name. Used to feed them good, too. Then his mama died, and he stayed with his mama's sister. He growed up to be a man, and when the war come, he saw fit to go off and fight in it. I didn't have nothing to give him except these things that told him who I was, and what he come from. If you know your pappy did something, you know you can do something too.

"Anyway, he went off to war, and I went off still playing and singing. 'Course by then I wasn't as much as I used to be, not without somebody to make it worth the while. You know what I mean?"

"Yeah," Greg nodded, not quite really knowing.

"I traveled around, and one time I come home, and there was this letter saying Jesse got killed in the war. Broke my heart, it truly did.

"They sent back what he had with him over there, and what it was is this old mouth fiddle and these clippings. Him carrying it around with him like that told me it meant something to him. That was my treasure, and when I give it to him, he treated it just like that, a treasure. Ain't that something?"

"Yeah, I guess so," Greg said.

"You *guess* so?" Lemon Brown's voice rose an octave² as he started to put his treasure back into the plastic. "Well, you got to guess, 'cause you sure don't know nothing. Don't know enough to get home when it's raining."

"I guess . . . I mean, you're right."

"You OK for a youngster," the old man said as he tied the strings around his leg, "better than those scalawags what come here looking for my treasure. That's for sure."

"You really think that treasure of yours was worth fighting for?" Greg asked. "Against a pipe?"

"What else a man got 'cepting what he can pass on to his son, or his daughter, if she be his oldest?" Lemon Brown said. "For a big-headed boy, you sure do ask the foolishest questions." ❻

> **RETELL**
> ❻ What do you learn about the treasure?

"If you know your pappy did something, you know you can do something too."

Lemon Brown got up after patting his rags in place and looked out the window again.

"Looks like they're gone. You get on out of here and get yourself home. I'll be watching from the window, so you'll be all right."

Lemon Brown went down the stairs behind Greg. When they reached the front door, the old man looked out first, saw the street was clear, and told Greg to scoot on home.

"You sure you'll be OK?" Greg asked.

"Now, didn't I tell you I was going to East St. Louis in the morning?" Lemon Brown asked. "Don't that sound OK to you?"

"Sure it does," Greg said. "Sure it does. And you take care of that treasure of yours."

"That I'll do," Lemon said, the wrinkles about his eyes suggesting a smile. "That I'll do."

The night had warmed and the rain had stopped, leaving puddles at the curbs. Greg didn't even want to think how late it was. He thought ahead of what his father would say and wondered if he should tell him about Lemon Brown. He thought about it until he reached his stoop, and decided against it. Lemon Brown would be OK, Greg thought, with his memories and his treasure.

Greg pushed the button over the bell marked "Ridley," thought of the lecture he knew his father would give him, and smiled. ❼

> **RETELL**
> ❼ Are Greg's problems resolved at the end?

---

2. **octave** (äk′tiv) *n.:* eight whole notes.

Meet the Writer

Walter Dean Myers

"He Gave Me the Most Precious Gift"

Walter Dean Myers (1937–   ) was born in Martinsburg, West Virginia; he was one of eight children. Myers's mother died when he was two, and when he was three, his father sent him and two of his sisters to New York City to be raised by foster parents, the Deans. When he became a published writer, Myers added their name to his to show how important they were to him.

❝My foster father was a wonderful man. He gave me the most precious gift any father could give to a son: He loved me. . . . My foster mother understood the value of education, even though neither she nor my father had more than a rudimentary education. She also understood the value of story, how it could serve as a refuge for people, like us, who couldn't afford the finer things in life or even all of what came to be the everyday things.❞

Myers has been an editor and a teacher as well as a writer of books for children and young adults. He says:

❝Every time I sit down to write, I think of television as a value setter. I may write about a moral kid. Good. But TV says being tough is better. The TV people know that a certain kind of value system—'cool' masculine—is what sells beer and blue jeans. I have to counter that.❞

For Independent Reading

Hoops is a novel about a Harlem teenager contending for a citywide basketball title against powerful opposition—both on and off the court.

After You Read Response and Analysis

First Thoughts

1. Why does Greg smile at the thought of the lecture he will get from his father?

Thinking Critically

2. In your opinion, why does Greg decide not to tell his father about Lemon Brown?

3. What do you think Greg has learned from Lemon Brown?

4. What does Lemon Brown mean when he says that everyone's got a treasure (page 734)?

5. Lemon Brown says, "If you know your pappy did something, you know you can do something too" (page 737). What does he mean? Do you agree? Explain.

6. Now that you've read the story, as well as Walter Dean Myers's own words about his life, how would you explain the way this **writer's background** is reflected in his story? Include details from the story and from Myers's personal background in your response.

Reading Check

Work out the main events that advance the **plot** of the story by filling in a diagram like this one. You should find at least three key events that lead to the **climax** and one key event before the **resolution.**

Extending Interpretations

7. Myers says that in his writing he has to "counter" values conveyed by TV (page 739). Is that a worthwhile goal? If Myers asked you whether his story challenges the values communicated by TV, what would you say?

WRITING

Writing a Story

Write a children's story that includes parts of your own background. Set your story in a location you know well. Base your characters on people you know, even if you turn them into elves or dragons or puppy dogs. Focus your plot on something that you treasure—a photograph, an old toy, a person, a place. Make your children's story sad or silly or sweet, but make it *yours.*

Vocabulary in Context

In "The Treasure of Lemon Brown," the words in the Word Bank are used in the context of an adventure in a Harlem tenement. The following questions ask you to think of other contexts for these words.

Word Bank

impromptu
tentatively
intently
brittle
ominous

PRACTICE

1. How would an actor use the word *impromptu*?
2. How would the director of a play use the word *tentatively* in telling you that you might have won a part?
3. How would you use the word *intently* in talking about a book you can't put down?
4. How would a doctor use the word *brittle* in talking about an elderly person's bones?
5. How would a weather forecaster use the word *ominous*?

Grammar Link

Don't or *Doesn't*?

When you use the contractions *don't* and *doesn't,* be sure they agree with their subjects.

- *Don't* is a contraction of *do not.* Use *don't* with plural subjects and with the pronouns *I* and *you.*

  Greg's dad said, "Get good grades or you don't play basketball."

  The thugs don't know where Greg and Lemon Brown are hiding.

- *Doesn't* is a contraction of *does not.* Use *doesn't* with singular subjects (except *I* and *you*).

  Lemon Brown doesn't want to lose his treasure.

  Something doesn't have to be worth a lot of money to be a treasure.

If you're unsure whether to use *don't* or *doesn't* in a sentence, try substituting *do not* and *does not* for the contractions. You can tell that *she does not* is correct and that *she do not* is incorrect.

PRACTICE

Copy the following sentences, and fill in each blank with the correct contraction: *don't* or *doesn't.*

1. Even though it's raining, Greg _____ want to go home.
2. At first, Greg and Lemon Brown _____ trust each other.
3. Their distrust _____ stop them from hiding together when the thugs enter.
4. The thugs _____ know what kind of treasure Lemon Brown has.
5. "I _____ want to hurt you, old man. Just give me your money."

For more help, see Contractions, 15b, in the Language Handbook.

SKILLS FOCUS

Vocabulary Skills
Use vocabulary words in context.

Grammar Skills
Understand contractions.

Understanding Logic, Coherence, and Consistency

Reading Focus

Logic, Coherence, and Consistency
What do you think of this brief response to "The Treasure of Lemon Brown"?

Text 1: An *Illogical* Response

Lemon Brown is a homeless person; therefore, he could not have been a good blues player. I once knew someone who played the harmonica really well. He had red hair and was on my baseball team. I think homeless people should all be given a place to stay so they don't have to sleep on the sidewalk. Lemon Brown should get a job so he could get an apartment.

A Text Should Be Logical

It's pretty obvious that Text 1 is not logical, but why is that? **Logic** means correct reasoning. To be logical, statements should be supported by reasons, evidence, and examples. Statements are *illogical* if the evidence does *not* support what is being said. The statement that Lemon Brown could not have been a good blues singer because he is now homeless is illogical. It is illogical because Lemon Brown's current living situation tells us nothing about his past achievements.

A Text Should Be Coherent

For a text to be logical, it also needs **coherence** (kō·hir′əns). That means that all of its parts must stick together and be clearly understood. Text 1 is not coherent because the writer jumps from one idea to another without making a connection between them.

Transitional words can help the reader follow the coherence of a text. Transitional words connect sentences and ideas. If you pay attention to transitional words when you read, you may find your text easier to understand. The following list shows some situations in which transitional words are used, as well as some transitional words used in these situations:

- connecting ideas **chronologically,** or in time sequence—*first, next, before, then, when, while, meanwhile, at last*

- connecting things in **space**—*above, across, among, before, below, here, in, near, there, under, next to*

- connecting ideas in **order of importance**—*first, mainly, more important, to begin with, then, last*

- **comparing** ideas—*also, and, another, just as, like, similarly*

- **contrasting** ideas—*although, but, however, still, yet, on the other hand*

A Text Should Be Consistent

If a text is logical and coherent, it also has **internal consistency,** which means that all of its parts are connected and agree with what came before. Because Text 1 has no internal consistency, we cannot tell what topic or main idea is intended.

Here is another brief response to "The Treasure of Lemon Brown":

Reading Skills
Understand logic, coherence, and consistency.

Text 2: A *Logical* Response

The character of Lemon Brown reminds us of the humanity of homeless people. They are not just misfits who embarrass us by sleeping on our sidewalks and begging for change. Before their problems left them with no place to live, they too had jobs and families. We should always remember that they are human beings with ideas, opinions, and a life history. We should treat them with concern and respect.

This second response *is* logical, because it is based on evidence in the text that shows us Lemon Brown's humanity. It is coherent, because the ideas follow logically from one to the other. It has internal consistency, because all of it is about why homeless people are worthy of our concern and respect.

Background
Informational Text and Music

"The Treasure of Lemon Brown" is a fictional story about a man who once played the harmonica and sang the blues. The article that follows is about Little Walter, a famous real-life blues singer and harmonica player. It's by the Pulitzer Prize–winning writer Studs Terkel, who often writes about life in Chicago. Terkel's text is taken from the jacket copy of a recording of Little Walter's music.

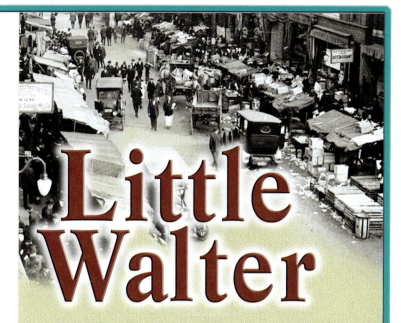

Little Walter

❶ Marion Walter Jacobs, age fourteen, stood on the corner blowing wildly into his harmonica.

❷ It was the colorful Chicago neighborhood known as the Maxwell Street Market. Here, wares, second- and thirdhand, were displayed out along the sidewalks or high on the open pushcarts. You could buy anything from used coffee grinders to slightly rusty fenders off a 1928 Cadillac to scratchy Victoria Spivey records. Here, too, wandering street musicians, blind and sighted, offered their wares: spirituals, blues, stomps, and pop tunes.

❸ Sunday mornings were the choice sessions. It was then the crowds were largest. From all over the city and its environs they came: to gawk,[1] to bargain, perchance to buy. They remained to listen.

❹ Young Jacobs ran his mouth and fingers across the harmonica like a magician performing sleight of hand. Passersby were . . . impressed. "Ooowee! Listen to Little

---

1. **gawk** (gôk) *v.*: stare.

Little Walter.

Walter!" It was this moniker[2] that stuck. Certainly, Marion was no name for a wild mouth harpist.

5 Little Walter had been playing the harmonica ever since he was six. Why did he take to this humble instrument? His reply is that of the bold spirit to whom all of life is a challenge: "If a guy could pick up a peanut and make something out of it (note: a reference to the deeds of George Washington Carver),[3] I figure I could take the harp an' make something out of it." (Artists of the harmonica seldom refer to it in this four-syllable manner. Always it's the "harp.")

6 He was born in Alexandria, Louisiana. . . . As a grocer's delivery boy, he offered the customers waltzes as well as vegetables—the harp was always in his back pocket. "Me an' my harp" were a love affair from way back.

7 In 1938, his family was part of the Deep South migration to Chicago. Our man was eight at the time. In this big, sprawling, booming city he heard new sounds. Here it was the great blues artists congregated: the legendary Big Bill, whose life and art were a saga in themselves; Big Maceo Merriwether, Tampa Red, Memphis Minnie. At first, the boy was not attuned to the blues; thus, his playing of polkas and waltzes and pop hits. Bit by bit, by a process of osmosis,[4] the richness of the blues found its way into his harp.

8 The young teenager tried to crash various clubs on Chicago's South and West Sides. Invariably he was booted out: "too young." But he was not to be denied, not for long. The veteran bluesmen took to the moans and cries that shouted their way out of his instrument. He was their man. During many of the personal appearances, his harmonica was heard italicizing the vocals of Big Bill, Muddy Waters, and many of their blues brethren. (Muddy insists that Little Walter accompany him on his recordings.)

9 His singing came out of Mother Necessity. He had no alternative. "I needed breathing time. If I blowed that harp without any rest, I'd never make it. Not the way *I* blow. So I began to sing in between my blowing, just to rest my lips an' my harp."

10 As much as any one man in recent years, . . . he's responsible for the resurgence[5] in the popularity of the blues harmonica. Says he wistfully: "Not so long ago, harp sold for a quarter. Now it cost two dollars. It'd be nice if that company'd remember who helped raise that price."

—Studs Terkel

---

2. **moniker** (män′i·kər) *n*.: slang for "nickname."
3. **George Washington Carver** (1864–1943): African American botanist famous for developing more than three hundred products from peanuts.
4. **osmosis** (äs·mō′sis) *n*.: in science, the passage of liquid through a membrane; here, absorption of ideas, feelings, and so on.
5. **resurgence** (ri·sʉr′jənts) *n*.: rising up again; re-emergence.

Analyzing an Article's Logic, Coherence, and Consistency

Little Walter

Test Practice

1. We can tell that this article has **internal consistency** because all of it is about —
   - A life on the streets of Chicago in 1938
   - B the different blues players in Chicago
   - C the development of Little Walter as a blues player
   - D the family history of Marion Walter Jacobs

2. Which of the following transitional expressions could make a **coherent** connection between these two sentences from paragraph 3?
   "Sunday mornings were the choice sessions. It was then the crowds were largest."
   - F in spite of
   - G although
   - H because
   - J eventually

3. Which of the following sentences would make a **logical** addition to the conclusion of paragraph 4?
   - A From then on he was Little Walter.
   - B Passersby ignored the street musicians.
   - C People could get great bargains on Maxwell Street.
   - D Harmonicas cost more now than when he began.

4. In paragraph 8, the writer says, "The veteran bluesmen took to the moans and cries that shouted their way out of his instrument." This means that —
   - F veteran bluesmen liked Little Walter's harmonica playing
   - G veteran bluesmen stole Little Walter's songs
   - H Little Walter was too much competition for the veteran bluesmen
   - J Little Walter became very sad

Constructed Response

1. When did Little Walter start playing the harmonica?

2. What do harmonica players call their instrument?

3. What happened when Little Walter and his family moved from Louisiana to Chicago?

4. Why did Little Walter start singing as well as playing his harmonica?

SKILLS FOCUS

Reading Skills
Analyze an article's logic, coherence, and consistency.

Idioms

In our ordinary, everyday conversation we use idioms without even noticing them. **Idioms** (id′ē·əmz) are expressions particular to a language or group. Idioms mean something other than the literal meanings of their words. *My heart is broken* is an idiom. So are these common expressions:

- It's raining cats and dogs.
- That book blew me away.
- The senator will twist some arms to pass the bill.
- I knocked myself out to finish on time.

PRACTICE 1

Take each idiom listed above, and tell what it means literally. Then, tell what it means figuratively. *My heart is broken,* for example, means literally "my heart is in at least two pieces" or "my heart can no longer pump blood." Figuratively it means "I am very sad and hurt."

Little Walter.

PRACTICE 2

Many of the titles and lyrics of blues songs are based on idioms. Below you will find three blues titles based on idioms, followed by an idiom used by Studs Terkel in the jacket notes for Little Walter's recording. What does each idiom mean literally? What does each one mean figuratively? (Notice how silly the literal meanings of the idioms are.)

1. A well-known blues song goes by the title "Nobody Knows You When You're Down and Out."

2. Little Walter uses some idioms as titles. "You Better Watch Yourself" is one.

3. "Off the Wall" is another of Little Walter's titles.

4. Terkel tells us that as a teenager, Little Walter tried to crash Chicago's blues clubs. (You might find this idiom more familiar in this form: *They weren't invited, so they tried to crash the party.*)

Chicago, 1924.

SKILLS FOCUS

Vocabulary Skills
Explain idioms.

Before You Read   The Short Story

A Smart Cookie / Bien águila

Make the Connection
Quickwrite ✏️

The mother in this story has hopes for her daughter. Write briefly about someone's hopes for you or about your own hopes for your future.

Literary Focus
Themes Cross Cultures

Whatever their heritage or traditions, people share certain dreams and fears. For example, people all over the world are likely to say, "I want my children to have everything I missed." In "A Smart Cookie" a mother talks about her missed opportunities and hopes that her daughter, Esperanza, will have a better future. (*Esperanza* means "hope" in Spanish.) As you read this story, look for a line spoken by the mother that expresses its **theme.** Remember that a theme reveals a truth about all our lives—often something that springs from our dreams or fears.

Reading Skills
Understanding Idioms

"A Smart Cookie" appears here in both English, the language in which Sandra Cisneros writes, and Spanish, her parents' language. When Elena Poniatowska translated the story into Spanish, the title posed a special problem because it is an **idiom,** an expression peculiar to a particular language. An idiom means something different from the literal meaning of each word. Do you know what the expression *smart cookie* means?

The translator could have simply used the Spanish words for *smart* and *cookie,* but in Spanish the phrase would just mean "intelligent pastry." To a Spanish speaker it would make no sense. She chose instead to change the title to "Bien águila" ("A Real Eagle"), a Spanish idiom that means something close to "smart cookie" in English.

INTERNET

More About Cisneros

Keyword: LE5 8-7

Background
Literature and Music

In this character sketch, the speaker is Esperanza, the young girl who narrates all the stories in Sandra Cisneros's book *The House on Mango Street.* In this sketch, Esperanza lets her mother do a lot of the talking.

Esperanza's mother refers to the tragic opera *Madama Butterfly* by Giacomo Puccini. Butterfly, the heroine of that opera, is a young Japanese woman who falls deeply in love with a U.S. naval officer and marries him. Shortly after their marriage her husband returns to America. Butterfly waits for years and years for him to come back to her and their child. When he does finally return, he has an American wife with him. Butterfly, in despair, gives them her beloved child and then takes her own life.

SKILLS FOCUS

Literary Skills
Understand universal themes.

Reading Skills
Understand idioms.

A Smart Cookie

Sandra Cisneros

I could've been somebody, you know? my mother says and sighs. She has lived in this city her whole life. She can speak two languages. She can sing an opera. She knows how to fix a TV. But she doesn't know which subway train to take to get downtown. I hold her hand very tight while we wait for the right train to arrive.

She used to draw when she had time. Now she draws with a needle and thread, little knotted rosebuds, tulips made of silk thread. Someday she would like to go to the ballet. Someday she would like to see a play. She borrows opera records from the public library and sings with velvety lungs powerful as morning glories.

Today while cooking oatmeal she is Madame Butterfly until she sighs and points the wooden spoon at me. I could've been somebody, you know? Esperanza, you go to school. Study hard. That Madame Butterfly was a fool. She stirs the oatmeal. Look at my comadres.° She means Izaura whose husband left and Yolanda whose husband is dead. Got to take care all your own, she says shaking her head.

Then out of nowhere:

Shame is a bad thing, you know. It keeps you down. You want to know why I quit school? Because I didn't have nice clothes. No clothes, but I had brains.

Yup, she says disgusted, stirring again. I was a smart cookie then.

° **comadres** (kô·mä**′**dräs) *n.*: Spanish for "close female friends" (literally, a child's mother and godmother).

Bien águila

Sandra Cisneros *translated by Elena Poniatowska*

Yo pude haber sido alguien, ¿sabes? dice mi madre y suspira. Toda su vida ha vivido en esta ciudad. Sabe dos idiomas. Puede cantar una ópera. Sabe reparar la tele. Pero no sabe qué metro tomar para ir al centro. La tomo muy fuerte de la mano mientras esperamos a que llegue el tren.

Cuando tenía tiempo dibujaba. Ahora dibuja con hilo y aguja, pequeños botones de rosa, tulipanes de hilo de seda. Algún día le gustaría ir al ballet. Algún día también, a ver una obra de teatro. Pide discos de ópera en la biblioteca pública y canta con pulmones aterciopelados y poderosos como glorias azules.

Hoy, mientras cuece la avena, es Madame Butterfly hasta que suspira y me señala con la cuchara de palo. Yo pude haber sido alguien, ¿sabes? Ve a la escuela, Esperanza. Estudia macizo. Esa Madame Butterfly era una tonta. Menea la avena. Fíjate en mis comadres. Se refiere a Izaura, cuyo marido se largó, y a Yolanda, cuyo marido está muerto. Tienes que cuidarte solita, dice moviendo la cabeza.

Y luego, nada más porque sí:

La vergüenza es mala cosa, ¿sabes? No te deja levantarte. ¿Sabes por qué dejé la escuela? Porque no tenía ropa bonita. Ropa no, pero cerebro sí.

¡Ufa! dice disgustada, meneando de nuevo. Yo entonces era bien águila.

Mercy (detail) (1992)
by Nick Quijano.

Meet the Writer

Sandra Cisneros

Crossing the Threshold

Like Esperanza, **Sandra Cisneros** (1954–   ) grew up in a Mexican American family in Chicago. She writes:

“I've managed to do a lot of things in my life I didn't think I was capable of and which many others didn't think me capable of either. Especially because I am a woman, a Latina, an only daughter in a family of six men. My father would've liked to have seen me married long ago. In our culture, men and women don't leave their father's house except by way of marriage. I crossed my father's threshold with nothing carrying me but my own two feet.”

For Independent Reading

"A Smart Cookie" comes from *The House on Mango Street,* a collection of short sketches narrated by Esperanza. It was published in Spanish as *La Casa en Mango Street.*

After You Read   Response and Analysis

First Thoughts

1. What connections, if any, do you see between what you wrote in your Quickwrite and "A Smart Cookie"?

Thinking Critically

2. When people use **verbal irony,** they mean just the opposite of what they say. When Esperanza's mother uses the **idiom** *smart cookie* to describe herself, what does she really mean?

3. What does Esperanza's mother mean when she says to her daughter, "Got to take care all your own"?

4. What lines in this sketch do you think express most strongly the **theme** of the mother's story? Be sure to compare your choices in class.

5. Read the biography of Sandra Cisneros carefully (see page 750). Can you find any links between the sketch of Esperanza's mother and Cisneros's life story? Refer to details from each text in your answer.

6. Describe Esperanza's mother's attitude toward education. Do you think it is an attitude people share across cultures? Do you agree with the mother about the effects of shame? Explain.

Reading Check

a. What is Esperanza's mother good at?

b. What has she never done?

c. What does she want Esperanza to do?

d. Why did Esperanza's mother quit school?

WRITING

Responding to an Opinion

Write two or three paragraphs responding to one of these opinions:

• Parents put pressure on children by wanting their children to have better lives than they had.

• Children need to know the mistakes their parents made so that they can avoid making the same mistakes.

• Education is the key to independence.

Use examples from real life (from your own life or from the lives of people you know), from literature, or from newspapers or magazines to support your response.

INTERNET
Projects and Activities
Keyword: LE5 8-7

Picnic en el Coche by Theresa Rosado.
Collection of Don Spyke.

SKILLS FOCUS

Literary Skills
Analyze themes.

Reading Skills
Analyze idioms.

Writing Skills
Respond to an opinion.

Idioms

An **idiom** is an expression that is peculiar to one language and means something different from the literal meaning of its words. *Hold your tongue* ("Don't speak") is an idiom of American English. If you didn't know this idiom, you might wonder why someone would want to hold on to a tongue! *Hold your horses* ("Be patient") is another idiom. If you didn't know this one, you might wonder, "What horses?"

PRACTICE

Each of the following statements contains an idiom, which is underlined. First, tell what the idiom means literally. Next, tell what the idiom means figuratively. The first item has been completed for you.

1. Joe has to stop <u>beating around the bush</u> and answer the question.

   Literal meaning: Joe is beating on some bushes
   with a stick.
   Figurative meaning: Joe is trying to avoid
   answering the question.

2. The rowdy class <u>clammed up</u> when the principal came in.

3. When I met you, I started <u>dancing on air</u>.

4. Shaquille <u>lost his head</u> when he decided to try out for varsity.

5. Liu couldn't <u>get a handle on</u> his math assignment.

6. Sharon <u>went overboard</u> decorating for her party.

7. The candidate <u>hit the nail on the head</u> when she said taxes are too high.

8. The surprise quiz was a <u>piece of cake</u>.

9. Luz <u>fell for</u> José the first time she saw him.

10. Our plans for vacation <u>went down the tube</u>.

SKILLS FOCUS

Vocabulary Skills
Analyze idioms.

Saying Yes

Make the Connection
Conduct a Survey

Most people living in the United States come from someplace else. You might have come to these shores as an immigrant yourself. Perhaps your parents or grandparents or great-grandparents came here from another place in the world. Even if your family has been here for many generations, chances are that they have moved around, from East to West, or from North to South, or from city to suburbs. Take a class poll to find out all the places your classmates and their families have come from. Think of a good way to display your findings graphically.

Literary Focus
Epilogue

An **epilogue** (ep′ə·lôg′), or afterword, is a brief closing section to a piece of literature. In a play the epilogue is often spoken directly to the audience by an actor. In a novel an epilogue might supply information about what happens to the characters after the novel ends. In nonfiction an epilogue might be a critical commentary. In this collection, selections have been chosen that reflect the heritage, traditions, attitudes, and beliefs of their authors. As you read "Saying Yes," see if you think it is an appropriate epilogue for this collection.

Reading Skills
Reading a Dialogue

The first part of "Saying Yes" is set up as a dialogue. A person asks questions, and a speaker answers—or tries to answer. The second part of the poem is a commentary on the questions. In lines 9–18, you will have to decide when to pause at the ends of lines and when to read on without pausing—in order to get the sense of the lines. Try reading this poem aloud with a partner.

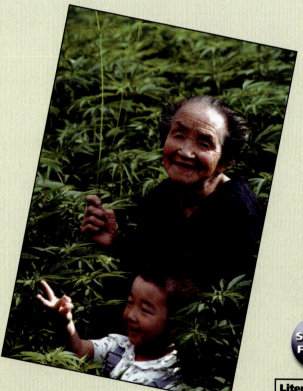

SKILLS FOCUS

Literary Skills
Understand epilogue.

Reading Skills
Read a dialogue.

Saying Yes

Diana Chang

"Are you Chinese?"
"Yes."

"American?"
"Yes."

5   "*Really* Chinese?"
"No . . . not quite."

"*Really* American?"
"Well, actually, you see . . ."

But I would rather say
10   yes

Not neither-nor,
not maybe,
but both, and not only

The homes I've had,
15   the ways I am

I'd rather say it
twice,
yes

Meet the Writer

Diana Chang

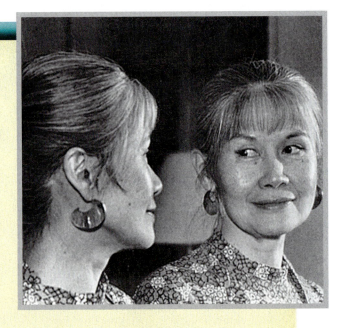

"Jot It Down on Anything!"
Born in the United States to a Eurasian mother and a Chinese father, **Diana Chang** (1934–   ) currently lives in New York. She has taught creative writing at Barnard College in New York City. Chang warns her students to be prepared to write down their ideas for poems at any time:

> As it comes, wherever it waylays you, jot it down. You may be writing when you are not writing—on the bus or while lugging groceries or avoiding cigarette smoke in an elevator. Jot it down on anything—the hem of a dress if necessary—or it'll leave with no trace, a snowflake on a warm skillet.

Chang's poems have appeared in many magazines. About "Saying Yes," Chang has written:

> To my surprise, 'Saying Yes' has been reprinted very often. I can only suppose it's because it is sincere and simple.

In addition to her poems, Chang has published novels, including *The Frontiers of Love*. That novel takes place in the Chinese city of Shanghai in 1945, a time when it was losing its distinctive cultural identity as its residents began to embrace Western values. Chang is also an accomplished painter and has exhibited her work in one-woman shows.

After You Read   Response and Analysis

First Thoughts

1. Do you think a person can identify equally with two different backgrounds? Or do you think a person has one primary identity? Explain your response.

Thinking Critically

2. How does the speaker answer when people ask if she is *really* Chinese and American?

3. In the second part of the poem, she reflects on her answers. What would she *like* to say?

Extending Interpretations

4. What do you think of Chang's comment about this poem in her biography?

5. Do you think this poem makes a fitting **epilogue** to this collection? Why or why not?

WRITING

Writing a Question-and-Answer Poem

Write a poem explaining how you feel about your own heritage or heritages. You could structure your poem, as Chang does, as a series of questions and answers. Display your poem, along with those of your classmates, as a mosaic representing your class. You could call your poetry display "Saying Yes." You might want to add photographs to the mosaic.

October Light by Diana Chang. Acrylic.
Photographer: Joan G. Anderson. Copyrighted and reproduced with the permission of Diana Chang, painter and poet.

Vermont Verge by Diana Chang. Acrylic.
Photographer: Joan G. Anderson. Copyrighted and reproduced with the permission of Diana Chang, painter and poet.

SKILLS FOCUS

Literary Skills
Analyze an epilogue.

Reading Skills
Read a dialogue.

Writing Skills
Write a poem.

Comparing Literature

Literary Focus

Plot: Moments of Recognition

The lightbulb above your head goes on, and you say, "Oh yeah!" You have realized something that changes the way you see things. This moment of recognition suddenly makes everything seem different somehow. The **plot** of a story can lead up to such a **moment of recognition.**

Plot is the driving force of fiction. The motor of plot is **conflict.** The conflict can be between opposing emotions within the mind of one character (**internal conflict**), between two characters, or between a character and forces beyond his or her control (**external conflicts**). The events that make up the plot flow from the conflict. The elements of plot are listed in the box on the right.

Reading Skills

Comparing and Contrasting

The two stories you are about to read both have a main character who takes an emotional journey that leads to a moment of recognition. After this moment, the characters don't see themselves or their families quite the same way again. As you read "The Medicine Bag" and "An Hour with Abuelo," pay attention to the similarities and differences in the main characters. Also pay attention to the similarities and differences in the ways the events unfold in these stories. A chart after each selection will help you compare and contrast these stories. When you **compare,** you look for ways in which things are alike. When you **contrast,** you look for ways in which things are different.

Elements of Plot

- **Introduction,** or **exposition,** tells who the characters are and what their conflict is.
- **Conflict** centers on the question of who or what is keeping the main character from getting what he or she wants.
- **Complications** are created when the characters take steps to resolve the conflict.
- **Climax** is the most exciting moment in the story, when the outcome of the conflict is decided.
- **Resolution** is the final part of the story, when the conflict is resolved and the story ends.

SKILLS FOCUS

Literary Skills
Analyze plot.

Reading Skills
Compare and contrast stories.

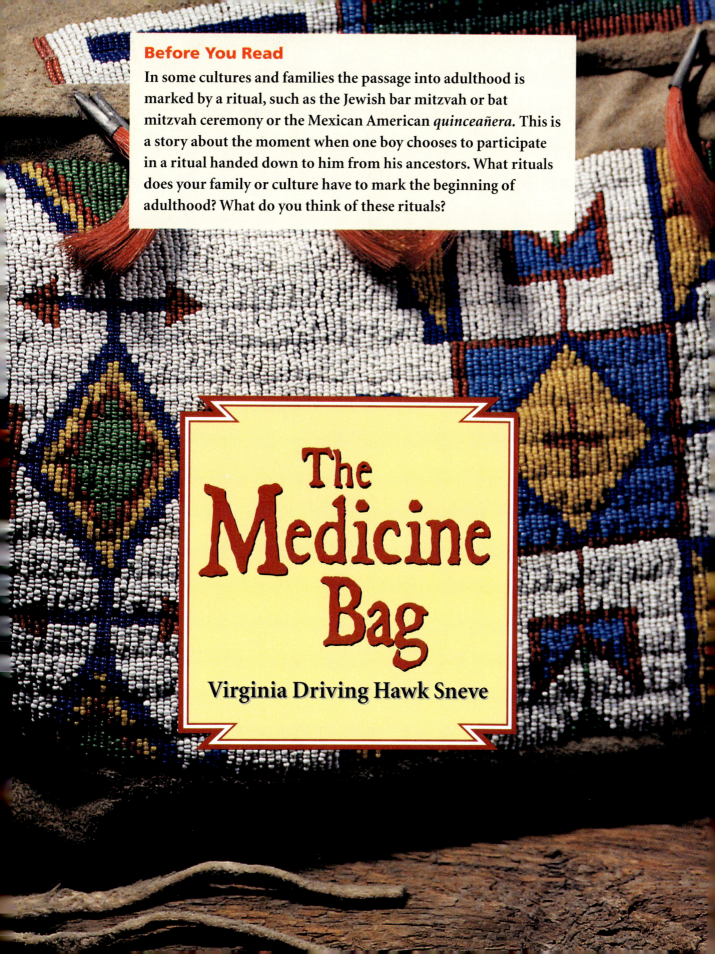

In some cultures and families the passage into adulthood is marked by a ritual, such as the Jewish bar mitzvah or bat mitzvah ceremony or the Mexican American *quinceañera*. This is a story about the moment when one boy chooses to participate in a ritual handed down to him from his ancestors. What rituals does your family or culture have to mark the beginning of adulthood? What do you think of these rituals?

The Medicine Bag

Virginia Driving Hawk Sneve

When the Eagle Spoke to Me (1979) by Jerry Ingram.

IDENTIFY

❶ List the things
you learn about this
narrator in the first
paragraph. Where
does he live? What is
his heritage? Does he
have siblings?

My kid sister Cheryl and I always bragged about our Sioux
grandpa, Joe Iron Shell. Our friends, who had always lived
in the city and only knew about Indians from movies and TV, were
impressed by our stories. Maybe we exaggerated and made Grandpa
and the reservation sound glamorous, but when we'd return home to
Iowa after our yearly summer visit to Grandpa, we always had some
exciting tale to tell. ❶

   We always had some authentic Sioux article to show our listeners.
One year Cheryl had new moccasins that Grandpa had made. On
another visit he gave me a small, round, flat rawhide drum which was
decorated with a painting of a warrior riding a horse. He taught me a

real Sioux chant to sing while I beat the drum with a leather-covered stick that had a feather on the end. Man, that really made an impression.

We never showed our friends Grandpa's picture. Not that we were ashamed of him, but because we knew that the glamorous tales we told didn't go with the real thing. Our friends would have laughed at the picture, because Grandpa wasn't tall and stately like TV Indians. His hair wasn't in braids but hung in stringy gray strands on his neck, and he was old. He was our great-grandfather, and he didn't live in a tepee, but all by himself in a part log, part tar-paper shack on the Rosebud Reservation in South Dakota. So when Grandpa came to visit us, I was so ashamed and embarrassed I could've died. ❷

There are a lot of yippy poodles and other fancy little dogs in our neighborhood, but they usually barked singly at the mailman from the safety of their own yards. Now it sounded as if a whole pack of mutts were barking together in one place.

I got up and walked to the curb to see what the commotion was. About a block away I saw a crowd of little kids yelling, with the dogs yipping and growling around someone who was walking down the middle of the street.

I watched the group as it slowly came closer and saw that in the center of the strange procession was a man wearing a tall black hat. He'd pause now and then to peer at something in his hand and then at the houses on either side of the street. I felt cold and hot at the same time as I recognized the man. "Oh, no!" I whispered. "It's Grandpa!"

I stood on the curb, unable to move even though I wanted to run and hide. Then I got mad when I saw how the yippy dogs were growling and nipping at the old man's baggy pant legs and how wearily he poked them away with his cane. "Stupid mutts," I said as I ran to rescue Grandpa.

When I kicked and hollered at the dogs to get away, they put their tails between their legs and scattered. The kids ran to the curb, where they watched me and the old man.

Dakota Sioux drum (c. 1910).

"Grandpa," I said, and felt pretty dumb when my voice cracked. I reached for his beat-up old tin suitcase, which was tied shut with a rope. But he set it down right in the street and shook my hand.

"Hau, Takoza, Grandchild," he greeted me formally in Sioux.

All I could do was stand there with the whole neighborhood watching and shake the hand of the leather-brown old man. I saw how his gray hair straggled from under his big black hat, which had a drooping feather in its crown. His rumpled black suit hung like a sack over his stooped frame. As he shook my hand, his coat fell open to expose a bright-red satin shirt with a beaded bolo tie[1] under the collar. His get-up wasn't out of place on the reservation, but it sure was here, and I wanted to sink right through the pavement. ❸

"Hi," I muttered with my head down. I tried to pull my hand away when I felt his bony hand trembling, and looked up to see fatigue[2] in his face. I felt like crying. I couldn't think of anything to say, so I picked up Grandpa's suitcase, took his arm, and guided him up the driveway to our house.

Mom was standing on the steps. I don't know how long she'd been watching, but her hand was over her mouth and she looked as if she couldn't believe what she saw. Then she ran to us.

"Grandpa," she gasped. "How in the world did you get here?"

She checked her move to embrace Grandpa, and I remembered that such a display of affection is unseemly to the Sioux and would embarrass him.

"Hau, Marie," he said as he shook Mom's hand. She smiled and took his other arm. ❹

As we supported him up the steps, the door banged open and Cheryl came bursting out of the house. She was all smiles and was so obviously glad to see Grandpa that I was ashamed of how I felt.

"Grandpa!" she yelled happily. "You came to see us!"

Grandpa smiled and Mom and I let go of him as he stretched out his arms to my ten-year-old sister, who was still young enough to be hugged.

"Wicincala, little girl," he greeted her, and then collapsed.

He had fainted. Mom and I carried him into her sewing room, where we had a spare bed.

---

1. **bolo tie:** cord with a decorated fastening, worn as a necktie.
2. **fatigue** (fə·tēg′) *n.:* exhaustion; tiredness.

Sioux war shield (c. 1850).

After we had Grandpa on the bed, Mom stood there helplessly patting his shoulder.

"Shouldn't we call the doctor, Mom?" I suggested, since she didn't seem to know what to do.

"Yes," she agreed, with a sigh. "You make Grandpa comfortable, Martin."

I reluctantly moved to the bed. I knew Grandpa wouldn't want to have Mom undress him, but I didn't want to, either. He was so skinny and frail that his coat slipped off easily. When I loosened his tie and opened his shirt collar, I felt a small leather pouch that hung from a thong[3] around his neck. I left it alone and moved to remove his boots. The scuffed old cowboy boots were tight and he moaned as I put pressure on his legs to jerk them off.

I put the boots on the floor and saw why they fit so tight. Each one was stuffed with money. I looked at the bills that lined the boots and started to ask about them, but Grandpa's eyes were closed again.

Mom came back with a basin of water. "The doctor thinks Grandpa is suffering from heat exhaustion," she explained as she bathed Grandpa's face. Mom gave a big sigh, "Oh hinh, Martin. How do you suppose he got here?"

We found out after the doctor's visit. Grandpa was angrily sitting up in bed while Mom tried to feed him some soup.

"Tonight you let Marie feed you, Grandpa," spoke my dad, who had gotten home from work just as the doctor was leaving. "You're not really sick," he said as he gently pushed Grandpa back against the pillows. "The doctor said you just got too tired and hot after your long trip."

---

3. **thong:** narrow strip of leather.

Sioux pipe bag.

Grandpa relaxed, and between sips of soup he told us of his journey. Soon after our visit to him Grandpa decided that he would like to see where his only living descendants lived and what our home was like. Besides, he admitted sheepishly, he was lonesome after we left. ❺

I knew everybody felt as guilty as I did—especially Mom. Mom was all Grandpa had left. So even after she married my dad, who's a white man and teaches in the college in our city, and after Cheryl and I were born, Mom made sure that every summer we spent a week with Grandpa.

I never thought that Grandpa would be lonely after our visits, and none of us noticed how old and weak he had become. But Grandpa knew and so he came to us. He had ridden on buses for two and a half days. When he arrived in the city, tired and stiff from sitting for so long, he set out, walking, to find us.

He had stopped to rest on the steps of some building downtown and a policeman found him. The cop, according to Grandpa, was a good man who took him to the bus stop and waited until the bus came and told the driver to let Grandpa out at Bell View Drive. After Grandpa got off the bus, he started walking again. But he couldn't see the house numbers on the other

IDENTIFY

❺ Why has Grandpa traveled to see Martin's family?

side when he walked on the sidewalk, so he walked in the middle of the street. That's when all the little kids and dogs followed him.

I knew everybody felt as bad as I did. Yet I was proud of this eighty-six-year-old man, who had never been away from the reservation, having the courage to travel so far alone. ❻

"You found the money in my boots?" he asked Mom.

"Martin did," she answered, and roused herself to scold. "Grandpa, you shouldn't have carried so much money. What if someone had stolen it from you?"

Grandpa laughed. "I would've known if anyone tried to take the boots off my feet. The money is what I've saved for a long time— a hundred dollars—for my funeral. But you take it now to buy groceries so that I won't be a burden to you while I am here."

"That won't be necessary, Grandpa," Dad said. "We are honored to have you with us and you will never be a burden. I am only sorry that we never thought to bring you home with us this summer and spare you the discomfort of a long trip."

Grandpa was pleased. "Thank you," he answered. "But do not feel bad that you didn't bring me with you, for I would not have come then. It was not time." He said this in such a way that no one could argue with him. To Grandpa and the Sioux, he once told me, a thing would be done when it was the right time to do it and that's the way it was.

"Also," Grandpa went on, looking at me, "I have come because it is soon time for Martin to have the medicine bag."

We all knew what that meant. Grandpa thought he was going to die and he had to follow the tradition of his family to pass the medicine bag, along with its history, to the oldest male child.

"Even though the boy," he said, still looking at me, "bears a white man's name, the medicine bag will be his."

I didn't know what to say. I had the same hot and cold feeling that I had when I first saw Grandpa in the street. The medicine bag was the dirty leather pouch I had found around his neck. "I could never wear such a thing," I almost said aloud. I thought of having my friends see it in gym class, at the swimming pool, and could imagine the smart things they would say. But I just swallowed hard and took a step toward the bed. I knew I would have to take it. ❼

But Grandpa was tired. "Not now, Martin," he said, waving his hand in dismissal, "it is not time. Now I will sleep."

ANALYZE

❻ How does Grandpa's story of his journey change the way Martin sees him?

ANALYZE

❼ A **conflict** can occur when two people want different things. What does Martin want? What does Grandpa want? Describe the conflict between Martin and Grandpa.

So that's how Grandpa came to be with us for two months. My friends kept asking to come see the old man, but I put them off. I told myself that I didn't want them laughing at Grandpa. But even as I made excuses, I knew it wasn't Grandpa that I was afraid they'd laugh at.

Nothing bothered Cheryl about bringing her friends to see Grandpa. Every day after school started, there'd be a crew of giggling little girls or round-eyed little boys crowded around the old man on the patio, where he'd gotten in the habit of sitting every afternoon.

Grandpa would smile in his gentle way and patiently answer their questions, or he'd tell them stories of brave warriors, ghosts, animals, and the kids listened in awed silence. Those little guys thought Grandpa was great.

Finally, one day after school, my friends came home with me because nothing I said stopped them. "We're going to see the great Indian of Bell View Drive," said Hank, who was supposed to be my best friend. "My brother has seen him three times, so he oughta be well enough to see us." **8**

When we got to my house, Grandpa was sitting on the patio. He had on his red shirt, but today he also wore a fringed leather vest that was decorated with beads. Instead of his usual cowboy boots he had solidly beaded moccasins on his feet that stuck out of his black trousers. Of course, he had his old black hat on—he was seldom without it. But it had been brushed and the feather in the beaded headband was proudly erect, its tip a brighter white. His hair lay in silver strands over the red shirt collar.

I stared just as my friends did and I heard one of them murmur, "Wow!"

Grandpa looked up and when his eyes met mine, they twinkled as if he were laughing inside. He nodded to me and my face got all hot. I could tell that he had known all along I was afraid he'd embarrass me in front of my friends.

"Hau, hoksilas, boys," he greeted, and held out his hand.

My buddies passed in a single file and shook his hand as I introduced them. They were so polite I almost laughed. "How, there, Grandpa," and even a "How do you do, sir."

"You look fine, Grandpa," I said as the guys sat on the lawn chairs or on the patio floor.

"Hanh, yes," he agreed. "When I woke up this morning, it seemed

PREDICT

8 What does Martin fear will happen when he brings his friends to see Grandpa? What do you think will happen?

Dakota Sioux vest (c. 1880–1900).

the right time to dress in the good clothes. I knew that my grandson would be bringing his friends."

"You guys want some lemonade or something?" I offered. No one answered. They were listening to Grandpa as he started telling how he'd killed the deer from which his vest was made.

Grandpa did most of the talking while my friends were there. I was so proud of him and amazed at how respectfully quiet my buddies were. Mom had to chase them home at suppertime. As they left, they shook Grandpa's hand again and said to me:

"Martin, he's really great!"

"Yeah, man! Don't blame you for keeping him to yourself." **❾**

EVALUATE

❾ How does the meeting between Martin's friends and Grandpa turn out? Do you think Martin's fears were justified? Why or why not?

10 Has Martin's atti-
tude about accepting
the medicine bag
changed since he
first heard about it?
Explain.

11 Who is Grandpa
telling a story about?
When and where does
the story take place?

"Can we come back?"

But after they left, Mom said, "No more visitors for a while, Martin. Grandpa won't admit it, but his strength hasn't returned. He likes having company, but it tires him."

That evening Grandpa called me to his room before he went to sleep. "Tomorrow," he said, "when you come home, it will be time to give you the medicine bag."

I felt a hard squeeze from where my heart is supposed to be and was scared, but I answered, "OK, Grandpa." **10**

All night I had weird dreams about thunder and lightning on a high hill. From a distance I heard the slow beat of a drum. When I woke up in the morning, I felt as if I hadn't slept at all. At school it seemed as if the day would never end and when it finally did, I ran home.

Grandpa was in his room, sitting on the bed. The shades were down and the place was dim and cool. I sat on the floor in front of Grandpa, but he didn't even look at me. After what seemed a long time, he spoke.

"I sent your mother and sister away. What you will hear today is only for a man's ears. What you will receive is only for a man's hands." He fell silent and I felt shivers down my back.

"My father in his early manhood," Grandpa began, "made a vision quest to find a spirit guide for his life. You cannot understand how it was in that time, when the great Teton Sioux were first made to stay on the reservation. There was a strong need for guidance from Wakantanka, the Great Spirit. But too many of the young men were filled with despair and hatred. They thought it was hopeless to search for a vision when the glorious life was gone and only the hated confines[4] of a reservation lay ahead. But my father held to the old ways. **11**

"He carefully prepared for his quest with a purifying sweat bath and then he went alone to a high butte[5] top to fast and pray. After three days he received his sacred dream—in which he found, after long searching, the white man's iron. He did not understand his vision of finding something belonging to the white people, for in that time they were the enemy. When he came down from the butte to cleanse himself at the stream below, he found the remains of a

---

4. **confines** (kän′finz′) *n.:* borders; boundaries.
5. **butte** (byo͞ot): steep, flat-topped hill standing alone on a plain.

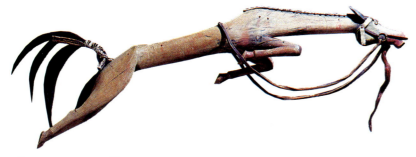

Sioux war pony effigy.
Robinson State Museum, Pierre, South Dakota.

campfire and the broken shell of an iron kettle. This was a sign which reinforced his dream. He took a piece of the iron for his medicine bag, which he had made of elk skin years before, to prepare for his quest.

"He returned to his village, where he told his dream to the wise old men of the tribe. They gave him the name Iron Shell, but neither did they understand the meaning of the dream. This first Iron Shell kept the piece of iron with him at all times and believed it gave him protection from the evils of those unhappy days.

"Then a terrible thing happened to Iron Shell. He and several other young men were taken from their homes by the soldiers and sent far away to a white man's boarding school. He was angry and lonesome for his parents and the young girl he had wed before he was taken away. At first Iron Shell resisted the teachers' attempts to change him and he did not try to learn. One day it was his turn to work in the school's blacksmith shop. As he walked into the place, he knew that his medicine had brought him there to learn and work with the white man's iron.

"Iron Shell became a blacksmith and worked at the trade when he returned to the reservation. All of his life he treasured the medicine bag. When he was old and I was a man, he gave it to me, for no one made the vision quest anymore." **12**

Grandpa quit talking and I stared in disbelief as he covered his face with his hands. His shoulders were shaking with quiet sobs and I looked away until he began to speak again.

"I kept the bag until my son, your mother's father, was a man and had to leave us to fight in the war across the ocean. I gave him the bag, for I believed it would protect him in battle, but he did not

EVALUATE

12 The Sioux believed that a medicine bag could provide protection and power. Do you think Iron Shell's medicine bag protected him? Why or why not?

take it with him. He was afraid that he would lose it. He died in a faraway place."

Again Grandpa was still and I felt his grief around me.

"My son," he went on after clearing his throat, "had only a daughter and it is not proper for her to know of these things."

He unbuttoned his shirt, pulled out the leather pouch, and lifted it over his head. He held it in his hand, turning it over and over as if memorizing how it looked.

"In the bag," he said as he opened it and removed two objects, "is the broken shell of the iron kettle, a pebble from the butte, and a piece of the sacred sage."[6] He held the pouch upside down and dust drifted down.

"After the bag is yours, you must put a piece of prairie sage within and never open it again until you pass it on to your son." He replaced the pebble and the piece of iron and tied the bag.

I stood up, somehow knowing I should. Grandpa slowly rose from the bed and stood upright in front of me, holding the bag before my face. I closed my eyes and waited for him to slip it over my head. But he spoke.

"No, you need not wear it." He placed the soft leather bag in my right hand and closed my other hand over it. "It would not be right to wear it in this time and place, where no one will understand. Put it safely away until you are again on the reservation. Wear it then, when you replace the sacred sage." **⓭**

Grandpa turned and sat again on the bed. Wearily he leaned his head against the pillow. "Go," he said, "I will sleep now."

"Thank you, Grandpa," I said softly, and left with the bag in my hands.

That night Mom and Dad took Grandpa to the hospital. Two weeks later I stood alone on the lonely prairie of the reservation and put the sacred sage in my medicine bag. **⓮**

---

6. **sage:** plant with fragrant leaves.

ANALYZE

⓭ What is surprising about the moment Martin receives the medicine bag from Grandpa?

ANALYZE

⓮ How is Martin's **internal conflict** over the medicine bag resolved?

Meet the Writer

Virginia Driving Hawk Sneve

Passing on the Heritage

Like Grandpa in "The Medicine Bag," **Virginia Driving Hawk Sneve** (1933–   ) was born on the Rosebud Reservation in South Dakota and is a member of the Rosebud Sioux. Sneve (snā ′vē) and her husband lived in Iowa for many years. Their children, like Martin and Cheryl, grew up knowing Rosebud only from summer visits. "The Medicine Bag" was inspired by Sneve's oldest son and his excitement over a great-uncle's visit, as she explains:

66 The day of my uncle's arrival, there were about a dozen little boys sitting on each side of our driveway waiting for this Indian uncle to show up. . . . My uncle came driving up in a great big blue air-conditioned Oldsmobile, and when he got out, he was wearing a pair of slacks and a sports shirt. My aunt, too, had on slacks and a blouse. We welcomed them, and in the bustle of the visit we didn't pay too much attention to the kids.

Later I found out from my neighbor, who was non-Indian, that my son had primed all the little boys to expect this uncle to come riding up on a horse, in a breechcloth. Those little boys were disgusted and upset because this uncle looked like anybody else. Until then, I hadn't thought about what my children thought about Indians. . . .

When I started writing for children, I did so with the specific purpose of informing my own children about their heritage and trying to correct some misconceptions about how they saw Indian people and how others thought about Indians. 99

First Thoughts

1. Finish this sentence: If I were Martin and I received the medicine bag, I would . . .

Thinking Critically

2. Why is Martin ashamed of Grandpa at the beginning of the story?

3. Martin's friends are impressed by Grandpa. Describe how Martin might feel about Grandpa if his friends laughed at him instead. Do you think his friends' opinion should make any difference?

4. What do you think Grandpa would do with the medicine bag if Martin were a girl? Why?

Reading Check

Use the following story map to outline the main elements of the story's plot:

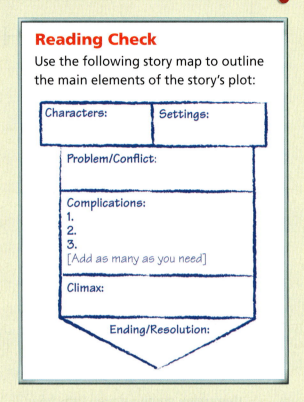

Characters: Settings:

Problem/Conflict:

Complications:
1.
2.
3.
[Add as many as you need]

Climax:

Ending/Resolution:

Comparing Literature

5. Fill in the first column of a chart like the one below. To identify the moment or moments of recognition (there may be more than one), ask yourself, *What does the main character learn that makes him see himself in a different way?* You can use your chart to help you write the comparison-contrast essay on page 781.

Comparing Moments of Recognition		
	"The Medicine Bag"	"An Hour with Abuelo"
Details about main character		
What he thinks of his grandfather at beginning of story		
What he thinks of his grandfather at end of story		
Moment(s) of recognition		

go.hrw.com

INTERNET

Projects and Activities

Keyword: LE5 8-7

SKILLS FOCUS

Literary Skills
Analyze plot.

Reading Skills
Compare and contrast stories.

Before You Read

This is a story about a boy who gets a lesson in what life was like for his family in Puerto Rico before he was born. How is the hour Arturo spends with his grandfather like one long moment of recognition?

An Hour with Abuelo

Judith Ortiz Cofer

"Just one hour, *una hora*,[1] is all I'm asking of you, son." My grandfather is in a nursing home in Brooklyn, and my mother wants me to spend some time with him, since the doctors say that he doesn't have too long to go now. I don't have much time left of my summer vacation, and there's a stack of books next to my bed I've got

---

1. **una hora** (ōō'nä ō'rä): Spanish for "one hour."

to read if I'm going to get into the AP English class I want. I'm going stupid in some of my classes, and Mr. Williams, the principal at Central, said that if I passed some reading tests, he'd let me move up. ❶

Besides, I hate the place, the old people's home, especially the way it smells like industrial-strength ammonia and other stuff I won't mention, since it turns my stomach. And really the abuelo[2] always has a lot of relatives visiting him, so I've gotten out of going out there except at Christmas, when a whole vanload of grandchildren are herded over there to give him gifts and a hug. We all make it quick and spend the rest of the time in the recreation area, where they play checkers and stuff with some of the old people's games, and I catch up on back issues of *Modern Maturity*. I'm not picky, I'll read almost anything.

Anyway, after my mother nags me for about a week, I let her drive me to Golden Years. She drops me off in front. She wants me to go in alone and have a "good time" talking to Abuelo. I tell her to be back in one hour or I'll take the bus back to Paterson. She squeezes my hand and says, *"Gracias, hijo,"*[3] in a choked-up voice like I'm doing her a big favor. ❷

I get depressed the minute I walk into the place. They line up the old people in wheelchairs in the hallway as if they were about to be raced to the finish line by orderlies who don't even look at them when they push them here and there. I walk fast to room 10, Abuelo's "suite." He is sitting up in his bed writing with a pencil in one of those old-fashioned black hardback notebooks. It has the outline of the island of Puerto Rico on it. I slide into the hard vinyl chair by his bed. He sort of smiles and the lines on his face get deeper, but he doesn't say anything. Since I'm supposed to talk to him, I say, "What are you doing, Abuelo, writing the story of your life?"

It's supposed to be a joke, but he answers, "Sí, how did you know, Arturo?"

His name is Arturo too. I was named after him. I don't really know my grandfather. His children, including my mother, came to New York and New Jersey (where I was born) and he stayed on the Island until my grandmother died. Then he got sick, and since nobody could leave their jobs to take care of him, they brought him to this

---

2. **abuelo** (äb·wä′lō): Spanish for "grandfather."
3. *Gracias, hijo* (grä′sē·äs′ ē′hō): Spanish for "Thank you, son."

nursing home in Brooklyn. I see him a couple of times a year, but he's always surrounded by his sons and daughters. My mother tells me that Don Arturo[4] had once been a teacher back in Puerto Rico, but had lost his job after the war. Then he became a farmer. She's always saying in a sad voice, *"Ay, bendito!*[5] What a waste of a fine mind." Then she usually shrugs her shoulders and says, *"Así es la vida."* That's the way life is. It sometimes makes me mad that the adults I know just accept whatever crap is thrown at them because "that's the way things are." Not for me. I go after what I want. ❸

Anyway, Abuelo is looking at me like he was trying to see inside my head, but he doesn't say anything. Since I like stories, I decide I may as well ask him if he'll read me what he wrote.

I look at my watch: I've already used up twenty minutes of the hour I promised my mother.

Abuelo starts talking in his slow way. He speaks what my mother calls book English. He taught himself from a dictionary, and his words sound stiff, like he's sounding them out in his head before he says them. With his children he speaks Spanish, and that funny book English with us grandchildren. I'm surprised that he's still so sharp, because his body is shrinking like a crumpled-up brown paper sack with some bones in it. But I can see from looking into his eyes that the light is still on in there.

---

4. **Don:** "Don" is a title of respect, like "Mr."
5. *bendito* (ben·dē′tō): Spanish for "bless him."

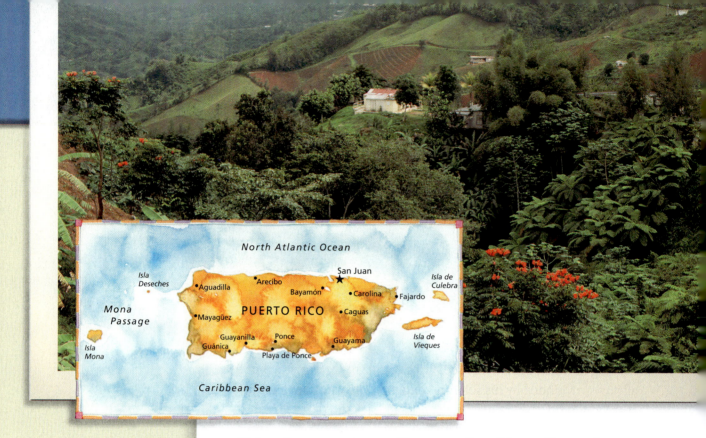

"It is a short story, Arturo. The story of my life. It will not take very much time to read it."

"I have time, Abuelo." I'm a little embarrassed that he saw me looking at my watch.

"Yes, hijo. You have spoken the truth. La verdad. You have much time."

Abuelo reads: "'I loved words from the beginning of my life. In the *campo*[6] where I was born one of seven sons, there were few books. My mother read them to us over and over: the Bible, the stories of Spanish conquistadors[7] and of pirates that she had read as a child and brought with her from the city of Mayagüez;[8] that was before she married my father, a coffee bean farmer; and she taught us words from the newspaper that a boy on a horse brought every week to her. She taught each of us how to write on a slate with chalks that she ordered by mail every year. We used those chalks until they were so small that you lost them between your fingers.

"'I always wanted to be a writer and a teacher. With my heart and

---

6. *campo* (käm′pō): Spanish for "country."
7. **conquistadors** (kän·kēs′tə·dörz′): any of the Spanish conquerors of Mexico, Peru, or other parts of America in the sixteenth century.
8. **Mayagüez** (mä′yä·gwes′): port city in western Puerto Rico.

soul I knew that I wanted to be around books all of my life. And so against the wishes of my father, who wanted all his sons to help him on the land, she sent me to high school in Mayagüez. For four years I boarded with a couple she knew. I paid my rent in labor, and I ate vegetables I grew myself. I wore my clothes until they were thin as parchment. But I graduated at the top of my class! My whole family came to see me that day. My mother brought me a beautiful *guayabera,* a white shirt made of the finest cotton and embroidered by her own hands. I was a happy young man.

"'In those days you could teach in a country school with a high school diploma. So I went back to my mountain village and got a job teaching all grades in a little classroom built by the parents of my students. ❹

"'I had books sent to me by the government. I felt like a rich man although the pay was very small. I had books. All the books I wanted! I taught my students how to read poetry and plays, and how to write them. We made up songs and put on shows for the parents. It was a beautiful time for me.

"'Then the war came, and the American President said that all Puerto Rican men would be drafted. I wrote to our governor and explained that I was the only teacher in the mountain village. I told him that the children would go back to the fields and grow up ignorant if I could not teach them their letters. I said that I thought I was a better teacher than a soldier. The governor did not answer my letter. I went into the U.S. Army.

"'I told my sergeant that I could be a teacher in the army. I could teach all the farm boys their letters so that they could read the instructions on the ammunition boxes and not blow themselves up. The sergeant said I was too smart for my own good, and gave me a job cleaning latrines. He said to me there is reading material for you there, scholar. Read the writing on the walls. I spent the war mopping floors and cleaning toilets.

"'When I came back to the Island, things had changed. You had to have a college degree to teach school, even the lower grades. My parents were sick, two of my brothers had been killed in the war, the others had stayed in Nueva York. I was the only one left to help the old people. I became a farmer. I married a good woman who gave me many good children. I taught them all

IDENTIFY

❹ What obstacles did Abuelo face? What sacrifices did he make to achieve his goal of becoming a teacher and a writer?

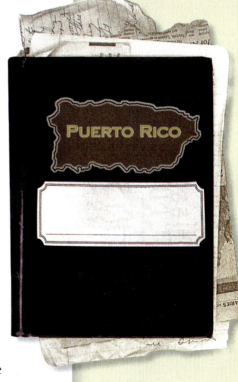

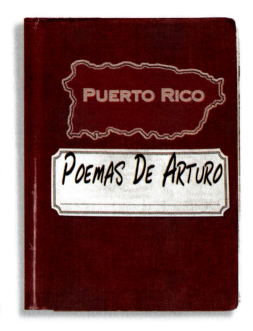

how to read and write before they started school.'"

Abuelo then puts the notebook down on his lap and closes his eyes.

"*Así es la vida* is the title of my book," he says in a whisper, almost to himself. Maybe he's forgotten that I'm there.

For a long time he doesn't say anything else. I think that he's sleeping, but then I see that he's watching me through half-closed lids, maybe waiting for my opinion of his writing. I'm trying to think of something nice to say. I liked it and all, but not the title. And I think that he could've been a teacher if he had wanted to bad enough. Nobody is going to stop me from doing what I want with my life. I'm not going to let la vida get in my way. I want to discuss this with him, but the words are not coming into my head in Spanish just yet. ❺ I'm about to ask him why he didn't keep fighting to make his dream come true, when an old lady in hot-pink running shoes sort of appears at the door.

She is wearing a pink jogging outfit too. The world's oldest marathoner, I say to myself. She calls out to my grandfather in a flirty voice, "Yoo-hoo, Arturo, remember what day this is? It's poetry-reading day in the rec room! You promised us you'd read your new one today."

I see my abuelo perking up almost immediately. He points to his wheelchair, which is hanging like a huge metal bat in the open closet. He makes it obvious that he wants me to get it. I put it together, and with Ms. Pink Running Shoes's help, we get him in it. Then he says in a strong deep voice I hardly recognize, "Arturo, get that notebook from the table, please."

I hand him another map-of-the-Island notebook—this one is red. On it in big letters it says, *POEMAS DE ARTURO*.

I start to push him toward the rec room, but he shakes his finger at me.

"Arturo, look at your watch now. I believe your time is over." He gives me a wicked smile.

COMPARE AND CONTRAST

❺ Recall the story Grandpa tells Martin in "The Medicine Bag." After hearing this story, Martin begins to respect Grandpa and his own heritage more. How does Arturo react to the story his grandfather tells him? Do you think he, like Martin, respects his grandfather more now? Explain.

Then with her pushing the wheelchair—maybe a little too fast—they roll down the hall. He is already reading from his notebook, and she's making bird noises. I look at my watch and the hour *is* up, to the minute. I can't help but think that my abuelo has been timing *me.* It cracks me up. I walk slowly down the hall toward the exit sign. I want my mother to have to wait a little. I don't want her to think that I'm in a hurry or anything. ❻

INFER

❻ Arturo says that he doesn't want his mother to think he's in a hurry. How has his attitude toward spending time with his grandfather changed?

Meet the Writer

Judith Ortiz Cofer

"A Home Where Two Cultures and Languages Became One"

Judith Ortiz Cofer (1952–   ) was born in Hormigueros, Puerto Rico. Because her father was in the military, she spent her childhood moving back and forth between a village in Puerto Rico and a city neighborhood in Paterson, New Jersey. She writes:

"I had spent my early childhood in the U.S., where I lived in a bubble created by my Puerto Rican parents in a home where two cultures and languages became one. I learned to listen to the English from the television with one ear while I heard my mother and father speaking in Spanish with the other. I thought I was an ordinary American kid—like the children on the shows I watched—and that everyone's parents spoke a secret second language at home."

Cofer later received her master of arts degree in English and went on to teach English at different schools, including the University of Georgia, where she is currently the Franklin Professor of English and Creative Writing. She reveals:

"It was a challenge not only to learn English, but to master it enough to teach it and—the ultimate goal—to write poetry in it."

For Independent Reading

The Latin Deli, a collection of fiction, poetry, and essays, describes more of Cofer's experiences growing up in two cultures.

After You Read   "An Hour with Abuelo"

First Thoughts

1. Finish this sentence: I understood how Arturo felt when . . .

Thinking Critically

2. Why doesn't Arturo want to visit his grandfather? (List as many reasons as you can think of.)

3. What do you think Arturo's grandfather means when he tells Arturo, "You have much time" (page 776)?

4. How is Arturo's life different from Abuelo's? What advantages does Arturo have that Abuelo didn't have? Can you think of any advantages Abuelo had?

5. **Irony** occurs when a situation turns out the opposite of how you expect. Do you sense any irony in the way Arturo's visit ends?

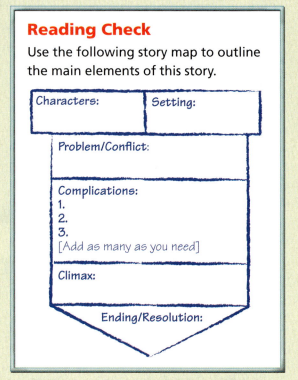

Reading Check

Use the following story map to outline the main elements of this story.

Characters:

Setting:

Problem/Conflict:

Complications:
1.
2.
3.
[Add as many as you need]

Climax:

Ending/Resolution:

Comparing Literature

6. Fill in the second column in a chart like the one below to help you identify the critical moments in Arturo's emotional journey. You can use your chart to help you write the comparison-contrast essay on the next page.

Comparing Moments of Recognition		
	"The Medicine Bag"	"An Hour with Abuelo"
Details about main character		
What he thinks of his grandfather at beginning of story		
What he thinks of his grandfather at end of story		
Moment(s) of recognition		

SKILLS FOCUS

Literary Skills
Analyze plot.

Reading Skills
Compare and contrast stories.

Comparing "The Medicine Bag" with "An Hour with Abuelo"

Assignment
1. Writing a Comparison-Contrast Essay

Compare the experiences of Martin from "The Medicine Bag" with those of Arturo from "An Hour with Abuelo." To help plan your essay, review the chart you completed after you read each story. The chart will help you focus on key elements in the stories and how they are similar and how they are different.

You can use the following outline to organize your essay:

I. **Main Characters**
    A. Martin
    B. Arturo
II. **Conflict**
    A. Martin's feelings about his great-grandfather
    B. Arturo's feelings about his grandfather
III. **Resolution**
    A. What Martin learned from his great-grandfather
    B. What Arturo learned from his grandfather

> Use the workshop on writing a Comparison-Contrast Essay, pages 516–521, for help with this assignment.

Assignment
2. Evaluating Oral History

Most cultures tell stories to pass down knowledge, traditions, and beliefs. The older generation tells stories to the younger generation to help them understand what has come before them. Interview an older relative or friend about an aspect of his or her life that you are not familiar with. Write down the story or stories you hear. With a partner or group, discuss what these stories tell you about your family's traditions, values, and beliefs.

Assignment
3. Writing a Persuasive Essay

Some people think that our society doesn't have ways of helping young people cross the threshold into adulthood. We need traditions and meaningful rituals for this important rite of passage, they say. In what ways do people today mark the passage into adulthood? Do you think there should be other ways of helping young people to accept the duties and responsibilities of adult life? Do you think, instead, that things are all right the way they are? In a brief essay, explain your point of view. Support your beliefs with details.

SKILLS FOCUS

Writing Skills
Write a comparison-contrast essay; evaluate oral history; write a persuasive essay.

The Old Grandfather and His Little Grandson

traditional European, retold by **Leo Tolstoy**

The grandfather had become very old. His legs would not carry him, his eyes could not see, his ears could not hear, and he was toothless. When he ate, bits of food sometimes dropped out of his mouth. His son and his son's wife no longer allowed him to eat with them at the table. He had to eat his meals in the corner near the stove.

Tolstoy with his grandson.

One day they gave him his food in a bowl. He tried to move the bowl closer; it fell to the floor and broke. His daughter-in-law scolded him. She told him that he spoiled everything in the house and broke their dishes, and she said that from now on he would get his food in a wooden dish. The old man sighed and said nothing.

A few days later, the old man's son and his wife were sitting in their hut, resting and watching their little boy playing on the floor. They saw him putting together something out of small pieces of wood. His father asked him, "What are you making, Misha?"

The little grandson said, "I'm making a wooden bucket. When you and Mama get old, I'll feed you out of this wooden dish."

The young peasant and his wife looked at each other and tears filled their eyes. They were ashamed because they had treated the old grandfather so meanly, and from that day they again let the old man eat with them at the table and took better care of him.

Meet the Writer

Leo Tolstoy

A Writer and a Reformer

When Count **Leo Nikolayevich Tolstoy** (lē′ō nē′kô·lä′ye·vich′ tôl′stoi′) (1828–1910) died in a railroad station at the age of eighty-two, he may have been the most famous man in the world. His death from pneumonia was front-page news in England and America. For, in addition to being the greatest living Russian novelist, Tolstoy was also a social and religious reformer.

Tolstoy was born to wealthy parents, but he became an orphan when he was nine. He and his siblings were raised by aunts on the family estate. At nineteen, Tolstoy split his inheritance with his brothers and became the master of his family's estate.

Within three years, Tolstoy managed to gamble away about one fourth of his inheritance. Looking for adventure, he joined the Russian army and fought bravely during the Crimean War (a war over southeastern Europe during the 1850s). The sufferings that he witnessed during the war helped bring out his serious nature.

In 1862, Tolstoy married Sonya Andreyevna Behrs. In addition to bearing him thirteen children, Sonya recopied her husband's unreadable manuscripts and took over the management of his estate, allowing Tolstoy to write his greatest works, *War and Peace* and *Anna Karenina.*

Later in life, Tolstoy spoke out against the Russian government, capitalism, and the Orthodox Church. He rejected much of his earlier writing for its focus on the Russian upper classes. Tolstoy became the leader of a movement that championed the poor. His ideas inspired later nonviolent reformers such as Mahatma Gandhi and Martin Luther King, Jr.

Writing Workshop

Assignment

Write a short story on a topic of your choice.

Audience

Children, teenagers, or adults.

RUBRIC
Evaluation Criteria

A good story

1. focuses on a conflict that the characters must resolve
2. includes a series of related events that lead to a climax
3. develops characters through dialogue and action
4. provides vivid details of the setting
5. ends with a resolution of the conflict
6. reveals a theme

Writing Skills
Write a short story.

NARRATIVE WRITING
Short Story

Reading stories is a pleasure most of us experience throughout our lives. Writing stories can also be enjoyable. Writing a story gives you a chance to unlock your imagination and let your ideas flow. In this workshop you will write a short story to share with others.

Prewriting

1 Choosing an Idea for a Story

A **prompt** can sometimes help you find a story idea. Read and respond to the following prompt:

> We generally write best about the things we know well. Even though a short story is a fictional narrative, the characters and events need to have points of contact with real life. Characters who occupy an imaginary world still need to remind us of our own thoughts and feelings. Create a short story that shows the connection between real and imaginary worlds.

If you're stuck, choose a story from this anthology or another story you have read, and jot down responses to one or more of the following questions:

- What would happen to the story's characters if they were placed in another setting?
- What would happen if other characters were placed in the story's setting?
- What might have happened before the events of the story? What might happen after?
- How would the story change if it were told from another character's point of view?

2 Planning Your Story Characters

Begin with characters. Use your imagination to flesh them out. Use the list of questions that appear under **Developing Characters** on page 785.

Plot

For your plot, plan four elements:

- A conflict, or struggle. The basis of your story will be how characters deal with this conflict.
- A series of related events set in motion by the conflict. Keep readers guessing by using suspense.
- A climax, or high point, when the conflict is settled.
- A resolution, or outcome, showing how things work out.

Setting

Use these questions to plan your setting:

- When and where does your story take place?
- What objects and scenery are important to the setting?
- What length of time does your story cover?
- Is the setting part of the conflict?

Point of View

All short stories have a narrator who tells the story. A story may be told from the first-person point of view or the third-person point of view. Be consistent in the point of view you choose for your story.

Drafting

1 Crafting a Strong Beginning

Your first sentence should catch the reader's attention. Arouse your reader's curiosity by creating suspense and by showing your characters in action.

2 Showing Cause and Effect

A plot is a series of events related by cause and effect. As you write, make sure that there is a logical connection in the sequence of events leading toward the climax.

3 Rounding Out the Ending

Show how characters are affected by the resolution of the conflict. Have they changed or learned something? Does your ending suggest an overall theme?

Developing Characters

Jot down answers to the following questions to bring your characters to life:

- How do the characters look?
- What do they think?
- What do they say?
- How do they act?
- What do others say about the characters?
- How do others act around them or react to them?

Writing Tip

Observing Setting

Try looking at your everyday surroundings as if you had never seen them before. What color are the desks in your classroom, for example? Where are the windows, and how many are there? For five minutes, write down as many details of a **setting** as you can.

Framework for a Short Story

Beginning

Describe setting and main character(s).

_____

_____

Introduce conflict.

_____

_____

Middle

Write events in time order, building toward a climax and keeping readers in suspense.

Event #1:

_____

Event #2:

_____

Event #3:

_____

End

Resolve story's conflict, and tie up loose ends.

_____

_____

go.
hrw
.com

INTERNET

More Writer's Models

Keyword: LE5 8-7

Student Model

Experiment 023681

"They're still regressing," said Martak, as he raised his head from the viewing screen. He wore a look of disappointment on his face. "I can't see much use in the continued funding of Experiment 023681. We have others which are working much better."

"Very well," rumbled the deep voice of Martak's supervisor. "It's too bad, though. They seemed so promising."

"I know, I know. Disappointing, isn't it?" commented Martak. "But living conditions are horrible, they insist on killing each other in these petty little things called 'wars,' and look at their life span: on the outside, ninety-five of their 'years'!"

"I agree. OK. You now officially have permission to terminate Experiment 023681."

Johnny gazed on his mostly finished sand castle and felt all the pride a four-year-old could have. He noticed it was getting dark, though, so he proceeded at top speed.

Martak looked at the small mass of swirling blues, greens, and whites for one last time. Then he slowly pushed the red button and entered his access code.

"Request?" questioned a tinny voice from a grille in the wall.

"Terminate Experiment 023681."

"Request confirmed . . ."

5—

Johnny looked up. Did he hear his mother calling him? He couldn't be sure, so he went back to playing in his sandbox.

"John!" screamed his mother from the house.

Suspense is created by the title.

Action and character conveyed through **dialogue.**

Shift to **point of view** of a new character.

Suspense is added by countdown, descriptive details, and mother's voice.

4—

Johnny sighed and dropped his shovel as he slowly trudged toward his house. He knew his mother meant it when she just said "John." He looked up at the darkening sky and saw the first stars.

3—

"*Now,* John!" yelled his mother.

"I'm coming!" he responded. He ambled to the porch, cleaned his shoes, and began to walk inside. On some unexplainable impulse, he turned and looked at the sky once more.

2—

Man, that's a bright star up there! Hmmm, it seems to be growing larger! I guess it's an airplane, he decided. He opened the door and went in.

He then moved to the window and looked out. Man, it's even bigger! It looked like a big flashlight had been shone on the house.

1—

He heard his mother yell at him to get away from the window, and his father yell something about invaders, but he was entranced.

0

Martak watched as the small, perfect sphere was engulfed in a yellow flame. The flame slowly turned orange, then red, then finally settled into a black cloud which died, leaving behind only dust. He sighed regretfully, as Johnny had done, and turned to the next experiment.

Climax of story and outcome.

    —Peter Leary
    Athens Academy
    Athens, GA

Strategies For Elaboration

To write realistic **dialogue,** listen closely to people talking. Take note of the following:

- use of contractions and slang
- use of half-finished sentences and phrases
- interruptions—how, when, and why speakers interrupt one another

Read your dialogue aloud. Keep revising it until it sounds real.

Communications Handbook
H E L P

See Proofreaders' Marks.

Evaluating and Revising

Use the following chart to evaluate and revise your essay.

Short Story: Content and Organization Guidelines		
Evaluation Questions	▶ **Tips**	▶ **Revision Techniques**
❶ Does your story contain an interesting, well-developed plot? Does the conflict create suspense?	▶ **Place a check mark** next to each element: beginning, conflict, complications, climax, and resolution.	▶ **Add** or **elaborate** on plot elements as necessary. **Delete** details that spoil the suspense.
❷ Are main characters complex and convincing?	▶ **Underline** character details, description, and dialogue.	▶ **Add** details about appearance, personality, or background. **Add** dialogue and actions that reveal character, if needed.
❸ Does the story establish a definite setting? Does the setting evoke a mood?	▶ **Highlight** details about the setting and mood.	▶ **Elaborate** on the setting, if necessary, by adding descriptive details.
❹ Are events arranged in a coherent order? Are transitions used to show order?	▶ **Number** the major events. **Put a star** next to transitional expressions.	▶ **Rearrange** any events that are out of order. **Add** transitional words and phrases, if necessary, to show the order of events.
❺ Is the point of view clear and consistent?	▶ **Circle** pronouns that show whether the point of view is first or third person.	▶ **Cut** pronouns or details that shift the point of view.
❻ Does the story reveal a theme?	▶ **Underline** clues that point to the theme.	▶ **Add** details or sentences that clarify your theme.

On page 789, you'll find the opening paragraphs of a short story that has been revised. Following the Revision Model are questions to help you evaluate the writer's revisions.

Revision Model

Greg looked out his bedroom window at the ^{gray, dismal} sky. It was

raining again. It had rained on those two other days also.

Perhaps it was ~~a bad sign~~ ^{an omen} that this day would end like

those others ^{—in failure}.

Around the kitchen table ^{that morning}, his mother and sister had ^{carefully}

avoided the topic that was on everyone's mind.

Would he be the only senior at Wilson High without a

driver's license? He had already failed the test twice.

"You're too uptight," the examiner told him ^{, after he had missed a stop sign on the second test}. Greg then

tried to relax behind the wheel when his father took him

out on practice sessions. ~~It didn't help.~~ Greg found that he

was ~~holding~~ ^{gripping} the steering wheel too tightly and pumping

the brake at every intersection. Greg ^{, however,} had a sinking feeling

that he would be a washout again. "You're ready," his

father said. "You'll be sure to pass the next time."

Evaluating the Revision

1. How has the writer elaborated on key details?

2. Where has the writer rearranged text? Does this improve
the passage?

PROOFREADING
TIPS

- *Exchange papers with a partner, and proofread each other's work. Find and correct errors in spelling, punctuation, capitalization, and grammar before you prepare your final draft. Use the spellchecker on your computer if you have one.*

- *If you're working on a computer, you may want to mark corrections on a printout, so you can have a record of your changes.*

- *If there is dialogue, check the rules for using quotation marks, 14c–j, in the Language Handbook.*

PUBLISHING
TIPS

- *Submit your story to the school literary magazine or another publication that accepts student writing.*

- *Consider adding illustrations to your story. Draw your own pictures, or use clip art from a computer.*

Test Practice

DIRECTIONS: Read the story. Then, answer each question that follows.

This excerpt is from a story that takes place during Hanukkah, the Jewish Festival of Lights, which usually begins in December. Hanukkah celebrates the rededication of the Temple in Jerusalem in 165 B.C. Another Jewish holiday, Purim, mentioned in the first paragraph, is a spring festival that honors Queen Esther.

from Just Enough Is Plenty: A Hanukkah Tale
Barbara Diamond Goldin

Malka's family lived in a village in Poland. They were poor, but not so poor. They had candles for the Sabbath, noisemakers for Purim, and spinning tops for Hanukkah.

Mama was busy preparing for tonight, the first of the eight nights of Hanukkah. She peeled onions and grated potatoes for the latkes, the potato pancakes.

Malka's younger brother Zalman carved a dreidel, a spinning top.

"This dreidel will spin the fastest of all," he boasted.

Papa was working long hours in his tailor shop so they could buy more food for the holiday. More potatoes, more onions, more flour, more oil.

For on the first night of Hanukkah, Malka's family always invited many guests. But this year only Aunt Hindy and Uncle Shmuel were coming to visit.

"Only two guests?" Malka asked. "Last year, we had so many guests that Papa had to put boards over the pickle barrels to make the table big enough."

"That was last year," Mama said gently. "This year has not been a good one for Papa in the shop. People bring him just a little mending here, a little mending there. He cannot afford to buy new material to sew fancy holiday dresses and fine suits."

"But it's Hanukkah," Malka reminded Mama.

Mama patted Malka's shoulder. "Don't worry, Malkaleh. We know how to stretch. We're poor, but not so poor. Now go. Ask Papa if he has a few more coins. I need more eggs for the latkes."

SKILLS FOCUS

Literary Skills
Analyze a story using a biographical approach to literary criticism.

Meet the Writer

When she wrote this story, **Barbara Diamond Goldin** was a preschool teacher and storyteller who lived with her husband and two children in Northampton, Massachusetts. Three of her grandparents came from Poland. It was only in doing research for this book that she learned how they probably lived before coming to America. Perhaps this fictional story could be *their* true story!

1. The setting, a village in Poland, reflects the writer's **heritage** because —

   A Poland is where she was born

   B some of her grandparents came from Poland

   C many Americans came from Poland

   D Poland is a good place for a story

2. "She peeled onions and grated potatoes for the latkes, the potato pancakes." **Context clues** in this sentence tell you that *latkes* are —

   F peeled onions

   G grated potatoes

   H potato pancakes

   J Polish lakes

3. Hanukkah **traditions** mentioned in this excerpt include —

   A eating potato pancakes

   B working long hours

   C blowing loud noisemakers

   D living in Poland

4. When Mama says, "We're poor, but not so poor," she is expressing the **belief** that —

   F they have enough

   G they are really rich

   H poverty doesn't matter

   J it's better to be poor

5. In doing research for this book, the writer learned more about —

   A teaching preschool

   B life in Massachusetts

   C Polish immigration

   D her Polish heritage

Constructed Response

6. Name at least two Hanukkah **traditions** that are mentioned in the story excerpt.

Test Practice

DIRECTIONS: Read the article. Then, answer each question that follows.

Blasting Through Bedrock: The Central Pacific Railroad Workers

Flo Ota De Lange

1 In the winter of 1866–1867, blizzards gripped the Sierra Nevada. Dwellings were buried in blowing, shifting, drifting, driving snow. Men who were building the western portion of the country's first transcontinental railroad had to tunnel from their camp to the mountainside, where they spent long, cold days digging out rock so tracks could be laid. The Central Pacific Railroad was building east from California to meet the Union Pacific Railroad, which was working west from Omaha, Nebraska.

2 Who were these hardy workers who survived the blizzards and helped build the nation's first transcontinental railroad? Most of them were immigrants from China. When other railroad hands saw the newly hired Chinese workers, they were scornful. How could these young men, averaging about four feet ten inches in height, heave a large shovelful of rock? The other workers either didn't know or had forgotten that the ancestors of

these men had built one of the Seven Wonders of the World—the Great Wall of China—which was begun in 221 B.C. The wall extends more than four thousand miles and averages about twenty-six feet high and twenty feet wide!

3 At the start the Central Pacific Railroad hired fifty Chinese laborers. These men knew little about railroad grading, but they learned quickly. Eventually the Chinese labor force grew to between ten thousand and twelve thousand workers. These men dug, blasted tunnels, and laid track up the Sierra Nevada, over the Donner Pass, and down through the deserts of Nevada.

4 People often credit the transcontinental railroad to men of vision—engineers, financiers, and politicians—without acknowledging the way their vision became a reality. As the president of the Central Pacific Railroad and former governor of California, Leland Stanford, wrote to

SKILLS FOCUS

Reading Skills
Analyze an article's logic, coherence, and consistency.

President Andrew Johnson on October 19, 1865, "The greater portion of the laborers employed by us are Chinese. . . . Without them it would be impossible to complete the western portion of this great national enterprise within the time required by the Acts of Congress."

5 Complete it these workers did! Cannons roared in New York City and San Francisco when the telegraph lines carried the news: The Union Pacific and the Central Pacific Railroad lines had met at Promontory, Utah, on May 10, 1869.

1. Which of the following details would be consistent with the **unity** of paragraph 1?

   A The Great Pyramids are also among the Seven Wonders of the World.

   B The Great Wall of China ascends steep ridges angled at seventy degrees.

   C Many people died from cave-ins and avalanches during the blizzards.

   D Building model trains is a rewarding and enjoyable hobby.

2. Read these sentences from paragraph 1. Which of the transition words that follow could be used to connect the two sentences **coherently**?

   "Dwellings were buried in blowing, shifting, drifting, driving snow. Men . . . had to tunnel from their camp to the mountainside. . . ."

   F before

   G however

   H although

   J therefore

3. Which of the following sentences could be added to this article without destroying its **internal consistency**?

   A During blizzards, people cannot see in front of them, and so they bump into things.

   B Chinese workers did backbreaking work from sunup to sundown six days a week.

   C Asa Whitney was the first to see the importance of a transcontinental railroad.

   D It took fourteen train lines to get Lincoln's body from Washington, D.C., to Illinois.

Constructed Response

4. What is the **main idea** of this article?

Test Practice

Multiple-Meaning Words

DIRECTIONS: Use context clues to identify the meaning of each underlined word as it is used in the sentence. (Sentences are taken from "Ribbons.")

1. "Dad's head was just disappearing as he leaned into the trunk of the car." In this sentence, *trunk* means —

   A   large stem of a tree

   B   long snout

   C   large suitcase

   D   compartment at the back of a car

2. "Because Grandmother's airfare and legal expenses had been so high, there wasn't room in the family budget for Madame Oblomov's ballet school." In this sentence, *high* means —

   F   tall

   G   lofty

   H   costly

   J   excited

3. "'Nice children don't drool on people,' she snapped at me." In this sentence, *snapped* means —

   A   bit suddenly

   B   snatched quickly

   C   spoke sharply

   D   broke apart

4. "Crouching, he used the cords to lift a box in each hand." In this sentence, *lift* means —

   F   raise

   G   ride

   H   steal

   J   elevator

5. "Suddenly I felt lost, and the following weeks only made me more confused." In this sentence, *lost* means —

   A   mislaid

   B   unseen

   C   bewildered

   D   wasted

6. "When I complained to Mom about how Grandmother was spoiling Ian, she only sighed." In this sentence, *spoiling* means —

   F   destroying

   G   decaying

   H   marring

   J   overindulging

SKILLS FOCUS

Vocabulary Skills
Analyze multiple-meaning words.

Collection 7: Skills Review

Writing Skills

Test Practice

DIRECTIONS: Read the following passage from a short story. Then, answer each question that follows.

(1) Jesse nervously approached the front porch of his house and stopped before climbing the steps. (2) His mother was probably in the kitchen preparing dinner. (3) His father wouldn't be home for another hour. (4) He knew his family's routine. (5) Wearily, Jesse slipped his backpack off and dropped it on the steps. (6) He froze in terror. (7) Inside the cover of his notebook, there was a letter addressed to his parents. (8) The letter was from the principal. (9) It claimed that Jesse had been caught plagiarizing a social studies report. (10) How was he going to face his parents?

1. The main character in this story is —
   A   the principal
   B   Jesse's mother
   C   Jesse's father
   D   Jesse

2. Which sentence is unnecessary and can be deleted?
   F   Sentence 4
   G   Sentence 7
   H   Sentence 8
   J   Sentence 9

3. A **cliché** is a phrase or expression that has been used so much it seems stale. Which sentence contains a cliché?
   A   Sentence 2
   B   Sentence 3
   C   Sentence 6
   D   Sentence 8

4. What would be the best way to combine Sentences 7 and 8?
   F   Inside the cover of his notebook, there was a letter addressed to his parents and it was from the principal.
   G   A letter that had been addressed to his parents and which was from the principal was inside the cover of his notebook.
   H   A letter from the principal addressed to his parents was inside the cover of his notebook.
   J   Having been signed by the principal, a letter addressed to his parents was inside the cover of his notebook.

5. To develop this story, the writer must do all of the following *except* —
   A   demonstrate motivation for the main character's actions
   B   provide a happy ending
   C   develop the internal and external conflicts
   D   bring events to a climax

SKILLS FOCUS

Writing Skills
Analyze a short story.

Fiction

Serious Consequences

Ailin's family resists breaking with ancient Chinese traditions in a time of social change. On the other hand, Ailin does not wish to have her feet bound and does not wish to be married to someone who has been selected for her. In Lensey Namioka's *Ties That Bind, Ties That Break,* Ailin must choose between pleasing her family and pleasing herself.

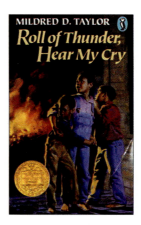

I'll Stand My Ground

Eight-year-old Cassie Logan does not understand the startling actions of white landowners in Depression-era Mississippi. Over the course of a year, she learns another lesson—why her family is desperately fighting to hold on to the land they call home. In *Roll of Thunder, Hear My Cry,* Mildred Taylor tells a story of pride and courage that all families can learn from.

A Blessing or a Curse?

Ella received a gift from a fairy on the day she was born. While this may sound exciting, Ella has never appreciated the gift because it is the gift of obedience. She has to do whatever anyone tells her to do. In Gail Carson Levine's Newbery Medal winner *Ella Enchanted,* Ella goes on a mission to change the way things are. She won't allow ogres, elves, or fairy godmothers to get in her way in this retelling of the Cinderella story.

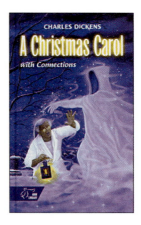

The Meaning of Christmas

During his lifetime, Charles Dickens was known for his acts of charity. Perhaps that aspect of Dickens's character inspired his holiday classic, *A Christmas Carol.* Ebenezer Scrooge, a bitter, selfish old man, is unmoved by the holiday season. With the help of three Christmas spirits, he is able to change the course of his life and discover the joys of giving and of love.

This title is available in the HRW Library.

Nonfiction

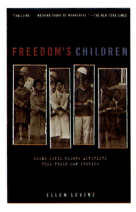

Oh, Freedom

What was it like to walk through angry, violent mobs to integrate an all-white school? to be arrested for refusing to give up a seat at the front of a bus? to fight for freedom when other people your age were going to sports practice or attending their first dance? In *Freedom's Children,* Ellen Levine presents oral histories by African Americans who were involved as children or teenagers in the civil rights movement of the 1950s and 1960s.

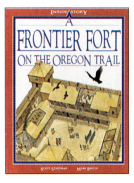

Settling Down

In *A Frontier Fort on the Oregon Trail,* Scott Steedman and Mark Bergin look at the way people lived in the Old West. Bergin's detailed illustrations present a typical day in the life of a soldier, a homemaker, and a trapper. Steedman fleshes out the illustrations with helpful text, including an explanation of how a cabin and a fort were built in the "New World."

Starting Out

Today, the only work most children in the United States have to worry about is schoolwork. Sadly, this was not always the case. In *Immigrant Kids,* Russell Freedman looks at how young people lived in the late nineteenth and early twentieth centuries, when children often had to take jobs and work under unsafe and exhausting conditions. Photographs from the period help us empathize with the sufferings of these children.

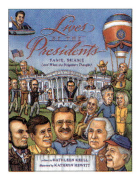

Not in the Newspapers

Are you ever curious about the hobbies of America's leaders? Do you want to know about their interesting quirks, favorite foods, and most beloved pets? Do you ever wonder where they grew up and how they lived after they left office? You can find out in *Lives of the Presidents* by Kathleen Krull. The book also contains a wealth of information about first ladies and the children of presidents.

Reading for Life

Informational Focus:

- **Using Documents to Solve a Problem**

- **Analyzing Consumer Materials**

- **Explaining How to Use Technical Devices**

INTERNET

Collection Resources

Keyword: LE5 8-8

Reading Informational Texts

Documents for Life

by Sheri Henderson

Read All About It

Life today can get pretty complicated as we race down the information superhighway. Let's say you want to do something easy, like go to a movie. There's nothing complicated about that. All you need to know is where and when the movie is playing. Actually there are many other choices you can make. Besides learning the time and place, you can read reviews by critics or by "regular" people like you, get in-depth information about the cast and director, reserve seats for yourself and your friends, view film clips and ads, purchase tie-in items like T-shirts, and even join a fan club. To do all this, you might use the telephone, TV, the Internet, e-mail, snail mail, instant messaging, or a fax. You might browse through a newspaper or magazine, a bookstore, a library, or a mall. In the process you would be reading a variety of information-based documents. Our world is full of them, and they come in three basic types.

Workplace Documents

The odds are good that in the next thirty years you will hold a variety of jobs. The job you volunteer for at age thirteen will probably be very different from the one you accept at age forty-three. Whether you are taking orders for fast food or giving orders to a staff of a thousand, your job will probably require you to **read for information.** When earning a living is involved, that information is important. **Workplace documents** serve two basic functions:

- **Communication.** E-mail, memorandums (memos), and reports will tell you about upcoming meetings, changes in policy, and other information you need to know in order to do your job. You will need to pay close attention to the information conveyed.

- **Instruction.** Employee manuals tell what is expected of you on the job. User's guides teach you how to operate the equipment you use. These, too, will be essential to your success at work.

Public Documents

Public documents consist of information concerning public agencies and not-for-profit groups. They can be about voting issues, health concerns, community decisions, and a host of other subjects. Public documents inform people of situations, decisions, responsibilities, schedules, occasions, and events that may interest them. If you become involved with a government agency, school, park, library, or volunteer group, you'll be using public documents. If you vote, drive, call the fire or police department, or address the city council, you'll use public documents. Public documents exist to tell people what is happening in their own community, city, state, and nation and even on the planet.

Consumer Documents

A **consumer** is someone who buys something or uses what someone else buys. That covers just about everyone: you, your friends—even a baby. The things we—consumers—buy fall into two basic categories: goods (stuff) and services (help). Many goods are simple to use: You don't need an instruction manual to show you what to do with a candy bar! More complicated goods may not be so easy to use. You buy a computer. Now what? You'll need some information to get your computer up and running. Therefore, your computer package will include some or all of the following documents:

- **product information** that tells what the computer will do

- a **contract** that spells out exactly what services will and will not be provided

- a **warranty** that spells out exactly what happens if the computer doesn't work properly and what you are required to do to receive service

- an **instruction manual** that tells how to set up and use the computer

- **technical directions** that give precise technical information about installing and assembling the computer and any peripheral devices, like printers

These **consumer documents** give you the information you need to select, purchase, and use your computer. They also define legal rights and responsibilities: yours, those of the company that made the computer, and those of the company that sold it.

Read the Fine Print

Have you ever heard someone say, "Read the fine print"? There's good reason for that warning. As a consumer you are responsible for understanding whether or not the goods are what you want or need before you buy them. If they aren't, you may run into difficulties getting a refund or an exchange. Company policies differ on returns and exchanges. Most stores will let you return clothes if you change your mind before you wear them, but they may not take back other goods. Before you buy, read the fine print.

Product information on the box or label is the first place to check to see that the item is really what you want. Is the dress washable? Does the CD player have all the features you want? Before you buy something, read all about it.

Contracts define what you are getting, what it costs, and how long the agreement lasts. Contracts are generally binding once you or your parent or guardian signs them (in most states you have to be eighteen or older to sign a legal contract). The signature shows that you have agreed to what the contract says. "I didn't know" is not an acceptable excuse if you become unhappy with the terms. Before you sign, read the fine print.

Warranties guarantee that the product will work for a specified period of time. Warranties give you an idea of how reliable the product is and what the company will do if it breaks. The company may repair a defective product or give you a new one. Before you buy, read the details.

Instruction manuals are also important. If you break an item because you didn't read the instructions for installation or proper use, you will be out of luck (and some money). Your warranty will not cover the loss. Before you operate a new product, read the manual.

Technical directions are often included when an item is complicated or mechanical in nature. They lay out the steps you must follow to assemble or operate a device. If a step is skipped or performed out of order, the device may not work or may even break. When

you're following technical directions, it's a good idea to

- read the directions all the way through before you begin
- check off the steps one by one as you complete them
- compare your work with the diagrams and drawings for each step

Take the Time to Read It

Reading an owner's manual and the fine print in a warranty and a contract requires discipline when you are just itching to use your new purchase and start having fun with it. Patience! Perseverance! It's better to spend a few minutes slogging through difficult reading than to get stuck with an item that doesn't suit your needs, costs more than it has to, or gets broken right out of the box.

You can see how important information-based documents are. The pages that follow will give you some practice with them. Remember: Patience! Perseverance! This is *your* life—and perhaps your allowance.

Reading Skills and Strategies

Information, Please *by* Kylene Beers

Long ago people painted pictures on cave walls. Sometimes those paintings told stories. Other times they conveyed information. Today we've traded cave walls for e-zines and e-books and have replaced cave paintings with word processing, but we're still doing the same thing as our ancestors—leaving behind stories and sharing information.

Reading informational texts is both similar to and different from reading stories. Think about what these similarities and differences might be.

Narrative Versus Informational Text

Whether reading a fictional **narrative** (writing that tells a story) or a nonfiction **informational** text (a text that explains something), you do the following things:

- Think about what the text tells you.
- Compare and contrast.
- Predict what will happen.
- Summarize what has happened.
- Sequence the events.
- Note cause-and-effect relationships.
- Make inferences.
- Draw conclusions.

So how do narrative texts differ from expository texts? The most basic difference is that almost all fiction follows a narrative structure and much of nonfiction follows an expository, or explanatory, structure.

Tips for Reading Informational Texts

1. If the text has **numbered steps,** think of someone telling you, "First, do this. Next, do that."

2. Look for **subheads.** Subheads are like someone saying, "Look here! This is a new topic!"

3. Watch for **boldface** or *italic* type. This signals something important.

4. Look for **graphics** like maps or charts. They give you additional information.

5. Look for words and phrases that signal a **comparison** (*similarly, likewise*) or a **contrast** (*on the other hand, however, others believe*).

6. Look for words and phrases that signal a **cause-and-effect** relationship (*as a result, therefore, consequently*).

Use these tips as you read "Tools of the Trade."

SKILLS FOCUS

Reading Skills
Understand how to read informational texts.

As you read, you'll find this open-book sign at certain points in the text: . Stop at these points, and think about what you've just read.

❶ The first paragraph begins with "In the old days." The second paragraph begins with "Nowadays." Why is it important to notice how those two paragraphs begin?

❷ Notice the word *however* in the first line of the third paragraph. What contrast does this word indicate?

❸ Scan this page. Notice the use of bullets and boldface subheads. Why do you think the writer decided to emphasize those subheads?

Tools of the Trade

from The Newspaper Designer's Handbook
Tim Harrower

In the old days, page designers spent a lot of time drawing boxes (to show where photos went). And drawing lines (to show where text went). And drawing *more* boxes (for graphics and sidebars and logos).

Nowadays, most designers do their drawing on computers. But those old tools of the trade are still handy: pencils (for drawing lines), rulers (for measuring lines), calculators (for estimating the sizes of those lines and boxes), and our old favorite, the proportion wheel (to calculate the dimensions of boxes as they grow larger or smaller). ❶

The electronic newsroom has arrived, however. So if you're serious about newspapering, get comfortable with computers. They're indispensable tools that improve performance and save time when it comes to ❷

- **Writing and editing stories.** Most newsrooms tossed out their typewriters years ago. Today, reporters and editors use computers to type, edit, file stories, fit headlines and search databases.

- **Producing photos.** Digital photography lets you adjust the size, shape, and quality of images electronically.

- **Pagination.** At most newspapers, pages are created electronically with desktop-publishing software.

- **Creating illustrations and graphics.** With a good drawing program, it's easy to create full-color artwork in any style. And even if you're not an artist, you can still buy clip art or subscribe to wire services, which provide first-class graphics you can rework, resize, or simply store in an electronic archive for later use. ❸

Some of the computer accessories newspaper people use are shown on the opposite page.

Computer Accessories

Floppy disks and CDs:
Information can be stored in a computer's internal memory drive, or it can be transported from computer to computer via portable disks. Floppy disks came first; they can hold a megabyte or two. Compact disks (CDs) are far more powerful, storing 600 megabytes of data— perfect for photos, video, and music.

Printer: *Once you design your news feature on the computer, how do you print the thing out? Many desktop publishers use laser printers like this one: high resolution devices that output near-typeset quality type and graphics.* ❹

ANALYZE

❹ Notice how the photos are integrated with the text. Why might it be important to place the photos of the machines beside the text that explains what they do?

Scanner: *This device can capture photos or artwork electronically. It scans images like a photocopying machine, after which you can adjust their size, shape and exposure on your computer screen—avoiding the traditional darkroom altogether.*

Modem: *A device that allows computers to communicate with each other and transmit data (text, images, page layouts) over telephone lines. Newer computers use their built-in modems to link users to electronic databases and information services.*

Before you can store your news story on a disk, you must format the disk, or prepare it to receive data. The following directions show how to accomplish this using a PC. Keep in mind, however, that operating systems are constantly being updated, so directions may vary slightly depending on the computer you're working on.

Formatting a Disk on a PC

If you have this type of computer, you can format a disk in two major ways.

Using DOS:

1. Turn on the computer.

2. Use the DOS commands when your screen displays the C prompt (C:\ or C:\>).

3. If Windows loads automatically when you turn on your computer, you can get back to the C prompt by double-clicking with the mouse or highlighting the arrow keys and pressing ENTER on the MS-DOS icon on the Main Windows window.

4. Insert a disk in Drive A to start formatting.

Using Format Disk Command:

1. Turn on the computer.

2. Insert a disk in Drive A.

3. Double-click on the File Manager icon, which will display the File Manager window on the screen.

4. Click and hold on Disk at the very top of the File Manager window.

5. Move the mouse's arrow down to the Format disk.

6. Release the mouse's button.

7. A Format Disk window will appear on the screen.

8. If it doesn't say Drive A, click on the arrow next to the Disk In Box.

9. Click on OK to start formatting. ❺

ANALYZE

❺ The writer presents the information in this section in lists instead of running it together in paragraphs. Is the numbered-list format helpful? Why or why not?

Reading Informational Texts

PRACTICE 1

Look back at "Tools of the Trade." Think about the tips you read on page 803 as you answer these questions:

1. Why did the author boldface some of the words on page 804?

2. What information do the pictures on pages 805–806 give you that the text doesn't? Is it important to look at the pictures? Explain.

3. Why were numbered lists used on the last page of the article?

PRACTICE 2

Authors try to make explanations in expository texts clearer by using words that signal a sequence, a comparison or a contrast, or a cause-and-effect relationship. Look through "Tools of the Trade" for the following signal words or phrases. What is each word or phrase signaling?

a) Before

b) The following

c) If . . . you

d) However

SKILLS FOCUS

Reading Skills
Use specific strategies for reading informational texts.

Using Documents to Solve a Problem

Reading Focus

Using Information from Documents to Solve a Problem

We live in a complex society. As a participant in that society, you'll often need to read a variety of documents in order to understand all sides of a situation or the reasons for a decision. Sometimes you'll vote on the solution you prefer. Sometimes you'll ask your government to listen to your views before making a decision. Either way you'll want to have your facts straight, and that means reading carefully.

■ In the following pages you'll find **consumer, public,** and **workplace documents** that concern specific problems faced by communities perhaps like your own. Pretend you are a member of these communities. What are the problems? What needs haven't been met? What concerns are voiced? The annotations beside each document show the kind of critical thinking you might do in order to understand the situation. Once you get your facts straight, you'll be able to find the right solution.

SKILLS FOCUS

Reading Skills
Use information from documents to solve a problem.

Skateboard Park Documents

MEMORANDUM

From: A. Longboard, Assistant Director of Parks and Recreation
To: J. Cool, Director of Parks and Recreation
Re: Establishment of a Permanent Skateboard Park

> The Parks and Recreation Department is thinking about building a skateboard park.

Critical Issues

A. Need. Ten percent of the families in this city, about seven thousand households, include at least one skateboarder. The city provides no designated space for skateboarding. Police reports show that citations for illegal skating are rising every month. This problem is particularly acute in downtown areas, leading to complaints from businesses. The nearest public skateboard park is twenty miles to the east in Mogul, where illegal skating dropped sharply when its park opened last year.

> There is a clear need: 7,000+ skaters, no existing park, business complaints, tickets. What about injuries?

B. Liability. California AB 1296 states that persons who skateboard on public property are expected to know that it is a potentially dangerous sport. They cannot sue the city, county, or state for their injuries as long as the city has passed an ordinance requiring

- helmet, kneepads, and elbow pads for all skaters in the park
- clear and visible signs warning citizens of this requirement
- citations for skaters who violate the ordinance

Such an ordinance was enacted by our city council on July 15, 2000. Therefore, building a skateboard park would not pose a liability risk to the city as long as the above requirements are met.

> Looks as if the city would not be at risk of injury lawsuits. Good. How would we keep kids safe, though?

C. Cost. Local groups have raised half the necessary $140,000. The Parks and Recreation Department's budget can fund the other half. Costs will be minimal— only inspection for damage and yearly maintenance.

> Looks as if we could afford it.

D. Location. The city already owns two sites:

- 1.3 acres of the park area between 180th Avenue and 360th Drive, bordered by Drab Street and Grinding Drive, two heavily used thoroughfares. On two sides of the park are neighborhood houses.

> Site 1: Automobile safety issues? Neighbors' complaints? What's on that site now?

- 2.1 acres in the 15-acre sports park at Ramp and Spin avenues. This site is set back from heavily traveled roads but still offers excellent access and visibility from service roads within the park. It is also three tenths of a mile from the fire station and paramedic aid. There are no residential neighborhoods bordering the complex.

> Site 2: No busy street or neighbors. Close to paramedics. Better choice.

The City Beat

by N. Parker

A lively debate occurred at last Tuesday's packed city council meeting on the subject of whether to establish a skateboard park. Mayor Gridlock made a few opening remarks and then turned the microphone over to J. Cool, Director of Parks and Recreation. Mr. Cool read from portions of a report prepared by his staff, who had investigated the need for and the liability, risks, cost, and possible location of a park. Several members of the community spoke.

> A packed meeting? Looks as if there's a lot of interest.

K. Skater said, "Skateboarding is a challenging sport. It's good for us. But right now we have no place to skate, and so kids are getting tickets for illegal skating. Lots of people say it's too dangerous, but that's not true. Kids get hurt in every sport, but you can make it a lot less dangerous for us if you give us a smooth place to practice. Still, we skaters have to be responsible and only take risks we can handle. That teaches us a lot."

> The right space would cut risks. Sports help kids learn to judge their strengths and limitations.

D. T. Merchant remarked, "I am a store owner downtown. These skaters use our curbs and handrails as their personal skating ramps. They threaten pedestrians and scare people. If we build them an alternative, I believe most will use it. Then the police can concentrate on the few who break the rules."

> Merchants need relief. Illegal skating is unsafe for everyone. Park may reduce police time spent citing skaters.

G. Homeowner had this to say: "Skaters are illiterate bums. They think safety gear means thick hair gel. They have no respect. They will disturb my neighborhood all night long with their subhuman noise. I would like to remind the city council—I pay taxes and I vote. A skateboard park?

> This guy really hates site 1.

Not in my backyard!"

F. Parent: "My son is an outstanding citizen. He is respectful and well behaved. He also lives to skateboard. This city has placed my son at risk by failing to give him a safe place to skate. If we were talking about building a basketball court, nobody would think twice before agreeing. I'm a voter too, and I expect the city council to be responsive to the needs of *all* citizens."

> Safety again. Good point.

Finally, S. B. Owner said, "I am the owner of the Skate Bowl. Skateboarding is not a fad. It is here to stay. You may not like the way some skaters act or look, but I know them all. They're great kids. Seems like most of the good folks here tonight are worried about safety. So here's what I propose: I will sell all safety gear in my store at 50 percent off. That's less than it costs me, folks. All that you parents have to do is fill out an emergency-information card for your skater and return it to me. I'll see that the information is entered in a database that paramedics, hospital workers, and police officers can access. I'll also make sure that everyone who comes to my store knows what the Consumer Product Safety Commission says: 'Kids who want to skate are going to skate. Let's help them skate safely.'"

> Affordable safety gear, emergency contacts, consumer education— I think I'll write a letter in support of this.

Mr. Owner's proposal was met with a standing ovation. Plans to move ahead with the skateboard-park project will be formally put to a vote at next month's regular session.

> It looks as if this could pass. Now they will have to decide where to put the park.

DISCOUNT COUPON FOR

50%OFF 50%OFF

S. B. Owner's

SKATE BOWL

This coupon entitles bearer,
_____,
to **50 PERCENT OFF**

the regular list price on all helmets, kneepads, and elbow pads.

Discount does not extend to shoes, padded clothing, boards, trucks, stickers, or any other equipment. Discount does not include state or local sales tax. Discount is not good in combination with any other discount or coupon. Bearer must show photo identification, such as a school ID or a yearbook photograph.

> Read the fine print. Not all protective items are reduced in price. Kids will need a photo ID too.

excerpts from

Consumer Product Safety Commission
Document 93

Approximately 26,000 persons go to hospital emergency rooms each year for skateboard-related injuries. Several factors— lack of protective equipment, poor board maintenance, and irregular riding surfaces—are involved in these accidents.

> Board maintenance? Nobody ever thinks about that.

Who gets injured. Six of every ten skateboard injuries happen to children under fifteen years of age. Skateboarders who have been skating for less than a week suffer one third of the injuries; riders with a year or more of

> Let's hold beginner safety classes.

experience have the next highest number of injuries.

Injuries to first-time skateboarders are, for the most part, caused by falls. Experienced riders suffer injuries mainly when they fall after their skateboards strike rocks and other irregularities in the riding surface, or when they attempt difficult stunts.

Environmental hazards. Irregular surfaces account for more than half the skateboarding injuries caused by falls. Before riding, skateboarders should check the surface for holes, bumps, rocks, and debris. Areas set aside for skateboarding generally have smoother riding surfaces. Skateboarding in the street can result in collisions with cars, causing serious injury or even death.

The skateboard. Before using their boards, riders should check them for hazards, such as loose, broken, or cracked parts; sharp edges; slippery top surfaces; and wheels with nicks and cracks. Serious defects should be corrected by a qualified repair person.

Protective gear. Protective gear—such as slip-resistant, closed shoes, helmets, and specially designed padding—may not fully protect skateboarders from fractures, but its use is recommended because such gear can reduce the number and severity of injuries.

The protective gear currently on the market is not subject to federal performance standards, and so careful selection by consumers is necessary. In a helmet, look for proper fit and a chin strap; make sure the helmet does not block the rider's vision and hearing. Body padding should fit comfortably. If it is tight, it can restrict circulation and reduce the skater's ability to move freely. Loose-fitting padding, on the other hand, can slip off or slide out of position.

Source: U.S. Consumer Product Safety Commission, Washington, D.C. 20207.

PRACTICE

Writing a Letter
Have you reached a decision? We're betting you have. Now all you have to do is write to your city council in support of the plan. Cite information from the Skateboard Park documents to support your position. Don't forget to include suggestions for yearly inspection clinics and beginner safety classes. By the way, which do you think is the better site (see page 810)? Can you explain why?

SKILLS FOCUS

Reading Skills
Analyze information from documents to solve a problem.

Leash-Free Dog Run Documents
You Decide

Here's another citywide problem to solve: Read the following **public, workplace,** and **consumer documents.** What's the situation? What decision must be made? What's the best solution? This time, make your own notes as you read.

Back   Forward   Reload   Home   Search

Location: http://www.sp.com/home

SouthPaws

Welcome to the SouthPaws Web site. SouthPaws is a not-for-profit group dedicated to creating and maintaining a leash-free space on the south side of our city for its 165,000 canine (that's dog) citizens. Please consider joining our 3,300+ members. Your membership fees are tax-deductible and will help give our dogs their own space! If you are interested in volunteering, please check out <u>Volunteer Want Ads.</u> Finally, you might want to consider SouthPaws T-shirts, sweats, caps, or leashes as a gift or for yourself. All proceeds support SouthPaws.

What's New?

Congratulations to the hundreds of volunteers who gathered signatures on the SouthPaws petition. All that hard work last spring paid off! The residents of our city have voted to establish a park or a beach where our dogs can run unleashed. This space will be jointly funded by the city and SouthPaws donations. SouthPaws volunteers will supervise the space during daylight hours and will be empowered to ticket dog owners who do not observe cleanup and safety rules. We will have one trial year after the space officially opens to prove that the idea works. Now we need your help more than ever.

We are working with the city Parks and Recreation Department to choose a location. These are the most likely locations:

Cameo Park

Pro
- is centrally located
- has convenient access roads
- has street parking

Con
- will incur high maintenance costs
- is smallest, at 1.2 residential acres
- is now a popular family park
- may lead nearby residents to object to noise, nuisances

Rocky Point Beach

Pro
- is little used
- consists of 5 nonresidential acres
- has ample parking
- will incur low start-up and maintenance costs

Con
- is inconveniently located
- has nonsand beach; smooth but potentially slippery rocks

Main Beach

Pro
- is centrally located
- consists of 7.3 nonresidential acres
- has sand beach

Con
- is heavily used all year
- may cause conflicts with businesses
- has limited, costly parking
- will require 24-hour security and maintenance staffing
- will incur high maintenance costs

Pick a Site

Click here to cast your vote in our survey.

SouthPaws

SouthPaws · 1111 South P Street · South City, CA · 90123

December 12, 2004

Ms. T. Wagger
Director of Parks and Recreation
2222 Central Avenue
South City, CA 90123

Dear Ms. Wagger,

SouthPaws members would like you to take their concerns into account when choosing the site of the proposed dog run. Here they are, in order of importance:

1. Space. Healthy dogs need ample space in which to run. The park needs to be large enough for a fair number of dogs to run around in it without colliding with one another. Ample size will minimize the possibility of dogfights.

2. Conflicts. A site that is already popular for sports, family activities, or tourism will likely be a problem.

3. Site. Our research shows that dog beaches are preferable to dog parks. Dogs are hard on park grass, which quickly turns to mud in rainy weather. Sand or shells can be brushed off a dog, but mud requires a bath. Dog beaches are also easier to supervise and clean.

Thank you for working with us to find a solution that is in the best interests of the most people. We are looking forward to meeting with you next week.

Sincerely,

A. K. Nine

A. K. Nine
Chairperson
SouthPaws Site Committee

Back

Forward

Reload

Home

Search

Location: http://www.sp.com/home

SouthPaws

Did You Know?

- In our city there are 165,000 licensed dogs.
- The city devotes a total of 10 acres to leash-free dog areas.
- The city devotes 1,050 acres to softball, 1,040 acres to golf, 287 acres to tennis.
- Eastside Leash-Free Dog Park accommodates 2,000 dogs per week on its 1-acre site.

SouthPaws Membership Information

Annual Tax-Deductible Membership Fees

Basic: $15 per year; entitles you to newsletter and voting rights

Deluxe: $25 per year; entitles you to the above plus one T-shirt or cap

Sponsor: $100 per year; entitles you to all of the above plus discounted dog-obedience classes and merchandise from local merchants

Angel: $250 per year; entitles you to all of the above plus your name on our Wall of Fame

New!

Help SouthPaws while you tell the world about your best friend. Buy a brick in the new Dog Walk of Fame. Your pet's name and a short message will be inscribed. Be sure to provide your pet's name, your name, and your message (up to 45 letter spaces). (Available to SouthPaws members only; $50 per pet's name.)

Membership in SouthPaws makes a great gift. Print out a membership application, complete it, and mail it with your donation.

Don't want to join? Then how about making a donation? We appreciate contributions in any amount.

Analyzing Documents to Solve a Problem

Leash-Free Dog Run Documents

Test Practice

1. The decision to build the dog run was made by —
   A   the city council
   B   Parks and Recreation
   C   SouthPaws
   D   voters

2. If you were not a SouthPaws member but wanted to buy a brick in the new Dog Walk of Fame, it would cost you a minimum of —
   F $15
   G $25
   H $50
   J $65

3. How many acres are already devoted to leash-free zones?
   A   1
   B   10
   C   287
   D   1,050

4. SouthPaws members are *most* concerned about —
   F   access
   G   conflicts
   H   space
   J   type of area

5. The site that *best* meets the needs and concerns of SouthPaws members is —
   A   Cameo Park
   B   Rocky Point Beach
   C   Main Beach
   D   either Rocky Point or Main Beach

Constructed Response

1. What problem is the SouthPaws Web site concerned with?

2. What three concerns do SouthPaws members have?

3. Which proposed site addresses *most* of SouthPaws' concerns? Why?

SKILLS FOCUS

Reading Skills
Analyze information from documents to solve a problem.

Understanding Consumer Materials

Reading Focus

Elements and Features of Consumer Materials

What has two wheels, pedals to make it go, and handles for steering the front wheel? A _____. That was easy to figure out, because the question names a bicycle's most basic elements. Still, is that all there is to a bicycle? Is that how you'd describe a bicycle you want? No way. You want stuff on your bike—maybe for mountain biking, maybe for racing, maybe for just looking cool. You want a bicycle that stands out in your crowd. You want features that make it unique.

Bicycles have common elements as well as special features. So do consumer documents. The **elements** that make up consumer materials define what the document is—warranty, contract, product information, or instruction manual. The **features** are what make consumer documents unique. For example, all contracts spell out what you get and what you give. Without those two elements a contract isn't really a contract. Features are described in the details. Some features may be to your advantage; others may not. Understanding the details of a contract before you sign it will help you avoid problems later.

■ Let's look at some **consumer materials.** The notes in the margin will help you identify the elements and features of each type of document.

WarpSpeedNet Documents

Choosing a High-Speed Internet Service Provider

Juan's family phone line is always busy, because everyone uses the Internet. They have decided that the family's big yearly purchase will be high-speed Internet access. The best price was offered by a cable company, and they decided to try it. The first **product information** they got was contained in the **advertisement** below:

Recognizing the Elements and Features of an Advertisement

With

You Get What You Want—*Now.*

Only WarpSpeedNet provides all the cable equipment and services you need for a lightning-fast Internet connection through your home computer. *Never wait again* to dial in, log on, or connect. WarpSpeedNet is always on, always ready to go. You'll never be disconnected in the middle of a download again!

WarpSpeedNet is point-and-click easy to use. Get weather reports *now*, news *now*, Web shopping *now*, music *now*, games *now*. Anything the World Wide Web offers, WarpSpeedNet brings to you—*Now!*

CALL DURING THE NEXT TWO WEEKS TO RECEIVE **FREE** INSTALLATION AND A RISK-FREE 30-DAY MONEY-BACK GUARANTEE

**Call now and mention priority code RIW.
1-555-WarpNet**

Service subject to availability in your area. Offer good in South and North County areas only. Minimum computer-system requirements apply. Offer expires 12/31/03.

Element—description of selling points.
Features—no equipment to buy; speedy, convenient, easy.

Element—enticements to buy.
Features—free installation, money-back guarantee, short-term offer.

Element—contact information.

Element—limitations.
Features—is not available everywhere, does not work with all computers, has expiration date.

PRACTICE

Analyzing an Advertisement

The purpose of an advertisement is, of course, to make you want a product. One of the ways it does this is to emphasize the good points and de-emphasize the limitations. Jot down on your own paper a few notes about how the emphasis and lack of emphasis were achieved in the advertisement above.

SKILLS FOCUS

Reading Skills
Analyze an advertisement.

Reading a Service Agreement

Let's say that Juan's family decides to give WarpSpeedNet a try. We'll assume that they live in South County, meet the minimum computer-system requirements, and call within the two-week deadline. Juan's family is now entitled to everything the company promised: free installation, thirty-day money-back trial, and all the necessary cable equipment. This is what they receive when they sign up, along with a few more consumer documents. Let's take a closer look at those documents.

Don't let the word *agreement* in the following example fool you. This is a **contract,** and like most contracts, it is long and complicated to read. We won't print the whole thing, but here are two important sections:

SERVICE AGREEMENT

1. Equipment

A. Equipment includes rental of cable modem and necessary connections to permit use of one (1) computer to WarpSpeedNet service.

B. WarpSpeedNet will install equipment. Subscriber will grant company reasonable access to install, inspect, repair, maintain, or disconnect the equipment. Refusal to do so may result in discontinued service.

C. Cable equipment remains the property of WarpSpeedNet. Upon termination of service, equipment shall be returned in original condition, ordinary wear and tear excepted.

2. Charges

A. Subscriber agrees to pay for the monthly service subscribed to, including charges for installation, in advance. Monthly charges are set forth on a separate price list and are subject to change.

B. Subscribers who discontinue service will be required to pay all due and past-due charges. If the subscriber reconnects service, a charge will apply.

C. If cable equipment is lost, damaged, or stolen, subscriber must pay $300 to WarpSpeedNet for replacement.

_____
Company representative signature and date

_____
Subscriber signature and date

Element— services (what Juan's family gets). **Features—** cable service and equipment for one computer, installation, and setup.

Element— costs (what Juan's family pays). **Features—** payments per agreement, including all fees, charges, and replacement costs.

Element— signatures (no contract is valid without them).

SKILLS FOCUS

Reading Skills
Analyze a service agreement.

PRACTICE

Comparing and Contrasting

1. Take a few minutes to jot down the ways in which the advertisement and the contract are similar and the ways in which they are different.

2. Did you notice a mismatch between the advertisement and item 2.A under "Charges" in the contract? What is it? Which do you think will apply to Juan's family?

Reading an Instruction Manual

Juan's family also received an instruction manual. Let's take a closer look.

WELCOME TO

> **Element**—table of contents.

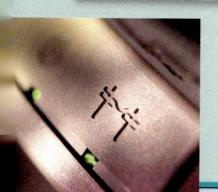

PRACTICE

Finding Information in an Instruction Manual

Some of the lights on the cable modem flash on and off, and Juan wonders if something is wrong. According to the table of contents, what page would tell him what he wants to know?

Cable Modem Lights

There are four lights on the front of your cable modem.

1. Power	**Steady green:** Power is on.
2. Cable	**Steady green:** Cable is ready to use.
	Flashing red-green: Cable is setting up connection. Wait.
	Flashing red: Connection has a problem. See Troubleshooting, page 33.
	No light: There is no cable connection. Call for service.
3. Computer link	**Steady green:** Connection is working.
	Flashing red: There is a connection problem. See Troubleshooting, page 33.
	No light: Computer has been turned off or disconnected.
4. Data	**Flashing light:** Modem is sending or receiving data.

15

Element—
explanation
of product.
Features—
specific meaning
of each light.

PRACTICE

Following Directions

1. Juan notices that lights 1 and 2 are always green. What does that mean?
2. Light 3 is on only sometimes. When should it be on?
3. Light 4 flashes on and off a great deal. Why is it flashing?
4. Is the cable modem working properly, or is there a problem? What do you think?
5. What is the **purpose** of the instruction manual? How is this purpose different from that of the contract and the advertisement? How is it the same?

SKILLS FOCUS

Reading Skills
Analyze an instruction manual.

Reading a Warranty

If the cable modem isn't working as promised, what can Juan's family do? Let's check the warranty.

The purpose of a warranty is _____. Yes! It tells when, how, and for how long you can get your money back. Take another look at WarpSpeedNet's warranty. What does it really offer? If the equipment fails during the first year, Juan's family can get a refund for the amount they paid. But hold on a minute! That doesn't really apply to Juan's family. Can you figure out why? (Hint: Go back and read the contract.)

This is all there is to it: product information, contract, instruction manual, warranty.

LIMITED WARRANTY

The WarpSpeedNet modem is guaranteed to be free of defects in material or workmanship under normal use for a period of one (1) year from the date of purchase. If the product malfunctions during this period, call WarpSpeedNet Customer Service to obtain a return authorization.

YOU MUST OBTAIN THIS AUTHORIZATION BEFORE RETURNING THE PRODUCT. PRODUCTS RECEIVED WITHOUT AUTHORIZATION WILL BE RETURNED TO SENDER. WHEN YOU CALL, BE PREPARED TO PROVIDE YOUR PROOF OF PURCHASE (RECEIPT NUMBER AND PRODUCT SERIAL NUMBER).

Clearly mark your return-authorization number on the box, and include sales receipt inside the box. In no event will WarpSpeedNet provide a refund in excess of the amount paid for the product.

Element—information on what is and is not guaranteed.
Features—specific information on when and how a refund may be obtained.

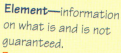

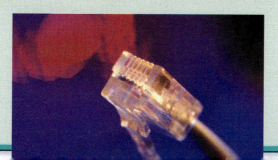

SweetPlayer Documents

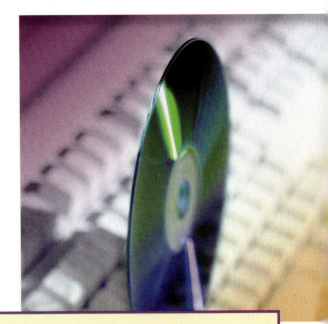

Now Juan is ready to use that high-speed modem. His first stop? MP3 and *fast* downloads!

MP3? What is that? MP3 is an audio format, a software code that turns sounds into information a computer can understand. MP3 is nonproprietary. That means no one can claim ownership—anyone who wants to write a software program using it can legally do so. MP3 squeezes good sound quality into a small package. The sound-size combination makes MP3 the most popular audio format used today.

Juan can't wait to start listening to music on the family's computer. He has a collection of CDs from which he wants to rip (copy) his favorite tracks. He wants to explore Web radio and find new artists with cool tunes on sites where music is posted for free downloading. He needs the right software and has narrowed his search to a product called SweetPlayer, but which version should he get? Let's look at the Internet **advertisement.**

Is it legal? The Internet is full of music. You can get your favorite hit in MP3 with a single click. It's easy, it's free—and it could be illegal. Many music sites contain music that someone has copied from a CD by digitizing it for use on computers and then placing it where other people can download it. It's a convenient and popular practice, but it is *not* legal. So what *is* legal?

1. You may rip tracks from a CD you own to a computer or to the Internet as long as they are for your own use and not for the use of other people.
2. You may download free promotional tracks. This is an increasingly popular way for artists to introduce their work to you. All music is legal on sites where the works are posted by the artists and record companies that created them. Free and promotional tracks are clearly marked, usually under the heading "Free Music." There are often CDs for sale by the artist too. Watch out, though. If a friend wants the same track, he or she will have to download it. It is not legal for you to copy a CD you downloaded from the Net.
3. You may buy the track for your own use. Many sites, including those of more and more record companies, are now offering tracks for sale in this manner.

Rule of thumb: If the way in which music is to be downloaded doesn't fit any of the three situations described above, the process probably isn't legal. When in doubt, check the copyright notice on the site.

SKILLS FOCUS

Reading Skills
Analyze consumer materials.

Reading an Internet Advertisement and Instructions

Back   **Forward**   **Reload**   **Home**   **Search**

Location: http://www.sweetplayer.com

SWEETPLAYER
The Best Free MP3 Player in Town!

SWEETPLAYER GIVES YOU

- fast and easy one-click downloading of MP3 files
- access to any of 2,500+ Web radio stations
- close to CD-quality sound with 128 Kbps sampling

And for a limited time you get

- SweetPlayer Deluxe for the introductory price of $19.95 (suggested retail price $29.95)*

Try it for 30 days, risk free.**

SweetPlayer Deluxe offers all the features of SweetPlayer *plus* it

- creates, edits, and organizes play lists
- rips CDs to MP3 files quickly and easily
- provides 256 Kbps, which means CD-quality sound
- personalizes your look with a choice of 100+ skins

*Special offer ends 6/15/04.
**After 30 days, software will require an activation code. Upon receipt of payment, purchaser will be sent the activation code by e-mail, fax, or U.S. mail.

Juan clicks on "SweetPlayer Deluxe." The following downloading directions appear on the screen:

DOWNLOAD DIRECTIONS

1. Shut down all open applications except your Internet browser.
2. Click on "Download Now."
3. Note where you are saving the download.
4. When download is complete, double-click on the saved file.
5. Fill in the requested registration information, and follow the instructions on your screen.
6. You must click "Accept" in the software-user's-agreement box to continue.
7. Click on "Yes" to reboot your computer once installation is complete. The computer will reboot automatically, and the program icon will appear on your desktop or on your "Start" menu.

Reading a Software User's Agreement and Warranty

Even though he plans to click on "Accept," Juan reads the software user's agreement carefully. (Remember that a user agreement is a form of **contract.**) It is long and complicated. Here are the parts that grab Juan's attention:

SOFTWARE USER'S AGREEMENT

IMPORTANT—READ CAREFULLY: This license agreement for SweetPlayer Deluxe is a legal agreement. By clicking on "Accept" or installing, copying, or using the software, you agree to abide by the terms and conditions of this license agreement. If you do not agree, click on "I Do Not Accept," and do not install the software.

1. License. The purchaser is granted a license to use this software on any single computer or on any two computers as long as the computers are not in use at the same time.

2. Use. In using this software, the purchaser agrees to comply with all laws, including applicable restrictions concerning copyright and other intellectual property rights.

3. This software is for *individual use only.* Files that are downloaded with this software, and are subject to copyright restrictions, may not be distributed to third parties or shared outside your normal circle of family and friends.

4. Title. The software is protected by copyright laws of the United States. This agreement relates to software use. Title and ownership rights and intellectual property rights remain with SweetPlayer, Inc.

Before clicking on "Accept," Juan also reads the **warranty.**

LIMITED WARRANTY

SweetPlayer, Inc., warrants that for a period of sixty (60) days from the date of purchase, the software will perform as described if operated as directed. SweetPlayer, Inc., makes no other warranties. This warranty will immediately terminate upon improper use or violations of the software user's agreement.

SweetPlayer, Inc., may, at its choice (1) replace defective media, (2) advise you how to achieve described performance, (3) refund the license-agreement fee. SweetPlayer, Inc., will be obligated to honor this warranty only if you inform SweetPlayer, Inc., of the problem during the warranty period and provide evidence of the date you acquired the software.

Under no circumstances will SweetPlayer, Inc., be held liable for more than the licensing cost of the product.

Now Juan is ready to go! He knows what he can legally do and what the company must legally provide. He clicks on "Accept." It is time to turn up the sound and— ba-boom, ba-boom, ba-dub-ba-duh-ba-BOOM.

Analyzing Consumer Materials

SWEETPLAYER Documents

Test Practice

1. Which of the following documents are the **download directions** *most* like?
   - **A** A warranty
   - **B** A contract
   - **C** Product information
   - **D** An instruction manual

2. The "Accept" button on the software user's agreement takes the place of a —
   - **F** description of services
   - **G** catalog of equipment
   - **H** signature on a contract
   - **J** feature of a warranty

3. By buying this product, Juan has purchased —
   - **A** the copyright and ownership title to the software
   - **B** shares of stock in the company
   - **C** the right to use the software
   - **D** the right to share the software with others

4. The **advertisement** and the **software user's agreement** are *alike* in that they both —
   - **F** offer important information about the product and its use
   - **G** entice the reader to buy the product
   - **H** discuss the legal terms and conditions of use
   - **J** tell the buyer how to get a refund

5. The **software user's agreement** and the **warranty** are *different* in that the first —
   - **A** describes the product, and the second describes the company
   - **B** is a legal document, but the second is not a legal document
   - **C** mainly outlines what the seller must do, and the second mainly outlines what the buyer must do
   - **D** mainly outlines what the buyer must do, and the second mainly outlines what the seller must do

Constructed Response

1. Describe the basic **elements** of the SweetPlayer **advertisement**.

2. What special **features** does the ad offer? When will Juan be required to pay for his software? What will happen if he fails to make a payment?

3. Describe the basic **elements** of the **software user's agreement**.

4. What special **features** does the agreement detail?

5. In a few sentences, explain the difference between the advertisement and the agreement. What happens if Juan does not agree to the terms of the software user's agreement?

SKILLS FOCUS

Reading Skills
Analyze consumer materials.

Understanding Technical Directions

Computers

Did you use a computer to wake up this morning? You might think of a computer as something you use to send e-mail or surf the Net, but computers are around you all the time. Computers are in automobiles, VCRs, and telephones. Even an alarm clock is a computer! An alarm clock, like the one in **Figure 1,** lets you program the time you want to wake up, and it will wake you up at that time.

Figure 1 *Believe it or not, this alarm clock is a computer!*

What Is a Computer?

A **computer** is an electronic device that performs tasks by processing and storing information. A computer performs a task when it is given a command and has the instructions necessary to carry out that command. Computers do not operate by themselves, or "think."

Following Technical Directions

When you want to make or do something new, you usually consult directions. To find out how long to boil spaghetti, you read the directions on the box. To do yoga exercises, you might follow the directions on a videotape. The directions for operating scientific and mechanical devices are called **technical directions.**

Figure 2
The Functions of a Computer

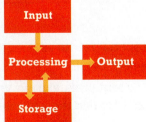

Basic Functions The basic functions a computer performs are shown in **Figure 2.** The information you give to a computer is called *input*. Setting your alarm clock is a type of input. To perform a task, a computer *processes* the input, changing it to a desirable form. Processing could mean adding a list of numbers, executing a drawing, or even moving a piece of equipment. Input doesn't have to be processed immediately; it can be stored until it is needed. Computers store information in their *memory*. For example, your alarm clock stores the time you want to wake up. It can then process this stored information by going off at the programmed time. *Output* is the final result of the task performed by the computer. What's the output of an alarm clock? The sound that wakes you up!

SKILLS FOCUS

Reading Skills
Understand technical directions.

Computer Hardware

For each function of a computer, there is a corresponding part of the computer where each function occurs. **Hardware** refers to the parts, or equipment, that make up a computer. As you read about each piece of hardware, refer to **Figure 3.**

Input Devices Instructions given to a computer are called input. An *input device* is the piece of hardware that feeds information to the computer. You can enter information into a computer using a keyboard, a mouse, a scanner, a digitizing pad and pen—even your own voice!

Central Processing Unit A computer performs tasks within an area called the *central processing unit,* or CPU. In a personal computer, the CPU is a microprocessor. Input goes through the CPU for immediate processing or for storage in memory. The CPU is where the computer does calculations, solves problems, and executes the instructions given to it.

Figure 3 Computer Hardware

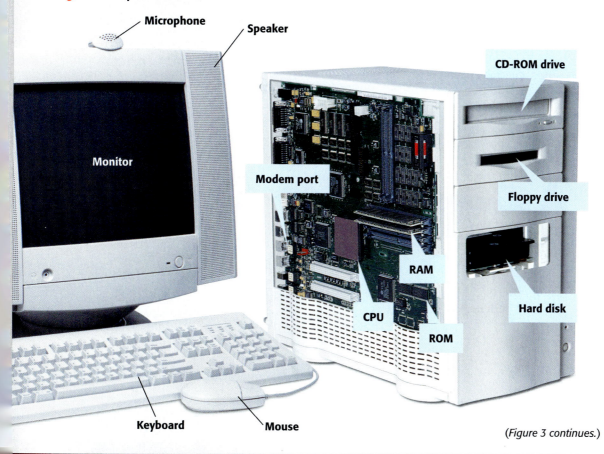

Microphone

Speaker

CD-ROM drive

Monitor

Modem port

Floppy drive

RAM

Hard disk

CPU

ROM

Keyboard

Mouse

(*Figure 3 continues.*)

Memory Information can be stored in the computer's memory until it is needed. Hard disks inside a computer and floppy disks or CD-ROMs inserted into a computer have memory to store information. Two other types of memory are *ROM* (read-only memory) and *RAM* (random-access memory).

ROM is permanent. It handles functions such as computer start-up, maintenance, and hardware management. ROM normally cannot be added to or changed, and it cannot be lost when the computer is turned off. On the other hand, RAM is temporary. It stores information only while that information is being used. RAM is sometimes called working memory. Large amounts of RAM allow more information to be input, which makes for a more powerful computer.

Output Devices Once a computer performs a task, it shows the results on an *output device*. Monitors, printers, and speaker systems are all examples of output devices.

Modems One piece of computer hardware that serves as an input device as well as an output device is a *modem*. Modems allow computers to communicate. One computer can input information into another computer over a telephone line, as long as each computer has its own modem. As a result, modems permit computers to "talk" with other computers.

Figure 3 Computer Hardware (*continued*)

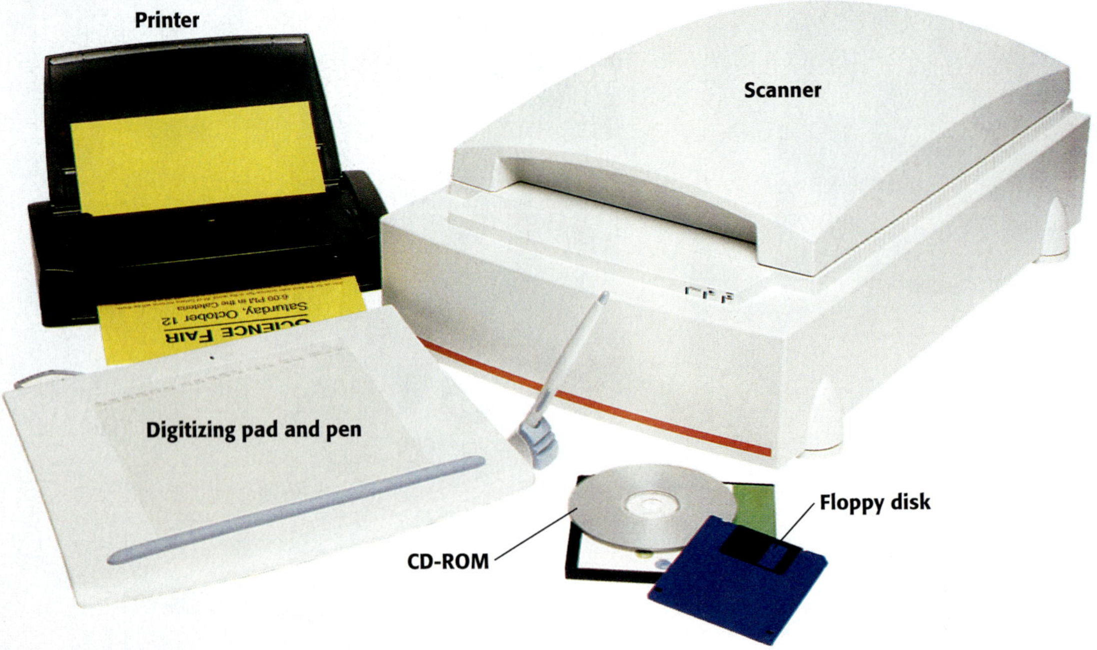

Printer

Scanner

Digitizing pad and pen

CD-ROM

Floppy disk

The Internet—A Global Network

Thanks to modems and computer software, it is possible to connect many computers and allow them to communicate with one another. That's what the **Internet** is—a huge computer network consisting of millions of computers that can all share information with one another.

How the Internet Works Computers can connect to one another on the Internet by using modems to dial into an Internet service provider, or ISP. A home computer connects to an ISP over a normal phone line. A school, business, or other group can have a local area network (LAN) that connects to an ISP using one phone line. As depicted in **Figure 4,** ISPs are connected globally by satellite. And that's how computers go global!

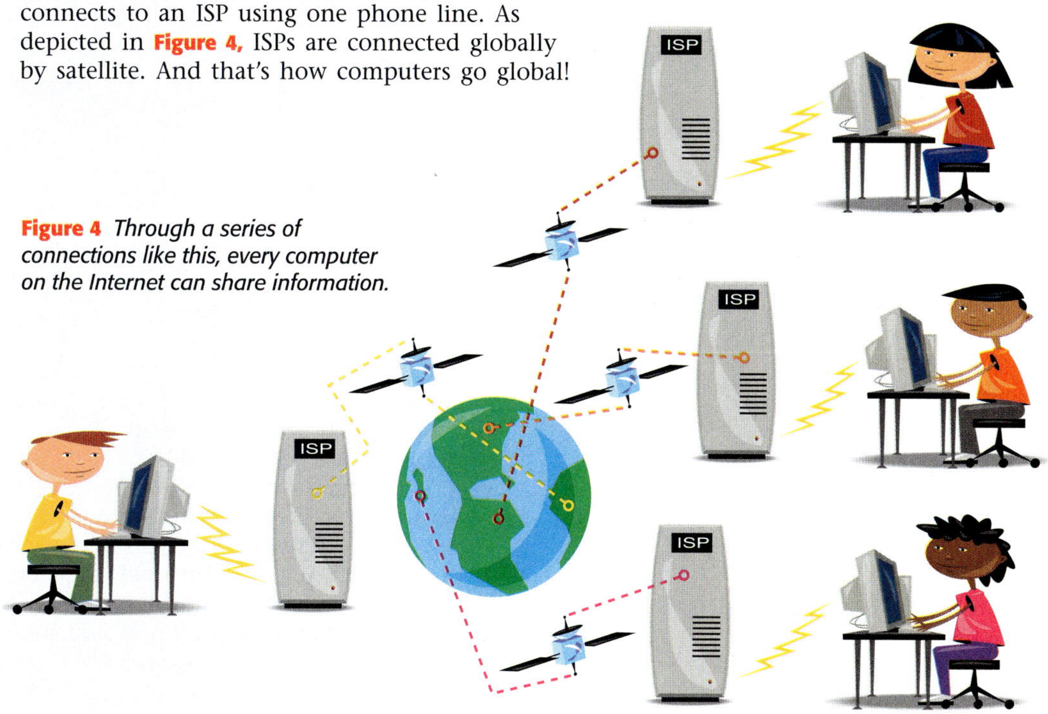

Figure 4 *Through a series of connections like this, every computer on the Internet can share information.*

—*From* Holt Science and Technology

How to Set Up a Computer

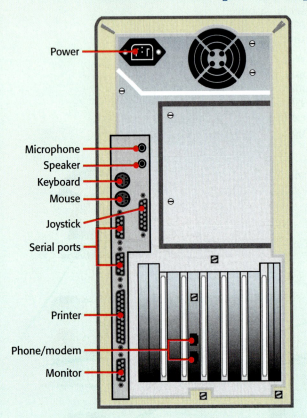

Power

Microphone
Speaker
Keyboard
Mouse
Joystick
Serial ports
Printer
Phone/modem
Monitor

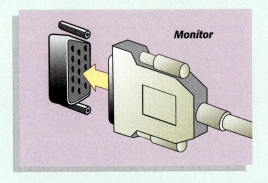

Monitor

Step 1
Connect the monitor to the computer.

The monitor has two cords: One cord, the **monitor interface cable,** lets the computer communicate with the monitor. It connects to the video port (the port designated for monitors) at the back of the computer. The connector on this cord is a plug with pins in it; the pins correspond to holes in the video port on the computer. This cable probably has screws to secure the connection. The other cord is the **monitor's power cord,** which plugs into the wall outlet or **surge protector,** a plug-in device that protects electronic equipment from high-voltage electrical surges (see Step 5).

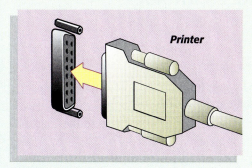

Step 2

Connect the printer to the computer.

The cable connectors that fit parallel ports, which your printer uses, have pins like those on the monitor cable and are usually secured with screws. Connect one end to the back of your printer and then connect the other end to the back of your computer where you see a **printer icon.**

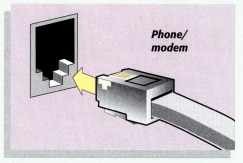

Step 4

Connect the phone line and phone to the modem.

Most computers come with **internal modems.** All you need to do is bring a line from the wall phone jack to the phone jack on the modem, which is visible on the back of your computer, and plug your telephone into the other jack on the modem.

Step 3

Connect the keyboard and mouse.

The connectors at the ends of the cords for the mouse and keyboard are round, and if you look inside them, you'll see small metal pins. These must be lined up correctly with the holes in the ports for the parts to fit together. Do not force the connectors together if they are not fitting properly; take another look to see whether you have them lined up correctly. Plug each connector into its labeled port on the back of your computer.

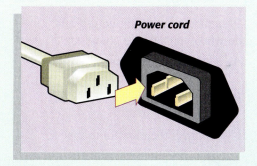

Step 5

Connect the power cords.

The **power cord** is a three-prong, grounded cord you attach to your computer. Attach the power cord to the computer first; then, plug it into a surge protector. Do the same with the monitor's power cord. The surge protector then plugs into a grounded wall outlet. Turn on the monitor first, then the computer, and you're ready to go!

Analyzing Technical Directions

Computers *from* Holt Science and Technology

Test Practice

1. According to the illustration on page 829, which of the following is *not* housed with the central processing unit?
   - **A** Modem port
   - **B** Monitor
   - **C** RAM
   - **D** CD-ROM drive

2. Which of the following parts is *not* an example of an **output device**?
   - **F** Monitor
   - **G** Printer
   - **H** Speaker system
   - **J** Mouse

3. What is the first thing you should do when you set up a computer?
   - **A** Connect the keyboard and mouse
   - **B** Connect the phone line to the modem
   - **C** Connect the monitor to the computer
   - **D** Connect the power cords

4. Why is it important to plug in the **surge protector**?
   - **F** It connects the keyboard to the mouse.
   - **G** It protects electronic equipment from high-voltage electrical surges.
   - **H** It hooks up the phone line to the modem.
   - **J** It turns the power off.

5. Which components of your computer do you *not* have to connect before you can use the Internet?
   - **A** Monitor to computer
   - **B** Printer to computer
   - **C** Keyboard and mouse
   - **D** Telephone line to modem

Constructed Response

1. What is the definition of a computer?
2. According to the chart on page 828, what are the four functions of a computer?
3. What is computer hardware?
4. What do modems allow computers to do?
5. What is the Internet?

SKILLS FOCUS

Reading Skills
Analyze technical directions.

Writing Workshop

PERSUASIVE WRITING
Problem-Solution Essay

Problem-solution essays usually focus on problems that are serious and that affect large numbers of people. For example, an essay might address a local problem, such as gridlock at a busy intersection, or an international problem, such as global warming. Your aim is to persuade your readers that your proposed solution is sensible, realistic, and workable.

Prewriting

 Choosing a Topic

The first step in writing a problem-solution essay is finding a problem that you want to solve. Consider this **prompt:**

> Problems exist in many places: in your school, in your community, in the nation, and throughout the world. The student body of a high school might have to deal with a student council that doesn't accomplish much. A town might have a problem with unhealthy levels of lead in the water supply. An increase in tax evasion might pose a national problem; malnutrition is a worldwide problem. Identify a problem that you believe is important to young people as well as to adults. Write an essay in which you present the problem and persuade your readers to accept your solution or solutions.

Working with a group of classmates, list as many problems as you can think of. Then, choose three topics that interest you the most. Fill in a chart like the one below with facts and opinions.

Facts and Opinions	Problem 1	Problem 2	Problem 3
Why it's a problem			
What and whom it affects			

Assignment

Write an essay describing a problem and offering one or more solutions.

Audience

Anyone affected by the problem

RUBRIC
Evaluation Criteria

A good problem-solution essay

1. identifies the problem clearly

2. provides evidence of the seriousness of the problem

3. proposes one or more solutions

4. considers opposing opinions and contradictory evidence

5. targets the audience and their point of view

6. makes a convincing argument for a change in thinking or action

SKILLS FOCUS

Writing Skills
Write a problem-solution essay.

Problem-Solution Essay   **835**

Strategies for Elaboration

Often the best way to convince an audience of something is to get them to picture it.

- Jot down examples of scenarios (story situations) involving the problem or your suggested solution.

- Choose one, and include it in your problem-solution essay. You might begin with "Imagine that . . ." or "Suppose that . . ."

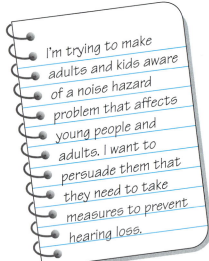

I'm trying to make adults and kids aware of a noise hazard problem that affects young people and adults. I want to persuade them that they need to take measures to prevent hearing loss.

2 Exploring Solutions

Brainstorm workable solutions to one of the problems you listed. Fill in a chart like the one below.

Problem	Possible Solutions
Exposure to very loud sounds for a short or prolonged period can lead to hearing loss.	Avoid noise levels above 120 decibels. Use protective devices such as earmuffs or earplugs. Alert others—especially children—to the hazards of noise.

Choose the most workable solution or solutions to the problem.

3 Targeting Your Audience

Whom do you want to persuade? Before you begin writing, make sure you've identified the audience for your essay. Your primary audience should include the following groups:

- people affected by the problem
- people responsible for causing the problem
- people who can act on your proposed solutions

Your tone, word choice, and approach should be adapted to your audience. Ask yourself, "What do they know about my topic? What are their concerns about it? What arguments would they find persuasive?"

Drafting

1 Using a Strong Beginning

Open your essay by grabbing the reader's attention with a quotation, an interesting statistic, or a vivid example of the problem. In the introduction, give a clear statement of the problem. You might provide evidence that the problem exists (in the form of statistics or anecdotes), discuss its causes, and identify its effects on your readers' lives.

2 Proposing Solutions

Summarize your solution or solutions to the problem. Describe each solution in detail. You might stress how practical your solution is, explain how it might be accomplished, and identify the consequences of failing to act.

3 Anticipating Objections

Be prepared to answer objections to your solution. Look for weaknesses in your proposed solution, and see if you can strengthen your arguments. Think of any objections to your ideas that might be raised so that you can anticipate and counter them. Deal with the possible objections by stressing the benefits of your approach.

4 Ending on a Strong Note

State what you want your readers to do. Do you want to change their thinking? Do you want them to take action? You might conclude with your strongest argument or with a prediction of what will happen if the problem remains unsolved.

In the following model the writer addresses the topic of a shortened school week and the effects it might have on students. Note how her intended audience influences her tone, her word choice, and the way she presents the issue.

Framework for a Problem–Solution Essay

Introduction (a strong example or statement):

_____

Problem:

_____

Details:

_____

Benefits:

_____

Possible objections:

_____

Your responses:

_____

Conclusion (a strong argument, a summary, or a call to action):

_____

Student Model

Members of the School Board:
Due to lack of money, schools in several states have decided to eliminate an entire day from the school week. I do not agree with this idea and believe that it creates a real problem.

    A shortened school week means a longer school day because five workdays are crammed into four. Although their week is shorter, students are still expected to accomplish school objectives within a

States problem.

INTERNET

More Writer's Models

Keyword: LE5 8-8

Strategies for Elaboration

To support your problem-solution essay, you can use

- facts and statistics
- anecdotes and examples from personal experience
- opinions from experts

As you think about your solution, ask yourself these questions:

- How will it work? Who is involved? What will happen?
- Why is this solution better than other possible solutions? (Give facts, examples, statistics.)
- How much will it cost, and who will pay for it?

particular time frame. This means that these students have to work harder, longer hours than the students who enjoy a five-day week. I would think that the quickened pace results in less quality instruction time for the teacher and exhausted students.

Provides first reason why it is a serious problem.

The school districts that have tried the shorter school week argue that it can save 200,000 dollars per year in the school's budget. I think, though, that the shortened school week causes more problems than it has advantages. A shorter school week also presents problems for working parents and the community. Younger children will need day care one day a week, which will be hard for day care centers to accommodate.

Considers opposing opinion.

Provides second reason why it is a serious problem.

Instead of cutting a day of school, I propose that the school districts solve their financial problems by greater collaboration among neighboring districts. This could mean sharing staff members, equipment, library resources and other services. Here in western New York, this solution has already been used successfully by local colleges for many years. It gives students more opportunities instead of taking them away.

States a proposed solution.

Provides specific details.

In conclusion, I think that it is important for schools to work together to find money to keep the fifth day rather than sacrifice the happiness and health of the students.

Concludes with a restatement of main idea.

—Maura C. Whitman
Martha Brown Middle School
Fairport, New York

Evaluating and Revising

Use the following chart to evaluate and revise your essay.

Problem–Solution Essay: Content and Organization Guidelines		
Evaluation Questions	▶ **Tips**	▶ **Revision Techniques**
❶ Do you open with a strong beginning? Does your introduction identify the problem?	▶ **Underline** the attention-getting opening. Highlight the statement of the problem.	▶ **Add** a strong statement, a statistic, or a vivid example of the problem, if needed.
❷ Do you provide evidence of the seriousness of the problem?	▶ **Put stars** next to the details that show the causes and effects of the problem.	▶ **Add** causes and effects that show the seriousness of the problem.
❸ Does your essay propose one or more solutions to the problem?	▶ **Circle** the statements that propose a solution.	▶ If necessary, **add** solutions.
❹ Do you examine the pros and cons of the solution?	▶ **Check** the descriptions of benefits and objections.	▶ If necessary, **elaborate** with details.
❺ Does your essay target your audience?	▶ **Bracket** phrases or sentences that identify your audience.	▶ **Adjust tone,** if necessary, to reach your audience.
❻ Does your conclusion make a convincing argument for change? Does it include a call to action?	▶ **Underline** your concluding argument. **Draw a wavy line** under the call to action.	▶ **Revise** your concluding statement to make it more specific. **Add** a call to action.

On the next page you'll find the opening paragraph of a problem-solution essay that has been revised. Following the Revision Model are questions that will help you evaluate the writer's revisions.

PROOFREADING
TIPS

- Make sure that any quotations or titles are correctly punctuated. For more help, see Quotation Marks, 14c–k, in the Language Handbook.

- After you proofread your paper, ask a classmate to double-check for errors.

Communications Handbook
H E L P

See Proofreaders' Marks.

PUBLISHING
TIPS

- Present your essay as a speech to your intended audience.

- Send your essay as a letter to the editor of your school or local newspaper.

Student Model

Before you turn up the volume on your stereo or CD player with earphones, you ought to know that ^*exposure to* sounds that are too loud can lead to hearing loss.

The loudness of sound is measured in units called decibels. Experts ~~say~~ *agree* that loud noises exceeding 120 decibels ^*, such as noise made by motorcycles or firecrackers,* can damage structures in the ear and result in hearing loss. ~~Some occupations are subject to high noise levels. Think about workers who use pneumatic drills and airline pilots who fly jets.~~

Every day we are subjected to loud noises, such as the sound of vacuum cleaners, car alarms, and blaring music. We need to take action to avoid or minimize the hazards of loud noise.

Evaluating the Revision

1. Which details have been added to help explain the problem?
2. Do you agree with the writer's decision to delete two sentences? Explain.
3. Has the writer created greater clarity by rearranging sentences? Tell why or why not.

Collection 8: Skills Review

Writing Skills

Test Practice

DIRECTIONS: Read the following passage from a problem-solution essay. Then, answer each question that follows.

(1) Plagiarism—taking someone else's idea or writing and presenting it as your own work—is a widespread problem among published writers as well as schoolchildren. (2) A number of prominent authors have been sued for literary theft, and some have been found guilty. (3) Although students are not likely to face a lawsuit for plagiarism, they may endanger their academic careers. (4) They may fail courses or even be expelled. (5) Plagiarism, whether intentional or unintentional, is dangerous. (6) Although the Internet can be a wonderful source of information, much of the material available online is not trustworthy. (7) In order to attack the problem of plagiarism, we need a better understanding of students' motives. (8) We also need practical, effective strategies that students, teachers, and parents can use to deal with the problem.

1. The subject this essay deals with is —
   A the different types of plagiarism
   B plagiarism by students
   C the history of plagiarism
   D plagiarism lawsuits

2. Which sentence is unnecessary and should be deleted?
   F Sentence 3
   G Sentence 4
   H Sentence 6
   J Sentence 8

3. The addition of details or examples would strengthen the claim in —
   A Sentence 2
   B Sentence 4
   C Sentence 6
   D Sentence 7

4. The probable audience for this essay is —
   F professional historians and other academics
   G textbook publishers
   H law-enforcement officials
   J students, teachers, and parents

5. Which topic is the rest of this essay likely to deal with?
   A Ways to spot plagiarism
   B The role of school authorities in discouraging plagiarism
   C The reasons for widespread plagiarism
   D All of the above

SKILLS FOCUS

Writing Skills
Analyze a problem-solution essay.

Reading for Life: Magazines *and* Web Sites

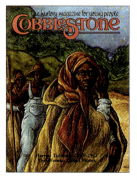

So Many Roads

Each issue of *Cobblestone* focuses on an important aspect of the history of the United States. You might read about a historic figure like Robert E. Lee, a famous event like the California gold rush, or a document like the Bill of Rights. There's even been an issue dedicated to American cartoons! *Cobblestone* brings history to life with informative feature stories, engaging activities, and riveting photographs.

Whatever You Want

Cricket magazine has been capturing the imagination of kids for more than twenty-five years. In a typical issue you'll find folk tales, poetry, biographies, and just about any other style of writing you can think of. *Cricket* also features word games, story contests, and plenty of illustrations.

All Over the Map

In *National Geographic Kids* magazine you will read reports of developments in technology and features on exotic animals. You'll find *Kids Did It!*, profiles of young people who are making great achievements in science, sports, and music. Check out the Web site at www.nationalgeographic.com/kids.

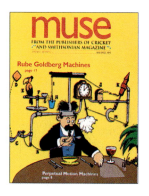

Musing About the World

Muse gets you to question the world around you and to wonder how and why things work the way they do. The articles (many of which are written by experts) cover a range of topics having to do with art, science, and history. There are also nine cartoon Muses (like the nine Muses in Greek mythology) who appear in the margins of each issue and add a little humor by making amusing comments and cracking jokes.

The Truth Is in Here

Have you ever wanted the inside scoop on outer space? Now you can find it on the Web at kids.msfc.nasa.gov/. You'll discover a three-dimensional map of the solar system, biographical pieces about astronauts, and information on how NASA keeps track of all those spaceships. The site is also loaded with games and even features an art gallery.

By Students, for Students

MidLink, an online magazine, fosters creativity in students around the globe through international poetry exchanges. Kids also build Web sites on topics such as favorite authors, historic landmarks, and camping experiences. With its links to sites on social studies, science, and more, *MidLink* can also serve as a research tool. You'll find *MidLink* at www.ncsu.edu/midlink.

The Door's Wide Open

Kids' Castle is an online magazine developed by *Smithsonian* magazine. You will discover a variety of worlds inside: air and space, history, the arts, animals, science, and personalities. Click on the history link, and you might learn the story behind postage stamps. Follow the sports links, and you could discover vintage baseball leagues, where the rules of the game were different from today's. That's just the beginning: For more, log on at www.kidscastle.si.edu.

Where Have We Been?

The Library of Congress has a Web site that offers an overview of America's past: *America's Story from America's Library*, at www.americaslibrary.gov, introduces you to famous Americans as diverse as Harry Houdini and Langston Hughes. It also invites you to jump back in time to join America at play. Check out "See, Hear, and Sing" if you want to watch a movie, hear a song, or play a tune from America's past at this lively, interactive site.

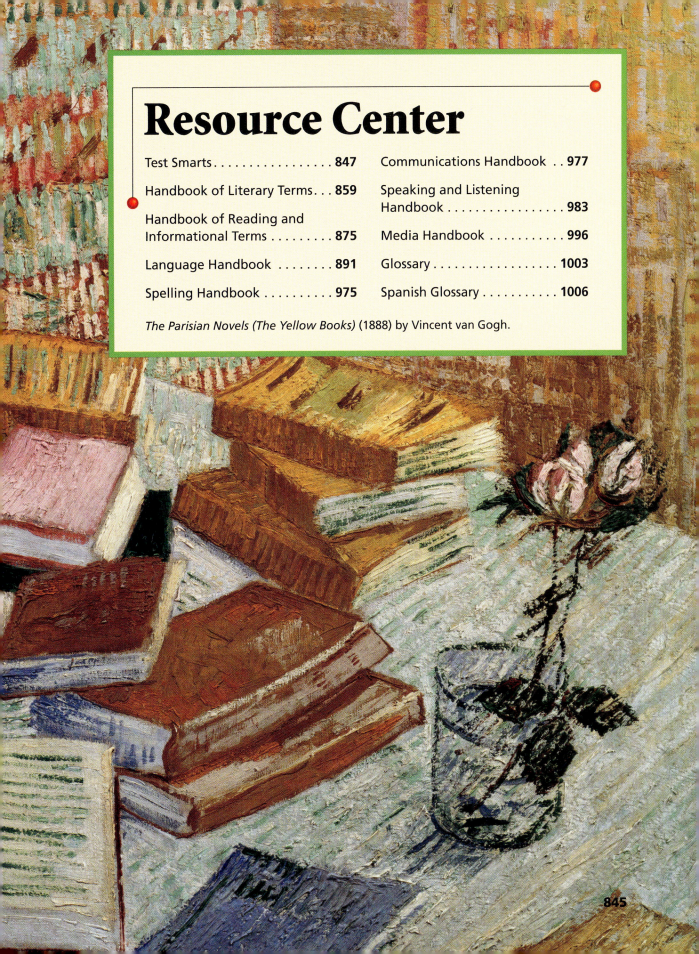

Resource Center

The Parisian Novels (The Yellow Books) (1888) by Vincent van Gogh.

Test Smarts

by **Flo Ota De Lange and Sheri Henderson**

Strategies for Taking Multiple-Choice Tests

If you have ever watched a quiz show on TV, you know how multiple-choice tests work. You get a question and (usually) four choices. Your job is to pick the correct one. Easy! (Don't you wish?) Taking multiple-choice tests will get a whole lot easier when you apply these Test Smarts:

Track your time.

Expect success.

Study the directions.

Take it all in.

Spot those numbers.

Master the questions.

Anticipate the answers.

Rely on 50/50.

Try. Try. Try.

Search for skips and smudges.

Track Your Time

You race through a test for fear you won't finish, and then you sit watching your hair grow because you finished early, or you realize you have only five minutes left to complete eleven zillion questions. Sound familiar? You can avoid both problems if you take a few minutes before you start to estimate how much time you have for each question. Using all the time you are given can help you avoid making errors. Follow these tips to set **checkpoints:**

- How many questions should be completed when one quarter of the time is gone? when half the time is gone?

- What should the clock read when you are halfway through the questions?

- If you find yourself behind your checkpoints, you can speed up.

- If you are ahead, you can—and should—slow down.

Expect Success

Top athletes know that attitude affects performance. They learn to deal with their negative thoughts, to get on top of their mental game. So can you! But how? Do you compare yourself with others? Most top athletes will tell you that they compete against only one person: themselves. They know they cannot change another person's performance. Instead, they study their own performance and find ways to improve it. That makes sense for you too. You are older and more experienced than you were the day you took your last big test, right? So review your last scores. Figure out just what you need to do to top that "kid" you used to be. You can!

What if you get anxious? It's OK if you do. A little nervousness will help you focus. Of course, if you're so nervous that you think you might get sick or faint, take time to relax for a few minutes. Calm bodies breathe slowly. You can fool yours into feeling calmer and thinking more clearly by taking a few deep breaths—five slow counts in, five out. Take charge, take five, and then take the test.

Study the Directions

You're ready to go, go, go, but first it's wait, wait, wait. Pencils. Paper. Answer sheets. Lots of directions. Listen! In order to follow directions, you have to know them. Read all test directions as if they contained the key to lifetime happiness and several years' allowance. Then, read them again. Study the answer sheet. How is it laid out? Is it

1

2

3

4

or

1   2   3   4 ?

What about answer choices? Are they arranged

A   B   C   D

or

A   B

C   D ?

Directions count. Be very, very sure you know exactly what to do and how to do it before you make your first mark.

Take It All In

When you finally hear the words "You may begin," briefly **preview the test** to get a mental map of your tasks:

- Know how many questions you have to complete.
- Know where to stop.
- Set your time checkpoints.
- Do the easy sections first; easy questions are worth just as many points as hard ones.

Spot Those Numbers

"I got off by one and spent all my time trying to fix my answer sheet." *Oops.* Make it a habit to

- match the number of each question to the numbered space on the answer sheet every time
- leave the answer space blank if you skip a question
- keep a list of your blank spaces on scratch paper or somewhere else—but *not* on your answer sheet. The less you have to erase on your answer sheet, the better.

Master the Questions

"I knew that answer, but I thought the question asked something else." Be sure—very sure—that you **know what a question is asking you.** Read the question at least twice before reading the answer choices. Approach it as you would a mystery story or a riddle. Look for clues. Watch especially for words like *not* and *except*—they tell you to look for the choice that is false or different from the other choices or opposite in some way. If you are taking a reading-comprehension test, read the selection, master all the questions, and then re-read the selection. The answers will be likely to pop out the second time around. Remember: A test isn't trying to trick you; it's trying to test your knowledge and your ability to think clearly.

Anticipate the Answers

All right, you now understand the question. Before you read the answer choices, **answer** the question yourself. **Then, read the choices.** If the answer you gave is among the choices listed, it is probably correct.

Rely on 50/50

"I . . . have . . . no . . . clue." You understand the question. You have an answer, but your answer is not listed, or perhaps you drew a complete blank. It happens. Time to **make an educated guess**—not a *wild* guess, but an *educated* guess. Think about quiz shows again, and you'll know the value of the 50/50 play. When two answers are eliminated, the contestant has a 50/50 chance of choosing the correct one. You can use elimination too.

Always read every choice carefully. **Watch out for distracters**—choices that may be true but are too broad, too narrow, or not relevant to the question. Eliminate the least likely choice. Then, eliminate the next, and so on until you find the best one. If two choices seem equally correct, look to see if "All of the above" is an option. If it is, that might be your choice. If no choice seems correct, look for "None of the above."

Try. Try. Try.

Keep at it. **Don't give up.** This sounds obvious, so why say it? You might be surprised by how many students do give up. Think of tests as a kind of marathon. Just as in any marathon, people get bored, tired, hungry, thirsty, hot, discouraged. They may begin to feel sick or develop aches and pains. They decide the test doesn't matter that much. They decide they don't care if it does—there'll always be next time; whose idea was this, anyway? They lose focus. Don't do it.

Remember: The last question is worth just as much as the first question, and the questions on a test don't get harder as you go. If the question you just finished was really hard, an easier one is probably coming up soon. Take a deep breath, and keep on slogging. Give it your all, all the way to the finish.

Search for Skips and Smudges

"Hey! I got that one right, and the machine marked it wrong!" If you have ever—ever—had this experience, pay attention! When this happens in class, your teacher can give you the extra point. On a machine-scored test, however, you would lose the point and never know why. So, listen up: All machine-scored answer sheets have a series of lines marching down the side. The machine stops at the first line and scans across it for your answer, stops at the second line, scans, stops at the third line, scans, and so on, all the way to the end. The machine is looking for a dark, heavy mark. If it finds one where it should be, you get the point. What if you left that question blank? A lost point. What if you changed an answer and didn't quite get the first mark erased? The machine sees two answers instead of one. A lost point. What if you made a mark to help yourself remember where you skipped an answer? You filled in the answer later but forgot to erase the mark. The machine again sees two marks. Another lost point. What if your marks are not very dark? The machine sees blank spaces. More lost points.

To avoid losing points, take time at the end of the test to make sure you

- did not skip any answers
- gave one answer for each question
- made the marks heavy and dark and within the lines

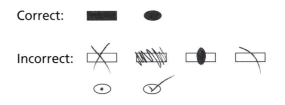

Get rid of smudges. Make sure there are no stray pencil marks on your answer sheet. Cleanly erase those places where you changed your mind. Check for little stray marks from pencil tapping. Check everything. You are the only person who can.

Reading Comprehension

Many tests have a section called **reading comprehension.** The good news is that you do not have to study for this part of the test. Taking a reading-comprehension test is a bit like playing ball. You don't know where the ball will land, so you have to stay alert to all possibilities. However, just as the ball can come at you in only a few ways, there are only a few kinds of questions that can be used on reading-comprehension tests. This discussion will help you identify the most common ones.

The main goal of the reading comprehension section is to test your understanding of a reading passage. Be sure to keep these suggestions in mind when you read a selection on a test:

- **Read the passage once** to get a general overview of the topic.

- If you don't understand the passage at first, keep reading. **Try to find the main idea.**

- Then, **read the questions** so that you'll know what information to look for when you **re-read the passage.**

Two kinds of texts are used here. The first one is an informational text. The second is an updated fairy tale.

DIRECTIONS: Read the following selection. Then, choose the best answer for each question. Mark each answer on your answer sheet in the square provided.

Stars and Stripes Forever

The U.S. flag defended by Barbara Frietchie during the Civil War had only thirty-four stars. Those stars stood for the thirty-four states that had been admitted to the Union by 1862. (Although the Southern states had seceded from the Union, President Abraham Lincoln refused to have their stars removed from the flag.)

Since 1960, the year after Hawaii became the fiftieth state, the U.S. flag has had fifty stars. Congress decided in 1818 that the number of stripes would be kept at thirteen, representing the original thirteen colonies. Known as the Stars and Stripes, the red, white, and blue flag has represented the United States at home, around the world, and even on the moon, where it was planted by astronauts in 1969.

ITEM 1 asks for vocabulary knowledge.

1. In the first paragraph, the word seceded means —

    A yielded

    B benefited

    C withdrawn

    D banished

Answer: Look at the surrounding sentences, or **context,** to see which definition fits.

A is incorrect. *Yield* means "to give in" and does not fit the context.

B is incorrect. If the Southern states had benefited, or helped, the Union, removing their stars would probably not have been an issue.

C is the best answer. Since the Southern states had withdrawn from the Union, some might have called for the removal of their stars from the flag.

D is incorrect. It doesn't fit the context.

ITEM 2 asks for close reading. Read carefully to see if the answer is stated directly in the text.

2. According to the passage, how many stars were on the U.S. flag in 1862?

   F Thirteen

   G Fifty

   H Twenty

   J Thirty-four

Answer: Read the passage carefully to see if the answer is directly stated.

J is the correct answer. The last sentence of the first paragraph of the passage indicates that there were thirty-four stars on the flag in 1862.

ITEM 3 asks for close reading. Read carefully to see if the answer is stated directly in the text.

3. In which year did Hawaii become a state?

   A 1818

   B 1862

   C 1959

   D 1960

Answer: Read the passage carefully to find the answer.

C is the correct answer. The first sentence of the second paragraph of the passage tells the year in which Hawaii became a state.

ITEM 4 asks for an inference.

4. What is this passage mainly about?

   F How the U.S. flag has changed over time

   G Why the Civil War was fought

   H How a territory becomes a state

   J When U.S. astronauts first reached the moon

Answer: Think about which statement covers the passage as a whole.

F is the best answer. It covers most of the details in the passage.

G is incorrect. The passage does not provide an explanation of why the war was fought.

H is incorrect. The passage does not tell how a territory becomes a state.

J is incorrect. It is only one detail in the passage.

ITEM 5 asks for a prediction.

5. What would happen if a U.S. territory or commonwealth, such as Puerto Rico, became a state?

   A Another star would be added to the flag.

   B Another red stripe would be added to the flag.

   C Another white stripe would be added to the flag.

   D Neither a star nor a stripe would be added to the flag.

Answer: Find the information in the passage that supports a probable future outcome.

A is the best answer. Since a new star is added for each new state, if Puerto Rico or some other territory becomes a state, Congress will add a fifty-first star.

B is incorrect. Since the passage indicates that the number of stripes is fixed at thirteen, there is no reason to think that another red stripe will be added.

C is incorrect. Since the passage indicates that the number of stripes is fixed at thirteen, there is no reason to think that another white stripe will be added.

D is incorrect. Although stripes are not added for new states, stars are.

ITEM 6 asks for a summary.

6. Which is the *best* summary of this passage?

   F The U.S. flag is known as the Stars and Stripes.

   G The U.S. flag has a unique design.

   H The U.S. flag has changed over the years but continues to represent the United States.

   J The fifty stars on the U.S. flag represent the fifty states in the Union.

Answer: Think about the answer that best sums up the passage as a whole.

F is incorrect. It states a fact and does not cover the passage as a whole.

G is incorrect. This statement simply describes the flag.

H is the best answer. This answer best sums up the content of the paragraph.

J is incorrect. This answer states a fact about the flag.

DIRECTIONS: Read the following selection. Then, choose the *best* answer for each question. Mark each answer on your answer sheet in the space provided.

Goldilocks and the Cyberbears

There was once a family of cyberbears who lived in a cozy cottage in the cyberwoods. There was gigasized Papa Bear, megasized Mama Bear, and byte-sized Baby Bear.

These three bears were <u>notables</u> because a wolf at their door had sold them a webcam which had turned them into media stars. Each morning, people all over the world went to their Web site to watch Mama Bear preparing the family's

breakfast porridge. Each morning she, of course, served it so hot the entire family had to go for a walk in the woods until the steam cleared.

One morning when the steam did clear, what did people see but Goldilocks doing her famous routine of "This porridge is too hot; this porridge is too cold; this porridge is just right" and eating it all up.

The fact that Goldilocks was a <u>trespasser on private property</u> prompted two hundred people to sign on to the Bears' chat room immediately. They protested the fact that this girl had broken into the Bears' cottage. The president of the Cyberwoods Conservancy also signed on. He warned that it was wise not to feed the humans.

Goldilocks, unaware of the webcam that was tracking her every movement, next went into the Bears' study. . . .

ITEM 1 is a vocabulary question. To identify the best definition of the underlined word as it is used in the context, consider the surrounding words and phrases.

1. In the fairy tale the underlined word <u>notables</u> means —

   A unknowns

   B typical folk

   C contestants

   D celebrities

A is incorrect. The Bears' star status makes choice A the opposite of *notables*.

B is incorrect. These are anything but ordinary, run-of-the-mill bears.

C is incorrect. Nothing in the text says they are on a quiz show.

D is the best answer. Celebrities have the star status of these fine bears.

ITEM 2 is another vocabulary question.

2. In the fairy tale the word trespasser means —

    F a person with a pass

    G an intruder

    H an unexpected guest

    J a building inspector

G is the best answer. Two hundred people wouldn't protest the presence of F, H, or J in the Bears' cottage. None of the other people would have "broken into" the cottage.

ITEM 3 is a factual question. Re-read the fairy tale to find the correct answer.

3. Where do the three Bears live?

    A In the forest

    B In a clearing

    C In the cyberwoods

    D In town

A is incorrect. It is close but not quite right. Read on.

B is incorrect. Nothing is said in the fairy tale about a clearing.

C is the best answer. This is what the story says.

D is incorrect. This is *way* off base.

ITEM 4 is another factual question.

4. What can viewers from around the world watch each morning?

    F Mama Bear preparing the family's breakfast porridge

    G The story of Goldilocks and the three bears

    H Goldilocks doing her famous song-and-dance routine

    J Goldilocks breaking Baby Bear's chair

F is the best answer. G, H, and J are incorrect for several reasons, including the fact that Goldilocks shows up at the Bears' house only once, not every morning.

ITEM 5 asks you to make a judgment based on details in the story.

5. The Bears could be described as leading which kind of life?

    A Hard

    B Wild

    C Exciting

    D Comfortable

A is incorrect. The only hard thing about the Bears' life was too-hot porridge.

B is incorrect. Life in the Bears' cottage was more tame than wild.

C is incorrect. The Bears followed a pretty ordinary daily routine.

D is the best answer. The Bears had all the comforts of home, plus a webcam.

ITEM 6 asks you to place events in chronological order, the order in which they occur.

6. Which event belongs in the blank?

    Goldilocks arrives at the cottage.

    _____ .

    Two hundred people sign on to the Bears' chat room in protest.

    F The Bears go for a walk.

    G The wolf sells the Bears a webcam.

    H Goldilocks tastes the porridge.

    J The Bears get a lesson in pet care.

H is the answer. F and G happen before Goldilocks arrives, and J never happens.

ITEM 7 asks you to make a judgment. You'll need to think carefully, but the information you need for the answer is in the story.

7. The Bears became media stars because —

A they tried out for a show

B a wolf sold them a webcam

C Goldilocks made them famous

D Papa Bear was a casting director

A is incorrect. No tryouts are mentioned.

B is the best answer. The wolf sells the Bears the webcam, which makes them famous.

C is incorrect. They are already stars when Goldilocks arrives.

D is incorrect. Little is said about Papa Bear in the story.

ITEM 8 If you read all the choices, you'll get the answer, even without any prior knowledge of the instructions.

8. The phrase "wise not to feed the humans" is a twist on what common instruction?

F Stop when the light is red.

G Don't talk to strangers.

H Keep off the grass.

J Do not feed the animals.

J is the best—and only reasonable—answer.

ITEM 9 asks you to analyze a character in the story.

9. In this cyberstory the behavior of Goldilocks can *best* be described as —

A thoughtful

B selfish

C scientific

D loving

B is the best answer. Goldilocks walks into the Bear family's house and eats their porridge. None of the other adjectives describe this behavior.

ITEM 10 requires you to have prior knowledge.

10. Based on the traditional fairy tale of Goldilocks and the three bears, what do you predict will happen next?

F Goldilocks gets arrested for trespassing.

G People get bored and stop watching the Web site.

H Goldilocks breaks Baby Bear's videogame.

J The wolf returns and eats Goldilocks.

H is the best answer. In the traditional tale, Goldilocks goes on to break Baby Bear's chair, which is similar to her breaking his videogame. F, G, and J could happen in this version, but they have no parallel in the traditional fairy tale.

Strategies for Taking Writing Tests

 ## Writing a Personal Narrative

Many of the most interesting stories you will read are true stories about people who impress others. In addition to reading such stories, you might be asked to write one. Writing tests sometimes include prompts for **personal narratives.** How would you answer a prompt like the one to the right?

> **Prompt**
>
> Think of someone you know who is important to you. Write a brief biography of that person's life, relating an incident that involved you. Use details to describe your subject and your feelings toward the subject.

▶ **STEP 1** **Read the prompt carefully, and identify the subject of your biography.**
I need to write about someone I know who is important to me. I'll write about my uncle Jared.

▶ **STEP 2** **Brainstorm details to describe the subject's appearance, actions, and feelings.** What makes your subject unique and memorable?
Uncle Jared looks just like my dad—blue eyes and light brown hair. He is always kidding around and making up silly games for my cousins and me. He loves to make people laugh.

▶ **STEP 3** **Outline the incident you will relate.** What is the sequence of events that make up the incident?
1. During a visit to my cousin's house, I got a bad ear infection. 2. My uncle stayed up with me all night because I was running a fever and was in a lot of pain. He read stories and played his guitar. 3. The next morning he took off from work to drive me back home.

▶ **STEP 4** **Jot down notes about the significance of the events.** How are the events important to your subject's life, to you, and to your audience?
I think my uncle felt bad because I was so sick. He doesn't like to see people unhappy. I really appreciate that he stayed up with me. That night my uncle showed how caring he could be.

▶ **STEP 5** **Use your notes to write a draft of your narrative.** Afterward, revise and proofread your draft, making sure you have organized your events so that readers can understand them.

Writing a Response to an Expository Passage

On a writing test, you may be asked to respond to an **expository,** or informative, reading selection. Such tests often give you both a selection and a writing prompt.

The steps and student responses below will help you respond to a prompt like the one to the right. "Home, Sweet Soddie" can be found on pages 180–182.

"Home, Sweet Soddie" can be found on pages 180–182.

Prompt

"Home, Sweet Soddie" by Flo Ota De Lange tells about the experiences pioneers had living on the prairie. Write an essay in which you explain what can be learned from reading about life on the prairie. Include details from the article to support your ideas.

▶ **STEP 1** **Read the prompt carefully, noting key words and phrases.**
The key words and phrases are "explain" and "include details."

▶ **STEP 2** **Read the selection at least twice.** Read first for the overall meaning of the work. Then, read the selection a second time, keeping the key words and phrases from the prompt in mind.

▶ **STEP 3** **Write a main idea statement.** Your main idea statement should give the title and author of the work and should directly address the task described in the prompt.
In "Home, Sweet Soddie," Flo Ota De Lange identifies several interesting things that can be learned from studying life on the prairie.

▶ **STEP 4** **Find specific details from the selection to support your main idea.** If you include quotations, remember to enclose them in quotation marks.
Pioneers had to cope with sod houses that leaked when it rained and that contained worms in the walls. They also had to deal with extreme weather and lots of bugs, including millions of grasshoppers that could eat through a whole farm in a few hours.

▶ **STEP 5** **Draft, revise, and proofread your response.** Be sure to organize your essay effectively, including a formal introduction, body, and conclusion. When you are finished writing, proofread to correct mistakes in spelling, punctuation, and capitalization.

Writing an Expository Essay

When you take a writing test, you may be asked to **explain** how to do something. Because you cannot do research during a test, you will already know all of the information you need to answer the prompt. How might you handle a prompt such as the one to the right?

Prompt

You have learned many skills that help you succeed in school. Write a letter to a younger child explaining how to do something that helps you succeed in school. Explain the steps involved, and provide details that elaborate on each step.

▶ **STEP 1 Identify the writing task.** The prompt gives you clues about the audience, purpose, and format of your answer.

▶ **STEP 2 Choose a topic, and write a thesis statement** that identifies your purpose—to explain how to perform the task you have chosen.

▶ **STEP 3 Organize your ideas** by jotting down the steps you want to explain. A time line can help you put your ideas in chronological order.

▶ **STEP 4 Write your response.** Keeping your audience and purpose in mind, list the steps in chronological order, and elaborate on each step. Be sure to include specific details that will be helpful to your audience.

Audience: a child in elementary school
Purpose: to explain how to do something
Format: a letter

Topic: finishing homework on time

Thesis: Finishing homework on time is important for success in school and only requires a few simple steps.

Time line for finishing homework on time

| 1. Write due date. | 2. Put work in notebook. | 3. Do work before watching TV. | 4. Bring work on due date. |

Possible elaborations:

Step 1: Tell students to do this so they will not forget when assignments are due.

Step 2: Explain that they should do this to keep from losing assignments.

Step 3: Tell them that doing homework right away will be easier than trying to do it late at night when they are sleepy.

Step 4: Explain that this will keep them from losing points for late work.

Using the M.E.E.T.S. Strategy to Develop a Persuasive Essay

In a writing test, you may be asked to write a **persuasive essay.** To generate reasons and evidence to support your position, use the M.E.E.T.S. strategy explained in the steps below. The student responses are based on the prompt to the right.

Prompt

Your principal has decided that students should complete twenty hours of community service during the school year. The two plans under consideration are assigning students a job during school hours or allowing students to choose a job and complete the hours on their own time. Decide which plan you prefer. Then, write an essay in which you defend your position.

▶ **STEP 1** **Identify your position on the topic given in the prompt.**
I think students should choose a job and complete the hours on their own time.

▶ **STEP 2** **Use the memory device M.E.E.T.S. (Money, Effort, Education, Time, Safety) to list the benefits of your position.**
M = The school may have to pay someone to find jobs for students.
E = Teachers will not have to make the effort to find jobs for students.
E = I'll learn more since I get to do the work I enjoy.
T = I can complete the hours when I want.
S = Students may leave school, saying they have work to do when they don't. Allowing students to complete the hours on their own time reduces the chances of students getting into trouble for lying.

▶ **STEP 3** **Identify the three strongest reasons you developed using M.E.E.T.S.** Your strongest reasons will be those for which you have the most evidence and those that address readers' concerns about the topic.
My three strongest reasons: Teachers will not have to find jobs for students. I'll learn more from a job I choose. I can complete the hours when it is convenient for me.
I think these are the issues my readers are most concerned about.

▶ **STEP 4** **Draft, revise, and proofread your essay.** Make sure you present your ideas in a logical order. Afterward, correct mistakes in spelling, punctuation, and capitalization.

Handbook of Literary Terms

For more information about a topic, turn to the page(s) in this book indicated on a separate line at the end of the entries. To learn more about *Alliteration*, for example, turn to pages 617 and 670 in this book.

On another line are cross-references to entries in the handbook that provide closely related information. For instance, at the end of *Autobiography* are cross-references to *Biography* and *Nonfiction*.

ALLITERATION **The repetition of consonant sounds in words that are close together**. Alliteration occurs mostly in poetry, though prose writers use it from time to time. Although alliteration usually occurs at the beginning of words, it can also occur within or at the end of words. In the following stanza, notice the repeated *s*, *m*, and *b* sounds:

> The sun was shining on the sea,
>   Shining with all his might:
> He did his very best to make
>   The billows smooth and bright—
> And this was odd, because it was
>   The middle of the night.
>
>   —Lewis Carroll, from "The Walrus
>   and the Carpenter"

The repetition of vowel sounds in words that are close together is called **assonance**.

See pages 617, 670.
See also *Poetry*.

ALLUSION **A reference to a statement, a person, a place, or an event from literature, the arts, history, religion, mythology, politics, sports, or science.** Allusions enrich the reading experience. Writers expect readers to recognize allusions and to think about the literary work and the allusions contained in it almost at the same time. For example, "I Have a Dream" (page 483) alludes to the song "My Country, 'Tis of Thee." A reader who is not familiar with that song will miss some of the speech's intended meaning.

See pages 482, 546.
See also *Literary Devices*.

ANALOGY **A comparison made between two things to show how they are alike.** Writers often make analogies to show how something unfamiliar is like something well known or widely experienced. Analogies are often used by scientific writers to explain difficult concepts.

See pages 274, 487.
See also *Literary Devices, Metaphor, Simile*.

ANECDOTE **A brief story told to illustrate a point.** Anecdotes are frequently found in memoirs, biographies, and autobiographies. In "In Trouble" (page 251), for example, Gary Paulsen uses two anecdotes about his huskies to illustrate their intelligence.

ANTAGONIST *See Protagonist.*

ASSONANCE *See Alliteration.*

ATMOSPHERE **The overall mood or feeling of a work of literature.** A work's atmosphere, or mood, can often be described in one or two adjectives, such as *scary, happy, sad,* or *nostalgic.* A writer produces atmosphere by creating images and using sounds that convey a particular feeling. "The Tell-Tale Heart" (page 537) is noted for its eerie atmosphere. The setting of a story can also contribute to its atmosphere. For example, the hot sun beating down on the farmworkers in "The Circuit" (page 281) contributes to a mood of oppression.

See pages 236–237.

AUTHOR **The writer of a literary work or document.** Toni Cade Bambara is the author of "Raymond's Run" (page 547); Abraham Lincoln is the author of the Gettysburg Address (page 480).

See page 729.

AUTOBIOGRAPHY **A person's account of his or her own life or of part of it.** "Camp Harmony" (page 469) is an example of autobiographical writing.

See page 185.
See also *Biography, Nonfiction.*

BALLAD **A song or songlike poem that tells a story.** Ballads usually tell stories of tragedy, love, or adventure, using simple language and a great deal of repetition. They generally have regular rhythm and rhyme patterns that make them easy to memorize. "The Dying Cowboy" (page 643) and "The Cremation of Sam McGee" (page 637) are both ballads.

See pages 618, 636.
See also *Narrative Poem, Poetry.*

BIOGRAPHY **An account of a person's life or of part of it, written or told by another person.** The excerpt from *Harriet Tubman* (page 143) is part of a longer biography.

See page 142.
See also *Autobiography, Nonfiction.*

CHARACTER **A person or an animal in a story, a play, or another literary work.** Characters can be classified according to the changes they undergo. A **static character** does not change much in the course of a work. Billy Weaver in "The Landlady" (page 72) is a static character. In contrast, a **dynamic character** changes as a result of a story's events. Squeaky in "Raymond's Run" (page 547) is a dynamic character.

A character's **motivation** is any force (such as love or fear or jealousy) that drives the character to behave in a particular way.

See pages 134–135, 142, 162, 185, 265.
See also *Characterization, Motivation, Protagonist.*

CHARACTERIZATION **The way a writer reveals the personality of a character.** A writer may simply tell readers that a character is amusing or evil or dull or brave. This method is called **direct characterization.** Most often, though, writers use **indirect characterization,** revealing personality in one or more of the following ways:

1. through the words of the character
2. through description of the character's looks and clothing
3. through description of the character's thoughts and feelings
4. through comments made about the character by other characters in the story
5. through the character's behavior

When a writer uses indirect characterization, we must use our own judgment and the evidence the writer gives to infer the character's **traits.**

See pages 134–135, 439.

CHRONOLOGICAL ORDER **The arrangement of events in the order in which they occurred.** Most stories are told in chronological order. Sometimes, however, a writer interrupts the chronological order to flash back to a past event or to flash forward to a future event. *The Diary of Anne Frank* (page 369), for example, begins in 1945, when Mr. Frank arrives at the hiding place. The main story, however, takes place from 1942 to 1944.

See page 724.
See also *Flashback.*

CLIMAX **The point in a story that creates the greatest suspense or interest.** At the climax something happens that reveals how the conflict will turn out.

See pages 2–3.
See also *Drama, Plot, Short Story.*

COMEDY **In general, a story that ends happily for its main characters.** The hero or heroine usually overcomes a series of obstacles to get what he or she wants. (In contrast, the main character in a **tragedy** comes to an unhappy end.) The word *comedy* is not always a synonym for *humor.* Some comedies are humorous; others are not.

See also *Tragedy.*

CONFLICT **A struggle between opposing characters or opposing forces.** In an **external conflict** a character struggles with an outside force, which may be another character, society as a whole, or a natural force. In contrast, an **internal conflict** takes place within a character's own mind. It is a struggle between opposing needs, desires, or emotions. Alfonso in "Broken Chain" (page 17) has an external conflict with his brother over borrowing his bike and an internal conflict over his fears of facing his date without a bike.

See pages 2–3, 16, 236.
See also *Plot.*

CONNOTATION **A meaning, association, or emotion suggested by a word, in addition to** its dictionary definition, or denotation. Words that have similar denotations may have different connotations. For example, suppose you wanted to describe someone who rarely changes plans in the face of opposition. You could use either *determined* or *pigheaded* to describe the person. The two words have similar denotations, but *determined* has positive connotations and *pigheaded* has negative connotations.

See page 461.
See also *Diction, Style, Tone.*

COUPLET **Two consecutive lines of poetry that rhyme.** Couplets are often used in humorous poems because they pack a quick punch. "Casey at the Bat" (page 650), "The Cremation of Sam McGee" (page 637), "Maiden-Savin' Sam" (page 644), and "Ode to a Toad" (page 659) are all written in four-line stanzas consisting of two couplets in each stanza. Shakespeare uses couplets in many of his plays, often for a more serious purpose, to give closure to a speech or an act.

See pages 617, 662.
See also *Poetry, Rhyme, Stanza.*

DENOTATION See *Connotation.*

DESCRIPTION **Writing intended to re-create a person, a place, a thing, an event, or an experience.** Description uses images that appeal to the senses of sight, smell, taste, hearing, or touch. It is often used to create a mood or emotion. Writers use description in all forms of fiction, nonfiction, and poetry. This description of the effect of extreme cold on a dog and its owner may make you feel cold, too:

> The frozen moisture of its breathing had settled on its fur in a fine powder of frost, and especially were its jowls, muzzle, and eyelashes whitened by its crystaled breath. The man's red beard and moustache were likewise frosted, but more

solidly, the deposit taking the form of ice and increasing with every warm, moist breath he exhaled. Also, the man was chewing tobacco, and the muzzle of ice held his lips so rigidly that he was unable to clear his chin when he expelled the juice. The result was that a crystal beard of the color and solidity of amber was increasing its length on his chin. If he fell down, it would shatter itself, like glass, into brittle fragments.

—Jack London, from "To Build a Fire"

See pages 250, 280.
See also *Imagery.*

DIALECT **A way of speaking that is characteristic of a certain geographical area or a certain group of people.** A dialect may have a distinct vocabulary, pronunciation system, and grammar. In a sense, we all speak a dialect. One dialect usually becomes dominant in a country or culture, however, and is accepted as the standard way of speaking and writing. In the United States, for example, the formal language is known as **standard English.** (It's the kind of English taught in schools, used in national newspapers and magazines, and spoken by newscasters on television.)

Writers often reproduce regional dialects or speech to bring a character to life and to give a story color. For example, the dialect Squeaky speaks in "Raymond's Run" (page 547) helps us see and hear her as a real person.

See pages 532, 546, 548.
See also *Literary Devices.*

DIALOGUE **Conversation between two or more characters.** Most stage dramas consist entirely of dialogue together with stage directions. The dialogue in a drama must move the plot along and reveal character. Dialogue

is also an important element in most stories and novels, as well as in some poems and nonfiction. By using dialogue, a writer can show what a character is like.

In the written form of a play, dialogue appears without quotation marks. In prose or poetry, however, dialogue is usually enclosed in quotation marks.

A **monologue,** or **soliloquy,** is a part of a drama in which one character who is alone onstage speaks aloud his or her thoughts and feelings.

See also *Drama.*

DICTION **A writer's or speaker's choice of words.** People use different types of words, depending on the audience they are addressing, the subject they are discussing, and the effect they are trying to produce. For example, slang words that would be suitable for a humorous piece like "Casey at the Bat" (page 650) would not be appropriate for a serious essay like "A Tragedy Revealed: A Heroine's Last Days" (page 445). Diction is an essential element of a writer's style and has a major effect on the tone of a piece of writing.

See also *Connotation, Style, Tone.*

DRAMA **A work of literature meant to be performed for an audience by actors.** (A drama, or **play,** can also be enjoyed in its written form.) The actors work from the **playwright's** script, which includes dialogue and stage directions. The script of a drama written for the screen is called a **screenplay** (if it's for TV, it's a **teleplay**), and it also includes camera directions.

The action of a drama is usually driven by a character who wants something and takes steps to get it. The main stages of a drama are often described as **exposition, complications, climax,** and **resolution.** Most dramas are divided into **acts** and **scenes.**

See page 364.

ELEGY A poem of mourning, usually about someone who has died. "O Captain! My Captain!" (page 667) is an elegy on the death of President Abraham Lincoln.

See pages 616, 666.
See also *Poetry.*

EPIC A long narrative poem that is written in heightened language and tells stories of the deeds of a heroic character who embodies the values of a society. One of the oldest surviving epics is *Gilgamesh,* which was written down around 2000 B.C. in ancient Mesopotamia. Homer's *Iliad* and *Odyssey,* dating from around 500 B.C. in Greece, are two of the best-known Western epics. *Beowulf* (page 648), from around A.D. 700, is the oldest surviving Anglo-Saxon epic. A mock epic, such as "Casey at the Bat" (page 650), imitates the epic style in a comical way in order to poke fun at its topic.

See pages 618, 647.
See also *Poetry.*

EPILOGUE A brief closing section to a piece of literature. Shakespeare's plays often have an epilogue spoken by an actor directly to the audience (see page 881, under *Meter,* for an example). In this textbook, "Saying Yes" (page 754) is an epilogue that sums up the selections in Collection 7.

See page 753.

ESSAY A short piece of nonfiction prose that examines a single subject. Most essays can be categorized as either personal or formal.

The **personal essay** generally reveals a great deal about the writer's personality and tastes. Its tone is often conversational, sometimes even humorous, and there may be no attempt to be objective. In fact, in a personal essay the focus is the writer's feelings and response to an experience. Personal essays are also called **informal** or **familiar** essays.

The **formal essay** is usually serious, objective, and impersonal in tone. Its purpose is to inform readers about a topic or to persuade them to accept the writer's views. The statements in a formal essay should be supported by facts and logic.

See pages 29, 533.
See also *Nonfiction, Objective Writing.*

EXAGGERATION Overstating something, usually for the purpose of creating a comic effect. *He's so thin that if he turned sideways, he'd disappear* is an example of exaggeration. Much of the humor in "The Cremation of Sam McGee" (page 637) comes from exaggeration.

See page 574, 636.
See also *Literary Devices, Understatement.*

EXPOSITION The kind of writing that explains or gives information. You'll find exposition in newspaper and magazine articles, encyclopedias and dictionaries, and textbooks and other nonfiction books. In fact, what you're reading right now is exposition.

In fiction and drama, **exposition** refers to the part of a plot that gives information about the characters and their problems or conflicts.

See pages 2–3, 16.
See also *Drama, Nonfiction, Plot, Short Story.*

FABLE A brief story told in prose or poetry that contains a moral, a practical lesson about how to get along in life. The characters of most fables are animals that speak and behave like people. Some of the most popular fables, such as "The Dog and The Wolf" (page 522), are attributed to Aesop, a storyteller of ancient Greece. Often a moral is stated at the end of a fable.

FICTION A prose account that is made up rather than true. The term *fiction* usually refers to **novels** and **short stories.** Fiction is often based on a writer's experiences or on historical events, but a writer may add or alter characters, events, and other details to create a desired effect. "The Landlady" (page 72) is entirely made up. "The Circuit" (page 281), on the other hand, is based to some extent on the writer's experiences.

See also *Historical Fiction, Nonfiction.*

FIGURE OF SPEECH A word or phrase that describes one thing in terms of another and is not meant to be understood as literally true. Figures of speech always involve some sort of imaginative comparison between seemingly unlike things.

The most common figures of speech are the **simile** (*The sun was shining like a new penny*), the **metaphor** (*The sun was a huge, unblinking eye*), and **personification** (*The sun smiled down on the bathers*).

See pages 530–532, 670.
See also *Literary Devices, Metaphor, Personification, Simile.*

FLASHBACK Interruption in the present action of a plot to show events that happened at an earlier time. A flashback breaks the normal forward movement of a narrative. Although flashbacks often appear in the middle of a work, they can also be placed at the beginning. They usually give background information the audience needs in order to understand the present action. The first scene of *The Diary of Anne Frank* (page 369) takes place about one year after the main action of the play. Almost the entire play, then, is a flashback to an earlier time. Flashbacks are common in stories, novels, and movies and sometimes appear in stage plays and poems as well.

See also *Plot.*

FOLK TALE A story that has no known author and was originally passed on from one generation to another by word of mouth. Unlike myths, which are about gods and heroes, folk tales are usually about ordinary people—or animals that act like people. Folk tales tend to travel, and you'll often find the same **motifs**—elements such as characters, images, or story lines—in the tales of different cultures. Cinderella, for example, appears as Aschenputtel in Germany, Yeh-Shen in China, Tam in Vietnam, and Little Burned Face among the Algonquin people of North America.

See also *Fable, Legend, Myth, Tall Tale.*

FORESHADOWING The use of clues or hints to suggest events that will occur later in the plot. Foreshadowing is used to build suspense or anxiety in the reader or viewer. A gun found in a bureau drawer in Act One of a drama may foreshadow violence later in the play. In the early part of "The Landlady" (page 72), details that hint at mystery and danger suggest what later happens to the main character, Billy.

See page 71.
See also *Suspense.*

FREE VERSE Poetry without a regular meter or rhyme scheme. Poets writing in free verse try to capture the natural rhythms of ordinary conversation—or, as in this free-verse poem, a very unusual conversation:

Love in the Middle of the Air

CATCH ME!
  I love you, I trust you,
  I love you
CATCH ME!
  catch my left foot, my right
  foot, my hand!
  here I am hanging by my teeth
  300 feet up in the air and

> CATCH ME!
>   here I come, flying without wings,
>   no parachute, doing a double triple
>   super flip-flop somersault
>   RIGHT UP HERE WITHOUT A
>   SAFETY NET AND
> CATCH ME!
>   you caught me!
>   I love you!
>
>   now it's *your* turn
>
>   —Lenore Kandel, from "Circus"

Poets writing in free verse may use **internal rhyme, repetition, alliteration, onomatopoeia,** and other sound effects. They also frequently use vivid imagery and striking metaphors and similes. "I Hear America Singing" by Walt Whitman (page 671) is a famous poem written in free verse.

> See pages 617, 670.
> See also *Meter, Poetry, Rhyme.*

HISTORICAL FICTION **A novel, story, or play set during a real historical era.** Historical events (such as battles that really happened) and historically accurate details give us an idea of what life was like during a particular period and in a specific setting.

> See also *Fiction.*

IAMBIC PENTAMETER **A line of poetry that contains five beats consisting of an unstressed syllable followed by a stressed syllable.** The iambic pentameter line is the most common in English poetry. Shakespeare's plays are written in iambic pentameter, and so is "On the Grasshopper and the Cricket" (page 663), as can be seen in the first line:

The poetry of earth is never dead

> See page 662.
> See also *Meter, Poetry, Sonnet.*

IDIOM **An expression peculiar to a particular language that means something different from the literal meaning of the words.** *Hold your tongue* (Don't speak) and *Bury your head in the sand* (Ignore a difficult situation) are idioms of American English, as is the title "A Smart Cookie" (page 748).

> See pages 746, 752.

IMAGERY **Language that appeals to the senses.** Most images are visual—that is, they create pictures in the reader's mind by appealing to the sense of sight. In "Mrs. Flowers" (page 186), Maya Angelou uses words to paint a picture of a smile: "A slow widening of her thin black lips to show even, small white teeth, then the slow effortless closing."

Images can also appeal to the senses of hearing, touch, taste, and smell, or even to several senses at once.

> See pages 532, 670.
> See also *Description.*

INVERSION **The reversal of the normal word order of a sentence.** For example, a writer might change *Her hair was long* to *Long was her hair,* inverting the sentence to emphasize the word *long* or to fit a poem's rhyme scheme (*Long was her hair—she had plenty to spare*).

IRONY **A contrast between expectation and reality.** Irony can create powerful effects, ranging from humor to strong emotion. The following terms refer to three common types of irony:

1. **Verbal irony** involves a contrast between what is said or written and what is really meant. If you were to call a baseball player who has just struck out "slugger," you would be using verbal irony.

2. **Situational irony** occurs when what happens is very different from what we expected would happen. When Casey

strikes out after we've been lead to believe he will save the day in "Casey at the Bat" (page 650), the poet is using situational irony.

3. **Dramatic irony** occurs when the audience or the reader knows something a character does not know. *The Diary of Anne Frank* (page 369) is filled with dramatic irony. We know about the tragic fate of the people in the Secret Annex, but they do not. Note the irony in the following words spoken by Mr. Frank to Mr. Van Daan. "Didn't you hear what Miep said? The invasion has come! We're going to be liberated! This is a time to celebrate!" (Act Two, Scene 3)

See pages 532, 536.

LEGEND **A story of extraordinary deeds that is handed down from one generation to the next.** Legends are based to some extent on fact. For example, George Washington did exist, but he did not chop down his father's cherry tree when he was a boy.

See also *Fable, Folk Tale, Myth, Tall Tale.*

LIMERICK **A very short humorous or non-sensical poem.** A limerick has five lines, a definite rhythm, and an *aabba* **rhyme scheme.** It tells a brief story. President Woodrow Wilson is said to have written this limerick:

> I sat next to the Duchess at tea;
> It was just as I feared it would be;
>   Her rumblings abdominal
>   Were truly phenomenal,
> And everyone thought it was me!

See also *Poetry, Rhyme.*

LITERARY DEVICES **The devices a writer uses to develop style and convey meaning.** Literary devices are a writer's tricks of the trade. They include allusion, analogy, dialect, exaggeration, figures of speech, imagery, irony, repetition, symbolism, and understatement. Literary devices that are used mostly in poetry include alliteration, assonance, meter, onomatopoeia, rhyme, and rhythm.

See pages 530–532, 536, 546, 562, 569.

LYRIC POEM **A poem that expresses the feelings or thoughts of a speaker rather than telling a story.** Lyric poems can express a wide range of feelings or thoughts. Both "A word is dead" and "The Word" (page 570) explore the speaker's feelings about words. Lyric poems are usually short and imply, rather than directly state, a single strong emotion or idea.

See pages 618, 624.
See also *Poetry.*

METAMORPHOSIS **A miraculous change from one shape or form to another one.** In myths and other stories, the change is usually from human or god to animal, from animal to human, or from human to plant. Greek and Roman myths contain many examples of metamorphosis. The myth of Narcissus, for example, tells how the vain youth Narcissus pines away for love of his own reflection and is finally changed into a flower.

METAPHOR **An imaginative comparison between two unlike things in which one thing is said to be another thing.** The metaphor is an important type of figure of speech. Metaphors are used in all forms of writing and are common in ordinary speech. When you say someone has a heart of stone, you do not mean that the person's heart is made of rock. You mean that the person is cold and uncaring.

Metaphors differ from **similes,** which use words such as *like, as, than,* and *resembles* to make comparisons. William Wordsworth's famous comparison "I wandered lonely as a cloud" is a simile because it uses *as*. If Wordsworth had written "I was a lonely, wandering cloud," he would have been using a metaphor.

Sometimes a writer hints at a connection instead of stating it directly. T. S. Eliot uses an **implied metaphor** in one of his poems when he describes fog as rubbing its back on windows, making a sudden leap, and curling around a house to fall asleep. By using words that we associate with a cat's behavior, Eliot implies a comparison without stating "The fog is a cat."

"I'm running a loose ship."

© The New Yorker Collection 1992 Victoria Roberts from cartoonbank.com. All Rights Reserved.

An **extended metaphor** is a metaphor that is extended, or developed, over several lines of writing or even throughout an entire work. "O Captain! My Captain!" (page 667) contains an extended metaphor in which the United States is compared to a ship and President Abraham Lincoln is compared to the captain of the ship.

See pages 531, 568, 569, 573, 624.
See also *Figure of Speech, Simile*.

METER **A pattern of stressed and unstressed syllables in poetry.** It is common practice to show this pattern in writing by using two

symbols. The symbol ´ indicates a stressed syllable. The symbol ˘ indicates an unstressed syllable. Indicating the metrical pattern of a poem in this way is called **scanning** the poem. The following lines by William Shakespeare have been scanned in part. (The lines make up the speech of the mischief-maker Puck, or Robin Goodfellow, at the end of the comedy *A Midsummer Night's Dream. Reprehend* means "criticize"; *serpent's tongue* means "hissing"; *Give me your hands* means "Clap.")

If we shadows have offended,
Think but this, and all is mended,
That you have but slumbered here
While these visions did appear,
And this weak and idle theme,
No more yielding but a dream,
Gentles, do not reprehend.
If you pardon, we will mend.
And, as I am an honest Puck,
If we have unearned luck
Now to scape the serpent's tongue,
We will make amends ere long,
Else the Puck a liar call.
So, good night unto you all.
Give me your hands, if we be friends,
And Robin shall restore amends.

—William Shakespeare,
from *A Midsummer Night's Dream*

See page 616.
See also *Poetry, Rhythm*.

MOOD See *Atmosphere*.

MOTIF See *Folk Tale*.

MOTIVATION **The reasons a character behaves in a certain way.** Among the many reasons for a person's behavior are feelings, experiences, and commands by others. In

"Too Soon a Woman" (page 170), Mary does not let the children eat the mushroom until she learns by eating it herself that it is not poisonous. Her motivation is her concern for their well-being.

See pages 135, 169.
See also *Character.*

MYTH **A story that explains something about the world and typically involves gods or other supernatural forces.** Myths reflect the traditions and beliefs of the culture that produced them. Almost every culture has **creation myths,** stories that explain how the world came to exist or how human beings were created. Other myths explain different aspects of life and the natural world. One of the ancient Greek myths, for instance, tells how Prometheus gave humans the gift of fire. Most myths are very old and were handed down orally before being put in written form. The exact origin of most myths is not known.

See also *Fable, Folk Tale, Legend, Tall Tale.*

NARRATION **The kind of writing that tells a story.** Narration is the main tool of writers of fiction. It is also used in any piece of nonfiction that relates a series of events in the order in which they happened (for example, in historical writing and science articles).

See page 536.
See also *Exposition, Fiction, Nonfiction.*

NARRATIVE POEM **A poem that tells a story.** "Paul Revere's Ride" (page 629) and "Casey at the Bat" (page 650) are narrative poems.

See pages 618, 628.
See also *Poetry.*

NONFICTION **Prose writing that deals with real people, things, events, and places.** Popu-

lar forms of nonfiction are the autobiography, the biography, and the essay. "Mrs. Flowers" (page 186) is an excerpt from Maya Angelou's autobiography. Other examples of nonfiction are newspaper stories, magazine articles, historical writing, science reports, and even diaries and letters.

See also *Autobiography, Biography, Essay, Fiction.*

NOVEL **A long fictional story, usually longer than one hundred book pages.** A novel uses all the elements of storytelling—plot, character, setting, theme, and point of view. It usually has more characters, settings, and themes and a more complex plot than a short story. A **novella** is a fictional story that is shorter than a novel and longer than a short story.

See also *Plot, Short Story.*

OBJECTIVE WRITING **Writing that presents facts without revealing the writer's feelings and opinions.** Most news reports in newspapers are objective writing.

See also *Essay, Subjective Writing.*

ODE **A lyric poem, rhymed or unrhymed, on a serious subject.** Odes are usually addressed to one person or thing. In "Oda a las gracias / Ode to Thanks" (pages 657–658), Pablo Neruda praises the word *thanks.*

See pages 618, 657.
See also *Poetry.*

ONOMATOPOEIA **The use of words whose sounds imitate or suggest their meaning.** *Buzz, rustle, boom, ticktock, tweet,* and *bark* are all onomatopoeic words. In the following lines the poet suggests the sound of sleigh bells in the cold night air by using onomatopoeia:

> Hear the sledges with the bells—
> Silver bells!

> What a world of merriment their melody
> foretells!
> How they tinkle, tinkle, tinkle,
> In the icy air of night!
> While the stars that oversprinkle
> All the Heavens, seem to twinkle
> With a crystalline delight.
> —Edgar Allan Poe,
> from "The Bells"

See pages 618, 670.

PARALLEL EPISODES **Repeated elements of the plot.** Three times the Big Bad Wolf goes to a little pig's house and says, "I'll huff and I'll puff and I'll blow your house in." Each time this happens, we have a parallel episode. Each of Melinda Alice's wishes in "Those Three Wishes" (page 122) is a parallel episode.

See pages 3, 32.
See also *Plot*.

PERSONIFICATION **A figure of speech in which an object or animal is spoken of as if it had human feelings, thoughts, or attitudes.** This poet writes about the moon as if it were a woman wearing silver shoes ("shoon"):

> Slowly, silently, now the moon
> Walks the night in her silver shoon;
> This way, and that, she peers, and sees
> Silver fruit upon silver trees.
> —Walter de la Mare, from "Silver"

See pages 531, 569, 572, 573.
See also *Figure of Speech*.

PERSUASION **A kind of writing intended to convince a reader to think or act in a certain way.** Examples of persuasive writing are found in newspaper editorials, in speeches, and in many essays and articles. The techniques of persuasion are widely used in advertising. Persuasion can use language that appeals to the emotions, or it can use logic to appeal to reason. When persuasive writing appeals to reason and not to the emotions, it is called **argument.** The Gettysburg Address (page 480) and "I Have a Dream" (page 483) are examples of persuasive writing.

PLAYWRIGHT **The author of a play, or drama.** Playwrights Frances Goodrich and Albert Hackett wrote *The Diary of Anne Frank* (page 369), which they based on Anne Frank's diary and life story.

See also *Author, Drama.*

PLOT **The series of related events that make up a story.** Plot is what happens in a short story, novel, play, or narrative poem. Most plots are built from these basic elements: An **introduction,** or **exposition,** tells us who the characters are and usually what their conflict is. **Complications** arise when the characters take steps to resolve the conflict. Eventually the plot reaches a **climax,** the most exciting moment in the story, when the outcome is decided one way or another. The final part of the story is the **resolution,** in which the conflict is resolved and the story is brought to a close.

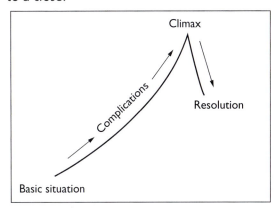

Not all works of fiction or drama have a traditional plot structure. Modern writers often experiment with plot. At times they eliminate some or almost all of the parts of a traditional plot in order to focus on other elements, such as character, point of view, or mood. In both "The Landlady" (page 72) and "Those Three Wishes" (page 122), the story ends with the climax. The reader infers the resolution.

See pages 2–3, 4, 250.
See also *Climax, Drama, Exposition, Parallel Episodes, Subplots.*

POETRY **A kind of rhythmic, compressed language that uses figures of speech and imagery designed to appeal to our emotions and imagination.** Poetry is usually arranged in lines. It often has a regular pattern of rhythm and may have a regular rhyme scheme. **Free verse** is poetry that has no regular pattern of rhythm or rhyme, though it is generally arranged in lines. Major forms of poetry include the **lyric,** the **narrative,** the **epic,** and the **ballad.**

See also *Ballad, Elegy, Epic, Figure of Speech, Free Verse, Imagery, Lyric Poem, Meter, Narrative Poem, Ode, Refrain, Rhyme, Rhythm, Sonnet, Speaker.*

POINT OF VIEW **The vantage point from which a story is told.** The most common points of view are the omniscient, the third-person limited, and the first person.

1. In the **omniscient** (all-knowing) **point of view,** the narrator knows everything about the characters and their problems. This all-knowing narrator can tell us about the past, the present, and the future of the characters. The narrator can also tell us what the characters are thinking and what is happening in several places at the same time. But the narrator does not take part in the story's action. Rather, the narrator stands above the action like a god. The omniscient is a familiar point of view; we have heard it in fairy tales since we were very young. "There Will Come Soft Rains" (page 266)

has an omniscient narrator, one who does not tell us everything.

2. In the **third-person limited point of view,** the narrator focuses on the thoughts and feelings of only one character. From this point of view, we observe the action through the eyes of only one of the characters in the story. "The Treasure of Lemon Brown" (page 730) is told from the third-person limited point of view.

3. In the **first-person point of view,** one of the characters, using the personal pronoun *I,* tells the story. We become familiar with the narrator, but we can know only what this person knows and observe only what this person observes. All of our information about the story comes from this narrator, who may be unreliable. "The Circuit" (page 281) is told from the first-person point of view.

See page 533.

PROSE **Any writing that is not poetry.** Essays, short stories, novels, newspaper articles, and letters are all written in prose. Unlike poetry, prose is usually composed in paragraphs.

See also *Fiction, Nonfiction, Poetry.*

PROTAGONIST **The main character in a work of literature.** The protagonist is involved in the work's central conflict. If there is another character opposing the protagonist, that character is called the **antagonist.** In "Flowers for Algernon" (page 33), Charlie is the protagonist. In a subplot of the story, Joe Carp and Frank Reilly are his antagonists.

See also *Character.*

PUN **A play on the multiple meanings of a word or on two words that sound alike but have different meanings.** Most often puns are used for humor; they turn up in jokes all the time. *Where does an elephant put suitcases?* Answer: *In its trunk.* This pun is called a **homographic pun**; it is a play on a word (*trunk*) that has two meanings ("proboscis of an elephant" and "compartment in an automobile"). *Is Swiss cheese good for you?* Answer: *Yes, it is holesome.* This pun is called a **homophonic pun**; it is a play on words that sound alike but are spelled differently and have different meanings (*hole* and *whole*).

REFRAIN **A repeated sound, word, phrase, line, or group of lines.** Refrains are usually associated with songs and poems but are also used in speeches and other forms of literature. Refrains are most often used to build rhythm, but they may also provide emphasis or commentary, create suspense, or help hold a work together. Refrains may be repeated with small variations in a work to fit a particular context or to create a special effect. "Fallen cold and dead" is a refrain in the poem "O Captain! My Captain!" (page 667).

See page 479.

RESOLUTION See *Plot.*

RHYME **The repetition of accented vowel sounds and all sounds following them in words that are close together in a poem.** *Mean* and *screen* are rhymes, as are *crumble* and *tumble.* The many purposes of rhyme in poetry include building rhythm, lending a songlike quality, emphasizing ideas, organizing poems (for instance, into stanzas or couplets), providing humor or pleasure for the reader, and aiding memory.

End rhymes are rhymes at the ends of lines. In the following poem, *ought* and *thought* form end rhymes, as do *afternoon* and *soon:*

> **Condition**
>
> I have to speak—I must—I should
>   —I ought . . .

> I'd tell you how I love you if I thought
> The world would end tomorrow afternoon.
> But short of that . . . well, it might be
>   too soon.
>
>   —Vikram Seth

Internal rhymes are rhymes within lines. The following line has an internal rhyme (*turning/burning*):

> Back into the chamber turning, all my soul
>   within me burning
>
>   —Edgar Allan Poe, from "The Raven"

Rhyming sounds need not be spelled the same way: *Gear/here,* for instance, is a rhyme. Rhymes can involve more than one syllable or more than one word; *poet/know it* is an example. Rhymes involving sounds that are similar but not exactly the same are called **approximate rhymes** (or **near rhymes** or **slant rhymes**). *Leave/live* is an example of an approximate rhyme. Poets writing in English often use this kind of rhyme because they believe it sounds less artificial and more like real speech than exact rhymes do. Also, it is difficult to come up with fresh, original exact rhymes. Poets interested in how a poem looks on the printed page sometimes use **eye rhymes,** or **visual rhymes**—"rhymes" involving words that are spelled similarly but pronounced differently. *Tough/cough* is an eye rhyme. (*Tough/rough* is a "real" rhyme.)

The pattern of end rhymes in a poem is called a **rhyme scheme.** To indicate the rhyme scheme of a poem, use a separate letter of the alphabet for each end rhyme. For example, the rhyme scheme of the opening of "Kubla Khan" (page 616) is *abaab.*

See pages 616–618.
See also *Free Verse, Poetry.*

RHYTHM **A musical quality produced by the repetition of stressed and unstressed**

syllables or by the repetition of certain other sound patterns. Rhythm occurs in all forms of language, both written and spoken, but is particularly important in poetry.

The most obvious kind of rhythm is the regular repetition of stressed and unstressed syllables found in some poetry. In the following lines, which describe a cavalry charge, the rhythm echoes the galloping of the attackers' horses:

> The Assyrian came down like the wolf on the
> fold,
> And his cohorts were gleaming in purple and
> gold;
> And the sheen of their spears was like stars on
> the sea,
> When the blue wave rolls nightly on deep
> Galilee.
>
> —George Gordon, Lord Byron, from
> "The Destruction of Sennacherib"

Writers also create rhythm by repeating words and phrases or even by repeating whole lines and sentences. The following passage by Walt Whitman is written in free verse and does not have a regular pattern of rhythm or rhyme. Yet the lines are rhythmical because of Whitman's use of repetition.

> I hear the sound I love, the sound of the
> human voice,
> I hear all sounds running together, combined,
> fused, or following,
> Sounds of the city and sounds out of the city,
> sounds of the day and night,
> Talkative young ones to those that like them,
> the loud laugh of work-people at their
> meals . . .
>
> —Walt Whitman, from "Song of Myself"

See pages 479, 616–618, 628, 670.
See also *Meter.*

SATIRE **Writing that ridicules something, often in order to bring about change.** Satire may poke fun at a person, a group of people, an attitude, a social institution, even all of humanity. Writers use satire to convince us of a point of view or to persuade us to follow a course of action.

SETTING **The time and place of a story, play, or narrative poem.** Most often the setting is described early in the story. For example, the story "Too Soon a Woman" (page 170) begins, "We left the home place behind, mile by slow mile, heading for the mountains, across the prairie where the wind blew forever." Setting often contributes to a work's emotional effect. It may also play an important role in the plot, especially in stories involving a conflict between a character and nature such as "In Trouble" (page 251).

See pages 236–237, 250, 265.

SHORT STORY **A short fictional prose narrative.** The first short stories were written in the nineteenth century. Early short story writers include Sir Walter Scott and Edgar Allan Poe. A short story's plot usually consists of these basic elements: the **introduction (basic situation** or **exposition), complications, climax,** and **resolution.** Short stories are more limited than novels. They usually have only one or two major characters and one important setting.

See pages 2–3.
See also *Fiction, Novel, Plot.*

SIMILE **A comparison between two unlike things, using a word such as** *like, as, than,* **or** *resembles. Her face was as round as a pumpkin* and *This steak is tougher than an old shoe* are similes.

See pages 531, 569, 573, 624.
See also *Figure of Speech, Metaphor.*

SONNET **A fourteen-line poem, usually written in iambic pentameter.** There are two kinds of sonnets: The **English,** or **Shakespearean, sonnet** has three four-line units and ends with a couplet. The **Italian,** or **Petrarchan, sonnet** (named after the fourteenth-century Italian poet Petrarch) poses a question or makes a point in the first eight lines. The last six lines respond to that question or point. "On the Grasshopper and the Cricket" (page 663) is in the form of an Italian sonnet.

See pages 618, 662.
See also *Iambic Pentameter, Poetry.*

SPEAKER **The voice talking to us in a poem.** The speaker is sometimes, but not always, the poet. It is best to think of the voice in the poem as belonging to a character the poet has created. The character may be a child, a woman, a man, an animal, or even an object.

See page 711.

STANZA **A group of consecutive lines in a poem that form a single unit.** A stanza in a poem is something like a paragraph in prose: It often expresses a unit of thought. A stanza may consist of any number of lines; it may even consist of a single line. The word *stanza* is an Italian word for "stopping place" or "place to rest." In some poems, such as "Casey at the Bat" (page 650), each stanza has the same rhyme scheme.

STEREOTYPE **A fixed idea about the members of a particular group of people that does not allow for any individuality.** Stereotypes are often based on misconceptions about racial, social, religious, gender, or ethnic groups. Some common stereotypes are the ideas that all football players are stupid, that all New Yorkers are rude, and that all politicians are dishonest.

STYLE **The way a writer uses language.** Style results from **diction** (word choice), sentence structure, and tone. One writer may use many figures of speech, for example; another writer may prefer straightforward language with few figures of speech.

See pages 530–532.
See also *Diction, Literary Devices, Tone.*

SUBJECTIVE WRITING **Writing in which the feelings and opinions of the writer are revealed.** Editorials, personal essays, and autobiographies are examples of subjective writing, as are many poems.

See also *Objective Writing.*

SUBPLOT **A minor plot that relates in some way to the main story.** In "Broken Chain" (page 17), Alfonso's problems with his brother are a subplot of the major story of his date with Sandra. In "Flowers for Algernon" (page 33), Charlie's relationship with Miss Kinnian and his problems at his job are subplots of the main plot, involving the surgery to make Charlie more intelligent.

See pages 2–3, 32.
See also *Plot.*

SUSPENSE **The uncertainty or anxiety that a reader feels about what will happen next in a story, novel, or drama.** In "The Tell-Tale Heart" (page 537), the suspense builds as the insane narrator describes his long vigil at his victim's door.

See page 71.
See also *Plot.*

SYMBOL **A person, a place, a thing, or an event that has meaning in itself and stands for something beyond itself as well.** Some symbols are so well known that we sometimes forget they are symbols. The bald eagle, for example, is a symbol of the United

States; the Star of David is a symbol of Judaism; and the cross is a symbol of Christianity. In literature, symbols are often personal and surprising. In "Suéter / Sweater" (page 565), for example, a sweater symbolizes the grandmother's love and caring.

See pages 531, 562.

TALL TALE **An exaggerated, far-fetched story that is obviously untrue but is told as though it should be believed.** Almost all tall tales are humorous. "The Cremation of Sam McGee" (page 637) is a tall tale told in the form of a poem.

See page 636.
See also *Exaggeration, Folk Tale.*

THEME **The general idea or insight about life that a work of literature reveals.** A theme is not the same as a subject. The subject of a work can usually be expressed in a word or two: *love, childhood, death.* A theme is an idea or message that the writer wishes to convey *about* that subject. For example, one theme of "Camp Harmony" (page 469) might be stated as *Innocent people often suffer in times of conflict.* The same themes, such as *Good will triumph over evil,* often recur in works from different cultures and times.

"If you were to boil your book down to a few words, what would be its message?"

© The New Yorker Collection 1986 Edward Koren from cartoonbank.com. All Rights Reserved.

A work's themes (there may be more than one) are usually not stated directly. Most often the reader has to think about all the elements of the work and use them to make an **inference,** or educated guess, about what the themes are.

See pages 354–355, 364, 468, 747.

TONE **The attitude a writer takes toward his or her subject, characters, and audience.** For example, a writer's tone might be humorous, as in "Ode to a Toad" (page 659), or passionate and sincere, as in "I Have a Dream" (page 483). When people speak, their tone of voice gives added meaning to what they say. Writers use written language to create effects similar to those that people create with their voices.

See pages 237, 280.
See also *Connotation, Diction, Style.*

TRAGEDY **A play, novel, or other narrative in which the main character comes to an unhappy end.** A tragedy depicts serious and important events. Its hero achieves wisdom or self-knowledge but suffers a great deal—perhaps even dies. A tragic hero is usually dignified and courageous and often high ranking. The hero's downfall may be caused by a **tragic flaw** (a serious character weakness) or by external forces beyond his or her control. *The Diary of Anne Frank* and Shakespeare's *Hamlet* are tragedies.

See also *Comedy, Drama.*

UNDERSTATEMENT **A statement that says less than what is meant.** Understatement is the opposite of exaggeration. It is usually used for comic effect. If you were to say that the Grand Canyon is a nice little hole in the ground, you would be using understatement.

See also *Exaggeration, Literary Devices.*

Handbook of Reading and Informational Terms

For more information about a topic, turn to the page(s) in this book indicated on a separate line at the end of the entries. To learn more about *Cause and Effect,* for example, turn to page 156.

On another line there are cross-references to entries in this Handbook that provide closely related information. For instance, *Chronological Order* contains a cross-reference to *Structural Patterns.*

ANALOGY An **analogy** (ə·nal′ə·jē) compares one thing with another thing to show, point by point, how they are alike. Writers often use analogies to show how something unfamiliar is like something well-known. Writers of scientific and technical texts often use analogies to explain difficult concepts.

Another kind of analogy is a **word analogy.** This kind of analogy is often used in tests. It asks you to compare two words and figure out how they are related to each other. To complete a word analogy,

1. figure out the relationship between the two words; then,

2. identify another pair of words that are related to each other in the same way.

In a word analogy, the symbol : means "is to." The symbol : : means "as." Once you get the hang of it, completing analogies is fun. Here's an example:

> Select the pair of words that best completes the analogy.

> STANZA : POEM : : _____
>
> **A** metaphor : simile
>
> **B** chapter : book
>
> **C** fiction : nonfiction
>
> **D** words : music

The correct answer is B. The completed analogy should read: Stanza is to poem as chapter is to book. The relationship between stanza and poem is one of *part* to *whole.* Just as a stanza is part of a poem, a chapter is part of a book.

In another kind of verbal analogy, the words might be opposites:

> DRY : WET : : cold : hot
>
> Dry is to wet as cold is to hot.

See pages 274, 557.

CAUSE AND EFFECT The **cause-effect pattern** is a text structure that writers use to explain how or why one thing leads to another. The **cause** is the reason that an action or reaction takes place. The **effect** is the result or consequence of the cause. A cause can have more than one effect, and an effect may have several causes. Writers may explain causes only or effects only. Sometimes a text is organized in a cause-and-effect chain. One cause leads to an effect, which causes another effect, and so on. Notice the cause-and-effect chain in the following paragraph from an interview with John Lewis in *The Power of Nonviolence* (another excerpt of which appears on page 489):

> In April, unknown people bombed the house of our attorney. It shook the whole area, and it shook us. How could we respond to the bombing and do something that would channel the frustration of the students in a nonviolent manner? We decided to have a march, and we sent the mayor a telegram letting him know that by noon we would march on city hall. And the next day, more than five thousand of us marched in twos in an orderly line to the city hall.

Cause:
House bombed.

↓

Effect/Cause:
It shook everyone.

↓

Effect/Causes:
People decided to march.
Telegram sent to mayor.

↓

Effect:
Nonviolent march.

Writers use the cause-effect pattern in both narrative and informational texts. In many stories, events in the plot are connected in a cause-and-effect chain. Some words and phrases that are clues to the cause-effect pattern are *because, depended on, inspired, produced, resulting in, led to,* and *outcome.* Never assume, either in your reading or in real life, that one event causes another just because it happens before it.

See pages 156, 289.
See also *Coherence, Organizational Patterns, Structural Patterns.*

CHRONOLOGICAL ORDER Writers use **chronological order,** or time order, when they put events in the sequence in which they happened, one after the other. Chronological order is a common text structure in narratives, both fictional and nonfictional. Chronological order is very important in history texts and in science texts. You will also find chronological order in directions, from directions for a simple process, such as making hot chocolate, to technical directions for using a complex mechanical device, such as an electric generator. Some words and phrases that signal the chronological-order pattern are *first, after, finally, in the meantime, as soon as,* and *at this point.*

See pages 156, 265.
See also *Coherence, Organizational Patterns, Structural Patterns.*

COHERENCE The word *cohere* means "stick together." A text has **coherence** (kō·hir′əns) when ideas stick together because they're arranged in an order that makes sense to the reader. To aid in coherence, writers often help you follow a text by using **transitions,** words and phrases that show how ideas are connected.

Common Transitional Words and Phrases	
Comparing Ideas also, and, moreover, too, similarly, another	**Contrasting Ideas** although, still, yet, but, on the other hand
Showing Cause-Effect for, since, as a result, therefore, so that	**Showing Importance** first, last, to begin with, mainly, more important
Showing Location above, across, over, there, inside, behind	**Showing Time** before, at last, when, eventually, at once

See pages 742–743.
See also *Cause and Effect, Chronological Order, Comparison and Contrast, Order of Importance, Spatial Order.*

COMPARISON AND CONTRAST When you **compare,** you look at how two or more things are similar, that is, alike. When you **contrast,** you look at how things are different. Comparison and contrast is a text structure that discusses similarities and differences. There are two basic ways to organize a comparison-and-contrast text.

1. **Block method.** Discuss all the features (sometimes called **points of comparison**) of Subject 1 first; then, all the features of Subject 2. For each subject, discuss the same features in the same order. A block comparison and contrast of the two subjects Earth and Mars (see page 278) would be organized by subject.

Subject	Features
Earth	• planet surface • weather • length of day and year
Mars	• planet surface • weather • length of day and year

2. **Point-by-point method.** Discuss one feature at a time. First, talk about a feature in Subject 1; then, discuss the same feature in Subject 2.

Features	Subject
planet surface	• Earth • Mars
weather	• Earth • Mars
length of day and year	• Earth • Mars

Expect to see transitions that help you follow the ideas in both block structure and point-by-point structure. The transitions *both* and *neither* help you find similarities.

Transitions such as *but* and *however* help you pinpoint differences.

A graphic organizer such as a Venn diagram, which uses overlapping circles to show relationships, can help you keep track of similarities and differences. See page 261 for an example of a Venn diagram.

See pages 156, 261, 439.
See also *Coherence, Organizational Patterns, Structural Patterns.*

CONCLUSION A **conclusion** is a final idea or judgment that you draw, or come to, after you've considered all the evidence. In "In Trouble," from his memoir *Woodsong* (page 251), Gary Paulsen tells how he observed his dog Columbia playing a joke on another dog. That observation leads him to a chain of reasoning based on what he knows about other animals. After he considers the evidence, he draws a conclusion.

> If Columbia could do that, I thought, if a dog could do that, then a wolf could do that. If a wolf could do that, then a deer could do that. If a deer could do that, then a beaver, and a squirrel, and a bird, and, and, and . . .
> And I quit trapping then.
> It was wrong for me to kill.

As you read, you draw conclusions based on information in the text combined with what you already know. You may or may not agree with Paulsen's reasoning and the conclusion it leads him to. Your own experiences with animals may tell you that a dog and a wolf may have a sense of humor—but that other animals might not. In that case, you might conclude that Paulsen's conclusion is valid (true and logical) for him, but not for you.

See page 294.

Handbook of Reading and Informational Terms

CONSISTENCY A text is **consistent** when its details focus on the main idea and are in agreement with it. Consistency is important because details that have little or nothing to do with the main idea of the text distract and confuse the reader. Why is the second sentence in the following passage inconsistent with the point of the passage?

> In the winter of 1866–1867 blizzards gripped the Sierra Nevada. Spring came early, and the weather was unusually warm on the East Coast. Dwellings were buried in blowing, shifting, drifting, driving snow.

See pages 742–743.

CONTEXT CLUE If you don't know the meaning of a word, **context clues,** the words and sentences surrounding it, can sometimes help you guess its meaning. The following chart gives you four types of context clues. In the examples the unfamiliar word appears in boldface (dark type). The context clue is underlined.

Definition: Look for words that define the unfamiliar word, often by giving a **synonym** for it.

> She peeled onions and grated potatoes for the **latkes,** the potato pancakes.

Restatement: Find words that restate the unfamiliar word's meaning.

> Ballet dancers perform on the **pointe** of their toeshoes—a platform about the size of a silver dollar.

Example: Look for examples that reveal the meaning of the unfamiliar word.

> Street vendors offered their **wares:** goods of all kinds were piled in their stalls.

Contrast: Find words that contrast the unfamiliar word with a word or phrase you already know.

> The land was **arid,** in contrast to the rich, fertile land we had left behind.

See pages 32, 192, 264, 297, 467, 728.

DETAIL The details that are most important in a text are called **critical details.** If you e-mail a faraway friend about a film you've seen, you have to make decisions about which details to include and which to leave out. A critical detail is one that you must include for the text to make sense. Being able to separate critical details from minor ones is especially important in writing a summary.

See pages 193, 488, 654.
See also *Summarizing.*

ENUMERATION Enumeration (ē · n $\overline{oo}$ 'mər · ā'shən) is a kind of text structure that organizes information into a list. The facts or events on the list may be cited in the order of size, location, importance, or any other order that will make sense to the reader. Some of the words and phrases that signal the enumeration text pattern are *to begin with, secondly, most important, for instance, another, for example,* and *in fact.* Social studies textbooks and science textbooks often use the enumeration text pattern. For an example of the enumeration pattern, see "The Fugitive Slave Acts of 1793 and 1850" (page 157).

See page 156.
See also *Coherence, Logic.*

FACT A **fact** is something that can be verified, or proved. It can be proved by direct observation or by checking a reliable reference source. The following statement is a fact:

> In 1860, Abraham Lincoln was elected president despite winning only 40 percent of the popular vote.

You can verify this fact by looking it up in a history book or in an encyclopedia. In fields where discoveries are still being made, you need to check facts in a recently published source. A Web site on the Internet may be current, but it may not be reliable. Remember that anybody can post a statement on the Internet. If you suspect that a statement given as a fact is not true, try to find the same fact in another source.

See page 67.
See also *Opinion*.

FALLACIOUS REASONING Statements that seem reasonable at first may, if examined closely, prove to be based on **fallacious** (fə · lā′shəs) **reasoning,** faulty reasoning, or mistakes in logic. (The word *fallacious* comes from a Latin word meaning "deceptive" or "tricky." The word *false* comes from the same root, as does the word *fallacy*.) Fallacious reasoning leads to false or incorrect conclusions. Here are some types of fallacious reasoning:

1. **Begging the question,** also called **circular reasoning,** assumes the truth of a statement before it has been proved. You appear to be giving a reason to support your opinion, but all you're doing is restating the same thing in different words.

> Everyone should be required to attend school sports events because mandatory attendance at such events is important.
>
> We can't control worldwide air pollution because every country in the world is guilty of polluting the air.

2. **Name-calling** uses labels to attack the person on the other side of the argument, instead of giving reasons or evidence to support the opposing point of view. This fallacy includes attacking the person's character, situation, or background.

> You're not seriously considering Latisha's childish ideas for the school dance, are you?
>
> Of course, Allen's not going to say that doctors make too much money. His mother's a doctor.

3. **Stereotyping** gives all members of a group the same (usually undesirable) characteristics. It assumes that everyone (or everything) in that group is alike. (The word *stereotype* comes from the word for a metal plate that was used to print the same image over and over.) Stereotypes are often based on misconceptions about racial, social, religious, gender, or ethnic groups.

> Smart kids are poor athletes.
>
> Actors are conceited.
>
> Big cities are dirty and dangerous.

4. **Hasty generalization** is a broad, general statement or conclusion that is made without sufficient evidence to back it up. A hasty generalization is often made on the basis of one or two experiences or observations.

> My brother is left-handed, and he's an artist. My aunt is left-handed, and she writes songs. I'm right-handed, and I have no artistic or musical talent at all.
>
> **Hasty generalization:** Left-handed people are more creative than right-handed people.

If any exceptions to the conclusion can be found, the generalization is not true.

5. **Either/or fallacy** assumes that there is only one correct choice or one solution, even though there may be many.

> Either we have free trade, or we return to the cold war.
>
> If you don't get good grades this year, you're not college material.

6. **False cause and effect** occurs when one event is said to be the cause of another event just because the two events happened in sequence. You cannot assume that an event caused whatever happened afterward.

> We got new uniforms, and our team won four straight games. The uniforms helped us win.
>
> Our mayor should be reelected. During her first term the crime rate in our city fell almost 10 percent.

See page 533.

GENERALIZATION A **generalization** is a broad statement that applies to many individuals, experiences, situations, or observations. A generalization is a type of conclusion that is drawn after considering as many of the facts as possible. A valid generalization is based on evidence, specific data, or facts. Here are some specific facts and a generalization based on them. Notice that each fact is one piece of evidence. The generalization then states what the evidence adds up to, drawing a conclusion that applies to all members of the group.

> **Specific Facts:** My dog wags her tail when she's happy. Kathy's dog, Soot, wags his tail when he is happy.
>
> **Generalization:** All dogs I've seen wag their tails when they're happy.

A generalization jumps from your own specific experiences and observations to a larger, general understanding. To be **valid,** or true, a generalization must apply to every specific individual or instance within the group—including the millions in the group that are not mentioned or listed in arriving at the generalization.

See pages 294, 468.

IDIOM An **idiom** (id′ē · əm) is an expression peculiar to a particular language that means something different from the literal (dictionary) meaning of the words. If your brother tells you he's fallen for Angela, you know that he means he likes her a lot. Despite what the words say, you know he hasn't fallen down. Every language has its own idioms. When you grow up speaking a language, you understand its idioms without even thinking about them. When you're learning a new language, it's hard to figure out what its idioms mean, and it's even harder to use them correctly.

See pages 746, 747, 752.

INFERENCE An **inference** is a guess based on clues. When you read, you make inferences based on clues that the writer provides. For example, you guess what will happen next in a story based on what the writer has already told you. You change your inferences as the writer gives you more information. Sometimes a writer will deliberately drop a clue that leads you, for a short time, to an incorrect inference about what is going to happen next. That's part of the fun of reading. Until you get to the end of a suspenseful story, you can never be sure about what will happen next.

When you're writing about a story or an informational text, you must be sure your inferences are supported by details in the text.

Supported inferences are based directly on evidence in the writer's text that you can point to and on reasonable prior knowledge. Some interpretation of the evidence is possible, but you cannot ignore or contradict facts in the text that the writer has given you.

Unsupported inferences are conclusions that are not logical. They ignore the facts in the text, or misinterpret them. Whenever you're asked to write an essay about a text, it's a good idea to re-read the text before and after you write your essay. Check each inference you make against the text to make sure you can find evidence for it. For example, if you write an analysis of a character in a story and you say that the character is self-centered, you should cite details from the text to support your inference.

See pages 142, 280, 294, 558.

INFORMATIVE TEXTS When you're reading for your own enjoyment, a mystery story, for instance, you can read at your own pace. You can speed up to see what happens next. If you get bored, you can move on to another story. When you're **reading for information,** you need to read slowly, looking for main ideas and important details. Slow and careful reading is especially important when you're trying to get meaning from consumer, workplace, and public documents. These documents are often not written by professional writers, so they may be difficult to read. **Consumer documents** are texts like warranties, contracts, product information, and instructional manuals. Here are some points to keep in mind when you read consumer documents:

1. Try to read the consumer document before you buy the product. Then you can ask the clerk to explain anything you don't understand.

2. Read all of the pages in whatever language comes most easily to you. (Many documents are printed in two or three languages.) You will often find important information where you least ex-

pect it, such as at the very end of the document.

3. Read the fine print; *fine,* here, means "tiny and barely readable." Some fine-print statements in documents are required by law. They are designed to protect you, the consumer, not the company that makes the product, so the company may not be interested in emphasizing these points.

4. Don't expect the document to be interesting or easy to read. If you don't understand a statement and you can't ask someone at the store that sold you the product, send an e-mail to the company that made it. It's OK to complain to the company if you find their consumer document confusing.

5. Before you sign anything, read everything on the page and be sure you understand what you're agreeing to. Ask to take the document home, and have your parent or guardian read it. If you are not of legal age in your state, an adult may be responsible for whatever you've signed. Make a copy of any document that you've put your signature to—and keep it in a place where you can find it.

Workplace documents include items like job applications, memos, instructional manuals, and employee handbooks. In addition to the points about reading consumer documents, you might want to keep these points in mind:

1. Take all the time you need to read and understand the document. Don't let anyone rush you or tell you that a document is not important, that it's just a formality.

2. Read technical directions carefully, even if they're just posted on the side of a device you're supposed to operate. Read all of the directions before you

start. Ask questions if you're not sure how to proceed. Don't try anything out before you know what will happen next.

3. An employee handbook contains the "rules of the game" at a particular business. It tells you about holidays, work hours, break times, and vacations, as well as other important company policies. Read an employee handbook from cover to cover. Pay special attention to information about health benefits, probationary periods, and policies on sexual harassment.

Public documents are texts put out by public agencies and not-for-profit groups such as community-action organizations and church groups. They might inform readers about matters like health concerns, schedules, and records. As you get older, this type of document will become increasingly important to you. Practice reading public documents now, and talk about your understanding of them with your family.

Question Sheet for Informational Texts

1. What is the topic? _____

2. Do I understand what I'm reading? _____

3. What parts should I re-read? _____

_____

4. What are the main ideas and details?

   Main idea: _____   Main idea: _____

   Details: _____   Details: _____

   Main idea: _____   Main idea: _____

   Details: _____   Details: _____

5. Summary of what I learned:

   _____

   _____

See pages 800–802, 809.

JUDGMENT When you make **judgments,** you form opinions. As you read a text or watch TV, you're constantly making judgments about what you read and see. When you express your opinions in writing, it's important to support your judgments with evidence. If you're writing about a story's plot or characters, you should support your judgments with references to the text, to other works, or to your own experiences. Before you make judgments about a TV show or a movie, here are some points to keep in mind:

1. Identify the purpose of the program or film. You need to know the writer's goal before you say to what extent the goal was reached. If the writer's purpose was humor, you should judge it for its humor, not for the credibility of its characters and plot.

2. Think about the beliefs and assumptions that the work represents. For example, is violence considered funny? tragic? ordinary? Does the program attack or ignore stereotypes?

3. Evaluate the information presented, especially in a nonfiction TV program. What are the program's sources? How reliable are they? What biases or prejudices do you notice? Be sure to distinguish between provable facts and someone's opinions.

4. Make your own judgment. After you've observed the work critically, draw your own conclusions and support them with references to the work itself, to other works of the same type and purpose, and to your personal knowledge.

See page 546.
See also *Fallacious Reasoning, Opinion, Purposes of Texts.*

KWL CHART Before you start reading a text, it's a good idea to review what you already know about the subject. As you think about

---

the subject, you'll come up with questions that the text may answer. Making a **KWL chart** can help you focus on a text. The following chart is based on the text from *Harriet Tubman: Conductor on the Underground Railroad* (page 143):

- In the **K** column, jot down what you already know about Harriet Tubman.

- In the **W** column, write any questions you have that the text might answer. Glancing through the text, looking at the pictures, if any, and reading subtitles and captions will help you come up with questions.

- As you read, note in the **L** column what you learn that supplements, answers, or contradicts what you wrote in the other two columns.

K	W	L
What I **K**now	What I **W**ant to Know	What I **L**earned
She was African American.	What underground railroad?	

See page 444.

LOGIC is correct reasoning. A **logical text** supports statements with reasons and evidence. A text is illogical when it does not provide reasons backed by evidence (facts and examples). Notice how each sentence in the following text, from "Blasting Through Bedrock: The Central Pacific Railroad Workers" (page 792), gives evidence that supports the sentence before it:

In the winter of 1866–1867, blizzards gripped the Sierra Nevada. Dwellings were buried in blowing, shifting, drifting, driving snow. Men who were building the western portion of the country's first transcontinental railroad had to tunnel from their camp to the mountainside, where they spent long, cold days digging out rock so tracks could be laid. The Central Pacific Railroad was building east from California to meet the Union Pacific Railroad, which was working west from Omaha, Nebraska.

See page 533.
See also *Logical Order.*

LOGICAL ORDER is a method of organization used in informational texts. In **logical order,** details are classified into related groups. Writers who use this order may use the **comparison-and-contrast** pattern to show similarities and differences among various groups. For an example of logical order, see "Fast, Strong, and Friendly Too" (page 261), an article about dogs.

See page 724.
See also *Comparison and Contrast.*

MAGAZINE A **magazine** is a publication, usually in paperback, that comes out at regular intervals, such as weekly, monthly, or even annually. There are all kinds of magazines that appeal to general or special interests—from groups that love dogs (the magazine *Bark*) to people who enjoy reading about celebrities (the magazine *People*). A growing number of magazines are written especially for teenagers. Magazines may seek to entertain, to inform, or to persuade readers. Most have certain structural features in common:

- An attractive cover gives you the title, price, and date of the magazine and usually some idea of what's inside. A brightly colored illustration is usually included on the cover to grab your attention.

- The table of contents page appears close to the beginning of the magazine.

You may also find a list of contributors and letters to the editor in the opening pages.

- Most magazines contain photographs and other kinds of illustrations. Many include cartoons. Graphic features such as color and headings and subheadings in different sizes and fonts (printing styles), along with charts and maps, organize the text visually and often highlight information. You'll often find stories and articles printed in columns, but each page is designed for maximum appeal to the reader. Sidebars, short articles set off within the article, develop a topic related in some way to the main story.

- Many magazines are supported financially not by the price of the publication but by advertising revenues. Advertisers choose to sell their products in magazines that appeal to the kind of buyer they are looking for. Some readers think the splashy ads in some magazines are almost as entertaining as the magazine's features.

See page 275.
See also *Purposes of Texts.*

MAIN IDEA The **main idea** of a nonfiction text is the writer's most important point, opinion, or message. The main idea may be stated directly, or it may be only suggested or implied. If the idea is not stated directly, it's up to you to look at the details and decide on the idea they all seem to support. Try to restate the writer's main idea in your own words.

In a **persuasive text,** the writer's main idea, or thesis, is called a **proposition.** It is usually presented as a positive statement of opinion.

> Middle-school students should be required to wear uniforms.

> The sale of junk food should be prohibited in public schools.
>
> Every kid should get an allowance.

A proposition should be supported by reasons that explain the writer's opinion. Each reason should be supported, in turn, by details and evidence. The evidence may include **facts** and **figures (statistics), examples, anecdotes** (especially those that tell about personal experiences), and statements or direct **quotations by experts** on the subject.

See pages 29, 185, 462, 488.
See also *Note Taking, Outlining, Summarizing.*

MAPS Maps show the natural landscape of an area. Shading may be used to show physical features, such as mountains and valleys. Colors are often used to show elevation (height above or below sea level). **Political maps** show political units, such as states and nations. The map of Europe before World War II on page 366 is a political map. **Special-purpose maps** present information that is related to geography, such as the route of the Underground Railroad (page 151).

How to Read a Map

1. **Identify the map's focus.** The map's title and labels tell you its focus—its subject and the geographical area it covers.

2. **Study the legend.** The **legend,** or key, explains the symbols, lines, colors, and shading used in the map.

3. **Check directions and distances.** Maps often include a **compass rose,** a diagram that shows north, south, east, and west. If you're looking at a map that doesn't have one, assume that north is at the top, west is to the left, and so on. Many maps also include a **scale** to help you relate distances on the map to actual

distances. One inch on a map may equal one, ten, or fifty miles or more.

4. **Look at the larger context.** The **absolute location** of any place on earth is given by its **latitude** (the number of degrees north or south of the equator) and **longitude** (the number of degrees east or west of the **prime meridian,** or zero degrees longitude). Some maps also include **locator maps,** which show the area depicted in relation to a larger area. Notice the locator map in the upper right corner of the map shown here:

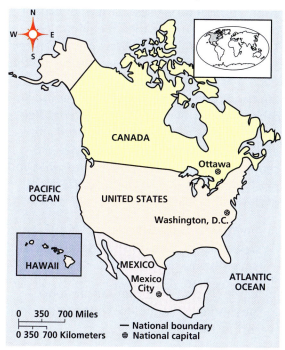

See page 366, 443.

MEANING The most important idea or message of an informational text is called its **underlying meaning.** When you're reading or summarizing a text, to find the underlying meaning, you need to ask yourself the following questions:

• What is the writer's point? What is his or her reason for writing this text?

• What idea do all the critical details add up to?

• What connection can I make between the meaning of this text and the meaning of other texts I have read?

• What connection can I make between this text and my own life? What special meaning does this text have for me? How do I feel about what the writer is saying? Do I agree or disagree? What reasons can I give for my opinion?

NOTE TAKING Taking notes is a good way to remember a writer's major ideas and interesting details. Notes are especially useful when you read an informational text such as a history or science assignment. You can jot down notes in a notebook such as the kind you might use for a reading log. Many students like to use three-by-five-inch note cards, which can be clipped together or filed in a small file box.

Tips for Taking Notes

1. **Your own words.** Notes don't have to be written in complete sentences. Put them in your own words, using phrases that will help you recall the text. When you take notes, it's a good idea to use either of the following techniques:

   • **Summarize** the information by writing only the important ideas.

   • **Paraphrase** by writing all the ideas in your own words.

   Taking notes in either of these ways will help you avoid using another writer's words. Copying information word for word and presenting it as your own is called **plagiarism** (plā′jə · riz′əm). When you want to copy another writer's words, you need to put quotation marks around the passage you copy and be sure to identify the writer.

2. **Main ideas.** Jot down each main idea at the top of its own page or note card. As

you keep reading, add details that relate to that idea page or to the note card.

3. **Write clearly.** Even though no one but you may ever see your notes (unless you become famous), try to write clearly for your own sake. You'll want to read your notes later, and decoding your own mysterious handwriting can take a lot of time. When you finish taking notes for the day, review them to make sure they make sense to you.

See page 488.
See also *Main Idea.*

OPINION An **opinion** is a belief or an attitude. An opinion cannot be proved to be true or false. The following statement is an opinion:

> Lincoln was the best president the United States has ever had.

People have different opinions about who was the best president.

A **valid opinion** is an opinion that is supported by facts. The following opinion is valid. It is supported by two verifiable facts.

> Lincoln was a great president because he freed the slaves and led our country through the Civil War.

When you read a persuasive text, remember that statements of opinion can't be proved, but they can and should be supported by facts.

See page 67.
See also *Fact.*

ORDER OF IMPORTANCE is a method of organization often used in informational texts. Writers of persuasive texts have to decide whether to give the strongest reason

first or to present the weakest reason first and end with the strongest point. News articles always begin with the most important details because they want to grab the readers' attention immediately. The structure of a news article looks like an upside-down triangle, with the least important details at the bottom.

See also *Details.*

ORGANIZATIONAL PATTERNS Writers of informational texts use a pattern of organization that will make their meaning clear. There are several ways writers can organize information. Don't expect a writer to use the same pattern throughout an entire text. Many writers switch from one pattern to another and may even combine patterns. Recognizing how a writer has organized a text—and noticing where and why the pattern changes—will help you understand what you read. Here are some of the organizational patterns you will find:

- **enumeration** (ē · noo'mər · ā'shən), also called **list**—citing a list of details: first, second, and so on

- **chronology,** time order, or sequence—putting events or steps in the order in which they occur

- **comparison-contrast**—pointing out and explaining similarities and differences

- **cause and effect**—showing how events happen as a result of other events

- **problem-solution**—explaining how a problem may be solved

- **question-answer**—asking questions, then giving the answers

See pages 156, 724.
See also *Cause and Effect, Chronological Order, Comparison and Contrast, Enumeration.*

OUTLINING If you've taken notes on a text, you may want to organize your notes into an outline. Outlining puts main ideas and details in a form that you can review quickly. An **informal outline,** sometimes called a working outline, should have at least three main ideas. You put supporting details under each main idea, like this:

Informal Outline

First main idea

Detail supporting first main idea

Another detail supporting first main idea

Third detail supporting first main idea

Second main idea

[etc.]

A **formal outline** is especially useful if you're writing a research paper. You might start with a working outline and then revise it into a formal one. Your teacher may ask you to submit a formal outline with your completed research paper, so you have to be sure that it has the correct form. When you create a formal outline, you revise it, making changes as you revise your paper.

Formal outlines use Roman numerals (I, II, III), capital letters (A, B, C), and Arabic numerals (1, 2, 3) to show order, relationship, and relative importance of ideas. The headings in a formal outline should have the same grammatical structure, and you must be consistent in your use of either phrases or sentences (you can't move back and forth between them). There are always at least two divisions under each heading or none at all.

Here is the beginning of a formal outline of "Memory a Matter of Brains and Brawn" (page 68):

Formal Outline

I. Importance of exercise in protecting brain function

A. Mental exercise

1. Reading

2. Learning a foreign language

B. Physical exercise

II. Preventing Alzheimer's disease

See page 488.
See also *Main Idea.*

PARAPHRASING Paraphrasing is usually used to restate a poem. In a **paraphrase,** you restate every line in your own words. A paraphrase is longer than a summary. In some cases, it may even be longer than the original text! A paraphrase can help you understand a difficult text. Here is a paraphrase of the poem "A word is dead" by Emily Dickinson (page 570):

> In the first three-line stanza, the speaker says that some people claim that a word is "dead," that is, it no longer has meaning or importance, after it is spoken. In the second three-line stanza the speaker states an opposing opinion, that a word only begins to "live" after it is spoken. This means that a word, especially a loving or hateful word, is like a living thing—it can hurt or bring hope or happiness to people.

PREDICTIONS As you read a story, you may keep guessing about what will happen next. That means you're already using a reading strategy called **making predictions.** To make predictions, look for clues that the writer gives you. Try to connect those clues with other stories you've read and with experiences in your own life. As you continue to read and more information comes in from the writer, you'll change, or adjust, your guesses. Making predictions as you read helps you become involved with the story and its characters and their conflicts.

See page 71.

PREVIEWING When you **preview** a text, you look over the material to see what lies ahead. **Scan** (look specifically for) chapter titles, headings, subheadings, and terms printed in boldface or italics. Glance at the illustrations and graphics (such as charts, maps, and time lines), and **skim** (read quickly) a paragraph or two to check the vocabulary level and writing style.

See page 536.

PRIOR KNOWLEDGE The knowledge you already have about a topic before you read a text is called your **prior knowledge.** (Prior means "before.")

See pages 443–444.

PURPOSES OF TEXTS Texts are written for different purposes. The writer may want to

- provide information

- influence the way you think or act

- express personal feelings

- entertain you

Readers also have different purposes: You read to get information, to enjoy a good story, to share an experience. Being aware of why you are reading helps you to **establish a purpose for reading,** which helps you to decide how you will read the text. If you are reading a science fiction novel just for fun, you might read quickly and eagerly to find out what happens next. If you decide to read that same novel for a book report, however, you would read more slowly and carefully.

You might even re-read some parts of the book to decide how you will evaluate it. Sometimes you read to find an answer to a particular question, such as "Where do penguins live?" To find the answer, you may need to use an index or table of contents first and then skim a text (read quickly) to locate the information you want.

See pages 29, 67, 178.
See also *Magazine.*

QUESTIONS One way to monitor your understanding is to ask **questions** as you read. Get in the habit of carrying on a dialogue (in your head or in a reading notebook) with the writer. Make comments, ask questions, and note what puzzles you. Jot down facts that you might want to look up and verify. Experiment with ways of noting questions, such as using sticky notes that you place by paragraphs. If you find yourself confused by a passage, try one of the following strategies:

- Re-read the passage more slowly.

- Read the passage aloud.

- Put the ideas into your own words.

- Look for context clues that might help you figure out the meaning of an unfamiliar word.

- Use a graphic organizer to jot down the text's ideas.

See page 711.
See also *Detail, Fallacious Reasoning.*

RETELLING A reading strategy called **retelling** helps you understand and recall what you read. As you're reading a text, stop often to retell the important events that have happened up to that point. You might want to tell a partner what has happened, or you can jot down notes in a reading note-book or journal. Retelling can be used in reading fiction and in reading historical and scientific texts.

See page 729.
See also *Detail*.

SOMEBODY WANTED BUT SO Stories are built on conflict. A good way to summarize a story's plot is to reduce it to the following formula:

Somebody (name the main character):

_____

Wanted (tell what the main character wants):

_____

But (tell what complications develop that get between the main character and what he or she wants):

_____

So (tell how it all comes out in the end):

_____

_____

See page 356.

SPATIAL ORDER Spatial (spā′shəl) order is one of the patterns writers use to organize their texts. **Spatial order** shows where things are located. (The word *spatial* is related to the word *space*. Spatial order shows where things are located in space.) Spatial order is often used in descriptive writing. Here is an example from "Camp Harmony" (page 469):

> Our home was one room, about eighteen by twenty feet, the size of a living room. There was one small window in the wall opposite the one door. It was bare

> except for a small, tinny wood-burning stove crouching in the center.

STORY MAP A graphic organizer like the following one can help you map the plot structure of a story:

Characters	What they want
Conflict (what keeps them from getting it):	
Complications 1. 2. 3.	
Climax (moments when conflicts are resolved):	

Resolution
(how it all
turns out):

See page 2–3, 16.

STRUCTURAL PATTERNS All texts have a structure. Without structure a piece of writing would fall apart—just as a house would fall down if its basic structure were faulty. The structure that holds a story together is called its **plot**. The structures that support the details in informative texts can be **chronology, order of importance, comparison and contrast,** or **cause and effect.**

See pages 156, 261, 265, 289, 724.

SUMMARIZING When you **summarize,** you mention and explain only the most important ideas of a work. Because a summary is much shorter than the original text, you have to decide which ideas to include and which ones to leave out. To summarize an informational text, start by naming the title, the author, and the subject. Then, go on to state the main ideas and the **key details,** those that support the main idea or underlying meaning. Follow the same order that the writer used. If you quote any of the writer's words, be sure to put quotation marks around them.

"Picking Strawberries: Could You Do It?" by Flo Ota De Lange gives information about picking strawberries for a living. The writer explains that strawberries are "easily bruised," but a worker has to pick about 840 strawberries every hour, or ten thousand strawberries in twelve hours to provide the worker's family "with the basics." To give readers some idea of how difficult it is to pick that many strawberries without damaging them, the writer describes a knot-tying experiment. She shows that picking strawberries is a difficult, repetitive job requiring a great deal of speed and coordination.

If you are summarizing a short story, you cite the story's title and author and the main events of the plot. You should mention the story's main characters, the conflict, and, of course, the resolution of the conflict.

See pages 16, 162, 169, 654, 674.
See also *Main Idea.*

TIME LINE Use a **time line** to find out when events happened.

A time line may show a vast span of time, such as thousands or millions of years.

Events on a time line are arranged in chronological order, with long-ago events at one end and more recent events at the other. The approximate date (year or century) of each event appears above, below, or beside the line.

See pages 367–368.

Language Handbook

1 THE PARTS OF SPEECH

THE NOUN

1a. A *noun* is a word used to name a person, a place, a thing, or an idea.

PERSONS	Maya Angelou, Dr. Strauss, children, team, baby sitter
PLACES	desert, neighborhood, outer space, New York City
THINGS	money, wind, animals, *Voyager 2,* Statue of Liberty
IDEAS	courage, love, freedom, equality, self-control

Compound Nouns

A **compound noun** is two or more words used together as a single noun. A compound noun may be written as one word, as separate words, or as a hyphenated word.

TIPS FOR SPELLING

When you are not sure how to write a compound noun, look in a dictionary.

ONE WORD	seafood, footsteps, videocassette, daydream, Iceland
SEPARATE WORDS	compact disc, police officer, John F. Kennedy, "Flowers for Algernon"
HYPHENATED WORD	self-esteem, great-grandparents, fourteen-year-old, sister-in-law

Collective Nouns

A **collective noun** is a word that names a group.

EXAMPLES faculty family herd team crew

Common Nouns and Proper Nouns

A **common noun** is a general name for a person, a place, a thing, or an idea. A **proper noun** names a particular person, place, thing, or idea. Proper nouns always begin with a capital letter. Common nouns begin with a capital letter in titles and when they begin sentences.

COMMON NOUNS	PROPER NOUNS
poem	"Paul Revere's Ride," "Oranges"
nation	Mexico, United States of America
athlete	Michael Jordan, Serena Williams
river	Rio Grande, Congo River

QUICK CHECK I

Identify each noun in the following sentences. Classify each noun as *common* or *proper*.

EXAMPLE **I.** Roald Dahl is the author of "The Landlady."

  I. *Roald Dahl—proper; author—common; "The Landlady"—proper*

1. Billy Weaver was going to The Bell and Dragon, an inn that was in Bath.
2. Was Billy wearing his brown suit and a navy-blue overcoat?
3. In his mind, briskness was a characteristic of businessmen.
4. "Big shots" in the company always seemed brisk to Billy.
5. How was the landlady like a jack-in-the-box?

Try It Out

For the following paragraph about "Jack and the Beanstalk," replace the vague nouns with exact, specific nouns.

[1] Have you read the story about the boy who traded an animal for seeds? [2] A huge vine grew from the seeds, and the boy climbed it. [3] At the top, he discovered a large man as well as a bird that laid golden eggs. [4] The boy stole the man's things. [5] The boy's parent forgave him for the foolish trade that he had made.

Using Specific Nouns

Whenever possible, use specific, exact nouns. Using specific nouns will make your writing more accurate and precise, as well as more interesting.

VAGUE People crowded into the building.
PRECISE **Men, women,** and **children** crowded into the **theater.**

VAGUE Following the young person was a small dog.
PRECISE Following the **child** was a **dachshund.**

THE PRONOUN

Ib. **A *pronoun* is a word used in place of one or more nouns or pronouns.**

EXAMPLES After Bill fed the dog and cat, Bill let the dog and cat go outside.
  After Bill fed the dog and cat, **he** let **them** go outside.

The word that a pronoun stands for is called its ***antecedent.*** Sometimes the antecedent is not stated.

STATED ANTECEDENT Mrs. Flowers opened the **book** and began reading **it.**
UNSTATED ANTECEDENT **Who** wrote the book?

Personal Pronouns

A ***personal pronoun*** refers to the one speaking (*first person*), the one spoken to (*second person*), or the one spoken about (*third person*).

PERSONAL PRONOUNS		
	SINGULAR	**PLURAL**
First Person	I, me, my, mine	we, us, our, ours
Second Person	you, your, yours	you, your, yours
Third Person	he, him, his, she, her, hers, it, its	they, them, their, theirs

EXAMPLES   **He** and **his** friends caught several frogs and put **them** in a bag.

Did **you** say that **it** is too cold for **us** to go outside?

Reflexive and Intensive Pronouns

A *reflexive pronoun* refers to the subject and directs the action of the verb back to the subject. An *intensive pronoun* emphasizes a noun or another pronoun. Reflexive pronouns and intensive pronouns have the same form.

REFLEXIVE AND INTENSIVE PRONOUNS	
First Person	myself, ourselves
Second Person	yourself, yourselves
Third Person	himself, herself, itself, themselves

REFLEXIVE   Alfonso asked **himself** why he had taken off the chain.

INTENSIVE   Mrs. Flowers made the tea cookies **herself.**

Demonstrative Pronouns

A *demonstrative pronoun* (*this, that, these, those*) points out a person, a place, a thing, or an idea.

EXAMPLE   **This** is Ernie's bike.

Interrogative Pronouns

An *interrogative pronoun* (*what, which, who, whom, whose*) introduces a question.

EXAMPLE   **Who** is the author of "Flowers for Algernon"?

Relative Pronouns

A *relative pronoun* (*that, what, which, who, whom, whose*) introduces a subordinate clause.

EXAMPLE   Mr. White received the two hundred pounds **that** he had wished for.

NOTE   The possessive pronouns *my, your, his, her, its, our,* and *their* are sometimes called *possessive adjectives.* Follow your teacher's instructions regarding these possessive forms.

NOTE   If you are not sure whether a pronoun is reflexive or intensive, read the sentence aloud, omitting the pronoun. If the meaning stays the same, the pronoun is intensive. If the meaning changes, the pronoun is reflexive.

EXAMPLES   Rachel painted the fence **herself.** [Without *herself,* the meaning stays the same. The pronoun is intensive.]

They treated **themselves** to a picnic. [Without *themselves,* the sentence doesn't make sense. The pronoun is reflexive.]

☞   *This, that, these,* and *those* can also be used as adjectives. See page 895.

☞   For more about subordinate clauses, see pages 929–932

NOTE Many indefinite pronouns can also serve as adjectives.

INDEFINITE PRONOUN
Both of the men regretted kidnapping Johnny.

ADJECTIVE **Both** men regretted kidnapping Johnny.

Indefinite Pronouns

An **indefinite pronoun** refers to a person, a place, or a thing that is not specifically named.

Common Indefinite Pronouns				
all	both	everybody	none	several
any	each	few	no one	some
anyone	either	many	one	something

EXAMPLES   **All** of them wanted to hear the story of Urashima Taro.
The travelers saw **someone.**

 QUICK CHECK 2

Identify each of the pronouns in the following sentences as *personal, reflexive, intensive, demonstrative, interrogative, relative,* or *indefinite.*

EXAMPLE   1. That was a very strange person!
          1. *That—demonstrative*

1. Who were her previous tenants, and what happened to them?
2. That is the guest book that they signed.
3. Had they themselves or anyone else been suspicious of her?
4. The house, which was brightly lit, had a sign in its window.
5. She brought a pot of tea for him and herself.

THE ADJECTIVE

 An *adjective* is a word used to modify a noun or a pronoun.

To *modify* a word means to describe the word or to make its meaning more definite. An adjective modifies a word by telling *what kind, which one, how much,* or *how many.*

WHAT KIND?	WHICH ONE?	HOW MUCH? *or* HOW MANY?
tall woman	*this* year	*less* time
steep mountain	*last* answer	*many* mistakes
exciting story	*middle* row	*few* marbles

An adjective may come before or after the word it modifies.

EXAMPLES   The **old** soldier told the **curious** couple that they could have **three** wishes.
The map, although **old** and **worn,** was **useful** to him.

Articles

The most frequently used adjectives are *a, an,* and *the.* The adjectives *a* and *an* are called **indefinite articles.** They indicate that the noun refers to someone or something in general. *A* is used before a word beginning with a consonant sound. *An* is used before a word beginning with a vowel sound.

EXAMPLE   He gave the salesclerk **a** nickel and **an** orange.

The adjective *the* is a **definite article.** It indicates that the noun refers to someone or something in particular.

EXAMPLE   Smiley went to **the** swamp to find **the** stranger a frog.

Proper Adjectives

A **proper adjective** is formed from a proper noun and begins with a capital letter.

PROPER NOUN	PROPER ADJECTIVE
Africa	**African** nations
Shakespeare	**Shakespearean** drama
Rio Grande	**Rio Grande** valley

Some proper nouns, such as *Rio Grande,* do not change spelling when they are used as adjectives.

Demonstrative Adjectives

This, that, these, and *those* can be used both as adjectives and as pronouns. When they modify a noun or a pronoun, these words are called **demonstrative adjectives**. When used alone, they are called **demonstrative pronouns**.

DEMONSTRATIVE ADJECTIVE   **This** poem was written by Amy Ling.
DEMONSTRATIVE PRONOUN   **This** is an example of personification.

☞ For more about demonstrative pronouns, see page 893.

 QUICK CHECK 3

In the following sentences, identify each adjective and the word that it modifies. Also, identify any articles, proper adjectives, or demonstrative adjectives.

EXAMPLE   **1.** Wasn't Christopher Mulholland a Cambridge undergraduate?

    1. *a (article)—undergraduate; Cambridge (proper)—undergraduate*

1. The houses were old and run-down but had once been grand.
2. This house looks like a nice, friendly place.
3. The room seems comfortable, with a large sofa and two pets.
4. The London train had been slow, and the weather was chilly.
5. What had happened to that Bristol man?

THE VERB

1d. A *verb* is a word used to express action or a state of being. The verb says something about the subject of a sentence.

EXAMPLES   Gary Soto **wrote** "Broken Chain."
"Oranges" **is** one of my favorite poems.

Action Verbs

1e. An *action verb* may express physical action or mental action.

PHYSICAL ACTION   jump, shout, search, carry, run

MENTAL ACTION   worry, think, believe, imagine, remember

Transitive and Intransitive Verbs

(1) A *transitive verb* is a verb that expresses an action directed toward a person or thing.

EXAMPLE   Alfonso **borrowed** Ernie's bike. [The action of *borrowed* is directed toward *bike*.]

With transitive verbs, the action passes from the doer—the subject—to the receiver of the action. Words that receive the action of a transitive verb are called **objects**.

EXAMPLE   Mr. White made three **wishes**. [*Wishes* is the object of the verb *made*.]

(2) An *intransitive verb* expresses action (or tells something about the subject) without passing the action to a receiver.

EXAMPLE   The broken chain **lay** beside the fence. [The action of *lay* is not directed toward a receiver.]

Linking Verbs

1f. A *linking verb* links, or connects, the subject with a noun, a pronoun, or an adjective in the predicate.

EXAMPLES   The winner of the race **is** Squeaky. [winner = Squeaky]
Gretchen **is** one of her opponents. [Gretchen = one]
Squeaky's brother **looks** happy. [happy brother]

COMMON LINKING VERBS	
Forms of the Verb *Be*	am, are, be, been, being, is, was, were
Other Linking Verbs	appear, become, feel, grow, look, remain, seem, smell, sound, stay, taste, turn

☞ For more about subjects and verbs, see pages 934–936.

NOTE A verb may be transitive in one sentence and intransitive in another.

TRANSITIVE   The teacher **read** "A Time to Talk."

INTRANSITIVE   The teacher **read** aloud.

☞ For more about objects, see pages 937–938.

☞ Linking verbs (*be, seem, feel,* etc.) never take direct objects. See pages 937–938 for more about linking verbs.

All linking verbs except forms of *be* and *seem* may also be used as action verbs. Whether a verb is used to link words or to express action depends on its meaning in a sentence.

LINKING   The tiger **looked** tame.

ACTION   The tiger **looked** for something to eat.

Helping Verbs

1g. A *helping verb (auxiliary verb)* helps the main verb to express an action or a state of being.

EXAMPLES   **should** be
might have won
will have been taken

A *verb phrase* consists of a main verb preceded by at least one helping verb.

EXAMPLE   Dr. Strauss and Dr. Nemur **are studying** Charlie. [The main verb is *studying*.]

COMMONLY USED HELPING VERBS	
Forms of *Be*	am, are, be, been, being, is, was, were
Forms of *Do*	do, does, did
Forms of *Have*	have, has, had
Other Helping Verbs	can, could, may, might, must, shall, should, will, would

Sometimes the verb phrase is interrupted by other words.

EXAMPLES   People **may** someday **communicate** with dolphins.
How much **do** you **know** about the writer Roald Dahl?
The narrator **could** not [*or* **couldn**'t] **see** the old man's "vulture eye."

 QUICK CHECK 4

Identify each verb in the following sentences as either an *action verb* or a *linking verb*. Identify each action verb as either *transitive* or *intransitive*.

EXAMPLE   **1.** A cold wind was blowing in Bath.
1. *was blowing—action, intransitive*

1. The glow of a street lamp lit up the window.
2. The landlady did not look strange.
3. Billy looked past the green curtains.
4. She could have been the mother of a friend of his.
5. Have you ever read a story like this one?

THE ADVERB

1h. An **adverb** is a word used to modify a verb, an adjective, or another adverb.

An adverb tells *where, when, how,* or *to what extent* (*how much* or *how long*).

EXAMPLES   **Quite stealthily,** the narrator opens the door. [*Quite* modifies the adverb *stealthily,* telling *to what extent; stealthily* modifies the verb *opens,* telling *how.*]

He is **extremely** cautious. [*Extremely* modifies the adjective *cautious,* telling *to what extent.*]

He buries the body **there.** [*There* modifies the verb *buries,* telling *where.*]

Police officers arrive **soon.** [*Soon* modifies the verb *arrive,* telling *when.*]

The police officers do **not** hear the noise. [*Not* modifies the verb phrase *do hear,* telling *to what extent.*]

Note in the examples above that adverbs may come before, after, or between the words they modify.

 NOTE   The word *not* is an adverb. When *not* is part of a contraction like *hadn't,* the *—n't* is an adverb.

☞ For more about modifiers, see Part 5: Using Modifiers.

Avoiding the Overuse of *Very*

The adverb *very* is often overused. In your writing, try to replace *very* with more descriptive adverbs or to revise the sentence so that other words carry more of the descriptive meaning.

EXAMPLE   Poe's stories are very suspenseful.

REVISED   Poe's stories are **extremely** suspenseful.

or

Poe's suspenseful stories **shock, frighten, and entertain readers.**

Try It Out ✎

For each of the following sentences, replace *very* with a more descriptive adverb, or rewrite the sentence to eliminate *very.*

1. The narrator in "The Tell-Tale Heart" is very deceitful.
2. At night, the old man's room is very dark.
3. This narrator seems very emotional.
4. Notice that Poe's use of italics is very effective.
5. When the heartbeat becomes very loud, the narrator confesses.

 QUICK CHECK 5

Identify the adverbs in the following sentences. After each adverb, write the word or phrase that the adverb modifies.

EXAMPLE   **1.** The landlady seemed almost familiar.

   1. *almost—familiar*

1. Suddenly, a woman appeared.
2. She spoke quite pleasantly to the young man.
3. Are eggs terribly expensive?
4. The young man had not taken his hat off.
5. Were other hats or coats there?

THE PREPOSITION

Ii. **A *preposition* is a word used to show the relationship of a noun or a pronoun to another word in the sentence.**

Notice how a change in the preposition changes the relationship between the cat and the house in the following examples.

The dog chased the cat **under** the house.
The dog chased the cat **around** the house.
The dog chased the cat **through** the house.
The dog chased the cat **out of** the house.

Common Prepositions

about	because of	for	of
above	before	from	on
according to	behind	in	out of
across	beneath	in front of	over
after	beside	inside	through
against	between	into	to
around	by	like	under
at	during	near	with

The Prepositional Phrase

A preposition is generally followed by a noun or a pronoun, called the **object of the preposition.** All together, the preposition, its object, and any modifiers of the object are called a **prepositional phrase.**

EXAMPLE   The wagon train slowly traveled **across the dusty prairie.**

A preposition may have more than one object.

EXAMPLE   Ms. Larson told us to look closely **at the poem's rhyme and rhythm.**

 QUICK CHECK 6

Identify the prepositional phrase or phrases in each of the following sentences. Then, underline each preposition.

EXAMPLE   **I.** Edgar Allan Poe died at an early age.

        I. *at an early age*

1. Much sadness and pain had come into his life.
2. He was a superb critic of other writers' works.
3. His small text on composition is still a classic.
4. His talent for terror is appreciated by millions of people.
5. His stories are in many textbooks and anthologies.

 For more about prepositional phrases, see pages 922 and 923–925.

NOTE Be careful not to confuse a prepositional phrase that begins with *to* (*to town*) with a verb form that begins with *to* (*to run*).

THE CONJUNCTION

1j. A *conjunction* is a word used to join words or groups of words.

(1) *Coordinating conjunctions* connect words or groups of words used in the same way.

Coordinating Conjunctions						
and	but	or	nor	for	so	yet

EXAMPLES Gretchen **or** Squeaky [two nouns]
small **but** comfortable [two adjectives]
down the track **and** across the finish line [two prepositional phrases]
The stars seem motionless, **but** actually they are moving rapidly through space. [two independent clauses]

(2) *Correlative conjunctions* are pairs of conjunctions that connect words or groups of words used in the same way.

Correlative Conjunctions		
both . . . and	either . . . or	neither . . . nor
not only . . . but also	whether . . . or	

EXAMPLES **Neither** Alfonso **nor** Sandra has a bike to ride. [two nouns]
Either leave a message on my answering machine, **or** call me after 7:00 P.M. tomorrow. [two independent clauses]

THE INTERJECTION

1k. An *interjection* is a word used to express emotion. It has no grammatical relation to other words in the sentence. Usually an interjection is followed by an exclamation point. Sometimes an interjection is set off by a comma.

Common Interjections					
aha	aw	hey	oh	ouch	whew
alas	gosh	hooray	oops	well	wow

EXAMPLES **Wow!** What an exciting race that was!
Well, he did his best.

 **QUICK CHECK 7**

Identify each *conjunction* and *interjection* in the following sentences.

EXAMPLE   **1.** Wow! Poe's rhythms are regular yet breathless.
              1. *Wow—interjection; yet—conjunction*

1. Notice the rich vocabulary and sentence structure in these stories by Edgar Allan Poe.
2. Oh, don't miss hearing a narration of "The Tell-Tale Heart."
3. Neither unfamiliar words nor long descriptive phrases should discourage you.
4. Skim them, but feel the speaker's emotions.
5. Let the sound and feeling of the poem fill you, and, pow, you will understand Poe.

DETERMINING PARTS OF SPEECH

The part of speech of a word is determined by the way that the word is used in a sentence. Many words can be used as more than one part of speech.

EXAMPLES   **Each** costs a dime. [pronoun]
               Each chocolate costs a dime. [adjective]

               He made a **wish.** [noun]
               For what did he **wish**? [verb]

               Mr. White makes his third wish, **for** he is afraid of what
                    he may find behind the door. [conjunction]
               Mrs. Flowers had made the tea cookies **for** her.
                    [preposition]

               The **well** has gone dry. [noun]
               Well, he seems to like Sandra. [interjection]
               He doesn't look **well** to me. [adjective]
               She writes **well.** [adverb]

 QUICK CHECK 8

Identify the part of speech of the italicized word in each sentence.

EXAMPLE   **1.** Each *beat* of the heart filled him with terror.
              1. *noun*

1. The heart *beat* on.
2. *That* was the heart of the old man.
3. Perhaps *that* terror was his own guilt.
4. Even *in* silence, he heard the sound.
5. The old man did not suspect the narrator *yet*.

2 AGREEMENT

NUMBER

Number is the form of a word that indicates whether the word is singular or plural.

2a. **When a word refers to one person, place, thing, or idea, it is *singular*. When a word refers to more than one, it is *plural*.**

SINGULAR	book	woman	one	I	he
PLURAL	books	women	many	we	they

 For more about forming plurals, see pages 968–969.

Agreement of Subject and Verb

2b. **A verb agrees with its subject in number.**

(1) Singular subjects take singular verbs.

EXAMPLES The **stranger shoots** the frog.
Johnny calls himself Red Chief.

(2) Plural subjects take plural verbs.

EXAMPLES Six **girls compete** in the race.
Many **people laugh** at Charlie.

The first auxiliary (helping) verb in a verb phrase must agree with its subject.

EXAMPLES **She is** helping Charlie.
They are helping Charlie.

Problems in Agreement

2c. **The number of a subject is not changed by a prepositional phrase following the subject.**

NONSTANDARD The sparse furnishings on the stage creates a somber atmosphere.

STANDARD The sparse **furnishings** on the stage **create** a somber atmosphere.

2d. **The following indefinite pronouns are singular: *anybody, anyone, each, either, everybody, everyone, neither, nobody, no one, one, somebody, someone.***

EXAMPLE **Each** of them **was sent** a bouquet.

2e. **The following indefinite pronouns are plural: *both, few, many, several.***

EXAMPLE **Both** of the stories **were written** by Shirley Jackson.

TIPS FOR SPELLING

Generally, nouns ending in s are plural (*candles, ideas, neighbors, horses*), and verbs ending in s are singular (*sees, writes, speaks, carries*). However, verbs used with the singular pronouns *I* and *you* generally do not end in s.

EXAMPLE **I walk** faster than **you do.**

2f. **The following indefinite pronouns may be either singular or plural:** *all, any, most, none, some.*

The number of *all, any, most, none,* or *some* is often determined by the number of the object in a prepositional phrase following the subject. If the subject refers to a singular object, the subject is singular. If the subject refers to a plural object, the subject is plural.

EXAMPLES   **All** of the **action occurs** on the top floor of a warehouse. [*All* refers to the singular object *action.*]

All of the **events occur** on the top floor of a warehouse. [*All* refers to the plural object *events.*]

Using indefinite pronouns correctly can be tricky. To help yourself, you may want to create an indefinite pronoun guide. First, summarize the information in rules 2d–2f and 2o–2r. Then, choose several examples to illustrate the rules. Create a "Help" file in which to store this information. Call up the file whenever you run into difficulty using indefinite pronouns.

2g. **Subjects joined by *and* usually take a plural verb.**

EXAMPLE   **Sam** and **Bill kidnap** Johnny.

A compound subject that names a single person or thing takes a singular verb. A compound noun used as a subject also takes a singular verb in most cases.

EXAMPLES   The **captain** and **quarterback** of the team **was** Lyle. [One person, Lyle, was both the captain and the quarterback.]

Rock and roll is my favorite kind of music. [*Rock and roll* is a compound noun naming one kind of music.]

2h. **When subjects are joined by *or* or *nor,* the verb agrees with the subject nearer the verb.**

EXAMPLES   Neither the **director** nor the **players were** on time for rehearsal.

Neither the **players** nor the **director was** on time for rehearsal.

QUICK CHECK I

For each of the following sentences, choose the correct form of the verb in parentheses.

EXAMPLE   **1.** Both of the girls (*love, loves*) running.

   1. *love*

1. My favorite story (*has, have*) always been "Raymond's Run."
2. Some of the story (*concern, concerns*) Squeaky's rival.
3. Neither Gretchen nor Mary Louise really (*smile, smiles*).
4. Squeaky's rival and schoolmate (*was, were*) Gretchen.
5. Insults and taunts directed at Raymond (*anger, angers*) his sister.

2i. **Collective nouns (such as *crowd*, *family*, and *team*) may be either singular or plural.**

A collective noun takes a singular verb when the noun refers to the group as a unit. A collective noun takes a plural verb when the noun refers to the individual parts or members of the group.

EXAMPLES   The Frank **family goes** into hiding. [The family as a unit goes into hiding.]

                 The Frank **family pack** their bags. [The individual members of the family pack bags.]

2j. **When the subject follows all or part of the verb, find the subject and make sure the verb agrees with it. The subject usually follows the verb in sentences beginning with *here* or *there* and in questions.**

EXAMPLES   There **is** a **frog** on that lily pad.

                 Have any other **frogs jumped** on?

The contractions *here's*, *there's*, and *where's* contain the verb *is* and should be used only with singular subjects.

NONSTANDARD   There's the books.

STANDARD   There **are** the **books**.

2k. **Use the contraction *don't* with plural subjects and with the pronouns *I* and *you*. Use the contraction *doesn't* with other singular subjects.**

EXAMPLES   The **police officers don't** hear the noise.

                 I don't like that song.

                 You don't have enough money to buy that.

                 The **frog doesn't** jump.

2l. **Words stating amounts are usually singular.**

A word or phrase stating a weight, a measurement, or an amount of money or time is usually considered one item. Such a word or phrase takes a singular verb.

EXAMPLE   **Twenty-five months is** the amount of time Anne kept the diary.

2m. **The title of a creative work or the name of an organization or country, even when plural in form, usually takes a singular verb.**

EXAMPLE   "Flowers for Algernon" **was made** into a movie.

2n. **A few nouns, though plural in form, are singular and take singular verbs.**

EXAMPLE   **Mathematics is** my best subject.

NOTE   When the subject of a sentence follows all or part of the verb, the word order is *inverted*. To find the subject of a sentence with inverted order, restate the sentence in normal word order.

INVERTED   Did Robert Frost **write** these poems?

NORMAL   Robert Frost **did write** these poems.

INVERTED   Into the clearing **stepped** a tiny **fawn**.

NORMAL   A tiny **fawn stepped** into the clearing.

☞ For more about contractions, see pages 962–963.

QUICK CHECK 2

In the following sentences, choose the form of the verb in parentheses that agrees with the subject.

EXAMPLE   **1.** The people in her family (*work, works*) hard.
                 1. *work*

1. *Hansel and Gretel* (*was, were*) the pageant that Squeaky was in.
2. Athletics (*has, have*) always interested Squeaky.
3. (*Don't, Doesn't*) she run well?
4. Fifty yards (*was, were*) the length of the run.
5. (*There's, There are*) not much dialogue in the story.

Agreement of Pronoun and Antecedent

A pronoun usually refers to a noun or another pronoun, called its *antecedent.*

2o.   A pronoun agrees with its antecedent in number and gender.

Some singular personal pronouns have forms that indicate gender. Masculine pronouns (*he, him, his*) refer to males. Feminine pronouns (*she, her, hers*) refer to females. Neuter pronouns (*it, its*) refer to things (neither male nor female) and sometimes to animals.

EXAMPLES   **Ernie** lent **his** bike to Alfonso.
                 Squeaky protects **her** brother.
                 The sergeant major took the **monkey's paw** and threw **it** into the fire.

Some antecedents may be either masculine or feminine. When referring to such antecedents, use both the masculine and the feminine forms.

EXAMPLE   **No one** on the committee gave **his or her** approval.

👉 For more about antecedents, see page 892.

NOTE The antecedent of a personal pronoun can be another kind of pronoun, such as *all* or *one.* To determine the gender of a personal pronoun in such cases, look at the phrase that follows the antecedent.

EXAMPLE   **Each** of the **girls** took **her** place at the starting line.

 **Revising Awkward Pronoun Agreement**

Sometimes, using both the masculine and the feminine forms to refer to an indefinite pronoun is awkward or confusing. To avoid such use, rephrase the sentence by using both a plural pronoun and a plural antecedent.

AWKWARD   **Everyone** except Fanny signed the petition because **he** or **she** did not like working with the "new" Charlie.

CLEAR   **All** of the workers except Fanny signed the petition because **they** did not like working with the "new" Charlie.

Try It Out

Revise the following sentences to eliminate the awkward use of *his or her.*

1. Each of the characters had his or her own motives.
2. One of the stagehands had forgotten his or her tools.
3. Everyone in the play knew his or her lines.
4. Either Anna or Fred will drive his or her van.
5. Nobody forgot his or her costume.

Problems in Agreement

2p. A singular pronoun is used to refer to *anybody, anyone, each, either, everybody, everyone, neither, nobody, no one, one, someone,* or *somebody.*

EXAMPLE   **Everybody** will have an opportunity to express **his or her** opinion.

2q. A plural pronoun is used to refer to *both, few, many,* or *several.*

EXAMPLE   **Both** of the novels by Mark Twain were on **their** shelf in the library.

2r. Either a singular or a plural pronoun may be used to refer to *all, any, most, none,* or *some.*

The number of the pronoun *all, any, most, none,* or *some* is determined by the number of the object of the preposition in the prepositional phrase following the pronoun.

EXAMPLES   Only **some** of the paint spilled, but **it** made a big mess. [*Some* refers to *paint.*]

Some of the children are ready for **their** naps. [*Some* refers to *children.*]

2s. A plural pronoun is used to refer to two or more antecedents joined by *and.*

EXAMPLE   When **Bill and Sam** wrote the ransom note, **they** asked for fifteen hundred dollars.

2t. A singular pronoun is used to refer to two or more singular antecedents joined by *or* or *nor.*

EXAMPLE   **Julio or Van** will bring **his** football.

A singular and a plural antecedent joined by *or* or *nor* can create an awkward sentence. Revise such a sentence to avoid the problem.

AWKWARD   Either Mr. Reyes or the Wilsons will be bringing their volleyball net.

REVISED   Either **Mr. Reyes** will be bringing **his** volleyball net, or the **Wilsons** will be bringing **theirs.**

Sentences with singular antecedents joined by *or* or *nor* also can sound awkward if the antecedents are of different genders. If the sentence sounds awkward, revise it to avoid the problem.

AWKWARD   Either Lori or Tony will read her or his poem about the Holocaust.

REVISED   Either **Lori** will read **her** poem about the Holocaust, or **Tony** will read **his.**

QUICK CHECK 3

For each blank in the following sentences, give a pronoun that will complete the meaning of the sentence.

EXAMPLE **1.** Both Alfonso and Ernie liked riding _____ bikes.
  1. *their*

1. Alfonso took good care of _____ bike.
2. Each of the boys had _____ own problems.
3. Neither of the girls from the Halloween party had kept _____ promise to Ernie.
4. Perhaps both of them had _____ reasons for not meeting Ernie and Frostie at the corner.
5. Did Ernie or Frostie keep _____ word?

2u. **Either a singular or a plural pronoun may be used with a collective noun (such as *committee*, *flock*, and *jury*).**

EXAMPLES   The **committee** has prepared **its** recommendation. [The committee as a unit has prepared the recommendation.]

The **committee** are sharing **their** ideas for the new recycling campaign. [The separate members of the committee have various ideas.]

2v. **A few nouns, though plural in form, are singular and take singular pronouns.**

EXAMPLE   All of them had expected the **news** to be bad, but **it** wasn't.

2w. **Words stating amounts usually take singular pronouns.**

EXAMPLE   Although the landlady charged **five and sixpence** a night for a room, **it** was much less than he had expected to pay.

NOTE The title of a creative work or the name of an organization or a country, even when plural in form, usually takes a singular pronoun.

EXAMPLE   I enjoyed reading ***The Outsiders*** because **it** had interesting characters.

 QUICK CHECK 4

For each blank in the following sentences, give a pronoun that will complete the meaning of the sentence.

EXAMPLE **1.** Father's team was playing, but _____ lost.
  1. *it*

1. The family were doing _____ chores.
2. "Oranges" is also by Gary Soto, and _____ is the next selection in the book.
3. He had only five cents, but _____ was enough for the candy.
4. Your checkers are all over the floor; please clean _____ up.
5. Checkers may be a good game, but I don't play _____ often.

3 USING VERBS

THE PRINCIPAL PARTS OF A VERB

The four basic forms of a verb are called the **principal parts** of a verb.

3a. **The principal parts of a verb are the *base form*, the *present participle*, the *past*, and the *past participle*.**

BASE FORM	PRESENT PARTICIPLE	PAST	PAST PARTICIPLE
return	(is) returning	returned	(have) returned
go	(is) going	went	(have) gone

Notice that the present participle and the past participle require helping verbs (forms of *be* and *have*).

Regular Verbs

3b. **A *regular verb* forms its past and past participle by adding –d or –ed to the base form.**

BASE FORM	PRESENT PARTICIPLE	PAST	PAST PARTICIPLE
use	(is) using	used	(have) used
attack	(is) attacking	attacked	(have) attacked
drown	(is) drowning	drowned	(have) drowned

Avoid the following common errors when forming the past or past participle of regular verbs:

1. leaving off the –d or –ed ending

EXAMPLE The innkeeper used [*not* use] to be a samurai.

2. adding unnecessary letters

EXAMPLE Fortunately, no one in the boating accident drowned [*not* drownded].

 QUICK CHECK I

For each of the following sentences, give the correct past or past participle form of the verb in parentheses.

EXAMPLE **1.** Two families (*share*) the house in China.

1. *shared*

For information about how participles are used as modifiers, see page 925.

In general, double the final consonant before adding –ed or –ing if the verb

(1) has only one syllable or has the accent on the last syllable

and

(2) ends in a single consonant preceded by a single vowel.

EXAMPLES   drop, dro**pp**ed, dro**pp**ing
refer, refe**rr**ed, refe**rr**ing

See page 967 for exceptions.

1. A relative of theirs living in the United States (*record*) a message to them.
2. They had (*live*) close to a river.
3. Xiaojun has (*carry*) water in buckets.
4. The families (*cook*) with the water.
5. They have (*use*) wheat stalks instead of wood for a fire.

Irregular Verbs

3c. An *irregular verb* forms its past and past participle in some other way than by adding *–d* or *–ed* to the base form.

An irregular verb forms its past and past participle

• by changing vowels or consonants

BASE FORM	PAST	PAST PARTICIPLE
sing	sang	(have) sung
build	built	(have) built

• by changing vowels and consonants

BASE FORM	PAST	PAST PARTICIPLE
see	saw	(have) seen
write	wrote	(have) written

• by making no changes

BASE FORM	PAST	PAST PARTICIPLE
cut	cut	(have) cut
cost	cost	(have) cost

Avoid the following common errors when forming the past or past participle of irregular verbs:

1. using the past form with a helping verb

NONSTANDARD	Coyote had stole the sun and the moon.
STANDARD	Coyote had **stolen** the sun and the moon.

2. using the past participle form without a helping verb

NONSTANDARD	They drunk the tea.
STANDARD	They **have drunk** the tea.

3. adding *–d* or *–ed* to the base form

NONSTANDARD	Brer Possum knowed not to trust Brer Snake.
STANDARD	Brer Possum **knew** not to trust Brer Snake.

NOTE If you are not sure about the principal parts of a verb, look in a dictionary. Entries for irregular verbs give the principal parts of the verb.

COMMON IRREGULAR VERBS

GROUP I: Each of these irregular verbs has the same form for its past and past participle.

BASE FORM	PRESENT PARTICIPLE	PAST	PAST PARTICIPLE
bring	(is) bringing	brought	(have) brought
find	(is) finding	found	(have) found
get	(is) getting	got	(have) got *or* gotten
hold	(is) holding	held	(have) held
keep	(is) keeping	kept	(have) kept
lead	(is) leading	led	(have) led
lend	(is) lending	lent	(have) lent
make	(is) making	made	(have) made
spend	(is) spending	spent	(have) spent
teach	(is) teaching	taught	(have) taught

 ## QUICK CHECK 2

For each of the following sentences, give the correct past or past participle form of the verb in parentheses.

EXAMPLE   **1.** The family (*keep*) chickens and a garden.
             1. *kept*

1. Finally, Xiaojun's father had (*make*) enough money for the trip.
2. The letter said that he had (*find*) an apartment.
3. They (*bring*) suitcases out to the car.
4. A friend had (*lend*) them the car.
5. In China, the teachers (*teach*) according to strict rules.

COMMON IRREGULAR VERBS

GROUP II: Each of these irregular verbs has a different form for its past and past participle.

BASE FORM	PRESENT PARTICIPLE	PAST	PAST PARTICIPLE
begin	(is) beginning	began	(have) begun
break	(is) breaking	broke	(have) broken
choose	(is) choosing	chose	(have) chosen
drink	(is) drinking	drank	(have) drunk
eat	(is) eating	ate	(have) eaten
fly	(is) flying	flew	(have) flown
go	(is) going	went	(have) gone
know	(is) knowing	knew	(have) known
ring	(is) ringing	rang	(have) rung
take	(is) taking	took	(have) taken

QUICK CHECK 3

For each of the following sentences, give the correct past or past participle form of the verb in parentheses.

EXAMPLE **1.** Xiaojun and her family (*go*) to the United States.
  1. went

1. They (*take*) boats, buses, and a train.
2. On the trip, she (*drink*) a soybean beverage.
3. They (*fly*) in an airplane from Hong Kong.
4. Their adventure had (*begin*).
5. She had not (*know*) about crayons and many other things.

COMMON IRREGULAR VERBS			
GROUP III: Each of these irregular verbs has the same form for its base form, past, and past participle.			
BASE FORM	**PRESENT PARTICIPLE**	**PAST**	**PAST PARTICIPLE**
burst	(is) bursting	burst	(have) burst
hit	(is) hitting	hit	(have) hit
hurt	(is) hurting	hurt	(have) hurt
let	(is) letting	let	(have) let
put	(is) putting	put	(have) put
read	(is) reading	read	(have) read
spread	(is) spreading	spread	(have) spread

 ## QUICK CHECK 4

For each of the following sentences, give the correct past or past participle form of the verb in italics.

EXAMPLE **1.** *read*   Xiaojun has _____ the encyclopedia.
  1. read

1. *put*   They had _____ their hopes for the future into the trip.
2. *burst*   When the match _____ into flames, they burned a string.
3. *hit*   In China, the teachers had _____ misbehaving students.
4. *hurt*   Discipline was strict, and penalties often _____.
5. *let*   Her mother has not _____ her go on dates yet.

VERB TENSE

3d. The *tense* of a verb indicates the time of the action or state of being expressed by the verb.

Most verbs have six tenses. Listing all the forms of a verb in the six tenses is called **conjugating** a verb.

CONJUGATION OF THE VERB *GO*	
PRESENT TENSE	
SINGULAR	**PLURAL**
I go	we go
you go	you go
he, she, *or* it goes	they go
PAST TENSE	
SINGULAR	**PLURAL**
I went	we went
you went	you went
he, she, *or* it went	they went
FUTURE TENSE	
SINGULAR	**PLURAL**
I will go	we will go
you will go	you will go
he, she, *or* it will go	they will go
PRESENT PERFECT TENSE	
SINGULAR	**PLURAL**
I have gone	we have gone
you have gone	you have gone
he, she, *or* it has gone	they have gone
PAST PERFECT TENSE	
SINGULAR	**PLURAL**
I had gone	we had gone
you had gone	you had gone
he, she, *or* it had gone	they had gone
FUTURE PERFECT TENSE	
SINGULAR	**PLURAL**
I will have gone	we will have gone
you will have gone	you will have gone
he, she, *or* it will have gone	they will have gone

NOTE In the future tense and in the future perfect tense, the helping verb *shall* is sometimes used in place of *will*.

NOTE The present tense is used to express an action or a state of being occurring now at the present time. It can also be used to express
- a customary action
- a general truth
- future time

EXAMPLES On Fridays, we **play** basketball**.** [customary action]

Jupiter **rotates** faster than Venus. [general truth]

The new theater **opens** two weeks from today. [future time]

This time line shows how the six tenses are related to one another.

Past	*Present*	*Future*
existing or happening in the past	existing or happening now	existing or happening in the future

Past Perfect	*Present Perfect*	*Future Perfect*
existing or happening before a specific time in the past	existing or happening sometime before now, or starting in the past and continuing now	existing or happening before a specific time in the future

Consistency of Tense

3e. Do not change needlessly from one tense to another.

When writing about events that take place in the present, use verbs in the present tense. Similarly, when writing about events that occurred in the past, use verbs in the past tense.

INCONSISTENT   Billy pressed the doorbell, and immediately a woman opens the door. [*Pressed* is past tense, and *opens* is present tense.]

CONSISTENT   Billy **pressed** the doorbell, and immediately a woman **opened** the door. [Both *pressed* and *opened* are past tense.]

CONSISTENT   Billy **presses** the doorbell, and immediately a woman **opens** the door. [Both *presses* and *opens* are present tense.]

Sometimes, changing verb tenses is necessary to show the order of events that occur at different times.

EXAMPLES   Tomorrow I **will read** aloud the story I **wrote** last week. [The action of reading will take place in the future; the action of writing took place in the past.]

She **guessed** that he **had won** the spelling bee. [The action of winning was completed before the action of guessing.]

By the time he **returns**, they **will have finished** all their chores. [The action of finishing will be completed before the action of returning.]

 ## QUICK CHECK 5

Read the following paragraph, and decide whether it should be rewritten in the present or past tense. Then, change the verb forms to make the verb tense consistent.

EXAMPLE   [1] Many Japanese families went to Camp Harmony and staying there for the duration of the war.

1. *Many Japanese families went to Camp Harmony and stayed there for the duration of the war.*

or

1. *Many Japanese families go to Camp Harmony and stay there for the duration of the war.*

[1] Monica Sone's mother sees the best in things and admired the dandelions. [2] She planned for a garden of them and is grateful for any type of beauty. [3] She is even happy about the nearness of the latrine, though the others were not so thrilled. [4] Like her mother, Sone's father has been grateful for good things, however small. [5] He finds a pile of lumber and loose nails and envisioned these scraps as the family's furniture.

Voice

3f. **Voice** **is the form a verb takes to indicate whether the subject of the verb performs or receives the action.**

When the subject performs the action, the verb is in the **active voice** and has an object. When the subject receives the action, the verb is in the **passive voice** and does not have an object.

ACTIVE   Saki **wrote** "The Open Window." [*"The Open Window"* is the direct object.]

PASSIVE   "The Open Window" **was written** by Saki. [no object]

Avoiding Passive Voice

Whenever possible, avoid using the passive voice, because it is less direct and less forceful. In some cases, in fact, a passive voice construction sounds awkward.

AWKWARD   The reason for the open window was explained to Framton by Vera. [passive voice]

IMPROVED   Vera explained to Framton the reason for the open window. [active voice]

SPECIAL PROBLEMS WITH VERBS

Sit and Set

(1) **The verb** *sit* **means "rest in an upright, seated position."** *Sit* **seldom takes an object.**

(2) **The verb** *set* **means "put (something) in a place."** *Set* **usually takes an object.**

BASE FORM	PRESENT PARTICIPLE	PAST	PAST PARTICIPLE
sit (rest)	(is) sitting	sat	(have) sat
set (put)	(is) setting	set	(have) set

EXAMPLES   Billy **sits** on the sofa. [no object]
Billy **sets** his suitcase in a chair. [Billy sets what? *Suitcase* is the object.]

Lie and Lay

(1) **The verb** *lie* **means "rest," "recline," or "be in a place."** *Lie* **never takes an object.**

(2) **The verb** *lay* **means "put (something) in a place."** *Lay* **usually takes an object.**

Try It Out ✎

Revise each of the following sentences by changing verbs in the passive voice to active voice.

1. The Gettysburg Address was delivered by Abraham Lincoln.
2. It has been admired by writers and imitated by speakers for more than one hundred years.
3. Those who died in the Civil War are honored by this short, eloquent speech.
4. The living are reminded of their "great task" by the address.
5. Freedom must be embraced and guarded by people.

BASE FORM	PRESENT PARTICIPLE	PAST	PAST PARTICIPLE
lie (rest)	(is) lying	lay	(have) lain
lay (put)	(is) laying	laid	(have) laid

EXAMPLES Zenta and Tokubei thought they **had lain** asleep for fifty years. [no object]

The boy **had laid** a nickel and an orange on the counter. [The boy had laid what? *Nickel* and *orange* are the objects.]

Rise and Raise

(1) **The verb *rise* means "go up" or "get up." *Rise* never takes an object.**

(2) **The verb *raise* means "lift up" or "cause (something) to rise." *Raise* usually takes an object.**

BASE FORM	PRESENT PARTICIPLE	PAST	PAST PARTICIPLE
rise (go up)	(is) rising	rose	(have) risen
raise (lift up)	(is) raising	raised	(have) raised

EXAMPLES The full moon **rose** slowly through the clouds last night. [no object]

The cheering crowd **raised** banners and signs over their heads. [The crowd raised what? *Banners* and *signs* are the objects.]

 QUICK CHECK 6

For each of the following sentences, choose the correct verb in parentheses.

EXAMPLE   **1.** As they (*set, sat*) in the car, Papa said nothing.
1. *sat*

1. Cardboard boxes full of their belongings (*sat, set*) on the floor.
2. He couldn't fall asleep and (*laid, lay*) wide awake in bed.
3. Roberto (*rose, raised*) the big boxes and (*lay, laid*) them in the car.
4. They started working each morning when the sun (*rose, raised*).
5. The sun had (*raised, risen*) high, and sweat poured off the workers.

COMPUTER NOTE Most word processors can help you check your writing to be sure that you've used verbs correctly. For example, a spellchecker feature will highlight misspelled verb forms such as *drownded* or *costed*. Style-checking software can point out inconsistent verb tense or overuse of passive voice. Such software may also highlight questionable uses of problem verb pairs such as *lie/lay* or *rise/raise*. Remember, though, that the computer is just a tool to help you improve your writing. As a writer, you need to make style and content choices to suit what you are writing.

4 USING PRONOUNS

CASE

Case is the form that a noun or a pronoun takes to show its use in a sentence. There are three cases: *nominative, objective,* and *possessive.* Unlike nouns, most personal pronouns have different forms for all three cases.

PERSONAL PRONOUNS		
SINGULAR		
NOMINATIVE	**OBJECTIVE**	**POSSESSIVE**
I	me	my, mine
you	you	your, yours
he, she, it	him, her, it	his, her, hers, its
PLURAL		
NOMINATIVE	**OBJECTIVE**	**POSSESSIVE**
we	us	our, ours
you	you	your, yours
they	them	their, theirs

> **NOTE** Many possessive pronouns (such as *my, your, his, her, its, our,* and *their*) are also called adjectives. Follow your teacher's directions in labeling these possessive forms.

The Nominative Case

4a. A subject of a verb is in the nominative case.

EXAMPLES **I** enjoy Gary Soto's stories. [*I* is the subject of *enjoy.*]

He and **she** sold tickets. [*He* and *she* are the subjects of *sold.*]

To choose the correct pronoun in a compound subject, try each form of the pronoun separately.

EXAMPLE: (*He, Him*) and (*I, me*) read "Paul Revere's Ride" to the class.

He read "Paul Revere's Ride" to the class.
Him read "Paul Revere's Ride" to the class.
I read "Paul Revere's Ride" to the class.
Me read "Paul Revere's Ride" to the class.

ANSWER: **He** and **I** read "Paul Revere's Ride" to the class.

> **NOTE** To choose the correct form of a pronoun used as a predicate nominative, remember that the pronoun could be used as the subject.
>
> **EXAMPLE** The fastest runners are **she** and **I.** [predicate nominatives]
> **She** and **I** are the fastest runners. [subjects]

> ☞ For more about predicate nominatives, see page 939.

4b. A *predicate nominative* is in the nominative case.

EXAMPLES The last one to leave was **he.** [*He* identifies the subject *one.*]

Do you think it may have been **they**? [*They* identifies the subject *it.*]

The Objective Case

4c. A *direct object* is in the objective case.

EXAMPLES   Ernie surprised **him.** [*Him* tells *whom* Ernie surprised.]
She read some Norse myths and enjoyed **them.** [*Them* tells *what* she enjoyed.]

To choose the correct pronoun in a compound direct object, try each form of the pronoun separately.

EXAMPLE: Charlie met Joe and (*he, him*) at the factory.
Charlie met *he* at the factory.
Charlie met *him* at the factory.
ANSWER: Charlie met Joe and **him** at the factory.

4d. An *indirect object* is in the objective case.

EXAMPLES   Mrs. Flowers lent **her** a book of poems. [*Her* tells *to whom* Mrs. Flowers lent a book.]
Lana takes good care of her cockatiel and often feeds **it** fresh spinach. [*It* tells *to what* Lana feeds spinach.]

To choose the correct pronoun in a compound indirect object, try each form of the pronoun separately.

EXAMPLE: Ebenezer Dorset sent Bill and (*he, him*) a note.
Ebenezer Dorset sent *he* a note.
Ebenezer Dorset sent *him* a note.
ANSWER: Ebenezer Dorset sent Bill and **him** a note.

4e. An *object of a preposition* is in the objective case.

EXAMPLES   Johnny wanted to stay with **them.** [object of the preposition *with*]
Laurie talked about **him** almost every day. [object of the preposition *about*]

To choose the correct pronoun when the object of a preposition is compound, try each form of the pronoun separately in the sentence.

EXAMPLE: Anne stood behind (*he, him*) and (*she, her*).
Anne stood behind *he.*
Anne stood behind *him.*
Anne stood behind *she.*
Anne stood behind *her.*
ANSWER: Anne stood behind **him** and **her.**

✔ QUICK CHECK I

For each of the sentences on the following page, choose the correct pronoun in parentheses.

☞ For more about direct objects, see pages 937–938.

☞ For more about indirect objects, see page 938.

☞ For a list of prepositions, see page 899. For more about prepositional phrases, see pages 922 and 923–924.

EXAMPLE   **1.** Mrs. Sappleton's niece would entertain (*he, him*).
            1. *him*

1. (*She, Her*) told (*him, he*) a story about a tragedy.
2. A very nervous gentleman was (*he, him*).
3. The story about (*they, them*) upset Mr. Nuttel.
4. Saki's story surprised (*us, we*) and amused (*I, me*).
5. The story was an inspiration to (*them, they*) and (*her, she*).

SPECIAL PRONOUN PROBLEMS

Who and Whom

The pronoun *who* has different forms in the nominative and objective cases. *Who* is the nominative form; *whom* is the objective form. When deciding whether to use *who* or *whom* in a question, follow these steps:

STEP 1:   Rephrase the question as a statement.

STEP 2:   Decide how the pronoun is used in the statement—as subject, predicate nominative, object of the verb, or object of a preposition.

STEP 3:   Determine the case of the pronoun.

STEP 4:   Select the correct form of the pronoun.

EXAMPLE: (*Who, Whom*) is that girl with Alfonso?

STEP 1:   The statement is *That girl with Alfonso is* (*who, whom*).

STEP 2:   The subject is *girl,* the verb is *is,* and the pronoun is a predicate nominative.

STEP 3:   A pronoun used as a predicate nominative should be in the nominative case.

STEP 4:   The nominative form is *who.*

ANSWER: **Who** is that girl with Alfonso?

When you are choosing between *who* or *whom* in a subordinate clause, follow these steps:

STEP 1:   Find the subordinate clause.

STEP 2:   Decide how the pronoun is used in the clause—as subject, predicate nominative, object of the verb, or object of a preposition.

STEP 3:   Determine the case of the pronoun.

STEP 4:   Select the correct form of the pronoun.

EXAMPLE: Mark Twain, (*who, whom*) I admire, wrote funny stories.

STEP 1:   The subordinate clause is (*who, whom*) I admire.

STEP 2:   In this clause, the subject is *I,* and the verb is *admire.* The pronoun is the direct object of the verb.

☞ For more about subordinate clauses, see pages 929–932.

STEP 3: A pronoun used as a direct object should be in the objective case.

STEP 4: The objective form is *whom.*

ANSWER: Mark Twain, **whom** I admire, wrote interesting books.

Pronouns with Appositives

To help you choose which pronoun to use before an appositive, omit the appositive and try each form of the pronoun separately.

EXAMPLE: (*We, Us*) students have memorized the Gettysburg Address. [*Students* is the appositive.]
We have memorized the Gettysburg Address.
Us have memorized the Gettysburg Address.

ANSWER: **We** students have memorized the Gettysburg Address.

👉 For more about appositives, see page 927.

Reflexive Pronouns

Reflexive pronouns (such as *myself, himself,* and *yourselves*) can be used as objects.

EXAMPLE: Brer Possum found **himself** in a dilemma. [*Himself* is the direct object and tells *whom* Brer Possum found in a dilemma.]

Do not use the nonstandard forms *hisself* and *theirself* or *theirselves* in place of *himself* and *themselves.*

EXAMPLE: Zenta figured out all by **himself** [*not* hisself] what was going on.

Do not use a reflexive pronoun where a personal pronoun is needed.

EXAMPLE: Leon and **I** [*not* myself] prefer hiking to rock climbing.

👉 For more about reflexive pronouns, see page 893.

 QUICK CHECK 2

For each of the following sentences, choose the correct pronoun in parentheses.

EXAMPLE 1. Mr. Nuttel need not wait by (*himself, hisself*).
1. *himself*

1. (*Who, Whom*) were they waiting for?
2. Mrs. Sappleton, (*who, whom*) was busy, would be down shortly.
3. (*We, Us*) girls wondered about the meanings of the characters' names.
4. Yes, they seemed meaningful to (*we, us*) boys, too.
5. Trish and (*myself, I*) will ask Ms. Reynolds about the names.

COMPUTER NOTE A computer can help you find pronoun problems in your writing. For example, a spellchecker will catch nonstandard forms such as *hisself* and *theirself.* To find other problems, you can use the "Search" command. If you sometimes use reflexive pronouns in place of personal pronouns, use the "Search" command to find each reflexive pronoun. Then, examine each pronoun to make certain that it is used correctly.

5 USING MODIFIERS

COMPARISON OF MODIFIERS

A *modifier* is a word, a phrase, or a clause that describes or limits the meaning of another word. Two kinds of modifiers—*adjectives* and a*dverbs*—take different forms when they are used to compare things.

5a. The three degrees of comparison of modifiers are *positive, comparative,* and *superlative*.

POSITIVE	weak	proudly	likely
COMPARATIVE	weaker	more proudly	more likely
SUPERLATIVE	weakest	most proudly	most likely

Regular Comparison

(1) Most one-syllable modifiers form their comparative and superlative degrees by adding *–er* and *–est*.

POSITIVE	near	bright	brave
COMPARATIVE	nearer	brighter	braver
SUPERLATIVE	nearest	brightest	bravest

(2) Some two-syllable modifiers form their comparative and superlative degrees by adding *–er* and *–est*. Other two-syllable modifiers form their comparative and superlative degrees by using *more* and *most*.

POSITIVE	gentle	healthy	clearly
COMPARATIVE	gentler	healthier	more clearly
SUPERLATIVE	gentlest	healthiest	most clearly

(3) Modifiers that have three or more syllables form their comparative and superlative degrees by using *more* and *most*.

POSITIVE	important	happily	accurately
COMPARATIVE	more important	more happily	more accurately
SUPERLATIVE	most important	most happily	most accurately

Irregular Comparison

Some modifiers do not form their comparative and superlative degrees by using the regular methods.

POSITIVE	bad	good *or* well	many *or* much
COMPARATIVE	worse	better	more
SUPERLATIVE	worst	best	most

NOTE To show decreasing comparisons, all modifiers form their comparative and superlative degrees with *less* and *least*.

POSITIVE
clear
neatly

COMPARATIVE
less clear
less neatly

SUPERLATIVE
least clear
least neatly

QUICK CHECK 1

Give the comparative and superlative forms for each of the following modifiers.

EXAMPLE   **1.** happy

          1. *happier, happiest*

1. lightly	**4.** silently	**7.** easy	**9.** furiously
2. luxurious	**5.** many	**8.** bad	**10.** safe
3. well	**6.** tall		

Uses of Comparative and Superlative Forms

5b. Use the comparative degree when comparing two things. Use the superlative degree when comparing more than two things.

COMPARATIVE   Squeaky is **faster** than Gretchen.

                         Luisa can perform the gymnastic routine **more gracefully** than I.

SUPERLATIVE   Mount Everest is the world's **highest** mountain.

                         Of all the children in the class, Charles behaves the **most aggressively.**

Avoid the common mistake of using the superlative degree to compare two things.

EXAMPLE   After reading both stories, I think "The Landlady" is the **more** [*not* most] interesting one.

5c. Include the word *other* or *else* when comparing a member of a group with the rest of the group.

NONSTANDARD   Smiley's frog can jump farther than any frog in Calaveras County. [Smiley's frog is one of the frogs in Calaveras County and cannot jump farther than itself.]

STANDARD   Smiley's frog can jump farther than any **other** frog in Calaveras County.

5d. Avoid using double comparisons and double negatives.

A *double comparison* is the use of both *–er* and *more* (*less*) or both *–est* and *most* (*least*) to form a comparison. A comparison should be formed in only one of these two ways, not both.

EXAMPLE   Matsuzo is **younger** [*not* more younger] than Zenta.

A *double negative* is the use of two negative words to express one negative idea.

EXAMPLE   I ca**n't** ever [*not* can't never] remember what the main character's name is.

Common Negative Words

barely	never	none	nothing
hardly	no	no one	nowhere
neither	nobody	not (–n't)	scarcely

 QUICK CHECK 2

For each of the following sentences, correct the error in comparison.

EXAMPLE   **1.** Brer Possum wasn't the most smartest critter.
        1. *Brer Possum wasn't the smartest critter.*

1. Apparently, Brer Snake was more smarter than Brer Possum.
2. Of the two, Brer Possum was the kindest.
3. Surely, Brer Snake was meaner than any critter in the woods.
4. He didn't seem to care about nobody.
5. He wasn't grateful, neither!

PLACEMENT OF MODIFIERS

5e. **Place modifying words, phrases, and clauses as close as possible to the words they modify.**

Prepositional Phrases

 For more about prepositions and prepositional phrases, see pages 899 and 923–925.

MISPLACED   I read a suspenseful story that Edgar Allan Poe wrote at lunch today.

CLEAR   **At lunch today** I read a suspenseful story that Edgar Allan Poe wrote.

Avoid placing a prepositional phrase where it can modify more than one word. Place the phrase so that it clearly modifies only one word.

MISPLACED   Gabriela said **in the morning** she was going home. [Does the phrase modify *said* or *was going*?]

CLEAR   Gabriela said she was going home **in the morning.** [The phrase modifies *was going.*]

CLEAR   **In the morning** Gabriela said she was going home. [The phrase modifies *said.*]

Participial Phrases

For more about participial phrases, see page 925.

MISPLACED   The narrator opened the door of the old man's room obsessed with the "vulture eye."

CLEAR   **Obsessed with the "vulture eye,"** the narrator opened the door of the old man's room.

A participial phrase that does not modify any word in the sentence is a ***dangling participial phrase.*** To correct a dangling phrase, supply a word that the phrase can modify, or add a subject and verb to the phrase.

DANGLING	Wishing for the money, the monkey's paw twisted in his hands.
CLEAR	Wishing for the money, **he** felt the monkey's paw twist in his hands.
CLEAR	**When he wished** for the money, the monkey's paw twisted in his hands.

Clauses

MISPLACED	My brother saw a hawk circling as he looked up.
CLEAR	**As my brother looked up,** he saw a hawk circling.

✓ QUICK CHECK 3

Some of the following sentences contain a misplaced modifier or a dangling participial phrase. Correct each error. If a sentence is correct, write *C.*

EXAMPLE   1. Brer Possum always helped others with kindness.
          1. *With kindness, Brer Possum always helped others.*

1. The possum saw a snake walking in the woods.
2. The snake was lying at the bottom of a hole which was trapped.
3. Calling for help, Brer Possum went to rescue the snake.
4. Brer Possum was bitten by the snake when he tried to help.
5. Reading the folk tale, the possum learns a lesson.

6 PHRASES

6a.   A *phrase* is a group of related words that is used as a single part of speech and does not contain a verb and its subject.

VERB PHRASE	should have been told [no subject]
PREPOSITIONAL PHRASE	for my sister and me [no subject or verb]

THE PREPOSITIONAL PHRASE

6b.   A *prepositional phrase* includes a preposition, a noun or a pronoun called the *object of the preposition,* and any modifiers of that object.

EXAMPLES   Robert Frost was born **in San Francisco.**
          The note **from Johnny's father** surprised Sam and Bill.

A computer can help you find and correct problems with modifiers. A spellchecker can find non-standard forms such as *baddest* and *carefuller.* However, you will need to examine phrase and clause modifiers yourself. If a phrase or a clause is misplaced, you can select it and move the whole phrase or clause closer to the word it modifies.

☞ For more about clauses, see Part 7: Clauses.

☞ For a list of commonly used prepositions, see page 899.

The Adjective Phrase

6c. **An *adjective phrase* is a prepositional phrase that modifies a noun or a pronoun.**

An adjective phrase tells *what kind* or *which one*.

EXAMPLES   Wang Wei was a talented painter **of landscapes.** [What kind of painter?]

Mike is the one **with the moustache.** [Which one?]

An adjective phrase always follows the word it modifies. That word may be the object of another prepositional phrase.

EXAMPLE   It is a poem **about a boy and a girl on their first date.** [The phrase *about a boy and a girl* modifies the noun *poem*. The phrase *on their first date* modifies the objects *boy* and *girl*.]

The Adverb Phrase

6d. **An *adverb phrase* is a prepositional phrase that modifies a verb, an adjective, or an adverb.**

An adverb phrase tells *how, when, where, why*, or *to what extent* (that is, *how long, how many*, or *how far*).

EXAMPLES   She treated him **with respect.** [How?]
The painting hangs **over the fireplace.** [Where?]
They arrived early **in the morning.** [When?]
He had been a samurai **for a long time.** [How long?]

An adverb phrase may come before or after the word it modifies.

EXAMPLES   The Sneve family lived in Iowa **for many years.**
For many years the Sneve family lived in Iowa.

An adverb phrase may be followed by an adjective phrase that modifies the object in the adverb phrase.

EXAMPLE   **In her poems about the Southwest,** Leslie Marmon Silko uses images that appeal to the senses. [*In her poems* modifies the verb *uses. About the Southwest* modifies the noun *poems.*]

 QUICK CHECK 1

Identify the prepositional phrase or phrases in each sentence in the following paragraph. Then, label each phrase as either an *adjective phrase* or an *adverb phrase*. Give the word (or words) the phrase modifies.

EXAMPLE   [1] Who is the author of "Paul Revere's Ride"?
   1. *of "Paul Revere's Ride"—adjective phrase—author*

[1] One of the most famous American historical events is the ride by Paul Revere through Middlesex. [2] In his poem, Henry Wadsworth

---

 NOTE More than one adjective phrase may modify the same word.

EXAMPLE   The box **of old magazines in the closet** is full. [The phrases *of old magazines* and *in the closet* modify the noun *box.*]

 NOTE More than one adverb phrase may modify the same word or words.

EXAMPLE   Yoshiko Uchida was born **in Alameda, California, in 1921.** [Both *in Alameda, California,* and *in 1921* modify the verb phrase *was born.*]

Longfellow immortalizes this heroic ride. [3] Across the river, Revere had waited for the signal about the British. [4] When it came, he rode into the night and called to the people to warn them. [5] With his vivid description of sights and sounds, Longfellow almost brings Revere's ride to life.

VERBALS AND VERBAL PHRASES

A **verbal** is a form of a verb used as a noun, an adjective, or an adverb. There are three kinds of verbals: the *participle,* the *gerund,* and the *infinitive.*

The Participle

6e. A *participle* is a verb form that can be used as an adjective.

(1) *Present participles* end in *–ing.*

EXAMPLES   The **creaking** floorboard bothered Anne.
Miep's news was **encouraging.**

(2) Most *past participles* end in *–d* or *–ed.* Others are irregularly formed.

EXAMPLES   The **oiled** hinge works smoothly.
Charlie Parker, **known** as Bird, was a talented musician.

☞ For lists of irregular past participles, see pages 909–911.

The Participial Phrase

6f. A *participial phrase* consists of a participle and all of the words related to the participle. The entire phrase is used as an adjective.

A participle may be modified by an adverb and may also have a complement.

EXAMPLES   **Defending Jabez Stone,** Daniel Webster proved again that he was a persuasive speaker. [The participial phrase modifies *Daniel Webster.* The noun *Jabez Stone* is the direct object of the participle *defending.*]
Squeaky noticed him **running swiftly alongside the fence.** [The participial phrase modifies *him.* The adverb *swiftly* and the adverb phrase *alongside the fence* modify the participle *running.*]

☞ For more about placement of participial phrases, see pages 922–923.

The Gerund

6g. A *gerund* is a verb form ending in *–ing* that is used as a noun.

SUBJECT	**Skating** can be good exercise.
PREDICATE NOMINATIVE	My hobby is **collecting** baseball cards.
OBJECT OF PREPOSITION	Lock the door before **leaving.**
DIRECT OBJECT	Did they enjoy **singing?**

The Gerund Phrase

6h. A *gerund phrase* consists of a gerund and all the words related to the gerund.

A gerund may be modified by an adverb and may have a complement. Because a gerund functions as a noun, it may also be modified by an adjective.

EXAMPLES **Minding Raymond** is Squeaky's only responsibility. [The gerund phrase is the subject of the verb *is*. The noun *Raymond* is the direct object of the gerund *minding*.]

The murderer heard **the beating of the old man's heart.** [The gerund phrase is the direct object of the verb *heard*. The adjective *the* and the adjective phrase *of the old man's heart* modify the gerund *beating*.]

The Infinitive

6i. An *infinitive* is a verb form that can be used as a noun, an adjective, or an adverb. An infinitive usually begins with *to*.

NOUNS **To learn** is **to grow.** [*To learn* is the subject of *is; to grow* is the predicate nominative referring to *to learn*.]

Squeaky likes **to run.** [*To run* is the direct object of the verb *likes*.]

ADJECTIVES He always has time **to talk.** [*To talk* modifies the noun *time*.]

If you like mystery stories, "The Inn of Lost Time" is a terrific one **to read.** [*To read* modifies the pronoun *one*.]

ADVERBS The landlady was eager **to please.** [*To please* modifies the adjective *eager*.]

Tokubei and Zenta stopped at the inn **to rest.** [*To rest* modifies the verb *stopped*.]

The Infinitive Phrase

6j. An *infinitive phrase* consists of an infinitive and its modifiers and complements.

An infinitive may be modified by an adjective or an adverb and may also have a complement. The entire infinitive phrase may act as a noun, an adjective, or an adverb.

EXAMPLES **To escape without a trace** was impossible. [The infinitive phrase is a noun used as the subject of the verb *was*. The prepositional phrase *without a trace* modifies the infinitive.]

NOTE The word *to* followed by a noun or a pronoun (*to class, to them, to the dance*) is a prepositional phrase, not an infinitive. Be careful not to confuse infinitives with prepositional phrases beginning with *to*.

EXAMPLE Matthew wants **to talk** [infinitive] **to Kim** [prepositional phrase].

Singing to them was one way **to boost their spirits.**
[The infinitive phrase is an adjective modifying *way*.
The noun phrase *their spirits* is the direct object of
the infinitive *to boost.*]

The crowd grew quiet **to hear President Lincoln.**
[The infinitive phrase is an adverb modifying the
adjective *quiet.* The noun *President Lincoln* is the
direct object of the infinitive *to hear.*]

☞ For more on com-
plements, see Part 9:
Complements.

 QUICK CHECK 2

Each of the following sentences contains at least one verbal phrase.
Identify each verbal phrase as *participial, gerund,* or *infinitive.*

EXAMPLE 1. Do you know the story of the Israelites fleeing Egypt?
1. *fleeing Egypt—participial phrase*

1. Who found baby Moses floating in the river?
2. Saved by the Pharaoh's daughter, Moses was taken to live at court.
3. Later, Moses went to the Pharaoh, warning him of the Lord's anger.
4. For decades, toiling for the Pharaoh had been the Israelites' fate.
5. To hear the song "Go Down, Moses" is to feel their sorrow.

APPOSITIVES AND APPOSITIVE PHRASES

6k. **An *appositive* is a noun or a pronoun placed beside
another noun or pronoun to identify or explain it.**

EXAMPLES   The poet **Langston Hughes** wrote "Refugee in America."
[The noun *Langston Hughes* identifies the noun *poet.*]

The explorers saw a strange animal, **something** with
fur and a bill like a duck's. [The pronoun *something*
refers to the noun *animal.*]

Two or more nouns or pronouns may be used as a compound appositive.

EXAMPLE   John James Audubon, an **artist** and a **naturalist,** painted
pictures of birds in their habitats. [The nouns *artist* and
naturalist explain the noun *John James Audubon.*]

6l. **An *appositive phrase* consists of an appositive and its
modifiers.**

EXAMPLES   Dana was always talking about Charles, **one of her
classmates.** [The adjective phrase *of her classmates*
modifies the appositive *one.*]

Black Hawk, **a famous chief of the Sauk,** fought hard
for the freedom of his people. [The article *a,* the adjective *famous,* and the adjective phrase *of the Sauk*
modify the appositive *chief.*]

QUICK CHECK 3

Identify the appositive phrase in each of the following sentences. Give the word or words each appositive phrase identifies.

EXAMPLE **1.** Read "Go Down, Moses," a favorite spiritual.

           1. *a favorite spiritual—"Go Down, Moses"*

1. Moses, Charlton Heston in the film, discovers his true identity.
2. He is really one of the Israelites, slaves to the Pharaoh's whims.
3. Moses decides to live with his true family, members of one tribe of the Israelites.
4. The Pharaoh, a father figure for Moses, rejects him.
5. Moses' name is removed from public record—all the monuments and scrolls—in Egypt.

Revising Choppy Sentences

Knowing how to use the different kinds of phrases can help you avoid writing short, choppy sentences. Simply turn at least one sentence into a phrase, and insert the phrase into another sentence.

CHOPPY	Roald Dahl was born in 1916. His birthplace was Wales.
PREPOSITIONAL PHRASE	Roald Dahl was born **in Wales** in 1916.
CHOPPY	Samuel Clemens wrote *Adventures of Huckleberry Finn*. Samuel Clemens is better known as Mark Twain.
PARTICIPIAL PHRASE	Samuel Clemens, **better known as Mark Twain**, wrote *Adventures of Huckleberry Finn*.
CHOPPY	Vera is Mrs. Sappleton's niece. She tells Mr. Nuttel a story.
APPOSITIVE PHRASE	Vera, **Mrs. Sappleton's niece**, tells Mr. Nuttel a story.

Try It Out

The following pairs of sentences are choppy. Revise each pair by turning one sentence into a phrase and inserting the phrase into the other sentence.

1. Casey was not at bat that day. Casey was known to all as an exceptionally strong player.
2. Jimmy Blake was up first. Blake was not a strong hitter.
3. He hit the ball hard. He ripped the hide from it.
4. The crowd roared. The crowd was in the bleachers.
5. Casey behaved arrogantly. He let two good balls go by.

7 CLAUSES

7a. A *clause* is a group of words that contains a verb and its subject and is used as a part of a sentence.

The two kinds of clauses are the *independent clause* and the *subordinate clause*.

THE INDEPENDENT CLAUSE

7b. An *independent* (or *main*) *clause* expresses a complete thought and can stand by itself as a sentence.

                   S   V

EXAMPLES   Amy Ling moved to the United States.

                   S   V

           This poem is about her grandmother.

THE SUBORDINATE CLAUSE

7c. A *subordinate* (or *dependent*) *clause* does not express a complete thought and cannot stand alone as a sentence.

                   S   V

EXAMPLES   when she was six years old

                 S   V

           whom Ling visited in Taiwan

The meaning of a subordinate clause is complete only when the clause is attached to an independent clause.

EXAMPLE   Amy Ling moved to the United States **when she was six years old.**

 QUICK CHECK 1

Identify each of the following groups of words as an *independent clause* or a *subordinate clause*.

EXAMPLE   **1.** if you have read Amy Ling's poem "Grandma Ling"
             1. *subordinate clause*

1. answer these questions
2. as soon as she met her grandmother
3. before she traveled to Taiwan
4. because Ling could not speak her grandmother's language
5. her footsteps were soft

The Adjective Clause

7d. An *adjective clause* is a subordinate clause that modifies a noun or a pronoun.

        ADJECTIVE   an **intelligent** man
ADJECTIVE PHRASE   a man **of intelligence**
ADJECTIVE CLAUSE   a man **who is intelligent**

For a list of relative pronouns, see page 893. For information on when to set off adjective clauses with commas, see page 953.

NOTE The relative pronouns *who* and *whom* are used to refer to people only. The relative pronoun *that* is used to refer both to people and to things. The relative pronoun *which* is used to refer to things only.

NOTE An adjective clause may be introduced by a relative adverb such as *when* or *where.*

EXAMPLES He finally returned to the cabin **where he had left Mary in charge of his children.**

The time period **when dinosaurs ruled** lasted millions of years.

An adjective clause usually follows the word it modifies and tells *which one* or *what kind.*

EXAMPLES Cheryl showed them the moccasins **that her grandfather had made.** [Which moccasins?]

Helen Keller was a remarkable woman **who could neither see nor hear.** [What kind of woman?]

An adjective clause is usually introduced by a ***relative pronoun,*** a word that relates an adjective clause to the word the clause modifies.

EXAMPLES "The Tell-Tale Heart," **which tells the story of a murderer's guilt,** is great to read aloud. [The relative pronoun *which* begins the adjective clause and relates it to the compound noun *"The Tell-Tale Heart."*]

Everything **that could be done** was done. [*That* relates the adjective clause to the pronoun *everything.*]

One author **whose stories I enjoy** is Amy Ling. [*Whose* relates the adjective clause to the noun *author.*]

In addition to relating a subordinate clause to the rest of the sentence, a relative pronoun also has a function in the subordinate clause.

EXAMPLES Is he the one **who wrote "The Moustache"**? [*Who* functions as subject of the verb *wrote.*]

She is a friend **on whom you can always depend.** [*Whom* functions as object of the preposition *on.*]

 QUICK CHECK 2

Identify the adjective clause in each of the following sentences. Underline the relative pronoun, and give the word or words the adjective clause refers to.

EXAMPLE 1. Davy Crockett, who is a legend, was born in Tennessee.
1. *who is a legend—Davy Crockett*

1. Irwin Shapiro's "Davy Is Born," which is in this book, is a tall tale.
2. Isn't it the story that is full of slang and dialect?
3. Mr. Shapiro, whose imagination is sizable, is an expert on dialect.
4. Was Davy Crockett one of the men who fought at the Alamo?
5. Crockett's father, whom Shapiro mentions, must have been proud.

The Adverb Clause

7e. An *adverb clause* is a subordinate clause that modifies a verb, an adjective, or an adverb.

ADVERB	You may sit **anywhere.**
ADVERB PHRASE	You may sit **in any chair.**
ADVERB CLAUSE	You may sit **wherever you wish.**

An adverb clause tells *where, when, how, why, to what extent,* or *under what condition.*

EXAMPLES   Put that package **wherever you can find room for it.**
[Where?]

Tokubei became furious **when he learned the truth.**
[When?]

My new friend and I talk **as if we've known each other for a long time.** [How?]

Because he dreads the cold grave, Sam McGee requests to be cremated. [Why?]

Johnny caused Sam and Bill more trouble **than they had expected.** [To what extent?]

If he sees two lanterns in the belfry, what will Paul Revere know? [Under what condition?]

Notice in these examples that an adverb clause does not always follow the word it modifies. When an adverb clause begins a sentence, the clause is followed by a comma.

An adverb clause is introduced by a *subordinating conjunction*—a word that shows the relationship between the adverb clause and the word or words that the clause modifies.

☞ For more information about using commas with adverb clauses, see page 955.

Common Subordinating Conjunctions

after	as though	once	when
although	because	since	whenever
as	before	so that	where
as if	even if	than	wherever
as long as	how	though	whether
as much as	if	unless	while
as soon as	in order that	until	

 QUICK CHECK 3

Identify the adverb clause in each of the following sentences. In each adverb clause, circle the subordinating conjunction, and underline the subject once and the verb twice.

EXAMPLE   **1.** I laughed out loud when Uncle Roarious used a rake for a comb.

1. (when) Uncle Roarious used a rake for a comb

1. Although kerosene oil is toxic, Uncle Roarious drank it.
2. Shapiro's Davy Crockett could talk when he was still a baby.
3. They planted Davy so that the child would grow.
4. While he was in the earth, the wind blew on him.
5. Davy talked as though he were a grown man.

The Noun Clause

7f. A *noun clause* is a subordinate clause used as a noun.

A noun clause may be used as a subject, a complement (predicate nominative, direct object, indirect object), or an object of a preposition.

SUBJECT	**That Jabez Stone is unlucky** is evident.
PREDICATE NOMINATIVE	A three-year extension was **what the stranger offered Jabez.**
DIRECT OBJECT	The judges determined **who won.**
INDIRECT OBJECT	The sheriff gave **whoever volunteered to help in the search** a flashlight.
OBJECT OF A PREPOSITION	He did not agree to **what the kidnappers demanded.**

Common Introductory Words for Noun Clauses

that	which	whoever
what	whichever	whom
whatever	who	whomever

In many cases, the word that introduces a noun clause has another function within the clause.

EXAMPLES A trophy will be given to **whoever wins the race.** [*Whoever* is the subject of the verb *wins.*]

Did anyone tell Alfonso **what he should do**? [*What* is the direct object of the verb *should do.*]

Their complaint was **that Charlie had changed.** [The word *that* introduces the noun clause but has no other function in the clause.]

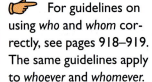 For guidelines on using *who* and *whom* correctly, see pages 918–919. The same guidelines apply to *whoever* and *whomever.*

 QUICK CHECK 4

Identify the noun clause in each of the following sentences. Tell whether the noun clause is a *subject*, a *predicate nominative*, a *direct object*, an *indirect object*, or an *object of a preposition*.

EXAMPLE 1. Laurie could not accept that he had done something bad.
1. *that he had done something bad—direct object*

1. Whatever went wrong must be someone else's fault.
2. Laurie's mother does not know that he has been making up stories about Charles.
3. Charles certainly gives whomever he can find a hard time.
4. The whole family is quite amused by what Laurie said about Charles.
5. Charles's true identity was what they didn't know.

8 SENTENCES

THE SENTENCE

8a. A *sentence* is a group of words that has a subject and a verb and expresses a complete thought.

A sentence begins with a capital letter and ends with a period, a question mark, or an exclamation point.

EXAMPLES   He told a story about Urashima Taro**.**
Have you read the novel *Shane***?**
What a dangerous mission it must have been**!**

Sentence or Sentence Fragment?

When a group of words either does not contain a subject and a verb or does not express a complete thought, it is a ***sentence fragment.***

SENTENCE FRAGMENT   The protagonist of the story. [What about the protagonist of the story?]

SENTENCE   The protagonist of the story is unnamed.

SENTENCE FRAGMENT   After reading the poem. [Who read the poem? What happened afterward?]

SENTENCE   After reading the poem, we asked the teacher several questions.

SENTENCE FRAGMENT   While Smiley was in the swamp. [What happened while Smiley was in the swamp?]

SENTENCE   While Smiley was in the swamp, the stranger filled the frog with quail shot.

> For information about end marks, see pages 951–952.

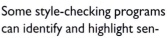

COMPUTER NOTE   Some style-checking programs can identify and highlight sentence fragments. Such programs are useful, but they aren't perfect. You still need to check each sentence yourself to be sure it has a subject and a verb and expresses a complete thought.

 QUICK CHECK 1

Tell whether each group of words is a *sentence* or a *sentence fragment*. If the word group is a sentence, correct it by adding a capital letter and end punctuation. If the word group is a sentence fragment, correct it by adding words, a capital letter, and end punctuation to make a complete sentence.

EXAMPLE   1. reading Robert Frost's poem "A Time to Talk"
1. *sentence fragment—I am reading Robert Frost's poem "A Time to Talk."*

1. a friend slowing down his horse on the road
2. he calls out
3. using a hoe for work on the hills near his home
4. to the walls made of stone comes the man
5. does he have time for a visit

THE SUBJECT AND THE PREDICATE

A sentence consists of two parts: a *subject* and a *predicate*.

8b. A *subject* **tells whom or what the sentence is about. The** *predicate* **tells something about the subject.**

Subject	Predicate

EXAMPLE   Laurie's mother / went to the meeting.

Finding the Subject

Usually, the subject comes before the predicate. Sometimes, however, the subject may appear elsewhere in the sentence. To find the subject of a sentence, ask *Who?* or *What?* before the predicate.

EXAMPLES   At the top of the tree, **a bird's nest** sat. [What sat? a bird's nest]

Lying beside the fence was **the broken chain.** [What was lying? the broken chain]

Does **Casey** strike out? [Who does strike out? Casey]

The Simple Subject

8c. A *simple subject* **is the main word or group of words in the complete subject.**

A **complete subject** consists of all the words that name and describe whom or what the sentence is about.

EXAMPLES   The long **trip** across the desert was finally over. [The complete subject is *the long trip across the desert.*]

One of my favorite poems is "The Cremation of Sam McGee." [The complete subject is *one of my favorite poems.*]

"The Cremation of Sam McGee" is a poem by Robert W. Service. [*"The Cremation of Sam McGee"* is both the simple subject and the complete subject.]

 QUICK CHECK 2

Identify the *complete subject* and the *simple subject* in each sentence of the following paragraph.

EXAMPLE   [1] Has your teacher read "Mrs. Flowers" yet?

    1. *complete subject—your teacher; simple subject—teacher*

[1] Maya Angelou's "Mrs. Flowers" characterizes a gentle woman. [2] Mrs. Flowers is a woman of great dignity and grace. [3] Out of kindness and genuine liking, she befriends young Marguerite. [4] A mutual love for literature links the two. [5] The warm respect of Mrs. Flowers' friendship gives Marguerite new self-esteem.

 NOTE   The subject of a sentence is *never* part of a prepositional phrase.

EXAMPLE   The **tips** of the rabbit's ears were sticking up behind the large cabbage. [What were sticking up? *Tips* were sticking up.]

 NOTE   In this book, the term *subject* refers to the simple subject unless otherwise indicated.

The Simple Predicate, or Verb

 8d. A *simple predicate,* or *verb,* is the main word or group of words in the complete predicate.

A **complete predicate** consists of a verb and all the words that describe the verb and complete its meaning.

EXAMPLES   The trees **sagged** beneath the weight of the ice. [The complete predicate is *sagged beneath the weight of the ice.*]

After the race, everyone **congratulated** Squeaky. [The complete predicate is *after the race . . . congratulated Squeaky.*]

In the roaring furnace **sat** Sam McGee. [The complete predicate is *in the roaring furnace sat.*]

The Verb Phrase

A simple predicate may be a one-word verb, or it may be a verb phrase. A **verb phrase** consists of a main verb and its helping verbs.

EXAMPLES   Our class **is reading** *The Diary of Anne Frank.*
Have you **done** your homework yet?

 QUICK CHECK 3

Identify the *complete predicate* and the *verb* in each of the following sentences. Keep in mind that parts of the complete predicate may come before and after the complete subject.

EXAMPLE   **1.** For no apparent reason, Mrs. Flowers asks Marguerite in.
1. *complete predicate—For no apparent reason . . . asks Marguerite in; verb—asks*

1. Surprisingly, she has made cookies especially for Marguerite.
2. Marguerite is delighted with the attention.
3. After their talk, Marguerite goes home.
4. She reads *A Tale of Two Cities* aloud.
5. How did the words of Charles Dickens help her?

The Compound Subject

 8e. A *compound subject* consists of two or more connected subjects that have the same verb. The usual connecting word is *and, or,* or *nor.*

EXAMPLES   Traveling together were **Zenta** and **Matsuzo.**
Smoked **turkey**, baked **ham**, or roast **goose** will be the main course for Thanksgiving dinner.
Neither the **trousers** nor the **shoes** that I want are on sale yet.

For more about verb phrases, see page 897.

Language Handbook

The Compound Verb

8f. A *compound verb* consists of two or more verbs that have the same subject. A connecting word—usually *and, or,* or *but*—is used between the verbs.

EXAMPLES   Mr. Nuttel **sat** down and **waited** for Mrs. Sappleton.
We **can go** forward, **go** back, or **stay** right here.

Both the subject and the verb of a sentence may be compound.

                              S   S   V   V
EXAMPLE   The **captain** and the **crew battled** the storm and **hoped** for better weather. [The captain battled and hoped, and the crew battled and hoped.]

 QUICK CHECK 4

Identify all *compound subjects* and *compound verbs* in the following sentences.

EXAMPLE   1. Mike and his sister had planned a visit to their grandmother.

   1. *compound subject—Mike, sister*

1. However, his sister wanted to go but fell ill.
2. Will his mother inspect his clothes or question him about his moustache?
3. Mike and his mother love and respect each other.
4. She does not like the moustache yet says little about it.
5. Mike's grandmother and the movie actress Ethel Barrymore look and sound alike.

Try It Out

Use a compound subject or a compound verb to combine each of the following sets of short sentences.

1. Grandmother greets her grandson. She thinks he is someone else.
2. According to Grandmother, blue jays come to the bird feeder. Chickadees come there, too.
3. A nurse enters the room. She offers Grandmother some juice.
4. Orange juice does not interest her. Neither does cranberry juice or grape juice.
5. Mike should tell Grandmother the truth. He cannot.

 TIPS FOR WRITERS

Using Compound Subjects and Verbs to Combine Ideas

Sometimes a writer will repeat a simple subject or verb for special emphasis. Often, though, such repetition serves no purpose. Using compound subjects and verbs, you can combine ideas and reduce wordiness in your writing. Compare these examples.

WORDY   Roald Dahl wrote eerie short stories. Saki and W. W. Jacobs were two other authors who wrote eerie short stories, too.

REVISED   **Roald Dahl, Saki,** and **W. W. Jacobs** wrote eerie short stories.

WORDY   Toni Cade Bambara studied mime and took acting lessons. She also worked in a hospital.

REVISED   Toni Cade Bambara **studied** mime, **took** acting lessons, and **worked** in a hospital.

9 COMPLEMENTS

RECOGNIZING COMPLEMENTS

9a. A *complement* is a word or a group of words that completes the meaning of a verb.

INCOMPLETE	Mr. White held [*what?*]
COMPLETE	Mr. White held the **paw.**
INCOMPLETE	Marguerite thanked [*whom?*]
COMPLETE	Marguerite thanked **her.**
INCOMPLETE	Squeaky is [*what?*]
COMPLETE	Squeaky is **confident.**

As you can see, a complement may be a noun, a pronoun, or an adjective. A complement is never in a prepositional phrase.

OBJECT OF A PREPOSITION	Benjamin is studying for his math **test.**
COMPLEMENT	Benjamin is studying his math **notes.**

 QUICK CHECK 1

Identify the *subject,* the *verb,* and the *complement* in each sentence in the following paragraph. [Remember: A complement is never in a prepositional phrase.]

EXAMPLE [1] Sandra Cisneros is a writer.
　　　　　　1. *subject—Sandra Cisneros; verb—is; complement—writer*

[1] She wrote "A Smart Cookie." [2] In the story, the writer describes her mother. [3] Her mother is quite skillful. [4] Yet, the older woman seems sad about many events in her life. [5] Nevertheless, she gives Esperanza her best advice.

DIRECT OBJECTS

9b. A *direct object* is a noun or a pronoun that receives the action of the verb or that shows the result of the action. A direct object tells *what* or *whom* after a transitive verb.

EXAMPLE We watched a **performance** of *The Diary of Anne Frank.* [The noun *performance* receives the action of the transitive verb *watched* and tells *what* we watched.]

A direct object never follows a linking verb.

LINKING VERB William Wordsworth **became** poet laureate of England in 1843. [The verb *became* does not express action; therefore, it has no direct object.]

 NOTE An adverb is never a complement.

ADVERB The frog is **outside.** [*Outside* modifies the verb by telling where the frog is.]

COMPLEMENT The frog is **heavy.** [The adjective *heavy* modifies the subject by describing the frog.]

☞ For more about transitive verbs, see page 896.

☞ For more about linking verbs, see pages 896–897.

For more about prepositional phrases, see pages 899 and 923–925.

 NOTE Direct objects and indirect objects may be compound.

EXAMPLES Mrs. Flowers served **tea cookies** and **lemonade.**

The sergeant major showed **Mr. White** and his **family** the monkey's paw.

A direct object is never part of a prepositional phrase.

OBJECT OF A PREPOSITION They walked for **miles** in the Japanese countryside. [*Miles* is not the direct object of the verb *walked;* it is the object of the preposition *for.*]

INDIRECT OBJECTS

9c. An *indirect object* is a noun or a pronoun that comes between the verb and the direct object and tells *to what* or *to whom* or *for what* or *for whom* the action of the verb is done.

EXAMPLE Smiley gave the **stranger** a frog. [The noun *stranger* tells *to whom* Smiley gave a frog.]

Linking verbs do not have indirect objects. Also, an indirect object is never in a prepositional phrase.

LINKING VERB Her mother **was** a collector of rare books.

INDIRECT OBJECT She sent her **mother** a rare book.

OBJECT OF A PREPOSITION She sent a rare book to her **mother.**

✓ QUICK CHECK 2

Identify the *direct objects* and the *indirect objects* in the following sentences. [Note: Not every sentence has an indirect object.]

EXAMPLE 1. Who gave Joe Iron Shell a ride?
 1. *indirect object—Joe Iron Shell; direct object—ride*

1. Grandfather had given Cheryl moccasins.
2. Didn't he teach his grandson Sioux chants?
3. The grandchildren loved him for these gifts and more.
4. Yet, they did not show friends his picture.
5. Instead, they told the boys and girls exaggerated stories about him.

SUBJECT COMPLEMENTS

A subject complement completes the meaning of a linking verb and identifies or describes the subject.

Common Linking Verbs					
appear	become	grow	remain	smell	stay
be	feel	look	seem	sound	taste

 For more about linking verbs, see pages 896–897.

The two kinds of subject complements are the *predicate nominative* and the *predicate adjective.*

Predicate Nominatives

9d. A *predicate nominative* is a noun or a pronoun that follows a linking verb and identifies the subject or refers to it.

EXAMPLES Denise is a good **friend.** [*Friend* is a predicate nominative that identifies the subject *Denise.*]

Enrique is **one** of the best players. [*One* is a predicate nominative that refers to the subject *Enrique.*]

Predicate nominatives never appear in prepositional phrases.

EXAMPLE The prize was a **pair** of tickets to the movies. [*Pair* is a predicate nominative that identifies the subject *prize. Tickets* is the object of the preposition *of,* and *movies* is the object of the preposition *to.*]

Predicate Adjectives

9e. A *predicate adjective* is an adjective that follows a linking verb and describes the subject.

EXAMPLES The landlady is very **pleasant.** [*Pleasant* follows the linking verb *is* and describes the subject *landlady.*]

This ground looks **swampy.** [*Swampy* follows the linking verb *looks* and describes the subject *ground.*]

Some verbs, such as *look, grow,* and *feel,* may be used as either linking verbs or action verbs.

LINKING VERB The field worker **felt** tired. [*Felt* is a linking verb because it links the adjective *tired* to the subject *field worker.*]

ACTION VERB The field worker **felt** the hot wind. [*Felt* is an action verb because it is followed by the direct object *wind,* which tells what the field worker felt.]

 QUICK CHECK 3

Identify the *predicate nominatives* and *predicate adjectives* in the following sentences.

EXAMPLE **1.** The old man did not seem tall enough or grand enough.
  1. *predicate adjectives—tall, grand*

1. For him, home was the Rosebud Reservation in South Dakota.
2. Were his hands leathery and brown?
3. Joe Iron Shell was Mother's grandfather and Martin and Cheryl's great-grandfather.
4. His most precious possession was his medicine bag.
5. With age, his dark hair had become gray and stringy.

NOTE Expressions such as *It is I* and *That was he* may sound awkward because in conversation people more frequently say *It's me* and *That was him.* These nonstandard expressions may one day become acceptable in writing as well as in speech. For now, however, it is best to follow the rules of standard English in your writing.

NOTE A predicate nominative may be compound.

EXAMPLE Miss Kinnian was Charlie's **teacher** and **friend.**

NOTE A predicate adjective may be compound.

EXAMPLE A computer can be **entertaining** and **helpful,** but sometimes **frustrating.**

 For more about verbs that may be used as either linking verbs or action verbs, see page 897.

Avoiding the Overuse of *Be* Verbs

Overusing the linking verb *be* can make writing dull and lifeless. Wherever possible, replace a dull *be* verb with a verb that expresses action.

BE VERB Edgar Allan Poe **was** a writer of poems, literary criticism, and short stories.

ACTION VERB Edgar Allan Poe **wrote** poems, literary criticism, and short stories.

10 KINDS OF SENTENCES

SENTENCES CLASSIFIED BY STRUCTURE

Sentences may be classified according to **structure**—the kinds and the number of clauses they contain. The four kinds of sentences are *simple, compound, complex,* and *compound-complex.*

The Simple Sentence

10a. A *simple sentence* has one independent clause and no subordinate clauses.

EXAMPLE Mr. Lema showed him the trumpet.

The Compound Sentence

10b. A *compound sentence* has two or more independent clauses but no subordinate clauses.

The independent clauses are usually joined by a comma and a coordinating conjunction, such as *and, but, for, nor, or, so,* or *yet.* The clauses are sometimes joined by only a semicolon.

EXAMPLES It was a large sum of money, but **Tokubei was willing to pay it.**
Zenta looked at the woman's left hand; it had six fingers.

The Complex Sentence

10c. A *complex sentence* has one independent clause and at least one subordinate clause.

A simple sentence may contain a compound subject, a compound verb, or both.

EXAMPLE Dr. Nemur

and **Dr. Strauss tested**

Charlie and **monitored** his progress.

EXAMPLE   Mary ate some of the mushroom before she gave any of it to the children.

> INDEPENDENT CLAUSE   **Mary ate** some of the mushroom
>
> SUBORDINATE CLAUSE   before **she gave** any of it to the children

EXAMPLE   Some of the sailors who took part in the mutiny on the British ship *Bounty* settled Pitcairn Island.

> INDEPENDENT CLAUSE   **some** of the sailors **settled** Pitcairn Island
>
> SUBORDINATE CLAUSE   **who took** part in the mutiny on the British ship *Bounty*

The Compound-Complex Sentence

10d.   A *compound-complex sentence* has two or more independent clauses and at least one subordinate clause.

EXAMPLE   I have read several stories in which the main characters are animals, but the story that I like best is "Brer Possum's Dilemma."

> INDEPENDENT CLAUSE   **I have read** several stories
>
> INDEPENDENT CLAUSE   the **story is** "Brer Possum's Dilemma"
>
> SUBORDINATE CLAUSE   in which the main **characters are** animals
>
> SUBORDINATE CLAUSE   that **I like** best

Using a Variety of Sentence Structures

By varying the length and the structure of your sentences, you can make your writing more interesting to read. As a rule, simple sentences are best used to express single ideas. To describe more complicated ideas and to show relationships between them, you will usually need to use compound, complex, and compound-complex sentences.

> SIMPLE SENTENCES   The cotton season began. He went to school. He met Mr. Lema.
>
> COMPOUND-COMPLEX SENTENCE   When the cotton season began, he went to school, and there he met Mr. Lema.

 QUICK CHECK I

Label each of the following sentences as *simple, compound, complex,* or *compound-complex.* Then, identify each of the clauses in the sentence as *independent* or *subordinate.*

Try It Out

Decide whether the information in each numbered item would be best expressed by a simple, compound, complex, or compound-complex sentence. Then, revise each item.

1. They took off their wings. There was not enough room on the ships.
2. The people had been able to fly. They had forgotten how.
3. The Master was a hard man. The Overseer was, too.
4. A slave collapsed in the heat. The Overseer whipped him.
5. She flew awkwardly at first. She soon soared freely. Everyone looked up to her.

EXAMPLE   **1.** Virginia Hamilton tells a story about people who could fly.

       1. *complex: independent—Virginia Hamilton tells a story about people; subordinate—who could fly*

1. In the Africa of long ago, people flew.
2. Sarah's baby was crying, but she couldn't quiet the child.
3. Although the Overseer chased her, he could not catch her.
4. Before they knew it, she had flown over the trees and disappeared.
5. Toby told others the magic words, and they flew away while many slaves on the ground called for help.

SENTENCES CLASSIFIED BY PURPOSE

Sentences may be classified according to **purpose.** The four kinds of sentences are *declarative, interrogative, imperative,* and *exclamatory.*

10e. A *declarative sentence* **makes a statement. It is followed by a period.**

EXAMPLE   According to Laurie, Charles was always causing trouble**.**

10f. An *interrogative sentence* **asks a question. It is followed by a question mark.**

EXAMPLE   Did Daniel Webster defeat the devil**?**

10g. An *imperative sentence* **gives a command or makes a request. It is followed by a period. A strong command is followed by an exclamation point.**

EXAMPLES   Look after the children while I'm gone**.** [mild command]
               Father, tell us a story**.** [request]
               Watch out**!** [strong command]

10h. An *exclamatory sentence* **shows excitement or expresses strong feeling. It is followed by an exclamation point.**

EXAMPLE   What a sad day in Mudville that was**!**

 ## QUICK CHECK 2

Classify each of the following sentences according to its purpose: *declarative, interrogative, imperative,* or *exclamatory.*

EXAMPLE   **1.** For Monday, read "The People Could Fly."
       1. *imperative*

1. Why did the people take off their wings?
2. Toby had not forgotten the magic words.
3. Listen to them.
4. Look up in the sky!
5. How the slaves must have imagined just such a scene!

> **NOTE** The "understood" subject of an imperative sentence is always *you.*
>
> **EXAMPLES** Father, (you) tell us a story. (You) Watch out!

> For more about end marks of punctuation, see pages 951–952.

11 WRITING EFFECTIVE SENTENCES

WRITING CLEAR SENTENCES

One of the easiest ways to make your writing clear is to use complete sentences. A **complete sentence** is a word group that has a subject, has a verb, and expresses a complete thought. Two of the stumbling blocks to the development of clear sentences are *sentence fragments* and *run-on sentences*. For information about sentence fragments, see page 933.

Run-on Sentences

11a. **Avoid using run-on sentences.**

If you run together two complete sentences as if they were one sentence, you get a **run-on sentence.**

RUN-ON	Margaret Bourke-White was a famous news photographer she worked for *Life* magazine during World War II.
CORRECT	Margaret Bourke-White was a famous news photographer. **S**he worked for *Life* magazine during World War II.
RUN-ON	Bourke-White traveled all over the world, she even went underground to photograph miners in South Africa.
CORRECT	Bourke-White traveled all over the world. **S**he even went underground to photograph miners in South Africa.

You can correct a run-on sentence

1. by making two sentences, as in the examples above

2. by using a comma and the coordinating conjunction *and, but,* or *or*

RUN-ON	Chinese people use kites in some religious ceremonies, they usually use them for sport.
CORRECT	Chinese people use kites in some religious ceremonies, **but** they usually use them for sport.

> **NOTE** To spot run-ons, try reading your writing aloud. A natural pause in your voice often marks the end of one thought and the beginning of another. If you pause at a place where you don't have any end punctuation, you may have found a run-on sentence.

COMBINING SENTENCES

11b. **Improve choppy sentences by combining them into longer, smoother sentences.**

You can combine sentences

1. by inserting words

ORIGINAL	Mrs. Flowers was an intelligent woman. She was generous, too.
COMBINED	Mrs. Flowers was an intelligent, **generous** woman.

2. by inserting phrases

ORIGINAL Henry David Thoreau lived at Walden Pond. He lived there for two years. He lived in a simple hut.

COMBINED **For two years** Henry David Thoreau lived **in a simple hut at Walden Pond.** [prepositional phrases]

ORIGINAL Harriet Tubman made the long journey to Philadelphia. She traveled at night.

COMBINED **Traveling at night,** Harriet Tubman made the long journey to Philadelphia. [participial phrase]

3. by using *and, but,* or *or*

ORIGINAL Eagle hunted for light. Coyote went with him.

COMBINED Eagle **and** Coyote hunted for light. [compound subject]

ORIGINAL The big box held the sun. The smaller box contained the moon.

COMBINED The big box held the sun, **and** the smaller box contained the moon. [compound sentence]

4. by using a subordinate clause

ORIGINAL Harriet Tubman did not believe that people should be slaves. She decided to escape.

COMBINED Harriet Tubman, **who believed no person should be a slave,** decided to escape. [adjective clause]

ORIGINAL Billy signed the guest book. He saw two other names.

COMBINED **When Billy signed the guest book,** he saw two other names. [adverb clause]

Try It Out ✎

Combine each of the following pairs of sentences. Make sure each revised sentence reads smoothly and shows the relationship you intend. If a pair of sentences should not be combined, write *C.*

1. Lemon Brown went to the window. Greg followed him.
2. The men were sitting down. They probably would not come back.
3. Greg asked about Lemon's injury. Lemon handed Greg the flashlight.
4. Lemon revealed his treasure. Greg stared at the strange package.
5. Greg was worried about Lemon. Lemon said that he would be fine.

TIPS FOR WRITERS

Combining Related Sentences

When you combine sentences, you show the relationships between ideas. Different combinations show different relationships. When combining sentences, be sure that each sentence you create shows the relationship you intend.

ORIGINAL Jan practiced the piano. Leon did his homework.

COMBINED After Jan practiced the piano, Leon did his homework.

COMBINED While Jan practiced the piano, Leon did his homework.

ORIGINAL Kim told a story. I wrote a poem.

COMBINED Kim told a story, and I wrote a poem.

COMBINED Kim told a story about which I wrote a poem.

QUICK CHECK 1

The following paragraph contains short, choppy sentences and run-on sentences. Use the methods you've learned in this section to make the sentences read smoothly.

EXAMPLE   [1] The building was dark. [2] It was scary.
1. *The building was dark and scary.*

[1] The room was dark. [2] There was a table. [3] An old mattress was there, too. [4] Greg heard sounds. [5] The sounds were coming from the wall. [6] He could not see the man. [7] The man stepped into the light. [8] The man's name was Lemon Brown he had been a blues singer. [9] Now, the blues had left him. [10] He was left alone, he had only his treasure for comfort.

IMPROVING SENTENCE STYLE

11c.   Improve *stringy* and *wordy* sentences by making them shorter and more precise.

Stringy sentences have too many independent clauses strung together with words like *and* or *but.*

STRINGY   Harriet Ross grew up as a slave in Maryland, and she worked on a plantation there, but in 1844, she married John Tubman, and he was a free man.

You can revise a stringy sentence

1. by breaking the sentence into two or more sentences

REVISED   Harriet Ross grew up as a slave in Maryland and worked on a plantation there. In 1844, she married John Tubman, a free man.

2. by turning some of the independent clauses into phrases or subordinate clauses

REVISED   Harriet Ross grew up as a slave in Maryland. She worked on a plantation there until, in 1844, she married John Tubman, who was a free man. [Notice that in addition to creating two separate sentences, this revision includes changing independent clauses into subordinate clauses.]

Wordy sentences tend to sound awkward and unnatural. You can revise a wordy sentence

1. by replacing a group of words with one word

WORDY   With great suddenness, the bicycle chain snapped.
REVISED   **Suddenly,** the bicycle chain snapped.

2. by replacing a clause with a phrase

WORDY After the play had come to an end, we walked over to a restaurant and treated ourselves to pizza.

REVISED **After the play,** we walked to a restaurant and treated ourselves to pizza.

3. by taking out a whole group of unnecessary words

WORDY Daniel Webster was a persuasive orator whose speeches were very convincing.

REVISED Daniel Webster was a persuasive orator.

✓ **QUICK CHECK 2**

The following paragraph is hard to read because it contains stringy and wordy sentences. Revise the paragraph to improve the sentence style.

EXAMPLE [1] Then something happened that was frightening.

1. *Then something frightening happened.*

[1] Some men called out and tromped around and called out again and wanted Lemon's treasure. [2] Lemon and Greg hid in the darkness and listened, and finally one man came upstairs, and Lemon went toward him. [3] With great fear, Greg heard the sounds of a fight. [4] Suddenly, the men ran away due to the fact that Greg had made a howling sound. [5] Then Greg asked Lemon about the treasure that he had.

12 CAPITAL LETTERS

12a. **Capitalize the first word in every sentence.**

EXAMPLE **S**he has written a report on Harriet Tubman.

The first word of a sentence that is a direct quotation is capitalized even if the quotation begins within a sentence.

EXAMPLE In her diary, Anne Frank wrote, "**I**n spite of everything, I still believe that people are really good at heart."

12b. **Capitalize the pronoun *I*.**

EXAMPLES "What should **I** do?" **I** asked.

12c. **Capitalize the interjection *O*.**

The interjection *O* is most often used on solemn or formal occasions. It is usually followed by a word in direct address.

EXAMPLES Exult **O** shores! and ring **O** bells!

—Walt Whitman, "O Captain! My Captain!"

NOTE Traditionally, the first word in a line of poetry, including song lyrics, is capitalized. Some poets and songwriters do not follow this style. When you are quoting, follow the capitalization used in the source of the quotation.

EXAMPLE

Go down, Moses,
Way down in Egypt land
Tell old Pharaoh
To let my people go.
——Traditional spiritual,
"Go Down, Moses"

For more about using capital letters in quotations, see page 959.

NOTE The interjection *oh* requires a capital letter only at the beginning of a sentence.

EXAMPLES **Oh,** that's all right.
I can't go, but, **oh,** I wish I could.

12d. **Capitalize proper nouns.**

A *common noun* is a general name for a person, a place, a thing, or an idea. A *proper noun* names a particular person, place, thing, or idea. A common noun is capitalized only when it begins a sentence or is part of a title. A proper noun is always capitalized. Some proper nouns consist of more than one word. In these names, short prepositions (those of fewer than five letters) and articles (*a, an, the*) are not capitalized.

COMMON NOUNS	holiday, man
PROPER NOUNS	Fourth of July, William the Conqueror

(1) Capitalize the names of persons and animals.

EXAMPLES   Sandra Cisneros, Toni Cade Bambara, John McEnroe, Frank Van den Akker, Algernon, Kermit, Black Beauty

(2) Capitalize geographical names.

TYPE OF NAME	EXAMPLES	
Towns, Cities	Grover's Corners	St. Louis
Counties, States	Orange County	Georgia
Countries	Mexico	Japan
Islands	Long Island	Molokai
Bodies of Water	Crystal River	Dead Sea
Forests, Parks	Argonne Forest	Palmetto State Park
Streets, Highways	Euclid Avenue	Route 66
Mountains	Mount Everest	Pikes Peak
Continents	Europe	North America
Regions	the Middle East	New England

 QUICK CHECK 1

For each of the following sentences, correct the word or words that have errors in capitalization.

EXAMPLE   **1.** Doesn't gary paulsen write about his dog columbia?
            1. *Gary Paulsen, Columbia*

1. Rose asked, "isn't the story set in the northwest territory?"
2. "no, i don't think so," will answered.
3. are you writing a poem about the dog obeah?
4. Yes, so far my best line is "o dog with heart for running sled."
5. Come to my house at 117 sixty-first street, and you can read it.

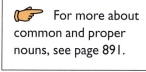 For more about common and proper nouns, see page 891.

 COMPUTER NOTE You may be able to use your spellchecker to help you capitalize people's names correctly. Make a list of the names you write most often. Then, add this list to your computer's dictionary or spelling feature.

 NOTE In a hyphenated street number, the second part of the number is not capitalized.

EXAMPLE
East Fifty-third Street

NOTE Words such as *north, east,* and *southwest* are not capitalized when they indicate direction.

EXAMPLES
traveling north
southwest of Austin

> **NOTE** The word *earth* is not capitalized unless it is used along with names of other heavenly bodies. The words *sun* and *moon* are not capitalized.
>
> **EXAMPLES** Water covers more than seventy percent of the surface of the earth.
>
> Mercury and Venus are closer to the sun than Earth is.

(3) Capitalize the names of planets, stars, and other heavenly bodies.

EXAMPLES Saturn, Canopus, Ursa Major

(4) Capitalize the names of teams, organizations, businesses, institutions, and government bodies.

TYPE OF NAME	EXAMPLES
Teams	Chicago Bulls Pittsburgh Pirates
Organizations	Future Farmers of America National Football League
Businesses	General Motors Corporation Kellogg Company
Institutions	Blake Memorial Hospital Lakeshore Junior High School
Government Bodies	Department of Education Governor's Council on Equal Opportunity

(5) Capitalize the names of historical events and periods, special events, and calendar items.

TYPE OF NAME	EXAMPLES	
Historical Events	Persian Gulf Conflict	the Crusades
Historical Periods	Paleozoic Era	Renaissance
Special Events	Kentucky State Fair	Olympic Games
Calendar Items	Monday	Memorial Day

(6) Capitalize the names of nationalities, races, and peoples.

EXAMPLES Italian, Japanese, African American, Caucasian, Hispanic

(7) Capitalize the names of religions and their followers, holy days, sacred writings, and specific deities.

TYPE OF NAME	EXAMPLES		
Religions and Followers	Christianity	Hindu	Judaism
Holy Days	Ramadan	Easter	Passover
Sacred Writings	Koran	Talmud	New Testament
Specific Deities	God	Allah	Vishnu

(8) Capitalize the names of buildings and other structures.

EXAMPLES Plaza Hotel   Eiffel Tower

> **NOTE** The name of a season is not capitalized unless it is part of a proper name.
>
> **EXAMPLES** first day of spring, Bluegrass Spring Festival

> **NOTE** The word *god* is not capitalized when it refers to a god of mythology. The names of specific gods, however, are capitalized.
>
> **EXAMPLE** The Egyptian sun god was Ra.

(9) Capitalize the names of monuments and awards.

TYPE OF NAME	EXAMPLES
Monuments	Washington Monument Vietnam Veterans Memorial
Awards	Newbery Medal Pulitzer Prize

(10) Capitalize the names of trains, ships, aircraft, and spacecraft.

TYPE OF NAME	EXAMPLES	
Trains	*California Zephyr*	*The Chief*
Ships	*Flying Cloud*	*Santa Maria*
Aircraft	*Spirit of St. Louis*	*Air Force One*
Spacecraft	*Voyager 2*	*Challenger*

(11) Capitalize the brand names of business products.

EXAMPLES   Reebok shoes, Ford station wagon, Bugle Boy jeans
[Notice that the names of the types of products are not capitalized.]

 QUICK CHECK 2

Correct each of the following expressions, using capital letters as needed. If an item is correct, write *C*.

EXAMPLE   **1.** the third reich
                    1. *the Third Reich*

1. north star
2. a ship called the *skimmer*
3. battle of the little bighorn
4. beliefs of muslims
5. a 1930 black plymouth
6. oglala sioux
7. the purple heart
8. largest animal on earth
9. camp harmony
10. the meeting on monday

12e.   **Capitalize proper adjectives.**

A *proper adjective* is formed from a proper noun and is almost always capitalized.

PROPER NOUN	PROPER ADJECTIVE
France	French cuisine
America	American heritage
William Shakespeare	Shakespearean actor

☞ For more about proper nouns and proper adjectives, see pages 891 and 895.

NOTE A title used alone in direct address is usually capitalized.

EXAMPLES Is everyone here, **R**everend?
May I help you, **S**ir [*or* sir]?

 NOTE Do not capitalize a word showing a family relationship when a possessive comes before the word.

EXAMPLES Barbara's **fa**ther and my **u**ncle Trent are the sponsors.

☞ For information on what titles to italicize (underline), see page 958.
For information on using quotation marks for titles, see page 961.

NOTE The article *the* before a title is not capitalized unless it is the first word of the title.

EXAMPLES Is that the late edition of the *Chicago Sun-Times*?
I am reading "**T**he Tell-Tale Heart."

12f. **Do not capitalize names of school subjects, except names of languages and of courses followed by a number.**

EXAMPLES **h**istory, **S**panish, **B**iology I

12g. **Capitalize titles.**

(1) **Capitalize a title of a person when it comes before a name.**

EXAMPLES They spoke to **G**overnor Adam and **D**r. Chang.

(2) **Capitalize a title used alone or following a person's name only when you want to emphasize the position of someone holding a high office.**

EXAMPLES Will the **S**ecretary of Labor hold a news conference?
The **s**ecretary of our scout troop has the measles.

(3) **Capitalize a word showing a family relationship when the word is used before or in place of a person's name.**

EXAMPLES Did **M**om invite **A**unt Frances and **U**ncle Ralph?

(4) **Capitalize the first and last words and all important words in titles of books, magazines, newspapers, poems, short stories, historical documents, movies, television programs, works of art, and musical compositions.**

Unimportant words in titles include
• prepositions of fewer than five letters (such as *at, of, for, from, with*)
• coordinating conjunctions (*and, but, for, nor, or, so, yet*)
• articles (*a, an, the*)

TYPE OF NAME	EXAMPLES
Books	*I Know Why the Caged Bird Sings* *Baseball in April*
Magazines	*Latin American Literary Review* *Field and Stream*
Newspapers	*Boston Herald* *USA Today*
Poems	"A Time to Talk" "Oranges"
Short Stories	"The Monkey's Paw" "The Inn of Lost Time"
Historical Documents	Bill of Rights Treaty of Ghent
Movies	*The Lion King* *Star Wars*
Television Programs	*Full House* *Murder, She Wrote*
Works of Art	*Mona Lisa* *I and the Village*
Musical Compositions	*West Side Story* *Rhapsody in Blue*

QUICK CHECK 3

Correct each of the following expressions, adding or deleting capital letters as needed.

EXAMPLE **1.** general George Armstrong Custer
 1. *General George Armstrong Custer*

1. parson walker
2. spanish class
3. the song "let me call you sweetheart"
4. st. bernard dogs
5. a hmong folk tale
6. the opera *pirates of penzance*
7. "Yes, captain."
8. a gift for my Uncle Ed
9. my Art Class
10. grandmother's dress

13 PUNCTUATION

END MARKS

An **end mark** is a mark of punctuation placed at the end of a sentence. The three kinds of end marks are the *period,* the *question mark,* and the *exclamation point.*

13a. **Use a period at the end of a statement.**

EXAMPLE   Jabez Stone sought the help of Daniel Webster**.**

13b. **Use a question mark at the end of a question.**

EXAMPLE   Did Paul Zindel write *Let Me Hear You Whisper***?**

13c. **Use an exclamation point at the end of an exclamation.**

EXAMPLE   What an exciting race that was**!**

13d. **Use a period or an exclamation point at the end of a request or a command.**

EXAMPLES   Kristi, please read the part of Miss Moray**.** [a request]
 Watch out**!** [a command]

13e. **Use a period after most abbreviations.**

TYPE OF ABBREVIATION	EXAMPLES			
Addresses	St**.**	Rd**.**	Blvd**.**	P**.**O**.** Box
Organizations and Companies	Co**.**	Inc**.**	Corp**.**	Assn**.**

(chart continued on next page)

Remember that correct capitalization of abbreviations is part of the proper spelling. Some abbreviations are capitalized.

EXAMPLES Mrs.   CD   Ky.   FBI

However, some abbreviations, especially those for measurements, are not capitalized.

EXAMPLES in.   yd   oz   cm   kg

Notice that abbreviations for most units of measurement are written without periods. (The abbreviation *in.* for *inch* needs a period so that it will not be confused with the word *in.*)

Consult a dictionary for the correct capitalization of an abbreviation.

For more about abbreviations, see the bottom of this page and page 952.

 NOTE A two-letter state abbreviation without periods is used only when it is followed by a ZIP Code.

EXAMPLE
Lodi, **CA** 95240

TYPE OF ABBREVIATION	EXAMPLES			
Personal Names	O. Henry		W. W. Jacobs	
Titles Used with Names	Mr.	Mrs.	Jr.	Dr.
States	Ky.	Fla.	Tenn.	Calif.
Times	A.M.	P.M.	B.C.	A.D.

When an abbreviation with a period ends a sentence, another period is not needed. However, a question mark or an exclamation point is used as needed.

EXAMPLES   This is my friend J. R.
           Have you met Nguyen, J. R.?

 ## QUICK CHECK I

For each of the following sentences, add periods, question marks, and exclamation points where they are needed.

EXAMPLE   1. What was your opinion of Dr Crocus
           1. *What was your opinion of Dr. Crocus?*

1. How that dolphin resisted them
2. The recipe on PBS called for 2 oz of milk
3. Hurry Call the fire department right now, C C
4. Contact him at P O Box 113, Fifth St, New York, NY
5. Was Robert W Service the poet laureate of Canada, T J

COMMAS

Items in a Series

13f. **Use commas to separate items in a series.**

Words, phrases, and clauses in a series are separated by commas to show the reader where one item in the series ends and the next item begins. Make sure there are three or more items in a series; two items often do not need a comma.

WORDS IN A SERIES	In late fall, the lake looked cold, gray, and calm.
PHRASES IN A SERIES	Tightening the spokes, checking the tire pressure, and oiling the gears, Carlos prepared his bike for the race.
CLAUSES IN A SERIES	I was late for school because my mother's car wouldn't start, my sister couldn't find her homework, and I forgot my lunch and had to go back to get it.

If all items in a series are joined by *and* or *or,* do not use commas to separate them.

EXAMPLE Have you read *The Friends* **or** *Summer of My German Soldier* **or** *Bridge to Terabithia?*

13g. **Use a comma to separate two or more adjectives that come before a noun.**

EXAMPLE Many ranchers depended on the small, tough, sure-footed mustang.

Sometimes the final adjective in a series is so closely linked to the noun that a comma is not used before the final adjective. If you aren't sure whether the final adjective and the noun are linked, use this test: Insert the word *and* between the adjectives. If *and* makes sense, use a comma.

EXAMPLE Training a frisky colt to become a gentle, dependable **riding horse** takes great patience. [*And* doesn't make sense between *dependable* and *riding*.]

Compound Sentences

13h. **Use a comma before *and, but, or, nor, for, so,* or *yet* when it joins independent clauses.**

EXAMPLE Outside, the wind was higher than ever, **and** the old man started nervously at the sound of a door banging upstairs.
　　　　　　　　　　　　　　—W. W. Jacobs, "The Monkey's Paw"

Interrupters

13i. **Use commas to set off an expression that interrupts a sentence.**

(1) **Use commas to set off a nonessential participial phrase or a nonessential subordinate clause.**

A *nonessential* (or *nonrestrictive*) phrase or clause adds information that can be omitted without changing the main idea of the sentence.

NONESSENTIAL PHRASE The spider web, **shining in the early light,** looked like sparkling lace.

NONESSENTIAL CLAUSE Edgar Allan Poe, **who wrote "The Tell-Tale Heart,"** is a master of the macabre.

Do not set off an *essential* (or *restrictive*) phrase or clause. Since such a phrase or clause tells *which one* or *which ones,* it cannot be omitted without changing the meaning of the sentence.

ESSENTIAL PHRASE The discovery **made by Zenta** saved Tokubei fifty gold pieces. [Which discovery?]

ESSENTIAL CLAUSE The book **that you recommended** is not in the library. [Which book?]

 NOTE A comma should never be used between an adjective and the noun immediately following it.

EXAMPLE Mary O'Hara wrote a tender, **suspenseful story** about a young boy and his colt.

 NOTE When the independent clauses are very short, the comma before *and, but,* or *or* may sometimes be omitted.

EXAMPLE They were hungry **and** they had nothing to eat.

☞ For more about compound sentences, see page 940.

☞ For more about participial phrases, see page 925. For more about subordinate clauses, see pages 929–932.

NOTE Do not set off an appositive that tells *which one* (or *ones*) about the word it identifies. Such an appositive is essential to the meaning of the sentence.

EXAMPLE My ancestor **Alberto Pazienza** immigrated to America on the ship *Marianna.* [Which ancestor? Which ship?]

☞ For more about appositives and appositive phrases, see page 927.

NOTE Some parenthetical expressions are not always used as interrupters. Use commas only when the expressions are parenthetical.

EXAMPLES What, **in your opinion,** would be the best solution? [parenthetical]
We all have faith **in your opinion.** [not parenthetical]

(2) Use commas to set off an appositive or an appositive phrase that is nonessential.

APPOSITIVE	Smiley's frog, **Dan'l Webster,** lost the contest.
APPOSITIVE PHRASE	Robert Frost, **my favorite poet,** won four Pulitzer Prizes.

(3) Use commas to set off words used in direct address.

EXAMPLE Do you know, **Elena,** who wrote "The Medicine Bag"?

(4) Use commas to set off a parenthetical expression.

A *parenthetical expression* is a side remark that adds information or relates ideas.

EXAMPLE Brer Possum should have known, **of course,** that Brer Snake would bite him.

Commonly Used Parenthetical Expressions

after all	for example	on the other hand
at any rate	for instance	I believe (hope, suppose, think)
by the way	generally speaking	in my opinion
in fact	of course	in the first place

Introductory Words, Phrases, and Clauses

13j. **Use a comma after certain introductory elements.**

(1) Use a comma after *yes, no,* or any mild exclamation such as *well* or *why* at the beginning of a sentence.

EXAMPLE Yes, I read "A Smart Cookie."

(2) Use a comma after an introductory prepositional phrase if the phrase is long or if two or more phrases appear together.

EXAMPLES **Underneath the moss-covered rock,** we found a shiny, fat earthworm.
By the end of the second day of the journey, they were exhausted.

(3) Use a comma after a participial phrase or an infinitive phrase that introduces a sentence.

PARTICIPIAL PHRASE	**Forced onto the sidelines by a sprained ankle,** Carlos was restless and unhappy.
INFINITIVE PHRASE	**To defend the honor of King Arthur's knights,** Sir Gawain accepted the Green Knight's challenge.

(4) Use a comma after an introductory adverb clause.

EXAMPLE   **As soon as he made the third wish,** the knocking stopped.

Conventional Situations

13k.   Use commas in certain conventional situations.

(1) Use commas to separate items in dates and addresses.

EXAMPLES   The delegates to the Constitutional Convention signed the Constitution on Monday, September 17, 1787, in Philadelphia, Pennsylvania.

Her address is 6448 Higgins Road, Chicago, IL 60607.

(2) Use a comma after the salutation of a friendly letter and after the closing of any letter.

EXAMPLES   Dear Mrs. Flowers,   Sincerely yours,

 QUICK CHECK 2

For each of the following sentences, add commas where they are needed.

EXAMPLE   **I.** With hope in the future they packed got in the wagon and rode away.

I. *With hope in the future, they packed, got in the wagon, and rode away.*

1. They didn't ride in a big Conestoga wagon but of course they did have a wagon.
2. Well his pa two sisters and he set out for the mountains.
3. Pa a wary man didn't know who Mary was where she came from or much about her.
4. Stranded they could starve or eat their horse or find food.
5. That mushroom which could have been poisonous saved them.

SEMICOLONS

A *semicolon* separates complete thoughts as a period does and also separates items within a sentence as a comma does.

13l.   Use a semicolon instead of a comma between closely related independent clauses when they are not joined by *and, but, or, nor, for, so,* or *yet.*

EXAMPLE   Motor activity is impaired; there is a general reduction of glandular activity; there is an accelerated loss of coordination.

—Daniel Keyes, "Flowers for Algernon"

☞   For more about prepositional phrases, see pages 923–925. For more about verbal phrases, see pages 925–927. For more about adverb clauses, see pages 930–931.

Try It Out ✎

Read each of the following sentences, and revise any sentence that you think is too heavily punctuated.

1. Mary was just eighteen years old, but she had nerve and stood her ground; in the days to come, the family would have reason to be grateful to her.

2. She had run away, she bore scars, and she wouldn't say much about herself; because the family had no money, little food, and too much work for one man, Pa did not want to take her along with them, and, once he did, he did not even speak to her.

3. Life on the prairie broke the spirits of many people, such as those that the family met along the way; the people were glum and frightened, and many of them were past despair, yet they would give their help.

4. As you can well imagine, it must have been hard for the homesteaders to share their venison; food was difficult to come by, and they had little for themselves.

5. Mary prepared the mushroom, frying it in a pan; then, she ate some and sat up all night, waiting to see if death would come.

NOTE When a conjunctive adverb or a transitional expression *joins* clauses, it is preceded by a semicolon and followed by a comma. When it *interrupts* a clause, however, it is set off by commas.

EXAMPLES You are entitled to your opinion; **however,** you can't ignore the facts.
You are entitled to your opinion; you can't, **however,** ignore the facts.

Tips for Writers

Avoiding the Overuse of Semicolons

Semicolons are most effective when they are not overused. Sometimes it is better to separate a compound sentence or a heavily punctuated sentence into two sentences than to use a semicolon.

ACCEPTABLE In the tropical jungles of South America, it rains almost every day, sometimes all day; the vegetation there, some of which is found nowhere else in the world, is lush, dense, and fast-growing.

BETTER In the tropical jungles of South America, it rains almost every day, sometimes all day. The vegetation there, some of which is found nowhere else in the world, is lush, dense, and fast-growing.

13m. **Use a semicolon between independent clauses joined by a *conjunctive adverb* or a *transitional expression*.**

A *conjunctive adverb* or a *transitional expression* shows how the independent clauses that it joins are related.

EXAMPLES Mr. Scratch was formidable; **however,** he was no match for Daniel Webster.
Dorset decided not to pay the ransom; **in fact,** he demanded money from the two kidnappers.

Commonly Used Conjunctive Adverbs

accordingly	furthermore	instead	nevertheless
besides	however	meanwhile	otherwise
consequently	indeed	moreover	therefore

Commonly Used Transitional Expressions

as a result	for example	that is	for instance
in addition	in spite of	in fact	in conclusion

13n. **Use a semicolon rather than a comma before a coordinating conjunction to join independent clauses that contain commas.**

EXAMPLE We will practice Act I on Monday, Act II on Wednesday, and Act III on Friday; and on Saturday we will rehearse the entire play.

13o. Use a colon before a list of items, especially after expressions like *as follows* or *the following.*

EXAMPLE   Robert Frost wrote the following: "Nothing Gold Can Stay," "The Road Not Taken," and "A Time to Talk."

13p. Use a colon before a statement that explains or clarifies a preceding statement.

When a list of words, phrases, or subordinate clauses follows a colon, the first word of the list is lowercase. When an independent clause follows a colon, the first word of the clause begins with a capital letter.

EXAMPLES   There are two kinds of people: cat lovers and dog lovers.

Our teacher asked us only one question: What had happened to the landlady's other boarders?

13q. Use a colon in certain conventional situations.

(1) Use a colon between the hour and the minute.

EXAMPLE   11:30 P.M.

(2) Use a colon after the salutation of a business letter.

EXAMPLES   Dear Sir or Madam: Dear Sales Manager:

(3) Use a colon between chapter and verse in referring to passages from the Bible and between a title and a subtitle.

EXAMPLES   John 3:16
"A Tragedy Revealed: A Heroine's Last Days"

 QUICK CHECK 3

For each of the following sentences, add commas, semicolons, and colons as needed.

EXAMPLE   **1.** There were no deer moreover all food was scarce.
1. *There were no deer; moreover, all food was scarce.*

1. Times were hard consequently some felt the emotions expressed in Psalm 22 1.
2. Daylight was precious by 7 00 A.M. travelers were on their way.
3. Their situation had become grave they had no food and the horse was worn out.
4. Mary a valiant woman found a mushroom a huge one and she cooked it.
5. The test tomorrow will cover the following setting theme and plot.

 NOTE   Never use a colon directly after a verb or a preposition that comes before a list of items.

INCORRECT   This marinara sauce is made of: tomatoes, bay leaves, onions, oregano, and garlic.
CORRECT   This marinara sauce is made of tomatoes, bay leaves, onions, oregano, and garlic.

INCORRECT   The main characters are: Sam, Bill, and Johnny.
CORRECT   The main characters are Sam, Bill, and Johnny.

14 PUNCTUATION

UNDERLINING (ITALICS)

COMPUTER NOTE If you use a computer, you may be able to set words in italics yourself. Most word-processing software and many printers are capable of producing italic type.

Italics are printed letters that lean to the right, such as *the letters in these words*. In your handwritten or typewritten work, indicate italics by underlining.

EXAMPLE *Monica Sone wrote <u>Nisei Daughter</u>.*

If this sentence were printed, it would look like this:

Monica Sone wrote *Nisei Daughter.*

14a. **Use underlining (italics) for titles of books, plays, periodicals, works of art, films, television programs, recordings, long musical compositions, ships, trains, aircraft, and spacecraft.**

NOTE The article *the* before the title of a magazine or a newspaper is usually neither italicized nor capitalized when it is written within a sentence. Some periodicals do include *the* as part of their titles.

EXAMPLES My parents subscribe to **the** *Chicago Tribune.*
He wrote for ***The New York Times.***

TYPE OF TITLE	EXAMPLES	
Books	*The Incredible Journey*	*Where the Red Fern Grows*
Plays	*Let Me Hear You Whisper*	*The Diary of Anne Frank*
Periodicals	*Newsweek*	*The Wall Street Journal*
Works of Art	*The Last Supper*	*Bird in Space*
Films	*The Wizard of Oz*	*Forrest Gump*
Television Programs	*The Simpsons*	*Law & Order*
Recordings	*Music Box*	*No Fences*
Long Musical Compositions	*A Sea Symphony*	*Peer Gynt Suite*
Ships	*Flying Cloud*	*Queen Elizabeth 2*
Trains	*Orient Express*	*Garden State Special*
Aircraft	*Spirit of St. Louis*	*Spruce Goose*
Spacecraft	*USS Enterprise*	*Voyager I*

☞ For examples of titles that are not italicized but, instead, are enclosed in quotation marks, see page 961.

14b. **Use underlining (italics) for words, letters, and figures referred to as such.**

EXAMPLES What is the difference between the words *emigrate* and *immigrate*?
Drop the final *e* before you add *-ing* to either of those words.
Is this number a *3* or an *8*?

 **QUICK CHECK 1**

For each of the following sentences, add underlining wherever necessary.

EXAMPLE   **1.** Who played Anne in The Diary of Anne Frank?

　　　　　　1. *Who played Anne in <u>The Diary of Anne Frank</u>?*

1. Paleoworld is a great television show.

2. Be certain to distinguish between the words to, too, and two.

3. That handwritten d looks like an a.

4. In formal writing, write and rather than &.

5. How did the movie King of the Wind differ from the book?

QUOTATION MARKS

14c. **Use quotation marks to enclose a *direct quotation*—a person's exact words.**

DIRECT QUOTATION　"Have you read *Let Me Hear You Whisper?*" asked Ms. Estrada.

Do not use quotation marks for an ***indirect quotation***—a rewording of a direct quotation.

INDIRECT QUOTATION　Ms. Estrada asked me whether I had read *Let Me Hear You Whisper*.

14d. **A direct quotation begins with a capital letter.**

EXAMPLE　Abe Lincoln said, "**T**he ballot is stronger than the bullet."

When the expression identifying the speaker interrupts a quoted sentence, the second part of the quotation begins with a lowercase letter.

EXAMPLE　"What are some of the things," asked Mrs. Perkins, "**t**hat the astronauts discovered on the moon?"

When the second part of a divided quotation is a sentence, it begins with a capital letter.

EXAMPLE　"Sandra and Alfonso went bike riding," remarked Mrs. Perkins. "**T**hey left an hour ago." [Notice that a period, not a comma, follows the interrupting expression.]

14e. **A direct quotation is set off from the rest of the sentence by a comma, a question mark, or an exclamation point, but not by a period.**

Set off means "separated." If a quotation appears at the beginning of a sentence, a comma follows it. If a quotation falls at the end of a sentence, a comma comes before it. If a quoted sentence is interrupted, a comma follows the first part and comes before the second part.

NOTE　When only part of a sentence is being quoted, the quotation generally begins with a lowercase letter.

EXAMPLE　Abe Lincoln described the ballot as "**s**tronger than the bullet."

EXAMPLES   "I've just finished reading a book about Harriet Tubman," Alison said.
Jaime said, "My favorite writer is Ray Bradbury."
"Did you know," asked Helen, "that O. Henry is the pseudonym of William Sydney Porter?"

14f.   **A period or a comma is always placed inside the closing quotation marks.**

EXAMPLES   Mr. Aaron said, "The story is set in Fresno, California."
"Mrs. Flowers reminds me of my aunt," Ruth added.

14g.   **A question mark or an exclamation point is placed inside the closing quotation marks when the quotation itself is a question or exclamation. Otherwise, the question mark or exclamation point is placed outside.**

EXAMPLES   "Did Marjorie Kinnan Rawlings write *The Yearling*?" asked Ken. [The quotation is a question.]
Sheila exclaimed, "I can't find my homework!" [The quotation is an exclamation.]
What did the captain mean when he said "Hard aport"? [The sentence, not the quotation, is a question.]

When both the sentence and the quotation at the end of the sentence are questions (or exclamations), only one question mark (or exclamation point) is used. It is placed inside the closing quotation marks.

EXAMPLE   Who wrote the poem that begins "How do I love thee?"

14h.   **When you write dialogue (conversation), begin a new paragraph each time you change speakers.**

EXAMPLE   "I'm listening," said the latter, grimly surveying the board as he stretched out his hand. "Check."
"I should hardly think that he'd come tonight," said his father, with his hand poised over the board.
"Mate," replied the son.
—W. W. Jacobs, "The Monkey's Paw"

14i.   **When a quotation consists of several sentences, place quotation marks at the beginning and at the end of the whole quotation.**

EXAMPLE   "Oh, please come in. I'm so happy to see you. Let me take your hat and coat," said Ms. Davis.

14j.   **Use single quotation marks to enclose a quotation within a quotation.**

EXAMPLE   "What Longfellow poem begins 'Listen, my children, and you shall hear'?" Carol asked.

NOTE   When a quotation ends with a question mark or with an exclamation point, no comma is needed.

EXAMPLES   "What were the Whites' three wishes?" asked Cynthia. "What a surprise that was!" exclaimed Meryl.

14k. Use quotation marks to enclose titles of short works such as short stories, poems, articles, songs, episodes of television programs, and chapters and other parts of books.

TYPE OF TITLE	EXAMPLES
Short Stories	"Raymond's Run" "Too Soon a Woman"
Poems	"O Captain! My Captain!" "Casey at the Bat"
Articles	"You and Your Computer" "The Best Word"
Songs	"Greensleeves" "The Streets of Laredo"
Episodes of Television Programs	"Tony Turns Fourteen" "An Englishman Abroad"
Chapters and Other Parts of Books	"Workers' Rights" "More Word Games"

☞ For examples of titles that are italicized (underlined), see page 958.

 ## QUICK CHECK 2

In the following dialogue, insert end marks, commas, and quotation marks. Correct any errors in capitalization, and begin new paragraphs as necessary.

EXAMPLE   [1] Aren't you the one who said Who, me?
         1. *Aren't you the one who said, "Who, me?"*

[1] Didn't you write music for the poem The Secret Heart Carl asked. [2] Yes, I had considered using music from the Beatles' song Yesterday Maria answered but it didn't work out. [3] I know what you mean, Carl replied. That reminds me of that poem To a Mouse. [4] Is that the one that says that plans don't always work? [5] Carl smiled and said yes, that's it!

 ## Using Quotations in Interviews

If you are writing a report and want to use material from an interview, you need to quote information from the source material. In general, you should follow these two rules:

- When you use someone else's ideas, give him or her credit.
- When you use someone else's words, quote them accurately.

Try It Out ✎

You have conducted an interview with a famous writer named F. A. Moss. During the interview, Mr. Moss made the statements listed below. Write a paragraph or two based on Mr. Moss's quotations. Be sure to use at least three direct quotations.

1. "A poem can come at any time, so I always carry a small notebook."
2. "Some of my best ideas occur to me in the middle of the night."
3. "Poetry is the heart of literature."
4. "I once wrote a haiku while waiting for a traffic light to change."
5. "Anyone can write poetry if only he or she speaks the truth."

15 PUNCTUATION

APOSTROPHES

Possessive Case

15a. The *possessive case* of a noun or a pronoun shows ownership or relationship.

(1) To form the possessive case of a singular noun, add an apostrophe and an *s*.

EXAMPLES   the boy's bike   Charles's father

(2) To form the possessive case of a plural noun ending in *s*, add only the apostrophe.

EXAMPLES   students' records   citizens' committee

(3) To form the possessive case of a plural noun that does not end in *s*, add an apostrophe and an *s*.

EXAMPLES   mice's tracks   children's voices

(4) To form the possessive case of most indefinite pronouns, add an apostrophe and an *s*.

EXAMPLES   everyone's opinion   somebody's umbrella

Contractions

15b. To form a contraction, use an apostrophe to show where letters have been left out.

A **contraction** is a shortened form of a word, a figure, or a group of words.

> **Common Contractions**
>
> | | | |
> |---|---|---|
> | he is.................he's | you will.....................you'll |
> | 1997...............'97 | of the clock.............o'clock |
> | let us................let's | they had....................they'd |
> | we are.............we're | where is...................where's |

The word *not* can be shortened to −*n't* and added to a verb, usually without changing the spelling of the verb.

EXAMPLES   are not.............aren't   have not ....haven't
does not ....doesn't   had not.............hadn't
do not..............don't   should not ....shouldn't
was not...........wasn't   were not...........weren't

EXCEPTIONS   will not............won't   cannot ....can't

Do not confuse contractions with possessive pronouns.

CONTRACTIONS	POSSESSIVE PRONOUNS
It's raining. [*It is*]	**Its** wing is broken.
Who's there? [*Who is*]	**Whose** turn is it?
There's only one left. [*There is*]	This car is **theirs.**
You're a good student. [*You are*]	**Your** story is interesting.

Plurals

15c. **Use an apostrophe and an *s* to form the plurals of letters, numerals, and signs and of words referred to as words.**

EXAMPLES   The word has two *r*'s, not one.
My brother is learning to count by *5*'s.
Don't use *&*'s in place of *and*'s.

 QUICK CHECK I

For each of the following sentences, insert apostrophes where they are needed.

EXAMPLE   **1.** Wont you please read "Paul Reveres Ride" aloud?
1. *Won't, Revere's*

1. Arent these Tesss pliers?
2. I cant tell if theyre *f*s or *t*s.
3. The kitten was following its mothers example.
4. Dont you use Los Angeles public transportation?
5. Because its raining, the childrens picnic has been canceled.

> **TIPS FOR SPELLING**
>
> You may notice that an apostrophe is not always used in forming the four kinds of plurals covered by rule 15c. Many writers omit the apostrophe if the plural meaning is clear without it. However, to make sure that your writing is clear, it is best to use an apostrophe.

HYPHENS

15d. **Use a hyphen to divide a word at the end of a line.**

EXAMPLE   How long had the new bridge been under construction before it was opened?

When dividing a word at the end of a line, remember the following rules.

(1) Divide a word only between syllables.

INCORRECT   Charlene began her report with a series of four questions about Shakespeare.

CORRECT   Charlene began her report with a series of four questions about Shakespeare.

> ☞ If you are not sure how to divide a word into syllables, look up the word in a dictionary.

COMPUTER NOTE Some word-processing programs will automatically break a word at the end of a line and insert a hyphen. Occasionally, such a break will violate one of the rules given in this section. Always check a printout of your writing to see how the computer has hyphenated words at the ends of lines. If a hyphen is used incorrectly, revise the line by moving the word or by rebreaking the word and inserting a "hard" hyphen (one that the computer cannot move).

(2) Do not divide a word so that one letter stands alone.

INCORRECT	Tokubei and his bodyguard Zenta stayed o-vernight in an unusual inn.
CORRECT	Tokubei and his bodyguard Zenta stayed overnight in an unusual inn.

(3) Divide an already hyphenated word at a hyphen.

INCORRECT	We are going to see my brother and my sis-ter-in-law tomorrow.
CORRECT	We are going to see my brother and my sister-in-law tomorrow.

(4) Do not divide a one-syllable word.

INCORRECT	Mr. White held the paw while he wish-ed for two hundred pounds.
CORRECT	Mr. White held the paw while he wished for two hundred pounds.

15e. **Use a hyphen with compound numbers from *twenty-one* to *ninety-nine* and with fractions used as adjectives.**

EXAMPLES   **twenty-five** dollars   **one-half** cup of flour

PARENTHESES

15f. **Use parentheses to enclose material that is added to a sentence but is not considered of major importance.**

EXAMPLES   Robert P. Tristram Coffin **(**1892–1955**)** wrote "The Secret Heart."
On the Sabbath we eat braided bread called challah **(**pronounced khä′ lə**)**.

A short sentence in parentheses may stand by itself or be contained within another sentence.

EXAMPLES   Fill in the order form carefully. **(Do not use a pencil.)**
The old fort **(it was used during the Civil War)** has been rebuilt and is open to the public.

DASHES

15g. **Use a dash to indicate an abrupt break in thought or speech.**

EXAMPLES   Alfonso don't—I mean, doesn't—want to face Sandra.
The murderer is—but I don't want to give away the ending.

 **QUICK CHECK 2**

For each of the following sentences, correct errors in the use of hyphens, and insert parentheses and dashes as needed.

EXAMPLE **1.** Test answers should be at least twenty five words long.

1. *Test answers should be at least twenty-five words long.*

1. The authors of all three stories that we've read excel in self-expression and in the use of imagery.
2. If I were in the same situation that you are, I would demand an apology from them.
3. Sixty five cents per pound is a good bargain.
4. Langston Hughes 1902–1967 is a major force in modern poetry.
5. The winner is oh, the envelope is empty!

16 SPELLING

USING WORD PARTS

Many English words are made up of two or more word parts. Some word parts have more than one form.

Roots

The **root** of a word is the part that carries the word's core meaning.

COMMONLY USED ROOTS		
WORD ROOT	**MEANING**	**EXAMPLES**
–port–	carry	portable, transport
–scrib–, –script–	write	describe, manuscript
–spec–	look	spectator, spectacles

Prefixes

A **prefix** is one or more letters or syllables added to the beginning of a word or word part to create a new word.

COMMONLY USED PREFIXES		
PREFIX	**MEANING**	**EXAMPLES**
dif–, dis–	away, off, opposing	differ, disagree
mis–	badly, not, wrongly	misbehave, misfortune
re–	back, again	rebuild, reclaim

Suffixes

A *suffix* is one or more letters or syllables added to the end of a word or word part to create a new word.

COMMONLY USED SUFFIXES		
SUFFIX	**MEANING**	**EXAMPLES**
–er, –or	doer, native of	actor, westerner
–ful	full of, characteristic of	joyful, truthful
–tion	action, condition	rotation, selection

SPELLING RULES

ie and ei

> **NOTE** This time-tested verse may help you remember the *ie* rule.
>
> *I* before *e*
> Except after *c*
> Or when sounded like *a,*
> As in *neighbor* and *weigh.*
>
> The rhyme above and rules 16a and 16b apply only when the *i* and the *e* are in the same syllable.

16a. **Except after c, write *ie* when the sound is long e.**

EXAMPLES achieve   shield   chief   field   piece
ceiling   conceit   deceit   deceive   receive
EXCEPTIONS either   leisure   neither
protein   seize   weird

16b. **Write *ei* when the sound is not long e, especially when the sound is long a.**

EXAMPLES foreign   forfeit   height   heir   their
freight   neighbor   reign   veil   weigh
EXCEPTIONS ancient   conscience   pie   patient
friend   mischief   lie   efficient

–cede, –ceed, and –sede

16c. **The only English word ending in *–sede* is *supersede.* The only words ending in *–ceed* are *exceed, proceed,* and *succeed.* Most other words that end with this sound end in *–cede.***

EXAMPLES concede   intercede   precede   recede   secede

Adding Prefixes

> **COMPUTER NOTE** Keep in mind that software for checking spelling will identify only misspelled words, not misused words. For example, if you used *their* when you should have used *there,* a spellchecker won't catch the error.

16d. **When adding a prefix to a word, do not change the spelling of the word itself.**

EXAMPLES over + see = **over**see
in + exact = **in**exact
mis + spell = **mis**spell
il + legal = **il**legal

Adding Suffixes

16e. **When adding the suffix –ly or –ness to a word, do not change the spelling of the word itself.**

EXAMPLES usual + ly = usual**ly**   eager + ness = eager**ness**
EXCEPTIONS For words that end in *y* and have more than one syllable, change the *y* to *i* before adding *-ly* or *-ness*.
  happy + ly = happ**ily**   lazy + ness = laz**iness**

16f. **Drop the final silent e before a suffix beginning with a vowel.**

EXAMPLES live + ing = liv**ing**   approve + al = approv**al**
EXCEPTIONS Keep the final silent *e* in a word ending in *ce* or *ge* before a suffix beginning with *a* or *o*.
  notice + able = notic**eable**
  courage + ous = courag**eous**

16g. **Keep the final silent e before a suffix beginning with a consonant.**

EXAMPLES hope + ful = hop**eful**   care + less = car**eless**
EXCEPTIONS true + ly = tru**ly**   judge + ment = judg**ment**

16h. **For words ending in y preceded by a consonant, change the y to i before any suffix that does not begin with i.**

EXAMPLES easy + ly = eas**ily**   cry + ing = cr**ying**

16i. **For words ending in y preceded by a vowel, keep the y when adding a suffix.**

EXAMPLES obey + ed = obe**yed**   boy + hood = bo**yhood**
EXCEPTIONS day—da**ily**   lay—la**id**   pay—pa**id**   say—sa**id**

16j. **Double the final consonant before a suffix beginning with a vowel if the word (1) has only one syllable or has the accent on the last syllable *and* (2) ends in a single consonant preceded by a single vowel.**

EXAMPLES occur + ed = occur**red**   forbid + en = forbi**dden**
EXCEPTIONS Do not double the final consonant in words ending in *w* or *x*.
  mow + ing = mo**wing**   wax + ed = wa**xed**

> **NOTE** When adding –*ing* to words that end in *ie*, drop the e and change the *i* to y.
>
> **EXAMPLES**
>   lie + ing = l**ying**
>   die + ing = d**ying**

> **NOTE** In some cases, the final consonant either may or may not be doubled.
>
> **EXAMPLE**   travel + er = trave**ler** *or* trave**ller**

✓ QUICK CHECK I

Each of the following sentences contains two misspelled words. Correct each misspelling.

EXAMPLE   **1.** Then he percieved the uniqueness of the expereince.
  1. *perceived, experience*

1. Many people beleive that biege creates a neutral background.
2. To sucede in business, you must not excede your funds.
3. Lonelyness saddly plagues many people, even in this crowded world.
4. My little brother is always taging along, manageing to ruin my fun.
5. The judgement went against him, causing arguements in the press.

Forming the Plurals of Nouns

16k. For most nouns, add –s.

SINGULAR	desk	idea	shoe	friend	camera	Wilson
PLURAL	desks	ideas	shoes	friends	cameras	Wilsons

16l. For nouns ending in s, x, z, ch, or sh, add –es.

SINGULAR	bus	fox	waltz	inch	dish	Suarez
PLURAL	buses	foxes	waltzes	inches	dishes	Suarezes

16m. For nouns ending in y preceded by a vowel, add –s.

SINGULAR	decoy	highway	alley	Riley
PLURAL	decoys	highways	alleys	Rileys

16n. For nouns ending in y preceded by a consonant, change the y to i and add –es.

SINGULAR	army	country	city	pony	ally	daisy
PLURAL	armies	countries	cities	ponies	allies	daisies

EXCEPTIONS   For proper nouns ending in *y*, just add -s.
Brady—Bradys   Murphy—Murphys

16o. For some nouns ending in f or fe, add –s. For others, change the f or fe to v and add –es.

SINGULAR	belief	thief	sheriff	knife	giraffe
PLURAL	beliefs	thieves	sheriffs	knives	giraffes

16p. For nouns ending in o preceded by a vowel, add –s.

SINGULAR	radio	patio	stereo	igloo	Matteo
PLURAL	radios	patios	stereos	igloos	Matteos

16q. For nouns ending in o preceded by a consonant, add –es.

SINGULAR	tomato	potato	echo	hero
PLURAL	tomatoes	potatoes	echoes	heroes

EXCEPTIONS   For musical terms and proper nouns, add -s.
alto—altos   Shapiro—Shapiros
solo—solos   Aquino—Aquinos

16r. The plural of a few nouns is formed in irregular ways.

SINGULAR	ox	goose	foot	tooth	woman	mouse
PLURAL	oxen	geese	feet	teeth	women	mice

16s. For most compound nouns, form the plural of the last word in the compound.

SINGULAR	bookshelf	push-up	sea gull	ten-year-old
PLURAL	bookshel**ves**	push-up**s**	sea gull**s**	ten-year-old**s**

16t. For compound nouns in which one of the words is modified by the other word or words, form the plural of the word modified.

SINGULAR	brother-in-law	maid of honor	eighth-grader
PLURAL	brother**s**-in-law	maid**s** of honor	eighth-grader**s**

16u. For some nouns the singular and the plural forms are the same.

SINGULAR	trout	sheep	Chinese	pliers
AND PLURAL	series	aircraft	Sioux	species

QUICK CHECK 2

Write the plural of each of the following items.

EXAMPLE	1. Native American
	1. *Native Americans*

1. species	6. mosquito
2. irony	7. child
3. cry	8. sergeant-at-arms
4. valley	9. shampoo
5. peach	10. scarf

In some names, marks that show pronunciation are just as important as the letters themselves.

PEOPLE Alemán Böll Ibáñez Khayyám Janáček Eugène

PLACES Açores Bogotá Camagüey Gîza Köln Sainte-Thérèse

If you're not sure about the spelling of a name, ask the person whose name it is, or check in a reference source.

16v. For numbers, letters, symbols, and words used as words, add an apostrophe and –*s*.

EXAMPLES	four *2*'s	two *m*'s
	missing *$*'s	too many *so*'s and *and*'s

Using Apostrophes with Plurals

In your reading, you may notice that some writers do not use apostrophes to form the plurals of numbers, capital letters, symbols, and words used as words.

EXAMPLES Laurence Yep grew up during the latter part of the 1900s.
Make sure that you put Xs or ✓s in all of the boxes on this form.

However, using an apostrophe is never wrong. Therefore, it is often best to use the apostrophe.

Try It Out ✎

For each of the following sentences, insert apostrophes where appropriate.

1. Do not use *its* to refer to people.
2. These *hers* should be written with *s*s.
3. As computer users know, */*s are very important in computing.
4. In the 1200s, several great romances were created.
5. How many *0*s are in a billion?

NOTE If you use several numbers, some short and some long, it is better to write them all as numerals.

EXAMPLE He wrote **37** plays and **154** poems.

Spelling Numbers

16w. Spell out a number that begins a sentence.

EXAMPLE **Five hundred** people went to see the game.

16x. Within a sentence, spell out numbers that can be written in one or two words. Use numerals for other numbers.

EXAMPLES In all, **fifty-two** people attended the family reunion.
More than **160** people were invited.

16y. Spell out numbers used to indicate order.

EXAMPLE She came in **second** [*not* 2nd] in the race.

 QUICK CHECK 3

The following sentences contain errors in spelling or the use of numbers. Correct each error.

EXAMPLE **1.** 1000's of ants rushed out.
1. *Thousands of ants rushed out.*

1. Why do these *t*s look like *f*s?
2. Hey! I sold my batch of tickets for fifty cents apiece, but he got 75 cents for each one of his.
3. In the 1st place, I don't know how to dance.
4. The satellite that was launched yesterday will travel one million one hundred fifty thousand miles.
5. 10 people showed up for the rehearsal.

17 GLOSSARY OF USAGE

This Glossary of Usage is an alphabetical list of words and expressions that are commonly misused in English. Throughout this section some examples are labeled *standard* or *nonstandard*. **Standard English** is the most widely accepted form of English. It is used in *formal* situations, such as in speeches and writing for school, and in *informal* situations, such as in conversation and everyday writing. **Nonstandard English** is language that does not follow the rules and guidelines of standard English.

a, an Use *a* before words beginning with consonant sounds. Use *an* before words beginning with vowel sounds. See page 895.

EXAMPLES He did not consider himself **a** hero.
Market Avenue is **a** one-way street.
An oryx is a large antelope.
We waited in line for **an** hour.

accept, except   *Accept* is a verb that means "receive." *Except* may be either a verb or a preposition. As a verb, *except* means "leave out" or "exclude"; as a preposition, *except* means "other than" or "excluding."

EXAMPLES   Squeaky **accepts** the responsibility.
Some students will be **excepted** from this assignment.
No one **except** Diego had finished the assignment.

affect, effect   *Affect* is a verb meaning "influence." The noun *effect* means "the result of some action."

EXAMPLES   His score on this test will **affect** his final grade.
The **effect** of the medicine was immediate.

ain't   Avoid this word in speaking and writing; it is nonstandard English.

all ready, already   *All ready* means "completely prepared." *Already* means "before a certain point in time."

EXAMPLES   We were **all ready** for the quiz on "The Monkey's Paw."
I had **already** read "Flowers for Algernon."

a lot   *A lot* should always be written as two words.

EXAMPLE   I spent **a lot** of time making this poster.

all together, altogether   The expression *all together* means "everyone or everything in the same place." The adverb *altogether* means "entirely."

EXAMPLES   The director called us **all together** for one final rehearsal.
He is **altogether** pleased with his victory.

at   Do not use *at* after *where*.

EXAMPLE   Where does she live? [*not* Where does she live at?]

bad, badly   *Bad* is an adjective. *Badly* is an adverb.

EXAMPLES   The tea tastes **bad**. [*Bad* modifies the noun *tea*.]
The boy's wrist was sprained **badly**. [*Badly* modifies the verb phrase *was sprained*.]

between, among   Use *between* when referring to two things at a time, even though they may be part of a group containing more than two.

EXAMPLE   Alfonso avoided Sandra **between** classes.

Use *among* when referring to a group rather than to separate individuals.

EXAMPLE   The money was divided **among** the four of them.

bust, busted   Avoid using these words as verbs. Use a form of either *burst* or *break*.

EXAMPLES   The balloon **burst** [*not* busted].
Alfonso's bicycle chain **broke** [*not* busted].

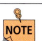 **NOTE**   Many writers overuse *a lot*. Whenever you run across *a lot* as you revise your own writing, try to replace it with a more exact word or phrase.

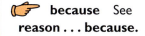 **among**   See **between, among.**

as   See **like, as.**

as if   See **like, as if, as though.**

☞ **because**   See **reason . . . because.**

choose, chose   *Choose* is the present tense form of the verb *choose*. It rhymes with *whose* and means "select." *Chose* is the past tense form of *choose*. It rhymes with *grows* and means "selected."

EXAMPLES   What did you **choose** as your topic?
Trish **chose** to do her report on Shel Silverstein.

could of   Do not write *of* with the helping verb *could*. Write *could have*. Also avoid *ought to of, should of, would of, might of,* and *must of*.

EXAMPLE   Mr. White **could have** [*not* could of] heeded his old friend's advice.

Of is also unnecessary with *had*.

EXAMPLE   If he **had** [*not* had of] seen it, he would have told me.

fewer, less   *Fewer* is used with plural words. *Less* is used with singular words. *Fewer* tells "how many"; *less* tells "how much."

EXAMPLES   I have **fewer** errors to correct than I thought.
The kidnappers asked for **less** money.

good, well   *Good* is always an adjective. Never use *good* as an adverb. Instead, use *well*.

EXAMPLE   She works **well** [*not* good] with the others.

Well may also be used as an adjective to mean "healthy."

EXAMPLE   Mary and the children didn't look **well**; they needed food.

had ought, hadn't ought   *Ought* is not used with *had*.

EXAMPLE   He **ought** [*not* had ought] to proofread more carefully.

he, she, they   Avoid using a pronoun along with its antecedent as the subject of a verb. This error is called the **double subject.**

NONSTANDARD   Toni Cade Bambara she is a famous writer.
STANDARD   Toni Cade Bambara is a famous writer.

hisself   *Hisself* is nonstandard English. Use *himself*.

EXAMPLE   Brer Possum finds **himself** [*not* hisself] in a dilemma.

how come   In informal situations, *how come* is often used instead of *why*. In formal situations, *why* should always be used.

INFORMAL   I don't know how come he told me that story.
FORMAL   I don't know **why** he told me that story.

kind of, sort of   In informal situations, *kind of* and *sort of* are often used to mean "somewhat" or "rather." In formal English, *somewhat* or *rather* is preferred.

INFORMAL   Alfonso was kind of shy.
FORMAL   Alfonso was **rather** shy.

👉 **doesn't, don't**
See page 904.

👉 **except**   See **accept, except.**

👉 **had of**   See **could of.**

👉 **its, it's**   See page 963.

---

learn, teach   *Learn* means "gain knowledge." *Teach* means "instruct" or "show how."

EXAMPLES   What did Brer Possum **learn** from Brer Snake?
What did Brer Snake **teach** Brer Possum?

like, as   In informal situations, the preposition *like* is often used instead of the conjunction *as* to introduce a clause. In formal situations, *as* is preferred.

EXAMPLE   Do you think Marguerite memorized a poem, **as** [*not* like] Mrs. Flowers had suggested?

like, as if, as though   In informal situations, the preposition *like* is often used for the compound conjunctions *as if* or *as though*. In formal situations, *as if* or *as though* is preferred.

EXAMPLE   Zenta acted **as if** [*not* like] he had never visited the inn.

 QUICK CHECK 1

Correct the errors in usage in each of the following sentences.

EXAMPLE   **1.** Anne Frank she lived for months in the Secret Annex.
1. *Anne Frank lived for months in the Secret Annex.*

1. It's hard to except the horrors of the concentration camps.
2. Alot of people reject the reality of these camps.
3. An visit to Majdanek learned Dara Horn about the camps.
4. Dara felt like the shoes in the huge pile there could of been hers.
5. Not surprisingly, Dara felt badly and claimed that a book doesn't teach as good as a visit to these camps.

of   Do not use *of* with other prepositions such as *inside, off,* and *outside*.

EXAMPLE   The sun is **inside** [*not* inside of] the larger box.

real   In informal situations, *real* is often used as an adverb meaning "very" or "extremely." In formal situations, *very* or *extremely* is preferred.

INFORMAL   Charlie became real intelligent.
FORMAL   Charlie became **extremely** intelligent.

reason . . . because   In informal situations, *reason . . . because* is often used instead of *reason . . . that*. In formal situations, use *reason . . . that,* or revise your sentence.

INFORMAL   The reason I like "Broken Chain" is because I identify with the protagonist, Alfonso.
FORMAL   The **reason** I like "Broken Chain" is **that** I identify with the protagonist, Alfonso.
or
I like "Broken Chain" **because** I identify with the protagonist, Alfonso.

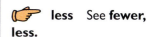 **less**   See **fewer, less.**

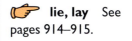 **lie, lay**   See pages 914–915.

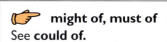 **might of, must of** See **could of.**

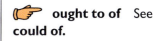 **ought to of**   See **could of.**

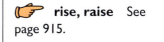 **rise, raise**   See page 915.

Language Handbook   **973**

☞ **should of** See **could of.**

☞ **sit, set** See page 914.

☞ **sort of** See **kind of, sort of.**

teach See **learn, teach.**

☞ **well** See **good, well.**

☞ **who's, whose** See page 963.

☞ **would of** See **could of.**

☞ **your, you're** See page 963.

some, somewhat Do not use *some* for *somewhat* as an adverb.

EXAMPLE The relationship between Squeaky and Gretchen improved **somewhat** [*not* some].

than, then *Than* is a conjunction used in making comparisons. *Then* is an adverb that means "at that time."

EXAMPLES Squeaky is a faster runner **than** Gretchen.
First we went to the store. **Then** we went to the library.

theirself, theirselves *Theirself* and *theirselves* are nonstandard English. Use *themselves.*

EXAMPLE They bought **themselves** [*not* theirself *or* theirselves] a telescope.

them *Them* should not be used as an adjective. Use *those.*

EXAMPLE Karen gave you **those** [*not* them] cassettes yesterday.

try and In informal situations, *try and* is often used instead of *try to.* In formal situations, *try to* should be used.

INFORMAL I will try and find you a picture of O. Henry.
FORMAL I will **try to** find you a picture of O. Henry.

when, where Do not use *when* or *where* incorrectly in stating a definition.

NONSTANDARD A flashback is when a writer interrupts the action in a story to tell about something that happened earlier.

STANDARD A flashback is an interruption of the action in a story to tell about something that happened earlier.

where Do not use *where* for *that.*

EXAMPLE I read **that** [*not* where] O. Henry spent time in prison.

 QUICK CHECK 2

Revise the following items according to the rules of formal English.

EXAMPLE 1. People did not have enough food for theirselves.
1. *People did not have enough food for themselves.*

1. The reason they had to be quiet was because someone outside of their hiding place might hear them.
2. Wherever she was, Anne would try and help people with they're problems.
3. She was often more cheerful then the others.
4. Her sister, Margot, had become real sick and than died, as others had.
5. You're lucky not to have suffered them brutalities that so many had to bear.

Spelling Handbook

COMMONLY MISSPELLED WORDS

No matter how many spelling rules you learn, you will find that it is helpful to learn to spell certain common words from memory. The fifty "demons" in the first list are words that you should be able to spell without any hesitation, even though they all contain spelling problems. Study them in groups of five until you are sure you know them.

The second, longer list contains words that you should learn if you do not already know them. They are grouped by tens so that you study them ten at a time. In studying each list, pay particular attention to the underlined letters. These letters are generally the ones that pose problems for students.

For more on spelling, see spelling rules 16a–y in the Language Handbook.

FIFTY SPELLING DEMONS

ache	cough	guess	ready	though
again	could	half	said	through
always	country	hour	says	tired
answer	doctor	instead	seems	tonight
blue	does	knew	shoes	trouble
built	don't	know	since	wear
busy	early	laid	straight	where
buy	easy	minute	sugar	women
can't	every	often	sure	won't
color	friend	once	tear	write

TWO HUNDRED SPELLING WORDS

absence	careless	field	mischief	separate
absolutely	carrying	fierce	muscle	shining
acceptance	ceased	finally	museum	similar
accommodate	ceiling	foliage	necessary	society
accumulate	choice	foreign	nervous	speech
achieve	college	fortunately	nineteen	strength
acquire	committee	forty	ninety	studying
across	completely	fourth	occasion	stupefy
advertisement	conceive	genius	occur	succeed
against	conscience	genuine	occurrence	success
aisles	conscious	government	opinion	surprise
among	control	governor	opportunity	suspicion
announce	correspondence	grammar	originally	sympathy
anxiety	courteous	guarantee	particularly	technique
apology	criticize	height	patience	temperament
apparent	curiosity	heir	perceive	temporary
appreciation	decision	heroes	performance	theory
arctic	definite	humorous	permanent	thorough
arguing	describe	hungrily	personal	tongue
argument	description	icicles	physical	tragedy
arithmetic	desirable	imaginary	picnic	transferred
assistance	divide	immediately	possess	treasury
associate	divine	independent	preferred	tries
attacked	efficiency	inoculate	privilege	university
attendance	eighth	intelligence	probably	unnecessary
attitude	eliminate	interest	professor	unusually
attorney	embarrass	interpret	pursue	useful
basis	equipment	judgment	realize	using
beginning	especially	knowledge	receive	vacuum
believe	exactly	laboratory	recommend	vague
benefit	excellent	leisure	referred	various
bicycle	execute	license	religion	veil
bough	existence	liquor	repetition	vicinity
bouquet	experience	loneliness	rhythm	villain
brief	experiment	luxury	safety	violence
brilliant	explanation	magazine	satisfy	warrior
bureau	extremely	marriage	scene	wholly
business	familiar	mathematics	schedule	whose
candidate	favorite	meant	seize	writing
career	February	medicine	sense	yield

Communications Handbook

Using a Media Center or Library

To find a book, audiotape, film, or video in a library, start by looking in the **catalog.** Most libraries use an **online,** or computer, **catalog.**

Online catalogs vary from library to library. With some you begin searching for resources by **title, author,** or **subject.** With others you simply enter **keywords** for the subject you're researching. With either system, you enter information into the computer and a new screen will show you a list of materials or subject headings relating to your request. When you find an item you want, write down the title, author, and **call number,** the code of numbers and letters that shows you where to find the item on the library's shelves.

Some libraries still use card catalogs. A **card catalog** is a collection of index cards arranged in alphabetical order by title and author. Nonfiction is also cataloged by subject.

Electronic Databases. **Electronic databases** are collections of information you can access by computer. You can use these databases to find such resources as encyclopedias, almanacs, and museum art collections.

There are two kinds of electronic databases: **Online databases** are accessed at a computer terminal connected to a modem. The modem allows the computer to communicate with other computers over telephone lines. **Portable databases** are available on CD-ROM.

A **CD-ROM** (compact disc–read only memory) is played on a computer equipped with a CD-ROM player. If you were to look up *Maya Angelou* on a CD-ROM guide to literature, for example, you could see and hear her reading passages from her books and also read critical analyses of her work.

Periodicals. Most libraries have a collection of magazines and newspapers. To find up-to-date magazine or newspaper articles on a topic, use a computerized index, such as *InfoTrac* or *EBSCO.* Some of these indices provide a summary of each article. Others provide the entire text, which you can read on-screen or print out. The *Readers' Guide to Periodical Literature* is a print index of articles that have appeared in hundreds of magazines.

Using the Internet

The **Internet** is a huge network of computers. Libraries, news services, government agencies, researchers, and organizations communicate and share information on the Net. The Net also lets you chat online with students around the world. For help in using the Internet to do research or to communicate with someone by computer, explore the options on the following page.

The Reference Section

Every library has materials you can use only in the library. Some examples are listed below. (Some reference works are available in both print and electronic form.)

Encyclopedias
Collier's Encyclopedia
The World Book Encyclopedia

General Biographical References
Current Biography Yearbook
The International Who's Who
Webster's New Biographical Dictionary

Special Biographical References
American Men & Women of Science
Biographical Dictionary of American Sports
Mexican American Biographies

Atlases
Atlas of World Cultures
National Geographic Atlas of the World

Almanacs
Information Please Almanac
The World Almanac and Book of Facts

Books of Quotations
Bartlett's *Familiar Quotations*

Books of Synonyms
Roget's International Thesaurus
Webster's New Dictionary of Synonyms

You've Got Mail!

E-mail is an electronic message sent over a computer network. On the Internet you can use e-mail to reach institutions, businesses, and individuals. When you e-mail places like museums, you may be able to ask **experts** about a topic you're researching. You can also use e-mail to chat with students around the country and around the world.

Internet forums, or newsgroups, let you discuss and debate lots of subjects with other computer users. You can write and send a question to a forum and get an answer from someone who may (or may not) know something about your topic.

Techno Tip

- If you get too few hits, use a more general word or phrase as your search term.

- If you get too many hits, use a more specific word or phrase as your search term.

The World Wide Web

The easiest way to do research on the Internet is on the World Wide Web. On the Web, information is stored in colorful, easy-to-access files called **Web pages.** Web pages usually have text, graphics, photographs, sound, and even video clips.

Using a Web Browser.   You look at Web pages with a **Web browser,** a program for accessing information on the Web. Every page on the Web has its own address, called a **URL,** or Uniform Resource Locator. If you know the address of a Web page you want to go to, just enter it in the location field on your browser.

Hundreds of millions of Web pages are connected by **hyperlinks,** which let you jump from one page to another. These links usually appear as underlined or colored words or images, or both, on your computer screen. With hundreds of millions of linked Web pages, how can you find the information you want?

Using a Web Directory.   If you're just beginning to look for a research topic, click on a **Web directory,** a list of topics and subtopics created by experts to help users find Web sites. Think of the directory as a giant index. Start by choosing a broad category, such as Literature. Then, work your way down through the subtopics, perhaps from Poetry to Poets. Under Poets, choose a Web page that looks interesting, perhaps one on Robert Frost.

Using a Search Engine.   If you already have a topic and need information about it, try using a **search engine,** a software tool that finds information on the Web. To use a search engine, just go to an online search form and enter a **search term,** or keyword. The search engine will return a list of Web pages containing your search term. The list will also show you the

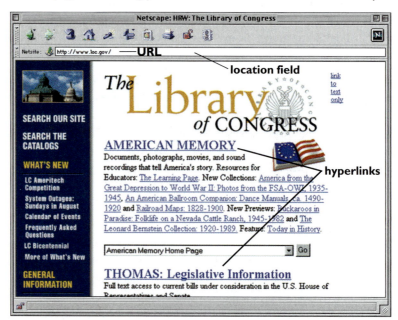

first few lines of each page. A search term such as *Frost* may produce thousands of results, or **hits,** including weather data on frost. If you're doing a search on the poet Robert Frost, most of these thousands of hits will be of no use. To find useful material, you have to narrow your search.

Refining a Keyword Search.   To focus your research, use **search operators,** such as the words AND or NOT, to create a string of keywords. If you're looking for material on Robert Frost and his life in Vermont, for example, you might enter the following search term:

Frost AND Vermont NOT weather

The more focused search term yields pages that contain both *Frost* and *Vermont* and nothing about weather. The chart on the right explains how several search operators work.

Evaluating Web Sources

Since anyone—you, for example—can publish a Web page, it's important to evaluate your sources. Use these criteria to evaluate a source:

Authority.   Who is the author? What is his or her knowledge or experience? Trust respected sources, such as the Smithsonian Institution, not a person's newsletter or home page.

Accuracy.   How trustworthy is the information? Does the author give his or her sources? Check information from one site against information from at least two other sites or print sources.

Objectivity.   What is the author's **perspective,** or point of view? Find out whether the information provider has a bias or a hidden purpose.

COMMON SEARCH OPERATORS AND WHAT THEY DO	
AND	Demands that both terms appear on the page; narrows search
+	Demands that both terms appear on the page; narrows search
OR	Yields pages that contain either term; widens search
NOT	Excludes a word from consideration; narrows search
–	Excludes a word from consideration; narrows search
NEAR	Demands that two words be close together; narrows search
ADJ	Demands that two words be close together; narrows search
" "	Demands an exact phrase; narrows search

Techno Tip

To evaluate a Web source, look at the top-level domain in the URL. Here is a sample URL with the top-level domain—a government agency—labeled.

top-level domain

http://www.loc.gov

COMMON TOP-LEVEL DOMAINS AND WHAT THEY STAND FOR	
.edu	Educational institution. Site may publish scholarly work or the work of elementary or high school students.
.gov	Government body. Information should be reliable.
.org	Usually a nonprofit organization. If the organization promotes culture (as a museum does), information is generally reliable; if it advocates a cause, information may be biased.
.com	Commercial enterprise. Information should be evaluated carefully.
.net	Organization offering Internet services.

Currency. Is the information up-to-date? For a print source, check the copyright date. For a Web source, look for the date on which the page was created or revised. (This date appears at the bottom of the site's home page.)

Coverage. How well does the source cover the topic? Could you find better information in a book? Compare the source with several others.

Listing Sources and Taking Notes

When you write a research paper, you must **document,** or identify, your sources so that readers will know where you found your material. You must avoid **plagiarism,** or presenting another writer's words or ideas as if they were your own.

Sample Source Card

> Reuben, Paul P. "Chapter 4: Early Nineteenth Century—Emily Dickinson."   3
>
> *PAL: Perspectives in American Literature—A Research and Reference Guide.*
>
> <http://www.csustan.edu/english/reuben/pal/chap4/dickinson.html>.

Listing Sources

List each source, and give it a number. (You'll use these source numbers later, when you take notes.) Here's where to find the publication information (such as the name of the publisher and the copyright date) you'll need for different types of sources:

- **Print sources.** Look at the title and copyright pages of the book or periodical.

- **Online sources.** Look at the beginning or end of the document or in a separate electronic file. For a Web page, look for a link containing the word *About.*

- **Portable electronic databases.** Look at the start-up screen, the packaging, or the disc itself.

There are several ways to list sources. The chart on page 981 shows the style created by the Modern Language Association.

Sample Note Card

> Dickinson's definition of poetry   3
> In letter to Thomas W. Higginson, editor *Atlantic Monthly*:
> "If I read a book and it makes my whole body so cold no fire can ever warm me, I know that is poetry."
>
> online source

Taking Notes

Here are some tips for taking notes:

- Put notes from different sources on separate index cards or sheets of paper or in separate computer files.

- At the top of each card, sheet of paper, or file, write a label that briefly gives the subject of the note.

- At the bottom, write the numbers of the pages on which you found the information.

- Use short phrases, and make lists of details and ideas. You don't have to write full sentences.

- Use your own words unless you find material you want to quote. If you quote an author's exact words, put quotation marks around them.

The sample note card at the left shows how to take notes.

Preparing a List of Sources

Use your source cards to make a **works cited** list at the end of your report. List your sources in alphabetical order, following the MLA guidelines for citing sources (see the chart below). Note the sample that follows.

Works Cited

"Emily Dickinson." The Academy of American Poets. 2003.
   @ http://www.poets.org/poets/poets.cfm?prmID=156.
Johnson, Thomas H., ed. Complete Poems of Emily Dickinson. Boston:
   Little, Brown, 1960.
Knapp, Bettina Liebowitz. Emily Dickinson. New York: Continuum, 1989.

The chart below shows citations of print, audiovisual, and electronic sources:

MLA GUIDELINES FOR CITING SOURCES	
Books	Give the author, title, city of publication, publisher, and copyright year. Knapp, Bettina Liebowitz. Emily Dickinson. New York: Continuum Publishing Co., 1989.
Magazine and newspaper articles	Give the author, title of article, name of the magazine or newspaper, date, and page numbers. Markiewicz, B. S. "Poets and Friends." American History Nov./Dec. 1995: 42–47.
Encyclopedia articles	Give the author (if named), title of the article, name of the encyclopedia, and edition (year). "Dickinson, Emily." Collier's Encyclopedia. 1996 ed.
Interviews	Give the expert's name, the words *Personal interview* or *Telephone interview,* and the date. Randy Souther. Telephone interview. 2 Jan. 2004.
Films, videotapes, and audiotapes	Give the title, producer or director, medium, distributor, and year of release. Emily Dickinson. Directed by Veronica Young. Annenberg/CPB project, 1988.
CD-ROMs and DVDs	In many cases, not all the information is available. Fill in what you can. Give the author, title of document or article; database title; publication medium (use the term *CD-ROM* or *DVD*); city of publication; publisher; date. "Dickinson, Emily." Microsoft Encarta 2003 Encyclopedia Deluxe Edition. CD-ROM. Redmond, WA: Microsoft Corporation, 1999–2003.
Online Sources	In many cases, not all the information is available. Fill in what you can. Give the author, title of document or article; title of complete work or database; name of editor; publication date or date last revised; name of sponsoring organization; date you accessed the site; the full URL in angle brackets. "Emily Dickinson." The Academy of American Poets. 2003. <@ http://www.poets.org/poets.cfm?prmID=156.>

PROOFREADERS' MARKS

Symbol	Example	Meaning
≡	New mexico	Capitalize lowercase letter.
/	next Spring	Lowercase capital letter.
∧	a book ⌃quotations *of*	Insert.
⌐	a good ~~good~~ idea	Delete.
⌒⌣	a grape fruit tree	Close up space.
∿	does'nt	Change order (of letters or words).
¶	¶ "Who's there?" she asked.	Begin a new paragraph.
⊙	Please don't forget⊙	Add a period.
⋏	Maya⋏did you call me?	Add a comma.
⋮	Dear Mrs. Mills⋮	Add a colon.
⋏;	Columbus, Ohio⋏; Dallas, Texas	Add a semicolon.
⌄ ⌄	⌄Are you OK?⌄he asked.	Add quotation marks.

Giving and Listening to a Personal Narrative

Choosing a Narrative

Your first step in preparing a presentation of an oral narrative is to choose the story you want to tell. You may tell a true story from your life or even a story from someone else's life. Here are some questions you can ask yourself when choosing a narrative to present.

- **Will the narrative appeal to my audience?** Once you have identified your listeners, choose a story that they are likely to understand and enjoy. For example, if you are going to tell your story to elementary school students, choose one that *they* might like to hear, such as a story about a person their age.

- **Is the narrative the right length?** If you have a time limit for your presentation, can the story be told within that amount of time?

- **Does the narrative have the characteristics of a good story?** Like a written personal narrative, an oral story should include the elements that will make it entertaining to its audience. Choose a story that relates an incident about which you can remember plenty of details and the significance of which you can effectively communicate to listeners.

Planning Your Presentation

Strategize Think about *how* to tell your story so that you will grab your audience. First, organize your ideas in a way that will make sense to listeners. (Most narratives should be told in chronological order to help listeners follow the series of events.) Then, plan to elaborate on those ideas using **narrative and descriptive strategies.**

The following chart lists some narrative and descriptive strategies that effective storytellers use:

NARRATIVE AND DESCRIPTIVE STRATEGIES	
Strategy	**Definition**
Relevant dialogue	the actual words of the people involved in the events that are important to your story
Specific action	events that are a necessary part of the story
Physical descriptions	vivid adjectives and precise nouns used to describe people, settings, and things
Action verbs	verbs that express either physical or mental activity (as opposed to *be* verbs such as *is, were, am,* and *been*)
Modifiers	words (or groups of words) that make the meaning of other words more specific
Sensory details	words that appeal to one or more of your five senses—sight, hearing, touch, taste, and smell
Background description	extra information listeners might need to understand your story
Comparing or contrasting characters	details showing how characters are similar to or different from each other

Acting out information is an effective way to communicate an idea. For example, instead of telling your audience that a character is angry, you can show them by using **facial expressions,** such as scowling or glaring. You can also raise the **modulation,** or pitch, of your voice to a shrill level and change the **tone** of your voice to sound irritated. Practice using your body and voice to communicate your message.

Make Notes To avoid finding yourself tongue-tied when you present your personal narrative, jot down some notes. Your notes should be brief and easy to read so that you can glance at them without losing eye contact with your audience.

Rehearsing and Delivering Your Presentation

Practice your presentation in front of a mirror. Then, try a rehearsal in front of friends. Listen to their **feedback,** and consider their ideas as you practice and improve your presentation. Here are some ways to make your presentation effective.

- Speak loudly enough for everyone to hear you.
- Keep an eye on your audience. Notice people's reactions, especially **nonverbal cues.** If they seem bored, it may be because they cannot hear you. If they nod and smile, then you know that you are on the right track.

Listening to Learn and Evaluate

Have a list of elements to evaluate as you listen to other narrative presentations. As you listen, jot down answers to the following questions:

- **Clarity and Coherence**—How well do you understand the events of the story? What does the speaker do to help you follow these events?
- **Narrative and Descriptive Strategies**—How effectively does the speaker use dialogue, specific action, physical descriptions, action verbs, modifiers, sensory details, background, and descriptive language?
- **Significance**—What is the significance, or meaning, of the story for the speaker? How does he or she make this meaning clear?
- **Delivery**—Does the speaker maintain eye contact with listeners and respond well to their reactions? How effectively does the speaker use his or her voice, face, and gestures?

Use this list of questions to evaluate your own presentation as you practice and to prepare a formal evaluation of a classmate's presentation.

Giving and Evaluating a Persuasive Speech

One way to convince others to accept your opinion is to give a persuasive speech. To give an effective speech, you will need to do much more than read a persuasive essay directly from the page; you will need to deliver the most important points in a solid presentation that will grab your audience.

Adapting a Persuasive Essay

To find material for your speech, you may want to consider the persuasive essays you wrote for the assignments on pages 338–343 or 835–840. Use the following instructions to develop your speech.

If your listening **audience** is different from your essay's audience, you will need to reconsider the content of your **message** to make sure that it relates to the listeners' backgrounds and interests. Consider what reasons, examples, and facts would appeal to those who will be listening. For example, if you are giving a speech to convince a group of parents to contribute to the creation of an art gallery in the school's hallways, you can connect with your audience by stressing the fact that the gallery would display the work of students—their children—not professionals. Making the content of your speech match your audience's backgrounds and interests will help you achieve your **purpose**—to persuade listeners that your opinion is the right one.

Organizing Your Speech   Even the best message can get lost in rambling sentences and wandering ideas. To make sure your speech is **coherent,** or easily understood, be certain that all your ideas are clearly related, given in an order that makes sense, and connected with **transitional words** and **phrases.**

Once you have identified which pieces of support from your essay you intend to keep and which need to be changed to fit your listening audience, you can start organizing your speech notes. The first step in organizing is to identify the most important points and write brief sentences and phrases about those points on note cards or in an **outline**. Once you have your points listed on note cards, you can number them in the order you want to present them. The chart below provides you with suggestions on how to organize the different elements of a persuasive speech.

ELEMENTS OF A PERSUASIVE SPEECH

Element	Location and Explanation
Preview	Preview what the speech will cover by presenting your *thesis statement* first. Your **thesis statement** identifies your issue and the position you will take. It will also guide the content of your speech, giving your speech **focus**.
Arguments	Arrange your arguments—your **reasons** and **evidence**—in **order of importance**. Begin your speech with the strongest reason for your opinion to get your audience's attention, or end with your strongest reason to leave a powerful impression. The body of your speech is no place for **opinions**, unless they come from an authority on the issue. **Facts, details**, and **examples** should make up the bulk of your support.
Counterarguments	A **counterargument** is any argument or concern your audience may have about the points you are trying to make. Think about where your audience might object to your ideas, and plan to address their main concern with a relevant reason at the appropriate point in your speech.
Definitions of Unfamiliar Words	Provide definitions of new and unfamiliar words as you use them.
Conclusion	The content of your conclusion depends on your purpose and audience. To try to sway listeners who still need convincing, briefly **summarize** your thesis and strongest reasons. If your audience seems to accept your opinion, include a **call to action** that tells the audience what they can do about the issue.

Delivering Your Speech

Since the purpose of your speech is to persuade others, your **delivery,** or *how* you give the speech, is critical. To ensure that your speech runs smoothly, practice giving it more than once. Keep the following suggestions in mind as you practice.

- **If possible, practice in front of an audience** so that you can get used to speaking in front of a group.
- **Practice using your note cards** just as you will use them on the day of your speech.

- **Use a timer or watch** to ensure that you stay within a certain time if your teacher has given you a time limit.
- **Review the evaluation guidelines below** before practicing. Knowing what your audience will be evaluating as you present will help you prepare.

Evaluating a Persuasive Speech

Before you evaluate a classmate's persuasive speech, keep in mind that most persuasive speakers have a **bias,** or a strong leaning toward a particular point of view. A speaker who reveals the reasons for his or her bias can seem more credible than one who does not. A speaker who does not reveal a bias may have a *hidden agenda.* A **hidden agenda** is a secret reason for speaking. For example, a speaker trying to convince classmates to establish an art gallery in the hallways may not tell his audience that he is really trying to make sure *his* artwork is displayed.

To evaluate a speech effectively, you must be a good listener. As you listen, take notes on the speaker's content, delivery, and credibility by answering the questions in the chart below.

QUESTIONS FOR EVALUATING A PERSUASIVE SPEECH	
Content	▪ What is the **purpose** of the presentation? Paraphrase the speaker's purpose.
	▪ What is the topic? Paraphrase the speaker's **point of view** on the topic. Does the speaker clearly state his or her opinion?
	▪ Which reasons are convincing and which are not? How are the reasons supported?
Delivery	▪ Describe the speaker's tone. Is it conversational or does it sound too formal?
	▪ Does the speaker speak loudly and slowly enough?
	▪ How often does the speaker make eye contact with the audience?
	▪ How do the speaker's nonverbal messages (such as gestures and facial expressions) match the verbal message? Are any of the gestures distracting? In what way are they distracting?
Credibility (Believability)	▪ What is the speaker's bias? How do you know?
	▪ What facts has the speaker used to support his or her opinion?
	▪ Does the speaker have unsupported opinions? What are they?

Giving and Listening to an Informative Speech

Preparing a Report for a Speech

To find material for your speech, you may want to adapt the report you wrote for the Writing Workshop on pages 218–223. As you get ready to make an informative speech, focus on these elements:

- **Think about the purpose and occasion.** Are you giving an informal speech to your class, or is your speech part of a formal evaluation? Think about how these factors affect your word choice and delivery.

- **Limit your speech to your report's major ideas and the evidence you need to clarify and support** those ideas. When giving evidence, make sure you tell your audience where you found that information.

- **Adjust your word choice** so that your audience can easily understand your ideas and learn from your speech.

- **Use a simple outline** to deliver your speech, rather than simply reading your report. Speaking from a simple outline will make your speech sound more conversational and natural.

- **Avoid speaking too fast or too slow or too loud or too soft.** In other words, use an effective **rate** and **volume** for your audience.

- **Use the pitch, or the highs and lows, of your voice to create an enthusiastic tone.** If the tone of your voice suggests that you do not care about your speech, your audience is likely to feel the same.

Using Visuals in an Informative Speech

Avoid getting caught up in "chartmania," the mysterious disease that affects speakers who use too many visuals. Having one or two well-chosen visuals is better than having too many. Whatever the number of visuals you decide to use, each one should have the same purpose: to complement and extend the meaning of an important point.

Posters, Pictures, Charts, and Graphs If you decide that using a poster, picture, chart, or graph is essential to your presentation, follow these tips:

- Make sure all words and pictures are large enough to be seen clearly from the back of the room.
- Be sure to describe in words what the visual means.
- When explaining a visual, face the audience.

Overhead Projectors or Presentation Software One of the best ways to use visuals that everyone can see is to use a projector. By creating transparencies of your visuals, you can make them large or small by moving the projector away from or closer to the screen. Some projectors even project images from a word-processing program or presentation software. If you choose to use a projector, consider these tips:

- Use dark colors for your text and pictures.
- Make your graphic simple. A cluttered design is confusing.
- Have a backup plan in case the projector breaks or is unavailable.

Video- or Audiotaped Segments Sometimes the best way to demonstrate your point is by using a video- or audiotaped segment. Here are some tips for using a video or audio clip:

- The clip should be fairly short; it should support your presentation, not replace it.
- Have your tape cued up before you speak, so that the audience does not have to wait for you to rewind or fast-forward it.
- Test your equipment before your audience arrives.

Running through your entire presentation—visuals and all—a few times will help you avoid making mistakes on speech day. Practice delivering your speech as if you were in front of the class. If you are using note cards or visuals, practice using them too. Keep practicing until you are able to get through the entire speech without stopping.

Listening to an Informative Speech

An informative speech often contains so much information that you might have trouble absorbing it all. To make the most of the informative speeches you hear, follow the steps listed in the chart on the next page.

QUESTIONS FOR EVALUATING AN INFORMATIVE SPEECH

Content	• **Determine your purpose.** Identify what you want to learn from listening to this speech.
	• **Make predictions.** Identify two or three points you expect the speaker to cover.
	• **Get ready.** Have pen or pencil and paper ready for taking notes.
Delivery	• **Devote your full attention to the speaker.** Looking around the room or doing another assignment is discourteous and will prevent you from learning all you can.
	• **Listen for cues that signal main points.** Cues can also include these words and phrases: *first, second,* and *finally; there are many reasons or causes; the most important thing is;* and *in conclusion.* Hearing these cues is the key to understanding, interpreting, and organizing the information you hear in the speech.
	• **Summarize the main points of the speech.** As you listen, take notes by summarizing the speaker's main points and supporting details.
Credibility (Believability)	• **Monitor your understanding.** Ask yourself if the speaker covered all of the points you expected. If not, what did he or she leave out? Ask the speaker to clarify.

Giving and Listening to an Oral Response to Literature

The information presented here will help you develop a focused and coherent oral presentation of a novel review. Your presentation will be **expository:** you will explain ideas about the novel. You will also listen to and evaluate your classmates' oral reviews and provide feedback.

Organizing Your Review

An effective oral response to a novel evaluates the novel on the basis of a set of criteria. In the process, the oral review

- presents a well-supported, insightful **interpretation** of the novel
- identifies and illustrates the writer's **technique**—how he or she chooses and arranges words in the novel.
- infers the **effects** of the book on its intended audience and provides support for the inference.

  As you consider what to include in your speech, think about your **audience.** Would they be most interested in the novel's characters? the plot? the themes? all three? Next, you will need to decide the order in which to present your main ideas. Follow a coherent **pattern of organization,** such as the one illustrated in the chart on the next page. It's a good idea to outline what you're going to say.

Rehearsing and Delivering Your Presentation

Practice delivering your presentation two or three times. As you rehearse, ask yourself the following questions, and keep them in mind as you practice.

ORGANIZATION OF AN ORAL REVIEW	
Introduction	Grab your audience's attention; introduce the novel you are reviewing by title, author, and a brief preview of the main points you will discuss; and state your thesis in a way that suggests whether or not you recommend the book.
Body	Provide support for your thesis with references to the text of the novel, to other works of literature, to other authors, or to personal knowledge.
Conclusion	Restate or echo your thesis, making your recommendation clear. Tell your audience what effect you believe the novel will have on readers.

- Are my **word choices** appropriate to my audience? Are there any technical terms I need to define? Is my vocabulary too simple or too advanced for my listeners?

- Am I enunciating clearly so that everyone can understand what I am saying? **Enunciation** refers to the distinctness of the sounds you make when you speak. Good enunciation is clear and precise. Poor enunciation often causes words to be slurred or word endings to be left off.

- Does the **pace** of my delivery sound unhurried, yet not so slow as to lull my listeners to sleep?

Evaluating a Review of a Novel

Answering the questions in the chart below as you listen to an oral presentation will help you provide valuable feedback.

QUESTIONS FOR EVALUATING AN ORAL REVIEW OF A NOVEL	
Content and Organization	- Is there an effective **introduction**? Explain why it is or is not effective. - How is the **body** of the speech developed? Identify one piece of evidence that supports each of the main points of the body. - How does the speaker restate, or echo, the main idea of the review in the **conclusion**? How does the speaker make his or her recommendation clear?
Delivery	- Is the speaker's choice of words appropriate? Explain. - Does the speaker maintain a lively but unhurried pace? Elaborate with examples. - Do the speaker's gestures and facial expressions add to the meaning of the presentation? Elaborate with examples.
Overall Effect	- What was the speaker's purpose? Did the speaker achieve it? Elaborate. - Were you able to visualize characters or events in the novel? Why or why not? - Did you agree with the speaker's point of view? Elaborate.

Interviewing

Interviews—conversations in which one person asks questions to obtain information—are more common than you might think.

You've probably been interviewed—by a teacher, the school nurse, or a neighbor wanting you to baby-sit or mow the lawn.

Sometime, you may need to conduct an interview yourself. Here's how to get off to a good start.

Preparing for the Interview

A good interviewer is well prepared. Before you take out your pencil and note pad, follow these steps:

- **Research your topic.** If your interview focuses on a topic—kayaking, say—go to the library and find out all you can about it. The more you know, the better your questions will be.

- **Know your subject.** If your interview focuses on the ideas and life of the person you're interviewing (your subject), see if any newspaper or magazine articles have been written about him or her. If your subject is a writer, read her latest book; if he's an architect, go see—or find a picture of—a building he designed.

- **Make a list of questions.** Ask obvious questions rather than pretend you know the answer. Don't ask questions that can be answered with a simple yes or no. Avoid questions that might influence your subject, like "You hate losing, don't you?"

- **Set up a time and place for the interview.** Choose a place that's comfortable and familiar to your subject—interview a horse trainer at her ranch or a chemistry teacher in his lab. Be on time.

Conducting the Interview

You're seated across from your subject, pencil poised. How do you make the most of your opportunity? Follow these guidelines:

- **Set the ground rules.** If you want to tape-record the interview, ask your subject's permission before you begin. If you plan to quote your subject's exact words in a newspaper article or in an essay, you must ask permission to do that too.

TIP Team up with a classmate, and come up with a situation in which an interviewer and a subject have opposing points of view (a dog hater interviews the director of the humane society; a vegetarian interviews the owner of a cattle ranch). Then, act out two versions of the interview. In the first version, the interview is tense and hostile, full of insults, interruptions, and accusations. In the second, the interview is polite and constructive, and the interviewer refrains from directly expressing a point of view. What did you learn from the two scenarios?

- **Be courteous and patient**. Allow your subject plenty of time to answer your questions. Try not to interrupt. Respect the person's ideas and opinions, even if you disagree.
- **Listen carefully.** Don't rush on to your next question. If you're confused, ask for an explanation. If an answer reminds you of a related question, ask it—even if it isn't on your list.
- **Focus on your subject, not on yourself.** Avoid getting off on tangents, such as "something like that happened to me...."
- **Wrap things up.** A good interview is leisurely but doesn't go on forever. Know when to stop. You can always phone later to check a fact or ask a final question. Be sure to thank your subject.

Following Up the Interview

Your notebook is filled, and your mind is bursting with ideas. How do you get your thoughts in order? Follow these steps:

- **Review your notes.** As soon as possible, read through your notes, and make sure your information is complete and clear.
- **Write a summary.** To make sure you understand what was said, write a summary of the main points of the interview.
- **Check your facts.** If you can, check the spelling of all names and technical facts against another source, such as an encyclopedia.

Turning the Tables: Being Interviewed

Sometime, someone may want to interview you. Here are some tips:

- **Stay relaxed.** Listen carefully to each question before you begin your answer. If a question confuses you, ask the interviewer to reword it or repeat it. Take your time. Long, thoughtful answers are better than short, curt ones.
- **Be accurate.** Don't exaggerate. If you're not sure of something, say so.
- **Keep a sense of humor.**

Evaluating Persuasive Images in the Media

Persuasive Images

When you look at a photograph of yourself, what do you see? You see yourself, right? Actually, the person in the picture is not the *real* you, but a representation of you. In fact, all media images are representations of reality that can shape people's ideas about the world. That is why you need to be a critical viewer of media images.

To view images critically, remember that an image is one person's version of reality. An image reflects the point of view of the person who created it. When you see an image, consider other points of view people might have about the image's subject. Image makers, from illustrators to photographers to graphic designers, make conscious choices about what an image will show and how it will show it. People who create all sorts of media images can use *content, color, light and shadow,* and *point of view* to make their images more persuasive.

Content   The **content** of an image is what it shows—everything included in the image. The way an image maker chooses to portray a subject is the most important persuasive choice he or she will make.

Look, for example, at the two images of the scientist Albert Einstein shown on the facing page. The image on the left is a caricature of Einstein that presents him as a comical figure. The oil painting on the right, on the other hand, portrays Einstein as wise, not humorous. The two images reflect the different purposes of the artists who created them. If you had seen only one of these portraits, how would you feel about Einstein? What opinion would you have of this scientist and of his life's work?

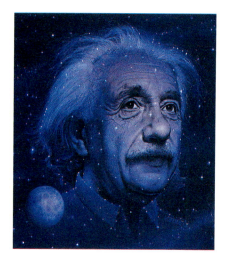

The other items in an image are also carefully chosen. An image maker may choose to include **persuasive symbols,** such as a bald eagle or an American flag. He or she may also add to a persuasive message by choosing to leave out certain things. For example, although President Franklin Roosevelt used a wheelchair, many portraits depict him from the waist up in order to leave out the wheelchair.

Color, Light, and Shadow   Image makers use **color** to create interest or to establish a mood. To create interest, an illustrator may use color to highlight the most important part of the image—by using a brighter color in that part of the image, for example. A photographer may use a computer, colored pencils, or paints to color one part of a black-and-white photograph to make it stand out.

Image makers can choose to create areas of **light** and **shadow** in their work. An image maker may carefully place shadows to make a subject look frightening or dramatic or romantic. Using plenty of even light with few or no shadows can make the subject look real and approachable. Sometimes photographers have to work with the light they have.

Point of View, or Angle   The **angle** at which you see the subject of an image can affect your impression of the subject. For example, seeing a subject from a direct angle may not affect your impression of it, but seeing it from above or below a normal angle can change your impression.

Look at the examples on the following page. In the picture on the left, the photographer stood on a ladder and shot the picture looking down at the boy. Do you see how the boy looks small and vulnerable? Now, look at the picture on the right taken from a low angle looking up at the same boy. From this angle the boy looks big and powerful, even a little intimidating.

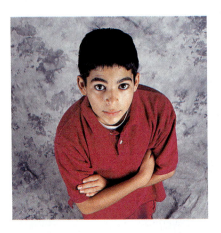

Medium

A **medium** is the means by which an image is created. All image makers use the techniques explained on pages 996–997, but each still medium—illustration and photography—also has its own unique characteristics and techniques. (The plural of *medium* is **media,** a term often applied to television, radio, newspapers, and the Internet.)

Illustration   An **illustration** is a picture created to explain something or to share a point of view. Drawings, cartoons, paintings, and computer-generated art are examples of illustrations. Each type of illustration lends itself to a different type of persuasive message.

Photography   Photographs are powerful partners to the written and spoken word. In a newspaper, for instance, you might read about an erupting volcano. Only when you see the picture that accompanies the article would you fully understand the massive destruction the volcano caused. Because photographs are so powerful and easy to reproduce, they are a popular medium, especially when they are used with the written word, as in newspapers and magazines.

The persuasive power of photographs is found in our belief that "photographs do not lie"—that they show reality. However, like illustrations, photographs only *resemble* an actual person, place, thing, or event. You should be aware that people can change or influence the information a photograph provides. As a photograph is being taken, a photographer can, under the right circumstances, use camera angle or lighting to alter the reality of a situation to suit his or her persuasive purposes. Even after developing a photo, a photographer can **crop,** or cut out, an unwanted part of a scene to make the image more persuasive.

Evaluating Media Images

To interpret and evaluate a media image, either still or moving, consider the following questions.

QUESTIONS FOR EVALUATING MEDIA IMAGES	
General Questions	• Who created the image? Do I know of a bias this source has—either positive or negative feelings toward the subject? Does this bias affect the message? • For what purpose was this image created?
Questions About Content	• What impression do I get from the image about its subject? Why? • How is this version of reality similar to or different from what I know from my own experience? • Does the image include any persuasive symbols? • What may have been left out of the image?
Questions About Color	• Is the image black-and-white, color, or both? What mood do the color choices create? • What parts of the image stand out because of color? Why might these parts be important?
Questions About Light and Shadow	• Is the light in the image even, or are there shadows? • What mood do the light and shadows create? Do shadows make the subject seem frightening or dramatic? What message does this send?
Questions About Point of View	• At what angle do you see the subject? a normal, direct angle? an angle above the subject? a low angle? • What impression of the subject does the angle give you? Does the subject seem powerful? vulnerable?
Questions About Medium	• What medium carries the image? • How do the characteristics of the medium add to the image's persuasive power?

Creating Graphics for Technical Documents

No matter how clear your technical document is, visuals such as flowcharts and diagrams can make an explanation even clearer to your readers. Providing such graphics helps readers create sharper mental pictures of the information you present.

Effective Graphics

An effective graphic in a technical document should be useful, not merely decorative. Useful graphics

- **add** to the information in the document or **clarify** something difficult to explain in words
- **focus** on a particularly important or potentially confusing part of an object or a process
- are **simple, clear,** and **uncluttered**

Features and Types of Graphics

For clarity, graphics need *titles* and often require *captions* and *labels*.

- **Titles** tell in just a few words exactly what the graphic shows.
- **Captions** explain the graphic using sentences placed near it.
- **Labels** briefly identify different parts of the graphic.

   Study the use of titles, captions, and labels in the following graphics.

   Three types of graphics are often used in technical documents to summarize information, to make complex information clearer, or to emphasize important points.

Water Wheel Variation 2

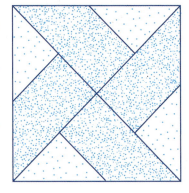

- **Illustrations,** such as digital photographs and computer drawings, show readers objects or events that are difficult to understand. For example, the computer-generated drawing on the previous page shows the pattern of a quilt.

- **Diagrams** use symbols, such as arrows, to illustrate how to do something or how something works. The following diagram shows how a canal lock works.

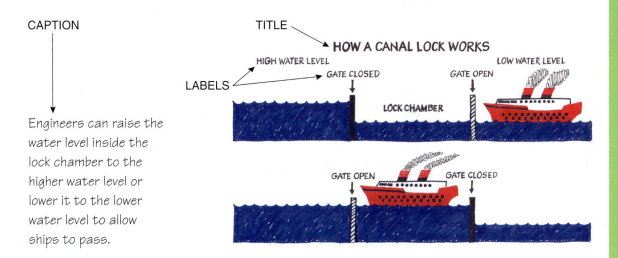

CAPTION

Engineers can raise the water level inside the lock chamber to the higher water level or lower it to the lower water level to allow ships to pass.

TITLE

HOW A CANAL LOCK WORKS

HIGH WATER LEVEL

LOW WATER LEVEL

LABELS

GATE CLOSED

GATE OPEN

LOCK CHAMBER

GATE OPEN

GATE CLOSED

- **Charts and graphs** offer a visual way to arrange ideas, showing trends or relationships. **Flowcharts,** such as the one below, show an order of events and can be particularly helpful in summarizing the information in a technical document.

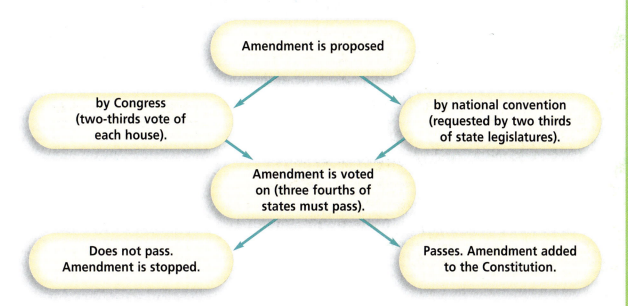

Amendment is proposed

by Congress (two-thirds vote of each house).

by national convention (requested by two thirds of state legislatures).

Amendment is voted on (three fourths of states must pass).

Does not pass. Amendment is stopped.

Passes. Amendment added to the Constitution.

Planning and Creating Graphics

Use the following steps to create computer-generated graphics for your technical document. To familiarize yourself with the variety of programs that are available, consult your computer lab instructor or browse the Internet for information.

1. **Decide what part of your report could be made clearer with the help of a graphic.** This decision is often made during the prewriting stage. A peer editor—someone who is unfamiliar with your topic—could also offer suggestions about where a graphic might be helpful.

2. **Select the best way to illustrate the part you have chosen.** Explore the software that is available to you. Options include scanning existing graphics, importing copyright-free digital photographs, or creating original tables, charts, graphs, and drawings. For example, you might create a table by entering information into a spreadsheet, using a word-processing program to paste certain shapes into a document, or using a drawing program to create a line drawing.

3. **By hand, make a rough sketch of your ideas to make sure the form you have chosen will work.** You may have to make several tries before you figure out the sizes and shapes of items that will work best in your graphic.

4. **Use a software tool to create the graphic.** Make your graphics bold and clear, not cluttered with unnecessary information or decorations. Use color only if it will make your message clearer. If you are working with an unfamiliar program, check any available self-tutoring functions or Help menus.

5. **Add an identifying title, labels, and captions to your graphic where needed.** Also, check the text of your document to be sure you have discussed the graphic. Remember to indicate the source of any information you have borrowed, even if you have created an original graphic using the information.

Glossary

The glossary below is an alphabetical list of vocabulary words found in the selections in this book. Use this glossary just as you use a dictionary—to find out the meanings of unfamiliar words. (Some technical, foreign, and more obscure words in this book are not listed here but instead are defined for you in the footnotes that accompany many of the selections.)

Many words in the English language have more than one meaning. This glossary gives the meanings that apply to the words as they are used in the selections in this book. Words closely related in form and meaning are usually listed together in one entry (for instance, *grudge* and *grudging*), and the definition is given for the first form.

The following abbreviations are used:

adj.	adjective
adv.	adverb
n.	noun
pl.	plural
v.	verb

Each word's pronunciation is given in parentheses. A guide to the pronunciation symbols appears at the bottom of this page. For more information about the words in this glossary or for information about words not listed here, consult a dictionary.

A

acute (ə·kyo͞ot′) *adj.:* sharp.
alleviate (ə·lē′vē·āt′) *v.:* relieve.
animation (an′i·mā′shen) *n.:* liveliness.
annihilation (ə·nī′ə·lā′shən) *n.:* complete destruction.
appall (ə·pôl′) *v.:* horrify. —**appalled** *v.* used as *adj.*
apparent (ə·per′ənt) *adj.:* visible.
audacity (ô·das′ə·tē) *n.:* boldness.

B

benign (bi·nīn′) *adj.:* kind.
breach (brēch) *n.:* opening.
brittle (brit′′l) *adj.:* having a sharp, hard quality; ready to break.

C

cavort (kə·vôrt′) *v.:* leap about.
chagrin (shə·grin′) *n.:* embarrassment.
circuit (sur′kit) *n.:* regular route of a person doing a certain job.
clamorous (klam′ər·əs) *adj.:* loud and demanding.
cognitive (käg′nə·tiv) *adj.:* having to do with the process of knowing and being able to remember.
conspicuous (kən·spik′yo͞o·əs) *adj.:* noticeable.
contention (kən·ten′shen) *n.:* conflict.
creed (krēd) *n.:* statement of belief or principles.
crucial (kro͞o′shəl) *adj.:* highly important.

---

at, āte, cär; ten, ēve; is, īce; gō, hôrn, lo͝ok, to͞ol; oil, out; up, fur; ə *for unstressed vowels, as* a *in* ago, u *in* focus; ′ *as in* Latin (lat′′n); chin; she; zh *as in* azure (azh′ər); thin; *the;* ŋ *as in* ring (riŋ)

D

derision (di·rizh′ən) *n.:* ridicule.

detect (dē·tekt′) *v.:* discover; notice.

deterioration (dē·tir′ē·ə·rā′shən) *n.:* worsening; decline.

discord (dis′kôrd′) *n.:* conflict.

disgruntle (dis·grunt′'l) *v.:* displease, annoy. —**disgruntled** *v.* used as *adj.*

dispel (di·spel′) *v.:* scatter; drive away.

dispirit (di·spir′it) *v.:* make sad; discourage. —**dispirited** *v.* used as *adj.*

drone (drōn) *n.:* continuous buzzing sound.

E

eloquence (el′ə·kwəns) *n.:* ability to write or speak gracefully and convincingly.

emaciate (ē·mā′shē·āt′) *v.:* make extremely thin, as from starvation or illness. —**emaciated** *v.* used as *adj.*

emerge (ē·murj′) *v.:* come out.

exalt (eg·zôlt′) *v.:* lift up.

exaltation (eg′zôl·tā′shen) *n.:* great joy.

exertion (eg·zur′shən) *n.:* hard work or effort.

exile (ek′sīl′) *n.:* living away from one's country or community. Exile is usually forced.

exotic (eg·zät′ik) *adj.:* foreign; strange in a fascinating way.

F

forlorn (fôr·lôrn′) *adj.:* abandoned and lonely.

fortify (fôrt′ə·fī′) *v.:* strengthen.

fugitive (fyōō′ji·tiv) *n.:* person fleeing danger.

G

gaunt (gônt) *adj.:* very thin and bony.

gesticulation (jes·tik′yōō·lā′shən) *n.:* energetic gesture.

gingerly (jin′jər′lē) *adv.:* cautiously.

grudge (gruj) *v.:* give reluctantly or unwilling. —**grudging** *v.* used as *adj.*

H

harass (har′əs) *v.:* trouble; bother. —**harassed** *v.* used as *adj.*

host (hōst) *n.:* army.

hypothesis (hī·päth′ə·sis) *n.:* theory to be proved.

I

illiteracy (i·lit′ər·ə·sē) *n.:* inability to read or write.

impromptu (im·prämp′tōō′) *adj.:* unplanned.

impulse (im′puls′) *n.:* urge.

inarticulate (in′är·tik′yōō·lit) *adj.:* unable to speak.

incentive (in·sent′iv) *n.:* reason to do something; motivation.

incomprehensible (in·käm′prē·hen′sə·bəl) *adj.:* impossible to understand.

indignant (in·dig′nənt) *adj.:* feeling anger because of something thought to be unjust. —**indignantly** *adv.*

indomitable (in·däm′i·tə·bəl) *adj.:* cannot be conquered.

inevitable (in·ev′i·tə·bəl) *adj.:* unavoidable.

inexplicable (in·eks′pli·kə·bəl) *adj.:* incapable of being explained.

infuse (in·fyōōz′) *v.:* fill.

instinctive (in·stiŋk′tiv) *adj.:* automatic. —**instinctively** *adv.*

intent (in·tent′) *adj.:* paying close attention. —**intently** *adv.*

intolerant (in·täl′ər·ənt) *adj.:* unwilling to put up with.

introspective (in′trə·spek′tiv) *adj.:* looking inward.

invariable (in·ver′ē·ə·bəl) *adj.:* not changing. —**invariably** *adv.*

irrevocable (i·rev′ə·kə·bəl) *adj.:* unable to be undone or changed. —**irrevocably** *adv.*

L

laborious (lə·bôr′ē·əs) *adj.:* hard; difficult.

laconic (lə·kän′ik) *adj.:* using few words. —**laconically** *adv.*

loathe (lō*th*) *v.:* hate.

M

mislead (mis·lēd′) *v.:* fool; lead to believe something that is incorrect.

O

oasis (ō·ā′sis) *n.:* place or thing offering relief.

oblivious (ə·bliv′ē·əs) *adj.:* unaware.

obscure (əb·skyoor′) *v.:* hide.

ominous (äm′ə·nəs) *adj.:* threatening.

ostentatious (äs′tən·tā′shəs) *adj.:* showy. —**ostentatiously** *adv.*

P

paranoia (par′ə·noi′ə) *n.:* mental disorder that causes people to feel unreasonable distrust and suspicion.

populate (päp′yə·lāt′) *v.:* live in. —**populated** *v.* used as *adj.*

premonition (prem′ə·nish′ən) *n.:* feeling that something bad will happen.

prodigious (prō·dij′əs) *adj.:* huge; amazing.

provocative (prə·väk′ə·tiv) *adj.:* stirring up thoughts or feelings.

R

raucous (rô′kəs) *adj.:* loud and rough.

reconciliation (rek′ən·sil′ē·ā′shən) *n.:* act of making up after arguments.

refrain (ri·frān′) *v.:* hold back.

refuge (ref′yooj) *n.:* place of safety.

refute (ri·fyoot′) *v.:* prove wrong using evidence.

regression (ri·gresh′ən) *n.:* return to an earlier or less advanced condition.

remorse (ri·môrs′) *n.:* deep feeling of guilt.

rend (rend) *v.:* tear. —**rent**

retrieve (ri·trēv′) *v.:* get back.

rivet (riv′it) *v.:* fasten, hold firmly.

rummage (rum′ij) *v.:* search through the contents of a box, a drawer, and so on.

S

sagacity (sə·gas′ə·tē) *n.:* intelligence and good judgment.

savor (sā′vər) *v.:* enjoy with great delight.

skimpy (skim′pē) *adj.:* less than enough.

staff (staf) *n.:* pole.

steep (stēp) *v.:* fill with. —**steeped** *v.* used as *adj.*

stir (stur) *v.:* wake up.

suavity (swäv′ə·tē) *n.:* smooth manner.

sublime (sə·blīm′) *adj.:* majestic; grand.

sullen (sul′ən) *adj.:* grumpy; resentful.

T

tangible (tan′jə·bəl) *adj.:* seen and felt.

taut (tôt) *adj.:* tightly stretched.

tentative (ten′tə·tiv) *adj.:* uncertain or hesitant. —**tentatively** *adv.*

terse (turs) *adj.:* brief and clear. —**tersely** *adv.*

tread (tred) *n.:* step.

tremulous (trem′yoo·ləs) *adj.:* trembling.

tyranny (tir′ə·nē) *n.:* cruel and unjust use of power.

U

unabashed (un′ə·basht′) *adj.:* unembarrassed.

V

vehement (vē′ə·mənt) *adj.:* forceful. —**vehemently** *adv.*

verify (ver′ə·fī′) *v.:* confirm.

vex (veks) *v.:* disturb.

vigil (vij′əl) *n.:* watch.

W

wary (wer′ē) *adj.:* cautious.

Z

zeal (zēl) *n.:* great enthusiasm; devotion to a cause.

Spanish Glossary

A

acute/agudo *adj.* penetrante; afilado; punzante.

alleviate/aliviar *v.* mitigar; calmar; tranquilizar.

annihilation/aniquilación *v.* destrucción; exterminación.

appall/espantar *v.* horrorizar; asombrar. **—appalled/espantado** *v.* usado como *adj.*

apparent/aparente *adj.* evidente; visible; manifiesto.

audacity/audacia *s.* osadía; intrepidez; valentía; coraje.

B

benign/benigno *adj.* favorable; sano; propicio; clemente.

breach/abertura *s.* ranura; hendidura.

brittle/quebradizo *adj.* frágil; quebradizo; delicado.

C

cavort/retozar *v.* juguetear; corretear.

chagrin/disgusto *s.* contrariedad; mortificación; desengaño.

circuit/circuito *s.* pista; trayecto rutinario.

clamorous/clamoroso *adj.* estruendoso; ruidoso; gritón.

cognitive/cognitivo *adj.* sapiente; conocedor; que trata del proceso asociado con el conocimiento y la memoria.

conspicuous/visible *adj.* obvio; llamativo; notable; patente; que llama la atención.

contention/contienda *s.* disputa; controversia; discusión.

creed/credo *s.* creencia; fe; dogma; declaración de principios o de fe.

crucial/crucial *adj.* crucial; decisivo; capital.

D

derision/mofa *s.* burla; broma; desprecio.

detect/detectar *v.* descubrir; revelar; observar; notar.

deterioration/deterioración *s.* daño; pérdida; menoscabo.

discord/discordia *s.* querella; conflicto; cizaña.

disgruntle/contrariar *v.* disgustar; fastidiar. **—disgruntled/contrariado** *v.* usado como *adj.*

dispel/disipar *v.* desvanecer; evaporar; esfumar.

dispirit/desalentar *v.* desanimar; abatir; deprimir. **—dispirited/desalenteado** *v.* usado como *adj.*

drone/zumbido *s.* ronroneo; sonido; rumor.

E

eloquence/elocuencia *s.* persuasión; palabra convincente y persuasiva.

emaciate/demacrar *v.* adelgazar; enflaquecer; debilitar. **—emaciated/demacrado** *adj.* extremadamente delgado; consumido.

emerge/emerger *v.* brotar; surgir; salir.

exalt/exaltar *v.* enaltecer; ensalzar; celebrar.

exaltation/exaltación *s.* entusiasmo; animación; ensalzamiento.

exertion/esfuerzo *s.* arranque; ardor.

exile/exilio *s.* destierro; vivir fuera de su país o comunidad.

exotic/exótico *adj.* extraño; raro; original; fascinante.

F

forlorn/triste *adj.* melancólico; desolado; afligido.

fortify/fortificar *v.* fortalecer; robustecer; consolidar.

fugitive/fugitivo *s.* evadido; fugado; persona que huye de un peligro.

G

gaunt/lúgubre *adj.* sombrío; taciturno.

gesticulation/gesticulación *s.* gesto; ademán; manoteo.

gingerly/cautelosamente *adv.* precavidamente; prudentemente.

grudge/resentir *v.* dar a regañadientes; envidiar; ver con malos ojos. —**grudging/ resentido** *v.* usado como *adj.*

H

harass/acosar *v.* hostigar; molestar.

host/multitud *s.* hueste; tropa; banda.

hypothesis/hipótesis *s.* suposición; conjetura; teoría por comprobar.

I

illiteracy/analfabetismo *s.* no poder leer o escribir.

impromptu/improvisado *adj.* espontáneo; imprevisto; intuitivo.

impulse/impulso *s.* deseo repentino; estímulo.

inarticulate/inarticulado *adj.* incapaz de expresarse; que no puede hablar.

incomprehensible/incomprensible *adj.* enigmático; denso; que no se comprende.

indignant/indignado *adj.* iracundo; colérico; encrespado; enojado por algo que parece injusto.

indomitable/indomable *adj.* indómito; rebelde; indócil; que no se puede conquistar.

inevitable/inevitable *adj.* necesario; irremediable; fijo.

inexplicable/inexplicable *adj.* misterioso; enigmático; incomprensible; que no se puede explicar.

infuse/infundir *v.* inspirar; imbuir; llenar.

instinctive/instintivo *adj.* involuntario; automático.

intent/atento *adj.* que presta atención; dispuesto; vigilante.

intolerant/intolerante *adj.* intransigente; inflexible; severo.

introspective/introspectivo *adj.* reflexivo; que observa su interior.

invariable/invariable *adj.* inmutable; inalterable; sin cambio.—**invariably/ invariablemente** *adv.* eternamente; perpetuamente.

irrevocable/irrevocable *adj.* inevitable; inapelable; que no se puede anular o deshacer. —**irrevocably/irrevocablemente** *v.* usado como *adv.*

L

laborious/laborioso *adj.* trabajoso; penoso; costoso.

laconic/lacónico *adj.* parco de palabras; breve; conciso.

loathe/detestar *v.* abominar; aborrecer; odiar.

M

mislead/engañar *v.* equivocar; descaminar.

O

oasis/oasis *s.* tregua; lugar o cosa que brinda alivio.

oblivious/inconsciente *adj.* despistado; negligente.

obscure/oscurecer *v.* ocultar; disimular; esconder.

ominous/siniestro *adj.* inquietante; adverso.

ostentatious/ostentoso *adj.* aparatoso; teatral; grandioso.

P

paranoia/paranoia *s.* paranoia; manía; demencia que causa desconfianza desmesurada.

populate/poblar *v.* habitar; ocupar; anidar.

premonition/premonición *s.* presentimiento; presagio; conjetura.

prodigious/prodigioso *adj.* maravilloso; enorme; fuera de serie.

provocative/provocativo *adj.* sugerente; insinuante; interesante.

R

raucous/ronco *adj.* estridente; desapacible; agitador.

reconciliation/reconciliación *s.* conciliación; acuerdo amistoso.

refrain/abstenerse *v.* callarse; tragar saliva; contenerse.

refuge/refugio *s.* protección; amparo.

regression/regresión *s.* retrocesión; retorno; regreso a una condición previa.

remorse/remordimiento *s.* culpabilidad profunda; contrición; arrepentimiento.

rend/rasgar *v.* rajar; hender; desgarrar.

retrieve/recuperar *v.* recobrar; rescatar; redimir.

rivet/remachar *v.* roblonar; sujetar; fijar.

rummage/hurgar *v.* curiosear; buscar en una caja o en un cajón.

S

sagacity/sagacidad *s.* perspicacia; prudencia; sensatez; lucidez.

savor/saborear *v.* paladear; probar; deleitarse.

skimpy/escaso *adj.* insuficiente; miserable; menos que bastante.

staff/bastón *s.* palo; báculo; apoyo.

steep/remojar *v.* empapar; impregnar; saturar.

stir/despertar *v.* avivar; animar.

suavity/afabilidad *s.* amabilidad; cortesía.

sublime/sublime *adj.* sin par; excelso; extraordinario; superior.

sullen/hosco *adj.* ceñudo; resentido; huraño; arisco.

T

tangible/tangible *adj.* que se puede tocar; palpable; asequible.

taut/tenso *adj.* tieso; rígido; tirante.

tentative/indeciso *adj.* vacilante; irresoluto; tímido.

terse/conciso *adj.* sucinto; lacónico; breve.

tread/pisar *v.* andar; pasar; marcar.

tremulous/trémulo *adj.* tembloroso; estremecido; palpitante.

tyranny/tiranía *s.* opresión; despotismo; absolutismo; abuso de poder.

U

unabashed/imperturbable *adj.* inalterable; tranquilo; descarado.

V

vehement/vehemente *adj.* violento; apasionado; elocuente.

verify/verificar *v.* comprobar; confirmar; cotejar.

vex/fastidiar *v.* molestar; disturbar; disgustar.

vigil/vela *s.* vigilia; vigilancia durante las horas de sueño.

W

wary/cauteloso *adj.* precavido; receloso; circunspecto.

Z

zeal/entusiasmo *s.* pasión; fervor; devoción.

Acknowledgments

For permission to reprint copyrighted material, grateful acknowledgment is made to the following sources:

Agencia Literaria Carmen Balcells on behalf of Fundación Pablo Neruda: From "Oda a las gracias" from *Odas Elementales* by Pablo Neruda. Copyright © 1954, 1995 by Pablo Neruda and Fundación Pablo Neruda.

Miriam Altshuler Literary Agency, on behalf of Walter Dean Myers: "The Treasure of Lemon Brown" by Walter Dean Myers from *Boys' Life Magazine,* March 1983. Copyright © 1983 by Walter Dean Myers. From "Walter Dean Myers" by Walter Dean Myers from *Speaking for Ourselves,* edited by Donald R. Gallo. Copyright © 2003 by Walter Dean Myers.

American Library Association: From "Starred Reviews: Books for Youth: *Parallel Journeys* by Eleanor H. Ayers" by Hazel Rochman from *Booklist,* vol. 91, no. 18, May 15, 1995. Copyright © 1995 by American Library Association.

Arte Público Press: From *Silent Dancing: A Partial Remembrance of a Puerto Rican Childhood* by Judith Ortiz Cofer. Copyright © 1990 by Judith Ortiz Cofer. Published by Arte Público Press–University of Houston, 1990.

The Associated Press: "Memory a Matter of Brains and Brawn" by Lauran Neergaard from *San Francisco Chronicle,* July 25, 2000. Copyright © 2000 by The Associated Press.

Bancroft Library, University of California, Berkeley: "The Wise Old Woman" from *The Sea of Gold and Other Tales from Japan,* adapted by Yoshiko Uchida. Copyright © 1965 by Yoshiko Uchida.

Susan Bergholz Literary Services, New York: From "Redwing Sonnets" from *Homecoming: New and Collected Poems* by Julia Alvarez. Copyright © 1984, 1996 by Julia Alvarez. Published by Plume, an imprint of The Penguin Group; originally published by Grove Press. Autobiographical comment by Sandra Cisneros. Copyright © 1987 by Sandra Cisneros. First published in *The Texas Observer,* September 1987. All rights reserved. "A Smart Cookie" and "Gil's Furniture Bought and Sold" from *The House on Mango Street* by Sandra Cisneros. Copyright © 1984 by Sandra Cisneros. Published by Vintage Books, a division of Random House, Inc., and in hardcover by Alfred A. Knopf in 1994. All rights reserved. "Bien águila" from *La casa en Mango Street* by Sandra Cisneros, translated by Elena Poniatowska. Copyright © 1984 by Sandra Cisneros; translation copyright © 1994 by Elena Poniatowska. Published by Vintage Español, a division of Random House, Inc. All rights reserved.

BOA Editions Ltd.: "Valentine for Ernest Mann" from *Red Suitcase: Poems* by Naomi Shihab Nye. Copyright © 1994 by Naomi Shihab Nye.

Brandt & Hochman Literary Agents, Inc.: "The Third Wish" from *Not What You Expected: A Collection of Short Stories* by Joan Aiken. Copyright © 1974, 2002 by Joan Aiken.

Curtis Brown, Ltd.: "The Panther" by Ogden Nash. Copyright © 1940, by Ogden Nash; copyright renewed.

Carus Publishing Company: From "Shipwreck at the Bottom of the World" by Jennifer Armstrong from *Muse,* vol. 4, no. 10, December 2000. Copyright © 2000 by Carus Publishing Company.

Diana Chang: "Saying Yes" by Diana Chang. Copyright © 2000 by Diana Chang.

Chronicle Books, LLC, San Francisco, www.Chronical Books.com: "Oranges" from *New and Selected Poems* by Gary Soto. Copyright © 1995 by Gary Soto.

Clarion/Houghton Mifflin Company: "Drumbeats and Bullets" from *The Boys' War* by Jim Murphy. Copyright © 1990 by Jim Murphy.

Jennifer Sibley Clement: "The Word" by Manuel Ulacia, translated by Jennifer Clement. Translation copyright © 1995 by Jennifer Clement.

Don Congdon Associates, Inc.: From "Ray Bradbury," an interview by Frank Filosa from *On Being a Writer,* edited by Bill Strickland. Copyright © 1967 by Frank Filosa. From "Drunk, and in Charge of a Bicycle" from *The Stories of Ray Bradbury.* Copyright © 1980 by Ray Bradbury. "The Drummer Boy of Shiloh" by Ray Bradbury. Copyright © 1960 by The Curtis Publishing Company; copyright renewed © 1988 by Ray Bradbury. Author's comments on "The Drummer Boy of Shiloh." Copyright © 2003 by Ray Bradbury. "The Flying Machine" by Ray Bradbury. Copyright 1953 and renewed © 1986 by Ray Bradbury. "The Fog Horn" by Ray Bradbury. Copyright © 1951 by The Curtis Publishing Company; copyright renewed © 1979 by Ray Bradbury. "There Will Come Soft Rains" by Ray Bradbury. Copyright 1950 by the Crowell-Collier Publishing Co.; copyright renewed © 1977 by Ray Bradbury.

Crown Publishers, a division of Random House, Inc.: From *Shipwreck at the Bottom of the World* by Jennifer Armstrong. Copyright © 1998 by Jennifer M. Armstrong.

Dial Books for Young Readers, a Member of Penguin Group (USA) Inc.: From the Foreword and "Brer Rabbit and Brer Lion" from *The Tales of Uncle Remus* by Julius Lester, illustrated by Jerry Pinkney. Copyright © 1987 by Julius Lester.

Doubleday, a division of Random House, Inc.: From *The Diary of a Young Girl: The Definitive Edition* by Anne Frank, edited by Otto H. Frank and Mirjam Pressler, translated by Susan Massoty. Copyright © 1995 by Doubleday, a division of Random House, Inc. From *The Cay* by Theodore Taylor. Copyright © 1969 by Theodore Taylor.

Dutton Signet, a Member of Penguin Group (USA) Inc.: From *Beowulf,* translated by Burton Raffel. Translation copyright © 1963 and renewed © 1991 by Burton Raffel.

Farrar, Straus & Giroux, LLC: "The Green Mamba" from *Going Solo* by Roald Dahl. Copyright © 1986 by Roald Dahl. All rights reserved. "The Puppy" from *Stories and Prose Poems* by Alexander Solzhenitsyn, translated by Michael Glenny. Translation copyright © 1971 by Michael Glenny.

Alberto Forcada: "Suéter" from *Despertar* by Alberto Forcada. Copyright © 1992 by Alberto Forcada. Published by Centro de Información y Desarrollo de la Literatura Infantiles (CIDCLI).

The Gale Group: From "Ann Petry" from *Contemporary Authors: Autobiography Series,* vol. 6, edited by Adele Sarkissian. Copyright © 1988 by Gale Research Company Inc. From "Gary Paulsen" from *Something About the Author: Autobiography Series,* vol. 54, edited by Anne Commire. Copyright © 1989 by Gale Research Company Inc. From "Walter Dean Myers" from *Something About the Author: Autobiography Series,* vol. 41, edited by Anne Commire. Copyright © 1985 by Gale Research Company. From "Yoshiko Uchida" from *Something About the Author: Autobiography Series,* vol. 1, edited by Adele Sarkissian. Copyright © 1986 by Gale Research Company Inc.

Marcia Ann Gillespie: From "Maya Angelou," an interview by Marcia Ann Gillespie from *Essence,* December 1992. Copyright © 1992 by Marica Ann Gillespie.

Judith Gorog: "Those Three Wishes" from *A Taste for Quiet and Other Disquieting Tales* by Judith Gorog. Copyright © 1982 by Judith Gorog.

Grolier Publishing Company: "Coming to America" from *New Kids on the Block: Oral Histories of Immigrant Teens* by Janet Bode. Copyright © 1989 by Janet Bode. Published by Franklin Watts.

Harcourt, Inc.: "The Naming of Cats" and illustration by Edward Gorey from "The Addressing of Cats" from *Old Possum's Book of Practical Cats* by T. S. Eliot. Copyright 1939 by T. S. Eliot; copyright renewed © 1967 by Esme Valerie Eliot. Illustration copyright © 1982 by Edward Gorey. "Broken Chain" from *Baseball in April and Other Stories* by Gary Soto. Copyright © 1990 by Gary Soto.

HarperCollins Publishers: From *No Pretty Pictures: A Child of War* by Anita Lobel. Copyright © 1998 by Anita Lobel. From "In Her Own Words" by Naomi Shihab Nye from *HarperChildrens* web site, accessed on October 5, 2000, at harperchildrens.com/hech/authorpage/index.asp?authorID=15255. Copyright © 2000 by Naomi Shihab Nye.

Harvard University Press and the Trustees of Amherst College: 1212 "A Word is Dead" and 1763 "Fame is a bee" from *The Poems of Emily Dickinson,* edited by Thomas H. Johnson. Copyright © 1951, 1955, 1979 by the President and Fellows of Harvard College. Published by The Belknap Press of Harvard University Press, Cambridge, Mass.

David Higham Associates: "The Landlady" from *Kiss, Kiss* by Roald Dahl. Copyright © 1959 by Roald Dahl.

Hill and Wang, a division of Farrar, Straus & Giroux, LLC: From *The Big Sea* by Langston Hughes. Copyright © 1940 by Langston Hughes; copyright renewed © 1968 by Arna Bontemps and George Houston Bass.

Gelston Hinds, Jr.: "Grandma Ling" by Amy Ling. Copyright © 1980 by Amy Ling. Originally published as "Grandma" in *Bridge: An Asian American Perspective,* vol. 7, no. 3, 1980. Photo caption by Amy Ling. Copyright © 1997 by Amy Ling.

Judith Infante: "Sweater" by Alberto Forcada, translated by Judith Infante. Copyright © 1995 by Judith Infante.

Lenore Kandel: "Love in the Middle of the Air" from "Circus" from *Word Alchemy* by Lenore Kandel. Copyright © 1960, 1966, 1967 by Lenore Kandel.

Daniel Keyes: "Flowers for Algernon" (short story version) by Daniel Keyes from *The Magazine of Fantasy & Science Fiction.* Copyright © 1959, 1987 by Daniel Keyes. Book length paperback version published by Harvest Books. Companion book, *Algernon, Charlie and I: A Writer's Journey,* published by Challenge Press, Challcrest Books, Boca Raton, Florida.

The Heirs to the Estate of Martin Luther King, Jr., c/o Writers House, Inc. as agent for the proprietor: "I Have a Dream" by Martin Luther King, Jr. Copyright © 1963 by Martin Luther King, Jr.; copyright renewed © 1991 by Coretta Scott King.

Alfred A. Knopf, a division of Random House, Inc.: "The People Could Fly" from *The People Could Fly* by Virginia Hamilton. Copyright © 1985 by Virginia Hamilton. "I, Too" and "Refugee in America" from *Collected Poems of Langston Hughes.* Copyright © 1994 by The Estate of Langston Hughes. "Condition" from *All You Who Sleep Tonight* by Vikram Seth. Copyright © 1987, 1990 by Vikram Seth.

Barbara S. Kouts on behalf of Joseph Bruchac: "Birdfoot's Grampa" by Joseph Bruchac. Copyright © 1978 by Joseph Bruchac.

Little, Brown and Company, Inc.: "Ode to Thanks" from *Odes to Opposites* by Pablo Neruda. Copyright © 1995 by Pablo Neruda and Fundación Pablo Neruda; English translation copyright © 1995 by Ken Krabbenhoft; illustrations and compilation copyright © 1995 by Ferris Cook. Excerpt (retitled "Camp Harmony") from *Nisei Daughter* by Monica Sone. Copyright © 1953 and renewed © 1981 by Monica Sone.

Little Simon, an imprint of Simon & Schuster Children's Publishing Division: "The Old Grandfather and His Little Grandson" from *Twenty-two Russian Tales for Young Children by Leo Tolstoy,* translated by Miriam Morton. English translation copyright © 1969 by Miriam Morton.

Liveright Publishing Corporation: "who are you,little i" from *Complete Poems, 1904–1962* by E. E. Cummings, edited by George J. Firmage. Copyright © 1963, 1991 by the Trustees for the E. E. Cummings Trust.

McIntosh and Otis, Inc.: "Too Soon a Woman" by Dorothy M. Johnson from *Cosmopolitan,* March 1953. Copyright © 1953 and renewed © 1981 by Dorothy M. Johnson.

Merlyn's Pen, Inc.: "Ode to a Toad" by Anne-Marie Wulfsberg from *Merlyn's Pen,* April/May 1991. Copyright © 1991 by Anne-Marie Wulfsberg. First appeared in *Merlyn's Pen: Fiction, Essays, and Poems by America's Teens.* All rights reserved. "Walking with Living Feet" by Dara Horn from *Merlyn's Pen,* October/November 1993. Copyright © 1993 by Merlyn's Pen, Inc. First appeared in *Merlyn's Pen: The National Magazines of Student Writing.* All rights Reserved.

Microsoft Corporation: "Shiloh, Battle of" from *Microsoft® Encarta® Online Encyclopedia 2002,* accessed October 30, 2002, at http://encarta.msn.com. Copyright © 1997–2004 by Microsoft Corporation. All rights reserved.

National Geographic Society: From "Destination: Mars" from *National Geographic World,* January 2000. Copyright © 2000 by National Geographic Society.

Dwight Okita: "In Response to Executive Order 9066" from *Crossing with the Light* by Dwight Okita. Copyright © 1992 by Dwight Okita. Published by Tia Chucha Press, Chicago.

Orchard Books, an imprint of Scholastic, Inc.: "An Hour with Abuelo" from *An Island Like You: Stories of the Barrio* by Judith Ortiz Cofer. Copyright © 1995 by Judith Ortiz Cofer.

Teresa Palomo Acosta: "My Mother Pieced Quilts" by Teresa Palomo Acosta from *Festival de Flor y Canto: An Anthology of Chicano Literature,* edited by Alurista et al. Copyright © 1976 by El Centro Chicano, University of Southern California.

Plimoth Plantation, Plymouth, Massachusetts, www.plimoth.org: From "The History of Thanksgiving" (retitled "Thanksgiving: A Meal Without Forks and Other Feast Facts"). 2002.

Leroy V. Quintana: "Legacy II" by Leroy V. Quintana from *The Face of Poetry,* edited by LaVerne Harrell Clark and Mary MacArthur. Copyright © 1979 by Leroy V. Quintana.

Random House, Inc.: Excerpts (retitled "Mrs. Flowers") from *I Know Why the Caged Bird Sings* by Maya Angelou.Copyright © 1969 and renewed © 1997 by Maya Angelou. "Raymond's Run" and from "A Sort of Preface" from *Gorilla, My Love* by Toni Cade Bambara. Copyright © 1971, 1972 by Toni Cade Bambara. *The Diary of Anne Frank* by Albert Hackett, Frances Goodrich Hackett. Copyright © 1956 by Albert Hackett, Frances Goodrich Hackett, and Otto Frank. "My Parents" from *Collected Poems: 1928–1985* by Stephen Spender. Copyright 1934 and renewed © 1962 by Stephen Spender.

Random House Children's Books, a division of Random House, Inc.: From *Green Eggs and Ham* by Dr. Seuss. TM and © 1960 and renewed © 1988 by Dr. Seuss Enterprises, L.P.

Russell & Volkening as agents for Ann Petry: "Go On or Die" and "The Railroad Runs to Canada" from *Harriet Tubman: Conductor on the Underground Railroad* by Ann Petry. Copyright © 1955 and renewed © 1983 by Ann Petry.

Salon.com: From "Ray Bradbury is on fire!" by James Hibberd from *Salon.com* web site, accessed December 23, 2002, at http://dir.salon.com/people/feature/2001/08/29/bradbury/index.html?pn=2. Copyright © 2002 Salon Media Group, Inc.

Scribner, a division of Simon & Schuster: "Green Gulch" from *The Night Country* by Loren Eiseley. Copyright © 1971 by Loren Eiseley.

Estate of Robert Service: From *Ploughman of the Moon* by Robert Service.

Simon & Schuster Books for Young Readers, an imprint of Simon & Schuster Children's Publishing Division: Excerpt (retitled "In Trouble") from *Woodsong* by Gary Paulsen. Copyright © 1990 by Gary Paulsen.

Virginia Driving Hawk Sneve: "The Medicine Bag" by Virginia Driving Hawk Sneve. From "Something to Be Proud of" by Virginia Driving Hawk Sneve from *Akwe:kon Journal,* vol. 10, no. 1, Spring 1993. Copyright © 1993 by Akwe:kon Press.

Gary Soto: Comment on "Broken Chain" by Gary Soto. Copyright © 1997 by Gary Soto.

Studs Terkel: Liner notes by Studs Terkel from *Little Walter,* LP-1428. Published by Sheldon Recording Studios, Inc.

Times Books, a division of Random House, Inc.: From "John Lewis: Hand in Hand Together" (retitled "The Power of Nonviolence") from *From Camelot to Kent State* by Joan Morrison and Robert K. Morrison. Copyright © 1987 by Joan Morrison and Robert K. Morrison.

Jackie Torrence: "Brer Possum's Dilemma" by Jackie Torrence from *Homespun: Tales from America's Favorite Storytellers,* edited by Jimmie Neil Smith. Copyright © 1988 by Jackie Torrence. Quote by Jackie Torrence.

Manuel Ulacia: "La Palabra" from *El rio y la piedra valencia* by Manuel Ulacia, published by Pretextos, Mexico. Copyright © 1989 by Manuel Ulacia.

University of Arkansas Press: "Introduction to Poetry" from *The Apple that Astonished Paris* by Billy Collins. Copyright © 1998 by Billy Collins.

Special Collections, University Library, University of California, Riverside: From "Memorial and Recommendations of the Grand Council Fire of American Indians" presented to the Hon. William Hale Thompson, mayor of Chicago, December 1, 1927" from *Textbooks and the American Indian* by the American Indian Historical Society, written by Jeannette Henry, edited by Rupert Costo. Copyright © 1970 by the Indian Historian Press, Inc.

University of New Mexico Press: "The Circuit" by Francisco Jiménez from *Cuentos Chicanos: A Short Story Anthology* edited by Rodolfo A. Anaya and Antonio Marquez. Copyright © 1984 by the University of New Mexico Press. Published for *New America* by the University of New Mexico Press. Comment on "The Circuit" by Francisco Jiménez. Copyright © 1997 by Francisco Jiménez

University of Utah Press: "Riding Lesson" from *An Afternoon of Pocket Billards* by Henry Taylor. Copyright © 1975 by Henry Taylor.

Viking Penguin, A Division of Penguin Books for Young Readers, A Member of Penguin Group (USA) Inc.: From *Just Enough Is Plenty: A Hanukkah Tale* by Barbara Diamond Goldin. Copyright © 1988 by Barbara Diamond Goldin.

Webb School of Knoxville, Knoxville, Tennessee: "Maiden-Savin' Sam (Ballad)" by Jenny Ellison from *Webb of Words, 1992–93.* Copyright © 1992 by Mary Jennifer Ellison. Published by the students of the Middle School of Webb School of Knoxville, TN.

Krishna Winston, literary executor, Estate of Richard and Clara Winston: "A Tragedy Revealed: A Heroine's Last Days" by Ernst Schnabel, translated by Richard and Clara Winston from *Life,* vol. 45, no. 7, August 18, 1958. Copyright © 1958 by Time, Inc.; copyright renewed © 1986 by Justina Winston Gregory and Krishna Winston.

World Book, Inc.: From "Olympic Games" from *The World Book Encyclopedia.* Copyright © 2004 by World Book, Inc. www.worldbook.com.

Laurence Yep: "Ribbons" by Laurence Yep from *American Girl* magazine, January/February 1992. Copyright © 1992 by Laurence Yep. An expanded version of "Ribbons" was published by G.P. Putnam in 1996.

Sources Cited:

From *My Life* by Golda Meir. Published by Dell Publishing Co., Inc., New York, NY, 1975.

From "Waiting for the Hmmm" by Jim Murphy from *Children's Book Council* web site, accessed November 25, 2002, at www.cbcbooks.org/html/jim_murphy.html.

Old Italian story quoted by Elly Shodell from *Particles of the Past: Sandmining on Long Island, 1870's–1980's* by Elly Shodell. Published by Port Washington Public Library, Port Washington, NY, 1985.

Picture Credits

The illustrations and/or photographs on the Contents pages are picked up from pages in the textbook. Credits for those can be found either on the textbook page on which they appear or in the listing below.

Page **17**, © Ronnie Kaufman/CORBIS; **20**, © Donna Day/ ImageState; **23**, David Young-Wolff/PictureQuest; **34**, Sellmur/Cinema Rel. Corp. (Courtesy The Kobal Collection); **35**, Bob Daemmrich/Stock Boston; **38**, Movie Still Archives; **43**, Culver Pictures, Inc.; **44, 46**, Kirchoff/Wohlberg, Inc.; **47, 48**, Movie Still Archives; **49**, Kirchoff/Wohlberg, Inc.; **50**, Movie Still Archives; **52**, Culver Pictures, Inc.; **54, 58**, Kirchoff/Wohlberg, Inc.; **61**, Movie Still Archives; **63**, (top) AP/Wide World Photos; **70**, Benelux Press/PictureQuest; **80**, Syndicated Features Limited/The Image Works; **99**, Mary Evans Picture Library; **101**, (swan) © Jose Azel/ Aurora/PictureQuest, (leaves) © PhotoDisc/Getty Images; **103**, © Jim Richardson/CORBIS; **104**, © PhotoDisc/Getty Images; **106**, © Adam Woolfitt/Woodfin Camp/PictureQuest; **107**, © Beth Gwinn; **110–111**, David Scott/Index Stock Photography; **115**, Mansell/TimePix; **130**, (top, left) Illustration by Joe DiCesare from *Jackaroo* by Cynthia Voight. Illustration copyright © 1995 by Scholastic Inc. Reprinted by permission. (top, right) Cover Illustration © 1990 by Steve Brennan., (bottom, left) Cover illustration by Joe DiCesare from *The Bloody Country* by James Lincoln Collier and Christopher Collier. Copyright © 1985 by Scholastic Inc. Reprinted by permission., (bottom, right) From *Kit's Wilderness* (jacket cover) by David Almond. Used by permission of Random House Children's Books, a division of Random House, Inc.; **131**, (top, left) Cover from *Farewell to Manzanar* by Jeanne Wakatsuki Houston and James D. Houston with Connections, © HRW, photograph by Camelot/Photonica., (top, right) Used by permission of Grolier Publishing Company., (bottom, left) From *We Shall Not Be Moved: The Women's Factory Strike of 1909* by Joan Dash. Cover copyright © 1996 by Scholastic Inc. Reprinted by permission, Photo by Brown Brothers., (bottom, right) Used by permission of HarperCollins Publishers.; **137**, **138–139**, © Newell Convers Wyeth/ PicturesNow!; **140**, © Chuck Savage/CORBIS; **153**, Thomas Y. Crowell; **163, 164, 165**, © Christian Michaels; **169, 170**, Kirchoff/Wohlberg, Inc.; **170**, (inset), **171, 172**, Solomon D. Butcher Collection/Nebraska State Historical Society.; **173**, Branson Reynolds/Index Stock Photography.; **174**, Lacy's Studio, Whitefish, Montana. Reprinted by permission of McIntosh and Otis, Inc.; **177**, (top) © Bettmann/CORBIS, (bottom, center) © David Muench/CORBIS, (bottom, right) © Archivo Iconografico S.A./CORBIS, (bottom, left) © COR-BIS, (right, center) © Bettmann/CORBIS; **178**, © Bettmann/ CORBIS; **178–179, 179**, © Arthur Rothstein/CORBIS; **180**, (top) © CORBIS, (bottom) Art Today; **181**, Artville; **182**, (top/bottom, right) © Academy of Natural Science of Philadelphia/CORBIS, (bottom, left) © CORBIS; **184**, © Tony Roberts/CORBIS; **186–187**, Pheobe Beasley. Courtesy of the artist.; **187**, Art Resource, NY; **188–189**, Pheobe Beasley. Courtesy of the artist.; **190**, AP/Wide World Photos; **192, 193** Pheobe Beasley. Courtesy of the artist.; **195**, © Tria Giovan/CORBIS; **196**, © Medford Historical Society Collection/CORBIS; **197**, (photo) Culver Pictures; **197**, (frame) © Bettmann/CORBIS; **198–199, 200**, © Bettmann/ CORBIS; **201**, (bottom) © Tria Giovan/CORBIS, (top)

© Arthur Cohen Photography/Scholastic Press; **209**, (blossoms) © George Lepp/CORBIS, (top) Culver Pictures; **210**, © David Muench/CORBIS; **211**, © Bassouls Sophie/CORBIS Sygma; **214–215**, © Joe McDonald/CORBIS; **216**, © Joseph Giannetti, Stock Boston/PictureQuest, (background) © PhotoDisc; **217**, (bottom) © Miriam Berkley, (top) From the Collections of the University of Pennsylvania Archives; **232** (top, left) Cover from *Bud, Not Buddy* by Christopher Paul Curtis with Connections, © HRW; Cover art by John Hull., (top, right) © Cover art Joe Curcio, (bottom, left) *North by Night* (jacket cover) by Katherine Ayres. Used by permission of Random House Children's Books, a division of Random House, Inc., (bottom, right) Cover from *The Glory Field* by Walter Dean Myers with Connections, © HRW.; **233**, (top, left) Cover from *The Boys' War* by Jim Murphy. Copyright © 1990 by Jim Murphy. Reprinted by permission of Clarion Books/Houghton Mifflin Company. All rights reserved. Cover photo courtesy of the Library of Congress., (top, right) Cover from *Behind Rebel Lines: The Incredible Story of Emma Edmonds, Civil War Spy,* by Seymour Simon, illustration copyright © by Darrel Milsap, reprinted by permission of Harcourt, Inc., (bottom, left) *North Star to Freedom, The Story of the Underground Railroad* by Gena K. Gorrell. Used by permission of Random House Children's Books, a division of Random House, Inc., (bottom, right) Jacket photo depicting Princess Ka'iulani courtesy of the Bernice P. Bishop Museum, Wm. B. Eerdmans Publishing Company.; **234–235**, © Scala/Art Resource, NY; **239, 240**, © CORBIS; **241**, © Dinodia Photo Library; **242–243, 243**, © CORBIS; **244–245**, © Carlos Adolfo Sastoque N./SuperStock; **246–247**, © CORBIS; **248**, © Lawrence Migdale/Stock, Boston Inc./PictureQuest; **258**, copyright Ruth Wright Paulsen; **261**, (left) © PhotoDisc/Getty Images, (top, right and bottom, right) © Layne Kennedy/CORBIS; **262**, © Layne Kennedy/CORBIS; **264**, (top) Pat O'Hara/CORBIS, (center) © YannArthus-Bertrand/CORBIS, (bottom) © Staffan Widstrand/CORBIS; **272**, Syndicated Features Limited/The Image Works; **273**, Kimberly Swift; **275**, National Geographic Society. Artwork © David B. Mattingly; **277**, (bottom) © Roger Ressmeyer/CORBIS; **278**, (top) Chip Simons Photography, (bottom left) © CORBIS, (bottom, right) © Reuters NewMedia/CORBIS, (background) © Roger Ressmeyer/CORBIS; **280–281**, Mark Richards/PhotoEdit; **282–283**, © PhotoDisc/Getty Images; **284**, Bob LeRoy/Index Stock Imagery; **286**, Charles Barry/ Santa Clara University, Santa Clara, CA.; **288**, © David Young-Wolff; **289**, (top) TIME Magazine, copyright TIME Inc./TimePix, (bottom) © Bettmann/CORBIS; **290**, (top) Arthur Schatz/TimePix, (bottom) © Bettmann/CORBIS; **290–291**, (background) Kirchoff/Wohlberg, Inc.; **291**, (top and center) © Bettmann/CORBIS, (bottom) UFW; **294**, © PhotoDisc/Getty Images; **295**, Bob LeRoy/Index Stock Imagery; **297**, AP/Wide World Photos; **299**, © Bassouls Sophie/CORBIS Sygma, (background) © Denis Scott/CORBIS; **300**, © Bettmann/CORBIS; **301**, © AP Photo/Mark Lennihan; **302**, © Douglas Kirkland/CORBIS; **303**, © Christie's Images/

CORBIS; **304,** Christie's Images/The Bridgeman Art Library; **307,** Mary Evans Picture Library; **308,** © David Forbert/SuperStock; **311,** © Lauros/Giraudon/The Bridgeman Art Library; **312–317,** From *The Ray Bradbury Chronicles, 1.* A Byron Preiss Book; **319,** © Guy Edwardes/Taxi/Getty Images; **320,** © Tony Freeman/PhotoEdit/PictureQuest; **320–321,** (bottom) © Lawson Wood/CORBIS; **322–323,** © Taxi/Getty Images; **326,** © CORBIS Images/PictureQuest; **327,** © Taxi/Getty Images; **328,** © Edward Cross/photolibrary/PictureQuest; **330,** From *The Ray Bradbury Chronicles, 1.* A Byron Preiss Book; **331,** © Frank Hurley/Royal Geographic Society, London.; **333,** Ortelius Design, Inc.; **334,** © Underwood & Underwood/CORBIS; **336,** © Frank Hurley/Royal Geographic Society, London.; **337,** © Emma Dodge Hanson; **350,** (top, left) Cover illustration copyright © 1992 by Richard Williams., (top, right) Cover from *The Call of the Wild* by Jack London with Connections, © HRW; illustration by Jerry Dadds/Deborah Wolfe Ltd., (bottom, left) Cover by Derek James, (bottom, right) *Purely Rosie Pearl* (jacket cover) by Patricia A. Cochrane. Used by permission of Random House Children's Books, a division of Random House, Inc.; **351,** (top, left) Cover, from *Travels with Charley* by John Steinbeck, copyright © 1961, 1962 by The Curtis Publishing Co., © 1962 by John Steinbeck, renewed © 1990 by Elaine Steinbeck, Thom Steinbeck, and John Steinbeck IV. Used by permission of Viking Penguin, a division of Penguin Group (USA) Inc., (top, right) Copyright Mankind/Holloway House Publishing Group, Los Angeles, CA., (bottom, left) L. Tom Perry Special Collections, Harold B. Lee Library, Brigham Young University, Provo, Utah., (bottom, right) Used by permission of HarperCollins Publishers.; **357,** From *The People Could Fly* by Virginia Hamilton, illustrated by Leo and Diane Dillon. Illustrations copyright © 1985 by Leo and Diane Dillon. Used by permission of Alfred A. Knopf, an imprint of Random House Children's Books, a division of Random House, Inc., (background) © Getty Images; **358, 361,** From *The People Could Fly* by Virginia Hamilton, illustrated by Leo and Diane Dillon. Illustrations copyright © 1985 by Leo and Diane Dillon. Used by permission of Alfred A. Knopf, an imprint of Random House Children's Books, a division of Random House, Inc.; **362,** Bruce Crippen; **366,** GEO Systems; **367,** (top, left and middle, left) © Anne Frank Fonds Basel/Anne Frank House/Getty Images, (right) Library of Congress; **368,** (right) © Bettmann/CORBIS; **369,** (inset) Movie Still Archives, (top and bottom) © Anne Frank Fonds Basel/Anne Frank House/Getty Images; **370,** Al Florentino; **372,** © Anne Frank Fonds Basel/Anne Frank House/Getty Images; **374, 377,** © Joan Marcus; **378,** © Anne Frank Fonds Basel/Anne Frank House/Getty Images; **380,** © Joan Marcus; **383, 386,** © Anne Frank Fonds Basel/Anne Frank House/Getty Images; **388,** © Joan Marcus; **391,** © Anne Frank Fonds Basel/Anne Frank House/Getty Images; **396,** National Archives, Washington, D.C.; **397, 399, 402,** © Joan Marcus; **407,** © Anne Frank Fonds Basel/Anne Frank House/Getty Images; **409,** © Joan Marcus; **411,** Trustees of the Imperial War Museum, London; **413, 421,** © Anne Frank Fonds Basel/Anne Frank House/Getty Images; **423,** © Joan Marcus; **427,** © Anne Frank Fonds Basel/Anne Frank House/Getty Images; **432,** © Joan Marcus; **434,** © Anne Frank Fonds Basel/Anne Frank House/Getty Images; **435,** © Bettmann/CORBIS; **439, 440–441,** © Anne Frank Fonds Basel/Anne Frank House/Getty Images; **443,** GEO Systems; **445,** Fotodienst, Utrecht, The Netherlands.; **449,** © Anne Frank Fonds Basel/Anne

Frank House/Getty Images; **454,** Brown Brothers; **457,** © Anne Frank Fonds Basel/Anne Frank House/Getty Images; **459,** Loomis Dean/TimePix; **462,** Netherlands Institute for War Documentation, Amsterdam, The Netherlands.; **463,** © M. Angelo/CORBIS; **464–465,** Photo used with permission from the U.S. Holocaust Memorial Museum, Washington, D.C.; **469,** © Museum of History and Industry/CORBIS; **471,** © Lawrence Migdale; **473,** © PhotoDisc/Getty Images; **474,** Courtesy of Monica Sone; **475,** © Ron Krisel/Getty Images; **476,** Photo courtesy of Dwight Okita; **478,** Alison J. Wright/Stock Boston; **480,** © H. Mark Weidman; **481,** Library of Congress; **483,** Don Uhrbrock/TimePix; **484,** © CORBIS; **485,** (top) Bob Fitch/BlackStar Picture Collection, (bottom, left) © Flip Schulke/CORBIS, (bottom, right) © Bettmann/CORBIS; **489,** (top) © CORBIS, (bottom) © Bettmann/CORBIS, (background) Matt Heron/Black Star Picture Collection; **490,** (top, left) Grey Villet/TimePix, (bottom, right and background.) Matt Heron/Black Star Picture Collection; **493,** © Bill Ross/CORBIS; **494,** (bottom) © Bettmann/CORBIS, (top) © Picture History; **497,** Yale Collection of American Literature, Beinecke Rare Book and Manuscript Library, Yale University, New Haven, CT. Photo by Carl Van Vechten, used with permission of the Van Vechten Estate.; **499,** © CORBIS; **500,** Michael Heron/Woodfin Camp & Associates; **501,** Kjell B. Snadved/Photo Researchers, Inc.; **501,** © Getty Images; **504,** (top, left) Culver Pictures, Inc., (center, left and bottom, left) By permission of the Watchorn Memorial Methodist Church, Alfreton, Derbyshire, England, (bottom, right) The American Jewish Joint Distribution Committee, Inc.; **504–505,** (photo left, background) Culver Pictures, Inc., (background) © Harcourt Index; **505,** (top) Brown Brothers, (bottom) Culver Pictures, Inc.; **506–507,** © Gary Brettnacher/Getty Images; **508,** (top, right) © Jonathan Kirn, (bottom, left) © Trevor Wood/Getty Images; **509,** (top, left) © Steve Leonard, (right) CORBIS; **510,** Overseas/© Envision; **511,** (left) ART WOLFE/ WWW.ARTWOLFE.COM, (right) Rene Burri/Magnum Photos, Inc.; **512,** George Holton/Photo Researchers, Inc.; **514,** Jeff Greenberg/Photo Researchers, Inc.; **515,** Tobe/Franklin Watts; **526,** (top, left) Cover from *The Clay Marble* by Minfong Ho with Connections, © HRW; illustration by Terry Hoff/Freda Scott Represents., (top, right) Cover from *Goodbye, Vietnam* by Gloria Whelan with Connections, © HRW; Postcard © Cameramann International, LTD; Rice field photo © Cliff Hollenbeck/International Stock., (bottom, left) *Tunes for Bears to Dance To* (jacket cover) by Robert Cormier. Used by permission of Dell Publishing, a division of Random House, Inc., (bottom, right) *Number the Stars* (jacket cover) by Lois Lowry. Used by permission of Random House Children's Books, a division of Random House, Inc.; **527,** (top, left) National Archives photo no. 210-G2C-160, (top, right) Cover art by George Pratt, (bottom, left) Used by permission of HarperCollins Publishers. Cover photo: Gerhard Gronefeld/Black Star., (bottom, right) Cover Art Copyright © 1990 by Sergio Giovine. Cover copyright © 1990 by HarperCollins Publishers; **528–529,** Art Resource, NY; **539–540, 541–542,** Culver Pictures, Inc.; **543,** © Bettmann/CORBIS; **545,** © Francesco Muntada/CORBIS; **547,** Kirchoff/Wohlberg, Inc.; **548, 549, 550, 552, 554,** Debra LaCappola and Charles Meier; **555,** Joyce Middler; **557,** © PhotoDisc, Inc./Getty Images; **558,** Copyright Vanni/Art Resource, NY; **559,** © Dimitri Lundt/TempSport/CORBIS; **560,** © Gianni Dagli Orti/CORBIS; **563,** (left, top & center) Tom Ridley/DK Images, (left, second & fourth fr.

top) © M. Angelo/CORBIS; (left, bottom) © PhotoDisc/Getty Images, (top) © Bettmann/CORBIS; **564,** (top) © M. Angelo/CORBIS; (2nd fr. top, 3rd, & last) © PhotoDisc/Getty Images; **565,** © Tony Arruza/CORBIS; **566,** (top) Courtesy of Teresa Palomo Acosta, (clockwise fr. bottom) © PhotoDisc/Getty Images, © M. Angelo/CORBIS, Tom Ridley/DK Images, © M. Angelo/CORBIS; **569,** © PhotoDisc/Getty Images; **570,** © Philadelphia Museum of Art/CORBIS; **574,** © PhotoDisc/Getty Images; **575,** From *The Tales of Uncle Remus: The Adventures of Brer Rabbit* as told by Julius Lester, illustrated by Jerry Pinkney. Dial Books, New York, art © 1987 by Jerry Pinkney.; **577,** (top) AP/Wide World Photos, (bottom) Courtesy of Davis Mather Folk Art Gallery, Santa Fe, NM.; **594,** Greensboro Historical Museum, Inc., Greensboro, NC.; **597,** Collection of the Charles E. and Eugenia C. Shannon Trust, Montgomery, AL.; **599,** Collection Charles Shannon, Montgomery, AL. Metropolitan Museum of Art, promised gift of Charles and Eugenia Shannon., photo by Irene Young; **612,** (top, left) © 1999 Smithsonian Institution. Hopi Pahlikmana (butterfly) Katsina Tihu (doll). Oraibi, Arizona. Photo by David Heald., (top, right) Jacket cover by Neil Waldman from *The Friends* by Rosa Guy. Used by permission of Bantam Books, a division of Random House, Inc., (bottom, left) From *Out of the Dust* by Karen Hesse. Published by Scholastic Press, a division of Scholastic Inc. Jacket illustration copyright © 1997 by Scholastic Inc. Used by permission. Jacket photograph courtesy of the Library of Congress Prints and Photographs Division, Farm Security Administration Collection., (bottom, right) Cover from *Hatchet* by Gary Paulsen with Connections, © HRW; illustration by Bill Schmidt/Hankins & Tebenborg LTD.; **613,** (top, left) Jacket illustration by Marc Tauss from *Black Hands, White Sails: The Story of African-American Whalers* by Patricia C. McKissack and Frederick L. McKissack. Published by Scholastic Press, a division of Scholastic Inc. Illustration copyright © 1999 by Scholastic Inc. Used by permission., (top, right) From *To Be a Slave* by Julius Lester, illustrated by Tom Feelings, copyright © 1968 by Tom Feelings, illustrations. Used by permission of Dial Books for Young Readers, A division of Penguin Young Readers Group, A Member of Penguin Group (USA) Inc., 345 Hudson St., New York, NY 10014. All right reserved., (bottom, left) Cover from *Babe Didrikson Zaharias: The Making of a Champion* by Russell Freedman. Copyright © 1999 by Russell Freedman. Reprinted by permission of Clarion Books/Houghton Mifflin Company. All rights reserved., (bottom, right) *The Story of My Life* (Bantam jacket cover) by Helen Keller. Used by permission of Bantam Books, a division of Random House, Inc.; **618,** © 1991 Reprinted courtesy of Bunny Hoest and Parade Magazine.; **620–621,** © Steve McDonough/CORBIS; **623,** (bottom) © Christopher Felver/CORBIS, (top) American University Publications; **625,** © PhotoDisc/Getty Images; **626,** © 1998 James McGoon; **627,** © PhotoDisc, Inc./Getty Images; **629–630,** © Paul Hurd/Getty Images; **631,** Private collection/Courtesy of Barbara Olsen.; **632,** © PhotoDisc/Getty Images; **637, 640,** Illustrations from "The Cremation of Sam McGee" by Robert W. Service and illustrated by Ted Harrison used by permission of Kids Can Press, Ltd., Toronto, Canada. Illustrations copyright © 1986 by Ted Harrison. Available in the United States through Greenwillow.; **642,** AP/Wide World Photos; **643,** The Bridgeman Art Library; **644,** © PhotoDisc/Getty Images; **646,** Illustrations from "The Cremation of Sam McGee" by Robert W. Service and illustrated by Ted Harrison used by

permission of Kids Can Press, Ltd., Toronto, Canada. Illustration copyright © 1986 by Ted Harrison. Available in the United States through Greenwillow.; **647,** Copyright The British Museum, London.; **649,** Lee Bolton; **649,** © Erich Lessing/Art Resource, NY; **650,** (right) © Richard Fukuhara/CORBIS; **652,** Courtesy of the Harvard University Archives.; **653,** Photo by Eirik Irgens Johnsen; **654,** United States Postal Service; **655,** © 2003 David Madison Sports Images, Inc.; **656,** United States Postal Service; **658,** © Orion Press/Black Sheep; **659,** (top and bottom) Jerry Jacka Photography, (top, right) Copyright Werner Forman/Art Resource, NY; **660,** (top) AP/Wide World Photos, (bottom) Photo by Michael Greenlar; **662,** © Orion Press/Black Sheep; **663,** The Bridgeman Art Library; **665,** AP/Wide World Photos; **666,** © Bettmann/CORBIS, (frame) © Dave Teel/CORBIS; **667,** © Frans Lanting, Inc.; **668,** Mansell/TimePix; **668,** Thomas D. McAvoy/TImePix; **669,** The National Museum of Health and Medicine, Armed Forces Institute of Pathology; **672,** Yale Collection of American Literature, Beinecke Rare Book and Manuscript Library, Yale University, New Haven, CT. Photo by Carl Van Vechten, used with permission of the Van Vechten Estate.; **675,** Robert W. Kelley/TimePix; **678,** © Alamy Images; **680,** Amy Ling; **683,** © LaVerne Harrell Clark; **686, 687,** Harcourt Brace & Company: "The Naming of Cats" and illustrations from *Old Possum's Book of Practical Cats* by T. S. Eliot, illustrated by Edward Gorey. Copyright 1939 by T. S. Eliot; copyright renewed © 1967 by Esme Valerie Eliot. Illustrations copyright © 1982 by Edward Gorey.; **688,** © Michael Newman/PhotoEdit, Inc.; **700,** (top, left) Little, Brown and Company, (top, right) Cover Page of *In the Eyes of the Cat: Japanese Poetry for All Seasons* selected and illustrated by Demi, translated by Tze-si Huang. Translation copyright © 1992 by Tze-si Huang. Reprinted by permission of Henry Holt and Company, LLC., (bottom, left) Cover from *Rainbows Are Made* by Carl Sandburg, illustration copyright © 1982 by Fritz Eichenberg, used with permission of Harcourt, Inc., (bottom, right) Cover painting by Leticia Tarrago; **701,** (top, left) Cover from *The Harlem Renaissance.* Cover painting: Barbecue (1934) by Archibald Motley, courtesy of Howard University Gallery of Art, Washington, D.C., (top, right) *A Great and Glorious Game: Baseball Writings of A. Bartlett Giamatti,* edited by Kenneth S. Robson. Copyright © 1998 by the author. Reprinted by permission of Algonquin Books of Chapel Hill, a division of Workman Publishing., (bottom, left) Cover from *Lincoln: A Photobiography* by Russell Freedman. Copyright © 1987 by Russell Freedman. Reprinted by permission of Clarion Books/Houghton Mifflin Company. All rights reserved., (bottom, right) From *A Nation Torn* by Delia Ray, copyright © 1990 by Laing Communications. Used by permission of Lodestar Books, an affiliate of Dutton Children's Books, A division of Penguin Young Readers Group, A Member of Penquin Group (USA) Inc., 345 Hudson St., New York, NY 10014. All rights reserved.; **707,** © Ivan Massar/Black Star Publishing/PictureQuest; **707,** © Richard T. Nowitz/CORBIS; **708–709,** © Stone/Getty Images; **712,** © Donald C. Johnson/CORBIS; **713,** ZEFA Zeitgeist/Photonica; **714,** Wilhelm Scholz/Photonica; **715,** © Jim Erickson/CORBIS; **716,** Tony Hutchings/© Getty Images; **719,** The Bridgeman Art Library; **720,** © Peter Beck/CORBIS; **721,** Rick Browne; **725,** © Christie's Images/SuperStock; **728,** © SuperStock; **739,** Ken Petretti/Bantam Doubleday Dell; **743,** © Bettmann/CORBIS; **744,** David Redfern/Retna; **746,** (bottom) © Bettmann/CORBIS; (top) © Ray Flerlage/

Illustrations

Index of Skills

The boldface page numbers indicate an extensive treatment of a subject.

LITERARY SKILLS

Actions, 142
Alliteration, 617, 645, 670, 859
Allusion, 166, **482,** 486, **546,** 556, 859
Analogy, 466, 525, **557,** 859
Anecdote, 859
Antagonist, 859
Approximate rhyme, **617**
Assonance, **617,** 859
Atmosphere, 859–860
Author, 311, 329, 654, 674, 860
    study, **298**
Autobiography, 191, 227
Background, writer's, **729,** 740
Ballad, **618, 636,** 645
Belief, 791
Big moments, 355
Biographical approach, **729**
Biography, **142,** 860
Cause and effect, 192, 785
Causes, 259, 346
Character, 14, 26, **134–135,** 154, **162, 185,** 191, 227, 298, 395, 410, 860
    in biography, **142**
    dynamic, 410
    main, 311, 329, 654, 774
    motivation, **135,** 142, **169,** 175, 544
    profile chart, 135
    setting as, **265,** 273
    theme and, 354
Characterization, **134–135,** 860
    comparing, **439**
    direct, **134**
    indirect, **134–135**
Chronological account, 460
Chronological order, **265,** 273, 346, 860–861
Cliché, 795
Climax, **2,** 14, 81, 98, 99, 125, 327, 329, 436, 544, 740, **758,** 861
Comedy, 861
Comic language, **574**
Comparing, 439, 677, 758
Comparing and contrasting
    characters, 395, 437
    Venn diagram, 437
Comparing literature, 84, 194, 492, 574, 677, 758
    historical comparison chart, 202, 212, 213
    humor comparison chart, 578, 595
    literature comparison chart, 202, 212, 213, 495, 498, 502, 578, 595, 772, 780
    moments-of-recognition
    comparison chart, 772, 780
    story comparison chart, 100, 108

Complications, **2,** 14, 94, 758
Conclusions, 346
Conflict, **2,** 14, **16,** 64, 97, 99, 105, 175, 236, 298, 307, 311, 327, 329, 395, 436, 556, 654, 722, **758,** 765, 861
    external, **16,** 26, 758
    internal, **16,** 26, 758, 762, 770
Connotation, 861
Context clues, 32, 50, 227
Contrasting, 439, 677, 758
Couplet, **617,** 662, 861
Cross-cultural themes, **747**
Customs, 236
Description, 861–862
Dialect, **532, 546,** 556, 609, 862
Dialogue, 862
Diction, 862
Drama, 862
Dramatic irony, 442, **532, 536,** 544
Dynamic character, 410
Effects, 259, 292
Elegy, 616, 669, 863
End rhyme, **617**
Epic, **618, 647,** 863
    hero, 653
    mock, 653
Epic hero, 653
Epilogue, **753,** 757, 863
Essay, 863
Exact rhyme, **617**
Exaggeration, **574, 636,** 646, 863
Exposition, 758, 774, 863
Extended metaphor, **531,** 669
External conflict, **16,** 26, 758
Fable, 863
Facts, 154
Factual reporting, **443**
Fiction, 864
Figures of speech, 206, **530–532, 569,** 609, 670, 864
    metaphors, 306, 330, **531,** 569, 619, 627, 653, 669
    personification, 273, **531,** 567, 569, 572, 627, 653
    similes, 323, **531,** 569, 572, 627, 653
    symbols, **531, 562,** 567, 609
Flashback, 118, 395, 864
Folk tale, 864
Foreshadowing, **71,** 81, 89, 321, 544, 595, 864
Free verse, **617, 670,** 673, 864
Generalizations, **298,** 330, **468,** 477
Graphic organizers
    character profile chart, 135
    cluster map, 482
    historical comparison chart, 202, 212, 213
    humor comparison chart, 578, 595
    literature comparison chart, 202, 212, 213, 495, 498, 502, 578, 595, 772, 780

message response chart, 311, 318, 329
moments-of-recognition
    comparison chart, 772, 780
outline, 202
plot diagram, 3, 81, 578, 595, 740
poetry comparison chart, 681, 684
Somebody Wanted But So chart, 318
story comparison chart, 100, 108
story map, 3, 81, 100, 175, 595, 722, 772, 780
theme comparison chart, 495, 498, 502
time line, 287
Venn diagram, 437
writer profile chart, 705
Graphic story, **330**
Heritage, writer's, 791
Historical fiction, **194,** 865
Humor, **574**
    comic language, **574**
    comparing, **596**
    comparison chart, 578, 595
    exaggeration, **574, 636,** 646
    situational irony, **574**
    understatement, **574**
    verbal irony, **574**
Iambic pentameter, **662,** 865
Idioms, 751, 865
Imagery, 203, 305, **532,** 670, 681, 865
Independent Reading, 13, 25, 63, 80, 107, 130, 153, 232, 258, 272, 337, 350, 435, 526, 543, 555, 577, 594, 612, 626, 642, 700, 721, 739, 750, 779, 796, 842
Inferences, **142,** 154, 166, **238,** 239, 248–249, 259, 273, **280,** 346, 567, 595
Internal conflict, **16,** 26, 758, 762, 770
Internal rhyme, **617,** 645
Introduction, 758, 774
Inversion, 865
Irony, 154, **532, 536,** 780, 865
    dramatic, 442, **532, 536,** 544, 866
    situational, **532, 536, 574,** 609, 865
    verbal, **532, 536, 574,** 609, 751, 865
Judgments, **546,** 556
Key passages, 443
Key statements, 443
Legend, 866
Limerick, 866
Literary criticism
    biographical approach, **729**
    imagination and fiction, **705**
    writer profile chart, 705
    writers' experience and fiction, **704–705**
Literary devices, 866
Lyric poetry, **618, 624,** 866

Main characters, 311, 329, 654, 774
Main events, 654
    time line, 287
Main idea, **185**, 191, 227, **443**, 460, 695, 697
Message, 125, **298**, 311, 318, 328, 329, 330
    response chart, 311, 318, 329
Metamorphosis, 866
Metaphor, 306, 330, **531**, 569, 619, 627, 653, 669, 866
    extended, 669
Meter, **616**, **628**, 635, 867
Mock epic, 653
Mock-heroic stories, **647**
Moment of recognition, **758**
    comparison chart, 772, 780
Mood, **237**, 250, 346, 410, 544, 867
Motif, **84**, 867
Motivation, **135**, 142, **169**, 175, 544, 606, 867
Motives, 135
Myth, 868
Narrative form, 191, **803**, 868
Narrative poetry, 166, **618**, **628**, 635, 868
Narrator, **536**, 544
Nonfiction, 868
Novel, 868
Objective writing, 868
Ode, **618**, **657**, 661, 868
Onomatopoeia, **618**, 670, 868
Parallel episodes, **3**, **32**, 64, 125, 869
Pentameter, **662**
Personification, 273, **531**, 567, 569, 572, 627, 653, 869
Persuasion, 869
Place, 236
Playwright, 869
Plot, **2–3**,16, 26, 100, 250, 298, 740, **758**, 869
    climax, **2**,125, 740, **758**
    complications, **2**, 758
    conflict, **2**, **758**
    diagram, 3, 81, 578, 595, 740
    exposition, 758
    moment of recognition, **758**
    parallel episodes **3**, **32**, 64, 125
    resolution, **2**, 740, 758
    Somebody Wanted But So chart, 318
    story map, 3, 81, 100, 175, 595, 722, 772, 780
    subplots, **3**
Poetry, **616–618**, 694, 870
    alliteration, **617**, 645, 670
    assonance, **617**
    ballad, **618**, **636**, 645
    comparison chart, 681, 684
    couplet, **617**, 662
    elegy, 616, 669
    epic, **618**, **647**
    extended metaphor, 669
    figures of speech, **569**, 670
    free verse, **617**, **670**, 673
    iambic pentameter, **662**
    imagery, 670, 681
    lyric, **618**, **624**

main idea, 695
metaphor, **569**, 619, 627, 653, 669
meter, **616**, **628**, 635
mock-heroic stories, **647**
narrative, 166, **618**, **628**, 635
ode, **618**, **657**, 661
onomatopoeia, **618**, 670
personification, 567, **569**, 572, 627, 653
rhyme, **616–617**, 619
rhythm, **616**, 619, **628**, 669, 670, 673
simile, **569**, 619, 627, 653
sonnet, **618**, **662**
symbol, **562**, 567
title, 619
    See also Rhyme.
Point of view, 64, 870
Predicting, **71**, 81, 395, 410
Primary source, 154, 364
Problems, 654
Prose, 870
Protagonist, 870
Pun, 870
Purpose, 460
Quest, 329
Recurring theme, **355**, 468
Refrain, **479**, 486, 669, 871
Resolution, **2**, 14, 64, 81, 125, 654, 740, 758
    theme and, 355, 871
Reversal, 410
Rhyme, **616–617**, 619
    approximate, **617**
    couplet, **617**
    end, **617**
    exact, **617**
    internal, **617**, 645
    See also Poetry.
Rhythm, **616**, 619, **628**, 669, 670, 673, 871
Satire, 872
Setting, **236–237**, 250, 259, 273, 280, 287, 298, 311, 320, 329, 346, 653, 707, 872
    as character, **265**, 273
    as conflict, **236**
    customs, 236
    mood, **237**, 250, 346
    place, 236
    role in plot, 250
    time, 236
    tone, 237, **280**, 287
Short story, 872
Simile, 323, **531**, 569, 572, 627, 653, 872
Situational irony, **532**, 536, **574**, 609
Sonnet, **618**, **662**, 873
    English, or Shakespearean, **662**
    Italian, or Petrarchan, **662**
Speaker, 707, **711**, 722, 873
Stanza, 873
Stereotype, 502, 873
Story, **84**
    comparison chart, 100, 108
Style, **530–532**, 873
    allusions, **546**
    dialect, **532**, **546**

figures of speech, **530–532**
imagery, **532**
irony, **532**
Subjective writing, 873
Subplot, **3**, 26, **32**, 64, 873
Summary, 477
    Somebody Wanted But So chart, 318
Suspense, 86, 873
Symbol, **531**, **562**, 567, 609, 873
Tall tale, 636, 874
Theme, **354–356**, **364**, 436, 468, 477, 486, **492**, 523, 654, **677**, **747**, 751, 874
    big moments and, 355
    characters and, 354
    comparison chart, 495, 498, 502
    cross-cultural, **747**
    recurring, **355**, 468
    resolution and, 355
    title and, 354
Title, 26, 31, 175, 287, 311, 329, 654
    theme and, 354
Time, 236
Tone, 127, 129, 229, 237, **280**, 287, 709, 874
Traditions, 791
Tragedy, 874
Trickster tales, 578, 595
Underlying meanings, 656, 697
Understatement, **574**, 874
Verbal irony, **532**, 536, **574**, 609, 751
Writer's background, **729**, 740

INFORMATIONAL READING SKILLS

Advertisement, **819**, 824, 827
    elements, 819, 827
    features, 819, 827
Analogy, 466, 875
Analyzing proposition and support, **29**, **67**
Anecdotes, 67
Attitude, 69
Author, 654, 674
Biased treatment, 178
Broad scope, 178
Caption, 275
Cause and effect, 156, 292, 654, 724, 875
    chart, 292
    false, **533**, 535
Causes, 292, 724
Chronological order, 156, **724**, 742, 876
Closing statement, 29
Coherence, **742–743**, 745, 793, 876
Comparing, 261, 263, 742
Comparing texts, **178**
Comparison and contrast, 156, **261**, 820, 877
    chart, 263
    Venn diagram, 261
Conclusions, 127, **294**, 296, 877
    valid, 294
Conflict, 654

opinions from experts as, 67
reasons, 29, 67
statistics as, 67
Supported inferences, **558**, 561
Supporting details, **462**, 674
Surge protector, 834
Symbol, 466
Technical directions, **801, 802, 828**
for basic functions, 828
for computers, 828–833
for connecting keyboard and mouse, 833
for connecting monitor, 832
for connecting phone line and modem, 833
for connecting power cords, 833
for connecting printer, 833
for CPU, 829
for hardware, 829
for input devices, 829
for Internet, 831
for memory, 830
for modems, 830
for output devices, 830
Text structure, **156**, 193, **724, 727**
cause and effect, 156, **724**
chronological order, 156, **724**
comparison and contrast, 156
enumeration or sequence, 156
logical order, **724, 727**
of magazines, **275**
order of importance, **724**
unity in, **724, 727**
Theme, 654, 656
Title, 275, 654, 674
Tone, 127, 183, 229
Topic, 674
Transitional words, **742**
for chronological connections, 742
for comparing, 742
for contrasting, 742
for order-of-importance connections, 742
for spatial connections, 742
Treatment of ideas, **178**
biased, 178
objective, 178
Underlying meaning, 656, 697
Unity, **724**, 727, 793
Unsupported inferences, **558**, 561
Valid conclusions, 294
Warranty, **801, 802, 823**, 826, 827
elements, **823**
features, **823**
Web sources
evaluating, 979
Workplace documents, **800**
communication, **800**
instruction, **800**
World Wide Web, 978

VOCABULARY SKILLS

Analogy, 466, 525, **557**
Antonyms, 192
British English, **82**
Cause and effect, 192

Comparison, 438
Connotations, **461**
Context, 192, 728, 741
Context clues, **192, 264,** 347, 467, 728, 762, 791
antonyms, 192
cause and effect, 192
chart, 264
definitions and restatements, 192
examples, 192
multiple meanings, 297
synonyms, 192
Definitions, 70, 192
Denotation, 461
Derivation, 66, **184**
Examples, 192, 723
Etymology, 66, 70
word map for, 66
Figures of speech, 545, **557**
analogy, **557**
metaphor, 557
simile, 557
Graphic organizers
context clues chart, 264
Spanish word chart, 293
time line, 186
word map, 66, 70
word tree, 155
History of the English language, **65–66, 155, 167, 176**
time line, 176
Homographs, **260**
Homophones, **260**
Idioms, **746, 752**
Indo-European roots, **167**
Latin roots, **27–28, 155, 160**
Latin words, **155, 160**
Old English, **65**, 176
Metaphor, 525, 557 **568, 573**
Middle English, **65**, 176
Modern English, 65, **66**, 176
Multiple-meaning words, 128, 167, 297, 524, 698, 794
Personification, **573**
Related words, 70, 155
Restatements, 192, 478
Romance language, **27**
Simile, 525, 557, **573**
Software, 545
Spanish words, 293
chart, 293
Synonym finder, 545
Synonyms, 192, 230, 348, **545**, 610
Thesaurus, 545
Time line, 176
Verifying meanings, 260
by comparison, 438
by example, 723
by restatement, 478
Word analogy, **274**, 487
Word map, 66, 70
for etymology, 66
Word tree, 155
Words in context, 467, 487

READING SKILLS

Analogy, 875
Asking questions, **711**
Biographical criticism, **706, 710**
It Says, I Say, And So chart, 710
Chronology, **265**
Comparing and contrasting, **84, 136,** 141, **261, 439, 492, 677, 758,** 877
H-map, 141
Comparing humorous styles, **574**
Comparing texts, **178**
Conclusions, **294**, 296, 877
Context clues, **32, 50,** 762, 791, 878
Dialogue
in poetry, **753**
with the text, **479**
Evaluating historical accuracy, **194,** 213
Fallacious reasoning, **533, 535,** 879
either/or fallacy, **533, 535,** 880
examples and, **533**
expert testimony and, **533**
facts and, **533**
false cause and effect, **533**, 535, 880
hasty generalizations, **533, 535,** 879
logic and, **533**, 879
name-calling, **533**, 534, **535,** 879
statistics and, **533**
stereotyping, **533, 535,** 879
Form, using to find meaning, **662**
Generalizations, **294**, 296, **298**, 330, **468**, 477, 880
hasty, **533, 535,** 880
Graphic organizers
H-map, 141
It Says, I Say, And So chart, 249, 710
KWL chart, **444**, 460
Somebody Wanted But So chart, 318, 363
Historical accuracy, evaluating, **194,** 213
Idioms, **747,** 751, 880
Inferences, **142,** 154, 166, **238,** 239, 248–249, 259, 273, **280, 294,** 296, 346, **558,** 567, 595, 880
It Says, I Say, And So strategy, 249
Informational texts, **803,** 881
It Says, I Say, And So strategy, **710**
chart, 249, 710
Judgments, **546,** 556, 882
Logic, 533, **742–743,** 745, 883
Magazine, text structure of, **275,** 883
Main idea, **185,** 191, 227, **443,** 460, 695, 697, 884
Meaning, 885
Metaphors in poetry, 619
Note-taking, **488,** 885
details and, 488
main ideas and, 488
note cards for, 488
Outlining, **488,** 491, 887
formal, **488**
informal, **488**
Paraphrasing, **162,**166, 887

SPEAKING AND LISTENING/MEDIA SKILLS

Index of Authors and Titles

STUDENT AUTHORS AND TITLES